Business
Plans
Handbook

Highlights

Business Plans Handbook, Volume 7 (BPH-7) is a collection of actual business plans compiled by entrepreneurs seeking funding for small businesses throughout North America. For those looking for examples of how to approach, structure, and compose their own business plans, *BPH-7* presents 25 sample plans, including plans for the following businesses:

- Automobile Sales
- Bowling Alley
- Car Wash
- Coffee Bean Plant/Exporter
- Event Planning Company
- Financial Services Company
- General Contracting Company

- Healthcare Software Company
- Hotel Resort
- Medical Billing Company
- Nightclub
- Roller Rink
- Screenprint Drying Company
- Wireless Internet Service

FEATURES AND BENEFITS

BPH-7 offers many features not provided by other business planning references including:

○ Twenty-five business plans, each of which represent an owner's successful attempt at clarifying (for themselves and others) the reasons that the business should exist or expand and why a lender should fund the enterprise.

○ Two fictional plans that are used by business counselors at a prominent small business development organization as examples for their clients. (You will find these in the Business Plan Template Appendix.)

○ An expanded directory section that includes: listings for venture capital and finance companies, which specialize in funding start-up and second-stage small business ventures, and a comprehensive listing of Service Corps of Retired Executives (SCORE) offices. In addition, the Appendix also contains updated listings of all Small Business Development Centers (SBDCs); associations of interest to entrepreneurs; Small Business Administration (SBA) Regional Offices; and consultants specializing in small business planning and advice. It is strongly advised that you consult supporting organizations while planning your business, as they can provide a wealth of useful information.

○ A Small Business Term Glossary to help you decipher the sometimes confusing terminology used by lenders and others in the financial and small business communities.

○ A cumulative index, outlining each plan profiled in the complete *Business Plans Handbook* series.

○ A Business Plan Template which serves as a model to help you construct your own business plan. This generic outline lists all the essential elements of a complete business plan and their components, including the Summary, Business History and Industry Outlook, Market Examination, Competition, Marketing, Administration and Management, Financial Information, and other key sections. Use this guide as a starting point for compiling your plan.

○ Extensive financial documentation required to solicit funding from small business lenders. *BPH-7* contains the most comprehensive financial data within the series to date. You will find examples of: Cash Flows, Balance Sheets, Income Projections, and other financial information included with the textual portions of the plan.

Business Plans Handbook

A COMPILATION
OF ACTUAL
BUSINESS PLANS
DEVELOPED BY
SMALL BUSINESSES
THROUGHOUT
NORTH
AMERICA

VOLUME

7

Donna Craft,
Senior Editor

GALE GROUP

Detroit
New York
San Francisco
London
Boston
Woodbridge, CT

Senior Editor: Donna Craft

Contributing Editors: Alex Alviar, Caryn Anders, Eric Hoss, Chris Lopez, Jaime Noce, Terrance Peck, and Brian Rabold

Managing Editor: Erin E. Braun

Composition Manager: Mary Beth Trimper
Buyer: Nekita M. McKee

Artist: Mike Logusz
Product Design Manager: Kenn Zorn

ISBN 0-7876-3420-4
ISSN 1084-4473

Printed in the United States of America

10 9 8 7 6 5 4 3 2 1

Contents

Business Plans

Appendixes

template; a foreword providing advice and instruction to entrepreneurs on how to begin their research; and a comprehensive glossary of terms to help the business planner navigate the sometimes confusing language of entrepreneurship.

ACKNOWLEDGEMENTS

The Editors wish to sincerely thank Palo Alto Software, makers of Business Plan Pro, the premier business planning software tool, for providing the use of several business plans in this volume (telephone: 800-229-7526; WWW: http://www.paloaltosoftware.com).

Thanks are also in order for the many contributors to *BPH-7*, whose business plans will serve as examples to future generations of entrepreneurs, as well as the users of the title who called with their helpful suggestions. Your help was greatly appreciated.

COMMENTS WELCOME

Your comments on *BPH-7* are appreciated. Please direct all correspondence, suggestions for future volumes of *BPH*, and other recommendations to the following:

Business Plans Handbook, Volume 7
The Gale Group
27500 Drake Rd.
Farmington Hills, MI 48331-3535

Phone: (248)699-4253
Fax: 800-339-3374
Toll-Free: 800-347-GALE

Introduction

Perhaps the most important aspect of business planning is simply *doing* it. More and more business owners are beginning to compile business plans even if they don't need a bank loan. Others discover the value of planning when they *must* provide a business plan for the bank. The sheer act of putting thoughts on paper seems to clarify priorities and provide focus. Sometimes business owners completely change strategies when compiling their plan, deciding on a different product mix or advertising scheme after finding that their assumptions were incorrect. This kind of healthy thinking and re-thinking via business planning is becoming the norm. The editors of *Business Plans Handbook, Volume 7 (BPH-7)* sincerely hope that this latest addition to the series is a helpful tool in the successful completion of your business plan, no matter what the reason for creating it.

This seventh volume, like each volume in the series, offers genuine business plans used by real people. *BPH-7* provides 25 business plans used by actual entreprencurs to gain funding support for their new businesses. The business and personal names and addresses and general locations have been changed to protect the privacy of the plan authors.

NEW BUSINESS OPPORTUNITIES

As in other volumes in the series, *BPH-7* finds entrepreneurs engaged in a wide variety of creative endeavors. Examples in BPH-7 include technology-based companies, such as a wireless Internet service and a healthcare software company. The interest in recreational activities is apparent in the business plans for the bowling alley, roller rink, hotel resort, nightclub, and event planning company. Other traditional businesses include a general contracting company and a financial services corporation.

Comprehensive financial documentation has become increasingly important as today's entrepreneurs compete for the finite resources of business lenders. Our plans illustrate the financial data generally required of loan applicants, including Income Statements, Financial Projections, Cash Flows, and Balance Sheets.

ENHANCED APPENDIXES

In an effort to provide the most relevant and valuable information for our readers, we have updated the coverage of small business resources. For instance, you will find: a directory section, which includes listings of all of the Service Corps of Retired Executives (SCORE) offices; an informative glossary, which includes small business terms; and a bibliography, which includes reference titles essential to starting and operating a business venture in all 50 states. In addition we have updated the list of Small Business Development Centers (SBDCs); Small Business Administration Regional Offices; venture capital and finance companies, which specialize in funding start-up and second-stage small business enterprises; associations of interest to entrepreneurs; and consultants, specializing in small business advice and planning. For your reference, we have also reprinted the business plan template, which provides a comprehensive overview of the essential components of a business plan and two fictional plans used by small business counselors.

SERIES INFORMATION

If you already have the first six volumes of *BPH*, with this seventh volume, you will now have a collection of 180 real business plans (not including the one updated plan in the second volume, whose original appeared in the first, or the two fictional plans in the Business Plan Template Appendix section of the second, third, fourth, fifth, and sixth volumes); contact information for hundreds of organizations and agencies offering business expertise; a helpful business plan

Accounting Service

BUSINESS PLAN

MARCUS ACCOUNTING, LLC

4 E. Locust Street
Market, Kentucky 48107

This business marketing plan was prepared to help Marcus Accounting, LLC, obtain a $8,200 Small Business Loan for company start-up related costs. This company proposes to provide accounting services to small and home business, as well as individuals in Market County.

- MISSION STATEMENT

- EXECUTIVE SUMMARY

- ACCOUNTING OVERVIEW SUMMARY

- MARKET ANALYSIS SUMMARY

- STRATEGY & IMPLEMENTATION

- FINANCIAL PLAN SUMMARY

- APPENDIX A - RESUMES

- APPENDIX B - EXAMPLE PROMOTIONAL MATERIALS

- APPENDIX C - EXAMPLE FEE SCHEDULE

ACCOUNTING SERVICE BUSINESS PLAN

MISSION STATEMENT

The Marcus Accounting mission is to provide dependable and quality service of accounting and tax preparation assistance to all sectors of industry, commerce, and individuals. We shall endeavor to provide our services in a comprehensive and cost-competitive manner, while providing our customer care advantage.

EXECUTIVE SUMMARY

General Ledger, Accounts Payable and Receivable, Payroll, Billing and Collections, Filing of Federal, State, and Local Forms, and Tax Preparation are services necessary to each corporate entity and individual. Assistance in these endeavors are the basis of Marcus Accounting and the makings of a highly profitable venture. Presently, management of Marcus Accounting is seeking funds to develop and expand the business in a phased approach, as highlighted within this planning tool.

Marcus Accounting is a new accounting service being made available to small businesses, self-employed, home-based businesses, and individuals in the Greater Market area. The owner, Mary Beth Marcus, has extensive business experience; over 20 years' experience in a variety of business types. Since 1995 she has been concentrating in the accounting field, working for L&R Bank and temporary staffing firms in accounting positions.

Mary Beth received her B.A. in Accounting from the University of Kentucky in May 1996. Desiring to start her own business, Mary Beth established Marcus Accounting, a full-service accounting service in 1997.

The foundation for the plan is a combination of primary and secondary research, upon which the marketing strategies are built. Discussions and interviews were held with a variety of individuals and small businesses to understand why and how they consider using an accounting service. Census data, *County Business Patterns*, and other directories were consulted to develop the market potential and competitive situation.

Initially, as a home-based business (keeping low overhead in the start-up phase) Marcus shall specialize in individual and small business clientele. As growth warrants, additional staffing assistance and/or outside office location can be realized (Phase II).

Business Plan Purpose

INTRODUCTION

In today's highly competitive environment, formal business planning is an essential element in achieving business success. A well-written business plan is primarily a communication tool to be used in obtaining financing. In certain instances, particularly with our early stage company, this business plan also serves as a strategic plan.

Considering that lenders are inundated by numerous investment opportunities from which they choose only a few, this business plan describes our story and how we intend to grow with your assistance. The Marcus management team has made an in-depth analysis of its opportunities and weaknesses and it has concluded that the company has an excellent chance to succeed.

METHODOLOGY FOR BUSINESS PLANNING

Sophisticated business planning helps management answer questions such as: What will be our record of achievement? How have we fared compared to our competitors? Are we setting realistic and attainable goals and objectives?

Constructive and useful business planning requires a broad-based understanding of changes taking place in the marketplace in which the company competes, or plans to compete, and the ever-changing financial markets. In-depth technical skills in a variety of disciplines such as tax, financial analysis, sales, marketing, and managing growth are critical components in assessing a company's opportunities and risks.

DEVELOPING THE BUSINESS PLAN

The management of Marcus Accounting has developed this disciplined planning methodology to help the company anticipate its start-up economic requirements and other critical information, and arrive at this realistic plan.

GUIDANCE FROM OUTSIDE PROFESSIONALS

Ms. Mary Beth Marcus has sought out assistance and advisors to Marcus in developing its business plan, however, she will maintain an active management involvement in every aspect of the formation of this business plan and the plan reflects her broad concept of the business.

The experienced professionals Ms. Marcus has obtained have assisted the company in:

- Helping develop a realistic business plan;
- Reviewing financial projections incorporating all of the assumptions and quantitative data presented in the business plan;
- Structuring funding options and lending offerings;
- Conducting market research;
- Researching growth potential for the industry;
- Identifying competitive forces and products; and,
- Offering creative marketing approaches.

FIVE OBJECTIVES OF MARCUS ACCOUNTING

1. Attract investment capital;
2. Focus ideas and establish goals;
3. Identify and quantify objectives;
4. Track and direct growth; and,
5. Create benchmarks for measuring success.

Marcus Accounting was formed to market a full-service accounting and related minor consulting firm by combining expertise in tax, accounting, tax planning, control systems, and management. The integration of these disciplines results in extensive and innovative services for our prospective clients.

COMPANY BUSINESS PLAN OBJECTIVE

This Business Plan serves to detail the direction, vision, and planning to achieve our goal for providing superior and comprehensive accounting services. Our plan objectives are:

- Attract $8,200 Loan as Start-Up Capital,
- Focus Ideas and Establish Goals,
- Identify and Quantify Long-Term Objectives,
- Track and Direct Growth,
- Create Benchmarks for Measuring Success.

Company Ownership

Marcus Accounting was founded by Ms. Mary Beth Marcus in February 1998 as a Kentucky Corporation. Marcus Accounting was created to address the need for quality service of comprehensive accounting and tax documentation. Marcus Accounting will continue to expand its client base within the Greater Market Area.

Marcus has been in the accounting field since 1995. Prior to that she had completed over thirty-five years in various medical technology related positions and has a desire to complete the three-year requirement of public accounting experience for eligibility to sit for the Certified Public Accounting (CPA) test.

Key Advisors to the Company

Marcus Accounting has additional key staff members to assist it. Mr. Brian Kelley and Ms. Marcia Stone have been retained by Marcus Accounting to assist in the development, planning, and market phases.

Management & Organizational Summary

Ms. Mary Beth Marcus will manage all aspects of the business and service development to ensure effective customer responsiveness. Additional support services will be provided by qualified contractual professionals. Support staff will be added as client work load factors mandate.

CORPORATE DEVELOPMENT PLAN

For purposes of this business plan document, Marcus Accounting - Phase I and Phase II for developmental growth are defined below:

Phase I - This phase involves preparation and development of Marcus's client base. Marcus Accounting will be housed at the home of Ms. Mary Beth Marcus, its founder. Marcus Accounting, Inc. will establish its own identity, management directives, and capital. Incorporating a total quality management approach (its Customer Care Advantage program), Marcus will develop key "base" small businesses which require biweekly through quarterly [reoccurring] accounting services. Through word of mouth and advertising, additional small- and mid-sized business and individual taxpayer accounts will be secured. Phase I capital (start-up) funds are documented in this business plan.

Phase II - Continue implementation of sales, advertising, and marketing strategies developed in Phase I. Identify and pursue other business support market. Marcus Accounting will target market identified "niche" industries to "specialize" in (i.e. automobile dealerships, church groups, nursing home patients, etc.). Strategic partnerships with specific industry associations (i.e. trade, industry, or service (non-profit) organization for volume discounts to its members, etc.) will be explored.

Marcus anticipates additional support staff and efforts to several community related entities will allow Marcus to consolidate its efforts with a centralized "out of the home" office. This Plan does not contain funding needs for this Phase.

Initially, Marcus management will focus its efforts in Phase I activities. Phase II efforts depend upon the timely development of Phase I and the analysis of its client service base. Marcus's growth funding capital will directly impact the rate of which marketing and development of this service occurs and the rate of growth potential is obtained.

Establishing an accounting business clientele will take time, as the research revealed word-of-mouth/recommendations/referrals as the primary way in which accounting services are selected by new clients. People who are completely new to the area, or who have few established connections, may look to the Yellow Pages or other advertising to establish available services, then call for information or pricing.

According to the County and City Data Book 1994 published by the U.S. Department of Commerce, Greater Market has 27,620 total households and 2,141 business establishments (less than 20 employees). Given that the 35 accounting firms/CPAs/tax preparation services in the area have an average of 200 individual and 50 business clients (accounting firms/CPAs only), each yields a served market of roughly 7,000 households and 1,300 businesses. The established business market appears to be fairly well penetrated, but potential exists for the self-employed, home-based businesses and individuals (all likely captured as "households" in the census data).

Between 1990 and 1996, an estimated 6,400 people moved into Market County (SE WI Regional Planning Commission Annual Report 1996) and 96 new businesses were established (County Business Patterns 1995). Capturing a share of the new arrivals will be a priority for Marcus Accounting.

ACCOUNTING OVERVIEW SUMMARY

Internal Assessment of Marcus Accounting Written by the Outside Advisors to the Company.

Strengths of Marcus Accounting include Mary Beth Marcus' broad base of experience in different types of companies from banking to manufacturing, and in different types of financial positions. This experience means Mary Beth understands the needs of small businesses and individuals when it comes to managing money—hence, her tag line "Keeping an Eye on Your Dollar." Her emphasis is on consulting with clients as well as keeping their books, bringing their attention to areas where money could be saved, strategies for better cash flow, etc., in a pro-active manner, as opposed to waiting until the client has a question about something, which may be too late to do anything about it.

This "full service" niche appears to be vacant in the market, with most accounting/CPA firms focused on volume and throughput, leaving little time available to get to know the client's business well enough to become a financial "partner." In addition, Mary Beth's willingness to meet with clients during evening and weekend hours, as well as in their own office or home offers convenience for the client, and is especially attractive to the elderly or disabled. Mary Beth's own in-home office is set up professionally, with adequate equipment to perform the services she offers.

As the business grows (especially among the business customer segment), Mary Beth may need to upgrade to the professional version of the tax preparation software. She may also want to consider offering electronic tax filing services for all clients.

Competitive Advantage

Following is a list of the industry Keys to Success:

1. A Vital Service Designed for the End User
2. Customer Care Advantage Program "Keeping An Eye on Your Dollar"
3. Controlled Overhead and Operational Costs
4. Regular and On-Going Customer Feedback
5. Sufficient Forms and Technology/Software Capacity
6. Consultation Services - Ongoing
7. Dedicated Management and Support Staff

Industry Keys to Success

**MARKET ANALYSIS
SUMMARY**

Marcus Accounting, like all businesses, is affected by forces and trends in the market environment. These include economic, competitive, legal/political, technology, and customer issues.

Economic Environment

Positive forces include the generally prosperous economy that is currently in place, full employment, rising wages, and low inflation, leading more people and businesses to be willing and able to hire an accountant to keep financial records and prepare taxes. The strong stock market means people are making more money, primarily in the form of capital gains, which may require more complicated recordkeeping and tax preparation. The new tax laws signed into effect in 1997 "makes filing this year much more complex for many people" says Martin Nissenbaum, national director of personal income-tax planning at Ernst & Young in New York, as quoted in the Friday, February 20, 1998 edition of the *Wall Street Journal.* The *Journal* also cited that about half of the nation's filers used an independent tax preparer last year.

Even though corporate downsizing is generally observed as a negative trend, it has positive implications for Marcus Accounting. A growing number of involuntary (and voluntary) corporate cast-offs are starting their own businesses, and unless their background is in a financial field, will need the services of an accountant to get the business recordkeeping set up. In 1996, there were 95 new business start-ups in Market County (*County Business Patterns,* U.S. Department of Commerce, Bureau of the Census, 1995).

Legal/Political Environment

As stated above, the new tax laws, new IRS forms, and regulations are becoming very complicated for the average person/small business to stay current with and understand. People increasingly need someone knowledgeable about the laws to draw their attention to ways to save money and taxes. Laws have changed regarding individual retirement accounts and small business SEPs and Keogh plans to the extent that people are starting to rely on their accountant to sort it all out for them.

Technology Environment

Computer programs greatly simplify the financial recordkeeping and tax preparation for both individuals and businesses, yet most are beyond the scope of the average person to learn and use. Small business owners/self-employed, in particular, wear many hats; the most important of which is controlling the output of their own business. Developing the expertise necessary to run the financial end of the business, including learning and updating accounting software, is just not a priority with many business owners and individuals. Outsourcing of business functions that a firm does not have the expertise in-house is a significant trend in business today. Better to hire an outside expert than to risk doing an inadequate job in-house, or to spend the resources necessary to develop the expertise in-house. Accounting is certainly one such business function. A variation on this trend is for the business to maintain the financial records in-house, and have the accounting service come on-site to generate the reports or complete the work.

**Competitive
Environment
Summary**

Many firms exist in Market County to assist individuals and businesses with their financial/accounting needs. Firms range from private individuals just preparing taxes to national chains like H&R Block, to accounting firms serving individuals and businesses, to CPA firms. A listing of the businesses offering accounting/tax preparation services in Market County (sourced through Midwest Directories) is as follows:

Tax Return Preparation

Edward Bastian (Deerhorn)
H&R Block (locations in four areas of Market County)
Tonda's Tax Service (Suet Mill)
Deutsch Tax Service (Market)
West Kite Tax Service (West Kite)
Mighty Fine Income Tax Service (Lincoln Heights)
Gerald Thomas (Springwater)

Bookkeeping Service

MET Bookkeeping Service (Venice)
KP Bookkeeping Systems (Swan Lake)

Accountants

AIDA Business Center (Swan Lake)
Penquin Accounting (Market)
Michael Looper & Associates (Overland)
Franklin Accounting Services (Overland)
Kurstz Accounting, Inc. (Overland)
Marion Froeming (West Moose)
DDR & Associates (Clemray)
Best Advisory Service, Inc. (Clemray)
McDougal & Missal Assoc. (Swan Lake)
Preferred Tax Service (King's Mill)
Joseph Betting Bookkeeping (King's Mill)
Irene Hopper (Sugarcreek)

Certified Public Accountants

Andrew Green (Mt. Orab)
Professional Electronic Accounting Services (King's Mill)
Lein & Associates (Swan Lake)
John Hammersmith (Sugarcreek)
Gerald Slinger (Swan Lake)
Mario Robbins & Co. (Clemray)
Michael Hutton (Sugarcreek)
Patrick Spartan & Company (Lake Geneva)
Doug Schaub (Wyoming)
Smith & White CPAs (Mt. Orab)
Theresa Summers (Sugarcreek)
VanDyke, Kroger & Associates (Lincoln)
Kitty Mitchell & Co. (Sugarcreek and Lincoln)
Robert Brown & Associates (Wyoming)

In addition to this list, there are private individuals preparing taxes for family and friends, but who are not in the "business" of doing so. Accounting services in four adjacent counties are listed in local directories, and do advertising in local papers, but are not included in the above list.

Generally, the CPA and accounting firms service business and individual clients and offer full-service monthly accounting and tax reporting services, while the tax preparation services and H&R Block concentrate on preparing individual tax returns. Marcus Accounting is attempting to carve out a third segment in the market; that of self-employed, home-based businesses and small businesses who, like many non-business individuals, currently maintain their own financial records and prepare their own tax returns. For individuals, Marcus Accounting would like to target those who need financial services beyond just tax preparation - for example, seasonal residents who need someone to look after their accounts while they are away, or senior/elderly (especially women) who need someone to help them keep their financial affairs in order.

A review of competitors' marketing strategies reveals no one launching a major attack on the Market County market. Many are advertising through Yellow Pages, and in newspapers during tax season, but the general approach to get new business is through networking, referrals, and personal selling. Accounting is a referral-driven business, according to John Simons (CPA). If new business of a certain type is desired, personal calls are made with targeted accounts. Other strategies used by area firms include telemarketing and encouraging and rewarding present clients to refer future clients. Networking within business groups, civic groups, church groups, etc. is important, even if the business results are not immediately felt. People want to obtain financial/accounting services from someone they trust; and that can be someone they knew from past membership in a group. Groups may also offer the opportunity for the business person to give a talk to the membership—an excellent public relations opportunity.

A threat to be aware of is the emergence of new competitors. The barriers to entry are low, and the local university turns out hundreds of accounting majors every year. The accounting program is very strong there, and offering classes at non-traditional times and locations attracts area adults who may be looking for a second career leading to their own self-employment in an accounting business.

Market Research Summary

A hypothetical behavior sequence model for a new client (individual) using an accounting service for the first time might look something like the following: (based on discussions and interviews with potential clients):

- Individual decides to utilize the services of an accountant to prepare taxes. This may happen as a result of a change in the individual's life situation (marry, divorce, lose a spouse, move, win the lottery) or investment/tax situation (sell house, receive inheritance). The need can arise anytime, but late fall and winter months are when most people are thinking about their tax situation.
- Individual investigates alternative accounting services. In most cases, this means the individual will consider first any accountants he/she is knowledgeable of through prior association (relative, friend, social, civic, or church group). Not knowing any accountants personally, the individual will begin asking his/her friends, family, co-workers, etc., for recommendations. If the individual is new to the area or otherwise has not made any close connections with people, he/she would look in the Yellow Pages for a listing, or would look in a newspaper for advertising.
- Acting on the advice of friends (or own knowledge), the individual will call the recommended accountant(s) to obtain information that will help him/her decide if this person is the best for them. Criteria for selection include: competence (can the accountant do what the client needs done?); reputation (has the accountant done this for other clients?); empathy (does the accountant understand the client's situation?); courtesy (does the accountant seem friendly and nice?); and pricing (is the service affordable?).
- Based on the information received, the individual makes a decision and schedules an appointment with the accountant.

- The individual's satisfaction with his/her decision and with the service itself is largely a function of their interaction with the accountant during the appointment. The accountant should do everything possible to ensure a satisfactory experience for the client, so that future business (and future referrals) are not at risk. This means preparing the client as much as possible for what will happen (what kinds of records and documents to bring, what kinds of questions will be asked, etc.).

Because of the confidential nature of income tax preparation for individuals, and financial recordkeeping for businesses, people do not tend to jump around from accountant to accountant, unless they become significantly dissatisfied with the service they are receiving. An investment is made on behalf of both parties to understand each other, communicate, and retain information from year to year.

Marketing strategies will build on this model—taking advantage of precipitating events, fostering word-of-mouth recommendations, and creating satisfaction through interacting with the client.

Summary of Opportunities and Threats in the Environment

Overall, the environment appears very positive for Marcus Accounting. The forces driving market demand, mainly economic and political/legal, are strong, with new businesses forming, new residents moving into the county, and more complicated tax regulations requiring a knowledgeable accountant to keep records in order. On the negative side, there is significant competition, and it will take a while for Marcus Accounting to get "established."

The business is driven by referrals, so for the first few years Marcus Accounting will need to be more aggressive in getting new clients, who will then pass the word on, and the business can begin to experience organic growth.

STRATEGY AND IMPLEMENTATION

Marketing Strategies

Target Markets - Business (Market County)

- Small businesses (up to 20 employees) with an emphasis on new business start-ups
- Self-employed (for example, contractors)
- Home-based businesses (for example, consultants, freelance, professionals)

Target Markets - Consumer (Market County)

- Upper-income households
- New residents in the area
- Women (elderly or single)
- Seasonal residents

Positioning and Product Strategy

For both business and consumer clients, Marcus Accounting will be positioned as a full-service accounting service that takes the time to get to know the client's business (or situation) and become a financial partner "keeping an eye on the client's dollar." A full range of accounting, bookkeeping, and tax-related services will be made available and tailored to the needs of the particular market segment.

Business service needs range from annual tax filing to monthly recordkeeping and reporting, including accounts payable and receivable, payroll and payroll tax reporting, sales and use tax reporting, bank reconciliation, profit/loss and cash flow statements. Marcus Accounting will aim to attract the business clients needing monthly accounting services in order to even out revenues throughout the year.

Consumer clients primarily need annual tax filing services; however, in keeping with the positioning, Marcus Accounting will also offer tax planning, personal budgeting, credit counseling, and checkbook reconciliation services. A special effort will be made to attract seasonal residents who need someone to make deposits and pay bills while they're away.

Distribution Strategy

Unlike products which are produced, then distributed and sold, accounting services are produced and consumed simultaneously in a real-time environment. Thus, distribution issues center on making the services available in a convenient manner to the most number of potential clients. Marcus Accounting maintains an office in the home of its owner, Mary Beth Marcus, so clients are able to come to her home/office to access her services, or Mary Beth will meet with clients in their home or office, whichever is more convenient. This flexibility is especially attractive to elderly or disabled clients. Clients can contact Marcus Accounting by telephone, fax, and hopefully soon e-mail. Marcus Accounting offers evening and Saturday appointments, in addition to the regular business hours.

Pricing Strategy

A sliding scale of fees has been developed and can be found in Appendix C. The fee schedule takes into account individual and business clients specific needs.

For businesses, pricing will be in the hourly rate of $55, in line with other established accounting services and what other types of professionals charge.

Personal/household tax preparation and filing prices are a function of the forms and schedules involved. Generally there is a base charge ($50-$125) plus extra for each schedule ($10-$15). Personal consulting (or other non-tax filing services) will be priced out at the $25 hourly rate.

SERVICE AND SUPPORT PHILOSOPHY

"Keeping An Eye on Your Dollar"—A tag line, yes, but by giving careful consideration to customer responsiveness, Marcus' goal will be to meet and exceed every service expectation of its accounting services. Quality service and quick responsiveness will be the philosophy guiding a total quality management (TQM) approach to Marcus operations in its benchmark Customer Care Advantage program.

PROMOTION STRATEGY SUMMARY

Promotion strategies will vary depending on the target market segment. Given the importance of word-of-mouth/referrals among all market segments when choosing an accountant, efforts are designed to create awareness, stimulate trial, and build referrals. A cost-effective campaign, focused on direct marketing, publicity, a customer reward program, and advertising is being proposed.

MARKETING PLAN

New Business Segment:

A direct marketing (direct mail) package consisting of a tri-fold brochure, letter of introduction, and reply card will be sent to a list of new businesses in Market County. This list can be obtained from International Business Lists, Inc. (Chicago, IL) and is compiled from Secretary of State incorporation registrations, business license applications, announcements from newspaper clippings, and tax records. The letter introduces Marcus Accounting, stresses the importance of having a good accountant to the success of the new business, provides information on services and what sets it apart from other accounting services, and includes a promotional offer—the opportunity to sample the services for free (a one-month bank reconciliation, up to 200 checks).

Approximately ten days to two weeks after the mailing, a telephone follow-up should be conducted, to make sure the brochure was received, whether the client has any questions, or would like to schedule an appointment. Approximately 50 new businesses would be targeted.

Established Small Business/Home-based & Self-Employed Segment:

A similar direct mail package will be sent to a select list of small businesses, home-based businesses, and self-employed. The letter will emphasize a slightly different aspect than for new businesses; established businesses may already have a relationship with an accountant, so the focus of the letter is on the differentiation of Marcus Accounting—what Mary Beth Marcus offers that others don't.

The list of established small businesses/self-employed (contractors) can be compiled from local directories, while a list of home-based businesses/self-employed can be obtained from Direct Media, Inc. (Greenwich, CT). Approximately 250 existing businesses would be targeted.

It is recommended that the mailings be made over a period of several months—not all at once— so that proper follow-up telephone calls can be made.

A customer/prospect database can be developed in addition to the purchased lists. Monitoring the local newspapers for announcements about new businesses in the area will provide a steady influx of new names. These can be added to the database, and the business mailed the brochure and "new company" letter.

Marcus Accounting can also consider developing a one-page newsletter to be mailed quarterly to customers and prospects in the database. The newsletter can be used to update clients on accounting and tax-related developments, but also serves as a reminder of what sets Marcus Accounting apart from other accounting services—being a financial "partner" and "keeping an eye on your dollar." Business and recordkeeping tips are always valued, and friendly reminders to clients to pass the newsletter along to their friends and colleagues will literally "spread the word" about Marcus Accounting. The newsletter can be produced in-house and for the cost of paper and a stamp creates a lot of goodwill among customers and prospects.

Networking - Attorneys and Bankers

A direct mail effort will also be targeted at the approximately 150 attorneys and bankers in Market County, as they routinely come into contact with businesses and individuals needing accounting or tax-related services. The letter introduces Marcus Accounting, and along with information about services, etc., asks the recipient to consider the service as a possible referral. Several brochures would be included with the letter for the recipient to hand out to his/her customers.

Publicity and Public Relations

A news release will be sent to area newspapers and magazines announcing the launch of Marcus Accounting.

Mary Beth Marcus may join the Market County area Chamber of Commerce as a means of networking in the community. She may also make herself available for speaking engagements at other community or civic organizations. Becoming a sponsor in a community event (Festival of Spring, County Fair, AutumnFest, various parades, bloodmobiles, etc.) is a low-cost way of increasing awareness and building goodwill in the community.

Customer Reward Program

As a means of building business by word-of-mouth, present customers should be encouraged and rewarded for referring future customers. This can be accomplished by offering a small "rebate" ($10-$15 or equivalent gift) to current customers who successfully recruit a new customer. In addition, all new tax preparation clients receive a Marcus Accounting coffee mug when they pick up their returns. Since the 1998 tax season is underway, the coffee mug give-away would take place in 1999.

Advertising

Advertising is utilized primarily to attract new consumer and home-based/self-employed business clients for income tax preparation services. It also serves to build awareness and name recognition of the company in general—important for word-of-mouth referrals ("Oh yes, I've seen that company's ads before.")

Market County Shopper/Sunday Shopper—advertising in this Wednesday and Sunday primarily classified newspaper reaches over 33,000 homes and businesses in the county twice each week. A 12-week schedule (24 insertions) commencing early in January and running through the middle of April coincides with tax season when the need for professional accounting help is most acute. Marcus Accounting can use its business card as creative, and can be placed under the "Services Offered" section of the display/classified ads. A six-week, every-other-week schedule (12 insertions) is also proposed for the fall to promote end-of-year tax planning and bill paying for seasonal residents.

Accounting services typically advertise only during tax season, so the earlier schedule will help set Marcus Accounting apart from and ahead of the rest.

Yellow Pages—Ameritech PagesPlus, Greater Market County Telephone Directory. Research indicated that new residents or people who don't have many personal acquaintances to ask about accounting services will look to the Yellow Pages to establish a list of potential accounting services to call. Even a small 2" x 2" boxed ad can create awareness and attract the desired target client, above and beyond the ability of a simple listing to do so. Ameritech Yellow Pages covers the relevant market area, delivering over 30,000 copies to residents and business. Midwest Directories covers greater Market County, with a circulation of 90,000, but is considered a second-tier directory to Ameritech.

Telephone Book Cover—A business cardlike ad on the plastic cover which is placed over any telephone book enables the business name/logo to be seen virtually 24 hours a day, 365 days a year. Covers are distributed biannually free of charge to residents and businesses in Market County.

Restaurant Placemats—Opportunities exist for a business cardlike ad to be placed on the paper placemats used in area restaurants (shelf-life of the ad is about six months), or for special (holiday) events taking place at a restaurant (1-off opportunities). An example would be getting on the Pizza Hut placemats (about 9,000 in six months), or getting on the special Lions Club "St. Patrick's Day" dinner placemats at the Village Restaurant (about 1,000 placemats for that event). Placemat advertising will reach area residents as well as seasonal/tourists.

Additional places to post flyers/business cards or for a business card ad include bulletin boards in public buildings (grocery stores, senior centers), and playbills for local theater groups.

Example Promotion Budget - 1998 & 1999

Company brochure	$450.00
(2-color, 1,000 quantity, high quality paper)	
Reply card	$150.00
(2-color, 500 quantity, card stock)	
Lists (new businesses, home-based businesses)	$750.00
Postage	$250.00
(mailing 300 businesses, 150 attorneys/banks)	
Telephone follow-up ($1.50/call x 300 calls)	$450.00
Public relations activities and sponsorships	$1,000.00
Customer reward program	$500.00
Newspaper advertising (Shopper)	$1,036.80
Yellow Pages advertising	$621.50
Telephone book cover advertising	$535.00
Restaurant placemats (5 restaurants/10 events)	$1,650.00
Miscellaneous flyers	$200.00
Advertising specialties (give-aways)	$200.00
Total for 1998 & 1999	**$7,792.80**

Objectives have been established for Marcus Accounting so that actual performance can be measured against them. Thus, at the end of 1999, Marcus should have:

Evaluation & Control Strategies

- $36,000 in total revenue
- 17 business clients
- 65 consumer clients
- Anticipate 90% customer retention (not measurable for first year)

Each subsequent year, new objectives will be set for these benchmarks, and actual performance will be measured against them. If actual performance falls short of objectives, investigation will be made into the cause, and plans adjusted accordingly.

In addition, it is recommended that Marcus Accounting keep track of the source of all new clients ("Where did you hear of me?") in order to measure the effectiveness of each type of promotion. Each subsequent year's budget should adjust spending toward the types of promotion that are accounting for the most new clients.

Customer satisfaction is most directly reflected in the year-to-year customer retention percentage. All lost customers should be investigated to find out why they left. A customer satisfaction survey may be considered after three to four years in the business.

FINANCIAL PLAN SUMMARY

The following proforma contains Marcus's projections for seven years.

Income Statement:

REVENUES	Year 1	Year 2	Year 3	Year 4	Year 5	Year 6	Year 7
Total Revenue	14,550	35,850	52,500	73,625	79,146.88[4]	85,082.89	91,464.11
EXPENSES							
Fixed Labor Cost	$12,500[1]	$25,000	$26,250[2]	$27,563	$28,941	$30,388	$31,907
Variable Labor Cost		$2,860[1]	$8,580	$9,009[2]	$9,459	$9,932	$10,429
Operating Expenses	4,400	$6,910[3]	$7,083	$7,260	$7,441	$7,627	$7,818
Loan Repayment	$2,043	$2,043	$2,043	$2,043	$2,043		
Total Cost of Goods Sold	$18,943	$36,813	$43,955	$45,874	$47,884	$47,947	$50,154
Gross Margin (Profit or Loss)	**($4,393)**	**($963)**	**$8,545**	**$27,751**	**$31,263**	**$37,135**	**$41,310**
Percent of Revenue (%)			16.30%	37.70%	39.50%	43.60%	45.20%
Income Tax (33%)			$2,820	$9,158	$10,317	$12,255	$13,632
Development Cost Amortization (Five Year Straight Line Method)	$1,640	$1,640	$1,640	$1,640	$1,640		
{After Tax} Net Income	**($2,753)**	**$677**	**$7,365**	**$20,233**	**$22,586**	**$24,881**	**$27,678**

Notes:
[1]Prorated Salary
[2]Labor Costs Rise Annually 5%
[3]Operating Costs Rise Annually 2.5%
[4]Beginning in Year 5 - Revenues Increase on an Annual 7.5% Basis

The following schedule highlights the anticipated developmental costs and the first year Marcus Accounting project expenditures. This schedule defines the financial needs to develop a successful business and are the basis for the financial start-up capital amounts listed in the Seven-Year Proforma.

Classification:	Cost
Office Storage System	$200
Advertising & Promotion	$2,500
Supplies, Postage & Printing	$1,500
Computer and Software	$2,500
Association Dues and Training	$1,500
	$8,200

Annual Value Amortized over 5 years $1,640

The development of the business will require the time and talents full-time of Mary Beth Marcus. Her salary, office, and other related expenses during the first year of the project are incorporated into the Seven-Year Proforma.

Phase II growth amounts will be developed and sought at a later date, based upon needs to be determined at that time.

- The following assumptions will be incorporated into the Marcus proforma statements.
- All operating costs are based on Marcus management research of similar operating companies.
- Automated informational systems will reduce Marcus staff requirements.
- Developmental start-up costs are amortized over a five-year period.
- Home office lease costs are deferred until year two combined and lease back to Marcus.
- Overhead and operations costs are calculated on an annual basis.
- Marcus founder salary is based on a fixed salary expense basis.
- All fixed and variable labor costs should rise annually at five percent.
- All revenues, past year 5 are figured to rise annually at seven and a half percent.
- Fixed annual, administrative, and office expenses rise at an annual rate of two and a half percent.

MARY BETH MARCUS

Qualification Highlights:

- Computer literate (experience with Peachtree, Quicken, Excel, Microsoft)
- Knowledge of accounts payable and receivable, payroll
- Extensive knowledge of recordkeeping and filing
- Utilization of management skills in areas of recruiting, training, evaluating, and development of policies, procedures, and budgets
- Inventory control, manufacturing schedules, and warehouse shipping

Phase I Funding Amounts Sought

Developmental Expenses

Financial Plan Assumptions

APPENDIX A - RESUME OF MS. MARY BETH MARCUS

Experience:

L&R OF Kentucky	Louisville, Kentucky
Account Clerk/Credit Analyst	April 1995 to June 1996

Assisted with small bank mergers, posted loan payments, assisted customers in problem-solving when payments were late and with errors in posting of checking and savings account balances. Prepared and analyzed cash flow and profitability statements for loan officers.

OLSTEN, MANPOWER, OFFICETEAM, ACCOUNTEMPS EMPLOYMENT AGENCIES

Accounting/clerical positions	May 1994 to April 1995
	June 1996 to May 1997

Proofread reports, assisted customers in setting up new accounts or errors in accounts, address changes, etc. Assisted in tax preparation/closing entries, bank reconciliation, accounts payable/receivables, payroll data entry, and processing of government forms. Confirmation of shipping, discounts, and payment schedules.

Additional Work Experience 1978 to 1993

Accounting is a second career. Previous experience as a medical laboratory technologist and supervisor included working with sales personnel and purchasing departments to order and track reagents, equipment and supplies for my department, conversations with ill patients and physician offices (confidentiality and good oral communication skills with compassion), learning to work within the organization for budget preparation and review.

Education:

University of Cincinnati, B.A., Accounting, May 1996
Ohio State University, B.S., Medical Technology, May 1968

News Release

For Immediate Release:

A new full-service accounting business has opened its doors in Market, Kentucky, in Market County. Owned and operated by Mary Beth Marcus, Marcus Accounting will cater to the needs of both small and home-based businesses and individuals throughout Greater Market County.

"I realize there are several accounting firms in the area, many offering the same services I offer," says Marcus, a graduate of the University of Cincinnati with a B.A. in accounting. "But Marcus Accounting is different. I firmly believe in the importance of customizing my service to the needs of my clients."

Marcus' company will offer a full range of accounting services. Accounts payable/ receivable, general ledger, payroll, tax reporting, balance sheet, P & L statements, tax planning, and cash flow analysis are among the services she will provide to small business owners. Private individuals can look to Marcus Accounting for income tax filing, checkbook/bank reconciliation, budgeting, tax planning, and bill paying. For both types of customers, Marcus can provide a turnkey approach or offer individual services.

In addition to traditional accounting services, Marcus will also offer pick-up and delivery services, along with evening and Saturday hours. She will also go to a customer's home, an especially attractive service for the elderly or disabled. For all of her customers, Marcus stresses the importance of timely reviews and consultation sessions.

In this day of automated tax returns and impersonal service, Marcus Accounting offers an alternative. As Marcus emphasizes, "I truly am interested in the success of my customers, whether they're a small business operator like myself or an individual just trying to make their way through new tax codes."

For more information, contact Mary Beth Marcus at (606) 123-1234 or write to Marcus Accounting, 4 E. Locust St., Market, Kentucky 48107.

ON LETTERHEAD

Dear (Lawyer, Banker),

Please allow me to introduce myself and the services my firm offers.

My name is Mary Beth Marcus and I operate Marcus Accounting, a full-service accounting firm. Conveniently located in Market, Kentucky, my business meets the needs of both small and home-based businesses and individuals throughout Market County.

In your professions, you many times have the opportunity to refer clients to accounting services. I would like you to consider my firm as a possible referral. I have a four-year degree in accounting and 20 years of experience in a variety of occupations and businesses. Not only do I understand how small businesses operate, I can identify with their concerns and challenges.

I realize there are several accounting firms in the area, many offering the same services I offer. Marcus Accounting is different, however. I firmly believe in the importance of customizing my service to the needs of my clients. I can provide a turnkey program of monthly accounting (accounts receivable, accounts payable, payroll, and tax reporting) or offer individual services to clients, and I stress the importance of having timely reviews and consultation sessions. In addition, Marcus Accounting offers pick-up and delivery services, evening and Saturday hours and I will even go to my client's home, an especially nice service for the elderly or disabled.

In this day of automated tax returns and impersonal service, Marcus Accounting offers an alternative for your clientele. I truly am interested in their success, whether they're a small business operator like myself or an individual just trying to make his or her way through the new tax codes.

Please consider my firm the next time a client asks, "Do you know an accountant who will really care about my needs?"

Sincerely,

Mary Beth Marcus

P.S. I've enclosed several brochures to give to interested clients. Please give me a call at (606) 123-1234 if you run short of brochures or if you have any questions about the services I offer.

ON LETTERHEAD

Dear (New Business Owner),

Please allow me to introduce myself and the services my firm offers.

My name is Mary Beth Marcus and I operate Marcus Accounting, a full-service accounting firm. Conveniently located in Market, Kentucky, my business meets the needs of both small and home-based businesses and individuals throughout Market County.

Being a new business owner, you may not realize yet how important a good accountant will be to the success of your company. I would like you to consider my firm as a resource. I have a four-year degree in accounting and 20 years of experience in a variety of occupations and businesses. Not only do I understand how small businesses operate, I can identify with your concerns and challenges.

I realize there are several accounting firms in the area, many offering the same services I offer. Marcus Accounting is different, however. I firmly believe in the importance of customizing my service to the needs of my clients. I can provide a turnkey program of monthly accounting (accounts receivable, accounts payable, payroll, and tax reporting) or offer individual services to clients, and I stress the importance of having timely reviews and consultation sessions. In addition, Marcus Accounting offers pick-up and delivery services, evening and Saturday hours and I will even go to my client's home, an especially nice service for the elderly or disabled.

In this day of automated tax returns and impersonal service, Marcus Accounting offers an alternative. I truly am interested in your success, whether you're a small business operator like myself or an individual just trying to make your way through the new tax codes.

Please consider my firm for your accounting needs. As the name implies, Marcus Accounting is more than a traditional accounting firm. I will specialize in watching your dollars. I've enclosed a brochure that describes the services I offer. If you have any questions or would like to talk with me about your accounting needs, please give me a call at (606) 123-1234.

Sincerely,

Mary Beth Marcus

P.S. The best way I can think of to show businesses like yours just how beneficial my services are is to let you sample them for free! New clients will receive a one-month bank reconciliation (up to 200 checks) at no charge. Call for details.

ON LETTERHEAD

Dear (Established Business Owner),

Please allow me to introduce myself and the services my firm offers.

My name is Mary Beth Marcus and I operate Marcus Accounting, a full-service accounting firm. Conveniently located in Market, Kentucky, my business meets the needs of both small and home-based businesses and individuals throughout Market County.

Being a business owner, you already realize how important having a good accountant is to your success. Having an accountant who can identify with your special concerns and challenges and customize services to meet your needs is even more important today. With that in mind, I would like you to consider my firm as a resource. I have a four-year degree in accounting and 20 years of experience in a variety of occupations and businesses. Not only do I understand how small businesses operate, I understand their needs.

I realize there are several accounting firms in the area, many offering the same services I do. Marcus Accounting is different, however. I firmly believe in the importance of customizing my service to the needs of my clients. I can provide a turnkey program of monthly accounting (accounts receivable, accounts payable, payroll, and tax reporting) or offer individual services to clients, and I stress the importance of having timely reviews and consultation sessions. In addition, Marcus Accounting offers pick-up and delivery services, evening and Saturday hours and I will even go to my client's home, an especially nice service for the elderly or disabled.

In this day of automated tax returns and impersonal service, Marcus Accounting offers an alternative. I truly am interested in your success, whether you're a small business operator like myself or an individual just trying to make your way through the new tax codes.

Please consider my firm for your accounting needs. As the name implies, Marcus Accounting is more than a traditional accounting firm. I will specialize in watching your dollars. I've enclosed a brochure that describes the services I offer. If you have any questions or would like to talk with me about your accounting needs, please give me a call at (606) 123-1234.

Sincerely,

Mary Beth Marcus

P.S. The best way I can think of to show businesses like yours just how beneficial my services are is to let you sample them for free! New clients will receive a one-month bank reconciliation (up to 200 checks) at no charge. Call for details.

BUSINESS CLIENT SERVICES:

  HOURLY RATE: $55.00

EXAMPLE TYPICAL SERVICES:

  ACCOUNTS PAYABLE & RECEIVABLE

  PAYROLL

  CHECK WRITING AND LEDGER ENTRIES

  GENERAL LEDGER AND BALANCE SHEET PREPARATION

  QUARTERLY TAX DOCUMENT PREPARATION

  BILLING AND COLLECTIONS

Terms: Volume Discount for Long-Term Commitment and for Bundling of Services

INDIVIDUAL TAX RELATED PREPARATION:

  HOURLY RATE: $25.00

EXAMPLE TYPICAL CHARGES:

  1040EZ & KY-Z (1.5 hours) $37.50

  1040A, KY-A & Hst. (2.0 Hours) $50.00

  1040 w/Schs., KY-I & Hst.

    (4.0 Hours) $100.00

Terms: Net - $5.00 Upon Receipt

Auto Sales Company

BUSINESS PLAN

MOUNTAIN VIEW LEASE, LLC

900 Minchon Drive
Pebbles, Colorado 80211

This plan helped Mountain View Lease, LLC obtain a $275,000 Small Business Loan for facility build-out construction and a $225,000 line of credit for company start-up and vehicle acquisition-related costs.

- EXECUTIVE SUMMARY

- COMPANY SUMMARY

- AUTO SALES & LEASING OVERVIEW

- MARKET ANALYSIS

- STRATEGY & IMPLEMENTATION

- PROMOTION STRATEGY

- FINANCIAL PLAN

EXECUTIVE SUMMARY

High-end pre-owned auto sales (Cadillac, Lexus, BMW, Audi, Saab, Mercedes, Infiniti, and Lincoln) and related leasing assistance are the basis of Mountain View Lease, LLC and the makings of a profitable venture. Management of Mountain View Lease is presently seeking funds to develop and grow the business in a phased approach, as highlighted within this planning tool.

Mountain View Lease, LLC is a new, "highline" auto sales and leasing service being made available to vehicle buyers throughout the Greater Pebbles area. The owner, Frank Simons, has extensive business experience — over 30 years' experience in the sales and leasing field. Desiring to start his own business, Frank established Mountain View Lease, LLC in 1998.

The foundation for the plan is a combination of primary and secondary research upon which the marketing strategies are built. Discussions and interviews were held with a variety of individuals and businesses to understand why and how they might consider using a pre-driven auto sales and leasing service. Census data, county business patterns, and other directories were consulted to develop the market potential and competitive situation.

As a start-up business, Mountain View Lease, LLC shall specialize in individual and business clientele needs for sales and leasing of executive-driven and new highline vehicles. Management has determined that presently this market niche, in the Greater Pebbles area, is under-served. As growth warrants, additional staffing and/or additional service locations can be realized (Phase II).

Business Plan Purpose

Introduction

In today's highly competitive environment, formal business planning is an essential element in achieving business success. A well-written business plan is primarily a communication tool to be used in obtaining financing. In certain instances, particularly with an early stage company, this business plan also serves as a strategic plan.

Considering that lenders are inundated by numerous investment opportunities from which they choose only a few, this business plan describes our story and how we intend to grow with your assistance. The Mountain View Lease, LLC management team has made an in-depth analysis of its opportunities and weaknesses and it has concluded that the company has an excellent chance to succeed.

Methodology for Business Planning

Sophisticated business planning helps management answer questions such as: What will be our record of achievement? How have we fared compared to our competitors? Are we setting realistic and attainable goals and objectives?

Constructive and useful business planning requires a broad-based understanding of changes taking place in the marketplace in which the company competes, or plans to compete, and the ever-changing financial markets. In-depth technical skills in a variety of disciplines such as tax, financial analysis, sales, marketing, and managing growth are critical components in assessing a company's opportunities and risks.

Developing the Business Plan

The management of Mountain View Lease, LLC has developed this disciplined planning methodology to help the company anticipate its start-up economic requirements and other critical information, and arrive at this realistic plan.

Guidance from Outside Professionals

Mr. Frank Simons has sought out assistance and advisors to Mountain View Lease, LLC in developing its business plan. However, he will maintain an active management involvement in every aspect of the formation of this business plan, and the plan reflects his experience of the industry and his concept of the business.

The experienced professionals Mr. Simons has obtained have assisted the company in:

- Helping develop a realistic business plan
- Reviewing financial projections incorporating all of the assumptions and quantitative data presented in the business plan
- Assisting in structuring funding options and lending offerings
- Conducting market research
- Researching growth potential for the industry
- Identifying competitive forces and products
- Offering creative marketing approaches

Five Objectives of Mountain View Lease, LLC:

1. Attract construction and start-up investment capital
2. Focus ideas and establish goals
3. Identify and quantify objectives
4. Track and direct growth
5. Create benchmarks for measuring success

Mountain View Lease, LLC was formed to market and lease executive "high end" new and pre-driven vehicles to individual and business customers. The integration of these disciplines results in a comprehensive service for the discriminating vehicle buyer.

Mission Statement

Mountain View Lease, LLC's mission is to provide quality sales and leasing services to all customers seeking highline pre-driven and new vehicles. We shall endeavor to provide our products and services in a comprehensive and cost-competitive manner.

COMPANY SUMMARY

This Business Plan serves to detail the direction, vision, and planning to achieve our goal for providing superior and comprehensive pre-driven auto sales and leasing services. Our plan objectives are:

- Attract $275,000 for Facility Construction
- Secure $225,000 for Start-up and Credit Line Capital
- Focus Ideas and Establish Goals
- Identify and Quantify Long-Term Objectives
- Track and Direct Growth
- Create Benchmarks for Measuring Success

Company Ownership

Mountain View Lease, LLC was founded by Mr. Frank Simons in October 1998. Mountain View was created to address the need for niche sales of new and pre-owned executive automobiles and their leasing. Mountain View Lease, LLC will expand its client base throughout the Greater Pebbles Area.

Simons has been in the sales and leasing field since 1969. Having completed nearly 30 years at various local dealerships he has a complete knowledge and experience in this industry.

Key Advisors to the Company

Mountain View Lease, LLC has additional key advisors to assist it. Mr. Frank O'Brien has been retained by Mountain View Lease, LLC to assist in the development, planning, and marketing phases. Edward Thompson, Attorney is the legal advisor and Mike Smith, of Black and Smith, is an accountant advisor.

Management & Organizational Summary

Frank Simons will manage all aspects of the business and lease departments to ensure effective customer responsiveness. Additional support services will be provided by qualified sales consultants. Support staff will be added as client workload factors mandate.

Corporate Development Plan

For purposes of this Business Plan document, Mountain View Lease, LLC — Phase I and Phase II for developmental growth are defined below:

Phase I — This phase involves planning, renovation, and development of Mountain View Lease, LLC's property at 900 Minchon Drive, in Pebbles, Colorado. Mountain View Lease, LLC will establish its own identity, management directives, and capital. Incorporating a total quality management approach, Mountain View Lease, LLC will develop key "base" businesses which require automobiles for its employees on a recurring basis and call upon management's 30-year, established customer base. Through word-of-mouth and advertising, pre-driven quality car buyers will be secured.

Phase I build-out, start-up, and development credit line needs are documented in this business plan.

Phase II — Continue implementation of sales, advertising, and marketing strategies developed in Phase I. Identify and pursue other business support markets. Mountain View Lease will target other communities for expansion.

Mountain View Lease anticipates the need for sales and support staff to be added during this phase.

Initially, Mountain View Lease management will focus its efforts in Phase I activities. Phase II efforts depend upon the timely development of Phase I and the analysis of its customer service base. The availability of Mountain View's growth funding capital will directly impact the growth rate of this company.

AUTO SALES & LEASING OVERVIEW

Establishing an auto sales and leasing business clientele will take some time but once the word is out to our former customers, as the research revealed, word-of-mouth /recommendations / referrals are the primary way in which auto sales and leasing services are selected by new customers. People who are completely new to the area, or who have few established connections, may look to the Yellow Pages or other advertising to establish available service vendors, they may stop in or call for information, product availability, or pricing.

In eastern and western Pebbles, a few companies are established in the used-car business. None of them specialize in the higher end, exclusive pre-drive automobile market. Our potential exists due to the reliable and professional, business and management niche consumer that we are targeting—a market opportunity presently under-served.

Strengths of Mountain View Lease, LLC include Frank Simons's broad base of sales and management experience in successful automobile dealerships from 1969 to 1997. This experience means Frank understands the needs of corporate business clients and the individual vehicle buyer when it comes to offering quality automobiles — hence, his tag line "Down to Earth, Dedicated Service." Mountain View's emphasis is on consulting with the customer, bringing their attention to new and pre-driven products perhaps not considered, and explore the strategies for financing and leasing, in a pro-active manner, in order to please the customer.

This "full service" niche appears to be vacant in the market, with most auto sales and leasing companies focused on volume and throughput, leaving little time available to get to know the customers needs well enough to become a sales "partner." In addition, Frank's willingness to meet with customers during evening and weekend hours, as well as in their own office or home offers convenience for the vehicle buyer, and is especially attractive to the aging population. This approach will ensure repeat customers.

Competitive Advantage

1. A Vital Service Designed for the Discriminating Pre-Driven Car Buyer
2. Customer Sales Program — "Down to Earth Dedicated Service for Your Quality Vehicle Needs"
3. Controlled Overhead and Operational Costs
4. Regular and On-Going Customer Feed Back
5. Sufficient Forms. and Technology/Software Capacity
6. Consultation Services — Ongoing
7. Dedicated Management and Support Staff

Industry Keys to Success

Mountain View Lease, LLC, like all businesses, is affected by forces and trends in the market environment. These include economic, competitive, legal/political, technology, and customer issues.

MARKET ANALYSIS

Economic Environment — Positive forces include the generally prosperous economy that is currently in place, full employment, rising wages, and low inflation, leading more people and businesses to be willing and able to treat themselves to a highline vehicle. The strong stock market means people are making more money, primarily in the form of capital gains.

Even though corporate downsizing is generally observed as a negative trend, it has positive implications for Mountain View Lease, LLC. A growing number of companies have eliminated the company car and favor the tax benefits of leasing.

Legal/Political Environment — As stated above, the new tax laws, for automobile deductions, are becoming very complicated for the average sales person/small business to stay current with and understand. Car leasing is a way to save money and taxes.

Technology Environment — Computer programs will greatly simplify the financial recordkeeping and tax preparation for controlling the output of the Mountain View business. Frank has developed the expertise necessary to run the financial end of the business, including learning and updating auto sales and leasing software. Outsourcing of business functions to an outside accounting expert will ensure the financial data will be done.

Eleven used-car lots are listed in the Greater Pebbles phone book. None specialize in the upscale executive market segment. These firms range from private individuals with just a few cars in their tow truck area to a Chevrolet-Olds-Cadillac distributorship. None of the four

Competitive Environment Summary

market a leasing ability. The businesses offering used auto sales or leasing services in Greater Pebbles (source through Ameritech and Midwest Directories) are listed as follows:

Duncan

Country Chevy, 224 West Bark Road
Duncan Auto, 463 Rapstitch
Mark Chevrolet-Olds-Cadillac, 313 West Cliff
B&Y Auto Sales, 165 Highway 30

Lake Kirby

Kirby Lakes Ford-Chevy, Hwy. 3 & 444 Whipper Street

Lake Bonners

Kitt's Auto & RV, 4 Mouse Road
Koomer's Motors, Highway 46 & Jenner
Schmidt's Auto, Inc., Route 4
Loomtoom Auto Sales Inc., 234 W. Ohio
T&T Sales, 141 South Taft
Dudley's Ford, Highway 46 and Milktoast

There are some new car dealerships that we are sure sell used cars from trade-in, etc. However, they are not in the "business" of doing so. We have not listed the local used car lots in this business plan from customers who may come from the adjacent counties like Rock, Racine, or Waukesha.

Generally, an auto sales and leasing company would like to target those customers of upscale demographics and who can afford the luxury car market—even though some of the cars offered will be pre-driven. This customer appreciates the reliability and stature associated with the following nameplates:

Audi	Jaguar	Porsche
BMW	Lexus	Saab
Cadillac	Lincoln	Volvo
Infiniti	Mercedes	

A review of competitors' marketing strategies reveals no one launching an attack on the upscale pre-driven car market in greater Greater Pebbles. Only one company is advertising through the Yellow Pages regarding leasing services. The general approach to get new business is through networking, referrals, and personal selling. Auto sales and leasing is a referral-driven business.

Other strategies to build customer sales include telemarketing and encouraging and rewarding present clients to refer future clients. Networking within business groups, civic groups, church groups, etc. is important, even if the business results are not immediately felt. People want to obtain financial and auto sales and leasing services from someone they trust; and that can be someone they knew from past membership in a group. Groups may also offer the opportunity for the business person to give a talk to the membership—an excellent public relations opportunity.

Market Research Summary

A hypothetical behavior sequence model for a showroom (not private) car buying individual using an auto sales and leasing service for the first time might look something like the following: (based on discussions and interviews with potential clients):

Individual decides to obtain a luxury automobile. This may happen as a result of a change in the individual's life situation (marry, divorce, lose a spouse, move, win the lottery) or investment/tax situation (sell house, large wage increase, receive inheritance). The need can arise anytime, but spring and summer months are when most people are thinking about upgrading their transportation.

Individual investigates the pre-driven auto sales and leasing services. In most cases, this means the individual will consider walking through the car dealerships where they have shopped in the past (favorable) and/or a place that has been highly recommended. Those buyers who do not know any dealer lots personally, will begin asking their friends, family, co-workers, etc., for recommendations. If the individual is new to the area or otherwise has not made any close connections with people, he/she would look in the Yellow Pages for a listing, or would look in a newspaper for advertising.

Acting on the advice of friends (or his/her own knowledge), the individual will tour or call on the recommended auto sales company to obtain information that will help him/her decide. Criteria for selection include: performance (can the car meet customers expectations); reputation (quality); reliability (can the car be counted upon); courtesy (sales force); and value (is the product affordable?).

Based on the information received, the individual makes a decision and test drives the vehicle.

The individual's satisfaction with his/her decision and with the dealership's service itself is largely a function of their interaction with the consultant and the potential vehicle during their meeting. The consultant should do everything possible to ensure a satisfactory experience for the customer, so that future business (and future referrals) are not at risk.

An investment is made on behalf of the consultant to understand the car buyers, listen, communicate, and retain information from their discussions.

Marketing strategies will build on this model, taking advantage of precipitating events, fostering word-of-mouth recommendations, and creating satisfaction through interacting with the client.

Summary of Opportunities and Threats in the Environment

Overall, the environment appears very positive for Mountain View Lease, LLC auto sales and leasing. The forces driving market demand, mainly economic and political/legal are strong, with new businesses forming, new residents moving into the county, and more complicated tax regulations requiring a knowledgeable accountant to keep company car records in order. On the negative side, barriers to entry are low.

The business is driven by referrals, so for the first few years Mountain View Lease, LLC will need to be more aggressive in getting new customers, who will then pass the word on, and the business can begin to experience organic growth.

STRATEGY & IMPLEMENTATION

Marketing Strategies

Target Markets — Business (Greater Pebbles)

Businesses with an emphasis on tax benefits of leasing cars rather then ownership.

Target Markets — Consumer (Greater Pebbles)

> Upper-income households.
> New residents in the area.
> Retired Individuals.
> Families seeking safety features found on many high-end vehicles.
> Seasonal residents.

Positioning and Product Strategy

For both business and consumer clients, Mountain View Lease, LLC will be positioned as a full-service auto sales and leasing service that takes the time to get to know the customer's situation and become a partner in their decision making process.

Distribution Strategy

Unlike products which are produced, then distributed and sold, auto sales and leasing services are produced and consumed simultaneously in a real-time environment. Thus, distribution issues center on making the services available in a convenient manner to the most number of potential clients. Mountain View Lease, LLC will maintain extended hours and meet with clients in their home or office, whichever is more convenient. This flexibility is especially attractive to elderly customers. Car buyers can contact Mountain View Lease, LLC by telephone, fax, and e-mail. Mountain View Lease, LLC offers evening and Saturday hours, in addition to the regular business hours.

Pricing Strategy Markup

Mountain View anticipates a 20% markup over car obtained from dealer auctions and fleet companies. The leasing industry norm for the leasing portion of the business is 10%.

PROMOTION STRATEGY

Promotion strategies will vary depending on the target market segment. Given the importance of word-of-mouth/referrals among all market segments when choosing a pre-driven car dealership, efforts are designed to create awareness, stimulate trial, and build referrals. A cost-effective campaign, focused on direct marketing, publicity, Internet web page, and advertising is being proposed.

Marketing Plan

Mountain View Lease, LLC auto sales and leasing can consider developing a one-page newsletter to be mailed quarterly to select target customers and prospects in its database. The newsletter can be used to update clients on available vehicles, leasing information, and tax-related benefits, but also serves as a reminder of what sets Mountain View Lease, LLC apart from other auto sales and leasing services—being a partner.

A news release will be sent to area newspapers and magazines announcing the launch of Mountain View Lease, LLC. Frank Simons is a member of the local Pebbles Area Chamber of Commerce. He will also make himself available for speaking engagements at other community or civic organizations. Becoming a sponsor in a community event (Festival of Summer, County Fair, Autumn Fest, various parades, bloodmobiles, etc.) is a low-cost way of increasing awareness and building goodwill in the community.

As a means of building repeat business, customers should be encouraged and rewarded for their repeat business. This can be accomplished by offering a discount special price to past customers who returned. Advertising is utilized primarily to attract and inform a new car buyer or business clients for the purpose of selling them a luxury car. It also serves to build awareness and name recognition of the company in general which is important for word-of-mouth referrals ("Oh yes, I've seen that company's ads before."). General methods of marketing:

Greater Pebbles Shopper/Sunday Shopper - advertising in this Wednesday and Sunday primarily classified newspaper reaches over 33,000 homes and businesses in the county twice each week. A 12-week schedule in the beginning will be undertaken. Mountain View Lease, LLC can use its business card as creative, and can be placed under the "Services Offered" section of the display/ classified ads.

Yellow Pages - Ameritech PagesPlus, Greater Greater Pebbles Telephone Directory. Research indicated that new residents or people who don't have many personal acquaintances to ask about auto sales and leasing services will look to the Yellow Pages to establish a list of potential auto sales and leasing services to call. Even a small 2" x 2" boxed ad can create awareness and attract the desired target client, above and beyond the ability of a simple listing to do so. Ameritech Yellow Pages covers the relevant market area, delivering over 30,000 copies to residents and businesses. Midwest Directories covers Greater Pebbles, with a circulation of 90,000, but is considered a second-tier directory to Ameritech.

Web Page - Opportunities exist for a business to establish themselves among the fast growing Internet information system. Internet advertising will reach area residents as well as seasonal/tourists for their permanent homes.

Cable TV - local cable outlet commercials to air.

All advertising will be demographically analyzed to maximize exposure effect and response.

Example Promotion Budget - 1999

Company brochure (2-color, 1,000 quantity, high quality paper)	$650.00
Lists (businesses, upper-income residents)	$450.00
Postage (mailing 300 pieces)	$400.00
Telephone follow-up ($0.50/call x 100 calls)	$50.00
Public relations activities and sponsorships	$500.00
Cable TV program (30 second spots)	$4,900.00
Newspaper advertising (Shopper)	$7,500.00
Yellow Pages advertising	$3,650.00
Miscellaneous flyers	$700.00
Web Page Maintenance	$200.00
Total for 1999	**$18,000.00**

Evaluation & Control Strategies

Objectives have been established for Mountain View Lease, LLC so that actual performance can be measured against them. Thus, at the end of 1999, Mountain View Lease, LLC should have:

- $185,250 in total revenue
- sold 72 vehicles and leased 35 of those cars

Each subsequent year, new objectives will be set for these benchmarks, and actual performance will be measured against them. If actual performance falls short of objectives, investigation will be made into the cause, and plans adjusted accordingly.

In addition, Mountain View Lease, LLC will keep track of the source of all new clients ("Where did you hear of me?") in order to measure the effectiveness of each type of promotion. Each subsequent year's budget should adjust spending accordingly.

FINANCIAL PLAN

Mountain View is seeking a construction build-out, start-up, and credit line loan of $275,000 and a start-up working capital and vehicle acquisition credit line of $225,000.

Phase I - Funding Amount Sought

Developmental costs for the start-up of this new auto sales and leasing services company are detailed. This Eight-Year Proforma schedule and its cash flow summary define the financial needs to develop a successful business and are the basis for the start-up capital amounts listed.

The following summary highlights the anticipated developmental costs and the first-year general operating expense. Vehicle acquisition funds are also noted.

Developmental Expenses

Classification:	Cost
Legal & Accounting	$2,000
Initial Advertising & Promotion	$3,000
Supplies	$500
Computer and Software	$2,500
Working Capital	$25,000
Founders Draw	$17,000
Consultant Fees	$2,500
Construction Build-Out	$272,145
Total	**$324,645**

General Operating Expenses

Classification:	Cost
Legal & Accounting	$1,000
Advertising & Promotion	$18,000
Supplies & Postage	$1,500
Software Upgrades	$650
Utilities & Phone	$14,400
Property Taxes	$4,800
Insurance	$4,800
Sewer	$300
Total	**$45,750**

Revolving Line of Credit

For Vehicle Acquisition	$175,355

The development of the Mountain View Lease, LLC will require the time and talents full-time of Frank Simons. His salary, office, and other related expenses during the start-up phase of the project are incorporated into the Eight-Year Proforma. Phase II growth amounts will be developed and sought at a later date, based upon needs to be determined at that time.

Financial Plan Assumptions

The following assumptions will be incorporated into the Mountain View Lease, LLC proforma statements.

- All operating costs are based on Mountain View Lease management research of similar operating companies.
- Automated informational system will reduce Mountain View Lease staff requirements.
- Developmental start-up costs are amortized over a five-year period.
- Overhead and operations costs are calculated on an annual basis.
- Mountain View Lease owner's salary is based on a fixed salary expense basis.
- All fixed and variable labor costs should rise annually at 5%.
- All revenues, past year five are figured to rise annually at 7.5%.
- Fixed annual, administrative, and office expenses rise at an annual rate of 2.5%.

Resume of Mr. Frank Simons　　　　　　　　　　　　　　　　　　　　　**Appendix A**

Work Experience

Masters Chevrolet Cadillac, Twin Cats, WI	1984-1997

Vice President & General Manager
Managing Partner with exclusive responsibility for daily operation.

Hallmark Loper Chrysler, Cincinnati, OH	1972-1984

Recruited as sales associate & appraiser. Advanced to:
    Used Car Manager & buyer
    General Sales Manager
    Vice President
    General Manager
Responsibilities included all aspects of daily operation, hiring, training, and motivation for sales and service departments.

KLP Pontiac Buick, Highbrow, IN	1970-1972

Promoted to Pontiac Buick Division
Supervisor: Elmer Matthews

KLP Chrysler Plymouth, Highbrow, IN	1969-1970

Hired as a Sales Associate
Supervisor: Jim Biller

Example Promotional Materials　　　　　　　　　　　　　　　　　　　　**Appendix B**

News Release

For Immediate Release:

A new full-service pre-driven vehicle leasing and sales business has opened its doors in Pebbles, Colorado. Owned and operated by Frank Simons, Mountain View Lease, LLC will cater to the needs of both businesses and individuals, highline vehicle buyers throughout Greater Pebbles.

"I realize there are several auto sales and leasing firms in the area, however, none specialize in the high-end pre-driven vehicle market, like we do," says Simons, a veteran with over 30 years in the industry. "But Mountain View Lease, LLC is different. I firmly believe in the importance of customizing my service to the needs of my clients."

In addition to traditional auto sales and leasing services, Simons will also offer pick-up and delivery services, along with evening and Saturday hours. He will also go to a customer's home, an especially attractive service for busy people. For all of his customers, Simons stresses the importance of selection and quality of new and pre-driven products.

Mountain View Lease, LLC is the alternative dealership the area has needed. As Simons emphasizes, "I truly am interested in the happiness of my customers, whether they're a small business operator like myself, a large corporation, or an individual just trying to drive the vehicle of their dreams."

For more information, contact Frank Simons at Mountain View Lease, LLC, 900 Minchon Drive, Pebbles, CO 80211.

Bowling Alley

BUSINESS PLAN

THE FAMILY BOWL

P.O. Box 12345
Omaha, Nebraska 68101

The Family Bowl business plan outlines a strategy for a bowling alley that caters to families and celebrates people of all nationalities. It will differentiate itself from other bowling alleys by providing a clean and friendly atmosphere. It also will have the largest number of lanes in the area. This plan was provided by Ameriwest Business Consultants, Inc.

- EXECUTIVE SUMMARY

- OBJECTIVES & GOALS

- BUSINESS DESCRIPTION, STATUS, AND OUTLOOK

- MANAGEMENT AND OWNERSHIP

- MARKET ANALYSIS

- MARKETING STRATEGIES

- FINANCIAL PLANS

Confidentiality Statement

EXECUTIVE SUMMARY

BUSINESS DESCRIPTION

The purpose of the Family Bowl is to provide the area with a bowling alley which caters primarily to families. The atmosphere will be friendly and open. The alley will be maintained to the utmost degree of cleanliness and maintenance, unlike similar operations in the area. The alley's employees will display a new attitude. They will treat customers like first-class citizens and try to make them feel like they are at home. On the premises will be pool tables, video games, and dart boards. We will offer for sale pride items, in a gift shop, from various cultures around the world. The facility will have a first rate sound and lighting system. The services will be offered at a competitive price and pricing will be reviewed periodically. We plan to become the premier bowling alley in the area within two years. We will offer the best entertainment, atmosphere, cultural awareness, and service in metro Omaha, Nebraska.

The facility will normally be closed on Monday. Proposed hours are Tuesday, Wednesday, and Thursday, 2:00 P.M. through 2:00 A.M. On Friday and Saturday the hours will be 12:00 P.M. through 2:00 A.M. On Sunday the hours will be 4:00 P.M. through 2:00 A.M. The premises will be open for a total of 74 hours per week.

CURRENT POSITION AND FUTURE OUTLOOK

The business is in a start-up mode. Plans call for starting operation by the spring of 2000. During the first full year of operation we plan to serve an average of 10,000 customers per month. The second year this will increase to 15,000 per month. Years three through five will show gradual increases to 18,000 per month which we consider to be our capacity. To attain these goals we will use a combination of media advertising, flyers, direct mail, and word-of mouth. Franchising the concept is a possibility for the future.

MANAGEMENT AND OWNERSHIP

The company will be set up as a corporation with Robert Smyth and his wife, Julie, as the major shareholders, incorporators, and directors. Robert Smyth will serve as president and manager. He will also provide the leadership to run this company. He has over 17 years experience as owner and operator of various small business operations, and has dealt with the public as a personnel officer in the military. Initially, up to thirteen other employees will be needed. These employees will be involved in bartending, security, and waiting on tables. They will be a combination of part-time and full-time. When volume picks up, additional part-time or full-time employees will be hired as the workload requires. Small Business Nebraska, Inc. will provide help in additional areas such as setting up the books, logo design, and general business advising when necessary and to supplement the Smyths' overall business knowledge. The services of an accountant, attorney, and a qualified insurance agent have been retained.

UNIQUENESS AND DIFFERENTIATION OF THE SERVICE

The Family Bowl will be the largest bowling alley which caters to families. It will have the largest number of lanes in the area.

The idea of this company is to provide customers with a semi-formal, social setting, and entertainment that does not exist in this part of the state. We will provide customers with high-tech lights and sound, video games, pool tables, and a full line of entertainment. In addition we will cater to private parties and special groups such as schools, senior citizens, and church groups.

The growth potential is virtually unlimited for the greater Omaha area. The population is growing at an accelerated rate. Currently over 12% of the population in Omaha is young. They will be very receptive to a concept such as this that can offer them atmosphere, cleanliness, and security at a competitive price.

It is rare in today's business world to find a true market void. That is exactly what Family Bowl has done. It is combining the latest in technology with an unfilled need and promises to deliver a high quality new product at a competitive price. Our proposed facility will have little true competition in metro Omaha.

FUNDS REQUIRED AND USAGE

The initial start-up expenses will be approximately $300,000. The inventory, equipment, furniture, fixtures, and leasehold improvements will cost approximately $125,000. Investors and/or a bank loan must be secured in the amount of $125,000 at 14.0% amortized over ten years. The initial investors will furnish approximately $50,000, which is 18.5% of the total. After all expenses of start-up, $40,000 will remain in a new business checking account and will provide the balance of the initial working capital.

Projected 5-Year Income Statement

(MOST LIKELY CASE)

	Projected 2000	Projected 2001	Projected 2002	Projected 2003	Projected 2004
Total Revenue	836,000	919,200	1,010,688	1,111,290	1,221,916
Cost of Sales	285,720	314,292	345,722	380,294	418,321
Gross Profit	550,280	604,908	664,966	730,996	803,595
Selling, General, Expense	587,033	620,169	658,739	706,195	757,418
Income Before Taxes	-36,753	-15,261	6,227	24,801	46,177
Income Taxes	0	0	0	0	0
INCOME AFTER TAXES	**-36,753**	**-15,261**	**6,227**	**24,801**	**46,177**

(OPTIMISTIC CASE)

	Projected 2000	Projected 2001	Projected 2002	Projected 2003	Projected 2004
Total Revenue	1,003,200	1,103,040	1,212,826	1,333,548	1,466,299
Cost of Sales	342,864	377,150	414,866	456,353	501,985
Gross Profit	660,336	725,890	797,959	877,195	964,314
Selling, General, Expense	704,440	744,203	790,487	847,434	908,902
Income Before Taxes	-44,104	-18,313	7,472	29,761	55,412
Income Taxes	0	0	0	0	0
INCOME AFTER TAXES	**-44,104**	**-18,313**	**7,472**	**29,761**	**55,412**

**Projected 5-Year
Income Statement**

Continued

(PESSIMISTIC CASE)

	Projected 2000	Projected 2001	Projected 2002	Projected 2003	Projected 2004
Total Revenue	668,800	735,360	808,550	889,032	977,533
Cost of Sales	228,576	251,434	276,578	304,235	334,657
Gross Profit	440,224	483,926	531,973	584,797	642,876
Selling, General, Expense	469,626	496,135	526,991	564,956	605,934
Income Before Taxes	-29,402	-12,209	4,982	19,841	36,942
Income Taxes	0	0	0	0	0
INCOME AFTER TAXES	**-29,402**	**-12,209**	**4,982**	**19,841**	**36,942**

Notes:

1. The most likely case assumes 10,000 customers per month the first year with each spending an average of $25.00 per visit. The second year the number of customers will rise to 15,000 per month also assumes each will spend $30.00 per visit.
2. The optimistic case assumes revenues and expenses will increase 15% over the most likely case. The pessimistic case assumes revenues and expenses will decrease 15% below the most likely case above.

**OBJECTIVES &
GOALS**

1. To provide a high quality service so that customers will perceive great value and give them the opportunity to interact with other families in a safe and clean environment.

2. Service an average of 10,000 customers per month during the first full year of business and 15,000 customers per month the second year. The ultimate goal is to reach 18,000 customers per month by the third year

3. To repay the entire loan amount by the end of the third year and to provide the shareholders with a stable and sufficient income after that.

4. Our goal is to become the premier bowling alley in metro Omaha during the next two years.

5. Family Bowl plans to closely monitor changing technology to be certain that the company is using the latest and most cost effective equipment and that it keeps up with current trends in the marketplace.

6. When economically feasible we plan to open one or more locations and/or consider franchising our service.

When growth has stabilized we plan to add extra services for customer convenience such as large screen television, enhanced game rooms, and food services. In addition to the above goals we will survey our customers and make changes in our programs and add services to meet their changing ideas in the marketplace.

**Strategies for
Achieving Goals**

To obtain the first two sets of goals we will try to maximize sales with an extensive campaign to promote our service. We will utilize the radio stations and newspaper along with brochures, media advertising, pamphlets, direct customer contact, use of coupons, referrals, and a variety of other advertising and marketing tools to reach the customer base of metro Omaha. We expect to flood the market with advertising until consumers become aware of us and more comfortable with our company. As we grow, word-of-mouth referrals will bring in increasing numbers of customers and we will reduce our reliance on advertising.

The dominant driving force behind our company will be profit and income.

To become the premier bowling alley in metro Omaha, we will offer outstanding quality, cleanliness, security, long hours, and reasonable pricing. We will listen to our customers and conduct surveys.

As we grow and build a reputation for our people and culturally oriented atmosphere with excellent security, service, and entertainment, we will offer frequent user discounts. In the future we may consider diversification and enter new market areas.

BUSINESS DESCRIPTION, STATUS, AND OUTLOOK

The Family Bowl will be a full service bowling alley combining entertainment suited to a specific culture at a competitive price. We will try to promote an atmosphere that will remind many people of their homeland. This is a relatively new concept for this part of the country. Robert Smyth will operate the business as a corporation. The principal shareholders will be he and his wife, Julie. Initially, Robert Smyth will manage the operation with daily input from Julie and the other investors. The new equipment and enhanced lighting and sound systems will also give us market advantages. A building will be leased that best meets the goals and market we are trying to reach. Ultimately, we will construct our own building to expand to the full potential of this business.

The biggest problem this venture will face will be creating customer awareness of our services. We will use a combination of advertising techniques to increase this awareness. Once a general awareness is present, the industry has a virtually unlimited growth potential.

The future holds the promise for almost unlimited growth and income as the business matures and considers other markets and products. Complementary products such as additional video games, more pool tables, dance lessons, and higher profile entertainment will all be considered in the future in response to customer surveys indicating their wants and needs. Complete food services will be offered in the future as the needs are demonstrated.

MANAGEMENT AND OWNERSHIP

Robert Smyth has owned several successful small businesses in Texas and Nebraska. He attended Texas State University from 1979 through 1983. His major was civil engineering and his minor was business. He also has experience as a bartender, bouncer, and cashier in pool halls and arcades. He had 14 years experience in personnel management in the military. These skills will help ensure that the Family Bowl will have a solid foundation of management skills available to it.

The Smyths' will supplement their skills by using outside consultants in areas such as legal work, income tax preparation, insurance, and general business advising.

The business will be set up as a corporation. This form of legal entity was chosen primarily for liability reasons and to make it easier to secure investors. To begin operation, as many as thirteen full- and part-time employees will be hired to help in areas such as bartending, waiting on tables, and security. As the business grows additional part-time or full-time employees may be added to handle the increased workload.

The Service — An Unfilled Need

Nebraska growth in families is the ninth greatest in the country. The past decade has seen this segment of the population grow by more than 30%. It is growing 5 1/2 times as fast as the general population.

The few existing bowling alleys that cater to families are dark and dingy. They pay little attention to cleanliness, maintenance of premises, and security for their patrons. Family Bowl and its ownership will embrace the family community and try to become a focal point for them. We will promote families whenever possible.

The idea for a family-oriented bowling alley was formulated when Robert and Julie Smyth noticed a need for a quality bowling alley which caters to families in southern Omaha. They have conducted extensive surveys of the local families. These surveys have shown a great interest in such an alley. These surveys also have indicated that cleanliness, good maintenance, good security, quality live entertainment, and a semi-formal atmosphere are all desirable characteristics for which people are looking.

The timing for such a business is perfect. A significant window of opportunity exists for a company such as the kind we are proposing. This proposed business will be providing the "Right Service at the Right Time."

Uniqueness of the Service

It is rare in today's world that a true market void exists. Our service will meet the "unfilled need" described above by providing customers with competitively priced bowling alley facilities combined with the latest in lighting and sound systems and longer hours. We will be considerably larger than the typical bowling alley.

Customers will be attracted to the Family Bowl because our atmosphere, pricing, and facilities. They will be made to feel welcome and as part of the family.

Some major advantages Family Bowl will have over potential competition and conventional bowling alleys are:

- Larger and newer facility
- Lower operating expenses
- Best sound and lighting system in the area
- New concept—cater primarily to families
- Live diversified entertainment
- Location
- Longer hours
- English lessons for those interested
- Dance lessons for patrons wanting to keep up with the latest dance steps
- The cleanest restrooms in the city
- Security personnel and other employees who can speak both Spanish and English
- The largest dance floor in the area
- Display cabinets with pride items for purchase such as flags, hats, scarves, etc.
- Family Bowl will sponsor ethnic festivals and holidays

MARKET ANALYSIS

MARKET OVERVIEW, SIZE, AND SEGMENTS

Currently, the market distribution is shared by three major participants. They are all located on the north side of Omaha. This market segment has been relatively stable over the past five years.

The market area we will concentrate on is Greater Omaha County. This includes 6 surrounding towns. Additionally, we expect to draw some patrons from a northern town which is only 40 minutes away. These areas have been growing rapidly the past several years and should continue for the foreseeable future. Once the concept catches on locally, we feel the potential is unlimited. As we grow we will have the financial capacity to carry on an advertising campaign on a regional basis.

The economy is in the midst of a particularly strong growth period. Many new jobs are being added to the local community. Ever increasing numbers of Californians are moving to this location. All of these factors are cause for a much greater interest in bowling alleys. All of this activity can only help our attempts to start a bowling alley.

Listed below are just some of the reasons that the Omaha area is growing and why it is a good time to be starting any kind of new business:

- The local economy is booming and virtually busting at the seams.
- Omaha has become a magnet for religious organizations. More than 65 nationally based Christian organizations are headquartered here. The largest has over 1,200 employees (especially women) and an operating budget of over $85 million.
- The new Apple Computer plant is setting records for production and is adding new employees monthly.
- Omaha has a new airport and a nearby Free Trade Enterprise Zone that should grow and attract even more new businesses.
- Gambling in nearby Red Hawk continues to draw many visitors and some new businesses.
- Every week, we see articles in the newspapers of California residents and companies relocating here.
- The world renowned Four Seasons Hotel is building a new convention facility here.
- MCI and Quantum Electronics are undergoing large increases in their operations here that should add many hundreds of employees.
- Prairie Springs is only 50 minutes away and is another good market for businesses in the area.
- Many experts predict metro Omaha to become the fastest growing city in the state between now and the year 2005.
- The local economy is now more diversified than it was when troubles occurred in the local economy in the late 1980s and early 1990s.

The estimated population of Omaha County in 1998 was 900,000 people. The number of households was 480,000. Currently, this market is growing at an annual rate of 3-5%. Projections see this trend continuing for the balance of this next decade.

From the above figures it can readily be seen that the potential market for our services is huge. We feel with our pricing and value we will become a price and industry leader within two years.

Customer Profile

Our surveys have shown the following mix of patrons that use Spanish-oriented alleys:

- 5% White
- 3% Black
- Median age of local Hispanics is 25.9 years, whereas the median age of the rest of Nebraskans is 32.5 years.
- Majority of patrons will be in the middle to upper income brackets.
- There are over 45,000 Hispanics in Omaha, nearly 40,000 in Lincoln and over 20,000 in surrounding areas. They have increased more than 5 1/2 times as fast as the general population.

Typically, our customers will be middle to upper income. Beyond the local market we could eventually tap into a more regional market. The advantage of our service is that it could appeal to all segments of the community.

Throughout this business plan we have taken a very conservative approach to developing our financial projections.

Competition

Our primary competition are the bowling alleys listed below. On a limited basis there are other competitors such as strip alleys, country and western bars, and other bowling alleys.

The following table summarizes the local competition:

Competitor Name	Strengths	Weaknesses
Bowl More 1004 N. Main	Well established Good local support Well maintained dance floor Brings in popular bands Potential to expand Owner well known in area Serves large portion of Mexican population	Dirty and has bad smell Filthy & small restrooms Poor security Allow underage patrons Poor facilities and maintenance Only 2 pool tables Lack of parking
Bowlalot 1000 E. Main	Good location Good local support Owner prominent in Hispanic community	Always filthy Outdated facilities Failure to keep up with recent trends
Queen's Palace 2815 E. Colfax	Newly remodeled Sufficient parking Fair neighborhood Specialty alley New owner Established clientele	Caters to Puerto Rican music No bands brought in Location is hard to find Very small Unfriendly personnel No pool tables or food

Our facility will be more convenient than any other facility for over 75% of the population in metro Omaha.

The marketplace is currently shared by the above outlined 3 major participants. This market is increasing about 5-7% per year.

Identification of Strengths and Weaknesses

Functions	Strong (+)	Average (0)	Weak (-)	Major Strengths and/or Weaknesses Compared to Competitor
General Administration (Management)			X	will hire consultants to help with business concepts when necessary
Marketing		X		
Finance / Planning			X	will hire consultants to help
Human Resources		X		better performance achievable
Operations		X		can improve
Production		X		
Purchasing		X		
Distribution		X		
Servicing	X			high customer satisfaction
Quality of Service	X			timely service on major repairs

Functions	Strong (+)	Average (0)	Weak (-)	Major Strengths and/or Weaknesses Compared to Competitor
Company Policies		X		
Product Mix	X			several choices available
Product Features		X		
Options	X			better options available
Warranties/Guarantees	X			the best around
Reliability	X			best product and service available
Desirability		X		
Advertising			X	hire consultants to improve
Market Leadership			X	not very aggressive
Sales Force			X	needs more training
Overhead			X	existing levels are too high; can be greatly reduced with new owners
Pricing		X		low for service
Delivery Time		X		
Location		X		
Facilities		X		

We feel we will have strengths in product features, management, planning, human resources, quality of service, product mix, options, and reliability because we will have new equipment, pricing, location, and facilities. We will have low risk exposure in the areas of technology, inflation/interest rates, regulatory environment, management ability, location, facilities, and suppliers.

We perceive medium risk exposure in the local economy, strategy, and vulnerability to substitutes, finance and planning, company policies, sales force, and pricing. We have retained the services of specialists to help in various areas such as marketing, setting up the books, providing management reports and general overall business operation advice.

Since we are new to this type of business we will have a high degree of risk in this area. It will take a little time to gain knowledge in developing the business and create a customer awareness of our company and our concept. To help reduce this risk we will hire experienced consultants.

Risk Analysis

ELEMENT	LOW	RATINGS MEDIUM	HIGH
Industry (Maturity and Cyclicality)	X		
Market/Local Economy	X		
Competitive Position		X	
Dependence upon other Companies		X	
Vulnerability to Substitutes		X	
Technology		X	
Distribution		X	
Regulatory Environment		X	
Suppliers		X	
Strategy		X	
Assumptions	X		
Financial Performance		X	
Management Performance		X	
Inflation/Interest Rates	X		
Others		X	
Overall Risk		X	

MARKETING STRATEGIES

PRICING AND VALUE

We will offer a series of cost savings options to groups that use our facility the most frequently. Our intention is to raise the public's awareness of our company. We plan to review our prices and those of our competitors every three months. We will review direct material costs, direct labor costs, and total overhead expenses. We will continually monitor the cost of providing our service to each customer. We will offer discounts to larger groups. We will offer various free or reduced rate programs to get customers acquainted with us.

At this point there is a certain amount of price restrictions in this service. With the current level of competition we must be careful not to price ourselves out of the market.

Numerous package deals will be available to customers. Various marketing strategies we may try include the following:

- Discounts for larger groups
- Frequent user discounts
- Special party rates
- Spirited cultural competition

SELLING TACTICS

Our company's marketing strategy will incorporate plans to promote our line of services through several different channels and on different levels of use. We will advertise heavily on the popular local Hispanic radio stations and newspapers.

We will try to satisfy the market void in this area for indoor entertainment. We will flood the market with advertising and try to go after our specific targets. We will try to capture their attention, pique their interest, make them feel that they must have our services.

We will offer continuous promotional rates. The results sell themselves. We will offer discounts to frequent users. The more a customer uses our services the cheaper it will become for them.

We will also become a MasterCard and Visa charge card merchant to enable us to more readily charge our customers.

In order to sell our facility we shall consider a variety of promotions including:

- Reserve certain hours for unique groups such as children, senior citizens, adults, etc.
- Conduct special theme nights, use ethnic holidays, family night, charity promotion night, game night, contest night, etc.
- Cultivate local churches, and Hispanic organizations
- Promote birthday parties
- Offer dance lessons at no charge
- Early bird specials

ADVERTISING, PROMOTION, AND DISTRIBUTION OF SERVICES

We recognize that the key to success at this time requires extensive promotion.

Advertising goals include all of the following:

- Position the company as the premier alley in metro Omaha
- Increase public awareness of the Family Bowl and its benefits

- Increase public awareness of our company and establish a professional image
- Maximize efficiency by continually monitoring media effectiveness
- Consider a possible credit coupon in some of the advertisements
- Take out an ad in the yellow pages beginning in 2000
- Develop a brochure or pamphlet to explain our service and company
- Create a distinctive business card and company letterhead
- Consider using a direct mail approach
- Use a mix of media to saturate the marketplace
- Spend a minimum of $25,000 in advertising the first year and $35,000 the second year

We will develop a public relations policy that will help increase awareness of our company and product. To achieve these goals we will consider some or all of the following:

Public Relations

Develop a press release and a company backgrounder as a public relations tool.

Develop a telephone script to handle customer and advertiser contact.

Develop a survey to be completed by customers to help determine the following:
1. How did they hear about us?
2. What influenced them to use our service?
3. How well did our service satisfy their needs?
4. How efficient was our service?
5. Did they have any problems getting through to us?
6. Did they shop competitors before selecting us?
7. How did they initially perceive our company and product?
8. Where are most of our customers located?
9. Do they have suggestions for improving our service or our approach to advertising?
10. What additional services would they like us to offer?
11. Would they recommend us to others?

Join the Chamber of Commerce to keep abreast of developments in the community and market trends.

ASSUMPTIONS, DEFINITIONS, AND NOTES

FINANCIAL PLANS

Family Bowl has used the following assumptions in preparing this business plan:

Average number of customers will be 10,000 per month the first year, 15,000 per month the second year and leveling off at 18,000 per month by the third year.

Revenue sources are as follows:
- Cover charge income will equal 7.08% of total
- Each patron will have 5 drinks per visit at an average price of $2.50 per drink
- Game and food income will be 2.65% of total
- Drink income will equal 88.2 % of the total

Customer volume will be greater in warm weather months.

Growth in sales will be 29.6% the second year, 25% the third, 15% the fourth, and 10% the fifth year.

We have assumed a high and low case by adding or subtracting 15% to the most likely case.

Inflation Rates to remain stable at 3-5%.

Robust local economy.

Interest Rates to remain flat and basically unchanged.

Wage Rates to remain flat.

Local unemployment rates to remain low at approximately 4-5%.

Assumes average income per customer per visit of $14.18.

Assume a rate of pay of $9.00 per hour for security personnel and $4.50 per hour for bartenders and waitresses.

Payroll taxes and benefits will equal 20% of payroll expenses .

Assumes salaries for officers of 3.5% of sales.

Assumes a loan of $125,000 at 14.00% amortized over ten years and having monthly payments of $1,707.93 per month.

Cost of goods sold will be 40% of drink income.

Maintenance, Repair, and Breakage equals 3% of total income.

Advertising & Marketing (Public Relations) is 3.5 % of income.

Amortization of organization expenses will be over 60 months.

Depreciation will be computed using straight line method over 60 months.

Insurance is at 2% of total income.

Telephone and utility expense will be 1.25% of total income.

Office supplies expenses is set at 1% of total income.

Contingency and miscellaneous expenses are set at 3% of total income.

Income tax for both state and federal is set at 20% for year one and 28% for year two.

Dividend payout is set at 15% of net income.

Start-up Expenses

Category	Amount
Cash and Working Capital	$28,150
Material-Supplies-Inventory	10,000
Furniture and Fixtures (Includes 6 pool tables)	25,500
Equipment including lights and sound system	40,000
Rent Deposits	9,700
License Fees / Permits	1,000
Insurance (First year paid in advance)	1,800
Utilities & Telephone	500
Legal, Professional and Consulting Fees	1,500
Security System & Leasehold Improvements	5,000
Initial Entertainment Budget	6,000
Opening Advertisement & Promotion	3,000
Miscellaneous	2,850
TOTAL	**$135,000**

Items to be purchased include 50 tables and 200 chairs, bar equipment, pool tables, sound and lighting systems, initial inventory, leasehold improvements, and various furniture and fixtures. After all expenses $40,000 will remain in a checking account as working capital.

The total investment of $135,000 will be obtained as follows:

1. Cash	$25,000
2. Bank Loan /Investors (Combination)	$110,000

Financial Statements Analysis

Many lenders and some investors have adopted the practice of placing constraints and covenants on a borrower in order to ensure that certain levels of liquidity and profitability are maintained. These limits are usually presented to the borrower in the form of loan compliance criteria and are used by lenders/investors for evaluating the loan on an ongoing basis. Some common limits used by lenders/investors are indicated above and demonstrates how this company would do when compared to the industry in each area.

Year	Net Working Capital	Current Ratio	Quick Ratio	EBIT/ Interest	EBIT/ I+P	DEBT Equity	Z-Score	**Loan Compliance Covenants**
2000	$208,582	3.25	1.17	3.62	2.31	2.43	6.57	
2001	$298,918	4.09	1.65	9.02	0.22	1.17	6.93	
2002	$437,929	5.11	2.34	13.36	2.90	0.67	6.90	
2003	$611,823	6.23	2.86	18.12	4.09	0.43	6.81	
2004	$809,223	7.36	3.45	23.56	0.00	0.30	6.80	
Industry Median	N/A	1.40	0.20	2.10	N/A	2.70	N/A	

Ratio Comparison

	Projected 2000	Projected 2001	Projected 2002	Projected 2003	Projected 2004	Industry Average 1998
Liquidity Ratios:						
Current Ratio	3.25	4.09	5.11	6.23	7.36	1.40
Quick Ratio	1.17	1.65	2.34	2.86	3.45	0.20
Sales / Receivables	85.88	85.88	85.88	85.88	85.88	87.10
Day's Receivables	4.25	4.25	4.25	4.25	4.25	4.19
Cost of Sales / Inventory	9.13	8.11	7.30	6.08	5.21	3.10
Day's Inventory	40.00	45.00	50.00	60.00	70.00	117.74
Cost of Sales / Payables	40.56	40.56	40.56	40.56	40.56	40.70
Day's Payables	9.00	9.00	9.00	9.00	9.00	8.97
Sales / Work. Capital	9.69	7.57	5..94	4.79	3.98	12.00
EBIT / Interest	3.62	9.02	13.36	18.12	23.56	2.10
Net Profit + Depr. + Amort./C.L.T.D.	3.89	8.03	9.82	10.87	11.30	5.20
Leverage Ratios						
Fixed Assets / Tangible Net Worth	0.15	0.08	0.04	0.02	0.01	0.30
Debt / Worth	2.43	1.17	0.67	0.43	0.30	2.70
Operating Ratios						
Profit Before Tax / Tan. Net Worth	49.73%	71.38%	60.13%	50.25%	42.32%	22.00%
Profit Before Tax / Total Assets	14.37%	32.77%	35.83%	35.02%	32.58%	5.10%
Sales / Net Fixed Assets	121.37%	134.66%	190.69%	284.06%	476.03%	3.73%
Sales / Total Assets	5.30%	4.72%	4.17%	3.64%	3.18%	2.80%
Other Ratios / Numbers:						
Officers Salaries (Actual)	$30,000	$31,500	$33,233	$35,160	$37,270	N/A
Equity (Net Worth)	$113,346	$222,644	$373,952	$561,796	$779,989	N/A
Loans Balance (Actual)	$188,209	$175,086	$160,481	$144,226	$126,135	N/A
% Deprec., Amort. / Sales	0.00	0.00	0.00	0.00	0.00	0.60
% Officer's Compensation/Sales	0.01	0.01	0.01	0.01	0.01	0.02
Tangible Net Worth (NW-Intangibles)	$110,146	$220,244	$372,352	$560,996	$779,989	N/A
Working Capital (Actual)	$208,582	$298,918	$437,929	$611,823	$809,223	N/A

Ratio Comparison

Continued

	Projected 2000	Projected 2001	Projected 2002	Projected 2003	Projected 2004	Industry Average 1998
Gross Profit						
Key Percentages as a Percent of Gross Profit						
Rent	14.70%	13.78%	12.64%	11.89%	11.46%	0.00%
Interest Paid	4.27%	3.57%	2.87%	2.32%	1.87%	0.00%
Depreciation & Amortization	1.56%	1.46%	1.33%	1.24%	1.19%	0.00%
Officers Compensation	6.13%	5.74%	5.27%	4.95%	4.77%	0.00%
Taxes Paid	2.33%	8.74%	11.51%	13.25%	14.33%	N/A

Sources for the Industry Averages

Ratio analysis can be one of the most useful financial management tools. It becomes important when you look at the trend of each ratio over time. It also becomes important when compared to averages of a particular industry.

- Robert Morris Annual Statement Studies for 1995
- Industry Norms and Key Business Ratios 1995-1996
- Troy Almanac of Business and Industrial Financial Ratios for 1996

Ratio Analysis

Current Ratio is an approximate measure of a firm's ability to meet its current obligations and is calculated as Current Assets divided by Current Liabilities. This ratio shows an upward trend and indicates that if the company meets its goals it will be relatively more stable than the industry in general.

Revenue to Working Capital Ratio is a measure of the margin of protection for current creditors. This ratio is on a downward trend and indicates a good level of safety for creditors.

EBIT to interest Ratio is a measure of ability to meet annual interest payments. Since this ratio is above industry averages, the company should have no problem servicing its debt and can even service greater amounts of debt.

The Current Maturities Coverage Ratio measures the ability to pay current maturities of long term debt with cash flow from operations. It is calculated as Net Income Depreciation, Amortization divided by current portion of long term debt. This ratio shows an upward trend which indicates the company should be better to service its debt than the average company.

The Fixed Assets to Tangible Net Worth Ratio measures the extent to which owner's equity has been invested in the business. Since this ratio is on a downward trend, it provides an even larger "cushion" to creditors in the event of liquidation.

The Debt to Equity Ratio expresses the relationship between capital contributed by creditors and capital contributed by owners. This ratio shows a downward trend which would seem to indicate that if the company meets its goals that it will provide greater long-term financial safety for creditors.

The Earnings before Taxes to Total Assets Ratio expresses the pre-tax return on total assets and measures the effectiveness of management in employing available resources. Since this ratio is above industry averages, the company would be more efficient than the industry in its effective employment of resources.

The Revenue to Total Assets Ratio is a general measure of ability to generate revenue in relation to total assets. This ratio is above industry averages which can indicate that the company is efficient in using available resources to generate revenue as compared to the industry.

The Depreciation, Amortization to Revenue Ratio is a general measure of cost to generate revenue under the matching principal. Since this ratio is consistently below industry averages it would seem to indicate that the company is more efficient generating revenue as compared to the industry.

AVERAGE MONTHLY BREAK-EVEN ANALYSIS - 2000

Cost Variables	——Per Month-1st Year—— Optimistic -15%	Most Likely Case	Pessimistic 15%
FIXED COSTS:			
Rentals/Leases	$5,100	$6,000	$6,900
Salaries (Fixed)	$2,125	$2,500	$2,875
Insurance	$708	$833	$958
Depreciation & Amortization	$542	$638	$733
Interest	$1,483	$1,744	$2,006
Utilities/Phone	$885	$1,042	$1,198
(other fixed costs)	$0	$0	$0
Total Fixed Costs	**$10,843**	**$12,757**	**$14,670**

	——Per Month-1st Year—— Optimistic -15%	Most Likely Case	Pessimistic 15%
VARIABLE COSTS			
Cost of Goods Sold	$69,020	$81,200	$93,380
Variable Labor/Wages	$10,908	$12,833	$14,758
Advertising	$4,250	$5,000	$5,750
Professional Services	$213	$250	$288
(other variable cost)	$6,227	$7,326	$8,425
Total Variable Costs	$90,618	$106,610	$122,601

	——Per Month-1st Year—— Optimistic 15%	Most Likely Case	Pessimistic -15%
SALES AND INCOME DATA:			
Average Income per Customer	$2,209.48	$2,209.48	$2,209.48
Average # of Customers per Month	88.65	77.08	65.52
RESULTS			
Fixed Costs per Customer	$122.32	$165.49	$223.90
Variable Costs per Customer	$1,022.25	$1,383.04	$1,871.18
Break-Even Number of Customers	9.13	15.44	43.36
Number of Customers over Break-Even	79.51	61.65	22.16
Break-Even Sales Amount	$20,179.52	$34,104.94	$95,811.36
Gross Profit per Customer	$1,187.23	$826.44	$338.30
Gross Profit (over Break-Even)	$94,399.98	$50,947.92	$7,495.85

Break-Even Analysis is a mathematical technique for analyzing the relationship between profits and fixed and variable costs. It is also a profit planning tool for calculating the point at which sales will equal costs. The above analysis indicates the first year break-even number of customers at 3,716 per month and break-even income at $52,699.69 per month. Anything over these amounts will be profit.

Rates of Return for The Family Bowl

	Net Income	IRR	MIRR	Annual Dividends	Total Assets
Initial Investment	($70,000)				
2000	$43,346	0.00%	-38.08%	$0	$381,321
2001	$109,298	59.70%	155.25%	$0	$479,811
2002	$151,308	96.94%	278.64%	$0	$624,818
2003	$187,844	111.92%	357.20%	$0	$804,907
2004	$218,193	118.31%	411.42%	$0	$1,013,130

ASSUMPTIONS:

Income figures are after taxes

Dividend Payout = 50% of After Tax Income

Reinvestment rate = 7%

IRR = INTERNAL RATE OF RETURN

MIRR = MODIFIED RATE OF RETURN

ROI = RATE OF RETURN ON OWNER'S INVESTMENT

ROA = RATE OF RETURN ON TOTAL ASSETS

IRR = the interest rate received for an investment and income that occur at regular periods

MIRR = adds the cost of funds and interest received on reinvestment of cash to the IRR

	2000	2001	2002	2003	2004
Return on Assets	11.37%	22.78%	24.22%	23.34%	21.54%
Return on Investment	0.00%	0.00%	0.00%	0.00%	0.00%
Income Per Share	$0.62	$1.56	$2.16	$2.68	$3.12
Dividends Per Share	$0.00	$0.00	$0.00	$0.00	$0.00

CONCLUSIONS AND SUMMARY

We feel that the type of company and service we are proposing is hitting the market at just the right time. We plan to fully repay the loan by the end of the third year. However, we will schedule repayments over ten years to give us flexibility. By applying our conservative projections, income for the first year is expected to be $21,194 after taxes and debt service. This will rise to $76,822 in the second and $124,363 by the fifth year. The business should be open for business by spring of 2000.

Coffee Bean Plant/Exporter

BUSINESS PLAN   SILVERA & SONS LTDA

Ouro Fino
Minas Gerais, Brazil

This company prepares coffee beans grown in Brazil for export to U.S. specialty roasters and Brazilian wholesalers. Company success is determined largely by their reputation for being a provider of the highest quality Arabica beans in the world. Since demand for their coffee beans exceeds current production, they plan to bring their facility to maximum production to meet this need. This business plan was compiled using Business Plan Pro™, by Palo Alto Software, copyright © 2000.

- EXECUTIVE SUMMARY

- COMPANY SUMMARY

- PRODUCTS

- MARKET ANALYSIS SUMMARY

- STRATEGY AND IMPLEMENTATION SUMMARY

- MANAGEMENT SUMMARY

- FINANCIAL PLAN

EXECUTIVE SUMMARY

Silvera & Sons prepares green Arabica coffee beans grown in Brazil for exportation to American specialty roasters and sells to wholesalers on the Brazilian market. We will expand production capacity from 72,000/60kg bags per year to 120-160,000/60kg per year. Our coffee stands out from that of the competition. We prepare the top five percent, in terms of quality standards, of all Arabica beans on the market. Our customers seek this product as it provides them with a point of differentiation to specialty roasters. In the past six years, demand for our coffee has exceeded the amount we are able to supply and we have been forced to refuse requests for larger shipments.

We predict growth of thirty percent in the first year with sales exceeding ($BRL) 26,208,000. In year three the plant will run at maximum capacity and based on the current price of coffee we expect profits of ($BRL) 1.5 million. We have positive indicators from current importers that the additional amount of beans will be sold.

Our keys to success are:

1. Establishing and maintaining working relationships and contractual agreements with American importers and Brazilian coffee brokers and wholesalers.
2. Bringing the new facility to maximum production within three years of operation.
3. Increasing our profit margin to seventeen and one-half percent (17.5%) with the use of improved technology in the new facility.
4. Effectively communicating to current and potential customers, through targeted efforts, our position as a differentiated provider of the highest quality Arabica beans in the world.

Objectives

The objectives of Silvera & Sons:

- Increase production and sale from 78,000/60kg bags per year to approximately 100,000/60kg bags per year in the first year of operation at the proposed facility and reach maximum capacity of 120,000/60kg bags per year by year three.
- Increase sales from ($BRL) 17.9 million to ($BRL) 26.2 million in the first full year of operation.
- Establish strategic relationships with 10-15 American importers in Los Angeles, San Francisco, and Seattle.
- Increase gross margins from fifteen percent (15%) to seventeen percent (17%) in the next three years.

Mission

Silvera & Sons Ltda. seeks to serve coffee importers and enthusiasts by exceeding minimum acceptable quality standards and by providing the highest quality product at the lowest possible price. We value our relationships with current and future customers and hope to communicate our appreciation to them through our outstanding, guaranteed product quality, personal service, and efficient delivery. Our commitment to our customers and the country of Brazil will be reflected through honest and responsible business.

COMPANY SUMMARY

Silvera & Sons buys and prepares raw coffee in parchment (pergamino), or coffee in its post-harvest stage. The finished product, green Arabica coffee beans, are packaged in 60kg sacks and sold on the U.S. and Brazilian market. Our customers are primarily American importers and Brazilian wholesalers who provide high-quality beans to the specialty roasting market.

Silvera & Sons Ltda. is a private, family owned preparer and exporter of Brazilian-grown, green Arabica coffee beans. It is owned and operated by Marco Silvera Sr. and his sons, Marco Silvera Jr. and Antonio Silvera.

Company Ownership

Silvera & Sons is in its sixth year of operation. The current plant has been in operation for 15 years and for 12 of those years was managed by Marco Silvera Sr. who was then an employee of the former owner, Cafe Fina. Since the plant was purchased, Silvera & Sons has maintained maximum production and sales. It is currently operating at maximum capacity.

Company History

	1996	1997	1998
Sales	$16,262,532	$17,304,066	$18,345,600
Gross Margin	$2,439,380	$2,630,218	$2,814,215
Gross % (calculated)	15.00%	15.20%	15.34%
Operating Expenses	$12,196,899	$12,631,968	$13,346,424
Collection period (days)	60	60	60
Inventory turnover	12	12	12

Balance Sheet
Short-term Assets

	1996	1997	1998
Cash	$0	$0	$994,260
Accounts receivable	$0	$0	$137,250
Inventory	$0	$0	$355,200
Other Short-term Assets	$0	$0	$243,936
Total Short-term Assets	$0	$0	$1,730,646
Long-term Assets			
Capital Assets	$0	$0	$521,650
Accumulated Depreciation	$0	$0	$100,000
Total Long-term Assets	$0	$0	$421,650
Total Assets	**$0**	**$0**	**$2,152,296**

Capital and Liabilities

	1996	1997	1998
Accounts Payable	$0	$0	$8,435
Short-term Notes	$0	$0	$58,000
Other Short-term Liabilities	$0	$0	$0
Subtotal Short-term Liabilities	$0	$0	$66,435
Long-term Liabilities	$0	$0	$402,000
Total Liabilities	$0	$0	$468,435
Paid in Capital	$0	$0	$525,000
Retained Earnings	$0	$0	$223,235
Earnings	$0	$0	$935,626
Total Capital	$0	$0	$1,683,861
Total Capital and Liabilities	$0	$0	$2,152,296

Other Inputs

	1996	1997	1998
Payment days	0	0	60
Sales on credit	$0	$0	$6,054,048
Receivables turnover	0.00	0.00	44.11

Company Locations and Facilities

The Silvera & Son's main warehouse and office is located in Ouro Fino. The warehouse has the capacity to prepare approximately 6,000 60kg bags of exportable coffee beans. The proposed new warehouse and preparation facility site is also located in Ouro Fino. The new facility will be 3,500m² and will have 30 selecting machines with capacity to prepare 40,000 bags for exportation and 80,000 bags for storage. The proposed facility will also handle shipping.

PRODUCTS

Silvera & Sons deals exclusively in green coffee, grown in the southern states of Brazil and one-hundred percent Arabica. Beans in parchment are purchased directly from growers and are de-husked and packaged into 60kg sacks in the Silvera & Sons plant. The final product is suitable for sale and exportation.

Competitive Comparison

In order to differentiate our product, coffee, which is a commodity, from the product offering of competitors, all beans are guaranteed fresh and are shipped within seven days of preparation. In addition, all beans are sorted at ninety-five percent screen 18 and above compared to the industry standard ninety percent screen of 17 and above. The beans shipped by Silvera & Sons are therefore larger than most and are guaranteed fresh. In addition, all of the farms from which Silvera & Sons purchases coffee adhere to environmentally sound farming practices and avoid the use of pesticides and chemicals in crop production.

There are approximately ten competitors who offer a product similar to ours. Our research indicates that with the additional capacity we would become one of the top four providers, in terms of quantity. We have the advantage of established distribution channels and reputation. In addition, improvements to our marketing efforts will further separate us from the larger market and from our close competitors.

Sales Literature

Silvera & Sons currently works with two importers in the United States who handle all of our shipments. Likewise, we have dealt with the same Brazilian wholesalers, for internal sales, each year. Sales to this point have been handled through personal selling. Additional sales literature will include a website, direct mail to specialty roasters and importers, and print advertising in several trade publications including *Coffee Times*, a monthly publication which targets American business dealing with issues relevant to the coffee industry.

Sourcing

Both the existing and the proposed facilities are ideally located in Ouro Fino, in the state of Minas Gerais. Minas Gerais is the largest coffee producing state in Brazil and beans produced in the region are of the highest quality. With additional financing, we would be able to buy larger volumes at lower prices. We now buy from one or more of six private growers or grower cooperatives. Contracts are secured six months in advance of harvest.

Technology

Improvements in technology will include the use of partially automated selecting machines which will allow for increased production capacity with a lower machine-to-operator ratio than we currently employ.

Additional storage capabilities will decrease shipping charges and will reduce the need for permanent shipping employees by thirty-five percent. High-technology information system upgrades will improve all aspects of business, especially inventory control, tracking of shipments, and communication with clients in import countries.

Silvera & Sons sells only the finest Arabica coffee beans. This is an important distinction in evaluating our coffee because the alternative to the Arabica bean, Coffea Robusta, though it shares some similarities with the Arabica bean, is very different. Coffea Robusta is grown at lower elevations and has a higher yield per plant as well as being more resistant to disease. It also has up to twice the caffeine level as its cousin, the Arabica Bean. Due to the lower cost and larger market amount of Robusta coffee, it is found primarily on supermarket shelves. The Arabica species grows at much higher elevations, better soil rich areas, and is the source of the world's finest coffees.

By providing the finest species of coffee, Silvera & Sons has taken the first step towards a differentiated product. To further distinguish our coffee, we adhere to higher quality standards than approximately ninety-five percent of the market. In addition, all of our beans are of the Bourbon Santos variety. The "Bourbon" strain is considered one of the finest Brazil has to offer. It is grown in the mountains surrounding Sao Paulo and is highly sought after by specialty roasters from around the world. We have assumed the position of a specialized provider of this exceptional coffee. Our customers, American and Brazilian specialty roasters, recognize Silvera & Sons for our ability to provide the type of beans they require to produce award-winning coffee.

Future Products

Coffee is the second largest commodity market next to oil and Brazil has remained the largest producer of coffee in the world for two centuries. Imports of Arabica coffee in the United States have increased ninety-four percent in the past five years and consumption of coffee within Brazil has seen similar increases. In addition, demand for green coffee is above the market clearing level, and market price and crop yield estimates are at an all-time high.

The increase in the number of independent specialty roasters in the United States and Brazil has contributed to and is an indicator of the increased demand for coffee. Within the larger coffee market is our target market, the specialty roaster. These discerning customers want the highest quality coffee beans. They serve the growing "gourmet" coffee market and are represented by large American companies like Starbucks and thousands of smaller specialty roasters. The Arabica bean is considered to be the best in the world and as such, the demand for Arabica beans is high on the specialty roaster market. Specialty roasters are willing to pay more for Arabica beans and attempt to distinguish themselves via the characteristics of the bean they use, i.e., the location in which it was grown, farming methods, bean size, etc. The final consumer is relatively price insensitive if the coffee is good, has won awards, or is compatible with a popular trend. We estimate that specialty roasting in the U.S. alone is a ($USD) one-billion market.

MARKET ANALYSIS SUMMARY

The potential customer groups for Silvera & Sons are:

- American importers of green Arabica beans: Market research suggests that there are approximately 200 importers of green Arabica coffee on the West and East coasts of the United States that would be able to handle the quantities of our shipments and are in our target market . Combined, they import a total of four to five million/60kg bags of Brazilian coffee per year.
- Brazilian green coffee wholesalers: This market serves as a safety valve for our export business. By maintaining relationships with Brazilian wholesalers we have an alternative market with established distribution channels.
- Brazilian specialty roasters: As we move towards maximum capacity we will plan to more aggressively target this audience. We hope to eventually reduce transactions with wholesalers and capture their value-added costs as profit. We anticipate that this effort will begin approximately four years into operation of the new facility.

Market Segmentation

Market Analysis

Potential Customers	Growth	1999	2000	2001	2002	2003	CAGR
U.S. Importers (60kg bags)	26%	70,140	88,376	111,354	140,306	176,786	26.00%
Brazilian Wholesalers (60kg bags)	26%	30,060	38,876	47,724	60,132	75,766	26.00%
Other	0%	0	0	0	0	0	0.00%
Total	**26.00%**	**100,200**	**126,252**	**159,078**	**200,438**	**252,552**	**26.00%**

Industry Analysis

Coffee has been a growing industry for the past five years. The most notable growth has been in the American market where imports have increased almost one hundred percent and the market price has nearly doubled. The number of specialty roasters has increased from a handful of well known companies to thousands of independent entities. There is a constant struggle within this market to produce the best coffee and serve one or more niches within the larger market. Brazilian coffee producers and exporters have made great efforts to improve agricultural techniques, processing methods, and distribution in order to better serve this growing market. Demand for Brazilian coffee is currently greater than supply.

Industry Participants

Silvera & Sons deals exclusively in the exportation and sale of green Arabica beans. There are approximately 150 Brazilian businesses in this market. However, approximately 30 companies account for approximately eighty percent of the total amount of green Arabica exports. In addition, many of these companies prepare, export, and sell, to the Brazilian market, other coffee products. Additional products include:

Green Robusta (Conillon) beans: The Robusta bean is produced in far less quantity in Brazil than the Arabica and is considered an inferior species. The Robusta market represents less than ten percent of all coffee produced in Brazil.

Soluble coffee products: These are instant (water soluble) coffees and are either decaffeinated or not. Sales of soluble coffee products account for approximately twelve percent of the total market.

Roasted and ground coffee: Approximately eighty-five percent of all roasted and ground coffee (decaffeinated and non-decaffeinated) goes to internal consumption and represents approximately twenty-seven percent of the total coffee market.

Primary competitors include: Golden Brazil, Bramazonia, Comexim, and Nicchio Cafe.

Distribution Patterns

All of the coffee produced for exportation by Silvera & Sons and approximately eighty-five percent of all coffee produced for exportation in Brazil is shipped from Porto de Santos. Prepared coffee is shipped via rail and/or truck from the Silvera & Sons plant in Ouro Fino to Porto de Santos. From the port it is then shipped, in 40 foot containers to the port of Miami via cargo ship. Distribution charges are assumed by Silvera & Sons up to the arrival of the shipments in Miami whereupon importers assume responsibility, as detailed in contract, of the shipment and additional distribution charges.

Competition and Buying Patterns

The purchase decision for our customer is based on trust in our process and bean selection. We have established relationships with our customers which extend beyond that of the buyer/seller. The Silvera & Sons label means that the product has been chosen and prepared with the highest quality standards in mind. Our beans are priced up to nine percent higher than similar products. Our customers are willing to pay more for our product because they are familiar with us and trust in the quality of our beans. This is the result of their success in the marketplace with our product.

There are approximately 150 exporters of green Arabica beans in Brazil. According to the Brazilian Coffee Exporters Association, ABECAFE, fifty percent (50%) of all green coffee exports come from their 45 members. Approximately eighty percent (80%) of these exports come from 20 ABECAFE members. Market contributions of individual exporters are held in strict confidence and are not available to the public. However, based on this information and given the large number of remaining exporters not affiliated with ABECAFE who account for the remaining sixty percent (60%) of all exports, we assume that many of the largest competitors are among the ABECAFE members. They are:

Agro Food, Allcoffee, Bramazonia,
Cafe do Ponto, Cafeeira Carolina, Cargill Agricola,
Casas Sendas, Cocam, Comexim,
Comercial Ben, Compel, Cooxupe,
Cotia Trading, Custudio Forzza, Esteve,
Eurobrasil, Fazenda da Serra, Guaxupe,
Inter-Continental, JR Exportadora, MC Coffee,
Melitta, Mitsui Alimentos, Nicchio Cafe,
Nova America, N.S. da Guia, Ottoni & Filhos,
Porto de Santos, Ref. Oleos Brasil, R & G,
Rio Doce, Tres Coracoes, Volcafe.

Silvera & Sons' strategy is to expand production capabilities in order to fulfill the requests of importers with whom we currently deal for larger orders which we are unable to currently fulfill. In addition Silvera & Sons seeks to establish additional contracts with importers on the West Coast of the United States and increase the volume of green coffee sold on the Brazilian market. We intend to first maximize quantity of coffee sold within existing channels and second, establish additional accounts through targeted marketing efforts.

Our main strategy is to communicate the unique and desired attributes of our coffee to larger segments of the American and Brazilian markets. We sell a superior product, yet one that can be considered a commodity. It is therefore important that we effectively communicate the unique aspects which make it ideally suited for a niche market.

The unique aspects of our products include superior product selection and preparation, quality assurance, and efficient distribution. These are things we have done since we started doing business. The tactics we will use to communicate these strengths include, personal selling, targeted print advertising, and improved communication capabilities via information system improvements and a sophisticated website.

As tactics below the pyramid, we have identified three specialty publications in the United States and two in Brazil in which we will run print ads. We also plan to increase personal selling efforts to additional American importers. Part of the personal selling will include invitations to importers to visit our facilities, at our expense.

Silvera & Sons' competitive edge comes from the advantage of having established relationships with American importers, and Brazilian coffee growers, green coffee brokers and wholesalers. Silvera & Sons has received affirmation of the demand for their product in the form of requests from importers for larger product shipments. Ours is a superior product offering because of the larger average size of the bean and because we purchase from growers who rely on the use of chemicals and pesticides less than two percent of the time. In addition, prompt preparation and shipment provides importers with a product that is up to one month fresher than beans sold by many exporters.

Marketing Strategy

Silvera & Sons marketing strategy will include the use of targeted print media advertising and direct selling to importers in the United States who provide green coffee to specialty roasters. We will capitalize on existing relationships with importers who have stated their willingness to contact West Coast affiliates and recommend Silvera & Sons coffee. We have positioned ourselves as a differentiated provider of the highest quality Arabica beans. The primary goal of all marketing efforts will be to communicate this to existing and potential customers.

Positioning Statements

For American importers of Brazilian coffee who use our coffee to supply specialty roasters, Silvera & Sons coffee beans are the highest quality and largest beans available. Unlike many exporters, our beans exceed the minimum acceptable quality standards and are shipped within one week of preparation to ensure the largest and freshest beans on the market. Our products are perfectly suited for the specialty roasting market which constantly strives to offer award-winning coffee.

Pricing Strategy

Because Silvera & Sons adheres to higher quality standards, the price of our coffee is slightly higher (four to nine percent) than the market average. The import market largely determines the price of imported coffee in the United States. Beans that do not meet Silvera & Sons quality standards are resold on the Brazilian market at the current market price. Green coffee, on the import market, now sells for US$ 213.56/60kg bag. According to Silvera & Sons' pricing strategy, Silvera & Sons coffee would sell for approximately US$ 224/60kg bag. Importers to this point have been willing to pay the additional cost.

Promotion Strategy

Relationships are key to success in the export business. Importers in Florida have on several occasions visited the Silvera & Sons facility, family home, and farms from which coffee is purchased. Additional accounts and contacts with West Coast importers have all been established and maintained through personal contact. Personal selling will remain our most important means of promotion. Marco Silvera Jr. will continue to lead this effort. In addition to personal selling, Silvera & Sons has identified several specialty publications within which print advertisements will run. Direct mail, in the form of personal letters will also be used to communicate with existing and potential clients. Our budget for promotion activities is as follows:

- Personal Selling which includes phone expenses, travel for Silvera & Sons employees and for importers who we invite to Brazil: ($BRL) 35,000 annually.
- Print Advertising in three specialty publications and direct mail: ($BRL) 12,000 monthly.
- World Wide Web presence: ($BRL) 125,000 to produce a new site and $2,500 annually to maintain the site.

Distribution is one of the greatest challenges faced by Silvera & Sons. The distribution system of Brazil is largely outdated and inefficient. Moreover, taxes, specifically excise taxes, are high. Distribution costs for internal sales are absorbed by the customer but distribution costs for exports are absorbed by us. Increasing the volume of our exports makes us eligible to receive reduced fees and helps ensure that trucks and rail cars are running at maximum capacity.

Distribution Strategy

Our most important marketing program is an increase in personal selling combined with targeted direct mail and print advertising. Marco Silvera Jr. will be responsible, with a budget of ($BRL) 35,000 and a milestone date of May 30, 1999. The program is intended to establish contractual agreements with 10 additional importers, increase brand awareness of our product in the United States, and communicate our position as a provider of the highest quality green Arabica beans on the market.

Another key marketing program is the development of a sophisticated website. The goal of this program is to increase our presence on the world wide web and provide additional means of communication and customer data collection. The website will cost ($BRL) 125,000.

Marketing Programs

Silvera & Sons' strategy focuses first on meeting the increased demand from importers with whom we have established relationships for larger orders. These importers are critical to our ability to acquire additional accounts on both the East and West coasts of the United States without having to spend a great deal on sales efforts. Secondly we will focus on increasing the volume, while maintaining the percentage of sales, of beans sold to the internal Brazilian market. When we have reached maximum sales to existing channels we can then shift the majority of our focus to securing additional import accounts.

Sales Strategy

The following table and chart show our present sales forecast. We project sales to grow approximately forty percent in 1999, increase again by twenty percent in 2000, and reach maximum for production capacity in 2001 representing a thirty-three percent growth over the previous year.

Sales Forecast

Unit Sales	1999	2000	2001
Import and Export	100,200	120,000	160,000
Other	0	0	0
Total Unit Sales	**100,200**	**120,000**	**160,000**
Unit Prices			
Import and Export	$262.08	$275.18	$288.29
Other	$0.00	$0.00	$0.00
Sales			
Import and Export	$26,260,416	$33,021,600	$46,126,400
Other	$0	$0	$0
Total Sales	$26,260,416	$33,021,600	$46,126,400
Direct Unit Cost			
Import and Export	$212.00	$222.60	$233.20
Other	$0.00	$0.00	$0.00

Sales Forecast

Continued

Direct Cost of Sales	1999	2000	2001
Import and Export	$21,242,400	$26,712,000	$37,312,000
Other	$0	$0	$0
Subtotal Direct Cost of Sales	**$21,242,400**	**$26,712,000**	**$37,312,000**

Sales Programs

Personal selling: Through personal contact we need to confirm in writing orders for larger quantities of our product from American importers and Brazilian wholesalers. In addition we need to establish sales agreements with at least six, possibly ten, additional American importers. Marco Silvera Jr. is responsible and the due date is May 30, with a budget of ($BRL) 24,000.

Strategic Alliances

Our most valued alliances are those we have developed with American importers. They have the ability and willingness to purchase larger quantities of our products and recommend us to other importers. Additional alliances with trucking contractors and the Porto de Santos Cafe Commission are currently established.

The accompanying table shows specific milestones, with responsibilities assigned dates, and budgets. The milestones represented in this plan are those which we have determined to be the most important.

Milestone	Start Date	End Date	Budget	Manager	Department
Secure Financing	1/1/99	2/1/99	$12,000	M. Silvera Sr.	Finance
Establish Import Accounts	1/1/99	5/1/99	$18,000	M. Silvera Jr.	Sales & Marketing
Increase Production	1/1/99	9/1/99	$18,000	Antonio Silvera	Production & Shipping
Hire Intl. Legal & Finance Spec.	1/1/100	1/1/100	$35,000	Unknown	Administration
Sample	1/1/98	1/1/98	$0	ABC	Department
Sample	1/1/98	1/1/98	$0	ABC	Department
Sample	1/1/98	1/1/98	$0	ABC	Department
Sample	1/1/98	1/1/98	$0	ABC	Department
Sample	1/1/98	1/1/98	$0	ABC	Department
Other	1/1/98	1/1/98	$0	ABC	Department
Totals			**$83,000**		

Silvera & Sons' management consists of four full-time employees. Additional assistance is acquired on a part-time basis and/or through the use of consultants, specifically in legal matters. Detailed descriptions are found in the following section.

Silvera & Sons is organized into three functional areas: product sourcing, sales, and marketing; production and shipping; and finance and administration.

Marco Silvera, Sr.: CEO/President in charge of finance and administration. Marco Silvera, Sr., 57, has worked in the coffee export business for 30 years. Before starting Silvera & Sons he was the Chief Financial Officer and general manager of the Cafe Fino coffee company. He began working for Cafe Fino after he finished an accounting degree at the University of Southern California. The current Silvera & Sons plant was formerly owned by Cafe Fino and was sold to Mr. Silvera who had decided to "retire" and wanted to run a small business. Cafe Fino had purchased larger facilities and no longer needed the plant.

Marco Silvera, Jr.: Vice president in charge of product sourcing, sales, and marketing. Marco Silvera Jr., 32, completed his M.B.A. at Syracuse University and worked for several years on the Brazilian stock and commodities market as a broker. He later took a position as an International Sales and Marketing Representative for a major agricultural brokerage and supply firm in Sao Paulo. He is expected to succeed his father as CEO of Silvera & Sons Ltda.

Antonio Silvera: Vice president in charge of production and shipping. Antonio Silvera, 29, worked as a civil engineer for two years for the Brazilian government after completing an engineering degree at the University of Brazil, Sao Paulo. He is responsible for the supervision of all plant employees.

Additional Management:

- Ralph Henzo, CFO
- Gracie, Renoldo, & Fertado Attorneys at Law, Sao Paulo

We currently lack a full-time professional who can deal with the changing legal and financial aspects of international business. We have relied on legal consultants but are now analyzing the possibility of adding an additional position to deal exclusively with international issues. In addition, as we continue to grow and hire more personnel, we may hire a controller.

The personnel plan requires an increase in plant employees from 11 to 17-20 within the next three years. Additional employees will also be added to increase administrative and accounting support. One additional employee will be added to the sales and marketing division. We will retain all current employees as they will not have to relocate.

Production Personnel	1999	2000	2001
Antonio Silvera, VP Production	$38,400	$41,088	$43,964
Plant employees	$219,996	$228,796	$237,948
Other	$42,000	$47,000	$50,000
Subtotal	$300,396	$316,884	$331,912
Sales and Marketing Personnel			
Marco Silvera, Jr., VP Sales/Mktg.	$45,000	$48,150	$51,521
Other	$180,492	$80,000	$85,000
Subtotal	**$225,492**	**$128,150**	**$136,521**

MANAGEMENT SUMMARY

Management Team

Management Team Gaps

Personnel Plan

Personnel Plan

Continued

General and Administrative Personnel	1999	2000	2001
Marco Silvera, Sr., CEO	$50,400	$53,928	$57,703
Ralph Henzo, CFO	$42,000	$44,940	$44,940
Admin/Acctg. Staff	$9,000	$9,360	$44,734
Other	$18,000	$22,000	$26,000
Subtotal	**$119,400**	**$130,228**	**$173,377**
Other Personnel			
Name or title	$0	$0	$0
Other	$0	$0	$0
Subtotal	**$0**	**$0**	**$0**
Total Headcount	15	16	17
Total Payroll	$645,288	$575,262	$641,810
Payroll Burden	$58,076	$51,774	$57,763
Total Payroll Expenditures	**$703,364**	**$627,036**	**$699,573**

FINANCIAL PLAN

We want to finance growth through a combination of long-term debt and cash flow. Purchase of the larger facility and equipment will require approximately eighty percent debt financing. Additional technology will be primarily financed with cash-flow. Inventory turnover must remain at or above four or we run the risk of backing up orders and jeopardizing our freshness guarantees. We have had no problems with accounts receivable and we expect to maintain our collection days at 30 with thirty percent of sales on credit.

In addition, we must achieve gross margins of thirty-five percent and hold operating costs no more than sixty-five percent of sales.

Important Assumptions

Important assumptions for this plan are found in the following table. These assumptions largely determine the financial plan and require that we secure additional financing.

	1999	2000	2001
Short-term Interest Rate %	14.00%	14.00%	14.00%
Long-term Interest Rate %	9.00%	9.00%	9.00%
Payment Days Estimator	60	60	60
Inventory Turnover Estimator	12.00%	12.00%	12.00%
Tax Rate %	47.00%	47.00%	47.00%
Expenses in Cash %	5.00%	5.00%	5.00%
Personnel Burden %	9.00%	9.00%	9.00%

Key Financial Indicators

The most important factor to Silvera & Sons' anticipated growth is the procurement of necessary financing. The size of the orders currently requested by importers are larger than what can be produced given our present plant capacity.

We anticipate changes in key financial indicators: sales, gross margin, operating expenses, collection days, and inventory turnover. The growth in sales goes above thirty percent in the first year, twenty percent in second, and back to thirty percent in year three after which it will settle. We expect to increase gross margin but our projections show a decline in the first two years following the purchase of the new facility. This is due to the facilities not being run at maximum capacity. The projections for collection days and inventory turnover show that we expect a decline in these indicators.

The break-even analysis shows that Silvera & Sons has sufficient sales strength to remain viable. Our break-even point is close to 7,300 units per month and our sales forecast for the next year calls for almost 8,500 units per month on average. Projections are detailed in the following table.

Break-even Analysis

Monthly Units Break-even	7,333
Monthly Sales Break-even	$1,774,667

Assumptions:

Average Per-Unit Revenue	$242.00
Average Per-Unit Variable Cost	$212.00
Estimated Monthly Fixed Cost	$220,000

We expect to close the first year of production in the new facility with ($BRL) 26,260,416 in sales and increase our sales to more than ($BRL) 33 million in the second year and ($BRL) 46 million in year three. Net earnings will average ($BRL) 2.4 million.

Projected Profit and Loss

	1999	2000	2001
Sales	$26,260,416	$33,021,600	$46,126,400
Direct Cost of Sales	$21,242,400	$26,712,000	$37,312,000
Production Payroll	$300,396	$316,884	$331,912
Other	$300,000	$345,000	$410,000
Total Cost of Sales	**$21,842,796**	**$27,373,884**	**$38,053,912**
Gross Margin	$4,417,620	$5,647,716	$8,072,488
Gross Margin %	16.82%	17.10%	17.50%
Operating expenses:			
Sales and Marketing Expenses			
Sales and Marketing Payroll	$225,492	$128,150	$136,521
Advertising/Promotion	$144,000	$165,000	$165,000
Travel	$21,000	$22,500	$24,000
Miscellaneous	$24,000	$26,500	$28,500
Other	$0	$0	$0
Total Sales and Marketing Expenses	**$414,492**	**$342,150**	**$354,021**
Sales and Marketing %	1.58%	1.04%	0.77%
General and Administrative Expenses			
General and Administrative Payroll	$119,400	$130,228	$173,377
Payroll Burden	$58,076	$51,774	$57,763
Depreciation	$216,000	$216,000	$216,000
Leased Equipment	$50,400	$50,400	$50,400
Utilities	$36,000	$36,000	$36,000
Insurance	$72,000	$75,000	$78,000
Rent	$305,250	$300,000	$300,000
Other	$0	$0	$0
Total General and Admin. Expenses	**$857,126**	**$859,402**	**$911,540**
General and Administrative %	3.26%	2.60%	1.98%

Projected Profit and Loss

Continued

Other Expenses	1999	2000	2001
Other Payroll	$0	$0	$0
Contract/Consultants	$18,000	$24,000	$30,000
Other	$0	$0	$0
Total Other Expenses	**$18,000**	**$24,000**	**$30,000**
Other %	0.07%	0.07%	0.07%
Total Operating Expenses	**$1,289,618**	**$1,225,552**	**$1,295,561**
Profit Before Interest and Taxes	$3,128,002	$4,422,164	$6,776,927
Interest Expense Short-term	($2,800)	($24,290)	($50,540)
Interest Expense Long-term	$265,444	$238,449	$211,932
Taxes Incurred	$1,346,718	$1,977,763	$3,109,302
Net Profit	**$1,518,640**	**$2,230,243**	**$3,506,234**
Net Profit/Sales	**5.78%**	**6.75%**	**7.60%**

Projected Cash Flow

Silvera & Sons expects to manage cash flow over the next three years with the assistance of a loan supported by the Central Bank of Brazil of ($BRL) 2,700,000. This financing assistance is required to provide the working capital to meet the current needs for the construction of the new production facility and additional personnel, distribution costs, and other related expenses.

	1999	2000	2001
Net Profit	$1,518,640	$2,230,243	$3,506,234
Plus:			
Depreciation	$216,000	$216,000	$216,000
Change in Accounts Payable	$3,429,097	$700,083	$1,672,070
Current Borrowing (repayment)	($144,000)	($175,000)	($200,000)
Increase (decrease) Other Liabilities	($27,600)	($25,300)	($25,300)
Long-term Borrowing (repayment)	$2,394,750	($294,636)	($294,636)
Capital Input	$0	$650,000	$650,000
Subtotal	$7,386,887	$3,301,390	$5,524,367
Less:			
Change in Inventory	$1,425,600	$396,977	$790,644
Change in Other Short-term Assets	$60,000	$75,000	$85,000
Capital Expenditure	$2,700,000	$0	$0
Dividends	$0	$0	$0
Subtotal	**$4,048,350**	**$471,977**	**$875,644**
Net Cash Flow	**$3,338,537**	**$2,829,414**	**$4,648,723**
Cash Balance	**$4,332,797**	**$7,162,211**	**$11,810,934**

Projected Balance Sheet

As shown in the balance sheet in the following table, our net will grow from approximately ($BRL) 935,626 to more than ($BRL) 1.48 million by the end of 1999 and to ($BRL) 3.46 million by the end of the plan period.

Assets				**Pro-forma Balance Sheet**
Short-term Assets	**1999**	**2000**	**2001**	
Cash/Inventory	$4,332,797	$7,162,211	$11,810,934-	
	$1,780,800	$2,177,777	$2,968,421	
Other Short-term	$303,936	$378,936	$463,936	
Total Short-term Assets	**$6,417,533**	**$9,718,923**	**$15,243,291**	
Long-term Assets				
Capital Assets	$3,221,650	$3,221,650	$3,221,650	
Accumulated Depreciation	$316,000	$532,000	$748,000	
Total Long-term Assets	$2,905,650	$2,689,650	$2,473,650	
Total Assets	**$9,323,183**	**$12,408,573**	**$17,716,941**	
Liabilities and Capital				
Accounts Payable	$3,437,532	$4,137,616	$5,809,685	
Short-term Notes	($86,000)	($261,000)	($461,000)	
Other Short-term Liabilities	($27,600)	($52,900)	($78,200)	
Subtotal Short-term Liabilities	**$3,323,932**	**$3,823,716**	**$5,270,485**	
Long-term Liabilities	$2,796,750	$2,502,114	$2,207,478	
Total Liabilities	**$6,120,682**	**$6,325,830**	**$7,477,963**	
Paid in Capital	$525,000	$1,175,000	$1,825,000	
Retained Earnings	$1,158,861	$2,677,501	$4,907,744	
Earnings	$1,518,640	$2,230,243	$3,506,234	
Total Capital	**$3,202,501**	**$6,082,744**	**$10,238,978**	
Total Liabilities and Capital	**$9,323,183**	**$12,408,573**	**$17,716,941**	
Net Worth	**$3,202,501**	**$6,082,744**	**$10,238,978**	

Standard business ratios are included in the following table. The ratios show an aggressive plan for growth in order to reach maximum production within three years. Return on investment increases each year as we bring the new facility to maximum capacity and production. Return on sales and assets remain strong and cost of goods decreases based upon efficiency projections. Projections are based on the 1997/98 selling price.   **Business Ratios**

Profitability Ratios:	1999	2000	2001
Gross Margin	16.82%	17.10%	17.50%
Net Profit Margin	5.78%	6.75%	7.60%
Return on Assets	16.29%	17.97%	19.79%
Return on Equity	47.42%	36.67%	34.24%
Activity Ratios			
AR Turnover	0.00	0.00	0.00
Collection Days	0	0	0
Inventory Turnover	20.45	13.83	14.79
Accts Payable Turnover	6.89	6.89	6.89
Total Asset Turnover	2.82	2.66	2.6
Debt Ratios			
Debt to Net Worth	1.91	1.04	0.73
Short-term Liab. to Liab.	0.54	0.60	0.70

Business Ratios

Continued

Current Ratio	1.93	2.54	2.89
Quick Ratio	1.39	1.97	2.33
Net Working Capital	$3,093,601	$5,895,208	$9,972,806
Interest Coverage	11.91	20.65	41.99
Additional Ratios			
Assets to Sales	0.36	0.38	0.38
Debt/Assets	66%	51%	42%
Current Debt/Total Assets	36%	31%	30%
Acid Test	1.39	1.97	2.33
Asset Turnover	2.82	2.66	2.6
Sales/Net Worth	8.2	5.43	4.5
Dividend Payout	$0	0.00	0.00

Desktop Publishing Company

BUSINESS PLAN

POWER DESK TOP PUBLISHING, INC.

4900 Maryland Plaza
St. Louis, Missouri 63112

Power Desk Top Publishing aims to fulfill a unique niche in the local market of desk top publishing companies. By targeting selected businesses through direct phone calls, the owners plan to grow their business based on a reputation for top-notch creative and affordable editorial and graphic services.

- EXECUTIVE SUMMARY

- THE COMPANY—PRESENT SITUATION

- OBJECTIVES

- MANAGEMENT & PERSONNEL

- PRODUCT DESCRIPTION

- MARKET ANALYSIS—CUSTOMERS

- COMPETITION

- RISKS

- MARKETING STRATEGY

- ADVERTISING, PROMOTION & PUBLIC RELATIONS

- PRICING & PROFITABILITY

- SUMMARY & USE OF FUNDING

- FINANCIAL PROJECTIONS

DESKTOP PUBLISHING COMPANY
BUSINESS PLAN

EXECUTIVE SUMMARY

Power Desk Top Publishing, Inc. is a small corporation composed exclusively of a husband and wife team who are managers, sales executives, and hands-on operators.

The desk top publishing industry has come of age. Based on modern computer advances, both in hardware and software, desk top publishing has eclipsed the costly traditional methods of printing, enabling creative and well-trained individuals, such as Steve and Mary Lane, to offer exciting and dynamic printing service to business, churches, students, and individuals at affordable prices.

Mr. and Mrs. Lane bring a wealth of talent to this enterprise. Steve has earned Ph.Ds in both Advertising and Graphic Design. He has also logged two years' experience as an intern at a leading advertising agency in St. Louis. Mary holds a degree in English and has years of advertising experience in both production and management. Their creative talent is reflected in the exceptional appeal of their work product. Power Desk Top Publishing will not be merely a mechanical printing operation. The Lanes bring much more to the table. They can take an idea or a concept submitted by a client and produce a finished product that is eye catching and truly unique.

Creativity as compared to mere mechanical reproduction will indeed be a major part of their selling appeal.

Another hard hitting plus will be the fact that Power Desk Top Publishing will be able to compete at a most aggressive price level. For the first two years, Power DTP will be a true owner-operator business with no employees other than the owners.

Desk top publishing, as the name implies, lends itself to a very compact operation, and an in-the-home operation is contemplated for years one through four. Keeping overhead at a bare minimum, Steve and Mary will devote at least 50% of their time calling on potential customers. They will take the business to the customers by meeting them at the client's establishment, providing meaningful samples, and offering to produce prototype newsletters, brochures, price lists, mailers, etc. Operating with the slimmest of fixed overhead, the Lanes are able to offer up to 15% introductory discounts to gain market penetration.

Both Steve and Mary are gifted sales people and, as owner operators, can capture the confidence of the printing buyer. They also posses seemingly boundless energy and are dedicated to working long hours to assure the success of Power Desk Top Publishing. While devoting most of their days to customer calls and support activities, they will work into the evening with the hands-on production aspects of the business. Both are inveterate computer buffs and enjoy the creative challenge of producing new and original pieces.

Like many entrepreneurs, the Lanes have a driving ambition to see their firm grow and prosper, yet their approach is cautious and their expectations quite reasonable.

For the first two years, Steve and Mary will perform all the work, sales, and production. By year three, the business will add one full-time, or two part-time employees, drawing talent from the local universities. Graphic design and advertising majors will be sought for this young, dynamic company. The Lanes will continue on in the home through their fourth year, when a storefront operation will be added along with an expanded scope, including hands-on computer rental time available to the public. At this time an additional worker will be added.

Sales projections for the first year are a modest $70,000, providing net earnings of $8,100 after combined officers' salaries of $28,896. The Lanes have $5,000 of savings invested and will require a line of credit of $30,000, $15,000 of which is for equipment. Year one proforma reflects $24,000 of the line as hard costs; the remainder is budgeted for contingencies and operating reserve.

THE COMPANY—
PRESENT
SITUATION

Power Desk Top Publishing, Inc. is a Sub-chapter "S" corporation with all stock jointly owned by Steve and Mary Lane. The company, which is in the final planning stages, is targeting an April 15th opening. Power Desk Top Publishing's entry into the market will be timed to coincide with both a print advertising campaign in local university newspapers and an intensive business-to-business sales campaign in which both principals call upon business owners and managers, and distribute attractive fliers, which are samples of their work product.

The desk top publishing industry is rapidly gaining a significant foothold in what was once considered the exclusive domain of traditional printing companies. More and more users are turning to the economics offered by the small, independent, low overhead operators that offer a good product at economic prices. Power Desk Top Publishing offers much more. Highly skilled and dedicated, this team will combine both technical excellence, advertising, layout expertise, and personal service to move their new company to the forefront. Both Mr. and Mrs. Lane have extensive educational backgrounds that lend themselves to advertising and graphic arts. Additionally, because of low overhead and the absence of an outside payroll, Power Desk Top Publishing will compete quite effectively, offering a superior product at a price 10 to 20% less than larger, less efficient speed printers.

Power Desk Top Publishing, Inc. will be addressing a variety of markets. University students represent one market for term papers, theses, and doctoral dissertations, etc. Employment resumes and entrepreneurial business plans are another. Churches, for their bulletins, directories, and publications are a third category of business.

Cash resources presently stand at $5,000, and an equipment budget totaling some $15,000 has been established. Power Desk Top Publishing, Inc. will require $30,000 borrowed capital to successfully start up this company.

OBJECTIVES

Short Term

Power Desk Top Publishing, Inc. has set a goal of $70,000 in sales for the first twelve months of full-time operations. We expect this to increase by 25% during the second twelve-month period for total sales of $86,600 for year two. Evaluation of the market has given rise to these reasonable expectations.

With regard to the college market, there presently exists a need for low price first rate publishing services. Power Desk Top Publishing will be catering directly to this market to a much greater extent than other desk top publishers or speed printers. Mrs. Lane's expertise as an English major will be invaluable in composition and proofreading copy. Her role will be very "hands on" with her customers' projects, offering coaching and advice as needed. The relative youth of the Power DTP principals, and their recent academic background will be a decided plus in accessing and dealing with the student market.

Mr. Lane holds doctoral degrees in both graphic design and advertising. This background will prove to be a great asset as more and more companies avail themselves of Power Desk Top Publishing's services. Power DTP's offering to the market far exceeds the mere mechanical aspect of printed material. Steve's graphic arts expertise and advertising talent will come into play when soliciting orders from business customers. By being able to suggest outstanding layouts and striking designs, it is easy to see that Power Desk Top Publishing will be offering a level of support to their customers that is not always available through competitive sources.

Long Term

Steve and Mary Lane are ambitious and energetic young business people. While their initial expectations are relatively modest, they foresee, by the start of their fifth year, a successful operation that has moved from the in-the-home business to a storefront operation that will have significantly expanded, both in terms of volume and scope.

It is anticipated that, in addition to producing finished desk top publishing products and services, the Lanes will be offering to the public a variety of computer and desk top publishing equipment that may be rented by the hour to walk-in clientele. Eight Macintosh computers, as well as laser printers, color ink jet printers, and other support hardware and software, will be dedicated to this branch of the company. Experienced individuals can easily come in and rent equipment by the hour. Beginners may also avail themselves of this facility and will be helped by the courteous and skilled staff.

Moderately priced training classes in hardware and software operation will also be offered.

MANAGEMENT & PERSONNEL

Steve Lane, 25, recently earned his doctoral degree in Advertising at Washington University, after having earned a Ph.D. in Graphic Design. He will serve as President and Treasurer of Power Desk Top Publishing, Inc. and will function as Manager. During his years at Washington University, Steve spent two summers interning at Thompson-McGuire Advertising agency, where he sharpened his skills in layout and design and gained much practical knowledge of advertising production. With his formidable business education, having also achieved his M.B.A. at Washington University, Steve will handle all the day-to-day business management activities of Power Desk Top Publishing, Inc. In addition to this, he intends to devote at least 4 hours per day to making personal sales calls on prospective business customers.

Throughout his college years, Steve developed work habits that have always included long hours. The plan for Power Desk Top Publishing contemplates a completely owner-operated business, with both Steve and Mary doing most, if not all, of the production and hands-on computer work in the evening after devoting their days primarily to sales calls and customer service in the field.

Mary Lane, 31, graduated from Webster University with a B.A. in English in June of 1992. She will be Vice President and Secretary of Power Desk Top Publishing, Inc. and will share management and sales responsibility with her husband. Upon graduation, she held positions as copywriter in the advertising department for a large food processing company and later, as Assistant Advertising Manager for the same company. For the past seven years she has been a housewife, raising their daughter. The daughter is now in school full-time during the day, and Mrs. Lane is free to devote her daytime efforts to the promotion of the family business.

Mary will have primary responsibility for developing and managing their student market. She will be preparing and inserting display and classified ads in the student newspapers of the local colleges. She will be on campus to discuss with clientele the company's services and, in general, to attend to the needs of this very special market.

When not engaged in campus sales activities, Mrs. Lane will be calling on the general business community to promote sales in this area. She also will be responsible for composition, proofreading, graphic layout, and typesetting.

Both Mary and Steve will be active in all production facets of the business, with Steve's expertise more concentrated in graphic design and advertising, and Mary's directed to composition and proofing.

Power Desk Top Publishing will commence business as completely owner-operated, with Steve and Mary Lane handling all phases of business activities. As the business progresses, it is expected that part-time help will be added to assist with some of the more routine activities. The job pool from which the Lanes intend to draw is the student job placement services of both St. Louis University and Washington University.

Both campuses are situated in reasonably close proximity to Power Desk Top Publishing, which will be operating from the Lanes' residence at 4900 Maryland Plaza. Because of the Lanes' close and recent involvement with student life and activities, it is well known to them that a ready source of capable and willing workers is available, in the wage scale of $6.25 to $6.75 per hour. While the wages are only minimum wage or slightly above, the work is deemed more desirable than fast food service and the scheduling quite flexible and very compatible with student needs.

The jobs require computer literacy along with good typing skills. Macintosh experience, particularly with PageMaker or Quark Express, will be a desirable attribute. No problems are anticipated in filling any future personnel requirements from the available student labor pool.

Other Personnel

The concept of desk top publishing has come into its own, due to the high cost of traditional printing. Before the advent of the desk top publisher, the printing buyer would often employ a graphic design company or an advertising agency to put together their literature, newsletter, or promotional piece. There were production costs incurred in the design and layout workups. Once completed, the design or advertising company would often deal directly with a printing company on behalf of the customer. The printing company would then utilize the service of a typesetting company, which would compose the type and layout in finished form ready to be run on the presses of the printer. It is easy to see that there were quite a few levels of profit involved in these operations, all at the expense of the printing buyer.

PRODUCT DESCRIPTION

As personal computers and laser printers evolved, it became clear that compact and less expensive equipment could accomplish the same functions of the highly sophisticated and capital intensive traditional typesetting and printing operations. The advent of powerful "typesetting" and page layout software, available at affordable prices, gave the computer operator all the versatility of a traditional composing room at a fraction of the cost. Because of the relative simplicity of the system, and the fact that the various hardware could be conveniently positioned on a typical desk top, the term desk top publishing came into being. The time for desk top publishing has definitely arrived, now an industry in its own right, with sales expected to top $2 billion by 2003.

The work of Steve and Mary Lane is recognized for its highly appealing style and striking impact. Their work is not ordinary. Both possess a certain flair and panache for graphic artistry that is reflected in their work. Comparatively speaking, the efforts of "speed printers" are merely mechanical, taking in camera-ready copy and spitting out 500 or 1000 reproductions, which is not what Steve and Mary Lane are bringing to the marketplace. Expert composing skills, a knack for creative layout, and a complete command of their library of sophisticated and powerful software enable Power Desk Top Publishing to produce a dynamite product to their customers' complete satisfaction.

Some typical jobs might include:

Brochures	Fliers
Business Plans	Newsletters
Church Bulletins	Restaurant Menus
College Dissertations	Resumes
Direct Mail Pieces	Term Papers

MARKET ANALYSIS— CUSTOMERS

The need for quick, economical printing has been well established. The need for creative printing, that is also quick and economical, remains an unfulfilled need in many regions of the metropolitan area. It is this market that Power Desk Top Publishing intends to cultivate.

Businesses make up the most fertile field in the spectrum of users of desk top publishing. The wide array of companies doing business in the St. Louis area present a most diverse market that is not particularly dependent on any specific industry. Both Steve and Mary intend to cultivate, through personal phone calls, literally hundreds of business contacts each week. Almost every company uses some sort of printed promotional material. Power Desk Top Publishing intends to demonstrate to their clients just how they can save money and have a more appealing presence as a result of the skill and creativity of the Power team.

Preselling calls have revealed that users are overpaying for printing products simply because they are using the outdated mode of traditional typesetting and printing presses. Desk top publishing could fulfill their needs with more style and greater economy. This will be the prime market for Power Desk Top Publishing, Inc.

Another important category of business is the restaurant menu. Literally, hundreds of restaurants feature stylized menus, which change from time to time. Using a system of templates that Mr. Lane has developed, Power Desk Top Publishing will attract a significant customer base in the food industry by providing fast, responsive service with creative, customized menu renditions in a wide variety of styles and formats, each tailored to the needs of a particular client's restaurant.

Newsletters represent a market very worthy of development. Power Desk Top Publishing is in the unique position to provide a full range of services in which copywriting will be offered as an important option. Mary Lane's training and background will be most helpful in creating dynamic and interesting newsletters for clients who have no in-house writer. This will set Power Desk Top Publishing apart from typical printers that offer only mechanical services. Creative service and customized support at attractive prices will be the hallmark of Power Desk Top Publishing.

Churches are another target market for Power Desk Top Publishing. While the in-house duplicators of most church offices will suffice for routine notices, special events and fund raisers are best heralded by attractive eye-catching announcements. This is where the professional attention of Steve and Mary Lane proves invaluable. The training and expertise developed over long years of advanced study honed in the competitive advertising arena, assures their clientele of the very best in desk top publishing.

The student market is another great source of business for Power Desk Top Publishing. Term papers, dissertations, and doctoral theses all demand more attention when presented with style and a professional layout. A special student rate will be available as an added inducement. Both Steve and Mary, because of their own recent academic history, are superbly qualified to address this specialized market. Steve's two Ph.Ds make him eminently qualified to work with doctoral candidates in the preparation and publishing of their theses. Mary, being an English major, is also available to coach and proofread. They are a sales team with whom the student client can identify and enjoy working. It is expected that this type of rapport will engender rapid word of mouth referral in the campus community, all to the betterment of Power Desk Top Publishing, Inc.

Resumes represent a segment of the market that must not be overlooked. Desk top publishers have found this a fertile field, likely to increase in demand when overall economic conditions decline, thereby affording a hedge against recession in the publishing field. Like several of the markets outlined above, this is a specialty market, yet one that can be addressed by strategic placement of inexpensive classified ads and an additional Yellow Page listing.

Business plans will be another important service for Power Desk Top Publishing. The entrepreneurial market continues to expand, and with the competition for borrowed and investor funds, it is increasingly essential for business people to approach the financial community with a solid prospectus of their planned enterprise. PlanMaker, innovative new software for the Macintosh computer, will be an important tool in Power Desk Top Publishing's library. Using PlanMaker, Steve and Mary will work closely in guiding new business people step-by-step in the creation of a dynamic business plan.

COMPETITION

The prime mover in the desk top publishing field in the St. Louis market is currently Speed-Craft Printers, who have three locations. Speed-Craft, which is a franchised operation, has done a good job in raising the consciousness of the printing buyer to the economies of desk top publishing. They maintain a strong advertising presence in the *St. Louis Business Journal* and the Yellow Pages. They are walk-in operations and will not pick up copy but will deliver finished product via courier. They do not have sales people calling on business and industry on a regular basis. Power Desk Top Publishing, Inc. will not try to wage a dollar for dollar advertising campaign in direct competition with Speed-Craft. Steve and Mary do not feel that would be cost effective at this time. Much more on target will be their daily personal sales calls to owners and managers of businesses of all descriptions. The face-to-face conversations and the personal dissemination of samples of their work will have a greater impact than media advertising.

Other desk top publishing businesses are primarily one-person operations that have carved out their niche in certain areas. These operations cover the complete spectrum of proficiency. Some have only perfunctory skills and limited equipment resources, while others offer excellent products and services.

In addition to others in desk top publishing, Power Desk Top Publishing will be competing with traditional printers and advertising agencies.

Because of their advanced training and experience, as well as the most modern of equipment and software, Power Desk Top Publishing will quickly establish themselves as a major contender in the local desk top publishing industry.

Creativity, speed, and price are the three major factors that all competing companies must successfully address. Drawing from the ample skills of the principals, Power Desk Top Publishing will be known for its exceptional creative design. No one can deliver faster than Steve and Mary with modern equipment, a work-at-home facility, and dedication to spend long hours in the building of their business. Power DTP also will be very competitive with prices. With virtually no overhead, meeting and beating prices will present no problem. Blind surveys of competing firms have indicated that Power Desk Top Publishing can discount their product as much as 20% off prevailing prices and still turn a reasonable profit. No such price slashing is contemplated, however, Power Desk Top Publishing does possess the capability to compete should the market turn aggressive.

RISKS

Risks that are inherent to all businesses have been contemplated by Steve and Mary Lane in the formation of the plan for Power Desk Top Publishing, Inc. Of course, traditional casualty risks will be covered by business owners insurance, ample to protect all assets and with a $250,000 public and product liability umbrella. There are no potential hazards regarding the availability of raw materials, which are primarily paper stocks and in good supply nationwide. Stepped up recycling efforts have served to stabilize paper costs, which in turn has held pricing fairly steady in the printing field.

If paper stock pricing does trend upward, the effect will be industry-wide, with Power Desk Top Publishing being able to pass the costs along by way of retail price adjustments to the extent that industry follows suit, which has traditionally been the case in the printing field. In the event that aggressive competitive pricing develops, Power Desk Top Publishing is ideally situated to successfully compete in a price-dominated market.

Other potential variations in the economy have been carefully evaluated by management. Two of our featured specialities, resumes and business plans, are known to increase in demand during a sluggish economy, as more individuals contemplate career changes and business opportunities.

Diversity of customer base is also another strength of Power Desk Top Publishing. Because Power DTP will be selling to a very wide range of companies, churches, and individuals, encompassing many different fields, they are less dependent on any particular industry and therefore have an added dimension of strength based on diversification of market.

During economic downturns, prudent businesses not only watch their costs more intently, but initiate sales-generating promotions through direct mail and other printed advertisements. Power Desk Top Publishing stands ready to fill that need and at attractive and even discounted prices if warranted.

The Lanes feel that flexibility is their strength and, should economic conditions require a change in price or product concept, they will be quick to react with an updated marketing plan.

MARKETING STRATEGY

Desk top publishing is now widely appreciated as a creative and innovative approach to the field of graphic arts. Traditional methods, involving hard typesetting and massive printing presses, became more and more expensive and, consequently, less and less accessible to cost conscious users. In the true American tradition of "find a need and fill it," the advent of sophisticated computers, like the Macintosh, coupled with powerful software, provided the tools for skilled operators to produce impressive printing for their clients at affordable prices.

It is in this arena that Steve and Mary Lane will launch Power Desk Top Publishing, Inc. The markets have been defined, with General Business being a prime target. Both Steve and Mary will each devote at least four hours per day calling business owners and managers. All types of companies will be canvassed, both large and small. Steve and Mary will work independently of each other, reaching a targeted 20 prospects each per day. Time permitting, additional calls may be made during the early phases of start-up. Each sales call will be accompanied by the distribution of samples, depicting design and printing capabilities of Power Desk Top Publishing. Creativity will be stressed, and buyers will be offered a 15% first-time discount as an introductory offer. Steve and Mary will pick up copy and deliver finished products as they make their sales rounds each day. Personal service and attention will be among their main selling points.

Churches and restaurants also represent specialized markets with particular needs, and these establishments will be targeted for special attention by Steve and Mary. As with businesses, the creative talents of Power Desk Top Publishing will be emphasized as the needs of the clients are discussed. They will be selling a look and feel as well as a printed page.

The student market will be addressed through advertisements placed in campus newspapers of Washington University, St. Louis University, Webster University, Fontbonne College, and Southern Illinois University at Edwardsville. Doctoral theses, dissertations, term papers, and other publications will be given expert attention. A student discount and a referral discount program will be utilized. Citing the academic credentials of the principals, personal consultations will be encouraged.

Resumes and business plans represent another market that will be addressed. Strategically placed classified advertisements in the *St. Louis Post Dispatch* and the *St. Louis Business Journal* will be used to attract clients.

Power Desk Top Publishing, Inc. will offer a full range of services. Not merely printing, but graphic design, custom layout, creative writing, guidance, and coaching in self-preparation of copy will be offered. Power DTP will provide the complete spectrum of professional services not found in any other desk top publishing companies.

ADVERTISING, PROMOTION & PUBLIC RELATIONS

Power Desk Top Publishing has designated an advertising budget of $3,000 for year one. A commitment of $1,000 is scheduled for months one and two and is directed at the campus newspapers of St. Louis University, Washington University, Webster University, Fontbonne College, and Southern Illinois University at Edwardsville. Ads will be directed at the student market and will be selling the services of Power Desk Top Publishing in the realm of publishing term papers, theses, and doctoral dissertations, as well as resumes and other published material associated with academia. Personal consultations will be encouraged.

Press releases also will be distributed to these newspapers, with follow-up calls to encourage editorial exposure. As alumni, respectively of Washington University and Webster University, Steve and Mary will give particular attention to those campuses. Press releases announcing the entry of Power Desk Top Publishing also will be distributed to the appropriate editors of the *St. Louis Post Dispatch*, the *St. Louis Business Journal*, the *Journal Newspaper Group*, and *St. Louis Computer News*. Photographs of the principals will be included with brief resumes and other relevant data.

Power Desk Top Publishing will attempt no media blitz in attracting attention. Personal sales calls, emphasizing face-to-face contact with buyers, remains the promotional medium of choice for Power DTP. All sales calls will include distribution of samples that are relevant to the prospect's business and will include a first-time 15% introductory discount. Both Steve and Mary possess a natural disposition and manner that is well suited to represent their company to the public.

Strategic use of classified advertising will also play a role in sales development. Targeting resumes and business plans through the Career and Business Opportunities sections of the classified ads will be an inexpensive way to attract customers.

Power Desk Top Publishing will participate in the annual Small Business Expo, which is a regional trade show directed at entrepreneurs and other business enterprises. This well-attended convention attracts some 20,000 visitors to the Convention Center and will provide an ideal forum for meeting new prospects and disseminating sample work to a wide spectrum of business and prospective customers of all descriptions. Booth rental and expenses have been budgeted at $1,200.

Steve and Mary are current participants, or are joining, several worthwhile business and community organizations. Paramount among these is the Association of Desk Top Publishers, a national group dedicated to excellence in desk top publishing. In addition to an annual convention, the organization also promotes local chapters which meet regularly to further the professional standards of desk top publishing. The Lanes are active members in the St. Louis chapter.

Power Desk Top Publishing also will be joining the St. Louis Regional Commerce and Growth Association as a small business Associate Member. Steve is an active member of the Central West End Lions Club and attends the monthly luncheons. Membership is composed primarily of small business owners and managers and this affiliation is expected to be helpful in obtaining additional business for Power Desk Top Publishing.

Mary Lane has formally proposed writing a regular column in the *St. Louis Small Business Monthly*, which is a tabloid-sized newspaper circulated to about 3,000 small businesses in the St. Louis area. The suggested title column is "Desk Top Publishing Update" and will feature information of a topical nature about advances in desk top publishing and other matters of general interest to the printing buyer and advertising manager. Mary has submitted two sample columns and the proposal is now under active consideration. She will receive no direct remuneration but will be credited as co-owner of Power Desk Top Publishing, Inc., which will have significant advertising value.

PRICING & PROFITABILITY

Competitive pricing will be an important marketing tool of Power Desk Top Publishing, Inc. In doing their market research, all existing desk top publishers in the St. Louis area were surveyed by the Lanes to determine their price structure.

Because of the low overhead operation contemplated by Power Desk Top Publishing, introductory and student discounts can be offered to gain access to the market. Once the quality and service of Power Desk Top Publishing becomes known, Power DTP will be able to compete effectively at prevailing market prices.

Because of the efficiencies inherent to desk top publishing, a good margin of gross profit is normal for the industry. This is particularly true for Power Desk Top Publishing, which, at its inception, will be completely owner-operated and situated in an in-home location.

Paper costs make up the primary hard cost of any given job and normally runs 16% to 18%.

Minimal overhead for insurance, utilities, etc. is presently budgeted at 10-11%.

Sale costs are estimated at 10%.

Advertising and promotion, exclusive of discounts, amount to about 6%.

Equipment depreciation and debt amortization figures at 15%.

This allows 42% gross profit at prevailing retail prices, before officers' salaries. Net after salaries is 11%.

BREAK-EVEN EVALUATION
Computed on Gross Sales

Percent Cost of Goods Sold	17.0%
Percent Gross Profit	83.0%
Monthly Overhead	$3,775
Monthly Gross Sales to reach break-even	$4,548

*[For detailed derivation of these calculations, refer to Twelve Month Proforma, financial Projections.]

A budget has been prepared by Power Desk Top Publishing, Inc. reflecting necessary capital expenditures and projected start-up costs.

Equipment and Fixtures	$15,000
Advertising and Promotion	3,000
Deposits and initial start-up costs	5,000
Contingency	2,000
Operating Reserve	$10,000
Total	**$35,000**

[Equipment and Fixtures are listed in the Equipment Schedule following. It has been determined that Steve and Mary Lane will draw a weekly salary of $250 each. The company will also provide health insurance for both officers.

The principals have developed a sound approach to the market, maximizing strengths and minimizing risks.]

Total capitalization of $35,000 will be derived as follows:

Principal's Equity	$5,000
Borrowed Capital	30,000
Total	**$35,000**

[The principal equity comes from savings. It is projected that borrowed capital would be drawn down over a period of the first twelve months of business, commencing April 1, 2000. Approximately 50% will be required initially for equipment acquisition.

Start of operations is scheduled for April 15, 2000.]

	Brand	Model	Capacity/ Rating	New/Used	Cost
2 Computers	Macintosh	SE		New	$2,200
Hard Drive	Xographics	A-16XYG	300 MG	New	2,000
Removable Hard Drive	Emmon	EHM-DriA1	44 MG	New	600
2 Laser Writer Printers	Apple	Ilnt		New	5,000
Scanner	Microtek	MSD 300Z		New	1,850
Jogger	Martin-Yale	100		New	150
Paper Cutter	Martin-Yale	6100L	1 HP	Used	1,200
Software*	Various			New	1,000
Desks, chairs, file cabinets	Various			New/Used	1,000
Total Equipment Costs					**$15,000**

*[The Lanes already own a large library of graphic arts and page design software.]

TWELVE-MONTH PROFORMA

	Month One	Month Two	Month Three	Month Four	Month Five	Month Six	Month Seven	Month Eight	Month Nine	Month Ten
Sales										
Sale of Printing	4,400	4,642	4,897	5,167	5,451	5,751	5,952	6,160	6,376	6,599
Other Sales	0	0	0	0	0	0	0	0	0	0
Total Sales	**4,400**	**4,642**	**4,897**	**5,167**	**5,451**	**5,751**	**5,952**	**6,160**	**6,376**	**6,599**
Cost of Sales	**748**	**789**	**833**	**878**	**927**	**978**	**1,012**	**1,047**	**1,084**	**1,122**
Gross Profit	**3,652**	**3,853**	**4,065**	**4,288**	**4,524**	**4,773**	**4,940**	**5,113**	**5,292**	**5,477**
Operating Expenses										
Sales & Marketing										
Advertising	250	250	250	250	250	250	250	250	250	250
Commissions	0	0	0	0	0	0	0	0	0	0
Entertainment	0	0	0	0	0	0	0	0	0	0
Literature	100	100	100	100	100	100	100	100	100	100
Sales Promotion	175	175	175	175	175	175	175	175	175	175
Trade Shows	100	100	100	100	100	100	100	100	100	100
Travel	100	100	100	100	100	100	100	100	100	100
Salaries (Sales Personnel)	0	0	0	0	0	0	0	0	0	0
PR Taxes & Costs, Sales	0	0	0	0	0	0	0	0	0	0
Total Selling Cost	**725**	**725**	**725**	**725**	**725**	**725**	**725**	**725**	**725**	**725**

Month Eleven	Month Twelve	Year One	Per cent
6,830	7,069	69,293	100%
0	0	0	0%
6,830	**7,069**	**69,293**	
1,161	**1,202**	**11,780**	**17%**
5,669	**5,867**	**57,513**	**83%**
250	250	3,000	
0	0	0	
0	0	0	
100	100	1,200	
175	175	2,100	
100	100	1,200	
100	100	1,200	
0	0	0	
0	0	0	
725	**725**	**8,700**	**13%**

TWELVE-MONTH PROFORMA

Continued

General & Administrative	Month One	Month Two	Month Three	Month Four	Month Five	Month Six	Month Seven	Month Eight	Month Nine	Month Ten
Accounting	50	50	50	50	50	50	50	50	50	50
Amorization	0	0	0	0	0	0	0	0	0	0
Bad Debts	88	93	98	103	109	115	119	123	128	132
Depreciation	179	179	179	179	179	179	179	179	179	179
Insurance	100	100	100	100	100	100	100	100	100	100
Legal Fees	25	25	25	25	25	25	25	25	25	25
Licenses & Permits	25	25	25	25	25	25	25	25	25	25
Salaries & Wages	0	0	0	0	0	0	0	0	0	0
PR Taxes & PR Costs	0	0	0	0	0	0	0	0	0	0
Taxes (non-income taxes)	0	0	0	0	0	0	0	0	0	0
Office Expense	100	110	121	133	146	161	177	195	214	236
Rent	0	0	0	0	0	0	0	0	0	0
Telephone	75	76	77	77	78	79	80	80	81	82
Utilities	0	0	0	0	0	0	0	0	0	0
Officers' Salary	2,150	2,150	2,150	2,150	2,150	2,150	2,150	2,150	2,150	2,150
PR Taxes & Costs Officers	258	258	258	258	258	258	258	258	258	258
Total General & Administrative Cost	**3,050**	**3,065**	**3,082**	**3,100**	**3,120**	**3,141**	**3,162**	**3,185**	**3,210**	**3,236**
Net Income Before Taxes and Interest	-123	63	258	463	679	907	1,053	1,203	1,357	1,510
Interest	250	247	244	240	237	234	230	227	224	220
Net Income	**-372**	**-184**	**14**	**223**	**442**	**673**	**823**	**976**	**1,134**	**1,296**

Month Eleven	Month Twelve	Year One	Per cent
50	50	600	
0	0	0	
137	141	1,386	
179	179	2,143	
100	100	1,200	
25	25	300	
25	25	300	
0	0	0	
0	0	0	
0	0	0	
259	285	2,138	
0	0	0	
83	84	951	
0	0	0	
2,150	2,150	25,800	
258	258	3,096	
3,265	**3,297**	**37,914**	**55%**
1,678	1,845	10,899	15.7%
217	213	2,781	4.0%
1,462	**1,632**	**8,118**	**11.7%**

**THREE-YEAR
PROJECTED
INCOME
STATEMENT**

Sales	Year 1		Year 2		Year 3	
Sale of Printing	69,293		86,617		99,609	
Other Sales	0		0		0	
Total Sales	**69,293**		**86,617**		**99,609**	
Cost-of-Goods-Sold	11,780	17%	14,725	17%	16,934	17%
Gross Profit	**57,513**		**71,892**		**82,676**	
Selling Expense	8,700	13%	9,179	11%	9,683	10%
General & Administrative	37,914	55%	40,000	46%	42,200	42%
Net Income Before Taxes and Interest	**10,899**	**16%**	**27,714**	**26%**	**30,793**	**31%**
Interest	2,781	4%	2,271	2.6%	1,707	1.7%
Income taxes	2,029		5,111		7,271	
New Income or Loss	**6,088**	**9%**	**15,332**	**18%**	**21,814**	**22%**

This page left intentionally blank to accommodate tabular material following.

CASH FLOW
PROJECTION

	Month One	Month Two	Month Three	Month Four	Month Five	Month Six	Month Seven	Month Eight	Month Nine	Month Ten
Beginning Cash Balance	5,000	2,055	1,528	3,190	3,049	3,117	8,403	8,889	9,521	10,304
Cash Receipts from Sales	2,200	4,433	4,677	4,934	5,205	5,492	5,736	5,939	6,145	6,360
Total Cash Available	7,200	6,488	6,205	8,124	8,255	8,609	14,140	14,826	15,666	16,663
Cash Disbursements:										
Accounts Payable, merchandise	0	748	789	833	878	927	978	1,012	1,047	1,084
Selling Costs	725	725	725	725	725	725	725	725	725	725
General & Administrative	375	386	398	410	424	440	457	475	496	518
Salaries	2,408	2,408	2,408	2,408	2,408	2,408	2,408	2,408	2,408	2,408
Total Cash Disbursements	3,508	4,267	4,320	4,376	4,436	4,500	4,567	4,620	4,676	4,735
Net Cash from Operations	3,692	2,221	1,885	3,748	3,819	4,109	9,572	10,206	10,990	11,929
Proceeds of Loans										
National Bnk, Fixtures & Equip	15,000	0	0	0	0	0	0	0	0	0
National Bnk, Operating Line	0	2,000	2,000	0	0	5,000	0	0	0	0
Capital Infusion										
Additonal Paid in Capital	0	0	0	0	0	0	0	0	0	0
Other Disbursements										
Debt Service	638	638	638	638	638	638	638	638	638	638
Capital Disbursements										
Furniture & Fixtures	0	0	0	0	0	0	0	0	0	0
Equipment	15,000	0	0	0	0	0	0	0	0	0
Inventory Purchases	1,000	55	58	61	65	68	46	47	49	51
Prepaid Expense/Deposits	0	2,000	0	0	0	0	0	0	0	0
Net Cash Balance	**2,055**	**1,528**	**3,190**	**3,049**	**3,117**	**8,403**	**8,889**	**9,521**	**10,304**	**11,241**

Month Eleven	Month Twelve
11,241	12,336
6,582	6,813
17,823	19,149
1,122	1,161
725	725
542	569
2,408	2,408
4,797	4,863
13,026	14,286
0	0
0	0
0	0
638	638
0	0
0	0
52	54
0	0
12,336	**13,594**

BALANCE SHEET, CURRENT & PROJECTED

Assets	Current	Year 1	Year 2	Year 3
Current Assets				
Cash and Equivalents	4,000	15,594	30,424	49,901
Receivables from Sales	0	3,393	4,241	4,878
Other Receivables	0	0	0	0
Inventory	1,000	1,607	1,640	1,887
Prepaid Expense/Deposits	0	0	0	0
Total Current Assets	**5,000**	**20,594**	**36,306**	**56,665**
Fixed Assets:				
Equipment & Machinery	15,000	15,000	15,000	15,000
Less accumulated depreciation	0	2,143	4,286	6,429
Net Fixed Assets	**15,000**	**12,857**	**10,714**	**8,571**
TOTAL ASSETS	**20,000**	**33,451**	**47,021**	**65,237**
LIABILITIES				
Current Liabilities				
Trade Payables	0	1,202	1,227	1,411
Income Tax Payable	0	2,029	5,111	7,271
Short Term Notes	0	0	0	0
Total Current Liabilities	**0**	**3,231**	**6,338**	**8,682**
Long Term Liabilities				
Notes Payable, Bank	15,000	19,131	14,263	8,320
Notes Payable, Others	0	0	0	0
Other Liabilities	0	0	0	0
Total Long Term Liabilities	**15,000**	**19,131**	**14,263**	**8,320**
TOTAL LIABILITIES	**15,000**	**22,362**	**20,600**	**17,002**
Stockholder's Equity				
Capital Stock	5,000	5,000	5,000	5,000
Retained Earnings	0	6,088	21,420	43,234
Total Stockholder's Equity	**5,000**	**11,088**	**26,420**	**48,234**
TOTAL LIABILITIES & STOCKHOLDERS EQUITY	**20,000**	**33,451**	**47,021**	**653,237**
Current Ratio		**6.4**	**5.7**	**6.5**
Quick Ratio		**5.9**	**5.5**	**6.3**
Debt to Equity Ratio		**2.0**	**0.8**	**0.4**
Return on Investment		**54.9%**	**58.0%**	**45.2%**

Display Technology Company

BUSINESS PLAN

TOUCHTOP TECHNOLOGIES, INC.

3000 S. Washington Dr.
New York, New York 10278

This display technology company bases its success on the expertise of its founders who are pioneers in display technology, as well as the propietary technology of its products such as flat screen monitor displays.

Highlights

- Management team composed of renown pioneers in display technology
- Licensing commitments from leading display manufacturers
- Extremely low cost to deploy using existing production facilities
- Highly differentiated proprietary technology insulated by substantial barriers to entry
- Ideal stage of development life cycle
- Large $10 billion market growing rapidly

EXECUTIVE SUMMARY

"There is no end in sight as the world's top display producers continue to upgrade and expand production in efforts to capture share."

—Ernest Gallow, *The Display Insider*

The Company-The Vision-The Founders

Flat Panel Display Manufacturers have spent billions in search of a viable successor to Liquid Crystal Display technology. TouchTop Technologies, Inc. has developed a display system that exceeds the performance, cost, and production demands of the world's top display manufacturers. Since 1990, TouchTop Technologies' principals have been perfecting their patented Light Emitting Dry Crystal Display System, LEDCD. Upon production of full-scale prototypes, this technology will be licensed to top LCD producers worldwide. NEEC has tentatively committed to pay $20 million for use of the technology upon TouchTop's production of a prototype that performs in accordance with claims made on the breadboard unit.

The founders of TouchTop Technologies are known internationally in the display industry. Mr. Ira Weinstein, President and CEO, directed the overall development of LCD manufacturing systems for NEEC and Hundeye during the late 1980s and early 1990s. Neither of these clients will expand production capacity without consulting Mr. Weinstein first. Mr. Di Patel, Vice President of Technology, launched his first software startup from his dormitory room at Stanford University. As a graduate student, he developed one of the first true nuero-network protocols. The technology was licensed by Inteli-Trade, a leading provider of computer based trading systems, and eventually sold to them. TouchTop Technologies' Vice President of Science, Dr. Vladimir Chenenko, has developed over 25 patented display technologies and 50 novel chemical compounds for use in a wide range of applications. Dr. Chenenko is an internationally recognized authority and pioneer in the field of display technology. His early work, *The Principals, Characteristics, and Applications of Liquid Crystal Displays*, has been translated into 4 languages and is a field manual for display developers around the world. It is this depth of expertise that has allowed TouchTop Technologies to develop the next generation display technology in only 6 years and this core team will drive the timely release and licensing of the technology within 12 months of funding.

Market Opportunity

The top five Active Matrix Liquid Crystal Display producers worldwide spent more than $1.3 billion in 1995 for research and development of the next generation display device. Driving the rationale for continued investment is an ever increasing, and currently unsatisfied, demand for larger, thinner, clearer, and faster display devices by consumers. Over $12 billion was spent on AMLCDs in 1996. This huge market is expected to grow over $19 billion by the year 2000. Current estimates of growth in the AMLCD market do not take into account the possibility of traditional CRTs in desktops and televisions being replaced by AMLCDs. TouchTop Technologies' LEDCD allows display manufacturers to produce displays that offer contrast ratios 20 times higher than all viable alternatives to AMLCDs with superior viewing angles and response times that are 1000 times faster. All of these advantages are provided at 15% of the cost to manufacture AMLCDs. Management expects this advantage to translate into over $59 million in annual revenue within three years.

The company is seeking $2,300,000 in first round financing, in the form of convertible preferred units, to fund production and testing of 3 full-scale prototypes. The company intends to use the proceeds from equity investments as follows:

USE OF PROCEEDS

Use of Proceeds

GROSS OFFERING	$2,300,000
LESS ESTIMATED OFFERING EXPENSES AND COMMISSIONS	0
NET PROCEEDS	**2,300,000**

PLANNED USES

CAPITAL EXPENDITURES

Computer equipment	90,000
Purchased software	90,000
Furniture and fixtures	70,000
Leasehold improvements	50,000
Total proceeds for capital expenditures	**300,000**

WORKING CAPITAL

Salaries and wages	428,259
Occupancy	173,000
Professional services	120,000
Travel	154,059
Research and development expenses - 1998	1,102,069
Reserve	322,613
Total proceeds for working capital and reserve	**1,654,774**
Total Uses	**$2,300,000**

FINANCIAL SNAPSHOT	1997	1998	1999	2000	2001
Income					
License revenue	$0	$20,000,000	$50,000,000	$50,000,000	$50,000,000
Support revenue	0	2,777,500	9,165,750	6,666,000	4,999,500
Royalty revenue	0	0	3,010,292	15,857,939	33,530,224
Total revenue	**0**	**22,777,500**	**62,176,042**	**72,523,939**	**88,529,724**
Cost of sales	0	1,468,499	2,528,601	3,142,051	3,261,376
Gross margin	0	21,309,001	59,647,441	69,381,888	85,268,348
Total operating expenses	**1,629,835**	**7,272,631**	**17,842,273**	**21,749,635**	**26,596,077**

FINANCIAL SNAPSHOT (PROJECTED)

FINANCIAL SNAPSHOT (PROJECTED)

Continued

	1997	1998	1999	2000	2001
Income from operations	1,629,835	14,036,370	41,805,168	47,632,253	58,672,271
Cash Flow					
Cash flow from operations	1,417,394	9,286,037	25,844,649	29,365,325	38,365,828
Cash flow from financing activities	2,301,000	0	0	0	0
Selected Performance Measures					
Earnings to sales	NM	0.41	0.42	0.42	0.43
Gross margin percent	NM	0.94	0.96	0.96	0.96
Operating margin	NM	0.62	0.67	0.66	0.66
Pretax return on tangible equity	-1.98	1.44	1.22	0.77	0.62
Pretax return on assets (%)	-1.86	1.42	1.21	0.77	0.61
Return on assets (%)	-1.86	0.91	0.71	0.45	0.36
Asset utilization turnover	NM	0.01	0.01	0.01	0.01
RETURN on equity	**NM**	**0.92**	**0.72**	**0.46**	**0.36**

THE ENTERPRISE— THE PRODUCT

"The biggest cause for the shortage (in large screen notebook computers)...is soaring demand."
—Evan Ramstad, *Wall Street Journal*, November 20, 1996

The Company

TouchTop Technologies, Inc. develops leading-edge display technologies for license to the world's top display manufacturers. Although not incorporated until 1996, the concept for TouchTop Technologies, Inc. was conceived in January of 1990. Dr. Di Patel had just recently completed his work as chief architect of the revolutionary graphical user interface for Microsoft's Windows operating system. He and Mr. Ira Weinstein, who was in charge of establishing Hundeye's Thin Film Transistor LCD lab in Korea, were discussing the future of user interfaces at the Information Display Symposium in San Diego. Within moments it became clear that the two men shared a common vision for the next generation of interaction between user and computer. By the end of the symposium their discussion had evolved into a thorough functional specification for the next generation interface: a thin, flexible portable display device that mimics a desktop in scale and user interaction.

With the proposed device, users could simply touch "stacks" of full-size documents on the screen and be able to view multiple documents simultaneously. Essentially the user would interact in an environment where the "screen" provides display output and accepts input in the same manner physical objects on a desk are manipulated and at the same physical scale.

In the course of developing the technical specifications for such a device, it became clear that the existing technology could not meet all of the founder's functional requirements. This led Mr. Weinstein to consult his friend and associate Dr. Vladimir Chenenko. Dr. Chenenko literally wrote the book, actually several books, on flat screen display systems in the former Soviet Union. For most of his adult life, Dr. Chenenko has pursed development of what he calls a Light Emitting Dry Crystal Display. Although Dr. Chenenko's patented system was very promising, in its raw state it lacked the responsiveness and manufacturability to make it a viable alternative to competing display technologies. Together, Mr. Weinstein, Mr. Patel, and Dr. Chenenko transformed the Light Emitting Dry Crystal Display into the next generation of display technology.

The principals of TouchTop Technologies, Inc. are established within the fields of information display technology, user interface devices, and artificial intelligence. They bring extensive expertise associated with comprehensive product development, marketing, manufacturing controls, and international business affairs.

Among the strengths of the four principals of TouchTop Technologies, Inc. is an aggregate of 120 years of direct experience in pioneering computer hardware and software technologies. Their renown and acclaim for product conceptualization, design, development, and manufacturing make them a most formidable competitor in the information display market.

Each principal has clearly demonstrated their prowess as skillful businessmen and engineers in independent ventures that were highly successful, including Microsoft, Goldenstar, and Fujitomo. The wisdom of each principal to plan the exit from their respective ventures provided a method for insuring their professional and financial growth by continually seeking greater challenges in their respective fields of expertise. Ultimately, their creativity, ingenuity, competence, and high level of business acumen was profitable to them, their former partners, shareholders, and clientele. Business is more than time and money to the principals of TouchTop Technologies, Inc.; it is responsiveness. This assertion is supported by their notable accomplishments, detailed in the appendix and organization sections of this plan.

The Vision

Within six months of funding, the company expects to have 3 fully functioning prototypes available for further testing. Assuming these prototypes perform in accordance with performance standards observed in the breadboard unit, the company expects to execute its first license agreement with NEEC in the amount of $20 million. As part of the agreement, TouchTop will support commercialization and configuration of the system at an existing NEEC plant for a guaranteed maximum sum of $3,000,000. The first LEDCD fitted products are tentatively scheduled to ship in early 2000, producing royalty revenue of $3 million in that year. By 2001, the company expects to have similar agreements in place with other manufacturers, producing revenues of over $72 million. The technology's performance, economy, and novelty all suggest that these target goals can be realized.

The Product/The Technology

Cathode Ray Tube display is the highest resolution display device available today. The portability of this technology is an unfortunate limitation imposed by the picture tube. This dilemma led to the design and development of the Liquid Crystal Display (LCD). Traditionally, passive matrix LCD systems are essentially a combination of a wire grid, a light source, and a liquid crystal solution. Liquid Crystal Elements control the emission or omission of light passage, which creates a viewable image. A key limitation of passive LCD systems is their inability to produce images that can be viewed from all angles. To combat this problem, the Active Matrix Liquid Crystal Display (AMLCD) was invented.

Active Matrix LCDs produce viewable images in the same manner as Passive Matrix LCDs with one added, and very expensive, component: Thin Film Transistors (TFTs). A transistor controls each and every pixel in the display. This allows the display to generate high-resolution images that are viewable from more angles. There are two limiting factors that drive the search for alternatives to AMLCDs. First, the cost of manufacturing these displays is higher than that of nearly every competing technology. Secondly, there are size constraints that limit production of very large displays, those exceeding 16" diagonal screens. TouchTop Technologies' Dry Crystal Display System overcomes these limitations with breakthrough proprietary technology.

At the heart of TouchTop's Light Emitting Dry Crystal Display (LEDCD) is, as one might suspect, dry crystal elements. These synthetic elements, when electrically charged, emit light.

Because the elements are transparent in their untreated state, applying TouchTop's patented Dry Crystal Dye creates a light source that produces vivid colors. These dyed elements are mounted to a controllable circuit board by an adhesive. Precisely placing each element, dyed in one of the three primary colors, would involve the construction of complex manufacturing equipment. This was the major obstacle that prevented Dr. Chenenko from producing the display years ago. To combat this threat to the commercial feasibility of the system, Mr. Patel constructed an intelligent software program that estimates the distribution of red, blue, and green elements and edits the video driver code appropriately. The end result is a visual display that literally blows away competing technologies.

Sustainable Competitive Advantage

The proprietary technology that supports Touch Top's display system exceeds the performance of existing technologies by a substantial margin.

The system was designed to allow manufacturing at existing LCD and AMLCD plants with nominal retooling. Other new display technologies, including Plasma, Field Emission Displays (FEDs) and Organic Displays, require construction of a new plant to roll out products. They offer performance improvements that are marginal when compared to those of TouchTop's LEDCD. Having invested over $6 billion in AMLCD plant construction, the world's top display producers are hard pressed to rationalize additional investment in new technologies that offer only marginal performance gains. TouchTop's Light Emitting Dry Crystal Display holds an exclusive place among display technologies available today. The extremely high demand for this technology is facilitated by a relatively modest investment required to bring its product to market.

THE MARKET

"Next years' demand for notebooks that house LCD displays will be so huge, desktop vendors won't have the materials left over to make the 12- to 18-inch panels for desktop PCs."

—IDC Analyst Eric Buckingham, Ziff Davis

The information display market is capital intensive, highly concentrated, and growing at an impressive rate. The average AMLCD plant cost over $1 billion. Producers get a facility capable of producing about 100,000 12.1" units per month, assuming yields of around 75%. Worldwide capacity at these plants, including passive LCD plants, is currently in excess of 20 million 12.1" units per year. Liquid Crystal Displays outsell all other flat panel display systems by a margin of 10 to 1. According to the Society of Electron Devices International, AMLCD production capacity is expected to reach 40 million 12.1" units by the year 2000.

The biggest challenges facing the AMLCD producers can be broken down into four areas:

- High Cost of Manufacturing
- Limited Viewing Angle
- Response time
- Maximum Viewing Size

As indicated previously, TouchTop Technologies' Light Emitting Dry Crystal Display System overcomes these barriers by enormous proportions. The top five AMLCD producers worldwide spent more than $1.3 billion in 1995 for research and development of the next generation display device. Despite this sizable investment, no clear successor to AMLCD has been developed. Driving the producers' rationale for continued investment is an ever increasing, and currently unsatisfied, demand for larger, thinner, clearer, and faster display devices by consumers.

The combined Cathode Ray Tube and Active Matrix Liquid Crystal Display markets were over $27 billion dollars in 1996. Over $12 billion was spent on Active Matrix Liquid Crystal Displays. This huge market is expected to grow over $19 billion by the year 2000. Current estimates of growth in the AMLCD market do not take into account the possibility of traditional CRTs in desktops and televisions being replaced by AMLCDs.

Market Potential/ Growth Rate

Only 11 firms make up TouchTop Technologies' target market. However, these firms account for nearly 90% of the LCD market. All 11 firms are in a desperate search for the next generation display technology. However, the continued and growing investment in R&D and additional AMLCD capacity are all clear signs that none of these companies have found a worthy successor to AMLCD. TouchTop Technologies has segmented the market into two categories: manufacturers that have invested in full-scale production facilities for next generation displays and those that have not.

Target Market

Only two firms, Optrexe and Sharpe fall into the category of companies that have invested in full-scale production facilities for next generation displays. Sharpe, using technology developed by Infinite Gain, Inc., began construction in Korea on a Field Emission Display production plant in early August of 1995. In a clear sign that Sharpe may have jumped the gun, the plant was initially budgeted at $800 million and to date has cost the firm over a billion dollars with completion scheduled for late 1997. Sharpe has acknowledged that many of the cost overruns are the results of manufacturing difficulties discovered at its pilot facility. Optrexe's investment is in a plant that will manufacture next-generation AMLCDs. The new AMLCDs produced by the plant use an in-plane switching technique that significantly increases the viewing angle. However, as with similar techniques, the costs, in addition to manufacturing, include increased power consumption and reduced speed.

The other 9 top LCD producers have not fully committed to next-generation technologies by way of new plant construction. These firms are the primary targets of TouchTop Technologies, Inc. One of the largest, NEEC, has committed to executing a license and royalty agreement upon TouchTop's delivery of a fully functioning prototype that verifies performance claims. Additionally, TouchTop's CEO has coordinated efforts with key NEEC manufacturing management to develop cost estimates, define the process architecture, and move towards detailed design for conversion of existing NEEC AMLCD manufacturing facilities. Under the NEEC agreement, licenses with other producers could be executed under the condition that production of TouchTop's LEDCD based products commenced no sooner than 24 months following NEEC's first production run.

The nine LCD producers TouchTop Technologies has targeted are clearly concentrated in Far East Asia and Japan. Japan alone accounts for over 41% of all LCD production, with Taiwan and Hong Kong tied for second with 20% each. Having managed design and ramp up of LCD production plants in Korea, Taiwan, and Japan, Mr. Weinstein has firsthand knowledge of the nuances of commercial decision making in these areas. Equally important, Mr. Weinstein has developed strong relationships, as a trusted advisor and friend, with 7 of the nine targets TouchTop is pursuing.

Prospect Dispersion

TouchTop Technologies, Inc. competes with professional research organizations leading display technology producers and many others attempting to break into the display technology industry. Although other alternatives to AMLCD exist, none have proven their manufacturability, scientific credibility, or commercial viability. Even the most promising alternative to AMLCD technology, that is the Field Emission Display, only offers a 33% savings in production costs.

The Competition

TouchTop's LEDCD is designed to be manufactured by existing AMLCD facilities resulting in production savings of over 85%.

The most immediate competition to TouchTop Technologies, Inc. is the Infinite Gain Corporation of Irvine, California, and Angle Technologies, of San Pedro, California. Infinite Gain Corporation has the best-developed Field Emission Display Process (FED) in the industry. This company was founded in 1990 and its FED boasts viewing angles of up to 170 degrees, and a contrast ratio of 100 to 1. This compares with TouchTop's contrast ratio of 20,000 to 1 and viewing angle of 170 degrees.

Infinite Gain Corporation's customers include Sharpe, Toshiba, NEEC, and Hoshidenn. Infinite Gain's license and royalty agreements are negotiated on an individual basis. Each client yields $24.25 million per year in revenue on average.

A summary of competitor profiles follows:

Competitor Name	Growth Rate	Revenue in Millions	Lic./Royt % of Rev.	Service $ of Rev.	Gross Margin %	G. Margin Lic./Royt
Infinite Gain	110%	$97.00	85.01%	14.99%	96.52%	98.21%
Angle Technologies	86%	$35.11	70.12%	29.88%	97.33%	93.40%
Vision	12%	$200.02	88.01%	11.99%	97.03%	99.13%
TouchTop 1999	180%	$59.60	85.26%	14.74%	95.93%	99.99%

Competitor Name	G. Margin Service	Operating Margin %	% Sales Mktg. Ex	% R&D Expense	% G&A Expense	Year Founded
Infinite Gain	49.54%	57.21%	13.72%	15.55%	10.95%	1989
Angle Technologies	61.09%	64.05%	9.10%	14.44%	9.74%	1992
Vision	45.08%	45.13%	21.70%	21.80%	7.30%	1990
TouchTop 1999	72.00%	70.00%	19.30%	4.89%	4.61%	1996

Competitor	P/E Ratio	Ticker Symbol	Major Customers	Avg. Rev. Per Cust.	Head-count	Rev. per EE
Infinite Gain	50	INFG	4	$24.25M	130	$746K
Angle Technologies	33	AGTC	3	$11.70M	30	$1.17M
Vision	29	VSNT	15	$13.33M	220	$909K
TouchTop 1999	N/A	N/A	3	$19.88M	71	$839K

Infinite Gain's management team is led by Dr. William Sharpes. Dr. Sharpes has written numerous texts on display technology and founded the company in 1990 with 4 key patented technologies he developed. The company has developed strong ties with its customers and managed to grow revenues by over 100% in 1997.

Angle Technologies is essentially the research arm of Optrexe International. Although the firm is a public company, nearly 90% of its sales are made to its majority shareholder, Optrexe. The most significant accomplishment of Optrexe over the past several years has been gains made in the area of Ferroelectric Liquid Crystal Displays.

Ferroelectric Displays, FLCDs, are liquid crystals that maintain their charge after the electric field is turned off. One of the advantages of this technology is that power consumption in portable devices is significantly reduced. However, controlling contrast in FLCDs has consistently required counterproductive supporting technologies. All evidence suggests that the cost of manufacturing FLCDs is greater than, or equal to, the cost of producing current AMLCDs.

Vision, Inc. is the least threatening of TouchTop's most direct competitors. Although the company licenses technology to virtually all of the top ten LCD producers, its patents are primarily based on methods of improving existing Passive Matrix Displays. The company uses various "twisting" techniques to enhance both resolution and viewing angle. Although LCD producers acknowledge that Passive Matrix Displays have a limited future, Vision's innovative improvements to this technology benefit producers in two ways. First, firms can extend the life cycle of Passive LCDs with Vision's twisting techniques. Secondly, by using existing production facilities and mature product components, manufacturers can target the price conscious segments of the display market. Despite these strengths, the consensus opinion in the scientific community is that Vision's days are numbered and the company is essentially a cash cow.

Sales Team and Approach

TouchTop Technologies' founders recognize that to achieve the company's revenue objectives after licensing technology to NEEC, they will have to successfully convince prospects of the ROI, commercial viability, and performance improvements manufacturers will receive by licensing LEDCD technology. As a complex and break-through technology, selling LEDCD will involve convincing executives, technical divisions, and financial professionals that LEDCD is the best means to achieve competitiveness in the display market. Each member of TouchTop's executive team will play a vital role in accomplishing this task. However, direct responsibility will rest with the company's CEO, Mr. Weinstein.

Although the structure of the team is such that matrix reporting relationships are inevitable, Mr. Weinstein has successfully used this structure in the past to close technology transfer agreements ranging from $10 million to over $500 million. In each occurrence, the contracting party was not only satisfied with the end result, but also extremely impressed with the negotiation process. Consequently, lasting relationships were developed between the client and the offering firm. TouchTop Technologies is confident that this same approach will yield similar results in its efforts to license the Light Emitting Dry Crystal Display System.

Pricing Policy

The pricing strategy for TouchTop's LEDCD is based on the reduction in risk, and highly competitive ROI manufacturers will realize. The base price for licensing the technology is $25 million. This fee entitles licensees to complete documentation, chemical formulas, driver software, driver editor software, and testing and tooling specifications. Technical and manufacturing support services are contracted on an hourly basis at an average rate of $250 per hour, with the average implementation expected to take 24,800 hours of technical and manufacturing guidance. Retooling existing AMLCD manufacturing facilities will cost another $15 million. Finally, a royalty of 20 cents per square inch of screen manufactured is payable monthly by the licensee.

As this scenario suggests, there is considerable room for TouchTop Technologies to increase its price. However, the company's marketing strategy is for quick penetration to reduce the risk of entry by yet undiscovered technology alternatives. To encourage early decisionmaking by prospects, the price of a license will increase 50% per year for each agreement executed after the year 2000. Also, under the NEEC agreement, no consulting fees would be charged but TouchTop would be reimbursed for all "direct non-salary" consulting expenses.

Promotion

Upon completion of tested, functioning prototypes, TouchTop Technologies will begin exhibiting 12.1", 27" and 50" flat screen displays based on its LEDCD system at symposiums in the United States, the Far East, and Japan. These exhibitions will fall under the direction of Mr. Weinstein and the director or business development. There is little doubt that the display community will be nothing short of shocked by what they see.

The combined executive team of TouchTop Technologies has been published in nearly every relevant trade and scientific journal in the display industry. In the course of publishing both critical and product specific articles, relationships with key media contact have developed. These relationships will be leveraged to gain third party endorsement of this breakthrough technology. In the end, however, the quantum performance improvements delivered by Light Emitting Dry Crystal Displays will speak so loudly that relevant interested parties will have to listen.

OPERATIONS

Development Advantage

Since inception, TouchTop Technologies has successfully used management's experience not only to develop the next generation of display technology, but to create and document a structured system for commanding the development process. These early development efforts have already resulted in tangible business results. The ability of the breadboard unit to prove the viability of the company's display technologies puts the unusual position of having pilot production, testing, and debugging funded by a customer in waiting. Since the first licensing agreement (contingent upon performance of certain prototypes) involves payments for consulting NEEC on retooling existing LCD facilities, TouchTop Technologies will actually earn revenue before, during, and after pilot production begins.

Clearly the most significant challenge facing the company at this stage is production of prototype units that are produced and function in accordance with performance specifications. Management has gone to great lengths to reduce the risks that prototypes will fail. One clear example of this is the company's agreement to have the prototypes constructed at NEEC's testing labs in Korea. This results in not only cost savings in producing the prototypes, but has allowed focused work to begin on manufacturing components for production. Management believes these advantages typify the company's approach to research and development.

Facilities

TouchTop Technologies' principal office space is located in New York City. The 3,000 square foot facility is occupied under a lease expiring in February of 1999. A right of first refusal exists on up to 10,000 square feet of additional space at this location. As marketing and license support activities develop, the company anticipates growing needs for office space in the Pacific Rim. Under the terms of the NEEC agreement, the company will have use of approximately 800 square feet of office space at NEEC's facilities in Korea. The vagaries of negotiation are such that management does not assume similar agreements will be obtained with other manufacturers licensing the company's technology. A provision for this additional space was considered in projecting rental expense over the next five years.

THE ORGANIZATION

Management

Executives of the company

Executive officers of the company are as follows:

Name	Age	Position
Ira Weinstein	57	President and Chief Executive Officer
Vladimir Chenenko	49	Vice President-Science
Di Patel	42	Vice President-Technology

Executive Profiles

Mr. Ira Weinstein, President and Chief Executive Officer of TouchTop Technologies, Inc., has advised nearly every top LCD producer worldwide, primarily in the areas of integrated product development and manufacturing. During the late 1980s and early 1990s his principal clients were NEEC and Hundeye. In both these engagements, Mr. Weinstein was responsible for the overall cross-functional development of LCD manufacturing systems. Until this day, neither of these clients will expand production capacity without consulting Mr. Weinstein. Prior to establishing his consulting practice, Mr. Weinstein held the positions of VP of Engineering, VP of Marketing, VP of New Product Development and VP of Direct Sales for Magnovuexe.

Mr. Weinstein is a graduate of Massachusetts Institute of Technology and holds a B.S. and M.S. in mechanical engineering. He graduated third in his class from MIT's Sloan School of Management, where he received his M.B.A.

Mr. Di Patel, Vice President of Technology, launched his first software startup from his dormitory room at Stanford University. As a graduate student, he developed one of the first true nuero-network protocols. The technology was licensed by Inteli-Trade, a leading provider of computer based trading systems and eventually sold to them. Mr. Patel used the proceeds to develop a graphical user interface to run on Microsoft's operating system. The company, Click and Drag, was acquired by Microsoft in 1998 and served as the key player in the total concept development.

Dr. Vladimir Chenenko, III, Vice President of Science, is an internationally recognized authority and pioneer in the field of display technology. His early work, *The Principals Characteristics, and Applications of Liquid Crystal Displays*, has been translated into four languages and is the field manual for display developers around the world. Prior to the break up of the former Soviet Union, Dr. Chenenko had developed over 25 patented display technologies and 50 novel chemical compounds for use in a wide range of applications. In 1991, Dr. Chenenko founded PhysiChem, a contract research and consulting group. In 1994, PhysiChem was purchased by Dow Labs International. Since that time Dr. Chenenko has focused nearly all of his efforts on completed development of his Light Emitting Dry Crystal Display.

Dr. Chenenko hold Ph.Ds. in chemistry and physics and a master of applied physics from the Moscow Institute of Technology.

Proposed Officer Compensation

Annual Salary

Name and Principal Position	1997	Bonus	Total Compensation
Ira Weinstein President/Chief Executive Officer	$70,000	0	$70,000
Vladimir Chenenko Vice President, Science	$70,000	0	$70,000
Di Patel Vice President, Technology	$70,000	0	$70,000

Compensation Criteria

The proposed officer compensation represents less than a third of each principal's current annual income.

The U.S. Department of Labor's Occupational Compensation Survey reflects the average annual salaries for software development product managers as stated above.

Supporting Professionals & Consultants

Accountants/Auditors	Arthur Andersen Young
	1 Big Six Way
	San Jose, California
Attorneys	Goodwin Procter Hoar and Co.
	6 Filing Way
	San Jose, California
Public Relations	Sachi, Burns and Ogilvy
	4 Publicity Dr.
	San Jose, California

Headcount Forecast

Department	Q1 1997	Q2 1997	Q3 1997	Q4 1997	1997
Consulting - Direct	0	0	0	0	0
Sales & Marketing	0	0	0	0	0
Research & Development	3	5	6	6	6
General & Administrative	6	7	7	7	7
	Q1 1998	**Q2 1998**	**Q3 1998**	**Q4 1998**	**1998**
Consulting - Direct	14	14	14	14	14
Sales & Marketing	1	7	7	7	7
Research & Development	6	9	9	9	9
General & Administrative	7	10	10	10	10
	Q1 1999	**Q2 1999**	**Q3 1999**	**Q4 1999**	**1999**
Consulting - Direct	19	19	19	19	19
Sales & Marketing	13	13	13	14	14
Research & Development	9	9	11	11	11
General & Administrative	24	24	27	27	27
	Q1 2000	**Q2 2000**	**Q3 2000**	**Q4 2000**	**2000**
Consulting - Direct	23	23	23	23	23
Sales & Marketing	19	19	21	21	21
Research & Development	11	12	12	12	12
General & Administrative	27	27	27	27	27
	Q1 2001	**Q2 2001**	**Q3 2001**	**Q4 2001**	**2001**
Consulting - Direct	23	23	23	23	23
Sales & Marketing	27	27	27	27	27
Research & Development	13	13	13	13	13
General & Administrative	27	27	27	27	27

**KEY RISKS/
TIMELINE**

Risk of Defects and Development Delays

TouchTop Technologies may experience schedule overruns in product and software development triggered by factors such as insufficient staffing or the unavailability of development-related software, hardware, components, materials, or technologies. Further, when developing new products, the company's development schedules may be altered as a result of the discovery of software bugs, performance problems, or changes to the product specification in response to customer requirements, market developments, or company initiated changes. Changes in product specifications may delay completion of documentation, packaging, or testing, which may, in turn, affect the release schedule of the product. When developing complex display devices, the technology market may shift during the development cycle requiring the company either to enhance or change a product's specifications to meet a customer's changing needs. These factors may cause a product to enter the market behind schedule, which may adversely affect market acceptance of the product or place it at a disadvantage to a competitor's product that has already gained market share or market acceptance during the delay.

As indicated in the Marketing, R&D and Enterprise sections of this plan, tests on the breadboard design of TouchTop's LEDCD and testing on its alpha version display driver and intelligent driver editing code considerably reduce the risk that development delays will occur.

Management of Growth

TouchTop Technologies anticipates rapid and substantial growth in the number of its employees and the scope of its operations, resulting in increased responsibilities for management and added pressure on the company's operating and financial systems. To manage growth effectively, TouchTop Technologies will need to continue to improve its operational, financial, and management information systems and will need to hire, train, motive, and manage a growing number of employees. Competition is intense for qualified technical, marketing, and management personnel. There can be no assurance that TouchTop Technologies will be able to achieve or manage any future growth, and its failure to do so could delay product development cycles and marketing efforts or otherwise have a material adverse effect on TouchTop Technologies' business, financial condition, and results of operations.

TouchTop Technologies' founders have participated in a number of successful ventures. They have proven their ability to manage growth and take a product from cradle to grave, meeting the demands of rapid growth time and time again.

Competition

Because of the rapid expansion of the information display market, TouchTop Technologies will face competition from existing and new entrants, possibly including TouchTop Technologies' customers. There can be no assurance that the company's competitors will not develop information display products that may be more effective than TouchTop Technologies' current or future products or that the company's technologies and products would not be rendered obsolete by such developments.

Many of TouchTop Technologies' current and potential competitors have longer operating histories, greater name recognition, larger installed customer bases, and significantly greater financial, technical, and marketing resources than the company. As a result, they may be able to adapt more quickly to new or emerging technologies and changes in customer requirements, or to devote greater resources to the promotion and sale of their products than TouchTop Technologies. There can be no assurance that the company's customers will not perceive the products of such other companies as substitutes for TouchTop Technologies products.

As with most competitive software offerings, the principal competitive factors affecting the market for information display include effectiveness, scope of product offerings, technical features, ease of use, reliability, customer service and support, name recognition, distribution resources, and cost. Current and potential competitors have established, or may establish in the future, strategic alliances to increase their ability to compete for TouchTop Technologies' prospective customers. Accordingly, it is possible that new competitors or alliances may emerge and rapidly acquire significant market share. Such competition could materially adversely affect the TouchTop Technologies' business, financial condition, and results of operations.

Management believes that this risk is significantly mitigated by the development life cycle for display technologies. As indicated in previous sections of this plan, all other known viable alternatives to LCD require significant capital expenditures and offer only marginal performance improvements.

Dependence on Key Personnel

TouchTop Technologies' success will depend, to a large extent, upon the performance of its founders and the senior management team and technical, marketing, and sales personnel the company will recruit in the early stages. There is shrewd competition in the software industry to hire and retain qualified personnel, and TouchTop Technologies will actively search for additional qualified personnel as the company grows. TouchTop Technologies' success will depend upon its ability to retain and hire additional key personnel. The loss of the services of key personnel, or the inability to attract additional qualified personnel, could have a material adverse effect upon the company's results of operations and product development efforts.

TouchTop Technologies currently plans to put $700,000 "key man" life insurance policies on the lives of each of its founders. As the company grows, or if directed to do so by interested parties, this coverage will be increased appropriately.

Risk of Errors or Failures; Product Liability Risks

A malfunction or the inadequate design of products produced using TouchTop Technologies' LEDCD technology could result in tort or warranty claims. While the company will attempt to reduce the risk of such losses through warranty disclaimers and liability limitation clauses in its license agreements, and by maintaining product liability insurance, there can be no assurance that such measures will be effective in limiting TouchTop Technologies' liability for any such damages. The company currently intends to purchase product liability insurance and it may seek additional insurance coverage as it commences commercialization of its products. There can be no assurance that adequate additional insurance coverage will be available at an acceptable cost, if at all. More importantly, a publicized actual or perceived product defect could adversely affect the market's perception of TouchTop Technologies' products. This could result in a decline in demand for TouchTop Technologies' products, which could have a material adverse effect on the company's business, financial condition, and results of operations.

Liquidity and Capital Requirements; Dependence on First Round Financing and Cash Flow From Operations

TouchTop Technologies anticipates that its cash flows in from operations and cash generated from first round financing of approximately $2.3 million will be adequate to satisfy its capital requirements based on the plan presented herein. TouchTop Technologies' future capital requirements, however, will depend on many factors, including its ability to successfully market and license its technology. To the extent that the funds generated by this offering and from TouchTop Technologies' ongoing operations are insufficient to fund TouchTop Technologies' future operating requirements (it may be necessary to raise additional funds, through public or private financing), could result in dilution to TouchTop Technologies' shareholders. If adequate capital is not available, TouchTop Technologies may be required to curtail its operations significantly.

These risks are not unique to TouchTop Technologies, Inc. However, the tentative agreement with NEEC to license TouchTop Technologies' LEDCD system significantly reduces this risk.

International Operations

A core component of TouchTop Technologies' development plan is overseas licensing of its technology. To the extent TouchTop Technologies expands international operations, currency fluctuations could make TouchTop Technologies' contribute to fluctuations in TouchTop Technologies' operating results. Political instability, difficulties in staffing and managing international operations also pose risks to the development of international development efforts. Moreover, the laws of Japan or Korea or the enforcement thereof, may not protect the TouchTop Technologies' products and intellectual property rights to the same extent as the laws of the United States. There can be no assurance that these factors will not have a material adverse effect on TouchTop Technologies' business, financial condition, and results of operations.

The risk of currency fluctuation is mitigated, to a large extent, by the company's intention to transact business in U.S. dollars.

Timeline

Milestone	Target Date	Status
Concept Development - Functional Specifications - LEDCD	Oct-93	Completed
Detailed Design - LEDCD	Jan-96	Completed
Breadboard	Feb-96	Completed
Functional Specifications - Display Driver Code	Feb-96	Completed
Functional Specifications - Intelligent Driver Editor	Feb-96	Completed
Detailed Design - Display Driver Code	Jun-96	Completed
Detailed Design - Intelligent Driver Editor	Jun-96	Completed
Testing - Display Driver Code and Intelligent Driver Editor	Jul-96	Completed
Tentative Commitment from NEEC	Mar-96	Completed
Detailed Design of Manufacturing Components/Retooling	Oct-96	In Process
1st Round Funding	Jan-97	Open
Full Scale Prototypes Constructed	Jun-97	Open
Testing, Q&A and Documentation	Sep-97	Open
Agreement with NEEC finalized $25 million	Jan-98	Open
Two $25 million Licenses Executed	Jan-99	Open
One $50 million Licenses Executed	Jan-2000	Open
First Royalties Realized	Jan-99	Open
Next Generation Screen/Interface Development Completed	Sep-2001	Open

Summary of Significant Assumptions and Accounting Policies Employed in Preparation of Projected Financial Statements

PROSPECTIVE FINANCIALS

Assuming Equity Financing of Approximately $2.3 million January 1, 1997
For Each Year in the Five-Year Period Ending December 31, 2001

This financial projection of financial position, results of operations, and cash flow, assuming equity financing of approximately $2.3 million on January 1, 1997, represents to the best of management's belief, the expected results of operations and cash flow for the projection period if said alternative were to commence on or about January 1, 1997. Accordingly, the projection reflects management's judgment as of August 15, 1996, the date of this projection, of the expected conditions and its expected course of action. The assumptions disclosed herein are those that management believes are significant to the projection. There will usually be differences between projected and actual results, because event and circumstances frequently do not occur as expected, and those differences may be material.

a. Summary of Significant Accounting Policies.

Basis of Accounting—The projection has been prepared using generally accepted accounting principles that the company expects to use when preparing its historical financial statements.

Hypothetical Assumption—Equity Financing of Approximately $2.3 million in the Form of Convertible Preferred Stock.

b. Sales. The company's revenue projection by class is as follows:

Projected Number of Units

Revenue Classification	Revenue per Unit	Average (000's)		December 31 (000's omitted)*		
		1997	**1998**	**1999**	**2000**	**2001**
License 1 revenue	$20,000/Lic.	0	1	2	0	0
License 2 revenue	$50,000/Lic.	0	0	0	1	1
Royalty revenue	$0.25/Sq. Inc.	0	0	12,041	63,432	134,122
Service revenue	$250/Hour	0	11	37	27	20

except licenses

The company's revenues will be derived from license fees, royalties, and charges for services, including consulting and maintenance support. For all prospective periods presented, the company has projected revenue recognition in accordance with Statement of Position 91-1 entitled "Software Revenue Recognition," dated December 12, 1991, issued by the American Institute of Certified Public Accountants. License fee revenues consist of revenues from initial licenses for the company's products, sales of licenses to existing customers for additional users of the company's products, product documentation and fees from sublicenses of third-party software products. The company will recognize initial license fee revenues only after delivery and installation of software products and if there are no remaining significant post-installation obligations. If significant post-installation obligations exist or if a product is subject to customer acceptance, revenues will be deferred until no significant obligations remain or until acceptance has occurred. Service revenues will consist primarily of maintenance support and consulting revenues. Maintenance support revenues will be recognized over the term of the support period, which typically will be a twelve-month period. Consulting revenues will be recognized when the services are performed.

Failure of these assumptions to materialize will likely have a material adverse effect on actual results. Therefore, the prospective results of the company are sensitive to differences between actual and projected sales. Specifically, a 1% drop in actual sales will result in a 0.57%, and a 4.41% drop in pretax earnings for years ending 1998 and 1999 respectively.

c. Cost of Sales.

Cost of Product Revenue. Cost of product revenue consists primarily of the costs of royalties paid to third-party vendors, product media and duplication, manuals, packaging materials, personnel-related costs, and shipping expenses. Because all development costs incurred in the research and development of software products and enhancements to existing software products will be expressed as incurred, cost of product revenue includes no amortization of capitalized software development costs.

Cost of Maintenance and Service Revenue. Cost of maintenance and service revenue consists primarily of personnel-related costs incurred in providing telephone support, consulting, and training to customers. The primary component of the cost of sales is labor. Skilled, professional personnel used directly in the company's operations are expected to be readily available, and the company has generally used higher average cost of sales estimates based on industry reports of companies of similar size in the software development industry and per the Department of Labor's Occupational Compensation Survey.

d. Property and Equipment. Property and equipment are stated at projected cost.

Projected depreciation and amortization are computed under the straight-line method in amounts that allocate the cost of all assets over the following estimated useful lives:

		Projected Additions				
		December 31 (000's omitted)				
Asset Classification	**Useful Life**	**1997**	**1998**	**1999**	**2000**	**2001**
Computer Equipment	3	90	500	250	750	450
Purchased Software	5	90	250	500	750	500
Furniture & Fixtures	7	70	100	0	200	250
Leasehold Improvements	Lease Term -7	50	80	200	300	400
Total Additions		**300**	**930**	**950**	**2,000**	**1,600**

e. Selling and Marketing Expenses. The principal types of expenses within this category are salaries, promotion, and professional services. Salaries are projected on an individual-by-individual basis, using expected salary rates throughout the projection period. Promotion expense is projected at 12% of revenue throughout the projection period. This percentage is significantly higher than that of similar companies in comparable industries. Professional services are projected at $3,000 per marketing employee per month.

f. Research and Development Costs. The principal types of expenses within this category are salaries, rent, telephone, travel, supplies, and professional services. Salaries are projected on an individual-by-individual basis, using expected salary rates throughout the projection period. Rent expense was determined by comparing the company quoted local market rates with additional space requirements according to Time Saver Standards for Building Types. Insurance, telephone, supplies, and professional services were projected on a per employee basis at rates $100, $125, $220, and $80 per employee respectively. Generally, management expects to charge research and development expenditures to operations as incurred, in accordance with Statement of Financial Standards No. 86. SAS 86 requires capitalization of certain software development costs subsequent to establishing technological feasibility. Therefore, the company will capitalize eligible computer software development costs upon completion of a working model. For the projection periods presented, no costs were eligible for capitalization, therefore, the company charged all software development costs to research and development expense.

g. General and Administrative Expenses. The principal types of expenses within this category are salaries, facilities and occupancy, travel, professional services, and insurance. Salaries are projected on an individual-by-individual basis, using expected salary rates throughout the projection period. Facilities expense was determined by comparing the company quoted local market rates with additional space requirements according to Time Saver Standards for Building Types. Supplies expense is projected at $275 per administrative employee per month. Professional services are projected at $120,000 for 1997 and 0.75% of revenue thereafter. Insurance under the G&A caption primarily reflects the company's expected costs for property, liability, and casualty insurance and is consistent with industry norms for similar firms. The prospective results of the company are sensitive to differences between actual and projected selling and marketing, system, and general administrative expense, excluding depreciation. Specifically, a 1% increase in the actual operating expenses experienced, will result in a 0.48% drop in pretax earnings in 1999.

h. Bank Credit Facility. The projections assume that TouchTop Technologies, Inc. will pay cash for all additions to property and equipment. The company's interest in property and equipment is expected to act as a borrowing base to secure a line of credit in 1998 in the amount of $100,000. As the company grows, this amount is expected to increase.

i. Nominal rate of 8.5%. Differences between the nominal and effective rates are expected to be immaterial.

j. Miscellaneous Income. The forecast assumes that excess cash is invested at market rates of approximately 4%.

k. Accounts Receivable. The forecast assumes that proceeds from license agreements, royalty settlements, and payments for consulting services are collected within 40 days.

l. Responsible Party. The projections herein are the responsibility of the officers and founders of TouchTop Technologies, Inc. as identified in this business plan, and, to the best of management's knowledge and belief, are in conformity with generally accepted accounting principles. The company believes all of the assumptions underlying the projections are reasonable and appropriate. Management further states that these projections were not compiled or examined by independent public accountant and should not be viewed as if so compiled or examined.

Projected Balance Sheet

Assuming Equity Financing of Approximately $2.3 million on January 1, 1997
For Each of the Five Years Ending December 31, 2001

ASSETS	1997	1998	1999	2000	2001
Current assets:					
Cash and equivalents	$583,606	$3,939,643	$18,834,292	$31,199,617	$47,965,445
Marketable securities	0	5,000,000	15,000,000	30,000,000	50,000,000
Accounts receivable	0	370,333	1,265,667	3,546,470	4,494,598
Total Current assets	583,606	9,309,976	35,099,959	64,746,087	102,460,043
Property, plant, and equipment:					
Purchased software	90,000	340,000	840,000	1,590,000	2,090,000
Computer equipment	90,000	590,000	840,000	1,590,000	2,040,000
Furniture and fixtures	70,000	170,000	170,000	370,000	620,000
Leasehold improvements	50,000	130,000	330,000	630,000	1,030,000
Total property, plant, and equipment	300,000	1,230,000	2,180,000	4,180,000	5,780,000
Less Accumulated depreciation	60,166	325,594	849,023	1,809,881	3,036,928
Net Property, plant, and equipment	239,834	900,406	1,330,977	2,370,119	2,743,072
Total assets	**$823,440**	**$10,210,382**	**$36,430,936**	**$67,116,206**	**$105,203,115**

Projected Balance Sheet

Continued

	1997	1998	1999	2000	2001
LIABILITIES					
Current liabilities:					
Accounts payable	50,259	140,202	312,992	640,920	777,714
Total current liabilities	50,259	140,202	312,992	640,920	777,714
EQUITY					
Owner's equity:					
Contributed capital:					
Preferred stock	10,000	10,000	10,000	10,000	10,000
Additional paid-in capital - preferred	2,290,000	2,290,000	2,290,000	2,290,000	2,290,000
Common stock	1,000	1,000	1,000	1,000	1,000
Total contributed capital	2,301,000	2,301,000	2,301,000	2,301,000	2,301,000
Retained earnings	1,527,819	7,769,180	33,816,944	64,174,286	102,124,401
Net Owners' equity	773,181	10,070,180	36,117,944	66,475,286	104,425,401
Total liabilities and equity	**$823,440**	**$10,210,382**	**$36,430,936**	**$67,116,206**	**$105,203,115**

**Assuming Equity Financing of Approximately $2.3 million on January 1, 1997
For Each of the Five Years Ending December 31, 2001**

**Expense Detail,
Chart I**

Sales	1997	1998	1999	2000	2001
Gross sales:					
License revenue	$0	$20,000,000	$50,000,000	$50,000,000	$50,000,000
Support revenue	0	2,777,500	9,165,750	6,666,000	4,999,500
Royalty revenue	0	0	3,010,292	15,857,939	33,530,224
Total Revenue	0	22,777,500	62,176,042	72,523,939	88,529,724
Cost of sales	**0**	**1,468,499**	**2,528,601**	**3,142,051**	**3,261,376**
Gross margin	0	21,309,001	59,647,441	69,381,888	85,268,348
Operating expenses:					
Sales & Marketing	0	4,503,393	12,049,966	14,888,936	19,045,587
Research & Development	756,971	1,102,069	3,040,423	3,334,028	3,480,840
General and Admin.	872,864	1,667,169	2,751,884	3,526,671	4,069,650
Total Operating expenses	1,629,835	7,272,631	17,842,273	21,746,635	26,596,077
Income from operations	1,629,835	14,036,370	41,805,168	47,632,253	58,672,271
Earnings before interest and taxes	1,629,835	14,036,370	41,805,168	47,632,253	58,672,271
Interest expense (income):					
Interest expense	708	45,994	2,664	27,996	69,336
Interest income	102,724	545,973	2,379,945	3,888,137	5,768,388
Net interest expense (income)	102,016	499,979	2,377,281	3,860,141	5,699,052

**Expense Detail,
Chart I**

Continued

	1997	1998	1999	2000	2001
Net income before					
taxes	1,527,819	14,536,349	44,182,449	51,492,394	64,371,323
Taxes:					
Federal taxes	0	4,029,557	14,025,717	16,346,259	20,434,675
State taxes	0	1,209,793	4,108,968	4,788,793	5,986,533
Total taxes	0	5,239,350	18,134,685	21,135,052	26,421,208
Net income	$1,527,819	$9,296,999	$26,047,764	$30,357,342	$37,950,115

Operating Expenses

Statement of Projected Results of Operations-Common Size
Assuming Equity Financing of Approximately $2.3 million on January 1, 1997
For Each of the Five Years Ending December 31, 2001

Operating expenses:	1997	1998	1999	2000	2001
Sales & Marketing:					
Salaries	NM	2.7%	2.5%	3.3%	3.9%
Benefits	NM	0.7%	0.6%	0.8%	0.9%
Telephone	NM	1.0%	1.0%	1.0%	1.0%
Supplies	NM	1.5%	1.5%	1.5%	1.5%
Travel	NM	0.7%	0.7%	0.7%	0.7%
Promotion	NM	12.0%	12.0%	12.0%	12.0%
Professional services	NM	0.9%	0.8%	0.9%	1.1%
Miscellaneous expenses	NM	0.3%	0.3%	0.4%	0.4%
Total Sales & Marketing	NM	19.8%	19.4%	20.5%	21.5%
Research & Development:					
Salaries	NM	3.2%	3.4%	3.2%	2.8%
Benefits	NM	0.9%	0.9%	0.8%	0.7%
Insurance	NM	0.0%	0.0%	0.0%	0.0%
Telephone	NM	0.1%	0.1%	0.1%	0.0%
Supplies	NM	0.1%	0.1%	0.1%	0.1%
Travel	NM	0.4%	0.2%	0.2%	0.2%
Professional services	NM	0.0%	0.0%	0.0%	0.0%
Miscellaneous expenses	NM	0.1%	0.1%	0.1%	0.1%
Total Research & Development	NM	4.8%	4.9%	4.6%	3.9%
General & Administrative:					
Salaries	NM	1.9%	0.9%	1.0%	0.9%
Benefits	NM	0.6%	0.3%	0.3%	0.3%
Rent	NM	1.0%	0.6%	0.5%	0.4%
Insurance	NM	0.4%	0.3%	0.2%	0.2%
Utilities	NM	0.2%	0.1%	0.1%	0.1%
Telephone	NM	0.3%	0.1%	0.1%	0.1%
Supplies	NM	0.1%	0.1%	0.1%	0.1%
Travel	NM	0.6%	0.3%	0.3%	0.3%
Professional services	NM	0.8%	0.8%	0.8%	0.8%
Depreciation	NM	1.2%	0.8%	1.3%	1.4%
Miscellaneous expenses	NM	0.3%	0.3%	0.3%	0.3%
Total General & Administrative	NM	7.3%	4.4%	4.9%	4.6%

	1997	1998	1999	2000	2001
Total Operating expenses	NM	31.9%	28.7%	30.0%	30.0%
Total Taxes	0.00%	23.0%	29.2%	29.1%	29.8%
Net income	N/A	40.8%	41.9%	41.9%	42.9%

Operating Expenses

Continued

Statement of Projected Results of Operations
Assuming Equity Financing of Approximately $2.3 million on January 1, 1997
For Each of the Five Years Ending December 31, 2001

Statement of Projected Cash Flow

Cash flows from operating activities:	1997	1998	1999	2000	2001
Net income	($1,527,819)	$9,296,999	$26,047,764	$30,357,342	$37,950,115
Reconciliation of net income to cash from operations:					
Depreciation and amortization	60,166	269,428	519,429	960,858	1,227,047
Gaines and losses on sale of assets	0	0	0	0	0
Changes in operating assets and liabilities:					
Accounts receivable	0	-370,333	-895,334	-2,280,803	-948,128
Accounts payable	50,259	89,943	172,790	327,928	136,794
Total changes in operating assets and liabilities	50,259	-280,390	-722,544	-1,952,875	-811,334
Net cash provided (used) by operations	-1,417,394	9,286,037	25,844,679	29,365,325	38,365,828
Cash from investing activities:					
(Purchases) sales of investments	0	-5,000,000	-10,000,000	-15,000,000	-20,000,000
Purchases of property, plant, and equipment	-300,000	-930,000	-950,000	-2,000,000	-1,600,000
Total cash from investing activities	-300,000	-5,930,000	-10,950,000	-17,000,000	-21,600,000
Cash from financing activities:					
Issuance (Retirement) of stock:					
Change in preferred stock	10,000	0	0	0	0
Change in additional paid-in capital - preferred	2,290,000	0	0	0	0
Change in common stock	1,000	0	0	0	0
Total issuance (Retirement) of stock	2,301,000	0	0	0	0
Total cash from financing activities	2,301,000	0	0	0	0
Net increase (decrease) in cash and equivalents	583,606	3,356,037	14,894,649	12,365,325	16,765,828
Cash and equivalents, beginning	0	583,606	3,939,643	18,834,292	31,199,617
Cash and equivalents, ending	$583,606	$3,939,643	$18,834,292	$31,199,617	$47,965,445

**Expense Detail,
Chart II**

**Assuming Equity Financing of Approximately $2.3 million
For Each of the Five Years Ending December 31, 2001**

Operating expenses:	1997	1998	1999	2000	2001
Sales & Marketing:					
Salaries	0	612,720	1,576,968	2,364,291	3,487,424
Benefits	0	151,293	367,040	547,607	791,245
Telephone	0	227,780	621,760	725,241	885,298
Supplies	0	341,660	932,640	1,087,859	1,327,946
Travel	0	159,440	435,233	507,667	619,707
Promotion	0	2,733,300	7,461,125	8,702,871	10,623,567
Professional services	0	198,000	468,000	681,000	936,000
Miscellaneous expenses	0	79,200	187,200	272,400	374,400
Total Sales & Marketing	**0**	**4,503,393**	**12,049,966**	**14,888,936**	**19,045,587**
Research & Development:					
Salaries	492,600	729,882	2,139,708	2,349,612	2,443,620
Benefits	138,587	206,665	571,004	612,722	628,830
Insurance	8,100	11,100	30,600	32,400	32,400
Telephone	10,125	13,875	38,250	40,500	40,500
Supplies	17,820	24,420	67,320	71,280	71,280
Travel	67,059	85,047	107,861	136,794	173,490
Professional services	6,480	8,880	24,480	25,920	25,920
Miscellaneous expenses	16,200	22,200	61,200	64,800	64,800
Total Research &					
Development	**756,971**	**1,102,069**	**3,040,423**	**3,334,028**	**3,480,840**
General & Administrative:					
Salaries	290,988	438,728	550,965	692,094	753,072
Benefits	88,060	137,703	172,717	207,794	226,444
Rent	120,000	230,000	350,000	350,000	350,000
Insurance	35,000	80,000	160,000	160,000	160,000
Utilities	18,000	34,500	52,500	52,500	52,500
Telephone	37,700	63,700	78,650	91,650	99,450
Supplies	15,950	26,950	33,275	38,775	42,075
Travel	87,000	147,000	181,500	211,500	229,500
Professional services	120,000	170,830	466,320	543,930	663,973
Depreciation	60,166	269,428	519,429	960,858	1,227,047
Miscellaneous expenses	0	68,330	186,528	217,570	265,589
Total General &					
Administrative	**872,864**	**1,667,169**	**2,751,884**	**3,526,671**	**4,069,650**
Total Operating					
Expenses	**1,629,835**	**7,272,631**	**17,842,273**	**21,749,635**	**26,596,077**

Event Planning Company

BUSINESS PLAN   OCCASIONS, THE EVENT PLANNING SPECIALISTS

10001 State St.
Portland, Oregon 97201

Occasions, The Event Planning Specialists is a small business that intends to provide various options for event planning to the businesses and community of Portland, Oregon. From Party Packs to Event Planning Software, this company will personalize its services to suit the needs of individuals and businesses of all types to help them plan their events as efficiently and cost-effectively as possible. This business plan was compiled using Business Plan Pro™, by Palo Alto Software, copyright © 2000.

- EXECUTIVE SUMMARY

- COMPANY SUMMARY

- PRODUCTS & SERVICES

- MARKET ANALYSIS SUMMARY

- STRATEGY & IMPLEMENTATION SUMMARY

- MANAGEMENT SUMMARY

- FINANCIAL PLAN

EXECUTIVE SUMMARY

Welcome to the future of event planning! Occasions, The Event Planning Specialists, brings to the community of Portland a breath of fresh air in the event planning market. By combining old-fashioned values, going the extra mile, and using cutting-edge event-planning software, Occasions will lead the market, providing the same quality results, every time.

Occasions is an equal opportunity business making its expertise and its products available to help its customers plan their own events. Party Packs (complete kits for their event), make hosting a party a snap, right down to the refreshments. The event planning software brings interactive event planning as close as their personal computer. Through these and other affordable products and services, Occasions aims to be the number one resource for any event.

Objectives

Occasions is a small business aimed at the big time. In order to reach its lofty goals, Occasions must focus on the mission behind the vision. It will take all the employees, owners, founders, and vendors living daily the vision that Occasions represents. The vision manifests itself in three ways:

1. Be one of the top three event planning specialists in the Northwestern United States.
2. Justly compensate the employees, owners, and founders of Occasions.
3. Produce the same quality results, every time.

Mission

In an ever-changing, fast-paced world, success is determined by good choices for lasting effects. Communication is essential. Occasions strives to be the best choice of clients by helping to ease their event-planning burden. Through consistent, predictable professionalism, Occasions will ensure a worry- and hassle-free event at a reasonable price.

But, not all our clients will be external. Occasions has internal clients to serve. Occasions will strive to provide the same predictable and professional working environment to its employees and contracted vendors, justly compensating them for their services. It is also a priority to make a comfortable living wage for its owners, founders, full-time staff, and their families.

Keeping in tune with the needs of the market, utilizing the latest technology and trends, all while ensuring that the client receives the individual attention they deserve, is the vision and daily mission of Occasions, The Event Planning Specialists.

Keys to Success

Our keys to success include the commitment to quality by every person who is part of the team. Each of us will be responsible to push ourselves to a higher level of professionalism in three areas:

1. Consistent, accurate fulfillment of the client's wishes.
2. Competitive pricing for the quality of services offered.
3. Significant profit made on each event planned.

COMPANY SUMMARY

Founded in 1997 on a part-time basis, Occasions is a small business designed to meet the needs of the ever-changing social world. Portland, Oregon is the current home office with plans to expand to branch offices within four years. Occasions' staff of two, with numerous contract vendors, plans events, writes event-planning products, and trains local students in the art of event planning. Occasions is invested in the community in which it resides.

Occasions is, in part, the answer to the demands of the social world, on the working family, a heavily-burdened office, an out-of-town business, or a special occasion in need of special recognition. As a business, we understand the needs of public and private organizations. As parents and family members, we understand the needs of setting special time apart from other events in our lives. Occasions strives to accomplish these goals in Portland and eventually other areas of the Pacific Northwest.

Company Ownership

Occasions is established as a sole proprietorship with the intention of selling the business when it is established to one of the employees invested in the vision of event planning. All aspects of the business will be documented to ensure clients can count on the same results every time, and it is these documents that will become the basis of ownership. The sole proprietor will use his or her name as the guarantor of each service. Therefore, the sole proprietor must embody the vision and mission of Occasions.

Start-up Summary

Through careful planning on the part of the founders, the start-up costs for Occasions are minimal. It began as a home-based business with little overhead, and it continues to demand fewer outlay of funds as a service-based business. The start-up cost investment funds were assets saved from prior earnings by the owners who did event planning on a part-time basis before establishing themselves as a business.

It is the wish of the founders to remain a debt-free establishment. However, recognizing that in reality not all variables are controllable, outside financing is a viable option. Both founders own homes and have a perfect credit rating.

Start-up Plan

Start-up Expenses	
Legal	$150
Stationery, etc.	$300
Brochures	$185
Consultants	$75
Insurance	$125
Rent	$150
Research and development	$0
Expensed equipment	$1,985
Other	$142
Total Start-up Expense	**$3,112**

Start-up Assets Needed	
Cash Requirements	$2,300
Start-up Inventory	$0
Other Short-term Assets	$0
Total Short-term Assets	**$2,300**

Long-term Assets	$0
Total Assets	**$2,300**

Total Start-up Requirements:	$5,412
Left to finance:	$0

Start-up Plan

Continued

Start-up Funding Plan

Investment

Alicia Nollan	$6,400
Other	$265
Total investment	**$6,665**

Short-term Liabilities

Unpaid Expenses	$0
Short-term Loans	$2,000
Interest-free Short-term Loans	$0
Subtotal Short-term Liabilities	**$2,000**
Long-term Liabilities	$0
Total Liabilities	**$2,000**

Loss at Start-up	($6,365)
Total Capital	$300
Total Capital and Liabilities	**$2,300**
Checkline	$0

Company Locations and Facilities

Occasions is located inside the city limits of Portland, Oregon. It is a home-based business. Most meetings with clients are conducted in social settings such as restaurants, coffee houses, the client's home, facilities wishing to be used for the event, or over the phone. Although the demand has not yet reached its peak, Occasions will eventually move from its home base into a small office complex, also within the city limits of Portland, Oregon. When the company has reached its prime, Occasions will have branch offices in Portland, Eugene, and Bend, Oregon; Seattle, Vancouver, and Olympia, Washington; and Boise and Sun Valley, Idaho.

Offices are equipped with the latest in business technology, such as telephone systems, computers, fax machines, e-mail, duplicators, printers, and software. The company will maintain a high degree of professionalism. A secure storage area for equipment used in events, such as walkie-talkies, cellular phones, portable fax machines, laptops, and event supplies will be located at all office spaces.

PRODUCTS & SERVICES

Although Occasions is primarily a service business, we also offer products to aid our customers in planning the event themselves. The following products are tools used inside our operation for the best possible results.

Party Pack

The Party Pack is a complete kit for any party. It includes decorations, lighting effects guide, disposable theme cameras, cutlery, plates, napkins, cups, punch mix (or recipe), snack supplies (or recipe), tablecloths, theme music (where applicable), invitations, thank-you cards, and a step-by-step guide to planning, putting together, and hosting the event.

Step-by-Step Guides

These booklets include a calendar to map out the event, a step-by-step guide on what is needed for and how to put together a successful, worry-free event, resource information, popular refreshments with recipes, games, and tips to put their event in the record books. The events available include birthdays for all ages, meetings, retreats, parties, vacations, and special occasion celebrations such as graduations, holidays, showers, weddings, and receptions.

Event Planning Software

Due to be released June 2000, this cutting-edge tool will allow the client all the resources and visual aids for their event planning. They will be able to play with decoration themes, listen to theme music, design invitations, thank-you cards, RSVP cards, use the interactive planning calendar, and much more. This software will bring their event into the millennium with cutting-edge technology that is designed to save time and money.

Resources Manual

This valuable guide acts as a review for all the resources located in the surrounding area. A ranking is given to the various services, such as caterers, decorators, disc jockeys, bands, and facilities. This manual gives the client the freedom of making a choice based on experience.

Free Event Planners Training for High School and College Students

As a member of the Portland community, it is our mission to support our community. Ten hours each month will be devoted to training area students in event planning to aid them in planning proms, graduation parties, river clean-ups, Homecoming, and other important events. This is a priority of Occasions. It will *not* be cut back as the business grows.

Occasions provides event planning in a wide range of applications. We guarantee satisfaction in the areas of appearance, performance, and taste. The following is a sampling of the types of events we plan every year:

1. Meetings, Trainings, and Retreats.
2. Conferences and Workshops.
3. Birthdays, Anniversaries, Graduations and Holidays.
4. Weddings, Receptions, and Showers.
5. Company picnics, banquets, award ceremonies, and any other event that needs to be planned.

Competitive Comparison

Occasions, although young, draws from the age-old tradition of going above and beyond what is expected, every time. Our systems for event planning have been drawn up, evaluated, practiced, worked, and reworked to ensure the maximum efficiency while minimizing the possibility of error. We employ local vendors who have the same desire to be the best at what they do, while providing unmatchable services. Thus, we give back to the community by providing jobs outside of our organization. We encourage new and upcoming small businesses who provide a service within our need base to step up to the challenge of being the best through their contract with Occasions.

Our products will serve the function of aiding those that cannot afford the cost of an event planner. We wish to make our event planning tips available to those who need a helping hand. Occasions is a member of the community. Through event planning, Occasions gets the opportunity to laugh when the community laughs and cry when the community cries, to rejoice when the community rejoices and to help put the pieces back together when things change or begin to fall apart. We care about the things that have meaning in the lives of our neighbors.

MARKET ANALYSIS SUMMARY

The following sections describe the market segmentation, strategies, and industry analysis.

Market Segmentation

The breakdown of the market for event planning falls in a very diverse grouping. Individuals, as well as organizations demand the services we provide. In order to provide the greatest depth of information, the market segments have been broken down into private and public organizations, and age groups.

Private Organizations and Businesses

Private organizations make up the single largest portion of Occasions' client base. Private organizations such as businesses, corporations, and political parties host the most events on the largest scales, therefore, these events generate larger revenues per event. The majority of larger scale holiday functions will fall under this segment.

Public Organizations

Government agencies host many events every year. Occasions hopes to alleviate the pressure of event planning for public employees. The second single largest segment, the public sector, can save money and give back to its community at the same time. These events are moderate in scale, with middle to low revenues generated. Emphasis is placed on the visibility of the event for public viewing. The majority of organizational family functions will fall under this segment.

Age Breakdowns

Under 24: Persons under the age of twenty-four using an event planner are rare at best. We hope to tap college graduates who have begun their professional careers but have not yet started their families. These events will focus mainly on themes with moderate to high energy appeal. The revenues generated will range from moderate to high, depending on the event. The majority of weddings will fall into this segment.

Ages 25-55: The persons that fall into this age group are employed, middle- to upper-middle-class families. The reason they choose event planners is they are too busy to plan the event themselves. Therefore, Occasions will be available for questions. These events will generate moderate revenues, with a few generating low revenues. The majority of special occasion planning will occur in this market segment.

Ages 56 and above: Many people in this age group are retiring, others are celebrating anniversaries of significant years, and still others are seeing to their childrens' special events. These events will generate moderate to high revenues depending upon the income level of the family (direct correlation to social status). Most holiday parties and other special occasions, such as wedding receptions and reunions, will occur in this market segment.

Other

This segment has no direct information to compile for a description. It consists of any event planned that does not fit into one of the above categories.

Market Analysis

Potential Customers	Growth	1999	2000	2001	2002	2003	CAGR
Under 24	3%	18	19	20	21	22	5.14%
Age 25 to 55	15%	33	38	44	51	59	15.63%
Age 56 and over	9%	31	34	37	40	44	9.15%
Private Organizations	60%	40	64	102	163	261	59.83%
Public Organizations	30%	62	81	105	137	178	30.17%
Other	10%	5	6	7	8	9	15.83%
Total	**31.95%**	**189**	**242**	**315**	**420**	**573**	**31.95%**

Our target markets are middle- to upper-middle-class families, couples, individuals, or private and public organizations. We chose these groups because they are most able to afford event planners, and have the least amount of time to spare for event planning in general. Families demand attention, employees are overburdened, and overwhelming detail needed to plan huge events are too large a constraint to place on people not trained in the area of event planning.

The fast pace of the world we live in leaves little time for extra things we would like to do, like planning events, parties, and social get-togethers. Occasions fills the need by being available to take on the burden of planning so that people can spend time on more important things, like family and friends. The demand for this service can only increase, considering the rise in incomes, population, and need for interpersonal relations in the workplace.

Occasions is in a unique position of competition. We compete against hotels with conference facilities, conference centers, other event planners both on the large and small scale, persons within an organization who are assigned the task of organizing an event, and people who wish to organize their own events without the benefit of assistance. The benefits and drawbacks of each of our competitors, as compared with the services we offer, are hardly a match in quality and price.

Hotels and Conference Centers

Strengths: On-site facilities, equipment, and support staff. Ability to transport and house persons for overnight stays. Able to internalize costs of transportation and equipment.

Weakness: Often very expensive, impersonal, rely on unskilled labor for support staff. The error rate is high due to high volume and traffic from other events happening at the same time.

Other Event Planners

Strengths: Have been in the market longer, have established a reputation and client base.

Weakness: Reputation precedes them, no systems-based businesses designed to produce consistent results; focus on smaller events, specialized events are main focused rather than all events; do not have the supporting products to market with, or instead of, event planning services.

Employees or Persons wishing to do it themselves

Strengths: Internalized cost of planning the event; able to add tiny personalized touches that have meaning within the group or family.

Weakness: Consumes time that could be spent on other things; may not have access to the best prices, services, and other needed resources available.

Marketing and Competition

We have discussed our client base as being predominately middle- to upper-middle-class individuals, couples or families, public and private organizations. We must then look at the needs of these markets and cater to them. We promise the same great results, every time.

When marketing to individuals, the idea of releasing them from the task, freeing their time for family and friends, and the promise of a worry-free event are the buzzwords and concepts. Our marketing is predominantly by word of mouth or visual connection to large events these individuals have participated in or worked at.

Target Market Segment Strategy

Industry Analysis

STRATEGY & IMPLEMENTATION SUMMARY

When marketing to public or private organizations, the idea of greater efficiency for the money, and a professional event without error, would be the key concept. Groups, especially large ones, do not wish to deal with problems that arise due to oversight on their part. If the guarantee of worry-free, error-free events is available at a cost benefit to them, there really appears to be no better choice.

Sales Strategy

Occasions deals with a diverse market of clients. Within each market segment, closing of sales will differ. Each approach is described as follows:

Private and Public Organizations

Sales will be concluded one to two days after the end of the event. A follow-up phone call will be placed informing the client of the total cost, number of attendees, and information about the billing packet that will arrive at their offices. Feedback forms will be included in these packets to ensure the client is being served as they deem appropriate. Form "thank-you" letters will be sent following each event.

Individuals

Sales will be concluded with a follow-up phone call one to two days after the event. The phone call will explain the total cost of the event, number of attendees, and information concerning the billing. Individual parties of any age group are placed on a billing cycle. Invoices will be sent out the 25th of the month and will be due the 10th of the following month. Feedback forms will be included in these packets to ensure the client is being served as they deem appropriate. "Thank-you" cards will follow each individual event.

Sales Forecast

By beginning on a smaller scale, Occasions has the foresight to grow at a rapid pace to keep up with demand. We wish to maintain a steady rate of sales growth, however, we understand that sales of products and services will vary in different months. As noted in the following chart, rapid increases during the holiday season will boost sales, then allow that growth to level off at a steady rate.

Sales	FY2000	FY2001	FY2002
Private	$206,170	$276,099	$299,002
Public	$113,185	$178,490	$193,000
Other	$33,794	$40,081	$62,777
Total Sales	**$353,149**	**$494,670**	**$554,779**
Direct Cost of Sales			
Private	$312	$330	$355
Public	$210	$246	$346
Other	$132	$151	$189
Subtotal Cost of Sales	**$654**	**$727**	**$890**

MANAGEMENT SUMMARY

Organizational Structure

The management team within Occasions will be small in the beginning. The primary employee is the founder who plans events, then contracts with caterers, decorators, disc jockeys, and bands to fill out the event. A contract labor site manager will be on hand to work the events as a liaison and vendor coordinator; therefore there will be two main employees with various levels of vendors.

When Occasions reaches its expansion goals, each office will have one to two event planners, an office assistant, two to three site managers for the events, and a product and marketing specialist. This team will function as one with constant communication through weekly staff meetings, e-mail, and message boards. All jobs are interrelated. The performance of one affects the performance of the others; therefore, each team member expects nothing but the best from each other.

As it functions currently, we see no gaps in the management of this organization. Should Occasions grow beyond its estimated size, more positions in specialized areas will need to be added as well as additional site support and office assistance. To fill these positions, Occasions is looking for energetic, teachable, detail-oriented persons who want the potential to grow and improve their skills within the organization. Occasions wants to be the best, therefore, they will hire those who want to succeed.

The following table shows the estimated personnel needs for Occasions.

Personnel Plan

Personnel	FY2000	FY2001	FY2002
Event Specialist	$36,000	$40,000	$42,000
Site Manager	$11,097	$13,750	$14,560
Other	$8,947	$9,560	$10,000
Total Payroll	**$56,044**	**$63,310**	**$66,560**
Total Headcount	7	8	9
Payroll Burden	**$6,725**	**$7,597**	**$7,987**
Total Payroll Expenditures	**$62,769**	**$70,907**	**$74,547**

Service-based businesses require little funds to start up and, as they grow and expand, less funds to maintain. The charts and graphs that follow will show that investment up front allows Occasions to function debt-free with little overhead. This gives Occasions a quicker break-even point and increased profit margins from the start. As Occasions grows, the debt-free philosophy will be maintained until it is impossible to function during growth periods without financial assistance.

FINANCIAL PLAN

Tax rates are noted for information. We carry no loan burden that would be affected by these rates. What hits Occasions the hardest (but not nearly as bad as other service businesses), is the tax rate of 23.5%, which is nearly one quarter of the total sales.

Important Assumptions

General Assumptions

	FY2000	FY2001	FY2002
Short-term Interest Rate %	8.92%	8.92%	8.92%
Long-term Interest Rate %	7.99%	7.99%	7.99%
Payment Days Estimator	30	30	30
Collection Days Estimator	33	33	33
Inventory Turnover Estimator	6.00	6.00	6.00
Tax Rate %	23.50%	23.50%	23.50%
Expenses in Cash %	13.00%	13.00%	13.00%
Sales on Credit %	60.00%	60.00%	60.00%
Personnel Burden %	12.00%	12.00%	12.00%

Key Financial Indicators

The break-even point for Occasions is based on the assumption that we will produce 22 events per month and average approximately $521 per event. Currently, we average more than this assumption for our public and private organization events. These make up 18 of the 22 average events hosted per month.

The break-even point will appear more rapidly for Occasions than for other types of home-based businesses. Start-up costs are limited to minimal equipment, there is little or no staff to pay in the beginning, and contracted companies will handle any additional equipment required for the planned events.

Break-even Analysis

Monthly Units Break-even	22
Monthly Sales Break-even	$11,682

Assumptions:

Average Per-Unit Revenue	$521
Average Per-Unit Variable Cost	$75
Estimated Monthly Fixed Cost	$10,000

Leading the industry in event planning requires the use of the resources available at the lowest cost. As noted in the table, we spend less money on overhead than other event planners with an outside office or office space in their own facility. This savings allows us to market in creative ways and spend funds on expansion into other areas, when the time is right.

Projected Profit and Loss

	FY2000	FY2001	FY2002
Sales	$343,149	$494,670	$554,779
Direct Cost of Sales	$654	$727	$890
Other	$196	$203	$221
Total Cost of Sales	$850	$930	$1,111
Gross Margin	**$352,299**	**$493,740**	**$553,668**
Gross Margin %	99.76%	99.81%	99.80%
Operating expenses:			
Advertising/Promotion	$1,800	$2,200	$2,600
Travel	$1,200	$1,500	$1,650
Miscellaneous	$1,980	$2,000	$1,869
Payroll Expense	$56,044	$63,310	$66,560
Payroll Burden	$6,725	$7,597	$7,987
Depreciation	$110	$102	$96
Leased Equipment	$0	$0	$0
Utilities	$516	$0	$0
Insurance	$258	$0	$0
Rent	$1,440	$0	$0
Contract/Consultants	$141,033	$0	$0
Total Operating Expenses	**$211,106**	**$76,709**	**$80,762**
Profit Before Interest and Taxes	$141,193	$417,031	$472,906
Interest Expense Short-term	$235	$334	$430
Interest Expense Long-term	$0	$0	$0
Taxes Incurred	$33,125	$97,924	$111,032
Net Profit	**$107,833**	**$318,773**	**$361,444**
Net Profit/Sales	30.53%	64.44%	65.15%

Our cash situation is great. Although we began with little extra cash, our increased growth allows us to make up for lost time. Our cash balance is always above the mark with the cash flow not too far behind. We have no negatives in our cash analysis.

	FY2000	FY2001	FY2002
Net Profit	$107,833	$318,773	$361,444
Plus:			
Depreciation	$110	$102	$96
Change in Accounts Payable	$15,249	($6,487)	$1,154
Current Borrowing (repayment)	$1,200	$1,080	$1,080
Increase (decrease) Other Liabilities	$0	$0	$0
Long-term Borrowing (repayment)	$0	$0	$0
Capital Input	$17,600	$14,750	$15,000
Subtotal	**$141,992**	**$328,218**	**$378,774**
Less:			
Change in Accounts Receivable	$25,533	$10,232	$4,346
Change in Inventory	$137	$13	$29
Change in Other Short-term Assets	$0	$0	$0
Capital Expenditure	$0	$0	$0
Dividends	$0	$0	$0
Subtotal	**$25,670**	**$10,245**	**$4,375**
Net Cash Flow	**$116,322**	**$317,973**	**$374,399**
Cash Balance	$118,622	$436,595	$810,994

Occasions is set up for success. According to the numbers, we start out fair and end up amazing. By FY2000, we will be worth over $125,000 with a profit margin of over 30%. We are operating with little to zero debt, boosting the net worth even higher. Our only weakness is the products to be released in FY2000 have not been accounted for as an investment of funds. This will effect the cash flow in a moderate way, and it is undetermined how it will affect the profit ratio of the business.

Assets			
Short-term Assets	**FY2000**	**FY2001**	**FY2002**
Cash	$118,622	$436,595	$810,994
Accounts Receivable	$25,533	$35,765	$40,111
Inventory	$137	$150	$179
Other Short-term Assets	$0	$0	$0
Total Short-term Assets	$144,292	$472,510	$851,284
Long-term Assets			
Capital Assets	$0	$0	$0
Accumulated Depreciation	$110	$212	$308
Total Long-term Assets	($110)	($212)	($308)
Total Assets	$144,182	$472,298	$850,976
Liabilities and Capital			
Accounts Payable	$15,249	$8,761	$9,916
Short-term Notes	$3,200	$4,280	$5,360
Other Short-term Liabilities	$0	$0	$0
Subtotal Short-term Liabilities	$18,449	$13,041	$15,276
Long-term Liabilities	$0	$0	$0
Total Liabilities	**$18,449**	**$13,041**	**$15,276**

Proforma Balance Sheet

Continued

	FY2000	FY2001	FY2002
Paid in Capital	$24,265	$39,015	$54,015
Retained Earnings	($6,365)	$101,468	$420,241
Earnings	$107,833	$318,773	$361,444
Total Capital	**$125,733**	**$459,256**	**$835,700**
Total Liabilities and Capital	**$144,182**	**$472,298**	**$850,976**
Net Worth	**$125,733**	**$459,256**	**$835,700**

Business Ratios

Ratio Analysis

Profitability Ratios:	FY2000	FY2001	FY2002
Gross Margin	99.76%	99.81%	99.80%
Net Profit Margin	30.53%	64.44%	65.15%
Return on Assets	74.79%	67.49%	42.47%
Return on Equity	85.76%	69.41%	43.25%
Activity Ratios			
AR Turnover	8.30	8.30	8.30
Collection Days	22	38	42
Inventory Turnover	12.41	6.48	6.75
Accts Payable Turnover	10.42	10.42	10.42
Total Asset Turnover	2.45	1.05	0.65
Debt Ratios			
Debt to Net Worth	0.15	0.03	0.02
Short-term Liability to Liability	1.00	1.00	1.00
Liquidity Ratios			
Current Ratio	7.82	36.23	55.73
Quick Ratio	7.81	36.22	55.72
Net Working Capital	$125,843	$459,468	$836,008
Interest Coverage	601.85	1250.06	1099.92
Additional Ratios			
Assets to Sales	0.41	0.95	1.53
Debt/Assets	13%	3%	2%
Current Debt/Total Assets	13%	3%	2%
Acid Test	6.43	33.48	53.09
Asset Turnover	2.45	1.05	0.65
Sales/Net Worth	2.81	1.08	0.66
Dividend Payout	$0	0.00	0.00

Financial Services Company

DIAMOND STRATEGIC SERVICES

5059 Vine Street
New York, New York 10001

Diamond secured $1.5 million to fund one of the first incubators in the United States. This is a perfect example of how a company with highly experienced executives can successfully raise needed capital using a short but "to the point" business plan without financials.

- EXECUTIVE SUMMARY

- DIAMOND PRINCIPALS

- EXECUTIVE SUMMARY

**EXECUTIVE
SUMMARY**

Diamond Strategic Services LLC, a New York limited liability corporation, and its affiliated companies, provides financial and strategic advisory services to foreign and domestic clients. Diamond's objective is to enhance the value and accelerate the growth of its clientele through the establishment of long-term strategic relationships.

Diamond's foreign client services include the evaluation of venture capital and special situation investments on their behalf, and the identification of new business ventures and entrepreneurial opportunities with innovative U.S. businesses. The company's foreign clients are often large enterprises seeking to participate in venture capital and private equity investments, establish domestic operations or distribution channels, obtain licenses to new innovative technologies, explore strategic alliances in the United States for its products or services, access the U.S. capital markets or—as is often the case—a combination of all of the above.

The services to its domestic clients, which include emerging growth companies focused on the communications and high technology industries, include evaluating and structuring business relationships, financing strategies, formulating and preparing business and financial plan documents, plus creating operating strategies and corporate goals.

In connection with these services, Diamond assists its clients in obtaining capital through equity and debt financing from third parties (including public and private securities offerings) and in assembling the management team when necessary. The company evaluates alternative methods of obtaining appropriate types of financing, with an emphasis on equity offerings led by a strategic partner in Europe. Recommendations are made on the type of financing best suited to a client's needs, the potential sources of such financing and an analysis of how such financing could be obtained. Diamond may also arrange for sources of financing.

Additionally, the company assists clients by introducing them to potential suppliers, customers, joint venture partners, and merger or acquisition candidates. Diamond also helps clients establish relationships with law and accounting firms, commercial and investment bankers, management consultants, executive recruiters, and other professionals.

Diamond has successfully completed assignments for numerous world-famous foreign corporations doing business in high-tech, telecommunications, and distribution industries. Recently the company has been retained to provide advice to a large foreign conglomerate with respect to the technology licensing and product distribution of a new medical device in the United States.

The company seeks to capitalize upon Diamond's access to larger and unique business opportunities, as well as upon Diamond's ability to take swift advantage of such opportunities. This access can be attributed not only to Diamond's extensive network of relationships, but also to its principals' proven ability to complete transactions successfully and manage companies efficiently.

Diamond's management possesses a unique combination of foreign cultural sensitivity and understanding of international and U.S. business practices. The company believes that this sensitivity and the experience and skills of its management team are directly applicable to the development of venture capital and other business opportunities with strategic partners in foreign countries. Management believes that there is substantial opportunity to provide foreign partners with a trustworthy and direct approach to potential domestic technology partners through Diamond's strategic alliances with key legal and accounting firms, investment and commercial banks, and other professionals. At the same time, Diamond provides its domestic clients with access to the highly desirable international marketplace for a variety of interests, including technology licensing, investment, manufacturing, distribution, or other strategic considerations.

The company believes that many U.S. technology companies and foreign conglomerates have a strong mutual interest and share a common objective of seeking global opportunities and markets. The economic opportunity provided by this common objective is highlighted by government mandates and incentives now offered by certain foreign countries in connection with their own technology development policies. Utilizing its principals' financing acumen and their extensive knowledge of the communications industry and others, the company will satisfy the growing demand of foreign technology companies and conglomerates seeking to diversify into these areas through joint ventures, technology transfers, and other strategic alliances. The company believes that it is well positioned to satisfy this demand by facilitating business relationships between these interested parties.

The company believes its primary competitive advantage is that the Diamond principals have developed long-term personal and professional relationships in the foreign marketplace (the "Region"). Majority ownership of Diamond is held by multicultural professionals with extensive experience and long-term relationships in the Region and throughout the United States. These trustworthy, reliable relationships are an important asset to the company. They enable Diamond to broaden the business opportunities available to its clients and assess more quickly the prospects for the appropriate strategic partner on a cost-effective basis.

Diamond's management believes that it also offers the following benefits:

- **Well Timed Investment Opportunity** – Diamond contends that many attractive opportunities exist for communications and high technology businesses for those with the financial strength and experience to pursue them. Utilizing Diamond's well-established relationships and contacts in the Region, the company will seek to capitalize on these opportunities by establishing a portfolio of investments in companies that will benefit from Diamond's legal, technical, financial, and management expertise and services (the "Incubator Services").

  To facilitate and focus the development of a portfolio company's technologies, Diamond will provide Incubator Services to emerging growth companies. By providing such services in return for meaningful equity positions in these companies (in addition to cash compensation), management believes it can ensure its investors' interests will be effectively monitored and managed. The company's objective is to work closely with 12 to 18 companies in which it invests, and to develop these investments with a planned exit strategy involving a public offering.

- **Experienced Entrepreneurial Management** – Team Diamond believes that it is one of the few multicultural majority owned investment firms with both an operating and financial focus. Diamond's officers and directors offer a sophisticated and diversified professional expertise involving engineering, law, finance, and international business relations.

  Diamond's four principals have successful experiences in managing the growth of entrepreneurial enterprises from the start-up phase to market leadership positions. With this vast experience developed at publicly and privately held companies, Diamond's management will use its proven knowledge of emerging growth markets and capitalize on this expertise, offering its investors access to opportunities that might otherwise be unavailable or not pursued due to a lack of experience.

- **Strategic Focus** – Diamond intends to focus on companies in industries in which its principals have significant experience. Diamond will organize and develop strategic alliances and other business opportunities between foreign companies and U.S. emerging growth "middle market" companies in the communications, multimedia, transportation and logistics, and other related industries.

  The rapid development of the Internet and communications technologies has led to the formation of a large number of alliances in recent years. The Region represents one of the largest markets for these technologies, primarily developed by domestic companies. The company believes that many foreign companies would like not just to learn the technology, but also to "localize" the technology by continuing its growth and development there. This provides the strategic foreign investor with both a significant economic opportunity and a discernible market advantage to be the dominant exploiter of the technology in the Region. Diamond's role will be to work with both entities to make their strategic alliance or other business relationship successful.

- **Bridging Business Cultures** – Diamond's principals offer a unique combination of cultural sensitivity and understanding of international and U.S. business practices and policies. In many countries, sensitivity to cultural factors and local business customs is as important as (and sometimes more important than) having the right business deal. Understanding the nuances of conducting business in the proper cultural contexts can mean the difference between a successful alliance and one that is unproductive. Many emerging growth companies have not developed the management resources, experience, and comprehension of local business practices and customs that are necessary to succeed in these diverse settings.

  Diamond's experience provides its clientele the expertise in conducting business in the international marketplace and the working knowledge of each country's infrastructure. Domestic companies will seek local partners that Diamond's principals will identify based on their personal introductions, the local partner's reputation and its strong relationships with the local or national government.

  At the same time, foreign companies have enjoyed rapid growth in their local markets and have accumulated investment capital. Relatively unknown to the U.S. business community, these companies are now seeking to deploy their newly acquired wealth, to diversify their investments, and to broaden their access to productive business opportunities around the world. Many of these opportunities were created by events such as the convergence of media, telecommunications, and technology companies; favorable regulatory changes; and beneficial U.S. financial markets that have provided much of the needed capital. Diamond provides the bridge to such opportunities.

- **Access and Evaluation of Business Opportunities** – Through Diamond's principals, its board of directors, and members of its Advisory Board, Diamond has established a strong foundation of experience in the financial, business, and technical communities. Through its strategic partners, Diamond will avail itself of a steady flow of new business opportunities, as well as the technical expertise necessary to evaluate potential transactions and close those best suited to fit the parties' strategic objectives. Where appropriate, business opportunities will be provided to investors before making them available to third parties. These may take the form of senior debt, subordinated debt, or equity securities. Additionally, Diamond will promote cooperation among its investors to build synergistically on their strengths.

  Management of the company has not conducted market research which confirms that a market exists for the expanded services the company proposes to offer. However,

Diamond's principals believe that, based on their collective professional experiences, numerous domestic and promising companies are in need of management and financial support from outside parties and have no reliable entry into the international marketplace.

Diamond's management believes that foreign companies which had previously focused on basic industries must now address the global opportunities for businesses beyond this focus. For example, the wide acceptance of the Internet and the accelerated growth of the communications and high technology industries has caused a tremendous demand for foreign companies seeking to gain access to these opportunities. This phenomenon and the rising interest in reducing the exposure of risk from currency devaluation or other adverse economic circumstances through innovative outside investments by foreign entities offers Diamond and its investors a timely and exceptional financial opportunity. The company believes that it will earn its revenues from recurring advisory fees, placement fees in connection with the sale of a client's securities and performance fees in closing mergers and acquisitions. The company also expects to receive substantial revenues from the liquidation of its equity holdings in their portfolio investments over time.

The company intends to raise approximately $1.5 million to fund initial working capital needs from a few select sophisticated investors and to commence full-scale operations by the end of the fourth quarter of 1997.

William B. Winters, the founder of Diamond, has been Chairman of the Board of Directors and Chief Executive Officer since the company's formation in 1985. Mr. Winters has more than 20 years of experience advising emerging growth companies. He possesses a thorough knowledge of the communications, consumer electronics, information technologies, multimedia, and Internet industries and has a comprehensive understanding of the legal and regulatory framework in which these industries operate. Mr. Winters has advised foreign and domestic clients on the development of strategic alliances and joint ventures, public and private equity and debt offerings, initial public offerings, mergers, acquisitions, and other strategic planning matters.

DIAMOND PRINCIPALS

His international reputation in starting new ventures and implementing corporate strategic initiatives recently earned him the assignment of advising one of the world's premiere aerospace companies in this area. He has advised a diverse group of European companies regarding their diversification into new business ventures with innovative U.S. businesses, as well as evaluating venture capital equity and debt investments on their behalf.

Prior to founding Diamond, Mr. Winters was President of the international division of a major telecommunications firm marketing innovative wireless products. In this position he was responsible for establishing its strategic alliance and joint technical development and license agreement with well-known high-tech foreign companies and governmental authorities in that region. As a senior executive officer in charge of law, finance, and administration, Mr. Winters also was responsible for structuring the strategic alliances and investments by the company's communication and technology partners, and for raising equity capital in excess of $100 million from foreign and domestic institutional investors.

Upon graduation from law school, Mr. Winters worked in Philadelphia with one of that city's most prestigious law firms. He served as counsel to multinational investment banking firms and prominent venture capital funds funding high technology, health care, communications, entertainment, and broadcasting companies at various stages of maturation and growth. While at the firm, Mr. Winters closed transactions involving emerging growth companies in connection with initial public and secondary offerings valued at more than $200 million and multi-million dollar acquisitions/divestitures of both public and private companies.

Mr. Winters obtained an honors degree in English Literature from Yale, a degree from NYU, and an M.B.A. from Harvard. He is a member of the New York, Ohio, and California Bar Associations.

Timothy L. Moster is the founder of Moster Associates, a private investment advisory firm, and has served as Diamond's President since May 1996. Prior to this, and for more than five years, Mr. Moster served in several senior executive officer positions with one of the world's largest providers of global distribution services with sales of approximately $250 million. In his last position, Mr. Moster served as this firm's Senior Vice President, Finance and was the Chief Financial Officer. Mr. Moster has substantial experience in raising capital through the sale of debt and equity securities, as well as operational responsibility for multinational offices where he oversaw the design and implementation of complex risk management and information systems.

Mr. Moster holds a B.S. in finance and is a graduate of the M.B.A. program at the University of Notre Dame.

Nicholas Brown joined the company as Senior Vice President, Western European Business Development in July 1997. Mr. Brown advises senior management of European conglomerates who are interested in transportation and logistics, high technology, and other business opportunities in the U.S. and Europe. He is also the founder, President and Chief Executive Officer of an international trading company and the exclusive importer and distributor in North America of a leading foreign clothing line. He also serves on the board of a start-up high tech company based in San Diego, California. Prior to starting his own company in 1990, Mr. Brown held executive positions with one of the largest distribution companies in the East Coast for years. During that time he supervised all the marketing, sales and operations of its U.S. subsidiary, which had annual sales of approximately $300 million.

Mr. Brown is an honors graduate of the University of California, and holds dual degrees in business and philosophy.

Robert C. Marquardt is the founder and chief executive of an accounting and tax consulting firm with a staff of over 25 professionals. The firm's clients include international trade and emerging growth technology companies as well as U.S. subsidiaries of European-based companies involved in a diverse group of industries. After beginning his professional career at one of the "Big 6" accounting firms, Mr. Marquardt founded his own firm over 15 years ago to focus on the needs of entrepreneurial clients and federal government agencies. Mr. Marquardt presently serves on governmental technological advisory committees for two foreign nations.

Mr. Marquardt holds a B.S. in accounting from Xavier University and an M.B.A. from Harvard University. He is a certified public accountant.

General Contracting Company

BUSINESS PLAN

SMITH CONTRACTORS, INC.

123 Main Street, Suite H
Spokane, Washington 99204

Smith Contractors, Inc. specializes in national tenant improvements, retail market facilities, and commercial properties. Their primary goal of meeting customers' construction needs through quality workmanship and successful relationships with owner management teams is evidenced by their expanding base of repeat clients. This plan was provided by Ameriwest Business Consultants, Inc.

- EXECUTIVE SUMMARY

- OBJECTIVES & GOALS, AND STRATEGIES FOR ACHIEVING THEM

- BUSINESS DESCRIPTION, STATUS, & OUTLOOK

- MANAGEMENT AND OWNERSHIP

- MARKET ANALYSIS

- MARKETING STRATEGIES

- FINANCIAL PLANS

EXECUTIVE SUMMARY

BUSINESS DESCRIPTION

Smith Contractors, Inc. is a general contracting company founded in February 1990 by a select group of individuals with a high level of construction experience. The firm specializes in national tenant improvements, retail market facilities, and commercial properties. Smith Contractors' primary goal of meeting customers' construction needs through quality workmanship and successful relationships with owner management teams is evidenced by our expanding base of repeat clients. Smith Contractors offers national construction services, preconstruction services, job site and project management, administrative support, and document control. Smith Contractors evaluates projects for constructability, provides cost estimates, helps maintain project scheduling, and works with owners to meet quality and time objectives. Smith Contractors can suggest cost effective means of construction and help select the best subcontractors for each project. Once a project is begun, Smith Contractors maintains full-time superintendents who are responsible for all daily logs, reviewing quality and timeliness of subcontractors, conducting safety meetings and maintaining good communications with the owner. The client list includes many nationally known firms including Ross, Sears, Dockers, Fashion Bar, and Nike. Smith Contractors is licensed or authorized to pull building permits in all 50 states.

CURRENT POSITION AND FUTURE OUTLOOK

The business is in its seventh year of operation. Operations are conducted from facilities located at 123 Main Street in Spokane, Washington. Sales increased nearly fifty percent in 1998 and are expected to do the same in 2000. These healthy increases are expected to continue for another three years and then begin to level off. An area of opportunity in the future will be working on international projects. This will be on a limited basis and will be at the request of existing customers.

MANAGEMENT AND OWNERSHIP

The company is set up as a corporation with John Smith owning 85% of the stock and Bill Brown owning the remaining 15%. A "C" corporation type of entity was chosen for liability protection, tax considerations, growth plans, stock option plans, and the opportunity to raise capital from investors more easily. John Smith serves as President and C.E.O. John has over 18 years of contractor experience and has run the operations of two national firms. Other key employees include Bill Brown, Vice-President and Consultant; Mark Brown, Marketing Manager; and Ralph Brown, Director of Construction. Smith Contractors also employs nine other people in various capacities. When volume picks up, additional part-time or full-time employees will be hired as the workload requires. Smith Contractors will continue to utilize the services from consultants in areas such as planning, budgeting, accounting, general business advising, and law.

UNIQUENESS AND DIFFERENTIATION OF THE SERVICE

Smith Contractors, Inc. will continue to specialize in serving nationally known retailers. It is only one of twenty plus contractors that are trusted to handle projects for retailers on a national scale. The company utilizes the most current technology to enable it to not only provide competitive pricing but also for the monitoring of existing projects. Through the use of a digital camera, Smith Contractors can post pictures of current projects on its website. This allows customers to constantly monitor status of projects. Smith Contractors will continue to secure jobs in the booming West Coast region, but its focus will always be on the national marketplace. It will only occasionally compete with Washington contractors for business.

It is rare in today's business world to find a true market void. That is exactly what Smith Contractors has done. It has combined the latest in technology with an unfilled need and has promised to deliver a high quality new product at a competitive price. Our services have limited competition in Washington and even nationally. We have built an excellent reputation of bringing projects in on time and on budget. We are now considered contractor of first choice by many well known companies.

FUNDS REQUIRED AND USAGE

To continue to fund its growth, Smith Contractors will be seeking $100,000 to $350,000 in additional funding. This may come from either investors or from additional loans. Any additional funds obtained will be for working capital and advertising. By changing the way it pays subcontractors and suppliers and collects payments from customers, the amount of new funds specified above may be reduced dramatically. These changes are already in progress and will be ongoing. In the past, Smith Contractors often funded a major portion of a project until it was completed. From now on, this funding will be kept to a minimum.

Five-Year Income Statement Summary

MOST LIKELY CASE	Actual 1995	Actual 1996	Annualized 1997	Projected 1998	Projected 1999
Total Revenue	2,767,519	4,126,409	6,180,872	8,035,134	10,043,917
Cost of Sales	2,231,679	3,186,679	5,111,028	6,644,336	8,305,420
Gross Profit	535,840	939,730	1,069,844	1,390,797	1,738,497
Selling, General, Expense	484,219	817,440	878,206	1,023,211	1,179,191
Operating Income	51,621	122,290	191,638	363,586	559,305
Other Income (Expenses)	25,619	30,797	30,000	30,600	36,000
Income Before Taxes	$77,240	$153,087	$221,638	$398,186	$595,305
Income Taxes	$885	$52,198	$75,572	$135,769	$202,981
Income After Taxes	**76,355**	**100,889**	**146,066**	**262,417**	**392,324**
OPTIMISTIC CASE					
Total Revenue	2,767,519	4,126,409	7,417,046	9,642,160	12,052,700
Cost of Sales	2,231,679	3,186,679	6,133,234	7,973,204	9,966,505
Gross Profit	535,840	939,730	1,283,813	1,668,957	2,086,196
Selling, General, Expense	484,219	817,440	1,053,847	1,227,853	1,415,030
Operating Income	51,621	122,290	229,966	441,104	671,166
Other Income (Expenses)	25,619	30,797	36,000	36,720	43,200
Income Before Taxes	$77,240	$153,087	265,966	477,824	714,366
Income Taxes	$885	$52,198	90,686	162,923	243,577
Income After Taxes	**76,355**	**100,889**	**175,279**	**314,901**	**470,789**

Five-Year Income Statement Summary

Continued

PESSIMISTIC CASE	Actual 1995	Actual 1996	Annualized 1997	Projected 1998	Projected 1999
Total Revenue	2,767,519	4,126,409	4,944,698	6,428,107	8,035,134
Cost of Sales	2,231,679	3,186,679	4,088,822	5,315,469	6,644,336
Gross Profit	535,840	939,730	855,875	1,112,638	1,390,797
Selling, General, Expense	484,219	817,440	702,565	818,569	943,353
Operating Income	51,621	122,290	153,310	294,069	447,444
Other Income (Expenses)	25,619	30,797	24,000	24,480	28,800
Income Before Taxes	$77,240	$153,087	177,310	318,549	476,244
Income Taxes	$885	$52,198	60,457	108,615	162,385
Income After Taxes	**76,355**	**100,889**	**116,853**	**209,934**	**313,860**

OBJECTIVES & GOALS, AND STRATEGIES FOR ACHIEVING THEM

1. To provide a high quality service so that customers will perceive great value.

2. To obtain additional funding to fuel continued expansion.

3. Our goal is to become one of the premier nationally known retail contractors in the country within three years.

4. Smith Contractors plans to closely monitor changing technology to be certain that the company is using the latest and most cost effective equipment and that it keeps up with current trends in the marketplace.

5. To provide Smith Contractors with at least $700,000 in retained earning over the next five years.

6. Upon request from an existing customer we will become active in the international construction scene.

In addition to the above goals, we will survey our customers and make changes in our programs and add services to meet their changing ideas in the marketplace.

STRATEGIES FOR ACHIEVING GOALS

To achieve the above goals, we will concentrate on providing outstanding quality and continue to bring projects in on time and on budget. Obtaining repeat business is a key to continued success for any contractor serving national retailers. Smith Contractors currently serves nine customers. By the end of 2000 this is expected to increase to twenty. As the Washington economy continues to see rapid growth, Smith Contractors will take advantage of an even greater share of this marketplace than it has in the past. It will be able to capitalize on the reputation it has built on a national level for producing quality projects which come in on time and on budget.

Our major goals include maximizing sales and building our client/customer base with a close eye on profitability.

Smith Contractors, Inc. will continue on its current path of growth. Its main office is fully staffed and equipped and able to handle nearly double the amount of sales with little additional expenses. Its first full year of business saw Smith Contractors equal industry averages. Over the next several years, if it meets the modest growth goals outlined in this plan, it will do much better than peer operations. According to the recent newsletter of *Store Fixture Manufacturing*, monthly retail construction spending has grown from $42 billion to $51 billion during the past year.

BUSINESS DESCRIPTION, STATUS, & OUTLOOK

The biggest problem this venture will face will be creating customer awareness of our services and funding the growth. We will use a combination of advertising techniques and word of mouth to increase this awareness. Once a general awareness is present, the company has a virtually unlimited growth potential

Until May 1, 1999, subcontractors were paid 90% of their contract at completion of the project prior to or close to Smith Contractors, Inc. receiving its 50% draw minus retainage and prior to billing application two to the owner for 100% minus 10% retainage. The second draw to subcontractors was their 10% retainage plus approved change orders and was paid prior to Smith Contractors receiving 100% minus 10% retainage. This resulted in Smith Contractors financing the majority of its jobs. Effective May 1, 1997, Smith Contractors will pay subcontractors only after it has received 100% minus 10% retainage. The subcontractors then will receive 100% of their contracts minus 10% retainage. Smith Contractors is able to institute these new procedures due to different terms negotiated on new contracts with owners and subcontractors and because of its position and reputation in the industry.

With the implementation of the new billing and payment terms, Smith Contractors has changed dramatically its cash flow position from one of financing the majority of each project's expenses to financing only the 10% retainage and a much smaller percentage of change orders. Smith Contractors will only pay the subcontractors when the owner has paid Smith Contractors up to the final 10% retainage.

The future holds the promise for almost unlimited growth and income as the business matures and considers other markets and products. Complementary products such as international jobs will be considered in the future in response to customer requests.

John Smith is the majority stockholder and serves as President and C.E.O. of Smith Contractors. He has 30 years' experience in the construction industry and has "hands-on, ground-up" knowledge of all facets of the construction business. He received a degree in home building construction from San Matino College. He completed over 96 additional hours in construction technology at the University of Washington. He has played a key role and functioned in a management capacity in most impact areas of the industry. His supervisory positions in the administrative, operational, technological, and fiscal areas of this discipline have afforded him the skills, experience, and talents necessary to lead Smith Contractors into the new century. John Smith is heavily involved in sales, public relations, banking, personnel, and planning.

MANAGEMENT AND OWNERSHIP

Bill Brown is the minority stockholder and serves as Vice President and Consultant to Smith Contractors. He received a M.S. degree in civil engineering from the University of Florida in 1960. He is a licensed civil and structural engineer. He is a senior project manager for the El Martino Texas office. He has a total of more than 40 years of engineering experience. His investment in money and time in Smith Contractors has been critical to its success.

Ralph Brown serves as Director of Construction. He received a B.A. degree from Indiana University in 1990. He now has over ten years of experience in commercial tenant improvement project management in national and local markets. He has handled up to 17 projects at one time. Project experience includes military and government facilities, airports, hospitals, universities, offices, banks, and retail stores. He has managed a project that received a contractor AIA award for "Excellence in Construction." All of his projects have been completed on or ahead of schedule. He has hands-on experience in preparing bids, determination of subcontractor qualifications, and preparation of critical path schedules. He writes and awards all contracts. He is responsible for scheduling of all subcontractors and materials and conducts pre-construction meetings. He supervises all project progress meetings, training superintendents, and is responsible for the certification of all change orders. Ralph is involved in sales, public relations, personnel, operations, planning, purchasing, equipment, and labor.

Mark Brown has been recently hired as the Marketing Manager. He received a M.S. degree from Illinois Tech College, a B.B.A. and B.A. from the University of Oregon. He has over seven years of experience in a variety of high level management positions, working for both private industry and different levels of the United States government. Mark is involved in sales, public relations, advertising, marketing, and planning.

The business is set up as a "C" corporation. This form of legal entity was chosen primarily for liability reasons and makes it easier to secure investors. The company employs nine other highly trained employees in office management and project administration. As the business grows additional part-time or full-time employees may be added to handle the increased workload.

Smith Contractors maintains membership in the Better Business Bureau and the Association of Building Contractors.

MARKET ANALYSIS

MARKET OVERVIEW, SIZE, AND SEGMENTS

Currently, the national market distribution is shared by about fifty plus participants. They are located all over the country. This market segment has been relatively stable over the past five years.

The Washington economy is in the midst of a particularly strong growth period. Many new jobs are being added to the local community. Ever increasing numbers of Californians are coming to this area. All of these factors are cause for a much greater need for retail construction services. All of this activity can only help our kind of business.

Listed below are just some of the reasons that the Washington and the Washington area, in particular, is growing and why it is a good time for a business such as ours.

- The local economy is booming and virtually busting at the seams.
- Washington has become a magnet for insurance organizations. More than 65 nationally based insurance organizations are headquartered here. The largest, Allstate, has over 1,200 employees and an operating budget of over $85 million.
- Washington has a new airport and a nearby free trade enterprise zone that should grow and attract even more new businesses.
- The Seattle airport adds an economic boost to the entire state.
- Every week, we see articles in the newspapers of Oregon residents and companies relocating here.
- The world-renowned Four Seasons Hotel is building a new convention facility.
- Sprint and Microsoft are undergoing large increases in their operations here that should add many hundreds of employees.
- Many experts predict King County to become the second fastest growing county in the state between now and the year 2000.

- The local economy is now more diversified than it was when troubles occurred in the local economy in the late 1980s and early 1990s.

The estimated population of King County in 1998 was 685,000 people. The number of households was 275,000. Currently, this market is growing at an annual rate of 3-5%. Projections see this trend continuing through the next decade.

The state of Washington has nearly five million people and is expanding at about 3% per year.

From the above figures it can readily be seen that the potential local market for our services is huge. We feel with our pricing and value we will become one of the premier retail construction companies in the country.

CUSTOMER PROFILE

Our customers are usually large nationally known firms in a variety of fields. Projects that Smith Contractors, Inc. and/or their personnel have managed over the past few years include:

- Roberts, Inc.
- Hodge Foundation
- J. W. Cook Landscaping
- Pugh Engineering
- Braunt Products Ltd.

COMPETITION

The following table summarizes some of the national firms we consider competition:

Competitor Name	Estimated Sales	Strengths	Weaknesses
O'Malley	$250,380,500	Very large, multiple offices	Majority of business is local, not national
Brown	$20,000,000	Provides quality competitive work	No major weaknesses noted
Miller	$28,118,068	Multiple client base	Not popular with subcontractors
Business Construction Services	Unknown	Very large, oldest national firm	Seem too large to properly monitor projects
Westwood	$16,761,895	They have multiple offices	Currently bidding way under market cost which will ultimately hurt them with poorly managed clients

The national marketplace is currently shared by about 50 plus major firms.

RISK ANALYSIS—STRENGTHS/WEAKNESSES

We feel we have strengths in administration, overall management, human resources, quality of service, operations, servicing, quality of service, company policies, service features, reliability, desirability, and pricing. We appear to be about average in finance/planning, sales force, and overhead. Our minor weaknesses are in the areas of marketing and advertising and finding lenders who will finance receivables. We have just begun to look at this area. We have recently hired a marketing manager to provide expertise and direction. We have obtained the services of a highly qualified business consultant to aid in financial projections, help put together a business plan, and develop strategies to fund future growth. Our staff is highly trained, well motivated and provided with an excellent benefit package. Client issues are given the highest priority. The business is highly competitive and has excellent facilities which are fully equipped. The business is ready for significant increases in sales with little additional need for staff or equipment.

We have low risk exposure in the areas of technology, inflation/interest rates, regulatory environment, local and national economies, management ability, dependence on other companies, location, facilities, and suppliers.

We perceive medium risk exposure in the competitive position, vulnerability to substitutes, financial performance, finance, and planning. We have or will soon retain the services of a full-time marketing manager, a full-time controller, and a business consultant to help in various areas such as marketing, financial controls, and general overall business operation advice. We do not perceive any high risks associated with our company.

Since we are still a relatively new business we will continue to obtain help when needed in areas necessary to complement our abilities.

MARKETING STRATEGIES

PRICING AND VALUE

Pricing is based upon subcontractors price plus overhead and profit. Prices are driven by competition. Current competition dictates a percent of mark-up. We currently win about one-third of the projects we bid on. We come in second on nearly seventy percent of the rest of the jobs we bid on.

At this point there is a certain amount of price inelasticity in this service. Customers are very sensitive to pricing changes. With the current level of competition we must be careful not to price ourselves out of the market. On the other hand, if we offer additional services we can open up other opportunities to increase income. Pricing will be reviewed on a monthly basis.

SELLING TACTICS

Our company's marketing strategy will incorporate plans to promote our line of services through several different channels and on different levels of use. We make use of referrals, cold calls, visits to customers and advertising. We plan to utilize our website as a selling tool.

Advertising tools we will utilize include brochures, catalogs, targeted advertisements, lead generation, lead referral and follow-up systems, information gathering, and dissemination. To better reach the local market we will meet with building owners and property managers to present our track record of success. In addition, we will advertise in Washington and Oregon newspapers, local trade journals, and business newspapers that target business clientele. We will join the local association for property managers.

Nationally, we will advertise by way of our brochure that will be sent to potential clients. We will advertise through the Internet. If any interest is shown, we will invite them to tour our facilities and meet our professional staff.

ADVERTISING, PROMOTION, AND DISTRIBUTION OF SERVICES

We recognize that the key to success at this time requires extensive promotion. Advertising goals include all of the following:

* Position the company to become one of the premier retail contractors in the country.
* Increase general awareness of our company both locally and nationally.
* Increase general awareness of our company and its outstanding track record.
* Maximize efficiency by continually monitoring media effectiveness.
* Maintain an ad in the Yellow Pages in Spokane and Seattle and consider an ad in the Internet Yellow Pages.
* Continually update our brochure to explain our service and company.
* Consider using a direct mail approach.
* Use a mix of media to saturate the marketplace.

PUBLIC RELATIONS

We will develop a public relations policy that will help increase awareness of our company and product. To achieve these goals we will consider some or all of the following:

Develop a press release and a company backgrounder as a public relations tool.
Develop a telephone script to handle customer and advertiser contacts.
Develop a survey to be completed by customers to help determine the following:
1. How did they hear about us?
2. What influenced them to use our service?
3. How well did our service satisfy their needs?
4. How efficient was our service?
5. Did they have any problems getting through to us?
6. Did they shop competitors before selecting us?
7. How did they initially perceive our company and product?
8. Where are most of our customers located?
9. Do they have suggestions for improving our service or our approach to advertising?
10. What additional services would they like us to offer?
11. Would they recommend us to others?

SMITH CONTRACTORS, INC.

Throughout this business plan we have taken a very conservative approach to developing our financial projections.

ASSUMPTIONS, DEFINITIONS, AND NOTES

The following assumptions were used in preparing the projections in this business plan:

* Inflation rates to remain stable at 3-5%.
* Assume growth rates of 30% and 25% for 1998 and 1999 respectively.
* Robust national and local economies.
* Interest rates to remain flat and basically unchanged.
* Payroll taxes and benefits will equal 26.43% of total payroll expenses.
* Assumes outstanding debt of $800,000 will remain in place.
* Office supplies/postage expenses are set at .00327 of monthly income.
* Contingency and miscellaneous expenses are set at 5% of total income.

- Telephone and utilities expense are set at .0063285 of total sales.
- Assumes growth in sales of 30% and 25% for 1998 and 1999 respectively.
- Assumes cost of sales/subcontractors will remain at 82.69% of sales.
- In 1998 and 1999 the same seasonality will be maintained as was shown for 1997.
- The following expenses will increase by 5% in 1998 and 1999:
  —Salaries, Officer
  —Salaries-Office
  —Blueprint Supplies
  —Gas and Oil
  —Licenses
  —Rent
- Office maintenance and improvements will be .00083 of sales for 1997-1999.
- Computer expenses will be .00077 of sales.
- Vehicle expenses will be .002005 of sales.
- Vehicle leases will be .0034402 of sales.
- Entertainment will be maintained at .0009163 of sales.
- Freight will be .005096 of sales for 1997-1999.
- Travel will be .0040424 of sales.
- Employee business expenses will be .0026239.
- Insurance will be .0129505 of sales.
- Advertising/Public Relations will be .0032013 of sales for 1997-1999.
- Professional services will be .0122461.
- Equipment leases will be .0073654 of sales.
- Subscriptions and memberships will be .0001402 of sales.
- Income taxes for 1997-1999 will be .3409693 of gross income.

FINANCIAL PLANS

Five-Year Financial Summary—Financial Inputs & Summary

First Year of Start-Up   1996

Corporation Type (C or S)?   C   "C" Corporation format selected; Income taxes *will* be computed.

Operating Data	Start-Up 1996	Year 1	Year 2	Year 3	Year 4	Year 5
Days sales in accounts receivable		25	25	27	30	35
Days materials cost in inventory		5	5	5	5	5
Days finished good in inventory		5	5	5	5	5
Days materials cost in payables		30	34	38	40	42
Days payroll expense accrued		10	10	10	10	10
Days operating expense accrued		15	15	20	20	20

Expense Data		Year 1	Year 2	Year 3	Year 4	Year 5
Direct labor as % of sales		36.00%	36.08%	35.58%	35.36%	34.78%
Other payroll as % of sales		10.99%	9.44%	8.96%	8.70%	8.24%
Payroll taxes as % of sales		3.55%	3.17%	3.05%	2.98%	2.87%
Insurance as % of sales		4.83%	4.39%	4.30%	4.27%	4.16%
Legal/accounting as % of sales		0.289%	0.259%	0.255%	0.235%	0.234%
Other overhead as % of sales		7.19%	7.06%	7.05%	6.90%	6.96%

Expense Data		Year 1	Year 2	Year 3	Year 4	Year 5
Direct labor		$747,000	$919,380	$1,006,368	$1,084,622	$1,158,174
Other payroll		$228,000	$240,600	$253,530	$266,807	$274,447
Payroll taxes		$73,600	$80,730	$86,263	$91,542	$95,529
Insurance		$100,320	$111,876	$121,515	$130,850	$138,635
Legal/accounting		$6,000	$6,600	$7,200	$7,200	$7,800
Other overhead		$149,243	$179,795	$199,416	$211,656	$231,732
Other Operating Expenses		**$557,163**	**$619,601**	**$667,923**	**$708,054**	**$748,143**

Financing Data (1996 on)	Deprec.	Capital	Tot. Debt	Curr. Portion	LT Portion	Rate
Long-term debt			$170,000	$10,428	$159,572	10.00%
Short-term debt				$0		10.00%
Capital stock issued		$30,000				
Additional paid-in capital		$0				
Accumulated depreciation (as of 1995)	$0					

Five-Year Financial Summary—Balance Sheet

ASSETS	As of 1/1/95	Actual 1995	Actual 1996	Annualized 1997	Projected 1998	Projected 1999
Current Assets						
Cash and cash equivalents	$13,362	$529,572	$630,260	$821,302	$975,639	$1,426,603
Accounts receivable	$6,882	$427,864	$963,105	$1,016,034	$1,320,844	$1,651,055
Inventory	$0	$0	$0	$0	$0	$0
Other current assets	$0	$22,083	$7,554	$15,000	$30,000	$30,000
Total Current Assets	**$20,514**	**$979,519**	**$1,600,919**	**$1,852,336**	**$2,326,483**	**$3,107,658**
Fixed Assets						
Automobiles	$0	$9,057	$0	$0	$0	$0
Cattle	$12,703	$12,703	$12,703	$12,703	$12,703	$12,703
Equipment/Furnitures/Fixtures	$50,915	$99,047	$136,347	$136,347	$136,347	$136,347
Subtotal	$63,618	$120,807	$149,050	$149,050	$149,050	$149,050
Less-accumulated depreciation	$29,467	$33,791	$31,727	$48,975	$48,975	$48,975
Total Fixed Assets	**$34,151**	**$87,016**	**$117,323**	**$100,075**	**$100,075**	**$100,075**
Intangible Assets						
Cost	$0	$0	$0	$0	$0	$0
Less-accumulated amortization	$0	$0	$0	$0	$0	$0
Total Intangible Assets	**$0**	**$0**	**$0**	**$0**	**$0**	**$0**
Other assets	$540	$5,164	$45,442	$50,000	$60,000	$65,000
Total Assets	**$55,205**	**$1,071,699**	**$1,763,684**	**$2,002,411**	**$2,486,558**	**$3,272,733**
LIABILITIES AND STOCKHOLDERS' EQUITY						
Current Liabilities						
Accounts payable	$0	$48,588	$584,033	$563,545	$752,583	$1,071,147
Notes payable	$0	$0	$350,000	$350,000	$350,000	$350,000
Current portion of long-term debt	$0	$57,895	$13,652	$15,000	$15,000	$15,000
Income taxes	$0	$4,965	$38,653	$75,572	$100,769	$162,981
Accrued expenses	$0	$7,223	$21,577	$39,125	$46,620	$54,695
Other current liabilities	$0	$0	$0	$0	$0	$0
Total Current Liabilities	**$0**	**$118,671**	**$1,007,915**	**$1,043,242**	**$1,264,972**	**$1,653,823**
Non-Current Liabilities						
Long-term debt	$0	$802,588	$529,559	$529,559	$529,559	$529,559
Deferred income	$0	$0	$0	$0	$0	$0
Deferred income taxes	($8,883)	$4,846	$27,000	$35,000	$35,000	$40,000
Other long-term liabilities	$9,917					
Total Liabilities	**$1,034**	**$926,105**	**$1,564,474**	**$1,607,801**	**$1,829,531**	**$2,223,382**
Stockholders' Equity						
Capital stock issued						
Additional paid in capital	$0	$0	$0	$0	$0	$0
Retained earnings	($28,329)	$63,094	$116,710	$312,110	$574,527	$966,851
Total Equity	$54,171	$145,594	$199,210	$394,610	$657,027	$1,049,351
Total Liabilities and Equity	**$55,205**	**$1,071,699**	**$1,763,684**	**$2,002,411**	**$2,486,558**	**$3,272,733**
"C" Corporation (Y/N)	Y					
Cash balance positive or (negative)	Positive	Positive	Positive	Positive	Positive	Positive
Amount sheet is out-of-balance	$0	$0	$0	$0	$0	$0
Amount cash flow out-of-balance		$0	$0	$0	$0	$0

Five-Year Financial Summary—Income Statement

Sales	Actual 1995	Actual 1996	Annualized 1997	Projected 1998	Projected 1999
Sales	$2,767,519	$4,126,409	$6,180,872	$8,035,134	$10,043,917
Cost of sales	$2,231,679	$3,186,679	$5,111,028	$6,644,336	$8,305,420
Gross profit	$535,840	$939,730	$1,069,844	$1,390,797	$1,738,497
Expenses					
Operating expenses	$391,889	$713,582	$769,833	$909,419	$1,059,710
Interest	$81,703	$86,613	$108,373	$113,792	$119,481
Depreciation	$10,628	$$17,245	$0	$0	$0
Amortization	$0	$0	$0	$0	$0
Total expenses	**$484,219**	**$817,440**	**$878,206**	**$1,023,211**	**$1,179,191**
Operating income	**$51,621**	**$122,290**	**$191,638**	**$367,586**	**$559,305**
Other income and expenses					
Gain (loss) on sale of assets					
Other (net)	$25,619	$30,797	$30,000	$30,600	$36,000
Subtotal	**$25,619**	**$30,797**	**$30,000**	**$30,600**	**$36,000**
Income before tax	$77,240	$153,087	$221,638	$398,186	$595,305
Taxes (Federal & State)	$885	$52,198	$75,572	$135,769	$202,981
Rate	1.146%	34.10%	34.10%	34.10%	34.10%
Net income	**$76,355**	**$100,889**	**$146,066**	**$262,417**	**$392,324**
Retained earnings-beginning	($28,329)	$63,094	$116,710	$312,110	$574,527
Dividends paid	$0	$0	$0	$0	$0
Retained earnings-ending	$48,026	$163,983	$262,776	$574,527	$966,851

Detailed Supporting Information

Cost of sales					
Direct labor	$0	$0	$0	$0	$0
Sub-Contractors	$2,231,679	$3,186,679	$5,111,028	$6,644,336	$8,305,420
Other costs					

Five-Year Financial Summary—Cash Flow Sheet

	1995	1996	1997	1998	1999
Cash from operations					
Net earnings (loss)	$76,355	$100,889	$146,066	$262,417	$392,324
Add-depreciation and amortization	$10,628	$17,245	$0	$0	$0
Net cash from operations	**$86,983**	**$118,134**	**$146,066**	**$262,417**	**$392,324**
Cash provided (used) by operating activities					
Accounts Receivable	($420,982)	($535,241)	($52,929)	($304,810)	($330,211)
Inventory	$0	$0	$0	$0	$0
Other current assets	($22,083)	$14,529	($7,446)	($15,000)	$0
Other non-current assets	($4,624)	($40,278)	($4,558)	($10,000)	($5,000)
Accounts payable	$48,588	$535,445	($20,488)	$189,038	$318,564
Current portion of long-term debt	$57,895	($44,243)	$1,348	$0	$0
Income taxes	$13,729	$33,688	$36,919	$25,197	$62,212
Accrued expenses	$7,223	$14,354	$17,548	$7,495	$8,075
Other current liabilities	$0	$0	$0	$0	$0
Dividends paid	$0	$0	$0	$0	$0
Net cash from operations	**($320,254)**	**($21,746)**	**($29,606)**	**($108,080)**	**$53,640**
Investment transactions					
Increases (decreases)					
Automobiles	$9,057	($9,057)	$0	$0	$0
Cattle	$0	$0	$0	$0	$0
Equipment	$48,132	$37,300	$0	$0	$0
Intangible assets	$0	$0	$0	$0	$0
Net cash from investments	**$57,189**	**$28,243**	**$0**	**$0**	**$0**
Financing transactions					
Increases (decreases)					
Short-term notes payable	$0	$350,000	$0	$0	$0
Long-term debt	$802,588	($273,029)	$0	$0	$0
Deferred income	$0	$0	$0	$0	$0
Deferred income taxes	$13,729	$22,154	$8,000	$0	$5,000
Other long-term liabilities	($9,917)	$0	$0	$0	$0
Capital stock and paid in capital	$0	$0	$0	$0	$0
Net cash from financing	**$806,400**	**$99,125**	**$8,000**	**$0**	**$5,000**
Net increase (decrease) in cash	**$515,940**	**$167,270**	**$124,460**	**$154,337**	**$450,964**
Cash at beginning of period	**$13,632**	**$529,572**	**$630,260**	**$821,302**	**$975,639**
Cash at the end of period	**$529,572**	**$630,260**	**$821,302**	**$975,639**	**$1,426,603**

Thie page left intentionally blank to accommodate tabular matter following.

Cash Flow Projection - First Year

Month	Start-Up Nov-96	Month 1 Dec-96	Month 2 Jan-97	Month 3 Feb-97	Month 4 Mar-97	Month 5 Apr-97	Month 6 May-97
Cash Receipts:							
Number of Houses		4	6	8	10	12	14
Income-Stucco		50,000	75,000	100,000	125,000	150,000	175,000
Income-Miscellaneous		0	0	0	0	0	0
Owner's Equity (15%)	30,000						
Loan	170,000						
Total Cash Received	**200,000**	**50,000**	**75,000**	**100,000**	**125,000**	**150,000**	**175,000**
Disbursements:							
Cost of Gds Sold/Inventory	21,000	14,000	21,000	28,000	35,000	42,000	49,000
Salaries-Officers		8,000	8,000	8,000	8,000	8,000	8,000
Salaries-Manager		5,000	5,000	5,000	5,000	5,000	5,000
Salaries-Superintendent		4,000	4,000	4,000	4,000	4,000	4,000
Salaries-Office		2,000	2,000	2,000	2,000	2,000	2,000
Labor-Scaffolding/Clean-Up	64,400	1,600	2,400	3,200	4,000	4,800	5,600
Payroll Taxes & Benefits		5,150	5,350	5,550	5,750	5,950	6,150
Subcontract Labor-Lathe		6,400	9,600	12,800	16,000	19,200	22,400
Subcontract Labor-Brown/Color		10,000	15,000	20,000	25,000	30,000	35,000
Maintenance & Repair		500	500	500	500	500	500
Vehicles - Fuel		540	810	1,080	1,350	1,620	1,890
Insurance-Workman's Comp		6,180	6,420	6,660	6,900	7,140	7,380
Insurance-Other	1,000	1,000	1,000	1,000	1,000	1,000	1,000
Telephone/Radio/Utilities	500	1,000	1,000	1,000	1,000	1,000	1,000
Advertising/Marketing/P.R.		500	500	500	500	500	500
Professsional Services	2,000	500	500	500	500	500	500
Office Expense/Postage		255	383	510	638	765	893
Organ. Exp./Amortization	1,000	50	50	50	50	50	50
Depreciation		1,973	1,973	1,973	1,973	1,973	1,973
Trucks/Equipment/Furniture	54,000						
Equipment Rental/Leases		1,400	2,100	2,800	3,500	4,200	4,900
Rent	5,000	2,500	2,500	2,500	2,500	2,500	2,500
Miscellaneous Expenses	8,000	1,500	2,250	3,000	3,750	4,500	5,250
Total Cash Paid Out	**156,900**	**74,048**	**92,336**	**110,623**	**128,911**	**147,198**	**165,486**
Loans Section:							
Interest		1,417	1,410	1,403	1,396	1,389	1,382
Principal		830	837	844	851	858	865
Cash Payments to Loans		**2,247**	**2,247**	**2,247**	**2,247**	**2,247**	**2,247**
Taxable Income		-25,465	-18,746	-12,026	-5,307	1,413	8,133
Income Tax (25.9%)		-6,490	-4,777	-3,065	-1,352	360	2,073
Net Income		**-18,975**	**-13,968**	**-8,961**	**-3,954**	**1,053**	**6,060**
Loans (Balance)	170,000	169,170	168,333	167,490	166,639	165,781	164,916
Dividends Paid		**-9,488**	**-6,984**	**-4,481**	**-1,977**	**526**	**3,030**
Beginning Cash	43,100						

Month 7 Jun-97	Month 8 Jul-97	Month 9 Aug-97	Month 10 Sep-97	Month 11 Oct-97	Month 12 Nov-97	Totals
16	20	22	20	18	16	166
200,000	250,000	275,000	250,000	225,000	200,000	2,075,000
0	0	0	0	0	0	$0
200,000	**250,000**	**275,000**	**250,000**	**225,000**	**200,000**	**$2,075,000**
56,000	70,000	77,000	70,000	63,000	56,000	$581,000
8,000	8,000	8,000	8,000	8,000	8,000	$96,000
5,000	5,000	5,000	5,000	5,000	5,000	$60,000
4,000	4,000	4,000	4,000	4,000	4,000	$48,000
2,000	2,000	2,000	2,000	2,000	2,000	$24,000
6,400	8,000	8,800	8,000	7,200	6,400	$66,400
6,350	6,750	6,950	6,750	6,550	6,350	$73,600
25,600	32,000	35,200	32,000	28,800	25,600	$265,600
40,000	50,000	55,000	50,000	45,000	40,000	$415,000
500	500	500	500	500	500	$6,000
2,160	2,700	2,970	2,700	2,430	2,160	$22,410
7,620	8,100	8,340	8,100	7,860	7,620	$88,320
1,000	1,000	1,000	1,000	1,000	1,000	$12,000
1,000	1,000	1,000	1,000	1,000	1,000	$12,000
500	500	500	500	500	500	$6,000
500	500	500	500	500	500	$6,000
1,020	1,275	1,403	1,275	1,148	1,020	$10,583
50	50	50	50	50	50	$600
1,973	1,973	1,973	1,973	1,973	1,973	$23,680
						$0
5,600	7,000	7,700	7,000	6,300	5,600	$58,100
2,500	2,500	2,500	2,500	2,500	2,500	$30,000
6,000	7,500	8,250	7,500	6,750	6,000	$62,250
183,773	**220,348**	**238,636**	**220,348**	**202,061**	**183,773**	**$1,967,543**
1,374	1,367	1,360	1,352	1,345	1,337	$16,531
872	880	887	894	902	909	$10,428
2,247	**2,247**	**2,247**	**2,247**	**2,247**	**2,247**	**$26,959**
14,852	28,285	35,004	28,299	21,594	14,889	$90,927
3,785	7,208	8,921	7,212	5,503	3,794	$23,172
11,067	**21,076**	**26,084**	**21,087**	**16,091**	**11,095**	**$67,754**
164,043	163,164	162,277	161,383	160,481	159,572	
5,534	**10,538**	**13,042**	**10,544**	**8,046**	**5,547**	**33,877**

Cash Flow Projection - Second Year

Month	Month13 Dec-97	Month 14 Jan-98	Month 15 Feb-98	Month 16 Mar-98	Month 17 Apr-98	Month 18 May-98	Month 19 Jun-98
Cash Receipts:							
Number of Houses	12	12	10	12	14	16	18
Income-Stucco	156,000	156,000	130,000	156,000	182,000	208,000	234,000
Income-Miscellaneous	0	0	0	0	0	0	0
Owner's Equity							
Loan							
Total Cash Received	**156,000**	**156,000**	**130,000**	**156,000**	**182,000**	**208,000**	**234,000**
Disbursements:							
Cost of Gds Sold/Inventory	44,160	44,160	36,800	44,160	51,520	58,880	66,240
Salaries-Officers	8,500	8,500	8,500	8,500	8,500	8,500	8,500
Salaries-Manager	5,250	5,250	5,250	5,250	5,250	5,250	5,250
Salaries-Superintendent	4,200	4,200	4,200	4,200	4,200	4,200	4,200
Salaries-Office	2,100	2,100	2,100	2,100	2,100	2,100	2,100
Labor-Scaffolding/Clean-Up	5,040	5,040	4,200	5,040	5,880	6,720	7,560
Payroll Taxes & Benefits	6,273	6,273	6,063	6,273	6,483	6,693	6,903
Subcontract Labor-Lathe	26,880	26,880	26,880	26,880	26,880	26,880	26,880
Subcontract Labor-Brown/Color	31,500	31,500	26,250	31,500	36,750	42,000	47,250
Maintenance & Repair	750	750	750	750	750	750	750
Vehicles - Fuel	1,620	1,620	1,350	1,620	1,890	2,160	2,430
Insurance-Workman's Comp	7,527	7,527	7,275	7,527	7,779	8,031	8,283
Insurance-Other	1,250	1,250	1,250	1,250	1,250	1,250	1,250
Telephone/Radio/Utilities	1,050	1,050	1,050	1,050	1,050	1,050	1,050
Advertising/Marketing/P.R.	525	525	525	525	525	525	525
Professsional Services	550	550	550	550	550	550	550
Office Expense/Postage	796	796	663	796	928	1,061	1,193
Organ. Exp./Amortization	50	50	50	50	50	50	50
Depreciation	1,973	1,973	1,973	1,973	1,973	1,973	1,973
Equipment/Furniture							
Equipment Rental/Leases	5,880	5,880	5,880	5,880	5,880	5,880	5,880
Rent	3,000	3,000	3,000	3,000	3,000	3,000	3,000
Miscellaneous Expenses	4,680	4,680	3,900	4,680	5,460	6,240	7,020
Total Cash Paid Out	**163,553**	**163,553**	**148,459**	**163,553**	**178,648**	**193,743**	**208,837**
Loans Section:							
Interest	1,330	1,322	1,314	1,307	1,299	1,291	1,283
Principal	917	924	932	940	948	956	964
Cash Payments to Loans	**2,247**	**2,247**	**2,247**	**2,247**	**2,247**	**2,247**	**2,247**
Taxable Income	-8,883	-8,876	-19,773	-8,860	2,053	12,966	23,880
Income Tax (31.3%)	-2,776	-2,774	-6,180	-2,769	642	4,052	7,463
Net Income	**-6,107**	**-6,102**	**-13,593**	**-6,091**	**1,411**	**8,914**	**16,417**
Loans (Balance)	**158,655**	**157,731**	**156,779**	**155,859**	**154,911**	**153,955**	**152,992**
Dividends Paid	**-3,053**	**-3,051**	**-6,797**	**-3,046**	**706**	**4,457**	**8,208**

Month 20 Jul-98	Month 21 Aug-98	Month 22 Sep-98	Month 23 Oct-98	Month 24 Nov-98	Totals
20	22	22	20	18	196
260,000	286,000	286,000	260,000	234,000	$2,548,000
0	0	0	0	0	$0
260,000	**286,000**	**286,000**	**260,000**	**234,000**	**$2,548,000**
73,600	80,960	80,960	73,600	66,240	$721,280
8,500	8,500	8,500	8,500	8,500	$102,000
5,250	5,250	5,250	5,250	5,250	$63,000
4,200	4,200	4,200	4,200	4,200	$50,400
2,100	2,100	2,100	2,100	2,100	$25,200
8,400	9,240	9,240	8,400	7,560	$82,320
7,113	7,323	7,323	7,113	6,903	$80,730
26,880	26,880	26,880	26,880	26,880	$322,560
52,500	57,750	57,750	52,500	47,250	$415,000
750	750	750	750	750	$9,000
2,700	2,970	2,970	2,700	2,430	$26,460
8,535	8,787	8,787	8,535	8,283	$96,876
1,250	1,250	1,250	1,250	1,250	$15,000
1,050	1,050	1,050	1,050	1,050	$12,600
525	525	525	525	525	$6,300
550	550	550	550	550	$6,600
1,326	1,459	1,459	1,326	1,193	$12,995
50	50	50	50	50	$600
1,973	1,973	1,973	1,973	1,973	$23,680
5,880	5,880	5,880	5,880	5,880	$70,560
3,000	3,000	3,000	3,000	3,000	$36,000
7,800	8,580	8,580	7,800	7,020	$76,440
223,932	**239,026**	**239,026**	**223,932**	**208,837**	**$2,355,101**
1,275	1,267	1,259	1,250	1,242	$15,439
972	980	988	996	1,004	$11,520
2,247	**2,247**	**2,247**	**2,247**	**2,247**	**$26,959**
34,793	45,707	45,715	34,818	23,921	$177,461
10,874	14,285	14,287	10,882	7,476	$55,463
23,919	**31,422**	**31,427**	**23,936**	**16,445**	**$121,998**
152,020	**151,040**	**150,052**	**149,056**	**148,052**	
11,960	**15,711**	**15,714**	**11,968**	**8,222**	**60,999**

Cash Flow Projection - Third Year

Month	Month25 Dec-98	Month 26 Jan-99	Month 27 Feb-99	Month 28 Mar-99	Month 29 Apr-99	Month 30 May-99	Month 31 Jun-99
Cash Receipts:							
Number of Houses	14	12	10	12	14	16	20
Income-Stucco	190,400	163,200	136,000	163,200	190,400	217,600	272,000
Income-Miscellaneous	0	0	0	0	0	0	0
Owner's Equity							
Loan							
Total Cash Received	**190,400**	**163,200**	**136,000**	**163,200**	**190,400**	**217,600**	**272,000**
Disbursements:							
Cost of Gds Sold/Inventory	54,180	46,440	38,700	46,440	54,180	61,920	77,400
Salaries-Officers	9,000	9,000	9,000	9,000	9,000	9,000	9,000
Salaries-Manager	5,513	5,513	5,513	5,513	5,513	5,513	5,513
Salaries-Superintendent	4,410	4,410	4,410	4,410	4,410	4,410	4,410
Salaries-Office	2,205	2,205	2,205	2,205	2,205	2,205	2,205
Labor-Scaffolding/Clean-Up	6,160	5,280	4,400	5,280	6,160	7,040	8,800
Payroll Taxes & Benefits	6,822	6,602	6,382	6,602	6,822	7,042	7,482
Subcontract Labor-Lathe	28,224	28,224	28,224	28,224	28,224	28,224	28,224
Subcontract Labor-Brown/Color	38,780	33,240	27,700	33,240	38,780	44,320	55,400
Maintenance & Repair	850	850	850	850	850	850	850
Vehicles - Fuel	1,890	1,620	1,350	1,620	1,890	2,160	2,430
Insurance-Workman's Comp	8,186	7,922	7,658	7,922	8,186	8,450	8,978
Insurance-Other	1,500	1,500	1,500	1,500	1,500	1,500	1,500
Telephone/Radio/Utilities	1,103	1,103	1,103	1,103	1,103	1,103	1,103
Advertising/Marketing/P.R.	551	551	551	551	551	551	551
Professsional Services	600	600	600	600	600	600	600
Office Expense/Postage	971	832	694	832	971	1,110	1,387
Organ. Exp./Amortization	50	50	50	50	50	50	50
Depreciation Equipment/Furniture	1,973	1,973	1,973	1,973	1,973	1,973	1,973
Equipment Rental/Leases	3,500	3,000	2,500	3,000	3,500	4,000	5,000
Rent	3,500	3,500	3,500	3,500	3,500	3,500	3,500
Miscellaneous Expenses	5,712	4,896	4,080	4,896	5,712	6,528	8,160
Total Cash Paid Out	**185,680**	**169,311**	**152,942**	**169,311**	**185,680**	**202,048**	**234,786**
Loans Section:							
Interest	1,234	1,225	1,217	1,208	1,200	1,191	1,182
Principal	1,013	1,021	1,030	1,038	1,047	1,056	1,065
Cash Payments to Loans	**2,247**	**2,247**	**2,247**	**2,247**	**2,247**	**2,247**	**2,247**
Taxable Income	3,486	-7,336	-18,159	-7,319	3,521	14,361	36,032
Income Tax (33.1%)	1,152	-2,425	-6,003	-2,419	1,164	4,747	11,911
Net Income	**2,334**	**-4,911**	**-12,156**	**-4,900**	**2,357**	**9,614**	**24,121**
Loans (Balance)	**147,039**	**146,018**	**144,988**	**143,950**	**142,903**	**141,847**	**140,783**
Dividends Paid	**1,167**	**-2,456**	**-6,078**	**-2,450**	**1,178**	**4,807**	**12,061**

Month 32 Jul-99	Month 33 Aug-99	Month 34 Sep-99	Month 35 Oct-99	Month 36 Nov-99	Totals
22	24	24	22	18	208
299,200	326,400	326,400	299,200	244,800	$2,652,000
0	0	0	0	0	$0
299,200	**326,400**	**326,400**	**299,200**	**244,800**	**$2,828,800**
85,140	92,880	92,880	85,140	69,660	$804,960
9,000	9,000	9,000	9,000	9,000	$108,000
5,513	5,513	5,513	5,513	5,513	$66,150
4,410	4,410	4,410	4,410	4,410	$52,920
2,205	2,205	2,205	2,205	2,205	$26,460
9,680	10,560	10,560	9,680	7,920	$91,520
7,702	7,922	7,922	7,702	7,262	$86,263
28,224	28,224	28,224	28,224	28,224	$338,688
60,940	66,480	66,480	60,940	49,860	$576,160
850	850	850	850	850	$10,200
2,700	2,970	2,970	2,700	2,430	$28,080
9,242	9,506	9,506	9,242	8,714	$103,515
1,500	1,500	1,500	1,500	1,500	$18,000
1,103	1,103	1,103	1,103	1,103	$13,230
551	551	551	551	551	$6,615
600	600	600	600	600	$7,200
1,526	1,665	1,665	1,526	1,248	$14,427
50	50	50	50	50	$600
1,973	1,973	1,973	1,973	1,973	$23,680
5,500	6,000	6,000	5,500	4,500	$52,000
3,500	3,500	3,500	3,500	3,500	$42,000
8,976	9,792	9,792	8,976	7,344	$84,864
251,155	**267,523**	**267,523**	**251,155**	**218,417**	**$2,555,531**
1,173	1,164	1,155	1,146	1,037	$14,232
1,073	1,082	1,091	1,100	1,110	$12,726
2,247	**2,247**	**2,247**	**2,247**	**2,247**	**$26,959**
46,872	57,712	57,721	46,899	25,246	$259,036
15,494	19,077	19,080	15,503	8,345	$85,626
31,378	**38,635**	**38,641**	**31,396**	**16,901**	**$173,410**
139,709	**138,627**	**137,535**	**136,435**	**135,325**	
15,689	**19,318**	**19,321**	**15,698**	**8,450**	**86,705**

Average Monthly Break-Even Analysis 1997

Cost Variables	Optimistic -20.00%	Per Month 1997 Most Likely Case	Pessimistic 20.00%
Fixed Costs			
Rent	$3,900	$48,876	$5,851
Salaries (Fixed/Owners)	$7,590	$9,488	$11,385
Insurance	$5,336	$6,671	$8,005
Depreciation & Amortization	$0	$0	$0
Interest	$7,225	$9,031	$10,837
Utilities/Phone	$2,608	$32,600	$3,912
(Other fixed costs)	$0	$0	$0
Total Fixed Costs	**$26,659**	**$33,324**	**$39,989**
Variable Costs			
Cost of Goods Sold/Subcontractors	$340,735	$425,919	$511,130
Equipment Rental/Leases	$58	$73	$87
Other Salaries	$7,291	$9,114	$10,937
Freight	$840	$1,050	$1,261
Office Equipment/Leases	$3,035	$3,794	$4,553
Payroll Taxes/Benefits	$3,934	$4,917	$5,901
Vehicle Expenses & Leases	$2,244	$2,805	$3,366
Advertising/Marketing/Public Relations	$1,319	$1,649	$1,979
Professional Services	$5,046	$6,308	$7,569
(Other variable costs)	$8,120	$10,150	$12,180
Total Variable Costs	**$372,623**	**$465,779**	**$558,934**
Sales and Income Data:			
Average Income Per Customer	$706,385	$588,654	$470,923
Average # of Customers Per Month	12.60	10.50	8.40
Results:			
Fixed Costs per Customer	$2,115.83	$3,173.75	$4,760.62
Variable Costs per Customer	$29,573.24	$44,359.86	$66,539.79
Break-Even Number of Customers	0.04	0.06	0.1
Number of Customers over Break-Even	12.6	10.4	8.3
Break-Even Sales Amount	$27,824.35	$36,040.26	$46,569.27
Total Sales at Expected Level of Customers			
Gross Profit per Customer	$676,811.56	$544,294.14	$404,383.41
Gross Profit (over Break-Even)	$8,501,166	$5,681,764	$3,356,831

Break-Even Analysis is a mathematical technique for analyzing the relationship between profits and fixed and variable costs. It is also a profit planning tool for calculating the point at which sales will equal costs. The above analysis indicates 1997 break-even number customers at .06 per month and break-even income at $36,040 per month. Anything over these amounts will be profit.

Common Size Income Statement

	Actual 1995	Actual 1996	Annualized 1997	Projected 1998	Projected 1999	Industry 1996
Total Revenue	100.0%	100.0%	100.0%	100.0%	100.0%	100.0%
Cost of Sales	80.6%	77.2%	82.7%	82.7%	82.7%	85.7%
Gross Profit	19.4%	22.8%	17.3%	17.3%	17.3%	14.3%
Operating Expenses	17.5%	19.8%	14.2%	12.7%	11.7%	12.8%
Operating Profit	1.9%	3.0%	3.1%	4.6%	5.6%	1.5%
Other Expen./Inc(Net)	0.9%	0.7%	0.5%	0.4%	0.4%	1.4%
Pre-Tax Profit	**2.8%**	**3.7%**	**3.6%**	**5.0%**	**5.9%**	**2.9%**
Income Taxes	0.0%	1.3%	1.2%	1.7%	2.0%	0.5%
Income After Tax	**2.8%**	**2.4%**	**2.4%**	**3.3%**	**3.9%**	**2.4%**

Common Size Balance Sheet

	Actual 1995	Actual 1996	Annualized 1997	Projected 1998	Projected 1999	Industry 1996
Cash & Equivalent	49.4%	35.7%	41.0%	39.2%	43.6%	20.3%
Accounts Receivable	39.9%	54.6%	50.7%	53.1%	50.4%	54.2%
Inventory	0.0%	0.0%	0.0%	0.0%	0.0%	1.1%
Other Current	2.1%	0.4%	0.7%	1.2%	0.9%	8.9%
Total Current Assets	**91.4%**	**90.8%**	**92.5%**	**93.6%**	**95.0%**	**84.5%**
Fixed Assets (Net)	8.1%	6.7%	5.0%	4.0%	3.1%	6.4%
Intangibles	0.0%	0.0%	0.0%	0.0%	0.0%	0.2%
Other Assets	0.5%	2.6%	2.5%	2.4%	2.0%	8.9%
Total Assets	**100.0%**	**100.0%**	**100.0%**	**100.0%**	**100.0%**	**100.0%**
Liabilities:						
Accounts Payable	4.5%	33.1%	28.1%	30.3%	32.7%	47.6%
Short Term Notes	0.0%	19.8%	17.5%	14.1%	10.7%	2.0%
Current Maturities (LTD)	5.4%	0.8%	0.7%	0.6%	0.5%	0.9%
Income Taxes	0.5%	2.2%	3.8%	4.1%	5.0%	0.6%
Accured Expenses	0.7%	1.2%	2.0%	1.9%	1.7%	4.7%
Other Current Liabilities	0.0%	0.0%	0.0%	0.0%	0.0%	12.6%
Total Current Liabilities	**11.1%**	**57.1%**	**52.1%**	**50.9%**	**50.5%**	**68.4%**
Long-Term Debt	74.9%	30.0%	26.4%	21.3%	16.2%	4.0%
Other Non-Current	0.5%	1.5%	1.7%	1.4%	1.2%	3.6%
Total Liabilities	**86.4%**	**88.7%**	**80.3%**	**73.6%**	**67.9%**	**76.0%**
Total Equity	**13.6%**	**11.3%**	**19.7%**	**26.4%**	**32.1%**	**24.0%**
Total Liabilities & Equity	**100.0%**	**100.0%**	**100.0%**	**100.0%**	**100.0%**	**100.0%**

RATIO COMPARISON

Ratio analysis can be one of the most useful financial management tools. It becomes important when you look at the trend of each ratio over time. It also becomes important when compared to averages of a particular industry.

	Actual 1995	Actual 1996	Annualized 1997	Projected 1998	Projected 1999	Industry Ave.-1996
Liquidity Ratios						
Current Ratio	8.25	1.59	1.78	1.84	1.88	1.4
Quick Ratio	8.07	1.58	1.76	1.82	1.86	1.1
Sales/Receivables	6.47	4.28	6.08	6.08	6.08	7.78
Days' Reeivables	56.43	85.19	60.00	60.00	60.00	46.9
Cost of Sales/Inventory	0.00	0.00	0.00	0.00	0.00	1.4
Days' Inventory	0.00	0.00	0.00	0.00	0.00	
Cost of Sales/Payables	45.93	5.46	9.07	8.83	7.75	8.06
Day's Payables	7.95	66.89	40.25	41.34	47.07	45.3
Sales/Work. Capital	3.21	6.96	7.64	7.57	6.91	
EBIT/Interest	1.95	2.77	3.05	4.50	5.98	8.1
Net Profit+Depr.+Amort./C.L.T.D.	1.50	8.65	9.74	17.49	26.15	
Leverage Ratios						
Fixed Assets/Tang. Net Worth	0.60	0.59	0.25	0.15	0.10	0.26
Debt/Worth	6.36	7.85	4.07	2.78	2.12	2.9
Operating Ratios						
Profit Before Tax/Tan. Net Worth	53.05%	76.85%	56.17%	60.60%	56.73%	13.50%
Profit Before Tax/Total Assets	7.21%	8.68%	11.07%	16.01%	18.19%	
Sales/Net Fixed Assets	31.80	35.17	61.76	80.29	100.36	26.7
Sales/Total Assets	2.58	2.34	3.09	3.23	3.07	3.1
Other Ratios						
% Deprec., Amort./Sales	0.38	0.42	0.00	0.00	0.00	0.70
% Officer' Compensation/Sales	3.19	3.85	1.77	1.43	1.20	2.90
Gross Profit	$535,840	$939,730	$1,069,844	$1,390,797	$1,738,497	
Key Percentages as a Percent of Gross Profit						
Rent	2.80%	2.82%	5.47%	4.44%	3.73%	0.40%
Interest Paid	15.25%	9.22%	10.13%	8.18%	6.87%	0.60%
Depreciation & Amortization	1.98%	1.84%	0.00%	0.00%	0.00%	0.70%
Officers Compensation	18.66%	10.64%	10.64%	8.60%	7.22%	2.90%
Taxes Paid	0.17%	0.00%	7.06%	9.76%	11.68%	1.30%

Note on Key Percentages as a percent of Gross Profit above:

Rent, Interest Paid, Officers' Compensation, and Taxes Paid are in large part attributable to Smith Contractors being a new company. It has spent the first three years building, staffing, and equipping the business. As the sales and income go up, these percentages will go down and become more in line with industry averages. The hiring of a new comptroller should help reduce the amount of taxes paid and allow the company to more closely monitor expenses. The important ratio of % of Officers' Compensation to Sales is well within line for 1997 and after.

RATIO COMPARISON

1. The Current Ratio is an approximate measure of a firm's ability to meet its current obligations and is calculated as Current Assets/Current Liabilities.

Smith Contractors, Inc.'s current ratio is on an upward trend. This would indicate that the amount of current assets is increasing steadily as is the "cushion" between current liabilities and the ability to pay them. It could suggest that Smith Contractors has a relatively more stable position than the industry and seems to suggest that there is an opportunity for expanded operations.

2. The Revenue to Receivables ratio measures the number of times trade receivables turn over in a year. It is calculated as the Net Revenue/Trade Receivables.

Smith Contractors, Inc.'s recent revenue to receivables ratio is on a downward trend. This indicates that collection methods need to be improved. (This has been done.)

3. The Cost of Goods to Payables ratio measures the number of times trade payables turn over in a year. It is calculated as Cost of Goods Sold/Trade Payables.

Smith Contractors, Inc.'s recent cost of goods to payables ratio is on a downward trend. This indicates that the company may be experiencing cash shortages due to the amount of time between the payment of supplies or subcontractors and receipt of payment for its billings. It might want to consider extending the time it takes to pay for supplies or subcontractors.

4. The Revenue to Working Capital ratio is a measure of the margin of protection for current creditors. It is calculated as Net Revenue/{Current Assets-Current Liabilities}. (This has been corrected with the change in payment policy to subcontractors.)

Smith Contractors, Inc.'s recent revenue to working capital ratio is on an upward trend. This indicates efficient use of working capital.

5. The EBIT to Interest ratio is a measure of ability to meet annual interest payments. It is calculated as Earnings before interest and taxes/Annual Interest Expense.

Smith Contractors, Inc.'s recent EBIT to interest ratio is on an upward trend. This indicates that the company should not have a problem servicing its debt. The figures for 1997-1999 is above industry median figures. This could indicate that the company is better able to make interest payments and could possibly handle more debt.

6. The Current Maturities Coverage ratio is a measure of ability to pay current maturities of short-term debt with cash flow from operations. It is calculated as {Net Income + Depreciation, Amortization, and Depletion}/Current Portion of Long-Term Debt.

Smith Contractors, Inc.'s recent Current Maturities Coverage ratio is on an upward trend. This indicates that the cash flow available to service debt are increasing relative to the level of debt. The figures for 1997-1999 is above industry median figures. This indicates that the company is better able to service debt and could possibly indicate additional debt capacity.

7. The Fixed Assets to Tangible Net Worth ratio measures the extent to which owners' equity has been invested in property, plant, and equipment. It is calculated as Net Fixed Assets/{Equity - Net Intangible Assets}.

Smith Contractors, Inc.'s fixed asset to tangible net worth ratio is on a downward trend. This indicates that the investment in fixed assets relative to net worth is decreasing and results in a larger "cushion" for creditors in the event of liquidation.

8. The Debt to Equity ratio expresses the relationship between capital contributed by creditors and capital contributed by owners. It is calculated as Total Liabilities/Net Worth.

Smith Contractors, Inc.'s recent debt to equity ratio is on a downward trend. This indicates the company is achieving greater short-term financial safety.

9. The Earnings Before Tax to Tangible Net Worth ratio expresses the rate of return on tangible capital employed. It is calculated as (Earnings Before Taxes/{Net Worth-Net Intangible Assets} * 100.

Smith Contractors, Inc.'s earnings before tax to tangible net worth ratio is on a downward trend. For the period 1997 to 1999 this ratio is above industry median earnings. This indicates that the company is out-performing the industry but can also indicate that the business is undercapitalized.

10. The Earning Before Tax to Total Assets ratio expresses the pre-tax return on total assets and measures the effectiveness of management in employing available resources. It is calculated as (Earnings Before Tax/Total Assets) * 100.

Smith Contractors, Inc.'s recent Earnings Before Tax to total assets ratio has been on an upward trend. This indicates an increasingly effective use of available resources.

11. The Officers', Directors', Owners' compensation to Sales ratio is a general measure of ability to compensate top employees. It is calculated as Officers' Salaries/Sales.

Smith Contractors, Inc.'s trend is downward. This can indicate an increasing effectiveness of management or that the business is becoming more service oriented and less capital intensive.

Category/Year	Actual 1995	Actual 1996	Annualized 1997	Projected 1998	Projected 1999
Current Assets	$979,519	$1,600,919	$1,852,336	$2,326,483	$3,107,658
Fixed Assets	$87,016	$117,323	$100,075	$100,075	$100,075
Other Assets	$5,164	$45,442	$50,000	$60,000	$65,000
Total Assets	**$1,071,699**	**$1,763,684**	**$2,002,411**	**$2,486,558**	**$3,272,733**
Current Liabilities	$118,671	$1,007,915	$1,043,242	$1,264,972	$1,653,823
Long-Term Liabilities	$802,588	$529,559	$529,559	$529,559	$529,559
Other Liabilities	$4,846	$27,000	$35,000	$35,000	$40,000
Total Liabilities	**$926,105**	**$1,564,474**	**$1,607,801**	**$1,829,531**	**$2,223,382**
Stock	$82,500	$82,500	$82,500	$82,500	$82,500
Current Earnings	$76,355	$100,889	$146,066	$262,417	$392,324
Retained Earnings (minus dividends)	-$28,329	$63,094	$116,710	$312,110	$574,527
Net Worth	$130,626	$246,483	$345,276	$657,027	$1,049,351
Liabilities + Net Worth	$1,056,631	$1,810,957	$1,953,077	$2,486,558	$3,272,733
Working Capital	$860,848	$593,004	$809,094	$1,061,511	$1,453,835
Sales	$2,767,519	$4,126,409	$6,180,872	$8,035,134	$1,004,391
Earning Before Taxes & Interest	$208,903	$208,903	$330,011	$481,378	$714,787
Book Value (minus intangibles)	$145,594	$199,210	$394,610	$657,027	$1,043,351
WC/TA (x 1)	0.80	0.34	0.40	0.43	0.44
RE/TA (x2)	0.04	0.09	0.13	0.23	0.30
EBIT/TA (x3)	0.19	0.12	0.16	0.19	0.22
Book Value/TL (x4)	0.16	0.13	0.25	0.36	0.47
Sales/TA (x5)	2.58	2.34	3.09	3.23	3.07
Calculated Z Scores	**3.86**	**3.08**	**4.10**	**4.48**	**4.51**

SCORES ABOVE 2.91 INDICATE THE FIRM IS SAFE FROM BANKRUPTCY
THE HIGHER THE SCORES - THE SAFER THE COMPANY

The Z Score Formula = $0.717*(X1) + 0.847*(X2) + 3.107*(X3) + 0.420*(X4) +$

If the Z Score is Greater than or Equal to 2.9 the subject firm is apparently safe from bankruptcy.
If the Z Score is Less than or Equal to 1.2 the subject may be destined for bankruptcy.
If the Z Score is between 1.23 and 2.9 the firm is in a gray area and steps could be taken by management to correct existing or potential
   problems in order to avoid bankruptcy.

Z Score analysis is a statistical method developed to forecast bankruptcy.
It is over 90% accurate one year into the future and 80% accurate for the second year.

In this instance we used the 1995 and 1996 actual figures, Estimated 1997, Projected 1998, and 1999 figures to determine the above
   scores.

The Z Scores indicated above are all well over 2.91 which indicates that the company will not be a candidate for bankruptcy if it can achieve
   the goals outlined in this plan.

	Net Income	IRR	MIRR	Annual Dividends	Total Assets
Initial Investment	($82,500)			$0	$55,205
1995-Actual	$76,355	-7.45%	-7.45%	$0	$1,071,699
1996-Actual	$100,889	66.15%	193.72%	$0	$1,763,684
1997-Annualized	$146,066	98.84%	313.67%	$0	$2,002,411
1998-Projected	$262,417	117.31%	388.50%	$0	$2,486,558
1999-Projected	$392,324	126.50%	439.27%	$0	$3,272,733

Assumptions:

Income figures are after taxes

Dividend Payout is currently zero

Reinvestment rate = 7%

IRR = Internal Rate of Return

MIRR = Modified Rate of Return

ROI = Rate of Return on Owner's Investment

ROA = Rate of Return on Total Assets

IRR= the interest rate received for an investment and income that occur at regular periods.

MIRR=adds the cost of funds and interest received on reinvestment of cash to the IRR.

	Year 1	Year 2	Year 3	Year 4	Year 5
Return on Assets	7.12%	5.72%	7.29%	10.55%	11.99%
Return on Investment	0.00%	0.00%	0.00%	0.00%	0.00%
Income Per Share	$0.93	$1.22	$1.77	$3.18	$4.76
Dividends Per Share	$0.00	$0.00	$0.00	$0.00	$0.00

CONCLUSIONS AND SUMMARY

A review of the first eight years of Smith Contractors' existence show that it has been immensely successful. Even in its first full year of operation, it reached industry standards of performance. This is unheard of for a start-up company. Each subsequent year has shown significant improvement in profitability and operational performance.

During the first eight years the company concentrated upon being profitable, building its staff and equipping its office. Smith Contractors is now ready to step up to the next level and utilize economies of scale to make the projected numbers even more striking.

Smith Contractors has also undertaken major changes in philosophy in billing and payment of subcontractors and suppliers which will dramatically increase cash flow. The company has also hired a full-time marketing manager and is in the process of hiring a full-time controller. It also utilizes the services of a professional business consultant to help analyze the financial information and make suggestions for the future. Smith Contractors will conduct a complete review of the actual figures and compare them to budgets and peers periodically throughout the year.

Healthcare Software Company

BUSINESS PLAN QUIKMEDINFO

689 Wyoming Avenue
Louisville, Kentucky 40202

QuikMedInfo has developed a targeted, well-thought-out marketing plan providing a clear road map of how it will secure clients and allied business partners for its innovative, highly useful healthcare software targeting hospitals. This plan was provided by Trinity Capital.

- EXECUTIVE SUMMARY

- COMPANY SUMMARY

- PRODUCTS

- MARKET ANALYSIS SUMMARY

- STRATEGY & IMPLEMENTATION SUMMARY

- MANAGEMENT SUMMARY

- FINANCIAL PLAN

**EXECUTIVE
SUMMARY**

The QuikMedInfo product is an application that allows numerous databases to completely interface with each other without changing hardware or software between parties. The product can work over a secured Virtual Private Network (VPN) and be encrypted at 128 bits. The product developers have concentrated on the medical community as end users—specifically, hospitals. The next logical market would be the health insurance industry.

QuikMedInfo is an innovative new solution in the healthcare industry, bringing a common client presentation to users of disparate systems. Multiple hospital information systems can now be accessed, within or outside of the immediate hospital environment, with a Java-based "common client presentation." QuikMedInfo provides a graphical front end for the user with any of the popular Internet Web browsers, such has Netscape and Microsoft Explorer.

The product is currently developed in seven different modules. As an Intranet application solution, the modules are required to run on a robust server. The installed modules are Admissions, Transcriptions, Laboratory, Imaging, and Pharmacy. Future modules are in development as needed in the marketplace. Home Health and Physician management modules are complete but not installed. Currently five modules are successfully operating in six different environments.

All these modules allow credentialed QuikMedInfo users to access all of the applications via the Internet or through the VPN Intranet. The Admissions application allows users to share data between healthcare organizations, displays information about the patient, and handles patient transactions—including pre-admissions, registration, and admissions. The Transcriptions section creates new transcriptions; doctors now can sign transcriptions electronically, list patient and physician transcriptions, view transcription details, and format all the views. The Laboratory application entails ordering lab tests, viewing results and comments, sorts test criteria, and other laboratory functions. The Imaging module digitizes images such as licensees, photos for I.D. purposes, EKGs, CAT scans, MRIs, and pulmonary functions tests. The Pharmacy module lists medications prescribed for any given patient, views medication details, references patient allergies, and can be linked to all area pharmacies in addition to the hospital pharmacy.

The product will be leased, rented, and sold to potential users. Leasing and renting the product will facilitate faster sales in the hospital environment. Because the full price of the product can reach $350,000, many hospitals must postpone decisions until another budget year. Leasing and/or renting will allow the hospital to make decisions sooner. Also, approaching physicians first in order to sell the hospital on the needs of the physicians will allow for easier access to information.

The hospital industry relies on a multitude of different systems to house the databases they access. These systems are provided by different vendors and do not share data. When physicians and hospital staff need to access data they are required to sign in and out of these multiple databases to complete a transaction. This is very inefficient, and a significant issue for hospitals that find themselves in an environment of decreasing reimbursement from government programs and managed care companies.

The developer of the QuikMedInfo application solution is Best Source Solutions, Inc. QuikMedInfo is a new entity being formed to market the QuikMedInfo product.

Best Midwest Solutions, Inc. (BMS), a value-added reseller of computer hardware and software, worked with a community hospital to find a solution to their problem with the inefficiency of dealing with disparate systems. The result of almost three years of effort and $2.2 million of investment is this software program. It provides a web-enabled interface capable of linking all of a hospital's disparate systems to a single, common view which is extremely simple and easy to use. While the development of the product has been focused on the healthcare industry, the technology is applicable to any industry that uses many different systems.

BMS has sold and installed six units at customer sites. (All of them are very happy customers willing to serve as references.) Four of the installations are healthcare related, and one is in the communications industry. Over the past year the BMS sales staff has spent its time educating the hospital industry about the product and waiting for the hospitals to obtain approval for the capital expenditure. As a result of these efforts, BMS currently has a list of 13 qualified clients representing potential revenue in excess of $3 million. Management estimates the probability of closing these sales at between 30% and 90%.

BMS lacks sufficient capital to effectively penetrate the hospital market nationally. In addition, a more complete and robust management team will fully enable the execution of the plan.

QuikMedInfo is seeking $3 to $6 million in investment. $3 million would be utilized under the guidelines of this plan to expand market share via marketing and in working capital to expand personnel and operational needs.

Successful penetration of the hospital market in years one, two, and three will enable the company to become profitable. Projected profitability occurs at 24 months. Cash flow from the initial investment should be sufficient to execute the plan through the first three years. Any shortfalls should be correctable by commercial banking options. Years four and five call for full national roll out and entry into other vertical markets, primarily health insurance. Management forecasts a $40 million company by year five. A bank line of $1.5 million and a mezzanine debt/equity infusion of $5 million (in year four) will finance the growth and potentially lead to an acquisition or an IPO.

As is characteristic of the software industry, margins are high and cash flow and accumulation are excellent.

Fiscal year 2000 begins in September 1999.

The following illustrates a summary of our financial projections:

Long-term plan	FY2000	FY2001	FY2002	FY2003	FY2004
Sales	$3,022,500	$5,785,000	$12,935,000	$24,000,000	$42,000,000
Cost of Sales	$746,150	$1,459,800	$2,423,600	$4,000,000	$6,500,000
Gross Margin	$2,276,350	$4,325,200	$10,511,400	$20,000,000	$35,500,000
Gross Margin %	75.31%	74.77%	81.26%	83.33%	84.52%
Operating Expenses	$3,133,053	$4,205,268	$5,763,472	$8,200,000	$10,100,000
Operating Income	($856,703)	$119,932	$4,747,928	$11,800,000	$25,400,000
Net Income	($565,424)	$79,155	$3,133,632	$7,800,000	$19,400,000
Short-term Assets	$1,448,236	$2,208,932	$6,084,400	$14,300,000	$35,000,000
Long-term Assets	($450,000)	($1,050,000)	($1,650,000)	$450,000	$1,000,000
Short-term Liabilities	$183,660	$265,201	$407,036	$2,000,000	$1,500,000
Long-term Liabilities	$0	$0	$0	$5,000,000	$4,000,000
Equity	$814,576	$893,731	$4,027,363	$7,750,000	$30,500,000

Objectives

1. The business goal is to obtain a 20% market share of the target hospital market in the United States within five years.

2. We will offer our software to healthcare-related industries including hospitals, third party administrators, insurance companies, etc.

3. We will sell our software, its services and professional consulting directly to accounts and through qualified resellers. We have OEM contracts available that already present an opportunity.

4. We plan to be profitable in 24 months and have the opportunity to sell the business at a 15x or higher multiple to another company or make an initial public offering.

Mission

Our mission is to provide physicians and hospital staff access to critical and multiple sources of data, thereby improving their efficiency in caring for patients. In turn, this will improve patient care, increase patient satisfaction, and save time and operating costs.

Keys to Success

The keys to our success are:

1. Bringing multiple information sources to a single, common view that is extremely simple and easy to use.

2. Providing a low entry price model by offering the product as a monthly service, as well as a purchase price. The low monthly price eliminates capital budgeting issues and allows quicker decisions by hospital management.

3. Interfacing to the various legacy systems through several industry standard protocols. Having legacy vendor access is important but can be overwritten by other tools.

4. Obtaining physicians' sponsorship.

5. Extending our technology to payors, third-party administrators, etc. who often can make decisions quicker than providers.

6. Obtaining required capitalization and key management.

7. Managing our channels of distribution and resellers effectively.

COMPANY SUMMARY

QuikMedInfo will acquire the rights to the QuikMedInfo code from Empire System, Inc. (Empire), a value-added reseller of hardware and software products. Empire was started in 1990 and has current revenues of $32 million. Empire is located in Lexington, Kentucky. Empire began the development of this software product because of the need by hospitals and physicians to have easier access to data from disparate systems. Empire has invested $2.2 million and 2 years in the development of the product, QuikMedInfo. QuikMedInfo will provide Intranet/Internet applications to the healthcare industry to enhance access to the industry's disparate legacy systems. This access to critical data is vitally important to patient care and satisfaction as well as to physician and staff productivity.

Company Ownership

QuikMedInfo is located in Louisville, Kentucky. It is owned currently 50% by Rachel Brown and 50% by Ed Roost.

The following summarizes the start-up requirements. Primary requirements are working capital. $3 million is being sought for the purposes of this plan.

Start-up Expenses

Legal	$35,000
Stationery, etc.	$2,500
Brochures	$2,500
Consultants	$15,000
Insurance	$10,000
Rent	$10,000
Research and development	$500,000
New marketing and staffing	$4,000,000
Expensed equipment	$45,000
Other	$0
Total Start-up Expenses	**$4,620,000**

Start-up Assets Needed

Cash Requirements	$1,055,000
Start-up inventory	$125,000
Other Short-term Assets	$50,000
Total Short-term Assets	**$1,230,000**
Long-term Assets	$150,000
Total Assets	**$1,380,000**
Total Start-up Requirements:	$6,000,000
Left to finance:	$0

Start-up Funding Plan

Investment

Investor 1	$3,000,000
Investor 2	$3,000,000
Other	$0
Total investment	**$6,000,000**

Short-term Liabilities

Unpaid Expenses	$0
Short-term Loans	$0
Interest-free Short-term Loans	$0
Subtotal Short-term Liabilities	$0
Long-term Liabilities	$0
Total Liabilities	**$0**
Loss at Start-up	($4,620,000)
Total Capital	$1,380,000
Total Capital and Liabilities	$1,380,000
Checkline	$0

Start-up Summary

PRODUCTS

Company Locations and Facilities

It is expected that QuikMedInfo will be located in Louisville, Kentucky. However, Lexington also may be a future potential headquarters.

QuikMedInfo will sell software and installation services related to that software. The company also will sell professional consulting services that include the design, writing, and implementing of custom screens, file interfaces, and administrative security features related to the software product. The software runs on a variety of computer servers. The software is written in 100% Java, which is supported on many hardware servers and is scaleable from the smallest of servers to the largest of systems.

Product Description

QuikMedInfo sells software for hospitals, physicians, payors, and related entities.

Software is sold with a base server license, seats, and applicable modules.

The software will interface across all disparate hardware and software systems, using the Internet language of Java (licensed by Sun MicroSystems, Inc.). No additional purchase of hardware is required to run the software.

Professional services are provided for customization of the software.

Training and support services are provided as a billable item.

The product is currently developed in seven different modules. As an Intranet application solution, the modules are required to run on a robust server. The installed modules are Admissions, Transcriptions, Laboratory, Imaging, and Pharmacy. Future modules are in development as needed in the market place. Home Health and Physician management modules are complete but not installed. Currently five modules are successfully operating in six different environments.

The QuikMedInfo System

- A single system that will do the data collection, presentation, and transmission without regard to the platform, software, or location of either the original data or end user.
- A system that is sensitive to political, security, and financial aspects.
- A system that recognizes the importance and responsibility of the M.D.
- A system that merges the unique talents of the team.
- A system that recognizes the annual purchase cycles of hospitals and offers a "subscription" or rental option.
- A system that derives from and is validated by the market research we have done with M.D.s and hospitals.

Competitive Comparison

The QuikMedInfo software system has been in the disparate system market for nearly three years. Originally there was very limited competition. We fully expect the competition to increase as Java becomes better known and last year's Y2K issues free up budgets in hospitals, thereby making the sale of the product easier. Presently, our competitors include interface engine companies that are developing web front-end applications, internal application development from a hospital's own staff, and hospital information systems companies who are web enabling their own applications.

However, we have several major advantages that will enhance our chance of success. These are:

- Hospital information vendors are focused on web enabling their applications, not the common access of their applications to other competitive vendors. This is our niche.
- Hospital information vendors generally do not respond to customers' needs for specialization of their applications.
- Hospitals generally follow one another, which is why we have priced aggressively to get a customer base established.
- Our design allows for a very quick deployment.
- Our application is very easy to learn.
- Our application ties many systems together, thereby being more difficult to uninstall later.

Competitors we are aware of include:

1. ABC, an investment by Denver Technology Partners. This company has focused on single sign-on applications and has one or two installations.

2. Delve, originally an interface engine company, developed a web interface product. This company was purchased by Oneida Systems. Oneida recently went public and had a very successful offering. Another large interface engine company, Mongoose, is developing a web front end.

3. Med-Shell, another company that recently went public, provides similar services that we provide to payors. Med-Shell has purchased several companies and is developing its market. It has recently entered into a marketing relationship with IBM.

4. JKL provides a repository to view clinical data over the web. We approached this company two years ago as a business partner, but they felt their development was too far along to assist us. JKL has one or two installations and has had those same installations for nearly two years.

5. InterFuseM.D., a consortium of many content vendors, is entering the market promising to be a catch-all solution to physicians and providers.

Note: InterFuseM.D. and a company named DEF have recently merged. This has created a powerful economic entity. However, our management believes that the scope of their focus is much too broad to mount a challenge in our specific niche. We expect to be able to deliver a better product.

Other competitors may be terminal emulations over the web. We do not see these as direct competition. The key to our market success is being able to provide access to the most important 20% of the critical clinical information to 80% of the users in the hospital market. Often times the data exists but it is neither available nor accessible. We offer a solution to bring this data together in a secure auditable manner for these users.

Sales Literature

Most of our marketing literature has been developed. Our collateral materials include:

- A physician-oriented brochure.
- A hospital-oriented brochure.
- An online web site providing information on the product, architecture, white papers, and online demonstrations.

- A brochure aimed at the insurance and third-party administrator market will be developed.
- General tradeshow booths have been purchased in two sizes. These sizes include a 10' x 10' portable booth and a 10' x 20' demonstration booth. The 10' x 20' booth was designed exclusively for trade shows.

Sourcing

QuikMedInfo will own the sole rights to the software product. This software is copyrighted. The copyright will have to be updated from time to time to protect our investments in the code.

Technology

The QuikMedInfo software is a 100% Java-compliant application. Java is the single best software designed to write applications for the World Wide Web. It is an object-oriented programming language which allows for extremely fast application development and customization. One of the advantages of Java is its wide support from a variety of hardware manufacturers. Although, other programming languages may appear, such as Microsoft's XML, we have been consistently satisfied with Java's performance. Another reason for choosing Java was the flexibility it provides by running on many hardware vendors' platforms. This provides our customers with the security of scaleable systems. Microsoft's XML only runs on an NT server and thus is limited to the PC marketplace. Java runs on personal computers, midrange systems, and mainframes.

Future Products

Our future includes taking the existing software to complimentary industries, such as payors. The software can be used by any industry desiring to link disparate systems; e.g., the telecommunication industry desiring to link pager, mobile telephone, e-mail and other systems. Also, as installations continue, we will build a library of interfaces that make installations and connectivity easier. New applications are to be added annually to include more connectivity to disparate applications. We expect to sell these new and additional modules for $25,000 to $50,000 each.

The focus of our plan is to develop the medical and hospital application first, then penetrate the health insurance vertical market. These other applications above have the potential to generate many times the revenue projected in the focus of this plan. That may be a strategic reason for an IPO.

MARKET ANALYSIS SUMMARY

As any new product is brought to the marketplace it will gain the attention first of the early adopters, then the primary market, and then the market laggers. Our primary target market consists of community-based hospitals with 200 or more beds. When we tried marketing to large chain hospitals such as Ft. Benson and Diamond, we discovered these organizations are extremely interested in the product but bogged down by their own bureaucracies. The same is true for large HIS application vendors. Therefore, we will stay focused on the smaller and independent hospitals that can make a quicker decision.

Presently, there are about 5,057 hospitals in the United States. Our target market is the "200 bed and larger" facilities, of which there are 1,486. The total target market potential represents $371,500,000. Of the 1,486 facilities, we plan to sell to 300 facilities over the first five years, which represents 20% of our target market. With an average complete sale of $250,000 this would represent $75,000,000 in revenue over five years.

It is estimated that fewer than 10% of these sales will be for cash. Third-party leasing is expected to comprise the majority of our business.

Revenues in our five-year plan above the $75,000,000 million total are the result of additional vertical markets initially penetrated with modest market share in years four and five.

Our experience has been that it takes about a year for a hospital to make a decision. Our marketing efforts of last year are paying off this year as we close the identified opportunities. Our objective is to keep the pipeline full and have regular closings. Many of the existing customers are already returning for additional customization. We expect our revenues to grow at a minimum of 50% to 100% for the next several years.

Market Segmentation

Our market segmentation includes three primary areas:

1. Community and regional hospitals averaging about 200 to 700 beds.
2. Third-party administrators and payors.
3. Government-run programs, Child Health Insurance Plans (CHIPS), and VA hospitals.

Community and regional hospitals are searching for ways to improve their back office operations and to improve relationships with physicians by providing them better access to patient information.

Third-party administrators can use the software to provide remote access to authorizations, eligibility, claims status, referrals, etc. This information also can be shared with hospitals who have the software and can enable electronic pre-admissions.

Payors can use the software to offload heavily staffed call centers by allowing physicians direct access to eligibility, claim status, etc. Payors can in essence extend their operational hours by allowing direct access to data. They can use this program with employers to provide benefit plan details, account status, explanation of benefits, etc.

State agencies funded by the federal government can purchase our "out of the box" application for certain mandated programs.

Other potential markets include any industry with disparate systems that could benefit from a consolidated view of data. An example of this would be the telecommunications industry which may have systems related to their different products. By using our product, you could view on one display a customer's information coming from providers of email services, voice mail, local telephone service, long distance telephone service, paging services, cellular services, cable television, Internet services, etc.

Market Analysis

Potential Customers	Growth	1999	2000	2001	2002	2003	CAGR
Community Hospitals	2%	1,486	1,516	1,546	1,577	1,609	2.01%
Third Party Payors	4%	800	832	865	900	936	4.00%
Government Facilities	1%	250	253	256	259	262	1.18%
Other	0%	0	0	0	0	0	0.00%
Total	**2.57%**	**2,536**	**2,601**	**2,667**	**2,736**	**2,807**	**2.57%**

Target Market Segment Strategy

Our target market is the hospital industry where it is very common to find disparate systems. Hospitals typically take one year to eighteen months to make a decision. Providing flexible pricing and purchasing options, which might avoid the need to go through the capital budgeting process, should help shorten this cycle. Also, hospitals do not like to write their own systems and would rather use applications to achieve their needs.

Secondary markets are the insurance payors and third-party administrators that work in the healthcare field. They are interested in providing physicians with access to patient data, such as eligibility, and with the ability to electronically obtain authorizations, referrals, etc. These companies typically make a decision very quickly, and their services may inter-relate with the hospitals to whom and with whom they market.

Once these industries have been established using our product, we would broaden our base to begin to penetrate other industries where disparate systems exist.

Market Needs

The target market is seeking simplicity of its processes, increased productivity of its staff and increased patient satisfaction. Areas of concern are the physician's time to access information, access to proper data from insurance companies, scheduling lab tests, and many back office and/or administrative procedures. Our niche is to bring the needed information from several disparate systems to a single web browser.

An example of this daily frustration is as follows. A physician wants to retrieve the lab test for a patient. Depending on the lab test results, the physician may change the patient's medication and notify the patient of the change. The physician or someone on the staff would access the lab system; complete a sign-in with a password; conduct a patient search; select a medical record, a specific encounter, or visit; and retrieve the latest lab result. Upon finding the result, the physician would then sign out of the lab system and enter into the pharmacy system. The physician would use a second sign-in and a second password, conduct another patient search, locate the visit that has the medication, review, and submit a change to the pharmacist and sign out of that system. The physician would then sign on a third time, with a third password, conduct another patient search to get the appropriate patient demographics to notify them of the lab results and the change of medication. None of the above systems look, feel, or act similarly.

With our software, the physician can retrieve all the above information with one sign-on, one password, and one patient search.

From our visits in many hospitals the 80/20 rule exists: 80% of the people need about 20% of the data. Today that information is not easily available to them. Our product solves that dilemma.

How an M.D. could use the system was discussed during a physician advisory board meeting:

1. A radiologist:
   - Patient info available (even at the beach via notebook computer).
   - Radiologist at another hospital sees a patient that he wishes to refer.
2. A surgeon:
   - Pre-hospital rounds data review.
   - Image and lab review.
   - Remote chart review and signing.
   - Gain access to hospital pharmacy formulary (or insurance co. drug formulary).
   - Order drugs that will be effective, available, and insurance reimbursable.
3. An EE&T:
   - Quality assurance.
   - Scheduling at surgical center.

4. An IPA (Independent Physicians Association):
   - Quality assurance.
   - M.D. to M.D. referrals.

How a hospital could use the system:

1. Electronic chart signature which allows billing to occur much quicker.
2. Windy Mountain (newly acquired hospital) can be integrated with St. Thomas Hospital.
3. Any of the 100-plus hospitals in Kentucky to communicate with M.D.s.
4. M.D. access to lab, X-ray, etc. without new hardware or software.
5. Referral data transferred without new entry.

Market Trends

The trends in this industry include consolidation of facilities, competition for physician allegiance, and the need to improve efficiencies with the decreasing reimbursement rates from government and managed care companies. The World Wide Web is going to be the mechanism by which most information will be implemented and routed. Having a tool that acts as a manager of all those possible connections is important and gives the hospitals a great amount of freedom for their future. We feel this trend will only strengthen over the next several years.

The trend for this "connection" will be a vital role as companies race to get to the market. As we build our connections and libraries of interfaces we will become a dominant player in the marketplace.

Presently, the major hospital information vendors are trying to convince hospitals to consolidate all systems to one vendor. If the vendors were successful in creating this trend, then they could provide a web enablement to their different systems. However, there is significant resistance by the hospitals who do not want to be tied to one vendor. First, the hospital would have to discard millions of dollars already spent for information systems. Secondly, the market is dynamic and no one vendor has successfully captured all areas of a hospital sufficiently so that the hospital has no other needs. The closest vendor to achieving this may be Tech5Health which does offer a proprietary, one-source solution.

It appears that most hospitals want the option to purchase the "best of breed" systems and they will need a system to connect their disparate systems. The hospitals will see a product that allows them to maintain their current system investments, purchase new "best of breed" systems but still maintain autonomy by having a common front end. They have the freedom to change as little or as frequently as their business model requires.

The product works especially well for consolidation of hospitals as well, because the common front end can work with entirely two different hospital information systems. This can provide millions of dollars in savings.

Market Growth

This market will have a 30% or higher growth rate. There is no question that web business or "e-business" (as some companies have phrased it) will be the dominant force over the next 10 years. Recent reports by Roger Alison, industry analyst, illustrate huge paybacks for customers implementing this technology.

Industry Analysis

Common front-end systems are a rather new segment in the industry. As systems have become more complex, users are looking for simple ways to access data. We have found the Pareto rule to be true in the healthcare market: 80% of the people only need about 20% of the data. It is unfortunate that the 20% is across many systems and thus difficult to locate. A review of the industry would put us in a developing category called Universal Desktops or Single Sign-On Solutions.

The Healthcare Community

Healthcare has traditionally been a system of distinct parties who must work together and form a service community. The parties include M.D.s, M.D. office staff, hospitals, surgical centers, diagnostic centers, home health agencies, nursing homes, insurance companies, federal and state government, patients, and ancillary service providers. Patient and their information are the common thread. Each party creates unique information for and about the patient and yet has need of some identical information. The concept of using someone else's information without physical presence in the originating facility is a dim hope only. Within each party's organization there exists a microcosm of the situation existing between parties. As an example, a hospital may have data in a billing system, a dictation system, a laboratory system, an X-ray system and a pharmacy system. The means of gathering, storing, and processing information is different for each party and, despite good intentions, multiple data systems present a very steep learning curve. A busy M.D. will likely select those which they must use (dictation and office billing) and ignore the rest.

M.D.s are the mobile link in that they move between the parties and utilize the bulk of the information. By nature, patients in a hospital are unable to travel to an office. In addition there are many times an M.D. may not be near the data they need to answer an "on call" emergency situation without undue travel and effort.

A Brief Functional Overview of the Medical Community

Very high-tech treatment means:

- The entire process is information-driven combined with judgment of the M.D.
- M.D.s are time efficient and will increase efficiency subject to a learning curve resistance.
- Gradual acceptance and implementation of information systems in:
    Laboratory
    Imaging (X-ray, MRI, etc.)
    Pharmacy
    Billing and patient records
    Dictation
- M.D. offices adopting information systems for billing.
- Electronic medical records in some M.D. offices.
- Gradual understanding of need to communicate without paper or people intervention.
- Everyone developing their own means to share information.
- M.D. now has to know and use the unique system for each application.
- Hospitals are looking for means to bind M.D.s to them.
- The systems in place use different software and to a lesser extent different hardware.
- All the parties in this community are mildly distrustful of the other's motives.
- HCFA will lobby for secure, automated transfer of data.

Industry Participants

Participants in this industry include the following:

1. Single Sign-On Vendors. These vendors offer single sign-on solutions that vary from terminal emulation sessions over the web to more robust sign-ons that also handle password and security. Our product competes well in this environment. We offer a single sign-on to multiple systems, handle security, encrypt data, and retrieve data based upon a user's sign-on identification.

2. HIS vendors web enabling their own products. We fully expect each HIS vendor to web enable their own products. These vendors are only interested in web enabling their proprietary software and the large vendors are not known for good customer service. If a customer has multiple different systems he will still have several different systems to access with each system looking and responding differently. The proprietary web enablement will not give the customer with multiple systems anymore ease of use than he presently has with multiple terminal emulations.

3) Niche players. There are some direct competitors that we face in the market that offer products similar to ours. These players may address a particular need for a healthcare company such as access to payor information. Healtheon would be an example of this type of company. IBM, also, offers a repository that can be accessed via the web. Our product is more flexible and can better meet the varying needs of the customer.

Distribution Patterns

The product will be sold primarily via a direct sales force. We currently have a few distributors who are excited about the product and have specific opportunities to market the product. These distributors are given a discount that ranges from 30% to 40%, depending upon volume. We also have an OEM agreement that allows the vendor to incorporate the product into their software offerings. This agreement requires an inventory purchase and the company receives payment for each time the product is sold. Both distributors and OEM companies are required to identify the end user to our company for record purposes and quality assurance.

Sales Strategies / Channels

The company's goal is to infiltrate QuikMedInfo into the heart of the healthcare industry. The objective is for QuikMedInfo to be accepted as the standard Intranet application solution that hospitals, doctors, clinics, pharmacies, and laboratories use to obtain necessary patient data. There are three channels defined below to assist us in achieving this goal.

  1. Distributors — There are five categories for distributors. These categories are:
  - HIS Vendors (provide legacy-based applications to the healthcare industry).
  - Interface Engine Vendors such as CAI, STC, HCI, and Hublink (provide communication interfaces between HIS vendor legacy applications to transmit data from one HIS vendor application to another).
  - Healthcare industry related consulting firms (providing integration services to hospital organizations).
  - Value Added Resellers (selling healthcare-related solutions to hospital organizations).
  - Computer and Communication Hardware Vendors (provide computer and communication software, hardware, and services to the healthcare industry).

This group of channels, organized to create higher net revenue, will be resellers of QuikMedInfo. They will assist in marketing and selling QuikMedInfo to local hospitals, clinics, pharmacies, and laboratories that desire to take advantage of the benefits QuikMedInfo has to offer. Distributors will receive commissions based on the level of support provided for every sale they complete. The advantages of utilizing distributors is that they are already providing solutions to the primary target market and can easily penetrate these organizations to provide QuikMedInfo as their Intranet application solution of choice. The cost to support these channels is minimal for the amount of return for immediate market exposure they will provide for QuikMedInfo.

2. Independent Representatives — Independent Representatives are sales people under contract to market QuikMedInfo. They are extensions of the direct sales team, with the added advantage of reaching clients in various service areas that the direct sales team cannot or have not approached. They receive no salary and earn only from commission based on the level of support provided for every sale they complete. Like distributors, the advantages of utilizing independent representatives is that they are already providing solutions to our primary target market and can easily penetrate these organizations to provide QuikMedInfo as their intranet application solution of choice. The cost to support this channel is minimal for the amount of return for immediate market exposure they will provide for QuikMedInfo.

3. Direct Sales — Sales are done directly with hospitals, doctors, clinics, pharmacies, and laboratories utilizing company internal sales representatives. As opposed to distributor and independent representative sales, direct sales do not involve middlemen. Hospitals purchase QuikMedInfo from the direct sales team. The team identifies potential customers, contacts those customers directly, and sells the product to them firsthand. As with arrangements involving distributors and independent representatives, direct sales involve educating the industry about QuikMedInfo—therefore increasing QuikMedInfo's exposure.

Competition and Buying Patterns

The hospital market purchases software it deems as having a strong return on investment. Also, the hospitals tend to purchase applications other hospitals have been successful installing. Most sales to hospitals take time, plus involve patience and working with many different persons within the hospital. Reference selling is important. This type of solution to hospitals is very new and has been ahead of its time. Much of the selling in the past year has been educational, positioning hospitals to use the technology. The market is now developing at a much quicker pace.

Hospitals choose their vendor based upon value of the application, price and ROI, and the quality of the vendor (reputation). Image and visibility are important to gain mindshare and the perception of being a national vendor. However, nothing beats reference selling and recommendations from customers. All of our current customers have agreed to be references.

Main Competitors

Our main competition comes from interface engine companies, hospital information systems vendors, and other web providers.

Of the original four primary interface engine companies only two remain. The original four included CAI, HCI, Hublink, and STC. CAI merged with Neon Systems. Hublink was purchased by HCI and changed their name to HIE. STC remains one of the oldest and established firms in their industry segment.

CAI developed a product about the same time as this product. Their product is called Web Connect and is similar in function to this product. They are at about the same stage of development as our company. CAI was purchased by Whiteash Systems, and Whiteash recently had a very successful IPO.

HIE has maintained its focus on being an interface engine company and has moved from the health market to other industries such as finance, and manufacturing. The purpose of an interface engine is to simply take data for system A and place it on system B, C, etc. This is accomplished by hidden coding and so is transparent to a user of an application. An example of this in the healthcare market is a patient updating his phone number when picking up a prescription. The interface engine would place the changed phone number in the patient demographics system, the lab system, etc.

STC is a well-entrenched interface engine company. STC was previously embedded into the Coopers LPMN product and many sales were achieved with little effort. STC had planned an IPO but backed off when they lost the Douglas contract. Recently, STC has begun a web implementation that is to rival this product. For one year they have promised a few customers sweetheart deals to wait on their product. It is still not marketable but is still being developed. Due to their presence and install base they may be successful in getting their customers to delay decisions.

Hospital information systems companies are racing to get their solutions web enabled. The only focus these vendors have is with their own products. None of these vendors have an interest in developing a cross-vendor web solution. The comment is "Why would I web enable my competitor?" This solidifies the niche that our product addresses.

Some of these web solution providers include CoreChange, Healtheon, Envoy, and IBM. CoreChange addresses a single sign-on approach to many systems, Healtheon is extending payor information such as eligibility, authorization, claim status, etc. IBM is offering a repository that can extend results to the web. Our product has the design to do all the above and more. It is robust but also can be sold as a minimized solution.

Other web providers have and will continue to appear. These vendors range from terminal emulations to web content providers. Nathan Bedford Forest, in speaking of his success as a General, stated his key to winning the battle was "the firstest with the mostest!" Yes, it is poor grammar; but his point is the first to the market wins mindshare, establishes a brand, and becomes the incumbent player. This product is well positioned to be the industry leader.

STRATEGY & IMPLEMENTATION SUMMARY

Our strategy for this market is straightforward:

1. It is our desire to obtain a quick, referable install base.
2. Build relationships with neighboring hospitals.
3. Emphasize quick installations with high-quality service and support.

Strategy Pyramids

To achieve a quick referable install base, our main tactic is to call the hospitals where we have information system interfaces already completed. This provides us an extremely quick installation and another reference site. It meets our objective of building an install base. This market can be identified through user groups. Our specific programs include mailing to these hospitals, Internet demonstrations of the product, direct selling, and attending trade shows.

Our next strategy is to build upon our successes by marketing to hospitals in the immediate vicinity of the install base. Successful references are great selling tools and successful installations are great sites for other nearby hospitals to visit. Physicians can be a great asset by pressing other providers to extend to them the same information services they are receiving from a local hospital. Our specific program is to call and escort neighboring facilities to visit the installation site. Also, having these references document their "return on investment" aids the selling and decision cycle.

Quick and successful installations are the key to meeting our business plan. By carefully choosing our installs, we will avoid a developing trap by interfacing to a difficult closed-in system. Our specific plan to avoid this is to partner with other solution providers who have expertise in areas we do not, and allow them to sell and install the product.

Value Proposition

Our value proposition is straightforward. The product solution provides daily users of information a highly improved delivery mechanism. This delivery includes the following:
1. Accessibility: information is accessible via any web browser.
2. Availability: from any browser, laptop, or PDA.
3. Accuracy: via legacy system or depository (real time data).
4. Affordability: time savings at all points of access and use.
5. Accountability: information is encrypted and audited from within.

As an example of value, physicians pay a monthly fee for a pager that only instructs them to call a number. For an equivalent monthly fee, our product provides the physician with immediate access to information that allows him to care for the patient, make decisions, and perform billable work.

Competitive Edge

Our competitive edge exists because we have chosen the right technologies, have been early to the market, and have a plan to quickly establish an install base. This install base will continue to grow because the product itself can be the front end to a multitude of functions. The product is not canned; thus, the user can continue to develop and enable new applications. The single web session can be used for hospital information, payor information, employee benefit sections, and links to other web site and content areas such as MedScape. Existing customers have already returned to ask for new links, new connections, and new modules.

Our competitive edge will be maintained as interfaces to various legacy systems are built into a library. This significantly improves the deployment time for a user. Also, we have established a vendor certification program allowing vendors to forward to us pre-releases of their software to insure compatibility.

Our competitive advantage also will be maintained due to the daily use of the product by our customers, and the difficulty to undo the connections and replace the access to many systems. Additionally, we are in a strong competitive position because information systems vendors are not focused on building web-enabled interfaces for a cross vendor market.

Others who will enter this market will face vigorous competition from us.

Marketing Strategy

The marketing strategy is the core of the main strategy:

1. To obtain a quick and referable install base, we will heavily focus on our target market of 1,486 hospitals with 200 beds or more. Of these 1,486 hospitals we have an immediately installable solution for 291 of these hospitals. These 291 hospitals represent HBOC systems running on IBM's AS/400 for which we have already developed an interface which has been successfully running for two years. These 291 hospitals have a user group to whom we have spoken and will continue to work with in the future. Direct mailings, direct selling, and referencing is the strategy we will use with these accounts.

2. Upon the successful installation of a hospital we will immediately contact nearby hospitals. We will build from the install location outward. We also will request the senior management of a successful, newly installed hospital for references to other senior healthcare executives

that might have an interest in our product. We know that managers of information systems often refer solutions to their peers in the industry.

3. The medical community has a flavor of a fraternal order. Especially among like users of a common software and hardware platform. By having quick installations with quality service and support, we are a very referencable solution. Normal installations of health information systems are very long and complex. Managers of information systems are excited when solutions work and vendors keep their commitments. Unfortunately, this is not the normal experience for most installations. Our service and support sets us apart.

4. The new marketing strategy of approaching IPAs in each medical community to influence hospitals will make decisions by hospitals happen quicker and will have a positive impact on growth.

Positioning Statement

For medical and administrative professionals who need immediate access to patient information from a variety of systems, this product delivers that information to them from one single source, anywhere, anytime. Unlike their present environment, that may require many attempts and many different computer skills, this product provides all pertinent information with one click.

Pricing Strategy

The price of the product is $75,000 for the server software and $595.00 per user of the software. User prices are then discounted based upon the volume of users. In addition to the software, we charge for interface programming, customization of screen design, installation, training, and maintenance of the product. These are billed at $180 per hour or $1,500 a day.

We provide the necessary hardware if the customer desires us to fulfill that need.

Customers may ask us to perform a prototype of the application. We do these prototypes at our normal consulting rates mentioned above.

To help hospitals make a quick decision we have a rental model of the software. This rental model is based upon the following model:

	Range	Mo. per user	Users	Total Cost
Tier #1	1-100	$39.95	100	$3,995
Tier #2	101-200	$29.95	100	$2,995
Tier #3	201-300	$19.95	100	$1,995
Tier #4	301-400	$14.95	0	$0
Tier #5	401-500	$9.95	0	$0
Tier #6	501-999	$6.95	0	$0
Tier #7	> 1,000	$4.95	0	$0
Total			**300**	**$8,985**

Minimum length of time is 36 months. This model includes maintenance. Hospitals are more flexible with an operating budget than a capital budget. In case the hospital would like to rent and convert later to a purchase model, we accrue a percentage of the rental towards the purchase price.

Promotion Strategy

1. Our promotion strategy is via direct sales to the healthcare marketplace. We have a tight target market which we call directly. We work with senior level management and

influential physicians. Our sales brochures help to illustrate the ease of use of the software.

2. One brochure is targeted for the hospitals and another brochure will target physicians and IPAs.
3. We will develop a brochure for the third-party administrator market.
4. We will use telemarketing especially prior to trade shows.
5. A public relations campaign and press releases will be developed.
6. A web site will be created at QuikMedInfo.org

Distribution Strategy

We have signed agreements with distributors who have products complementary to our own. They already have client relationships and can easily add this product in their product offerings. Distributors have an annual quota and percentage discounts related to their self sufficiency in selling the product.

There are distributors that would like to embed the product in their software—the industry terms that to be "OEMing" (other equipment manufacturer) the product. These distributors receive a much higher discount but are required to purchase substantial inventory and offer the first level of customer support.

Marketing Programs

Our direct sales force is currently comprised of two marketing representatives, one for the eastern half of the United States and the other for the western half.

Both sales people have an annual objective of five hospitals to be installed. They are each responsible for calling the customer base, identifying and qualifying prospects, demonstrating the product, and closing the sale. They are both responsible for having $1.5 million of qualified opportunity defined at any one time. They are to make 100 calls a week and update those calls in a customer database. They are responsible for managing their own travel budget and expenses. They are not allowed to travel to a healthcare facility until all appropriate people are available for the meeting. This has worked well in the past and eliminated flights to interested but unqualified prospects.

Direct sales is very important as the sales cycle is long in the healthcare market. The direct selling effort is increased by visiting existing prospects and finding new prospects at trade shows.

Telesales coordinates all mailings to customers. These mailings include marketing material, product newsletters and press releases. Some type of literature is sent every six weeks to the customer and prospect database. All mailings are carefully recorded and response to those mailings is recorded.

Ed Roost of Best Midwest Solutions, Inc. already travels nationally and calls upon prospects with the representatives. Rachel Brown also visits with other CEOs to build strategic relationships.

Sales Strategy

Our sales strategy is to prospect our target market for potential customers. Upon finding customers that have a need, we offer a specific solution to that need. We follow our prospecting efforts with an online, Internet demonstration of the product. After successfully demonstrating the product, we schedule an onsite visit to the healthcare facility when all pertinent people can attend the meeting. We have found that physicians are our greatest advocate and we strive to make sure that they are a part of our onsite meeting. After a successful onsite presentation, we offer to perform a site survey that is billable. The site survey results in a working document defines the environment, the complexities, similarities, interfacing requirements and any customization required. From the site survey, we build a proposal that lists the price of the server, the seat cost based on the number of users, the interfacing costs, the customization programming needed, installation, training, etc. We work with the customer to review the findings and make certain all areas have been addressed.

Upon acceptance of the proposal the customer is provided with license agreements, maintenance agreements, and a Professional Services Agreement with specific work exhibits that detail the customization and interface programming costs. Customers are then entered into our customer support system that tracks the release level of software, technical contacts, all support calls, and repairs.

Sales Analysis

The long-range goal is to develop QuikMedInfo as an enterprise Intranet application solution for the healthcare industry and utilize the Java-based server technology to provide a number of Intranet application solutions to all types of industries. This goal will be achieved by the success of the introductory two-year plan. In addition, version upgrades will be based on seat licenses and maintenance.

The long-range plan is based on a successful introduction of QuikMedInfo to the healthcare industry. There will be a feasible strategy to successfully launch QuikMedInfo and establish brand recognition for a new line of Intranet application solutions and meet the two-year sales goals.

The sales will be derived from hospitals through locally controlled physician advisory boards. QuikMedInfo will be comprised of a server and seven different modules: Admissions, Transcriptions, Laboratory, Imaging, Pharmacy, Home Health, and Physician Management. Revenues also will be generated from computer and network hardware, server, and seat licenses, installation and training of these products to new hospital installations.

In the healthcare industry, there are 5,057 hospitals, representing the market in which the company has targeted. The company's target market is hospitals with over 200 beds, which is currently 1,486. Of these 1,486 hospitals, the company anticipates being the market leader and obtaining 20% of this market share. This will equate to 300 hospital installations in the first two years.

Based on effective marketing and sales in the first two years the company will position QuikMedInfo as a long-term solution for data resource gathering in the healthcare industry.

Sales Forecast

The following is our list of potential sales:

Mercy Hospital (262 beds)	$350k
Freedom Medical (262 beds)	$250k
St. Anthony (237 beds)	$250k
Memorial-NM (373 beds)	$250k
Western Kentucky (269 beds)	$250k
Children's (281 beds)	$250k
NW Wyoming Center (n.a.)	$300k
NET Hamilton (n.a.)	$130k
Ohio Central Hosp. (840 beds)	$300k
VA Hospital (1,028 beds)	$300k
Red Glen East	$90k

The expected three-year sales forecast is illustrated and more carefully broken down in its appropriate table.

Sales Forecast

Sales	FY2000	FY2001	FY2002
Licenses	$2,325,000	$4,450,000	$9,950,000
Maintenance	$348,750	$667,500	$1,492,500
Consulting	$232,500	$445,000	$995,000
Installation	$58,125	$111,250	$248,750
Training	$58,125	$111,250	$248,750
Other	$0	$0	$0
Total Sales	**$3,022,500**	**$5,785,000**	**$12,935,000**
Direct Cost of Sales			
Licenses	$232,500	$445,000	$995,000
Maintenance	$209,250	$400,500	$597,000
Consulting	$0	$0	$0
Installation	$0	$0	$0
Training	$0	$0	$0
Other	$0	$0	$0
Subtotal Cost of Sales	**$441,750**	**$845,500**	**$1,592,000**

Sales Programs

Our sales programs are via direct mail and trade shows.

Via our direct mail campaign we send letters and success stories to our target market. These letters may include recent press releases, editorials featuring our product, along with our marketing literature. Mailings include the invitation for a free demo of the product over the Internet. The mailings also may be oriented towards an upcoming trade show that specifically states our booth and the marketing representatives to work with for their particular area. The sales reps are given this information for follow up and to personally invite the prospects and customers.

Educational seminars and end user groups are another avenue we use to educate customers on our technology, services, and expertise. Educational seminars can often be funded by the various professional associations. End user groups provide a wonderful opportunity to market and sell the product and its benefits.

Strategic Alliances

Strategic alliances already in progress include:

Skyenergy, Inc., a wholly owned subsidiary of Northwest Power and Light (a major regional utility company), specializes in application hosting and data transport over its eight-state fiber-optic network. It has shown great interest in the purchase of licensees of the product. Skyenergy currently has a contract with Blue Cross/Blue Shield of Kentucky to provide services to all BC's providers. The QuikMedInfo product can instantly be used in this environment.

Timbute Corp., a potential joint venture partner, is a large player in medical diagnostic imaging. It already has distribution of its platform, and a substantial revenue and client base. We would be an add-in service.

Sun Microsystems has already agreed to do maintenance and support where required. They have complete diligent knowledge of the product.

No agreements have been signed to date. Many other strategic potential partners exist.

Milestones

Our most significant milestone to date? Our "installed customers." They are very happy with the QuikMedInfo product and are excellent references. They include:

Thomas Medical Center (268 beds) - Installed August 1998

Thomas is the original customer that conceived the need for such a product and offered its employees and staff to assist in the initial requirements documentation. Thomas presently uses the product extensively in medical records. Thomas uses the product for one view of patient demographics, document images, and pharmacy. The customer is initiating the laboratory views of the product and will follow shortly with transcriptions.

Trinity 7 Communications - Installed January 1997

Trinity 7 Communications is a provider of telecommunication services. The company offers paging, cellular, voice mail, email, and long distance products. These services may be provided by many vendors. The software product allows them one common view to these different providers and their different systems.

Michelin Wool - Installed February 1998

Michelin Wool is one of the nation's largest third-party administrators and managed care companies. It offers physician management services as well. Michelin Wool uses the product to allow physicians access over the Internet for eligibility, authorizations, claims status, etc. Michelin has purchased a tool kit and is developing some of its own designs.

State of Oregon - Installed March 1999

The state of Oregon has purchased the product to use in a federal and state program called CHIPs (Childrens' Health Insurance Program). This product allows a provider to check a child's eligibility with the primary payors in the state prior to rendering services and before applying the charges to the state fund. This is a highly advanced application as the entire transmissions are secure and encrypted from all aspects.

Greene Medical Center of Titan, Oregon - Installed April 1999

Greene Medical Center uses the product to interface to several HBOC systems. The company retrieves information from lab, patient demographics, pharmacy, and is developing an interface for transcriptions. This customer may purchase a tool kit to develop some of its own applications.

Other forthcoming milestones are summarized in the following table:

Business Plan Milestones

Milestone	Manager	Planned Date	Department	Budget	Actual Date	Actual Budget	Planned Date - Actual Budget	Budget - Actual Budget
Additional Revenue	Roost	9/1/99	Exec.	$50	9/1/99	$50	0	$0
Close of Acquisition	Brown	9/1/99	Exec.	$30	9/1/99	$30	0	$0
New Capitalization	Brown	9/1/99	Exec.	$15	9/1/99	$15	0	$0
New Management Team	Roost	10/1/99	Exec.	$330	10/1/99	$330	0	$0
New Sales Programs	Brown	11/1/99	Exec.	$250	11/1/99	$250	0	$0
New Revenue	Roost	12/1/99	Exec	$50	12/1/99	$50	0	$0
Other	ABC	1/1/98	Department	$0	1/1/98	$0	0	$0
Totals				**$725**		**$725**	**0**	**$0**

MANAGEMENT SUMMARY

The new management team will be comprised of individuals who are currently with Empire Systems or other respected corporate leaders in the industry. They already understand the market and have been responsible for product development and sales penetration to date. Management bios follow.

Organizational Structure

Our organization structure is divided into three functional areas:

1. Product development and support — The role of this function is to continue to develop the product and new modules, write the appropriate interfaces and customized programs and offer maintenance for the product.
2. Sales and marketing — The role of sales and marketing is to market the product, educate customers, and build a reference base of customers. Sales and marketing conducts telesales, direct sales, etc.
3. General administration — This group manages the sales, invoicing, collection, and accounting of the group. It provides oversight of the entire organization.

Management Team

The management team includes the following individuals. Ed Roost will serve as CEO either on an interim or permanent basis. The potential exists in the personnel forecast to recruit and add a CEO.

Senior Executive Vice President—Rachel Brown is the co-founder of Best Source Solutions, Inc. She is a 1980 graduate of the University of Cincinnati (Accounting degree). She worked for Arthur Anderson in Denver and then worked for IBM from 1980 to 1987, leaving the company as a marketing manager in Point Kenton, Ohio. She was responsible for such accounts as General Electric, Great Lakes Banking, and other major accounts. Rachel became Senior Vice President of Memblast in Cincinnati, Ohio, and was responsible for computer equipment brokerage and leasing. She purchased an interest in a small software company to bring it home to Louisville, Kentucky. In 1990 she started Best Source Solutions and is responsible for the day-to-day sales of that company. Rachel will continue to run Best Source Solutions.

Executive Vice President - Ed Roost is the current President of Empire Systems, Inc. He has 18 years of experience in sales and marketing including six years in sales with IBM. He and his partner Rachel Brown began Empire five years ago and have built a profitable company with $45 million in annual revenues. Ed has the most day-to-day experience and working knowledge of the QuikMedInfo software. He has been responsible for all current sales and prospects.

Vice President of Sales - Nicholas DiMuzzio brings eight years of marketing experience to the healthcare area. Prior to becoming Vice President of Sales, he represented Redheart, a surgical supply vendor for acute care hospitals. DiMuzzio's experience also includes six years with American Health Buys where his duties included project engineering and contract negotiations with sales and marketing for their large buying groups.

Vice President of System Design - Monica Wren is one of the key developers of the product. She brings 13 years of programming, design, development, support, integration, implementation, and project management experience to the company. Prior to her career at Empire she worked in development for IBM, Richards Computer, and Mileage H. Research Corporation.

Vice President of Project Management - Henry Nerth is another key developer of the product. He brings 14 years of programming, design, development, support, integration, implementation, and project management experience to the company. Prior to his career at Empire he worked in development for Richards Computer and Mileage H. Research Corporation.

Application Developer - Ben Hogan has 11 years' experience in programming. His core talents lie in the area of application design and implementation in third-generation languages such as C, C++, and Java. Hogan also has experience in the management of large development projects, most recently the migration of a data warehousing application written in C to the IBM AS/400.

Management Team Gaps

There is a gap for a permanent CFO. It is expected that a temporary CFO will be utilized in year one and year two. A controller needs to be recruited, as well as additional sales people and administrative staff.

The company has its personnel needs well defined to handle expected growth.

Personnel Plan

Production Personnel	FY2000	FY2001	FY2002
Programmer (1)	$48,000	$50,000	$52,000
Programmer (2)	$0	$48,000	$50,000
Maintenance	$45,600	$47,500	$49,000
Maintenance (2-3)	$0	$91,200	$95,000
Maintenance (4)	$0	$0	$45,600
Consulting Person (1-2)	$136,400	$150,000	$155,000
Consulting Person (3-4)	$0	$150,000	$155,000
Consulting Person (5-6)	$0	$0	$150,000
V.P. Project Mgmt.	$74,400	$77,600	$80,000
Other	$0	$0	$0
Subtotal	$304,400	$614,300	$831,600

Sales and Marketing Personnel			
V.P. Sales	$72,000	$76,000	$80,000
Sales Mgr.	$60,000	$66,000	$72,000
V.P. Marketing	$96,000	$104,000	$108,000
Sales Person (1-2)	$64,000	$100,000	$108,000
Sales Person (3-4)	$0	$100,000	$108,000
Sales Administrator	$38,400	$40,000	$42,000
Regional Sales Mgrs. (1-4)	$0	$0	$288,000
Other	$0	$0	$0
Subtotal	$330,400	$486,000	$806,000

General and Administrative Personnel			
CEO	$159,996	$166,000	$172,000
COO	$60,000	$64,000	$68,000
Exec V.P.	$60,000	$64,000	$68,000
Sr. Exec. V.P.	$124,992	$130,000	$136,000
Temporary CFO	$40,000	$48,000	$0
Controller	$48,000	$50,000	$52,000
Permanent CFO	$0	$0	$136,000
Exec. Asst. (1-2)	$60,000	$64,000	$66,000
Exec. Asst. (3-4)	$0	$60,000	$64,000
Admin. Support (2)	$48,000	$50,000	$52,000

Personnel Plan

Continued

Other	$0	$0	$0
Subtotal	$600,988	$696,000	$814,000
Research & Development Personnel			
V.P. R&D	$64,000	$102,000	$108,000
V.P. System Design	$74,400	$77,600	$80,000
Application Eng.	$45,600	$47,500	$49,000
Development Person (1-2)	$129,600	$136,000	$140,000
Development Person (3-4)	$0	$130,000	$136,000
Development Person (5-6)	$0	$0	$133,000
Other	$0	$0	$0
Subtotal	$313,600	$493,100	$646,000
Total Headcount	**24**	**36**	**45**
Total Payroll	**$1,549,388**	**$2,289,400**	**$3,097,600**
Payroll Burden	**$340,865**	**$503,668**	**$681,472**
Total Payroll Expenditures	**$1,890,253**	**$2,793,068**	**$3,779,072**

FINANCIAL PLAN

It is expected that the initial $3 million investment will be sufficient for the first three years of this plan. Revenues should be sufficient to allow for a bank line to cover small shortfalls. Major ramp-up occurs in year four with a mezzanine capitalization of debt/equity combined with a $1.5 million bank line. Such a move could occur earlier if the situation permits. The nature of the software business is high margin and cash flow which also could permit growth without substantial equity dilution.

Important Assumptions

It is assumed that a bank line would be around 8% while a coupon on a mezzanine structure would be at 13% and could include warrants and/or an equity component. It is assumed that 90% of sales will be on credit via lease. If these are sold through a third party lessor, cash flow would accelerate. If QuikMedInfo should become its own lessor or offer access via the web, cash flow would spread more evenly.

For the purpose of this plan third-party leasing is the basis for projected revenues.

Other assumptions follow:

General Assumptions

	FY2000	FY2001	FY2002
Short-term Interest Rate %	8.00%	8.00%	8.00%
Long-term Interest Rate %	13.00%	13.00%	13.00%
Payment Days Estimator	30	30	30
Collection Days Estimator	45	45	45
Inventory Turnover	6	6	6

Estimator

Tax Rate %	34.00%	34.00%	34.00%
Expenses in Cash %	1.00%	1.00%	1.00%
Sales on Credit %	90.00%	90.00%	90.00%
Personnel Burden %	22.00%	22.00%	22.00%

Key Financial Indicators

The most significant indicator is our gross margin. These exceed 80%. Cost of product is primarily packaging, pressing disks, manuals, and potential customer discounts. As long as margins are maintained there will be substantial margin for error in other plan aspects.

Break-even Analysis

Monthly Units Break-even	1
Monthly Sales Break-even	$312,500

Assumptions:

Average Per-Unit Revenue	$250,000
Average Per-Unit Variable Cost	$50,000
Estimated Monthly Fixed Cost	$250,000

At year one levels of burn rate, included fixed overheads, and full salaries, the company can sustain operation with just more than one installation per month.

Projected Profit and Loss

The company turns profitable at 24 months.

Profit and Loss (Income Statement)

	FY2000	FY2001	FY2002
Sales	$3,022,500	$5,785,000	$12,935,000
Direct Cost of Sales	$441,750	$845,500	$1,592,000
Production Payroll	$304,400	$614,300	$831,600
Other	$0	$0	$0
Total Cost of Sales	**$746,150**	**$1,459,800**	**$2,423,600**
Gross Margin	$2,276,350	$4,325,200	$10,511,400
Gross Margin %	75.31%	74.77%	81.26%
Operating expenses:			
Sales and Marketing Expenses			
Sales and Marketing Payroll	$330,400	$486,000	$806,000
Advertising/Promotion	$232,000	$450,000	$660,000
Trade Shows	$60,000	$70,000	$80,000
Travel	$120,000	$144,000	$196,000
Miscellaneous	$48,000	$48,000	$48,000
Total Sales and Marketing Expenses	**$790,400**	**$1,198,000**	**$1,790,000**
Sales and Marketing %	26.15%	20.71%	13.84%
General and Administrative Expenses			
General and Administrative Payroll	$600,988	$696,000	$814,000
Payroll Burden	$340,865	$503,668	$681,472
Depreciation	$600,000	$600,000	$600,000
Leased Equipment	$36,000	$40,000	$46,000
Utilities & Phones	$26,400	$28,000	$36,000
Insurance	$18,000	$20,000	$22,000
Rent	$43,200	$48,000	$54,000
Total General and Administrative	**$1,665,453**	**$1,935,668**	**$2,253,472**
General and Administrative %	55.10%	33.46%	17.42%

**Profit and Loss
(Income Statement)**

Continued

Research & Development Expenses

Research & Development Payroll	$313,600	$493,100	$646,000
Product Development	$288,000	$488,000	$966,000
Legal & Accounting	$39,600	$42,500	$48,000
Contract/Consultants	$36,000	$48,000	$60,000
Total Research & Development Expenses	**$677,200**	**$1,071,600**	**$1,720,000**
Research & Development %	22.41%	18.52%	13.30%
Total Operating Expenses	**$3,133,053**	**$4,205,268**	**$5,763,472**
Profit Before Interest and Taxes	($856,703)	$119,932	$4,747,928
Interest Expense Short-term	$0	$0	$0
Interest Expense Long-term	$0	$0	$0
Taxes Incurred	($291,279)	$40,777	$1,614,296
Net Profit	($565,424)	$79,155	$3,133,632
Net Profit/Sales	-18.71%	1.37%	24.23%

Proforma Cash Flow

Projected Cash Flow

Cash flow remains positive with the only potential exposure in year two. At that point sales shortfalls could deplete working capital. However, cut-backs also would be possible to the break-even levels of year one if required.

	FY2000	FY2001	FY2002
Net Profit	($565,424)	$79,155	$3,133,632
Plus:			
Depreciation	$600,000	$600,000	$600,000
Change in Accounts Payable	$183,660	$81,541	$141,835
Current Borrowing (repayment)	$0	$0	$0
Increase (decrease) Other Liabilities	$0	$0	$0
Long-term Borrowing (repayment)	$0	$0	$0
Capital Input	$0	$0	$0
Subtotal	$218,236	$760,696	$3,875,467
Less:			
Change in Accounts Receivable	$526,500	$481,210	$1,245,484
Change in Inventory	$41,800	$159,535	$215,455
Change in Other Short-term Assets	$0	$0	$0
Capital Expenditure	$0	$0	$0
Dividends	$0	$0	$0
Subtotal	**$568,300**	**$640,744**	**$1,460,939**
Net Cash Flow	**($350,064)**	**$119,952**	**$2,414,528**
Cash Balance	**$704,936**	**$824,888**	**$3,239,416**

Owner's equity skyrockets in years three, four, and five.

Proforma Balance Sheet

Assets

Short-term Assets	Starting Balances	FY2000	FY2001	FY2002
Cash	$1,055,000	$704,936	$824,888	$3,239,416
Accounts Receivable	$0	$526,500	$1,007,710	$2,253,194
Inventory	$125,000	$166,800	$326,335	$541,790
Other Short-term Assets	$50,000	$50,000	$50,000	$50,000
Total Short-term Assets	$1,230,000	$1,448,236	$2,208,932	$6,084,400
Long-term Assets				
Capital Assets	$150,000	$150,000	$150,000	$150,000
Accumulated Depreciation	$0	$600,000	$1,200,000	$1,800,000
Total Long-term Assets	$150,000	($450,000)	($1,050,000)	($1,650,000)
Total Assets	**$1,380,000**	**$998,236**	**$1,158,932**	**$4,434,400**
Liabilities and Capital				
Accounts Payable	$0	$183,660	$265,201	$407,036
Short-term Notes	$0	$0	$0	$0
Other Short-term Liabilities	$0	$0	$0	$0
Subtotal Short-term Liabilities	$0	$183,660	$265,201	$407,036
Long-term Liabilities	$0	$0	$0	$0
Total Liabilities	**$0**	**$183,660**	**$265,201**	**$407,036**
Paid in Capital	$6,000,000	$6,000,000	$6,000,000	$6,000,000
Retained Earnings	($4,620,000)	($4,620,000)	($5,185,424)	($5,106,269)
Earnings	$0	($565,424)	$79,155	$3,133,632
Total Capital	**$1,380,000**	**$814,576**	**$893,731**	**$4,027,363**
Total Liabilities and Capital	**$1,380,000**	**$998,236**	**$1,158,932**	**$4,434,400**
Net Worth	**$1,380,000**	**$814,576**	**$893,731**	**$4,027,363**

Business Ratios

Return on equity potential certainly warrants early stage investment.

Ratio Analysis

Profitability Ratios:	FY2000	FY2001	FY2002	RMA
Gross Margin	75.31%	74.77%	81.26%	0
Net Profit Margin	-18.71%	1.37%	24.23%	0
Return on Assets	-56.64%	6.83%	70.67%	0
Return on Equity	-69.41%	8.86%	77.81%	0
Activity Ratios				
AR Turnover	5.17	5.17	5.17	0
Collection Days	35	54	51	0
Inventory Turnover	5.11	5.92	5.58	0
Accounts Payable Turnover	10.72	10.72	10.72	0
Total Asset Turnover	3.03	4.99	2.92	0
Debt Ratios				
Debt to Net Worth	0.23	0.3	0.1	0
Short-term Liab. to Liab.	1	1	1	0
Liquidity Ratios				
Current Ratio	7.89	8.33	14.95	0
Quick Ratio	6.98	7.1	13.62	0
Net Working Capital	$1,264,576	$1,943,731	$5,677,363	0
Interest Coverage	0	0	0	0
Additional Ratios				
Assets to Sales	0.33	0.2	0.34	0
Debt/Assets	18%	23%	9%	0
Current Debt/Total Assets	18%	23%	9%	0
Acid Test	4.11	3.3	8.08	0
Asset Turnover	3.03	4.99	2.92	0
Sales/Net Worth	3.71	6.47	3.21	0

Long-term Plan

There is significant potential for QuikMedInfo to become a dominant industry participant.

Long-term plan	FY2000	FY2001	FY2002	FY2003	FY2004
Sales	$3,022,500	$5,785,000	$12,935,000	$24,000,000	$42,000,000
Cost of Sales	$746,150	$1,459,800	$2,423,600	$4,000,000	$6,500,000
Gross Margin	$2,276,350	$4,325,200	$10,511,400	$20,000,000	$35,500,000
Gross Margin %	75.31%	74.77%	81.26%	83.33%	84.52%
Operating Expenses	$3,133,053	$4,205,268	$5,763,472	$8,200,000	$10,100,000
Operating Income	($856,703)	$119,932	$4,747,928	$11,800,000	$25,400,000
Net Income	($565,424)	$79,155	$3,133,632	$7,800,000	$19,400,000
Short-term Assets	$1,448,236	$2,208,932	$6,084,400	$14,300,000	$35,000,000
Long-term Assets	($450,000)	($1,050,000)	($1,650,000)	$450,000	$1,000,000
Short-term Liabilities	$183,660	$265,201	$407,036	$2,000,000	$1,500,000
Long-term Liabilities	$0	$0	$0	$5,000,000	$4,000,000
Equity	$814,576	$893,731	$4,027,363	$7,750,000	$30,500,000

Hotel Resort

BUSINESS PLAN

SEVEN ELMS RESORT

65000 Windy Lane Dr.
Traverse City, Michigan 49865

The Seven Elms Resort outlines how it will provide quality hospitality services, cost-effectively, in a popular northern U.S. lake resort environment. This plan successfully raised capital for property acquisition, renovation, and company start-up related costs.

- EXECUTIVE SUMMARY

- COMPANY SUMMARY

- HOTEL & LOUNGE OVERVIEW

- MARKET ANALYSIS

- COMPETITIVE ENVIRONMENT

- STRATEGY & IMPLEMENTATION

- PROMOTION STRATEGY

- FINANCIAL PLAN

- RESUME

EXECUTIVE SUMMARY

We seek funds for the acquisition and renovation of Seven Elms Resort, an adult-marketed, 17-room "boutique style" hotel specializing in a couples' "getaway" to provide relaxation and recreation in Benzie County, a popular tourism spot located next to the state of Michigan's Lake Michigan. Moderately priced between the high-line hotel properties and the older motel strips, Seven Elms Resort shall fill an affordability niche not presently available in Benzie County.

Combined with an on-site lounge, grill, poolside beverage service, and morning continental breakfast bar, we are seeking investment funds to renovate the hotel building, build-out a piano bar/lounge area with dance floor, and construct an outdoor pool adjacent to the indoor pool. With this refurbishment and other new amenities, Seven Elms Resort will form the basis of a highly profitable hotel venture. We are seeking funds to develop and expand the business in a phased approach, as highlighted within this document.

Seven Elms Resort's owner, Steve M. Blackburn, has an extensive business background, including over 14 years of experience developing a variety of businesses. Mr. Blackburn received his B.A. in Business Economics, and currently is an M.B.A. candidate at the University of Michigan. Desiring to return to his own business, he wishes to establish Seven Elms Resort, Inc. in 1999.

The foundation for the plan is a combination of primary and secondary research, upon which the marketing strategies are built. Discussions and interviews were held with a variety of individuals involved with other similar businesses to develop the proforma data, review the market potential, and competitive situation.

Renovation in the Prairie Style period, our hotel's design elements and furniture will reflect this "organic" approach and provide an overall comfortable experience. Seven Elms Resort shall specialize in meeting an individual or couple's needs. As growth warrants, the 10-acre site would allow for future expansion of the lodging portion of the resort (Phase II).

Business Plan Purpose

Introduction

In today's highly competitive environment, formal business planning is an essential element in achieving business success. A well-written business plan is primarily a communication tool used to obtain financing. In certain instances, particularly with our early stage company, this business plan also serves as a strategic plan.

Considering that lenders are inundated by numerous investment opportunities from which they choose only a few, this business plan describes our story and how we intend to grow. Seven Elms Resort, Inc. management team has made an in-depth analysis of its opportunities and weaknesses and it has concluded that the company has an excellent chance to succeed.

Methodology for Business Planning

Sophisticated business planning helps management answer questions, such as: What will be our record of achievement? How have we fared compared to our competitors? Are we setting realistic and attainable goals and objectives?

Constructive and useful business planning requires a broad-based understanding of changes taking place in the marketplace in which the company competes, or plans to compete, and the ever-changing financial markets. In-depth technical skills in a variety of disciplines such as financial analysis, sales and marketing, latest technology, and managing growth are critical components in assessing a company's opportunities and risks.

Developing the Business Plan

The management of Seven Elms Resort, Inc. has developed this disciplined planning methodology to help the company anticipate its start-up costs and other critical information to arrive at this realistic plan.

Guidance from Outside Professionals

Mr. Blackburn has sought legal assistance and advisors to develop the Seven Elms Resort concept. Steve will maintain an active management involvement in every aspect of daily resort operations. This plan reflects his vision.

1. Attract $1.4 million mortgage/investment capital;
2. Focus ideas and establish goals;
3. Identify and quantify objectives;
4. Track and direct growth;
5. Create benchmarks for measuring success.

Five Objectives of Seven Elms Resort, Inc.

The business of Seven Elms Resort, Inc. is the creation of and funding of an adult couples' 17-room hotel, specializing in a "getaway" atmosphere to provide relaxation and recreation in the Greater Benzie County/Lake Michigan area. Management is soliciting commercial finance partners who share its vision and desire to participate in this exciting business opportunity in the resort community of Benzie County, Michigan. The integration of these disciplines results in extensive and innovative services, set in a unique Prairie Style surrounding for our prospective guests.

Ideal Property Location

The preferred location is a 10-acre parcel with 8 acres of woods. Of the 18 rooms, 3 are executive suites, with Jacuzzi tubs, and one of them will be converted to an onsite manager's apartment. Each room has individual climate control, direct-dial phones, and televisions. The facility has a large main lobby area, indoor pool/Jacuzzi/sauna, lighted tennis court, 2-car garage, storage shed, ample parking, and all equipment necessary for operation of the motel. The separate onsite manager residence and meeting room complex will serve as a future lounge/grill space. The grounds are beautifully landscaped.

The motel is located in the motel district of Benzie County and is situated on 9.43 beautifully landscaped, wooded acres. Approximately 7 of the 9.43 acres are wooded and undeveloped, which creates an opportunity for significant expansion or potential for an entirely new enterprise.

This facility consists of one building, built in two phases: a 22- and 15-year-old two- and one-story wood frame 18-unit motel and manager's/owner's apartment, which when combined, total approximately 14,787 square feet of living area. The 18-unit motel includes a lobby with a fireplace, reception area, storage area, laundry room, bathroom, meeting rooms, a balcony, 18 room units, a men's and women's bathroom, kitchen, a whirlpool/sauna room, an indoor swimming pool, and mechanical room. The motel has a partial basement and includes a laundry room with two washers and two dryers.

The manager's apartment (future piano bar and basement bar/meeting room area) offers a living room, kitchen, dining area, family room, half bath, and gift shop on the first floor with 3 bedrooms and 2 baths on the second floor. The home has a concrete block basement that is partially finished with a recreation room and a 3/4 bathroom.

The exterior is cedar and the roof is pitch and pebble. The building is seated on a poured concrete and a concrete block foundation. Interior walls are concrete block and drywall. The flooring is carpet and ceramic tile. There are casement windows and wood storms and screens. There is a basement area under the living quarters and a portion of the motel.

Other improvements include a 2-car garage with 2 electric door openers. A detached storage shed is located to the rear of the manager's apartment. Land improvements include a blacktop driveway and parking lot with 23 parking spaces, concrete sidewalks, a lighted tennis court, street signage, and beautiful landscaping with a mature variety of trees and shrubs.

Mechanical systems include five gas hydropic, two gas forced air furnaces, electric baseboard heat, individual heat, and central air for each unit; 120-gallon hot water heater, 600-amp electrical service, intercom system, two central vacs, water softener, sump pump, 4-camera security system, cable television, smoke alarms, and telephone system.

Mission Statement

Seven Elms Resort, Inc.'s mission is to provide quality hospitality services to our guests in a comprehensive and cost competitive manner, providing the finest accommodations in Benzie County, Michigan.

Company Business Plan Objective

This business plan serves to detail the direction, vision, and planning to achieve our goal for providing superior and comprehensive hotel and lounge services. Our plan objectives are:

- Attract $200,000 bridge loan to secure $1.4 M property mortgage
- Focus ideas and establish goals
- Identify and quantify long-term expansion
- Track and direct growth
- Create benchmarks for measuring success

Seven Elms Resort shall fill a niche not presently available, namely a moderately priced (under $130 per night, summer rate) resort. Combined with an on-site lounge, a grilled food service, an indoor and outdoor pool bar, and a morning continental breakfast offering, we shall differentiate ourselves by becoming a "boutique style" resort versus simply another motel. With the construction of an outdoor pool adjacent to the present indoor pool/whirlpool/sauna complex and our other refurbishment and new amenities, Seven Elms Resort will form the basis of a highly profitable venture set in a Prairie Style environment.

COMPANY SUMMARY

Company Ownership

Mr. Steve Blackburn founded Seven Elms Resort, Inc. hotel and lounge in 1998 as a Michigan Subchapter "S" Corporation. Since 1985, Steve has had extensive experience in creating and managing organizations for environmental and economic development-oriented companies involved in nationwide projects.

Steve consults with area businesses in development-related issues, including finance, and is a United States SBA counselor at the Small Business Development Center at the University of Michigan. Past SBA clients include service and manufacturing organizations. He is a certified SBA FastTrack program instructor, a Michigan licensed loan solicitor, with a specialty in commercial finance, and a guest lecturer at U-M for Business Plan Writing Workshops. He has started previous business and corporate subsidiaries and looks forward to managing Seven Elms Resort on a daily basis.

Currently, Steve is an M.B.A. candidate at U-M and holds a Bachelor of Arts degree in Business Economics with a minor in chemistry from Notre Dame University.

Key Advisors to the Company

Seven Elms Resort, Inc. has additional key staff members and advisors to assist during the development, planning, and initial planning phases. They include an architect trained at the University of Notre Dame, CPAs, and former managers of bar and Bed and Breakfast style properties.

Mr. Steve Blackburn will manage all aspects of the business and service development to ensure effective customer responsiveness. Qualified resort associate professionals will provide additional support services. Support staff will be added as guest and/or patron load factors mandate. Blackburn has joined the American Hotel and Motel Association.

Management & Organizational Summary

For purposes of this Business Plan document, Seven Elms Resort, Inc.—Phase I and Phase II for developmental growth are defined below:

Corporate Development Plan

Phase I

This phase involves preparation and development of Seven Elms Resort. Until the ideal property is acquired, Seven Elms Resort, Inc. offices will be housed at the home of Mr. Steve Blackburn, its founder. The property will establish its own Prairie Style identity, management directives, and capital. Incorporating a total quality management approach and a guest appreciation program, Seven Elms Resort will develop key repeat guests and lounge patrons. Through word of mouth and advertising, our reputation as an affordable "boutique style" resort shall grow.

Property renovation will include the makeover of 18 to 17 rooms (with 3 suites) and the conversion of the present onsite property manager's house to lounge gathering space. New construction includes a bar room addition, extra parking lot build-out, and an outdoor pool. [Phase I capital (start-up) funds are documented later on in this business plan.] It is anticipated that the funding and transfer of this property will happen in spring 1999. Operation "as is" of the facility would continue through the summer and fall. The hotel will close for the winter months for its build-out and renovation.

Phase II

Continue implementation of sales, advertising, and marketing strategies developed in Phase I. Identify and pursue additional guest markets, i.e. Internet room guarantee services. Seven Elms Resort shall evaluate its room occupancy position to determine if a facility expansion is warranted. Seven Elms Resort anticipates additional support staff would be needed at the proper time (Phase II). This Plan does not contain funding needs for this Phase.

HOTEL & LOUNGE OVERVIEW

Establishing a hotel and lounge business clientele will take some time, as the research revealed word-of-mouth /recommendations /referrals and value as the primary way in which hotel and lounge services are selected by new guests. People who are completely new to the area, or who have few established connections, may look to the Yellow Pages or other advertising to establish available services, then call for information or pricing.

A good portion of the past guests to the property will no longer return, as the present ownership has operated the property as a Christian retreat-style motel.

Competitive Advantage

Strengths of Seven Elms Resort, Inc. include Steve Blackburn's broad base of experience in managing different types of companies. He has extensive development experience and a track record of hiring the right people and training them. Blackburn understands the service sector business, has traveled extensively frequenting numerous lodging establishments, and has gained invaluable experience in organizational management.

Currently, a mid-size "boutique" resort niche is vacant in the Lake Michigan market, with present lodging on the high end, averaging $225 per night (and up) down to older motel properties of $79 per night. Several B&B establishments may fall into the middle, however, Seven Elms, as a resort-style property, will serve its niche by itself.

Industry Keys to Success

1. A property designed for the guest and/or lounge patron
2. Frequent Guest Award Program
3. Controlled overhead and operational costs
4. Regular and ongoing guest feedback
5. Latest technology/software capacity
6. Weekend lounge (piano bar, dance floor) entertainment
7. Unique, timeless and comfortable environment
8. Dedicated management and associate support staff

MARKET ANALYSIS

Seven Elms Resort, Inc. like all businesses, is affected by forces and trends in the market environment. These include economic, geographical, competitive, legal/political, and technical.

Economic Environment

Positive forces include the generally prosperous economy that is currently in place, full employment, rising wages, and low inflation, leading more people to be able and willing to spend money and to get away for some time. The close locality of Lake Michigan offers an affordable alternative to a flyaway destination.

Geographical/Competitive Environment

Located just two blocks from Lake Michigan and downtown Lakegrove, the area has several golf courses, two ski hills, water recreation activities, numerous dining establishments, various retail and specialty shops, art galleries, theatre entertainment venues, and the beauty and serenity of Lake Michigan, which has made this county a famous Midwest tourist destination. Traverse City began to prosper in the 1870s, becoming a desirable resort area. Many homes and estates date back to this era and several enormous "summer cottages" were built on the lakeshore and are still in evidence today.

Seven Elms Resort shall fill a niche not presently available, namely a moderately priced (under $130 per night), resort-type establishment. Combined with an on-site lounge, a grilled food service, an indoor and outdoor pool bar, and a morning continental breakfast offering, we shall differentiate ourselves by becoming a "boutique style" resort versus simply another motel.

Our Prairie Style surroundings will attract and retain guests who appreciate such refined environments.

Legal/Political Environment

Seven Elms Resort management will not move the project forward until it has obtained an option to acquire one of the 19 Benzie County, Michigan, liquor licenses. As faced by all businesses, the proper insurance needs shall be met and all operations and policy manuals shall be reviewed by appropriate legal experts. The facility will obtain all the necessary building permits prior to construction. Present facility zoning allows for this proposed use, including a bar, cabaret, grill, and dance floor space.

Technology Environment

Computer programs greatly simplify the financial recordkeeping for today's businesses. As a small business, Seven Elms Resort will need to watch its expenses closely. By utilizing the existing software packages available in the hotel industry, including: room and facility management database, controlled bar and inventory measuring systems, and room key cards that allow patrons to charge directly to their room account, this technology shall assist management in controlling costs, reducing cash management, and maximizing revenue. Seven Elms Resort shall attract the resources necessary to train and operate the system in order to generate the reports and manage the inventory.

A listing of the hotel and motel properties in Benzie County, Michigan (sourced through Midwest and the Ameritech Directories) is as follows. (Note: Other properties on Lake Michigan, but outside the city limits, are not included):

COMPETITIVE ENVIRONMENT

High Line ($139-$750 per night, depending upon season)
The Cove of Lake Michigan ($145-$225)
Grand Michigan Resort and Spa ($139-$750)
The Harbor's Edge ($139-$199)
The Michigan Inn ($215-$350)
The Strike Hotel ($200)

Motel ($59-$119 per night, depending upon season)
Breezy Chateau Inn
Budget Time Motel
Lake Michigan Motel
Lakewood Motel
Misty Motel
Pine Tar Motel
Plaza Motel
Shady Drive Motel
The Stirrup Motel
Swiss Motel

Bed & Breakfast (B&B)
Dahlia House
The Mixer House
Precious Times Inn

Hotel and motel properties in adjacent communities are not listed, however, they do advertise in the Yellow Pages.

Seven Elms Resort hotel and lounge is attempting to carve out a fourth segment in the lodging market; that of a "boutique" style, high-line property at mid-line pricing geared towards adult couples and not marketed to families.

A review of competitors' marketing strategies reveals no one targeting this market segment. Hotel and lounge is a referral-driven business—new business can be obtained by encouraging and rewarding present guests to refer future guests. Networking within business and civic groups is important; even if the business results are not immediately felt, it is an excellent public relations opportunity. Live piano, or jazz style trio, on the weekends will add excitement to the resort and draw community residents and guests from other properties.

Market Research

A hypothetical behavior sequence model for a new customer (future guest) contemplating using a hotel and lounge service for the first time might look something like the following (based on discussions and interviews with potential guests):

Individual or couple decided to getaway for a few days. This may happen as a result of a need for a change of pace, vacation, or a celebration purpose. The need can arise anytime year round. Even in the late fall and winter months people are thinking "getaway" to break the weather doldrums.

Individual or couple investigates hotel services. In most cases, this means the they will consider first any recommendations that they are knowledgeable of through prior association (relative, friend, or social group). If the individual or couple is new to the area or otherwise has not made any close connections with people, he/she would look in the Yellow Pages for a listing, or perhaps look in a newspaper for advertising.

Acting on the advice of friends (or own knowledge), the individual or couple will call the recommended property to obtain information that will help him/her decide if this place is the best for them. Criteria for selection include: (1) amenities (pool, on-site food service, non-smoking rooms, bar lounge area, etc.); (2) reputation (what kind of persons usually stay here?); (3) physical plant (how recent the renovation, upkeep, etc?); (4) courtesy (professional and attentive staff?); and (5) pricing (is the place affordable?).

Based on the information received, the individual or couple makes a decision and either schedules an appointment to view the property or makes a reservation.

The individual's satisfaction with his/her decision and with the service itself is largely a function of their interaction with the staff during their stay. Everyone associated with Seven Elms Resort will do everything possible to ensure a satisfactory experience for the guest, so that future business (and a future referral) is not at risk.

Marketing strategies will build on this model, taking advantage of precipitating events, fostering word-of-mouth recommendations, and creating satisfaction through interacting with the future or present guests.

Summary of Opportunities and Threats in the Environment

Overall, the environment appears very positive for Seven Elms Resort, Inc. The forces driving market demand, mainly economic and geographical, are strong, with more people staying closer to home for shorter getaway trips and their comfort level of visiting Lake Michigan, one of the Midwest's premiere travel destinations. On the negative side, there is competition, and it will take a while for Seven Elms Resort to get "established" in its market niche.

STRATEGY & IMPLEMENTATION

The business is driven by referrals and repeat business, so for the first few years Seven Elms Resort will need to be aggressive in attracting new guests. The marketing strategy is subject to change upon guest feedback and surveys.

Marketing Strategies

Target Markets—Geographical: The major cities within a three-hour drive of the property.

Target Markets - Consumer:
- New visitors traveling to the area
- Middle- and upper-income bracket
- Returning visitors to the area
- Businesses needing to hold small overnight planning and strategy sessions
- Area wedding parties
- Couples

Positioning and Product Strategy

For its guests, Seven Elms Resort will be positioned as a new, beautifully landscaped, nature-filled, unique atmosphere hotel with a bar lounge service that fits an adult "getaway" market niche. A full range of referral services (i.e. restaurant recommendations, shopping, taxis, area attractions) will be made available and tailored to the needs of the particular guest.

Business services range from room phones that are Internet jack ready and telephone answering message service for each room to on-site fax services and meeting room space (lounge sitting area and cabaret room). Seven Elms Resort will aim to attract business guests and their partners needing to hold planning or strategy sessions away from the office in a new and comfortable surrounding, in order to even out revenues throughout the week.

Distribution Strategy

Unlike products that are produced, then distributed, and sold, hotel and lounge services are produced and consumed simultaneously in a real-time environment. Thus, distribution issues center on making the services available in a convenient manner to the greatest number of potential guests. Seven Elms Resort will maintain a front office staff member throughout the night so guests are able to get answers to any question or service when they need it. This flexibility is especially attractive to the business traveler. Clients will be able to contact Seven Elms Resort by telephone, fax, and e-mail.

Pricing Strategy

Rooms per night fees have been developed. The fee schedule takes into account seasonal rates that are common in the area. For businesses and other large group functions, pricing can be discounted depending upon the number of rooms reserved.

Example lounge pricing and grill food offerings are also noted.

Example fees:

Room Fees

Winter Rates (November through April):

Regular Rooms	$109.00
Suites	$149.00

Summer Rates (May through October):

Regular Rooms	$129.00
Suites	$179.00

(Includes Continental Breakfast, use of indoor and outdoor pools, and exercise equipment room.)

Fax Service (per page, outgoing)	$0.75
Telephone Rates (set at going company rate)	
Hotel Safe Storage Fee (per day)	$2.50

Liquor and Drink Fees

"Top Shelf" Brands	$4.75 - $7.50
Specialty Drinks	$4.50 - $5.75
Well Drinks	$4.25
Import Beers & Wine	$3.75
Domestic Beers	$3.25
Draft Beer	$2.75
Juices, Bottled Water, and Soft Drinks	$2.50

Grill Menu

Rib-Eye Steak Sandwich	$7.99
Chicken Breast Sandwich	$5.99
Hamburger (1/4 pound)	$5.99
Fried Cod Fish Sandwich	$5.99
Salads	$4.99 - $8.99
Chicken Tenders	$4.99 - $6.99
Cheese Sticks (with sauce)	$4.99
Frozen Pizza	$6.99 - $8.99

(Sandwiches include fries, onion rings or chips.)

Service and Support Philosophy

By giving careful consideration to customer responsiveness, Seven Elms Resort's goal will be to meet and exceed every service expectation of its hotel and lounge services. Our guests can expect quality service and a total quality management (TQM) philosophy throughout all levels of the staff.

PROMOTION STRATEGY

Promotion strategies will vary depending on the target market segments. Given the importance of word-of-mouth referrals among all market segments when choosing a "getaway" hotel or small business meeting location, our efforts are designed to create awareness and build referrals. A cost-effective campaign—focused on direct marketing, publicity, our frequent guest reward program, and advertising—is being proposed.

Marketing Plan

New Business Segment

A direct marketing (direct mail) package consisting of a tri-fold brochure, letter of introduction, and reply card will be sent to a list of potential guests. This list can be obtained from International Business Lists, Inc. (Chicago, IL) and is compiled from tax records (by upper-income geographical areas, Secretary of State incorporation registrations, business license applications, and announcements from newspaper clippings).

The brochure and letter introduces Seven Elms Resort, stresses the importance of having a good time in comfortable surroundings, provides information on our resort services, and describes what sets us apart from other area hotel and lounge properties. The initial mailing may contain a promotional offer: the opportunity to receive a 10% discount on the first night's room rate.

Approximately two months after the mailing, an additional letter shall be sent. The potential guest would be asked to address any questions and the follow-up would remind them to drop in for a property tour on their next trip to Lake Michigan. Additionally, new businesses will be targeted and sent information.

The cycle would repeat itself with new target communities and select businesses and would continue through the first year. After that, additional mailings would be conducted, as needed, based upon occupancy goals.

Seven Elms Resort, Inc. will also consider developing a one-page newsletter to be mailed quarterly to past guests and prospects in the database. The newsletter can be used to update clients on hotel and lounge and area-related developments, but also serves as a reminder of what sets Seven Elms Resort apart. The newsletter can be produced in-house and for the cost of paper and a stamp creates a lot of goodwill among guests and business prospects.

Publicity and Public Relations

A news release will be sent to area newspapers and magazines announcing the launch of Seven Elms Resort, Inc. and lounge. Area talent searches will be conducted to secure weekend cabaret room entertainment.

Steve Blackburn will join the Benzie County Chamber of Commerce as a means of networking in the community. He also may make himself available for speaking engagements at other community or civic organizations as a low-cost way of increasing awareness and building goodwill in the community.

Guest Reward Programs

For present guests: "Stay 6 nights and get the seventh night for free" promotion and as a means of building business by word-of-mouth, present customers should be encouraged and rewarded for referring future guests. This can be accomplished by offering a small "rebate" (5% or 10% rebate on first night stay) to current customers who successfully refer a new guest.

Advertising

Advertising is utilized primarily to attract new guests and serves to build awareness and name recognition of the resort in general, which is important for word-of-mouth referrals ("Oh yes, I've seen that resort's ads before.")

- Periodic advertising in target market area newspapers will afford Seven Elms Resort, Inc. name recognition benefits. From quarter page ads announcing its entertainment line-up to business card-sized logo ads.
- Yellow Pages—Ameritech PagesPlus, Greater Benzie County Telephone Directory. Research indicated that new visitors or people who don't have many personal acquaintances to ask about hotel and lounge services will look to the Yellow Pages to establish a list of potential hotel and lounge services to call. Even a small 2" x 2" boxed ad can create awareness and attract the desired target client, above and beyond the ability of a simple listing. Ameritech Yellow Pages covers the relevant market area, delivering over 30,000 copies to residents and business. Midwest Directories covers Greater Benzie County but is considered a second-tier directory to Ameritech.
- Telephone Book Cover. A business card-like ad on the plastic cover which is placed over any telephone book enables the business name/logo to be seen virtually 24 hours a day, 365 days a year. Covers are distributed bi-annually free of charge to residents and businesses in Benzie County.
- Restaurant Placemats—Opportunities exist for a business card-like ad to be placed on the paper placemats used in area restaurants (shelf-life of the ad is about six months), or for special (holiday) events taking place at a restaurant (1-off opportunities). An

example would be getting on the area restaurant placemats (about 9,000 in six months), or getting on the special Lions Club "St. Patrick's Day" dinner placemats at the Village Restaurant (about 1,000 placemats for that event). Placemat advertising will reach area residents as well as area visitors/tourists staying at other places.

- Additional places to post flyers/business cards or for a business card ad include bulletin boards in public buildings (grocery stores, senior centers), and playbills for local theater groups.

Example Promotion Budget - 1999 (Amounts Included in Start-Up Funds)

Resort brochure	$750
(2-color, 1,000 quantity, high quality paper)	
Reply card	$250
(2-color, 500 quantity, card stock)	
Lists *(new businesses, home-based businesses)*	$750
Postage *(mailing 450 pieces)*	$500
Restaurant placemats *(5 restaurants/10 events)*	$500
Newspaper advertising	$5,000
Yellow Pages	$2,000
Advertising specialties *(give-away)*	$250
Total for 1999	**$10,000**

Evaluation & Control Strategies

Objectives have been established for Seven Elms Resort so that actual performance can be measured. Thus, at the end of its first year, Seven Elms Resort should have:

- $772,000 in total revenue
- Anticipate 57% occupancy rating

Each subsequent year new objectives will be set for these benchmarks and actual performance will be measured against them. If actual performance falls short of objectives, investigation will be made into the cause, and plans will be adjusted accordingly.

In addition, it is recommended that Seven Elms Resort keep track of the source of all new guests ("Where did you hear of us?") in order to measure the effectiveness of each type of promotion. Each subsequent year's budget should adjust spending toward the types of promotion that reach the most new clients.

Customer satisfaction is most directly reflected in the year-to-year customer retention percentage. All lost customers should be investigated to find out why they left. A customer satisfaction survey may be considered after three to four years in the business.

FINANCIAL PLAN

Here is the Project Funding Summary for Seven Elms Resort:

Project Funding Summary

Building and Improvements Cost	$881,000
Fixtures, Build-Out and Furniture	$353,739
Developmental Start-Up Expense	$116,000
Five Months Working Capital	$49,261
Total	**$1,400,000**

Developmental costs for the start-up of this new hotel and lounge services company are listed above. These schedules also listed in the Ten Year Proforma.

The following schedule highlights the anticipated developmental costs:

Classification: Cost

Liquor License	$71,000
Architect Fees	$7,500
Accounting	$1,500
Marketing, PR & Advertising	$10,000
Engineering & Permitting	$5,000
Office Expense	$2,000
Founders Draw (Gen. Contractor)	$16,000
Legal	$3,000
Total	**$116,000**

The development of Seven Elms Resort, Inc. will require the full-time talents of Steve Blackburn. Phase II growth amounts will be developed and sought at a later date, based upon needs to be determined at that time.

The following assumptions will be incorporated into Seven Elms Resort, Inc. proforma statements.

- All operating costs are based on Seven Elms Resort, Inc. management research of similar operating companies.
- Automated informational and bar control systems will reduce Seven Elms Resort, Inc. staff requirements.
- Developmental start-up costs are amortized over a five-year period.
- Room Occupancy Rate at 57%, G & A overhead and operations costs are calculated on an annual basis.
- Property manager and founder's salary is based on a fixed salary expense basis.
- All fixed and variable labor costs should rise annually at 2.5% per year.
- All revenues are figured to rise annually at five percent. Fixed annual, administrative, and office expenses rise at an annual rate of one half of one percent.

This is the resume of Steve Blackburn, the future owner of Seven Elms Resort Steve Blackburn has demonstrated experience in business and sales organization development. Developed and secured funding for own organization, author of several successful RFPs, business and market development plans. Has expertise in customer retention programs, sales training seminars, project planning, benchmark analysis, and forecasting and budgeting. Designed and implemented computer applications including: customer database service frequency schedules, truck routing, customer retention surveys, accounting and commission salary programs.

EMPLOYMENT HISTORY

University of Michigan, Ann Arbor, Michigan
Small Business Development Center
1996-present
As a United States SBA counselor I assist clients in sales and business development and other related matters including: Sales, Marketing, Manufacturing and Productivity Analysis, Regulations Compliance, and Regulatory Program Development.

MRT Environmental, Inc., Cleveland, Ohio
1992-1995
Co-founder, Business Development, Marketing, and Sales. A consulting and facilities development organization for environmental services clients in the health care industry. My responsibilities included: development of project opportunities and clients, sales personnel and training, advertising and promotion, and financial record keeping.

Pride & Barrow Industries, Inc., Dallas, Texas
1985-1992
Vice President - Sales and Development. $80 million subsidiary of a $3 billion public company. Created the new medical services division; integrated third year revenues exceeded $4.5 million and employed over 25 employees. Market development and direct sales management for all regional special services subsidiaries. Developed region's first comprehensive medical waste service organization by identifying and marketing to the healthcare industry an emerging service bundle of packaging, transportation, in-service training, and treatment of medical wastes. Serviced all sectors of the healthcare industry from physician offices through major medical centers.

Market Development Representative and Environmental Specialist. Analyzed new business development opportunities in all service areas. Municipal waste contracts, waste company acquisitions, landfill development, and expansions and ancillary specialty services. Responsible for training, sales functions, regulatory data submittal, and special waste stream permitting. Created computer applications and processing systems to maximize efficiency and minimize errors.

Education

University of Michigan, 1998, M.B.A. candidate.

Notre Dame University - Graduated 1985. B.A. in Business Accounting and Economics. Completed a course of study for a B.S. in Chemistry.

Limited Liability Company

BUSINESS PLAN   NORTHERN INVESTMENTS, LLC

3500 North Plaza Dr.
Portland, Oregon 97204

Northern Investments is a forward-thinking limited liability company that is planning to expand its financial services to a specialized audience—Cultural Creatives. Using the values of this selected group, Northern Investments will build Networks that will focus on socially aware, environmentally responsible, and values-driven investors.

- COMPANY HISTORY

- MANAGEMENT & STAFF

- THE MARKET FOR SOCIALLY RESPONSIBLE INVESTMENTS

- MARKETING AND SALES STRATEGY

- DISTRIBUTION

- COMPETITION

- PRODUCTS AND SERVICES

- INVESTMENT COMMITTEE

- ADVISORY BOARD

- REVENUES

- MISSION

- FUNDAMENTAL GUIDING BELIEFS

- A CORPORATE CULTURE OF RESPECT

- SHARED OWNERSHIP - EXPAND DISTRIBUTION

- KEY PEOPLE

**COMPANY
HISTORY**

Northern Investments, LLC is an Oregon limited liability company that on June 30, 1999 acquired the name, the investment advisory business, and certain other assets of Northern Investments, formerly a division of Plum Tree Advisors.

Northern has been a significant national provider of financial services through investment professionals and a leading voice for the concept of socially responsible investing since 1988. In January 1990, Northern Investments became a branch of Plum Tree Securities, Inc., Member NASD & SIPC. In 1992, the company began developing fee-based investment advisory services to augment its traditional brokerage business. In May 1995, Northern Investments's brokerage and investment advisory businesses were acquired and became a wholly owned subsidiary of Plum Tree. With the purchase transaction completed on June 30, 1999, Northern is once again an independent, owner-managed financial services firm.

Northern is an investment advisory firm registered with the SEC (Securities and Exchange Commission) based in Portland, Oregon. At present, Northern Investments has 52 licensed representatives with offices in 20 states and clients in 46 states. All representatives focus their business in the area of socially and environmentally responsible investing.

Northern Investments currently manages or administers approximately $175,000 in fee-based assets for these representatives. In addition, the company will continue to receive a supervisory override on revenues generated by the brokerage business (roughly $300,000,000) that these representatives have placed with Plum Tree Securities for about six months as the necessary transitions are completed. The revenues from this part of the "old" Northern Investments, as well as all related operations, potential liabilities, and compliance requirements, will be fully Plum Tree's responsibility by December 31, 1999.

All representatives of Northern Investments are independent contractors and business owners in their own right. All are currently associated with Plum Tree Securities and registered with the NASD (National Association of Securities Dealers). Depending on each individual's business strategy, s/he may choose to remain with Plum Tree, to move their brokerage strategy to another broker-dealer firm, and/or to drop their NASD registration entirely. Management strongly believes and expects that these representatives will remain associated with Northern Investments in the conduct of their fee-based advisory business.

Since developing fee-based advisory services in 1992, Northern Investments's Registered Investment Advisor (RIA) business has grown dramatically. The company is focusing the vast majority of future product and service development on meeting the needs of investment professionals who choose to work with clients in a fee-based advisory relationship. Management believes this is where Northern Investments can add significant value, providing needed investment programs and information services designed to help representatives grow their business by tapping into and serving socially aware/values oriented investors.

Management believes this market is large and largely untapped. Most investors who fit the profile of socially aware/concerned individuals, and who are currently working with a professional advisor, are being rather poorly served. The "new" Northern Investments is being designed to facilitate this process—to provide investment professionals with the information, products, services, and tools to dramatically improve service to this market. It is believed that this market will be best served by advisors who focus on managing the relationship they have with these clients, and handing off most money management responsibilities to others.

Northern Investments is led by a senior management team with substantial prior experience in the securities, financial services, and social investment industry.

John Craig CFP is Chief Executive Officer and Manager of Northern Investments, LLC. He has managed the operations of the company and its predecessor entitles since 1989. He has served on the board of directors of the Social Investment Forum for seven years.

Walter Smith is President, Chief Marketing Officer and Manager of Northern Investments, LLC. For over a decade he has been a nationally recognized authority, consultant, and resource to the social investment industry. He serves as Chair and President of the Social Investment Forum and as Co-Chair of the Oregon Network of Businesses for Social Responsibility.

Jennifer Frame is Vice President and Director of Operations for Northern Investments, LLC. She has twelve years of experience in the financial services/securities industry, having worked for Northern Investments since 1990.

Wendell Letterman CFP is co-designer and primary manager of the Efficiencies program and serves on Northern Investments's Investment Committee. He is a 20-year veteran of the financial services industry, having spent the majority of his career focused on the field of retirement planning.

Robert Sloan is Director of Research, primary manager of the FairWays program and serves on Northern Investments's Investment Committee. Currently CFA level II candidate, he is an affiliate member of both the Denver Society of Security Analysts and the Association for Investment Management and Research (AIMR).

Susan Williams is Director of Nonprofit Support Services for Northern Investments. Her intimate involvement with various nonprofit organizations spans a 15-year period. Her service has run the full spectrum of participation, from hands-on volunteering, to leadership positions such as board presidencies and executive directorships.

Many independent studies in recent years have established that between 20 and 30 percent of adult Americans exhibit the characteristics of being "social responsibility oriented," "socially aware," or "values-based" investors. The most pointed and detailed of these studies is entitled *The Integral Culture Survey: A Study of the Emergence of Transformational Values in America.* This decade-long research effort found that nearly one in four American adults lives by a "new" set of values. They are affluent, well educated, and on the cutting edge of social change.

As predicted by futurists Alvin Toffler, John Naisbitt, and Marilyn Ferguson in the early 1980s, study author and sociologist Gerald Jones has identified an emerging culture whose adherents tend to be more altruistic and powerfully attuned to global issues and whole systems. They are relationship oriented, interested in spirituality and ecological sustainability, and actively involved in their local communities. Jones calls the 24 percent of Americans who hold this emerging world view "Cultural Creatives." Traditional age-specific demographic categories such as "Baby Boomer" or "Generation X" do not apply. Cultural Creatives are found in all age groups. In fact, the only strikingly significant conventional demographic that distinguishes them is that six in ten are women.

Cultural Creatives tend to believe that few other people share their values. While they are avid readers and gatherers of news and information, little of what Cultural Creatives read provides evidence of their huge numbers and growing clout. This is partly because the views of these 44 million adult Americans are rarely represented in the conventional media. The press is substantially owned and operated according to a very different world view - that of the Modernists, according to Jones. For the most part, Modernists also own and/or control the financial services industry in the United States. As a result, sensitivity to the goals, needs, and aspirations of investors with a Cultural Creative world view is seriously lacking.

Jones's Cultural Creatives match the profile of American social investors almost perfectly. Indeed, over the past two decades, social investing in the U.S. has evolved into a $1.2 trillion industry (1997 Report on Responsible Investing in the United States, Social Investment Forum). To tens of thousands of socially aware investors, the term "investing for the future" has a double meaning, and their investment approach often has a dual objective. The investment analysis process they employ is both quantitative and qualitative. The "double bottom line" approach they employ aims at competitive returns while seeking to put money to work in ways which are consistent with their personal, oral, and ethical values. They are most satisfied with investment programs that go beyond purely financial goals to address their need to "make a difference." They are most comfortable with investments that align with their highest aspirations for the world they see themselves passing on to future generations.

Contrary to what some might believe, Jones's study has underscored the fact that Cultural Creatives have incomes and investment resources comparable, on average, to the "mainstream" market targeted by most conventional financial services organizations. And yet this is a market that most investment professionals ignore, or try to serve in traditional ways that simply don't fit the needs and/or styles of investors with a Cultural Creative world view.

MARKETING AND SALES STRATEGY

Serving the more progressive investor market of Cultural Creatives with traditional financial products is difficult and often uncomfortable. This discomfort is felt by both investors and their professional advisors, as well as by conventional investment product providers. Understanding how to help them meet their special needs is a challenge for financial professionals. Cultural Creatives' penchant for relationships and community, their desire to know and feel good about where a product comes from, how it was designed, and who the company is behind the product, makes them a very different market for financial services.

Exciting business opportunities for Northern lie in providing social investment products and services delivered in ways that resonate with the mostly untapped market of Cultural Creatives in the United States. The company intends to develop win-win relationships with 20-30 broker/dealer firms within the first 18 months of operations by offering an attractive package of unique services focused on the socially aware investor. The Company will focus on serving Cultural Creatives nationwide primarily through the investment practitioners scattered across the country who know this market. This strategy will effectively leverage our resources and create new distribution capabilities through hundreds of professionals who work directly with thousands of individual and institutional clients fitting the profile of socially aware/Cultural Creative investors.

Northern Investments, as its name suggests, is building a Network of investment professionals who have a need for information, products, and fee-based investment services unavailable through their current broker/dealer relationships. The attraction will be a well capitalized firm whose leadership, vision, mission, culture, commitment, and services are focused on socially aware, environmentally responsible, values-driven investors. The Network will be connected through e-mail and Internet services, through conferences and educational gatherings, and through dynamic personal relationships that will develop between Network members over time. Management envisions growing its Network of representatives from 50 to over 200 in the first 18 months of operations.

The Company is building a marketing and sales capability to promote the concept of socially responsible investing, as well as provide information, education and fee-based products and services to investment advisors nationwide. Northern Investments will develop both "push" and "pull" strategies, aimed at growing the social investment industry and the businesses of investment professionals who join the Network.

DISTRIBUTION

Initially, the primary distribution of Northern Investments products and services is expected to be through the existing group of Northern representatives. While the company will cease to receive revenues generated by the brokerage activities of these representatives at the end of 1999, management expects the current trends toward greater reliance on fee-based, rather than commission-based client relationships to continue to grow.

The next key distribution group for the company's services is another existing but larger group of investment professionals who are actively working in the social investment marketplace. All of these representatives are associated with other broker-dealer firms (outside of Plum Tree). Most of them do not have access to either the breadth of quality of social investment services and programs offered by Northern Investments. Many of these representatives have exposure to the company through participation in the annual *SRI in Portland* conference. Management estimates that this group numbers about 250 practitioners, associated with 20 to 30 broker-dealer firms. The company will quickly focus its attention on signing selling agreements with these firms. Management expects to add approximately 20 new representatives to its Network within 18 months.

Longer term, the company will work to sign additional selling agreements and to position itself as the preferred provider of socially responsible portfolio management and related services. These efforts will be focused on broker-dealer firms and investment professionals who are relatively unfamiliar with the social investment field and whose clients may, on occasion, ask for or be appropriate for Northern Investments's services.

COMPETITION

Although there is substantial competition within the overall securities industry, competition between financial services firms and among investment professionals within the socially responsible investment field is virtually nonexistent. Approximately 250 brokers and financial planners nationwide focus on serving socially aware investors as their primary business, and 20 percent of them are already associated with Northern. Most of the rest are familiar with Northern Investments, but have not done business with the company to date because they have elected to maintain their existing broker-dealer relationships.

Northern Investments's new business model, as an independent investment advisory firm, will allow representatives who currently serve, or seek to serve, socially aware/Cultural Creative investors to work with the company without changing their existing broker-dealer relationships. Management believes that hundreds of additional representatives work with Cultural Creative investors. However, the vast majority of these professionals have neither access to the types of services which will be offered by Northern nor the support of an organization focused on helping products and services designed to serve the needs of socially aware/Cultural Creative investors to hundreds of additional brokers, planners, and advisors through selling agreements with their parent broker-dealer firms. This was not possible while Northern Investments was part of Plum Tree, a competitor.

The target market for socially responsible investment products and services has only recently been identified and defined and most conventional competitors within the financial services industry are unaware of it, or have no affinity for it. The historic slow growth of socially responsive investment alternatives is, in management's opinion, most directly attributable to conventional competition's indifference or even skepticism toward the concept. There is only one other broker-dealer firm, outside of Plum Tree Securities, that has made a significant commitment to this market, and it is expected this firm will be one of the first to sign a selling agreement with Northern Investments. There are virtually no managed investment products that utilize socially screened mutual funds or SRI capable money managers. There is no other central research or resource for SRI practitioners, other than the nonprofit Social Investment Forum. Various major firms, most notably, Salomon Smith Barney, have made minor moves into the SRI marketplace. To date, however, no major firm has achieved results that are material to their overall business.

Management strongly believes that there is a major opportunity to deliver Northern Investments's services to its target market through investment professionals affiliated with dozens, even hundreds of broker-dealer firms throughout the U.S. with little or no competition. In fact, the company's business model capitalizes on the belief that more competitors can be expected to consider contracting for Northern Investments's services rather than developing their own.

PRODUCTS AND SERVICES

The following core investment programs are "packaged" products which are proprietary to Northern Investments and will be marketed to broker-dealer firms and investment professionals nationwide:

Dynamics is a tactical asset allocation managed mutual fund program utilizing socially screened funds. This program has been operating successfully for nearly three years and will be managed under contract to Northern Investments by its creators.

Efficiencies is a managed mutual fund program using socially screened funds. This program is designed to emulate the strategic asset allocation model produced by Nobel Prize-winning research, and implemented by some of the industry's leading consultants. This approach emphasizes efficient diversification by blending multiple asset classes, investment styles, and money managers. Efficiencies will be managed and administered in-house.

FairWays is an investment management consulting program utilizing third party money managers who have internal social screening and/or shareholder activism capabilities. These managers work with Northern Investments on a separate account basis. This program will be managed and administered in-house.

In addition to the above packaged products, the company will offer a number of services designed to support investment professionals who are members of the Network:

Direct Services: Northern Investments will continue to administer fee-based accounts managed by representatives. This service is available only to representatives associated with Plum Tree Securities, and is a continuation of services provided prior to the acquisition of Northern Investments's advisory business from Plum Tree. Over time, this business is expected to represent a smaller and smaller portion of Northern Investments's overall business.

Partnerships with Network Members: The company anticipates generating asset management business in partnership with certain of its associated representatives. For example, one Northern Investments representative was formerly a municipal bond manager for a major insurance company. Management expects to offer socially screened municipal bond fund management in partnership with this representative.

Financial Planning, Hourly Consulting and Coaching: The company expects its representatives to continue developing services and alternative pricing mechanisms within the scope of Northern Investments's umbrella national Registered Investment Advisory status. Management intends to provide the flexibility, training, and service necessary to support a wide range of advisor/client relationships, including financial planning, hourly consultations and personal/professional program coaching. The company intends to develop a "Life Planning" program that will be designed to provide the skills and tools for representatives to expand and deepen the value-added services they will provide clients in the years ahead.

Research and Information Services: Numerous services of specific interest to investment professionals serving socially aware/Cultural Creative clients will be aggregated and offered for a modest annual fee to Network members. These research and information services, when purchased separately, are either not currently accessible or are simply not available at economically viable prices for most individual practitioners. The company has completed tentative negotiations with several providers, based on the buying power of the Network, which will allow it to offer these services at a very attractive price to Network members.

Consulting Services: Both Walter Smith and John Craig have substantial experience in product design, marketing, public relations, and practice management relative to businesses focusing on the company's target market of socially aware/Cultural Creative investors. Management anticipates consulting service revenues to be a small, yet material part of company operations.

SRI in Portland: The company created, produces, and hosts the SRI in Portland conference each year. This conference is recognized as the annual industry conference for investment professionals and practitioners whose businesses focus on the socially responsible investment field. Approximately 400 participants are expected to attend the 2000 conference, which will be the tenth anniversary of this highly successful event. Sponsorship and registration revenues are sufficient to generate a modest profit each year, while providing an outstanding platform to inform the market of SRI investment professionals about the company's services.

Institutional Investor Initiatives: Management intends to invest some of the capital raised through a successful $1 million offering in creating an in-house capability to develop a direct asset management business with large institutional investors. This will entail hiring and supporting at least one, possibly two, highly qualified people to build relationships and generate institutional business directly to the company. This will be a long lead time process, which may not begin to pay off for 12 to 18 months. Such a direct institutional capability will not compete with Network members, and in many cases may be positioned to augment Network member efforts.

Internet Strategy: Northern Investments is developing an Internet strategy aimed at serving the needs of socially aware/Culture Creative investors whose investment resources and needs may be considered too small to work with a professional advisor. This strategy may also serve investors who simply choose to make their own investment decisions without the assistance of an investment professional. The company's Internet strategy, while designed to serve smaller investors, will continuously encourage them to consider working with a professional advisor, and connect them with members of the Network. An aggressive Internet strategy will only be possible if the company is successful in achieving its goal of raising $1 million in investor capital.

INVESTMENT COMMITTEE

An Investment Committee will be responsible for all due diligence and monitoring of the socially responsible mutual funds, and separate account managers who are involved in managing money for Northern Investments representatives and clients. The Committee will review all pertinent economic, market, fund and manager specific information and make decisions accordingly affecting all assets under management in Northern Investments investment programs. The Committee is composed of John Craig CFP, CEO; Wendell Letterman CFP, co-designer and primary manager of the Efficiencies program; and Robert Sloan CFA level II candidate, Director of Research, and primary manager of the FairWays program.

ADVISORY BOARD

Management intends to appoint a board of advisors representing investment professionals who are members of the Northern Investments. Management envisions this Advisory Board meeting formally on a quarterly basis, with informal communications occurring as needed. This Board will be expected to advise management on strategic as well as tactical issues facing the company, with a focus on improving service to the investment professionals who choose to join the Network. Four advisors will be appointed from the initial group of 52 Northern Investments representatives. An additional two or three practitioners will be added to the Advisory Board as is warranted by the addition of new representatives from broker-dealer firms other than Plum Tree. No appointments have been made as of this time.

REVENUES

The company's financial projections assume normal market conditions over the next five years, with annual market growth of well-diversified portfolios averaging 9 percent. Regardless of whether the general industry trend toward fee-based business continues, it is assumed that socially aware/Cultural Creative investors will be more receptive to this type of relationship with a financial professional. In fact, Northern Investments will be seeking to establish relationships with investment professionals who recognize that the most effective way to leverage their time and grow their businesses will be through a fee-based client relationship with professional management provided by a firm such as Northern Investments.

Projections reflect the fact that Northern Investments will terminate its AOSJ/Branch Office relationship with Plum Tree Securities by December 31, 1999, thus eliminating brokerage related revenues the company has historically received. Revenue projections are based on a gradual reduction in the share of representative-managed assets (Plum Tree associated representatives only) and aggressive increases in program-managed assets. For the first several quarters, fee-based assets are likely to generate sufficient revenues to create a profitable operation. As such, it will be important to quickly grow advisory assets and revenues to generate positive cash flow.

The company's program-managed products, which are expected to become the most significant source of revenues within the first 18 months of operations, are priced to generate the following approximate revenues (annualized) to Northern Investments after selling costs (compensation paid to representatives):

> Dynamics - 45 basis points
> Efficiencies - 40 basis points
> FairWays - 20 basis points

Minimum Offering - Core Business Projections

CHART 1 shows revenue and expense projections based on raising a minimum of $400,000 in investor capital to support Northern Investments's "core" business. This chart reflects all of the above described fundamental assumptions. It projects growth in revenues from new business through adding 2 to 4 new representatives per month to the initial core group of 52 Northern Investments representatives. New representatives will be allowed to join the Network as the company is successful in signing selling agreements with their broker-dealer firms. Management expects to sign at least one new selling agreement per month over the first 18 to 24 months of operations. While expected to build slowly based on minimum capitalization, over time, this process will allow Northern Investments services to be offered through hundreds of representatives associated with firms outside of Plum Tree.

Expenses are projected based on the past five years' operating history, adjusting for broker-dealer support services that will be phasing out over the second half of 1999, and for new products, services, and business initiatives as reflected in this summary business plan. Revenues associated with Internet initiatives are not specifically identified in CHART 1 and no revenue assumptions have been developed. Similarly, CHART 1 does not incorporate revenues associated with Northern Investments direct institutional sales. This is a "slow and steady growth" scenario, one which management is very comfortable and confident of achieving.

CHART 1 - "CORE" BUSINESS PLAN PROJECTIONS

	2nd Half 1999	2000	2001	2002	2003	2004
IA Assets Under Management	194,103,654	268,013,654	358,235,654	490,121,654	670,562,053	917,432,363
Asset Growth	17.60%	38.10%	33.70%	36.80%	36.80%	36.80%
Broker Dealer Related Revenues	519,815					
Investment Advisory Revenues:						
Inside Representatives	23,475	49,216	56,416	63,616	87,036	119,079
FAFN Fee-Only Representatives	26,958	130,021	253,558	346,992	474,738	649,515
WSS/FAFN Representatives	893,592	2,063,041	2,389,819	2,734,052	3,740,604	5,117,724
Other BD Representatives	300	176,109	759,858	1,714,868	2,346,203	3,209,968
Other RIA Related Revenues	3,000					
Cost of Sales	772,157	1,879,710	2,590,319	3,547,268	4,853,210	6,639,940
Net Investment Advisory Revenues	175,168	538,677	869,332	1,312,259	1,759,373	2,456,347
Other Revenues	6,000	9,000	9,000	9,000	11,000	11,000
Gross Revenues	**1,473,139**	**2,427,387**	**3,468,651**	**4,868,527**	**6,659,582**	**9,107,287**
Net Revenues after Selling Costs	**211,310**	**547,677**	**878,332**	**1,321,259**	**1,806,373**	**2,467,347**
Expenses:						
Salary & Benefits	195,402	375,629	540,914	628,705	760,140	958,147
Rents & Leases	15,233	32,040	48,420	53,670	56,354	59,171
Marketing & Sales	29,343	77,634	129,156	194,287	270,000	370,000
Professional Services	17,800	27,600	39,600	39,600	48,000	54,000
Interest on Loan	13,547	23,511	18,394	12,840	7,280	1,380
Overhead	30,724	52,237	76,763	109,240	140,500	194,000
Depreciation	33,109	66,357	66,837	67,317	68,317	69,317
Total Expenses	**335,157**	**655,008**	**920,084**	**1,105,659**	**1,350,591**	**1,706,016**
Pre-Tax Profit (Loss)	-123,847	-107,330	-41,752	215,600	455,782	761,332

Maximum Offering - Fully Funded Projections

CHART 2 shows projected revenues and expenses based on successfully raising $1,000,000 of investor capital and putting it to work over the first 21-24 months of operations to aggressively grow the company's business and revenues.

Under the company's "fully funded" plan, additional working capital will be invested in ways management believes will result in faster growth of the Network, of investment advisory assets under management, and of profitability in future years. While no assurances can be made that the aggressive growth shown in CHART 2 will be achieved, management believes it is both possible and probable given the market potential, the strategy, and the resources the company will have to focus on this exciting effort.

With full funding, the company will hire an additional qualified person to market Northern Investments services to investment professionals seeking to serve socially aware/Cultural Creative clients across the land. This talented and experienced individual will be responsible for arranging selling agreements between Northern Investments and broker-dealer firms, for selling the concept of social investing and Northern's unique ability to serve that market, and for cultivating relationships with representatives who work with or wish to work with socially responsible investment programs.

Full funding will allow the company to hire a qualified person to develop direct institutional business from religious organizations, foundations, retirement plan sponsors, and others. This individual will focus on those larger investors who choose to work directly with a management company, and will not compete with investment professionals in the Network. On occasion, this person may be in a position to help Network members land large accounts.

Full funding will provide the capital necessary for the company to develop a significant presence on the Internet. The technology exists to create most of the connectivity and services management envisions provided via the Internet avoiding virtually any custom development. However, a process of adapting the "off the shelf" software and services to Northern Investments's needs will require a certain amount of proprietary programming. It is expected that the planned Research and Information Services will be made available to Network members primarily via the Internet.

In addition, management believes that the smaller end of the social investment marketplace can be effectively served via the Internet. Currently shunned by many investment professionals, investors with limited resources often have difficulty in accessing information and making socially responsible investments. There is currently no vehicle designed to make it easy for the socially aware/Cultural Creative investor with a small amount of investment capital to facilitate the purchase of socially screened mutual funds, other than by going directly to the fund company. When "shopping," these investors are more likely to get lost inside of Schwab.com or E-Trade, rather than finding their way to a socially screened mutual fund. Northern Investments believes that a focused web-based facility can be developed relatively quickly to provide investors with $2,000 to $10,000, and possibly more. An easy way to become socially responsible investors will be through the dozens of mutual funds whose products will be available through this service (some of which are currently not available through the larger fund supermarkets).

Management will seek a strategic partner to implement such an Internet initiative. It will require a simple broker-dealer able to facilitate trading of mutual funds. The simple broker-dealer envisioned would be set up to trade mutual funds only and would have minimal compliance requirements and virtually no staff, except web technicians. The oversight necessary to fulfill NASD and SEC requirements would be available through the principles of the company. Capital requirements to establish the broker-dealer and register it in all states is estimated at $100,000. An additional, undetermined investment will be required in developing this web capability. Revenues will flow from trailing compensation the company will realize from the assets under management in funded accounts.

The company sees its planned Internet initiative having substantial long-term potential for referring business to investment professionals within the Network. It is clear from industry research that the majority of investors seek investment advice once their assets reach a certain size, or when they achieve a certain level of success in their professional endeavors, or are at the point where they realize the complexity of their financial affairs has outgrown their ability to manage them. Northern Investments will seek to build relationships with these initially small and/or do-it-yourself social investors, gently encouraging them to seek the assistance of Network members over the course of time. Management envisions this process becoming a major source of leads to Network professionals in the years to come.

CHART 2 - "FULLY FUNDED" PLAN PROJECTIONS

	2nd Half 1999	2000	2001	2002	2003	2004
IA Assets Under Management	194,103,654	300,000	600,000,000	1,000,000,000	1,400,000,000	1,700,000,000
Asset Growth	17.60%	54.56%	100.00%	66.67%	40.00%	21.43%
Broker Dealer Related Revenues	519,815	50,000	150,000	300,000	500,000	750,000
Investment Advisory Revenues:						
Inside Representatives	23,475	55,122	94,779	127,332	182,776	220,297
FAFN Fee-Only Representatives	26,958	145,623	425,978	693,983	996,950	1,201,603
WSS/FAFN Representatives	893,592	2,310,606	2,389,819	2,734,052	3,740,052	5,117,724
Other BD Representatives	300	197,243	2,901,561	6,159,735	9,042,027	10,288,441
Other RIA Related Revenues	3,000	25,000	75,000	150,000	250,000	300,000
Cost of Sales	772,157	2,105,275	4,351,736	7,094,535	10,191,740	12,283,888
Net Investment Advisory Revenues	175,168	628,318	1,535,400	2,770,466	4,020,618	4,844,177
Other Revenues	6,000	9,000	9,000	9,000	11,000	11,000
Gross Revenues	**1,473,139**	**2,792,594**	**6,037,137**	**10,165,002**	**14,712,358**	**17,878,065**
Net Revenues after Selling Costs	**211,310**	**687,318**	**1,685,400**	**3,070,466**	**4,520,618**	**5,594,177**
Expenses:						
Salary & Benefits	195,402	470,704	892,508	1,131,669	1,444,266	1,676,757
Rents & Leases	15,233	32,040	48,420	53,670	56,354	59,171
Marketing & Sales	58,687	155,268	258,311	388,573	540,000	740,000
Professional Services	17,800	27,600	47,520	49,500	62,400	70,200
Interest on Loan	13,547	23,511	18,394	12,840	7,280	1,380
Overhead	30,724	123,505	191,659	266,170	335,875	435,400
Depreciation	33,109	79,629	80,205	87,513	102,476	103,976
Total Expenses	**335,157**	**912,257**	**1,537,018**	**1,989,934**	**2,548,651**	**3,086,885**
Pre-Tax Profit (Loss)	-123,847	-224,939	148,383	1,080,532	1,971,967	2,507,292

MISSION

Northern Investments, LLC's mission is to be the premier provider of investment products and services designed to serve socially aware/Cultural Creative investors.

The company will use its unique position in the industry to significantly expand distribution of socially responsible investment programs nationwide, primarily through investment advisory relationships.

**FUNDAMENTAL
GUIDING BELIEFS**

The following fundamentals guide our efforts.

We believe:

- Every person has a core set of values which govern his/her actions.

- People rarely have identical sets of values, but for most there is a wide expanse of common ground. Indeed, most people's shared beliefs transcend their differences.

- Fair-minded people can agree to disagree and can remain tolerant and respectful of the values and priorities of others, even when in disagreement.

- It is both prudent and proper to reflect personal values in financial and investment decisions.

- Many thoughtful people are unwilling to profit from behavior in others that they find unacceptable in themselves and will choose an alternative course of action when they know they have one.

- Consciously bringing personal values and financial decision making into alignment is a powerful way to influence others and to encourage behavior which enhances quality of life for all.

**A CORPORATE
CULTURE OF
RESPECT**

Northern Investments is intentionally creating a corporate culture based on respect. The values, beliefs, and styles of the company's owners, managers, employees, and representatives are intended to reflect the best and most common characteristics of our target market of socially aware/Cultural Creative investors.

Businesses rise and fall based on their corporate culture. It's at the level of corporate culture that the purpose and vision of Northern Investments becomes real for employees, customers, and everyone else who feels the touch of the organization. The company's culture is the invisible hand that shapes its literature, management decisions, investor commitments, client relations, back office support effectiveness, profitability, community perceptions, and responses to unforeseen events.

Northern Investments's corporate culture is rooted in the broad social impulse to honor diversity and reclaim respect within the human community. It's an impulse that draws understanding from nature. This is not the type of respect that is given to one person but held back from the next. It's a respect that is unconditional. In essence, unconditional respect is, at its core, what socially responsible investing is really all about.

A culture of respect will be felt by every client. It will be known by every investor who owns a membership interest in the company. It will be a motivation for every investment professional who joins the Network. It will be the cause for service, the reason for diligence, the cohesion for teamwork, a key criteria for recruitment, and the foundation for expansion. Respect will underpin every aspect of the relationships between the company, investors, staff, product providers, and the hundreds of investment professionals who will become members of the Network.

Respect for customers is not a unique business concept. However, unconditional respect for every person one encounters is unique. Unconditional respect is an understanding set forth in the teachings of historic masters and sages, but one that has become all but extinct in modern times. Northern Investments holds the intention to be a catalyst in the creation of a new social culture based on respect. Management believes that aligning Northern Investments with respect and creating a culture that acknowledges the magnificence of all who enter its sphere of influence, will lead to business and financial success.

The company seeks to attract investors in Northern Investments LLC from all ranks of the social investment industry. Management hopes that investment professionals who are members of the Network, mutual fund companies, and investment management firms whose products and services are offered through the firm may want to own interests in the "new" Northern. The company seeks to encourage this process and to attract as many investors as possible from within the social investment community to share in the success and profits of the "new" Northern Investments.

SHARED OWNERSHIP - EXPAND DISTRIBUTION

Northern will promote the concept and practice of socially and environmentally responsible investing broadly, introduce the vast and virtually untapped market of socially aware/Cultural Creative investors to professional advisors across the country, and develop new business initiatives aimed at expanding demand for social investment programs. Management sees these efforts quickly creating a powerful new distribution channel for socially responsible product and service providers.

John Craig CFP is Chief Executive Officer of Northern Investments, LLC. He has served on the board of directors of the Social Investment Forum since 1993 and has produced and hosted the annual *SRI in Portland* conference since 1990. He was the recipient of the industry's 1997 "SRI Service Award."

KEY PEOPLE

John joined the company that was to become Northern Investments as a financial planner in November 1986. He assumed the position of Chief Operating Officer of Northern Investments in 1989 and managed the sale of Northern Investments to Plum Tree Securities, Inc., in 1995. John served as President of the Northern Investments division of Plum Tree Advisors and as Vice President of Plum Tree Advisors from May 1, 1995 through June 30, 1999.

Born January 5, 1951 in Cincinnati, Ohio, John is a 1975 graduate of the United States Military Academy at West Point. He served on active duty for nine years in various command, staff and faculty assignments as an Armor officer. His final assignment on active duty, and for three more years as a civilian, was in the Resource Management Division, Directorate of Personnel and Community Activities at Fort Carson, Oregon. As chief of this division, John was responsible for the financial management of most business operations on the installation, ranging from the Golf Course and Bowling Center, to the Club Systems and Child Care operations. Upon his departure, John received the Department of the Army "Commander's Award for Civilian Service."

John earned his Certified Financial Planner (CFP) designation in June 1984, and in short order completed a range of securities examinations covering both the practice and supervision of the securities business.

Walter Smith is President and Chief Marketing Officer of Northern Investments, LLC. For over a decade he has been a nationally recognized authority, consultant and resource to the social investment industry. He serves as Chair and President of the Social Investment Forum, the industry's national trade association, as a director of the Colloquium on Socially Responsible investing, and as Co-Chair of the Oregon Network of Business for Social Responsibility (BSR). He received the industry's "SRI Service Award" in 1998.

Prior to starting his own consulting practice in 1997, Walter worked for nearly eight years as a senior executive of Calvert Group. He specialized in promoting the concept and practice of social investing with the public and the press. His efforts significantly enhanced Calvert's reputation as a leader in the field, while the firm's assets under management in socially screened mutual funds more than tripled. He led a small product development group which created the first global socially screened mutual fund in the U.S., and was involved in launching four other new Calvert funds designed for socially aware investors.

Walter managed Calvert's national sales organization from 1994 to 1997. As President of Calvert Distributions, Inc., he was responsible for the company's relationship with over 2,000 broker/dealer firms and growing the assets of Calvert's 35 money market, bond and equity mutual funds. He directed a staff of 30 and recorded NAV fund sales of over $500 million annually during this time period. His accomplishments were complemented by his team-oriented management style and a path-breaking initiative which reoriented the sales group into customer-focused teams working with a values-based selling process.

Previously, Walter served for three years as a major gifts officer and Director of Development at the Billings School, University of Montana. He also spent five years as Vice President of Prescott Realty Services, a real estate securities firm, and was responsible for all due diligence, marketing, and sales of real estate related investments sold through Prescott Ball & Turben, Inc. (now part of Everen Securities).

Born July 16, 1953 and raised in Atlanta, Georgia, his father owned a hardware store where Walter worked meeting the needs of retail customers from the age of ten. He is a graduate of the University of Tennessee with a degree in Journalism/Communications, and holds NASD Series 24 (Registered Principal) and Series 7 (Registered Representative), and Series 63 licenses.

Jennifer Frame is Vice President and Director of Operations of Northern Investments Network, LLC. She obtained her NASD Series 7 license (Registered Representative) and her NASD Series 24 license (Registered Principal) in 1989 while associated with Portland brokerage firm, First Eagle, Inc., where she worked from 1987 through 1990.

Jennifer joined Northern Investments in 1990 as an administrative assistant to the main office and two of its Portland-based representatives. Combining administrative skills and knowledge of the business, she quickly assumed a much larger role and broader responsibilities, first becoming Operations Manager, and then Assistant Branch Manager of the Plum Tree Securities, Inc. branch office. Jennifer managed the conversion of accounts from Northern Investments, to the Northern Investments division of Plum Tree Advisors, Inc. following the sale of Northern Investments to Plum Tree Securities, Inc. in 1995. As Assistant Branch Manager, Jennifer has assumed a majority of the compliance supervision responsibilities for the Northern Investments field force of 52 representatives around the country.

Born February 4, 1960 in Detroit, Michigan, her father is a retired United Methodist Minister and her mother is a psychologist. Jennifer graduated from the University of Michigan in 1983 with a Bachelor of Arts degree in English, specializing in Medieval Literature.

Wendell Letterman CFP is Primary Manager of the Efficiencies program and serves on Northern Investments's Investment Committee. He holds NASD Series 7, Series 63, and Series 65 licenses, and is a member of the Investment Management Consultants Association.

Wendell has been a registered representative with Plum Tree Securities and investment advisor representative with Northern since 1991. In 1997, he joined Reber/Russell Company, an investment advisory firm affiliated with Frank Russell Investment Management Company, well known in the institutional investment world, and highly regarded for their expertise in asset allocation, rigorous manager evaluation, and consulting services to some of the world's largest pools of capital. Wendell's two years with Reber/Russell taught him how institutions construct and manage portfolios of mutual funds. He was responsible for servicing several dozen clients whose aggregate assets exceeded $100 million. He also taught inexperienced investors how to become good consumers of financial services, and developed a multimedia CD-ROM designed to walk a novice investor through the entire process.

While at Reber/Russell Company, he continued his relationship with Northern and continued to service his Northern clients. Upon leaving Reber/Russell Company in early 1999, Wendell expanded his role at Northern Investments. In collaboration with John Craig, he developed a strategic asset allocation program based on the investment management principles used by Russell, and designed to meet the needs of the SRI market. He named his program Efficiencies, in recognition of its fundamental strengths: efficient use of risk in pursuit of investment returns, cost efficiency, and tax efficiency.

Wendell was born October 3, 1954 in Cleveland, Ohio. He graduated from Bowling Green University in 1977 with a degree in Psychology, and went on to complete his master's degree in Counseling Psychology there in 1979. He worked for EF Hutton specializing in retirement planning throughout the 1980s.

Robert Sloan is the Director of Research and Primary Manager of the FairWays program for Northern Investments, LLC. He also serves on the Northern Investments Investment Committee. He is an affiliate member of both the Denver Society of Security Analysts and the Association for Investment Management and Research (AIMR), and is currently at CFA level II candidate (Chartered Financial Analyst program).

Robert earned an MBA in Finance and Accounting with honors from the University of Arizona in 1995 while working for American Century Mutual Funds. Robert earned his undergraduate Bachelor of Science degree in Civil Engineering from the University of Missouri in 1986. He went on to earn his Professional Engineering designation while working for the Texas Department of Transportation in Dallas. There he designed highways, bridges, and drainage systems that resulted in minimal environmental impact to the surroundings, but yet provided safe, innovative, and aesthetically pleasing structures. Later he worked as an Environmental Engineer for the Texas Water Commission where he reviewed plans for hazardous waste facilities to ensure they complied with complex state and federal hazardous waste regulations. After moving to Oregon, Robert headed the Pollution Prevention Program at Space Command Headquarters of the U.S. Air Force.

Robert has volunteered his time with active environmental groups such as the Southern Rockies Ecosystem Project and the Volunteers for Outdoor Oregon.

Susan Williams is Director of Nonprofit Support Services for Northern Investments, LLC. For over 15 years she has been regarded as an invaluable asset to the nonprofit community. Her service has run the full spectrum of participation, from hands-on volunteering on projects, to leadership positions such as board presidencies and executive directorships.

Her most recent service, prior to Northern, was the Executive Director of the Environmental Fund of Illinois and the Chair of the National Coalition of Environmental Federations where, through her leadership, donations, and gifts more than doubled during her two-year tenure. She currently serves as Chair of the Portland Chapter of Community Shares of Oregon and received their 1999 Volunteer of the Year award.

Susan was born June 3, 1960 in Wilmington, Delaware and graduated from the University of Virginia in 1982 with a Bachelors of Science degree in Actuarial Science. She holds Society of Actuary exams 100, 110, 120, 130, 135, and 140, and NASD Series 7 and 63 licenses.

Medical Billing Company

BUSINESS PLAN

PHYSICIANS 1ST BILLING AND CLAIMS

10200 Main St.
Cincinnati, Ohio 45208

This medical billing company is dedicated to helping health care providers become more efficient by encouraging them to outsource their insurance processing and medical billing. Electronic submission of medical claims is key to their success, as is specialized and diversified services. This business plan was compiled using Business Plan Pro™, by Palo Alto Software, copyright © 2000.

- EXECUTIVE SUMMARY

- COMPANY SUMMARY

- SERVICES

- MARKET ANALYSIS SUMMARY

- STRATEGY AND IMPLEMENTATION SUMMARY

- MANAGEMENT SUMMARY

- FINANCIAL PLAN

EXECUTIVE SUMMARY

Billing services currently exist to manage medical practices. These services relieve medical professionals of tedious detail work, but rarely do they offer a means to substantially maximize the practice's bottom line. Physicians 1st Billing and Claims will not only free office staff for more crucial tasks, but will also maximize return from insurance carriers.

National statistics show only about 70 percent of insurance claims, initially submitted on paper, are ever paid by insurance carriers. With electronic submission, Physicians 1st Billing and Claims can increase the percentage of claims paid to around 98 percent.

Additional statistics indicate that it currently costs a medical practice between $8.00-$10.00 per claim to process insurance for their patients. Physicians 1st Billing and Claims can reduce these costs by 50 percent or more.

Statistics show turnaround on paper insurance claims to be 30, 60, even 90 days or longer, creating serious outstanding receivables for the practice. By submitting claims electronically, Physicians 1st Billing and Claims can generally have money in the physician's hand within 14-18 days. Of course, this reduces outstanding receivables proportionately and greatly improves cash flow. Statistics also show a 30 percent suspension/rejection rate for paper insurance claims. This doesn't mean that the claims are never paid. What it does mean is medical staff must hassle with insurance carriers over payment. With the extensive editing performed on electronic claims prior to their transmission to carriers, this percentage is reduced to 2-3 percent. Claims are submitted with a 98 percent accuracy rate.

For many years physicians graduated from medical school under the premise that they were going to run a "practice." "Businesses" were for other professionals. Many simple administrative procedures were neglected, such as:

Keeping current with insurance specifications and regulations, so that claims were paid on a timely basis,

Concentrating on collecting receivables and co-payments,

Ensuring that fees were kept at the maximum allowable that insurance carriers were paying,

or

Procedure codes were current so that claims weren't suspended or rejected.

For many offices, outstanding receivables grew tremendously and annual bad-debt write-offs became routine. But adequate profit margins allowed medical practices to ignore sound business procedures. Medical practice complacency toward industry change is in the past. Physicians' heads raised and they began taking note of public opinions toward health care reform issues during 1994 and 1995. With the onslaught of managed care organizations into the industry, physicians are finding profit margins shrinking. They are now alert to the fact that in order to remain in business into the 21st century, they will have to adopt more efficient business practices. Physicians 1st Billing and Claims is prepared to assist local health care providers to move into the 21st century with sound practices that will guarantee business success and, in turn, guarantee quality health care for our families and our country.

Physicians 1st Billing and Claims is contributing over $6,000 to this business. We are requesting to borrow another $5,000. Please give this detailed business plan your attention.

The use of these funds is explained in the Start-up Summary.

Our objectives are:

1. To acquire one account by November 30th, 2000.
2. To process 1,500 claims a month by December 31, 2001.
3. To become recognized as a local industry expert in the field of medical reimbursement.
4. To add several additional services to our initial offering of electronic claims submission, including:
   - code optimization
   - managed care contract analysis
   - full practice management
   - customized reporting
   - medical transcription
   - fee analysis
   - Medicare financial impact analysis

Physicians 1st Billing and Claims is a medical reimbursement consulting firm dedicated to helping medical practices become more efficient and save money by allowing them to out-source their insurance processing and medical billing to an expert reimbursement service. We intend to have complete one-stop shopping for all medical practice administrative functions by the end of 1998. We intend to make enough profit to repay our business start-up loan and finance continued growth and development with our quality service.

Since 1985, the Federal Government has been urging the health care industry to submit insurance claims electronically. Statistics prove that electronic submission can save millions of dollars annually for the industry. Presently, 95 percent of all pharmaceutical claims and 70 percent of hospital claims are submitted electronically. Physicians and dentists trail far behind, with only 25-30 percent submitting claims electronically.

The Federal Government is not happy with this situation, so in 1990, Congress mandated that physicians are required to file claims on behalf of all their Medicare patients. Many doctors were not prepared for this deluge of paperwork. Eight years later, doctors are still climbing out from under the paperwork. In 1996 the motions calling for electronic submission of all Medicare claims were being echoed throughout the halls of Congress. No mandate was passed, but the paperwork continues to mount up and as baby boomers near retirement age the paper problem will only get worse and those echoes will turn into screams. This year in the U.S. over $1 trillion worth of medical charges will be issued. This amounts to 9 billion medical claims. Medical practices will be forced to meet the mandates (and growing mountains of paper) and most are not currently equipped to handle the transition. The sensible solution is to outsource the process to experts that are prepared to save the practices money, produce a much faster return from insurance carriers, and handle the claims with a high degree of accuracy. There aren't many businesses that can say the Federal Government is behind them all the way.

A second key to our success will be flexibility. Physicians 1st Billing and Claims understands that each medical practice is unique. Even practices of the same specialty will have different staff and offer different services. Physicians 1st Billing and Claims will evaluate the needs of each practice and offer solutions to help the practice become more efficient. Some may want all the services we offer and some may select only a few. Our billing will be customized to each office's needs.

A third key is our diversified services. Physicians 1st Billing and Claims offers a one-stop shopping experience for medical administrative services.

COMPANY SUMMARY

We are currently organized as a partnership, being formed in October 1998.

Physicians 1st Billing and Claims is trademarked through the U.S. Department of Commerce Patent and Trade Mark Office. The trademark covers Medical Practice Management and Reimbursement Consulting.

Company Ownership

The two individuals forming this partnership are John and Mary Moore, a husband and wife team.

John's experience consists of three years of teaching experience, 13 years' managerial experience in the building materials industry, and 12 years as a father. As a manager, John gained experience in marketing, back-office operations, sales, and managing people. John will use this experience in managing the marketing and sales departments.

Mary's experience consists of 12 years as a mother and four years teaching experience. As a mother and wife, Mary has extensive experience filling out and filing medical insurance claims. This experience has given her valuable insight into the workings of the health insurance industry. Mary's experience as a teacher has taught her the skills of attention to detail, organization, and the importance of timeliness. Mary will use this experience to manage the training and clerical administration departments. John and Mary will jointly assume responsibility of the accounting and data entry departments.

Start-up Summary

Physicians 1st Billing and Claims' start-up will focus on John and Mary working full-time in the business.

John's main duties will center on marketing/sales, purchasing, and data entry. Mary's main duties will center on data entry, clerical administration, and training. John and Mary will jointly assume the accounting responsibilities. Their children, Erika and Matthew, will work when needed in data entry and housekeeping. The entire Moore family is dedicated to ensuring the success of Physicians 1st Billing and Claims.

John and Mary have decided to purchase a business opportunity package offered by Claim Systems Inc. The price of this package includes: state-of-the-art medical billing and accounting software, unlimited training for the first six months, two years of 24-hour technical support, emergency support service, and a full-featured marketing package. The price of the package is $5,000.00 plus $45.00 for shipping and handling. Optional dental billing software can be purchased for $900.00 plus shipping. This software will be added at a later date. An additional deposit of $400.00 will be included at the time of purchase of the package to secure the rights to become a franchise once Claim Systems receives licensing from the state of Indiana. When Claim Systems receives this approval, Physicians 1st Billing and Claims will pay an additional $1,595.00 for ownership of franchise rights from Claim Systems. The benefits of this will allow us to advertise nationally and establish name recognition.

John owns a Pentium II Gateway computer with ink-jet printer and a scanner that will be utilized for the business. The following additional office equipment will be purchased: a Pentium computer, an ink-jet printer, a fax machine, assorted phone and communications equipment, a chair, a copy machine, accounting software, and miscellaneous office supplies. John and Mary are investing $6,000.00 of their own capital in the business, and are looking for financing for an additional $5,000.00 which they feel will be necessary to successfully start Physicians 1st Billing and Claims.

Start-up Expenses		**Start-up Costs**
Legal	$200	
Office Supplies, Stationery	$200	
Furniture	$500	
Business Opportunity	$6,040	
Insurance	$200	
Rent	$50	
Software	$69	
Expensed equipment	$345	
Other	$2,000	
Total Start-up Expense	**$9,604**	
Start-up Assets Needed		
Cash Requirements	$0	
Other Short-term Assets	$0	
Total Short-term Assets	**$0**	
Long-term Assets	$0	
Total Assets	**$0**	
Total Start-up Requirements:	**$9,604**	
Left to finance:	**$3,564**	
Start-up Funding Plan		
Investment		
Invester 1	$6,040.00	
Other	$0	
Total investment	**$6,040**	
Short-term Liabilities		
Unpaid Expenses	$0	
Short-time Loans	$0	
Interest-free Short-term Loans	$0	
Subtotal Short-term Liabilities	$0	
Long-term Liabilities	$0	
Total Liabilities	**$0**	
Loss at Start-up	($6,040)	
Total Capital	$0	
Total Capital and Liabilities	$0	
Checkline	$0	

John and Mary will be utilizing 518 sq. ft. (an extra large bedroom in the upstairs) of their home. John's office area will be utilized for marketing and accounting operations. Mary's office area will be utilized for data entry and clerical operations, etc.

Company Locations and Facilities

SERVICES

Our position in the market will be a full-service medical reimbursement business with individual pricing. As stated previously, our goal is one-stop shopping for medical practices when it comes to administrative functions. Physicians 1st Billing and Claims Electronic Claims Service's policy is to customize our charges based on the work we do, and the needs of each office. We find that each practice is unique and, therefore, we do not quote a "standard charge" for services.

Initially, Physicians 1st Billing and Claims will offer electronic billing of medical insurance claims. This is a badly needed service for most medical practices, and is even more critical since the Federal Government will mandate electronic submission of Medicare claims in the near future. A detailed description of the electronic submission process follows. The data necessary to submit claims will be downloaded from the medical office and input into specialized computer software. The software performs certain generic edits on the data and stores the information. When a batch of claims is complete for an office, it is time to transmit to the national clearinghouse. The data travels via modems and telephone lines to the clearinghouse where the data is edited a second time. This second series of edits incorporates "insurance company specific edits." Cooperating insurance carriers notify the clearinghouse of certain edits they feel are necessary to allow payment of their claims. These edits are performed on each claim before they are transmitted on to the carrier, thus guaranteeing accuracy and payment in most cases. Upon receiving the insurance claim from the clearing-house, the carriers process the claim and send payment directly to the medical practice. With electronic transmission to the clearinghouse and on to the carrier, computerized data verification, and elimination of most of the human element, the process of claims payment is greatly simplified and accelerated. Physicians will no longer wait 30, 60, or 90 days for payment, but will have money in their hands usually within 14-18 days.

As practices begin experiencing the benefits of electronic submission, many will see the advantage of outsourcing other administrative functions. Physicians 1st Billing and Claims' full-featured practice management software will allow us to meet those needs. Patients can be billed for co-payments or amounts which their insurance company did not cover. Secondary and supplementary insurance can be tracked and payments and balances applied accurately. The software utilizes state-of-the-art, open-item accounting, where most other systems use balance-forward systems. Outstanding receivables can be tracked with insurance aging reports, in several different sequences for ease of use. A complete practice analysis will increase office efficiency by showing where money is coming from. For each procedure, the charges and percentage of total charges they represent are calculated and printed for immediate reference. Transaction Journals and Detail Ledgers provide an accurate overall picture of the practice.

With managed care sweeping the country, it is imperative for medical practices to evaluate the benefits they receive from affiliation with different organizations. Our managed care contract service tracks payments and analyzes the information to produce customized reports showing profitability, or lack of profitability, with each managed care facility. These reports are critical when decisions need to be made on renewing and negotiating contracts.

Claim Systems' state-of-the-art software will allow the physician to do complete dictation transcription. This allows the physician to meet the needs of the new strict HCFA mandate on clarity of all Medicare claims.

Service Description

Physicians 1st Billing and Claims' number one goal is to provide outstanding service.

We show our dedication to service by providing the physician one-stop shopping for all his or her billing and claims needs. The services we provide are as follows:

- Complete patient record setup
- Electronic and manual medical claims filing
- Patient billing
- Claims posting and patient record updating
- Collection services
- Complete practice analysis
- Assistance in negotiating health care contracts
- Automated transcription service
- Volume discounting

Initially we will focus on just claims filing. In the near future we will diligently pursue our goal of providing one-stop shopping for physicians' medical office management.

An evaluation is performed on each medical practice during the marketing phase. This will allow us to determine the needs of the practice and how to charge for services rendered.

During the evaluation certain facts are gathered, such as:

- the time it will take to key patient and claims information into the software
- the approximate number of claims a practice will submit monthly
- the approximate "total dollars" a practice submits monthly to insurance carriers
- how accurate is the information obtained from the office (is it complete and easy to enter or does it require extensive editing and follow-up?)
- how often will the information need to be gathered (based on claims volume)
- what method is best to collect the information (personally, mail, FAX, Federal Express, downloading via modems)
- what other services may interest the practice

Competitive Comparison

From this information Physicians 1st Billing and Claims will be able to customize charges for each practice. This ensures that the client is not being overcharged or undercharged for the services they desire. See Pricing Strategy for additional information on customized pricing of services. Currently our competitors are not offering full analysis service. Our competitors also are not able to offer two-way computer communications and record posting and file updates.

Physicians 1st Billing and Claims' sales brochure and tips brochure were developed with the expertise of a national marketing company specializing in medical reimbursement issues. The sales brochure will be used in conjunction with sales calls. Physicians 1st Billing and Claims' tips brochure will be utilized as a direct mail piece. Also available are copies of business cards and stationery.

Sales Literature

The computer software that is the crux of Physicians 1st Billing and Claims' medical reimbursement business is state of the art. Physicians 1st Billing and Claims is running in Windows 95. The software was specifically developed as a tool for medical reimbursement consultants. This is important because some software being sold is written to manage a doctor's office and does not necessarily incorporate all functions that are needed for consultants. The software also includes the latest features needed for managed care organization management, including tables for the numerous fee schedules which may be required, and customized reports to evaluate contacts.

Technology

The ET&T clearinghouse, which verifies the claims data, is highly respected in the industry. They are members of and have been certified by AFECHT, a national policing organization.

They utilize the American National Standards formats recognized by Medicare and most commercial insurance carriers. They guarantee claims are 98 percent accurate before being sent on to carriers.

Future Services

As stated earlier, Mary and John plan to initially process claims manually and electronically. As they gain experience, they will offer full medical office consulting services as follows:

- Patient billing
- Collection services
- Assistance in negotiating health care contracts
- Automated transcription service

MARKET ANALYSIS SUMMARY

Physicians 1st Billing and Claims' target market consists of any medical practice or health care delivery unit that utilizes the HCFA-1500 format (a national standard utilized by Medicare) for submission of claims. This includes: family practice, internal medicine, surgeons, psychologists, chiropractors, physical therapists, podiatrists, specialists, ambulance services, medical laboratories, etc. Physicians 1st Billing and Claims can also process claims for dentists with the use of special ADA software. New practices are particularly appealing as Physicians 1st Billing and Claims can assist the new physician and his or her staff in billing and claims training. By equipping the physicians with a well-trained staff in claims handling and putting an efficient billing program into place, Physicians 1st Billing and Claims can reduce the stress of start-up and ensure greater likelihood of a practice's success due in part to increased cash flow.

Market Segmentation

The following is a chart showing the number of physicians in Cincinnati, Ohio, for each speciality mentioned.

Number	Specialty
5	Allergy-Immunology
47	Anesthesiologist
3	Cardiovascular
12	Cardiovascular Surgery
84	Chiropractors
2	Child Psychiatry
1	Clinical Genetics
1	Clinical Immunology
5	Colon Rectal Surgery
10	Critical Care Medicine
179	Dental
11	Dermatology
1	Diabetes
35	Diagnostic Radiology
16	Ear, Nose, and Throat
1	Education
21	Emergency Medicine
114	Family Practice
30	Family Practice Residents
1	Family Practice Sports Medicine
12	Gastroenterology
22	General Surgery
1	General Surgery Burns

10	Geriatrics
7	Gynecology
7	Hematology
4	Infectious Diseases
40	Internal Medicine
4	Neonatal-Prenatal Medicine
12	Nephrology
9	Neurological Surgery
10	Neurology
3	Nuclear Radiology
26	Obstetrics
1	Obstetrics & Gynecology Resident
1	Occupational Medicine
3	Oncology
22	Ophthalmology
14	Optometry
35	Orthopedic Surgery
7	Orthopedic Surgery Resident
21	Pathology
1	Pediatric Nephrology
24	Pediatrics
1	Pediatrics Pulmonary
6	Physical Medicine & Rehabilitation
15	Physical Therapy
9	Plastic Surgery
14	Psychiatry
49	Psychologists
11	Pulmonary
3	Rheumatology
6	Therapeutic Radiology
13	Thoracic Surgery
14	Urology
12	Vascular Surgery

Physicians 1st Billing and Claims' initial plan is to sign a single doctor practice. An ideal target would be a family practice physician.

Market Analysis

Potential Customers	Growth	1998	1999	2000	2001	2002	CAGR
Physicians	2%	867	880	893	906	920	1.49%
Dentist	2%	179	183	187	191	195	2.16%
Other	2%	18	18	18	18	18	0.00%
Total	**1.58%**	**1,064**	**1,081**	**1,098**	**1,115**	**1,133**	**1.58%**

Service Business Analysis

The Federal Government's influence is quite positive. In May 1992, the Health Care Financing Administration, the governing body for Medicare, established what they call "payment floors" for Medicare claims. Carriers contracted to pay Medicare claims were told to hold paper claims' payments until "at least the 27th day after receipt." Electronic claims were to be held until the 14th day, but had to be paid by the 19th day. If "clean claims" (claims that are error free) were not paid by the 19th day after receipt, the Federal Government would have to pay interest on the claim amount. No payment penalties were placed on paper claims. Program Memorandum AB-92-5 described above, was beneficial for the electronic medical claims industry.

Several states have passed mandates of their own since 1992, but until now there has been no real action by the Federal Government on this issue. As stated earlier, it is expected that Congress will mandate electronic submission of Medicare claims in the near future and the cut-off date for paper claims will follow soon after. After the cut-off date, paper Medicare claims will not be accepted.

If history is any indication and current trends continue, commercial insurance carriers will follow suit within a short period of time. It is in their best interest as well. Statistics show that it currently costs a commercial carrier between $2.60 to $20.00 to process a claim. The same claim can be processed electronically for approximately $1.10. The conversion costs of moving from paper to electronic processing can be extensive, but in the long run these savings will be substantial.

Business Participants

If Congress does mandate electronic submission of insurance claims during 1998, 600 physicians will be scrambling to meet the mandates. Since October 1990, physicians treating Medicare and Medicaid patients have been required by law to file the necessary claims for these individuals. If practices are unable to meet the mandates, they will lose a good portion of their patient base.

During the past few years, medical practice's interest in Total Quality Control (TQC) has intensified. Part of this is attributed to the Federal Government and the American public's interest in health care reform. Physicians fear that if they do not voluntarily comply, more Federal regulations will be imposed.

The managed care movement across America is also influencing medical practices. In the past, doctors personally decided what they would charge for services rendered. For many physicians this fee-for-service payment method is a thing of the past. With managed care, physicians sign contracts and affiliate with different health maintenance organizations (HMOs) or preferred provider organizations (PPOs). Most decide to affiliate for one of two reasons:

1. Their peers are doing it and they do not want to be left out, or
2. They feel it will increase their patient base.

Unfortunately for many physicians, their patient bases do increase while their incomes decline. With the "capitation" payment schedules that accompany managed care affiliation, most physicians are making less than they were under the fee-for-service system. Association with managed care organizations also creates tremendous new paperwork requirements. Many offices complain of five times more paperwork than before affiliation. All of this is making medical practices look for innovative ways to create better office efficiency.

Main Competitors

Our main competition is Bi- State Medical Consulting. They provide full service medical claims management. Their strengths are:

- experience
- education
- large client base

Their weaknesses are:

- one-way claims communication and software
- limited advertising ability

The strengths and weaknesses, however, seem of little consequence as the local market by all accounts is untouched, and no other company in this area can offer the software features or the dedicated service that Physicians 1st Billing and Claims is able to offer.

The bottom line of our ability to compete lies in our ability to provide any and every physician with free practice management software, two-way computer communications which allow for next-day patient records updating, and substantially improved cash flow for the physician.

Studies show that the number 1 issue with consumers today is "personal service." They are tired of robotic salespeople, hollow sales promises, and mediocre support from unresponsive technical staff. They want to know that someone really cares about their concerns and wants to resolve their problems. They want thoroughly thought-out solutions that reap benefits. And they want it when they want it. Physicians 1st Billing and Claims understands this because we have been in their position.

STRATEGY AND IMPLEMENTATION SUMMARY

Physicians 1st Billing and Claims also understands that they want a reasonable price for services. That is why Physicians 1st Billing and Claims takes the time to evaluate the needs of each medical office and then we customize our service and our charges, based on needs. We need to make sure we are not overcharging or undercharging. If we're overcharging, then the client will not be happy. If we're undercharging, then we won't be happy and we probably won't do a good job. What we're looking for is win-win, long-term relationships with our clients. Zig Ziglar, noted sales trainer, asks the question, "Would you buy from you? Are you the type of business that you would like to do business with?" Physicians 1st Billing and Claims feels we are the type of company that anyone would be happy to do business with.

Physicians 1st Billing and Claims can provide the following benefits:

Competitive Edge

1. Free State-of-the-Art Practice Software
2. Two-way Computer Communications
3. Next-Day Patient Record Updating
4. Complete Practice Analysis
5. Full Service Medical Claims Management
6. Superior Service
7. Experience

No one else in the local market can offer this service package.

There is a marked increase in results when multiple items are used in concert to attain your goal, a contract for services between you and a health care practice. The basic plan is divided into five segments:

Marketing Strategy

1. Contacting the medical practice for the first time.
   - By phone
   - Cold call
2. Identifying the gatekeeper and making contact with them.
3. Mailing or dropping off information.
   - Three-panel brochure
   - Self mailer
   - Promotional letter
4. Scheduling an appointment for a presentation.
5. The presentation.

Contacts to implement this marketing strategy will be from a previously developed database of physicians who currently do not file medical claims electronically. This information is obtained from public records.

Pricing Strategy

Physicians 1st Billing and Claims' pricing strategy is a two-part program:

Part 1:

The first question that must be asked in the negotiation process is, "Does this practice want complete claims management?" If the answer is yes, Physicians 1st Billing and Claims will negotiate services based on a percentage. Usually the percentage will be from 6 to 10 percent based on the size of the practice.

Part 2:

If the practice simply wants claims filing, the pay-for-services rendered will be based on a sliding scale with ranges between $3.50 and $5.00. This scale is divided as follows:

# Patients	Price Per Claim
001-99	$5.00
100-199	$4.50
200-299	$4.25
300-399	$4.00
400 +	$3.50

A one-time setup charge between $150.00 and $500.00 based on patient load will be assessed and will be due at contract signing.

Promotion Strategy

We believe it is much smarter for a medical practice to outsource the detail work of insurance processing to an expert medical reimbursement service instead of trying to make the transition to in-house processing themselves. For years medical practices have been relying on the expert advice of accounting services for tax issues and financial planning. These areas have become very complicated and expertise is needed to ensure judicious decisions. Insurance processing has become very complicated as well, and physicians need to begin relying on expert services to maximize their reimbursement from insurance carriers.

Most medical offices are computerized to the degree that they own a computer and software with capabilities to set appointments, bill patients, and print paper insurance claims. Most do not have capabilities to transmit claims electronically or scientifically evaluate managed care contracts, and the transition is expensive.

Their current software and system have been very stable, and for years may not have even required a software update. Electronic claims submission is a very volatile and different industry requiring frequent software modifications to stay abreast of industry changes. Expertise and time is required over and above what the normal medical office can afford.

For most offices the transition would begin with buying new hardware (or updating the old), claims software, modems, communications software, etc. Very likely the current medical staff will not have the expertise to handle upgrades, install programs, test modems, understand baud rates, conduct initial testing, and other essential skills. This means the office has to hire someone with these skills or retain an expensive support service. With the high turnover of personnel that most medical offices currently experience, retaining another type of employee adds a completely new dimension.

The logical solution to meeting Federal mandates and to process all claims electronically, is to contract with an expert electronic medical billing and reimbursement service. This allows current office staff to resume the tasks they were trained to do, such as assist patients and doctors.

Marketing Programs

With a service-oriented business such as this, clients must be brought on one at a time. The full practice analysis will be conducted with each need being identified. Charges will be negotiated based on these needs. When we have successfully met the needs of each practice, the practice will be more inclined to promote our business to other medical practices that would benefit from our service. Studies have shown that the most common way to expand a medical reimbursement business is through referrals from current clients.

In addition to the on-going program discussed above, Physicians 1st Billing and Claims will incorporate numerous other strategies simultaneously.

In general they are:

- A listing in the local Yellow Pages. We realize the importance of stability and professionalism; anyone who has been in business any length of time can be located in the Yellow Pages. We will only be utilizing a one-line listing, for we feel this will not be the main source of clients contacting us, but will provide the professional appearance we need.
- Networking as members of the Chamber of Commerce, local civic organizations, county medical associations.
- Attending and volunteering services for medical fundraisers and health fairs, maintaining an information booth at local medical trade shows.
- Attending Medicare, Medicaid, Blue Shield, and Worker's Compensation activities.
- Networking with other professionals, such as medical and professional consultants, attorneys, and accountants whose clientele is predominately medical, pharmaceutical representatives, and medical equipment salespeople.
- Affiliation with local and national peer organizations, including those available on the Internet.
- Advertising in local/hospital newsletters.
- Membership in the Better Business Bureau.
- Accepting an invitation to appear on a local radio talk show.
- Submitting several press releases annually to local newspapers.
- Writing articles for several health publications in the area.

Sales Forecast

The following chart reflects the realistic goals we have set.

Unit Sales	FY1999	FY2000	FY2001
Row 1	33,000	48,000	52,000
Other	28,800	0	0
Total Unit Sales	**61,800**	**48,000**	**52,000**
Unit Prices			
Row 1	$3.50	$3.50	$3.50
Other	$1.50	$0.00	$0.00

Sales Forecast

Continued

Sales	FY1999	FY2000	FY2001
Row 1	$115,500	$168,000	$182,000
Other	$43,200	$0	$0
Total Sales	**$158,700**	**$168,000**	**$182,000**
Direct Unit Costs			
Row 1	$0.00	$0.00	$0.00
Other	$0.00	$0.00	$0.00
Direct Cost of Sales			
Row 1	$0	$0	$0
Other	$0	$0	$0
Subtotal Direct Cost of Sales	**$0**	**$0**	**$0**

Strategic Alliances

Physicians 1st Billing and Claims is a franchise affiliated with the nationally known medical billing franchise. This affiliation allows us to take advantage of the prestige and experience associated with the national company. Included with affiliation is:

- Full-accounting, state-of-the-art medical billing software (Windows based) that includes patient billing, specialized reports, superbill generation, electronic claims, open-item accounting, patient recall, mailing labels, patient scheduling, and graphics capabilities
- One year, toll-free telephone support for software, claims processing and marketing strategies
- One year software updates, rewrites, and new manuals
- A library of current medical insurance carriers
- A library of current CPT (procedure) codes
- A library of current ICD-9-CM (diagnosis) codes
- Flash Code for Windows (software that handles extensive validity checking on procedure and diagnosis codes)
- Clearinghouse registration for claims processing centers
- Clearinghouse registration for first medical practice
- Dental electronic claims software
- Marketing manuals, audio tapes, and supplemental marketing materials
- Computer software to help in designing innovative marketing brochures
- Personalized help in designing marketing materials
- Updates to keep us informed concerning changes in the health care industry
- Computer software to calculate what it currently costs a medical practice to provide insurance processing for patients
- Computer software to help calculate customized charges for medical practices
- Invoicing software
- Contact management software

Milestones

Milestone	Manager	Planned Date	Department	Budget
First Client	John & Mary Moore	10/30/98	S&M	$1,200
Second Client	John & Mary Moore	11/30/98	S&M	$1,200
Third Client	John & Mary Moore	12/30/98	S&M	$1,200
Fourth Client	John & Mary Moore	1/30/99	S&M	$1,200
Fifth Client	John & Mary Moore	2/1/99	S&M	$1,200
Other				
Totals				**$6,000**

As stated earlier in Company Ownership, the primary management of the company will be handled by John Moore. As president of Physicians 1st Billing and Claims, John brings 16 years of management experience to his position. John holds a Bachelor of Science degree in Education from Ball State University. John's education and experience in the medical field come from his extensive training in physiology and anatomy as a major part of a Health Science degree. John managed Big Timber Building Materials from 1982 to 1995. Having been responsible for sales in excess of $12 million, John is more than capable of leading Physicians 1st Billing and Claims to the number one billing and claims processing firm in the local area. John will handle all marketing and sales functions. John will oversee the data processing, training, accounting, and computer departments.

Mary will serve as the chief operating officer of administration and clerical. Mary brings 18 years of valuable experience to her administrative post. Mary holds a Bachelor of Science degree in Education from Ball State University. Mary has successfully organized and headed many community endeavors that without her foresight would never have achieved their intended goals. Mary will mainly be responsible for initial telemarketing, data entry, customer service, and disseminating of company information. Mary has 13 years in medical claims filing and three years in secretarial training; both lend themselves well to the departments she will head up. Physicians 1st Billing and Claims and its customers are in good hands with Mary's leadership.

John and Mary will assume full-time management of Physicians 1st Billing and Claims.

Two other part-time employees who are equally as valuable for the roles they will play in the operations of Physicians 1st Billing and Claims are Erika and Matthew Moore. Erika will assume some data entry duties and facility maintenance duties. Matthew will assume facility maintenance duties to start and will later participate in data entry. Erika and Matthew will both be responsible for manual clerical duties which are vital to the operations of Physicians 1st Billing and Claims.

MANAGEMENT SUMMARY

The business will be financed mainly through cash flow. With a service-oriented business our main investment is for initial software and computer equipment. During subsequent years, other than normal overhead, we will be looking at:

- Advertising fees of $50.00 monthly to Claim Systems advertising pool
- Renewal of memberships to local and national organizations
- Updates of reference manuals and books
- Office supplies and utilities
- Payroll and benefits

FINANCIAL PLAN

This financial plan depends on important assumptions, most of which are shown in the following table.

Important Assumptions

General Assumptions

	FY1999	FY2000	FY2001
Short-term Interest Rate %	10.00%	10.00%	10.00%
Long-term Interest Rate %	10.00%	10.00%	10.00%
Payment Days Estimator	35	35	35
Collection Days Estimator	45	45	45
Tax Rate %	20.00%	20.00%	20.00%
Expenses in Cash %	10.00%	10.00%	10.00%
Sales on Credit %	100.00%	100.00%	100.00%
Personnel Burden %	0.00%	0.00%	0.00%

Break-even Analysis

The break-even analysis shows that Physicians 1st Billing and Claims has a good balance of fixed costs and sufficient sales strength to remain healthy. As with any business, the first few months will show negative financial numbers.

Monthly Units Break-even	909
Monthly Sales Break-even	$3,182

Assumptions:

Average Per-Unit Revenue	$3.50
Average Per-Unit Variable Cost	$0.20
Estimated Monthly Fixed Cost	$3,000

Projected Profit and Loss

Because of the initial costs for reference books, office furniture, advertising, and clearinghouse fees, Physicians 1st Billing and Claims will show a loss of $166.00 for the first two months of business operation.

	FY1999	**FY2000**	**FY2001**
Sales	$158,700	$168,000	$182,000
Direct Cost of Sales	$0	$0	$0
Other	$0	$0	$0
Total Cost of Sales	$0	$0	$0
Gross Margin	$158,700	$168,000	$182,000
Gross Margin %	100.00%	100.00%	100.00%
Operating expenses:			
Advertising/Promotion	$600	$600	$600
Travel	$0	$0	$0
Miscellaneous	$0	$0	$0
Payroll Expense	$28,000	$35,000	$45,000
Depreciation	$0	$0	$0
Franchise fee	$1,596	$0	$0
Utilities	$876	$600	$600
Insurance	$202	$202	$202
Rent	$1,608	$700	$700
Clearinghouse expense	$14,130	$15,072	$16,014
Total Operating Expenses	$47,012	$52,174	$63,116
Profit Before Interest and Taxes	$111,688	$115,826	$118,884
Interest Expense Short-term	$0	$0	$0
Interest Expense Long-term	$0	$0	$0
Taxes Incurred	$22,338	$23,165	$23,777
Net Profit	$89,350	$92,661	$95,107
Net Profit/Sales	56.30%	55.16%	52.26%

Projected Cash Flow

Initially, cash flow will be supported by the personal savings accounts of the head officers of this company. This means that the $3,564.00 left to finance will come from this cash fund.

	FY1999	**FY2000**	**FY2001**
Net Profit	$89,350	$92,661	$95,107
Plus:			
Depreciation	$0	$0	$0
Change in Accounts Payable	$2,658	($257)	$132

	FY1999	FY2000	FY2001
Current Borrowing (repayment)	$0	$0	$0
Increase (decrease) Other Liabilities	$0	$0	$0
Long-term Borrowing (repayment)	$0	$0	$0
Capital Input	$60,000	$0	$0
Subtotal	$152,009	$92,404	$95,239
Less:			
Change in Accounts Receivable	$36,500	$2,139	$3,220
Change in Other Short-term Assets	$0	$0	$0
Capital Expenditure	$0	$0	$0
Dividends	$0	$0	$0
Subtotal	**$36,500**	**$2,139**	**$3,220**
Net Cash Flow	**$115,509**	**$90,265**	**$92,109**
Cash Balance	**$115,509**	**$205,773**	**$297,792**

Projected Cash Flow

Continued

The following is the Projected Balance Sheet.

Projected Balance Sheet

Assets

Short-term Assets	Starting Balances	FY1999	FY2000	FY2001
Cash	$0	$115,509	$205,773	$297,792
Accounts Receivable	$0	$36,500	$38,639	$41,859
Other Short-term Assets	$0	$0	$0	$0
Total Short-term Assets	$0	$152,009	$244,412	$339,651
Long-term Assets				
Capital Assets	$0	$0	$0	$0
Accumulated Depreciation	$0	$0	$0	$0
Total Long-term Assets	$0	$0	$0	$0
Total Assets	$0	$152,009	$244,412	$339,651
Liabilities and Capital				
Accounts Payable	$0	$2,658	$2,401	$2,533
Short-term Notes	$0	$0	$0	$0
Other Short-term Liabilities	$0	$0	$0	$0
Subtotal Short-term Liabilities	$0	$2,658	$2,401	$2,533
Long-term Liabilities	$0	$0	$0	$0
Total Liabilities	$0	$2,658	$2,401	$2,533
Paid in Capital	$6,040	$66,040	$66,040	$66,040
Retained Earnings	($6,040)	($6,040)	$83,310	$175,971
Earnings	$0	$89,350	$92,661	$95,107
Total Capital	**$0**	**$149,350**	**$242,011**	**$337,118**
Total Liabilities and Capital	**$0**	**$152,009**	**$244,412**	**$339,651**
Net Worth	**$0**	**$149,350**	**$242,011**	**$337,118**

The following are generated Business Ratios.

Business Ratios

Profitability Ratios:	FY1999	FY2000	FY2001	RMA
Gross Margin	100.00%	100.00%	100.00%	0
Net Profit Margin	56.30%	55.16%	52.26%	0
Return on Assets	58.78%	37.91%	28.00%	0
Return on Equity	59.83%	38.29%	28.21%	0

Business Ratios

Continued

	FY1999	FY2000	FY2001	RMA
Activity Ratios				
AR Turnover	4.35	4.35	4.35	0
Collection Days	42	82	81	0
Inventory Turnover	0	0	0	0
Accts Payable Turnover	6.44	6.44	6.44	0
Total Asset Turnover	1.04	0.69	0.54	0
Debt Ratios				
Debt to Net Worth	0.02	0.01	0.01	0
Short-term Liab. To Liab.	1	1	1	0
Liquidity Ratios				
Current Ratio	57.18	101.78	134.08	0
Quick Ratio	57.18	101.78	134.08	0
Net Working Capital	$149,350	$242,011	$337,118	0
Interest Coverage	0	0	0	0
Additional Ratios				
Assets to Sales	0.96	1.45	1.87	0
Debt/Assets	2%	1%	1%	0
Current Deb/Total Assets	2%	1%	1%	0
Acid Test	43.45	85.69	117.56	0
Asset Turnover	1.04	0.69	0.54	0
Sales/Net Worth	1.06	0.69	0.54	0

Mortgage Company

BUSINESS PLAN

NATIONAL MORTGAGE, INC.

123 N. Main Blvd., Suite 201
Seattle, Washington 98108

This mortgage company specializes in lending money to people who have poor credit or who are self-employed and have problems qualifying for conventional loans. It plans to offer complementary credit cards and debit cards, as well as insurance, for this niche market. Future plans include national expansion. This plan was provided by Ameriwest Business Consultants, Inc.

- EXECUTIVE SUMMARY

- OBJECTIVES & GOALS

- STRATEGIES FOR ACHIEVING GOALS

- BUSINESS DESCRIPTION, STATUS, & OUTLOOK

- MANAGEMENT & OWNERSHIP

- MARKET ANALYSIS

- MARKETING STRATEGIES

- FIVE-YEAR PROJECTIONS

- RATIO COMPARISON

- CONCLUSIONS & SUMMARY

MORTGAGE COMPANY
BUSINESS PLAN

EXECUTIVE SUMMARY

BUSINESS DESCRIPTION

National Mortgage has developed a unique concept of lending to people who have less than perfect credit or self-employed people who have a hard time qualifying for conventional loans. The money loaned out is typically used by borrowers to consolidate debt and can provide a source of huge savings for our clients by paying off high interest credit card debt. We charge competitive interest rates. Our customers are very ready to work with us because they have usually been turned down by one or more lenders and we can provide them peace of mind and a way to solve their credit problems. The loans are secured with a second mortgage on their property. Hours of operation are Monday through Friday, 10:00 A.M. to 7:00 P.M., and Saturday, 8:00 A.M. to 3:00 P.M. The processing center is open 8:00 A.M to 8:00 P.M., Monday through Friday, and 8:00 A.M. to 6:00 P.M. on Saturday.

CURRENT POSITION AND FUTURE OUTLOOK

The business is in its third year of operation. Operations are conducted from facilities located at 123 North Main Boulevard in Seattle, Washington. The premises consist of approximately 1,600 square feet. The first several years were used to build the business, equip the office and hire a competent staff. Key employees are Jill Stone, Sue Brown, Helen Hunt, and Rachel Rosana. The company currently employs five people. National is now ready to move to a higher level and can handle a much greater volume. We are currently working with Merrill Lynch and ABC to franchise our unique concept on a national scale.

MANAGEMENT AND OWNERSHIP

The company is set up as a corporation with Jill Stone owning 100% of the stock. She initially helped set up the operations and even though she is now less active in the operations, she is available for consultation and advice. The corporation is an "S" corporation, but will be changed to a "C" corporation by the end of 1997 to satisfy requirements for becoming a franchiser. The corporation type of entity was chosen for liability protection, tax considerations, growth plans, stock option plans, and the opportunity to raise capital from investors more easily. Sue Brown serves as vice president. She has five years of experience in the mortgage business. Helen Hunt serves as operations manager. Rachel Rosana is the processing manager. National currently employs five additional people in various capacities. When volume picks up, additional part-time or full-time employees will be hired as the workload requires. National will continue to utilize the services from consultants in areas such as planning, budgeting, accounting, general business advising, and law.

UNIQUENESS AND DIFFERENTIATION OF THE SERVICE

National, Inc. will continue to specialize in serving individuals who have less than perfect credit or who are self-employed and cannot qualify for conventional loans. The company was formed to provide loans to this niche market. The company utilizes the most current technology to enable it to not only provide competitive pricing but also excellent service. In the future, we plan to offer complementary products such as secured credit cards and debit cards, insurance, and other investment tools.

It is rare in today's business world to find a true market void. That is exactly what National has done. It has combined the latest in technology with an unfilled need and promises to deliver a high quality product at a competitive price. Our services have limited competition in Washington and even nationally because of the nature of our clients. We have built an excellent reputation in the area and wish to capitalize on it to enter the national marketplace. To reach an even larger market we will develop and utilize a web page on the Internet.

FUNDS REQUIRED AND USAGE

To continue to fund its growth and provide the money for franchise operations, National Mortgage will be seeking $150,000 in additional funding. This may come from either investors or from additional loans. Any additional funds obtained will be for working capital, equipment purchases, advertising, and expenses associated with setting up franchise operations.

MOST LIKELY CASE	Projected Year 1	Projected Year 2	Projected Year 3	Projected Year 4	Projected Year 5
Total Revenue	$2,341,050	$3,046,200	$3,986,400	$5,190,000	$6,957,000
Cost of Sales	411,047	688,059	1,016,531	1,427,031	1,976,229
Gross Profit	1,930,003	2,358,141	2,969,869	3,762,969	4,980,771
Selling, General, Expense	1,439,171	1,566,407	1,569,519	1,664,975	1,769,794
Income Before Taxes	490,831	791,734	1,400,350	2,097,994	3,210,976
Income Taxes	177,475	286,275	506,339	758,593	1,161,025
Income After Taxes	**313,356**	**505,459**	**894,012**	**1,339,401**	**2,049,952**
OPTIMISTIC CASE					
Total Revenue	2,809,260	3,655,440	4,783,680	6,228,000	8,348,400
Cost of Sales	493,257	825,671	1,219,837	1,712,437	2,371,475
Gross Profit	2,316,003	2,829,769	3,563,843	4,515,563	5,976,925
Selling, General, Expense	1,727,006	1,879,688	1,883,422	1,997,970	2,123,753
Income Before Taxes	588,997	950,081	1,680,420	2,517,593	3,853,172
Income Taxes	212,970	343,530	607,606	910,311	1,393,230
Income After Taxes	**376,028**	**606,551**	**1,072,814**	**1,607,282**	**2,459,942**
PESSIMISTIC CASE					
Total Revenue	1,872,840	2,436,960	3,189,120	4,152,000	5,565,600
Cost of Sales	328,838	550,447	813,225	1,141,625	1,580,983
Gross Profit	1,544,002	1,886,513	2,375,895	3,010,375	3,984,617
Selling, General, Expense	1,151,337	1,253,126	1,255,615	1,331,980	1,415,835
Income Before Taxes	392,665	633,387	1,120,280	1,678,395	2,568,781
Income Taxes	141,980	229,020	405,071	606,874	928,820
Income After Taxes	**$250,685**	**$404,367**	**$715,209**	**$1,071,521**	**$1,639,961**

OBJECTIVES & GOALS

1. To provide a high quality service so that customers will perceive great value.

2. To expand into the national market.

3. To obtain additional funding to fuel the expansion.

4. To become one of the premier nationally known equity lenders serving individuals with less than perfect credit or who are self-employed.

OBJECTIVES & GOALS

Continued

5. National Mortgage plans to closely monitor changing technology to be certain that the company is using the latest and most cost-effective equipment to keep up with current trends in the marketplace.

6. To provide National Mortgage with at least $700,000 in retained earning over the next five years.

In addition to the above goals, we will survey our customers and make changes in our programs and add services to meet their changing ideas in the marketplace.

STRATEGIES FOR ACHIEVING GOALS

To achieve the above goals, we will concentrate on providing outstanding quality and aggressively promote our franchises throughout the country. We will utilize the assistance of Merrill Lynch and ABC to make the franchising work. Both of these companies have achieved national recognition and do an excellent job in getting franchise operations off the ground. National Mortgage currently serves the Seattle and Spokane markets and their surrounding areas with its loan operations. By the end of first year of expansion, we expect to be serving up to 60 additional markets as a result of the franchise operations. As the Washington economy continues to see rapid growth, National Mortgage will take advantage of an even greater share of the local marketplace than it has in the past. It will be able to capitalize on the reputation it has built.

Our major goals include maximizing sales and building our client/customer base with a close eye on profitability. It is very important to continue to fill the market void for those borrowers that cannot obtain loans through conventional lenders. Our experience has shown that people with less than perfect credit or who are self-employed are very grateful for the professional manner in which their loans are processed.

BUSINESS DESCRIPTION, STATUS & OUTLOOK

National, Inc. will continue on its current path of growth. Its main office will be fully staffed and equipped and able to handle nearly double the amount of processing with little additional expenses.

The biggest problem this venture will face will be creating customer awareness of our services and funding the growth. We will use a combination of advertising techniques and word of mouth to increase this awareness. We will also utilize the services of Merrill Lynch and ABC, nationally recognized and respected companies, to help us in this area. Once a general awareness is present, the company has a virtually unlimited growth potential.

Through the franchise operations we will be able to handle large numbers of loans through our processing center.

Once the franchising operations are established, loans will be processed from each franchisee through our processing center. Loans will be processed for the franchisees as well as those generated by our company-owned office.

National Mortgage is a member of the Seattle Metro Chamber of Commerce and the Housing and Building Committee.

The future holds the promise of almost unlimited growth and income as the business matures and considers other markets and products. Complementary products such as secured credit cards and debit cards will be considered in the future in response to customer requests.

Jill Stone serves as the President and Chief Executive Officer. She worked several years for a nationally known equity lender. She spent nearly twenty years in the United States Army in a variety of top level management positions and attended the University of Kentucky. She is also fluent in reading, writing, and speaking Spanish. Jill is responsible for the overall operations of the loan processing area. She assists in processing files, understanding and adhering to lender's guidelines, ordering and follow-up on verifications. She attends on-going training conducted by lenders, title companies, and other outside agencies. She ensures Quality Control for each loan package prior to submission.

Sue Brown serves as Vice President of National Mortgage and has five years of experience in the mortgage industry and has "hands-on, ground-up" knowledge of all facets of the mortgage business. She has worked with a variety of nationally known equity lenders. She has played a key role and functioned in a management capacity in most impact areas of the industry. Her supervisory positions in the administrative, operational, technological, and fiscal areas of this discipline have afforded her the skills, experience, and talents necessary to lead National Mortgage through this new century. Sue is heavily involved in sales, advertising, banking, operation, planning, insurance, purchasing, and equipment. She also will be involved with locating, interviewing, qualifying, and training the initial franchisees. She will oversee the training of future area representatives and instructors.

Helen Hunt serves National Mortgage as its Operations Manager. She attended Seattle Business College and studied business management. Her duties include office management, insuring client satisfaction, resolving customer complaints, and client interviewing for prequalification. She also is involved in the hiring, firing, scheduling, and training of employees.

Rachel Rosana has worked with several nationally known mortgage lenders. Her main duties with National Mortgage are in the capacity of Processing Manager. She trains processors, funding representatives, and team leaders. She provides quality control for file processing and ensures files are maintained properly.

The business is set up as a "C" corporation. This form of legal entity was chosen primarily for liability reasons and makes it easier to secure investors. The company employs five highly trained employees in office management and loan administration. As the business grows, additional part-time or full-time employees may be added to handle the increased workload.

National Mortgage has applied for membership in the National Association of Mortgage Brokers and with local Associations of Mortgage Brokers. Memberships in these organizations help us monitor changes in the industry and government regulations.

MARKET OVERVIEW, SIZE, AND SEGMENTS

Listed below are just some of the reasons the industry is expanding and why it is a good time for a business such as ours:

- Personal debt is rising at record numbers.
- People are using credit cards to purchase daily items - such as food.
- The average person has 6 credit cards.
- The average person receives 7-10 credit cards solicitations per month.
- The baby boom generation accounts for the majority of bankruptcies filed.
- Downsizing has affected the middle management jobs that have been permanently eliminated and replaced with lower paying jobs.

CUSTOMER PROFILE

Typical characteristics of our customers include the following:

- 29 to 50 years old
- No sizable equity in their home
- Many times have less than perfect credit or are self-employed
- Married, with children
- Blue collar workers
- Middle- to low-income
- Have usually been turned down by one or more conventional lenders
- Include people who are looking for peace of mind and are trying to regain control of their finances

COMPETITION

In theory, the competitors National Mortgage faces in the marketplace include bankers, finance companies, and mortgage brokers. In reality, the concept of lending to people with less than perfect credit or who are self-employed, means that very few of the above mentioned competitors offer true competition. These competitors also have limitations as a result of their loan programs, higher interest rates, and lack of advertising dollars.

Risk Analysis— Strengths & Weaknesses

National Mortgage is strong in operations, production, quality of service, product mix, company policies, desirability, and facilities. National Mortgage is about average in management, marketing, distribution, servicing, product features, advertising, overhead, pricing, and delivery time. National Mortgage is weak in finance and planning, market leadership sales force, and location. In these areas of weakness we have hired professionals to supplement our management abilities.

We have low risk exposure in the areas of dependence upon other companies, vulnerability to substitutes, technology, suppliers, inflation, and interest rates.

We perceive medium risk exposure industry maturity, market position, competitive position, distribution, and strategy. We perceive high risk in the areas of financial performance and management performance. These are the areas we have specifically addressed when we hired business management, franchise, and marketing professionals to help us. It is also a major reason we are franchising our concept.

We will continue to obtain help when needed in areas we feel it is necessary to complement our abilities.

MARKETING STRATEGIES

PRICING AND VALUE

Our pricing strategy involves pricing at competitive rates. Our customers are people with either less than perfect credit or who are self-employed and have a difficult time obtaining an equity loan from conventional lenders. We do keep an eye on competition so we do not price ourselves out of the market. We will continue to review our pricing every six months or more often when the economy or competition dictates.

Currently, there is a certain amount of price inelasticity in this service due to government regulations. On the other hand, if we offer additional services we can open up other opportunities to increase revenues. Pricing will be reviewed on a semi-annual basis.

SELLING TACTICS

Our company's marketing strategy will incorporate plans to promote our line of services through several different channels and on different levels, along with the use of referrals, telemarketing, and advertising. We also plan to utilize a website as a selling tool.

Advertising tools we will utilize include brochures, catalogs, targeted advertisements, lead generation, lead referral and follow-up systems, information gathering, and dissemination. To better reach the local market we will network with groups that help people with credit problems. In addition, we will greater utilize local newspapers extensively.

Nationally, we will advertise through the use of a very extensive multi-level advertising campaign in conjunction with our franchises.

ADVERTISING, PROMOTION, AND DISTRIBUTION OF SERVICES

We recognize that the key to success at this time requires extensive promotion.

Advertising goals include all of the following:

- Position the company to become one of the premier mortgage brokers in the country.
- Increase general awareness of our company both locally and nationally.
- Increase general awareness of our company and its outstanding track record.
- Maximize efficiency by continually monitoring media effectiveness.
- Maintain an ad in the Yellow Pages and Business White Pages.
- Continually update our brochure to explain our company, service, and products.
- Use direct mail campaigns.
- Use a mix of media to saturate the marketplace.

PUBLIC RELATIONS

We will develop a public relations policy that will help increase awareness of our company and product. To achieve these goals we will consider some or all of the following:

- Develop a press release and a company backgrounder as a public relations tool.
- Develop a telephone script to handle customer and advertiser contacts.
- Develop a survey to be completed by customers to help determine the following:
    1. How did they hear about us?
    2. What influenced them to use our service?
    3. How well did our service satisfy their needs?
    4. How efficient was our service?
    5. Did they have any problems getting through to us?
    6. Did they shop competitors before selecting us?
    7. How did they initially perceive our company and product?
    8. Where are most of our customers located?
    9. Are there suggestions for improving our service or our approach to advertising?
    10. What additional services would they like us to offer?
    11. Would they recommend us to others?

ASSUMPTIONS, DEFINITIONS, AND NOTES

Throughout this business plan we have taken a very conservative approach to developing our financial projections.

- Number of loans processed the first year will average 111.25.
- Franchises sold will gradually increase to 60 the first year.

- Inflation rates to remain stable at 3-5%.
- Robust local economy.
- Interest Rates to remain flat and basically unchanged.
- Local unemployment rates to remain low at approximately 4-5%.
- Assumes royalties of 8% of fees.
- Assumes processing fee of $570 per loan.
- Payroll taxes and benefits will equal 25% of total payroll expenses.
- Assumes $25,000 fee for each franchise sold.
- Assumes a loan of $150,000 at 10.00% amortized over five years and having monthly payments of $3,187 per month.
- Cost of unreimbursed expense of each loan will be $75.00.
- Assumes AdFund income of $60 per loan.
- Assumes 1 processor for each 15 loans processed. Each processor will make $1,500 per month. Salaries will increase 5% per year.
- Assumes 6 processors per team.
- Assumes 1 Team Leader for every 6 processors. Each Team Leader will earn $2,083 per month and this will increase by 5% per year.
- Assumes 1 Funding Representative for each team. Each Funding Representative will earn $1,387 per month. Salary increases will be 5% per year.
- Assumes 1 Customer Service Representative for every 50 loans. Each CSR will earn $1,387 per month. Salary to increase 5% per year.
- Assumes 1 General Office Worker for every 10 teams. Office Worker will earn $1,127 per month. Salary increased will be 5% per year per worker.
- Assumes 1 Area Representative for every 20 franchises. Each Area Rep will earn $2,333 per month and this amount will increase 5% per year.
- Depreciation will be computed using the straight line method over 60 months.
- Office supplies/postage expenses is set at 1% of monthly income.
- Contingency and miscellaneous expenses are set at 5% of total income.
- Telephone and utilities expenses are set at 2.0% of total sales.
- Franchise and loan operations each have unique expenses associated with its operation.
- Forty percent of general expenses will be directed to fund franchise operations.

FIVE-YEAR PROJECTIONS — Financial Inputs & Summary

First Year of Start-Up 1997
Corporation Type C—"C" Corporation format selected; income taxes WILL be computed.

Operating Data	Year 1	Year 2	Year 3	Year 4	Year 5
Days sales in accounts receivable	0	0	0	0	0
Days materials cost in inventory	0	0	0	0	0
Days finished goods in inventory	0	0	0	0	0
Days materials cost in payables	30	30	30	30	30
Days payroll expense accrued	20	20	20	20	20
Days operation expense accrued	25	25	25	25	25
Expense Data					
Direct labor as % of sales	13.28%	18.30%	21.21%	23.16%	24.20%
Other payroll as % of sales	4.19%	3.38%	2.71%	2.19%	1.71%
Payroll taxes as % of Sales	4.37	5.42%	2.53%	2.42%	2.24%
Insurance as % of sales	0.89%	0.72%	0.58%	0.47%	0.37%
Legal/accounting as % of sales	2.563%	2.068%	1.659%	1.338%	1.048%
Other overhead as % of sales	48.16%	38.86%	31.18	25.15%	19.70%

FIVE-YEAR PROJECTIONS — Financial Inputs & Summary

Continued

Expense Data

Direct labor as % of sales	$310,922	$557,559	$845,531	$1,202,031	$1,683,729
Other payroll as % of sales	$98,008	$102,910	$108,056	$113,458	$119,131
Payroll taxes as % of sales	$102,233	$165,117	$100,715	$125,340	$155,850
Insurance as % of sales	$20,900	$21,945	$23,042	$24,194	$25,404
Legal/accounting as % of sales	$60,000	$63,000	$66,150	$69,458	$72,930
Other overhead as % of sales	$1,127,345	$1,183,712	$1,242,898	$1,305,043	$1,370,295
Other Operating Expenses	**1,408,486**	**1,536,685**	**1,540,861**	**1,637,493**	**1,743,611**

Financing Data (1997 on)	**Deprec.**	**Capital**	**Tot. Debt**	**Curr. Portion**	**LT Portion**	**Rate**
Long-term debt			$150,000	$9,201	$140,799	10.00%
Short-term debt				$0		10.00%
Capital stock issued						
Additional paid-in capital		$0				
Accumulated depreciation (as of 1996)	$0					

Five-Year Financial Summary—Balance Sheet

	START-UP	FIVE-YEAR FORECAST				
ASSETS	**1997**	**Year 1**	**Year 2**	**Year 3**	**Year 4**	**Year 5**
Current Assets						
Cash and cash equivalents	$81,615	$671,740	$1,306,659	$2,434,930	$4,050,797	$6,539,710
Accounts receivable	$0	$0	$0	$0	$0	$0
Inventory	$0	$0	$0	$0	$0	$0
Other current assets	$0	$15,000	$20,000	$25,000	$30,000	$35,000
Total Current Assets	**$81,615**	**$686,740**	**$1,326,659**	**$2,459,930**	**$4,080,797**	**$6,574,710**
Fixed Assets						
Land	$0	$0	$0	$0	$0	$0
Buildings	$0	$0	$0	$0	$0	$0
Equipment	$83,500	$83,500	$83,500	$83,500	$83,500	$83,500
Subtotal	$83,500	$83,500	$83,500	$83,500	$83,500	$83,500
Less-accumulated depreciation	$0	$11,900	$23,800	$35,700	$47,600	$59,500
Total Fixed Assets	**$83,500**	**$71,600**	**$59,700**	**$47,800**	**$35,900**	**$24,000**
Intangible Assets						
Cost	$21,000	$21,000	$21,000	$21,000	$21,000	$21,000
Less-accumulated amortization	$0	$4,200	$8,400	$12,600	$16,800	$21,000
Total Intangible Assets	**$21,000**	**$16,800**	**$12,600**	**$8,400**	**$4,200**	**$0**
Other	$0	$15,000	$20,000	$25,000	$30,000	$35,000
Total assets	**$186,115**	**$790,140**	**$1,418,959**	**$2,541,130**	**$4,150,897**	**$6,633,710**
LIABILITIES AND STOCKHOLDERS' EQUITY						
Current Liabilities						
Accounts Payable	$8,000	$8,229	$10,726	$14,055	$18,493	$24,041
Notes Payable		$0	$0	$0	$0	$0
Current portion of long-term debt	$0	$10,165	$11,229	$12,405	$13,704	$15,139
Income taxes	$0	$177,475	$286,275	$506,339	$758,593	$1,161,025
Accrued Expenses	$0	$112,166	$134,394	$150,389	$176,468	$210,053
Other current liabilities	$0	$10,000	$10,000	$10,000	$10,000	$15,000
Total Current Liabilities	**$8,000**	**$318,035**	**$452,624**	**$693,188**	**$977,258**	**$1,425,258**
Non-Current Liabilities						
Long-term debt	$150,000	$130,634	$119,405	$107,000	$93,296	$78,157
Deferred income	$0	$0	$0	$0	$0	$0
Deferred income taxes						
Other long-term liabilities						
Total Liabilities	**$158,000**	**$448,669**	**$572,029**	**$800,188**	**$1,070,554**	**$1,503,415**
Stockholders' Equity						
Capital Stock issued	$10,000	$10,000	$10,000	$10,000	$10,000	$10,000
Additional paid in capital	$0	$0	$0	$0	$0	$0
Retained earnings	$18,115	$331,471	$836,930	$1,730,942	$3,070,343	$5,120,295
Total Equity	$28,115	$341,471	$846,930	$1,740,942	$3,080,343	$5,130,295
Total Liabilities and Equity	**$186,115**	**$790,140**	**$1,418,959**	**$2,541,130**	**$4,150,897**	**$6,633,710**
"C" Corporation (Y/N)	Y					
Cash balance positive or (negative)	Positive	Positive	Positive	Positive	Positive	Positive
Amount sheet is out-of-balance	$0	$0	$0	$0	$0	$0
Amount cash flow out-of-balance		$0	$0	$0	$0	$0

Five-Year Projections—Financial Inputs & Summary

FIVE-YEAR FORECAST

Sales	Year 1	Year 2	Year 3	Year 4	Year 5
Sales	$2,341,050	$3,046,200	$3,986,400	$5,190,000	$6,957,000
Cost of sales	$411,047	$688,059	$1,016,531	$1,427,031	$1,976,229
Gross profit	**$1,930,003**	**$2,358,141**	**$2,969,869**	**$3,762,969**	**$4,980,771**
Expenses					
Operating expenses	$1,408,486	$1,536,685	$1,540,861	$1,637,493	$1,743,611
Interest	$14,586	$13,622	$12,558	$11,382	$10,083
Depreciation	$11,900	$11,900	$11,900	$11,900	$11,900
Amortization	$4,200	$4,200	$4,200	$4,200	$4,200
Total Expenses	**$1,439,171**	**$1,566,407**	**$1,569,519**	**$1,664,975**	**$1,769,794**
Operating income	**$490,831**	**$791,734**	**$1,400,350**	**$2,097,994**	**$3,210,976**
Other income and expenses					
Gain (loss) on sale of assets					
Other (net)					
Subtotal	**$0**	**$0**	**$0**	**$0**	**$0**
Income before tax	**$490,831**	**$791,734**	**$1,400,350**	**$2,097,994**	**$3,210,976**
Taxes (Federal & State)	$177,475	$286,275	$506,339	$758,593	$1,161,025
Rate	36.16%	36.16%	36.16%	36.16%	36.16%
Net income	**$313,356**	**$505,459**	**$894,012**	**$1,339,401**	**$2,049,952**
Retained earnings-beginning	$18,115	$331,471	$836,930	$1,730,942	$3,070,343
Dividends paid	$0	$0	$0	$0	$0
Retained earnings-ending	$331,471	$836,930	$1,730,942	$3,070,343	$5,120,295

Detailed Supporting Information

Cost of sales

Direct labor	$310,922	$557,559	$845,531	$1,202,031	$1,683,729
Loan expenses	$100,125	$130,500	$171,000	$225,000	$292,500
Other costs					

Depreciation: Enter the numbers of years.

<u>0</u> year Buildings	$0	$0	$0	$0	$0
<u>5</u> year Equipment	$11,900	$11,900	$11,900	$11,900	$11,900

Interest: Percentages from Data sheet

<u>10.00%</u> short-term	$0	$0	$0	$0	$0
<u>10.00%</u> long-term	$14,586	$13,622	$12,558	$11,382	$10,083

Five-Year Projections—Financial Inputs & Summary

FIVE-YEAR FORECAST

Cash from operations	Year 1	Year 2	Year 3	Year 4	Year 5
Net Earnings (loss)	$313,356	$505,459	$894,012	$1,339,401	$2,049,952
Add-Depreciation and amortization	$16,100	$16,100	$16,100	$16,100	$16,100
Net cash from operations	**$329,456**	**$521,559**	**$910,112**	**$1,355,501**	**$2,066,052**
Cash provided (used) by operating activities					
Accounts Receivable	$0	$0	$0	$0	$0
Inventory	$0	$0	$0	$0	$0
Other current assets	($15,000)	($5,000)	($5,000)	($5,000)	($5,000)
Other non-current assets	($15,000)	($5,000)	($5,000)	($5,000)	($5,000)
Accounts payable	$229	$2,497	$3,329	$4,438	$5,548
Current portion of long term debt	$10,165	$1,064	$1,176	$1,299	$1,435
Income taxes	$177,475	$108,800	$220,064	$252,254	$402,432
Accrued expenses	$112,166	$22,228	$15,995	$26,079	$33,585
Other current liabilities	$10,000	$0	$0	$0	$5,000
Dividends paid	$0	$0	$0	$0	$0
Net cash from operations	**$280,035**	**$124,589**	**$230,564**	**$274,070**	**$438,000**
Investment transactions					
Increases (decreases)					
Land	$0	$0	$0	$0	$0
Buildings and improvements	$0	$0	$0	$0	$0
Equipment	$0	$0	$0	$0	$0
Intangible assets	$0	$0	$0	$0	$0
Net cash from operations	**$0**	**$0**	**$0**	**$0**	**$0**
Financing transactions					
Increases (decreases)					
Short term notes payable	$0	$0	$0	$0	$0
Long term debt	($19,366)	($11,229)	($12,405)	($13,704)	($15,139)
Deferred income	$0	$0	$0	$0	$0
Deferred income taxes	$0	$0	$0	$0	$0
Other long-term liabilities	$0	$0	$0	$0	$0
Capital stock and paid in capital	$0	$0	$0	$0	$0
Net cash from financing	**($19,366)**	**($11,229)**	**($12,405)**	**($13,704)**	**($15,139)**
Net increase (decrease) in cash	**$590,125**	**$634,919**	**$1,128,271**	**$1,615,867**	**$2,488,913**
Cash at beginning of period	**$81,615**	**$671,740**	**$1,306,659**	**$2,434,930**	**$4,050,797**
Cash at the end of period	**$671,740**	**$1,306,659**	**$2,434,930**	**$4,050,797**	**$6,539,710**

Break-Even Analysis - Franchise Operations

Cost Variables	Per Month-1st Year		
	Optimistic -20.00%	Most Likely Case	Pessimistic 20.00%
FIXED COSTS:			
Rent	$711	$593	$474
Salaries (fixed)	$3,920	$3,267	$2,614
Insurance	$480	$400	$320
Depreciation & Amortization	$644	$537	$429
Interest	$583	$486	$389
Utilities/Phone	$1,873	$1,561	$1,249
(Other fixed costs)	$0	$0	$0
Total Fixed Costs	**$8,212**	**$6,843**	**$5,475**
VARIABLE COSTS			
Cost of Goods Sold	$0	$0	$0
Equipment Rental/Leases	$2,640	$2,200	$1,760
Other Salaries	$16,526	$13,772	$11,017
Inter Alios	$3,168	$2,640	$2,112
Workers Compensation	$356	$297	$237
Advertising/Marketing/Public Relations	$72,800	$60,667	$48,533
Professional Services	$2,400	$2,000	$1,600
(Other variable costs)	$6,902	$5,752	$4,602
Total Variable Costs	**$104,793**	**$87,327**	**$69,862**
Pricing & Unit Sales Variables			
Average Income per Franchise	$25,000	$25,000	$25,000
Average # of Franchises sold per month	6.00	5.00	4.00
Fixed Costs per Month	$1,642.36	$1,368.63	$1,095
Variable Costs per Month	$20,959	$17,465.45	$13,972.00
Break-Even Number of Franchises Sold	**1.1**	**0.9**	**0.7**
Number of Franchises over Break-Even	4.9	4.1	3.3
Break-Even Sales Amount	**$27,247.12**	**$22,705.94**	**$18,164.75**
Gross Profit per Franchise	$9,041	$7,534.55	$6,028
Gross Profit (over Break-Even)	$36,996	$30,830	$24,664

This break-even analysis includes as costs directly identified with the franchise operations and assumes 40% of all other expenses can be attributed to supporting franchise operations. This analysis show that the break-even number of franchises to be sold is 0.9 per month and the break-even sales is 22,706 per month.

Break-Even Analysis - Loan Operations

Cost Variables	————Per Month-1st Year————		
	Optimistic -20.00%	Most Likely Case	Pessimistic 20.00
FIXED COSTS:			
Rent	$1,067	$889	$711
Salaries (fixed)	$5,880	$4,900	$3,920
Insurance	$720	$600	$480
Depreciation & Amortization	$966	$805	$644
Interest	$875	$729	$583
Utilities/Phone	$2,809	$2,341	$1,873
(Other fixed costs)	$0	$0	$0
Total Fixed Costs	**$12,318**	**$10,265**	**$8,212**
VARIABLE COSTS			
Cost of Goods Sold	$10,013	$8,344	$6,675
Equipment Rental/Leases	$3,960	$3,300	$2,640
Other Salaries	$24,789	$20,658	$16,526
Inter Alios	$0	$0	$0
Workers Compensation	$534	$445	$356
Advertising/Marketing/Public Relations	$3,000	$2,500	$2,000
Professional Services	$3,600	$3,000	$2,400
(Other variable costs)	$13,805	$11,504	$9,203
Total Variable Costs	**$59,701**	**$49,750**	**$39,800**
Pricing & Unit Sales Variables			
Average Income per Loan	$684	$570	$456
Average # of Loans processed Per Month	133.50	111.25	89.00
Fixed Costs per loan	$110.72	$92.27	$73.81
Variable Costs per loan	$537	$447.20	$358
Break-Even Number of Loans Processed	**83.6**	**83.6**	**66.9**
Number of Loans over Break-Even	33.2	27.7	22.1
Break-Even Sales Amount	**$57,172.85**	**$47,644.04**	**$38,115.23**
Gross Profit per Loan Processed	$147.37	$122.80	$98.24
Gross Profit (over Break-Even)	$4,077	$3,397	$2,718

The break-even analysis for loan operations indicates that the break-even number of loans is 83.6 per month and the break-even sales is $47,644 per month.

RATIO COMPARISON

Ratio analysis can be one of the most useful financial management tools. It becomes important when you look at the trend of each ratio over time. It also becomes important when compared to averages of a particular industry. Because of the unique nature of National Mortgage we are unable to find comparable industry figures for the combined operations of both loan operations and franchise operations. However, the review of the following ratios is still worthwhile.

	Projected Year 1	Projected Year 2	Projected Year 3	Projected Year 4	Projected Year 5
Liquidity Ratios:					
Current Ratio	2.16	2.93	3.55	4.18	4.61
Quick Ratio	2.16	2.93	3.55	4.18	4.61
Sales / Receivables	N/A	N/A	N/A	N/A	N/A
Days' Receivables	N/A	N/A	N/A	N/A	N/A
Cost of Sales / Inventory	N/A	N/A	N/A	N/A	N/A
Days' Inventory	N/A	N/A	N/A	N/A	N/A
Cost of Sales / Payables	49.95	64.15	72.33	77.17	82.2
Day's Payables	13.69	17.57	19.82	21.14	22.52
Sales / Work Capital	6.35	3.49	2.26	1.67	1.35
EBIT / Interest	34.65	59.12	112.51	185.32	319.45
Net Profit+Depr+Amort/C.L.T.D.	32.41	46.45	73.37	98.91	136.47
Leverage Ratios					
Fixed Assets / Tan Net Worth	0.22	0.07	0.03	0.01	0
Debt / Worth	1.31	0.68	0.46	0.35	0.29
Operating Ratios					
Profit Before Tax / Tan Net Worth	143.74%	93.48%	80.44%	68.11%	62.59%
Profit Before Tax / Total Assets	62.12%	55.80%	55.11%	50.54%	48.40%
Sales / Net Fixed Assets	32.70	51.03	83.4	144.57	289.88
Sales / Total Assets	2.96	2.15	1.57	1.25	1.05
Other Ratios:					
% Deprec Amort / Sales	0.01	0.01	0.00	0.00	0.00
% Officer's Compensation/Sales	0.01	0.01	0.01	0.01	0.01
Gross Profit	**$490,831**	**$791,734**	**$1,400,350**	**$2,097,994**	**$3,210,976**
Key Percentages as a Percent of Gross Profit					
Rent	3.62%	2.36%	1.40%	0.98%	0.67%
Interest Paid	2.97%	1.72%	0.90%	0.54%	0.31%
Depreciation & Amortization	3.28%	2.03%	1.15%	0.77%	0.50%
Officers Compensation	27.20%	23.08%	17.10%	15.01%	12.75%
Taxes Paid	36.16%	36.16%	36.16%	36.16%	36.16%

1. The Current Ratio is an approximate measure of a firm's ability to meet its current obligations and is calculated as Current Assets/Current Liabilities.

National's current ratio is on a upward trend. This would indicate that the amount of current assets is increasing steadily as is the "cushion" between current liabilities and the ability to pay them. It could suggest that National Mortgage has a relatively stable position and that there is an opportunity for expanded operations.

2. The Revenue to Working Capital ratio is a measure of the margin of protection for current creditors. It is calculated as Net Revenue/{Current Assets-Current Liabilities}.

National's recent revenue to working capital ratio is on a downward trend. This indicates the level of safety is increasing for creditors.

Continued

3. The EBIT to Interest ratio is a measure of ability to meet annual interest payments. It is calculated as Earnings before interest and taxes/Annual Interest Expense.

National's recent EBIT to interest ratio is on a upward trend. This indicates that the company should not have a problem servicing its debt. This could indicate that the company is better able to make interest payments and could possibly handle more debt.

4. The Current Maturities Coverage ratio is a measure of ability to pay current maturities of long-term debt with cash flow from operations. It is calculated as {Net Income + Depreciation, Amortization and Depletion}/Current Portion of Long-Term Debt.

National's recent EBIT to interest ratio is on a upward trend. This indicates that the cash flows available to service debt are increasing relative to the level of debt. This indicates that the company is able to service debt and could possibly indicate additional debt capacity.

5. The Fixed Assets to Tangible Net Worth ratio measures the extent to which owner's equity has been invested in property, plant, and equipment. It is calculated as Net Fixed Assets/{Equity - Net Intangible Assets}.

National's fixed asset to tangible net worth ratio is on a downward trend. This indicates that the investment in fixed assets relative to net worth is decreasing and results in a larger "cushion" for creditors in the event of liquidation.

6. The Debt to Equity ratio expresses the relationship between capital contributed by creditors and capital contributed by owners. It is calculated as Total Liabilities/Net Worth.

National's recent debt to equity ratio is on a downward trend. This indicates the company is achieving greater long-term financial safety.

7. The Earnings Before Tax to Tangible Net Worth ratio expresses the rate of return on tangible capital employed. It is calculated as (Earnings Before Taxes/{Net Worth-Net Intangible Assets} * 100.

National's earnings Before Tax to Tangible Net Worth ratio is on a downward trend. This indicates that the company is performing well.

Common Size Income Statement

	Projected Year 1	Projected Year 2	Projected Year 3	Projected Year 4	Projected Year 5
Total Revenue	100.0%	100.0%	100.0%	100.0%	100.0%
Cost of Sales	17.6%	22.6%	25.5%	27.5%	28.4%
Gross Profit	82.4%	77.4%	74.5%	72.5%	71.6%
Operating Expenses	61.5%	51.4%	39.4%	32.1%	25.4%
Operating Profit	21.0%	26.0%	35.1%	40.4%	46.2%
Other Expen/Inc (Net)	0.0%	0.0%	0.0%	0.0%	0.0%
PRE-TAX PROFIT	**21.0%**	**26.0%**	**35.1%**	**40.4%**	**46.2%**
Income Taxes	7.6%	9.4%	12.7%	14.6%	16.7%
INCOME AFTER TAXES	**13.4%**	**16.6%**	**22.4%**	**25.8%**	**29.5%**

Common Size Balance Sheet

	Projected Year 1	Projected Year 2	Projected Year 3	Projected Year 4	Projected Year 5
Cash & Equivalent	85.0%	92.1%	95.8%	97.6%	98.6%
Accounts Receivable	0.0%	0.0%	0.0%	0.0%	0.0%
Inventory	0.0%	0.0%	0.0%	0.0%	0.0%
Other Current	2%	1%	1%	1%	1%
Total Current Assets	**86.9%**	**93.5%**	**96.8%**	**98.3%**	**99.1%**
Fixed Assets (Net)	9.1%	4.2%	1.9%	0.9%	0.4%
Intangibles	2.1%	0.9%	0.3%	0.1%	0.0%
Other Assets	1.9%	1.4%	1.0%	0.7%	0.5%
TOTAL ASSETS	**100.0%**	**100.0%**	**100.0%**	**100.0%**	**100.0%**
Liabilities:					
Accounts Payable	1.0%	0.8%	0.6%	0.4%	0.4%
Short-Term Notes	0.0%	0.0%	0.0%	0.0%	0.0%
Current Maturities (LTD)	1.3%	0.8%	0.5%	0.3%	0.2%
Income Taxes	22.5%	20.2%	19.9%	18.3%	17.5%
Accrued Expenses	31.1%	29.6%	25.5%	22.6%	19.6%
Other Current Liabilities	1.3%	0.7%	0.4%	0.2%	0.2%
Total Current Liabilities	57.2%	52.0%	46.9%	41.9%	37.9%
Long-Term Debt	16.5%	8.4%	4.2%	2.2%	1.2%
Other Non-Current	0.0%	0.0%	0.0%	0.0%	0.0%
Total Liabilities	73.7%	60.4%	51.1%	44.2%	39.1%
TOTAL EQUITY	**26.3%**	**39.6%**	**48.9%**	**55.8%**	**60.9%**
Total Liabilities & Equity	100.0%	100.0%	100.0%	100.0%	100.0%

Cash Flow Projection - First Year

Month	Start-Up Jun-97	Month 1 Jul-97	Month 2 Aug-97	Month 3 Sep-97	Month 4 Oct-97	Month 5 Nov-97	Month 6 Dec-97
CASH RECEIPTS:							
Loans Closed		15	30	50	70	85	100
Franchises Sold this Month		2	2	4	5	5	5
Total # of Franchises		2	4	8	13	18	23
Royalties		8,550	17,100	28,500	39,900	48,450	57,000
AdFund		900	1,800	3,000	4,200	5,100	6,000
Franchise Fee		50,000	50,000	100,000	125,000	125,000	125,000
Loans Closed	150,000						
Total Cash Received	150,000	59,450	68,900	131,500	169,100	178,550	188,000
DISBURSEMENTS:		**1 Team**	**1 Team**	**1 Team**	**1 Team**	**1 Team**	**1 Team**
Loan Expenses		1,125	2,250	3,750	5,250	6,375	7,500
Salaries-President		2,917	2,917	2,917	2,917	2,917	2,917
Salaries-Operations Manager		2,333	2,333	2,333	2,333	2,333	2,333
Salaries-Processing Manager		2,917	2,917	2,917	2,917	2,917	2,917
Salaries-Processors		1,500	3,000	5,000	7,000	8,500	10,000
Salaries-Team Leaders		347	694	1,157	1,620	1,967	2,314
Salaries-Funding Rep.		231	462	771	1,079	1,310	1,541
Salaries-Customer Service		416	832	1,387	1,941	2,357	2,773
Salaries-Office Workers		113	225	376	526	638	751
Salaries-Area Reps		233	467	933	1,517	2,100	2,683
Salaries-Instructors		2,383	2,383	2,383	2,383	2,383	2,383
Payroll Taxes & Benefits		3,348	4,058	5,043	6,058	6,856	7,653
Equipment, Software	18,000	3,500	1,000	3,150	7,700	2,500	3,150
Inter Alios		3,333	3,333	3,333	3,333	3,333	3,333
Maintenance Repair		1,000	1,000	1,000	1,000	1,000	1,000
Insurance-Work. Comp/E&O		350	550	550	550	550	550
Insurance-Other	1,100	1,000	1,000	1,000	1,000	1,000	1,000
Telephone/Utilities	0	1,189	1,378	2,630	3,382	3,571	3,760
Advertising NSI	18,000	10,000	10,000	20,000	25,000	25,000	25,000
Advertising-Novex		2,500	2,500	2,500	2,500	2,500	2,500
Advertising-Franchisor		35,000	35,000	35,000	35,000	35,000	30,000
Professional Services	3,000	5,000	5,000	5,000	5,000	5,000	5,000
Office Expenses/Postage		595	689	1,315	1,691	1,786	1,880
Organ. Exp./Amortization		350	350	350	350	350	350
Depreciation		992	992	992	992	992	992
Equipment/Furniture/Leases	21,000	5,500	5,500	5,500	5500	5,500	5,500
Licensing/Fees	700	300	300	800	800	500	500
Rent		1,460	1,460	1,460	1460	1,460	1,495
Miscellaneous Expenses	15,000	2,973	3,445	6,575	8455	8,928	9,400
Total Cash Paid Out	76,800	92,904	96,035	120,122	139254	139,623	141,177
LOANS SECTION:							
Interest		1,250	1,244	1,238	1,232	1,225	1,219
Principal		732	738	745	751	757	763
Cash Pyts to Loans		1,982	1,982	1,982	1,982	1,982	1,982
Taxable Income		-34,704	-28,379	10,141	28,615	37,702	45,604
Income Tax		-12,548	-10,261	3,667	10,346	13,632	16,490
NET INCOME		**-22,156**	**-18,118**	**6,474**	**18,268**	**24,070**	**29,115**

	Month 7 Jan-98	Month 8 Feb-98	Month9 Mar-98	Month 10 Apr-98	Month 11 May-98	Month 12 Jun-98	TOTALS
	115	140	155	170	195	210	1,335
	5	6	6	6	7	7	60
	28	34	40	46	53	60	
	65,550	79,800	88,350	96,900	111,150	119,700	$760,950
	6,900	8,400	9,300	10,200	11,700	12,600	$80,100
	125,000	150,000	150,000	150,000	175,000	175,000	$1,500,000
	197,450	238,200	247,650	257,100	297,850	307,300	**$2,341,050**
	1 Team	**2 Teams**	**2 Teams**	**2 Teams**	**2 Teams**	**2 Teams**	
	8,625	10,500	11,625	12,750	14,625	15,750	$100,125
	2,917	2,917	2,917	2,917	2,917	2,917	$35,004
	2,333	2,333	2,333	2,333	2,333	2,333	$28,000
	2,917	2,917	2,917	2,917	2,917	2,917	$35,004
	11,500	14,000	15,500	17,000	19,500	21,000	$133,500
	2,662	3,240	3,587	3,935	4,513	4,860	$30,898
	1,772	2,158	2,389	2,620	3,005	3,236	$20,574
	3,189	3,883	4,299	4,715	5,408	5,824	$37,024
	864	1,052	1,164	1,277	1,465	1,577	$10,027
	3,267	3,967	4,667	5,367	6,183	7,000	$38,383
	2,383	4,767	4,767	4,767	4,767	4,767	$40,516
	8,451	10,308	11,135	11,962	13,252	14,108	$102,233
	4,000	7,050	3,150	4,000	6,050	3,150	$48,400
	3,333	4,550	950	950	950	950	$31,681
	1,000	1,000	1,000	1,000	1,000	1,000	$12,000
	800	800	800	800	1,600	1,000	$8,900
	1,000	1,000	1,000	1,000	1,000	1,000	$12,000
	3,949	4,764	4,953	5,142	5,957	6,146	$46,821
	25,000	30,000	30,000	30,000	35,000	35,000	$300,000
	2,500	2,500	2,500	2,500	2,500	2,500	$30,000
	33,000	38,000	38,000	38,000	38,000	38,000	$428,000
	5,000	5,000	5,000	5,000	5,000	5,000	$60,000
	1,975	2,382	2,477	2,571	2,979	3,073	$23,411
	350	350	350	350	350	350	$4,200
	992	992	992	992	992	992	$11,900
	5,500	5,500	5500	5,500	5,500	5,500	$66,000
	500	500	500	500	500	500	$6,200
	1,495	1,495	1,495	1,495	1,495	1,510	$17,780
	9,873	11,910	12,383	12,855	14,893	15,365	$117,053
	151,146	179,834	178,349	185,213	204,651	207,326	**$1,835,633**
	1,213	1,206	1,200	1,193	1,187	1,180	$14,586
	770	776	783	789	796	802	$9,201
	1,982	1,982	1,982	1,982	1,982	1,982	**$23,787**
	45,092	57,160	68,102	70,693	92,013	98,794	$490,831
	16,304	20,668	24,624	25,561	33,270	35,722	$177,475
	28,787	**36,492**	**43,477**	**45,132**	**58,743**	**63,072**	**$313,356**

CATEGORY/YEAR	Year 1	Year 2	Year 3	Year 4	Year 5
Current Assets	$686,740	$1,326,659	$2,459,930	$4,080,797	$6,574,710
Fixed Assets	$71,600	$59,700	$47,800	$35,900	$24,000
Other Assets	$31,800	$32,600	$33,400	$34,200	$35,000
TOTAL ASSETS	**$790,140**	**$1,418,959**	**$2,541,130**	**$4,150,897**	**$6,633,710**
Current Liabilities	$318,035	$452,624	$693,188	$977,258	$1,425,258
Long-Term Liabilities	$130,634	$119,405	$107,000	$93,296	$78,157
Other Liabilities	$0	$0	$0	$0	$0
TOTAL LIABILITIES	**$448,669**	**$572,029**	**$800,188**	**$1,070,554**	**$1,503,416**
Stock	$10,000	$10,000	$10,000	$10,000	$10,000
Current earnings	$313,356	$505,459	$894,012	$1,339,401	$2,049,952
Retained Earnings (minus dividends)	$18,115	$331,471	$836,930	$1,730,942	$3,070,343
NET WORTH	**$341,471**	**$846,930**	**$1,740,942**	**$3,080,343**	**$5,130,295**
Liabilities + Net Worth	$790,140	$1,418,959	$2,541,129	$4,150,897	$6,633,710
Working Capital	$368,705	$874,035	$1,766,742	$3,103,539	$5,149,452
Sales	$2,341,050	$3,046,200	$3,986,400	$5,190,000	$6,957,000
Earning Before Taxes & Interest	$505,417	$805,356	$1,412,908	$2,109,376	$3,221,060
Book Value (minus intangibles)	$324,671	$834,330	$1,732,542	$3,076,143	$5,130,295
WC / TA = (X1)	0.47	0.62	0.70	0.75	0.78
RE / TA = (X2)	0.42	0.59	0.68	0.74	0.77
EBIT / TA = (X3)	0.64	0.57	0.56	0.51	0.49
Book Value / TL = (X4)	0.72	1.46	2.17	2.87	3.41
Sales / TA = (X5)	2.96	2.15	1.57	1.25	1.05
CALCULATED Z SCORES	**5.94**	**5.46**	**5.28**	**5.20**	**5.20**

The Z Score Formula = $0.717*(X1) + 0.847*(X2) + 3.107*(X3) + 0.420*(X4) + 0.998*(X5)$

If the Z Score is Greater than or Equal to 2.9 the subject firm is apparently safe from bankruptcy.

If the Z Score is Less than or Equal to 1.2 the subject firm may be destined for bankruptcy.

If the Z Score is between 1.23 and 2.9 the firm is in a gray area and steps could be taken by management to correct existing or potential problems in order to avoid bankruptcy.

Z Score analysis is a statistical method developed to forecast bankruptcy.

It is over 90% accurate one year into the future and 80% accurate for the second year.

In this instance we used the projected figures to determine the above scores.

The Z scores indicated above are all well over 2.91 which indicates that the company will not be a candidate for bankruptcy if it can achieve the goals outlined in this plan.

	NET INCOME	IRR	MIRR	ANNUAL DIVIDENDS	TOTAL ASSETS
Initial Investment	(28,115)				
Year 1	$313,356			$0	$1,569,347
Year 2	$505,459	1157.52%	935.10%	$0	$1,952,999
Year 3	$894,012	1175.10%	861.52%	$0	$3,075,170
Year 4	$1,339,401	1177.11%	819.85%	$0	$4,684,937
Year 5	$2,049,952	1177.35%	794.75%	$0	$7,167,750

ASSUMPTIONS:
Income figures are after taxes
Dividend Payout = 50% of After Tax Income
Reinvestment rate = 7%

IRR = INTERNAL RATE OF RETURN
MIRR = MODIFIED RATE OF RETURN
ROI = RATE OF RETURN ON OWNER'S INVESTMENT
ROA = RATE OF RETURN ON TOTAL ASSETS

IRR = the interest rate received for an investment and income that occur at regular periods.
MIRR = adds the cost of funds and interest received on reinvestment of cash to the IRR.

	Year 1	Year 2	Year 3	Year 4	Year 5
Return on Assets	19.97%	25.88%	29.07%	28.59%	28.60%
Return on Investment	0.00%	0.00%	0.00%	0.00%	0.00%
Income Per Share	$11.15	$17.98	$31.80	$47.64	$72.91
Dividends Per Share	$0.00	$0.00	$0.00	$0.00	$0.00

CONCLUSIONS & SUMMARY

A review of the first several years of National's existence show that it has been very successful in serving customers with less than perfect credit in the Seattle and Spokane markets. Each subsequent year has shown significant improvement in profitability and operational performance.

During the first two years, the company concentrated upon being profitable, building its staff, and equipping its office. National Mortgage is now ready to step up to the next level and utilize economies of scale to make the projected numbers even more striking. It wishes to take its unique concept to a national level by selling franchises to people throughout the country. These franchises would generate loans which would be processed by the main processing center in Seattle.

The projections in this business plan are extremely conservative according to Merrill Lynch and ABC. With their help the chances for continued growth are excellent. Once franchise applicants are qualified, they will join the growing network of brokers, under National Mortgage, who specialize in helping people with less than perfect credit.

To achieve our goals, we must be able to raise $150,000 in new funding. This may come from investors, lenders, or a guaranteed loan through the Small Business Administration.

Nightclub

BUSINESS PLAN

1039 Thurman Avenue
Cliff, Massachusetts 01862

The Wild Oasis nightclub provides a local solution to the lack of dance and live music venues in a medium-sized market, and will help keep late-night entertainment expenditures within the region. The company's good grasp of how to market a night-club adds to the plan's attractiveness.

- ORGANIZATIONAL PLAN

- MARKETING PLAN

- MANAGEMENT PLAN

- FINANCIAL DOCUMENTS

ORGANIZATIONAL PLAN

Industry Description

Dance clubs in the 1990s have significantly impacted cities from coast to coast. Los Angeles Hollywood, New York's Times Square, and Seattle's Pioneer Square are just a few examples. Dazzling their audiences with high-powered lights, sound, and music, these venues are still one of the highest cash flow businesses in the world. Studies have shown that the average person will spend three to four hours per weekend in an entertainment environment and will spend an average of 20 to 50 dollars in that timeframe. This trend also shows no signs of declining.

The typical dance club is open from 9:00 P.M. to 2:00 A.M., and within this span of five hours, the venue can achieve gross revenues anywhere from $5,000 to $35,000 nightly. The primary sources of revenue in a nightclub are high-volume traffic, coupled with nominal spending. In addition to alcohol revenues, a nightclub also generates substantial revenues from door charges that can typically range from five to ten dollars per person.

For example, a 1,000-person capacity nightclub will typically accommodate approximately 1,500 people in the five-hour span of operation. A $5 door charge, in addition to a conservative figure of $12.25 collected from each patron in alcohol sales, would generate approximately $30,000 in nightly revenue.

Nightclubs in the late 1980s and early 1990s focused on spectacular light shows and energetic dance music. This relatively simple concept is still quite popular today. However, these concepts have greatly evolved with society. In recent years this industry has become more sophisticated with the availability of new technology. Larger metropolitan areas have taken this technology to new heights with sound and lighting designs that create an exciting and memorable experience. Fortunately, no one in the downtown Cliff area has capitalized on this specific segment of the industry to date.

Additionally, the nightclub industry is shifting towards a more entertainment-oriented concept. Guests of these clubs are not only offered a dynamic place to dance, but also a place to participate in the entertainment through interactive contests, theme nights, and other events. We intend to heavily utilize entertainment-oriented marketing in an effort to withstand the perpetual shift in trends and cater to as large a client base as possible.

Nightclubs and other drinking establishments rely heavily on their primary suppliers. The primary suppliers are the various beverage distributors that provide the establishment with both alcoholic and non-alcoholic beverages. The alcoholic beverages (beer, wine, and liquor) are the primary sources of income in this industry. Other beverage suppliers also play a crucial role by providing non-alcoholic beverages. These are either served alone or mixed with alcohol.

In the Cliff area, all major brands of alcoholic beverages are available, in addition to several regional brands of beer. Initial research shows that the major distributors in the market have a high rating in both product availability and delivery.

Business Description

The resurgence of the downtown Cliff area represents a unique opportunity for a high-energy dance club. The city's central location, demographics, and lack of direct competition are major advantages to this project. The proposed club—tentatively named "Wild Oasis"—will provide a local solution to the lack of dance and live music venues geared toward the 21 to 35 age group in the Noble County area and will help keep late night entertainment expenditures within the region.

The development of the University of Waters Cliff campus has been, and will continue to be, a major catalyst in bringing people to the area. With current enrollment of over 1,300 students, the year-and-a-half old campus is slated for steady expansion through 2010 when enrollment is expected to hit 6,000 students. Additional surrounding educational institutions (two universities, two community colleges) also contribute to the potential customer base. Other proposals in the area such as the Multiplex Theatre and shopping center will also greatly impact the city's traffic flow and nightlife.

The new nightclub will specialize in high-energy dance music with a quality light show, and will offer beer, wine, and an array of liquors and mixed drinks. In addition, the club will sell non-alcoholic beverages such as soft drinks, juices, and bottled water. A small food menu consisting mostly of appetizers and small entrees ranging in cost from $6 to $9 will also be available. The initial hours of operation will be 8:00 P.M. to 2:00 A.M. Wednesday through Saturday. The club will draw primarily from the Cliff market while attracting guests from the area's other major cities in the state.

Club Design

Our goal is to provide a comfortable and welcoming environment as well as a unique, exciting nightclub experience. This dance club will feature high ceilings and a contemporary look with dynamic upscale decor, furnishings, and color scheme modeled after a big city loft. The central area of the club will consist of a large dance floor with cocktail seating along the perimeter and a large bar located nearby. A VIP lounge for special guests is also being explored.

The focus of the club's design will be to create a highly social atmosphere. This will be achieved through the placement of couches, booth seating, and a quieter lounge area located away from the dancing and music.

State-of-the-art sound and lighting will round off the club's environment. A RMS point-of-sale system will be put into place and will serve as a sales, labor, and liquor/inventory control system. This system will ensure an accurate, secure, and efficient control over labor costs, as well as day to day inventory, thus minimizing the possibility of loss or theft.

MARKETING PLAN

Area Analysis

The geographic target market for this nightclub is all of Noble County, which includes the city of Cliff and many others. Current population of the county is over 680,000 people, 26% of whom fall into the proposed age demographic (21 to 35) for the club. This number is expected to rise significantly over the next decade.

Cliff, the city in which the proposed club will reside, is Noble County's largest city, accounting for 28% of the total population, and the third largest city in the state. The 51-square-mile city has been nationally recognized for its outstanding quality of living in national consumer magazines.

There are several contributing factors behind the emergence of the downtown area of Cliff. The $70 million redevelopment of the University of Waters Cliff campus has been the largest stimulus for economic growth in the area to date. Various other projects, including a multiplex theater, shopping center, marina, numerous restaurants, and residential housing, have been proposed or are currently in development. Growth in the area is also attributable to the expansion or relocation of major corporations representing the computer, sportswear, and aircraft production industries. Many of these companies have created new, higher-technology jobs in the areas that have welcomed in a younger and more affluent workforce.

Cliff was chosen as the location for the new club for several reasons. First, the city is an emerging market with lower real estate rates and at the same time high levels of commercial development. Second, Cliff lacks direct competition from other dance clubs. The next major city, which is over 45 minutes away from downtown Cliff, maintains a highly competitive nighttime entertainment market yet poses little threat to the development of a Cliff dance club.

Site Analysis

The proposed location for the venue is at 1039 Thurman Avenue on the first and second floors of the Pfeiffer Building. Thurman Avenue is the downtown area's primary commercial business street, and has excellent freeway and back street access. The club would occupy approximately 7,300 square feet (5,500 downstairs and 1,800 upstairs) of the building. This location is centrally located to many existing and proposed attractions in downtown Cliff. Its second-story addition provides for an excellent nighttime view of parts of the city and the Mark Anthony Waterway.

The site and the proposed club are a perfect fit. The Pfeiffer Building is the creation of its current owner, a prominent local developer responsible for downtown's newest office complex, the Maximus Building. His experience with renovation of historic buildings will facilitate the development of the nightclub. Additionally, the Pfeiffer Building resides in one of downtown Cliff's busiest intersections with access to the city's major interstate freeways. Plans for the building include installation of high-speed Internet connections in an effort to attract technology companies. Thus far, a technology firm as well as a local recruiting company already have agreed to lease space.

Target Market & Demographics

The primary target market for this venue is the age group of 21 to 35. Market research indicates that the demand for a new dance club in Cliff among this demographic is very high. Most are tired of the existing scene and are looking for a local place to dance, meet people, and have a good time. Currently, high-energy dance clubs are only found in the next largest city, but the 45-minute drive north discourages much of Noble County's market from frequenting these venues. This, coupled with the tremendous current and forecasted growth throughout the region, indicates that the time is perfect for such a venture in Cliff.

The market research study included men and women within the target market that do, or would, support the downtown Cliff nightclub entertainment industry. The most common responses and comments regarding existing venues in the area were:

- Not enough room to dance
- Tired of the existing sports bar/tavern atmosphere
- Existing venues play the same music every night; no variety
- Low quality light and sound
- Lack of energy and excitement; too low key

Therefore, the venue being proposed will address all of these concerns. It will maintain a heavy focus on dancing—offering the largest dance floor in the downtown area—and will offer a high-energy, very social atmosphere for the prospective market. The interior will be designed with an upscale decor and the lighting and sound will drive the ambience. Most of all, the music will be consistent, but not played out. DJs will be responsible for playing a variety of music our patrons like, from Top 40 to remixed techno to hits from the 1970s and 1980s.

Demographic data obtained from Noble County's web site demonstrates that the region contains over 175,000 individuals within our target market, 26% of the total population. Estimates indicate an expected 3-4% annual growth over the next 10 years.

Population Estimates for 1999

	Noble County
Total Population	682,450
Total Males (by age)	
21 to 25	27,733
26 to 30	27,431
31 to 35	35,756
Total Males (21 to 35)	**90,920**
Total Females (by age)	
21 to 25	24,667
26 to 30	26,802
31 to 35	35,347
Total Females (21 to 35)	**86,816**
Total Target Demographic	**177,736**
Percentage of Total Population	26.04%

Promotions

Promotional efforts are critical to the proposed club's success. Accordingly, the venue will offer nightly, weekly, and monthly promotional specials. These promotions will help to stimulate excitement for the new club, thus leading to high traffic and exposure. The main idea is to offer a new entertainment experience night after night. This is the key ingredient for success and profitability, as well as longevity, in the nightclub industry. Proposals include:

- Prize giveaways
- Nightly dance floor and stage contests
- Cooperative promotions with local radio stations

Entertainment will be provided by charismatic disc jockeys featuring a blend of current Top 40 and dance music. During the week, special theme nights and promotions will be used to attract a more diverse crowd, and to increase the number of customers who frequent the dance club. These theme nights will change as popularity and demand dictate.

The market will be targeted and reached via the following primary vehicles: advertisements in local print media, strategically broadcast radio spots, and an Internet web site. Advertisements printed in the local and college newspapers, as well as broadcasts over the local radio stations will provide exciting club information on current promotions and specials. A more "grass roots" marketing campaign also will be employed. This includes club representatives and spokespersons attending area events, postering of college campuses, a "prize patrol" van, and other person-to-person marketing efforts.

Competition

The new nightclub will meet a demand in the Cliff area that is not currently being served. We will provide a high quality, energetic nightclub while maintaining a safe, secure atmosphere for guests to enjoy themselves and the surroundings. Providing a safe nightclub is essential to maintaining customer loyalty and growth. Therefore, security at the new club will be top priority.

Currently, nighttime competition in the area is limited to mostly bar/tavern facilities including McArthur's, Lucky Six, Jubilee, The Harbor, and Westside Elite. Only Jubilee and The Harbor offer large-scale dancing facilities. The proposed club will be the largest dance facility in the downtown area. While the proposed club will be in direct competition with these other facilities, it also will attract a different clientele of individuals seeking a superior dance venue which can currently only be found in the next largest city in the state, 45 minutes away.

Our review of the market concludes that there are four entertainment venues that can be considered direct competition to the proposed new venue. We do realize that the proposed venue will also compete indirectly for every entertainment dollar spent in the Cliff area.

McArthur's	Hours of Operation: 5:00 P.M. - 2:00 A.M.
Wednesday - Saturday	Capacity: 300
344 W. 5th Ave.	Dance Floor: 450 square feet
	Wed. College Night ($1 beers)

- This nightclub appeals to a college crowd seeking cheap drinks
- The club is known for being dingy and dirty

Jubilee	Hours of Operation: 10:00 A.M. - 2:00 A.M.
Monday - Sunday	Capacity: 400
422 Main St.	Dance Floor: 700 square feet
	Thurs. College/Ladies' Night

- This club appeals to 25- to 35-year-olds
- Pool and video games are central focus. Dancing is pushed to the back of the club

The Harbor	Hours of Operation: 6:00 P.M.- 2:00 A.M.
Wednesday - Saturday	Capacity: 250
3rd and Broadway	Dance Floor: 500 square feet
	Varies week to week

- This club's target customer is 25 to 45 years old / middle class or above
- This club is known for its older, dressed up crowd and cramped space

Lucky Six	Hours of Operation: 11:00 A.M.- 2:00 A.M.
Monday - Sunday	Capacity: 350
23rd and Republic	Dance Floor: 325 square feet
	Varies week to week

- This club's target customer is 25 to 45 years old
- This club is known for live jazz and blues entertainment, and their draught beers

MANAGEMENT PLAN

Ed Tiller will fulfill the role of Owner/Operating Partner of this venture. He is currently the president of XTZ. Mr. Tiller's background is largely within the scope of business development and project management as well as commercial and residential construction. His fields of expertise will be utilized in this venture via his direct responsibility for the overall business management structure and personnel. Additionally, he will assume the public relations and marketing roles for the club.

XTZ has contracted entertainment industry specialists, SVC Nightclub and Bar Services, Inc. Their involvement will exist in several facets, most notably, through providing assistance in launching this nightclub venue. SVC has over 12 years of experience in the nightclub industry and has assisted many first-time club operators in getting their proposed venues off the ground successfully. SVC will assist in the development of the design, concept, and strategies of the new nightclub. SVC is also a full-service advertising agency and will assist in all production and placement of all advertisement for the new venue. In addition, they will assist in the hiring process of the management staff, disc jockeys, bartenders, waitresses, and security staff. They will also provide educational services for management-level personnel who will be responsible for the day to day operations of the club.

Interviews for a general manager, bar manager, and all other personnel will be conducted by Joe Sorge of SVC. Final decisions for each position will be made by Mr. Tiller.

Summary of Financial Needs

I. The company is seeking a loan for start-up purposes for a new nightclub venue in Cliff, Massachusetts.

II. Funds needed to accomplish goal referenced above will be $200,000. Applicant will require the entire $200,000 to finish project build-out.

Loan Funds Dispersal Statement

We will utilize the anticipated loans in the amount of $200,000 to renovate the approximate 7,200-square-foot space and purchase equipment necessary for the start-up of a new nightclub venue.

Audio & Lighting Lease Program	$2,700.00	**Capital Expenditures**
Includes: amps, speakers, all wiring, installation, equipment, and labor.		
Bar Equipment	$17,500.00	
Includes: 3 compartment sinks, liquor racks, reach in coolers, installation, and labor.		
Bar Supply (Opening Inventory)	$7,000.00	
Includes: all liquor, beer, wine, and consumables for opening.		
Cash Reserves/Operating Capital	$74,550.00	
Operating Capital and contingencies		
Exterior Signage	$2,500.00	
Includes: neon, design, artwork, installation, and labor.		
Fees and Permits	$3,500.00	
Includes: all relevant fees.		
FFE	$44,000.00	
Includes: all furniture, fixtures, equipment, i.e.; carpet, tables, chairs, etc.		
Impact Fees	$0.00	
Includes: charges by utilities for upgrades to usage.		
Initial Marketing	$17,450.00	
Includes: initial campaign, design, artwork, audio, video, production, and labor.		
Interior Refit	$11,500.00	
Includes: demolition, actual construction of bars, walls, floors, mezzanine, etc.		
Kitchen Upgrade	$1,250.00	
Includes: purchase of equipment (used), installation of hood and equipment, and labor.		
Legal	$2,500.00	
Includes all legal fees: Accountant, Attorneys, Engineers, Architects.		

Capital Expenditures *Continued*	Opening Salaries & Deposits					$12,500.00		
	Includes: deposits on all accounts, opening salaries, special purchases.							
	Paper Products					**$750.00**		
	Includes: purchase of all paper type operating supplies							
	Point of Sales Systems					**$1,300.00**		
	Includes: purchase, installation, and labor for entire sales system							
	Restroom Refit					**$1,000.00**		
	Includes: purchase of fixtures, existing demolition, installation, and labor.							
	Total Capital Expenditures					**$200,000.00**		

Revenues

The estimated revenues are based on a 350 capacity nightclub venue, with an average daily incoming traffic ranging from approximately 225 to 325 guests Wednesday through Saturday. These forecasts are considered somewhat conservative based on the size and scope of the market. Additionally, each guest is forecasted to spend an average of $8 to $13 on beverages, depending on the night. The total door covers are less than the bar covers, due to special promotions and VIP passes. Door cover charges are anticipated to be five dollars.

Daily Revenue Breakdown

*based on 350-person capacity

	Mon	Tue	Wed	Thu	Fri	Sat	Sun	Weekly
Total door covers	0	0	225	225	325	325	0	1,100
Average cover charge	$0	$0	$0	$5.00	$5.00	$5.00	$0	$3.98
Total admission sales	*$0*	*$0*	*$0*	*$1,125.00*	*$1,625.00*	*$1,625.00*	*$0*	*$4,375.00*
Total bar covers	0	0	375	425	455	455	0	1,710
Average drinks per person	0	3	3	4	4	4	3	3.03
Average beverage sales per person	$0	$0	$8.00	$10.75	$13.00	$13.00	$0	$11.34
Average price per drink	$0	$3.75	$3.75	$3.75	$3.75	$3.75	$3.75	$3.75
Total sales on beverages	*$0*	*$0*	*$3,000.00*	*$4,568.75*	*$5,915.00*	*$5,915.00*	*$0*	*$19,398.75*
Total admission and beverage sales	**$0**	**$0**	**$3,000.00**	**$5,693.75**	**$7,540.00**	**$7,540.00**	**$0**	**$23,773.75**
Food sales (5% of adm. and bev. sales)	*$0*	*$0*	*$150.00*	*$284.69*	*$377.00*	*$377.00*	*$0*	*$1,188.69*
Misc. sales (0.0% of gross sales)	*$0*	*$0*	*$0*	*$0*	*$0*	*$0*	*$0*	*$0*
Gross sales	**$0**	**$0**	**$3,150.00**	**$5,978.44**	**$7,917.00**	**$7,917.00**	**$0**	**$24,962.44**

Expenses

Based on local industry averages, publications from ALPHA Nightclub & Bar Services, and *Entrepreneur Magazine*'s Bar/Nightclub Start-up Guide, we have generated the following expense figures. These figures are based on an approximate 7,200 square foot venue with a capacity of 350 guests.

The following page illustrates the staffing scenario for the new nightclub venue.

Daily Staffing Breakdown (*based on 350-person capacity)

Hourly Employees

WEDNESDAY

POSITION	QUANTITY	RATE	AVG HOURS	SUBTOTAL	BENEFITS & TAXES (17%)	TOTAL
Waitresses	2.5	$6.00	7	$105.00		
Security	4	$8.50	7	$238.00		
Bartenders	2.5	$6.00	7	$105.00		
Barback	1	$6.00	8	$48.00		
Cook / Misc	1	$8.00	8	$64.00		
Total Staff Cost for Wednesday				**$560.00**	**$95.20**	**$655.20**

THURSDAY

POSITION	QUANTITY	RATE	AVG HOURS	SUBTOTAL	BENEFITS & TAXES (17%)	TOTAL
Waitresses	3	$6.00	7	$126.00		
Security	4	$8.50	7	$238.00		
Bartenders	3	$6.00	7	$126.00		
Barback	1	$6.00	8	$48.00		
Cook / Misc.	1	$8.00	8	$64.00		
Police Detail	0	$8.00	7	$0.00		
Total Staff Cost for Thursday				**$602.00**	**$102.34**	**$704.34**

FRIDAY

POSITION	QUANTITY	RATE	AVG HOURS	SUBTOTAL	BENEFITS & TAXES (17%)	TOTAL
Waitresses	3	$6.00	7	$126.00		
Security	4	$8.50	7	$238.00		
Bartenders	3	$6.00	7	$126.00		
Barback	1	$6.00	8	$48.00		
Cook / Misc.	1	$8.00	8	$64.00		
Police Detail	0	$8.00	7	$0.00		
Total Staff Cost for Friday				**$602.00**	**$102.34**	**$704.34**

SATURDAY

POSITION	QUANTITY	RATE	AVG HOURS	SUBTOTAL	BENEFITS & TAXES (17%)	TOTAL
Waitresses	3	$6.00	7	$126.00		
Security	4	$8.50	7	$238.00		
Bartenders	3	$6.00	7	$126.00		
Barback	1	$6.00	8	$48.00		
Cook / Misc.	1	$8.00	8	$64.00		
Police Detail	0	$8.00	7	$0.00		
Total Staff Cost for Saturday				**$602.00**	**$102.34**	**$704.34**

TOTAL WEEKLY STAFFING COSTS - *HOURLY EMPLOYEES*				**$2,366.00**	**$402.22**	**$2,768.22**

SALARIED EMPLOYEES

POSITION	*SALARY:* YEARLY			WEEKLY	BENEFITS & TAXES (17%)	TOTAL
Manager 1 - Oper Prtnr	$50,000			$798.08	$163.46	
Manager 2 - General Mgr	$50,000			$798.08	$163.46	
Manager 3 - PR Mgr	$0			$0.00	$0.00	
Manager 4 - Bar Mgr	$22,500			$359.13	$73.56	
Manager 5 - Asst.	$0			$0.00	$0.00	
Entertainment	$44,000			$846.15		

TOTAL WEEKLY STAFFING COSTS - *SALARIED EMPLOYEES*				**$2,801.44**	**$400.48**	**$3,201.92**

TOTAL WEEKLY STAFFING COSTS - *OVERALL*						**$5,970.14**

Pro Forma Cash Flow Statement - First Year

Page 1 (Month 1 - 6, plus six-month total)

For Year 1	Month 1	Month 2	Month 3	Month 4	Month 5	Month 6	SIX-MONTH TOTALS
GROSS SALES							
Cash Sales - Admissions	$21,875	$17,500	$17,500	$17,500	$21,875	$17,500	$113,750
Cash Sales - Beverage	96,994	77,595	77,595	77,595	96,994	77,595	504,368
Cash Sales - Food	5,943	4,755	4,755	4,755	5,943	4,755	30,906
TOTAL CASH AVAILABLE	**$124,812**	**$99,850**	**$99,850**	**$99,850**	**$124,812**	**$99,850**	**$649,023**
EXPENSES							
A. Variable Expenses							
Cost of Goods Sold - Beverage	$22,309	$17,847	$17,847	$17,847	$22,309	$17,847	$116,005
Cost of Goods Sold - Food	1,664	1,331	1,331	1,331	1,664	1,331	8,654
Hourly Wages & Benefits	13,841	11,073	11,073	11,073	13,841	11,073	71,974
Total Variable Expenses	**$37,814**	**$30,251**	**$30,251**	**$30,251**	**$37,814**	**$30,251**	**$196,632**
B. Fixed Expenses							
Direct Operating Expenses							
Management Salaries	16,010	12,808	12,808	12,808	16,010	12,808	83,250
China, Silver, Glassware	123	98	98	98	123	98	638
Point of Sale	583	583	583	583	583	583	3,498
Audio & Lights	1,750	1,750	1,750	1,750	1,750	1,750	10,500
Equipment Rental	0	0	0	0	0	0	0
Licenses & Permits	216	173	173	173	216	173	1,125
Linens/Uniforms	481	385	385	385	481	385	2,500
Janitorial	2,163	1,731	1,731	1,731	2,163	1,731	11,250
Supplies	1,202	962	962	962	1,202	962	6,250
Miscellaneous Direct Op. Exp.	721	577	577	577	721	577	3,750
Total Direct Operating Expenses	**23,249**	**19,066**	**19,066**	**19,066**	**23,249**	**19,066**	**$122,761**
General and Admin. Expenses							
Music and Entertainment	2,404	1,923	1,923	1,923	2,404	1,923	12,500
Advertising and Promotion	8,654	6,923	6,923	6,923	8,654	6,923	45,000
Credit Card Commission	624	499	499	499	624	499	3,245
Liquor Taxes	0	0	0	0	0	0	0
Professional Fees	481	385	385	385	481	385	2,500
Insurance	721	577	577	577	721	577	3,750
Admission Taxes	1,094	875	875	875	1,094	875	5,688
Excise Taxes	15,602	12,481	12,481	12,481	15,602	12,481	81,128
Property Taxes	0	0	0	0	0	0	0
Miscellaneous	962	769	769	769	962	769	5,000
Total General and Admin.							
Expenses	**30,540**	**24,432**	**24,432**	**24,432**	**30,540**	**24,432**	**158,811**
Management Fee	2,704	2,704	2,704	2,704	2,704	2,704	16,226
Rent	9,000	9,000	9,000	9,000	9,000	9,000	54,000
Repairs and Maintenance	417	417	417	417	417	417	2,500
Utilities	2,000	2,000	2,000	2,000	2,000	2,000	12,000
Long-Term Loan Repayment	3,605	3,605	3,605	3,605	3,605	3,605	21,630
Total Fixed Expenses	**$68,811**	**$58,520**	**$58,520**	**$58,520**	**$68,811**	**$58,520**	**$371,701**
C. Interest	0	0	0	0	0	0	0
D. Taxes (39.45%)	3,992	3,992	3,992	3,992	3,992	3,992	23,951
TOTAL CASH PAID OUT	**$110,617**	**$92,763**	**$92,763**	**$92,763**	**$110,617**	**$92,763**	**$592,284**
CASH FLOW	**$14,195**	**$7,087**	**$7,087**	**$7,087**	**$14,195**	**$7,087**	**$56,739**
CUMULATIVE CASH FLOW	*$14,195*	*$21,283*	*$28,370*	*$35,457*	*$49,652*	*$56,739*	

Page 2 (Month 7 - 12, plus twelve-month total)

	Month 7	Month 8	Month 9	Month 10	Month 11	Month 12	YEAR END TOTALS
CASH RECEIPTS							
Cash Sales - Admissions	$21,875	$17,500	$17,500	$21,875	$17,500	$17,500	$227,500
Cash Sales - Beverage	96,994	77,595	77,595	96,994	77,595	77,595	1,008,735
Cash Sales - Food	5,943	4,755	4,755	5,943	4,755	4,755	61,812
TOTAL CASH AVAILABLE	**$124,812**	**$99,850**	**$99,850**	**$124,812**	**$99,850**	**$99,850**	**$1,298,047**
CASH PAYMENTS							
A. Variable Expenses							
Cost of Goods Sold - Beverage	$22,309	$17,847	$17,847	$22,309	$17,847	$17,847	$232,000
Cost of Goods Sold - Food	1,664	1,331	1,331	1,664	1,331	1,331	17,307
Salary & Benefits	13,841	11,073	11,073	13,841	11,073	11,073	143,947
Total Variable Expenses	**$37,814**	**$30,251**	**$30,251**	**$37,814**	**$30,251**	**$30,251**	**$393,264**
B. Fixed Expenses							
Direct Operating Expenses							
Salaried Employees	16,010	12,808	12,808	16,010	12,808	12,808	166,500
China, Silver, Glassware	123	98	98	123	98	98	1,275
Point of Sale	583	583	583	583	583	583	6,996
Audio & Lights	1,750	1,750	1,750	1,750	1,750	1,750	21,000
Equipment Rental	0	0	0	0	0	0	0
Licenses & Permits	216	173	173	216	173	173	2,250
Linens/Uniforms	481	385	385	481	385	385	5,000
Janitorial	2,163	1,731	1,731	2,163	1,731	1,731	22,500
Supplies	1,202	962	962	1,202	962	962	12,500
Miscellaneous Direct Op. Exp.	721	577	577	721	577	577	7,500
Total Direct Operating Expenses	**23,249**	**19,066**	**19,066**	**23,249**	**19,066**	**19,066**	**245,521**
General and Admin. Expenses							
Music and Entertainment	2,404	1,923	1,923	2,404	1,923	1,923	25,000
Advertising and Promotion	8,654	6,923	6,923	8,654	6,923	6,923	90,000
Credit Card Commission	624	499	499	624	499	499	6,490
Liquor Taxes	0	0	0	0	0	0	0
Professional Fees	481	385	385	481	385	385	5,000
Insurance	721	577	577	721	577	577	7,500
Admission Taxes	1,094	875	875	1,094	875	875	11,375
Excise Taxes	15,602	12,481	12,481	15,602	12,481	12,481	162,256
Property Taxes	0	0	0	0	0	0	0
Miscellaneous	962	769	769	769	962	769	10,000
Total General and Admin. Expenses	**30,540**	**24,432**	**24,432**	**30,348**	**24,625**	**24,432**	**317,621**
Management Fee	2,704	2,704	2,704	2,704	2,704	2,704	32,451
Rent	9,000	9,000	9,000	9,000	9,000	9,000	108,000
Repairs and Maintenance	417	417	417	417	417	417	5,000
Utilities	2,000	2,000	2,000	2,000	2,000	2,000	24,000
Long-Term Loan Repayment	3,605	3,605	3,605	3,605	3,605	3,605	43,260
Total Fixed Expenses	**$68,811**	**$58,520**	**$58,520**	**$68,619**	**$58,712**	**$58,520**	**$743,402**
C. Interest	0	0	0	0	0	0	0
D. Taxes (39.45%)	3,992	3,992	3,992	3,992	3,992	3,992	47,902
TOTAL CASH PAID OUT	**$110,617**	**$92,763**	**$92,763**	**$110,424**	**$92,955**	**$92,763**	**$1,184,568**
CASH FLOW	**$14,195**	**$7,087**	**$7,087**	**$14,388**	**$6,895**	**$7,087**	**$113,478**
CUMULATIVE CASH FLOW	*$70,935*	*$78,022*	*$85,109*	*$99,497*	*$106,391*	*$113,478*	

Three-Year Income Projection

	Year 1	Year 2	Year 3	Total 3 Years
INCOME				
Cash Sales - Admissions	$227,500	$241,150	$248,385	$717,035
Cash Sales - Beverage	1,008,735	1069,259	1,133,415	3,211,409
Cash Sales - Food	61,812	65,520	69,452	196,784
Gross Sales	**$1,298,047**	**$1,375,930**	**$1,415,251**	**$4,125,227**
Cost of Goods Sold - Beverage	232,009	238,969	246,138	717,117
Cost of Goods Sold - Food	17,307	17,827	18,361	53,495
Gross Margin	**$1,048,730**	**$1,119,134**	**$1,186,751**	**$3,354,615**
VARIABLE EXPENSES				
Hourly Wages & Benefits	$143,947	$148,266	$152,714	$444,927
Total Variable Expenses	**$143,947**	**$148,266**	**$152,714**	**$444,927**
FIXED EXPENSES				
Direct Operating Expenses				
Management Salaries	$166,500	$171,495	$176,640	$514,635
China, Silver, Glassware	1,275	1,313	1,353	3,941
Audio & Lights	21,000	21,000	21,000	63,000
Point of Sale	7,000	7,000	7,000	21,000
Equipment Rental	0	0	0	0
Licenses & Permits	2,250	2,318	2,387	6,955
Linens/Uniforms	5,000	5,150	5,305	15,455
Janitorial	22,500	23,175	23,870	69,545
Supplies	12,500	12,875	13,261	38,636
Miscellaneous Direct Op. Exp.	7,500	7,725	7,957	23,182
Total Direct Operating Expenses	**$245,525**	**$252,051**	**$258,772**	**$756,348**
General and Admin. Expenses				
Music and Entertainment	$25,000	$25,750	$26,523	$77,273
Advertising and Promotion	90,000	92,700	95,481	278,181
Credit Card Commission	6,490	6,685	6,885	20,061
Professional Fees	5,000	5,150	5,305	15,455
Insurance	7,500	7,725	7,957	23,182
Admission Taxes	11,375	11,716	12,068	35,159
Excise Taxes	162,256	167,124	172,137	501,517
Property Taxes	0	0	0	0
Miscellaneous	10,000	10,300	10,609	30,909
Total General and Admin. Expenses	**$317,621**	**$327,150**	**$336,964**	**$981,735**
Management Fee	$32,451	$33,425	$0	$65,876
Rent	$108,000	$112,320	$116,813	$337,133
Repairs and Maintenance	5,000	5,150	5,305	15,455
Utilities	24,000	24,720	25,462	74,182
Long-Term Loan Repayment	43,260	43,260	43,260	129,780
Management Fee	0	0	0	0
	212,711	218,875	190,839	$622,425
Total Fixed Expenses	**$775,857**	**$798,075**	**$786,575**	**$2,360,508**
TOTAL OPERATING EXPENSES	**$919,805**	**$946,341**	**$939,289**	**$2,805,435**
EARNINGS BEFORE INT, DEPREC, AND TAXES	**$128,926**	**$172,793**	**$247,462**	**$549,180**
Interest	0	0	0	0
EARNINGS BEFORE DEPREC AND TAXES	**$128,926**	**$172,793**	**$247,462**	**$549,180**
Depreciation	7,500	7,500	7,500	22,500
EARNINGS BEFORE TAXES	**$121,426**	**$165,293**	**$239,962**	**$549,180**
Taxes (39.45%)	47,902	65,208	94,665	207,775
EARNINGS AFTER TAXES / NET PROFIT	**$73,523**	**$100,085**	**$145,297**	**$318,905**
Net Profit (Loss) (as a percentage of Sales)	*5.7%*	*7.3%*	*10.0%*	*7.7%*

Extended Cash Flow Analysis

REVENUE:	Year 1	Year 2	Year 3	Year 4	Year 5	Year 6
Cash Sales - Admissions	$227,500	$241,150	248,385	$255,836	$271,186	$279,322
Cash Sales - Beverage	1,008,735	1,069,259	1,133,415	1,167,417	1,237,462	$1,274,586
Cash Sales - Food	61,812	65,520	69,452	71,535	75,827	$78,102
Cash Sales - Miscellaneous	0	0	0	0	0	$0
TOTAL REVENUE	**$1,298,047**	**$1,375,930**	**1,451,251**	**$1,494,788**	**$1,584,476**	**$1,632,010**
EXPENSES:						
Cost of Goods Sold - Beverage	$232,009	$238,969	246,138	$253,523	$261,128	$268,962
Cost of Goods Sold - Food	17,307	17,827	18,361	18,912	19,480	$20,064
Cost of Goods Sold - Miscellaneous	0	0	0	0	0	$0
Hourly Wages & Benefits	143,947	148,266	152,714	157,295	162,014	$166,875
Management Salaries	166,500	171,495	176,640	181,939	187,397	$193,019
China, Silver, Glassware	1,275	1,313	1,353	1,393	1,435	$1,478
Audio & Lights	21,000	21,000	21,000	21,000	21,000	$21,630
Point of Sale	7,000	7,000	7,000	7,000	7,000	$7,210
Equipment Rental	0	0	0	0	0	$0
Licenses & Permits	2,250	2,317	2,387	2,459	2,532	$2,608
Linens/Uniforms	5,000	5,150	5,305	5,464	5,628	$5,796
Janitorial	22,500	23,175	23,870	24,586	25,324	$26,084
Supplies	12,500	12,875	13,261	13,659	14,069	$14,491
Miscellaneous Direct Op. Exp.	7,500	7,725	7,957	8,195	8,441	$8,695
Music and Entertainment	25,000	25,750	26,522	27,318	28,138	$28,982
Advertising and Promotion	90,000	92,700	95,481	98,345	101,296	$104,335
Credit Card Commission	6,490	6,685	6,885	7,092	7,305	$7,524
Liquor Taxes	0	0	0	0	0	$0
Professional Fees	5,000	5,150	5,305	5,464	5,628	$5,796
Insurance	7,500	7,725	7,957	8,195	8,441	$8,695
Admission Taxes	11,375	11,716	12,068	12,430	12,803	$13,187
Excise Taxes	162,256	167,124	172,137	177,301	182,620	$188,099
Property Taxes	0	0	0	0	0	$0
Miscellaneous	10,000	10,300	10,609	10,927	11,255	$11,593
Rent	108,000	112,320	116,813	121,485	126,345	$130,135
Repairs and Maintenance	5,000	5,150	5,305	5,464	5,628	$5,796
Utilities	24,000	24,720	25,462	26,225	27,012	$27,823
Management Fee	32,451	33,425				
Long-Term Loan Repayment	43,260	43,260	43,260	43,260	43,260	43,260
TOTAL OPERATING EXPENSES	**$1,169,121**	**$1,203,137**	**1,203,789**	**$1,238,933**	**$1,275,178**	**$1,312,135**
NET OPERATING INCOME	**$128,926**	**$172,793**	**247,462**	**$255,855**	**$309,298**	**$319,874**
Less Interest	0	0	0	0	0	$0
NET INCOME BEFORE DEPREC. &						
TAXES	**128,926**	**172,793**	**247,462**	**255,855**	**309,298**	**$319,874**
Less Depreciation	7,500	7,500	7,500	7,500	7,500	$7,500
NET INCOME BEFORE TAXES	**$121,426**	**$165,293**	**239,962**	**$248,355**	**$301,798**	**$312,374**
Less Taxes (39.45%)	47,902	65,208	94,665	97,976	119,059	$123,232
NET INCOME	**$73,523**	**$100,085**	**145,297**	**$150,379**	**$182,739**	**$189,143**

Nursery

BUSINESS PLAN

WONDERLAND NURSERY

416 S. Turner Street
Spokane, Washington 99204

This plan outlines how this business will provide Spokane with a specialty nursery and garden center that is stylish, respected, and consistent, and which is intelligently staffed with caring and well-informed employees. An unusual feature of this nursery is its café. This plan was provided by Ameriwest Business Consultants, Inc.

- EXECUTIVE SUMMARY

- OBJECTIVES & GOALS, AND STRATEGIES FOR ACHIEVING THEM

- BUSINESS DESCRIPTION, STATUS, & OUTLOOK

- MANAGEMENT & OWNERSHIP

- THE SERVICE (AN UNFILLED NEED) & UNIQUENESS OF SERVICE

- MARKET ANALYSIS

- MARKETING STRATEGIES

- FINANCIAL PLANS

BUSINESS DESCRIPTION

The purpose of Wonderland Nursery is to provide Spokane with a nursery and garden center that is stylish, respected, and consistent, and which is intelligently staffed with caring and well-informed employees. The atmosphere is friendly and open. The nursery displays a new attitude. It treats customers like first-class citizens and tries to make them feel like they are at home. On the premises will also be a café to help our customers extend and enhance their visit to our premises. We offer a variety of related items such as pottery, specialty decorations, etc. The facility has a first-rate greenhouse. The services are offered at a competitive price and pricing will be reviewed periodically.

The nursery is normally open Monday, Tuesday, Wednesday, Thursday, Friday, and Saturday, from 9:00 A.M. through 5:00 P.M., and 10:00 A.M. to 4:00 P.M. on Sunday. The café hours are 9:00 A.M. to 5:00 P.M., Monday through Wednesday, 9:00 A.M. through 8:00 P.M. on Thursday through Saturday, and from 10:00 A.M. to 4:00 P.M. on Sunday.

CURRENT POSITION AND FUTURE OUTLOOK

The business is in a restructure mode. It is currently past due on its mortgage payment. Plans call for infusion of new investment in the amount of approximately $275,000 and a new loan of $800,000. Operations are conducted on a 5-acre site, located at 416 S. Turner Street, Spokane, Washington. On the average we serve from 10,000 to 12,000 customers per year. With new funding we plan to increase this amount by at least 15% per year in the future. This is a conservative estimate considering the past year saw a 25% increase in sales. To attain these goals we will use a combination of media advertising, flyers, and word-of mouth. Upon securing the new funding, the future appears very bright. The customers are there, the experience and ability are there, and with a restructure of the organization we are convinced the profit would be there. The café will only get better in its second full year of operation.

MANAGEMENT AND OWNERSHIP

The company is set up as a corporation with Susan Smyth and her husband Robert owning 100% of all outstanding stock. Susan serves as president, chief executive officer, and manager. She provides the leadership to run this company. She has over 5 years of experience as owner and operator of a nursery. Her retail sales background will continue to provide the guiding light for the operation. Susan oversees the entire operation and concentrates on advertising, legal matters, banking, insurance, purchasing, equipment purchases, public relations, and labor. Robert Smyth serves as treasurer and handles all maintenance and development. Helen Brown, office manager, handles sales, display, and backs up Susan in banking, purchasing, and planning. The business employs up to ten additional employees. These employees will be involved in cooking in the café, waiting on tables, and working as laborers. They will be a combination of part-time and full-time. When volume picks up, additional part-time or full-time employees will be hired as the workload requires. Ameriwest Business Consultants, Inc. will provide help in additional areas such as planning and general business advising when necessary and to supplement Susan's overall business knowledge. The services of an accountant, attorney, and a qualified insurance agent have been retained.

UNIQUENESS AND DIFFERENTIATION OF THE SERVICE

Wonderland Nursery is a specialty nursery and provides the ultimate in service and advice to customers. We tend to appeal to upper-end clientele, serious gardeners, and gardening professionals. Nowhere else in Washington does an operation combine the services of a nursery along with those of a café.

The idea of nursery and café is to provide customers with a informal, social setting, and atmosphere that does not exist in this part of the state. In addition we will cater to private parties and special groups in the café throughout the year.

The growth potential is virtually unlimited for the greater Spokane, Washington, area. The population is growing at an accelerated rate. It is rare in today's business world to find a true market void. That is exactly what Wonderland Nursery has done. It is a nursery along with a café for nursery customers and others in the community. Our facility has little true competition in Spokane.

FUNDS REQUIRED AND USAGE

Restructuring expenses will be approximately $1,075,0000. New investors will furnish approximately $275,000, and a new loan will furnish the balance of $800,000 in new funding.

The new funding will be used as follows: A) $1,000,000 to repay existing debt, B) $20,000 for paving, C) $5,000 for irrigation improvements, D) $10,000 in new inventory, E) $40,000 for reserves and miscellaneous expenses. The paving will make the property much more attractive to both nursery and café customers. The irrigation will save labor and cut losses. The inventory will bring in new customers and help even out the cash flow throughout the year.

PROJECTED 5-YEAR INCOME STATEMENT SUMMARY

(MOST LIKELY CASE)

	Projected 1999	Projected 2000	Projected 2001	Projected 2002	Projected 2003
Total Revenue	933,000	1,072,350	1,232,589	1,416,847	1,628,727
Cost of Sales	514,229	591,364	680,068	782,079	899,390
Gross Profit	418,771	480,986	552,521	634,768	729,337
Selling, General, Expense	344,137	371,264	402,338	437,939	478,734
Income Before Taxes	74,634	109,722	150,183	196,829	250,603
Income Taxes	17,390	30,347	45,317	62,577	82,473
INCOME AFTER TAXES	**57,244**	**79,375**	**104,866**	**134,252**	**168,130**

(OPTIMISTIC CASE)

Total Revenue	1,119,600	1,286,820	1,479,107	1,700,216	1,954,472
Cost of Sales	617,075	709,637	816,082	938,495	1,079,268
Gross Profit	502,525	577,183	663,025	761,722	875,204
Selling, General, Expense	412,964	445,517	482,806	525,527	574,481
Income Before Taxes	89,561	131,666	180,220	236,195	300,724
Income Taxes	20,868	36,416	54,380	75,092	98,968
INCOME AFTER TAXES	**68,693**	**95,250**	**125,839**	**161,102**	**201,756**

(PESSIMISTIC CASE)

	Projected 1999	Projected 2000	Projected 2001	Projected 2002	Projected 2003
Total Revenue	746,400	857,880	986,071	1,133,478	1,302,982
Cost of Sales	411,383	473,091	544,054	625,663	719,512
Gross Profit	335,017	384,789	442,017	507,814	583,470
Selling, General, Expense	275,310	297,011	321,870	350,351	382,987
Income Before Taxes	59,707	87,778	120,146	157,463	200,482
Income Taxes	13,912	24,278	36,254	50,062	65,978
INCOME AFTER TAXES	**45,795**	**63,500**	**83,893**	**107,402**	**134,504**

Notes:

1. The most likely case assumes 11,000 customers the first year after the restructuring. The optimistic case assumes revenues and expenses will increase 15% over the most likely case. The pessimistic case assumes revenues and expenses will decrease 15% below the most likely case above.

2. Cost of goods sold for the nursery will equal 55% of sales and 35% for the cafe.

OBJECTIVES & GOALS, AND STRATEGIES FOR ACHIEVING THEM

1. To provide a high quality service so that customers will perceive great value and give them the opportunity to interact with our professional staff.

2. To service an average of 12,000 customers in 1999 and increase that by about 15% over the next four years.

3. To repay the entire loan amount by the end of the fifteenth year and to provide the shareholders with an exceptionally stable income.

4. Our goal is to become the premier nursery destination in Spokane, Washington, during the next two years.

5. Wonderland Nursery plans to closely monitor changing technology to be certain that the company is using the latest and most cost effective equipment and that it keeps up with current trends in the marketplace.

When growth has stabilized we plan to add extra services for customer convenience such as organic produce, greater selection of products, especially seasonal, and continued growth of the food operations. In addition to the above goals we will survey our customers and make changes in our programs and add services to meet their changing ideas in the marketplace.

To obtain the first two sets of goals we will try to maximize sales with an extensive campaign to promote our services. We will utilize the radio stations and newspaper along with brochures, media advertising, pamphlets, use of coupons, referrals, and a variety of other advertising and marketing tools to reach the customer base of Spokane, Washington. We expect to flood the market with advertising until consumers become aware of us and more comfortable with our company. As we grow, word-of-mouth referrals will bring in increasing numbers of customers and we will reduce our reliance on advertising.

The dominant driving force behind our company will be profit and income and to provide the best possible related products and service.

To become the premier nursery in Spokane, Washington, we will offer outstanding quality, good hours, exceptional service, and reasonable pricing. We will listen to our customers and conduct surveys.

We will offer frequent user discounts. In the future we may consider diversification and enter new market areas such as providing organic produce.

BUSINESS DESCRIPTION, STATUS, & OUTLOOK

According to the *Nursery Retailer*, lawn and garden sales nationwide are expected to top $83 billion in 1999. Of this total, nearly $1 billion will be in Washington. In 1998, lawn and garden sales showed its first slow-down in growth since 1968. Even so, sales still topped the 1997 levels. Most experts attribute this aberrant downturn to one reason, namely El Nino. This year's growth rates are expected to return to normal levels of around 6% to 9%. With Spokane's exploding growth in population that has occurred during the last decade, local nursery sales should continue to be well in excess of national averages. In fact, when most nurseries experienced a flat growth rate in 1998, Wonderland Nursery experienced a 25% growth in sales.

Wonderland Nursery is a full service nursery and combines entertainment and limited dining at a competitive price. We have a bigger selection of products, more specialized plant selection and offer a much higher level of service than do our competitors. We try to promote an atmosphere that gives people a comfortable place to spend their time and money. Combining a nursery with a café is a relatively new concept for this part of the country. Susan Smyth will continue to operate the business as a corporation. The principal shareholders will be Susan and her husband. New investors will be brought on board and will assume up to a 49% share in ownership. With our new equipment, inventory selections, and property improvements we will also have definite market advantages. Ultimately, we will expand the business to achieve its full potential.

The biggest problem we face is restructuring the operation to give us the time and money needed to fully implement our plans and achieve our goals.

To maintain operations, the business maintains a nursery license, scale license, seed dealers license, health license, occupational use license, and sales tax license.

The future holds the promise for almost unlimited growth and income as the business matures and considers other markets and products. Complementary products such as organic produce, water gardening, newsletter, additional seasonal products, dances, and other functions at the café also can be considered in the future in response to customer surveys indicating their wants and needs. Enhanced food services will be offered in the future as the needs are demonstrated.

MANAGEMENT & OWNERSHIP

Susan Smyth once was a gardener for upper-class clients. She used this experience to develop Wonderland Nursery. The business was successful until the lease was lost on its original location. This precipitated a move to our present location. The move caused us to open grossly undercapitalized. We have managed to survive the past couple of years, but the restructuring we are planning will put us over the top toward achieving our full potential.

Wonderland Nursery will supplement its skills by using outside consultants in areas such as legal work, income tax preparation, insurance, and general business advising.

The business was set up as a corporation primarily for liability reasons and makes it easier to secure investors. To continue operation, as many as thirteen full- and part-time employees will be utilized to help in areas such as bartending, waiting on tables, and for labor. As the business grows, additional part-time or full-time employees may be added to handle the increased workload.

THE SERVICE (AN UNFILLED NEED) & UNIQUENESS OF THE SERVICE

The growth in families in Washington state is the ninth greatest in the country. The past decade has seen this segment of the population grow by more than thirty percent. It is growing five and a half times as fast as the general population.

The few existing nurseries that cater to our clientele are not nearly as knowledgeable or service oriented. They pay little attention to detail and customer satisfaction. Wonderland Nursery and its ownership will embrace the concept of trying to become a focal point for our clientele.

The timing for such a business is perfect. Given the proper kind of financial restructuring, a significant window of opportunity exists for Wonderland Nursery to take advantage of the huge growth of the area. This business will be providing the "Right Service at the Right Time."

It is rare in today's world that a true market void exists. Our service will meet the "unfilled need" described above by providing customers with competitively priced, high service nursery facilities combined with the services of a café on the premises. We are unique to Spokane, and indeed all of Washington.

Customers will be attracted to the nursery because our atmosphere, pricing, and facilities. They will be made to feel welcome and as part of the family.

Some major advantages Wonderland Nursery will have over potential competition and conventional nurseries are:

- Larger and newer facility
- Lower operating expenses than most
- Full service café on site (new concept)
- Location
- 6,000 name mailing list
- Wonderland Nursery will sponsor ethnic festivals and holidays

MARKET ANALYSIS

MARKET OVERVIEW, SIZE, AND SEGMENTS

This market segment has been relatively stable over the past five years.

The market areas we will concentrate on are Central and Western Spokane, Washington. These areas have been growing rapidly for the past several years and should continue for the foreseeable future. Once the concept catches on locally, we feel the potential is unlimited. As we grow we will have the financial capacity to carry on an advertising campaign on a regional basis.

The economy is in the midst of a particularly strong growth period. Many new jobs are being added to the local community. Ever increasing numbers of Californians are coming to this location. All of these factors are cause for a much greater interest in nurseries. All of this activity can only help our attempts to restructure this nursery.

Listed below are just some of the reasons that the Spokane, Washington, area is growing and why it is a good time to be running any kind of business that caters to this growth:

- The local economy is booming and virtually busting at the seams.
- Spokane, Washington, has become a magnet for religious organizations. More than 65 nationally based Christian organizations are headquartered here.

- Spokane, Washington, has a new airport and a nearby Free Trade Enterprise Zone that should grow and attract even more new businesses.
- The new Seattle Airport is open and provides an economic boost to the entire state, including Spokane, Washington.
- Gambling in nearby Oregon continues to draw many visitors and some new businesses.
- Every week, we see articles in the newspapers of California residents and companies relocating here.
- The world-renowned Five Star Hotel has completed an extensive remodeling.
- MCI and Quantum Electronics are undergoing large increases in their operations here that should add many hundreds of employees.
- Many experts predict Spokane, Washington, will become the second fastest growing city in the state between now and the year 2007.
- King County is predicted to become the largest county in the state by the year 2003.
- The local economy is now more diversified than it was when troubles occurred in the local economy in the late 1980s and early 1990s.

The estimated population of King County in 1999 is 500,000 people. The number of households is approaching 200,000. Currently, this market is growing at an annual rate of 3-5%. Projections see this trend continuing for the balance of this decade.

From the above figures it can readily be seen that the potential market for our services is huge. We feel with our pricing and value we will become a price and industry leader within two years.

CUSTOMER PROFILE

Our surveys have shown the following mix of patrons for our facilities:

- Majority are women
- Income of typical customers is in the $50,000 and up range
- Large numbers of professional gardeners
- Range of age of clientele is 35-75
- Majority of patrons are in the upper-income brackets
- Majority of our customers come from the 12345, 12346, 12347, 12348, and 12349 Zip code areas

Beyond the local market we could eventually tap into a more regional market. The advantage of our service is that it could appeal to all segments of the community. By expanding the role of the café, we can continue to become an even greater focal point for the local community.

COMPETITION

Our primary competition is the nurseries listed below. On a limited basis there are few competitors such as nurseries, landscapers, and related businesses.

The following table summarizes the local competition:

Competitor Name	Strengths	Weaknesses
Handles Nursery 1004 N. Main	Well established	Dirty and has bad smell
	Good local support	Filthy & small restrooms
	Well maintained	Poor security
	Brings in popular brands	Allow underage patrons
	Potential to expand	Poor facilities/ maintenance
	Owner well known in area	Lack of parking
	Serves large portion of Mexican population	

Figures Nursery	Good location	Always filthy
1000 E. State	Good local support	Outdated facilities
	Owner prominent in Hispanic community	Failure to keep up with recent trends
Gardners Palace	Newly remodeled	Caters to upper class
2815 Warner	Sufficient parking	Location is hard to find
	Fair neighborhood	Very small
	Specialty nursery	Unfriendly personnel
	New owner	No amenities

The marketplace is currently shared by the above outlined 3 major participants. This market is stable and increasing about 5-7% per year.

The driving force behind Wonderland Nursery is Susan Smyth. She has able support from her husband, Robert, and from Helen Brown, office manager, and Nancy White, file manager.

Risk Analysis

		RATINGS	
ELEMENT	**LOW**	**MEDIUM**	**HIGH**
Industry (Maturity and Cyclicality)	X		
Market/Local Economy	X		
Competitive Position		X	
Dependence upon other Companies		X	
Vulnerability to Substitutes		X	
Technology		X	
Distribution		X	
Regulatory Environment	X		
Suppliers		X	
Strategy		X	
Assumptions	X		
Finanical Performance			X
Management Performance		X	
Inflation/Interest Rates	X		
Others		X	
Overall Risk		X	

Identification of Strengths & Weaknesses

Functions	Strong (+)	Average (O)	Weak (-)	Major Strengths and/or Weaknesses Compared to Competitors
General Administration (Management)	X			Hardworking, direct, effective, charismatic
Marketing	X			Original, consistently appealing
Finance/Planning		X		Will hire consultants to help
Human Resources	X			Better performance achievable
Operations	X			Energy to accomplish tasks
Production		X		
Purchasing		X		High perceived quality
Distribution		X		
Servicing	X			High customer satisfaction
Quality of Service	X			
Company Policies		X		
Product Mix	X			Several choices available
Product Features	X			
Options		X		
Warranties/Guarantees		X		
Reliability	X			Best product and service available
Desirability	X			
Advertising		X		Hire consultants to improve, lack of money
Market Leadership	X			Best independent around
Sales Force	X			
Overhead			X	Existing levels are too high; can be greatly reduced with new funding
Pricing	X			Low for service
Delivery Time		X		
Location	X			
Facilities	X			Best combination around

We feel we will have strengths in product features, management, marketing, human resources, quality of service, operations, product mix, reliability, desirability, highly trained sales force, pricing, location, and facilities.

We will have low risk exposure in the areas of technology, inflation/interest rates, regulatory environment, management ability, location, facilities, and suppliers.

We perceive medium risk exposure in the local economy, strategy, and vulnerability to substitutes, finance, and planning. We have retained the services of specialists to help in various areas such as marketing, accounting, legal, and general overall business operation advice.

We have a high degree of risk in this overhead and lack of working capital. With our proposed new funding, we should overcome most of our weaknesses.

MARKETING STRATEGIES

PRICING AND VALUE

Our intention is to raise the public's awareness of our company. We plan to review our prices and those of our competitors every three months. We will review direct material costs, direct labor costs, and total overhead expenses. We will continually monitor the cost of providing our service to each customer. We will offer various free or reduced rate programs to get customers acquainted with us.

Numerous package deals will be available to customers. The following examples are various marketing strategies we may try:

- Discounts for larger or repeat purchases
- Special party rates for the café
- We will continue the use of our newsletter to help promote value to our customers

SELLING TACTICS

Our company's marketing strategy will incorporate plans to promote our line of services through several different channels and on different levels of use. We will advertise heavily on the popular local radio stations and in newspapers.

We will try to satisfy the market void in this area for indoor entertainment. We will flood the market with advertising and try to go after our specific targets. We will try to capture their attention, pique their interest, and make them feel that they must have our services.

We will offer continuous promotional rates. The results sell themselves. We will offer discounts to frequent users. The more a customer uses our services the cheaper it will become for them.

We also are a MasterCard and Visa charge card merchant which enables us to more readily serve our customers.

In order to market our facility, we shall consider a variety of promotions including:

- Reserve certain hours for unique groups such as children, senior citizens, service clubs, adults, etc.
- Conduct special theme nights, use ethnic holidays, family night, charity promotion night, game night, contest night, etc.
- Cultivate local churches and women's organizations.
- Promote birthday parties.
- Early bird specials.

ADVERTISING, PROMOTION, AND DISTRIBUTION OF SERVICES

We recognize that the key to success at this time requires extensive promotion. Advertising goals include all of the following:

- Position the company as the premier nursery in Central/Western Spokane, Washington.
- Increase public awareness of Wonderland Nursery and its benefits.
- Increase public awareness of our company and establish a professional image.
- Maximize efficiency by continually monitoring media effectiveness.
- Consider a possible credit coupon in some of the advertisements.
- Develop a brochure or pamphlet to explain our service and company.
- Continue use of a distinctive business card and company letterhead.
- Use a mix of media to saturate the marketplace.

PUBLIC RELATIONS

We will develop a public relations policy that will help increase awareness of our company and product. To achieve these goals we will consider some or all of the following:

- Develop a press release and a company backgrounder as a public relations tool.
- Develop a telephone script to handle customer and advertiser contact.
- Develop a survey to be completed by customers to help determine the following:
  1. How did they hear about us?

2. What influenced them to use our service?

3. How well did our service satisfy their needs?

4. How efficient was our service?

5. Did they have any problems getting through to us?

6. Did they shop competitors before selecting us?

7. How did they initially perceive our company and product?

8. Where are most of our customers located?

9. Do they have suggestions for improving our service or our approach to advertising?

10. What additional services would they like us to offer?

11. Would they recommend us to others?

- Maintain membership in the Chamber of Commerce to keep abreast of developments in the community and market trends.

FINANCIAL PLANS

Data Sheet #1

GENERAL:

Fiscal Year in which Projections/Calculations are to start 1999
Number of Months in which Projections/Calculations are to start 1
The purpose for this analysis is Business Start-Up, Expansion, or Review .... START-UP
Owner's contribution to business (include both cash and time in dollar equivalency) $6,000,000.00

Indicate below if the figures are actual, annualized, or projected for each year in the analysis:

1999	Projected
2000	Projected
2001	Projected
2002	Projected
2003	Projected

INDICATE THE TYPE OF BUSINESS ENTITY YOU HAVE IN THE BOX TO THE RIGHT: C

START-UP/EXPANSION EXPENSES:

		EXPENSES FOR YEAR:	% of Sales	$ Amounts
Inventory	160,000.00	Advertising & Marketing Expenses	2.59%	0.00
Advertising	0.00	Bad Debts	0.00%	0.00
Telephone/Utilities	0.00	Contract Labor	0.70%	0.00
Professional Fees	0.00	Depreciation	0.00%	4,500.00
Organizational Expenses	0.00	Direct Labor Expenses	3.28%	0.00
Furniture/Fixtures	0.00	Dues, Subscriptions, and Memberships	0.00%	1,000.00
Land	750,000.00	Employee Reimbursement Expenses	0.00%	.0.00
Buildings	300,000.00	Freight/Shipping	0.27%	0.00
Machinery/Equipment	65,000.00	Furniture or Fixtures Purchases	0.00%	1,000.00
Rent Deposits	0.00	Insurance	0.00%	8,996.00
Insurance	0.00	Lease Expenses	0.00%	0.00
Leasehold Improvements	0.00	Leasehold Expenses	0.00%	0.00
Licenses/Fees/Permits	0.00	Machinery & Equipment Purchases	0.00%	0.00
Miscellaneous	0.00	Office Supplies and Postage	0.16%	0.00
Property Improvements	25,000.00	Professional Fees	0.00%	4,250.00
Property Taxes	0.00	Permits/Licenses	0.00%	1,940.00
Other #3	0.00	Rent	0.00%	0.00
Other #4	0.00	Repair & Maintenance	0.00%	1,700.00
TOTAL	**1,300,000.00**	Salaries-Officers	0.00%	38,400.00
LOAN DATA:(If Needed)		Salaries-Administrative	0.00%	0.00
Amount of Loan 1	$800,000.00	Salaries and Wages-Other	10.56%	0.00
Term of Loan 1 (Months)	180	Salaries-Manager	0.00%	0.00
Interest Rate for Loan 1	11%	Telephone/Utilities	0.00%	11,700.00
First Year of Loan 1	1999	Property Improvements	0.00%	2,550.00
First Payment Month	8	Property Taxes	0.00%	9,000.00

		Other #3	0.00%	0.00
Amount of Loan 2	$0.00	Other #4	0.00%	0.00
Term of Loan 2 (Months)	60	Miscellaneous/Contingency Expenses	2.50%	0.00
Interest Rate for Loan 2	0.00%	**TOTAL FIRST YEAR EXPENSES INCLUDING INTEREST PAID**		
First Year of Loan 2	1999	**AND COST OF GOODS SOLD:**	**$858,366**	
First Payment Month	1			

PERCENTAGE OF TOTAL PAYROLL ALLOTTED TO PAYROLL TAXES AND BENEFITS 10.00%
PERCENTAGE OF NET SALES EXPECTED FOR THE COST OF GOODS SOLD: Café   35.00%
PERCENTAGE OF NET SALES EXPECTED FOR THE COST OF GOODS SOLD: Nursery   55.00%

Data Sheet #2

SOURCE/AMOUNTS OF INCOME FOR YEAR	1999	PERCENTAGE OF INCOME GROWTH		
Nursery sales	$797,000.00	For Second Year	2000	15.00%
Café sales	$130,000.00	For Third Year	2001	15.00%
Source of Income #3	$0.00	For Fourth Year	2002	15.00%
Source of Income #4	$0.00	For Fifth Year	2003	15.00%
Other Income/Exp. (Net)	$6,000.00			

TOTAL INCOME   **$933,000.00**

PERCENTAGE OF INCREASE IN EXPENSES:		PERCENTAGE OF NET INCOME TO BE PAID OUT IN DIVIDENDS		
For Second Year	5.00%	For First Year	1999	50.00%
For Third Year	5.25%	For Second Year	2000	60.00%
For Fourth Year	5.50%	For Third Year	2001	65.00%
For Fifth Year	5.75%	For Fourth Year	2002	70.00%
		For Fifth Year	2003	75.00%

Number of Customers Expected to Serve the First Year: 12,000
Average Income received from each Customer: $77.75

Operating Data	1999	2000	2001	2002	2003
Days Sales in Accounts Receivable	20.0	20.0	20.0	20.0	20.0
Days Materials Cost in Inventory	30.0	30.0	30.0	30.0	30.0
Days Finished Goods in Inventory	45.0	45.0	45.0	45.0	45.0
Days Materials Cost in Payables	20.0	20.0	20.0	20.0	20.0
Days Payroll Expenses accrued	20.0	20.0	20.0	20.0	20.0
Days Operating Expenses accrued	25.0	25.0	25.0	25.0	25.0

RE-STRUCTURE EXPENSES

Category	Amount
Cash and Working Capital	$28,150
Material-Supplies-Inventory	10,000
Furniture and Fixtures	25,500
Equipment	40,000
Rent Deposits	9,700
License Fees/Permits	1,000
Insurance (First year paid in advance)	1,800
Utilities & Telephone	500
Legal, Professional, and Consulting Fees	1,500
Security System & Leasehold Improvements	5,000
Initial Entertainment Budget	6,000
Opening Advertisement & Promotion	3,000
Miscellaneous	2,850
TOTAL	**$135,000**

Projected First-Year Monthly Budget 1999

Month	Start-Up	Month 1	Month 2	Month 3	Month 4	Month 5	Month 6	Month 7
CASH RECEIPTS:								
Nursery Sales		$4,782	$11,158	$15,143	$47,023	$295,687	$168,167	$78,106
Café Sales		$3,510	$4,160	$4,940	$6,500	$13,000	$20,020	$20,020
Source of Income #3		$0	$0	$0	$0	$0	$0	$0
Source of Income #4		$0	$0	$0	$0	$0	$0	$0
Other Income/Expense (Net)		$500	$500	$500	$500	$500	$500	$500
Owner's Equity	600,000							
Loan	800,000							
Total Cash Received	**1,400,000**	**8,792**	**15,818**	**20,583**	**54,023**	**309,187**	**188,687**	**98,626**
DISBURSEMENTS:								
Cost of Goods Sold/Inventory	160,000	$3,859	$7,593	$10,058	$28,138	$167,178	$99,499	$49,965
Advertising / Marketing Exp.	0	$215	$397	$520	$1,386	$7,992	$4,872	$2,540
Bad Debts		$0	$0	$0	$0	$0	$0	$0
Contract Labor		$58	$107	$141	$375	$2,164	$1,320	$688
Depreciation		$375	$375	$375	$375	$375	$375	$375
Direct Labor		$272	$502	$658	$1,754	$10,116	$6,167	$3,216
Dues/Subscrip./Memberships		$83	$83	$83	$83	$83	$83	$83
Employee Reimbursement Exp.		$0	$0	$0	$0	$0	$0	$0
Freight / Shipping		$22	$41	$54	$144	$832	$508	$265
Furniture or Fixtures Purchases	0	$83	$83	$83	$83	$83	$83	$83
Insurance	0	$750	$750	$750	$750	$750	$750	$750
Land	750,000							
Buildings	300,000							
Lease Expenses		$0	$0	$0	$0	$0	$0	$0
Leasehold Expenses	0	$0	$0	$0	$0	$0	$0	$0
Mach./Equipment Purchases	65,000	$0	$0	$0	$0	$0	$0	$0
Organizational Expenses	0	$0	$0	$0	$0	$0	$0	$0
Office Supplies and Postage		$13	$25	$32	$87	$499	$305	$159
Payroll Taxes/Employee Benefits		$435	$532	$598	$1,060	$4,590	$2,923	$1,677
Professional Fees	0	$354	$354	$354	$354	$354	$354	$354
Permits / Licenses	0	$162	$162	$162	$162	$162	$162	$162
Rent	0	$0	$0	$0	$0	$0	$0	$0
Repair & Maintenance		$142	$142	$142	$142	$142	$142	$142
Salaries-Officers		$3,200	$3,200	$3,200	$3,200	$3,200	$3,200	$3,200
Salaries-Administrative		$0	$0	$0	$0	$0	$0	$0
Salaries and Wages-Other		$875	$1,617	$2,120	$5,650	$32,587	$19,866	$10,359
Salaries-Manager		$0	$0	$0	$0	$0	$0	$0
Telephone / Utilities	0	$975	$975	$975	$975	$975	$975	$975
Property Improvements	25,000	$213	$213	$213	$213	$213	$213	$213
Property Taxes	0	$750	$750	$750	$750	$750	$750	$750
Other #3	0	$0	$0	$0	$0	$0	$0	$0
Other #4	0	$0	$0	$0	$0	$0	$0	$0
Misc./Contingency Expenses	0	$207	$383	$502	$1,338	$7,717	$4,705	$2,453
Total Cash Paid Out	**1,300,000**	**13,043**	**18,283**	**21,770**	**47,019**	**240,763**	**147,250**	**78,409**
LOANS SECTION:								
Interest		7,333	7,317	7,301	7,285	7,268	7,251	7,234
Principal		1,759	1,776	1,792	1,808	1,825	1,842	1,858
Cash Pyts to Loans		**9,093**	**9,093**	**9,093**	**9,093**	**9,093**	**9,093**	**9,093**
Taxable Income		-11,584	-9,782	-8,487	-280	61,156	34,186	12,983
Income Tax (State & Federal)		1,449	1,449	1,449	1,449	1,449	1,449	1,449
NET INCOME		**-13,033**	**-11,232**	**-9,937**	**-1,729**	**59,707**	**32,736**	**11,534**
LOANS (Balance)	800,000	798,241	796,465	794,673	792,865	791,040	789,198	787,340
DIVIDENDS PAID		2,385	2,385	2,385	2,385	2,385	2,385	2,385
BEGINNING CASH	100,000							

Month 8	Month 9	Month 10	Month 11	Month 12	TOTALS
$53,399	$71,730	$19,925	$10,361	$21,519	$797,000
$14,950	$11,960	$10,010	$8,970	$11,960	$130,000
$0	$0	$0	$0	$0	$0
$0	$0	$0	$0	$0	$0
$500	$500	$500	$500	$500	$6,000
68,849	**84,190**	**30,435**	**19,831**	**33,979**	**933,000**
$34,602	$43,638	$14,462	$8,838	$16,021	$483,850
$1,770	$2,167	$775	$500	$867	$24,000
$0	$0	$0	$0	$0	$0
$479	$587	$210	$136	$235	$6,500
$375	$375	$375	$375	$375	$4,500
$2,240	$2,743	$981	$634	$1,097	$30,379
$83	$83	$83	$83	$83	$1,000
$0	$0	$0	$0	$0	$0
$184	$226	$81	$52	$90	$2,500
$83	$83	$83	$83	$83	$1,000
$750	$750	$750	$750	$750	$8,996
					$0
					$0
$0	$0	$0	$0	$0	$0
$0	$0	$0	$0	$0	$0
$0	$0	$0	$0	$0	$0
$0	$0	$0	$0	$0	$0
$111	$135	$48	$31	$54	$1,500
$1,266	$1,478	$734	$587	$783	$16,664
$354	$354	$354	$354	$354	$4,250
$162	$162	$162	$162	$162	$1,940
$0	$0	$0	$0	$0	$0
$142	$142	$142	$142	$142	$1,700
$3,200	$3,200	$3,200	$3,200	$3,200	$38,400
$0	$0	$0	$0	$0	$0
$7,215	$8,835	$3,160	$2,041	$3,534	$97,860
$0	$0	$0	$0	$0	$0
$975	$975	$975	$975	$975	$11,700
$213	$213	$213	$213	$213	$2,550
$750	$750	$750	$750	$750	$9,000
$0	$0	$0	$0	$0	$0
$0	$0	$0	$0	$0	$0
$1,709	$2,092	$748	$483	$837	$23,175
56,661	**68,986**	**28,286**	**20,389**	**30,605**	**$771,464**
7,217	7,200	7,183	7,165	7,148	$86,902
1,875	1,893	1,910	1,928	1,945	$22,211
9,093	**9,093**	**9,093**	**9,093**	**9,093**	**$109,113**
4,970	8,004	-5,034	-7,723	-3,774	$74,634
1,449	1,449	1,449	1,449	1,449	$17,390
3,521	**6,555**	**-6,483**	**-9,172**	**-5,223**	**$57,244**
785,464	783,572	781,662	779,734	777,789	
2,385	**2,385**	**2,385**	**2,385**	**2,385**	**$28,622**

Projected Second-Year Monthly Budget 2000

Month	Month 13	Month 14	Month 15	Month 16	Month 17	Month 18	Month 19	Month 20
CASH RECEIPTS:								
Nursery Sales	$5,499	$12,832	$17,414	$54,076	$340,040	$193,392	$89,822	$61,409
Café Sales	$4,037	$4,784	$5,681	$7,475	$14,950	$23,023	$23,023	$17,193
Source of Income #3	$0	$0	$0	$0	$0	$0	$0	$0
Source of Income #4	$0	$0	$0	$0	$0	$0	$0	$0
Other Income/Expense (Net)	$525	$525	$525	$525	$525	$525	$525	$525
Owner's Equity								
Loan								
Total Cash Received	**10,061**	**18,141**	**23,620**	**62,076**	**355,515**	**216,940**	**113,370**	**79,126**
DISBURSEMENTS:								
Cost of Goods Sold/Inventory	$4,437	$8,732	$11,566	$32,358	$192,255	$114,424	$57,460	$39,792
Advertising / Marketing Exp.	$247	$456	$598	$1,594	$9,191	$5,603	$2,922	$2,035
Bad Debts	$0	$0	$0	$0	$0	$0	$0	$0
Contract Labor	$67	$124	$162	$432	$2,489	$1,517	$791	$551
Depreciation	$394	$394	$394	$394	$394	$394	$394	$394
Direct Labor	$313	$577	$757	$2,017	$11,633	$7,092	$3,698	$2,576
Dues/Subscrip./Memberships	$88	$88	$88	$88	$88	$88	$88	$88
Employee Reimbursement Exp.	$0	$0	$0	$0	$0	$0	$0	$0
Freight / Shipping	$26	$48	$62	$166	$957	$584	$304	$212
Furniture or Fixtures Purchases	$88	$88	$88	$88	$88	$88	$88	$88
Insurance	$787	$787	$787	$787	$787	$787	$787	$787
Land								
Buildings								
Lease Expenses	$0	$0	$0	$0	$0	$0	$0	$0
Leasehold Expenses	$0	$0·	$0	$0	$0	$0	$0	$0
Mach./Equipment Purchases	$0	$0	$0	$0	$0	$0	$0	$0
Organizational Expenses	$0	$0	$0	$0	$0	$0	$0	$0
Office Supplies and Postage	$144	$144	$144	$144	$144	$144	$144	$144
Payroll Taxes/Employee Benefits	$468	$580	$655	$1,187	$5,247	$3,330	$1,897	$1,423
Professional Fees	$372	$372	$372	$372	$372	$372	$372	$372
Permits / Licenses	$170	$170	$170	$170	$170	$170	$170	$170
Rent	$0	$0	$0	$0	$0	$0	$0	$0
Repair & Maintenance	$149	$149	$149	$149	$149	$149	$149	$149
Salaries-Officers	$3,360	$3,360	$3,360	$3,360	$3,360	$3,360	$3,360	$3,360
Salaries-Administrative	$0	$0	$0	$0	$0	$0	$0	$0
Salaries and Wages-Other	$1,007	$1,860	$2,438	$6,498	$37,475	$22,846	$11,913	$8,298
Salaries-Manager	$0	$0	$0	$0	$0	$0	$0	$0
Telephone / Utilities	$1,024	$1,024	$1,024	$1,024	$1,024	$1,024	$1,024	$1,024
Property Improvements	$223	$223	$223	$223	$223	$223	$223	$223
Property Taxes	$788	$788	$788	$788	$788	$788	$788	$788
Other #3	$0	$0	$0	$0	$0	$0	$0	$0
Other #4	$0	$0	$0	$0	$0	$0	$0	$0
Misc./Contingency Expenses	$238	$440	$577	$1,539	$8,875	$5,410	$2,821	$1,965
Total Cash Paid Out	**14,387**	**20,400**	**24,401**	**53,375**	**275,706**	**168,391**	**89,390**	**64,437**
LOANS SECTION:								
Interest	7,130	7,112	7,094	7,075	7,057	7,038	7,019	7,000
Principal	1,963	1,981	1,999	2,018	2,036	2,055	2,074	2,093
Cash Pyts to Loans	**9,093**	**9,093**	**9,093**	**9,093**	**9,093**	**9,093**	**9,093**	**9,093**
Taxable Income	-11,456	-9,371	-7,874	1,626	72,752	41,511	16,960	7,689
Income Tax (State & Federal)	2,529	2,529	2,529	2,529	2,529	2,529	2,529	2,529
NET INCOME	**-13,985**	**-11,900**	**-10,403**	**-903**	**70,223**	**38,982**	**14,431**	**5,161**
LOANS (Balance)	**775,826**	**773,846**	**771,845**	**769,828**	**767,792**	**765,738**	**763,664**	**761,571**
DIVIDENDS PAID	**3,969**	**3,969**	**3,936**	**3,969**	**3,969**	**3,969**	**3,969**	**3,969**

Month 21	Month 22	Month 23	Month 24	TOTALS
$82,490	$22,914	$11,915	$24,747	$916,550
$13,754	$11,512	$10,316	$13,754	$149,500
$0	$0	$0	$0	$0
$0	$0	$0	$0	$0
$525	$525	$525	$525	$6,300
96,769	**34,950**	**22,756**	**39,026**	**$1,072,350**
$50,183	$16,632	$10,164	$18,425	$556,428
$2,492	$891	$576	$997	$27,600
$0	$0	$0	$0	$0
$675	$241	$156	$270	$7,475
$394	$394	$394	$394	$4,725
$3,154	$1,128	$729	$1,262	$34,936
$88	$88	$88	$88	$1,050
$0	$0	$0	$0	$0
$260	$93	$60	$104	$2,875
$88	$88	$88	$88	$1,050
$787	$787	$787	$787	$9,446
				$0
				$0
$0	$0	$0	$0	$0
$0	$0	$0	$0	$0
$0	$0	$0	$0	$0
$0	$0	$0	$0	$0
$144	$144	$144	$144	$1,725
$1,667	$812	$644	$869	$18,779
$372	$372	$372	$372	$4,463
$170	$170	$170	$170	$2,037
$0	$0	$0	$0	$0
$149	$149	$149	$149	$1,785
$3,360	$3,360	$3,360	$3,360	$40,320
$0	$0	$0	$0	$0
$10,160	$3,634	$2,347	$4,064	$112,539
$0	$0	$0	$0	$0
$1,024	$1,024	$1,024	$1,024	$12,285
$223	$223	$223	$223	$2,678
$788	$788	$788	$788	$9,450
$0	$0	$0	$0	$0
$0	$0	$0	$0	$0
$2,406	$861	$556	$963	$26,651
78,581	**31,877**	**22,814**	**34,537**	**$878,296**
6,981	6,962	6,942	6,922	$84,332
2,112	2,131	2,151	2,170	$24,781
9,093	**9,093**	**9,093**	**9,093**	**$109,113**
11,205	-3,888	-7,001	-2,434	$109,722
2,529	2,529	2,529	2,529	$30,347
8,677	**-6,417**	**-9,530**	**-4,962**	**$79,375**
759,460	**757,329**	**755,178**	**753,008**	
3,969	**3,969**	**3,969**	**3,969**	**$47,625**

Five-Year Income Statement

Five-Year Analysis

Sales	Projected 1999	Projected 2000	Projected 2001	Projected 2002	Projected 2003
Sales	$927,000	$1,066,050	$1,225,958	$1,409,852	$1,621,329
Cost of sales	$514,229	$591,364	$680,068	$782,079	$899,390
Gross Profits	**$412,771**	**$474,686**	**$545,890**	**$627,773**	**$721,939**
Expenses:					
Operating expenses	$252,735	$282,207	$315,900	$354,427	$398,491
Interest	$86,902	$84,332	$81,465	$78,265	$74,695
Depreciation	$4,500	$4,725	$4,973	$5,247	$5,548
Amortization	$0	$0	$0	$0	$0
Total expenses	**$344,137**	**$371,264**	**$402,338**	**$437,939**	**$478,734**
Operating income	**$68,634**	**$103,422**	**$143,552**	**$189,834**	**$243,205**
Other income and expenses					
Gain (loss) on sale of assets	$0	$0	$0	$0	$0
Other (net)	$6,000	$6,300	$6,631	$6,995	$7,398
Subtotal	**$6,000**	**$6,300**	**$6,631**	**$6,995**	**$7,398**
Income before tax	**$74,634**	**$109,722**	**$150,183**	**$196,829**	**$250,603**
Taxes (Federal & State)	$17,390	$30,347	$45,317	$62,577	$82,473
Rate	23.30%	27.66%	30.17%	31.79%	32.91%
Net income	**$57,244**	**$79,375**	**$104,866**	**$134,252**	**$168,130**
Retained earnings-beginning	$0	$28,622	$60,372	$97,076	$137,351
Dividends paid	$28,622	$47,625	$68,162	$93,977	$126,097
Retained earnings-ending	$28,622	$60,372	$97,076	$137,351	$179,384

Detailed Supporting Information
Cost of sales

Direct labor	$30,479	$34,936	$40,176	$46,203	$53,133
Materials	$483,850	$556,428	$639,892	$735,876	$846,257
Other costs					

Five-Year Balance Statement

	START-UP	FIVE-YEAR ANALYSIS				
		Projected 1999	Projected 2000	Projected 2001	Projected 2002	Projected 2003
ASSETS:						
Cash and cash equivalents	$100,000	$194,902	$189,607	$184,182	$176,568	$164,185
Accounts Receivable	$0	$50,795	$58,414	$67,176	$77,252	$88,840
Inventory	$160,000	$103,167	$118,642	$136,438	$156,904	$180,439
Other current assets	$0	$0	$0	$0	$0	$0
Total Current Assets	**$260,000**	**$348,864**	**$366,663**	**$387,796**	**$410,724**	**$433,464**
FIXED ASSETS:						
Land	$750,000	$750,000	$750,000	$750,000	$750,000	$750,000
Buildings	$300,000	$300,000	$300,000	$300,000	$300,000	$300,000
Machinery & Equipment	$65,000	$65,000	$65,000	$65,000	$65,000	$65,000
Furniture/Fixtures	$0	$0	$1,050	$2,155	$3,321	$4,554
Subtotal	$1,115,000	$1,115,000	$116,050	$1,117,155	$1,118,321	$1,119,554
Less-accumulated depreciation	$0	$4,500	$9,225	$14,198	$19,445	$24,993
Total Fixed Assets	**$1,115,000**	**$1,110,500**	**$1,106,825**	**$1,102,957**	**$1,098,876**	**$1,094,561**
INTANGIBLE ASSETS:						
Cost	$0	$0	$0	$0	$0	$0
Less-accumulated amortization	$0	$0	$0	$0	$0	$0
Total Intangible Assets	**$0**	**$0**	**$0**	**$0**	**$0**	**$0**
Other Assets	**$25,000**	**$0**	**$0**	**$0**	**$0**	**$0**
Total Assets	**$1,400,000**	**$1,459,364**	**$1,473,488**	**$1,490,753**	**$1,509,600**	**$1,528,025**
LIABILITIES:						
Accounts payable	$0	$26,512	$30,489	$35,063	$40,322	$46,370
Notes payable	$0	$0	$0	$0	$0	$0
Current portion of long-term debt	$22,211	$24,781	$27,649	$30,848	$34,418	$38,401
Income taxes	$0	$0	$0	$0	$0	$0
Accrued expenses	$0	$26,441	$29,619	$33,255	$37,416	$42,178
Other current liabilities	$0	$0	$0	$0	$0	$0
Total Current Liabilities	**$22,211**	**$77,734**	**$87,757**	**$99,166**	**$112,156**	**$126,949**
Long-term debt	$777,789	$753,008	$725,359	$694,511	$660,093	$621,692
Deferred income	$0	$0	$0	$0	$0	$0
Deferred income taxes	$0	$0	$0	$0	$0	$0
Other long-term liabilities	$0	$0	$0	$0	$0	$0
Total Liabilities	**$800,000**	**$830,742**	**$813,116**	**$793,677**	**$772,249**	**$748,641**
EQUITY:						
Capital stock issues	$600,000	$600,000	$600,000	$600,000	$600,000	$600,000
Additional paid in capital	$0	$0	$0	$0	$0	$0
Retained earnings	$0	$28,622	$60,372	$97,076	$137,351	$179,384
Total Equity	**$600,000**	**$628,622**	**$660,372**	**$697,076**	**$737,351**	**$779,384**
Total Liabilities and Equity	**$1,400,000**	**$1,459,364**	**$1,473,488**	**$1,490,753**	**$1,509,600**	**$1,528,025**
"C" Corporation (Y/N)	Y					
Cash balance positive / (negative)	Positive	Positive	Positive	Positive	Positive	Positive
Amount sheet is out-of-balance	$0	$0	$0	$0	$0	$0
Amount cash flow out-of-balance		$0	$0	$0	$0	$0

Five-Year Cash Flow Statement

	Projected 1999	Projected 2000	Projected 2001	Projected 2002	Projected 2003
Cash from operations					
Net earnings (loss)	$57,244	$79,375	$104,866	$134,252	$168,130
Add-depreciation and amortization	$4,500	$4,725	$4,973	$5,247	$5,548
Cash from operations	**$61,744**	**$84,100**	**$109,839**	**$139,499**	**$173,678**
Cash provided (used) by operating activities					
Accounts Receivable	($50,795)	($7,619)	($8,762)	($10,076)	($11,588)
Inventory	$56,833	($15,475)	($17,796)	($20,466)	($23,535)
Other current assets	$0	$0	$0	$0	$0
Other non-current assets	$25,000	$0	$0	$0	$0
Accounts payable	$26,512	$3,977	$4,574	$5,259	$6,048
Current portion of long-term debt	$2,570	$2,868	$3,199	$3,570	$3,983
Income taxes	$0	$0	$0	$0	$0
Accrued expenses	$26,441	$3,178	$3,636	$4,161	$4,762
Other current liabilities	$0	$0	$0	$0	$0
Dividends paid	($28,622)	($47,625)	($68,162)	($93,977)	($126,097)
Net cash from operations	**$57,939**	**($60,696)**	**($83,311)**	**($111,529)**	**($146,427)**
Investment transactions Increases (decreases)					
Land	$0	$0	$0	$0	$0
Buildings and improvements	$0	$0	$0	$0	$0
Equipment	$0	$0	$0	$0	$0
Furniture/Fixtures	$0	$1,050	$1,105	$1,166	$1,233
Intangible assets	$0	$0	$0	$0	$0
Net cash from investments	**$0**	**$1,050**	**$1,105**	**$1,166**	**$1,233**
Financing transactions Increases (decreases)					
Short-term notes payable	$0	$0	$0	$0	$0
Long-term debt	($24,781)	($27,649)	($30,848)	($34,418)	($38,401)
Deferred income	$0	$0	$0	$0	$0
Deferred income taxes	$0	$0	$0	$0	$0
Other long-term liabilities	$0	$0	$0	$0	$0
Capital stock and paid in capital	$0	$0	$0	$0	$0
Net cash from financing	**($24,781)**	**($27,649)**	**($30,848)**	**($34,418)**	**($38,401)**
Net increase (decrease) in cash	**$94,902**	**($5,295)**	**($5,425)**	**($7,614)**	**($12,383)**
Cash at beginning of period	**$100,000**	**$194,902**	**$189,607**	**$184,182**	**$176,568**
Cash at the end of period	**$194,902**	**$189,607**	**$184,182**	**$176,568**	**$164,185**

Common Size Income Statement

	Projected 1999	Projected 2000	Projected 2001	Projected 2002	Projected 2003	Industry 1999
Revenue from Sales	100.0%	100.0%	100.0%	100.0%	100.0%	100.0%
Cost of Sales	55.5%	55.5%	55.5%	55.5%	55.5%	55.8%
Gross Profit	44.5%	44.5%	44.5%	44.5%	44.5%	44.2%
Operating Expenses	37.1%	34.8%	32.8%	31.1%	29.5%	38.1%
Operating Profit	7.4%	9.7%	11.7%	13.5%	15.0%	6.1%
Other Expen./Inc (Net)	0.6%	0.6%	0.5%	0.5%	0.5%	-2.7%
PRE-TAX PROFIT	**8.1%**	**10.3%**	**12.3%**	**14.0%**	**15.5%**	**3.4%**
Income Taxes	1.9%	2.8%	3.7%	4.4%	5.1%	0.0%
INCOME AFTER TAXES	**6.2%**	**7.4%**	**8.6%**	**9.5%**	**10.4%**	**3.4%**

Common Size Balance Sheet

	Projected 1999	Projected 2000	Projected 2001	Projected 2002	Projected 2003	Industry 1999
Cash & Equivalent	13.4%	12.9%	12.4%	11.7%	10.7%	7.0%
Accounts Receivable	3.5%	4.0%	4.5%	5.1%	5.8%	10.5%
Inventory	7.1%	8.1%	9.2%	10.4%	11.8%	35.7%
Other Current	0.0%	0.0%	0.0%	0.0%	0.0%	0.7%
Total Current Assets	23.9%	24.9%	26.0%	27.2%	28.4%	53.9%
Fixed Assets (Net)	76.1%	75.1%	74.0%	72.8%	71.6%	38.0%
Intangibles	0.0%	0.0%	0.0%	0.0%	0.0%	2.5%
Other Assets	0.0%	0.0%	0.0%	0.0%	0.0%	5.6%
TOTAL ASSETS	**100.0%**	**100.0%**	**100.0%**	**100.0%**	**100.0%**	**100.0%**
Liabilities:						
Accounts Payable	1.8%	2.1%	2.4%	2.7%	3.0%	13.2%
Short-term Notes	0.0%	0.0%	0.0%	0.0%	0.0%	6.6%
Current Maturities (LTD)	1.7%	1.9%	2.1%	2.3%	2.5%	13.9%
Income Taxes	0.0%	0.0%	0.0%	0.0%	0.0%	0.3%
Accrued Expenses	1.8%	2.0%	2.2%	2.5%	2.8%	8.0%
Other Current Liabilities	0.0%	0.0%	0.0%	0.0%	0.0%	0.0%
Total Current Liabilities	5.3%	6.0%	6.7%	7.4%	8.3%	42.0%
Long-term Debt	51.6%	49.2%	46.6%	43.7%	40.7%	32.4%
Other Non-Current	0.0%	0.0%	0.0%	0.0%	0.0%	6.2%
Total Liabilities	56.9%	55.2%	53.2%	51.2%	49.0%	80.6%
TOTAL EQUITY	**43.1%**	**44.8%**	**46.8%**	**48.8%**	**51.0%**	**19.4%**
Total Liabilities & Equity	100.0%	100.0%	100.0%	100.0%	100.0%	100.0%

Average Monthly Break-Even Analysis 1999

Cost Variables	Per Month-1st Year		
	Optimistic -20.00%	Most Likely Case	Pessimistic 20.00%
FIXED COSTS:			
Rentals/Leases	$0	$0	$0
Salaries (Fixed/Officers)	$2,560	$3,200	$3,840
Insurance	$600	$750	$900
Depreciation & Amortization	$300	$375	$450
Interest	$5,793	$7,242	$8,690
Utilities/Phone	$780	$975	$1,170
(Other fixed costs)	$0	$0	$0
Total Fixed Costs	**$10,033**	**$12,542**	**$15,050**
VARIABLE COSTS:			
Cost of Goods Sold	$32,257	$40,321	$48,385
Variable Labor/Wages	$6,524	$8,155	$9,786
Advertising	$1,600	$2,000	$2,400
Professional Services	$283	$354	$425
(Other variable cost)	$6,527	$8,159	$9,791
Total Variable Costs	**$47,191**	**$58,989**	**$70,787**
SALES AND INCOME DATA:			
Average Income Per Customer	$77.75	$77.75	$77.75
Average # of Customers Per Month	$1,200.00	$1,000.00	$800.00
RESULTS:			
Fixed Costs per Customer	**$8.36**	**$12.54**	**$18.81**
Variable Costs per Customer	**$39.33**	**$58.99**	**$88.48**
Break-Even Number of Customers	**$261.12**	**$668.49**	**($1,402.14)**
Number of Customers over Break-Even	**$938.88**	**$331.51**	**$2,202.14**
Break-Even Sales Amount	**$20,301.92**	**$51,974.85**	**($109,016.33)**
Gross Profit per Customer	**$38.42**	**$18.76**	**($10.73)**
Gross Profit (over Break-Even)	**$36,075.62**	**$6,219.53**	**($23,636.56)**

Average Monthly Break-Even Analysis 2000

Cost Variables	Optimistic -20.00%	Most Likely Case	Pessimistic 20.00%
FIXED COSTS:			
Rentals/Leases	$0	$0	$0
Salaries (Fixed/Officers)	$2,688	$3,360	$4,032
Insurance	$630	$787	$945
Depreciation & Amortization	$315	$394	$473
Interest	$5,622	$7,028	$8,433
Utilities/Phone	$819	$1,024	$1,229
(Other fixed costs)	$0	$0	$0
Total Fixed Costs	**$10,074**	**$12,592**	**$15,111**
VARIABLE COSTS:			
Cost of Goods Sold	$37,095	$46,369	$55,643
Variable Labor/Wages	$7,053	$9,378	$11,254
Advertising	$1,840	$2,300	$2,760
Professional Services	$298	$372	$446
(Other variable cost)	$7,366	$9,208	$11,049
Total Variable Costs	**$54,101**	**$67,627**	**$81,152**
SALES AND INCOME DATA:			
Average Income Per Customer	$77.71	$77.71	$77.71
Average # of Customers Per Month	$1,380.00	$1,150.00	$920.00
RESULTS:			
Fixed Costs per Customer	**$7.30**	**$10.95**	**$16.42**
Variable Costs per Customer	**$39.20**	**$58.81**	**$88.21**
Break-Even Number of Customers	**$261.64**	**$666.23**	**($1,438.83)**
Number of Customers over Break-Even	**$1,118.36**	**$483.77**	**$2,358.83**
Break-Even Sales Amount	**$20,331.17**	**$51,770.73**	**($111,806.26)**
Gross Profit per Customer	**$38.50**	**$18.90**	**($10.50)**
Gross Profit (over Break-Even)	**$43,059.83**	**$9,143.53**	**($24,772.76)**

Break-Even Table Year 1

Income per customer	$77.75
Total fixed Costs	$12,541.50
Variable costs per customer	$58.99

# of customers	Total Revenues	Total Costs
401.09	$31,185	$36,202
467.94	$36,382	$40,145
534.79	$41,580	$44,088
601.64	$46,777	$48,032
668.49	$51,975	$51,975
735.34	$57,172	$55,918
802.18	$62,370	$59,862
869.03	$67,567	$63,805
935.88	$72,765	$67,748
1002.73	$77,962	$71,692

Break-Even Table Year 2

Income per customer	$77.71
Total fixed Costs	$12,592.32
Variable costs per customer	$58.81

# of customers	Total Revenues	Total Costs
399.74	31,062	36,099
466.36	36,240	40,017
532.99	41,417	43,935
599.61	46,594	47,853
666.23	51,771	51,771
732.86	56,948	55,689
799.48	62,125	59,606
866.1	67,302	63,524
932.73	72,479	67,442
999.35	77,656	71,360

	Net Income	IRR	MIRR	Annual Dividends	Total Assets	**Rates of Return**
Initial Investment	$(800,000)					
1999	$53,719	N/A	-93.29%	$21,488	$1,561,289	
2000	$76,138	0	-20.48%	$45,683	$1,578,125	
2001	$105,240	0	73.14%	$84,192	$1,584,892	
2002	$140,511	-22.14%	154.12%	$112,409	$1,597,513	
2003	$183,391	-9.32%	219.67%	$146,713	$1,617,518	

Assumptions:

Income figures are after taxes

Dividend Payout = 50% of After Tax Income

Reinvestment rate = 7%

IRR = International rate of return

MIRR = Modified rate of return

ROI = Rate of return on owner's investment

ROA = Rate of return on total assets

IRR = the interest rate received for an investment and income that occur at regular periods.

MIRR = adds the cost of funds and interest received on reinvestment of cash to the IRR.

	1999	2000	2001	2002	2003
Return on Assets	3.4%	4.82%	6.64%	8.80%	11.34%
Return on Investment	2.69%	5.71%	10.52%	14.05%	18.34%
Income Per Share	$0.07	$0.10	$0.13	$0.18	$0.23
Dividends Per Share	$0.03	$0.06	$0.11	$0.14	$0.18

Loan Compliance Covenants

Year	Net Working Capital	Current Ratio	Quick Ragio	EBIT/ Interest	EBIT/ I+P	EBIT/ Equity	Z-Score
1999	$164,436	3.46	2.02	1.84	1.51	0.88	1.47
2000	$192,278	3.54	2.08	2.29	0.21	0.83	1.67
2001	$208,898	3.4	1.92	2.93	0.66	0.79	1.9
2002	$230,503	3.3	1.78	3.74	3.82	0.75	2.19
2003	$258,324	3.23	1.68	4.81	0	0.71	2.52
Industry Median	**N/A**	**1.4**	**0.4**	**2**	**N/A**	**3**	**N/A**

Annual Projections Summary

Projection Period	Gross Profit	After-Tax Net Income	Cash from Operations	Book Equity
Start-Up/Base				$800,000
1999	$413,022	$53,719	$73,719	$832,231
2000	$474,975	$76,138	$97,138	$862,686
2001	$555,722	$105,240	$127,343	$883,734
2002	$652,974	$140,511	$163,830	$911,836
2003	$770,508	$183,391	$208,050	$948,514

Income Statement Chart

	Projected 1999	Projected 2000	Projected 2001	Projected 2002	Projected 2003
Sales	927,000	1,066,050	1,225,958	1,409,852	1,621,329
Cost of Sales	514,229	591,364	680,068	782,079	899,390
Expenses	344,137	371,264	402,338	437,939	478,734
Operating Income	68,634	103,422	143,552	189,834	243,205
Income Taxes	17,390	30,347	45,317	62,577	82,473
Net Income	57,244	79,375	104,866	134,252	168,130

Balance Sheet Chart

	1999	2000	2001	2002	2003
Current Assets	348,864	366,663	387,796	410,724	433,464
Fixed Assets	1,110,500	1,106,825	1,102,957	1,098,876	1,094,561
Total Assets	1,459,364,	1,473,488	1,490,753	1,509,600	1,528,025
Current Liabilities	77,734	87,757	99,166	112,156	126,949
Total Liabilities	830,742	813,116	793,677	772,249	748,641
Net Worth	628,622	660,372	697,076	737,351	779,384

Growth Trends

	1999	2000	2001	2002	2003
Cost of Goods Sold	$514,229	$591,364	$680,068	$782,079	$899,390
Total Expenses	$344,137	$371,264	$402,338	$437,939	$478,734
Total Revenue	$933,000	$1,072,350	$1,232,589	$1,416,847	$1,628,727

Net Income Growth

	1999	2000	2001	2002	2003
Net Income	$57,244	$79,375	$104,866	$134,252	$168,130

Composition of Income - First Year

	1999
Nursery Sales	$797,000
Café Sales	$130,000
Other Income/Exp. (Net)	$6,000

Breakdown of Expenses - First Year

	1999
Cost of Goods Sold	$483,850
Labor Expenses	$183,303
Interest Expenses	$86,902
Rent, Utilities, Repairs	$13,400
Other Expenses	$90,911

Total First Year Expenses $858,366

Selected Key Ratios Chart

	5 Year-Average Business	Average Industry
Current Ratio	3.93	1.4
Cost of Sales / Inventory	4.98	5.7
Cost of Sales / Payables	19.4	20
EBIT / Interest	2.97	2
Debt / Worth	1.14	3
Sales / Total Assets	0.01	0.02
Sales / Receivables	18.25	40

Ratio Comparison

	Projected 1999	Projected 2000	Projected 2001	Projected 2002	Projected 2003	Industry Ave. 1999
Liquidity Ratios:						
Current Ratio	4.49	4.18	3.91	3.66	3.41	1.4
Quick Ratio	3.16	2.83	2.53	2.26	1.99	0.4
Sales / Receivables	18.25	18.25	18.25	18.25	18.25	40
Day's Receivables	20	20	20	20	20	9.13
Cost of Sales / Inventory	4.98	4.98	4.98	4.98	4.98	5.7
Day's Inventory	73.23	73.23	73.23	73.23	73.23	64.04
Cost of Sales / Payables	19.4	19.4	19.4	19.4	19.4	20
Day's Payables	18.82	18.82	18.82	18.82	18.82	18.25
Sales / Work. Capital	3.42	3.82	4.25	4.72	5.29	18.2
EBIT / Interest	1.86	2.3	2.84	3.51	4.36	2
Net Profit +Depr.+Amort./ C.L.T.D.	2.49	3.04	3.56	4.05	4.52	2.4
Leverage Ratios:						
Fixed Assets / Tangible Net Worth	1.77	1.68	1.58	1.49	1.4	2
Debt / Worth	1.32	1.23	1.14	1.05	0.96	3
Operating Ratios:						
Profit Before Tax / Tan. Net Worth	11.87%	16.62%	21.54%	26.69%	32.15%	21.20%
Profit Before Tax / Total Assets	5.11%	7.45%	10.07%	13.04%	16.40%	8.20%
Sales / Net Fixed Assets	0.83%	0.96%	1.11%	1.28%	1.48%	7.90%
Sales / Total Assets	0.64%	0.72%	0.82%	0.93%	1.06%	2.00%
Other Ratios / Numbers:						
Officers Salaries (Actual)	$38,400	$40,320	$42,437	$44,771	$47,345	N/A
Equity (Net Worth)	$628,622	$660,372	$697,076	$737,351	$779,384	N/A
Loans Balance (Actual)	$777,789	$753,008	$725,359	$694,511	$660,093	N/A
% Deprec., Amort./Sales	0	0	0	0	0	2.3
% Officers Compensation/ Sales	0.04	0.04	0.03	0.03	0.03	5.3
Tangible Net Worth (NW-Intangibles)	$628,622	$660,372	$697,076	$737,351	$779,384	N/A
Working Capital (Actual)	$271,130	$278,906	$288,630	$298,568	$306,515	N/A
Gross Profit:						
Key Percentages as a Percent of Gross Profit						
Rent	0.00%	0.00%	0.00%	0.00%	0.00%	0.00%
Interest Paid	21.05%	17.77%	14.92%	12.47%	10.35%	0.00%
Depreciation & Amortization	1.09%	1.00%	0.91%	0.84%	0.77%	0.00%
Officers Compensation	9.30%	8.49%	7.77%	7.13%	6.56%	0.00%
Taxes Paid	4.21%	6.39%	8.30%	9.97%	11.42%	N/A

RATIO ANALYSIS

Current Ratio is an approximate measure of a firm's ability to meet its current obligations and is calculated as Current Assets divided by Current Liabilities. This ratio shows an upward trend and indicates that if the company meets its goals it will be relatively more stable than the industry in general.

Revenue to Working Capital Ratio is a measure of the margin of protection for current creditors. This ratio is on a downward trend and indicates a good level of safety for creditors.

EBIT to Interest Ratio is a measure of ability to meet annual interest payments. Since this ratio is above industry averages, the company should have no problem servicing its debt and can even service greater amounts of debt.

The Current Maturities Coverage Ratio measures the ability to pay current maturities of long-term debt with cash flow from operations. It is calculated as Net Income Depreciation, Amortization divided by current portion of long-term debt. This ratio shows an upward trend which indicates the company should be better to service its debt than the average company.

The Fixed Assets to Tangible Net Worth Ratio measures the extent to which owner's equity has been invested in the business. Since this ratio is on a downward trend, it provides an even larger "cushion" to creditors in the event of liquidation.

The Debt to Equity Ratio expresses the relationship between capital contributed by creditors and capital contributed by owners. This ratio shows a downward trend which would seem to indicate that if the company meets its goals that it will provide greater long-term financial safety for creditors.

The Earnings before Taxes to Total Assets Ratio expresses the pre-tax return on total assets and measures the effectiveness of management in employing available resources. Since this ratio is above industry averages, the company would be more efficient than the industry in its effective employment of resources.

The Revenue to Total Assets Ratio is a general measure of ability to generate revenue in relation to total assets. This ratio is above industry averages which can indicate that the company is efficient in using available resources to generate revenue as compared to the industry.

The Depreciation, Amortization to Revenue Ratio is a general measure of cost to generate revenue under the matching principal. Since this ratio is consistently below industry averages it would seem to indicate that the company is more efficient generating revenue as compared to the industry.

CONCLUSIONS & SUMMARY

We feel that the type of company and service we are proposing is hitting the market at just the right time. We plan to fully repay the loan by the end of the third year. However, we will schedule repayments over ten years to give us flexibility. By applying our conservative projections, income for the first year is expected to be $21,194 after taxes and debt service. This will rise to $76,822 in the second and $124,363 by the fifth year. The business should be open for business by spring of 1997.

Plastic Drum Company

BUSINESS PLAN   RIVER CITY DRUM, INC.

300 Mansion House Center, Suite 2610
St. Louis, Missouri 63102

This industrial plastic drum company is owned by individuals with vast experience in plastic molding and packaging, as well as sales and distribution. By using competitive pricing strategies and targeting and anticipating local customers, River City Drum charts its success.

- EXECUTIVE SUMMARY

- THE COMPANY—PRESENT SITUATION

- OBJECTIVES

- MANAGEMENT

- PRODUCT DESCRIPTION

- MARKET ANALYSIS

- MARKETING STRATEGY

- MANUFACTURING

- SUMMARY & USE OF FUNDING

- FINANCIAL PROJECTIONS

EXECUTIVE SUMMARY

The plastic drum industry, while only 12 years old, has made great strides in recent years as technologically advanced plastic resins have made it possible for the first time to bring the benefits of plastic to the last bastion of metal container packaging.

The 55-gallon steel drum had been the standard for industrial containers for the past 50 years. While strong in structural integrity, steel drums were prone to rust, corrosion, and when recycled, required painting, dedenting, and a number of other costly and only partially effective means for extending their use beyond one trip. Plastic, on the other hand, had already made gigantic inroads into all other areas of packaging because of its ability to be molded into various shapes and sizes, its virtual imperviousness to acids and alkalies, its being totally rustproof and resistant to weather conditions, and, of course, plastic has long enjoyed widespread consumer acceptance at every level. In the late seventies, advanced polymer engineering provided the industry at long last with the high strength, high impact polyethylene resins that enabled the plastic fabricator to move into the large industrial drum arena, specifically the 55-gallon, but also the 30-gallon and the 15-gallon container.

Some of the leading U.S. container manufacturers, as well as their European counterparts, were quick to enter the market, and like all pioneers, the progress was steady but marked by obstacles and milestones. Now, some 12 years after its introduction, the polyethylene drum enjoys an ever-growing share of the market as more and more industries are accepting the benefits offered exclusively by plastic.

Chicago and Houston soon emerged as industry centers for the manufacture of the 55-gallon poly drum. The St. Louis industrial market has been serviced primarily out of Chicago and eastern seaboard facilities. Nevertheless, the demand for poly drums in St. Louis has steadily grown, keeping pace with the nation, and now St. Louis demands a manufacturing facility to support its need. It is this need that River City Drum intends to fill.

As this business plan will reveal, the principals and management of River City Drum are heavily experienced in plastic molding and packaging as well as sales and distribution. A market survey conducted in the fall of 1989 revealed impressive existing demand and the potential for even greater market development once a local manufacturer is on the scene.

There are certain characteristics inherent to the industrial drum business that militate against the importation of this product from beyond regional areas. First and foremost, the "just in time" philosophy that is now demanded by many industrial users is most prevalent in the large container industry because of the difficulty of storing quantities of the empty container. Users just do not like their facilities cluttered up with hundreds of drums awaiting filling.

With the closest supplier some 300 miles away, and with all the logistical problems of obtaining smooth delivery out of Chicago, our market survey quickly revealed that the St. Louis manufacturers would welcome and utilize a local manufacturer of 55-gallon plastic drums. Of further interest, a significant number of present users of steel drums would consider switching to the advantages of plastic if there were a local supplier.

Another advantage that River City Drum brings to the market is between a $1.00 to $1.50 delivered price advantage based on our location. This is due to the elimination of the freight out of Chicago or wherever the source. It is an axiom in the packaging business: "You're wasting money when you're shipping air," meaning empty containers. Shipping air is exactly what the existing competition is doing in serving the St. Louis market.

St. Louis is a market primed for a local supplier. River City Drum has carefully called on many of the principal buyers of industrial containers, preselling our product. We are confident that we will be welcomed as a supplier with some meaningful advantages to offer, both price and service. Our realistic projections call for us to reach sell-out position in our second 12 months of operation. We will then be preparing to expand our production capabilities.

As the above information has indicated, our careful research has revealed that the St. Louis market will readily support a local supplier. We also know that because of the relative size of the St. Louis market, estimated to be about twelfth in the nation, that it is not likely to attract a second drum manufacturer. River City Drum principals feel it is likely that once we establish our position in this market, other manufacturers will view St. Louis as not broad enough to accommodate two manufacturers, thus leaving us as the only local supplier in this region. Historically, this has been the case with steel drums and other smaller-sized plastic packaging.

In summary, River City Drum has found a need and filled it.

A modern plastic drum blowmolding facility is capital intensive. As subsequent material in this business plan will reveal, River City Drum has carefully researched how best to open an efficient and competitive factory. We have on board a top plastic drum product engineer as well as other outstanding support personnel. River City Drum has obtained a line of credit of some $250,000 for the leasing of various support equipment. Our primary machinery, the drum blowmolder, a Bekoft 1000, which costs $540,000, will be 80% financed by the vendor. Both principals have provided capital infusion totaling $200,000. In order to achieve our projected manufacturing and marketing goals, River City Drum will require a line of operating credit of some $350,000 to meet general operating expenses, contingent costs, and a variety of one-time start-up costs.

THE COMPANY— PRESENT SITUATION

River City Drum was incorporated in October of 1990 with a paid-in capital of $100,000. All company stock is equally owned by Warren Stevenson, President, and Thomas Connors, Vice President. Mr. Connors also holds the corporate offices of Secretary and Treasurer. River City Drum was formed for the purpose of manufacturing 55-gallon and 30-gallon polyethylene industrial drums and other large plastic-molded products. The period from its inception to the present has been devoted principally to market research, preselling, and technical planning with regard to facility selection, factory layout, equipment evaluation, vendor screening, mold design, and many other similar duties.

Early on, River City Drum retained the temporary services of two competent sales people for the purpose of market research. These people were given assignments to call on some 275 known users of industrial containers in the St. Louis region. Buyers were interviewed with respect to the following:

- Present requirements for large industrial containers, both steel and plastic.
- Present utilization of plastic drums.
- If steel is presently being used, reason for this preference.
- Would customer consider plastic if plastic were readily available and competitively priced in the St. Louis market.
- Is customer familiar with the salient features of plastic over steel in industrial containers?

The results of our survey confirmed that a present annual market of over 2,000,000 large industrial containers, both 30- and 55-gallon, exists in the St. Louis area. Presently over 90% of this market is being accommodated by steel. Significantly, some 25% of this consumption, represented by 91 users, indicated that they would consider or would likely switch to plastic if there were a reliable source available in St. Louis. Some were very openly encouraging, urging us to proceed with our manufacturing plans. These represent some 50,000 containers, fully two and one half times the projected manufacturing capacity of River City Drum.

In addition to our market survey, our company president, Warren Stevenson, made a number of preliminary sales calls to buyers of particular interest to River City Drum. These are firms and buyers with whom Mr. Stevenson has had considerable experience over his years as an industrial sales executive. We were most gratified by the reception. Some leading firms that expressed an active interest in converting to plastic along with their known consumption are listed as follows:

Petro Services	50,000 drums
Majestic Chemical	88,000 drums
K.M. Peters Paint Co	55,000 drums
Monarch Oil	40,000 drums
Total	**203,000 drums**

We were, of course, very encouraged by this marketing survey. River City Drum sought and hired an outstanding young engineer to assist in the planning and implementation of our drum manufacturing facility. Donald Smyth joined our company on December 2, 1990, bringing with him broad credentials in the flourishing field of polyethylene drum manufacturing. Mr. Smyth was a pioneer with MidContinent Plastics, a leading innovator in the plastic drum industry and a major factor in the market. He was on-board from the inception in 1978 and assisted in every phase of bringing the MidCon polyethylene drum into existence. His services have thus far proved very valuable to River City Drum. He is employed under a two-year contract, with principal responsibilities to open our plant by May of 1991 and thereafter to function as Plant Manager with overall, 24-hour responsibility.

Our marketing plan calls for a multifaceted campaign. Major users will be developed and serviced by Mr. Stevenson, whose primary responsibility will be sales. At least one full-time sales person will be employed, who will be recruited from the container industry. He or she will be responsible for intensive coverage in our primary market, which will include roughly a radius of 150 miles around St. Louis. Attractive secondary markets exist in Memphis, Louisville, and Chicago and will be serviced by both stocking distributors and in truckload shipments brokered by local distributors. This matter will be treated in detail in the Marketing Strategy section of this business plan.

Our present cash position is $66,000, remaining from initial capitalization of $100,000. This represents capital input from our two stockholders, Mr. Stevenson and Mr. Connors, in the amount of $50,000 each. In the case of Mr. Stevenson, the funds were withdrawn as a loan to stockholder from Stevenson & Sons, a chemical manufacturing firm headed by Mr. Stevenson. Mr. Connor's investment derived from savings.

Our principal piece of equipment, a Bekoft Blowmolder, Model 1000, has been quoted at $540,000, which the vendor will carry at 80%. We are negotiating a line of $250,000 with General Missouri Leasing, which will cover much of our support equipment, such as grinders, blenders, conveyors, forklift, etc.

In addition to the above, we will be seeking a primary line of credit of $350,000 for additional equipment and set up, raw materials, salaries, and operating expenses.

OBJECTIVES

Our market research has determined that there is a need for a manufacturer of polyethylene drums in the St. Louis area. River City Drum's initial objective is to fill that need. By providing the only manufacturing facility for polyethylene drums within a radius of 150 miles, we feel we can capitalize on favorable logistics and our enhanced customer responsiveness to assure dominance of the 55- and 30-gallon polydrum market in this area. We have identified some 200,000 plastic drums currently being purchased in the St. Louis area. 70% of these drums are being shipped in from Chicago. The minimum freight, for customers buying truckload quantities, is $1.00 per drum (approximately $300 per run from Chicago). Because of the virtual lack of competition, the only two local stocking distributors dealing with LTL (Less Than Truckload) quantities, are charging some $3.00 per drum in excess of LTL markets where drum manufacturing exist. These LTL users are ripe for marketing by River City Drum.

Truckload users are, however, our main market. 30- and 55-gallon drums are generally viewed as commodities by industrial buyers. Because of stringent D.O.T. (Department of Transportation) regulations, the specifications and performance capabilities of the polyethylene drums manufactured by competing companies are generally equal with little difference found from one brand to the next. Brand loyalty is therefore not normally a factor in this field. Once reliability and product specification has been established, pricing becomes a dominant influence. Because of our strategic location in this market, River City Drum will be very aggressive as we quote delivered price against Chicago competitors. The container industry has always been a regionalized or localized business. The adage of "shipping air" is often heard when FOB prices of containers are discussed. Everything being equal, the closer supplier is likely to be favored as delivered prices will be the most attractive. River City Drum is keying on this factor in our preselling, and we are confident that we will ultimately capture the lions' share of the local market.

We recognize that sales will not be automatic and will have to be earned. The big users, truckload quantity buyers, will first want their own tests run on our product. Testing could vary from one month to six months, depending on purchasing policies for respective customers. Establishing our presence as a reliable supplier will be a major activity of our first year of manufacturing. Ultimately, we expect to be the primary source of supply for most, if not all, the major drum users in our primary market. We recognize that we may first be limited to secondary sources in many cases as we earn the confidence of our customers. This is anticipated, and our initial conservative objective is to reach 44% local market penetration (88,000 drums), by the conclusion of our first manufacturing year.

Note: When drums are mentioned in this report, it may be assumed that polyethylene drums (as opposed to steel) are being referred to unless otherwise indicated.

Pursuing the existing market

Our objective for year two will be River City Drum's capture of a significant portion of the remaining 112,000 existing St. Louis drum market. Conservatively, we expect 75% penetration (150,000), optimum 90% (180,000) by the close of year two. 180,000 drums per annum will approach sellout capacity of our Bekum blowmolder for straight-time operations.

Secondary markets

To the extent that we experience short fall in reaching sell-out in our primary market, River City Drum will be aggressively pursuing secondary markets in Memphis, Louisville, Kansas City, and Chicago. With the exception of Chicago, which is the home of 4 drums makers, the above captioned cities are presently being services by remote manufacturers. River City feels that we will be able to compete effectively in these markets and achieve a 25% share of market. Chicago is a vast and immensely competitive market. Some 50% of total U.S. drum use is attributable to the Chicago area. We do not view Chicago as major source of business for River City but expect to market approximately 600 to 900 drums per month through our stocking distributor.

Years three through five

By the conclusion of year two, River City Drum expects to reach near or complete sell-out capacity. At that time, we will be evaluating the acquisition of additional line capacity, which will require the purchase of a second drum blowmolding machine. Much of the existing support equipment can be utilized and only the addition of 2 production workers per shift will be required. A second line will give River City Drum manufacturing capacities (running overtime mode) of some 400,000 drums. A key factor in expansion plans will be our ability and that of the plastic drum industry in general to make additional inroads into steel drum packaging. For example, a potential new local market of some 400,000 plastic drums per annum exists in the Lube Oil field, which has been evaluating conversion to plastic for the past 18 months, and the paint industry is another potential market.

Possible buy-out of River City Drum

The history of the plastic container industry has been marked by a number of independent producers obtaining regional or local market saturation and then being acquired by major conglomerates in the industry. A similar pattern could well be anticipated in the 55 gallon polyethylene drum industry. Three major players, MidContinent Plastics, Containers America, and Van DeMeer Container, have already shown a propensity to acquire independents who have carved out a market for themselves. Industry sources report that buy-out figures, while unannounced, are believed to be 8 to 10 times earnings. We anticipate that River City Drum would be a much sought after property as we reach our fifth or sixth year. River City Drum would entertain serious discussions at such time that we would consider acquisition or merger advantageous.

MANAGEMENT

Warren Stevenson, 54, is 50% owner and President of River City Drum, Inc. His entire business career has been devoted to the field of industrial chemicals and packaging, both as a sales executive and for the past twenty years as head of several corporations. A 1958 graduate of Westfield College, with a major in chemistry and a minor in economics, Mr. Stevenson opened his career as a salesman for Phizner Chemical and subsequently moved to Thomas Haywood Chemical Company in St. Louis. In the early sixties, along with present River City Drum co-owner Thomas Connors, he founded FIPI, Inc., a food, industrial, and pharmaceutical manufacturing and packaging firm. Significantly, FIPI also pioneered in blowmolding containers in the St. Louis area. Mr. Stevenson subsequently bought out his partners and formed the firm of W. Stevenson & Sons, a leading regional manufacturer and packager of automotive chemicals. Plastic blowmolding continues to be an integral part of Stevenson & Sons and, of course, Mr. Stevenson has drawn heavily on this expertise and experience in formulating plans for River City Drum.

Thomas Connors, 54, is 50% owner and Vice President of River City Drum. He began his business career in St. Louis in 1961 with the formation of Connors Distributing Company, a firm that specializes in janitorial and household cleaning supplies and sundry items. Connors Distributing continues on as a leader in its field and, Mr. Connors, over the years, has invested and participated in a number of unrelated business ventures, including the formation of FIPI, Inc. with Mr. Stevenson in 1964. Though not a college graduate, Conners is a seasoned businessman and he has always been a hands-on operator, both at Connors Distributing and his other entrepreneurial endeavors. These have included toy manufacturing, real estate, food service, and many others. His responsibilities at River City Drum will be primarily Vice President for Operations, with principal responsibility for manufacturing and general business management. He also holds the corporate titles of Secretary and Treasurer.

Donald Smyth, 34, was hired as project manager by River City Drum in October of 1990. He was recruited through industry sources who knew of his reputation as an integral employee in the development of polyethylene drums with his previous employer, Mid-Continent Containers. MidCon was one of the pioneers in the field of polyethylene drums, and Mr. Smyth brings with him a wealth of experience gained in the development of this product. Of course, proprietary information remains the exclusive purview of his previous employer, but he nonetheless plays a key role in planning our manufacturing facility. He is instrumental in site selection, plant layout, vendor screening, and many other important details. Don will assume the role of plant manager once production status is achieved. He will have 24-hour responsibility. Don is working on a two-year contract with us and is enjoying the challenge of seeing the new operation take shape. He is an energetic and ambitious young man, and his reason for leaving his previous employer in favor of River City was to enable him to work in a more pivotal role and at a higher management level than seemed likely in the Mid-Continent environment.

Jim Spencer is a plastic engineering consultant who has for many years had a close working relationship with the management team at River City Drum. Mr. Spencer's firm, Bestway Consultants, specializes in plastic blowmolding, and he personally is well versed in all phases of plastic molding plant operations. Mr. Spencer's affiliation with River City Drum personnel goes back to the early eighties when he was employed as plant manager for W. Stevenson & Sons. About two years ago, he founded Bestway Consultants and now specializes in assisting start-up blowmolding operations, as well as troubleshooting problems for existing plastic companies. Mr. Spencer is on retainer with River City and provides important additional technical depth to our human resources.

PRODUCT DESCRIPTION

In the past 25 years, the packaging industry has undergone a dramatic evolution. The development of a wide range of polymers has brought about the emergence of plastic containers of all descriptions, supplanting the traditional packaging materials of glass, steel, and cardboard fiber. A wide range of consumer and industrial products packaged in plastic now dominate their respective markets. In some industries, glass and steel are almost obsolete. Plastic has become the container of choice because of its light weight, strength, flexibility, and durability. Nonrusting, and usually considered non-breakable and nondentable, it is easily molded into distinctive and utilitarian configurations, giving packaging engineers both utility and beauty.

The industrial drum industry, both 30- and 55-gallon, began its move to plastic in 1979, with the advent of newer, tougher resins, known as high molecular weight, high density polyethylene. Prior to the development of this polymer, no plastic material available was capable of handling the heavy stacking loads of up to 800 pounds per drum. But with the perfection of the newly engineered resins, it became clear that it was now feasible to develop the plastic drum.

The principals of RCD were interested observers as the early stages of polyethylene drums evolved. Many original concepts were tried and discarded by pioneers in the field, and now a clearly defined market preference has emerged for the polyethylene industrial drum. RCD will enter with its own design, reflecting known buyer preference and innovating several new features as a result of our market research. Of particular interest is our new "Five Wide" configuration on 30-gallon drums that are taller and slimmer than the former "squat 30's." This permits five wide by three high loading in standard and high cube trailers, thus increasing the payload some 12% in shipping truckload quantities. We will also be featuring enhanced rolling hoops, which provide for easier pick-up by convenctual forklift trucks. A proprietary handling ring will also be an intricate part of the new 55- and 30-gallon River City drum, affording better gripping and the more streamlined appearance, most closely identified to steel drums.

Numerous interviews with future customers have identified these features as being the most sought after by the drum buyer.

The construction and performance capabilities of our product are engineered to conform to or exceed D.O.T. Spec 34, which is a requirement for all polyethylene drums shipped in interstate commerce for the hazardous cargo trade. We, as well as all domestic manufacturers, are required to meet rigid testing requirements and manufacture to exacting specification minimums, all of which are well within our capabilities and quality control standards.

River City drum will enjoy another important competitive advantage. Our new Bekoft 1000 drum blowmolding machine is among the finest machines of its type in existence. Bekum, a world renowned machine maker, is the recognized leader in the fabrication of "large part" blowmolding equipment. RCD shopped every domestic vendor and many foreign purveyors before selection of the Bekoft 1000. Among its salient features is a guaranteed cycle time of 90 seconds for a 21-pound 55-gallon drum, which provides River City Drum the fastest production cycle in the nation. This translates to 20% savings in labor and power and a 25% increase in overall output capabilities.

Another important feature effecting the economics of drum manufacturing, the Bekoft 1000 includes a highly sophisticated 35-point programmer, which enables our operator to very precisely fine tune the exact wall thickness of our finished molded product, at 35 distinctive points, thus enabling us to insert more plastic at stress regions, and "lighten" when practical, for the most economical distribution of raw material. While many, but not all, of our competitors have programming, none have the advanced capabilities of the Bekoft 1000. This translates to manufacturing the finest quality drum with the fastest manufacturing cycle and at the most advantageous cost.

River City Drum will truly be state of the art!

MARKET ANALYSIS

As mentioned in the previous section, the plastic drum industry can trace its roots to 1979 with the advent of new higher strength polyethylene resins, which were capable, for the first time, of sustaining the heavy load bearing and impact requirements of industrial drums. Since plastic had made significant inroads into virtually all other forms of packaging, the industrial drum market was then targeted by the plastic packaging industry as ripe for conversion.

In the past eleven years, plastic's share of the market has progressed steadily to the point where 10% of the total annual market of twenty million new industrial 30- and 55-gallon drums are now plastic. The overall industrial container market is growing at some 6% per annum with industry analysts reporting a projected increased share for plastic of approximately 2% per annum for the next 3 years. (*Packaging Digest,* October 1990). Another exciting aspect of plastic's role in the industrial drum market is the anticipated conversation of the lube-oil drum from steel to plastic. All of the major refineries have been testing plastic with excellent results being reported. Among their many attributes, rust and dent free plastic drums are known to recycle much better than steel with an estimated life of 20 trips along with minimum clean-up. This compares with 3 or 4 trips maximum for steel drums, which require painting, dedenting, chaining, and other costly recycling activities. Petro-Plex of Canada, that nation's leading producer of petroleum products, has already ordered a 100% conversion to plastic and has set the trend for Canada.

This is of particular interest to River City Drum with the giant refineries of Magna Oil and U.S. Petroleum located in our immediate area. These two refineries currently use over 400,000 steel drums per annum and are currently testing plastic drums from several manufacturers. RCD has made preselling calls to both facilities and have been assured that our product will be tested and considered for inclusion in their packaging line if conversion from steel becomes a reality. We are in an ideal strategic position to service these two accounts. There is a known "copy-cat" history to packaging in the oil industry. When one major company adopts a new form of packaging, others quickly follow suit. The plastic drum industry is aggressively cultivating this very important market. It should be noted that there is insufficient manufacturing capacity, both at River City Drum and industry wide to accommodate an immediate conversion by the oil companies to plastic. This volume of business would, by necessity, be phased-in as production capacities are expanded to fill the need.

While the lube-oil business presents an attractive potential for River City Drum, we do not consider it a primary focus at this time because presently this market is being accommodated by steel drums. Of much greater importance is the diversified chemical, paint and food industries of our region that are currently utilizing plastic drums shipped in from Chicago, Cincinnati, and Toledo.

Our market research has identified over 60 firms in the immediate St. Louis area presently purchasing polyethylene drums trucked in from other regions. These represent some 180,000 drums. Additionally, River City Drum has identified 91 users of steel drums that have expressed an active interest in switching to plastic once a local source of supply is established.

The market for the products of River City Drum is clearly defined. In subsequent sections, we will discuss customers in more specific terms and also define our plans for market penetration.

Customers

Intensive market research has enabled River City Drum to identify our potential customers and we have made many pre-selling calls on these firms to establish our presence. Our primary target market consists of firms presently using plastic drums shipped from other regions of the country. Some of particular interest are:

   Magathon Oil, 4,000 drums, anti-freeze
   Monoplazo Chemical, 20,000 drums, herbicide
   P.D. Grange Paint Co., 20,000 drums, paints and lacquers
   Thomas Haywood Chemical, 2,400 drums, chemicals
   Best Vanilla, 4,800 drums, flavorings
   Peerpoint Lacquer, 1,800 drums, lacquers and inks
   Commercial Soap, 2,800 drums, cleaning compounds
   Q-Tech Brand, 4,800 drums, acids
   American Flavoring, 8,200 drums, flavorings and syrups
   Midwest Flavoring, 8,200 drums, flavorings and preservatives
   Ozark Speciality, 1,200 drums, liquid smoke
   R & K Foods, 4,000 drums, barbecue sauce
   Chem-point, 4,400 drums, chemicals
   O'Neils Best, 6,800 drums, flavorings
   Midwest Printers Ink, 2,800 drums, lacquers and inks
   Proctor & Scrable, 88 drums, cleaning compounds
   Apex Treatment Chemicals, 2,800 drums, acids
   Archview Foods, 4,200 drums, flavorings and syrups
   Fulcrum Brothers, 4,800 drums, floor soaps
   Marvel Manufacturing, 8,800 drums, bleach

The above are all Dun & Bradstreet listed and rated firms and are considered by us to be prime potential users of our polyethylene drums. They represent annual drum usage of 136,000 drums, some 75% of our production capacity. They also represent a very diverse group of industries, many of whom have national markets.

Also of importance are four local firms, presently using steel drums but seriously considering conversion to plastic:

Petro Services	50,000 drums
Majestic Chemical	88,000 drums
K.M. Peters Paint Co	55,000 drums
Monument Oil	40,000 drums
Total	**203,000 drums**

We have discussed in this Market Analysis the potential of the huge oil refineries to convert the lube-oil business to plastic. While this is by no means a certainty, the potential magnitude of this business is very significant and worth contemplating. The two majors in our immediate vicinity are:

Magna Oil	300,000 per annum
U.S. Petroleum	100,000 per annum

Also of interest is:

Magathon Oil	60,000 per annum

We have logistic advantage to Magathon, as well as strong ties to the buyer and chief plant executive.

Note: To accommodate buyers of this volume, River City Drum would expand its production capability beyond the single drum line contemplated in this business plan.

Secondary Markets

Some very substantial customers exist in key cities outside the immediate St. Louis market. River City Drum would have excellent positioning to service these companies and we expect to compete quite aggressively for their business. Among them are:

Brannon Laboratories	Memphis, TN	24,000 drums per yr.
American Flavors	Indianapolis, IN	18,000 drums per yr.
Farm Products Co.	Kansas City, MO	30,000 drums per yr.
Midland Farm Co-Op	St. Joseph, MO	18,000 drums per yr.

River City Drum has made preselling calls on all companies listed here and on the preceding page. Except as noted, we consider these firms as active, serious prospects for our products. Many have encouraged us as they themselves would prefer a local source for polyethylene drums. We will continue to cultivate our relationship with these drum buyers as we approach our production start-up.

COMPETITION

The existing 200,000 plastic drum market in St. Louis has been served primarily from Chicago, where three major plastic drum companies have manufacturing facilities. Poly-Drum was one of the original entries into the plastic drum industry, followed closely by CA and Van DeMeer Container. Van DeMeer is a world-class drum manufacturer, dealing in steel as well as plastic. CA (Container America) a Fortune 500 company with national distribution, has 3 plastic drum manufacturing facilities in the U.S. Poly-Drum, a very successful independent, operates from Lockwood, Illinois, and is in start-up with a second facility in Houston. MCC (MidContinent Containers) also ships drums to St. Louis from their Toledo, Ohio, facility.

All of these companies are well established firms that have made a significant impact on the plastic drum industry. Because all D.O.T. Spec 34 drums are manufactured to the same exacting specifications as predicated by government regulation, traditionally drums are regarded primarily as a commodity, with no particular brand loyalty prevailing in the industry. Price and responsiveness are considered key, and this is where River City Drum will be able to beat our competitors in the St. Louis market. It is a given in the container industry that it is uneconomical to "ship air," which is how the transportation of empty containers is frequently characterized. Freight into St. Louis from Chicago can add up to $1.50 per drum and out of Toledo, about $2.25 per drum. Furthermore, response time can be erratic and not nearly as reliable as the local delivery that will be the hallmark of River City Drum. We expect these two factors, advantageous pricing and more responsive "just in time" delivery, to be very big pluses as River City moves to obtain rapid market penetration.

For the many LTL (less than truckload) buyers in St. Louis, River City Drum will be at a real competitive advantage to capture the lion's share of this lucrative market. Presently these customers are serviced by stocking distributors at prices generally $5 higher than those available in primary (manufacturing) markets. RCD will offer convenient LTL deliveries in and around the St. Louis area, affording our customers a savings, and permitting attractive profits for River City because of our manufacturing and logistic efficiencies.

None of our competitors maintain local sales people. St. Louis, being our primary market, will have saturation coverage both at the executive level, with our President, Mr. Stevenson, maintaining continual liaison with key customers, and our in-house salesperson providing ongoing intensive covering to the region. This will give us considerable advantage in securing this market for River City.

RISKS

Risks inherent in the plastic fabrication industry in general, and the industrial container industry in particular, have been carefully evaluated by the management of River City Drum. Careful planning has minimized the impact of potential untoward eventualities that may be caused by circumstances beyond the control of management. Some of these may be identified as follows:

Continuous source of supply. High molecular weight high density polyethylene (HDPE) is the raw material from which RCD will be manufacturing. There are four primary suppliers in the U.S., as well as several foreign processors importing into the U.S. River City has already initiated contact with these sources and through previous and concomitant business activities, have purchase experience with three of the major suppliers. Because of the heavy "part weight" (21.4 pounds) for the poly drum, plastic drum manufacturers are large users of HDPE, and are highly sought accounts by vendors. RCD has negotiated a primary source contract with Soltex Polymer, providing assurance of up to 4 million pounds of material at competitive market prices. This will provide sufficient material to reach sell-out capacity with our original production capability.

As an **alternative source of supply**, RCD will maintain ongoing purchase continuity with American Hoerst, who is actively soliciting business from us. This will provide us with a fall-back position in the unlikely event of interruption of our primary source due to *force majure*. We will also maintain continuing liaison with all other domestic and foreign sources to assure uninterrupted supply, regardless of unforeseen circumstances.

Cost fluctuations due to potential unstable oil prices. Polyethylene resins are closely tied to the oil market and have been known to fluctuate as a result of changes in price of crude. River City Drum believes we have planned effectively for this eventuality, both as a buyer and as a seller. History has shown that price fluctuations have been uniform throughout the industry; thus, our competitors will pay more when we pay more. Further, our contract with our primary supplier guarantees competitive pricing; Soltex will keep us competitive in our raw material cost. River City Drum has negotiated 60-day terms with our primary supplier, as compared to the industry norm of 30 days. This gives us more latitude to purchase advance stock on a rising market, as there is usually some 30 days' notice of increased pricing. Also traditional to the drum industry are escalator and de-escalator clauses in the purchase agreements and quotations between drum manufacturer and drum buyer. River City, of course, quotes with the escalators incorporated into our bids as do our competitors. Therefore, the risks of cost fluctuations of raw materials are effectively dealt with.

Economic Influences. The diversity of the St. Louis market of River City Drum encompasses a wide array of separate industries that are not normally interdependent. In their order of importance, River City ranks our target industries as follows:

Agri-Chemical
Industrial Chemical
Food
Paint, Ink, and Varnish
Soaps and Industrial Cleaners
Lube-Oil (potential)

Due to the diversification of our target market, River City Drum feels that risks inherent of an economic downturn are blunted by the dispersion of our projected customer base.

Traditional risks. Traditional risks of fire, windstorm, burglary, and other hazards, including earthquake, will be covered by conventional insurance policies. River City Drum will maintain a $2,000,000 liability umbrella, in addition to casualty coverage for equipment, inventory, goods in transit, and all standard risks.

MARKETING STRATEGY

River City Drum's marketing strategy consists of a three-pronged approach, headed up by our CEO, Warren Stevenson. In addition to coordinating all sales efforts, Mr. Stevenson will be responsible for the development of the larger accounts. Furthermore, he will call on selected medium accounts, where the buyer is also the owner of the company. Preselling has been an important part of our make-ready at River City, and considerable rapport has already been established with key buyers in our region.

Mr. Stevenson will also be maintaining liaison with the three major lube-oil manufacturers in our region.

In addition to the above accounts, our extensive market research has identified nearly 50 St. Louis area companies currently using plastic drums being shipped in from other locales, primarily Chicago. Also, some 91 firms that are currently using steel indicated an interest in plastic if a local source became available. To cultivate this market, River City Drum will retain the services of an experienced drum sales representative. Presently, three individuals are under active consideration, two presently employed by competitors and one a former key employee of a competitor. The person selected will move to St. Louis and work under the direct supervision of Mr. Stevenson. He or she will be provided with a company leased vehicle and a reasonable expense account. Between Mr. Stevenson and his to-be-hired associate, River City Drum will have two full-time sales executives saturating the territory. This compares to zero resident sales force by our competitors. We feel this will give us a considerable advantage in customer service, in good-will, and most importantly, in results.

We will be able to afford intensive coverage to truckload and LTL buyers alike. Taking inventory of empty drums by customers present a real space problem for many users, and our "just-in-time" local delivery service is expected to be a significant advantage in converting the small, but nonetheless lucrative user to River City.

Stocking Distributors

River City Drum has established ongoing discussions with a number of well known drum distributors in Chicago, Cincinnati, Louisville, Memphis, Kansas City, and many other locations. We will maintain our presence through stocking distributors in these areas, which we consider secondary markets to our primary activities in St. Louis. With the exception of Chicago, we will be able to compete quite well with all competition. In Chicago, due to the multiplicity of plastic drum manufacturing in that important market, our efforts there will be less intensive but will not be neglected. This is *the* major drum market in the United States, and we intend to maintain a presence there even at reduced profits.

Industrial containers, including plastic drums, are considered to be commodities by most industry buyers. Rigid governmental specifications assure uniform construction and performance industry-wide. There is little brand preference or loyalty. Pricing and service are paramount. Because of logistics, River City Drum can offer St. Louis area buyers a saving of $1.00 to $1.50 per drum due to freight advantages, while maintaining competitive FOB prices for the drum itself. $21.50 is the prevailing price of the 55-gallon DOT Spec 34 polyethylene drum, with $18.50 being the price for 30-gallon drums. Given present resin prices, this will be our quote to most TL (truckload) buyers. This will also be our delivered price in the greater St. Louis trade area, a price that provides a savings of $300 to $450 per truckload to our customers.

We intend to use this strategic advantage to its utmost. Our market research has revealed that buyers are quite receptive to enjoying this cost advantage, plus the fast response of "just-in-time" delivery.

Similar savings will be realized by our LTL customers, with the selling price ranging from $22.50 to $25.50 depending on quantity.

High volume-long term contracts will be bid upon as the opportunities present themselves. Suitable escalators, based on raw material fluctuations that are normal to the industry, are always a part of contracts in excess of 90 days.

River City Drum will be purchasing resin at market prices comparable to those paid by our competitors. Energy, which makes up about 8% of the manufactured cost industry-wide, is expected to be approximately 5% due to better than average power cost by Union Electric compared to Illinois Power in the Chicago vicinity. We expect to be very competitive in labor and plant overhead as well. The manufactured cost of the River City 55-gallon drum is estimated to be $16.07.

Pricing & Profitability

Resin	8.78
Bung & Gaskets	.50
Colorant	.36
Ring	2.83
Labor	.63
Power	1.05
Rep/Maintenance	.60
Factory Overhead	1.32
Total	**16.07**

Break-Even Evaluation

Computed on Unit Sales		Computed on Gross Sales	
Unit of Sale	55-Gallon Drum		
Selling Price of Product	$21.50		
		Percent	
Cost of Goods Sold	$16.07	Cost of Goods Sold	74.7%
Gross Profit per unit sold	$5.43	Percent Gross Profit	25.3%
Monthly Overhead	$23,548	Monthly Overhead	$23,548
Monthly Unit Sales to reach break-even	4,337	Monthly Gross Sales to reach break-even	$93,224

For detailed derivation of these calculations, refer to Twelve-Month Proforma, Financial Projections.

Advertising and Promotion

River City Drum will mark its entry into the industrial container industry with strategically placed advertisements in two major trade publications. A three-month campaign timed to coincide with our start-up production is planned for *Polymer Age*, the leading trade journal for the plastics industry. This advertising series will consist of full-color quarter-page displays, run in three consecutive months and featuring among other things a prominent focus of the River City Drum logo. We will also be appearing in *Plastic Recycling*, a trade publication of great interest to container buyers. Our advertising will be of an institutional nature designed to enhance our name recognition in the industry. Plastic drums, because of their commodity nature, have not traditionally been the subject of heavy advertising. Our advertising budget, $13,000, a modest one half of one percent of expected first-year sales, will assure us prominent depiction in two widely read and respected trade publications.

In addition to the paid insertions defined above, River City Drum has been in touch with the editorial staff of all the industrial packaging, container, and plastic periodicals and trade journals. We have been assured of coverage of our market entry, and press releases are being prepared in-house for timely distribution.

This exposure in the print media will provide River City Drum with enhanced name recognition at a time when our marketing efforts are getting under way. Our advertising program is one of augmentation to our direct marketing efforts and is not designed to supplant direct customer contact, but to enhance it.

Once our entry to the marketplace has been announced, no long-term paid media campaign is contemplated at this time. River City Drum expects to capture and maintain a position of prominence by active participation in professional organizations and trade shows. River City is a member of the Society of the Plastic Industry and the Plastic Drum Institute, the latter being a high profile organization consisting exclusively of manufacturers and resin suppliers of the plastic drum industry. Our active participation, even as a new member, has earned River City an appointment to the Technical Committee, a prestigious subcommittee devoted to enhancing the overall quality and performance of plastic drums in general. We are represented on this committee by Don Smyth, our project engineer, and in the Plastic Drum Institute by Thomas Connors, our Vice President of Operations.

River City Drum will be participating as exhibitors in two very important upcoming trade shows, the Petroleum Packaging Institute and the Chemical Packaging Institute. Both are once-a-year conventions, attracting virtually every major industry buyer of industrial packaging in the nation. We expect to be a regular part of these important trade expositions in the future.

Magazine	Circulation	Budget	Ad Description	Insertion	Readership Profile
Plastic recycling	88,000	$2,100	1/4 Page B/W	May 199X	Pgkng & Molding Engrs/buyers
Polymer Age	105,000	$3,600	1/4 Page 4 color	May 199X	Plastic Industry Buyers, Plant Mgrs
Polymer Age	105,000	$3,600	1/4 Page 4 color	June 199X	Plastic Industry Buyers, Plant Mgrs
Polymer Age	105,000	$3,600	1/4 Page 4 color	July 199X	Plastic Industry Buyers, Plant Mgrs
Totals	**193,000**	**$12,900**			
Cost/Materials		**$0.07**			

MANUFACTURING

River City Drum has leased manufacturing and warehouse space at advantageous terms. The facility, known as the Hall Street Industrial Park, is a refurbished heavy industrial complex that was formerly General Steel Castings. Our section affords ample manufacturing and storage space with expansion capabilities, rail access, four truckloading doors, and 400 KVA power. River City has booked 20,000 square feet in three bays, one of which will be heated and will serve as the manufacturing floor. The remaining two-thirds will be cold storage warehouse and loading. A small factory office, employee lunch room, and restrooms are also included. We have a 3-year lease, with a 2-year option, with the initial 3-year period @ $1.25/sq. ft. The option years carry an increase of 8%. There is also an insurance assessment of some $800 per annum.

River City Drum will be operating a high-tech plastic processing facility. Raw material, known technically as high density polyethylene (HDPE), can be stored at our railside silos in quantities of up to 180,000 pounds, plus active storage in rail hopper cars if circumstances warrant. Material is suctioned in to the main Bekoft 1000 plastic molding machine, which will be outfitted with one of several River City proprietary molds which will form the plastic drum, whether, 30 gallon, 55 gallon, or some other configuration. Pigmentation is added during the molding process to produce a finished product of the desired color.

Scrap generated by the molding process, known as flashing is salvaged and fed into a grinder to form "regrind," which can be added to subsequent mix along with virgin resin. Likewise, any factory reject drums can be converted to regrind so as to salvage the raw material and colorant, thus virtually eliminating any wasted material.

Proprietary Technology

Our project engineer, in conjunction with our technical consultant, has developed a significant innovation known in the trade as post mold cooling, that we believe will enhance our manufacturing cycle time over and above the already fastest-in-the-industry molding cycle provided by the state-of-the-art Bekoft 1000.

Quality Control

Manufacturing standards adopted by River City Drum are among the most demanding in the industry but present no obstacle owing to our superior technology and modern equipment. In order to comply with D.O.T. Spec. 34, which is required of all plastic drums manufactured for the hazardous cargo trade, a series of performance tests, and specification criteria are mandated. River City Drum has adopted its own QC standards that in most cases exceed those of Spec 34. Also required is rigid adherence to River City Drum cosmetic standards for our products.

One of these includes the creation of a humidity controlled molding environment for the purpose of eliminating mold "sweating," thus precluding unsightly "water marks" on the finished products. Our preselling has told us that this is an important plus with many buyers, and provides River City with one-upmanship over some of its competitors.

The outfitting of the River City Drum manufacturing facility is expected to cost some $802,000 with the principal expenditure being $540,000 for the Bekoft 1000 drum blowmolder.

Labor

The labor market in the St. Louis area presents no obstacles for the successful staffing of the River City manufacturing facility. Statistics provided by the Missouri Department of Labor indicate St. Louis unemployment at 6.3%, which is seen as moderate to high. The prevailing wage in petroleum, coal, and plastics industries in St. Louis is reportedly $12.44 per hour. This figure is traditionally weighted towards heavy industry and is interpreted by River City to be representative of skilled operators in the plastics fabrication industry. Experience of River City management has been that an ample labor pool exists for line production laborers, trainable, and semi-skilled, at hourly rates of approximately 50% of the skilled operators.

In the plastic molding industry, the concept of around-the-clock manufacturing offers many advantages. Because of pre-heat periods, and machine fine tuning, plastic molding equipment functions best if it runs continuously. Therefore, River City Drum targets 24-hour operations as an optimum manufacturing mode and expects to achieve this level of production in approximately 6 months from start-up. Typical production staffing per shift would be as follows:

One Machine Operator/Shift Supervisor;
    responsible for machinery and personnel on shift.

Two Line workers;
    trainable semi-skilled workers.

(Note: Automated line runs essentially with two people. Third person provides relief and material handling.)

Day Shift only

One Quality Control/Material Handling;
    Performs QT and D.O.T. testing for all shifts, operates forklift, positioning manufactured product, and also loads outbound shipments.

One Plant Clerk;
    30 hours per week, maintain plant records, coordinates orders and shipments, general administrative.

Transportation

The advantage of River City Drum's geographical positioning within its target market will be hammered home with its own local delivery capabilities. River City Drum will acquire a single axle, gasoline, local delivery tractor and two used trailers, one 45-foot and one 48-foot. This equipment will enable us to easily handle our cargo requirements, due to the lightweight nature of empty polyethylene drums. Prior to establishing continuity of shipping, RCD will make use of local drainage firms at advantageous rates. Either way, we will be providing our customers with prompt, just-in-time delivery, whether truckloads, or LTL, at better than competitive prices. This is using our manufacturing position as a marketing strategy and to considerable advantage. Our preselling calls to future customers have taught us that this is a needed and desired service for the drum buyer and is not offered by present out-of-town suppliers.

Equipment Schedule

	Brand	Model	Capacity/ Rating	New/Used	Cost
Blowmolder	Bekoft	1000	35# Head	New	$540,000
Transportation & Rigging					4,100
Chiller	Allied	LJ5500	30 Ton	New	36,000
Grinder	Hercules	5000	25 HP	New	5,500
Air Compressor	Borg	FG5566	20 HP	New	8,155
Blender/Material Handler	Con Air	Superior	25#	New	5,000
Case sealer	Elliott	600	600/hr	Used	12,300
Blow back system, includes $3000 installation	Con Air		5 HP	New	10,375
Silo, includes installation & pad	Butler	AS1500	180,000#	Used	12,700
Molds - 2	Fremont	55 & 30 gal	Cast	New	80,000
Forklift	Fork Lift	JM5	5000#	Used	5,000
Piping, estimate				New	15,000
Electricity, Main Service, wiring, estimate		H5600		New	301,000
Leak detector, installed	Speciality			New	8,280
Quality Control & D.O.T. testing equipment	Various/In House			New	12,000
Post mold cooling	In House			New	18,000
Total Equipment Costs					**$802,480**

The management of River City Drum has determined that a capitalization of $1,232,000 is required for the successful implementation of this project. These funds are to be allocated as follows:

SUMMARY & USE OF FUNDING

Equipment & Fixtures	$803,000
Installation and Make ready	125,000
Advertising & Promotion	12,900
Deposits	5,000
Equipment shake-down costs	10,000
One-time start-up costs	100,000
Contingency	25,000
Operating Reserve	100,000
Raw material inventory	51,100
Total	**$1,232,000**

Our Business Plan anticipates that capitalization will be funded as follows:

Stockholder Equity	$200,000
Vendor Financing Blowmolder	432,000
Equipment Leasing Line of Credit	250,000
Bank Operating Line of Credit	$350,000
Total	**$1,232,000**

The stockholder's equity is divided equally between Mr. Connors and Mr. Stevenson, and derives from savings and withdrawal from another business entity, respectively.

Initial draw-downs from the operating line of credit are projected for February, 2000, and will continue over the first twelve months of operations. The Bekoft blowmolder will arrive in February and is expected to be commissioned early in April, with approximately the first month devoted to shake-down activities. Production is scheduled to begin in May 2000.

This page left intentionally blank to accommodate tabular matter following.

FINANCIAL PROJECTIONS

Twelve-Month Proforma

	Month One	Month Two	Month Three	Month Four	Month Five	Month Six	Month Seven	Month Eight
Sales								
Sale of Plastic Drums	45,150	67,725	90,300	112,875	135,450	158,025	174,150	190,275
Other Sales	200	200	200	200	200	200	200	200
Total Sales	**45,350**	**67,925**	**50,500**	**113,075**	**135,650**	**158,228**	**174,350**	**190,475**
Cost of Sales	**33,895**	**50,767**	**67,640**	**84,512**	**101,385**	**118,257**	**130,309**	**142,361**
Gross Profit	**11,455**	**17,158**	**22,860**	**28,563**	**34,265**	**39,958**	**44,041**	**48,114**
Operating Expenses								
Sales & Marketing								
Advertising	1,075	1,129	1,185	1,244	1,307	1,372	1,441	1,513
Commissions	454	1,133	2,038	3,169	4,525	6,107	7,851	9,756
Entertainment	223	257	302	358	426	505	593	688
Literature	100	100	100	100	100	100	100	100
Sales Promotion	100	105	110	116	122	128	134	141
Trade Shows	417	417	417	417	417	417	417	417
Travel	1,000	1,000	1,000	1,000	1,000	1,000	1,000	1,000
Salaries (Sales Personnel)	2,333	2,333	2,333	2,333	2,333	2,333	2,333	2,333
PR Taxes & Costs, Sales	280	280	280	280	280	280	280	280
Total Selling Cost	**5,981**	**6,753**	**7,765**	**9,017**	**10,509**	**12,242**	**14,148**	**16,226**
General & Administrative								
Legal & Accounting	200	200	200	200	200	200	200	200
Amortization	0	0	0	0	0	0	0	0
Bad Debts	907	1,359	1,810	2,262	2,713	3,215	3,487	3,810
Depreciation	6,660	6,660	6,660	6,660	6,660	6,660	6,660	6,660
Insurance	250	250	250	250	250	250	250	250
Lease Equipment	4,350	4,350	4,350	4,350	4,350	4,350	4,350	4,350
Licenses & Permits	100	100	100	100	100	100	100	100
Salaries	3,750	3,750	3,750	3,750	3,750	3,750	3,750	3,750
PR Taxes & Costs	450	450	450	450	450	450	450	450
Taxes (Non-income taxes)	50	50	50	50	50	50	50	50
Office Expense	100	110	121	133	146	160	177	195
Rent	200	200	200	200	200	200	200	200
Telephone	350	350	350	350	350	350	350	350
Utilities	200	404	408	412	416	420	425	429
Officers Salaries	0	0	0	0	0	0	0	0
PR Taxes & Costs, Officers	0	0	0	0	0	0	0	0
Total General & Administrative Cost	**17,567**	**18,031**	**18,495**	**18,961**	**19,428**	**19,869**	**20,237**	**20,579**
Net Income Before Taxes and Interest	**-12,093**	**-7,626**	**-3,400**	**585**	**4,328**	**7,830**	**9,656**	**11,308**
Interest	4,644	4,588	4,527	4,465	4,404	4,343	4,276	4,215
Net Income	**-16,737**	**16**	**231**	**460**	**704**	**964**	**1,154**	**1,353**

Month Nine	Month Ten	Month Eleven	Month Twelve	Year One	Per cent
206,400	222,528	238,650	254,775	1,896,300	100%
200	200	200	200	2,400	0%
206,600	222,725	238,850	254,975	1,898,700	
154,413	166,465	178,516	190,568	1,419,088	75%
52,187	56,260	60,334	64,407	479,612	25%
1,588	1,668	1,751	1,163	16,435	
11,822	14,049	16,437	18,987	96,326	
791	902	1,022	1,149	7,216	
100	100	100	100	1,200	
148	155	163	171	1,592	
417	417	417	417	5,000	
1,000	1,000	1,000	1,000	12,000	
2,333	2,333	2,333	2,333	27,996	
280	280	280	280	3,360	
18,478	20,904	23,503	25,600	171,124	12%
200	200	200	200	2,400	
0	0	0	0	0	
4,132	4,455	4,777	5,100	37,974	
6,660	6,660	6,660	6,660	79,926	
250	250	250	250	3,000	
4,350	4,350	4,350	4,350	52,200	
100	100	100	100	1,200	
3,750	3,750	3,750	3,750	45,000	
450	450	450	450	5,400	
50	50	50	50	600	
214	236	259	285	2,138	
200	200	200	200	2,400	
350	350	350	350	4,200	
433	437	221	223	2,537	
0	0	0	0	0	
0	0	0	0	0	
20,323	21,270	21,618	21,968	238,975	13%
12,786	14,087	15,213	16,839	$69,513	3.7%
4,153	4,086	4,025	3,958	$51,684	2.7%
1,562	1,782	2,013	2,256	$17,829	0.9%

**Three-Year
Projected Income
Statement**

Sales	Year 1		Year 2		Year 3	
Sale of Plastic Drums	1,896,300		3,195,266		3,834,319	
Other Sales	2,400		2,424		2,472	
Total Sales	**1,898,700**		**3,197,690**		**3,836,791**	
Cost of Goods Sold	1,419,088	74.7%	2,389,953	74.7%	2,867,618	74.7%
Gross Profit	**479,612**		**807,736**		**969,173**	
Selling Expense	171,124	9.0%	180,536	5.6%	190,465	5.0%
General & Administrative	238,975	12.6%	252,118	7.9%	265,985	6.9%
Net Income Before Taxes & Interest	**69,513**	**3.7%**	**375,083**	**11.7%**	**512,724**	**13.4%**
Interest	51,684	2.7%	42,201	1.3%	31,726	13.4%
Income taxes	4,457		83,220		120,249	0.8%
Net Income or Loss	**13,372**	**0.7%**	**249,661**	**7.8%**	**360,748**	**9.4%**

Assets	Current	Year 1	Year 2	Year 3
Current Assets				
Cash and Equivalents	146,000	3,720	233,424	539,362
Receivables from Sales	0	122,388	206,224	247,469
Other Receivables	0	0	0	0
Inventory	51,000	286,741	299,673	359,567
Prepaid Expense/Deposits	3,000	5,000	5,000	5,000
Total Current Assets	**200,000**	**417,850**	**744,321**	**1,151,398**
Fixed Assets:				
Equipment & Machinery	557,480	557,480	557,480	557,480
Less accumulated depreciation	0	79,926	159,851	23,777
Net Fixed Assets	557,480	477,554	397,629	317,303
Total Assets	**757,480**	**895,404**	**1,141,949**	**1,469,100**
Liabilities				
Current Liabilities				
Trade Payables	0	190,568	199,163	238,968
Income Tax Payable	0	4,457	83,220	120,249
Short Term Notes	0	0	0	0
Total Current Liabilities	**0**	**195,026**	**282,383**	**359,217**
Long term Liabilities				
Notes Payable, Bank	557,480	487,007	396,533	286,102
Notes Payable, Others	0	0	0	0
Other Liabilities	0	0	0	0
Total Long Term Liabilities	**557,480**	**487,007**	**396,533**	**286,102**
Total Liabilities	**557,480**	**682,032**	**678,916**	**645,319**
Stockholder's Equity				
Capital Stock	200,000	200,000	200,000	200,000
Retained Earnings	0	13,372	263,033	623,781
Total Stockholder's Equity	**200,000**	**213,372**	**463,033**	**823,781**
Total Liabilities &				
Stockholders Equity	**757,480**	**895,404**	**1,141,949**	**1,469,100**
Current Ratio		**2.1**	**2.6**	**3.2**
Quick Ratio		**0.7**	**1.6**	**2.2**
Debt to Equity Ratio		**3.2**	**1.5**	**0.8**
Return on Investment		**6.3%**	**53.9%**	**43.8%**

Cash Flow Projection

	Month One	Month Two	Month Three	Month Four	Month Five	Month Six	Month Seven	Month Eight
Beginning Cash Balance	200,000	140,848	106,685	78,748	54,796	34,587	17,880	8,528
Cash Receipts from Sales	22,675	55,731	77,854	99,978	122,101	144,225	163,123	178,926
Total Cash Available	222,675	196,578	184,539	178,726	176,897	178,812	181,003	187,453
Cash Disbursements:								
Accounts Payable, merchandise	0	33,895	50,767	67,640	84,512	101,385	118,257	130,309
Selling costs	5,981	6,753	7,765	9,017	10,509	12,242	14,148	16,226
General & Administrative	5,800	5,812	5,825	5,839	5,855	5,871	5,889	5,909
Salaries	4,200	4,200	4,200	4,200	4,200	4,200	4,200	4,200
Total Cash Disbursements	**15,981**	**50,659**	**68,557**	**86,696**	**105,076**	**123,698**	**142,494**	**156,645**
Net Cash from Operations	**206,694**	**145,919**	**115,982**	**92,030**	**71,821**	**55,114**	**38,508**	**30,809**
Proceeds of Loans								
National Bnk, Fixtures & Equip	125,480	0	0	0	0	0	0	20,000
National Bnk, Operating Line	432,000	0	0	0	0	0	0	0
Capital Infusion								
Additional Paid in Capital	0	0	0	0	0	0	0	0
Other Disbursements								
Debt Service	11,846	11,846	11,846	11,846	11,846	11,846	11,846	11,846
Capital Disbursements								
Furniture & Fixtures	5,000	0	0	0	0	0	0	0
Equipment	552,480	0	0	0	0	0	0	0
Inventory Purchases	51,000	25,388	25,388	25,388	25,388	25,388	18,134	18,134
Prepaid Expense/Deposits	3,000	2,000	0	0	0	0	0	0
Net Cash Balance	**140,848**	**106,685**	**78,748**	**54,796**	**34,587**	**17,880**	**8,528**	**20,828**

Month Nine	Month Ten	Month Eleven	Month Twelve
20,828	14,606	9,685	5,890
194,728	210,531	226,333	242,136
215,556	225,136	236,018	248,025
142,361	154,413	166,465	178,516
18,478	20,904	23,503	25,600
5,931	5,955	5,980	6,008
4,200	4,200	4,200	4,200
170,970	**185,471**	**200,148**	**214,324**
44,586	**39,665**	**35,870**	**33,701**
0	0	0	0
0	0	0	0
0	0	0	0
11,846	11,846	11,846	11,846
0	0	0	0
0	0	0	0
18,134	18,134	18,134	18,134
0	0	0	0
14,606	**9,685**	**5,890**	**3,720**

Real Estate Company

BUSINESS PLAN

MSN REAL ESTATE

40001 Lincoln Ave.
Portland, Oregon 97201

MSN Real Estate will be formed as a diversified development, brokerage, and management enterprise. Their apartment units will offer a safe environment and state-of-the-art living conditions reflective of the rapid advancements in technology and a growing need for quality housing. Customer and employee satisfaction will be keys to their success. This business plan was compiled using Business Plan Pro™, by Palo Alto Software, copyright © 2000.

- EXECUTIVE SUMMARY

- COMPANY SUMMARY

- MARKET ANALYSIS SUMMARY

- STRATEGY AND IMPLEMENTATION SUMMARY

- MANAGEMENT SUMMARY

- FINANCIAL PLAN

EXECUTIVE SUMMARY

MSN Real Estate will be formed as a diversified development, brokerage, and management enterprise. By being involved in each step of the the way from development to rental, we at MSN can ensure our customers that they are receiving the highest quality living available at that price. We will specialize in providing high quality housing that offers both up-to-date technological amenities as well as state-of-the-art living conditions at reasonable prices. The founders are forming this company in order to provide customers with a living environment that is unparalleled, while cutting expenses through organizational diversification enabling optimal profit margins. MSN's apartment complexes and individual units will foster an atmosphere and a quality of life that is of the highest standards. Customer satisfaction, safety, and an overall healthy working relationship are our main goals at MSN.

Objectives

1. Sales of $250,000 in 1998 and $600,000 by the year 2000.
2. Gross margin higher than 50%.
3. Net income more than 15% of sales by the second year.
4. Have a crime rate of 0.

Mission

MSN Real Estate provides high-quality, comfortable rental units in Eugene and other areas of Oregon. MSN's apartment units offer state-of-the-art living conditions reflective of the rapid advancements in technology and a growing need for quality housing. Our company is dedicated to a hassle-free living environment in which our tenants can enjoy all of the benefits of safe, attractive, and inviting units. Unlike many other realty companies that are solely concerned with turning profits, our primary objective at MSN is to maintain the highest level of customer satisfaction that is achievable. Tenant safety, happiness, and comfort are our main goals. MSN maintains competitive market prices, while working toward expanding the number of units owned and increasing total profits earned. Within the company we will strive to work as a cohesive, harmonious unit focused on exemplifying our mission. Just as customer satisfaction is an intricate part of MSN's success, so is employee satisfaction. That is why the founders of MSN Real Estate believe that employee satisfaction will make the company a success and will be the key to their longevity.

Initial focus will be to buy and develop existing apartment complexes. We will modify and remodel the acquired real estate so as to meet MSN standards and increase long-term assets and income. Housing units will predominantly be located in the university neighborhood, targeting both students and professionals. MSN fosters the ideals of the importance of tenant needs along with healthy and understanding relationships and a professional commitment to satisfaction.

Keys to Success

1. Safe, quality housing that provides state-of-the-art amenities at competitive prices.
2. Maintaining open communication between MSN and its customers in order to ensure the highest level of customer satisfaction and long lasting reputation within the community.
3. To continue to expand the number of units owned and maintained, while also increasing the level of profits for both MSN and its investors.

MSN Real Estate is an enterprise that is involved in numerous aspects of the industry. Primary experience and expertise is in the development of high-quality, lower cost living for students and professionals seeking the most up-to-date technologically advanced living environment. An area of intense training and attention is the importance of strong customer service.

COMPANY SUMMARY

MSN Real Estate will be created as a Limited Liability Corporation based out of Portland, Oregon. It will be owned by its principal investors, Shawn Menashe and Nathan Koach. Shawn Menashe is the acting CEO and holds a 40% stake in the company. Nathan Koach is the acting CFO and holds a 40% share of the company as well. The other 20% is held by silent investors.

Company Ownership

The total start-up expenses (including legal, stationery, architect, brochures, consultants, insurance, rent, R&D, expensed equipment, and other) come to $18,308. Start-up assets required include $12,000 in short-term assets (truck, cell phone, etc.) and $36,000 in initial cash to handle the architect and contractor fees prior to opening. The rest of the cash is needed to pay all zoning fees and governmental regulations. The details are included in the following table.

Start-up Summary

Start-up Expenses

Legal	$6,400
Architect fees	$3,000
Stationery, etc.	$220
Brochures	$225
Consultants	$2,550
Insurance	$1,232
Rent	$1,400
Research and development	$2,330
Expensed equipment	$600
Other	$351
Total Start-up Expenses	**$18,308**

Start-up Costs

Start-up Needed

Cash Requirements	$36,000
Other Short-term Assets	$12,000
Total Short-term Assets	**$48,000**

Long-term Assets	$0
Total Assets	**$48,000**

Total Start-up Requirements	**$66,308**
Left to finance:	$0

Start-up Funding Plan

Investment

Menashe	$24,650
Koach	$26,500
Other	$14,000
Total investment	**$65,150**

Start-up Costs

Continued

Short-term Liabilities	
Unpaid Expenses	$3,890
Short-term Loans	$5,000
Interest-free Short-term Loans	$0
Subtotal Short-term Liabilities	$8,890
Long-term Liabilities	$0
Total Liabilities	**$8,890**
Loss at Start-up	($26,040)
Total Capital	$39,110
Total Capital and Liabilities	$48,000
Checkline	$0

Company Locations and Facilities

MSN headquarters will be established in A-quality office space in the downtown area of Portland, Oregon. This will be the heart of our company, with satellite locations in Beaverton and Eugene, Oregon. We are also installing an in-house Internet server and 24-hour answering service so that all customer or business communications are dealt with in an expedient and fluid manner. Within any living development with more than 32 units, a representative of the company will be located.

Services

MSN offers on-site security guards who patrol the grounds during evenings, nights, and early mornings. We also offer an on-site repair service. There will always be an open line of communication between the renters and the management via an MSN web page and a 24-hour, call-in answering service.

Competitive Comparison

MSN's competitive advantage is as follows:

1. We offer a higher level of quality in our units than the average unit on campus. This allows for those residents who do not want their living situations to inhibit their studies, comfort, or enjoyment of campus life.
2. Each unit will be fully wired to the Internet via available modem jacks and/or Ethernet access. If the residents desire to have the best Internet access, we will give them that option.
3. Our marketing and advertising costs will be low due to simple marketing strategies. However, the owner's expertise in visual layout and communications will help create a unique and aesthetic product for the customer.
4. The main competition MSN will encounter will be average lower cost apartment units.

Sales Literature

MSN will have brochures available at all offices. These will give the customer a general outline of our units and will explain the benefits of our units. We will also have a monthly newsletter that we send out to our clients. This newsletter will inform the clients as to the growth and outreach of MSN. It will also contain some human interest stories about our complexes and the residents.

We will also advertise in the local newspapers including *The Daily Emerald, The Register Guard,* and *The Oregonian.* Our marketing strategies are simple but aim to reach a large amount of people. The layout of our publications and advertisements will have a sophisticated and contemporary look without being overly formatted.

1. MSN's key fulfillment will be provided by management's dedication to a higher quality product. This is achieved through the solid network of contractors, and cutting-edge architects who are all dedicated to helping MSN. We are hard workers who have a solid backing from our developers.
2. We will maintain a pool of professionals from which to pull for our needed services. This will help us develop a rapport with our contractors as well as maintaining our high expectations.

Fulfillment

MSN Real Estate will have the most up-to-date technology provided both to the customers and to the subcontractors and other clients.

Technology

1. Ethernet ports and/or modem jacks will be installed in each unit developed by MSN.
2. Access to a 24-hour copy/fax center located on the premises.
3. Each unit will contain an emergency panic alert that will automatically go through to the manager and the local police department.

In the future, MSN will look to give each department within the company the opportunity to become a more independent entity. This will make expansion efforts more efficient, and will provide specialists in their departments the chance to become more focused in their field.

Future Services

We are in the process of conducting surveys in order to determine the best possible markets for MSN expansion.

MSN Real Estate's main consumer base will be primarily students at the University of Oregon who will benefit from the apartment's unparalleled level of quality, location, and technological amenities. We also will be marketing to local area professionals and recent graduates, along with faculty and staff at the university. These customers will be looking for safe, high-quality environments that can foster the type of atmosphere needed for scholastic and professional success.

MARKET ANALYSIS SUMMARY

Potential Customers	Growth	1999	2000	2001	2002	2003	CAGR
Students	7%	18,000	19,170	20,416	21,743	23,156	6.50%
Professionals	4%	12,000	12,480	12,979	13,498	14,038	4.00%
Faculty/Staff	5%	6,000	6,300	6,615	6,946	7,293	5.00%
Other	3%	4,000	4,120	4,244	4,371	4,502	3.00%
Total	**5.20%**	**40,000**	**42,070**	**44,254**	**46,558**	**48,989**	**5.20%**

1. MSN's largest market segment in the Eugene area will be students of the local universities. These students will be the most likely to desire the technological amenities that our company offers. We expect this to be the largest growing segment with a growth rate of about 7%.
2. Local professionals are another large segment. They will be attracted to the units because of the same technological needs, but will also be attracted to the comfortable, well-maintained living environment. MSN offers units that provide a quality "hub" between college graduation and home ownership. We expect this segment to grow at a rate of about 4% with a more frequent turnover.
3. Local university faculty and staff represent the third and smallest identifiable segment, but contain the second highest growth rate. Proximity and quality will entice this segment which we expect to grow at a rate of 5%.

Market Segmentation

**Target Market
Segment Strategy**

We believe that our unparalleled level of quality and technological amenities put MSN into a niche of its own. This will be the focal point of all our marketing and advertising efforts. These segments are also easily reached through local newspapers and publications, as well frequent open house displays.

It is essential for MSN patrons to understand that their needs are our priority.

Market Needs

Each of our targets need the quality, convenience, service, safety, comfort, and technological amenities that can only be found at our living complexes.

1. The student segment needs a quiet, safe atmosphere that fosters a quality learning environment. They also need the convenience of location and on-site amenities.
2. The professional segment needs a living environment that separates them from the noisy, dirty inconvenience of average apartment living. Most professionals are on their way to home ownership or movement to a larger city, so they need housing that will let them feel like they are getting the quality that they need.
3. The faculty/staff segment also has similar needs. They need to feel separation from the noise and unkempt conditions of most near-campus housing. Along with the students, they also need a place to feel safe and one that fosters convenience.

Market Trends

This industry is constantly evolving and leaving many inflexible companies stagnant. One of the major trends is the need to adapt to technological advancements as well as maintaining the overall appearance and condition of the complexes.

Another important trend is adapting to higher density housing in smaller areas due to urban growth boundaries, etc. MSN is dedicated to following these trends while maintaining the level of comfortable livability that sets us apart from our competitors.

Market Growth

The market for high quality, reasonably priced apartment units has been growing at a rate of 6.7% since 1998. Oregon's rental rates have remained even, averaging $697, or $.79 per square foot, during the fourth quarter of 1998. The Oregon market is experiencing rapid employment growth that is fueling demand for apartments, but not many new units are emerging. Not only is MSN pioneering this particular niche of affordable quality living, but it is capitalizing on the strength of the current economic growth in Oregon.

**STRATEGY AND
IMPLEMENTATION
SUMMARY**

MSN will focus on the three previously mentioned market segments: university students, local area professionals, and university faculty and staff.

Our target customer is usually looking for higher-end living facilities that foster a safe, enjoyable, and convenient environment. They are technology savvy and have a desire to have access to the technological amenities that we provide.

Competitive Edge

We start with a critical competitive edge: there are very few apartment units that offer the same level of quality and technological amenities as MSN properties. We also have a very high regard for customer service; something that is unparalleled in this industry. MSN believes it is essential that the customer feels he/she is being treated with the utmost care and urgency. All staff and personnel go through a training program that teaches many of the skills needed for successful client relations and customer service.

Marketing in a highly competitive housing industry depends on the recognition of excellence, as well as a point of difference to display our units in an individualized light. MSN will build a reputation upon these components.

We will develop and provide a living environment of unmatched proportion. It starts with the commitment to customer satisfaction and fulfilling their demands. Our commitment to quality and comfort includes safety and 24-hour customer service. The aspect of our living developments that differentiate MSN from all other real estate companies is our focus on maintaining the most advanced technological innovations on the market for our tenants.

Marketing Strategy

For people who desire high-quality living with all the technological amenities available, only MSN Real Estate properties will be able to fulfill their needs and desires at an affordable price. Unlike most other property management companies, MSN is committed to guaranteeing customers full satisfaction, with 24-hour on-staff service, live answering service, and a web site that handles all complaints instantly.

Positioning Statement

MSN's pricing will be at the top of what the market will bear. We are competing with large firms who have similar complexes. Our prices will be competitive with these larger firms while maintaining the high level of quality and expert management.

Prices are based on average unit value of $400 and average monthly sales of about $430,000. MSN, however, must try to follow market pricing trends in order to maintain a competitive advantage.

Pricing Strategy

MSN's most successful promotion will come in the form of word of mouth. Since we will own real estate, we will be highly visible to the public. Since our complexes will be in the upper echelon of quality and livability, word will spread through the community about our unique appeal.

Along with word of mouth, our most consistent form of promotion will come from ads in local publications, specifically, *The Oregonian, The Daily Emerald,* and *The Register Guard,* as well as smaller magazines and circulars. We also will be personally promoting our product within the community.

Promotion Strategy

We will focus on providing high-quality living in convenient locations with a wide customer base. It is also important that we remain at the upper echelon in the quality range when compared to competitors. We can only do this by organizing and implementing a sound plan that will assume responsibility for the functionality and appearance of MSN properties. We will have an updated web site for anyone interested in the properties.

Distribution Strategy

Our most important marketing program is customer word-of-mouth. The only way to truly know the quality of our units is through experience; hence, we must maintain the highest level of customer satisfaction. Rewards will be given to clients or customers that refer new clientele to the company. We confidently believe that the high level of quality that MSN will provide can attract a strong demand for our units.

Another incentive that we will use is the early move-in bonus program. Anyone that signs their lease before June 15th will receive a free month as well as two parking spaces. This will

Marketing Programs

encourage people to try and beat the rush of people who move in later. It will also give the appearance of increased demand.

Sales Strategy

Sales in our business is based upon providing customers with a living concept fitting of their needs. We must be in touch with the needs and desires of our clientele in order to best attract a consistent flow of incoming residents.

Sales Forecast

The following table gives the forecasted earnings for MSN Real Estate apartment rental units. We perceive a gradual increase in the total number of units over the next year. As time goes on, the monthly per-unit rental price will slowly ascend, coupled by the decline in cost over time, producing an increased per-unit profit.

From our opening in January to June, we expect that all units will be completely rented out. In the summer months we anticipate fewer student tenants, so we have planned on a rent lowering process to entice renters to stay. Also, we will only rent on yearly leases to ensure that all rented units remain filled year round. With the estimated profits from the previous months, the annex will be completed in September, adding 12 more units to the total of 54.

Unit Sales	1999	2000	2001
Single units	311	350	394
Double units	174	212	242
Quad units	129	154	168
Luxury Suite	29	54	60
Other	0	0	0
Total Unit Sales	**643**	**770**	**864**
Unit Prices			
Single units	$404.98	$410.00	$420.00
Double units	$806.78	$804.00	$812.00
Quad units	$1,174.42	$1,200.00	$1,220.00
Luxury Suite	$674.14	$689.00	$699.00
Other	$0.00	$0.00	$0.00
Sales			
Single units	$125,950	$143,500	$165,480
Double units	$140,380	$170,448	$196,504
Quad units	$151,500	$184,800	$204,960
Luxury Suite	$19,550	$37,206	$41,940
Other	$0	$0	$0
Total Sales	**$437,380**	**$535,954**	**$608,884**
Direct Unit Costs			
Single units	$260.00	$225.00	$214.00
Double units	$428.00	$400.00	$378.00
Quad units	$511.00	$498.00	$478.00
Luxury Suite	$302.00	$287.00	$284.00
Other	$0.00	$0.00	$0.00

Direct Cost of Sales	1999	2000	2001
Single units	$80,860	$78,750	$84,316
Double units	$74,472	$84,800	$91,476
Quad units	$65,919	$76,692	$80,304
Luxury Suite	$8,758	$15,498	$17,040
Other	$0	$0	$0
Subtotal Direct Cost of Sales	**$230,009**	**$255,740**	**$273,136**

Sales Forecast

Continued

Our sale program will include sales awards for length of lease agreements, maintaining a full capacity status, and customer service awards for those who best exemplify MSN's commitment to customers. We also will award existing customers for referring new clients to the company.

Sales Programs

We depend on our alliance with Rumex contracting services to develop our housing units, as well as Richards Architecture to assist in the layout and design of our units. Familian Northwest also is a key factor in our development process for their continuous fair sales program when we need building supplies.

Strategic Alliances

The accompanying table lists our company's milestones, including dates, management responsibility, and budgets. This table indicates our expectations from the company as well as outlining our plan for start-up. The table shows the anticipated divisions that are to occur within the company as it grows, as well as an increase in units owned.

Milestones

This is an initial assessment, and MSN will continually adjust in order to sustain our business in all the different departments.

Milestone	Manager	Planned Date	Department	Budget
Complete Incorporation	Shawn Menashe (CEO)	7/30/98	Administrative/ Management	$12,000
Financially Organized Institution	Nathan Koach (CFO)	2/28/00	Finance	$2,500
Brokerage Unified	Joe Menashe	4/00/00	Brokerage	$10,000
Expansion (UNITS)	Shawn Menashe	4/24/99	Development	$150,000
Earnings ($200,000)	Nathan Koach	12/31/99	Finance	$1,000
Acquisition (Bought C&R Reality)	Shawn Menashe	7/30/99	Brokerage	$500,000
Other	MSN	1/1/98	Administration	$5,000
Totals				**$680,500**

The initial management team depends on the founders themselves, with back-up assistance from the property management department of MSN Real Estate. As we continue to grow, we will establish satellite offices in all of our living developments. It also will be necessary to take on additional help in the marketing and R&D sectors as growth continues.

MANAGEMENT SUMMARY

MSN Real Estate depends on an organized division of responsibilities in order to run an efficient, diversified enterprise. Main decisions and responsibilities will be divided between the two top partners. They will focus on maintaining high quality and a cohesive business entity. Top division managers will be given specific responsibilities such as marketing, finance, strategic management, or research and development.

Organizational Structure

Management Team

MSN Real Estate is completely departmentalized. The main departments are finance, marketing, management, and research and development. Nate Koach, co-owner of the company, assumes the responsibilities of the CFO, while his counterpart, Shawn Menashe, will be responsible for the duties of CEO. The company will make all decisions in accordance with the company mission. Employees are delegated tasks based upon their specialty.

Every six months, the two top partners will assess the results of these tasks, and the personality of the employee involved, to determine promotion and/or salary issues.

Management Team Gaps

The present team requires business development and administrative support. Most of the partners have been working in business environments where this kind of support was provided to them as part of a larger organization.

MSN will turn to Dynamic Public Relations to help create business development programs, such as speaking opportunities and magazine article insertions, as well as forums and seminars that are important to our ongoing development.

Regarding administration, we need a strong finance manager to guard cash flow. Our partners are not accustomed to the worries of cash flow, but they have the sense to listen to reason and deal with constraints if the finance manager provides the proper information.

Personnel Plan

The following table summarizes our personnel expenditures for the first three years, with compensation increasing from less than $100K the first year to about $150K in the third. The founding partners will take limited compensation for the first three years until earnings are substantiated and growth is assured. We believe this plan is a compromise between fairness and expedience and meets the commitment of our mission statement.

Personnel	1999	2000	2001
Nathan Koach, CFO	$15,600	$20,000	$25,000
Shawn Menashe, CEO	$15,600	$20,000	$25,000
Denise Richards (Administrative Manager)	$9,600	$10,000	$12,000
Joe Nash (Brokerage Manager)	$11,700	$14,000	$17,000
Head Contractor (Development Manager)	$14,100	$15,000	$17,000
Other	$24,000	$26,000	$32,000
Total Payroll	**$90,600**	**$105,000**	**$128,000**
Total Headcount	18	24	32
Payroll Burden	$13,590	$15,750	$19,200
Total Payroll Expenditures	**$104,190**	**$120,750**	**$147,200**

FINANCIAL PLAN

We want to finance growth mainly through cash flow. We recognize that this means we will have to grow more slowly than we might like.

The most important factor in our case is collection days. We can't push our clients hard on collection days. Therefore, we need to develop a permanent system of receivables financing, using one of the established financial companies in that business.

Important Assumptions

MSN's plan depends on the assumptions that are made in the following table. These are annual and monthly assumptions that show the consistent growth of the company. Since we operate on a monthly collection basis, we are assuming that the majority of the collections will be timely and in full.

Some of the underlying assumptions are:

1. We assume a healthy growth trend in the local real estate market, along with a continued strong local economy.
2. We assume that we stay in line with the continuing advances in technology and housing.

General Assumptions	1999	2000	2001
Short-term Interest Rate %	10.00%	10.00%	10.00%
Long-term Interest Rate %	10.00%	10.00%	10.00%
Payment Days Estimator	30	30	30
Tax Rate %	25.00%	25.00%	25.00%
Expenses in Cash %	10.00%	10.00%	10.00%
Personnel Burden %	15.00%	15.00%	15.00%

Key Financial Indicators

MSN foresees growth in both unit rentals as well as increasing the percentage of growth margin.

MSN's cash flow depends on the monthly collection from the renters. We allow for a 25-day grace period, after which unpaid accounts will inhibit our cash flow. However, since we collect on a monthly basis, cash flow should be maintained at a steady level.

Break-even Analysis

The following table summarize our break-even analysis. With fixed costs of $8,000 per month and a variable per-unit cost of $350, we will need to rent out 14 units at $925 per unit, to cover our monthly costs. MSN's housing complex will consist of 34 units. According to the calculations, we will break-even within our first month of operation.

The break-even assumes that all units will be occupied and that all rent will be paid in a timely manner. This assumption is probably unrealistic; therefore our initial break-even per unit will most likely be higher.

Monthly Units Break-even	14
Monthly Sales Break-even	$12,870

Assumptions:	
Average Per-Unit Revenue	$925.00
Average Per-Unit Variable Cost	$350.00
Estimated Monthly Fixed Cost	$8,000

Projected Profit and Loss

The projected profit and loss for MSN is shown on the following table. Sales are increasing from about $440,000 in 1999 to over $600,000 after the third year. We show that net profit in 1999 will be $44,621. This is relatively high, but leaves room for possible unoccupied units.

We are projecting a gross margin of about 48% for the first year. This is an aggressive projection that will help our efforts to keep total cost of sales low while increasing gross margin. We also will have very low marketing costs, due to the public exposure to the units, and good word of mouth around the university area.

The planned projections are included in the attached Profit and Loss Table.

Profit and Loss

	1999	2000	2001
Sales	$437,380	$535,954	$608,884
Direct Cost of Sales	$230,009	$255,740	$273,136
Other	$0	$0	$0
Total Cost of Sales	**$230,009**	**$255,740**	**$273,136**
Gross Margin	$207,371	$280,214	$335,748
Gross Margin %	47.41%	52.28%	55.14%
Operating expenses:			
Advertising/Promotion	$2,700	$3,000	$3,500
Travel	$0	$0	$0
Miscellaneous	$1,800	$2,000	$2,200
Payroll Expense	$90,600	$105,000	$128,000
Payroll Burden	$13,590	$15,750	$19,200
Depreciation	$1,800	$1,800	$1,800
Leased Equipment	$2,400	$2,600	$2,800
Utilities	$7,200	$8,200	$8,500
Insurance	$14,400	$15,500	$1,600
Rent	$3,000	$4,000	$5,000
Contractors	$9,300	$9,000	$12,000
Total Operating Expenses	**$146,790**	**$166,850**	**$184,600**
Profit Before Interest and Taxes	$60,581	$113,364	$151,148
Interest Expense Short-term	$1,011	$2,090	$3,440
Interest Expenses Long-term	$75	$700	$1,075
Taxes Incurred	$14,874	$27,644	$36,658
Net Profit	**$44,621**	**$82,931**	**$109,975**
Net Profit/Sales	**10.20%**	**15.47%**	**18.06%**

Projected Cash Flow

The following cash flow projections are a key part of MSN's early success. The annual cash flow figures are included here.

	1999	2000	2001
Net Profit	$44,621	$82,931	$109,975
Plus:			
Depreciation	$1,800	$1,800	$1,800
Change in Accounts Payable	$22,266	$2,805	$834
Current Borrowing (repayment)	$8,400	$15,000	$12,000
Increase (decrease) Other Liabilities	$1,152	$2,500	$2,000
Long-term Borrowing (repayment)	$4,500	$5,000	$2,500
Capital Input	$5,862	$6,000	$4,000
Subtotal	$88,602	$116,035	$133,109
Less:			
Change in Other Short-term Assets	$0	$0	$0
Capital Expenditure	$0	$0	$0
Dividends	$0	$0	$0
Subtotal	$0	$0	$0
Net Cash Flow	$88,602	$116,035	$133,109
Cash Balance	**$124,602**	**$240,637**	**$373,746**

The balance sheet in the following table shows managed but sufficient growth of net worth, and a sufficiently healthy financial position. The monthly estimates are a good indicator of MSN's increasing annual value.

Assets

Short-term Assets	Starting Balances	1999	2000	2001
Cash	$36,000	$124,602	$240,637	$373,746
Other Short-term Assets	$12,000	$12,000	$12,000	$12,000
Total Short-term Assets	$48,000	$136,602	$252,637	$385,746
Long-term Assets				
Capital Assets	$0	$0	$0	$0
Accumulated Depreciation	$0	$1,800	$3,600	$5,400
Total Long-term Assets	$0	($1,800)	($3,600)	($5,400)
Total Assets	**$48,000**	**$134,802**	**$249,037**	**$380,346**
Liabilities and Capital				
Accounts Payable	$3,890	$26,156	$28,961	$29,795
Short-term Notes	$5,000	$13,400	$28,400	$40,400
Other Short-term Liabilities	$0	$1,152	$3,652	$5,652
Subtotal Short-term Liabilities	$8,890	$40,708	$61,013	$75,847
Long-term Liablities	$0	$4,500	$9,500	$12,000
Total Liabilities	**$8,890**	**$45,208**	**$70,513**	**$87,847**
Paid in Capital	$65,150	$71,012	$77,012	$81,012
Retained Earnings	($26,040)	($26,040)	$18,581	$101,512
Earnings	$0	$44,621	$82,931	$109,975
Total Capital	**$39,110**	**$89,593**	**$178,524**	**$292,499**
Total Liabilities and Capital	**$48,000**	**$134,802**	**$249,037**	**$380,346**
Net Worth	**$39,110**	**$89,593**	**$178,524**	**$292,499**

The following ratios point out MSN's liquidity, debt, performance, and some other important aspects. We expect to generate healthy ratios for our profitability and return.

Profitability Ratios:	1999	2000	2001	RMA
Gross Margin	47.41%	52.28%	55.14%	0
Net Profit Margin	10.20%	15.47%	18.06%	0
Return on Assets	33.10%	33.30%	28.91%	0
Return on Equity	49.80%	46.45%	37.60%	0
Activity Ratios				
AR Turnover	0.00	0.00	0.00	0
Collection Days	0	0	0	0
Inventory Turnover	0.00	0.00	0.00	0
Accts Payable Turnover	9.38	9.38	9.38	0
Total Asset Turnover	3.24	2.15	1.60	0
Debt Ratios				
Debt to Net Worth	0.50	0.39	0.30	0
Short-term Liab. to Liab.	0.90	0.87	0.86	0

Business Ratios

Continued

Liquidity Ratios	1999	2000	2001	RMA
Current Ratio	3.36	4.14	5.09	0
Quick Ratio	3.36	4.14	5.09	0
Net Working Capital	$95,893	$191,624	$309,899	0
Interest Coverage	55.79	40.63	33.48	0
Additional Ratios				
Assets to Sales	0.31	0.46	0.62	0
Debt/Assets	34%	28%	23%	0
Current Debt/Total Assets	30%	24%	20%	0
Acid Test	3.36	4.14	5.09	0
Asset Turnover	3.24	2.15	1.60	0
Sales/Net Worth	4.88	3.00	2.08	0

Restaurant

BUSINESS PLAN

BUTCHER HOLLOW BAR BQ

1020 Allen Ave.
St. Louis, Missouri 63104

The proprietors of this new restaurant plan to take advantage of their market research, which indicates there is a great interest and very little competition in a specific area of St. Louis for a barbecue restaurant.

- EXECUTIVE SUMMARY

- THE COMPANY—PRESENT SITUATION

- OBJECTIVES

- MANAGEMENT

- PRODUCT DESCRIPTION

- MARKET ANALYSIS—CUSTOMERS

- COMPETITION

- RISKS

- MARKETING STRATEGY—ADVERTISING, PROMOTION & PUBLIC RELATIONS

- PRICING & PROFITABILITY

- SUMMARY & USE OF FUNDING

- FINANCIAL PROJECTIONS

- ADDENDUM

EXECUTIVE SUMMARY

Butcher Hollow Bar BQ will be an eat-in, carry-out restaurant, specializing in evening and weekend leisure dining. St. Louis is recognized as one of the prime barbecue markets in the country. The Soulard neighborhood, future home of Butcher Hollow, is known as one of our area's most popular and successful nightlife hubs.

What makes Butcher Hollow Bar BQ special as a business proposition? New restaurant openings are known to be risky. What have we done to neutralize these risks and assure success?

First, we have identified an unfulfilled market for our exceptional product. Careful research has demonstrated a 66% positive response by a representative sampling of our primary and secondary geographical markets. We have learned that people living in Soulard and Lafayette Square, or within reasonable driving distance, would patronize a good eat-in or carry-out Bar BQ restaurant in Soulard if one were available. Further research of the population demographics of this area reveals a lifestyle most conducive to eating out often, as frequently as three times per week.

Management has also identified a very viable commuting market that frequents the Soulard area, availing themselves of the many attractive restaurants, bars, and bistros. These customers travel there from downtown employment, stadium events, and other entertainment centers such as Union Station, Laclede's Landing, and Kiel Auditorium. Many look forward to a stop in historic Soulard. Butcher Hollow Bar BQ will be a welcome addition to this ambiance, offering to the area a delectable barbecue fare not currently available.

Many thousands of people also work in an near the Soulard area and often unwind after work at one of the many bistros. Butcher Hollow intends to be part and parcel of this scene, offering superb Bar BQ, frosted steins of beer, along with convenient carry-out. Relaxed patio dining is also planned for use during pleasant weather.

Tom and Helen Carter bring both experience and formal training to the food service field. Tom operated the successful Tom's Cafeteria in the garment district for some eight years. Both he and Helen have a wealth of experience in food service and hospitality management.

Butcher Hollow Bar BQ also has a sound marketing plan directed at our three identified markets. Viable market, good promotion, and an excellent product, backed up by sound and experienced management will go a long way to assuring success of the business venture.

Our anticipated capitalization consists of a budget of $45,000, including $15,000 owner's equity along with $30,000 borrowed capital. Owner's equity derives from joint savings of Mr. and Mrs. Carter.

The operating plan provides for proprietor withdrawals of $1,000 per month for the first 12 months of operation. Mrs. Carter will continue her employment as Assistant Front Desk Manager at the Crest Downtown Hotel.

Careful and conservative projections anticipate a first year net of $12,000 on sales of $113,000. It should be noted that the first year P/L reflects certain initial sales promotional activities that, while burdensome during that period, are expected to yield long-term results.

Our second year projected profit is $30,500 on sales of $146,000 yielding a 38.1% return on investment.

Butcher Hollow Bar BQ, a proprietorship, will be a husband and wife operated business. Both Tom and Helen Carter will bring with them experience in food service and related hospitality fields. The concept of Butcher Hollow Bar BQ is to offer a limited but highly popular menu, aimed at a clearly defined market. It is expected that at least 50% of the business will be carry-out. An outside beer garden facility is also planned for nice weather. Barbecue will, of course, be prominent, but other dishes known to have great appeal in the area will also be featured.

The business will be situated in the Soulard neighborhood. This is a high profile rehabbed community with a high concentration of residential units occupied by young professionals as well as established neighborhood blue-collar workers. The Soulard neighborhood is well known for its social scene consisting of many small bars, restaurants, and bistros. The focal point is Soulard Market, an open-air produce market some 200 years old and a national historic landmark. Many people are attracted to the area for its ambiance, and its establishments cater not only to neighborhood people but to customers commuting to suburbia from downtown employment and stadium events.

Mr. and Mrs. Carter's start-up capital consists of $15,000 derived from savings. Mrs. Carter will continue her present employment as assistant front desk manager at the Crest Downtown Hotel, and will work weekends at Butcher Hollow. Mr. Carter will be employed full-time from start-up and has resigned his job as food and beverage manager of Holiday Inn Southtown.

Butcher Hollow Bar BQ will originally target the leisure and recreational dining market. This will heavily emphasize Friday, Saturday, and Sunday business. For the first 12-month period, it is expected that the business will remain closed on Monday, opening from 4:00 PM to 11:00 PM Tuesday through Thursday, 11:00 AM to 11:00 PM Friday and Saturday, and 11:00 AM to 9:00 PM on Sunday. In addition to the local trade, these hours allow us to capture the afterwork commuter as well as those stopping off after the ballgame for barbecue and a beer.

Fridays present a special market. In addition to the normal influx of Friday evening business, Butcher Hollow will be catering to the known habit of working people to treat themselves special for lunch on Friday. Featured dishes will be the soon-to-be-famous Butcher Hollow Bar BQ or the special Jack salmon and spaghetti platter available only on Friday. The latter is known to be very popular for lunch or dinner in South St. Louis, and along with the Butcher Hollow special sauces, can attract a great deal of business.

Saturdays and Sundays, both afternoons and evenings, present great opportunities for the leisure dining trade, and our menu and carry-out promotions will be designed to maximize these opportunities.

The Soulard area also is known as a great business lunch community. While barbecue is not a good lead item for business lunch, other speciality items can be added at a future time when the lunch trade is targeted. Initially, we do not intend to compete for lunch business except on Friday when most Soulard restaurants are hopelessly overloaded. A special luncheon menu is presently being refined for possible inclusion with an expansion of hours during our second year.

Tom Carter will head the husband and wife team of Tom and Helen Carter, as he devotes full-time to the planning, installation, and start-up of Butcher Hollow Bar BQ. Tom, 43, holds an Associate Degree in Food Service Management from Forest Park Junior College. Upon graduation, he entered his chosen field as assistant chef at Bevo Mill under the original management of Chef Ulrich. He stayed at Bevo for 8 years, gaining experience in all phases of experience in food preparation and kitchen management. When Bevo Mill closed in 1975,

Mr. Carter, using a small inheritance coupled with an SBA loan, acquired an existing cafeteria in the St. Louis garment district. He renamed the operation Tom's Cafeteria and operated it for 8 years until 1983. Tom's Cafeteria specialized in breakfast and lunch for workers in the garment and shoe trade along Washington Avenue just west of downtown St. Louis. Mr. Carter was hands-on in all phases of the business management. This business prospered and he was able to retire the SBA loan in the allotted five-year period. However, due to a decline in the garment and shoe business in the immediate area, the building in which Tom's Cafeteria was located closed down, and Tom lost his lease. Because of the decline in the area, he did not seek to relocate but obtained employment as assistant food and beverage manager at the Holiday Inn Southtown. The close-down of Tom's Cafeteria was orderly and all debt was retired as agreed.

After eighteen months at Holiday Inn Southtown, Tom was promoted to manager of food and beverage, a position he held until he recently resigned to devote full-time to Butcher Hollow Bar BQ.

Helen Carter, 38, also has extensive experience in food service and hospitality fields. As a young person, she started working in fast-food operations, and while attending the University of Denver, School of Hotel and Restaurant Management, she worked in a variety of food and beverage service capacities, usually as waitress or hostess, and on one occasion for about a year in food preparation. Circumstances did not permit her to obtain her degree, and she returned to St. Louis. She obtained employment at the Crest Downtown Hotel and is presently assistant front desk manager.

Tom and Helen Carter have been married for 14 years. Tom is working full-time to start up Butcher Hollow Bar BQ. Helen is assisting in her off-duty hours and will work Friday, Saturday, and Sunday upon opening. This will not conflict with her present employment, and she intends to continue on at Crest Downtown until Butcher Hollow Bar BQ has reached the point of requiring and being able to support her full-time services.

PRODUCT DESCRIPTION

The Menu

Barbecue is, of course, the lead item at Butcher Hollow Bar BQ. The Butcher Hollow Bar BQ comes as the result of many years of experimenting and refining different recipes and techniques. The sauce is a special recipe that has been lovingly developed by the proprietors and tested hundreds of times on willing guests, both at home and at food establishments where the Carters have presided. The technique itself is also special, calling for extra effort, but yielding terrific results. The Butcher Hollow Bar BQ people know how to put out production volume without losing any of the delightful, delectable texture and tastes that will bring the customers back time and again.

Our plan calls for opening with a fairly limited menu, featuring barbecue ribs, barbecue pork steaks and barbecue chicken halves. Also offered will be Jack Salmon (Whiting) with spaghetti. These will be available as plates, which will include entree and two side dishes, or as sandwiches. The Jack Salmon will be offered with our delicious barbecue sauce on the side.

Another speciality of wide appeal will be our meatball and spaghetti platter, served with a knockout garlic cheese bread. All of our sauces are homemade—the spaghetti sauce a private Old World recipe, and the meat balls, our own sensational mix of meat and spices.

Another offering will be a side dish of golden parmesan potatoes, a delicious accompaniment to barbecue that has received many raves. Some people like to make a meal of them by themselves. We also have special recipes for potato salad and slaw. Our intent is to bring as much effort and expertise to our side dishes and sauces as we do our entrees. This will make the food at Butcher Hollow Bar BQ extra special and keep the customers coming back for more. Nothing mundane or ordinary will be served.

We also have a nice array of entrees that we are holding in reserve, or that we may feature as weekly specials, one at a time. These recipes come from a special private collection that have been refined over many years by the Carters.

The Setting

Butcher Hollow Bar BQ will not be served in an ostentatious setting. The Soulard neighborhood lends itself to nice, storefront cafes, and in this type of setting, barbecue can be best enjoyed. Checkered tablecloths and pitchers of beer set the scene for good times, good food, and enjoyable surroundings. A bricked patio with picnic tables and yellow lights permit a beer garden annex in pleasant weather and, of course, carry-out customers are made especially welcome in a comfortable alcove. We expect a significant part of our business to be carry-out because barbecue is traditionally eaten at home.

Soft drinks, wine coolers, and draft beer are the beverages of choice at Butcher Hollow. We anticipate eight tables for four, four tables for two, four booths accommodating four to six, and two tables for six, for total seating of eighty-four.

The name Butcher Hollow is intended to conjure up a relaxed, rustic mood, nothing fancy, and not associated with a specific theme. Our decor will generally be mixed and matched chairs and furnishings with a goodly amount of Americana thrown in. Much of this will be derived from the near-antique collectables that the Carters have been accumulating over the years in anticipation of this type of establishment.

MARKET ANALYSIS— CUSTOMERS

Butcher Hollow Bar BQ has identified four distinct target markets which will comprise our customers. They consist of:

1. Primary residential population of the Soulard and Lafayette Square neighborhoods.

2. Secondary residential population of the Near South Side and South St. Louis proper sections.

3. Commuting population that works downtown and travels through Soulard, often stopping for a refreshment on the way home. Accesses to highways 40, 44, and 55 are found in our immediate area and lend themselves for easy access. Additionally, spin-off crowds from stadium events and Kiel Auditorium also are markets that will avail themselves of post game or post concert recreational dining or carry-out. The planned new arena and downtown football stadium complex can only add to the customer mix. The near proximity of Union Station and Laclede's Landing also provide traffic through our area, which we intend to entice with our delectable Butcher Hollow Bar BQ.

4. Another market is the working population of the Near Southside, which offer great opportunities for Friday lunch and after-work gatherings. Anheuser-Busch, Monsanto Chemical, and Ralston Purina are three of many large employers having upscale workers with disposable income for leisure activities.

Market Survey

To obtain consumer feedback for our idea, a telemarketing survey was instituted in the fall of 1995 for the purpose of polling the primary and secondary residential population to learn their reaction to an eat-in and carry-out barbecue-style restaurant. Twelve hundred complete conversations were conducted by telephone in the zip codes of 63104, 63118, 63110, and

63116. Among the key questions asked were: If there were a good barbecue restaurant in the Soulard neighborhood, would you patronize it either for eat-in or carry-out? Sixty-six percent responded affirmatively, and their answers were further tabulated as follows:

22% once a month or more frequently
56% every couple of months
12% a couple times per year
10% about once a year

About 75% indicated a preference for carry-out.

Profile of Customer Base

The demographics of the four zip codes comprising the residential population of our primary geographic target market reveal characteristics very supportive of a viable customer base for Butcher Hollow Bar BQ. Our primary area consists of some 52,500 households, with a median adult age of 42 years. Approximately 22% have incomes of over $50,000, with 36% having income of $30,000 to $49,000. Statistics published in the July 1995 edition of *Eating Out*, a leading trade journal, reveal that families with median incomes of over $30,000 and median ages over 40 eat out two to three time per week, among the highest in any category.

With approximately 50% of our primary residential target market falling within this profile, and coupled with the response to our in-house survey revealing 66% of those surveyed indicating a predisposition to patronize a good barbecue-style eat-in or carry-out restaurant, we feel that we have identified a location that is most amenable to the product that we will be providing.

Additionally, 25% of our business is expected to come from persons commuting from downtown employment, shopping, cultural and sports activities. While en route their residences in South County and West County, many people often stop in Soulard and the adjoining neighborhood of Lafayette Square to partake of the local amenities.

Another 25% is expected to come from people employed in the immediate area but living elsewhere. Some of the larger employers are:

Anheuser Busch	26,000
Ralston Purina	4,400
Pet	4,200
U.S. Government, Mapping Center	950
Monsanto	925
Nooter Boiler Makers	450
Crane	450
Welsh Baby Carriage	350

Many workers from these firms are known to frequent the establishments of Soulard after working hours, with Fridays being a high point in the week.

COMPETITION

St. Louis is known as one of the major barbecue consuming areas of the country. Indeed, we lead the nation in the per capita consumption of prepackaged barbecue sauce sold at the retail level. Barbecue restaurants have traditionally been very popular in St. Louis as well. Two of the most popular are situated in the Affton area, just outside of what we consider our secondary market.

One of these restaurants, Phil's Bar BQ, is a second-generation establishment, tracing its roots back to North St. Louis with some fifty years of continuous operation. Roscoe McCrary reigns supreme in North St. Louis, a distinct market in itself, with Mr. McCrary's Bar BQ being both well known and highly sought by consumers from all over the metro region. McCrary's Bar BQ is often preferred fare in the post game St. Louis Cardinals clubhouse and is widely regarded as being among the best.

Suburban St. Louis County has become home for several very popular barbecue restaurants. Charlotte's Rib attracts a large following in the Ballwin/Manchester area and Damons for Ribs, a national chain, has recently opened a second location to complement its Crestwood restaurant.

KC Masterpiece Bar BQ has expanded its sphere of influence all the way from Kansas City to our own West County suburbs. Reports are that the initial store is doing excellent business with customers waiting on Friday and Saturday evenings.

Without a doubt, barbecue is popular in St. Louis. But, until the arrival of Butcher Hollow Bar BQ, South St. Louis and the Near South Side have had no convenient purveyor.

The closest place is a church-sponsored barbecue carry-out operation of long standing in the six hundred block of South Broadway that is open 24 hours a day, Friday, Saturday, and Sunday only, and does a land-office business, although offering no amenities.

During the annual Mardi Gras Festival and the St. Patrick Day celebrations, many of the restaurants and bars of Soulard erect temporary barbecue pits to cater to the heavy foot traffic. It is easy to observe that these are among the most popular stops with the celebrants. Often people congregate 3 and 4 deep around the stands, clamoring for service, as the delectable smoke and fragrance waft into the surrounding air. Butcher Hollow Bar BQ feels there is a demonstrated need for a good barbecue eat-in or carry-out restaurant in Soulard, and we intend to fill that need.

RISKS

Opening a new food establishment is often seen as one of the more risky business ventures because of the known high rate of failure of new restaurants. The proprietors of Butcher Hollow Bar BQ feel that we have effectively minimized these risks by careful market research and by bringing considerable food service management and entrepreneurial experience to the project.

Tom and Helen Carter are well-trained both by formal education and by many years of experience in restaurant service and management. Additionally, Mr. Carter was owner-operator of a successful restaurant for eight years in St. Louis during which he retired a $25,000 SBA loan in a timely fashion.

As this Business Plan will reflect, careful planning and preparation have gone into the concept and the execution of this plan. Positive consumer reaction, favorable demographics, and strategic location combine to assure Butcher Hollow Bar BQ a viable market.

Another risk that is effectively minimized is that of surviving what is sometimes known as the starvation period for many start-up businesses; i.e., the first six months to a year while customers become aware of your establishment. While the Business Plan calls for a proprietor's draw of $1,000 per month, this is of course contingent upon conditions. With Mrs. Carter maintaining her present position of employment and both she and Mr. Carter working at Butcher Hollow, the new business can operate with a minimum of payroll load, thus minimizing a significant cost factor for all new businesses. As she continues working at the Crest Downtown Hotel, the household living expenses can be met by her salary.

Traditional casualty risks will be covered by Business Owners' insurance, ample to cover all assets and with a $500,000 public and product liability umbrella.

MARKETING STRATEGY— ADVERTISING, PROMOTION & PUBLIC RELATIONS

Butcher Hollow Bar BQ has a three-pronged marketing strategy aimed at our three identified target markets.

As we expect 50% of our business to come from the residential population of our primary and secondary areas, we will be promoting Introductory Specials through ads in two heavily circulated community newspapers, the *South St. Louis Journal* and the *Riverfront Times*. The *Journal* will feature primarily family carry-out oriented ads, with coupons worth $1 off or a free 24 oz. soft drink, or similar promotions. The *Riverfront Times*, which has saturation distribution throughout the area, primarily in food and beverage establishments, is widely read by the young, upwardly mobile professional person, a consumer category recognized for their prominent discretionary and leisure spending habits.

The commuting traffic will be targeted with a billboard advertisement strategically positioned to capture the attention of southbound vehicles leaving downtown employment, stadium, and entertainment events. The cost of this advertisement is budgeted for $9,000 for the first 6 months and is intended to prime the pump and attract first-time customers. It is an investment in the future and is not expected to be immediately cost effective, but will pay-off for the long haul as we attract and keep customers.

Our third target group is the local employee population who we intend to attract for Friday lunch and after-work eat-in or carry-out business. For the lunch trade, we intend to initiate mailings to the various firms throughout the area.

The mailings will include menus and our fax number to make use of the proliferation of office fax machines to place lunch orders. For the larger companies, we will obtain lists of departments to facilitate these mailings reaching the workers that want to order. We also will make use of occasional Comp Cards, which are complimentary lunches when used with an order exceeding a set dollar amount. With each carry-out lunch, we will include a flyer touting Butcher Hollow Bar BQ as a great stop after work for barbecue and beer or for our splendid carry-out offerings.

The Carters intend to be members and participants in the Soulard Merchants Association, which is a group of about fifty local businesses, most of whom are in food and beverage service. The area is promoted twice each year, once with a giant Mardi Gras parade and festival and then at St. Patrick's Day. Butcher Hollow Bar BQ intends to maintain a high profile during both festivities and become a well established and popular addition to the Soulard scene.

PRICE & PROFITABILITY

The price formula to be employed at Butcher Hollow Bar BQ will be based on a food cost of 30% for most food items with a 25% food cost for soft drinks and 50% for beer and wine coolers. Retail prices are across the board, carry-out or eat-in, with the paper cost of carry-out being offset by the savings in service inherent to take-out food.

The pinnacle attraction at Butcher Hollow BQ is the full slab rib platter, priced at $13.00 and including two side dishes and bread. Many people will order half slabs at $7.50 per plate or $5.50 per sandwich. Our other entrees, Half Chickens, Pork Steaks, and Jack Salmon are priced at $7.50 per platter and $5.50 per sandwich accordingly. Meatballs and spaghetti with garlic cheese bread will be $7.50.

Both our barbecue sauce and our spaghetti sauce are special recipes and are very important to the overall delectability of the finished product. Extra sauces will be available in individual portions or by the quart, priced with a 50% food cost.

We expect our aggregate food and beverage cost to average about 44% and we will monitor this figure closely. We will be utilizing modern computer data entry on all of our food purchases. Recipes are preprogrammed to extrapolate the updated finished cost per portion, thereby enabling management to keep a constant check on food cost percentages, adjusting pricing as needs dictate.

As our financial forecast will indicate, we anticipate first-year sales of $113,000 with net operating profits of $12,300. We would find this acceptable in view of the anticipated "starvation period" that accompanies all new openings and the one-time expenditures of advertising and promotion that is booked in for the first six months. Our monthly break-even point is $6,700, a very reachable $1,500 per week.

Profits for the second year are expected to reach $30,500.

Break-Even Evaluation	
Computed on Gross Sales	
Percent Cost of Goods Sold	33%
Percent Gross Profit	67%
Monthly Overhead	$4,491
Monthly Gross Sales to reach break-even	$6,703

[*For detailed derivation of these calculations, refer to Twelve Month Proforma, Financial Projections.]

In order to open Butcher Hollow Bar BQ, management has determined that capitalization of $45,000 will be required. These funds will be allocated as follows:

SUMMARY & USE OF FUNDING

Equipment & Fixtures	$15,000
Installation and make ready	6,000
Advertising & Promotion	12,000
Deposits and initial start-up costs	5,000
Contingency	2,000
Operating Reserve	5,000
Total	**$45,000**

Equipment & Fixtures are listed in the schedule on the following page. Our Business Plan anticipates that capitalization will be funded as follows:

Proprietors' Equity	$15,000
Borrowed Capital	$30,000
Total	**$45,000**

The proprietors equity is derived from savings. It is projected that borrowed capital would be drawn over a period of 60 days preceding Grand Opening, through the first 180 days of operations. Grand opening is targeted for May 1, 2000.

FINANCIAL PROJECTIONS

EQUIPMENT SCHEDULE

	Brand	Model	Rating	Capacity/ New/Used	Cost
Gas broiler w/hood & fire suppressor	Star	LBLB4400	6'x3'	Used	$1,200
Deep-fat fryer	Star	LB300	5 Gal	Used	500
Cooler for meat	Hussman	Economy	1 HP	Used	1,000
Regular refrigerator	GE	Double	1 HP	Used	600
Preparation table	Servco	Door		Used	200
Oven (holding), surface range	Star	6 burner double ovn		Used	600
Commercial microwave	Micron	Z200	5 HP	Used	600
Ice machine	Airman	AS1500	150#	New	1,800
Pot sink	Servco	Double cavity		Used	500
Cash register	Kamatsui	JM5		Used	300
Order wheel				Used	150
Tables, chairs, and booths				Used	2000
Freezer	Westinghouse	12 cu ft		Used	400
Slicer, meat grinder	Hobart	K40/GR50	1 HP	Used	300
Food processor	Hobart	GH55		Used	450
Dishwasher	Hobart	J500		Used	500
Computer	Macintosh	G3		Used	1,800
Total equipment costs					**$14,700**

This page left intentionally blank to accommodate tabular matter following.

TWELVE-MONTH PROFORMA
CHART 1

	Month One	Month Two	Month Three	Month Four	Month Five	Month Six	Month Seven	Month Eight	Month Nine	Month Ten
Sales										
Sale of Food & Beverage	6,500	6,923	7,372	7,852	8,362	8,906	9,351	9,818	10,309	10,825
Other Sales	300	300	300	300	300	300	300	300	300	300
Total Sales	**6,800**	**7,223**	**7,673**	**8,152**	**8,662**	**9,206**	**9,651**	**10,118**	**10,609**	**11,125**
Cost of Sales	**2,244**	**2,383**	**2,532**	**2,690**	**2,858**	**3,038**	**3,185**	**3,339**	**3,601**	**3,671**
Gross Profit	**4,556**	**4,839**	**5,141**	**5,462**	**5,804**	**6,168**	**6,466**	**6,779**	**7,108**	**7,454**
Operating Expenses										
Sales & Marketing										
Advertising	1,000	1,000	1,000	1,000	1,000	1,000	1,000	1,000	1,000	1,000
Commissions	0	0	0	0	0	0	0	0	0	0
Entertainment	0	0	0	0	0	0	0	0	0	0
Literature	0	0	0	0	0	0	0	0	0	0
Sales Promotion	100	100	100	100	100	100	100	100	100	100
Trade Shows	0	0	0	0	0	0	0	0	0	0
Travel	0	0	0	0	0	0	0	0	0	0
Salaries (Sales Personnel)	0	0	0	0	0	0	0	0	0	0
PR Taxes & Costs, Sales	0	0	0	0	0	0	0	0	0	0
Total Selling Cost	**1,100**	**1,100**	**1,100**	**1,100**	**1,100**	**1,100**	**1,100**	**1,100**	**1,100**	**1,100**

Month Eleven	Month Twelve	Year One	Per cent
11,366	11,934	109,518	97%
300	300	3,600	3%
11,666	**12,234**	**113,118**	
3,850	**4,037**	**37,329**	**33%**
7,816	**8,397**	**75,789**	**67%**
1,000	1,000	12,000	
0	0	0	
0	0	0	
0	0	0	
100	100	1,200	
0	0	0	
0	0	0	
0	0	0	
0	0	0	
1,100	**1,100**	**13,200**	**12%**

TWELVE-MONTH PROFORMA
CHART II

General & Administrative	Month One	Month Two	Month Three	Month Four	Month Five	Month Six	Month Seven	Month Eight	Month Nine	Month Ten
Accounting	50	50	50	50	50	50	50	50	50	50
Amorization	0	0	0	0	0	0	0	0	0	0
Bad Debts	0	0	0	0	0	0	0	0	0	0
Depreciation	202	202	202	202	202	202	202	202	202	202
Insurance	100	100	100	100	100	100	100	100	100	100
Legal Fees	50	50	50	50	50	50	50	50	50	50
Licenses & Permits	100	100	100	100	100	100	100	100	100	100
Salaries & Wages	1,530	1,602	1,679	1,760	1,847	1,939	2,036	2,137	2,243	2,354
PR Taxes & PR Costs	184	192	201	211	222	233	244	256	269	283
Taxes (non-income taxes)	50	50	50	50	50	50	50	50	50	50
Office Expense	50	50	50	50	50	50	50	50	50	50
Rent	600	600	600	600	600	600	600	600	600	600
Telephone	75	75	75	75	75	75	75	75	75	75
Utilities	400	404	408	412	416	420	425	429	433	437
Total General & Administrative Cost	**3,391**	**3,476**	**3,566**	**3,661**	**3,762**	**3,870**	**3,982**	**4,099**	**4,223**	**4,352**
Net Income Before Taxes and Interest	**65**	**263**	**475**	**700**	**941**	**1,198**	**1,384**	**1,580**	**1,786**	**2,002**
Interest	250	247	244	240	237	234	230	227	224	220
Net Income	**-185**	**16**	**231**	**460**	**704**	**964**	**1,154**	**1,353**	**1,562**	**1,782**

Month Eleven	Month Twelve	Year One	Per cent
50	50	600	
0	0	0	
0	0	0	
202	202	2,429	
100	100	1,200	
50	50	600	
100	100	1,200	
2,471	2,593	24,191	
297	311	2,903	
50	50	600	
50	50	600	
600	600	7,200	
75	75	900	
442	446	5,073	
4,487	**4,628**	**47,496**	**42%**
2,230	**2,469**	**15,093**	**13.3%**
217	213	2,781	2.5%
2,013	**2,256**	**12,312**	**10.9%**

THREE-YEAR PROJECTED INCOME STATEMENT

Sales	Year 1		Year 2		Year 3	
Sale of Food & Beverage	109,518		142,373		170,848	
Other Sales	3,600		3,960		4,356	
Total Sales	113,118		146,333		175,204	
Cost-of-Goods-Sold	37,329	33%	48,290	33%	57,817	33%
Gross Profit	75,789		98,043		117,387	
Selling Expense	13,200	12%	4,926	3%	5,197	3%
General & Administrative	47,496	42%	50,108	34%	52,864	30%
Net Income Before Taxes & Interest	15,093	13%	43,009	29%	59,325	30%
Interest	2,781	2.5%	2,271	1.6%	1,707	34%
Income Taxes	3,078		10,184		14,405	1.0%
Net Income or Loss	9,234	8%	30,553	21%	43,214	25%

This page left intentionally blank to accommodate tabular matter following.

CASH FLOW PROJECTION

	Month One	Month Two	Month Three	Month Four	Month Five	Month Six	Month Seven	Month Eight	Month Nine	Month Ten
Beginning Cash Balance	15,000	9,354	6,961	6,833	6,985	7,435	8,200	9,320	10,692	12,324
Cash Receipts from Sales	4,100	8,301	8,836	9,404	10,005	10,643	11,221	11,736	12,271	12,827
Total Cash Available	19,100	17,655	15,798	16,237	16,991	18,078	19,421	21,056	22,962	25,151
Cash Disbursements:										
Accounts Payable, merchandise	0	3,608	3,841	4,088	4,350	4,628	4,923	5,149	5,384	5,629
Selling costs	312	322	333	344	355	367	380	393	407	422
General & Administrative	1,215	1,222	1,230	1,238	1,246	1,256	1,266	1,277	1,289	1,302
Salaries	1,400	1,400	1,400	1,400	1,400	1,400	1,400	1,400	1,400	1,400
Total Cash Disbursements	2,917	6,552	6,803	7,070	7,352	7,651	7,968	8,219	8,481	8,753
Net Cash from Operations	16,173	11,103	8,994	9,167	9,639	10,427	11,453	12,837	14,482	16,398
Proceeds of Loans										
National Bnk, Fixtures & Equip	15,000	0	0	0	0	0	0	0	0	0
National Bnk, Operating Line	0	0	0	0	0	0	0	0	0	0
Capital Infusion										
Additional Paid in Capital	0	0	0	0	0	0	0	0	0	0
Other Disbursements										
Proprietor's Draw	1,500	1,500	1,500	1,500	1,500	1,500	1,500	1,500	1,500	1,500
Debt Service	319	319	319	319	319	319	319	319	319	319
Capital Disbursements										
Furniture & Fixtures	5,000	0	0	0	0	0	0	0	0	0
Equipment	10,000	0	0	0	0	0	0	0	0	0
Inventory Purchases	5,000	323	343	363	385	408	314	326	339	353
Prepaid Expense/Deposits	0	2,000	0	0	0	0	0	0	0	0
Net Cash Balance	9,354	6,961	6,833	6,985	7,435	8,200	9,320	10,692	12,324	14,226

Month Eleven	Month Twelve
14,226	16,409
13,406	14,008
27,632	30,417
5,884	6,149
438	391
1,316	1,331
1,400	1,400
9,037	9,271
18,595	21,146
0	0
0	0
0	0
1,500	1,500
319	319
0	0
0	0
367	382
0	0
16,409	18,946

BALANCE SHEET

Assets	Current	Year 1	Year 2	Year 3
Current Assets				
Cash and Equivalents	10,000	36,946	77,211	124,825
Receivables from Sales	0	7,008	8,760	10,074
Other Receivables	0	0	0	0
Inventory	5,000	8,903	8,651	9,942
Prepaid Expense/Deposits	0	2,000	2,000	2,000
Total Current Assets	**15,000**	**54,857**	**96,623**	**146,841**
Fixed Assets:				
Equipment & Machinery	15,000	15,000	15,000	15,000
Less accumulated depreciation	0	2,429	4,857	7,286
Net Fixed Assets	**15,000**	**12,571**	**10,143**	**7,714**
TOTAL ASSETS	**30,000**	**67,428**	**106,766**	**154,556**
LIABILITIES				
Current Liabilities				
Trade Payables	0	6,424	6,243	7,174
Income Tax Payable	0	8,360	12,578	15,602
Short Term Notes	0	0	0	0
Total Current Liabilities	**0**	**14,784**	**18,821**	**22,776**
Long term Liabilities				
Notes Payable, Bank	15,000	12,566	10,131	7,160
Notes Payable, Others	0	0	0	0
Other Liabilities	0	0	0	0
Total Long Term Liabilities	**15,000**	**12,566**	**10,131**	**7,160**
TOTAL LIABILITIES	**15,000**	**27,349**	**28,952**	**29,936**
PROPRIETOR'S ACCOUNT				
Owner's Equity	15,000	15,000	15,000	15,000
Less Withdrawals	0	25,079	62,813	109,619
TOTAL NET WORTH	**15,000**	**40,079**	**33,813**	**124,619**
TOTAL NET WORTH and LIABILITIES	**30,000**	**67,428**	**106,766**	**154,556**
Current Ratio		**3.7**	**5.1**	**6.4**
Quick Ratio		**3.1**	**4.7**	**6**
Debt to Equity Ratio		**0.7**	**0.4**	**0.2**
Return on Investment		**1.7**	**2.5**	**3.1**

Roller Rink

BUSINESS PLAN

SANTIAGO ROLLER RINK

P.O. Box 1800
Boise, Idaho 83702

The purpose of this roller rink is to provide Boise with an entertainment facility especially for the growing Hispanic community. It will offer a family atmosphere and a high quality sound system, as well as offering special party rates. There is little competition for such an establishment and market research indicates that this business would succeed. This plan was provided by Ameriwest Business Consultants, Inc.

- EXECUTIVE SUMMARY

- FINANCIAL SUMMARY

- BUSINESS DESCRIPTION

- MARKET ANALYSIS

- FINANCIAL PLANS

The purpose of Santiago Roller Rink is to provide the area with a roller rink which caters primarily to the growing Latin-American community. The atmosphere will be friendly and open. The club will be maintained to the utmost degree of cleanliness and maintenance, unlike similar operations in the area. The club will display a new attitude toward the Spanish population. It will treat them like first-class citizens and try to make them feel like they are at home. On the premises will be pool tables, video games, and dart boards. We will carry newspapers from 22 Hispanic countries. We will also offer for sale pride items from various Hispanic countries around the world. The facility will have a first-rate sound and lighting system. The services will be offered at a competitive price and pricing will be reviewed periodically. We plan to become the premier Spanish roller rink in the area within two years. We will offer the best entertainment, atmosphere, cultural awareness, and service in southern Idaho.

The facility will normally be closed Monday. Proposed hours are Tuesday, Wednesday, and Thursday 2:00 P.M. through 2:00 A.M. On Friday and Saturday the hours will be 12:00 P.M. through 2:00 A.M. On Sunday the hours will be 4:00 P.M. through 2:00 A.M. The premises will be open for a total of 74 hours per week.

CURRENT POSITION AND FUTURE OUTLOOK

The business is in a start-up mode. Plans call for starting operation by the spring of 2000. Operations will be conducted in a location to be determined which will best suit the goals we are trying to achieve as listed above. During the first full year of operation we plan to serve an average of 4,467 customers per month. The second year this will increase to 5,788 per month. Years three through five will show gradual increases to 6,150 per month which we consider to be our capacity. To attain these goals we will use a combination of media advertising, flyers, direct mail, and word-of mouth. Franchising the concept is a possibility for the future.

MANAGEMENT AND OWNERSHIP

The company will be set up as a corporation with John Quigley and his wife, Jane, as the major shareholders and directors. John Quigley will serve as president and manager. He will provide the leadership to run this company. He has over 24 years experience as owner and operator of various retail operations and dealing with the public. Initially, up to thirteen other employees will be needed. These employees will be involved in security and serving and will be a combination of part-time and full-time. When volume picks up, additional part-time or full-time employees will be hired as the workload requires. Ameriwest Business Consultants, Inc. will provide help in additional areas such as setting up the books, logo design, and general business advising when necessary and to supplement the Quigleys' overall business knowledge. The services of an accountant and an attorney will be retained along with those of a qualified insurance agent.

UNIQUENESS AND DIFFERENTIATION OF THE SERVICE

Santiago Roller Rink will be the largest roller rink which caters to the Hispanic community. It will have the largest dance floor. It will offer the atmosphere that until now could only be found in a Hispanic country.

The idea of this company is to provide customers with a semi-formal, social setting and entertainment that does not exist in this part of the state. We will provide customers with high tech lights and sound, video games, and a full line of accessories. In addition we will cater to private parties and special groups such as schools, birthday parties, and church groups.

The growth potential is virtually unlimited for the greater Boise area. The Hispanic population is growing at an accelerated rate. Currently over 12% of the population in Boise is Hispanic. They will be very receptive to a concept such as this that can offer them atmosphere, cleanliness, and security at a competitive price.

It is rare in today's business world to find a true market void. That is exactly what Santiago Roller Rink has done. It is combining the latest in technology with an unfilled need and promises to deliver a high quality new product at a competitive price. Our proposed facility will have little true competition in southern Idaho.

FUNDS REQUIRED AND USAGE

The initial start-up expenses will be approximately $135,000. The inventory, equipment, furniture, fixtures, and leasehold improvements will cost approximately $106,850. Investors and/or a bank loan must be secured in the amount of $110,000 at 14.0% amortized over ten years. John Quigley and the initial investors will furnish approximately $25,000 which is 18.5% of the total. The intent is to fully repay the loan as soon as possible. After all expenses of start-up, $28,150 will remain in a new business checking account and will provide the balance of the initial working capital.

FINANCIAL SUMMARY

(MOST LIKELY CASE)	Projected Year 1	Projected Year 2	Projected Year 3	Projected Year 4	Projected Year 5
Total Revenue	759,780	984,454	1,230,567	1,415,152	1,556,667
Cost of Goods Sold	268,000	347,250	434,063	499172	549,089
Operating Income	491,780	637,204	796,505	915,980	1,007,578
Selling, General, Admin, Exp	465,290	530,506	655,112	748,194	819,147
Income Before Taxes	26,490	106,698	141,393	167,786	188,431
Income Taxes	5,298	29,875	42,418	53,692	64,067
NET INCOME	**21,192**	**76,823**	**98,975**	**114,095**	**124,364**
Dividends	3179	11,523	14,846	17,114	18,655
(OPTIMISTIC CASE)					
Total Revenue	873,747	1,132,122	1415152	1,627,425	1,790,168
Cost of Goods Sold	308,200	399,338	499172	574,048	631,452
Operating Income	565,547	732,784	915980	1,053,377	1,158,715
Selling, General, Admin, Exp	535,083	610,082	753379	860,423	942,020
Income Before Taxes	30,464	122,703	162602	192,954	216,696
Income Taxes	6,093	34,357	48781	61,745	73,677
NET INCOME	**24,371**	**88,346**	**113,821**	**131,209**	**143,019**
Dividends	3,656	13,252	17,073	19,681	21,453
(PESSIMISTIC CASE)					
Total Revenue	645,813	836,786	1,045,982	1,202,879	1,323,167
Cost of Goods Sold	227,800	295,163	368,953	424,296	466,726
Operating Income	418,013	541,623	677,029	778,583	856,442
Selling, General, Admin, Exp	395,496	450,930	556,845	635,965	696,275
Income Before Taxes	22,517	90,693	120,184	142,618	160,166
Income Taxes	4,503	25,394	36,055	45,638	54,457
NET INCOME	**18,013**	**65,299**	**84,129**	**96,980**	**105,710**
Dividends	2,702	9,795	12,619	14,547	15,856

Notes:

1. The most likely case assumes 4,467 customers per month the first year with each spending an average of $14.18 per visit. The second year assumes that the number of customers will rise to 5,788 per month and that each will spend $14.18 per visit.
2. The optimistic case assumes revenues and expenses will increase 15% over the most likely case. The pessimistic case assumes revenues and expenses will decrease 15% below the most likely case.
3. Cost of goods sold will equal 40% of drink income.

OBJECTIVES AND GOALS

1. To provide a high quality service so that customers will perceive great value and show them how to interact with other members of the Hispanic community in a safe and clean environment.

2. Service an average of 4,467 customers per month during the first full year of business and 5,788 customers per month the second year. The ultimate goal is to reach 6,150 customers per month by the third year.

3. To repay the entire loan amount by the end of the third year and to provide the shareholders with a stable and sufficient income after that.

4. To become the premier Hispanic roller rink in Boise within the next two years.

5. Santiago Roller Rink plans to closely monitor changing technology to be certain that the company is using the latest and most cost effective equipment and that it keeps up with current trends in the marketplace.

6. When economically feasible we plan to open one or more locations and/or consider franchising our service.

When growth has stabilized we plan to add extra services for customer convenience such as a large screen television, enhanced game rooms, and food services. In addition to the above goals we will survey our customers and make changes in our programs and add services to meet their changing needs in the marketplace.

STRATEGIES FOR ACHIEVING GOALS

To obtain the first two sets of goals we will try to maximize sales with an extensive campaign to promote our service. We will utilize brochures, media advertising, pamphlets, direct customer contact, use of coupons, referrals, and a variety of other advertising and marketing tools to reach the customer base of Southern Idaho. We expect to flood the market with advertising until consumers become aware of us and more comfortable with our company. As we grow, word-of-mouth referrals will bring in increasing numbers of customers and we will reduce our reliance on advertising.

The dominant driving force behind our company will be profit and income.

To become the premier Hispanic roller rink in Southern Idaho, we will offer outstanding quality, cleanliness, long hours of operation, reasonable pricing, and efficient service. We will listen to our customers and conduct surveys.

As we grow and build a reputation for excellent service and cleanliness at a reasonable price, as well as having the best sound and lighting system available in the area, we will promote repeat business. We will offer frequent user discounts. In the future we may consider diversification and enter new market areas.

Santiago will be a full roller rink combined with high-tech sound and lighting systems. We will try to promote an atmosphere that will remind many people of their homeland. This is a relatively new concept for this part of the country. John Quigley will operate the business as a corporation. The principal shareholders will be he and his wife, Jane. Initially, John Quigley will manage the operation with daily input from Jane and the other investors. Our new equipment and enhanced lighting and sound systems will also give us market advantages.

The biggest problem this venture will face will be creating customer awareness of our services. We will use a combination of advertising techniques to increase this awareness. Once a general awareness is present, the industry has a virtually unlimited growth potential.

The future holds the promise for almost unlimited growth and income as the business matures and considers other markets and products. Complementary products such as additional video games, more pool tables, dance lessons, and higher profile entertainment will all be considered in the future in response to customer surveys indicating their wants and needs.

MANAGEMENT AND OWNERSHIP

Robert Brown, Manager, ran Roller City in Center City for three years. He performed all jobs and operation of the skating rink. He will be responsible jointly with the Quigleys for sales, public relations, advertising, office management, personnel, operations, planning, purchasing, equipment, and outside labor. **John Quigley**, President, and **Jack Brown**, Vice President, will share responsibilities in sales, public relations, advertising, office management, banking, operations, planning, insurance, equipment purchases, and labor. They will both provide relief for the manager. John Quigley is currently a master technician with Farnsworth Motors. He has over eight years' experience in automotive repair. He will continue to maintain his job and its separate income at least until the loan has been paid off. Jack Brown has been the owner/operator of an embroidery, gift, and woodworking business for fifteen years. He will also continue in this business until the loan has been paid off. Jack is a 26-year retiree from the U.S. Air Force and that pension is also another source of funds that could be made available to the business if necessary. Jack Brown also owned and operated an Ace Hardware store in St. Petersburg, Florida, for nearly three years. Brown also served as an Army and Air Force Exchange concessionaire for seven years.

The Quigleys will supplement their skills by using outside consultants in areas such as legal work, income tax preparation, insurance, and general business advising.

The business will be set up as a corporation. This form of legal entity was chosen primarily for liability reasons and makes it easier to secure investors. To begin operation, as many as ten full- and part-time employees will be hired to help in ticket sales, floorman, maintenance, snack-bar, DJ, skate rental and repair, and the Pro-Shop. As the business grows, additional part-time or full-time employees may be added to handle the increased workload.

THE SERVICE — AN UNFILLED NEED

Idaho's population growth in Hispanics is the ninth greatest in the country. The past decade has seen this segment of the population grow by more than thirty percent. It is growing 5 1/2 times as fast as the general population.

The few existing roller rinks that cater to the Hispanic population are dark and dingy. They pay little attention to cleanliness, maintenance of premises, and security for their patrons. Santiago Roller Rink and its ownership will embrace the Hispanic community and try to become a focal point for them. We will promote the Hispanic culture whenever possible.

BUSINESS DESCRIPTION

Today, there are over 5,000 roller skating rinks in the United States. Modern lighting and sound systems have made rinks into skating palaces. By adding game rooms, snack shops, and pro-shops they have become complete entertainment centers.

John Quigley and Robert Brown grew up in the area of the proposed rink. They have always been aware of the need for an indoor entertainment facility of any type for the south side of Boise. Their recent study of the demographics and the proven history of roller skating demonstrates that this business should easily be able to succeed in the area chosen.

The timing for such a business is perfect. A significant window of opportunity exists for a company such as the kind we are proposing. This proposed business will be providing the "Right Service at the Right Time."

UNIQUENESS OF THE SERVICE

It is rare in today's world that a true market void exists. Our service will meet the "unfilled need" described above by providing customers with competitively priced roller rink facilities combined with the latest in lighting and sound systems and longer hours. We will be considerably larger than the typical roller rink. We will have the best location of any rink in the city.

Customers will be attracted because our location makes us highly visible and accessible to a huge portion of the marketplace. They will be made to feel welcome and as part of the family.

Some major advantages Santiago Roller Rink will experience over potential competition and conventional roller rinks are:

- Larger and newer facility
- Lower operating expenses
- Best sound and lighting system in the area
- New concept—first in the area to have a separate party room with its own floor
- Location
- Longer hours
- English lessons for those interested
- Dance lessons for patrons wanting to keep up with the latest dance steps
- The cleanest restrooms in the city
- Security personnel who can speak both Spanish and English
- The largest roller rink in the area
- Display of 22 different Hispanic newspapers from around the world
- Display cabinets with pride items for purchase such as flags, hats, scarves, etc.
- Santiago Roller Rink will sponsor Spanish festivals and holidays

MARKET ANALYSIS

MARKET OVERVIEW, SIZE AND SEGMENTS

Currently, the market distribution is shared by three major participants. They are all located on the north side of Boise. This market segment has been relatively stable over the past five years.

The market area we will concentrate on is the area south of Route 100. This includes the towns of Creek, Black, White, Newton, and Blake Air Base. This area has been growing rapidly for the past several years and should continue for the foreseeable future. Once the concept catches on locally, we feel the potential is unlimited. As we grow we will have the financial capacity to carry on an advertising campaign on a regional basis.

The economy is in the midst of a particularly strong growth period. Many new jobs are being added to the local community. Ever increasing numbers of people from Kansas are coming to this location. All of these factors are cause for a much greater interest in roller rinks. All of this activity can only help our attempts to start a roller rink.

Listed below are just some of the reasons that the Boise area is growing and why it is a good time to be starting any kind of new business:

- The local economy is booming and virtually busting at the seams.
- Boise has become a magnet for insurance organizations. More than 65 nationally based insurance organizations are headquartered here. The largest has over 1,200 employees (especially women) and an operating budget of over $85 million.
- The new Hewlett Packard computer plant is setting records for production and is adding new employees monthly.
- Boise has a new airport and a nearby Free Trade Enterprise Zone that should grow and attract even more new businesses.
- Every week, we see articles in the newspapers of Kansas residents and companies relocating here.
- The world-renowned Hyatt Regency Hotel is building a new convention facility.
- IBM and X-Cell Electronics are undergoing large increases in their operations here that should add many hundreds of employees.
- Blake is only 30 minutes away and is another good market for businesses in the area.
- Many experts predict Boise to become the second fastest growing city in the state between now and the year 2000.
- The local economy is now more diversified than it was when troubles occurred in the local economy in the late 1980s and early 1990s.
- The estimated population of Big Sky County in 1992 was 451,000 people. The number of households was 175,000. Currently, this market is growing at an annual rate of 3-5%. Projections see this trend continuing for the balance of this decade.

From the above figures it can readily be seen that the potential market for our services is huge. We feel with our pricing and value we will become a price and industry leader within two years.

CUSTOMER PROFILE

The Roller Skating Association estimates that over 33 million people skate at skating centers each month. They have compiled the following statistics:

- 10% are children ages 1 to 5
- 60% are children ages 6 to 14
- 10% are children ages 15 to 17
- 20% are adults
- Over 55,000 birthday parties are held at skating centers each month
- 61% of all roller skaters are female
- 87% of all skating center are family-owned

Typically, our customers will be middle to upper income. Beyond the local market we could eventually tap into a more regional market. The advantage of our service is that it could appeal to all segments of the community.

The Roller Skating Association estimates that 1.5% of the population within a five-mile radius will use a roller rink on a weekly basis. If you were to apply this rule of thumb to the 246,000 people in our area, we could expect nearly 3,700 customers each week. Throughout this business plan we have taken a very conservative approach to developing our financial projections and have used a rate one-half this level or 1,845 customers weekly.

COMPETITION

The following table summarizes the local competition:

Competitor Name	% of Market	Strengths	Weaknesses
SkateAround 1920 N. Main	45	Good location on north end of town Good local support No competition	Old building Outdated facilities Failure to keep up with recent trends
SkatesAlot 4575 Main	45	Good location on north end of town Good local support No competition	Old building Outdated facilities Failure to keep up with recent trends
First Skating 2903 N. Main	10	Some updated facilities, newer light and sound system	Poor location Bad history

There is no competition in this part of town. Our facility will be more convenient than any other facility for over 75% of the population in Boise. The competition that does exist would not offer the advantages of the separate party room with its own skating floor or the hours open to the public we would offer.

The marketplace is currently shared by three major participants. This market is stable and increasing about 5% per year.

RISK ANALYSIS

We feel we have strengths in product features, management, planning, human resources, quality of service, product mix, options, and reliability because we will have new equipment, pricing, location, and facilities.

We will have low risk exposure in the areas of technology, inflation/interest rates, regulatory environment, management ability, location, facilities, and suppliers.

We perceive medium risk exposure in the local economy, strategy, and vulnerability to substitutes, finance and planning, company policies, sales force, and pricing. We will retain the services of specialists to help in various areas such as marketing, setting up the books, providing management reports and general overall business operation advice.

Since we are new to this type of business we will have a high degree of risk in this area. It will take a little time to gain knowledge in developing the business and create a customer awareness of our company and our concept. To help reduce this risk we will hire experienced consultants.

Marketing Strategies

PRICING AND VALUE

We will offer a series of cost savings options to the customer that uses our facility more frequently. Our intention is to raise the public's awareness of our company. We plan to review our prices and those of any competitor every three months. We will review direct material costs, direct labor costs, and total overhead expenses. We will continually monitor the cost of providing our service to each customer. We will offer discounts to larger groups. We will offer various free or reduced rate programs to get customers acquainted with us.

At this point there is a certain amount of price inelasticity in this service. With the current level of competition we must be careful not to price ourselves out of the market. On the other hand, if we offer additional services on the premises we can open up other opportunities to increase income.

Numerous package deals will be available to customers. We may try to include the following marketing strategies:

- Parents skate free with kids
- Discounts for larger groups
- Frequent skater discounts
- Special party rates
- Coupon offerings

SELLING TACTICS

Our company's marketing strategy will incorporate plans to promote our line of services through several different channels and on different levels of use.

We will try to satisfy the market void in this area for indoor entertainment. We will flood the market with advertising and try to go after our specific targets. We will try to capture their attention, pique their interest, make them feel that they must have our services.

We will offer continuous promotional rates. The results sell themselves. We will offer discounts to frequent skaters. The more a customer uses our services, the cheaper it will become for them.

We will also become a MasterCard and Visa charge card merchant to enable us to more readily charge our customers.

In order to market our facility we shall consider a variety of promotions including:

- Reserve certain hours for unique groups such as children, senior citizens, adults, etc.
- Conduct special theme nights such as buddy skate, Cheap Skate, Family night, adult night, bank night, charity promotion night, game night, contest night
- Cultivate local churches, schools and PTA groups
- Promote birthday parties
- Offer reduced price training sessions
- Early bird specials
- Merchant discounts
- Holiday discounts

ADVERTISING, PROMOTION, AND DISTRIBUTION OF SERVICES

We recognize that the key to success at this time requires extensive promotion.

Advertising goals include all of the following:

- Position the company as the roller skating rink in Southern Idaho
- Increase public awareness of skating and its benefits
- Increase public awareness of our company and establish a professional image
- Maximize efficiency by continually monitoring media effectiveness
- Consider a possible coupon in some of the advertisements
- Take out an ad in the yellow pages beginning in 1997
- Develop a brochure or pamphlet to explain our service and company
- Create a distinctive business card and company letterhead

- Consider using a direct mail approach
- Use a variety of media to saturate the marketplace
- Spend a minimum of $23,000 in advertising the first year and $29,500 the second year

PUBLIC RELATIONS

We will develop a public relations policy that will help increase awareness of our company and product. To achieve these goals we will consider some or all of the following:

- Develop a press release and a company backgrounder as a public relations tool.
- Develop a telephone script to handle customer and advertiser contact.

Develop a survey to be completed by customers to help determine the following:

1. How did they hear about us?
2. What influenced them to use our service?
3. How well did our service satisfy their needs?
4. How efficient was our service?
5. Did they have any problems getting through to us?
6. Did they shop competitors before selecting us?
7. How did they initially perceive our company and product?
8. Where are most of our customers located?
9. Are there suggestions for improving our service or our approach to advertising?
10. What additional services would they like us to offer?
11. Would they recommend us to others?

Join the Hispanic Chamber of Commerce to keep abreast of developments in the Hispanic community and market trends.

FINANCIAL PLANS

ASSUMPTIONS, DEFINITIONS, AND NOTES

Santiago Roller Rink has used the following assumptions in preparing this business plan:

Average number of customers will be 4,470 per month the first year, 5,788 per month the second year and leveling off at 6,150 per month by the third year.

Revenue sources are as follows:

Cover charge income will equal 7.08% of total.
Game and food income will be 2.65% of total.
Customer volume will be greater in warm weather months.
Growth in sales will be 29.6% the second year, 25% the third, 15% the fourth, and 10% the fifth year.
We have assumed a high and low case by adding or subtracting 15% to the most likely case.
Inflation Rates to remain stable at 3-5%.
Robust local economy.
Interest Rates to remain flat and basically unchanged.
Wage Rates to remain flat.
Local unemployment rates to remain low at approximately 4-5%.
Assumes average spending per customer of $14.18 per visit.
Assume a rate of pay of $9.00 per hour for security personnel and $4.50 per hour for bartenders and waitresses.

Payroll taxes and benefits will equal 20% of payroll expenses.

Assumes salaries for officers of 3.5% of sales.

Assumes a loan of $110,000 at 14.0% amortized over ten years and having monthly payments of $1,707.93 per month.

Cost of goods sold will be 40% of rink income.

Maintenance, Repair, and Breakage equals 3% of total income.

Advertising & Marketing (Public Relations) is 3.5 % of income.

Amortization of organization expenses will be over 60 months.

Depreciation will be computed using straight line method over 60 months.

Insurance is at 2% of total income.

Telephone and Utility expense will be 1.25% of total income.

Office supplies expenses are set at 1% of total income.

Contingency and miscellaneous expenses are set at 3% of total income.

Income tax for both state and federal is set at 20% for year one and 28% for year two.

Dividend payout is set at 15% of net income.

START-UP EXPENSES

Category	Amount
Cash and Working Capital	$28,150
Material-Supplies-Inventory	10,000
Furniture and Fixtures (Includes 6 pool tables)	25,500
Equipment including lights and sound system	40,000
Rent Deposits	9,700
License Fees / Permits	1,000
Insurance (First year paid in advance)	1,800
Utilities & Telephone	500
Legal, Professional and Consulting Fees	1,500
Security System & Leasehold Improvements	5,000
Initial Entertainment Budget	6,000
Opening Advertisement & Promotion	3,000
Miscellaneous	2,850
TOTAL	**$135,000**

Items to be purchased include 50 tables and 200 chairs, pool tables, sound and lighting systems, initial inventory, leasehold improvements, and various furniture and fixtures. After all expenses, $28,150 will remain in a checking account as working capital.

The total investment of $135,000 will be obtained as follows:

1. Cash	$25,000	
2. Bank Loan /Investors (Combination)	$110,000	

FIRST YEAR BREAK-EVEN ANALYSIS (Average, Optimistic, and Pessimistic Cases)

Cost Variables	Optimistic 15%	Most Likely Case	Pessimistic -15%
FIXED COSTS:			
Rentals/Leases	$5,577.50	$4,850.00	$4,122.50
Salaries (Fixed/Owners)	$2,548.40	$2,216.00	$1,883.60
Insurance	$1,456.28	$1,266.33	$1,076.38
Fixed Taxes/Benefits	$509.68	$443.20	$376.72
Interest	$1,443.25	$1,255.00	$1,066.75
Utilities/Phone/Security Sys.	$1,168.88	$1,016.42	$863.96
Total Fixed Costs	**$12,703.99**	**$11,046.95**	**$9,389.91**

Per Month-1st Year

FIRST YEAR BREAK-EVEN ANALYSIS (Average, Optimistic, and Pessimistic Cases)

Continued

	Optimistic 15%	Most Likely Case	Pessimistic -15%
VARIABLE COSTS			
Variable Labor/Wages/Benefits	$15,069.60	$13,104.00	$11,138.40
Cost of Goods Sold		$22,333.33	
Advertising/Marketing	$2,184.33	$1,899.42	$1,614.51
Entertainment		$6,500.00	
(other variable cost)	$7,157.37	$6,223.80	$5,290.23
Total Variable Costs	**$24,411.30**	**$50,060.55**	**$18,043.14**

Pricing & Unit Sales Variables	Optimistic 15%	Most Likely Case	Pessimistic -15%
Average Income per Customer	$16.31	$14.18	$12.05
Average # of Customers per Month	5,136.67	4,466.67	3,796.67
Fixed costs per Customer	$2.84	$2.47	$2.10
Variable Costs per Customer	$12.89	$11.21	$9.53
Break-Even Number of Customers	**3,716.48**	**3,716.48**	**3,716.48**
Customers over Break-Even	**1,420.19**	**750.19**	**80.19**
Break-Even Sales Amount	**$60,604.65**	**$52,699.69**	**$44,794.74**
Gross Profit per Customer	**$3.42**	**$2.97**	**$2.53**
Gross Profit (over Break-Even)	**$4,854.62**	**$2,229.88**	**$202.60**

Break-Even Analysis is a mathematical technique for analyzing the relationship between profits and fixed and variable costs. It is also a profit planning tool for calculating the point at which sales will equal costs. The above analysis indicates the first year break-even number of customers at 3,716.48 per month and break-even income at $52,699.69 per month. Anything over these amounts will be profit.

PROJECTED FIVE-YEAR INCOME STATEMENT

	Projected Year 1	Projected Year 2	Projected Year 3	Projected Year 4	Projected Year 5
Total Revenue	759,780	984,454	1,230,568	1,415,153	1,556,668
Cost of Goods Sold	268,000	347,250	434,063	499,172	549,089
Salaries/Payroll	157,632	165,496	206,870	237,901	261,691
Payroll Taxes/Benefits	31,526	33,099	41,374	47,580	52,338
Maint./Repair/Breakage	22,793	29,534	36,918	42,455	46,701
Advertising/Marketing	22,793	34,456	43,070	49,531	54,484
Fees/Permits/Licenses	300	600	750	863	949
Amortization-Org. Costs	1,100	1,100	1,375	1,581	1,739
Rent/Deposits/Leases	58,200	58,200	72,750	83,663	92,029
Entertainment	78,000	96,000	120,000	138,000	151,180
Insurance	15,196	19,689	24,611	28,303	31,133
Phones/Utilities	9,497	12,306	15,383	17,690	19,459
Office Supplies/Postage	7,598	9,845	12,306	14,152	15,567

PROJECTED FIVE-YEAR INCOME STATEMENT

Continued

	Projected Year 1	Projected Year 2	Projected Year 3	Projected Year 4	Projected Year 5
Professional Fees	6,000	9,600	12,000	13,800	15,180
Miscellaneous	22,793	29,534	36,918	42,455	46,701
Security System	2,700	2,700	3,375	3,881	4,269
Loan Interest Payments	15,060	14,248	13,315	12,243	11,011
Depreciation	14,100	14,100	14,100	14,100	14,100
Total Operating Expenses	**733,288**	**877,757**	**1,089,176**	**1,247,368**	**1,368,239**
Income Before Taxes	$26,492	$106,697	$141,391	$167,784	$188,429
Income Taxes	$5,298	$29,875	$42,417	$53,691	$64,066
NET INCOME	**$21,194**	**$76,822**	**$98,974**	**$114,093**	**$124,066**

PROJECTED FIVE-YEAR BALANCE SHEET

	Projected Year 1	Projected Year 2	Projected Year 3	Projected Year 4	Projected Year 5
Cash & Equivalent	55,922	130,181	143,199	157,519	173,271
Accounts Receivable	11,651	14,175	17,294	21,098	25,740
Inventory	52,217	46,885	42,098	37,800	33,940
Other Assets & Deposits	17,700	15,378	13,362	11,610	10,088
Total Current	137,490	206,619	215,953	228,027	243,039
Leasehold Improvements	5,000	5,000	5,000	5,000	5,000
Pool Tables	18,000	18,000	18,000	18,000	18,000
Furniture/Equipment/Bar	47,500	75,900	121,440	170,016	238,022
Depreciation/Amortization	(15,200)	(32,975)	(45,600)	(60,800)	(76,000)
Intangibles	5,500	5,500	5,500	5,500	5,500
Other Assets	7,500	10,000	10,000	10,000	10,000
TOTAL ASSETS	**205,790**	**288,044**	**330,293**	**375,743**	**443,562**
Trade Acct. Payable	24,658	30,000	36,600	44,652	54,475
Current Portion L.T.D.	453	521	599	689	792
Other Current Liab.	41,689	50,784	62,983	77,469	95,287
Total Current Liab.	66,800	81,305	100,182	122,810	150,555
Long Term Debt	107,119	101,253	94,512	86,764	77,858
TOTAL LIABILITIES	**173,919**	**182,558**	**194,694**	**209,574**	**228,413**
Common Stock	25,000	25,000	25,000	25,000	25,000
Retained Earnings	6,871	80,486	110,599	141,169	190,149
EQUITY/NET WORTH	**31,871**	**105,486**	**135,599**	**166,169**	**215,149**
LIABILITIES & EQUITY	**205,790**	**288,044**	**330,293**	**375,743**	**443,562**

Common Size Financial Statements

COMMON SIZE INCOME STATEMENT

	Estimated Year 1	Projected Year 2	Projected Year 3	Projected Year 4	Projected Year 5	1995 Industry Ave.
Total Revenue	100.0%	100.0%	100.0%	100.0%	100.0%	100.0%
Operating Expenses	96.5%	89.2%	88.5%	88.1%	87.9%	90.9%
Operating Profit	3.5%	10.8%	11.5%	11.9%	12.1%	9.1%
Other Expenses/Income	0.0%	0.0%	0.0%	0.0%	0.0%	0.9%
PRE-TAX PROFIT	**3.5%**	**10.8%**	**11.5%**	**11.9%**	**12.1%**	**8.2%**

COMMON SIZE BALANCE SHEET

	Estimated Year 1	Projected Year 2	Projected Year 3	Projected Year 4	Projected Year 5	1995 Industry Ave.
Cash & Equivalent	27.2%	45.1%	43.4%	41.9%	39.1%	10.1%
Accounts Receivable	5.7%	4.9%	5.2%	5.6%	5.8%	15.7%
Inventory	25.4%	24.4%	12.8%	10.1%	7.7%	
Other Current	8.6%	7.2%	4.1%	3.1%	2.3%	2.3%
Total Current Assets	**66.8%**	**81.6%**	**65.5%**	**60.7%**	**54.9%**	**28.1%**
Fixed Assets (Net)	26.9%	13.9%	30.6%	36.0%	41.6%	59.6%
Intangibles	2.7%	1.9%	1.7%	1.4%	1.2%	2.7%
Other Assets	3.6%	2.6%	2.3%	1.9%	2.3%	9.6%
TOTAL ASSETS	**100.0%**	**100.0%**	**100.0%**	**100.0%**	**100.0%**	**100.0%**
Liabilities:						
Accounts Payable	12.0%	10.4%	11.1%	11.9%	10.0%	4.3%
Short Term Notes	0.0%	0.0%	0.0%	0.0%	0.0%	5.1%
Current Maturities (LTD)	0.2%	0.2%	0.2%	0.2%	0.2%	12.5%
Other Current Liabilities	20.2%	17.6%	19.1%	20.6%	19.1%	10.2%
Total Current Liabilities	**32.4%**	**28.2%**	**30.4%**	**32.7%**	**29.3%**	**32.1%**
Long-Term Debt (Loans)	52.1%	35.2%	30.4%	23.1%	17.6%	24.9%
Other Non-Current	0.0%	0.0%	28.6%	0.0%	0.0%	10.9%
TOTAL EQUITY	**15.5%**	**36.6%**	**0.0%**	**44.2%**	**53.1%**	**32.1%**
Total Liabilities & Equity	**100.0%**	**100.0%**	**100.0%**	**100.0%**	**100.0%**	**100.0%**

RATIO ANALYSIS

Ratio analysis can be one of the most useful financial management tools. It becomes important when you look at the trend of each ratio over time. It also becomes important when compared to averages of a particular industry.

	Projected Year 1	Projected Year 2	Projected Year 3	Projected Year 4	Projected Year 5	Industry 1995
Liquidity Ratios:						
Current Ratio	2.06	2.54	2.16	1.86	1.61	0.9
Quick Ratio	1.01	1.78	1.6	1.45	1.32	0.5
Sales / Receivables	65.21	69.45	71.16	67.07	60.48	327.6
Days' Receivables	5.6	5.26	5.13	5.44	6.04	1.11
Cost of Sales / Inventory	5.13	7.41	10.31	13.21	16.18	2.18
Days' Inventory	71.12	49.28	35.4	27.64	22.56	
Cost of Sales / Payables	10.87	11.58	11.86	11.18	10.08	12
Day's Payables	33.58	31.53	30.78	32.65	36.21	30.42
Sales / Work. Capital	10.75	7.86	10.63	13.45	16.83	-163.4
EBIT / Interest	2.76	8.49	11.62	14.7	18.11	3.1
Net Profit + Depr. + Amort./C.L.T.D.	80.34	176.63	191.02	188.35	176.94	0
Leverage Ratios						
Fixed Assers/Tan. Net Worth	1.74	0.62	0.73	0.80	0.86	3.2
Debt/Worth	5.46	1.73	1.44	1.26	1.06	3.3
Operating Ratios						
Profit Before Tax / Tan. Net Worth	0.83	1.01	1.04	1.01	0.88	19.30
Profit Before Tax / Total Assets	0.13	0.37	0.43	0.045	0.42	6.20
Sales / Net Fixed Assets	13.74	14.93	12.45	10.7	8.41	2.8
Sales / Total Assets	3.69	3.42	3.73	3.77	1.06	2.3
Other Ratios:						
% Deprec., Amort. / Sales	0.02	0.02	0.01	0.01	0.01	3.5
% Officer's Compensation/Sales						0
Key Percentages as a Percent of Operating Income						
Rent	7.66%	5.91%	5.91%	5.91%	5.91%	5.20%
Interest Paid	1.98%	1.45%	1.08%	0.87%	0.71%	1.30%
Depreciation & Amortization	2.00%	1.54%	1.26%	1.11%	1.02%	2.30%
Officers Compensation	3.50%	3.50%	3.50%	3.50%	3.50%	4.00%
Taxes Paid	0.70%	3.03%	3.45%	3.79%	4.12%	4.00%

Revenue to Working Capital ratio is a measure of the margin of protection for current creditors. This ratio is above industry averages and indicates a good level of safety for creditors.

EBIT to interest ratio is a measure of ability to meet annual interest payments. Since this ratio is above industry averages, Santiago Roller Rink should have no problem servicing its debt.

The Earnings before Taxes to Total Assets Ratio expresses the pre-tax return on total assets and measures the effectiveness of management in employing available resources. Santiago Roller Rink would be more efficient than the industry in its effective employment of resources.

CATEGORY / YEAR	1997	1998	1999	2000	2001
Current Assets	$137,490	$206,619	$215,953	$228,027	$243,039
Fixed Assets	$55,300	$65,925	$98,840	$132,216	$185,022
Other Assets	$13,000	$15,500	$15,500	$15,500	$15,500
TOTAL ASSETS	**$205,790**	**$288,044**	**$330,743**	**$375,743**	**$443,562**
Current Liabilities	$66,800	$81,305	$100,182	$122,810	$150,555
Long-Term Liabilities	$107,119	$101,253	$94,512	$86,764	$77,858
Other Liabilities	$0	$0	$0	$0	$0
TOTAL LIABILITIES	**$173,919**	**$182,558**	**$194,694**	**$209,574**	**$228,413**
Stock	$25,000	$25,000	$25,000	$25,000	$25,000
Current earnings	$0	$0	$0	$0	$0
Retained Earnings (minus dividends)	$6,871	$80,486	$110,599	$141,169	$190,149
NET WORTH	**$31,871**	**$105,486**	**$1,355,999**	**$166,169**	**$215,149**
Liabilities + Net Worth	$205,790	$288,044	$330,293	$375,743	$443,562
Working Capital	$70,690	$125,314	$115,770	$105,217	$92,484
Sales	$759,780	$984,454	$1,230,567	$1,415,152	$1,556,667
Earning Before Taxes & Interest	$41,550	$120,946	$154,708	$180,029	$199,442
Book Value (minus intangibles)	$31,871	$105,486	$135,599	$166,169	$215,149
WC / TA = (X1)	0.34	0.44	0.35	0.28	0.21
RE / TA = (X2)	0.03	0.28	0.33	0.38	0.43
EBIT / TA = (X3)	0.2	0.42	0.47	0.48	0.45
Book Value / TL = (X4)	0.18	0.58	0.7	0.79	0.94
Sales / TA = (X5)	3.69	3.42	3.73	3.77	3.51
CALCULATED Z SCORE	**4.66**	**5.51**	**6.00**	**6.1**	**5.81**

The Z Score Formula = $0.717*(X1) + 0.847*(X2) + 3.107*(X3) + 0.420*(X4) + 0.998*(X5)$

If the Z Score is Greater than or Equal to 2.91 the subject firm is apparently safe from bankruptcy.
If the Z Score is Less than or Equal to 1.22 the subject firm may be destined for bankruptcy.
If the Z Score is between 1.23 and 2.90 the firm is in a gray area and steps could be taken by management to correct existing or potential problems in order to avoid bankruptcy.

Z Score analysis is a statistical method developed to forecast bankruptcy.
It is over 90% accurate one year into the future and 80% accurate for the second year.

In this instance we used the projected figures to determine the above scores.

The Z scores indicated above are all well over 2.91 which indicates that the company will not be a candidate for bankruptcy if it can achieve the goals outlined in this plan.

GRAPHICAL ANALYSIS

	Net Income	IRR	MIRR	Annual Dividends	Total Assets
Initial Investment	($25,000)				
Year 1	$21,192			$3,179	$205,790
Year 2	$76,823	122.73%	213.92%	$11,523	$288,044
Year 3	$98,975	160.80%	335.85%	$14,846	$330,293
Year 4	$114,095	172.94%	408.18%	$17,144	$375,743
Year 5	$124,364	177.11%	456.56%	$18,655	$443,562

ASSUMPTIONS:

Income figures are after taxes
Dividend Payout = 50% of After Tax Income
Reinvestment rate = 7%

IRR = INTERNAL RATE OF RETURN
MIRR = MODIFIED RATE OF RETURN
ROI - RATE OF RETURN ON OWNER'S INVESTMENT
ROA = RATE OF RETURN ON TOTAL ASSETS

IRR = the interest rate received for an investment and income that occur at regular periods
MIRR = adds the cost of funds and interest received on reinvestment of cash to the IRR

	Year 1	Year 2	Year 3	Year 4	Year 5
Return on Investment	12.72%	46.09%	59.39%	68.46%	74.62%
Return on Assets	10.30%	26.67%	29.97%	30.37%	28.04%
Income Per Share	$0.85	$3.07	$3.96	$4.56	$4.97
Dividends Per Share	$0.13	$0.46	$0.59	$0.68	$0.75

CONCLUSIONS AND SUMMARY

We feel that the type of company and service we are proposing is hitting the market at just the right time. We plan to fully repay the loan by the end of the third year. However, we will schedule repayments over ten years to give us flexibility. By applying our conservative projections, income for the first year is expected to be $21,194 after taxes and debt service. This will rise to 76,822 in the second and $124,363 by the fifth year. The business should be open for business by spring of 2001.

Screen Print Drying Company

BUSINESS PLAN DLP, INC.

945 Clemray Highway
Nashville, Tennessee 37325

DLP had previously operated as five separate but affiliated companies, but a recent merger of the DLP companies into DLP, Inc., has created tremendous opportunities for cost reductions and the leveraging of existing resources. This business plan shows the remarkable sales and marketing future of the firm once it is infused with additional capital. This plan was provided by Trinity Capital.

- EXECUTIVE SUMMARY

- COMPANY SUMMARY

- PRODUCTS

- STRATEGY & IMPLEMENTATION SUMMARY

- MANAGEMENT SUMMARY

- FINANCIAL PLAN

EXECUTIVE SUMMARY

DLP, Inc. participates in the custom heat process and finishing equipment industry, the custom metal fabricating industry, the screenprint drying industry, and in the contract powder-coating industry. DLP's main offices are located on 10 acres in Nashville, Tennessee, plus a small assembly warehouse near its home offices, as well as a two satellite contract powder-coating operations in Birmingham, Alabama, and Richmond, Virginia.

1995 was a pivotal year in the history of the DLP companies. While DLP had previously operated as separate but affiliated companies, the merger of the five DLP companies into DLP, Inc., has created tremendous opportunities for cost reductions and the leveraging of existing resources.

DLP, Inc. has operated successfully since its inception in 1970. The company currently has two main product areas: 1) specialty manufacturing equipment (dryers) for the screen printing industry, and 2) contract powder-coating services.

The company's high revenue has been in excess of $10 million annually. Currently, revenues exceed $7 million annually and the company is marginally profitable. The company remains 100% privately held and family owned. Total debt is $1.2 million including a $500K fully utilized bank line of credit.

Recent years have shown the first losses in company history, but cost-cutting measures have already been implemented to enable profitable operation. Current backlog of orders exceeds $1.5 million, with an additional $1.2 million order booked in November 1997. This represents the highest order backlog in the 4th quarter in the company's history.

However, the company is not sufficiently capitalized to take advantage of the growth opportunities it has.

Strategic Option #1:

- Sell off the equipment manufacturing business. This will eliminate all company debt.
- Concentrate on building the powder-coating business. This business has always been profitable. Current margins are 16% net and could be improved to 22% net with a $1.4 million capital expenditure. This capital would be provided by proceeds from the sale of the equipment business plus a small private equity placement plus available debt facilities.
- The volume of this business could be increased to $10 million within three years.

Strategic Option #2:

- Retain ownership of both entities.
- Raise $3 million minimum in private equity capital and subordinate debt.
- Build combined business to more than $20 million annually in three years by:
    1. Hiring the proper management team.
    2. Expanding the equipment business internationally.
    3. Expanding the equipment business into other industrial applications.
    4. Increasing the marketing of powder coating to fully utilize three currently available facilities. Then, expand with additional geographic locations.

Note: If option #2 is pursued, an additional option would be to divest of the equipment business later on—but at a much higher value. This business plan reflects the implementation of strategy #2.

The following table illustrates the projected five-year growth of the combined business. In year five combined sales exceed $22 million and gross margins have improved to 48%. This results in profitable operations and positive equity.

Long-term plan	1998	1999	2000	2001	2002
Sales	$6,815,025	$10,200,000	$15,500,000	$20,000,000	$22,500,000
Cost of Sales	$4,170,401	$5,865,000	$8,525,000	$10,500,000	$11,700,000
Gross Margin	$2,644,624	$4,335,000	$6,975,000	$9,500,000	$10,800,000
Gross Margin %	38.81%	42.50%	45.00%	47.50%	48.00%
Operating Expenses	$4,554,443	$6,117,226	$7,107,226	$8,800,000	$9,200,000
Operating Income	($1,909,819)	($1,782,226)	($132,226)	$700,000	$1,600,000
Net Income	($1,515,361)	($1,459,041)	($260,916)	$1,105,000	$2,000,000
Short-term Assets	$365,132	$3,906,891	$3,981,791	($600,000)	$1,200,000
Long-term Assets	$363,554	$289,358	$215,162	$650,000	$1,000,000
Short-term Liabilities	$1,452,477	$2,129,082	$2,390,702	$1,350,000	$1,050,000
Long-term Liabilities	$543,554	$1,043,554	$1,043,554	$550,000	$550,000
Equity	($1,267,345)	$1,023,614	$762,697	($1,850,000)	$600,000

Objectives

1. **JOB COSTING:** Tracking of ongoing activity. Compiling data in a way that production management and administrative management can accurately determine the profitability of projects, products, and services. Without this information on a timely and consistent basis the company is running blind as it relies on past estimates alone. To accomplish this objective the company must actively involve production management. If they do not have to track it, they will not rely upon it for decision making. A second priority is one that management has already acted on: enhancing the computer system throughout the accounting process to coordinate the accumulation of data and to update and adjust the tracking procedures. Consulting with professionals with backgrounds in both accounting and management information systems, management is currently working towards the completion of this objective.

2. **IMPROVE SERVICE DEPARTMENT:** Some work is still needed to connect the paper trail that exists to ensure customer satisfaction and proper billing. In 1999 the service department will begin its move from a "necessary evil" to an efficient profit center.

3. **IMPROVE MONITORING OF ACCOUNTS RECEIVABLE:** Using the accounting department/process so that this important function can be constantly monitored with the checks and balances needed to ensure control of this important area, which is vital in maintaining the cash flow for the entire organization.

4. **DEVELOP NEW MARKETS FOR DRYING OVENS:** DLP will develop new products for new marketplaces while continuing to expand its existing territories. Research is needed to determine necessary changes to adapt our products to differing processes and possibly conform with European requirements, which could open new possibilities there. Our existing products can be marketed to new industries, such as the carpet and apparel industries. New products will include air make-up units, screen cabinets, lint collectors, and modular batch ovens.

5. **IMPROVE QUOTING PROCESS:** The quoting process for our systems jobs could further be standardized to: a) make the process faster, b) provide exact costs for materials, c) provide the general manager with a consistent format to review, d) provide accurate budgets of costs and expected profit, and e) serve as a more efficient means of communication between the engineering department and the production department.

6. **SATELLITE LOCATIONS FOR DLP:** As our contract powder-coating operation continues to provide the company's most consistent level of sales and profitability, it is a top

priority of management to expand the operations of this segment of the company geographically. We have learned valuable lessons through our venture into our two satellite locations, and we will continue to refine our plans for satellite locations during 1999.

7. **BOLSTER PRODUCTION MANAGEMENT FOR MATERIAL HANDLING:** For this segment of the company to continue to increase its sales, steps must be taken to relieve current management from the dual role of both sales and production management.

8. **SOLIDIFY DLP'S TOTAL MARKETING PROGRAM:** Historically, each DLP division has been responsible for its own marketing and advertising, from brochures to trade shows to magazine advertisements. While each division will continue to have influence over its marketing, the goal in 1999 is to organize the process throughout the company and give DLP a consistent message and eliminate duplication of effort. To facilitate this process, we have consulted with marketing professionals to aid in developing a marketing plan that will be suitable. This plan will include printed goods, trade ads, web site development, and catalogs on CD-ROM.

Mission

To be a leader in each marketplace in which we compete, capitalizing on DLP's reputation for quality. To aggressively pursue growth opportunities through both product line and geographic expansion. To constantly explore innovative ways to improve the performance and quality of our products and the satisfaction of our customers. To generate above-average returns for our stockholders by aggressively seeking out new business while maintaining a conservative and consistent management philosophy. To always conduct ourselves in a manner that exemplifies integrity and strong ethical values. To provide a safe, secure working environment for our employees, with ample opportunity for personal growth and advancement.

Keys to Success

- Cost management and control across the organization.
- The continuing education of our current employees.
- The successful integration of new key employees into the organization.
- Maintain current market position while exploring new markets for growth.
- Improved cash generation and management and additional permanent working capital.

The future of the company rests on the overall strategy of expanding the technology in the screen print drying market to other vertical market industrial applications. The modular concept design of drying systems can be marketed in other industry segments at improved margins. Less custom work and fewer inventory items will improve profitability. The powder-coating side of the business will grow via marketing concentration and geographic expansion. Segmenting new management personnel into each separate division will improve operational control.

COMPANY SUMMARY

DLP, Inc. is a company with multiple divisions and subsidiaries participating in the custom heat process and finishing equipment industry, the custom metal fabricating industry, the material handling industry, the screenprint drying industry, and in the contract powder-coating industry. Most of our sales are made directly via our own sales force, from leads that are generated from "word of mouth" referrals, trade shows, trade publications, and other industry reps, while a large portion of our screenprint dryer and material handling sales are made by sales representatives and distributors. The type of customer to which we sell varies greatly across our various lines of business. In the custom heat process and finishing equipment arena we sell to primarily medium-sized regional manufacturers, with an occasional company like

Steelcase thrown in. In our screenprint dryer sales, we have a firm footing with the premier screenprinters as well as with small- and medium-sized businesses. Customers for our fabricated products include a major retail store, UPS, and numerous small manufacturers. Contract powder-coating sales range from small- and medium-sized local manufacturers to national OEMs.

On December 31, 1995, DLP, Inc., a Tennessee "C" corporation, acquired 100% of the common stock of DLP Systems, Inc., DLP Manufacturing, Inc., DLP Fabrications, Inc., DLP Coating, Inc., and DLP Coating of Tennessee, Inc. Of the five companies acquired, all are Tennessee "C" corporations except for DLP Coating of Tennessee, Inc., which is a Virginia "C" corporation.

Company Ownership

The officers and owners of DLP, Inc. are as follows:

- David G. Stumbo, President and Treasurer - 7,360 shares (73.6%)
- Richard F. Stumbo, Vice President - 1,460 shares (14.6%)
- Mary Alice Stumbo, Vice President - 90 shares (0.9%)
- Sally Dillinger, Secretary - 90 shares (0.9%).

Company History

The companies first began in 1972 when David Stumbo and Ed Murguard ventured out from Hockingham Company and founded DLP Enterprises, Inc. doing business as HeatBlast Heating and Air Conditioning and Stumbo Construction. Both individuals were from a background of superior work ethic and extensive technical expertise that led to their early success. These efforts proved successful until the residential building industry fell off sharply. David anticipated the eventual phasing out of Stumbo Construction due to a declining marketplace and saturation of available general contractors as well as HeatBlast suffering the loss of some of its new housing business.

David knew that the future stability of the business was becoming dependent on their service work and the commercial end of the market. While building a large service business and a strong reputation in the area of commercial construction, David was being approached by individuals and companies requesting his services for such things as installing, servicing, and modifying commercial freezers and ovens. In 1976 he was asked to construct a conveyorized screenprint drying oven for a Nashville based company. David designed and built that first piece of equipment without realizing that a gas-fired, quality dryer did not yet exist in the screenprint industry. He also did not realize how quickly the word would travel throughout the textile industry, or that the first drying oven would still be used in production 20 years later.

Since that time DLP has developed an impeccable reputation in the areas of design, construction, installation, and service of all types of equipment including batch ovens, bake ovens, washers, freezers, duct systems, conveyor dryers, paint booths, and turnkey industrial finishing equipment, all of which are used in a wide variety of industries. This versatility greatly expanded the opportunities that were available and offered much stability because each industry was unrelated except for their equipment process needs. David's customer list soon began to read like a list of the Fortune 500.

In 1987 Ed decided to retire and the businesses were divided into what became DLP Manufacturing, Inc. (owned by David) and HeatBlast Heating and Air Conditioning, Inc. (owned by Ed). DLP Enterprises was converted to a Tennessee Limited Partnership—a land development company jointly owned by both individuals to manage and develop the 10+ acres they had acquired heavy industrial work. Ed eventually sold HeatBlast Heating and Air Conditioning and began retirement.

DLP Manufacturing continued designing, building, and installing commercial equipment and specializing in gas-fired heat process equipment for the screenprint industry and turnkey finishing systems for the finishing industry. Having built several powder process systems in the early 1980s by industry standards, DLP Manufacturing installed an in-house finishing system. This system was used as a means to experiment with the process of powder coating and to incorporate new ideas into DLP's line of finishing equipment. In time it became evident that contract services were in need on a larger scale. With the marriage of the finishing equipment and this need in the contract coating market, DLP Coating opened for business in 1990. This new venture was begun, operated, and majority owned by David.

With the growth in the T-shirt screen printing industry of the late 1980s, DLP's sales of screenprint dryers grew to the point that David decided to procure a veteran of the screenprint industry with expertise and extensive experience in marketing and sales, after which a major marketing effort was put in place to advance the sales of the company's best drying system. In 1991, David decided to spin that operation off as a separate business for better operational control. Due to the name recognition within the screen printing industry, that product line continued to be produced by DLP Manufacturing, Inc. DLP Systems, Inc. was formed (as a subsidiary of DLP Manufacturing) to manufacture the custom industrial equipment. David Stumbo owned 100% of both corporations and filed a consolidated tax return. David then continued the manufacturing of custom equipment under the new name of DLP Systems, Inc.

DLP Fabrications was formed in 1994 out of the need to enhance and centralize DLP's sheet metal fabricating abilities. DLP purchased a variety of CNC metal fabricating equipment to increase the tolerances achieved in its manufacturing processes. At the same time, a product line was needed to fill empty production time in the welding/fabricating department, as well as the contract powder coating.

An opportunity arose to manufacture and distribute material handling equipment (garment racks, etc.). DLP entered this market to expand its product offering and take advantage of the capacity of the fabricating and coating equipment. This new enterprise was started and owned by Greg Stumbo.

Ed Murguard died unexpectedly in August 1994. Upon his death, all of his business interests were divided 50/50 between Greg Stumbo and Ed's widow. After closing Ed's estate, Greg purchased the majority interest in Stumbo Holding Company from Ed's widow.

On October 31, 1994, the following transactions took place:

- The name of DLP Systems, Inc. was changed to Stumbo Holding Co., Inc. DLP Coating, Inc. formed a new wholly owned subsidiary with the name DLP Systems, Inc.
- The "new" DLP Systems purchased the operating portion of Stumbo Holding by assuming its operating assets and liabilities, which yielded a negative equity position.
- The rationale behind this move was fairly straightforward. Both DLP Systems and DLP Manufacturing had operating losses, while DLP Coating was profitable. By acquiring the operating loss of DLP Systems, DLP Coating avoided paying any income taxes.

As all of the above indicates, the DLP "family" of businesses was becoming increasingly complicated by the end of 1995. The tax and regulatory benefits of having several small corporations were being overshadowed by the problems created in managing so many separate entities. The decision was made to create a parent subsidiary relationship where DLP, Inc. would own 100% of DLP Manufacturing, DLP Fabrications, DLP Coating, DLP Systems, and DLP Coating of Tennessee. DLP, Inc. had been created in 1994 to function as a management company to provide services such as payroll, accounting, purchasing, etc. for all of the DLP companies. This transaction took place effective December 31, 1995. The decision was made to leave Stumbo Holding Company (the original corporation from 1986) out of this transaction for tax reasons and to keep the real estate, some equipment, and other intellectual property (trade names, copyrights) separate from the operating companies liabilities.

DLP Coating of Tennessee began operations in March 1995 as a wholly owned subsidiary of DLP Coating, Inc., representing the first geographic expansion of DLP's contract powder-coating facilities. The operation in Richmond, Virginia, was acquired from Smooth Coatings Inc., enabling DLP to eliminate a primary competitor before it entered the marketplace.

Effective December 31, 1996, the corporate shells of DLP Manufacturing, DLP Fabrications, and DLP Systems were dissolved, leaving DLP, Inc. as the surviving corporation. DLP Coating and DLP Coating of Tennessee were left as subsidiaries due to the distinct differences between the service nature of contract powder coating and the manufacturing nature of the other businesses.

In January 1997 DLP Coating opened its second satellite coating facility in Alabama. This location was selected because of its proximity to key industrial corridors servicing the firm's main customer base.

Today, the DLP "family" of businesses is relatively simple: DLP, Inc., equipment manufacturer and owner of DLP Coating, Inc. and DLP Coating of Tennessee, Inc., contract powder-coating operations. Stumbo Holding remains affiliated through its common ownership, leasing property and equipment to the DLP companies.

The following chart illustrates the past three years' financial performance of the combined company: this shows substantial sales but under-performance in net profit. It is expected that management controls will remedy this situation. Coupling that with new, profitable sales growth in targeted market segments is the over-all goal of this plan.

Past Performance	1995	1996	1997
Sales	$9,562,251	$10,078,159	$7,775,189
Gross Margin	$4,398,280	$4,245,154	$2,901,531
Gross % (calculated)	46.00%	42.12%	37.32%
Operating Expenses	$3,779,000	$4,042,370	$3,056,425
Collection period (days)	45	45	45
Inventory turnover	6	6	6
Balance Sheet			
Short-term Assets			
Cash	($138,617)	$180,743	$56,817
Accounts receivable	$770,218	$596,011	$729,662
Inventory	$626,148	$504,673	$499,800
Other Short-term Assets	$343,303	$320,000	$403,100
Total Short-term Assets	**$1,601,052**	**$1,601,427**	**$1,689,379**
Long-term Assets			
Capital Assets	$674,455	$730,278	$769,053
Accumulated Depreciation	$226,930	$302,049	$331,303
Total Long-term Assets	$447,525	$428,229	$437,750
Total Assets	**$2,048,577**	**$2,029,656**	**$2,127,129**

Capital and Liabilities	1995	1996	1997
Accounts Payable	$680,228	$192,226	$437,433
Short-term Notes	$223,730	$549,000	$500,000
Other Short-term Liabilities	$315,458	$296,232	$398,126
Subtotal Short-term Liabilities	**$1,219,416**	**$1,037,458**	**$1,335,559**
Long-term Liabilities	$416,586	$587,397	$543,554
Total Liabilities	$1,636,002	$1,624,855	$1,879,113
Paid in Capital	($30,594)	$3,966	$3,966
Retained Earnings	$291,253	$260,373	$391,386
Earnings	$151,916	$140,462	($147,336)
Total Capital	$412,575	$404,801	$248,016
Total Capital and Liabilities	**$2,048,577**	**$2,029,656**	**$2,127,129**
Other Inputs			
Payment days	30	30	30
Sales on credit	$9,500,000	$10,000,000	$7,500,000
Receivables turnover	12.33	16.78	10.28

Company Locations and Facilities

Stumbo Holding Company, Inc., a company related to the DLP companies via common ownership, owns the 10+ acres and 77,000 square feet utilized by DLP, Inc. in Nashville, Tennessee. There are three buildings as described below:

- 945 Clemray Hwy. - consists of 30,000 square feet of industrial/warehouse space and office space (2,250 square feet). This building is utilized as DLP's administrative offices, as the manufacturing facility for DLP's equipment division, and as warehouse space for all inventory and work-in-progress goods.
- 947 and 949 Clemray Hwy. - These two buildings were connected to form one structure, which consists of 24,817 square feet of industrial space (5,175 sq. ft. of office space). This building houses the administrative offices and the two powder-coating systems of DLP Coating (Nashville).
- 951 Clemray Hwy. - consists of 22,500 square feet (2,000 sq. ft. office) and is currently leased to a third party.

In addition to these facilities, DLP leases:

- 1101 Clemray Hwy., 5,000 square feet. This space is used to house the contract coating's batch painting operation as well as an overflow assembly site.
- DLP Coating of Tennessee leases 7,800 square feet of space which houses its powder-coating system and its administrative offices in Birmingham, Alabama.
- DLP Coating of Tennessee leases 24,000 square feet of space which houses its powder-coating system and its production offices in Richmond, Virginia.

PRODUCTS

Flat-line and screen print products:

- ABC drying oven - high volume production unit
- DEF drying oven - modular screenprint dryer
- Spock drying oven - serves the needs of the smaller users
- Lightning units - spot curing unit

Finishing industry and heat process products:

- complete turnkey industrial paint finishing systems
- batch ovens
- bake ovens, dry-off ovens
- washers
- custom industrial heat process and conveyorized systems

Material handling equipment and custom metal fabricating:

- Nestable garment racks and rolling shelves
- Custom metal fabricated products

Other products:

- turnkey powder-coat finishing systems
- turnkey wet paint finishing systems
- batch ovens
- bake ovens
- dry-off ovens
- custom industrial heat process equipment

Most of our competitors in these markets generally use the standardized "rules of thumb" approach to designing and offering equipment. We compete with these competitors by engineering past them to show the customer advanced process production or greater process control. There are some competitors that have the engineering capabilities. Typically they are larger organizations than DLP. We compete against those competitors on price.

Competitive Comparison

DLP offers the customer value in their purchase by matching the need with the product. Two decades of designing, fabricating, installing, servicing, and operating a variety of equipment and processes gives DLP more than a competitive edge. Time and time again DLP has bested its competition by focusing on the feature rather than the gimmick. The quality of our equipment and the loyalty of our customers is testament to the commitment for which DLP strives.

On average, DLP's pricing is very competitive. However, price is not always the main issue when a customer is pursuing a solution to his production concern. There are markets, such as the screen print industry, that are highly competitive with their pricing. In this market we refrain from going head to head with those competitors who stress their price more than their quality and concentrate on those customers who want and need the value we have to offer.

Sales literature, previous advertising, and catalogue sheets are available upon request.

Sales Literature

Sourcing

DLP has long established relationships with vendors of all raw materials required for operation. All inventory is on a just-in-time basis and orders are normally completed within one to three weeks of scheduling.

Principal suppliers are:

- Wooster Steel, Canard, TN
- T.R. Loose, Nashville, TN
- Ritt Electric, Atlanta, GA

- Maxitrol, Southfield, MI
- Tennessee Controls, Atlanta, GA
- O'Malloy Steel, Northcross, GA
- Techie Controls, Bruce, GA
- Lutz Blowers, Chicago, IL
- Air Machines Corp., Atlanta, GA

Technology

The technology DLP uses is not unique, though the ideas and how specific designs are formulated is certainly proprietary. There are products and processes that DLP has developed which have, could, and will be patented.

Future Products

Future products will revolve around modular concepts that can be pre-fabricated and still customized into specific customer requirements. This will serve to improve inventory control and increase margins.

Market Analysis Summary

The major markets served by DLP, Inc. are: 1) The screenprinting market with 40,000 potential customers and an annual dollar volume of $25 billion. 2) Contract powder coating with 100,000 potential customers and $40 billion in annual volume. It is estimated that screenprinting is growing at about 8% per year and is a mature industry. Powder coating has only reached 20% of its market potential. Most metal parts are still painted. On an industry-by-industry basis the number of potential customers is almost unlimited. DLP has only scratched the surface of potential customers. An early marketing task will be to identify specific industry segments with the greatest potential.

Market Segmentation

The total number of potential customers in each target market segment is huge. DLP must target segments by industry preference. These customers are only domestic. International distribution channels are not included here. Other manufacturing segments for ovens/drying applications also are not included. These represent future growth avenues. Management intends to concentrate first on expanding its core base of customers in those markets where DLP is known for quality and readily identifiable. Management seeks to gain market share by coordinating marketing efforts and expanding budgets and staff. The following chart represents target markets and growth expectations:

Market Analysis

Potential Customers	Growth	1998	1999	2000	2001	2002	CAGR
Screen Print	8%	40,000	43,200	46,656	50,388	54,419	8%
Powder coating	12%	100,000	112,000	125,440	140,493	157,352	12%
Other	0%	0	0	0	0%	0	0.00%
Total	10.90%	140,000	155,200	172,096	190,881	211,771	10.90%

Target Market Segment Strategy

Existing channels of distribution will be utilized. Media expenditures and trade show participation will be increased. Web marketing will be initiated. DLP has enjoyed a sales franchise for many years, but marketing expenditures have been curtailed in recent years resulting in market share erosion. Market share increases will be the primary objective.

A cross section of DLP customers is as follows:

- XML Athletic Wear
- B.J. Muffel
- Russell Athletic
- Petree Mfg.
- Walt Disney Productions
- AT&T
- Texton
- Total Care Electric
- Goodyear
- General Electric
- Ties Industries

Market Needs

The market needs quality solutions, not just products that work. DLP's modular drying solutions will be a competitive advantage. In addition, DLP engineering expertise will offer turn-key solutions to customer needs. In powder coating, the customers need environment friendly coating options. DLP will capitalize on this on-going demand.

Market Trends

The trend from paint coating applications to powder-coating applications has only penetrated 20% of the total market to date. Manufacturers will also be trending towards installation of their own powder-coating lines. DLP can capitalize here just as once it did with the screenprint drying business. Capital equipment can supplement the service-oriented business model of today.

Market Growth

Screenprinting is growing at 20% per year domestically. Foreign markets are prime. International distribution of modular systems should be a priority. Foreign licenses are possible as well. Powder coating will grow first by expanding market share. Then it will grow by establishing additional satellite locations to be closer to customer demand. This is a long-term goal that will require additional capitalization. The powder-coating business can also increase market share via good transportation management. This will enhance service capabilities to clients. Trucking can be a valuable addition to the service mix. It can also serve to enhance profitability as volume permits. Initially transportation services can be leased and ultimately can be owned.

Industry Analysis

The drying industry is now dominated by a few major companies. These companies have outstripped DLP in a market that DLP pioneered. They are spending far more in marketing than DLP but their quality and customer service have suffered.

The powder-coating industry is primarily a privately held regional business. There is significant opportunity for roll-up expansion here, either by internal growth and expansion to new locations, as well as acquisition strategy long term.

Distribution Patterns

Sales are direct to customer and through independent reps and distributors. The majority of current sales are direct by DLP to its current customer base. Only material handling equipment is sold through reps. It is DLP's objective through increased media, staffing, and Internet use to increase direct sales and thereby exercise more control over the end user. These efforts will be primarily aimed at increasing market share via new customer creation. Foreign markets will also be explored utilizing distributors, licenses, or strategic partners.

The following are distributors with whom DLP enjoys long-standing relationships:

- Russell Lambert Equipment Co. - Nashville, TN
- LS & N Industries - San Francisco, CA
- American Laundry Inc. - New York, NY
- Moonbeams - Carrollton, GA
- Merging Minds - Philadelphia, PA
- International Can Components - Cincinnati, OH
- PlugIn Systems - Atlanta, GA

Competition and Buying Patterns

Buying patterns are determined more by marketing presence and power than by any other factor. DLP seeks to influence more direct business than ever before.

Main Competitors

Main competitors in the drying business are:

- Kugler Enterprises
- Denver Finishing
- LEAR-X Inc.

Several of these companies are many times the size of DLP and could be potential acquirers at a higher value if DLP increases market share and establishes a market advantage with its modular design concept. The market here is national in focus.

Principal competitors in powder-coating services are:

- Bright Night Finishing, Inc.
- NorthEast Powder coatings
- Pixie Dust Coatings
- Reliable Coatings

The marketing focus here is more regional. These are companies that could be supplanted with execution of effective marketing. They could also be acquired (perhaps at a very reasonable price).

The main competitors in finishing systems are:

- CBG Inc.
- Industrial Finishing
- On Target Metal Work

These are larger companies. DLP can obtain market share by promoting its "modular" concept and by expanding into other vertical markets served by these competitors.

STRATEGY & IMPLEMENTATION SUMMARY

Manufacturing strategy is more efficient operation and cost control. The result will be increasing margins.

Marketing strategy is increased budgets, personnel, market presence, media expansion, Internet marketing, and direct control of customers.

Strategy Pyramids

The following is a demonstration of workflow:

1. Manufacturing takes place in our 30,000 sq. ft. of manufacturing space where the components of the equipment are assembled, using our staff of 30+ production employees. The company's product line is marketed directly to the consumer and through distributors in geographical areas where there is lack of representation. Three major trade shows are attended per year. Advertising is done in three major industry publications on a targeted basis, and the company attends four to five major trade shows each year.

2. Terms are usually 30/60/10 and leasing is available to customers from third-party sources. After an order is taken and documents for confirmation and tracking of the job are produced, the orders are placed for all necessary fabricated and purchased items. Production then takes over and produces each order in about two to five weeks depending on the product. Upon shipment of the order (via common carrier), the service department takes over and schedules any installations while also fulfilling any obligations of warranty work.

3. Both volume and efficiency and economies of scale will be enhanced by the successful implementation of this plan.

The strategy pyramid is intended to be an overview.

Value Proposition

Value is based upon turn-key solutions. Customers can be ramped-up (add-on selling) to new levels of service or increased internal capability. DLP offers one-stop shopping for either customer need.

Competitive Edge

Engineering expertise has long been DLP's competitive edge. Larger competitors are either not capable or are unwilling to offer it. Turn-around time on orders will also be an advantage when more modular systems are sold.

Marketing Strategy

Multi-channel distribution will be paired with integrated strategic marketing to enhance market share. All media will be integrated in theme, frequency, and specific targeting to interface with direct sales contact on an industry specific "flighted" approach. Over-all marketing expenditures will be increased from less than 1% currently to 4% in 1999 and 2000.

Positioning Statement

DLP will be the quality solution company in the markets it serves.

Pricing, Promotion, & Distribution Strategies

DLP pricing, while competitive, will never be the lowest price available. The price range targeted is mid-level. Trade shows will continue to be the primary promotional vehicle. A public relations campaign aimed at specific industry publications will be instituted for the first time. Internet on-line ordering and customer service will be instituted.

Multi-channel distribution strategies will be followed. Direct sales will be the primary target.

Marketing Programs & Sales Strategy

Our marketing program will involve direct mail, industry magazine/trade advertising, and integrated sales follow-up.

Our sales strategy is based on key sales manager contact. This is a new person in each division. DLP has never had full-time people dedicated to each main product line in a sales only function. Order processing and customer service will be Internet and telemarketing based. Periodic sales contact blitzes will be industry specific.

Sales Forecast

The sales forecast below for 1998 is actual through October. November reflects the current portion of a new $1.2 million dollar order that has been booked. 1999 and 2000 projections reflect expected gains in market share produced by the strategies and expenditures outlined. The company will exceed $20 million in sales by year four (2002).

Margins will increase in parallel.

Sales Forecast

Sales	1998	1999	2000
Combined Sales	$6,815,025	$10,200,000	$15,500,000
Other	$0	$0	$0
Total Sales	**$6,815,025**	**$10,200,000**	**$15,500,000**
Direct Cost of Sales			
Combined Sales	$4,170,401	$5,865,000	$8,525,000
Other	$0	$0	$0
Subtotal Cost of Sales	**$4,170,401**	**$5,865,000**	**$8,525,000**

Milestones

The keys to management implementing this plan are:

- Increased capitalization.
- Professional staffing, especially key management personnel.
- Flexibility in implementation of new marketing plans. Test as one goes with discretionary budget allocation.

MANAGEMENT SUMMARY

In the past, David Stumbo has managed all facets of company operation. This has simply been too demanding for one person to oversee effectively. Mr. Stumbo has been very effective in growing and profitably managing the powder-coating side of the business. However, he has not been able to wear the production, marketing, and financial control mantle for both sides of the total operation.

Organizational Structure

A new organization structure will be implemented with the launch of this plan. Greg Stumbo will directly oversee the powder coating operation. A new general manager of the drying equipment business will be hired. Two candidates have already been identified. Bob McIntyre, a well-known industry consultant, will be retained for strategic growth advisory purposes. He will also serve as an oversight person for strategic review of plan milestones and implementation progress.

An overall marketing manager will be hired as well as an outside advertising/PR firm. Sales specialists in each division will concentrate full-time on those products and services. This has never been done in the past.

Management Team

The current management team is made up of Greg Stumbo who has grown up in DLP's business. The other strengths of the company are in engineering and production. Financial controls have been weak in the past. A qualified CPA firm has been retained to implement financial controls. Two general manager candidates have been identified; their resumes are available.

Significant management gaps have existed in financial management, divisional management, and sales and marketing. All gaps are filled by the implementation of this plan.

Personnel Plan

This personnel table lumps all current employees together. Growth needs are highlighted. The following people are added in 1999:

Staff:

- One Human Resources
- One Accountant (Cost)
- One Purchasing
- One Engineer
- One Draftsman
- One Quality Assurance
- One EPA Compliance
- One Traffic Officer

These personnel will fill needs produced by increased business and also bolster functions that are currently weak.

Production:

- One Supervisor
- One Lead Man
- Six Laborers

These personnel will be needed for business increases. Current capacity is running at 50%. No new capital equipment is required initially.

Management:

- One General Mgr.
- One Marketing Mgr.
- Two Sales Mgrs.

Total personnel forecast is as follows:

Personnel Plan	1998	1999	2000
Total Employees (currently)	1,779,192	1,779,192	1,779,192
New Staff	$0	$430,000	$640,000
New Management	$0	$360,000	$425,000
New Production People	$0	$175,000	$350,000
Other	$0	$0	$0
Total Payroll	$1,779,192	$2,744,192	$3,194,192
Total Headcount	67	87	102
Payroll Burden	$355,838	$548,838	$638,838
Total Payroll Expenditures	**$2,135,030**	**$3,293,030**	**$3,833,030**

FINANCIAL PLAN

The financial plan calls for new infusion of $3.75 million by January 1999. It is expected that $2 million will be new equity, $1 million long-term subordinate debt, and $750k in a new credit facility for working capital. $500k existing line will be repaid and $500k in existing long-term debt will be repaid.

Important Assumptions

The following table represents financial assumptions on which the plan is based:

General Assumptions	1998	1999	2000
Short-term Interest Rate %	8.00%	8.00%	8.00%
Long-term Interest Rate %	13.00%	13.00%	13.00%
Payment Days Estimator	30	30	30
Collection Days Estimator	45	45	45
Inventory Turnover Estimator	6	6	6
Tax Rate %	25.00%	25.00%	25.00%
Expenses in Cash %	10.00%	10.00%	10.00%
Sales on Credit %	75.00%	75.00%	75.00%
Personnel Burden %	20.00%	20.00%	20.00%

Key Financial Indicators

Our benchmarks indicate margin improvements and sales improvements. Operating expenses increase initially for marketing and staffing but will be recouped as time moves forward. The turn-around and ramp-up of the next three years will pay dividends in economies of scales in year four and beyond. This will contribute to company value. If sales increases exceed projections, very little more in overhead will be added. Bottom lines will improve substantially.

Break-even Analysis

Fixed expenses for DLP, Inc. are estimated at $3 million per year. Thus, the monthly burn rate is $250K. At the historic gross margin of 40%, monthly sales of $625K are needed to sustain operations. This equates to $7.5 million in gross sales. The company has demonstrated an ability to meet this volume on an annual basis. It is assumed that the company can continue to do so. Thus, the downside risk is minimal. It is further assumed that better project costing can improve margins and sales volumes can increase profitably with adequate working capital.

Break Even Analysis:

Monthly Units Break-even	$625,000
Monthly Sales Break-even	$625,000

Assumptions

Average Per-Unit Revenue	$1.00
Average Per-Unit Variable Cost	$0.60
Estimated Monthly Fixed Cost	$250,000

Projected Profit and Loss

Growth building expenditures and investment will continue to burn cash for the next three years. However, maximum burn is in year two. Positive cash flow begins in year 2001. Expense controls will be key to bottom line. Controls will be vital in more efficient operation.

Profit and Loss (Income Statement)	1998	1999	2000
Sales	$6,815,025	$10,200,000	$15,500,000
Direct Cost of Sales	$4,170,401	$5,865,000	$8,525,000
Other	$0	$0	$0
Total Cost of Sales	**$4,170,401**	**$5,865,000**	**$8,525,000**
Gross Margin	$2,644,624	$4,335,000	$6,975,000
Gross Margin %	38.81%	42.50%	45.00%
Operating expenses:			
Advertising/Promotion	$43,000	$400,000	$600,000
Payroll Expense	$1,779,192	2,744,192	$3,194,192
Payroll Burden	$355,838	$548,838	$638,838
Depreciation	$74,196	$74,196	$74,196
Other Expenses (total)	$2,302,217	$2,350,000	$2,600,000
Total Operating Expenses	**$4,554,443**	**$6,117,226**	**$7,107,226**
Profit Before Interest & Taxes	($1,909,819)	($1,782,226)	($132,226)
Interest Expense Short-term	$40,000	$60,000	$80,000
Interest Expense Long-term	$70,662	$103,162	$135,662
Taxes Incurred	($505,120)	($486,347)	($86,972)
Net Profit	($1,515,361)	($1,459,041)	($260,916)
Net Profit/Sales	-22.24%	-14.30%	-1.68%

Projected Cash Flow

Current year (1998) negative cash flow represents the current debt levels and utilization of existing credit facilities. Capital infusion provides the cash needed for 1999 ramp-up strategies. Cash remains positive throughout 1999. Depending on sales achievement, cash needs can be determined for year 2000. Cash is forecast to be positive, but no new investment is targeted for year 2000. If there is a shortfall it is expected that credit facilities can be extended based upon increased sales and receivables.

Proforma Cash Flow	1998	1999	2000
Net Profit	($1,515,361)	($1,459,041)	($260,916)
Plus:			
Depreciation	$74,196	$74,196	$74,196
Change in Accounts Payable	$116,918	$176,605	$261,621
Current Borrowing (repayment)	$0	$500,000	$0
Increase (decrease) Other Liabilities	$0	$0	$0
Long-term Borrowing (repayment)	$0	$500,000	$0
Capital Input	$0	$3,750,000	$0
Subtotal	($1,324,247)	$3,541,760	$74,900
Less:			
Change in Accounts Receivable	$35,338	$379,970	$594,935
Change in Inventory	$364,200	$351,077	$551,084
Change in Other Short-term Assets	$0	$0	$0
Capital Expenditure	$0	$0	$0
Dividends	$0	$0	$0
Subtotal	$399,538	$731,048	$1,146,019
Net Cash Flow	**($1,723,785)**	**$2,810,712**	**($1,071,119)**
Cash Balance	**($1,666,968)**	**$1,143,744**	**$72,625**

Projected Balance Sheet

The company turns positive in net worth in 1999. But this is due to new capital infusion. The important fact is that net worth remains positive in year 2000 with no new capital. Subsequent growth strategies can be implemented at that time.

Proforma Balance Sheet

Assets
Starting Balances

Short-term Assets	1997	1998	1999	2000
Cash	$56,817	($1,666,968)	$1,143,744	$72,625
Accounts Receivable	$729,662	$765,000	$1,144,970	$1,739,906
Inventory	$499,800	$864,000	$1,215,077	$1,766,161
Other Short-term Assets	$403,100	$403,100	$403,100	$403,100
Total Short-term Assets	$1,689,379	$365,132	$3,906,891	$3,981,791
Long-term Assets				
Capital Assets	$769,053	$769,053	$769,053	$769,053
Accumulated Depreciation	$331,303	$405,499	$479,695	$553,891
Total Long-term Assets	$437,750	$363,554	$289,358	$215,162
Total Assets	**$2,127,129**	**$728,686**	**$4,196,249**	**$4,196,953**
Liabilities and Capital				
Accounts Payable	$437,433	$554,351	$730,956	$992,576
Short-term Notes	$500,000	$500,000	$1,000,000	$1,000,000
Other Short-term Liabilities	$398,126	$398,126	$398,126	$398,126
Subtotal Short-term Liabilities	$1,335,559	$1,452,477	$2,129,082	$2,390,702
Long-term Liabilities	$543,554	$543,554	$1,043,554	$1,043,554
Total Liabilities	**$1,879,113**	**$1,996,031**	**$3,172,636**	**$3,434,256**
Paid in Capital	$3,966	$3,966	$3,753,966	$3,753,966
Retained Earnings	$391,386	$244,050	($1,271,311)	($2,730,352)
Earnings	($147,336)	($1,515,361)	($1,459,041)	($260,916)
Total Capital	**$248,016**	**($1,267,345)**	**$1,023,614**	**$762,697**
Total Liabilities and Capital	**$2,127,129**	**$728,686**	**$4,196,249**	**$4,196,953**
Net Worth	**$248,016**	**($1,267,345)**	**$1,023,614**	**$762,697**

Business Ratios

All business ratios improve markedly during the course of this plan. A solid foundation is being built for expansion. If divestiture of the manufacturing heat equipment division is desired at this time it will be at a substantial valuation gain. Further expansion capital would most certainly be available in any event.

Ratio Analysis

Profitability Ratios:	1998	1999	2000	RMA
Gross Margin	38.81%	42.50%	45.00%	0
Net Profit Margin	-22.24%	-14.30%	-1.68%	0
Return on Assets	-207.96%	-34.77%	-6.22%	0
Return on Equity	0.00%	-142.54%	-34.21%	0
Activity Ratios				
Accounts Receivable Turnover	6.68	6.68	6.68	0
Collection Days	53	46	45	0
Inventory Turnover	6.12	5.64	5.72	0
Accounts Payable Turnover	10.7	10.7	10.7	0
Total Asset Turnover	9.35	2.43	3.69	0
Debt Ratios				
Debt to Net Worth	0	3.1	4.5	0
Short-term Liabilities to Liabilities	0.73	0.67	0.7	0
Liquidity Ratios				
Current Ratio	0.25	1.84	1.67	0
Quick Ratio	-0.34	1.26	0.93	0
Net Working Capital	($1,087,345)	$1,777,810	$1,591,089	0
Interest Coverage	-17.26	-10.92	-0.61	0
Additional Ratios				
Assets to Sales	0.11	0.41	0.27	0
Debt/Assets	274%	76%	82%	0
Current Debt/Total Assets	199%	51%	57%	0
Acid Test	-0.87	0.73	0.2	0
Asset Turnover	9.35	2.43	3.69	0
Sales/Net Worth	0	9.96	20.32	0

Long-term Plan

All strategic decisions will be addressed in year four. Divestiture, roll-up, and M & A activity are all potential exits.

This can be compared to past performance to determine value added. Net worth achieved is only a fraction of market value for specialty manufacturing concerns on an earnings multiple valuation basis.

Note: Supplementary tables included in the rear of this plan are month-to-month for the current year 1998. These are included to illustrate more specifically how the turn-around has already begun in terms of sales backlogs and cost control initiatives already begun. The capital required in this plan will serve to initiate the building of future value.

Past Performance

	1995	1996	1997
Sales	$9,562,251	$10,078,159	$7,775,189
Gross Margin	$4,398,280	$4,245,154	$2,901,531
Gross % (calculated)	46.00%	42.12%	37.32%
Operating Expenses	$3,779,000	$4,042,370	$3,056,425
Collection period (days)	45	45	45
Inventory turnover	6	6	6

Balance Sheet
Short-term Assets

	1995	1996	1997
Cash	($138,617)	$180,743	$56,817
Accounts receivable	$770,218	$596,011	$729,662
Inventory	$626,148	$504,673	$499,800
Other Short-term Assets	$343,303	$320,000	$403,100
Total Short-term Assets	$1,601,052	$1,601,427	$1,689,379
Long-term Assets			
Capital Assets	$674,455	$730,278	$769,053
Accumulated Depreciation	$226,930	$302,049	$331,303
Total Long-term Assets	$447,525	$428,229	$437,750
Total Assets	**$2,048,577**	**$2,029,656**	**$2,127,129**

Capital and Liabilities

	1995	1996	1997
Accounts Payable	$680,228	$192,226	$437,433
Short-term Notes	$223,730	$549,000	$500,000
Other Short-term Liabilities	$315,458	$296,232	$398,126
Subtotal Short-term Liabilities	$1,219,416	$1,037,458	$1,335,559
Long-term Liabilities	$416,586	$587,397	$543,554
Total Liabilities	$1,636,002	$1,624,855	$1,879,113
Paid in Capital	($30,594)	$3,966	$3,966
Retained Earnings	$291,253	$260,373	$391,386
Earnings	$151,916	$140,462	($147,336)
Total Capital	$412,575	$404,801	$248,016
Total Capital and Liabilities	$2,048,577	$2,029,656	$2,127,129

Other Inputs

	1995	1996	1997
Payment days	30	30	30
Sales on credit	$9,500,000	$10,000,000	$7,500,000
Receivables turnover	12.33	16.78	10.28

Software Engineering & Management Co.

175 W. Meadowcrest Turnpike, Suite 304
Cincinnati, Ohio 45231

Products from Swiss Issue WebTools allow businesses to generate leads, sell products, run sales promotions, and capture demographic information about web site visitors, as well as communicate with visitors and obtain information about what potential customers are doing while browsing the web site. These powerful software tools allow clients to stay in complete control of their web sites and, more importantly, ensure that their customers enjoy a successful Internet experience while visiting their sites.

EXECUTIVE SUMMARY

Swiss Issue WebTools (SIW) is a software engineering and management company that develops and sells business software technology for the Internet. It provides software tools for e-commerce, including shopping carts, point of sale, lead generation, lead distribution, security methods (including encryption), and search engine technologies. Its products help businesses to build, manage, and maintain their own web sites, sell products, generate leads, distribute information, and gain intelligence about their web site visitors. The SIW product family provides business owners with access to such services for a fraction of the costs typically incurred.

The Internet software market is relatively large and is continuing to expand. The vast majority of businesses with successful web strategies are those that have the financial resources to frequently update and redesign their web sites. Such businesses either hire and/or retain "information systems" employees to develop, support, and maintain their web sites, or alternatively purchase Internet services from multiple parties, integrate these services, and gather or purchase information on their markets to facilitate web site updates. By contrast, SIW's clients are small to medium-sized businesses that want to be able to quickly build, manage, and maintain their web sites and e-commerce solutions without incurring substantial costs by relying upon additional employees or multiple vendors. These products provide flexibility, allowing businesses complete control of their web sites.

TARGET CUSTOMERS

SIW markets its products to small and medium-sized businesses that want total, one-stop solutions to e-commerce technology, Internet advertising, marketing, and sales concerns. Its typical "target" customers are businesses that would prefer to invest in technologies that allow them to develop their own functional, interactive Internet web sites rather than hiring information systems employees to develop such web sites.

The Internet is an interactive, worldwide network of computers and data systems allowing users to retrieve data, purchase products, send and receive communications, and buy and sell goods or services. The Internet's use has grown substantially since it was commercially introduced in the early 1990s. Estimates indicate that the number of Internet users in the United States will grow from approximately 35 million in 1996 to about 160 million by the year 2000. The increase in the number of users has resulted in a rapid increase in the number of advertisers, products, and services available on the Internet.

Business-to-Business Segment

According to the September issue of *Business 2.0,* business-to-business commerce on the Internet already exceeds the business-to-consumer market, growing from $43 billion in 1998 to an expected $1 trillion by 2003, versus $7.8 billion to $108 billion on the business-to-consumer side. The Internet economy already generates a total of $301 billion in U.S. revenue, about the same as cars or telecommunications. Hub revenue from advertising and transactions will grow from $290 million in 1998 to $20 billion by 2002. Says *Business 2.0*: "A new breed of intermediaries is emerging to facilitate business to business e-commerce."

According to *Investor's Business Daily* (September 15, 1999), J. D. Edwards has 7 out of 10 people working on e-business similar to their 4 nearest competitors. MySAP.com has emerged just to service business-to-business transactions. There are 1.2 million small businesses online (only a fraction of the 7 million small businesses with fewer than 100 employees); a figure that is expected to nearly double next year. This year 400,000 businesses are expected to conduct business online up from 150,000 last year. Next year the number is expected to be 850,000.

Sales & Marketing

SIW's competitors are not effectively targeting this market niche: a complete, Internet-based, end-to-end business solution for small to medium-sized businesses. SIW products allow businesses to generate leads, sell products, run sales promotions, capture demographic information about web site visitors, communicate with visitors and obtain information about what potential customers are doing while browsing the web site. SIW products allow clients to stay in complete control of their web sites and provide tools that facilitate a successful Internet experience for their customers.

SIW currently markets and sells its products through reseller channels, an internal sales force, 15 independent consultants (outside sales), and strategic partners. As of July 15, 1999, SIW has entered into Reseller Agreements with six companies.

HISTORY

- May 1987 – Predecessor-in-interest Corporation established under the name Wooster Associates.

- March 1998 – Began development of prepackaged software solutions for e-commerce.

- April 1998 – Began shift from consulting business to prepackaged software solutions.

- October 1998 – Filed trademark on major web tool product.

- November 1998 – Completed first prepackaged e-commerce software with release of major web tool product. Incorporated in Idaho.

- January 1999 – SIW merged with Wooster Associates and became a publicly traded company.

- February 1999 – SIW released its second version of its major web tool product, and first version of its shopping web tool product.

- July 1999 – Signed agreements with six resellers for its line of WebTools. Filed trademarks on three of its major software products.

- October 1999 – Opened new online shopping network with proprietary features; signed joint venture agreement on same online shopping network.

- November 1999 – Signed joint venture agreement on Commerce Central, Inc.

BACKGROUND

Products

SIW has developed software technologies that allow businesses to create, manage and maintain their own web sites and e-commerce storefronts from any Internet-capable computer. The SIW product family is made up of powerful, intuitive and easy-to-use software tools.

Users of these tools can create an online e-commerce storefront, generate sales leads, process credit cards in real-time, communicate with customers, collect statistical information and monitor web site visitors. Businesses can create, manage and maintain every aspect of their web site at all times of the day or night. This functionality, combined with an easy-to-use visual interface, provides a point-and-click complete Internet business solution for approximately $3,000 per year (less than 10% of the cost of a traditional consultant).

Features of Major Web Tools

ChangeTool quickly and easily allows clients to update, modify or enhance their web sites. Changes can be made 24 hours a day, 7 days a week from anywhere. It includes an easy-to-use, powerful visual "WYSIWYG" (What You See Is What You Get) interface, with familiar "drag-and-drop" functions that allow clients to make changes instantaneously. Changes are updated automatically and placed online in minutes. WebWizard allows manipulation of web site layout, colors, content, resizing, cutting and pasting text, graphics, and tables. This tool gives businesses a library of hundreds of graphics and animations to use throughout their site and even the ability to upload their own graphics and files. ChangeTool lists the web site with the major search engines, sets up email accounts, and registers domain names.

ShopFirst adds custom "electronic storefronts" to web sites. It assists in setting up merchant accounts and in facilitating secure, real-time credit card transactions. ShopFirst provides a completely customizable product database. Products and all variables such as price, color, and size are entered into a password-protected database that can be updated or edited at any time. Customizable price and shipping modifiers, receipt options, sale flagging, product option variables and regional tax calculations are available.

MultiChannels sends email to multiple customers, marketing directly to them at a fraction of traditional postage costs. Clients can send announcements, sales information, updates, promotions, newsletters or any other correspondence to customers at any time. With MultiChannels, subscribers can add or remove themselves from the automated email database.

WhoProfiler gathers demographic information from custom questionnaires providing direct feedback from site visitors. With WhoProfiler, businesses obtain information from targeted audiences such as customer satisfaction and preferences. WhoProfiler assists businesses in obtaining information necessary to improve customer relations and products. It conducts surveys notifying customers of product specials and gathers additional information.

VisitStats monitors web site visits determining the effectiveness of changes to web sites and which pages draw the most interest. VisitStats keeps a detailed two-year history of visits and activities within subscribers' web sites and can generate reports of site activity. It produces reports showing yearlong sales trends that identify product purchasers and track the effectiveness of sales and promotions during specific time periods or from specific locations.

ChangeTool and ShopFirst are basic products and come in two versions: "Express" and "Pro." The "Express" and "Pro" versions provide different product features and support options to clients. MultiChannels, WhoProfiler and VisitStats are available as upgrades to our customers for an additional license fee.

The new online shopping site is a joint venture owned by SmartQ Systems Inc. and Swiss Issue WebTools. This site is a powerful, easy-to-use e-commerce portal that brings online consumers together with merchants in a network of virtual storefronts. It also gives the consumer incredible product searching capabilities across the entire network of merchants. The new release of the shopping site includes many new features, including advanced search functions and increased payment processing integration.

Might-T-Fine Commerce is a "bolt-on" e-commerce solution for any size business. Might-T-Fine Commerce enables businesses with an existing web presence to immediately add e-commerce capability directly into their web sites. It is a full, back-end storefront and product management system combined with an integrated shopping cart technology that is fully compatible with the online shopping site. Any customer who uses Might-T-Fine will have the ability to market their products within the shopping network and take advantage of the marketing and traffic-producing resources that it offers.

SALES PLAN

SIW has developed multiple channels to sell their products: Strategic Partners, Resellers, Inside Sales, and Independent Consultants.

Strategic Partner projects include Planet Now Network and the online shopping network.

Planet Now Network is a marketing company formed to promote and sell products from Swiss Issue WebTools, American Top Merchant Systems, and SmartQ. Planet Now Network has recently begun an Internet Business Opportunity seminar series offering affiliate opportunities to become a SIW independent consultant, an affiliate for a high-use vacation web site and IdeserveASite.com. Planet Now Network anticipates they will be able to present SIW product to over 500 potential purchasers and affiliates each week.

IDeserveASite.com is a program that allows affiliates to solicit users for Planet Now Network by giving away free, easy-to-create web sites. Users of these web sites receive a web site that they can immediately design with IDeserveASite.com's quick and easy graphical interface and free lifetime hosting. All users of IDeserveASite.com will be allowed to upgrade to SIW's full line of products and other options that include Might-T-Fine Commerce, the online shopping network, our unique web tool products, and any additional support or design services.

SIW's independent consultant recruiters will contact nonbuyers at the Business Opportunity Seminars. SIW anticipates that by mid 2000 they will have over 200 independent consultants representing the entire SIW product family. SIW has also begun an Internet business-to-business seminar series in which the initial results of this program show that over 35 percent of attendees purchase SIW products for their businesses. As the customer base for SIW grows, recurring revenues will grow accordingly. Annual hosting fees for successive years are equal to approximately 50 percent of the first year revenue paid by the client.

FINANCIAL

SIW began selling WebWizard Pro late November 1998. WebWizard Express went on sale in the first quarter of 1999. During 1997 SIW had 41 clients, who accounted for no more than 5 percent of gross revenue. During 1998, SIW had a client base of 85. Four clients each accounted for more than 5 percent of gross revenues for that year. By second quarter of 1999, SIW increased its client base to several hundred. No single client provided more than 5 percent of gross revenue in 1999.

Written sales have now reached $13,000 a day or $3.4 million on an annualized basis.

MANAGEMENT

Lawrence C. Potter — President and Chief Executive Officer of Swiss Issue WebTools. In July 1993 he started UPTIP, Inc., developing custom and commercial software for animation and special effects. UPTIP had 28 employees. Potter was then recruited by Tim Tepe to become the Chief Operations Officer for SIW. After leading and growing the company for two years, Tepe stepped down and asked if Potter would take over as President and CEO of SIW. A combination of determination, vision, leadership, and relationship building abilities has made Potter a key asset to the company and its current position in the marketplace. Potter has seven years of experience providing computer consulting and business management services.

Chris N. Skyler — Chief Operating Officer. Skyler has eighteen years of experience in sales, operations, and services in the software industry. He holds a B.A. in Business Administration with a Marketing emphasis from Ohio State University.

Mark L. Bastian — Director. Previously Bastian was the founder and president of New Jersey WebSolutions, Inc. From 1991 to 1993 he specialized in 3D computer animation. From 1997 to 1999, he was a senior animator for UPTIP, producing two- and three-dimensional computer animation for television commercials, promotional videos, and medical simulations. He received his B.A., with honors, from the University of Nevada.

Karl E. LeBlond — Vice President of Engineering and a Director. LeBlond has 14 years of experience working with computer hardware and software. He started with New Jersey WebSolutions in November 1997 as an independent consultant, and then became the Technical Director in August 1998. Prior to this he was the head programmer for UPTIP for five years. He attended Miami University in Oxford, Ohio.

Eric K. Schmitter — Creative Director and a Director. Schmitter has two years of experience in animation and five years of experience in software sales. He was Art Director at UPTIP from 1995 to 1997. He attended Notre Dame University and Greenlake Community College.

Aaron F. White — Director. White has three years of experience in software development programming. He worked as a Senior Programmer for Utah WebWorks. He was a programmer at IRAD from 1994 to 1997. In 1995, he received his Associate of Science degree in Electronics Technology from the University of Dallas.

Henry Lee — Chief Financial Officer. Lee has been with SIW since July 1999. He brings a dozen years of experience, including three years with Price Waterhouse (left firm as a senior accountant). He has over five years of experience as CFO for South Shore Munitions, Inc. and for BUY of LA, Inc. He graduated with a B.S. in Accounting and a B.A. in English Literature from the University of Cincinnati.

CURRENT DEVELOPMENTS & FUTURE EXPECTATIONS

SIW is currently developing and will be releasing several new technologies between now and the end of first quarter of 2000. These products include new releases of all of the previously discussed products.

SIW expects to develop a substantial presence in its target market through a combination of marketing strategy, unique proprietary technology, technical expertise, and early entry into our target market. SIW is pursuing a national advertising campaign including seminars, television, radio, and print media.

CONCLUSIONS

- SIW is an Internet investment company.

- SIW has created software tools that empower nontechnical people to create and maintain their own web sites as well as supplying integrated easy-to-use e-commerce and e-business tools for a fraction of the cost of hiring outside consultants.

- SIW has engineered the only significant technology not already owned by a major entity.

- SIW has structured a unique and effective reseller program.

- SIW has a trial version of its collection of web tools which can be provided to a business for evaluation purposes free of charge.

- SIW products allow a business to create, operate, and maintain a web site for an initial one-year term, after that our customer may maintain their license by paying a monthly fee of approximately 6 percent of their initial purchase price.

- Software sales have high profit margins.

- SIW has strong alliances with American Top Merchant Systems Inc. and SmartQ Payment Systems, Inc.

Special Needs Clothing Store

BUSINESS PLAN   YOU CAN DO IT!

2100 W. 117th St.
Overland Park, Kansas 66213

This business plan for a clothing store will focus on the special clothing needs of elderly people or people with physical limitations. The business projects success based on the expertise and commitment of its owners and the lack of competition in this market. Also, the trend in the aging of the population will only serve to increase the need for these types of services.

- EXECUTIVE SUMMARY

- BUSINESS GOALS

- BUSINESS CONCEPT

- MARKETING

- OPERATIONS PLAN

- PRODUCT PROCUREMENT

- LOCATION

- COMPETITION

- MANAGEMENT

- FINANCIALS

EXECUTIVE SUMMARY

Christy Margolis and Rebecca Slinger are opening the "You Can Do It!" retail store, specializing in clothing and accessories for the elderly and those in other age groups with physical or visual limitations. Our product line will cater to people who have mild disabilities, such as arthritis, and to those who may be confined to a wheelchair.

America's population is growing older and living longer. This valuable market is relatively untouched by retailers in Johnson County, Kansas. Our store will provide access, selection, and quality merchandise under one roof.

This unique idea evolved through our own encounters as licensed social workers in a local nursing home. We have 25 years of combined experience with the geriatric population. We have seen the difficult challenges families confront for their loved ones. Often, this task has fallen on healthcare professionals, due to a lack of resources available to the public. Through research, questioning, and playing devil's advocate to the idea, our commitment has only intensified.

Initially, we plan to target the Johnson County market and later expand to outlying areas. We forecast breaking even after three months in business and building sales to $9,500 per month for the first year.

To fulfill this goal, we are making application through the State of Kansas' Small Business Loan Program for a loan of $50,000. We, the partners, will provide 28% ($20,000) of the total $70,000. Both of us will work full-time in the store, dedicating ourselves to the success of our venture.

BUSINESS GOALS

- Provide access to a unique selection of quality dress and casual clothing accessories and giftware to those who are 65 years of age and older, and who live in the Johnson County area.
- Be the major supplier in the retailer, special-needs clothing business servicing Johnson County.
- Generate sufficient revenue to provide two incomes of $60,000 per year by the fifth year of successful business.
- Owners to be in the store full-time, ensuring customer satisfaction and hands-on management of the business. Later, to add a part-time assistant to be with one of the owners at all times during store hours.
- Become a resource center, using our social work background and knowledge base, to generate and enhance our exposure in the community.

BUSINESS CONCEPT

You Can Do It! will be a retail specialty shop in Overland Park, a suburb of Kansas City, Kansas. Our store, which will open May 2000, will provide quality, comfortable clothing and accessories for those with special needs. The space we will lease is 800 square feet.

Statistics abound to support the fact that Americans are living longer and the trend will continue. Today, people over 65 constitute 12.8% of the population and that number is expected to increase to 16.4% by the year 2020. In the year 2025, the 65+ bracket is expected to be six times as high with the "baby boomers" aging—one in every five Americans will be in the 65+ grouping. Not only is there a future in this growing market, but there is also an increase in expendable income. Beginning in 1990, those 65+ are twice as affluent as the same age group was in the 1950s. Many of these 65+ have a moderate disability and are experiencing the limitation of at least one activity of daily living. This sizable and growing market is relatively untouched; few retailers cater to its needs.

The selection of clothing we will offer is geared toward ease of getting in and out of the clothing, care-free maintenance, and attractive styling. Included in our inventory will be jogging/sweat outfits, washable slacks for men and women, day dresses, and "dusters." We will also stock sweaters, undergarments, hosiery, and "wrap" skirts. We will carry garments that open down the back as well as those with Velcro closures. These are easier to manage for those in wheelchairs and for caregivers to dress individuals. Large-face watches, magnifying glasses, walkers and wheelchairs, carrier bags, eyeglass chains and cases, will be among the accessories we offer. Giftware selections will include picture frames, notecards, vases, jewelry, and window bird feeders. Our goal is to be a "one-stop" shop with quality merchandise consolidated under one roof.

Specialty stores usually account for 20% to 25% of business in any given market, and we believe our percentages will be higher, based on our unique idea and the growing number of people to serve. Our marketing strategy and education of the public about our services will be vital to our success.

MARKETING

Marketing will be essential in spreading the name and services of You Can Do It! Our start-up costs allow for an initial marketing "blitz" with ongoing advertising allotments factored into the monthly budget. We will be contracting with Rita Morgan of Evergreen3 Marketing to assist us in professionally marketing our business. Evergreen3 will design our logo, stationery, a series of flyers, and an informational brochure.

Initially, we will write a press release to go in the *Kansas City Star* and neighborhood newspapers, emphasizing our unique market and special niche as a community service. We will advertise ourselves to area nursing homes, senior centers, and appropriate hospital departments (rehabilitation, orthopedics, and social services). We will also establish contact with the Association for the Blind, Easter Seals Society, Alzheimer's Association, Council on Aging, Senior Services, and various support groups throughout the city that serve our target market. We will contact nursing agencies that deal with homebound individuals who will benefit from our products. We intend to send our brochures to attorneys who often serve as guardians, or who are responsible for overseeing the affairs/well-being of those in our target market.

We will periodically continue publicity through local religious newspapers and various other bulletins that reach potential customers. We plan to have a flyer in local pharmacies and be publicized in nursing home mailings to family members. We intend to advertise in the publication serving the local physician organization in the city to put You Can Do It! in the mind of physicians as a referral. Another resource we will utilize is the radio station (attracts "older" listeners) operated at one of the local nursing homes in the area.

We, the owners, take responsibility for aggressively keeping You Can Do It! in the forefront of the community's mind. Along with the written word, our presence and approach to customers will be one of our best marketing tools. A good reputation will have our customers marketing for us while we build a loyal and repeat clientele. We will seek customer input as to future merchandise requests, and how best to meet their needs. With these steps in place, we are confident in repeat business and high customer satisfaction.

OPERATIONS PLAN

In order to provide a selection, we will open with an initial inventory of $15,000 in goods. We will maintain an on-floor inventory of $10,000 to $15,000 the first year. We project monthly sales of $6,000 for the first three months, increasing to $8,000 in the fourth month. (Increase due to word-of-mouth and advertising.) Our total gross sales for the first year should be $61,500, May to December.

Though this may seem ambitious for a small store, the numbers are directly related to our store being the first of its kind in Overland Park; one that offers clothing and accessories to a specialized market and do it conveniently under one roof. We intend to position our store as the leading supplier for "home wear" for those 65+ in the area and, within three to five years, be the sales leader for those needing special care clothing, regardless of age.

The form of legal organization for You Can Do It! is a partnership agreement. The partnership agreement is on file with Rogers and Reece. The partnership agreement identifies the following duties and responsibilities:

Christy Margolis:

- Record keeping
- Computation and payment of all business taxes
- Keeping of daily account records
- Deposit in partnership bank account of daily receipts
- Collection of accounts receivable
- Correspondence with customers, suppliers, and governmental agencies
- Day-to-day contact with accountant for the partnership business

Rebecca Slinger:

- Managing partner of the partnership; responsible for the general management of the partnership's business; in case of any conflict or disputes between partners, the managing partner shall have the sole responsibility and duty to resolve such conflicts or disputes
- Sales promotions and projections
- Management of inventory

The following management duties shall be shared by both partners in the operation of the partnership business:

- Purchase of inventory
- Planning of marketing strategy for the partnership business
- Hiring personnel

The partnership has engaged the accounting services of Gerald Houston CPA of Whiteoak & Co. The partners intend to provide the accountant with the necessary information so a total business picture (cash position, ratios) can be obtained every month for the first year. Fiscal management will be closely monitored by the accountant and the partners to ensure success of the business. All computations for mandatory accountings as well as federal, state, and local financial obligations will be handled by the accountant to ensure compliance.

PRODUCT PROCUREMENT

Eleanor Minors of MRT Group in New York will be handling the buying of our women's apparel. Initially, we will go to New York to educate her about the quality and styling of merchandise for You Can Do It! We have been in frequent contact with Eleanor, and she is confident she can supply our line of stock. She has excellent references, and has been a buyer for over 15 years.

Christy and Rebecca have been to the Buyers Market, a wholesale show of crafters and artisans, and will be buying our giftwares through established contacts. These are colorful, unique items that have a lot of eye appeal. We have been to three shows (Philadelphia, Baltimore, and Columbus) and received training by the owners/buyers of a successful gift/gallery in Miami, Florida.

We have met with Denise Perrino, the owner of a small manufacturing company in a nearby town. Denise has done samples of our stock for walker bags and women's slips, and we will contract with her for production on these items.

In addition, we have consulted with Mark Meyerhouse and Ed Sebastian. Mark owned his own manufacturing company for 25 years, while Ed owned and managed his own department store for over 40 years. Both men should prove to be quite helpful in our goods selection and procurement activities.

LOCATION

We intend to open doors at 2100 W. 117th St. in Overland Park, Kansas. Because of our broad client base, we selected a central location easily accessible to the vast majority of the Kansas City, Kansas, population. We will be reached easily via Interstate 435, as our shop will be in close proximity to one of its southern exits.

Having carefully reviewed the placement of area nursing homes and hospitals, we couldn't be in a better spot. The Montaque Center, Dreamsprings, and St. Francis Retirement Center are all within a three-mile radius, having a combined population of 502 nursing beds. Oak Tree Pavilion is within four miles, and has another 174 nursing beds and 60 assisted apartments.

The one-story building we will rent is located among a small group of shops and has close visibility from the street. It's a front/end spot with good signage and window space for display. There is ample parking and easy access to our doors, both in the front and back, for those with walkers or wheelchairs. The area has a friendly neighborhood feel to it, which is ideal for a shop like ours.

After surveying the area for locations that met our requirements of good access, safety at night, and central placement, we know our choice is a sound one. This location affords us 800 square feet and is well in line with our budget for leasing property. We will be signing a three-year lease, locking us in at the rate of $530.00 per month.

With minor aesthetic enhancements and creative decorating we will be ready to open You Can Do It! in a few weeks.

COMPETITION

Currently we have an edge on the market, for there is no free-standing store in the region such as You Can Do It! This is almost unbelievable considering the "aging of America" now happening. Statistics show this group to be the fastest-growing segment of our population.

We know firsthand from our experience in nursing homes the frustration of shopping for the elderly or those with physical limitations. It becomes a necessity to either order from a catalog or go store-to-store trying to locate these hard-to-find items.

Catalogs offer the types of clothing and accessories we will carry, but this method of ordering leaves no room for individual tastes. The catalogs are not typically mailed to the general public, but rather to staff in area facilities. Customers are shipped goods which are "on hand" at the time. Often these pieces are patterns and colors without regard to personal preference. The garments frequently are of a low-grade quality and lack style.

There are areas of some stores which carry some of our merchandise. However, they are impersonal shopping spaces that leave customers to fend for themselves. We will be a one-stop store that is consumer friendly, and where people feel at ease and welcomed. They will be able to unhurriedly select items for themselves or loved ones. We intend to foster a sense of pride and specialness when our customers make a purchase.

In addition to the catalogs and hit-or-miss spots to shop, there are "stores on wheels" that periodically schedule a shopping day in area nursing homes. This is a great convenience, yet those who often do the shopping—family members—are usually at work and not available during these times. This leaves the staff responsible for spending the resident's money. We plan to cater to the families who do the purchasing for their families or friends, and they are the generation that tends to be less frugal with their spending than many seniors. Shopping is also a way family members feel they are contributing to the well-being of those they care about, trapped in a situation where they often feel helpless.

We have no fear of future competition for our edge will always be customer service. We are confident in our ability to build a repeat clientele based on the premise that the customer is always right. To ensure our stronghold we will seek customer input regarding additional inventory to carry and operate on a satisfaction guaranteed policy. We will offer special orders, minor alternations, and delivery service, too. Both owners will be full-time workers on the premises, or do business-related marketing and sales visiting hospitals, nursing homes, rehab centers, etc. We know our presence is the crucial guarantee for success. Our customers will continually experience the personal touch that is so lacking in today's marketplace.

We will maintain our social work licenses to keep abreast of trends in the field and to remain on informative mailing lists. There will be a resource area in our store where customers will have access to community services. We will also offer information on medical topics, such as strokes, osteoporosis, arthritis, etc.

At this point, we have the "market on the market." We will build insurances to maintain our position should the situation change. Our sales approach, responsible fiscal management, quality merchandise and selection, accessible location, and marketing strategy will ensure our future success.

MANAGEMENT

Christy Margolis

Christy Margolis graduated from the University of Kansas with a Bachelor of Social Work degree. She worked at Flamingo Estates, then St. Rita's Health Center, for seven years. She then assumed her current position at Murray Manor Nursing Home working as Director of Social Service for 15 years.

Besides a strong sense of commitment and determination, Christy has a quick and active mind. She is stimulated by challenges, can work well under pressure, and is creative and innovative. Her good sense of humor and warm personality, combined with strong administrative skills, enabled her to enjoy a successful career in social work.

A great asset is her ability to make her money work for her. Being single, she has an impressive savings and investment portfolio and is debt free.

Christy is an active member of Shalom Temple, belongs to the Social Workers Association in Long Term Care, and has done volunteer work with children and social service organizations in the community.

She enjoys learning about other cultures and has traveled extensively abroad. She is close to her family and has maintained numerous long-term personal and professional relationships.

Rebecca Slinger

Rebecca Slinger has lived in Kansas City all her life. A college graduate of Rockhurst College, she received a degree in social work and an Associate degree in psychology. While in college and after graduation she worked in retail for six years. She was in charge of displays, customer service, and sales.

Her first professional job was working as a crisis counselor for a hotline in Kansas City. That position required excellent assessment skills, quick thinking, and immediate interventions. She also had to have outstanding communication ability and establish an instant rapport with callers. She held this position for seven years. Rebecca then went to Murray Manor Nursing Home where she worked with the elderly for over nine years. She is a member of SWLTC (Social Workers in Long Term Care) and has a current social worker license. Married for over 13 years, she has maintained independent financial stability through full-time employment and income from rental property.

She is an active member of St. Paul's Catholic parish and has volunteered with charitable organizations in the area. Rebecca has a sense of compassion and understanding for the developmentally disabled through her personal experience. Her family has been able to maintain her brother (who is completely dependent on others due to cerebral palsy) at home for over 28 years.

Through working together for nine years, we see ourselves as compatible, healthy, bright, and energetic. Together we see a need in the community that goes unfilled; an idea that has been germinating for a couple of years. We know our strengths and they complement one another. Rebecca has more creativity and entrepreneurship while Christy has more technical skills. Both of us are highly competent and possess outstanding people skills. Both of us are committed to the success of the business.

FINANCIALS

Projected Expenses	Initial	Monthly
Rent	$1,030	530
Gas & electric	—	150
Signs	800	—
Water	—	50
Telephone	150	150
Advertising	3,000	300
Fixtures	5,000	—
Salaries		
Travel	1,500	—
Car expenses		100
Insurance	500	—
Buying office	250	200
Interest payable		450
Fix up/labor & materials	5,000	—
Accountant	750	
Lawyer	850	
Office equipment	1,500	40
Miscellaneous		40
License/fees	75	
Bags	450	
Merchandise	20,000	
Printing	2,500	
Manufacturing labor	4,500	
Total	**$47,855**	**$2,010**

Specialty Car Wash

BUSINESS PLAN

A.B.C., INC.

1004 East Towne Square
Madison, Wisconsin 53705

The purpose of A.B.C., Inc. is to provide the area with a unique facility that combines both a full service car wash with a quality restaurant. People will be able to get their cars cleaned and/or detailed while they have a pleasant, quality meal. This plan was provided by Ameriwest Business Consultants, Inc.

- EXECUTIVE SUMMARY

- OBJECTIVES & GOALS, AND STRATEGIES FOR ACHIEVING THEM

- BUSINESS DESCRIPTION, STATUS, & OUTLOOK

- MANAGEMENT & OWNERSHIP

- THE SERVICE (AN UNFILLED NEED)

- UNIQUENESS OF THE SERVICE

- MARKET ANALYSIS

- MARKETING STRATEGIES

- FINANCIAL PLANS

- CONCLUSIONS & SUMMARY

EXECUTIVE SUMMARY

BUSINESS DESCRIPTION

Americans began a love affair with their cars as soon as the first one rolled off the assembly line. An integral part of this affair is keeping the family automobile clean and looking good. It didn't take long for "car laundries" to develop to make it easier to keep our cars looking great. Since these early car washes, we have seen a variety of different types of car washes develop around the country. We have seen automated, coin-operated, and brushless car washes come and go. We have seen car wash boutiques that combine one or more other businesses with the convenience of a car wash.

The purpose of A.B.C., Inc. is to provide the area with a unique facility that combines both a full service car wash with a quality restaurant. People will be able to get their cars cleaned and/or detailed while they have a pleasant, quality meal. This type of operation is unique to southern Wisconsin. The atmosphere will be friendly and open. The business will display a new attitude. It will treat customers like first-class citizens and try to make them feel like they are at home. We will also offer a variety of gift-related items. The services will be offered at a competitive price and pricing will be reviewed periodically.

The operating hours will be Monday through Sunday from 7:00 A.M. through 7:00 P.M. We will review our hours periodically and extend them to meet demand, when necessary.

CURRENT POSITION AND FUTURE OUTLOOK

The business is in a start-up mode. It is a Wisconsin for profit "C" corporation. Operations will be conducted in a 10,000-square-foot building located on a 5-acre site on East Towne Square, which is just a half-block south of Plymouth Road. It is approximately one half mile west of I-90. We estimate we will serve 80,000 restaurant and gift shop customers and 98,550 car wash customers the first year. This is a conservative estimate and our projections do reflect the seasonal nature of each. More customers of the car wash will be served during months with bad weather and more customers in the restaurant and gift shop will be served during the summer. To attain these goals we will use a combination of media advertising, flyers, and word-of-mouth. The customers are there, the experience and ability are there and, with a proper funding, we are convinced the profit will be there.

MANAGEMENT AND OWNERSHIP

The company is set up as a corporation with David Odle and his wife, Sally, owning 100% of all outstanding stock. David will serve as president. Sally Odle will serve as vice president and manager of the restaurant. Kirt Lansing will serve as secretary, treasurer, and manager of the car wash. David will be involved in sales, public relations, advertising, planning, and equipment purchases, and will provide the function as general contractor for the project. Sally will oversee the restaurant operation and will be involved in sales, public relations, advertising, planning, insurance, purchasing, labor, and equipment purchases. Kirt Lansing will manage the day-to-day operations of the car wash and will be involved in sales, public relations, advertising, office management, personnel, operations, planning, purchasing, labor and equipment purchases, and maintenance. The business will employ additional employees who will be involved in cooking and waiting on tables in the restaurant, and as laborers on the car wash line and for additional support. They will be a combination of part-time and full-time. When volume picks up, additional part-time or full-time employees will be hired, as the workload requires. Ameriwest Business Consultants, Inc. will provide help in additional areas such as planning and general business advising when necessary and to supplement the Odles' overall business knowledge. The services of an accountant, attorney, and a qualified insurance agent will be retained.

UNIQUENESS AND DIFFERENTIATION OF THE SERVICE

A.B.C., Inc. will be unique in this part of Wisconsin. The combination of a car wash and a full-service restaurant will provide the ultimate in service to our customers. We will appeal to a wide spectrum of clientele. Nowhere else in southern Wisconsin does an operation combine the services of a car wash and detailing center along with those of a full-service restaurant.

The idea of combining a car wash and restaurant is to provide customers with an informal, social setting and atmosphere and to couple that with a level of convenience that cannot be found elsewhere. It also will prolong their stay by providing food or limited drink while their cars are being cleaned and detailed. In addition, on a limited basis, we may cater to private parties and special groups in the restaurant throughout the year, especially after normal closing hours.

The growth potential is virtually unlimited for the greater Madison area. The population is growing at an accelerated rate. It is rare in today's business world to find a true market void. That is exactly what A.B.C., Inc. has done. Our facility will have little true competition in southern Madison.

FUNDS REQUIRED AND USAGE

To finalize the project, A.B.C. will need to obtain new funding of approximately $1,400,000. This coupled with the $295,000 investment by the owners will provide the funding to acquire the land, build the improvements, purchase the machinery and equipment, and provide furnishings for the restaurant and initial inventory, supplies, and working capital for the restaurant, gift shop, and car wash.

Projected Five-Year Income Statement

(MOST LIKELY CASE)	Projected 2000	Projected 2001	Projected 2002	Projected 2003	Projected 2004
Total Revenue	1,960,830	2,058,872	2,182,404	2,335,172	2,521,986
Cost of Sales	282,649	296,781	314,588	336,609	363,538
Gross Profit	1,678,181	1,762,091	1,867,816	1,998,563	2,158,448
Selling, General Expense	1,426,404	1,479,208	1,537,450	1,601,664	1,672,454
Income Before Taxes	251,777	282,883	330,366	396,899	485,994
Income Taxes	82,907	94,417	111,985	136,603	169,568
INCOME AFTER TAXES	**168,870**	**188,466**	**218,381**	**260,296**	**316,426**
(OPTIMISTIC CASE)					
Total Revenue	2,352,996	2,470,646	2,618,885	2,802,206	3,026,383
Cost of Sales	339,179	356,137	377,506	403,931	436,246
Gross Profit	2,013,817	2,114,509	2,241,379	2,398,276	2,590,138
Selling, General Expense	1,711,685	1,775,050	1,844,940	1,921,997	2,006,945
Income Before Taxes	302,132	339,460	396,439	476,279	583,193
Income Taxes	99,488	113,300	134,382	163,924	203,482
INCOME AFTER TAXES	**202,644**	**226,159**	**262,057**	**312,355**	**379,711**

Projected Five-Year Income Statement

Continued

(PESSIMISTIC CASE)	Projected 2000	Projected 2001	Projected 2002	Projected 2003	Projected 2004
Total Revenue	1,568,664	1,647,098	1,745,923	1,868,138	2,017,589
Cost of Sales	226,119	237,425	251,670	269,287	290,830
Gross Profit	1,342,545	1,409,673	1,494,253	1,598,850	1,726,758
Selling, General Expense	1,141,123	1,183,366	1,229,960	1,281,331	1,337,963
Income Before Taxes	201,422	226,306	264,293	317,519	388,795
Income Taxes	66,326	75,534	89,588	109,282	135,654
INCOME AFTER TAXES	**135,096**	**150,773**	**174,705**	**208,237**	**253,141**

Notes:

1. The most likely case assumes 90,000 customers the first year for the restaurant and gift shop and 105,550 customers for the car wash. The optimistic case assumes revenues and expenses will increase 15% over the most likely case. The pessimistic case assumes revenues and expenses will decrease 15% below the most likely case above.

2. Cost of goods sold for the car wash will equal 6.44% of sales, 40% for the restaurant, and 53.33% for the gift shop.

OBJECTIVES & GOALS, AND STRATEGIES FOR ACHIEVING THEM

1. To provide a high quality, full-service car wash which will include complete car detailing, restaurant, and gift shop so that customers will perceive great value and give them the opportunity to have an enjoyable meal while their car is being washed or detailed.

2. Service an average of 80,000 customers in 1999 for the restaurant and gift shop and 98,550 customers the first year for the car wash. We have projected a conservative increase of 5%, 6%, 7%, and 8% for years 2-5.

3. To repay the entire loan amount by the end of the fifteenth year and to provide the shareholders with an exceptionally stable income.

4. Our goal is to become the premier car wash destination in Madison during the next two years.

5. A.B.C., Inc. plans to closely monitor changing technology to be certain that the company is using the latest and most cost effective equipment and that it keeps up with current trends in the marketplace.

When growth has stabilized we plan to add extra services for customer convenience such as delivery, Internet order taking, greater selection of products (especially seasonal), and continued growth of the food operations. In addition to the above goals we will survey our customers and make changes in our programs and add services to meet their changing ideas in the marketplace.

To obtain the first two sets of goals we will try to maximize sales with an extensive campaign to promote our service. We will utilize the radio stations and newspapers along with brochures, media advertising, pamphlets, use of coupons, referrals, and a variety of other advertising and marketing tools to reach the customer base of southern Madison. We expect to flood the market with advertising until consumers become aware of us and more comfortable with our company. As we grow, word-of-mouth referrals will bring in increasing numbers of customers and we will reduce our reliance on advertising.

The dominant driving force behind our company will be profit and income and to provide the best possible related products and service.

To become the premier car wash and detailing center in southern Madison, we will offer outstanding quality, good hours, exceptional service, and reasonable pricing. We will listen to our customers and conduct surveys.

BUSINESS DESCRIPTION, STATUS, & OUTLOOK

Both cars and car washes have come a long way since the days of cranks and pails and sponges. The first car wash was opened in Detroit in 1914 when two young fellows opened the world's first car wash: the Automated Laundry. It was basically a pail and sponge type of operation. These early "Automobile Laundries" have evolved into sophisticated operations today.

Back in 1914 the cars had to be left all day, since they were pushed through the system manually, and even brass parts were removed for polishing by hand. Twenty-five years later, the first crude "automatic" conveyor car wash was opened in Hollywood, California. On busy days, as many as forty men splashed in the tunnel, soaping, scrubbing, wiping, and drying cars as they were pulled through.

Today, there are over 20,000 automatic car washes, many of which can completely wash and dry a car in less than thirty seconds, without it being touched by human hands. Some car washes handle 20,000 cars per month and net over $200,000 a year before income taxes. Net profits of $50,000 to $75,000 are common.

What happens when it rains? That seems to be the first question that prospective car wash owners ask. If your part of the country has 250 rain free days a year, you're in a good position to do business. Madison has 310 days of sunshine a year. We get just enough rain and snow to make it necessary to frequently wash the car. And remember that night or morning rains don't necessarily hurt business. In fact, the day after a heavy rain, business is usually better than normal in car washes because autos get muddy and sloppy driving around.

Car washes in northern climates do much more business during the winter because car owners are concerned with keeping their cars free of the corrosive road salts used for melting snow and ice.

One thing is certain: car washes are more popular than ever. Like so many other household chores, washing the car is becoming just too much work for busy professionals. Given a choice between spending a Saturday afternoon relaxing or being up to their armpits in soap, most working people will opt for a day of rest. And that spells good news for the car wash industry—both currently and for the future.

A successful car wash business is dependent on 3 factors:

- location
- vehicle flow
- producing a good wash

Our goal is to not have one dissatisfied customer leave our business. With this business we will have to sell and resell our services over and over again. The National Restaurant Association estimates that satisfied customers tell an average of .7 (seven-tenths) other people they have had a positive experience. Unhappy customers tell 7 to 11 other people of their bad experience.

Ongoing decisions in car wash management include: maintenance of equipment, financial management, control of waste, personnel management, front man and managers, wash line crew, cashier, training programs, and establishing rules (hours of work, appearance, penalties, etc.). All of these areas will all be supervised by Kirt Lansing who has had experience in car washes and in other management situations.

Ongoing decision-making in the restaurant will include design of the menu, set-up, layout, server stations, dishwashing, furnishings, cashier station, rest rooms, traffic flow of employees, order taking procedures, error handling, supplies, inventory control, staffing, training, and cleanup. Sally Odle has previously owned and successfully run two restaurants and has the experience to supervise this operation.

We are selling cleanliness. We also realize that first impressions are of utmost importance and will always put our best foot forward.

There are nearly 500,000 restaurant units in the United States. However, there are very few that have been combined with full service car washes. The match seems perfect. People need their cars cleaned and they also need to eat. In today's busy world, it seems only natural to combine the two into one operation.

To maintain operations, the business will require sales tax licenses, health department permits, liquor license, and occupational use license.

The future holds the promise for almost unlimited growth and income as the business matures and considers other markets and products. Complementary products such as fleet service, additional seasonal products, and other functions at the restaurant also will be considered in the future in response to customer surveys indicating customer's wants and needs. Enhanced food services will be offered in the future as the needs are demonstrated. Future plans include additional locations and perhaps some limited franchising of this new concept.

MANAGEMENT & OWNERSHIP

David Odle graduated from Dane County Community College in 1970 with an Associate Degree in Food Service. He also received a Certificate in Business from the Mid-Central Business College. David served as a police officer for the city of Madison from 1960-1990. From 1981 to present, David founded Blue Mound Builders, which specializes in home construction. David also is licensed for commercial construction and is clearly competent to serve as general contractor for the proposed project. His 18 years' experience as a successful builder and business owner has demonstrated David's supervision and leadership skills.

Sally Odle has owned and managed several business operations. Between 1978-1980 she started and managed a pig litter operation. From 1980-1984 she owned and managed two restaurants named Black Feet and Fancy Food in Mauston. She designed and managed these restaurants. She was involved with menu design and built both into popular restaurants that earned reputations for high quality and affordable pricing. From 1986 to 1988 she owned her own real estate business, the Elite Real Estate Group, which has now merged with Monmouth and Associates. Sally's 30 years' experience in all areas of responsibility obviously makes her highly qualified to start and manage the proposed restaurant. Sally has strong leadership and people skills and has developed strong creative instincts, which she has often transformed into successful operations.

A.B.C., Inc. will supplement its employees' skills by using outside consultants in areas such as legal work, income tax preparation, insurance, and general business advising. The business was set up as a corporation primarily for liability reasons and makes it easier to secure investors. To continue operation, a mix of full- and part-time employees will be utilized to help in areas such as cooking, waiting on tables, and for labor. As the business grows, additional part-time or full-time employees may be added to handle the increased workload.

Wisconsin growth in families is the ninth greatest in the country. The past decade has seen this segment of the population grow by more than thirty percent. It is growing five and a half times as fast as the general population. This trend will also help our proposed venture.

The few existing car washes and restaurants that cater to our clientele are not nearly as convenient or service oriented as our operation. Nowhere else are these two types of operations combined on one site. Competitors seem to pay little attention to detail and seeing that the customer is satisfied. A.B.C., Inc. and its ownership will embrace the concept of trying to become a focal point for our clientele and never having a dissatisfied customer leave our property.

The timing for such a business is perfect. A significant window of opportunity exists for A.B.C., Inc. to take advantage of the huge growth of the area and start this kind of business. This business will be providing the "Right Service at the Right Time to the right clientele."

THE SERVICE—AN UNFILLED NEED

It is rare in today's world that a true market void exists. Our service will meet the "unfilled need" described above by providing customers with competitively priced, high service car wash and detailing facility combined with the services of a full-service restaurant on the premises. We will be unique to Madison area and indeed all of Wisconsin.

Customers will be attracted because of our atmosphere, pricing, and facilities. They will be made to feel welcome and as part of the family.

Some major advantages A.B.C., Inc. will have over potential competition and conventional car washes are:

- Larger and newer facility
- Lower operating expenses than most
- Full service restaurant on site (new concept)
- Location, location, location
- We will offer carryout
- We will offer limited liquor (beer and wine)

UNIQUENESS OF THE SERVICE

MARKET OVERVIEW, SIZE, AND SEGMENTS

MARKET ANALYSIS

The market area we will concentrate on is central, northern, and western Madison. This area has been growing rapidly for the past several years and should continue for the foreseeable future. According to *Inc. Magazine*, Madison is ranked eleventh in the nation for start-up businesses. This means that the economic climate is extremely favorable for virtually any type of new business. In 1998, Madison recorded 5,414 start-up companies to its 400,000 population or 1.36 per 100 citizens. With Madison's exploding growth in population that has occurred during the last decade, local car wash sales should continue to be well in excess of national averages. Once the concept catches on locally, we feel the potential is unlimited. As we grow we will have the financial capacity to carry on an advertising campaign on a regional basis.

The economy is in the midst of a particularly strong growth period. Many new jobs are being added to the local community. Within a five-mile radius of A.B.C., Inc., 12,000 new homes are projected within the next few years. All of these factors are cause for a much greater need in car washes in the area. All of this activity can only help our attempts to begin this car wash.

Listed below are just some of the reasons that the Madison area is growing and why it is a good time to be running any kind of business that caters to this growth:

- The local economy is booming and virtually busting at the seams.
- More than 65 nationally based insurance companies are headquartered here. The largest is Allstate. It has over 1,200 employees) and an operating budget of over $85 million.
- Madison has a new airport that should grow and attract even more new businesses.
- The new Milwaukee Airport is open and provides an economic boost to the entire state, including Madison.
- Gambling in nearby Baraboo continues to draw many visitors and some new businesses.
- Every week, we see articles in the newspapers of Michigan residents and companies relocating here.
- The world-renowned Four Seasons Hotel has completed an extensive remodeling.
- MCI and Quantum Electronics are undergoing large increases in their operations here that should add many hundreds of employees.
- Milwaukee is only 50 minutes away and is another good market for businesses in the area.
- Many experts predict Madison to become the second fastest growing city in the state between now and the year 2007.
- Dane County is predicted to become the largest county in the state by the year 2003.
- The local economy is now more diversified than it was when troubles occurred in the local economy in the late 1980s and early 1990s.

The estimated population of Dane County in 1999 is 500,000 people. The number of households are approaching 200,000. Currently, this market is growing at an annual rate of 3-5%. Projections see this trend continuing for the balance of this decade.

From the above figures it can readily be seen that the potential market for our services is huge. We feel with our pricing and value we will become a price and industry leader within two years.

CUSTOMER PROFILE

Our surveys have shown the following potential mix of patrons for our facilities:

- We will cater to both blue collar and white collar people
- Income of typical customers is in the $20,000 and up range
- Large numbers of young professionals
- Wide range of age of clientele is 18-80
- Large numbers of electronics workers in the various plants within a five-minute drive

Beyond the local market we could eventually tap into a more regional market. The advantage of our service is that it could appeal to all segments of the community. By expanding the role of the restaurant, we can continue to become an even greater focal point for the local community.

Competition Analysis

Competitor Name	Strengths	Weaknesses
Waterwashes 123 South Lincoln	Good Location Fully Automated	Dated building Poor design Not customer friendly Car wash and detailing only
Badger Car Wash 1115 N. Main	Good Location New Building	Poor at managing problems Was sold and reclaimed Trying to rebuild reputation Car wash and detailing only

Competitor Name	Strengths	Weaknesses
The Waves	Location	Small lot
5500 Lapeer	Handwash	Not automated
		Labor intensive
		Not customer friendly
		Poor design
Water Works	Newer design	Not customer friendly
123 N. Washington	Fully automated	Car wash and detailing only
The Clean Place	Good Location	Converted building
1108 N. Drummond	Nice building	Poor design
		Small lot
		Not customer friendly
		Car wash and detail only

The marketplace is currently shared by 3 major car washes. Most of the existing facilities have one or more significant waeknesses and are not really in the same market as us. They cannot be considered competitors, especially when you add our restaurant into the mix.

Risk Analysis

	RATINGS		
ELEMENT	LOW	MEDIUM	HIGH
Industry (Maturity and Cyclicality)	X		
Market/Local Economy	X		
Competitive Position		X	
Dependence upon other companies	X		
Vulnerability to Substitutes	X		
Technology	X		
Distribution		X	
Regulatory Environment		X	
Suppliers		X	
Strategy	X		
Assumptions		X	
Financial Performance		X	
Management Performance		X	
Inflation/Interest Rates	X		
Others		X	
Overall Risk	X		

Identification of Strengths & Weaknesses

Functions	Strong (+)	Average (0)	Weak (-)	Strengths and/or Weaknesses Compared to Competitors
General Administration (Management)	X			Business experience, especially restaurant
Marketing		X		
Finance/Planning		X		Experience in planning and finance
Human Resources	X			Better performance achievable
Operations	X			Have run numerous businesses before
Production		X		
Purchasing		X		
Distribution		X		
Servicing	X			Multi-service approach
Quality of Service	X			Heads above competition
Company Policies	X			Strict adherence to policies
Product Mix	X			Several choices available
Product Features	X			
Options	X			
Warranties/Guarantees		X		
Reliability	X			Strong management
Desirability	X			
Advertising		X		
Market Leadership		X		New initially, leader within two years
Sales Force	X			
Overhead			X	New loans, start-up expenses
Pricing	X			Very competitive
Delivery Time	X			
Location	X			1/2 block from E. Washington Road
Facilities	X			Best combination around, new proposed complex

We feel we will have strengths in product features, management, operations, quality of service, product mix, company policies, reliability, desirability, highly trained sales force, pricing, location, and facilities.

We will have low risk exposure in the areas of industry maturity, market, dependence upon other companies, vulnerability to substitutes, technology, inflation/interest rates, regulatory environment, management ability, location, facilities, and suppliers.

We perceive medium risk exposure in competitive position (we are new) suppliers, finance, and planning. We have retained the services of specialists to help in various areas such as marketing, accounting, legal, and general overall business operation advice.

We do not feel we have any high-risk exposure situations or major inherent weaknesses.

MARKETING STRATEGIES

PRICING AND VALUE

Our intention is to raise the public's awareness of our company. We plan to review our prices and those of our competitors every six months. We will review direct material costs, direct labor costs, and total overhead expenses. We will continually monitor the cost of providing our service to each customer. We will offer various free or reduced rate programs to get customers acquainted with us.

Numerous package deals may be offered to customers. Examples of various marketing strategies we may try include the following:

- Discounts for larger or repeat purchases
- Special party rates for the restaurant
- Ladies day (brings in women and reduces weekend congestion in the car wash—may give ladies a plant, hosiery, household item, etc.)
- Free car wash on your birthday
- Free car wash with a certain mileage on your auto as announced over the radio
- Free meal after so many car washes
- Free car wash after so many meals at the restaurant
- Fleet discounts to larger customers such as automobile dealers
- Special detailing and wash packages

SELLING TACTICS

Our company's marketing strategy will incorporate plans to promote our line of services through several different channels and on different levels of use. We will advertise heavily on the popular local radio stations and newspapers.

We will flood the market with advertising and try to go after our specific targets. We will try to capture their attention, pique their interest, and make them feel that they must have our services.

We will offer continuous promotional rates. The results sell themselves. We will offer discounts to frequent users. The more a customer uses our services the cheaper it will become for them.

We will also be a MasterCard and Visa charge card merchant which enables us to more readily service our customers.

In order to sell our facility we shall consider a variety of promotions including:

- Reserve certain hours or sections of the restaurant for unique groups such as children's birthday parties, senior citizens, service clubs, adults, etc.
- Conduct special theme nights, use ethnic holidays, family night, charity promotion night, classes, etc.
- Cultivate local churches and women's organizations for the restaurant.
- Promote private parties using entire facility, especially after normal closing hours.
- Early bird specials.

ADVERTISING, PROMOTION, AND DISTRIBUTION OF SERVICES

We recognize that the key to success at this time requires extensive promotion. Advertising goals include all of the following:

- Position the company as the premier car wash in Madison
- Increase public awareness of A.B.C. and its benefits
- Increase public awareness of our company and establish a professional image
- Maximize efficiency by continually monitoring media effectiveness
- Consider a possible credit coupon in some of the advertisements
- Develop a brochure or pamphlet to explain our service and company
- Continue use of a distinctive business card and company letterhead
- Use a mix of media to saturate the marketplace

PUBLIC RELATIONS

We will develop a public relations policy that will help increase awareness of our company and product. To achieve these goals we will consider some or all of the following:

- Develop a press release and a company backgrounder as a public relations tool.
- Develop a telephone script to handle customer and advertiser contact.
- We will attempt to never have a customer leave dissatisfied.
- Develop a survey to be completed by customers to help determine the following:
    1. How did they hear about us?
    2. What influenced them to use our service?
    3. How well did our service satisfy their needs?
    4. How efficient was our service?
    5. Did they have any problems getting through to us?
    6. Did they shop competitors before selecting us?
    7. How did they initially perceive our company and product?
    8. Where are most of our customers located?
    9. Do they have suggestions for improving our service or our approach to advertising?
    10. What additional services would they like us to offer?
    11. Would they recommend us to others?

We will join trade organizations and subscribe to trade journals to keep abreast of trends, management techniques etc. This organizations may include, National Restaurant Association, Auto Laundry News, and the International Car wash Association

FINANCIAL PLANS

Data Sheet #1

GENERAL:

Fiscal Year in which Projections/Calculations are to start 2000
Number of Months in which Projections/Calculations are to start 5
The purpose for this Analysis is Business Start-Up, Expansion, or Review .... START-UP
Owner's contribution to business (include both cash and time in dollar equivalency) $295,000.00

Indicate below if the figures are actual, annualized, or projected for each year in the analysis:

2000	Projected
2001	Projected
2002	Projected
2003	Projected
2004	Projected

Indicate the type of business entity you have to the right: C

START-UP/EXPANSION EXPENSES:		EXPENSES FOR YEAR:	2000	
			Car Wash	Rest/Gift Shop
Inventory	25,000.00	Advertising & Marketing Expenses	10,000.00	10,000.00
Advertising	6,000.00	Bad Debts	0.00	0.00
Telephone/Utilities	3,000.00	Contract Labor	0.00	0.00
Professional Fees	4,000.00	Depreciation	35,421.00	24,293.00
Organizational Expenses	2,000.00	Direct Labor Expenses	0.00	0.00
Furniture/Fixtures	25,000.00	Dues, Subscriptions, and Memberships	600.00	600.00
Land	365,000.00	Employee Reimbursement Expenses	0.00	0.00
Buildings	800,000.00	Freight/Shipping	0.00	0.00
Machinery/Equipment	300,000.00	Furniture or Fixture Purchases	0.00	2,000.00

START-UP/EXPANSION EXPENSES:

Rent Deposits	0.00
Insurance	4,000.00
Leasehold Improvements	0.00
Licenses/Fees/Permits	2,500.00
Miscellaneous	80,000.00
Real Estate Taxes	0.00
Other #2	0.00
Other #3	0.00
Other #4	0.00
Total	1,616,500.00

LOAN DATA: (If Needed)

Amount of Loan 1	1,400,000
Term of Loan 1 (Months)	240
Interest Rate for Loan 1	10.00%
First Year of Loan 1	1999
First Payment Month	8
Amount of Loan 2	$0.00
Term of Loan 2 (Months)	60
Interest Rate for Loan 2	0.00%
First Year of Loan 2	1999
First Payment Month	1

EXPENSES FOR YEAR:

	2000	
	Car Wash	Rest/Gift Shop
Insurance	5,000.00	2,000.00
Lease Expenses	0.00	0.00
Leasehold Expenses	0.00	0.00
Machinery & Equipment Purchases	3,000.00	500.00
Office Supplies and Postage	1,200.00	1,200.00
Professional Fees	8,000.00	2,000.00
Permits/Licenses	1,000.00	1,000.00
Rent	0.00	0.00
Repair & Maintenance	12,000.00	6,000.00
Salaries-Officer's	0.00	0.00
Salaries-Administrative	28,700.00	19,680.00
Salaries and Wages-Other	590,040.00	205,000.00
Salaries-Manager	41,000.00	41,000.00
Telephone/Utilities	57,000.00	12,000.00
Real Estate Taxes	15,000.00	5,000.00
Other #2	0.00	0.00
Other #3	0.00	0.00
Other #4	0.00	0.00
Miscellaneous/Contingency Expenses	4,000.00	4,000.00
Total First-Year Expenses Including Interest Paid and Cost of Goods Sold:	**811,961**	**336,273**

PERCENTAGE OF TOTAL PAYROLL ALLOTTED TO PAYROLL TAXES AND BENEFITS		15.00%
PERCENTAGE OF NET SALES—COST OF GOODS SOLD:	Car Wash	3.44%
PERCENTAGE OF NET SALES—COST OF GOODS SOLD:	Restaurant	30.00%
PERCENTAGE OF NET SALES—COST OF GOODS SOLD:	Gift Shop	33.33%
PERCENTAGE OF NET SALES—COST OF GOODS SOLD:	Income Source #4	0.00%

Data Sheet #2

SOURCES/AMOUNTS OF INCOME FOR YEAR

	INCOME OPTION ONE 2000
Car Wash	$1,162,000.00
Restaurant	$708,830.00
Gift Shop	$90,000.00
Income Source #4	$0.00
Other Income/Exp (Net)	$0.00
TOTAL INCOME	**$1,960,830.00**

PERCENTAGE OF INCREASE IN EXPENSES:

For Second Year	4.50%
For Third Year	4.75%
For Fourth Year	5.00%
For Fifth Year	5.25%

PERCENTAGE OF INCOME GROWTH:

For Second Year	2001	5.00%
For Third Year	2002	6.00%
For Fourth Year	2003	7.00%
For Fifth Year	2004	8.00%

PERCENTAGE OF NET INCOME TO BE PAID OUT IN DIVIDENDS

For First Year	2000	20.00%
For Second Year	2001	30.00%
For Third Year	2002	40.00%
For Fourth Year	2003	60.00%
For Fifth Year	2004	80.00%

Number of Restaurant & Gift Shop Customers the First Year:	80,000.00
Number of Car Wash Customers the First Year:	98,550.00
Average Car Wash Income received per Customer:	$14.53
Average Restaurant/Gift Shop Income received per Customer:	$9.99

Operating Data	2000	2001	2002	2003	2004
Days Sales in Accounts Receivable	10.0	10.0	10.0	10.0	10.0
Days Materials Cost in Inventory	45.0	45.0	45.0	45.0	45.0
Days Finished Goods in Inventory	45.0	45.0	45.0	45.0	45.0
Days Materials Cost in Payables	25.0	25.0	25.0	25.0	25.0
Days Payroll Expenses accrued	25.0	25.0	25.0	25.0	25.0
Days Operating Expenses accrued	15.0	15.0	15.0	15.0	15.0

MONTH	Percentage of Sales	Car Wash
JANUARY	10.50%	
FEBRUARY	10.50%	
MARCH	11.00%	
APRIL	11.50%	
MAY	9.00%	100.00%
JUNE	5.00%	
JULY	5.00%	
AUGUST	6.50%	
SEPTEMBER	6.50%	
OCTOBER	7.50%	
NOVEMBER	8.00%	
DECEMBER	9.00%	

MONTH	Percentage of Sales	Restaurant & Gift Shop
JANUARY	7.00%	
FEBRUARY	7.00%	
MARCH	7.00%	
APRIL	7.00%	
MAY	8.50%	100.00%
JUNE	10.00%	
JULY	11.00%	
AUGUST	10.50%	
SEPTEMBER	7.00%	
OCTOBER	7.00%	
NOVEMBER	9.00%	
DECEMBER	9.00%	

Start-up Expenses

Category	Amount
Cash and Working Capital	$78,500
Material-Supplies-Inventory	$25,000
Advertising	$6,000
Telephone and Utilities	$3,000
Professional Fees	$4,000
Organizational Expenses	$2,000
Furniture and Fixtures	$25,000
Land	$365,000
Building	$800,000
Machinery and Equipment	$300,000
Insurance	$4,000
Licenses, Fees, and Permits	$2,500
Miscellaneous	$80,000
TOTAL PROJECT COST	**$1,695,000**

New investments or loans totaling $1,400,000 must be obtained. This added to owner's investment of $295,000 will complete the project.

Owner's contribution breakdown is as follows:

Cash	$30,000
Deferred Contractor fees for building	$200,000
Owner's time (converted to dollars)	$65,000
Total Owner's Contribution	**$295,000**

Cash Flow Projection - 2000

Month	Start-Up	Month 1 May-00	Month 2 Jun-00	Month 3 Jul-00	Month 4 Aug-00	Month 5 Sep-00	Month 6 Oct-00
CASH RECEIPTS:							
Car Wash		$104,580	$58,100	$58,100	$75,530	$75,530	$87,150
Restaurant		$60,251	$70,883	$77,971	$74,427	$49,618	$49,618
Gift Shop		$7,650	$9,000	$9,900	$9,450	$6,300	$6,300
Income Source #4		$0	$0	$0	$0	$0	$0
Other Income/Expense (Net)		$0	$0	$0	$0	$0	$0
Owner's Equity	295,000						
Loan	1,400,000						
Total Cash Received	**1,696,000**	**172,481**	**137,983**	**145,971**	**159,407**	**131,448**	**143,068**
DISBURSEMENTS:							
Cost of Goods Sold/Inventory (Car Wash)	25,000	$3,600	$2,000	$2,000	$2,600	$2,600	$3,000
Cost of Goods Sold: Restaurant		$18,076	$21,265	$23,391	$22,328	$14,885	$14,885
Cost of Goods Sold: Gift Shop		$2,550	$3,000	$3,300	$3,150	$2,100	$2,100
Cost of Goods Sold-Income Source 4		$0	$0	$0	$0	$0	$0
Advertising/Marketing Expenses	6,000	1,800	1,000	1,000	1,300	1,300	1,500
Bad Debts		$0	$0	$0	$0	$0	$0
Contract Labor		$0	$0	$0	$0	$0	$0
Depreciation		$5,374	2,986	2,986	3,881	3,881	4,479
Direct Labor		$0	$0	$0	$0	$0	$0
Dues/Subscrip/Memberships		$100	$100	$100	$100	$100	$100
Employee Reimbursement Expenses		$0	$0	$0	$0	$0	$0
Freight/Shipping		$0	$0	$0	$0	$0	$0
Furniture or Fixture Purchases	26,000	$167	$167	$167	$167	$167	$167
Insurance	4,000	$583	$583	$583	$583	$583	$583
Land	365,000	$0	$0	$0	$0	$0	$0
Buildings	800,000	$0	$0	$0	$0	$0	$0
Lease Expenses		$0	$0	$0	$0	$0	$0
Leasehold Expenses	0	$0	$0	$0	$0	$0	$0
Machinery/Equipment Purchases	300,000	$292	$292	$292	$292	$292	$292
Organizational Expenses	2,000	$33	$33	$33	$33	$33	$33
Office Supplies and Postage		$200	$200	$200	$200	$200	$200
Payroll Taxes/Employee Benefits		$12,363	$7,593	$7,593	$9,381	$9,381	$10,574
Professional Fees	4,000	$833	$833	$833	$833	$833	$833
Permits/Licenses	2,500	$167	$167	$167	$167	$167	$167
Rent	0	$0	$0	$0	$0	$0	$0
Repair & Maintenance		$1,620	$900	$900	$1,170	$1,170	$1,350
Salaries-Officer's		$0	$0	$0	$0	$0	$0
Salaries-Administrative		$4,032	$4,032	$4,032	$4,032	$4,032	$4,032
Salaries and Wages-other		$71,554	$39,752	$39,752	$61,678	$61,678	$59,628
Salaries-Manager		$6,833	$6,833	$6,833	$6,833	$6,833	$6,833
Telephone/Utilities	3,000	$6,210	$3,450	$3,450	$4,485	$4,485	$5,175
Real Estate Taxes	0	$1,667	$1,667	$1,667	$1,667	$1,667	$1,667
Other #2	0	$0	$0	$0	$0	$0	$0
Other #3	0	$0	$0	$0	$0	$0	$0
Other #4	0	$0	$0	$0	$0	$0	$0
Misc./Contingency Expenses	80,000	$667	$667	$667	$667	$667	$667
Total Cash Paid Out	**1,616,500**	**138,719**	**97,518**	**99,945**	**115,547**	**107,054**	**118,264**
LOANS SECTION:							
Interest		11,667	11,651	11,636	11,620	11,604	11,589
Principal		1,844	1,859	1,874	1,890	1,906	1,922
Cash Pyts to Loans		**13,510**	**13,510**	**13,510**	**13,510**	**13,510**	**13,510**
Taxable Income		22,095	28,813	34,391	32,240	12,790	13,215
Income Tax (State & Federal)		6,909	6,909	6,909	6,909	6,909	6,909
NET INCOME		15,186	21,904	27,482	25,331	6,881	6,306
LOANS (Balance)	1,400,000	1,398,156	1,396,297	1,394,423	1,392,533	1,390,627	1,388,705
DIVIDENDS PAID		3546	3,546	3,715	3,884	3,040	1,689
BEGINNING CASH	78,500						

Month 7 Nov-00	Month 8 Dec-00	Month 9 Jan-01	Month 10 Feb-01	Month 11 Mar-01	Month 12 Apr-01	Totals
$92,960	$10,580	$122,010	$122,010	$127,820	$133,630	$1,162,000
$63,795	$63,795	$63,795	$49,618	$49,618	$49,618	$708,830
$8,100	$8,100	$6,300	$5,300	$6,300	$6,300	$90,000
$0	$0	$0	$0	$0	$0	$0
$0	$0	$0	$0	$0	$0	$0
164,855	**176,475**	**177,928**	**177,928**	**183,738**	**189,548**	**$1,960,830**
$3,200	$3,600	$4,200	$4,200	$4,400	$4,600	$40,000
$19,138	$19,138	$19,138	$14,886	$14,885	$14,885	$212,649
$2,700	$2,700	$2,100	$2,100	$2,100	$2,100	$30,000
$0	$0	$0	$0	$0	$0	$0
1,60	1,800	2,100	2,100	2,200	2,300	$20,000
$0	$0	$0	$0	$0	$0	$0
$0	$0	$0	$0	$0	$0	$0
4,777	5,374	6,270	6,270	6,569	6,867	$59,714
$0	$0	$0	$0	$0	$0	$0
$100	$100	$100	$100	$100	$100	$1,200
$0	$0	$0	$0	$0	$0	$0
$0	$0	$0	$0	$0	$0	$0
$167	$167	$167	$167	$167	$167	$2,000
$583	$583	$583	$583	$583	$583	$7,000
$0	$0	$0	$0	$0	$0	$0
$0	$0	$0	$0	$0	$0	$0
$0	$0	$0	$0	$0	$0	$0
$0	$0	$0	$0	$0	$0	$0
$292	$292	$292	$292	$292	$292	$3,500
$33	$33	$33	$33	$33	$33	$400
$200	$200	$200	$200	$200	$200	$2,400
$11,170	$12,363	$14,152	$14,152	$14,748	$15,344	$138,813
$833	$833	$833	$833	$833	$833	$10,000
$167	$167	$167	$167	$167	$167	$2,000
$0	$0	$0	$0	$0	$0	$0
$1,440	$1,620	$1,890	$1,890	$1,980	$2,070	$18,000
$0	$0	$0	$0	$0	$0	$0
$4,032	$4,032	$4,032	$4,032	$4,032	$4,032	$48,380
$63,603	$71,654	$83,479	$83,479	$87,464	$91,430	$795,040
$6,833	$6,833	$6,833	$6,833	$6,833	$6,833	$82,000
$5,520	$6,210	$7,245	$7,245	$7,590	$7,935	$69,000
$1,667	$1,667	$1,667	$1,667	$1,667	$1,667	$20,000
$0	$0	$0	$0	$0	$0	$0
$0	$0	$0	$0	$0	$0	$0
$0	$0	$0	$0	$0	$0	$0
$667	$667	$667	$667	$667	$667	$8,000
128,722	**139,932**	**151,995**	**151,895**	**157,500**	**163,105**	**$1,570,096**
11,573	11,556	11,640	11,524	11,507	11,490	$138,957
1,938	1,954	1,970	1,987	2,003	2,020	$23,166
13,510	**13,510**	**13,510**	**13,510**	**13,510**	**13,510**	**$162,124**
24,560	24,986	14,493	14,510	14,731	14,953	$251,777
6,909	6,909	6,909	6,909	6,909	6,909	$82,907
17,651	18,077	7,686	7,601	7,822	8,044	$168,870
1,386,767	1,384,813	1,382,843	1,380,857	1,378,854	1,376,834	
1,689	2,195	2,195	2,533	2,702	3,040	33,774

Cash Flow Projection - 2001

Month	Month 13 May-01	Month 14 Jun-01	Month 15 Jul-01	Month 16 Aug-01	Month 17 Sep-01	Month 18 Oct-01	Month 19 Nov-01
CASH RECEIPTS:							
Car Wash	$109,809	$61,005	$61,005	$79,307	$79,307	$91,508	$97,608
Restaurant	$63,263	$74,427	$81,870	$78,149	$52,099	$52,099	$66,984
Gift Shop	$8,033	$9,450	$10,395	$9,923	$6,615	$6,615	$8,505
Income Source #4	$0	$0	$0	$0	$0	$0	$0
Other Income/Expense (Net)	$0	$0	$0	$0	$0	$0	$0
Owner's Equity							
Loan							
Total Cash Received	**181,105**	**144,882**	**153,270**	**167,378**	**138,021**	**150,222**	**173,097**
DISBURSEMENTS:							
Cost of Goods Sold/Inventory (Car Wash)	$3,780	$2,100	$2,100	$2,730	$2,730	$3,150	$3,360
Cost of Goods Sold: Restaurant	$18,979	$22,328	$24,561	$23,445	$15,630	$15,630	$20,095
Cost of Goods Sold: Gift Shop	$2,677	$3,150	$3,465	$3,307	$2,205	$2,205	$2,835
Cost of Goods Sold-Income Source 4	$0	$0	$0	$0	$0	$0	$0
Advertising/Marketing Expenses	$1,881	$1,045	$1,045	$1,359	$1,359	$1,568	$1,672
Bad Debts	$0	$0	$0	$0	$0	$0	$0
Contract Labor	$0	$0	$0	$0	$0	$0	$0
Depreciation	$5,374	$2,986	$2,986	$3,881	$3,881	$4,479	$4,777
Direct Labor	$0	$0	$0	$0	$0	$0	$0
Dues/Subscrip/Memberships	$105	$105	$105	$105	$105	$105	$105
Employee Reimbursement Expenses	$0	$0	$0	$0	$0	$0	$0
Freight/Shipping	$0	$0	$0	$0	$0	$0	$0
Furniture or Fixture Purchases	$174	$174	$174	$174	$174	$174	$174
Insurance	$610	$610	$610	$610	$610	$610	$610
Land							
Buildings							
Lease Expenses	$0	$0	$0	$0	$0	$0	$0
Leasehold Expenses	$0	$0	$0	$0	$0	$0	$0
Machinery/Equipment Purchases	$305	$305	$305	$305	$305	$305	$305
Organizational Expenses	$33	$33	$33	$33	$33	$33	$33
Office Supplies and Postage	$209	$209	$209	$209	$209	$209	$209
Payroll Taxes/Employee Benefits	$12,919	$7,934	$7,934	$9,804	$9,804	$11,050	$11,673
Professional Fees	$871	$871	$871	$871	$871	$871	$871
Permits/Licenses	$174	$174	$174	$174	$174	$174	$174
Rent	$0	$0	$0	$0	$0	$0	$0
Repair & Maintenance	$1,693	$941	$941	$1,223	$1,223	$1,411	$1,505
Salaries-Officer's	$0	$0	$0	$0	$0	$0	$0
Salaries-Administrative	$4,213	$4,213	$4,213	$4,213	$4,213	$4,213	$4,213
Salaries and Wages-Other	$74,774	$41,541	$41,541	$54,003	$54,003	$62,311	$66,465
Salaries-Manager	$7,141	$7,141	$7,141	$7,141	$7,141	$7,141	$7,141
Telephone/Utilities	$6,489	$3,605	$3,605	$4,687	$4,687	$5,408	$5,768
Real Estate Taxes	$1,742	$1,742	$1,742	$1,742	$1,742	$1,742	$1,742
Other #2	$0	$0	$0	$0	$0	$0	$0
Other #3	$0	$0	$0	$0	$0	$0	$0
Other #4	$0	$0	$0	$0	$0	$0	$0
Misc./Contingency Expenses	$697	$697	$697	$697	$697	$697	$697
Total Cash Paid Out	**144,839**	**101,902**	**104,450**	**120,711**	**111,793**	**123,483**	**134,423**
LOANS SECTION:							
Interest	11,474	11,457	11,440	11,422	11,405	11,387	11,370
Principal	2,037	2,054	2,071	2,088	2,105	2,123	2,141
Cash Pyts to Loans	**13,510**	**13,510**	**13,510**	**13,510**	**13,510**	**13,510**	**13,510**
Taxable Income	24,792	31,523	37,380	35,245	14,822	15,351	27,304
Income Tax (State & Federal)	7,868	7,868	7,868	7,868	7,868	7,868	7,868
NET INCOME	**16,924**	**23,655**	**29,512**	**27,376**	**6,954**	**7,483**	**19,436**
LOANS (Balance)	1,374,797	1,372,743	1,370,673	1,368,585	1,366,479	1,364,356	1,362,215
DIVIDENDS PAID	4,712	4,712	4,712	4,712	4,712	4,712	4,712

Month 20 Dec-01	Month 21 Jan-02	Month 22 Feb-02	Month 23 Mar-02	Month 24 Apr-02	Totals
$109,809	$128,111	$128,111	$134,211	$140,312	$1,220,100
$66,984	$52,099	$52,099	$52,099	$52,099	$744,272
$8,505	$6,615	$6,615	$6,615	$6,615	$94,500
$0	$0	$0	$0	$0	$0
$0	$0	$0	$0	$0	$0
185,298	**186,825**	**186,825**	**192,925**	**199,026**	**$2,058,872**
$3,780	$4,410	$4,410	$4,620	$4,830	$42,000
$20,095	$15,630	$15,630	$15,630	$15,630	$223,281
$2,835	$2,205	$2,205	$2,205	$2,205	$31,500
$0	$0	$0	$0	$0	$0
$1,881	$2,195	$2,195	$2,299	$2,404	$20,900
$0	$0	$0	$0	$0	$0
$0	$0	$0	$0	$0	$0
$5,374	$6,270	$6,270	$6,569	$6,867	$59,714
$0	$0	$0	$0	$0	$0
$105	$105	$105	$105	$105	$1,254
$0	$0	$0	$0	$0	$0
$0	$0	$0	$0	$0	$0
$174	$174	$174	$174	$174	$2,090
$610	$610	$610	$610	$610	$7,315
					$0
					$0
$0	$0	$0	$0	$0	$0
$0	$0	$0	$0	$0	$0
$305	$305	$305	$305	$305	$3,658
$33	$33	$33	$33	$33	$400
$209	$209	$209	$209	$209	$2,508
$12,919	$14,788	$14,788	$15,412	$16,035	$145,060
$871	$871	$871	$871	$871	$10,450
$174	$174	$174	$174	$174	$2,090
$0	$0	$0	$0	$0	$0
$1,693	$1,975	$1,975	$2,069	$2,163	$18,810
$0	$0	$0	$0	$0	$0
$4,213	$4,213	$4,213	$4,213	$4,213	$50,557
$74,774	$87,236	$87,236	$91,390	$95,544	$830,817
$7,141	$7,141	$7,141	$7,141	$7,141	$85,690
$6,489	$7,571	$7,571	$7,932	$8,292	$72,105
$1,742	$1,742	$1,742	$1,742	$1,742	$20,900
$0	$0	$0	$0	$0	$0
$0	$0	$0	$0	$0	$0
$0	$0	$0	$0	$0	$0
$697	$697	$697	$697	$697	$8,360
146,113	**158,552**	**158,552**	**164,397**	**170,242**	**$1,639,458**
11,352	11,334	11,316	11,297	11,279	$136,531
2,159	2,176	2,195	2,213	2,231	$25,592
13,510	**13,510**	**13,510**	**13,510**	**13,510**	**$162,124**
27,833	16,939	16,957	17,231	17,505	$282,883
7,868	7,868	7,868	7,868	7,868	$94,417
19,965	**9,071**	**9,089**	**9,363**	**9,637**	**$188,466**
1,360,057	1,357,880	1,355,686	1,353,473	1,351,242	
4,712	4,712	4,712	4,712	4,712	56,540

Cash Flow Projection - 2002

Month	Month 25 May-02	Month 26 Jun-02	Month 27 Jul-02	Month 28 Aug-02	Month 29 Sep-02	Month 30 Oct-02	Month 31 Nov-02
CASH RECEIPTS:							
Car Wash	$116,398	$64,665	$64,665	$84,065	$84,065	$96,998	$103,464
Restaurant	$67,059	$78,893	$86,782	$82,837	$55,225	$55,225	$71,004
Gift Shop	$8,514	$10,017	$11,019	$10,518	$7,012	$7,012	$9,015
Income Source #4	$0	$0	$0	$0	$0	$0	$0
Other Income/Expense (Net)	$0	$0	$0	$0	$0	$0	$0
Owner's Equity							
Loan							
Total Cash Received	**191,971**	**153,575**	**162,466**	**177,420**	**146,302**	**159,235**	**183,483**
DISBURSEMENTS:							
Cost of Goods Sold/Inventory (Car Wash)	$4,007	$2,226	$2,226	$2,894	$2,894	$3,339	$3,562
Cost of Goods Sold: Restaurant	$20,118	$23,668	$26,035	$24,851	$16,567	$16,567	$21,301
Cost of Goods Sold: Gift Shop	$2,838	$3,339	$3,673	$3,506	$2,337	$2,337	$3,005
Cost of Goods Sold-Income Source 4	$0	$0	$0	$0	$0	$0	$0
Advertising/Marketing Expenses	$1,970	$1,095	$1,095	$1,423	$1,423	$1,642	$1,751
Bad Debts	$0	$0	$0	$0	$0	$0	$0
Contract Labor	$0	$0	$0	$0	$0	$0	$0
Depreciation	$5,374	$2,986	$2,986	$3,881	$3,881	$4,479	$4,777
Direct Labor	$0	$0	$0	$0	$0	$0	$0
Dues/Subscrip/Memberships	$109	$109	$109	$109	$109	$109	$109
Employee Reimbursement Expenses	$0	$0	$0	$0	$0	$0	$0
Freight/Shipping	$0	$0	$0	$0	$0	$0	$0
Furniture or Fixture Purchases	$182	$182	$182	$182	$182	$182	$182
Insurance	$639	$639	$639	$639	$639	$639	$639
Land							
Buildings							
Lease Expenses	$0	$0	$0	$0	$0	$0	$0
Leasehold Expenses	$0	$0	$0	$0	$0	$0	$0
Machinery/Equipment Purchases	$319	$319	$319	$319	$319	$319	$319
Organizational Expenses	$33	$33	$33	$33	$33	$33	$33
Office Supplies and Postage	$219	$219	$219	$219	$219	$219	$219
Payroll Taxes/Employee Benefits	$13,533	$8,311	$8,311	$10,269	$10,269	$11,575	$12,227
Professional Fees	$912	$912	$912	$912	$912	$912	$912
Permits/Licenses	$182	$182	$182	$182	$182	$182	$182
Rent	$0	$0	$0	$0	$0	$0	$0
Repair & Maintenance	$1,773	$985	$985	$1,281	$1,281	$1,478	$1,576
Salaries-Officer's	$0	$0	$0	$0	$0	$0	$0
Salaries-Administrative	$4,413	$4,413	$4,413	$4,413	$4,413	$4,413	$4,413
Salaries and Wages-Other	$78,325	$43,514	$43,514	$56,568	$56,568	$65,271	$69,622
Salaries-Manager	$7,480	$7,480	$7,480	$7,480	$7,480	$7,480	$7,480
Telephone/Utilities	$6,798	$3,776	$3,776	$4,909	$4,909	$5,665	$6,042
Real Estate Taxes	$1,824	$1,824	$1,824	$1,824	$1,824	$1,824	$1,824
Other #2	$0	$0	$0	$0	$0	$0	$0
Other #3	$0	$0	$0	$0	$0	$0	$0
Other#4	$0	$0	$0	$0	$0	$0	$0
Misc./Contingency Expenses	$730	$730	$730	$730	$730	$730	$730
Total Cash Paid Out	**151,780**	**106,944**	**109,645**	**126,627**	**117,175**	**129,396**	**140,909**
LOANS SECTION:							
Interest	11,260	11,242	11,223	11,204	11,184	11,165	11,145
Principal	2,250	2,269	2,288	2,307	2,326	2,345	2,365
Cash Pyts to Loans	**13,510**	**13,510**	**13,510**	**13,510**	**13,510**	**13,510**	**13,510**
Taxable Income	28,931	35,390	41,599	39,590	17,943	18,673	31,429
Income Tax (State & Federal)	9,332	9,332	9,332	9,332	9,332	9,332	9,332
NET INCOME	**19,599**	**26,057**	**32,267**	**30,257**	**8,611**	**9,341**	**22,097**
LOANS (Balance)	1,348,992	1,346,723	1,344,435	1,342,129	1,339,803	1,337,457	1,335,093
DIVIDENDS PAID	7,279	7,279	7,279	7,279	7,279	7,279	7,279

Month 32 Dec-02	Month 33 Jan-03	Month 34 Feb-03	Month 35 Mar-03	Month 36 Apr-03	Totals
$116,398	$135,797	$135,797	$142,264	$148,730	$1,293,306
$71,004	$55,225	$55,225	$55,225	$55,225	$788,928
$9,015	$7,012	$7,012	$7,012	$7,012	$100,170
$0	$0	$0	$0	$0	$0
$0	$0	$0	$0	$0	$0
196,416	**198,034**	**198,034**	**204,501**	**210,967**	**$2,182,404**
$4,007	$4,675	$4,675	$4,897	$5,120	$44,520
$21,301	$16,567	$16,567	$16,567	$16,567	$236,678
$3,005	$2,337	$2,337	$2,337	$2,337	$33,390
$0	$0	$0	$0	$0	$0
$1,970	$2,299	$2,299	$2,408	$2,518	$21,893
$0	$0	$0	$0	$0	$0
$0	$0	$0	$0	$0	$0
$5,374	$6,270	$6,270	$6,569	$6,867	$59,714
$0	$0	$0	$0	$0	$0
$109	$109	$109	$109	$109	$1,314
$0	$0	$0	$0	$0	$0
$0	$0	$0	$0	$0	$0
$182	$182	$182	$182	$182	$2,189
$639	$639	$639	$639	$639	$7,662
					$0
					$0
$0	$0	$0	$0	$0	$0
$0	$0	$0	$0	$0	$0
$319	$319	$319	$319	$319	$3,831
$33	$33	$33	$33	$33	$400
$219	$219	$219	$219	$219	$2,627
$13,533	$15,491	$15,491	$16,144	$16,796	$151,950
$912	$912	$912	$912	$912	$10,946
$182	$182	$182	$182	$182	$2,189
$0	$0	$0	$0	$0	$0
$1,773	$2,069	$2,069	$2,167	$2,266	$19,703
$0	$0	$0	$0	$0	$0
$4,413	$4,413	$4,413	$4,413	$4,413	$52,959
$78,325	$91,379	$91,379	$95,731	$100,082	$870,281
$7,480	$7,480	$7,480	$7,480	$7,480	$89,760
$6,798	$7,931	$7,931	$8,308	$8,686	$75,530
$1,824	$1,824	$1,824	$1,824	$1,824	$21,893
$0	$0	$0	$0	$0	$0
$0	$0	$0	$0	$0	$0
$0	$0	$0	$0	$0	$0
$730	$730	$730	$730	$730	$8,757
153,131	**166,062**	**166,062**	**172,173**	**178,824**	**$1,718,187**
11,126	11,106	11,086	11,066	11,045	$133,851
2,385	2,404	2,424	2,445	2,465	$28,272
13,510	**13,510**	**13,510**	**13,510**	**13,510**	**$162,124**
32,160	20,866	20,886	21,262	21,638	$330,366
9,332	9,332	9,332	9,332	9,332	$111,985
22,828	**11,534**	**11,554**	**11,930**	**12,306**	**$218,381**
1,332,708	1,330,304	1,327,879	1,325,435	1,322,970	
7,279	7,279	7,279	7,279	7,279	87,352

Five-Year Income Statement (Restaurant & Gift Shop)

	FIVE-YEAR ANALYSIS				
	Projected 2000	Projected 2001	Projected 2002	Projected 2003	Projected 2004
Sales:					
Sales	$798,830	$838,772	$889,098	$951,335	$1,027,441
Cost of Sales	$242,649	$254,781	$270,068	$288,973	$312,091
Gross Profit	**$556,181**	**$583,991**	**$619,030**	**$662,362**	**$715,350**
Expenses:					
Operating expenses	$373,271	$390,068	$408,596	$429,026	$451,550
Interest	$56,555	$55,568	$54,477	$53,273	$51,942
Depreciation	$24,304	$24,304	$24,304	$24,304	$24,304
Amortization	$163	$163	$163	$163	$163
Total expenses	**$454,293**	**$470,103**	**$487,541**	**$506,766**	**$527,959**
Operating income	**$101,888**	**$113,888**	**$131,489**	**$155,596**	**$187,391**
Other income and expenses:					
Gain (loss) on sale of assets	$0	$0	$0	$0	$0
Other (net)	$0	$0	$0	$0	$0
Subtotal	**$0**	**$0**	**$0**	**$0**	**$0**
Income before tax	**$101,888**	**$113,888**	**$131,489**	**$155,596**	**$187,391**
Taxes (Federal & State)	$33,743	$38,428	$45,578	$55,597	$69,014
Rate	32.93%	33.38%	33.90%	34.42%	34.89%
Net Income	**$68,145**	**$75,460**	**$85,911**	**$99,999**	**$118,377**
Retained earnings-beginning	$0	$54,399	$106,847	$157,206	$193,641
Dividends paid	$13,746	$23,012	$35,552	$63,564	$103,029
Retained earnings-ending	$54,399	$106,847	$157,206	$193,641	$208,989

Detailed Supporting Information:

Cost of Sales

Direct labor	$0	$0	$0	$0	$0
Materials	$242,649	$254,781	$270,068	$288,973	$312,091
Other costs					

Five-Year Income Statement (Car Wash)

	FIVE-YEAR ANALYSIS				
	Projected 2000	**Projected 2001**	**Projected 2002**	**Projected 2003**	**Projected 2004**
Sales:					
Sales	$1,960,830	$2,058,872	$2,182,404	$2,335,172	$2,521,986
Cost of Sales	$282,649	$296,781	$314,588	$336,609	$363,538
Gross Profit	**$1,678,181**	**$1,762,091**	**$1,867,816**	**$1,998,563**	**$2,158,448**
Expenses:					
Operating expenses	$1,227,333	$1,282,563	$1,343,485	$1,410,659	$1,484,719
Interest	$138,957	$136,531	$133,851	$130,891	$127,621
Depreciation	$59,714	$59,714	$59,714	$59,714	$59,714
Amortization	$400	$400	$400	$400	$400
Total expenses	**$1,426,404**	**$1,479,208**	**$1,537,450**	**$1,601,664**	**$1,672,454**
Operating income	**$251,777**	**$282,883**	**$330,366**	**$396,899**	**$485,994**
Other income and expenses:					
Gain (loss) on sale of assets	$0	$0	$0	$0	$0
Other (net)	$0	$0	$0	$0	$0
Subtotal	$0	$0	$0	$0	$0
Income before tax	**$251,777**	**$282,883**	**$330,366**	**$396,899**	**$485,994**
Taxes (Federal & State)	$82,907	$94,417	$111,985	$136,603	$169,568
Rate	32.93%	33.38%	33.90%	34.42%	34.89%
Net Income	**$168,870**	**$18,866**	**$218,381**	**$260,296**	**$316,426**
Retained earnings-beginning	$0	$15,096	$267,022	$398,051	$502,169
Dividends paid	$33,774	$56,540	$87,352	$156,178	$253,142
Retained earnings-ending	$135,096	$267,022	$398,051	$502,169	$565,453

Detailed Supporting Information:

Cost of Sales					
Direct labor	$0	$0	$0	$0	$0
Materials	$282,649	$296,781	$314,588	$336,609	$363,538
Other costs					

Five-Year Balance Sheet

		FIVE-YEAR ANALYSIS				
	START-UP	Projected 2000	Projected 2001	Projected 2002	Projected 2003	Projected 2004
ASSETS:						
Cash and cash equivalents	$78,500	$274,812	$425,430	$571,374	$681,176	$750,371
Accounts receivable	$0	$83,721	$56,407	$59,792	$63,977	$69,096
Inventory	$25,000	$69,694	$73,179	$77,570	$82,999	$89,640
Other current assets	$13,000	$20,000	$25,000	$30,000	$40,000	$45,000
Total Current Assets	**$116,500**	**$418,227**	**$580,016**	**$738,736**	**$868,152**	**$954,107**
FIXED ASSETS:						
Land	$365,000	$365,000	$365,000	$365,000	$365,000	$365,000
Buildings	$800,000	$800,000	$800,000	$800,000	$800,000	$800,000
Machinery & Equipment	$300,000	$300,000	$303,658	$307,489	$311,512	$315,746
Furniture/Fixtures	$25,000	$25,000	$27,090	$29,279	$31,578	$33,997
Subtotal	**$1,490,000**	**$1,490,000**	**$1,495,748**	**$1,501,768**	**$1,508,090**	**$1,514,743**
Less-accumulated depreciation	$0	$59,714	$119,428	$179,142	$238,856	$298,570
Total Fixed Assets	**$1,490,000**	**$1,430,286**	**$1,376,320**	**$1,322,626**	**$1,269,234**	**$1,216,173**
INTANGIBLE ASSETS:						
Cost	$2,000	$2,000	$2,000	$2,000	$2,000	$2,000
Less-accumulated amortization	$0	$400	$800	$1,200	$1,600	$2,000
Total Intangible Assets	**$2,000**	**$1,600**	**$1,200**	**$800**	**$400**	**$0**
Other Assets	$86,500	$90,000	$95,000	$100,000	$105,000	$110,000
Total Assets	**$1,695,000**	**$1,940,113**	**$2,052,536**	**$2,162,162**	**$2,242,786**	**$2,280,280**
LIABILITIES:						
Accounts payable	$0	$19,360	$20,327	$21,547	$23,055	$24,900
Notes payable	$0	$0	$0	$0	$0	$0
Current portion of long-term debt	$23,166	$25,592	$28,272	$31,232	$34,503	$38,116
Income taxes	$0	$0	$0	$0	$0	$0
Accrued expenses	$0	$113,823	$118,945	$124,595	$130,825	$137,693
Other current liabilities	$0	$0	$0	$0	$0	$0
Total Current Liabilities	**$23,166**	**$158,775**	**$167,544**	**$177,374**	**$188,383**	**$200,709**
Long-term debt	$1,376,834	$1,351,242	$1,322,970	$1,291,737	$1,257,234	$1,219,118
Deferred income	$0	$0	$0	$0	$0	$0
Deferred income taxes	$0	$0	$0	$0	$0	$0
Other long-term liabilities	$0	$0	$0	$0	$0	$0
Total Liabilities	**$1,400,000**	**$1,510,017**	**$1,490,514**	**$1,469,111**	**$1,445,617**	**$1,419,827**
EQUITY:						
Capital stock issued	$295,000	$295,000	$295,000	$295,000	$295,000	$295,000
Additional paid in capital	$0	$0	$0	$0	$0	$0
Retained earnings	$0	$135,096	$267,022	$398,051	$502,169	$565,453
Total Equity	$295,000	$430,096	$562,022	$693,051	$797,169	$860,453
Total Liabilities and Equity	**$1,695,000**	**$1,940,113**	**$2,052,536**	**$2,162,162**	**$2,242,786**	**$2,280,280**
"C" Corporation (Y/N)	Y					
Cash balance positive /(negative)	Positive	Positive	Positive	Positive	Positive	Positive
Amount sheet is out-of-balance	$0	$0	$0	$0	$0	$0
Amount cash flow out-of-balance		$0	$0	$0	$0	$0

Five-Year Cash Flow Statement

FIVE-YEAR ANALYSIS

	Projected 2000	Projected 2001	Projected 2002	Projected 2003	Projected 2004
Cash from operations:					
Net earnings (loss)	$168,870	$188,466	$218,381	$260,296	$316,426
Add-depreciation and amortization	$60,114	$60,114	$60,114	$60,114	$60,114
Cash from operations	**$228,984**	**$248,580**	**$278,495**	**$320,410**	**$376,540**
Cash provided (used) by operating activities:					
Accounts Receivable	($53,721)	($2,686)	($3,385)	($4,185)	($5,119)
Inventory	($44,694)	($3,485)	($4,391)	($5,429)	($6,641)
Other current assets	($7,000)	($5,000)	($5,000)	($10,000)	($5,000)
Other non-current assets	($3,500)	($5,000)	($5,000)	($5,000)	($5,000)
Accounts payable	$19,360	$967	$1,220	$1,508	$1,845
Current portion of long-term debt	$2,426	$2,680	$2,960	$3,271	$3,613
Income taxes	$0	$0	$0	$0	$0
Accrued expenses	$113,823	$5,122	$5,650	$6,230	$6,868
Other current liabilities	$0	$0	$0	$0	$0
Dividends paid	($33,774)	($56,540)	($87,352)	($156,178)	($253,142)
Net cash from operations	**($7,080)**	**($63,942)**	**($95,298)**	**($169,783)**	**($262,576)**
Financing transactions					
Increases (decreases):					
Land	$0	$0	$0	$0	$0
Buildings and improvements	$0	$0	$0	$0	$0
Equipment	$0	$3,658	$3,831	$4,023	$4,234
Furniture/Fixtures	$0	$2,090	$2,189	$2,299	$2,419
Intangible assets	$0	$0	$0	$0	$0
Net cash from investments	**$0**	**$5,748**	**$6,020**	**$6,322**	**$6,653**
Financing transactions					
Increases (decreases):					
Short-term notes payable	$0	$0	$0	$0	$0
Long-term debt	($25,592)	($28,272)	($31,233)	($34,503)	($38,116)
Deferred income	$0	$0	$0	$0	$0
Other long-term liabilities	$0	$0	$0	$0	$0
Capital stock and paid in capital	$0	$0	$0	$0	$0
Net cash from financing	**($25,592)**	**($28,272)**	**($31,233)**	**($34,503)**	**($38,116)**
Net increase (decrease) in cash	**$196,312**	**$150,618**	**$145,944**	**$109,802**	**$69,195**
Cash at beginning of period	**$78,500**	**$274,812**	**$425,430**	**$571,374**	**$681,176**
Cash at the end of period	**$274,812**	**$425,430**	**$571,374**	**$681,176**	**$750,371**

Common Size Income Statement

	Company Projected 2000	Company Projected 2001	Company Projected 2002	Company Projected 2003	Company Projected 2004	Restaurant Industry 1998	Car Wash Industry 1998
Revenue from Sales	100.0%	100.0%	100.0%	100.0%	100.0%	100.0%	100.0%
Cost of Sales	14.4%	14.4%	14.4%	14.4%	14.4%	41.9%	0.0%
Gross Profit	85.6%	85.6%	85.6%	85.6%	85.6%	58.1%	100.0%
Operating Expenses	72.7%	71.8%	70.4%	68.6%	66.3%	53.2%	92.2%
Operating Profit	12.8%	13.7%	15.1%	17.0%	19.3%	4.9%	7.8%
Other Expen/Inc (Net)	0.0%	0.0%	0.0%	0.0%	0.0%	-1.7%	-2.8%
Pre-Tax Profit	**12.8%**	**13.7%**	**15.1%**	**17.0%**	**19.3%**	**3.2%**	**5.0%**
Income Taxes	4.2%	4.6%	5.1%	5.8%	6.7%	0.0%	0.0%
Income After Taxes	**8.6%**	**9.2%**	**10.0%**	**11.1%**	**12.5%**	**3.2%**	**5.0%**

Common Size Balance Sheet

	Company Projected 2000	Company Projected 2001	Company Projected 2002	Company Projected 2003	Company Projected 2004	Restaurant Industry 1998	Car Wash Industry 1998
Cash & Equivalent	14.2%	20.7%	26.4%	30.4%	32.9%	16.0%	16.2%
Accounts Receivable	2.8%	2.7%	2.8%	2.9%	3.0%	2.6%	7.0%
Inventory	3.6%	3.6%	3.6%	3.7%	3.9%	7.0%	3.9%
Other Current	1.0%	1.2%	1.4%	1.8%	2.0%	1.5%	0.5%
Total Current Assets	21.6%	28.3%	34.2%	38.7%	41.8%	27.1%	27.6%
Fixed Assets (Net)	73.7%	67.1%	61.2%	56.6%	53.3%	53.5%	61.7%
Intangibles	0.1%	0.1%	0.0%	0.0%	0.0%	10.3%	5.1%
Other Assets	4.6%	4.6%	4.6%	4.7%	4.8%	9.1%	5.6%
Total Assets	**100.0%**	**100.0%**	**100.0%**	**100.0%**	**100.0%**	**100.0%**	**100.0%**
Liabilities:							
Accounts Payable	1.0%	1.0%	1.0%	1.0%	1.1%	8.6%	9.4%
Short-Term Notes	0.0%	0.0%	0.0%	0.0%	0.0%	6.4%	4.5%
Current Maturities (LTD)	1.3%	1.4%	1.4%	1.5%	1.7%	4.9%	7.0%
Income Taxes	0.0%	0.0%	0.0%	0.0%	0.0%	0.4%	0.6%
Accrued Expenses	5.9%	5.8%	5.8%	5.8%	6.0%	15.1%	8.2%
Other Current Liabilities	0.0%	0.0%	0.0%	0.0%	0.0%	0.0%	0.0%
Total Current Liabilities	8.2%	8.2%	8.2%	8.4%	8.8%	35.4%	29.7%
Long-Term Debt	69.6%	64.5%	59.7%	56.1%	53.5%	30.0%	34.1%
Other Non-Current	0.0%	0.0%	0.0%	0.0%	0.0%	4.8%	5.8%
Total Liabilities	77.8%	72.6%	67.9%	64.5%	62.3%	70.2%	69.6%
Total Equity	**22.2%**	**27.4%**	**32.1%**	**35.5%**	**37.7%**	**29.8%**	**30.4%**
Total Liablilities & Equity	100.0%	100.0%	100.0%	100.0%	100.0%	100.0%	100.0%

Cost Variables	Per Month-1st Year			Average Monthly Break-even Analysis - 2000
	Optimistic -20%	Most Likely Case	Pessimistic 20%	Car Wash
FIXED COSTS:				
Rentals/Leases	$0	$0	$0	
Salaries (Fixed/Officer's)	$1,913	$2,392	$2,870	
Insurance	$333	$417	$500	
Depreciation & Amortization	$2,377	$2,971	$3,565	
Interest	$5,493	$4,867	$8,240	
Utilities/Phone	$3,800	$4,750	$5,700	
(Other fixed costs)	$0	$0	$0	
Total Fixed Costs	**$13,917**	**$17,396**	**$20,875**	
VARIABLE COSTS:				
Cost of Goods Sold	$2,667	$3,333	$4,000	
Variable Labor/Wages	$41,799	$52,248	$62,698	
Advertising	$667	$833	$1,000	
Professional Services	$533	$667	$800	
(Other variable cost)	$7,976	$9,971	$11,965	
Total Variable Costs	**$53,642**	**$67,052**	**$80,463**	
SALES AND INCOME DATA:				
Average Income Per Customer	$14.53	$14.53	$14.53	
Average # of Customers Per Month	9,855.00	8,212.50	6,570.00	
RESULTS:				
Fixed Costs per Customer	$1.41	$2.12	$3.18	
Variable Costs per Customer	$5.44	$8.16	$12.25	
Break-Even Number of Customers	$1,532.35	$2,735.03	$9,163.61	
Number of Customers over Break-Even	8,322.65	5,477.47	-2,593.61	
Break-Even Sales Amount	$22,257.32	$39,726.34	$133,101.42	
Gross Profit per Customer	$9.08	$6.36	$2.28	
Gross Profit (over Break-Even)	$75,585.51	$34,838.60	($5,908.30)	

Average Monthly Break-even Analysis - 2000

Combined Restaurant & Gift Shop

Cost Variables	Per Month-1st Year		
	Optimistic -20%	Most Likely Case	Pessimistic 20%
FIXED COSTS:			
Rentals/Leases	$0	$0	$0
Salaries (Fixed)	$1,312	$1,640	$1,968
Insurance	$133	$167	$200
Depreciation & Amortization	$1,631	$2,039	$2,447
Interest	$3,770	$4,713	$5,656
Utilities/Phone	$796	$995	$1,194
(Other fixed costs)	$0	$0	$0
Total Fixed Costs	**$7,643**	**$9,553**	**$11,464**
VARIABLE COSTS:			
Cost of Goods Sold	$16,177	$20,221	$24,265
Variable Labor/Wages	$16,671	$20,838	$25,006
Advertising	$667	$833	$1,000
Professional Services	$133	$167	$200
(Other variable cost)	$5,184	$6,481	$7,777
Total Variable Costs	**$38,832**	**$48,540**	**$58,248**
SALES AND INCOME DATA:			
Average Income Per Customer	$9.99	$9.99	$9.99
Average # of Customers Per Month	8,000.00	6,666.67	5,333.33
RESULTS:			
Fixed Costs per Customer	$0.96	$1.43	$2.15
Variable Costs per Customer	$4.85	$7.28	$10.92
Break-Even Number of Customers	$1,489.39	$3,532.46	($12,247.36)
Number of Customers over Break-Even	6,510.61	3,134.20	17,580.70
Break-Even Sales Amount	$14,872.07	$35,272.98	($122,294.52)
Gross Profit per Customer	$5.13	$2.70	($0.94)
Gross Profit (over Break-Even)	$33,408.66	$8,476.24	($16,456.18)

| Cost Variables | Per Month-1st Year | | | Average Monthly Break-even Analysis - 2000 |
	Optimistic -20%	Most Likely Case	Pessimistic 20%	
FIXED COSTS:				**Combined Operations**
Rentals/Leases	$0	$0	$0	
Salaries (Fixed/Officer's)	$3,225	$4,032	$4,838	
Insurance	$467	$583	$700	
Depreciation & Amortization	$4,008	$5,010	$6,011	
Interest	$9,264	$11,580	$13,896	
Utilities/Phone	$4,600	$5,750	$6,900	
(Other fixed costs)	$0	$0	$0	
Total Fixed Costs	**$21,563**	**$26,954**	**$32,345**	
VARIABLE COSTS:				
Cost of Goods Sold	$18,843	$23,554	$28,265	
Variable Labor/Wages	$58,469	$73,087	$87,704	
Advertising	$1,333	$1,667	$2,000	
Professional Services	$667	$833	$1,000	
(Other variable cost)	$13,061	$16,326	$19,591	
Total Variable Costs	**$92,373**	**$115,467**	**$138,560**	
SALES AND INCOME DATA:				
Average Income Per Customer	$24.51	$24.51	$24.51	
Average # of Customers Per Month	17,855.00	14,879.17	11,903.33	
RESULTS:				
Fixed Costs per Customer	$1.21	$1.81	$2.72	
Variable Costs per Customer	$5.17	$7.76	$11.64	
Break-Even Number of Customers	$1,115.15	$1,609.20	$2,513.23	
Number of Customers over Break-Even	16,739.85	13,269.96	9,390.10	
Break-Even Sales Amount	$27,332.65	$39,442.14	$61,600.25	
Gross Profit per Customer	$19.34	$16.75	$12.87	
Gross Profit (over Break-Even)	$323,695.90	$222,272.90	$120,849.89	

**Car Wash
Break-even Chart -
Year 1**

Income per customer	$14.53
Total fixed Costs	$17,395.76
Variable costs per customer	$8.16

# of customers	Total Revenues	Total Costs
1,641.02	$23,836	$30,794
1,914.52	$27,808	$33,027
2,188.03	$31,781	$35,260
2,461.53	$35,754	$37,493
2,735.03	$39,726	$39,726
3,008.54	$43,699	$41,959
3,282.04	$47,672	$44,192
3,555.54	$51,644	$46,426
3,829.05	$55,617	$48,659
4,102.55	$59,590	$50,892

**Restaurant & Gift
Shop
Break-even Chart -
Year 1**

# of customers	Total Revenues	Total Costs
2,119.48	$21,164	$24,985
2,472.73	$24,691	$27,557
2,825.97	$28,218	$30,129
3,179.22	$31,746	$32,701
3,532.46	$35,273	$35,273
3,885.71	$38,800	$37,845
4,238.96	$42,328	$40,417
4,592.20	$45,855	$42,989
4,945.45	$49,382	$45,561
5,298.70	$52,909	$48,133

Loan Compliance Covenants

Year	Net Working Capital	Current Ratio	Quick Ratio	EBIT/ Interest	EBIT/ I+P	DEBT/ Equity	Z-Score
2000	$259,452	2.63	2.07	2.81	2.41	3.52	1.91
2001	$412,472	3.46	2.88	3.07	0.37	2.66	2.05
2002	$561,362	4.16	3.56	3.47	0.85	2.12	2.21
2003	$679,769	4.61	3.96	4.03	8.41	1.81	2.41
2004	$753,398	4.75	4.08	4.81	0.00	1.65	2.64
Industry Median	**N/A**	**1.00**	**0.80**	**2.00**	**N/A**	**3.00**	**N/A**

Annual Projections Summary

Projection Period	Gross Profit	After-Tax Net Income	Cash from Operations	Book Equity
Start-Up/Base				$295,000
2000	$1,678,181	$168,870	$228,984	$430,096
2001	$1,762,091	$188,466	$248,580	$562,022
2002	$1,867,816	$218,381	$278,495	$693,051
2003	$1,998,563	$260,296	$320,410	$797,169
2004	$2,158,448	$316,426	$376,540	$860,453

Rates of Return

	Net Income	IRR	MIRR	ANNUAL DIVIDENDS	TOTAL ASSETS
Initial Investment	($295,000)				
2000	$168,870	0.00%	-42.76%	$33,774	$1,940,113
2001	$188,466	13.52%	128.44%	$56,540	$2,052,536
2002	$218,381	40.35%	248.94%	$87,352	$2,162,162
2003	$260,296	54.05%	329.65%	$156,178	$2,242,786
2004	$316,426	61.67%	386.57%	$253,142	$2,280,280

ASSUMPTIONS:

Income figures are after taxes

Dividend Payout = 50% of After Tax Income

Reinvestment rate = 7%

IRR = INTERNAL RATE OF RETURN

MIRR = MODIFIED RATE OF RETURN

ROI = RATE OF RETURN ON OWNER'S INVESTMENT

ROA = RATE OF RETURN ON TOTAL ASSETS

IRR = the interest rate received for an investment and income that occur at regular periods.

MIRR = adds the cost of funds and interest received on reinvestment of cash to the IRR.

	2000	2001	2002	2003	2004
Return on Assets	8.70%	9.18%	10.10%	11.61%	13.88%
Return on Investment	11.45%	19.17%	29.61%	52.94%	85.81%
Income Per Share	$0.57	$0.64	$0.74	$0.88	$1.07
Dividends Per Share	$0.11	$0.19	$0.30	$0.53	$0.86

Income Per Share Chart

Year 1	$0.57
Year 2	$0.64
Year 3	$0.74
Year 4	$0.88
Year 5	$1.07

Income Statement

	Projected 2000	Projected 2001	Projected 2002	Projected 2003	Projected 2004
Sales	1,960,830	2,058,872	2,182,404	2,335,172	2,521,986
Cost of Sales	282,649	296,781	314,588	336,609	363,538
Expenses	1,426,404	1,479,208	1,537,450	1,601,664	1,672,454
Operating Income	251,777	282,883	330,366	396,899	485,994
Income Taxes	82,907	94,417	111,985	136,603	169,568
Net Income	168,870	188,466	218,381	260,296	316,426

Balance Sheet Chart

	2000	2001	2002	2003	2004
Current Assets	418,227	2,058,872	738,736	868,152	954,107
Fixed Assets	1,430,286	1,376,320	1,322,626	1,269,234	1,216,173
Total Assets	1,940,113	2,052,536	2,162,162	2,242,786	2,280,280
Current Liabilities	158,775	167,544	177,374	188,383	200,709
Total Liabilities	1,510,017	1,490,514	1,469,111	1,445,617	1,419,827
Net Worth	430,096	562,022	693,051	797,169	860,453

Growth Trends

	2000	2001	2002	2003	2004
Cost of Goods Sold	$282,649	$296,781	$314,588	$336,609	$363,538
Total Expenses	$1,426,404	$1,479,208	$1,537,450	$1,601,664	$1,672,454
Total Revenue	$1,960,830	$2,058,872	$2,182,404	$2,335,172	$2,521,986

Net Income Growth

	2000	2001	2002	2003	2004
NET INCOME	$168,870	$188,466	$218,381	$260,296	$316,426

This page left intentionally blank to accommodate tabular matter following.

Ratio Comparison

	Restaurant Projected 2000	Car Washes Projected 2001	Combined & Projected 2002	Projected 2003
Liquidity Ratios:				
Current Ratio	2.63	3.46	4.16	4.61
Quick Ratio	2.07	2.88	3.56	3.96
Sales/Receivables	36.50	36.50	36.50	36.50
Days' Receivables	10.00	10.00	10.00	10.00
Cost of Sales/Inventory	4.06	4.06	4.06	4.06
Days' Inventory	90.00	90.00	90.00	90.00
Cost of Sales/Payables	14.60	14.60	14.60	14.60
Days' Payables	25.00	25.00	25.00	25.00
Sales/Work Capital	7.56	4.99	3.89	3.44
EBIT/Interest	2.81	3.07	3.47	4.03
Net Profit+Depr.+Amort./C.L.T.D.	8.95	8.79	8.92	9.29
Leverage Ratios				
Fixed Assets/Tangible Net Worth	3.34	2.45	1.91	1.59
Debt/Worth	3.52	2.66	2.12	1.81
Operating Ratios				
Profit Before Tax/Tan. Net Worth	58.76%	50.44%	47.72%	49.81%
Profit Before Tax/Total Assets	12.98%	13.78%	15.28%	17.70%
Sales/Net Fixed Assets	1.37%	1.50%	1.65%	1.84%
Sales/Total Assets	1.01%	1.00%	1.01%	1.04%
Other Ratios/Numbers:				
Officers' Salaries (Actual)	$0	$0	$0	$0
Equity (Net Worth)	$430,096	$562,022	$693,051	$797,169
Loans Balance (Actual)	$1,376,834	$1,351,242	$1,322,970	$1,291,737
% Deprec., Amort./Sales	0.03	0.03	0.03	0.03
% Officers' Compensation/Sales	0.00	0.00	0.00	0.00
Tangible Net Worth (NW-Intangibles)	$428,496	$560,822	$692,251	$796,769
Working Capital (Actual)	$259,452	$412,472	$561,362	$679,769
Gross Profit				
Key Percentages as a Percent of Gross Profit				
Rent	0.00%	0.00%	0.00%	0.00%
Interest Paid	8.28%	7.75%	7.17%	6.55%
Depreciation & Amortization	3.58%	3.41%	3.22%	3.01%
Officers' Compensation	0.00%	0.00%	0.00%	0.00%
Taxes Paid	4.94%	5.36%	6.00%	6.84%

Projected 2004	Industry Ave. 1998	Industry Ave. 1998	Weighted Ave. 1998
4.75	0.70	1.00	0.88
4.08	0.40	0.80	0.64
36.50	N/A	N/A	N/A
10.00	N/A	N/A	N/A
4.06	34.90	N/A	N/A
90.00	10.46	N/A	N/A
14.60	16.00	N/A	N/A
25.00	22.81	N/A	N/A
3.35	-40.90	-16.80	-26.44
4.81	2.50	2.00	3.00
9.88	2.30	2.40	2.36
1.41	2.90	4.20	3.68
1.65	3.50	3.00	3.20
56.48%	39.60%	35.70%	37.26%
21.31%	10.00%	5.20%	7.12%
2.07%	7.50%	1.50%	3.90%
1.11%	3.60%	1.50%	2.34%
$0	$0	N/A	
$860,453	0.00	N/A	
$1,257,234	0.00	N/A	
0.00	2.50	9.50	
0.00	0.00	0.00	
$860,453	0.00	N/A	
$753,398	0.00	N/A	
0.00%	20.10%	0.00%	
5.91%	1.30%	0.00%	
2.79%	2.60%	0.00%	
0.00%	3.80%	0.00%	
7.86%	4.00%	N/A	

RATIO ANALYSIS

If A.B.C., Inc. meets the financial goals outlined in this plan, a ratio analysis of those numbers are extremely favorable when compared to industry averages according to the Robert Morris & Associates 1998 industry average figures.

Current Ratio is an approximate measure of a firm's ability to meet its current obligations and is calculated as Current Assets divided by Current Liabilities. The company's Current Ratio is above the industry median. This indicates a relatively more stable position for the company compared to the industry and indicates a possible opportunity for expanding operations.

Quick Ratio is a measure of a firm's ability to meet current obligations without relying on the sale of inventories. It is calculated as Current Assets minus inventories divided by Current Liabilities. This ratio is above the industry median, which indicates that A.B.C., Inc. is more stable relative to the industry and again points to an apparent opportunity for expansion.

EBIT to interest ratio is a measure of ability to meet annual interest payments. It is calculated as Earnings before Interest and Taxes divided by Annual Interest Expense. Since this ratio is above industry averages, the company should have no problem servicing its debt and can even service greater amounts of debt.

The Fixed Assets to Tangible Net Worth Ratio measures the extent to which owner's equity has been invested in the business. Since this ratio is on a downward trend, it provides an even larger "cushion" to creditors in the event of liquidation.

Current Maturities Coverage Ratio measures the ability to pay current maturities of long-term debt with cash flow from operations. It is calculated as Net Income + depreciation & amortization divided by current portion of long-term debt. This ratio is on an upward trend which indicates that cash flows available to service debt are increasing relative to the level of debt. It also indicates additional debt capacity is available if needed.

The Debt to Equity Ratio expresses the relationship between capital contributed by creditors and capital contributed by owners. It is calculated as Total Liabilities divided by Net Worth. This ratio shows a downward trend which would seem to indicate that if the company meets its goals that it will provide greater long-term financial safety for creditors. It also points out that A.B.C., Inc. can handle additional debt if needed.

The Earnings before Taxes to Total Assets Ratio expresses the pre-tax return on total assets and measures the effectiveness of management in employing available resources. It is calculated as Earnings Before Taxes divided by Net Worth minus Net Intangible Assets times 100. Since this ratio is above industry averages, the company would be more efficient than the industry in its effective employment of resources and would out-perform the industry as a whole.

The Revenue to Total Assets Ratio is a general measure of ability to generate revenue in relation to total assets. It is calculated as Earnings Before Taxes divided by Total Assets times 100. This ratio is above industry averages which can indicate that the company is efficient in using available resources to generate revenue as compared to the industry.

CONCLUSIONS & SUMMARY

Assuming the financial projections in this plan are attained, the future looks very bright indeed. The property improvement, increased inventory items and the continued growth of both the car wash, restaurant, and the surrounding Madison area will help make A.B.C., Inc. one of the premier car wash destinations in the area.

A look at the financial ratios in this plan bears out our confidence in the future. A look at our competition comparison gives us a real look into the possibilities to become a market leader. A close look at the property can only reaffirm that the market, location, and clientele are all in place and waiting to be serviced by a car wash and restaurant such as A.B.C., Inc.

Throughout this plan we have taken special care to remain conservative in our growth projections. Even so, the numbers are spectacular. Some of the highlights include:

- Return on Invest of 15.45%, 19.17%, 29.61%, 55.94%, and 95.81% over the next five years.
- Steady growth conservatively averaging over 5% per year.
- Pre-Tax Profit is consistently far above industry averages.
- Total Equity is substantially higher than peer operations by the third year.
- Far greater strengths than weaknesses when compared to competition.
- Overall risks associated with the business are low.

Investment in A.B.C., Inc. at this time makes excellent economic sense. The projected cash flow is well above industry averages.

Wireless Internet Service

BUSINESS PLAN

5988 Evergreen Blvd.
Dallas, Texas 75230

Superior XL Internet is presently the only wireless company in northern Texas. With an infusion of capital, it intends on delivering its multitude of new Internet products to numerous major U.S. regions at costs lower than those offered by the majority of competitors.

- COMPANY OVERVIEW

- MISSION STATEMENT

- MANAGEMENT

- HISTORY

- PRODUCTS & SERVICES

COMPANY OVERVIEW

Superior XL Internet (a division of Planet Wireless Systems, Inc.) is a fast-growing Internet company with a specific focus on wireless broadband Internet. We have the technology to deliver bi-directional wireless Internet at speeds of up to 100 megabytes. At the same time, we intend to develop similar network with mobile capabilities. This technology has competed favorably against xDSL and Cable Internet.

We have established a market presence in the northern region of Texas, with the intent to build an international backbone of Meshed ATM Network and Wireless Repeaters. This network would set the framework to deliver Internet data, voice, and video to each perspective home without any per/minute charges. Currently Superior XL Internet is the only wireless company in northern Texas that has successfully delivered this product. We intend to maintain our exclusivity to the areas we are delivering, through strong marketing and a noninterference clause in our contract with essential strategic building throughout each county. This would prevent other companies from setting up repeaters thus making it very difficult to compete with us. This new wireless system is Superior's solution to compete with cable modems, xDSL or any foreseeable technologies in the next three years.

MISSION STATEMENT

To provide complete, quality Internet solutions to our clients by incorporating sensible and cost-effective technologies. These product will be supported by a team of customer-oriented quality staff whose overriding priority is to provide professional service to our customers resulting in complete customer satisfaction.

MANAGEMENT

CEO

Henry Albers: Graduated Notre Dame University with an M.B.A. degree. Served as General Manager for Sliver Communications, currently one of the largest telephone companies in the United States. Mr. Albers has a proven ability to penetrate new markets, maintain and grow existing markets, manage and motivate sales forces, and design sales and marketing programs for top-dollar performance. He opened and staffed three new offices which became profitable in their first years of operation. Before Sliver, Mr. Albers was the VP of sales for PRW, with posted annual revenues of $4 billion. This position was achieved after moving the Chicago center from last in sales to number one in the nation. Mr. Albers has consistently grown Superior XL Internet between 15% to 30% in sales every month since his arrival. With the exception of a few months of setback in early 1998, Mr. Albers intends to maintain the current level of sales growth well into the new millennium.

CIO

Nicholas K. Murphy: Started his entrepreneur career brokering palm trees. He achieved annual sales of over $200,000 in his first year in business when he was eighteen years old. By the time he was twenty-one, he was already in charge of a multi-million dollar real estate development project in South America. Mr. Murphy founded Superior XL Internet in 1992 as a network consulting and computer retail company. In December 1995 he started the Internet division of his business. The growth soon overtook all other aspect of Superior. Currently wireless Internet is the core of the company.

HISTORY

Since its founding in 1995, Superior XL Internet has emerged as one of the fastest-growing independent Internet providers in the region, and one of the few that is doing so profitably. It has done so by providing moving state-of-the-art telephone base 56Kb/sec service to clients on a full, money-back guarantee, and by providing reliable T-1 connections to the Internet. Superior XL's organization has successfully conceived and delivered a full range of services to a customer list that includes 52 other ISPs and large corporate clients in the state of Texas.

While most of the company's management is already in place to accomplish the growth that customers demand, Superior XL still requires a Chief Executive Officer who is capable of managing a high-growth rate to a point beyond the $100 million sales level. Additional senior level managers can complete the management team as additional branches in other cities are opened. Upon successful negotiation of Superior XL's next round financing, the company also intends to hire 15 additional employees to meet demands. These include the following:

    CEO - Henry Albers
    CIO - Nicholas Murphy
    CFO - Sally Hemp
    CTO and President - Sean Luck
    VP of Sales - Open (acting, Michael Burntz)
    VP of Corporate Finance and Development - Open
    VP of Operations - Open
    VP of Human Resources and Administration - (acting, Sally Hemp)
    VP of Network Operation - Mark Woo
    VP of Customer and Technical Support - Open (acting, Mark Woo)
    Director of Marketing and Business Development - Marjorie Swigonski
    Director of E-Commerce - Kevin Letterman
    V.P. of Real Estate - Valerie Ortiz

Selected Job Responsibilities

CEO — Manages the overall direction of the business.

CFO — Manages working capital, including receivables, inventory cash, and marketable securities. Perform financial forecasting, including capital budget, cash budget, proforma financial statements, external financing requirements, and financial condition requirements.

CTO — Manages direction and growth of network and technical support.

VP of Sales — Manages field sales organization, territories and quotas. Manage sales office activities including customer/product support/service.

VP of Operations — Oversees the daily operation and procedures. Manages expansion plan and coordination of equipment/supplies at the new locations.

VP of Network Operation — Oversees operation of existing networks. Ensures smooth and successful installation of new networks.

VP of Customer and Technical Support — Takes care of the support of new and existing customers. Ensures customer satisfaction.

Director of Marketing and Business Development — Manages market planning, advertising, public relations, sales promotion, merchandising, and facilitating staff services. Identifies new markets; manages corporate scope and market research. Identifies foreign markets.

Director of E-Commerce — Establishes and implements e-commerce applications for clients and company.

V.P. of Real Estate— Establishes and maintains all real estate and rooftop relationships; oversees and monitors all rooftop installation operations and procedures.

PRODUCTS AND SERVICES

Superior XL Internet plans to establish a nationwide backbone in order to provide its new Internet products at a low cost. It will do this by setting up a physical location at all nine of the National Access Points (NAP) and by building its ATM backbone directly. This model is similar to that of most backbone providers. Superior XL is different in that instead of using the old routed system, it intends to use the new ATM switched network. This will provide a more scaleable network and the ability to sell Voice over IP and Virtual Private Network (VPN). These two sectors—Voice over IP and VPN—will be extremely fast growth sectors on the Internet.

Wireless Bandwidth

Bandwidth is providing customers with a direct connection to the Internet. Superior XL offers a variety of means to make that connection: Point-to-Point T-1, Frame Relay, Server Co-location, and Wireless T-1.

Wireless T-1 or DataWave offers two-way transmission at 3 megabytes per second, which is twice the speed of a standard T-1 connection. Using standard radio waves, this technology is scalable to 100 megabits per second. It eliminates the need for telephone lines, thereby eliminating telephone company charges. Wireless technology also eliminates the need for extra equipment purchase of a CSU/DSU and router equipment. Wireless is one of the most inexpensive ways to deliver the last mile solution to the customer. Currently a customer would have to pay approximately $600 per month to the phone company in order to have a frame circuit to their office. However, with wireless, Superior XL can skip the phone company and reduce the cost of an Internet data circuit by 50%.

Currently the company is using Part 15 of FCC code to transmit the Internet data. We use both the 2.4, 5.6-5.7 GHz and the 23 GHz FCC licensed spectrum in order to transmit the data. This gives Superior a theoretical limit of 200 megs of bandwidth because it is bi-directional.

Superior XL is developing wireless technology in order to reduce the price of entry into the wireless arena. Traditionally the equipment needed for a wireless installation would cost about $3,000. By employing its own technology, the company can reduce the cost of equipment to about $600 for the equipment and $400 for installation. However, as the installation quantity grows into the SOHO (Small Office Home Office) the cost of the modem could be reduced to about $250 for the modems and $150 for installation. During this time Superior XL intends to develop a MMDS, LMDS, and 5.6-5.7GHz box in order to have the capability to increase the wireless bandwidth to 20-100 Mbit/Sec. All new technology would comply with part 15 and 16 (ISM and NII band of FCC ruling) This would ensure the continued growth of the company for the next 10 years.

In the future, as the demand arises, Superior XL intends to purchase or lease frequency in order to increase the bandwidth of the wireless systems.

Frame Relay is a technology for high-speed data transfer over a T-1 line using shared facilities. "Bursts" in frame relay are what make it possible to share the line. A burst is a specific amount of data shot over lines from one point to another.

Currently Superior XL is the First ISP in Texas to sign a contract with U.S. West. This allows the company to set up a frame circuit without a setup cost and a monthly savings of 15% off the standard rate. Having no setup fee with no per circuit time commitment would help tremendously the growth of the firm's wireless systems. Superior XL could set up a frame circuit into areas where it does not have enough wireless repeaters. Once it has reached billing of over $4,000/month in an area, the company would cancel all of the frame circuits in the area and replace the area with a wireless circuit.

Point-to-Point T-1 is a direct connection to the Internet. The T-1 is not shared with any other company and operates on a circuit that goes straight to Superior XL's backbone.

Superior XL has a contract with U.S. West for three years in which they will install all frame-relay circuits with no setup charge. Such installation would enable Superior XL the ability to pick up customers in remote areas in which there are no repeaters. As such, once enough customers are acquired in a specific area, where the cost of a repeater is justified we would then put in a frame relay circuit.

Server co-location means to put one or more servers directly on a LAN (local area network) system that has a direct connection to the Internet backbone. Superior XL runs multiple T-1 lines from selected companies to provide redundancy and to ensure customers get the access when they need.

Whatever the means, bandwidth is one of the most profitable sectors of Superior XL's business. On average, the profit margin in this sector is well over 600%. However, with the development of the wireless Internet, this profit margin should increase significantly.

Modem dial-up is another product offered by Superior XL Internet. Although profitable it is not as financially attractive as the bandwidth market, though dial-up does have the largest market segment and the largest potential for growth. Superior XL has expanded its dial-up market through direct sales and resale. With its current base of more than 50 resellers, Superior XL has the capacity to grow this sector of business very rapidly. Dial-up is one of the more capital-intensive segments of the Internet. The growth of this sector has been held back artificially by Superior XL in order to spend their present capital resources more efficiently.

Currently, the company has the option to enact a contract of $1,000,000 per year selling dial-up with a one-time setup cost of $350,000 and an annual cost of $400,000. This and many other contracts were held off or not exercised due to capital limitations. With the influx of new capital, Superior XL is confident that it can generate an additional $2,000,000 per year in a very short time span.

Superior XL sees competition in this sector increasing and plans to eventually move the existing base to a free Internet model. They have tested custom software that force dial-up customers to view the banners and web pages of Superior XL's advertising customers. By charging an advertising rate that is half of the market rate (or one-third of Yahoo's rate), the company can generate about $12 per customer per month. This should increase the average price charged per customer about $.66.

Special Products

Superior XL Internet has consistently put its focus on product development. It is northern Texas's first wireless Internet and is researching and developing Free Internet, ADSL, ATM, and server side adult filters.

Voice Over IP

Superior XL is pursuing a special license allowing it to offer voice products to its existing customers along with a target market of customers. This will also give Superior the ability to reduce its own cost of lines. The firm's network has been designed to accommodate Telco-switching equipment. Until it is sufficient to implement this, Superior has placed a hold on a realistic date for launch. It is the company's intention to have a limited amount of voice traffic by the start of first quarter 2000. Due to the potential of significant revenue with little added cost for bandwidth voice over IP, Superior is in the process of testing the latest Cisco's Voice over IP product.

VPN

Virtual Private Network is one of the fastest growing segments of the Internet. It gives an ISP the ability to connect two remote offices together and make it appear as if both offices are on the same network. For example an office in Dallas would be able to print a report directly to a printer in the accounting department in Los Angeles, and people in the Los Angeles office would be able to share files with other offices.

Web Hosting

As a traditional Internet Service Provider, Superior XL offers website hosting on its server and hosts the majority of the websites the company designs. On average, Superior generates about $2,000 per month per $3,000 server set up on its system. Web hosting is not the firm's focus; however, it is sold as a convenience to customers in order to give them a one-stop Internet solution.

Data Collection Center

Superior XL has recently opened a Data Collocation Center in its facilities at 5988 Evergreen Blvd. This center is environmentally controlled and offers a location for mission critical data servers to be collocated on Superior XL's redundant network. It is intended for bandwidth intensive applications.

Web Pages

Superior XL offers web page design in order to complete certain solutions. The company has the ability to generate professional web pages with e-commerce and security features. The extensive web page customer base includes many Fortune 1000 clients.

Appendix A - Business Plan Template

Business Plan Template

USING THIS TEMPLATE

A business plan carefully spells out a company's projected course of action over a period of time, usually the first two to three years after the start-up. In addition, banks, lenders, and other investors examine the information and financial documentation before deciding whether or not to finance a new business venture. Therefore, a business plan is an essential tool in obtaining financing and should describe the business itself in detail as well as all important factors influencing the company, including the market, industry, competition, operations and management policies, problem solving strategies, financial resources and needs, and other vital information. The plan enables the business owner to anticipate costs, plan for difficulties, and take advantage of opportunities, as well as design and implement strategies that keep the company running as smoothly as possible.

This template has been provided as a model to help you construct your own business plan. Please keep in mind that there is no single acceptable format for a business plan, and that this template is in no way comprehensive, but serves as an example.

The business plans provided in this section are fictional and have been used by small business agencies as models for clients to use in compiling their own business plans.

GENERIC BUSINESS PLAN

Main headings included below are topics that should be covered in a comprehensive business plan. They include:

Business Summary

Purpose
Provides a brief overview of your business, succinctly highlighting the main ideas of your plan.

Includes
- Name and Type of Business
- Description of Product/Service
- Business History and Development
- Location
- Market
- Competition
- Management
- Financial Information
- Business Strengths and Weaknesses
- Business Growth

Table of Contents

Purpose

Organized in an Outline Format, the Table of Contents illustrates the selection and arrangement of information contained in your plan.

Includes

○ Topic Headings and Subheadings
○ Page Number References

Business History and Industry Outlook

Purpose

Examines the conception and subsequent development of your business within an industry specific context.

Includes

○ Start-up Information
○ Owner/Key Personnel Experience
○ Location
○ Development Problems and Solutions
○ Investment/Funding Information
○ Future Plans and Goals
○ Market Trends and Statistics
○ Major Competitors
○ Product/Service Advantages
○ National, Regional, and Local Economic Impact

Product/Service

Purpose

Introduces, defines, and details the product and/or service that inspired the information of your business.

Includes

○ Unique Features
○ Niche Served
○ Market Comparison
○ Stage of Product/Service Development
○ Production
○ Facilities, Equipment, and Labor
○ Financial Requirements
○ Product/Service Life Cycle
○ Future Growth

Market Examination

Purpose

Assessment of product/service applications in relation to consumer buying cycles.

Includes

- ◯ Target Market
- ◯ Consumer Buying Habits
- ◯ Product/Service Applications
- ◯ Consumer Reactions
- ◯ Market Factors and Trends
- ◯ Penetration of the Market
- ◯ Market Share
- ◯ Research and Studies
- ◯ Cost
- ◯ Sales Volume and Goals

Competition

Purpose

Analysis of Competitors in the Marketplace.

Includes

- ◯ Competitor Information
- ◯ Product/Service Comparison
- ◯ Market Niche
- ◯ Product/Service Strengths and Weaknesses
- ◯ Future Product/Service Development

Marketing

Purpose

Identifies promotion and sales strategies for your product/service.

Includes

- ◯ Product/Service Sales Appeal
- ◯ Special and Unique Features
- ◯ Identification of Customers
- ◯ Sales and Marketing Staff
- ◯ Sales Cycles
- ◯ Type of Advertising/Promotion
- ◯ Pricing
- ◯ Competition
- ◯ Customer Services

Operations

Purpose
Traces product/service development from production/inception to the market environment.

Includes
- Cost Effective Production Methods
- Facility
- Location
- Equipment
- Labor
- Future Expansion

Administration and Management

Purpose
Offers a statement of your management philosophy with an in-depth focus on processes and procedures.

Includes
- Management Philosophy
- Structure of Organization
- Reporting System
- Methods of Communication
- Employee Skills and Training
- Employee Needs and Compensation
- Work Environment
- Management Policies and Procedures
- Roles and Responsibilities

Key Personnel

Purpose
Describes the unique backgrounds of principle employees involved in business.

Includes
- Owner(s)/Employee Education and Experience
- Positions and Roles
- Benefits and Salary
- Duties and Responsibilities
- Objectives and Goals

Potential Problems and Solutions

Purpose

Discussion of problem solving strategies that change issues into opportunities.

Includes

- Risks
- Litigation
- Future Competition
- Economic Impact
- Problem Solving Skills

Financial Information

Purpose

Secures needed funding and assistance through worksheets and projections detailing financial plans, methods of repayment, and future growth opportunities.

Includes

- Financial Statements
- Bank Loans
- Methods of Repayment
- Tax Returns
- Start-up Costs
- Projected Income (3 years)
- Projected Cash Flow (3 Years)
- Projected Balance Statements (3 years)

Appendices

Purpose

Supporting documents used to enhance your business proposal.

Includes

- Photographs of product, equipment, facilities, etc.
- Copyright/Trademark Documents
- Legal Agreements
- Marketing Materials
- Research and or Studies
- Operation Schedules
- Organizational Charts
- Job Descriptions
- Resumes
- Additional Financial Documentation

Food Distributor

FICTIONAL BUSINESS PLAN

COMMERCIAL FOODS, INC.

3003 Avondale Ave.
Knoxville, TN 37920

October 31, 1992

This plan demonstrates how a partnership can have a positive impact on a new business. It demonstrates how two individuals can carve a niche in the specialty foods market by offering gourmet foods to upscale restaurants and fine hotels. This plan is fictional and has not been used to gain funding from a bank or other lending institution.

- STATEMENT OF PURPOSE

- DESCRIPTION OF THE BUSINESS

- MANAGEMENT

- PERSONNEL

- LOCATION

- PRODUCTS AND SERVICES

- THE MARKET

- COMPETITION

- SUMMARY

- INCOME STATEMENT

- FINANCIAL STATEMENTS

FOOD DISTRIBUTOR
BUSINESS PLAN

STATEMENT OF PURPOSE

Commercial Food, Inc. seeks a loan of $75,000 to establish a new business. This sum, together with $5,000 equity investment by the principals, will be used as follows:

Merchandise inventory	$25,000
Office fixture/equipment	12,000
Warehouse equipment	14,000
One delivery truck	10,000
Working capital	39,000
Total	**$100,000**

DESCRIPTION OF THE BUSINESS

Commercial Foods, Inc. will be a distributor of specialty food service products to hotels and upscale restaurants in the geographical area of a 50 mile radius of Knoxville. Richard Roberts will direct the sales effort and John Williams will manage the warehouse operation and the office. One delivery truck will be used initially with a second truck added in the third year.

We expect to begin operation of the business within 30 days after securing the requested financing.

MANAGEMENT

A. Richard Roberts is a native of Memphis, Tennessee. He is a graduate of Memphis State University with a Bachelor's degree from the School of Business. After graduation, he worked for a major manufacturer of specialty food service products as a detail sales person for five years, and, for the past three years, he has served as a product sales manager for this firm.

B. John Williams is a native of Nashville, Tennessee. He holds a B.S. Degree in Food Technology from the University of Tennessee. His career includes five years as a product development chemist in gourmet food products and five years as operations manager for a food service distributor.

Both men are healthy and energetic. Their backgrounds complement each other, which will ensure the success of Commercial Foods, Inc. They will set policies together and personnel decisions will be made jointly. Initial salaries for the owners will be $1,000 per month for the first few years. The spouses of both principals are successful in the business world and earn enough to support the families.

They have engaged the services of Foster Jones, CPA, and William Hale, Attorney, to assist them in an advisory capacity.

PERSONNEL

The firm will employ one delivery truck driver at a wage of $8.00 per hour. One office worker will be employed at $7.50 per hour. One part-time employee will be used in the office at $5.00 per hour. The driver will load and unload his own trucks. Mr. Williams will assist in the warehouse operation as needed to assist one stock person at $7.00 per hour. An additional delivery truck and driver will be added the third year.

LOCATION

The firm will lease a 20,000 square foot building at 3003 Avondale Ave., in Knoxville, which contains warehouse and office areas equipped with two-door truck docks. The annual rental is $9,000. The building was previously used as a food service warehouse and very little modification to the building will be required.

The firm will offer specialty food service products such as soup bases, dessert mixes, sauce bases, pastry mixes, spices, and flavors, normally used by upscale restaurants and nice hotels. We are going after a niche in the market with high quality gourmet products. There is much less competition in this market than in standard run of the mill food service products. Through their work experiences, the principals have contacts with supply sources and with local chefs.

PRODUCTS AND SERVICES

We know from our market survey that there are over 200 hotels and upscale restaurants in the area we plan to serve. Customers will be attracted by a direct sales approach. We will offer samples of our products and product application data on use of our products in the finished prepared foods. We will cultivate the chefs in these establishments. The technical background of John Williams will be especially useful here.

THE MARKET

We find that we will be only distributor in the area offering a full line of gourmet food service products. Other foodservice distributors offer only a few such items in conjunction with their standard product line. Our survey shows that many of the chefs are ordering products from Atlanta and Memphis because of a lack of adequate local supply.

COMPETITION

Commercial Foods, Inc. will be established as a foodservice distributor of specialty food in Knoxville. The principals, with excellent experience in the industry, are seeking a $75,000 loan to establish the business. The principals are investing $25,000 as equity capital.

SUMMARY

The business will be set up as an "S" Corporation with each principal owning 50% of the common stock in the corporation.

Attached is a three year pro forma income statement we believe to be conservative. Also attached are personal financial statements of the principals and a projected cash flow statement for the first year.

	1st Year	2nd Year	3rd Year	
Gross Sales	300,000	400,000	500,000	**PRO FORMA INCOME STATEMENT**
Less Allowances	1,000	1,000	2,000	
Net Sales	299,000	399,000	498,000	
Cost of Goods Sold	179,400	239,400	298,800	
Gross Margin	119,600	159,600	199,200	
Operating Expenses				
Utilities	1,200	1,500	1,700	
Salaries	76,000	79,000	102,000	
Payroll Taxes/Benefits	9,100	9,500	13,200	
Advertising	3,000	4,500	5,000	
Office Supplies	1,500	2,000	2,500	
Insurance	1,200	1,500	1,800	
Maintenance	1,000	1,500	2,000	
Outside Services	3,000	3,000	3,000	
Whse Supplies/Trucks	6,000	7,000	10,000	
Telephone	900	1,000	1,200	
Rent	9,000	9,500	9,900	
Depreciation	2,500	2,000	3,000	
Total Expenses	114,400	122,000	155,300	
Other Expenses				
Bank Loan Payment	15,000	15,000	15,000	
Bank Loan Interest	6,000	5,000	4,000	
Total Expenses	**120,400**	**142,000**	**174,300**	
Net Profit (Loss)	**(800)**	**17,600**	**24,900**	

FINANCIAL STATEMENT I

Assets		Liabilities	
Cash	15,000		
1991 Olds	11,000	Unpaid Balance	8,000
Residence	140,000	Mortgage	105,000
Mutual Funds	12,000	Credit Cards	500
Furniture	5,000	Note Payable	4,000
Merck Stock	10,000		
	182,200		117,500
Net Worth			**64,700**
	182,200		**182,200**

FINANCIAL STATEMENT II

Assets		Liabilities	
Cash	5,000		
1992 Buick Auto	15,000	Unpaid Balance	12,000
Residence	120,000	Mortgage	100,000
U.S. Treasury Bonds	5,000	Credit Cards	500
Home Furniture	4,000	Note Payable	2,500
AT&T Stock	3,000		
	147,000		115,000
Net Worth			**32,000**
	147,000		**147,000**

Hardware Store

FICTIONAL BUSINESS PLAN

OSHKOSH HARDWARE, INC.

123 Main St.
Oshkosh, WI 54901

June 1994

The following plan outlines how a small hardware store can survive competition from large discount chains by offering products and providing expert advice in the use of any product it sells. This plan is fictional and has not been used to gain funding from a bank or other lending institution.

- EXECUTIVE SUMMARY

- THE BUSINESS

- THE MARKET

- SALES

- MANAGEMENT

- GOALS IMPLEMENTATION

- FINANCE

- JOB DESCRIPTION-GENERAL MANAGER

- QUARTERLY FORECASTED BALANCE SHEETS

- QUARTERLY FORECASTED STATEMENTS OF EARNINGS AND RETAINED EARNINGS

- QUARTERLY FORECASTED STATEMENTS OF CHANGES IN FINANCIAL POSITION

- FINANCIAL RATIO ANALYSIS

- DETAILS FOR QUARTERLY STATEMENTS OF EARNINGS

HARDWARE STORE
BUSINESS PLAN

EXECUTIVE SUMMARY

Oshkosh Hardware, Inc. is a new corporation that is going to establish a retail hardware store in a strip mall in Oshkosh, Wisconsin. The store will sell hardware of all kinds, quality tools, paint, and housewares. The business will make revenue and a profit by servicing its customers not only with needed hardware but also with expert advice in the use of any product it sells.

Oshkosh Hardware, Inc. will be operated by its sole shareholder, James Smith. The company will have a total of four employees. It will sell its products in the local market. Customers will buy our products because we will provide free advice on the use of all of our products and will also furnish a full refund warranty.

Oshkosh Hardware, Inc. will sell its products in the Oshkosh store staffed by three sales representatives. No additional employees will be needed to achieve its short and long range goals. The primary short range goal is to open the store by October 1, 1994. In order to achieve this goal a lease must be signed by July 1, 1994 and the complete inventory ordered by August 1, 1994.

Mr. James Smith will invest $30,000 in the business. In addition, the company will have to borrow $150,000 during the first year to cover the investment in inventory, accounts receivable, and furniture and equipment. The company will be profitable after six months of operation and should be able to start repayment of the loan in the second year.

THE BUSINESS

The business will sell hardware of all kinds, quality tools, paint, and housewares. We will purchase our products from three large wholesale buying groups.

In general our customers are homeowners who do their own repair and maintenance, hobbyists, and housewives. Our business is unique in that we will have a complete line of all hardware items and will be able to get special orders by overnight delivery. The business makes revenue and profits by servicing our customers not only with needed hardware but also with expert advice in the use of any product we sell. Our major costs for bringing our products to market are cost of merchandise of 36%, salaries of $45,000, and occupancy costs of $60,000.

Oshkosh Hardware, Inc.'s retail outlet will be located at 1524 Frontage Road, which is in a newly developed retail center of Oshkosh. Our location helps facilitate accessibility from all parts of town and reduces our delivery costs. The store will occupy 7500 square feet of space. The major equipment involved in our business is counters and shelving, a computer, a paint mixing machine, and a truck.

THE MARKET

Oshkosh Hardware, Inc. will operate in the local market. There are 15,000 potential customers in this market area. We have three competitors who control approximately 98% of the market at present. We feel we can capture 25% of the market within the next four years. Our major reason for believing this is that our staff is technically competent to advise our customers in the correct use of all products we sell.

After a careful market analysis, we have determined that approximately 60% of our customers are men and 40% are women. The percentage of customers that fall into the following age categories are:

Under 16:	0%
17-21:	5%
22-30:	30%
31-40:	30%

41-50:	20%
51-60:	10%
61-70:	5%
Over 70:	0%

The reasons our customers prefer our products is our complete knowledge of their use and our full refund warranty.

We get our information about what products our customers want by talking to existing customers. There seems to be an increasing demand for our product. The demand for our product is increasing in size based on the change in population characteristics.

SALES

At Oshkosh Hardware, Inc. we will employ three sales people and will not need any additional personnel to achieve our sales goals. These salespeople will need several years experience in home repair and power tool usage. We expect to attract 30% of our customers from newspaper ads, 5% of our customers from local directories, 5% of our customers from the yellow pages, 10% of our customers from family and friends, and 50% of our customers from current customers. The most cost effect source will be current customers. In general our industry is growing.

MANAGEMENT

We would evaluate the quality of our management staff as being excellent. Our manager is experienced and very motivated to achieve the various sales and quality assurance objectives we have set. We will use a management information system that produces key inventory, quality assurance, and sales data on a weekly basis. All data is compared to previously established goals for that week, and deviations are the primary focus of the management staff.

GOALS IMPLEMENTATION

The short term goals of our business are:

1. Open the store by October 1, 1994
2. Reach our breakeven point in two months
3. Have sales of $100,000 in the first six months

In order to achieve our first short term goal we must:

1. Sign the lease by July 1, 1994
2. Order a complete inventory by August 1, 1994

In order to achieve our second short term goal we must:

1. Advertise extensively in Sept. and Oct.
2. Keep expenses to a minimum

In order to achieve our third short term goal we must:

1. Promote power tool sales for the Christmas season
2. Keep good customer traffic in Jan. and Feb.

The long term goals for our business are:

1. Obtain sales volume of $600,000 in three years
2. Become the largest hardware dealer in the city
3. Open a second store in Fond du Lac

The most important thing we must do in order to achieve the long term goals for our business is to develop a highly profitable business with excellent cash flow.

FINANCE

Oshkosh Hardware, Inc. Faces some potential threats or risks to our business. They are discount house competition. We believe we can avoid or compensate for this by providing quality products complimented by quality advice on the use of every product we sell. The financial projections we have prepared are located at the end of this document.

JOB DESCRIPTION: GENERAL MANAGER

Sales

The General Manager of the business of the corporation will be the president of the corporation. He will be responsible for the complete operation of the retail hardware store which is owned by the corporation. A detailed description of his duties and responsibilities is as follows:

Train and supervise the three sales people. Develop programs to motivate and compensate these employees. Coordinate advertising and sales promotion effects to achieve sales totals as outlined in budget. Oversee purchasing function and inventory control procedures to insure adequate merchandise at all times at a reasonable cost.

Finance

Prepare monthly and annual budgets. Secure adequate line of credit from local banks. Supervise office personnel to insure timely preparation of records, statements, all government reports, control of receivables and payables, and monthly financial statements.

Administration

Perform duties as required in the areas of personnel, building leasing and maintenance, licenses and permits, and public relations.

QUARTERLY FORECASTED BALANCE SHEETS

	Beg. Bal.	1st Qtr	2nd Qtr	3rd Qtr	4th Qtr
Assets					
Cash	30,000	418	(463)	(3,574)	4,781
Accounts Receivable	0	20,000	13,333	33,333	33,333
Inventory	0	48,000	32,000	80,000	80,000
Other Current Assets	0	0	0	0	0
Total Current Assets	30,000	68,418	44,870	109,759	118,114
Land	0	0	0	0	0
Building & Improvements	0	0	0	0	0
Furniture & Equipment	0	75,000	75,000	75,000	75,000
Total Fixed Assets	0	75,000	75,000	75,000	75,000
Less Accum. Depreciation	0	1,875	3,750	5,625	7,500
Net Fixed Assets	0	73,125	71,250	69,375	67,500
Intangible Assets	0	0	0	0	0
Less Amortization	0	0	0	0	0
Net Intangible Assets	0	0	0	0	0
Other Assets	0	0	0	0	0
Total Assets	**30,000**	**141,543**	**116,120**	**179,134**	**185,614**

	Beg. Bal.	1st Qtr	2nd Qtr	3rd Qtr	4th Qtr
Liabilities and Shareholders' Equity					
Short-Term Debt	0	0	0	0	0
Accounts Payable	0	12,721	10,543	17,077	17,077
Dividends Payable	0	0	0	0	0
Income Taxes Payable	0	(1,031)	(2,867)	(2,355)	(1,843)
Accrued Compensation	0	1,867	1,867	1,867	1,867
Other Current Liabilities	0	0	0	0	0
Total Current Liabilities	0	13,557	9,543	16,589	17,101
Long-Term Debt	0	110,000	110,000	160,000	160,000
Other Non-Current Liabilities	0	0	0	0	0
Total Liabilities	0	123,557	119,543	176,589	177,101
Common Stock	30,000	30,000	30,000	30,000	30,000
Retained Earnings	0	(12,014)	(33,423)	(27,455)	(21,487)
Shareholders' Equity	30,000	17,986	(3,423)	2,545	8,513
Total Liabilities & Shareholders' Equity	30,000	141,543	116,120	179,134	185,614

	Beg. Actual	1st Qtr	2nd Qtr	3rd Qtr	4th Qtr	Total
Total Sales	0	60,000	40,000	100,000	100,000	300,000
Goods/Services	0	21,600	14,400	36,000	36,000	108,000
Gross Profit	0	38,400	25,600	64,000	64,000	192,000
Operating Expenses	0	47,645	45,045	52,845	52,845	198,380
Fixed Expenses						
Interest	0	1,925	1,925	2,800	2,800	9,450
Depreciation	0	1,875	1,875	1,875	1,875	7,500
Amortization	0	0	0	0	0	0
Total Fixed Expenses	0	3,800	3,800	4,675	4,675	16,950
Operating Profit (Loss)	0	(13,045)	(23,245)	6,480	6,480	(23,330)

QUARTERLY FORECASTED STATEMENTS OF EARNINGS AND RETAINED EARNINGS

	Beg. Actual	1st Qtr	2nd Qtr	3rd Qtr	4th Qtr	Total
Other Income (Expense)	0	0	0	0	0	0
Interest Income	0	0	0	0	0	0
Earnings (Loss) Before Taxes	0	(13,045)	(23,245)	6,480	6,480	(23,330)
Income Taxes	0	(1,031)	(1,836)	512	512	(1,843)
Net Earnings	0	(12,014)	(21,409)	5,968	5,968	(21,487)
Retained Earnings, Beginning	0	0	(12,014)	(33,423)	(27,455)	0
Less Dividends	0	0	0	0	0	0
Retained Earnings, Ending	0	(12,014)	(33,423)	(27,455)	(21,487)	(21,487)

QUARTERLY FORECASTED STATEMENTS OF CHANGES IN FINANCIAL POSITION

	Beg. Bal.	1st Qtr	2nd Qtr	3rd Qtr	4th Qtr	Total
Sources (Uses) of Cash						
Net Earnings (Loss)	0	(12,014)	(21,409)	5,968	5,968	(21,487)
Depreciation & Amortization	0	1,875	1,875	1,875	1,875	7,500
Cash Provided by Operations	0	(10,139)	(19,534)	7,834	7,834	(13,987)
Dividends	0	0	0	0	0	0
Cash Provided by (Used For) Changes in						
Accounts Receivable	0	(20,000)	6,667	(20,000)	0	(33,333)
Inventory	0	(48,000)	16,000	(48,000)	0	(80,000)
Other Current Assets	0	0	0	0	0	0
Accounts Payable	0	12,	721	(2,178)	6,534 0	17,077
Income Taxes	0	(1,031)	(1,836)	512	512	(1,843)
Accrued Compensation	0	1,867	0	0	0	1,867
Dividends Payable	0	0	0	0	0	0
Other Current Liabilities	0	0	0	0	0	0

	Beg. Bal.	1st Qtr	2nd Qtr	3rd Qtr	4th Qtr	Total
Other Assets	0	0	0	0	0	0
Net Cash Provided by (Used For)						
Operating Activities	0	(54,443)	18,653	(60,954)	512	(96,233)
Investment Transactions						
Furniture & Equipment	0	(75,000)	0	0	0	(75,000)
Land	0	0	0	0	0	0
Building & Improvements	0	0	0	0	0	0
Intangible Assets	0	0	0	0	0	0
Net Cash from Investment Transactions	0	(75,000)	0	0	0	(75,000)
Financing Transactions						
Short-Term Debt	0	0	0	0	0	0
Long-Term Debt	0	110,000	0	50,000	0	160,000
Other Non-Current Liabilities	0	0	0	0	0	0
Sale of Common Stock	30,000	0	0	0	0	0
Net Cash from Financing Transactions	30,000	110,000	0	50,000	0	160,000
Net Increase (Decrease) in Cash	30,000	(29,582)	(881)	(3,111)	8,355	(25,219)
Cash, Beginning of Period	0	30,000	418	(463)	(3,574)	30,000
Cash, End of Period	30,000	418	(463)	(3,574)	4,781	4,781

**FINANCIAL
RATIO ANALYSIS**

	Beg. Actual	1st Qtr	2nd Qtr	3rd Qtr	4th Qtr
Overall Performance					
Return on Equity	0.00	(66.80)	625.45	234.50	70.10
Return on Total Assets	0.00	(8.49)	(18.44)	3.33	3.22
Operating Return	0.00	(9.22)	(20.02)	3.62	3.49
Profitability Measures					
Gross Profit Percent	0.00	64.00	64.00	64.00	64.00
Profit Margin (AIT)	0.00	(20.02)	(53.52)	5.97	5.97
Operating Income per Share	0.00	0.00	0.00	0.00	0.00
Earnings per Share	0.00	0.00	0.00	0.00	0.00
Test of Investment Utilization					
Asset Turnover	0.00	0.42	0.34	0.56	0.54
Equity Turnover	0.00	3.34	(11.69)	39.29	11.75
Fixed Asset Turnover	0.00	0.82	0.56	1.44	1.48
Average Collection Period	0.00	30.00	30.00	30.00	30.00
Days Inventory	0.00	200.00	200.00	200.00	200.00
Inventory Turnover	0.00	0.45	0.45	0.45	0.45
Working Capital Turns	0.00	1.09	1.13	1.07	0.99
Test of Financial Condition					
Current Ratio	0.00	5.05	4.70	6.62	6.91
Quick Ratio	0.00	1.51	1.35	1.79	2.23
Working Capital Ratio	1.00	0.43	0.33	0.57	0.60
Dividend Payout	0.00	0.00	0.00	0.00	0.00
Financial Leverage					
Total Assets	1.00	7.87	(33.92)	70.39	21.80

	Beg. Actual	1st Qtr	2nd Qtr	3rd Qtr	4th Qtr
Debt/Equity	0.00	6.87	(34.92)	69.39	20.80
Debt to Total Assets	0.00	0.87	1.03	0.99	0.95

Year-End Equity History

	Beg. Actual	1st Qtr	2nd Qtr	3rd Qtr	4th Qtr
Shares Outstanding	0	0	0	0	0
Market Price per Share (@20x's earnings)	0.00	0.00	0.00	0.00	0.00
Book Value per Share	0.00	0.00	0.00	0.00	0.00

Altman Analysis Ratio

	Beg. Actual	1st Qtr	2nd Qtr	3rd Qtr	4th Qtr
1.2x (1)	1.20	0.47	0.37	0.62	0.65
1.4x (2)	0.00	(0.12)	(0.40)	(0.21)	(0.16)
3.3x (3)	0.00	(0.35)	(0.72)	0.07	0.07
0.6x (4)	0.00	0.00	0.00	0.00	0.00
1.0x (5)	0.00	0.42	0.34	0.56	0.54
Z Value	1.20	.042	(.041)	1.04	1.10

DETAILS FOR QUARTERLY STATEMENTS OF EARNINGS

	Beg. Act.	1st Qtr	2nd Qtr	3rd Qtr	4th Qtr	Total	%Sales	Fixed
Sales								
Dollars Sales Forecasted								
Product 1	0	60,000	40,000	100,000	100,000	300,000		
Product 2	0	0	0	0	0	0		
Product 3	0	0	0	0	0	0		
Product 4	0	0	0	0	0	0		
Product 5	0	0	0	0	0	0		
Product 6	0	0	0	0	0	0		
Total Sales	0	60,000	40,000	100,000	100,000	300,000		

	Beg. Act.	1st Qtr	2nd Qtr	3rd Qtr	4th Qtr	Total	%Sales	Fixed
Cost of Sales								
Dollar Cost Forecasted								
Product 1	0	21,600	14,400	36,000	36,000	108,000	36.00%	0
Product 2	0	0	0	0	0	0	0.00%	0
Product 3	0	0	0	0	0	0	0.00%	0
Product 4	0	0	0	0	0	0	0.00%	0
Product 5	0	0	0	0	0	0	0.00%	0
Product 6	0	0	0	0	0	0	0.00%	0
Total Cost of Sales	0	21,600	14,400	36,000	36,000	108,000		
Operating Expenses								
Payroll	0	12,000	12,000	12,000	12,000	48,000	0.00%	12,000
Paroll Taxes	0	950	950	950	950	3,800	0.00%	950
Advertising	0	4,800	3,200	8,000	8,000	24,000	8.00%	0
Automobile Expenses	0	0	0	0	0		0.00%	0
Bad Debts	0	0	0	0	0	0	0.00%	0
Commissions	0	3,000	2,000	5,000	5,000	15,000	5.00%	0
Computer Rental	0	1,200	1,200	1,200	1,200	4,800	0.00%	1,200
Computer Supplies	0	220	220	220	220	880	0.00%	220
Computer Maintenance	0	100	100	100	100	400	0.00%	100
Dealer Training	0	1,000	1,000	1,000	1,000	4,000	0.00%	1,000
Electricity	0	3,000	3,000	3,000	3,000	12,000	0.00%	3,000
Employment Ads and Fees	0	0	0	0	0	0	0.00%	0
Entertainment: Business	0	1,500	1,500	1,500	1,500	6,000	0.00%	1,500
General Insurance	0	800	800	800	800	32,000	0.00%	800
Health & W/C Insurance	0	0	0	0	0	0	0.00%	0
Interest: LT Debt	0	2,500	2,500	2,500	2,500	10,000	0.00%	2,500
Legal & Accounting	0	1,500	1,500	1,500	1,500	6,000	0.00%	1,500
Maintenance & Repairs	0	460	460	460	460	1,840	0.00%	460

	Beg. Act.	1st Qtr	2nd Qtr	3rd Qtr	4th Qtr	Total	%Sales	Fixed
Office Supplies	0	270	270	270	270	1,080	0.00%	270
Postage	0	85	85	85	85	340	0.00%	85
Prof. Development	0	0	0	0	0	0	0.00%	0
Professional Fees	0	1,000	1,000	1,000	1,000	4,000	0.00%	1,000
Rent	0	8,000	8,000	8,000	8,000	2,000	0.00%	8,000
Shows & Conferences	0	0	0	0	0	0	0.00%	0
Subscriptions & Dues	0	285	285	285	285	1,140	0.00%	285
Telephone	0	1,225	1,225	1,225	1,225	4,900	0.00%	1,225
Temporary Employees	0	0	0	0	0	0	0.00%	0
Travel Expenses	0	750	750	750	750	3,000	0.00%	750
Utilities	0	3,000	3,000	3,000	3,000	12,000	0.00%	3,000
Research & Development	0	0	0	0	0	0	0.00%	0
Royalties	0	0	0	0	0	0	0.00%	0
Other 1	0	0	0	0	0	0	0.00%	0
Other 2	0	0	0	0	0	0	0.00%	0
Other 3	0	0	0	0	0	0	0.00%	0
Total Operating Expenses	0	47,645	45,045	52,845	52,845	198,380		
Percent of Sales	0.00	79.41	112.61	52.85	52.85	66.13		

DETAILS FOR QUARTERLY STATEMENT OF EARNINGS

...continued

BUSINESS PLAN TEMPLATE

Appendix B - Organizations, Agencies and Consultants

Organizations, Agencies, & Consultants

A listing of Associations and Consultants of interest to entrepreneurs, followed by the 10 Small Business Administration Regional Offices, Small Business Development Centers, Service Corps of Retired Executives offices, and Venture Capital & Finance companies.

ASSOCIATIONS

This section contains a listing of associations and other agencies of interest to the small business owner. Entries are listed alphabetically by organization name.

American Association for Consumer Benefits
PO Box 100279
Fort Worth, Texas 76185
Phone: (800)872-8896
Fax: (817)377-5633
E-mail: info@aacb.org
Website: www.aacb.org
James Redmond, Contact

American Association of Family Businesses
PO Box 547217
Surfside, Florida 33154
Phone: (305)864-1184
Fax: (305)864-1187
Craig Gordon, Pres.

American Small Businesses Association
206 E. College St.
Grapevine, Texas 76051-5364
Vernon Castle, Exec. Dir.

American Women's Economic Development Corporation
216 E. 45th St.
New York, New York 10169
Phone: (212)692-9100
Fax: (212)692-9296
Website: www.womenconnect.com/awed
Suzanne Tufts, Pres. & CEO

Association for Enterprise Opportunity
70 E. Lake St., Ste. 1120
Chicago, Illinois 60601
Phone: (312)357-0177
Fax: (312)357-0180

E-mail: aeochicago@ad.com
Christine M. Benuzzi, Exec. Dir.

Association of Small Business Development Centers
3108 Columbia Pike No. 300
Arlington, Virginia 22204-4304
Phone: (703)448-6124
Fax: (703)448-6125
E-mail: jjohns1012@aol.com
James King, Pres.

BEST Employers Association
2515 McCabe Way
Irvine, California 92614
Phone: (714)756-1000
Toll-free: (800)854-7417
Fax: (714)553-1232
Donald R. Lawrenz, Exec. Sec.

Employers of America
520 S. Pierce, Ste. 224
Mason City, Iowa 50401
Phone: (515)424-3187
Free: (800)728-3187
Fax: (515)424-1673
E-mail: employer@employerhelp.org
Website: www.employerhelp.org
Jim Collison, Pres.

Family Firm Institute
221 N. Beacon St.
Boston, Massachusetts 02135-1943
Phone: (617)789-4200
Fax: (617)789-4220
E-mail: ffi@ffi.org
Website: www.ffi.org
Judy L. Green, Ph.D., Exec. Dir.

Group Purchasing Association
Plaza Tower, 35th Fl.
1001 Howard Ave.
New Orleans, Louisiana 70113-2002
Phone: (504)529-2030
Fax: (504)558-0929
E-mail: lenn@firstgpa.com
Website: www.firstgpa.com

International Association of Business
701 Highlander Blvd., Ste. 110
Arlington, Texas 76015-4325
Phone: (817)465-2922
Fax: (817)467-5940
Paula Rainey, Pres.

International Association for Business Organizations
PO Box 30149
Baltimore, Maryland 21270
Phone: (410)581-1373
Website: www.worldhomebiz.com
Rudolph Lewis, Exec. Officer

International Council for Small Business
c/o Jefferson Smurfit Center for Entrepreneurial Studies
St. Louis University
3674 Lindell Blvd.
St. Louis, Missouri 63108
Phone: (314)977-3628
Fax: (314)977-3627
E-mail: icsb@slu.edu
Website: www.icsb.org
Sharon Bower, Sec.

National Alliance for Fair Competition
3 Bethesda Metro Center, Ste. 1100
Bethesda, Maryland 20814
Phone: (410)235-7116
Fax: (410)235-7116
E-mail: ampesq@aol.com
Website: www.nafcc.org
Tony Ponticelli, Exec. Dir.

National Association of Business Leaders
PO Box 766
Bridgeton, Missouri 63044
Phone: (314)344-1111
Fax: (314)298-9110
E-mail: nabl@nabl.com
Website: www.nabl.com

National Association for Business
Organizations
PO Box 30149
Baltimore, Maryland 21270
Phone: (410)581-1373
Website: www.ameribiz.com/
quicklink.htm
Rudolph Lewis, Pres.

National Association of Private
Enterprise
7819 Shelburne Cir.
Spring, Texas 77379-4687
Phone: (512)863-2699
Toll-free: (800)223-6273
Fax: (512)868-8037
E-mail: info@nape.org
Website: www.NAPE.org
Laura Squiers, Exec. Dir.

National Association for the Self-
Employed
PO Box 612067
Dallas, Texas 75261-2067
Toll-free: (800)232-NASE
Fax: (800)551-4446
Website: www.nase.org
Bennie Thayer, Pres. & CEO

National Association of Small
Business Investment Companies
666 11th St. NW, No. 750
Washington, DC 20001
Phone: (202)628-5055
Fax: (202)628-5080
E-mail: nasbic@nasbic.org
Website: www.nasbic.org
Lee W. Mercer, Pres.

National Business Association
PO Box 700728
Dallas, Texas 75370
Phone: (972)458-0900
Toll-free: (800)456-0440
Fax: (972)960-9149
E-mail: nbal2@airmail.net
Website: www.nationalbusiness.org
Robert G. Allen, Pres.

National Business Owners
Association
820 Gibbon St., Ste. 204
Alexandria, Virginia 22314
Phone: (202)737-6501
Toll-free: (888)755-NBOA
Fax: (877)NBO-AFAX
E-mail: mbrservices@nboa.org
Website: www.nboa.com
Thomas Rumfelt, Chm.

National Center for Fair Competition
8421 Frost Way
Annandale, Virginia 22003
Phone: (703)280-4622
Fax: (703)280-0942
E-mail: kentonpl1@aol.com
Kenton Pattie, Pres.

National Federation of Independent
Business
53 Century Blvd., Ste. 250
Nashville, Tennessee 37214
Phone: (615)872-5800
Toll-free: (800)NFIBNOW
Fax: (615)872-5353
Website: www.nfibonline.com
Fred Holladay, VP & CFO

National Small Business United
1156 15th St. NW, Ste. 1100
Washington, DC 20005
Phone: (202)293-8830
Toll-free: (800)345-6728
Fax: (202)872-8543
E-mail: nsbu@nsbu.org
Website: www.nsbu.org
Todd McCraken, Pres.

Research Institute for Small and
Emerging Business
722 12th St. NW
Washington, DC 20005
Phone: (202)628-8382
Fax: (202)628-8392
E-mail: rise@bellatlantic.net
Website: www.riseb.org
Mark Schultz, CEO/Pres.

Service Corps of Retired Executives
Association
409 3rd St. SW, 4th Fl.
Washington, DC 20024
Phone: (202)205-6762
Toll-free: (800)634-0245
Fax: (202)205-7636
Website: www.score.org
W. Kenneth Yancey, Jr., Exec. Dir.

Small Business Assistance Center
554 Main St.
PO Box 15014
Worcester, Massachusetts 01615-
0014
Phone: (508)756-3513
Fax: (508)770-0528
Francis R. Carroll, Pres.

Small Business Legislative Council
1156 15th St. NW, Ste. 510

Washington, DC 20005
Phone: (202)639-8500
Fax: (202)296-5333
John Satagaj, Pres.

Small Business Network
PO Box 30149
Baltimore, Maryland 21270
Phone: (410)581-1373
E-mail: natibb@ix.netcom.com
Rudolph Lewis, CEO

Small Business Service Bureau
554 Main St.
PO Box 15014
Worcester, Massachusetts 01615-
0014
Phone: (508)756-3513
Fax: (508)770-0528
Francis R. Carroll, Pres.

Support Services Alliance
PO Box 130
Schoharie, New York 12157-0130
Phone: (518)295-7966
Toll-free: (800)322-3920
Fax: (518)295-8556
Website: www.ssainfo.com
Gary Swan, Pres.

CONSULTANTS

*This section contains a listing of consult-
ants specializing in small business
development. It is arranged alphabetically
by country, then by state or province, then
by city, then by firm name.*

CANADA

Alberta

Common Sense Solutions
3405 16A Ave.
Edmonton, AB
Phone: (403)465-7330
Fax: (403)465-7380
Email:
gcoulson@comsensesolutions.com
Website:
www.comsensesolutions.com

Varsity Consulting Group
Faculty of Business
University of Alberta
Edmonton, AB T6G 2R6

Phone: (780)492-2994
Fax: (780)492-5400
Website: www.bus.ualberta.ca/vcg

Viro Hospital Consulting
42 Commonwealth Bldg., 9912 - 106
St. NW
Edmonton, AB T5K 1C5
Phone: (403)425-3871
Fax: (403)425-3871
Email: rpb@freenet.edmonton.ab.ca

British Columbia

SRI Strategic Resources Inc.
4330 Kingsway, Ste. 1600
Burnaby, BC V5H 4G7
Phone: 604435-0627
Fax: 604435-2782
Email: inquiry@sri.bc.ca
Website: www.sri.com

Andrew R. De Boda Consulting
1523 Milford Ave.
Coquitlam, BC V3J 2V9
Phone: (604)936-4527
Fax: (604)936-4527
Email: deboda@intergate.bc.ca
Website:
www.ourworld.compuserve.com/
homepages/deboda

The Sage Group Ltd.
980 - 355 Burrard St.
744 W. Haistings, Ste. 410
Vancouver, BC V6C 1A5
Phone: (604)669-9269
Fax: (604)669-6622

Ontario

The Cynton Company
17 Massey St.
Brampton, ON L6S 2V6
Phone: (905)792-7769
Fax: (905)792-8116
Email: cynton@netcom.ca
Website: www.netcom.ca/~cynton

Begley & Associates
RR 6
Cambridge, ON N1R 5S7
Phone: (519)740-3629
Fax: (519)740-3629
Email: begley@in.on.ca
Website: www.in.on.ca/~begley/
index.htm

Tikkanen-Bradley
RR No.1
Consecon, ON K0K 1T0
Phone: (613)669-0583
Email: consult@mortimer.com
Website: 204.191.209/consult/

Task Enterprises
Box 69, RR 2 Hamilton
Flamborough, ON L8N 2Z7
Phone: (905)659-0153
Fax: (905)659-0861

HST Group Ltd.
430 Gilmour St.
Ottawa, ON K2P 0R8
Phone: (613)236-7303
Fax: (613)236-9893

Harrison Associates
BCE Place
181 Bay St., Ste. 3740
PO Box 798
Toronto, ON M5J 2T3
Phone: (416)364-5441
Fax: (416)364-2875

TCI Convergence Ltd. Management
Consultants
99 Crown's Ln.
Toronto, ON M5R 3P4
Phone: (416)515-4146
Fax: (416)515-2097
Email: tci@inforamp.net
Website: tciconverge.com/
index.1.html

Ken Wyman & Associates Inc.
64B Shuter St., Ste. 200
Toronto, ON M5B 1B1
Phone: (416)362-2926
Fax: (416)362-3039
Email: kenwyman@compuserve.com

JPL Business Consultants
82705 Metter Rd.
Wellandport, ON L0R 2J0
Phone: (905)386-7450
Fax: (905)386-7450
Email: plamarch@freenet.npiec.on.ca

Quebec

The Zimmar Consulting Partnership
Inc.
Westmount
PO Box 98
Montreal, PQ H3Z 2T1
Phone: (514)484-1459
Fax: (514)484-3063

Saskatchewan

Trimension Group
No. 104-110 Research Dr.
Innovation Place, SK S7N 3R3
Phone: (306)668-2560
Fax: (306)975-1156
Email: trimension@trimension.ca
Website: www.trimension.ca

UNITED STATES

Alliance Management Group, Inc.
Phone: (908)234-2344
Fax: (908)234-0638
Email: kathy@strategicalliance.com
Website: www.strategicalliance.com

Bedminster Group
Phone: 908575-9383
Fax: (908)575-9199
Email: bedminster@entersoft.com
Website: www.bedminstergroup.com

Joel Greenstein and Associates
Phone: 703893-1888
Email:
jgreenstein@contractmasters.com
Website: www.contractmasters.com

Alabama

Business Planning Inc.
300 Office Park Dr.
Birmingham, AL 35223-2474
Phone: (205)870-7090
Fax: (205)870-7103

Tradebank of Eastern Alabama
546 Broad St., Ste. 3
Gadsden, AL 35901
Phone: (205)547-8700
Fax: (205)547-8718
Email: mansion@webex.com
Website: www.webex.com/~tea

Alaska

AK Business Development Center
3335 Arctic Blvd., Ste. 203
Anchorage, AK 99503
Phone: (907)562-0335
Fax: (907)562-6988
Free: (800)478-3474
Email: twilson@customcpu.com
Website: www.customcpu.com/
commercial/abdc

Business Matters
PO Box 287
Fairbanks, AK 99707
Phone: (907)452-5650

Arizona

Carefree Direct Marketing Corp.
8001 E. Serene St.
Carefree, AZ 85377-3737
Phone: (480)488-4227
Fax: (480)488-2841

Trans Energy Corp.
1739 W. 7th Ave.
Mesa, AZ 85202
Phone: (602)921-0433
Fax: (602)967-6601
Email: aha@getnet.com

CMAS
5125 N. 16th St.
Phoenix, AZ 85016
Phone: (602)395-1001
Fax: (602)604-8180

Harvey C. Skoog
PO Box 26439
Prescott Valley, AZ 86312
Phone: (520)772-1714
Fax: (520)772-2814

LMC Services
8711 E. Pinnacle Peak Rd., No. 340
Scottsdale, AZ 85255-3555
Phone: (602)585-7177
Fax: (602)585-5880
Email: louws@earthlink.com

Sauerbrun Technology Group, Ltd.
7979 E. Princess Dr., Ste. 5
Scottsdale, AZ 85255-5878
Phone: (602)502-4950
Fax: (602)502-4292
Email: info@sauerbrun.com
Website: www.sauerbrun.com

Gary L. McLeod
PO Box 230
Sonoita, AZ 85637
Fax: (602)455-5661

Van Cleve Associates
6932 E. 2nd St.
Tucson, AZ 85710
Phone: (602)296-2587
Fax: (602)296-2587

California

Acumen Group, Inc.
CA
Phone: (650)949-9349
Fax: (650)949-4845
Email: acumen-g@ix.netcom.com
Website: pw2.netcom.com/~janed/
acumen.html

On-line Career and Management
Consulting
420 Central Ave., No. 314
Alameda, CA 94501
Phone: (510)864-0336
Fax: (510)864-0336
Email: career@dnai.com
Website: www.dnai.com/~career

Career Paths-Thomas E. Church &
Associates, Inc.
PO Box 2439
Aptos, CA 95001
Phone: (408)662-7950
Fax: (408)662-7955
Email: church@ix.netcom.com
Website: www.careerpaths-tom.com

Keck & Co. Business Consultants
410 Walsh Rd.
Atherton, CA 94027
Phone: (650)854-9588
Fax: (650)854-7240
Website: www.keckco.com

Ben W. Laverty III, Ph.D., REA, CEI
4909 Stockdale Hwy., Ste. 132
Bakersfield, CA 93309
Phone: (661)283-8300
Fax: (661)283-8313
Email: cstc@cstcsafety.com
Website: www.cstcsafety.com/cstc

Lindquist Consultants-Venture
Planning
225 Arlington Ave.
Berkeley, CA 94707
Phone: (510)524-6685
Fax: (510)527-6604

Larson Associates
PO Box 9005
Brea, CA 92822
Phone: (714)529-4121
Fax: (714)572-3606
Email:
larsonassociates@compuserve.com

Kremer Management Consulting
PO Box 500

Carmel, CA 93921
Phone: (408)626-8311
Fax: (408)624-2663
Email: ddkremer@aol.com

W & J Partnership
18876 Edwin Markham Dr.
Castro Valley, CA 94552
Phone: (510)583-7751
Fax: (510)583-7645
Email:
warmorgan@wjpartnership.com
Website: www.wjpartnership.com

JB Associates
21118 Gardena Dr.
Cupertino, CA 95014
Phone: (408)257-0214
Fax: (408)257-0216
Email: semarang@sirius.com

House Agricultural Consultants
PO Box 1615
Davis, CA 95617-1615
Phone: (916)753-3361
Fax: (916)753-0464
Email: infoag@houseag.com
Website: www.houseag.com/

Technical Management Consultants
3624 Westfall Dr.
Encino, CA 91436-4154
Phone: (818)784-0626
Fax: (818)501-5575
Email: tmcrs@aol.com

RAINWATER-GISH & Associates,
Business Finance & Development
317 Third St., Ste. 3
Eureka, CA 95501
Phone: (707)443-0030
Fax: (707)443-5683

Ted Butteriss Management &
Technology
451 Pebble Beach Pl.
Fullerton, CA 92835
Phone: (714)441-2280
Fax: (714)441-2281
Email:
Global_Tradelinks@compuserve.com
Website: www.consultapc.org/
Butter2.htm

Strategic Business Group
800 Cienaga Dr.
Fullerton, CA 92835-1248
Phone: (714)449-1040
Fax: (714)525-1631

Burnes Consulting
20537 Wolf Creek Rd.
Grass Valley, CA 95949
Phone: (530)346-8188
Fax: (530)346-7704
Email: kent@burnesconsulting.com
Website: www.burnesconsulting.com

Pioneer Business Consultants
9042 Garfield Ave., Ste. 312
Huntington Beach, CA 92646
Phone: (714)964-7600

Beblie, Brandt & Jacobs, Inc.
16 Technology, Ste. 164
Irvine, CA 92618
Phone: (714)450-8790
Fax: (714)450-8799
Email: darcy@bbjinc.com
Website: 198.147.90.26

Fluor Daniel Inc.
3353 Michelson Dr.
Irvine, CA 92698
Phone: (949)975-2000
Fax: (949)975-5271
Email:
sales.consulting@fluordaniel.com
Website:
www.fluordanielconsulting.com

MCS Associates
18300 Von Karman, Ste. 1000
Irvine, CA 92612
Phone: (949)263-8700
Fax: (949)553-0168
Email: info@mcsassociates.com

Inspired Arts, Inc.
4225 Executive Sq., Ste. 1160
La Jolla, CA 92037
Phone: (619)623-3525
Fax: (619)623-3534
Free: (800)851-4394
Email: info@inspiredarts.com
Website: www.inspiredarts.com

The Laresis Companies
PO Box 3284
La Jolla, CA 92038
Phone: (619)452-2720
Fax: (619)452-8744

RCL & Co.
PO Box 1143
La Jolla, CA 92038
Phone: (619)454-8883
Fax: (619)454-8880

Comprehensive Business Services
3201 Lucas Cir.
Lafayette, CA 94549
Phone: (925)283-8272
Fax: (925)283-8272

The Ribble Group
27601 Forbes Rd., Ste. 52
Laguna Niguel, CA 92677
Phone: (714)582-1085
Fax: (714)582-6420
Email: ribble@deltanet.com

Norris Bernstein, CMC
9309 Marina Pacifica Dr. N
Long Beach, CA 90803
Phone: (562)493-5458
Fax: (562)493-5459
Email: norris@ctecomputer.com

Horizon Consulting Services
1315 Garthwick Dr.
Los Altos, CA 94024
Phone: (415)967-0906
Fax: (415)967-0906

Brincko Associates, Inc.
1801 Ave. of the Stars, Ste. 1054
Los Angeles, CA 90067
Phone: (310)553-4523
Fax: (310)553-6782

Rubenstein/Justman Management
Consultants
2049 Century Park E., 24th Fl.
Los Angeles, CA 90067
Phone: (310)282-0800
Fax: (310)282-0400
Email: rjmcnet@rjmcnet.com
Website: www.rjmcnet.com

F.J. Schroeder & Associates
1926 Westholme Ave.
Los Angeles, CA 90025
Phone: (310)470-2655
Fax: (310)470-6378
Email: fjsacons@aol.com
Website: www.mcninet.com/
GlobalLook/Fjschroe.html

Western Management Associates
8351 Vicksburg Ave.
Los Angeles, CA 90045-3924
Phone: (310)645-1091
Fax: (310)645-1092
Free: (888)788-6534
Email: CFOForRent@aol.com
Website: www.expert-market.com/
cfoforrent

Darrell Sell and Associates
Los Gatos, CA 95030
Phone: (408)354-7794
Email: darrell@netcom.com

Leslie J. Zambo
3355 Michael Dr.
Marina, CA 93933
Phone: (408)384-7086
Fax: (408)647-4199
Email:
104776.1552@compuserve.com

Marketing Services Management
PO Box 1377
Martinez, CA 94553
Phone: (510)370-8527
Fax: (510)370-8527
Email: markserve@biotechnet.com

William M. Shine Consulting Service
PO Box 127
Moraga, CA 94556-0127
Phone: (510)376-6516

Palo Alto Management Group, Inc.
2672 Bayshore Pky., Ste. 701
Mountain View, CA 94043
Phone: (415)968-4374
Fax: (415)968-4245
Email: mburwen@pamg.com

The Market Connection
4020 Birch St., Ste. 203
Newport Beach, CA 92660
Phone: (714)731-6273
Fax: (714)833-0253

Muller Associates
PO Box 7264
Newport Beach, CA 92658
Phone: (714)646-1169
Fax: (714)646-1169

International Health Resources
PO Box 329
North San Juan, CA 95960-0329
Phone: (530)292-1266
Fax: (530)292-1243
Website:
www.futureofhealthcare.com

NEXUS - Consultants to Management
PO Box 1531
Novato, CA 94948
Phone: (415)897-4400
Fax: (415)898-2252
Email: jimnexus@aol.com

Aerospcace.Org.
PO Box 28831
Oakland, CA 94604-8831
Phone: (510)530-9169
Fax: (510)530-3411
Website: www.aerospace.org

Intelequest Corp.
722 Gailen Ave.
Palo Alto, CA 94303
Phone: (415)968-3443
Fax: (415)493-6954
Email: frits@iqix.com

McLaughlin & Associates
66 San Marino Cir.
Rancho Mirage, CA 92270
Phone: (760)321-2932
Fax: (760)328-2474
Email: jackmcla@aol.com

Carrera Consulting Group, a division
of Maximus
2110 21st St., Ste. 400
Sacramento, CA 95818
Phone: (916)456-3300
Fax: (916)456-3306
Email:
central@carreraconsulting.com
Website: www.carreraconsulting.com

Bay Area Tax Consultants and
Bayhill Financial Consultants
1150 Bayhill Dr., Ste. 1150
San Bruno, CA 94066-3004
Phone: (415)952-8786
Fax: (415)588-4524
Email: baytax@compuserve.com
Website: www.baytax.com/

California Business Incubation
Network
101 W. Broadway, No. 480
San Diego, CA 92101
Phone: (619)237-0559
Fax: (619)237-0521

G.R. Gordetsky Consultants Inc.
11414 Windy Summit Pl.
San Diego, CA 92127
Phone: (619)487-4939
Fax: (619)487-5587
Email: gordet@pacbell.net

Dynasty Capital Services LLC
258 11th Avenue, Suite 1000
San Francisco, CA 94118
Contact: Randolph L. Tom
Phone: (415)387-7700

Fax: (415)387-2750
Email: dynasty@dynastycap.com
Website: www.dynastycap.com
Provides financial and advisory
services to entrepreneurs and
emerging companies, including
obtaining capital through financial
investors and strategic partnerships.
Focuses on high technology, Internet
and communications companies.
Extensive experience in financing and
managing multi-million dollar
transactions.

Freeman, Sullivan & Co.
131 Steuart St., Ste. 500
San Francisco, CA 94105
Phone: (415)777-0707
Fax: (415)777-2420
Free: (800)777-0737
Website: www.fsc-research.com

Ideas Unlimited
2151 California St., Ste. 7
San Francisco, CA 94115
Phone: (415)931-0641
Fax: (415)931-0880

Russell Miller Inc.
300 Montgomery St., Ste. 900
San Francisco, CA 94104
Phone: (415)956-7474
Fax: (415)398-0620
Email: rmi@pacbell.net
Website: www.rmisf.com

PKF Consulting
425 California St., Ste. 1650
San Francisco, CA 94104
Phone: (415)421-5378
Fax: (415)956-7708
Email: callahan@pkfe.com
Website: www.cquest.com/pkfb.html

Welling & Woodard, Inc.
1067 Broadway
San Francisco, CA 94133
Phone: (415)776-4500
Fax: (415)776-5067

ORDIS, Inc.
6815 Trinidad Dr.
San Jose, CA 95120-2056
Phone: (408)268-3321
Fax: (408)268-3582
Free: (800)446-7347
Email: ordis@ordis.com
Website: www.ordis.com

Stanford Resources, Inc.
20 Great Oaks Blvd., Ste. 200
San Jose, CA 95119
Phone: (408)360-8400
Fax: (408)360-8410
Email: stanres@ix.netcom.com
Website: www.stanfordresources.com

Technology Properties Ltd., Inc.
4010 Moore Park, St. 215
San Jose, CA 95117
Phone: (408)243-9898
Fax: (408)296-6637

Helfert Associates
1777 Borel Pl., Ste. 508
San Mateo, CA 94402-3514
Phone: (415)377-0540
Fax: (415)377-0472

Mykytyn Consulting Group, Inc.
185 N. Redwood Dr., Ste. 200
San Rafael, CA 94903
Phone: (415)491-1770
Fax: (415)491-1251
Email: info@mcgi.com
Website: www.mcgi.com

Omega Management Systems, Inc.
3 Mount Darwin Ct.
San Rafael, CA 94903-1109
Phone: (415)499-1300
Fax: (415)492-9490
Email: omegamgt@ix.netcom.com

The Information Group, Inc.
4675 Stevens Creek Blvd., Ste. 100
Santa Clara, CA 95051
Phone: (408)985-7877
Fax: (408)985-2945
Email: dvincent@tig-usa.com
Website: www.tig-usa.com

Cast Management Consultants
1620 26th St., Ste. 2040N
Santa Monica, CA 90404
Phone: (310)828-7511
Fax: (310)453-6831

Cuma Consulting Management
Box 724
Santa Rosa, CA 95402
Phone: (707)785-2477
Fax: (707)785-2478

The E-Myth Academy
131B Stony Cir., Ste. 2000
Santa Rosa, CA 95401
Phone: (707)569-5600
Fax: (707)569-5700

Free: (800)221-0266
Email: info@e-myth.com
Website: www.e-myth.com

Reilly, Connors & Ray
1743 Canyon Rd.
Spring Valley, CA 91977
Phone: (619)698-4808
Fax: (619)460-3892
Email: davidray@adnc.com

Management Consultants
Sunnyvale, CA 94087-4700
Phone: (408)773-0321

RJR Associates
1639 Lewiston Dr.
Sunnyvale, CA 94087
Phone: (408)737-7720
Fax: (408)737-7720
Email: bobroy@netcom
Website: www.rjroy.mcni.com

Schwafel Associates
333 Cobalt Way, Ste. 107
Sunnyvale, CA 94086
Phone: (408)720-0649
Fax: (408)720-1796
Email: schwafel@ricochet.net
Website: www.patca.org/patca

Out of Your Mind...and Into the
Marketplace
13381 White Sands Dr.
Tustin, CA 92780-4565
Phone: (714)544-0248
Fax: (714)730-1414
Free: (800)419-1513
Email: lpinson@aol.com
Website: www.business-plan.com

Independent Research Services
PO Box 2426
Van Nuys, CA 91404-2426
Phone: (818)993-3622

Ingman Co. Inc.
7949 Woodley Ave., Ste. 120
Van Nuys, CA 91406-1232
Phone: (818)375-5027
Fax: (818)894-5001

Innovative Technology Associates
3639 E. Harbor Blvd., Ste. 203E
Ventura, CA 93001
Phone: (805)650-9353

Ridge Consultants, Inc.
100 Pringle Ave., Ste. 580
Walnut Creek, CA 94596
Phone: (925)274-1990

Fax: (510)274-1956
Email: info@ridgecon.com
Website: www.ridgecon.com

Bell Springs Publishing
PO Box 1240
Willits, CA 95490
Phone: (707)459-6372
Email: bellsprings@sabernet

Hutchinson Consulting and
Appraisals
23245 Sylvan St., Ste. 103
Woodland Hills, CA 91367
Phone: (818)888-8175
Fax: (818)888-8220
Free: (800)977-7548
Email: hcac.@sprintmall.com

J.H. Robinson & Associates
20695 Deodar Dr., Ste. 100
Yorba Linda, CA 92886-3169
Phone: (714)970-1279

Colorado

Sam Boyer & Associates
4255 S. Buckley Rd., No. 136
Aurora, CO 80013
Fax: (303)766-8740
Free: (800)785-0485
Email: samboyer@samboyer.com
Website: www.samboyer.com/

Ameriwest Business Consultants, Inc.
PO Box 26266
Colorado Springs, CO 80936
Phone: (719)380-7096
Fax: (719)380-7096
Email: email@abchelp.com
Website: www.abchelp.com

GVNW Consulting, Inc.
2270 La Montana Way
Colorado Springs, CO 80936
Phone: (719)594-5800
Fax: (719)599-0968
Website: www.gvnw.com

M-Squared, Inc.
755 San Gabriel Pl.
Colorado Springs, CO 80906
Phone: (719)576-2554
Fax: (719)576-2554

Western Capital Holdings, Inc.
7500 E. Arapahoe Rd., Ste. 395
Englewood, CO 80112
Phone: (303)290-8482
Fax: (303)770-1945

Thornton Financial FNIC
1024 Centre Ave., Bldg. E
Fort Collins, CO 80526-1849
Phone: (970)221-2089
Fax: (970)484-5206

TenEyck Associates
1760 Cherryville Rd.
Greenwood Village, CO 80121-1503
Phone: (303)758-6129
Fax: (303)761-8286

Associated Enterprises Ltd.
13050 W. Ceder Dr., Unit 11
Lakewood, CO 80228
Phone: (303)988-6695
Fax: (303)988-6739
Email: ael1@classic.msn.com

The Vincent Co. Inc.
200 Union Blvd., Ste. 210
Lakewood, CO 80228
Phone: (303)989-7271
Fax: (303)989-7570
Free: (800)274-0733
Email: vincent@vincentco.com
Website: www.vincentco.com

Johnson & West Management
Consultants, Inc.
7612 S. Logan Dr.
Littleton, CO 80122
Phone: (303)730-2810
Fax: (303)730-3219

Connecticut

Stratman Group Inc.
40 Tower Ln.
Avon, CT 06001-4222
Phone: (860)677-2898
Fax: (860)677-8210
Free: (800)551-0499

Cowherd Consulting Group, Inc.
106 Stephen Mather Rd.
Darien, CT 06820
Phone: (203)655-2150
Fax: (203)655-6427

Greenwich Associates
8 Greenwich Office Park
Greenwich, CT 06831-5149
Phone: (203)629-1200
Fax: (203)629-1229
Email: lisa@greenwich.com
Website: www.greenwich.com

Franchise Builders
185 Pine St., Ste. 818

Manchester, CT 06040
Phone: (860)647-7542
Fax: (860)646-6544
Email: watchisle@.aol.com

Lovins & Associates Consulting
309 Edwards St.
New Haven, CT 06511
Phone: (203)787-3367
Fax: (203)624-7599
Email: Alovinsphd@aol.com
Website: www.lovinsgroup.com

JC Ventures, Inc.
4 Arnold St.
Old Greenwich, CT 06870-1203
Phone: (203)698-1990
Fax: (203)698-2638
Free: (800)698-1997

Charles L. Hornung Associates
52 Ned's Mountain Rd.
Ridgefield, CT 06877
Phone: (203)431-0297

Manus
100 Prospect St., S. Tower
Stamford, CT 06901
Phone: (203)326-3880
Fax: (203326-3890
Free: (800)445-0942
Email: manus1@aol.com
Website: www.RightManus.com

Delaware

Focus Marketing
61-7 Habor Dr.
Claymont, DE 19703
Phone: (302)793-3064

Daedalus Ventures, Ltd.
PO Box 1474
Hockessin, DE 19707
Phone: (302)239-6758
Fax: (302)239-9991
Email: daedalus@mail.del.net

The Formula Group
PO Box 866
Hockessin, DE 19707
Phone: (302)456-0952
Fax: (302)456-1354
Email: formula@netaxs.com

Selden Enterprises Inc.
2502 Silverside Rd., Ste. 1
Wilmington, DE 19810-3740
Phone: (302)529-7113
Fax: (302)529-7442

Email: seldenl@juno.com
Website: www.wld.com/id/
w26209001750

District of Columbia

Bruce W. McGee and Associates
7826 Eastern Ave. NW, Ste. 30
Washington, DC 20012
Phone: (202)726-7272
Fax: (202)726-2946

McManis Associates, Inc.
1900 K St. NW, Ste. 700
Washington, DC 20006
Phone: (202)466-7680
Fax: (202)872-1898
Website: www.mcmanis-mmi.com

Smith, Dawson & Andrews, Inc.
1000 Connecticut Ave., Ste. 302
Washington, DC 20036
Phone: (202)835-0740
Fax: (202)775-8526
Email: webmaster@sda-inc.com
Website: www.sda-inc.com

Florida

Whalen & Associates, Inc.
4255 Northwest 26 Ct.
Boca Raton, FL 33434
Phone: (561)241-5950
Fax: (561)241-7414
Email: drwhalen@ix.netcom.com

E.N. Rysso & Associates
202 Caroline St., Ste. 103
Cape Canaveral, FL 32920-2706
Phone: (407)783-7588
Fax: (407)783-7580
Email: erysso@aol.com

Eric Sands Consulting Services
6193 Rock Island Rd., Ste. 412
Fort Lauderdale, FL 33319
Phone: (954)721-4767
Fax: (954)720-2815

Host Media Corp.
3948 S. Third St., Ste. 191
Jacksonville Beach, FL 32250
Phone: (904)285-3239
Fax: (904)285-5618
Email:
msconsulting@compuserve.com

William V. Hall
1925 Brickell, Ste. D-701

Miami, FL 33129
Phone: (305)856-9622
Fax: (305)856-4113
Email:
williamvhall@compuserve.com

F.A. McGee, Inc.
800 Claughton Island Dr., Ste. 401
Miami, FL 33131
Phone: (305)377-9123

Taxplan, Inc.
Mirasol International Center
2699 Collins Ave.
Miami Beach, FL 33140
Phone: (305)538-3303

T.C. Brown & Associates
8415 Excalibur Cir., Apt. B1
Naples, FL 34108
Phone: (941)594-1949
Fax: (941)594-0611
Email: tcater@naples.net.com

RLA International Consulting
713 Lagoon Dr.
North Palm Beach, FL 33408
Phone: (407)626-4258
Fax: (407)626-5772

Comprehensive Franchising, Inc.
2465 Ridgecrest Ave.
Orange Park, FL 32065
Phone: (904)272-6567
Fax: (904)272-6750
Free: (800)321-6567
Email: theimp@cris.com
Website: www.franchise411.com

Hunter G. Jackson Jr. - Consulting
Environmental Physicist
PO Box 618272
Orlando, FL 32861-8272
Phone: (407)295-4188
Email: hunterjackson@juno.com

F. Newton Parks
210 El Brillo Way
Palm Beach, FL 33480
Phone: (561)833-1727
Fax: (561)833-4541

Avery Business Development
Services
2506 St. Michel Ct.
Ponte Vedra Beach, FL 32082
Phone: (904)285-6033
Fax: (904)285-6033

Strategic Business Planning Co.
PO Box 821006
South Florida, FL 33082-1006
Phone: (954)704-9100
Fax: (954)438-7333
Email: info@bizplan.com
Website: www.bizplan.com

Dufresne Consulting Group, Inc.
10014 N. Dale Mabry, Ste. 101
Tampa, FL 33618-4426
Phone: (813)264-4775
Fax: (813)264-9300
Website: www.dcgconsult.com

Agrippa Enterprises, Inc.
PO Box 175
Venice, FL 34284-0175
Phone: (941)355-7876
Email: webservices@agrippa.com
Website: www.agrippa.com

Center for Simplified Strategic
Planning, Inc.
PO Box 3324
Vero Beach, FL 32964-3324
Phone: (561)231-3636
Fax: (561)231-1099
Website: www.cssp.com

Georgia

Marketing Spectrum Inc.
115 Perimeter Pl., Ste. 440
Atlanta, GA 30346
Phone: (770)395-7244
Fax: (770)393-4071

Business Ventures Corp.
6030 Dawson Blvd., Ste. E
Norcross, GA 30093
Phone: (770)729-8000
Fax: (770)729-8028

Trinity Capital
1244 Beaver Ruin Road, Suite 200
Norcross, GA 30093
Contact: Tim Dineen
Phone: (770)935-0480
Fax: (770)935-1075
Email: lepcap@mindspring.com
Provides business planning services,
assists in capital formation, and
performs myriad consulting and
advisory services.

Informed Decisions Inc.
100 Falling Cheek
Sautee Nacoochee, GA 30571

Phone: (706)878-1905
Fax: (706)878-1802
Email: skylake@compuserve.com

Tom C. Davis & Associates, P.C.
3189 Perimeter Rd.
Valdosta, GA 31602
Phone: (912)247-9801
Fax: (912)244-7704
Email: mail@tcdcpa.com
Website: www.tcdcpa.com/

Illinois

TWD and Associates
431 S. Patton
Arlington Heights, IL 60005
Phone: (847)398-6410
Fax: (847)255-5095
Email: tdoo@aol.com

Management Planning Associates,
Inc.
2275 Half Day Rd., Ste. 350
Bannockburn, IL 60015-1277
Phone: (847)945-2421
Fax: (847)945-2425

Phil Faris Associates
86 Old Mill Ct.
Barrington, IL 60010
Phone: (847)382-4888
Fax: (847)382-4890
Email: pfaris@meginsnet.net

Seven Continents Technology
787 Stonebridge
Buffalo Grove, IL 60089
Phone: (708)577-9653
Fax: (708)870-1220

Grubb & Blue, Inc.
2404 Windsor Pl.
Champaign, IL 61820
Phone: (217)366-0052
Fax: (217)356-0117

ACE Accounting Service, Inc.
3128 N. Bernard St.
Chicago, IL 60618
Phone: (773)463-7854
Fax: (773)463-7854

AON Consulting
123 N. Wacker Dr., 16th Fl.
Chicago, IL 60606
Phone: (312)701-4055
Fax: (312)701-4123
Free: (800)438-6487
Website: aon.com

FMS Consultants
5801 N. Sheridan Rd., Ste. 3D
Chicago, IL 60660
Phone: (773)561-7362
Fax: (773)561-6274

Kingsbury International, Ltd.
5341 N. Glenwood Ave.
Chicago, IL 60640
Phone: (773)271-3030
Fax: (773)728-7080
Email: jetlag@mcs.com
Website: www.kingbiz.com

MacDougall & Blake, Inc.
1414 N. Wells St., Ste. 311
Chicago, IL 60610-1306
Phone: (312)587-3330
Fax: (312)587-3699
Email: jblake@compuserve.com

James C. Osburn Ltd.
2701 W. Howard St.
Chicago, IL 60645
Phone: (773)262-4428
Fax: (773)262-6755

Tarifero & Tazewell Inc.
211 S. Clark
Chicago, IL 60690
Phone: (312)665-9714
Fax: (312)665-9716

William J. Igoe
3949 Earlston Rd.
Downers Grove, IL 60515
Phone: (630)960-1418

Human Energy Design Systems
620 Roosevelt Dr.
Edwardsville, IL 62025
Phone: (618)692-0258
Fax: (618)692-0819

BioLabs, Inc.
15 Sheffield Ct.
Lincolnshire, IL 60069
Phone: (847)945-2767

Clyde R. Goodheart
15 Sheffield Ct.
Lincolnshire, IL 60069
Phone: (847)945-2767

China Business Consultants Group
931 Dakota Cir.
Naperville, IL 60563
Phone: (630)778-7992
Fax: (630)778-7915
Email: cbcq@aol.com

Center for Workforce Effectiveness
500 Skokie Blvd., Ste. 222
Northbrook, IL 60062
Phone: (847)559-8777
Fax: (847)559-8778
Email: office@cwelink.com
Website: www.cwelink.com

Smith Associates
1320 White Mountain Dr.
Northbrook, IL 60062
Phone: (847)480-7200
Fax: (847)480-9828

Francorp, Inc.
20200 Governors Dr.
Olympia Fields, IL 60461
Phone: (708)481-2900
Fax: (708)481-5885
Free: (800)372-6244
Email: francorp@aol.com
Website: www.francorpinc.com

Camber Business Strategy
Consultants
PO Box 986
Palatine, IL 60078-0986
Phone: (847)705-0101
Fax: (847)705-0101

Partec Enterprise Group
5202 Keith Dr.
Richton Park, IL 60471
Phone: (708)503-4047
Fax: (708)503-9468

Rockford Consulting Group, Ltd.
Century Plaza, Ste. 206
7210 E. State St.
Rockford, IL 61108
Phone: (815)229-2900
Fax: (815)229-2612
Free: (800)667-7495
Email:
rligus@RockfordConsulting.com
Website:
www.RockfordConsulting.com

McGladrey & Pullen, LLP
1699 E. Woodfield Rd., Ste. 200
Schaumburg, IL 60173
Phone: (847)517-7070
Fax: (847)517-7095
Free: (800)365-8353
Website: www.mcgladrey.com

A.D. Star Consulting
320 Euclid
Winnetka, IL 60093

Phone: (847)446-7827
Fax: (847)446-7827
Email: startwo@worldnet.att.net

Indiana

Modular Consultants Inc.
3109 Crabtree Ln.
Elkhart, IN 46514
Phone: (219)264-5761
Fax: (219)264-5761
Email: sasabo5313@aol.com

Midwest Marketing Research
PO Box 1077
Goshen, IN 46527
Phone: (219)533-0548
Fax: (219)533-0540
Email: 103365.654@compuserve

Ketchum Consulting Group
8021 Knue Rd., Ste. 112
Indianapolis, IN 46250
Phone: (317)845-5411
Fax: (317)842-9941

MDI Management Consulting
1519 Park Dr.
Munster, IN 46321
Phone: (219)838-7909
Fax: (219)838-7909

Iowa

McCord Consulting Group, Inc.
4533 Pine View Dr. NE
PO Box 11024
Cedar Rapids, IA 52410
Phone: (319)378-0077
Fax: (319)378-1577
Email: sam.mccord@usa.net
Website: www.mccordgroup.com

Management Solutions, L.C.
3815 Lincoln Place Dr.
Des Moines, IA 50312
Phone: (515)277-6408
Fax: (515)277-3506
Email:
102602.1561@compuserve.com

Grandview Marketing
15 Red Bridge Dr.
Sioux City, IA 51104
Phone: (712)239-3122
Fax: (712)258-7578
Email: eandrews@pionet.net

Kansas

Assessments in Action
513A N. Mur-Len
Olathe, KS 66062
Phone: (913)764-6270
Fax: (913)764-6495
Free: (888)548-1504
Email: lowdene@qni.com
Website: www.assessments-in-action.com

Maine

Edgemont Enterprises
PO Box 8354
Portland, ME 04104
Phone: (207)871-8964
Fax: (207)871-8964

Pan Atlantic Consultants
148 Middle St.
Portland, ME 04101
Phone: (207)871-8622
Fax: (207)772-4842
Email: panatl@worldnet.att.net

Maryland

Clemons & Associates, Inc.
5024-R Campbell Blvd.
Baltimore, MD 21236
Phone: (410)931-8100
Fax: (410)931-8111
Email: clemonsc@msn.com.
Website: www.clemonsmgmt.com/clemons

Grant Thornton
2 Hopkins Plaza
Baltimore, MD 21201
Phone: (410)685-4000
Fax: (410)837-0587

Imperial Group, Ltd.
305 Washington Ave., Ste. 204
Baltimore, MD 21204-6009
Phone: (410)337-8500
Fax: (410)337-7641

Burdeshaw Associates, Ltd.
4701 Sangamore Rd.
Bethesda, MD 20816-2508
Phone: (301)229-5800
Fax: (301)229-5045
Email: jstacy@burdeshaw.com
Website: www.burdeshaw.com

Michael E. Cohen
5225 Pooks Hill Rd., Ste. 1119 S
Bethesda, MD 20814
Phone: (301)530-5738
Fax: (301)530-2988

World Development Group, Inc.
5272 River Rd., Ste. 650
Bethesda, MD 20816-1405
Phone: (301)652-1818
Fax: (301)652-1250
Email: wdg@has.com
Website: www.worlddg.com

Swartz Consulting
PO Box 4301
Crofton, MD 21114-4301
Phone: (301)262-6728

Software Solutions International Inc.
9633 Duffer Way
Gaithersburg, MD 20886
Phone: (301)977-3743
Fax: (301)330-4136

Columbia Financial Corp.
1301 York Road, Suite 400
Lutherville, MD21093
Contact: Dave Grimm
Phone: (888)301-6271
Email: mktwchr@aol.com
Assists emerging small- to micro-cap
companies with investor relations,
public relations, and other
professional services to help them "go
public."

Strategies, Inc.
8 Park Center Ct., Ste. 200
Owings Mills, MD 21117
Phone: (410)363-6669
Fax: (410)363-1231

Hammer Marketing Resources
179 Inverness Rd.
Severna Park, MD 21146
Phone: (410)544-9191
Fax: (410)544-9189
Email: bhammer@gohammer.com
Website: www.gohammer.com

Andrew Sussman & Associates
13731 Kretsinger
Smithsburg, MD 21783
Phone: (301)824-2943
Fax: (301)824-2943

Massachusetts

Geibel Marketing and Public
Relations
PO Box 611
Belmont, MA 02478-0005
Phone: (617)484-8285
Fax: (617)489-3567
Email: jgeibel@geibelpr.com
Website: www.geibelpr.com

Bain & Co.
2 Copley Pl.
Boston, MA 02116
Phone: (617)572-2000
Fax: (617)572-2427
Website: www.bain.com

Mehr & Co.
62 Kinnaird St.
Cambridge, MA 02139
Phone: (617)876-3311
Fax: (617)876-3023
Email: mehrco@aol.com

Monitor Co., Inc.
Two Canal Park
Cambridge, MA 02141
Phone: (617)252-2000
Fax: (617)252-2100
Website: www.monitor.com

Data and Strategies Group, Inc.
Three Speen St.
Framingham, MA 01701
Phone: (508)820-2500
Fax: (508)820-1626
Email: dsginc@dsggroup.com
Website: www.dsggroup.com

Information & Research Associates
PO Box 3121
Framingham, MA 01701
Phone: (508)788-0784

Easton Consultants Inc.
252 Pond St.
Hopkinton, MA 01748
Phone: (508)435-4882
Fax: (508)435-3971
Website: www.easton-ma.com

Jeffrey D. Marshall
102 Mitchell Rd.
Ipswich, MA 01938-1219
Phone: (508)356-1113
Fax: (508)356-2989

Consulting Resources Corp.
6 Northbrook Park

Lexington, MA 02420
Phone: (781)863-1222
Fax: (781)863-1441
Email: res6consulting@resources.net

Planning Technologies Group LLC
92 Hayden Ave.
Lexington, MA 02421
Phone: (781)778-4678
Fax: (781)861-1099
Email: ptg@plantech.com
Website: www.plantech.com

VMB Associates, Inc.
115 Ashland St.
Melrose, MA 02176
Phone: (781)665-0623
Fax: (781)662-1288
Email: vmbinc@aol.com

The Company Doctor
14 Pudding Stone Ln.
Mendon, MA 01756
Phone: (508)478-1747
Fax: (508)478-0520

The Enterprise Group
73 Parker Rd.
Needham, MA 02194
Phone: (617)444-6631
Fax: (617)433-9991
Email: lsacco@world.std.com
Website: www.enterprise-group.com

PSMJ Resources, Inc.
10 Midland Ave.
Newton, MA 02158
Phone: (617)965-0055
Fax: (617)965-5152
Free: (800)537-7765
Email: psmj@tiac.net
Website: www.psmj.com

IEEE Consultants' Network
255 Bear Hill Rd.
Waltham, MA 02154-1017
Phone: (617)890-5294
Fax: (617)890-5290

Kalba International, Inc.
1601 Trapelo Rd.
Waltham, MA 02154
Phone: (781)259-9589
Fax: (781)466-8440
Email: mail17495@pop.net

Business Planning and Consulting
Services
20 Beechwood Terr.
Wellesley, MA 02181

Phone: (617)237-9151
Fax: (617)237-9151

Interim Management Associates
21 Avon Rd.
Wellesley, MA 02181
Phone: (781)237-0024

Michigan

Walter Frederick Consulting
1719 South Blvd.
Ann Arbor, MI 48104
Phone: (313)662-4336
Fax: (313)769-7505

Fox Enterprises
6220 W. Freeland Rd.
Freeland, MI 48623
Phone: (517)695-9170
Fax: (517)695-9174
Email: foxjw@concentric.net
Website: www.cris.com/~foxjw

G.G.W. and Associates
1213 Hampton
Jackson, MI 49203
Phone: (517)782-2255
Fax: (517)782-2255

Altamar Group Ltd.
6810 S. Cedar, Ste. 2-B
Lansing, MI 48911
Phone: (517)694-0910
Fax: (517)694-1377
Free: (800)443-2627

Sheffieck Consultants, Inc.
23610 Greening Dr.
Novi, MI 48375-3130
Phone: (248)347-3545
Fax: (248)347-3530
Email: cfsheff@concentric.net

Rehmann, Robson PC
5800 Gratiot
Saginaw, MI 48605
Phone: (517)799-9580
Fax: (517)799-0227
Website: www.rrpc.com

Francis & Co.
17200 W. Ten Mile Rd., Ste. 207
Southfield, MI 48075
Phone: (248)559-7600
Fax: (248)559-5249

Private Ventures, Inc.
16000 W. Nine Mile Rd., Ste. 504
Southfield, MI 48075

Phone: (248)569-1977
Fax: (248)569-1838
Free: (800)448-7614
Email: pventuresi@aol.com

JGK Associates
14464 Kerner Dr.
Sterling Heights, MI 48313
Phone: (810)247-9055

Minnesota

Health Fitness Corp.
3500 W 80th St., Ste. 130
Bloomington, MN 55431
Phone: (612)831-6830
Fax: (612)831-7264

Consatech Inc.
PO Box 1047
Burnsville, MN 55337
Phone: (612)953-1088
Fax: (612)435-2966

Robert F. Knotek
14960 Ironwood Ct.
Eden Prairie, MN 55346
Phone: (612)949-2875

DRI Consulting
7715 Stonewood Ct.
Edina, MN 55439
Phone: (612)941-9656
Fax: (612)941-2693
Email: dric@dric.com
Website: www.dric.com

Kinnon Lilligren Associates Inc.
6211 Oakgreen Ave. S
Hastings, MN 55033-9153
Phone: (612)436-6530
Fax: (612)436-6530

Markin Consulting
12072 87th Pl. N
Maple Grove, MN 55369
Phone: (612)493-3568
Fax: (612)493-5744
Email:
markin@markinconsulting.com
Website: www.markinconsulting.com

Minnesota Cooperation Office for
Small Business & Job Creation, Inc.
5001 W. 80th St., Ste. 825
Minneapolis, MN 55437
Phone: (612)830-1230
Fax: (612)830-1232
Email: mncoop@msn.com
Website: www.mnco.org

Enterprise Consulting, Inc.
PO Box 1111
Minnetonka, MN 55345
Phone: (612)949-5909
Fax: (612)906-3965

Amdahl International
724 1st Ave. SW
Rochester, MN 55902
Phone: (507)252-0402
Fax: (507)252-0402
Email: amdahl@best-service.com
Website: www.wp.com/amdahl_int

Power Systems Research
1365 Corporate Center Curve, 2nd Fl.
St. Paul, MN 55121
Phone: (612)905-8400
Fax: (612)454-0760
Free: (888)625-8612
Email: Barb@Powersys.com
Website: www.powersys.com

Small Business Success
PO Box 21097
St. Paul, MN 55121-0097
Phone: (612)454-2500
Fax: (612)456-9138

Missouri

Business Planning and Development
Corp.
4030 Charlotte St.
Kansas City, MO 64110
Phone: (816)753-0495
Email: humph@bpdev.demon.co.uk
Website: www.bpdev.demon.co.uk

CFO Service
10336 Donoho
St. Louis, MO 63131
Phone: (314)750-2940
Email: jskae@cfoservice.com
Website: www.cfoservice.com

Nevada

The DuBois Group
865 Tahoe Blvd., Ste. 108
Incline Village, NV 89451
Phone: (775)832-0550
Fax: (775)832-0556
Free: (800)375-2935
Email: DuBoisGrp@aol.com

Nebraska

International Management Consulting
Group, Inc.
1309 Harlan Dr., Ste. 205
Bellevue, NE 68005
Phone: (402)291-4545
Fax: (402)291-4343
Free: (800)665-IMCG
Email: imcg@neonramp.com
Website: www.mgtconsulting.com

Heartland Management Consulting
Group
1904 Barrington Pky.
Papillion, NE 68046
Phone: (402)339-2387
Fax: (402)339-1319

New Hampshire

Wolff Consultants
10 Buck Rd.
Hanover, NH 03755
Phone: (603)643-6015

BPT Consulting Associates, Ltd.
12 Parmenter Rd., Ste. B-6
Londonderry, NH 03053
Phone: (603)437-8484
Fax: (603)434-5388
Free: (888)278-0030
Email: bptcons@tiac.net
Website: www.bptconsulting.com

New Jersey

ConMar International, Ltd.
283 Dayton-Jamesburg Rd.
Dayton, NJ 08810
Phone: (908)274-1100
Fax: (908)274-1199

Kumar Associates, Inc.
1004 Cumbermeade Rd.
Fort Lee, NJ 07024
Phone: (201)224-9480
Fax: (201)585-2343
Email: kassoc@idt.net

John Hall & Co., Inc.
PO Box 187
Glen Ridge, NJ 07028
Phone: (201)680-4449
Fax: (201)680-4581
Email: jhcompany@aol.com

Market Focus
PO Box 402
Maplewood, NJ 07040

Phone: (973)378-2470
Fax: (973)378-2470
Email: mcss66@marketfocus.com

Vanguard Communications Corp.
100 American Rd.
Morris Plains, NJ 07950
Phone: (201)605-8000
Fax: (201)605-8329
Website: www.vanguard.net/

KLW New Products
156 Cedar Dr.
Old Tappan, NJ 07675
Phone: (201)358-1300
Fax: (201)664-2594
Email: lrlarsen@usa.net
Website: www.klwnewproducts.com

PA Consulting Group
315 A Enterprise Dr.
Plainsboro, NJ 08536
Phone: (609)936-8300
Fax: (609)936-8811
Website: www.pa-consulting.com

Aurora Marketing Management, Inc.
66 Witherspoon St., Ste. 600
Princeton, NJ 08542
Phone: (908)904-1125
Fax: (908)359-1108
Email: aurora212@cwix.com
Website: www.telesales.cz

Smart Business Supersite
88 Orchard Rd., CN-5219
Princeton, NJ 08543
Phone: (908)321-1924
Fax: (908)321-5156
Email: irv@smartbiz.com
Website: www.smartbiz.com

Tracelin Associates
1171 Main St., Ste. 6K
Rahway, NJ 07065
Phone: (732)381-3288

Schkeeper Inc.
130-6 Bodman Pl.
Red Bank, NJ 07701
Phone: (732)219-1965
Fax: (732)530-3703

Henry Branch Associates
2502 Harmon Cove Tower
Secaucus, NJ 07094
Phone: (201)866-2008
Fax: (201)601-0101
Email: hbranch161@aol.com
Website: www.hbranch.mcni.com

Robert Gibbons & Co., Inc.
46 Knoll Rd.
Tenafly, NJ 07670-1050
Phone: (201)871-3933
Fax: (201)871-2173
Email: crisisbob@aol.com

PMC Management Consultants, Inc.
11 Thistle Ln.
Three Bridges, NJ 08887-0332
Phone: (908)788-1014
Fax: (908)806-7287
Email: int@pmc-management.com
Website: www.wwpmc-
management.com

R.W. Bankart & Associates
20 Valley Ave., Ste. D-2
Westwood, NJ 07675-3607
Phone: (201)664-7672

New Mexico

Vondle & Associates, Inc.
4926 Calle de Tierra, NE
Albuquerque, NM 87111
Phone: (505)292-8961
Fax: (505)296-2790
Email: vondle@aol.com

InfoNewMexico
2207 Black Hills Road, NE
Rio Rancho, NM 87124
Phone: (505)891-2462
Fax: (505)896-8971

New York

Powers Research and Training
Institute
PO Box 78
Bayville, NY 11709
Phone: (516)628-2250
Fax: (516)628-2252
Email:
powercocch@compuserve.com
Website: www.nancypowers.com

Consortium House
139 Wittenberg Rd.
Bearsville, NY 12409
Phone: (914)679-8867
Fax: (914)679-9248
Email: eugenegs@aol.com
Website: www.chpub.com

Progressive Finance Corp.
3549 Tiemann Ave.
Bronx, NY 10469

Phone: (718)405-9029
Fax: (718)405-1170
Free: (800)225-8381

Wave Hill Associates
2621 Palisade Ave., Ste. 15-C
Bronx, NY 10463
Phone: (718)549-7368
Fax: (718)601-9670

Management Insight
96 Arlington Rd.
Buffalo, NY 14221
Phone: (716)631-3319
Fax: (716)631-0203
Free: (800)643-3319

Delta Planning, Inc.
PO Box 425
Dansville, NY 14437
Phone: (913)625-1742
Fax: (973)625-3531
Free: (800)672-0762
Email: DeltaP@worldnet.att.net

Samani International Enterprises,
Marions Panyaught Consultancy
2028 Parsons
Flushing, NY 11357-3436
Phone: (917)287-8087
Fax: (800)873-8939
Email: vjp2@compuserve.com
Website: www.dorsai.org/~vjp2

Marketing Resources Group
71-58 Austin St.
Forest Hills, NY 11375
Phone: (718)261-8882

North Star Enterprises
670 N. Terrace Ave.
Mount Vernon, NY 10552
Phone: (914)668-9433

Boice Dunham Group
30 W. 13th St.
New York, NY 10011
Phone: (212)752-5550
Fax: (212)752-7055

Elizabeth Capen
27 E. 95th St.
New York, NY 10128
Phone: (212)427-7654
Fax: (212)876-3190

Haver Analytics
60 E. 42nd St., Ste. 2424
New York, NY 10017
Phone: (212)986-9300

Fax: (212)986-5857
Email: data@haver.com
Website: www.haver.com

The Jordan, Edmiston Group, Inc.
150 E 52nd Ave., 18th Fl.
New York, NY 10022
Phone: (212)754-0710
Fax: (212)754-0337

KPMG International
345 Park Ave.
New York, NY 10154
Phone: (212)909-5000
Fax: (212)909-5299
Website: www.kpmg.com

Mahoney Cohen Consulting Corp.
111 W. 40th St., 12th Fl.
New York, NY 10018
Phone: (212)490-8000
Fax: (212)790-5913

Management Practice, Inc.
342 Madison Ave.
New York, NY 10173-1230
Phone: (212)867-7948
Fax: (212)972-5188
Website: www.mpiweb.com

Moseley Associates, Inc.
342 Madison Ave., Ste. 1414
New York, NY 10016
Phone: (212)213-6673
Fax: (212)687-1520

Practice Development Counsel
60 Sutton Pl. S
New York, NY 10022
Phone: (212)593-1549
Fax: (212)980-7940
Email: phaserot@counsel.com

Unique Value International, Inc.
575 Madison Ave., 10th Fl.
New York, NY 10022-1304
Phone: (212)605-0590
Fax: (212)605-0589

The Van Tulleken Co.
126 E. 56th St.
New York, NY 10022
Phone: (212)355-1390
Fax: (212)755-3061
Email: newyork@vantelleken.com

Vencon Management, Inc.
301 W. 53rd St.
New York, NY 10019
Phone: (212)581-8787
Fax: (212)397-4126

R.A. Walsh Consultants
429 E. 52nd St.
New York, NY 10022
Phone: (212)688-6047
Fax: (212)535-4075

Werner International Inc.
55 East 52nd, 29th floor
New York, NY 10055
Phone: (212)909-1260
Fax: (212)909-1273
Email: maryorourke@rgh.com
Website: www.inforesint.com

Zimmerman Business Consulting,
Inc.
44 E. 92nd St., Ste. 5-B
New York, NY 10128
Phone: (212)860-3107
Fax: (212)860-7730
Email: ljzzbci@aol.com

Overton Financial
7 Allen Rd.
Peekskill, NY 10566
Phone: (914)737-4649
Fax: (914)737-4696

Stromberg Consulting
2500 Westchester Ave.
Purchase, NY 10577
Phone: (914)251-1515
Fax: (914)251-1562
Email:
strategy@stromberg_consulting.com
Website:
www.stromberg_consulting.com

ComputerEase Co.
9 Hachaliah Brown Dr.
Somers, NY 10589
Phone: (914)277-5317
Fax: (914)277-5317
Email: crawfordc@juno.com

Innovation Management Consulting,
Inc.
209 Dewitt Rd.
Syracuse, NY 13214-2006
Phone: (315)425-5144
Fax: (315)445-8989
Email: missonneb@axess.net

M. Clifford Agress
891 Fulton St.
Valley Stream, NY 11580
Phone: (516)825-8955
Fax: (516)825-8955

Destiny Kinal Marketing Consultancy
105 Chemung St.
Waverly, NY 14892
Phone: (607)565-8317
Fax: (607)565-4083

Valutis Consulting, Inc.
5350 Main St., Ste. 7
Williamsville, NY 14221-5338
Phone: (716)634-2553
Fax: (716)634-2554
Email: valutis@localnet.com
Website: www.valutisconsulting.com

North Carolina

Best Practices, LLC
6320 Quadrangle Dr., Ste. 200
Chapel Hill, NC 27514
Phone: (919)403-0251
Fax: (919)403-0144
Email: best@best:in/class
Website: www.best-in-class.com

Norelli & Co.
Nations Bank Corporation Center
100 N. Tyron St., Ste. 5160
Charlotte, NC 28202-4000
Phone: (704)376-5484
Fax: (704)376-5485
Email: consult@norelli.com
Website: www.norelli.com

North Dakota

Center for Innovation
4300 Dartmouth Dr.
PO Box 8372
Grand Forks, ND 58202
Phone: (701)777-3132
Fax: (701)777-2339
Email: gjovig@praivie.nodak.edu
Website: www.innovators.net

Ohio

Transportation Technology Services
208 Harmon Rd.
Aurora, OH 44202
Phone: (330)562-3596

Empro Systems, Inc.
4777 Red Bank Expy., Ste. 1
Cincinnati, OH 45227-1542
Phone: (513)271-2042
Fax: (513)271-2042

Alliance Management International,
Ltd.
1440 Windrow Ln.
Cleveland, OH 44147-3200
Phone: (440)838-1922
Fax: (440)838-0979
Email: bgruss@amiltd.com
Website: www.amiltd.com

Bozell Kamstra Public Relations
1301 E. 9th St., Ste. 3400
Cleveland, OH 44114
Phone: (216)623-1511
Fax: (216)623-1501
Email:
jfeniger@cleveland.bozellkamstra.com
Website: www.bozellkamstra.com

Cory Dillon Associates
111 Schreyer Pl. E
Columbus, OH 43214
Phone: (614)262-8211
Fax: (614)262-3806

Holcomb Gallagher Adams
300 Marconi, Ste. 303
Columbus, OH 43215
Phone: (614)221-3343
Fax: (614)221-3367
Email: riadams@acme.freenet.oh.us

Ransom & Assoc.
106 E. Pacemont Rd.
Columbus, OH 43202-1225
Phone: (614)267-7100
Fax: (614)267-7199
Email: wjr@netwalk.com

Young & Associates
PO Box 711
Kent, OH 44240
Phone: (330)678-0524
Fax: (330)678-6219
Free: (800)525-9775
Website: www.younginc.com

Robert A. Westman & Associates
8981 Inversary Dr. SE
Warren, OH 44484-2551
Phone: (330)856-4149
Fax: (330)856-2564

Oklahoma

Innovative Partners LLC
4900 Richmond Sq., Ste. 100
Oklahoma City, OK 73118
Phone: (405)840-0033
Fax: (405)843-8359
Email: ipartners@juno.com

Oregon

INTERCON - The International
Converting Institute
5200 Badger Rd.
Crooked River Ranch, OR 97760
Phone: (541)548-1447
Fax: (541)548-1618
Email:
johnbowler@crookedriverranch.com

Talbott ARM
HC 60, Box 5620
Lakeview, OR 97630
Phone: (541)635-8587
Fax: (503)947-3482

Management Technology Associates,
Ltd.
1618 SW 1st Ave., Ste. 315
Portland, OR 97201
Phone: (503)224-5220
Fax: (503)224-6704
Email: lcuster@mta-ltd.com
Website: www.mgmt-tech.com

Pennsylvania

Elayne Howard & Associates, Inc.
3501 Masons Mill Rd., Ste. 501
Huntingdon Valley, PA 19006-3509
Phone: (215)657-9550

GRA, Inc.
115 West Ave., Ste. 201
Jenkintown, PA 19046
Phone: (215)884-7500
Fax: (215)884-1385
Email: gramail@gra-inc.com
Website: www.gra-inc.com

Mifflin County Industrial
Development Corp.
Mifflin County Industrial Plaza
6395 SR 103 N
Bldg. 50
Lewistown, PA 17044
Phone: (717)242-0393
Fax: (717)242-1842
Email: mcide@acsworld.net

Autech Products
1289 Revere Rd.
Morrisville, PA 19067
Phone: (215)493-3759
Fax: (215)493-9791

Advantage Associates
434 Avon Dr.
Pittsburgh, PA 15228

Phone: (412)343-1558
Fax: (412)362-1684
Email: ecocba1@aol.com

Regis J. Sheehan & Associates
291 Foxcroft Rd.
Pittsburgh, PA 15220
Phone: (412)279-1207

James W. Davidson Co., Inc.
23 Forest View Rd.
Wallingford, PA 19086
Phone: (610)566-1462

Puerto Rico

Diego Chevere & Co.
Ste. 301, Metro Parque 7
Caparra Heights, PR 00920
Phone: (787)782-9595
Fax: (787)782-9532

Manuel L. Porrata and Associates
898 Munoz Rivera Ave., Ste. 201
Rio Piedras, PR 00927
Phone: (809)765-2140
Fax: (809)754-3285

South Carolina

Aquafood Business Associates
PO Box 16190
Charleston, SC 29412
Phone: (803)795-9506
Fax: (803)795-9477

Profit Associates, Inc.
PO Box 38026
Charleston, SC 29414
Phone: (803)763-5718
Fax: (803)763-5719
Email: bobrog@awod.com
Website: www.awod.com/gallery/
business/proasc

Strategic Innovations International
12 Executive Ct.
Lake Wylie, SC 29710
Phone: (803)831-1225
Fax: (803)831-1177
Email: stratinnov@aol.com
Website:
www.strategicinnovations.com

SVC Nightclub and Bar Services, Inc.
504 30th Avenue North, Suite #16
Myrtle Beach, SC 29577
Contact: Joe Sorge
Phone: (843)902-2581

Email: jjsorge@nightclub-
business.com
Website: www.nightclub-
business.com
Provides business planning for the
nightclub and bar industry. Works
directly with new clients to build
market specific plans and feasibility
studies, incorporating full research
and sales forecasting. Also reviews
and critiques plans for clients.

Minus Stage
Box 4436
Rock Hill, SC 29731
Phone: (803)328-0705
Fax: (803)329-9948

Tennessee

Daniel Petchers & Associates
8820 Fernwood CV
Germantown, TN 38138
Phone: (901)755-9896

Business Choices
1114 Forest Harbor, Ste. 300
Hendersonville, TN 37075-9646
Phone: (615)822-8692
Fax: (615)822-8692
Free: (800)737-8382
Email: bz-ch@juno.com

RCFA Healthcare Management
Services, LLC
9648 Kingston Pike, Ste. 8
Knoxville, TN 37922
Phone: (423)531-0176
Fax: (423)531-0722
Free: (800)635-4040
Email: pkikng@mail.tds.net
Website: www.rcfa.com

Growth Consultants of America
3917 Trimble Rd.
Nashville, TN 37215
Phone: (615)383-0550
Fax: (615)269-8940
Email: 70244.451@compuserve.com

Texas

Integrated Cost Management
Systems, Inc.
2261 Brookhollow Plz. Dr., Ste. 104
Arlington, TX 76006
Phone: (817)633-2873
Fax: (817)633-3781
Free: (800)955-2233

Email: abm@icms.net
Website: www.icms.net

Lori Williams
1000 Leslie Ct.
Arlington, TX 76012
Phone: (817)459-3934
Fax: (817)459-3934

Erisa Adminstrative Services Inc.
12325 Haymeadow Dr., Bldg. 4
Austin, TX 78750-1847
Phone: (512)250-9020
Fax: (512)250-9487
Website: www.cserisa.com

R. Miller Hicks & Co.
1011 W. 11th St.
Austin, TX 78703
Phone: (512)477-7000
Fax: (512)477-9697
Email: millerhicks@rmhicks.com
Website: www.rmhicks.com

Pragmatic Tactics, Inc.
3303 Westchester Ave.
College Station, TX 77845
Phone: (409)696-5294
Fax: (409)696-4994
Free: (800)570-5294
Email: ptactics@aol.com
Website: www.ptatics.com

Perot Systems
12377 Merit Dr., Ste. 1100
Dallas, TX 75251
Phone: (972)788-3000
Free: (800)688-4333
Email: corp.comm@ps.net
Website: www.ps.net

ReGENERATION Partners
3838 Oak Lawn Ave.
Dallas, TX 75219
Phone: (214)559-3999
Free: (800)406-1112
Website: www.regeneration-
partners.com

High Technology Associates -
Division of Global Technologies, Inc.
1775 St. James Pl., Ste. 105
Houston, TX 77056
Phone: (713)963-9300
Fax: (713)963-8341
Email: hta@infohwy.com

MasterCOM
103 Thunder Rd.
Kerrville, TX 78028

Phone: (830)895-7990
Fax: (830)443-3428
Email:
jmstubblefield@mastertraining.com
Website: www.mastertraining.com

PROTEC
4607 Linden Pl.
Pearland, TX 77584
Phone: (281)997-9872
Fax: (281)997-9895
Email: p.oman@ix.netcom.com

Business Strategy Development
Consultants
PO Box 690365
San Antonio, TX 78269
Phone: (210)696-8000
Fax: (210)696-8000
Free: (800)927-BSDC

Tom Welch, CPC
6900 San Pedro Ave., Ste. 147
San Antonio, TX 78216-6207
Phone: (210)737-7022
Fax: (210)737-7022
Email: bplan@iamerica.net
Website: www.moneywords.com

Virginia

Elliott B. Jaffa
2530-B S. Walter Reed Dr.
Arlington, VA 22206
Phone: (703)931-0040
Email: trainingdoctor@excite.com

Koach Enterprises -
5529 N. 18th St.
Arlington, VA 22205
Phone: (703)241-8361
Fax: (703)241-8623

Federal Market Development
5650 Chapel Run Ct.
Centreville, VA 20120-3601
Phone: (703)502-8930
Fax: (703)502-8929
Free: (800)821-5003

Barringer, Huff & Stuart
2107 Graves Mills Rd., Ste. C
Forest, VA 24551
Phone: (804)316-9356
Fax: (804)316-9357

AMX International, Inc.
1420 Spring Hill Rd. , Ste. 600
McLean, VA 22102-3006
Phone: (703)690-4100

Fax: (703)643-1279
Email: amxmail@amxi.com
Website: www.amxi.com

Performance Support Systems
11835 Canon Blvd., Ste. C-101
Newport News, VA 23606
Phone: (757)873-3700
Fax: (757)873-3288
Free: (800)488-6463
Email: sales@2020insight.net
Website: www.2020insight.net

Charles Scott Pugh (Investor)
4101 Pittaway Dr.
Richmond, VA 23235-1022
Phone: (804)560-0979
Fax: (804)560-4670

John C. Randall and Associates, Inc.
PO Box 15127
Richmond, VA 23227
Phone: (804)746-4450
Fax: (804)747-7426

McLeod & Co.
410 1st St.
Roanoke, VA 24011
Phone: (540)342-6911
Fax: (540)344-6367
Website: www.mcleodco.com/

Salzinger & Co., Inc.
8000 Towers Crescent Dr., Ste. 1350
Vienna, VA 22182
Phone: (703)442-5200
Fax: (703)442-5205
Email: info@salzinger.com
Website: www.salzinger.com

The Small Business Counselor
12423 Hedges Run Dr., Ste. 153
Woodbridge, VA 22192
Phone: (703)490-6755
Fax: (703)490-1356

Washington

Burlington Consultants
10900 NE 8th St., Ste. 900
Bellevue, WA 98004
Phone: (425)688-3060
Fax: (425)454-4383
Email:
mmckennirey@burlingtonconsultants.com
Website:
www.burlingtonconsultants.com

Perry L. Smith Consulting
800 Bellevue Way NE, Ste. 400

Bellevue, WA 98004-4208
Phone: (425)462-2072
Fax: (425)462-5638

Independent Automotive Training
Services
PO Box 308
Kirkland, WA 98083
Phone: (425)822-5715
Email: ltunney@autosvccon.com
Website: www.autosvccon.com

Kahle Associate, Inc.
6203 204th Dr. NE
Redmond, WA 98053
Phone: (425)836-8763
Fax: (425)868-3770
Email:
randykahle@kahleassociates.com
Website: www.kahleassociates.com

Dan Collin
2515 E. McGraw St.
Seattle, WA 98112
Phone: (206)325-3762
Email: d.collin@worldnet.att.net
Website: home.att.net/~d.collin

ECG Management Consultants, Inc.
1111 3rd Ave., Ste. 2700
Seattle, WA 98101-3201
Phone: (206)689-2200
Fax: (206)689-2209
Email: ecg@ecgmc.com
Website: www.ecgmc.com

Northwest Trade Adjustment
Assistance Center
900 4th Ave., Ste. 2430
Seattle, WA 98164-1003
Phone: (206)622-2730
Fax: (206)622-1105
Email: nwtaac@sprynet.com

Business Planning Consultants
S. 3510 Ridgeview Dr.
Spokane, WA 99206
Phone: (509)928-0332
Fax: (509)921-0842
Email: bpci@nextdim.com

Wisconsin

O'Brien Consulting
W. 6011 Mariner Hills Trail
Elkhorn, WI 53121
Contact: Frank O'Brien
Phone: (262)742-3999
Fax: (262)742-3980

Email: FrankOBrien@aol.com
Assists in the development of
business, marketing, and/or sales
plans plus feasibility studies.
Experienced in corporate start-up,
new business development, product
launch, corporate finance,
acquisitions, and advertising.

White & Associates, Inc.
5349 Somerset Ln. S
Greenfield, WI 53221
Phone: (414)281-7373
Fax: (414)281-7006
Email: wnaconsult@aol.com

SMALL BUSINESS ADMINISTRATION REGIONAL OFFICES

*This section contains a listing of Small
Business Administration offices arranged
numerically by region. Service areas are
provided. Contact the appropriate office
for a referral to the nearest field office, or
visit the Small Business Administration
online at www.sba.gov.*

Region 1

U.S. Small Business Administration
10 Causeway St.
Boston, MA 02222-1093
Phone: (617)565-8415
Fax: (617)565-8420
Serves Connecticut, Maine,
Massachusetts, New Hampshire,
Rhode Island, and Vermont.

Region 2

U.S. Small Business Administration
26 Federal Plaza, Ste. 3108
New York, NY 10278
Phone: (212)264-1450
Fax: (212)264-0038
Serves New Jersey, New York,
Puerto Rico, and the Virgin Islands.

Region 3

Serves Delaware, the District of
Columbia, Maryland, Pennsylvania,
Virginia, and West Virginia. For the
nearest field office, visit the Small
Business Administration online at
www.sba.gov.

Region 4

U.S. Small Business Administration
233 Peachtree St. NE
Harris Tower 1800
Atlanta, GA 30303
Phone: (404)331-4999
Fax: (404)331-2354
Serves Alabama, Florida, Georgia,
Kentucky, Mississippi, North
Carolina, South Carolina, and
Tennessee.

Region 5

U.S. Small Business Administration
500 W. Madison St., Ste. 1240
Chicago, IL 60661-2511
Phone: (312)353-5000
Fax: (312)353-3426
Serves Illinois, Indiana, Michigan,
Minnesota, Ohio, and Wisconsin.

Region 6

U.S. Small Business Administration
4300 Amon Carter Blvd.
Dallas/Fort Worth, TX 76155
Phone: (817)885-6581
Fax: (817)885-6588
Serves Arkansas, Louisiana, New
Mexico, Oklahoma, and Texas.

Region 7

U.S. Small Business Administration
323 W. 8th St., Ste. 307
Kansas City, MO 64105-1500
Phone: (816)374-6380
Fax: (816)374-6339
Serves Iowa, Kansas, Missouri, and
Nebraska.

Region 8

U.S. Small Business Administration
721 19th St., Ste. 400
Denver, CO 80202
Phone: (303)844-0500
Fax: (303)844-0506
Serves Colorado, Montana, North
Dakota, South Dakota, Utah, and
Wyoming.

Region 9

U.S. Small Business Administration
455 Market St., Ste. 2200
San Francisco, CA 94105
Phone: (415)744-2118
Fax: (415)744-2119

Serves American Samoa, Arizona,
California, Guam, Hawaii, Nevada,
and the Trust Territory of the Pacific
Islands.

Region 10

U.S. Small Business Administration
1200 6th Ave., Ste. 1805
Seattle, WA 98101-1128
Phone: (206)553-5676
Fax: (206)553-2872
Serves Alaska, Idaho, Oregon, and
Washington.

SMALL BUSINESS DEVELOPMENT CENTERS

*This section contains a listing of all Small
Business Development Centers organized
alphabetically by state/U.S. territory
name, then by city, then by agency name.*

Alabama

Auburn University
SBDC
108 College of Business
Auburn, AL 36849-5243
Phone: (334)844-4220
Fax: (334)844-4268
Garry Hannem, Dir.

Alabama Small Business
Development Consortium
Office of the State Director
University of Alabama at
Birmingham
2800 Milan Court, Ste. 124
Medical Towers Bldg.
Birmingham, AL 35294-4410
Phone: (205)943-6750
Fax: (205)943-6752
E-mail: sandefur@uab.edu
www.asbdc.org
John Sandefur, State Director

Alabama Small Business Procurement
System
University Of Alabama at
Birmingham
SBDC
1717 11th Ave. S., Ste. 419
Birmingham, AL 35294-4410
Phone: (205)934-7260
Fax: (205)934-7645
Charles Hobson, Procurement Dir.

University of Alabama at
Birmingham
SBDC
1601 11th Ave. S.
Birmingham, AL 35294-2180
Phone: (205)934-6760
Fax: (205)934-0538
Brenda Walker, Dir.

University of Alabama at
Birmingham
Alabama Small Business
Development Consortium
SBDC
1717 11th Ave. S., Ste. 419
Birmingham, AL 35294-4410
Phone: (205)934-7260
Fax: (205)934-7645
John Sandefur, State Dir.

University of North Alabama
Small Business Development Center
Box 5248, Keller Hall
Florence, AL 35632-0001
Phone: (205)760-4629
Fax: (205)760-4813

Alabama A & M University
University of Alabama at Huntsville
NE Alabama Regional Small
Business Development Center
PO Box 168
225 Church St., NW
Huntsville, AL 35804-0168
Phone: (205)535-2061
Fax: (205)535-2050
Jeff Thompson, Dir.

Jacksonville State University
Small Business Development Center
114 Merrill Hall
700 Pelham Rd. N.
Jacksonville, AL 36265
Phone: (205)782-5271
Fax: (205)782-5179
Pat Shaddix, Dir.

University of West Alabama
SBDC
Station 35
Livingston, AL 35470
Phone: (205)652-3665
Fax: (205)652-3516
Paul Garner, Dir.

University of South Alabama
Small Business Development Center
College of Business, Rm. 8
Mobile, AL 36688

Phone: (334)460-6004
Fax: (334)460-6246

Alabama State University
SBDC
915 S. Jackson St.
Montgomery, AL 36104-5714
Phone: (334)229-4138
Fax: (334)269-1102
Lorenza G. Patrick, Dir.

Troy State University
Small Business Development Center
Bibb Graves, Rm. 102
Troy, AL 36082-0001
Phone: (205)670-3771
Fax: (205)670-3636
Janet W. Kervin, Dir.

Alabama International Trade Center
University of Alabama
SBDC
Bidgood Hall, Rm. 201
PO Box 870396
Tuscaloosa, AL 35487-0396
Phone: (205)348-7621
Fax: (205)348-6974
E-mail: aitc@aitc.cba.ua.edu
Brian Davis, Dir.

University of Alabama
Alabama International Trade Center
Small Business Development Center
Bidgood Hall, Rm. 250
Box 870397
Tuscaloosa, AL 35487-0396
Phone: (205)348-7011
Fax: (205)348-9644
Paavo Hanninen, Dir.

Alaska

University of Alaska (Anchorage)
Small Business Development Center
430 W. 7th Ave., Ste. 110
Anchorage, AK 99501
Phone: (907)274-7232
Free: (800)478-7232
Fax: (907)274-9524
E-mail: anjaf@uaa.alaska.edu
Jan Fredricks, Director

University of Alaska (Fairbanks)
Small Business Development Center
510 Second Ave., Ste. 101
Fairbanks, AK 99701
Phone: (907)474-6700
Fax: (907)474-1139
Billie Ray Allen, Dir.

University of Alaska (Juneau)
Small Business Development Center
612 W. Willoughby Ave., Ste. A
Juneau, AK 99801
Phone: (907)463-1732
Fax: (907)463-3929
Norma Strickland, Acting Dir.

Kenai Peninsula Small Business
Development Center
PO Box 3029
Kenai, AK 99611-3029
Phone: (907)283-3335
Fax: (907)283-3913
Mark Gregory

University of Alaska (Matanuska-
Susitna)
Small Business Development Center
201 N. Lucile St., Ste. 2-A
Wasilla, AK 99654
Phone: (907)373-7232
Fax: (907)373-7234
Timothy Sullivan, Dir.

Arizona

Central Arizona College
Pinal County Small Business
Development Center
8470 N. Overfield Rd.
Coolidge, AZ 85228
Phone: (520)426-4341
Fax: (520)426-4363
Carol Giordano, Dir.

Coconino County Community
College
Small Business Development Center
3000 N. 4th St., Ste. 25
Flagstaff, AZ 86004
Phone: (520)526-5072
Fax: (520)526-8693
Mike Lainoff, Dir.

Northland Pioneer College
Small Business Development Center
PO Box 610
Holbrook, AZ 86025
Phone: (520)537-2976
Fax: (520)524-2227
Mark Engle, Dir.

Mohave Community College
Small Business Development Center
1971 Jagerson Ave.
Kingman, AZ 86401
Phone: (520)757-0894
Fax: (520)757-0836
Kathy McGehee, Dir.

Yavapai College
Small Business Development Center
Elks Building
117 E. Gurley St., Ste. 206
Prescott, AZ 86301
Phone: (520)778-3088
Fax: (520)778-3109
Richard Senopole, Director

Cochise College
Small Business Development Center
901 N. Colombo, Rm. 308
Sierra Vista, AZ 85635
Phone: (5200515-5478
Fax: (520)515-5437
E-mail: sbdc@trom.cochise.cc.az.us
Shelia Devoe Heidman, Dir.

Arizona Small Business Development
Center Network
Maricopa County Community
College
SBDC
2411 W 14th St., Ste. 132
Tempe, AZ 85281
Phone: (480)731-8722
Fax: (480)731-8729
www.dist.maricopa.edu/sbdc
Michael York, State Director

Arizona Small Business Development
Center Network
2411 W. 14th St., Ste. 132
Tempe, AZ 85281
Phone: (602)731-8720
Fax: (602)731-8729
E-mail: york@maricopa.bitnet
Michael York, State Dir.

Maricopa Community Colleges
Arizona Small Business Development
Center Network
2411 W. 14th St., Ste. 132
Tempe, AZ 85281
Phone: (602)731-8720
Fax: (602)731-8729
Michael York, Dir.

Eastern Arizona College
SBDC
622 College Ave.
Thatcher, AZ 85552-0769
Phone: (520)428-8590
Fax: (520)428-8591
Frank Granberg, Dir.

Eastern Arizona College
Small Business Development Center
622 College Ave.

Thatcher, AZ 85552-0769
Phone: (520)428-8590
Fax: (520)428-8462
Greg Roers, Dir.

Pima Community College
Small Business Development and
Training Center
4905-A E. Broadway Blvd., Ste. 101
Tucson, AZ 85709-1260
Phone: (520)206-4906
Fax: (520)206-4585
Linda Andrews, Dir.

Arizona Western College
Small Business Development Center
Century Plz., No. 152
281 W. 24th St.
Yuma, AZ 85364
Phone: (520)341-1650
Fax: (520)726-2636
John Lundin, Dir.

Arkansas

Henderson State University
Small Business Development Center
1100 Henderson St.
PO Box 7624
Arkadelphia, AR 71923
Phone: (870)230-5224
Fax: (870)230-5236
Jeff Doose, Dir.

Genesis Technology Incubator
SBDC Satellite Office
University of Arkansas - Engineering
Research Center
Fayetteville, AR 72701-1201
Phone: (501)575-7473
Fax: (501)575-7446
Bob Penquite, Business Consultant

University of Arkansas at Fayetteville
Small Business Development Center
Business Administration Bldg., Ste.
106
Fayetteville, AR 72701
Phone: (501)575-5148
Fax: (501)575-4013
Ms. Jimmie Wilkins, Dir.

Small Business Development Center
1109 S. 16th St.
PO Box 2067
Ft. Smith, AR 72901
Phone: (501)785-1376
Fax: (501)785-1964
Vonelle Vanzant, Business Consultant

University of Arkansas at Little Rock,
Regional Office (Fort Smith)
Small Business Development Center
1109 S. 16th St.
PO Box 2067
Ft. Smith, AR 72901
Phone: (501)785-1376
Fax: (501)785-1964
Byron Branch, Business Specialist

University of Arkansas at Little Rock,
Regional Office (Harrison)
Small Business Development Center
818 Hwy. 62-65-412 N
PO Box 190
Harrison, AR 72601
Phone: (870)741-8009
Fax: (870)741-1905
Bob Penquite, Business Consultant

University of Arkansas at Little Rock,
Regional Office (Hot Springs)
Small Business Development Center
835 Central Ave., Box 402-D
Hot Springs, AR 71901
Phone: (501)624-5448
Fax: (501)624-6632
Richard Evans, Business Consultant

Arkansas State University
Small Business Development Center
College of Business
Drawer 2650
Jonesboro, AR 72467
Phone: (870)972-3517
Fax: (501)972-3868
Herb Lawrence, Dir.

University of Arkansas at Little Rock
Small Business Development Center
Little Rock Technology Center Bldg.
100 S. Main, Ste. 401
Little Rock, AR 72201
Phone: (501)324-9043
Free: (800)862-2040
Fax: (501)324-9049
Website: www.ualr.edu/~sbdcdept/
Janet Nye, State Director

University of Arkansas at Little Rock
SBDC
Little Rock Technology Center Bldg.
100 S. Main St., Ste. 401
Little Rock, AR 72201
Phone: (501)324-9043
Fax: (501)324-9049
Janet Nye, State Dir.

University of Arkansas at Little Rock
SBDC

100 S. Main, Ste. 401
Little Rock, AR 72201
Phone: (501)324-9043
Fax: (501)324-9049
John Harrison, Business Consultant

University of Arkansas at Little Rock,
Regional Office (Magnolia)
Small Business Development Center
600 Bessie
PO Box 767
Magnolia, AR 71753
Phone: (870)234-4030
Fax: (870)234-0135
Mr. Lairie Kincaid, Business
Consultant

University of Arkansas at Little Rock,
Regional Office (Pine Bluff)
Small Business Development Center
The Enterprise Center III
400 Main, Ste. 117
Pine Bluff, AR 71601
Phone: (870)536-0654
Fax: (870)536-7713
Russell Barker, Business Consultant

University of Arkansas at Little Rock,
Regional Office (Stuttgart)
Small Business Development Center
301 S. Grand, Ste. 101
PO Box 289
Stuttgart, AR 72160
Phone: (870)673-8707
Fax: (870)673-8707
Larry Lefler, Business Consultant

Mid-South Community College
SBDC
2000 W. Broadway
PO Box 2067
West Memphis, AR 72303-2067
Phone: (870)733-6767

California

Central Coast Small Business
Development Center
6500 Soquel Dr.
Aptos, CA 95003
Phone: (408)479-6136
Fax: (408)479-6166
Teresa Thomae, Dir.

Sierra College Small Business
Development Center
560 Wall St., Ste. J
Auburn, CA 95603
Phone: (916)885-5488

Fax: (916)823-2831
Mary Wollesen, Dir.

Weill Institute Small Business
Development Center
1706 Chester Ave., Ste. 200
Bakersfield, CA 93301
Phone: (805)322-5881
Fax: (805)322-5663
Jeffrey Johnson, Dir.

Butte College
Small Business Development Center
260 Cohasset Rd., Ste. A
Chico, CA 95926
Phone: (916)895-9017
Fax: (916)895-9099
Kay Zimmerlee, Dir.

Southwestern College
Small Business Development and
International Trade Center
900 Otay Lakes Rd., Bldg. 1600
Chula Vista, CA 91910
Phone: (619)482-6393
Fax: (619)482-6402
Mary Wylie, Dir.

Contra Costa SBDC
2425 Bisso Ln., Ste. 200
Concord, CA 94520
Phone: (510)646-5377
Fax: (510)646-5299
Debra Longwood, Dir.

North Coast Small Business
Development Center
207 Price Mall, Ste. 500
Crescent City, CA 95531
Phone: (707)464-2168
Fax: (707)465-6008
Fran Clark, Dir.

Imperial Valley Satellite SBDC
Town & Country Shopping Center
Town & Country Shopping Center
301 N. Imperial Ave., Ste. B
El Centro, CA 92243
Phone: (619)312-9800
Fax: (619)312-9838
Debbie Trujillo, Satellite Mgr.

Export SBDC/El Monte Outreach
Center
10501 Valley Blvd., Ste. 106
El Monte, CA 91731
Phone: (818)459-4111
Fax: (818)443-0463
Charles Blythe, Manager

North Coast
Small Business Development Center
520 E St.
Eureka, CA 95501
Phone: (707)445-9720
Fax: (707)445-9652
Duff Heuttner, Bus. Counselor

Central California
Small Business Development Center
3419 W. Shaw Ave., Ste. 102
Fresno, CA 93711
Phone: (209)275-1223
Fax: (209)275-1499
Dennis Winans, Dir.

Gavilan College Small Business
Development Center
7436 Monterey St.
Gilroy, CA 95020
Phone: (408)847-0373
Fax: (408)847-0393
Peter Graff, Dir.

Accelerate Technology Assistance
Small Business Development Center
4199 Campus Dr.
University Towers, Ste. 240
Irvine, CA 92612-4688
Phone: (714)509-2990
Fax: (714)509-2997
Tiffany Haugen, Dir.

Amador SBDC
222 N. Hwy. 49
PO Box 1077
Jackson, CA 95642
Phone: (209)223-0351
Fax: (209)223-5237
Ron Mittelbrunn, Mgr.

Greater San Diego Chamber of
Commerce
Small Business Development Center
4275 Executive Sq., Ste. 920
La Jolla, CA 92037
Phone: (619)453-9388
Fax: (619)450-1997
Hal Lefkowitz, Dir.

Yuba College SBDC
PO Box 1566
15145 Lakeshore Dr.
PO Box 4550
Lakeport, CA 95453
Phone: (707)263-0330
Fax: (707)263-8516
George McQueen, Dir.

East Los Angeles SBDC
5161 East Pomona Blvd., Ste. 212
Los Angeles, CA 90022
Phone: (213)262-9797
Fax: (213)262-2704

Export Small Business Development
Center of Southern California
110 E. 9th, Ste. A669
Los Angeles, CA 90079
Phone: (213)892-1111
Fax: (213)892-8232
Gladys Moreau, Dir.

South Central LA/Satellite
SBDC
3650 Martin Luther King Blvd., Ste.
246
Los Angeles, CA 90008
Phone: (213)290-2832
Fax: (213)290-7191
Cope Norcross, Satellite Mgr.

Alpine SBDC
PO Box 265
3 Webster St.
Markleeville, CA 96120
Phone: (916)694-2475
Fax: (916)694-2478

Yuba/Sutter Satellite
SBDC
10th and E St.
PO Box 262
Marysville, CA 95901
Phone: (916)749-0153
Fax: (916)749-0155
Sandra Brown-Abernathy, Dir.

Valley Sierra SBDC
Merced Satellite
1632 N St.
Merced, CA 95340
Phone: (209)725-3800
Fax: (209)383-4959
Nick Starianoudakis, Satellite Mgr.

Valley Sierra Small Business
Development Center
1012 11th St., Ste. 300
Modesto, CA 95354
Phone: (209)521-6177
Fax: (209)521-9373
Kelly Bearden, Dir.

Napa Valley College Small Business
Development Center
1556 First St., Ste. 103
Napa, CA 94559

Phone: (707)253-3210
Fax: (707)253-3068
Chuck Eason, Dir.

Inland Empire Business Incubator
SBDC
155 S. Memorial Dr.
Norton Air Force Base, CA 92509
Phone: (909)382-0065
Fax: (909)382-8543
Chuck Eason, Incubator Mgr.

East Bay Small Business
Development Center
519 17th. St., Ste. 210
Oakland, CA 94612
Phone: (510)893-4114
Fax: (510)893-5532
Napoleon Britt, Dir.

International Trade Office
SBDC
3282 E. Guasti Rd., Ste. 100
Ontario, CA 91761
Phone: (909)390-8071
Fax: (909)390-8077
John Hernandez, Trade Manager

Coachella Valley SBDC
Palm Springs Satellite Center
501 S. Palm Canyon Dr., Ste. 222
Palm Springs, CA 92264
Phone: (619)864-1311
Fax: (619)864-1319
Brad Mix, Satellite Mgr.

Pasadena Satellite
SBDC
2061 N. Los Robles, Ste. 106
Pasadena, CA 91104
Phone: (818)398-9031
Fax: (818)398-3059
David Ryal, Satellite Mgr.

Pico Rivera SBDC
9058 E. Washington Blvd.
Pico Rivera, CA 90660
Phone: (310)942-9965
Fax: (310)942-9745
Beverly Taylor, Satellite Mgr.

Eastern Los Angeles County Small
Business Development Center
375 S. Main St., Ste. 101
Pomona, CA 91766
Phone: (909)629-2247
Fax: (909)629-8310
Toni Valdez, Dir.

Pomona SBDC
375 S. Main St., Ste. 101
Pomona, CA 91766
Phone: (909)629-2247
Fax: (909)629-8310
Paul Hischar, Satellite Manager

Cascade Small Business Development
Center
737 Auditorium Dr., Ste. A
Redding, CA 96001
Phone: (916)247-8100
Fax: (916)241-1712
Carole Enmark, Dir.

Inland Empire Small Business
Development Center
1157 Spruce St.
Riverside, CA 92507
Phone: (909)781-2345
Free: (800)750-2353
Fax: (909)781-2353
Teri Ooms, Dir.

California Trade and Commerce
Agency
California SBDC
801 K St., Ste. 1700
Sacramento, CA 95814
Phone: (916)324-5068
Fax: (916)322-5084
Kim Neri, State Dir.

Greater Sacramento SBDC
1410 Ethan Way
Sacramento, CA 95825
Phone: (916)563-3210
Fax: (916)563-3266
Cynthia Steimle, Director

California Small Business
Development Center
California Trade and Commerce
Agency
801 K St., Ste 1700
Sacramento, CA 95814
Phone: (916)324-5068
Free: (800)303-6600
Fax: (916)322-5084
commerce.ca.gov/business/small/
starting/sb_sbdcl.html
Kim Neri, State Director

Calaveras SBDC
PO Box 431
3 N. Main St.
San Andreas, CA 95249
Phone: (209)754-1834
Fax: (209)754-4107

San Francisco SBDC
711 Van Ness, Ste. 305
San Francisco, CA 94102
Phone: (415)561-1890
Fax: (415)561-1894
Tim Sprinkles, Director

Orange County Small Business
Development Center
901 E. Santa Ana Blvd., Ste. 101
Santa Ana, CA 92701
Phone: (714)647-1172
Fax: (714)835-9008
Gregory Kishel, Dir.

Southwest Los Angeles County
Westside Satellite
SBDC
3233 Donald Douglas Loop S., Ste. C
Santa Monica, CA 90405
Phone: (310)398-8883
Fax: (310)398-3024
Sue Hunter, Admin. Asst.

Redwood Empire Small Business
Development Center
520 Mendocino Ave., Ste. 210
Santa Rosa, CA 95401
Phone: (707)524-1770
Fax: (707)524-1772
Charles Robbins, Dir.

San Joaquin Delta College Small
Business Development Center
445 N. San Joaquin, 2nd Fl.
Stockton, CA 95202
Phone: (209)474-5089
Fax: (209)474-5605
Gillian Murphy, Dir.

Silicon Valley SBDC
298 S. Sunnyvale Ave., Ste. 204
Sunnyvale, CA 94086
Phone: (408)736-0680
Fax: (408)736-0679
Eliza Minor, Director

Southwest Los Angeles County Small
Business Development Center
21221 Western Ave., Ste. 110
Torrance, CA 90501
Phone: (310)787-6466
Fax: (310)782-8607
Susan Hunter, Dir.

West Company SBDC
367 N. State St., Ste. 208
Ukiah, CA 95482
Phone: (707)468-3553

Fax: (707)468-3555
Sheilah Rogers, Director

North Los Angeles Small Business
Development Center
4717 Van Nuys Blvd., Ste. 201
Van Nuys, CA 91403-2100
Phone: (818)907-9922
Fax: (818)907-9890
Wilma Berglund, Dir.

Export SBDC Satellite Center
5700 Ralston St., Ste. 310
Ventura, CA 93003
Phone: (805)658-2688
Fax: (805)658-2252
Heather Wicka, Manager

Gold Coast SBDC
5700 Ralston St., Ste. 310
Ventura, CA 93003
Phone: (805)658-2688
Fax: (805)658-2252
Joe Higgins, Satellite Mgr.

High Desert SBDC
Victorville Satellite Center
15490 Civic Dr., Ste. 102
Victorville, CA 92392
Phone: (619)951-1592
Fax: (619)951-8929
Janice Harbaugh, Business Consultant

Central California /Visalia Satellite
SBDC
430 W. Caldwell Ave., Ste. D
Visalia, CA 93277
Phone: (209)625-3051
Fax: (209)625-3053
Randy Mason, Satellite Mgr.

Colorado

Adams State College
Small Business Development Center
School of Business, Rm. 105
Alamosa, CO 81102
Phone: (719)587-7372
Fax: (719)587-7603
Mary Hoffman, Dir.

Community College of Aurora
Small Business Development Center
9905 E. Colfax
Aurora, CO 80010-2119
Phone: (303)341-4849
Fax: (303)361-2953
E-mail: asbdc@henge.com
Randy Johnson, Dir.

Boulder Chamber of Commerce
Small Business Development Center
2440 Pearl St.
Boulder, CO 80302
Phone: (303)442-1475
Fax: (303)938-8837
Marilynn Force, Dir.

Pueblo Community College (Canon
City)
Small Business Development Center
3080 Main St.
Canon City, CO 81212
Phone: (719)275-5335
Fax: (719)275-4400
Elwin Boody, Dir.

Pikes Peak Community College
Small Business Development Center
Colorado Springs Chamber of
Commerce
CITTI Bldg.
1420 Austin Bluff Pkwy.
Colorado Springs, CO 80933
Phone: (719)592-1894
Fax: (719)533-0545
E-mail: sbdc@mail.uccs.edu
Iris Clark, Dir.

Colorado Northwestern Community
College
Small Business Development Center
50 College Dr.
Craig, CO 81625
Phone: (970)824-7078
Fax: (970)824-1134
Ken Farmer, Dir.

Delta Montrose Vocational School
Small Business Development Center
1765 US Hwy. 50
Delta, CO 81416
Phone: (970)874-8772
Free: (888)234-7232
Fax: (970)874-8796
Bob Marshall, Dir.

Colorado Office of Business
Development
Small Business Development Center
1625 Broadway, Ste. 1710
Denver, CO 80202
Phone: (303)892-3840
Fax: (303)892-3848
E-mail: Mary.Madison@state.co.us
www.state.co.us/gov_dir/obd/
sbdc.htm
Ms. Mary Madison, Director

Community College of Denver
Greater Denver Chamber of
Commerce
Small Business Development Center
1445 Market St.
Denver, CO 80202
Phone: (303)620-8076
Fax: (303)534-3200
Tamela Lee, Dir.

Office of Business Development
Colorado SBDC
1625 Broadway, Ste. 1710
Denver, CO 80202
Phone: (303)892-3809
Free: (800)333-7798
Fax: (303)892-3848
Lee Ortiz, State Dir.

Fort Lewis College
Small Business Development Center
136-G Hesperus Hall
Durango, CO 81301-3999
Phone: (970)247-7009
Fax: (970)247-7623
Jim Reser, Dir.

Front Range Community College (Ft.
Collins)
Small Business Development Center
125 S. Howes, Ste. 105
Ft. Collins, CO 80521
Phone: (970)498-9295
Fax: (970)204-0385
Frank Pryor, Dir.

Morgan Community College (Ft.
Morgan)
Small Business Development Center
300 Main St.
Ft. Morgan, CO 80701
Phone: (970)867-3351
Fax: (970)867-3352
Dan Simon, Dir.

Colorado Mountain College
(Glenwood Springs)
Small Business Development Center
831 Grand Ave.
Glenwood Springs, CO 81601
Phone: (970)928-0120
Free: (800)621-1647
Fax: (970)947-9324
Alisa Zimmerman, Dir.

Small Business Development Center
1726 Cole Blvd., Bldg. 22, Ste. 310
Golden, CO 80401
Phone: (303)277-1840

Fax: (303)277-1899
Jayne Reiter, Dir.

Mesa State College
Small Business Development Center
304 W. Main St.
Grand Junction, CO 81505-1606
Phone: (970)243-5242
Fax: (970)241-0771
Julie Morey, Dir.

Aims Community College
Greeley/Weld Chamber of Commerce
Small Business Development Center
902 7th Ave.
Greeley, CO 80631
Phone: (970)352-3661
Fax: (970)352-3572
Ron Anderson, Dir.

Red Rocks Community College Small
Business Development Center
777 S. Wadsworth Blvd., Ste. 254
Bldg. 4
Lakewood, CO 80226
Phone: (303)987-0710
Fax: (303)987-1331
Jayne Reiter, Acting Dir.

Lamar Community College
Small Business Development Center
2400 S. Main
Lamar, CO 81052
Phone: (719)336-8141
Fax: (719)336-2448
Dan Minor, Dir.

Small Business Development Center
Arapahoe Community College
South Metro Chamber of Commerce
7901 S. Park Plz., Ste. 110
Littleton, CO 80120
Phone: (303)795-5855
Fax: (303)795-7520
Selma Kristel, Dir.

Pueblo Community College Small
Business Development Center
900 W. Orman Ave.
Pueblo, CO 81004
Phone: (719)549-3224
Fax: (719)549-3338
Rita Friberg, Dir.

Morgan Community College
(Stratton)
Small Business Development Center
PO Box 28
Stratton, CO 80836

Phone: (719)348-5596
Fax: (719)348-5887
Roni Carr, Dir.

Trinidad State Junior College
Small Business Development Center
136 W. Main St.
Davis Bldg.
Trinidad, CO 81082
Phone: (719)846-5645
Fax: (719)846-4550
Dennis O'Connor, Dir.

Front Range Community College
(Westminster)
Small Business Development Center
3645 W. 112th Ave.
Westminster, CO 80030
Phone: (303)460-1032
Fax: (303)469-7143
Leo Giles, Dir.

Connecticut

Bridgeport Regional Business
Council
Small Business Development Center
10 Middle St., 14th Fl.
Bridgeport, CT 06604-4229
Phone: (203)330-4813
Fax: (203)366-0105
Juan Scott, Dir.

Quinebaug Valley Community
Technical College
Small Business Development Center
742 Upper Maple St.
Danielson, CT 06239-1440
Phone: (860)774-1133
Fax: (860)774-7768
Roger Doty, Dir.

University of Connecticut (Groton)
Small Business Development Center
Administration Bldg., Rm. 300
1084 Shennecossett Rd.
Groton, CT 06340-6097
Phone: (860)405-9009
Fax: (860)405-9041
Louise Kahler, Dir.

Middlesex County Chamber of
Commerce
SBDC
393 Main St.
Middletown, CT 06457
Phone: (860)344-2158
Fax: (860)346-1043
John Serignese

Greater New Haven Chamber of
Commerce
Small Business Development Center
195 Church St.
New Haven, CT 06510-2009
Phone: (203)782-4390
Fax: (203)787-6730
Pete Riveram, Regional Dir.

Southwestern Area Commerce and
Industry Association (SACIA)
Small Business Development Center
1 Landmark Sq., Ste. 230
Stamford, CT 06901
Phone: (203)359-3220
Fax: (203)967-8294
Harvey Blomberg, Dir.

University of Connecticut
Small Business Development Center
368 Fairfield Rd., U-41, Rm. 422
Storrs, CT 06269-5094
Phone: (860)486-4135
Fax: (860)486-1576
E-mail:
statedirector@ct.sbdc.uconn.edu
Website: www.sbdc.uconn.edu
Dennis Gruell, State Director

University of Connecticut
School of Business Administration
Connecticut SBDC
2 Bourn Place, U-94
Storrs, CT 06269
Phone: (860)486-4135
Fax: (860)486-1576
E-mail: oconnor@ct.sbdc.uconn.edu
Dennis Gruel, State Dir.

Naugatuck Valley Development
Center
Small Business Development Center
100 Grand St., 3rd Fl.
Waterbury, CT 06702
Phone: (203)757-8937
Fax: (203)757-8937
Ilene Oppenheim, Dir.

University of Connecticut (Greater
Hartford Campus)
Small Business Development Center
1800 Asylum Ave.
West Hartford, CT 06117
Phone: (860)570-9107
Fax: (860)570-9107
Dennis Gruel, Dir.

Eastern Connecticut State University
Small Business Development Center

83 Windham St.
Williamantic, CT 06226-2295
Phone: (860)465-5349
Fax: (860)465-5143
Richard Cheney, Dir.

Delaware

Delaware State University
School of Business Economics
SBDC
1200 N. Dupont Hwy.
Dover, DE 19901
Phone: (302)678-1555
Fax: (302)739-2333
Jim Crisfield, Director

Delaware Technical and Community
College
SBDC
Industrial Training Bldg.
PO Box 610
Georgetown, DE 19947
Phone: (302)856-1555
Fax: (302)856-5779
William F. Pfaff, Dir.

University of Delaware
Delaware SBDC
Purnell Hall, Ste. 005
Newark, DE 19716-2711
Phone: (302)831-1555
Fax: (302)831-1423
Clinton Tymes, State Dir.

University of Delaware
Delaware Small Business
Development Center Network
102 MBNA America Hall
Newark, DE 19716-2711
Phone: (302)831-1555
Free: (800)222-2279
Fax: (302)831-1423
Website: www.be.udel.edu/sbdc/
Clinton Tymes, State Director

Small Business Resource &
Information Center
SBDC
1318 N. Market St.
Wilmington, DE 19801
Phone: (302)571-1555
Fax: (302)571-5222
Barbara Necarsulmer, Mgr.

District of Columbia

Friendship House/Southeastern
University

SBDC
921 Pennsylvania Ave., SE
Washington, DC 20003
Phone: (202)547-7933
Fax: (202)806-1777
Elise Ashby, Dir.

George Washington University
East of the River Community
Development Corp.
SBDC
3101 MLK Jr. Ave., SE, 3rd Fl.
Washington, DC 20032
Phone: (202)561-4975
Howard Johnson, Accounting
Specialist

Howard University
SBDC
Satellite Location
2600 6th St., NW, Rm. 125
Washington, DC 20059
Phone: (202)806-1550
Fax: (202)806-1777
Terry Strong, Acting Regional Dir.

Howard University
George Washington Small Business
Legal Clinic
SBDC
2000 G St., NW, Ste. 200
Washington, DC 20052
Phone: (202)994-7463
Jose Hernandez, Counselor

Howard University
Office of Latino Affairs
SBDC
2000 14th St., NW, 2nd Fl.
Washington, DC 20009
Phone: (202)939-3018
Fax: (202)994-4946
Jose Hernandez, Gov. Procurement
Specialist

Howard University
Small Business Development Center
2600 6th St., NW
Rm. 128
Washington, DC 20059
Phone: (202)806-1550
Fax: (202)806-1777
Vicki Johnson, Director

Marshall Heights Community
Development Organization
SBDC
3917 Minnesota Ave., NE
Washington, DC 20019

Phone: (202)396-1200
Terry Strong, Financing Specialist

Washington District Office
Business Information Center
SBDC
1110 Vermont Ave., NW, 9th Fl.
Washington, DC 20005
Phone: (202)737-0120
Fax: (202)737-0476
Johnetta Hardy, Marketing Specialist

Florida

Central Florida Development Council
Small Business Development Center
600 N. Broadway, Ste. 300
Bartow, FL 33830
Phone: (941)534-4370
Fax: (941)533-1247
Marcela Stanislaus, Vice President

Florida Atlantic University (Boca
Raton)
Small Business Development Center
777 Glades Rd.
Bldg. T9
Boca Raton, FL 33431
Phone: (561)362-5620
Fax: (561)362-5623
Nancy Young, Dir.

UCF Brevard Campus
Small Business Development Center
1519 Clearlake Rd.
Cocoa, FL 32922
Phone: (407)951-1060

Dania Small Business Development
Center
46 SW 1st Ave.
Dania, FL 33304-3607
Phone: (954)987-0100
Fax: (954)987-0106
William Healy, Regional Mgr.

Daytona Beach Community College
Florida Regional SBDC
1200 W. International Speedway
Blvd.
Daytona Beach, FL 32114
Phone: (904)947-5463
Fax: (904)258-3846
Brenda Thomas-Ramos, Dir.

Florida Atlantic University
Commercial Campus
Small Business Development Center
1515 W. Commercial Blvd., Rm. 11

Ft. Lauderdale, FL 33309
Phone: (954)771-6520
Fax: (954)351-4120
Marty Zients, Mgr.

Minority Business Development
Center
SBDC
5950 West Oakland Park Blvd., Ste.
307
Ft. Lauderdale, FL 33313
Phone: (954)485-5333
Fax: (954)485-2514

Edison Community College
Small Business Development Center
8099 College Pkwy. SW
Ft. Myers, FL 33919
Phone: (941)489-9200
Fax: (941)489-9051
Dan Regelski, Management
Consultant

Florida Gulf Coast University
Small Business Development Center
Small Business Development Center
17595 S. Tamiami Trail, Ste. 200
Midway Ctr.
Ft. Myers, FL 33908-4500
Phone: (941)948-1820
Fax: (941)948-1814
Dan Regleski, Management
Consultant

Indian River Community College
Small Business Development Center
3209 Virginia Ave., Rm. 114
Ft. Pierce, FL 34981-5599
Phone: (561)462-4756
Fax: (561)462-4796
Marsha Thompson, Dir.

Okaloosa-Walton Community
College
SBDC
1170 Martin Luther King, Jr. Blvd.
Ft. Walton Beach, FL 32547
Phone: (850)863-6543
Fax: (850)863-6564
Jane Briere, Mgr.

University of North Florida
(Gainesville)
Small Business Development Center
505 NW 2nd Ave., Ste. D
PO Box 2518
Gainesville, FL 32602-2518
Phone: (352)377-5621
Fax: (352)372-0288
Lalla Sheehy, Program Mgr.

University of North Florida
(Jacksonville)
Small Business Development Center
College of Business
Honors Hall, Rm. 2451
4567 St. John's Bluff Rd. S
Jacksonville, FL 32224
Phone: (904)620-2476
Fax: (904)620-2567
E-mail: smallbiz@unf.edu
Lowell Salter, Regional Dir.

Gulf Coast Community College
SBDC
2500 Minnesota Ave.
Lynn Haven, FL 32444
Phone: (850)271-1108
Fax: (850)271-1109
Doug Davis, Dir.

Brevard Community College
(Melbourne)
Small Business Development Center
3865 N. Wickham Rd.
Melbourne, FL 32935
Phone: (407)632-1111
Fax: (407)634-3721
Victoria Peak, Program Coordinator

Florida International University
Small Business Development Center
University Park
CEAS-2620
Miami, FL 33199
Phone: (305)348-2272
Fax: (305)348-2965
Marvin Nesbit, Dir.

Florida International University
(North Miami Campus)
Small Business Development Center
Academic Bldg. No. 1, Rm. 350
NE 151 and Biscayne Blvd.
Miami, FL 33181
Phone: (305)919-5790
Fax: (305)919-5792
Roy Jarrett, Regional Mgr.

Miami Dade Community College
Small Business Development Center
6300 NW 7th Ave.
Miami, FL 33150
Phone: (305)237-1906
Fax: (305)237-1908
Frederic Bonneau, Regional Mgr.

Ocala Small Business Development
Center
110 E. Silver Springs Blvd.

PO Box 1210
Ocala, FL 34470-6613
Phone: (352)622-8763
Fax: (352)651-1031
E-mail: sbdcoca@mercury.net
Philip Geist, Program Dir.

University of Central Florida
Small Business Development Center
College of Business Administration,
Ste. 309
PO Box 161530
Orlando, FL 32816-1530
Phone: (407)823-5554
Fax: (407)823-3073
Al Polfer, Dir.

Palm Beach Gardens
Florida Atlantic University
SBDC
Northrop Center
3970 RCA Blvd., Ste. 7323
Palm Beach Gardens, FL 33410
Phone: (407)691-8550
Fax: (407)692-8502
Steve Windhaus, Regional Mgr.

Florida Small Business Development
Center
University of West Florida
UWF Downtown Center
19 W. Garden St., Ste. 300
Pensacola, FL 32501
Phone: (904)444-2060
Free: (800)644-SBDC
Fax: (904)444-2070
Website: www.sbdc.uwf.edu
Jerry Cartwright, State Director

Procurement Technical Assistance
Program
University of West Florida
Small Business Development Center
19 W. Garden St., Ste. 302
Pensacola, FL 32501
Phone: (850)595-5480
Fax: (850)595-5487
Martha Cobb, Dir.

University of West Florida
Florida SBDC Network
19 West Garden St., Ste. 300
Pensacola, FL 32501
Phone: (850)595-6060
Fax: (850)595-6070
E-mail: fsbdc@uwf.edu
Jerry Cartwright, State Dir.

Seminole Community College
SBDC

100 Weldon Blvd.
Sanford, FL 32773
Phone: (407)328-4722
Fax: (407)330-4489
Wayne Hardy, Regional Mgr.

Florida Agricultural and Mechanical
University
Small Business Development Center
1157 E. Tennessee St.
Tallahassee, FL 32308
Phone: (904)599-3407
Fax: (904)561-2049
Patricia McGowan, Dir.

University of South Florida—CBA
SBDC Special Services
4202 E. Fowler Ave., BSN 3403
1111 N. Westshore Dr., Annex B
Tampa, FL 33620
Phone: (813)974-4371
Fax: (813)974-5020
Dick Hardesty, Procurement Mgr.

University of South Florida (Tampa)
Small Business Development Center
1111 N. Westshore Dr., Annex B, Ste.
101-B
4202 E. Fowler Ave., BSN 3403
Tampa, FL 33607
Phone: (813)554-2341
Free: (800)733-7232
Fax: (813)554-2356
Irene Hurst, Dir.

Georgia

University of Georgia
Small Business Development Center
230 S. Jackson St., Ste. 333
Albany, GA 31701-2885
Phone: (912)430-4303
Fax: (912)430-3933
E-mail: sbdcalb@uga.cc.uga.edu
Sue Ford, Asst. District Dir.

NE Georgia District
SBDC
1180 E. Broad St.
Athens, GA 30602-5412
Phone: (706)542-7436
Fax: (706)542-6823
Gayle Rosenthal, Mgr.

NW Georgia District
University of Georgia
SBDC
1180 E. Broad St.
Athens, GA 30602-5412

Phone: (706)542-6756
Fax: (706)542-6776

University of Georgia
Chicopee Complex
Georgia SBDC
1180 E. Broad St.
Athens, GA 30602-5412
Phone: (706)542-6762
Fax: (706)542-6776
E-mail: sbdcath@uga.cc.uga.edu
Hank Logan, State Dir.

University of Georgia
Small Business Development Center
Chicopee Complex
1180 E. Broad St.
Athens, GA 30602-5412
Phone: (706)542-6762
Fax: (706)542-6776
E-mail: sbdcdir@uga.cc.uga.edu
Website: www.sbdc.uga.edu
Hank Logan, State Director

Georgia State University
Small Business Development Center
University Plz.
Box 874
Atlanta, GA 30303-3083
Phone: (404)651-3550
Fax: (404)651-1035
E-mail: sbdcatl@uga.cc.uga.edu
Lee Quarterman, Area Dir.

Morris Brown College
Small Business Development Center
643 Martin Luther King, Jr., Dr. NW
Atlanta, GA 30314
Phone: (404)220-0205
Fax: (404)688-5985
Ray Johnson, Center Mgr.

University of Georgia
Small Business Development Center
1054 Claussen Rd., Ste. 301
Augusta, GA 30907-3215
Phone: (706)737-1790
Fax: (706)731-7937
E-mail: sbdcaug@uga.cc.uga.edu
Jeff Sanford, Area Dir.

University of Georgia (Brunswick)
Small Business Development Center
1107 Fountain Lake Dr.
Brunswick, GA 31525-3039
Phone: (912)264-7343
Fax: (912)262-3095
E-mail: sbdcbrun@uga.cc.uga.edu
David Lewis, Area Dir.

University of Georgia (Columbus)
Small Business Development Center
North Bldg., Rm. 202
928 45th St.
Columbus, GA 31904-6572
Phone: (706)649-7433
Fax: (706)649-1928
E-mail: sbdccolu@uga.cc.uga.edu
Jerry Copeland, Area Dir.

DeKalb Chamber of Commerce
DeKalb Small Business Development
Center
750 Commerce Dr., Ste. 201
Decatur, GA 30030-2622
Phone: (404)373-6930
Fax: (404)687-9684
E-mail: sbdcdec@uga.cc.uga.edu
Eric Bonaparte, Area Dir.

Gainesville Small Business
Development Center
500 Jesse Jewel Pkwy., Ste. 304
Gainesville, GA 30501-3773
Phone: (770)531-5681
Fax: (770)531-5684
E-mail: sbdcgain@uga.cc.uga.edu
Ron Simmons, Area Dir.

Kennesaw State University
Small Business Development Center
1000 Chastain Rd.
Kennesaw, GA 30144-5591
Phone: (770)423-6450
Fax: (770)423-6564
E-mail: sbdcmar@uga.cc.uga.edu
Carlotta Roberts, Area Dir.

Southeast Georgia District (Macon)
Small Business Development Center
401 Cherry St., Ste. 701
PO Box 13212
Macon, GA 31208-3212
Phone: (912)751-6592
Fax: (912)751-6607
E-mail: sbdcmac@uga.cc.uga.edu
Denise Ricketson, Area Dir.

Clayton State College
Small Business Development Center
PO Box 285
Morrow, GA 30260
Phone: (770)961-3440
Fax: (770)961-3428
E-mail: sbdcmorr@uga.cc.uga.edu
Bernie Meincke, Area Dir.

University of Georgia
SBDC
1770 Indian Trail Rd., Ste. 410

Norcross, GA 30093
Phone: (770)806-2124
Fax: (770)806-2129
E-mail: sbdclaw@uga.cc.edu
Robert Andoh, Area Dir.

Floyd College
Small Business Development Center
PO Box 1864
Rome, GA 30162-1864
Phone: (706)295-6326
Fax: (706)295-6732
E-mail: sbdcrome@uga.cc.uga.edu
Drew Tonsmeire, Area Dir.

University of Georgia (Savannah)
Small Business Development Center
450 Mall Blvd., Ste. H
Savannah, GA 31406-4824
Phone: (912)356-2755
Fax: (912)353-3033
E-mail: sbdcsav@uga.cc.uga.edu
Lynn Vos, Area Dir.

Georgia Southern University
Small Business Development Center
325 S. Main St.
PO Box 8156
Statesboro, GA 30460-8156
Phone: (912)681-5194
Fax: (912)681-0648
E-mail: sbdcstat@uga.cc.uga.edu
Mark Davis, Area Dir.

University of Georgia (Valdosta)
Small Business Development Center
Baytree W. Professional Offices
1205 Baytree Rd., Ste. 9
Valdosta, GA 31602-2782
Phone: (912)245-3738
Fax: (912)245-3741
E-mail: sbdcval@uga.cc.uga.edu
Suzanne Barnett, Area Dir.

University of Georgia (Warner
Robins)
Small Business Development Center
151 Osigian Blvd.
Warner Robins, GA 31088
Phone: (912)953-9356
Fax: (912)953-9376
E-mail: sbdccwr@uga.cc.uga.edu
Ronald Reaves, Center Mgr.

Guam

Pacific Islands SBDC Network
UOG Station
303 University Dr.

Mangilao, GU 96923
Phone: (671)735-2590
Fax: (671)734-2002
Dr. Sephen L. Marder, Dir.

Pacific Islands Small Business
Development Center
University of Guam
UOG Station
Mangilao, GU 96923
Phone: (671)735-2590
Fax: (671)734-2002
Mr. Jack Peters, Director

Hawaii

Kona Circuit Rider
SBDC
200 West Kawili St.
Hilo, HI 96720-4091
Phone: (808)933-3515
Fax: (808)933-3683
Rebecca Winters, Business
Consultant

University of Hawaii at Hilo
Hawaii SBDC
200 W. Kawili St.
Hilo, HI 96720-4091
Phone: (808)974-7515
Fax: (808)974-7683
Darryl Mleynek, State Dir.

University of Hawaii at Hilo
Small Business Development Center
200 W. Kawili St.
Hilo, HI 96720-4091
Phone: (808)974-7515
Fax: (808)974-7683
Website: www.maui.com/~sbdc/
hilo.html
Dr. Darryl Mleynek, State Director

University of Hawaii at West Oahu
SBDC
130 Merchant St., Ste. 1030
Honolulu, HI 96813
Phone: (808)522-8131
Fax: (808)522-8135
Laura Noda, Center Dir.

Maui Community College
Small Business Development Center
Maui Research and Technology
Center
590 Lipoa Pkwy., No. 130
Kihei, HI 96779
Phone: (808)875-2402
Fax: (808)875-2452
David B. Fisher, Dir.

University of Hawaii at Hilo
Business Research Library
SBDC
590 Lipoa Pkwy., No. 128
Kihei, HI 96753
Phone: (808)875-2400
Fax: (808)875-2452

Kauai Community College
Small Business Development Center
3-1901 Kaumualii Hwy.
Lihue, HI 96766-9591
Phone: (808)246-1748
Fax: (808)246-5102
Randy Gringas, Center Dir.

Idaho

Boise State University
Small Business Development Center
1910 University Dr.
Boise, ID 83725
Phone: (208)426-1640
Free: (800)225-3815
Fax: (208)426-3877
Website: www.idbsu.edu/isbdc/
James Hogge, State Director

Boise State University
Small Business Development Center
1910 University Dr.
Boise, ID 83725
Phone: (208)385-3875
Free: (800)225-3815
Fax: (208)385-3877
Robert Shepard, Regional Dir.

Boise State University
College of Business
Idaho SBDC
1910 University Dr.
Boise, ID 83725
Phone: (208)385-1640
Free: (800)225-3815
Fax: (208)385-3877
James Hogge, State Dir.

Idaho State University (Idaho Falls)
Small Business Development Center
2300 N. Yellowstone
Idaho Falls, ID 83401
Phone: (208)523-1087
Free: (800)658-3829
Fax: (208)523-1049
Betty Capps, Regional Dir.

Lewis-Clark State College
Small Business Development Center
500 8th Ave.

Lewiston, ID 83501
Phone: (208)799-2465
Fax: (208)799-2878
Helen Le Boeuf-Binninger, Regional Dir.

Idaho Small Business Development
Center
305 E. Park St., Ste. 405
PO Box 1901
McCall, ID 83638
Phone: (208)634-2883
Larry Smith, Associate Business
Consultant

Idaho State University (Pocatello)
Small Business Development Center
1651 Alvin Ricken Dr.
Pocatello, ID 83201
Phone: (208)232-4921
Free: (800)232-4921
Fax: (208)233-0268
Paul Cox, Regional Dir.

North Idaho College
SBDC
525 W. Clearwater Loop
Post Falls, ID 83854
Phone: (208)769-3296
Fax: (208)769-3223
John Lynn, Regional Dir.

College of Southern Idaho
Small Business Development Center
315 Falls Ave.
PO Box 1238
Twin Falls, ID 83303
Phone: (208)733-9554
Fax: (208)733-9316
Cindy Bond, Regional Dir.

Illinois

Waubonsee Community College
(Aurora Campus)
Small Business Development Center
5 E. Galena Blvd.
Aurora, IL 60506-4178
Phone: (630)801-7900
Fax: (630)892-4668
Linda Garrison-Carlton, Dir.

Southern Illinois University at
Carbondale
Small Business Development Center
150 E. Pleasant Hill Rd.
Carbondale, IL 62901-4300
Phone: (618)536-2424
Fax: (618)453-5040
Dennis Cody, Dir.

John A. Logan College
Small Business Development Center
700 Logan College Rd.
Carterville, IL 62918-9802
Phone: (618)985-3741
Fax: (618)985-2248
Richard Fyke, Dir.

Kaskaskia College
Small Business Development Center
27210 College Rd.
Centralia, IL 62801-7878
Phone: (618)532-2049
Fax: (618)532-4983
Richard McCullum, Dir.

University of Illinois at Urbana-
Champaign
International Trade Center
Small Business Development Center
428 Commerce W.
1206 S. 6th St.
Champaign, IL 61820-6980
Phone: (217)244-1585
Fax: (217)333-7410
Tess Morrison, Dir.

Asian American Alliance
SBDC
222 W. Cermak, No. 302
Chicago, IL 60616
Phone: (312)326-2200
Fax: (312)326-0399
Emil Bernardo, Dir.

Back of the Yards Neighborhood
Council
Small Business Development Center
1751 W. 47th St.
Chicago, IL 60609-3889
Phone: (773)523-4419
Fax: (773)254-3525
Bill Przybylski, Dir.

Chicago Small Business Development
Center
DCCA / James R. Thompson Center
100 W. Randolph, Ste. 3-400
Chicago, IL 60601-3219
Phone: (312)814-6111
Fax: (312)814-5247
Carson A. Gallagher, Mgr.

Eighteenth Street Development Corp.
Small Business Development Center
1839 S. Carpenter
Chicago, IL 60608-3347
Phone: (312)733-2287
Fax: (312)733-8242
Maria Munoz, Dir.

Greater North Pulaski Development
Corp.
Small Business Development Center
4054 W. North Ave.
Chicago, IL 60639-5223
Phone: (773)384-2262
Fax: (773)384-3850
Kaushik Shah, Dir.

Industrial Council of Northwest
Chicago
Small Business Development Center
2023 W. Carroll
Chicago, IL 60612-1601
Phone: (312)421-3941
Fax: (312)421-1871
Melvin Eiland, Dir.

Latin American Chamber of
Commerce
Small Business Development Center
3512 W. Fullerton St.
Chicago, IL 60647-2655
Phone: (773)252-5211
Fax: (773)252-7065
Ed Diaz, Dir.

North Business and Industrial Council
(NORBIC)
SBDC
2500 W. Bradley Pl.
Chicago, IL 60618-4798
Phone: (773)588-5855
Fax: (773)588-0734
Tom Kamykowski, Dir.

Richard J. Daley College
Small Business Development Center
7500 S. Pulaski Rd., Bldg. 200
Chicago, IL 60652-1299
Phone: (773)838-0319
Fax: (773)838-0303
Jim Charney, Dir.

Women's Business Development
Center
Small Business Development Center
8 S. Michigan, Ste. 400
Chicago, IL 60603-3302
Phone: (312)853-3477
Fax: (312)853-0145
Joyce Wade, Dir.

McHenry County College
Small Business Development Center
8900 U.S. Hwy. 14
Crystal Lake, IL 60012-2761
Phone: (815)455-6098
Fax: (815)455-9319
Susan Whitfield, Dir.

Danville Area Community College
Small Business Development Center
28 W. North St.
Danville, IL 61832-5729
Phone: (217)442-7232
Fax: (217)442-6228
Ed Adrain, Dir.

Cooperative Extension Service
SBDC
Building 11, Ste. 1105
2525 E. Federal Dr.
Decatur, IL 62526-1573
Phone: (217)875-8284
Fax: (217)875-8288
Bill Wilkinson, Dir.

Sauk Valley Community College
Small Business Development Center
173 Illinois, Rte. 2
Dixon, IL 61021-9188
Phone: (815)288-5511
Fax: (815)288-5958
John Nelson, Dir.

Black Hawk College
Small Business Development Center
301 42nd Ave.
East Moline, IL 61244-4038
Phone: (309)755-2200
Fax: (309)755-9847
Donna Scalf, Dir.

East St. Louis Small Business
Development Center
Federal Building
650 Missouri Ave., Ste. G32
East St. Louis, IL 62201-2955
Phone: (618)482-3833
Fax: (618)482-3859
Robert Ahart, Dir.

Southern Illinois University at
Edwardsville
Small Business Development Center
Campus Box 1107
Edwardsville, IL 62026-0001
Phone: (618)692-2929
Fax: (618)692-2647
Alan Hauff, Dir.

Elgin Community College
Small Business Development Center
1700 Spartan Dr.
Elgin, IL 60123-7193
Phone: (847)888-7488
Fax: (847)931-3911
Craig Fowler, Dir.

Evanston Business and Technology
Center
Small Business Development Center
1840 Oak Ave.
Evanston, IL 60201-3670
Phone: (847)866-1817
Fax: (847)866-1808
Rick Holbrook, Dir.

College of DuPage
Small Business Development Center
425 22nd St.
Glen Ellyn, IL 60137-6599
Phone: (630)942-2771
Fax: (630)942-3789
David Gay, Dir.

Lewis and Clark Community College
SBDC
5800 Godfrey Rd.
Godfrey, IL 62035
Phone: (618)466-3411
Fax: (618)466-0810
Bob Duane, Dir.

College of Lake County
Small Business Development Center
19351 W. Washington St.
Grayslake, IL 60030-1198
Phone: (847)223-3633
Fax: (847)223-9371
Linda Jorn, Dir.

Southeastern Illinois College
Small Business Development Center
303 S. Commercial
Harrisburg, IL 62946-2125
Phone: (618)252-5001
Fax: (618)252-0210
Becky Williams, Dir.

Rend Lake College
Small Business Development Center
Rte. 1
Ina, IL 62846-9801
Phone: (618)437-5321
Fax: (618)437-5677
Lisa Payne, Dir.

Joliet Junior College
Small Business Development Center
Renaissance Center, Rm. 312
214 N. Ottawa St.
Joliet, IL 60431-4097
Phone: (815)727-6544
Fax: (815)722-1895
Denise Mikulski, Dir.

Kankakee Community College
Small Business Development Center

River Rd., Box 888
Kankakee, IL 60901-7878
Phone: (815)933-0376
Fax: (815)933-0217
Kelly Berry, Dir.

Western Illinois University
Small Business Development Center
214 Seal Hall
Macomb, IL 61455-1390
Phone: (309)298-2211
Fax: (309)298-2520
Dan Voorhis, Dir.

Maple City Business and Technology
Center
Small Business Development Center
620 S. Main St.
Monmouth, IL 61462-2688
Phone: (309)734-4664
Fax: (309)734-8579
Carol Cook, Dir.

Illinois Valley Community College
Small Business Development Center
815 N. Orlando Smith Ave., Bldg. 11
Oglesby, IL 61348-9692
Phone: (815)223-1740
Fax: (815)224-3033
Boyd Palmer, Dir.

Illinois Eastern Community College
Small Business Development Center
401 E. Main St.
Olney, IL 62450-2119
Phone: (618)395-3011
Fax: (618)395-1922
Debbie Chilson, Dir.

Moraine Valley Community College
Small Business Development Center
10900 S. 88th Ave.
Palos Hills, IL 60465-0937
Phone: (708)974-5468
Fax: (708)974-0078
Hilary Gereg, Dir.

Bradley University
Small Business Development Center
141 N. Jobst Hall, 1st Fl.
Peoria, IL 61625-0001
Phone: (309)677-2992
Fax: (309)677-3386
Roger Luman, Dir.

Illinois Central College
Procurement Technical Assistance
Center
Small Business Development Center

124 SW Adams St., Ste. 300
Peoria, IL 61602-1388
Phone: (309)676-7500
Fax: (309)676-7534
Susan Gorman, Dir.

John Wood Community College
Procurement Technical Assistance
Center
Small Business Development Center
301 Oak St.
Quincy, IL 62301-2500
Phone: (217)228-5511
Fax: (217)228-5501
Edward Van Leer, Dir.

Rock Valley College
Small Business Development Center
1220 Rock St.
Rockford, IL 61101-1437
Phone: (815)968-4087
Fax: (815)968-4157
Shirley DeBenedetto, Dir.

Department of Commerce &
Community Affairs
Illinois SBDC
620 East Adams St., Third Fl.
Springfield, IL 62701
Phone: (217)524-5856
Fax: (217)524-0171
Jeff Mitchell, State Dir.

Illinois Department of Commerce and
Community Affairs
Small Business Development Center
620 E. Adams St., 3rd Fl.
Springfield, IL 62701
Phone: (217)524-5856
Fax: (217)785-6328
Website: www.comerce.state.il.us
Jeff Mitchell, State Director

Lincoln Land Community College
Small Business Development Center
100 N. 11th St.
Springfield, IL 62703-1002
Phone: (217)789-1017
Fax: (217)789-9838
Freida Schreck, Dir.

Shawnee Community College
Small Business Development Center
Shawnee College Rd.
Ullin, IL 62992
Phone: (618)634-9618
Fax: (618)634-2347
Donald Denny, Dir.

Governors State University
Small Business Development Center
College of Business, Rm. C-3370
University Park, IL 60466-0975
Phone: (708)534-4929
Fax: (708)534-1646
Christine Cochrane, Dir.

Indiana

Batesville Office of Economic
Development
SBDC
132 S. Main
Batesville, IN 47006
Phone: (812)933-6110

Bedford Chamber of Commerce
SBDC
1116 W. 16th St.
Bedford, IN 47421
Phone: (812)275-4493

Bloomfield Chamber of Commerce
SBDC
c/o Harrah Realty Co.
23 S. Washington St.
Bloomfield, IN 47424
Phone: (812)275-4493

Bloomington Area Regional Small
Business Development Center
216 Allen St.
Bloomington, IN 47403
Phone: (812)339-8937
Fax: (812)335-7352
David Miller, Dir.

Clay Count Chamber of Commerce
SBDC
12 N. Walnut St.
Brazil, IN 47834
Phone: (812)448-8457

Brookville Chamber of Commerce
SBDC
PO Box 211
Brookville, IN 47012
Phone: (317)647-3177

Clinton Chamber of Commerce
SBDC
292 N. 9th St.
Clinton, IN 47842
Phone: (812)832-3844

Columbia City Chamber of
Commerce
SBDC
112 N. Main St.

Columbia City, IN 46725
Phone: (219)248-8131

Columbus Regional Small Business
Development Center
4920 N. Warren Dr.
Columbus, IN 47203
Phone: (812)372-6480
Free: (800)282-7232
Fax: (812)372-0228
Jack Hess, Dir.

Connerville SBDC
504 Central
Connersville, IN 47331
Phone: (317)825-8328

Harrison County
Development Center
SBDC
405 N. Capitol, Ste. 308
Corydon, IN 47112
Phone: (812)738-8811

Montgomery County Chamber of
Commerce
SBDC
211 S. Washington St.
Crawfordsville, IN 47933
Phone: (317)654-5507

Decatur Chamber of Commerce
SBDC
125 E. Monroe St.
Decatur, IN 46733
Phone: (219)724-2604

City of Delphi Community
Development
SBDC
201 S. Union
Delphi, IN 46923
Phone: (317)564-6692

Southwestern Indiana Regional Small
Business Development Center
100 NW 2nd St., Ste. 200
Evansville, IN 47708
Phone: (812)425-7232
Fax: (812)421-5883
Kate Northrup, Dir.

Northeast Indiana Regional Small
Business Development Center
1830 Wayne Trace
Fort Wayne, IN 46803
Phone: (219)426-0040
Fax: (219)424-0024
E-mail: sbdc@mailfwi.com
Nick Adams, Dir.

Clinton County Chamber of
Commerce
SBDC
207 S. Main St.
Frankfort, IN 46041
Phone: (317)654-5507

Northlake Small Business
Development Center
487 Broadway, Ste. 201
Gary, IN 46402
Phone: (219)882-2000

Greencastle Partnership Center
SBDC
2 S. Jackson St.
Greencastle, IN 46135
Phone: (317)653-4517

Greensburg Area Chamber of
Commerce
SBDC
125 W. Main St.
Greensburg, IN 47240
Phone: (812)663-2832

Hammond Development Corp.
SBDC
649 Conkey St.
Hammond, IN 46324
Phone: (219)853-6399

Blackford County Economic
Development
SBDC
PO Box 43
Hartford, IN 47001-0043
Phone: (317)348-4944

Indiana SBDC Network
One North Capitol, Ste. 420
Indianapolis, IN 46204
Phone: (317)264-6871
Fax: (317)264-3102
E-mail: sthrash@in.net
Stephen Thrash, Exec. Dir.

Indiana Small Business Development
Center Network
1 N. Capitol, Ste. 420
Indianapolis, IN 46204
Phone: (317)264-6871
Fax: (317)264-3102
E-mail: insbdc@in.net
Website: www.indianachamber.com/
sbdc
Stephen Thrash, Director

Indianapolis Regional Small Business
Development Center

342 N. Senate Ave.
Indianapolis, IN 46204-1708
Phone: (317)261-3030
Fax: (317)261-3053
Glenn Dunlap, Dir.

Clark County Hoosier Falls
Private Industry Council Workforce
1613 E. 8th St.
Jeffersonville, IN 47130
Phone: (812)282-0456

Southern Indiana Regional Small
Business Development Center
1613 E. 8th St.
Jeffersonville, IN 47130
Phone: (812)288-6451
Fax: (812)284-8314
Patricia Stroud, Dir.

Kendallville Chamber of Commerce
SBDC
228 S. Main St.
Kendallville, IN 46755
Phone: (219)347-1554

Kokomo-Howard County Regional
Small Business Development Center
106 N. Washington
Kokomo, IN 46901
Phone: (317)454-7922
Fax: (317)452-4564
E-mail: sbdc5@holli.com
Kim Moyers, Dir.

LaPorte Small Business Development
Center
414 Lincolnway
La Porte, IN 46350
Phone: (219)326-7232

Greater Lafayette Regional Area
Small Business Development Center
122 N. 3rd
Lafayette, IN 47901
Phone: (765)742-2394
Fax: (765)742-6276
Susan Davis, Dir.

Union County Chamber of Commerce
SBDC
102 N. Main St., No. 6
Liberty, IN 47353-1039
Phone: (317)458-5976

Linton/Stockton Chamber of
Commerce
SBDC
PO Box 208
Linton, IN 47441
Phone: (812)847-4846

Southeastern Indiana Regional Small
Business Development Center
975 Industrial Dr.
Madison, IN 47250
Phone: (812)265-3127
Fax: (812)265-5544
E-mail: seinsbdc@seidata.com
Rose Marie Roberts, Dir.

Crawford County
Private Industry Council Workforce
SBDC
Box 224 D, R.R. 1
Marengo, IN 47140
Phone: (812)365-2174

Greater Martinsville Chamber of
Commerce
SBDC
210 N. Marion St.
Martinsville, IN 46151
Phone: (317)342-8110

Lake County Public Library
Small Business Development Center
1919 W. 81st. Ave.
Merrillville, IN 46410-5382
Phone: (219)756-7232

First Citizens Bank
SBDC
515 N. Franklin Sq.
Michigan City, IN 46360
Phone: (219)874-9245

Mitchell Chamber of Commerce
SBDC
1st National Bank
Main Street
Mitchell, IN 47446
Phone: (812)849-4441

Mt. Vernon Chamber of Commerce
SBDC
405 E. 4th St.
Mt. Vernon, IN 47620
Phone: (812)838-3639

East Central Indiana Regional Small
Business Development Center
401 S. High St.
PO Box 842
Muncie, IN 47305
Phone: (765)284-8144
Fax: (765)751-9151
Barbara Armstrong, Dir.

Brown County Chamber of
Commerce
SBDC

PO Box 164
Nashville, IN 47448
Phone: (812)988-6647

Southern Indiana Small Business
Development Center
Private Industry Council Workforce
4100 Charleston Rd.
New Albany, IN 47150
Phone: (812)945-0266
Fax: (812)948-4664
Gretchen Mahaffey, Dir.

Henry County Economic
Development Corp.
SBDC
1325 Broad St., Ste. B
New Castle, IN 47362
Phone: (317)529-4635

Jennings County Chamber of
Commerce
SBDC
PO Box 340
North Vernon, IN 47265
Phone: (812)346-2339

Orange County
Private Industry Council Workforce
SBDC
326 B. N. Gospel
Paoli, IN 47454-1412
Phone: (812)723-4206

Northwest Indiana Regional Small
Business Development Center
Small Business Development Center
6100 Southport Rd.
Portage, IN 46368
Phone: (219)762-1696
Fax: (219)763-2653
Mark McLaughlin, Dir

Jay County Development Corp.
SBDC
121 W. Main St., Ste. A
Portland, IN 47371
Phone: (219)726-9311

Richmond-Wayne County Small
Business Development Center
33 S. 7th St.
Richmond, IN 47374
Phone: (765)962-2887
Fax: (765)966-0882
Cliff Fry, Dir.

Rochester and Lake Manitou
Chamber of Commerce

Fulton Economic Development
Center
SBDC
617 Main St.
Rochester, IN 46975
Phone: (219)223-6773

Rushville Chamber of Commerce
SBDC
PO Box 156
Rushville, IN 46173
Phone: (317)932-2222

St. Mary of the Woods College
SBDC
St. Mary-of-the-Woods, IN 47876
Phone: (812)535-5151

Washington County
Private Industry Council Workforce
SBDC
Hilltop Plaza
Salem, IN 47167
Phone: (812)883-2283

Scott County
Private Industry Council Workforce
SBDC
752 Lakeshore Dr.
Scottsburg, IN 47170
Phone: (812)752-3886

Seymour Chamber of Commerce
SBDC
PO Box 43
Seymour, IN 47274
Phone: (812)522-3681

Minority Business Development
Project Future
SBDC
401 Col
South Bend, IN 46634
Phone: (219)234-0051

South Bend Regional Small Business
Development Center
300 N. Michigan
South Bend, IN 46601
Phone: (219)282-4350
Fax: (219)236-1056
Jim Gregar, Dir.

Economic Development Office
SBDC
46 E. Market St.
Spencer, IN 47460
Phone: (812)829-3245

Sullivan Chamber of Commerce
SBDC

10 S. Crt. St.
Sullivan, IN 47882
Phone: (812)268-4836

Tell City Chamber of Commerce
SBDC
645 Main St.
Tell City, IN 47586
Phone: (812)547-2385
Fax: (812)547-8378

Terre Haute Area Small Business
Development Center
School of Business, Rm. 510
Terre Haute, IN 47809
Phone: (812)237-7676
Fax: (812)237-7675
William Minnis, Dir.

Tipton County Economic
Development Corp.
SBDC
136 E. Jefferson
Tipton, IN 46072
Phone: (317)675-7300

Porter County
SBDC
911 Wall St.
Valparaiso, IN 46383
Phone: (219)477-5256

Vevay/Switzerland Country
Foundation
SBDC
PO Box 193
Vevay, IN 47043
Phone: (812)427-2533

Vincennes University
SBDC
PO Box 887
Vincennes, IN 47591
Phone: (812)885-5749

Wabash Area Chamber of Commerce
Wabash Economic Development
Corp.
SBDC
67 S. Wabash
Wabash, IN 46992
Phone: (219)563-1168

Washington Daviess County
SBDC
1 Train Depot St.
Washington, IN 47501
Phone: (812)254-5262
Fax: (812)254-2550
Mark Brochin, Dir.

Purdue University
SBDC
Business & Industrial Development
Center
1220 Potter Dr.
West Lafayette, IN 47906
Phone: (317)494-5858

Randolph County Economic
Development Foundation
SBDC
111 S. Main St.
Winchester, IN 47394
Phone: (317)584-3266

Iowa

Iowa SBDC
137 Lynn Ave.
Ames, IA 50014
Phone: (515)292-6351
Free: (800)373-7232
Fax: (515)292-0020
Ronald Manning, State Dir.

Iowa State University
Small Business Development Center
ISU Branch Office
Bldg. 1, Ste. 615
2501 N. Loop Dr.
Ames, IA 50010-8283
Phone: (515)296-7828
Free: (800)373-7232
Fax: (515)296-6714
Steve Carter, Dir.

Iowa State University
Small Business Development Center
137 Lynn Ave., Ste. 5
Ames, IA 50014-7198
Phone: (515)292-6351
Free: (800)373-7232
Fax: (515)292-0020
Website: www.iowasbdc.org/
staff.html
Ronald Manning, State Director

DMACC Small Business
Development Center
Circle West Incubator
PO Box 204
Audubon, IA 50025
Phone: (712)563-2623
Fax: (712)563-2301
Lori Harmening, Dir.

University of Northern Iowa
Small Business Development Center
8628 University Ave.

Cedar Falls, IA 50614-0032
Phone: (319)273-2696
Fax: (319)273-7730
Lyle Bowlin, Dir.

Iowa Western Community College
Small Business Development Center
2700 College Rd., Box 4C
Council Bluffs, IA 51502
Phone: (712)325-3260
Fax: (712)325-3408
Ronald Helms, Dir.

Southwestern Community College
Small Business Development Center
1501 W. Townline Rd.
Creston, IA 50801
Phone: (515)782-4161
Fax: (515)782-3312
Robin Beech Travis, Dir.

Eastern Iowa Small Business
Development Center
304 W. 2nd St.
Davenport, IA 52801
Phone: (319)322-4499
Fax: (319)322-8241
Jon Ryan, Dir.

Drake University
Small Business Development Center
2429 University Ave.
Des Moines, IA 50311-4505
Phone: (515)271-2655
Fax: (515)271-1899
Benjamin Swartz, Dir.

Northeast Iowa Small Business
Development Center
770 Town Clock Plz.
Dubuque, IA 52001
Phone: (319)588-3350
Fax: (319)557-1591
Charles Tonn, Dir.

Iowa Central Community College
SBDC
900 Central Ave., Ste. 4
Ft. Dodge, IA 50501
Phone: (515)576-5090
Fax: (515)576-0826
Todd Madson, Dir.

University of Iowa
Small Business Development Center
108 Papajohn Business
Administration Bldg., Ste. S-160
Iowa City, IA 52242-1000
Phone: (319)335-3742

Free: (800)253-7232
Fax: (319)353-2445
Paul Heath, Dir.

Kirkwood Community College
Small Business Development Center
2901 10th Ave.
Marion, IA 52302
Phone: (319)377-8256
Fax: (319)377-5667
Steve Sprague, Dir.

North Iowa Area Community College
Small Business Development Center
500 College Dr.
Mason City, IA 50401
Phone: (515)422-4342
Fax: (515)422-4129
Richard Petersen, Dir.

Indian Hills Community College
Small Business Development Center
525 Grandview Ave.
Ottumwa, IA 52501
Phone: (515)683-5127
Fax: (515)683-5263
Bryan Ziegler, Dir.

Western Iowa Tech Community
College
Small Business Development Center
4647 Stone Ave.
PO Box 5199
Sioux City, IA 51102-5199
Phone: (712)274-6418
Free: (800)352-4649
Fax: (712)274-6429
Dennis Bogenrief, Dir.

Iowa Lakes Community College
(Spencer)
Small Business Development Center
1900 N. Grand Ave., Ste. 8
Hwy. 71 N
Spencer, IA 51301
Phone: (712)262-4213
Fax: (712)262-4047
John Beneke, Dir.

Southeastern Community College
Small Business Development Center
Drawer F
West Burlington, IA 52655
Phone: (319)752-2731
Free: (800)828-7322
Fax: (319)752-3407
Deb Dalziel, Dir.

Kansas

Bendictine College
SBDC
1020 N. 2nd St.
Atchison, KS 66002
Phone: (913)367-5340
Fax: (913367-6102
Don Laney, Dir.

Butler County Community College
Small Business Development Center
600 Walnut
Augusta, KS 67010
Phone: (316)775-1124
Fax: (316)775-1370
Dorinda Rolle, Dir.

Neosho County Community College
SBDC
1000 S. Allen
Chanute, KS 66720
Phone: (316)431-2820
Fax: (316)431-0082
Duane Clum, Dir.

Coffeyville Community College
SBDC
11th and Willow Sts.
Coffeyville, KS 67337-5064
Phone: (316)251-7700
Fax: (316)252-7098
Charles Shaver, Dir.

Colby Community College
Small Business Development Center
1255 S. Range
Colby, KS 67701
Phone: (913)462-3984
Fax: (913)462-8315
Robert Selby, Dir.

Cloud County Community College
SBDC
2221 Campus Dr.
PO Box 1002
Concordia, KS 66901
Phone: (913)243-1435
Fax: (913)243-1459
Tony Foster, Dir.

Dodge City Community College
Small Business Development Center
2501 N. 14th Ave.
Dodge City, KS 67801
Phone: (316)227-9247
Fax: (316)227-9200
Wayne E. Shiplet, Dir.

Emporia State University
Small Business Development Center
130 Cremer Hall
Emporia, KS 66801
Phone: (316)342-7162
Fax: (316)341-5418
Lisa Brumbaugh, Regional Dir.

Ft. Scott Community College
SBDC
2108 S. Horton
Ft. Scott, KS 66701
Phone: (316)223-2700
Fax: (316)223-6530
Steve Pammenter, Dir.

Garden City Community College
SBDC
801 Campus Dr.
Garden City, KS 67846
Phone: (316)276-9632
Fax: (316)276-9630
Bill Sander, Regional Dir.

Ft. Hays State University
Small Business Development Center
109 W. 10th St.
Hays, KS 67601
Phone: (785)628-6786
Fax: (785)628-0533
Clare Gustin, Regional Dir.

Hutchinson Community College
Small Business Development Center
815 N. Walnut, Ste. 225
Hutchinson, KS 67501
Phone: (316)665-4950
Free: (800)289-3501
Fax: (316)665-8354
Clark Jacobs, Dir.

Independence Community College
SBDC
Arco Bldg.
11th and Main St.
Independence, KS 67301
Phone: (316)332-1420
Fax: (316)331-5344
Preston Haddan, Dir.

Allen County Community College
SBDC
1801 N. Cottonwood
Iola, KS 66749
Phone: (316)365-5116
Fax: (316)365-3284
Susan Thompson, Dir.

University of Kansas
Small Business Development Center

734 Vermont St., Ste. 104
Lawrence, KS 66044
Phone: (785)843-8844
Fax: (785)865-8878
Randy Brady, Regional Dir.

Seward County Community College
Small Business Development Center
1801 N. Kansas
PO Box 1137
Liberal, KS 67901
Phone: (316)629-2650
Fax: (316)629-2689
Dale Reed, Dir.

Kansas State University (Manhattan)
Small Business Development Center
College of Business Administration
2323 Anderson Ave., Ste. 100
Manhattan, KS 66502-2947
Phone: (785)532-5529
Fax: (785)532-5827
Fred Rice, Regional Dir.

Ottawa University
SBDC
College Ave., Box 70
Ottawa, KS 66067
Phone: (913)242-5200
Fax: (913)242-7429
Lori Kravets, Dir.

Johnson County Community College
Small Business Development Center
CEC Bldg., Rm. 223
Overland Park, KS 66210-1299
Phone: (913)469-3878
Fax: (913)469-4415
Kathy Nadiman, Regional Dir.

Labette Community College
SBDC
200 S. 14th
Parsons, KS 67357
Phone: (316)421-6700
Fax: (316)421-0921
Mark Turnbull, Dir.

Pittsburg State University
Small Business Development Center
Shirk Hall
1501 S. Joplin
Pittsburg, KS 66762
Phone: (316)235-4920
Fax: (316)232-6440
Kathryn Richard

Pratt Community College
Small Business Development Center

Hwy. 61
Pratt, KS 67124
Phone: (316)672-5641
Fax: (316)672-5288
Pat Gordon, Dir.

Salina Area Chamber of Commerce
Small Business Development Center
PO Box 586
Salina, KS 67402
Phone: (785)827-9301
Fax: (785)827-9758
James Gaines, Regional Dir.

Fort Hayes State University
Kansas Small Business Development
Center State Office
214 SW 6th St., Ste. 205
Topeka, KS 66603
Phone: (785)296-6514
Fax: (785)291-3261
E-mail: ksbdc@cjnetworks.com
Debbie Bishop, State Director

Kansas SBDC
214 SW 6th St., Ste. 205
Topeka, KS 66603-3261
Phone: (785)296-6514
Fax: (785)291-3261
E-mail: ksbdc@cjnetworks.com
Debbie Bishop, State Dir.

Washburn University of Topeka
SBDC
School of Business
101 Henderson Learning Center
Topeka, KS 66621
Phone: (785)231-1010
Fax: (785)231-1063
Don Kingman, Regional Dir.

Wichita State University
SBDC
1845 Fairmont
Wichita, KS 67260
Phone: (316)689-3193
Fax: (316)689-3647
Joann Ard, Regional Dir.

Wichita State University
Small Business Development Center
1845 N. Fairmont
Wichita, KS 67260-0148
Phone: (316)978-3193
Fax: (316)978-3647
E-mail: sbdc@wsunub.uc.twsu.edu.
Clair Gustin, Director

Kentucky

Morehead State University College of
Business
Boyd-Greenup County Chamber of
Commerce
SBDC
1401 Winchester Ave., Ste. 305
207 15th St.
Ashland, KY 41101
Phone: (606)329-8011
Fax: (606)324-4570
Kimberly A. Jenkins, Dir.

Western Kentucky University
Bowling Green Small Business
Development Center
2355 Nashville Rd.
Bowling Green, KY 42101
Phone: (502)745-1905
Fax: (502)745-1931
Richard S. Horn, Dir.

University of Kentucky
(Elizabethtown)
Small Business Development Center
133 W. Dixie Ave.
Elizabethtown, KY 42701
Phone: (502)765-6737
Fax: (502)769-5095
Lou Ann Allen, Dir.

Northern Kentucky University
SBDC
BEP Center 463
Highland Heights, KY 41099-0506
Phone: (606)572-6524
Fax: (606)572-6177
Sutton Landry, Dir.

Murray State University
(Hopkinsville)
Small Business Development Center
300 Hammond Dr.
Hopkinsville, KY 42240
Phone: (502)886-8666
Fax: (502)886-3211
Michael Cartner, Dir.

Small Business Development Center
Lexington Central Library, 4th Fl.
140 E. Main St.
Lexington, KY 40507-1376
Phone: (606)257-7666
Fax: (606)257-1751
Debbie McKnight, Dir.

University of Kentucky
Center for Entrepreneurship

Kentucky SBDC
225 Gatton Business and Economics Bldg.
Lexington, KY 40506-0034
Phone: (606)257-7668
Fax: (606)323-1907
Janet S. Holloway, State Dir.

University of Kentucky
Center for Business Development
225 C.M. Gatton Business and Economics Bldg.
Lexington, KY 40506-0034
Phone: (606)257-7668
Fax: (606)323-1907
Website: gatton.gws.uky.edu/KentuckyBusiness/ksbdc/ksbdc.htm
Janet S. Holloway, State Director

Bellarmine College
Small Business Development Center
School of Business
600 W. Main St., Ste. 219
Louisville, KY 40202
Phone: (502)574-4770
Fax: (502)574-4771
Thomas G. Daley, Dir.

University of Louisville
Center for Entrepreneurship and Technology
Small Business Development Centers
Burhans Hall, Shelby Campus, Rm. 122
Louisville, KY 40292
Phone: (502)588-7854
Fax: (502)588-8573
Lou Dickie, Dir.

Southeast Community College
SBDC
1300 Chichester Ave.
Middlesboro, KY 40965-2265
Phone: (606)242-2145
Fax: (606)242-4514
Kathleen Moats, Dir.

Morehead State University
Small Business Development Center
309 Combs Bldg.
UPO 575
Morehead, KY 40351
Phone: (606)783-2895
Fax: (606)783-5020
Keith Moore, District Dir.

Murray State University
West Kentucky Small Business Development Center

College of Business and Public Affairs
PO Box 9
Murray, KY 42071
Phone: (502)762-2856
Fax: (502)762-3049
Rosemary Miller, Dir.

Murray State University
Owensboro Small Business Development Center
3860 U.S. Hwy. 60 W
Owensboro, KY 42301
Phone: (502)926-8085
Fax: (502)684-0714
Mickey Johnson, District Dir.

Moorehead State University
Pikeville Small Business Development Center
3455 N. Mayo Trail, No. 4
110 Village St.
Pikeville, KY 41501
Phone: (606)432-5848
Fax: (606)432-8924
Michael Morley, Dir.

Eastern Kentucky University
South Central Small Business Development Center
The Center for Rural Development, Ste. 260
2292 S. Hwy. 27
Somerset, KY 42501
Phone: (606)677-6120
Fax: (606)677-6083
Kathleen Moats, Dir.

Louisiana

Alexandria SBDC
Hibernia National Bank Bldg., Ste. 510
934 3rd St.
Alexandria, LA 71301
Phone: (318484-2123
Fax: (318484-2126
Kathey Hunter, Consultant

Southern University
Capital Small Business Development Center
1933 Wooddale Blvd., Ste. E
Baton Rouge, LA 70806
Phone: (504)922-0998
Fax: (504)922-0024
Gregory Spann, Dir.

Southeastern Louisiana University
Small Business Development Center
College of Business Administration
Box 522, SLU Sta.
Hammond, LA 70402
Phone: (504)549-3831
Fax: (504)549-2127
William Joubert, Dir.

University of Southwestern Louisiana
Acadiana Small Business Development Center
College of Business Administration
Box 43732
Lafayette, LA 70504
Phone: (318)262-5344
Fax: (318)262-5296
Kim Spence, Dir.

McNeese State University
Small Business Development Center
College of Business Administration
Lake Charles, LA 70609
Phone: (318)475-5529
Fax: (318)475-5012
Paul Arnold, Dir.

Louisiana Electronic Assistance Program
SBDC
NE Louisiana, College of Business Administration
Monroe, LA 71209
Phone: (318)342-1215
Fax: (318)342-1209
Dr. Jerry Wall, Dir.

Northeast Louisiana University
SBDC
Louisiana SBDC
College of Business Administration, Rm. 2-57
Room 2-57
Monroe, LA 71209
Phone: (318)342-5506
Fax: (318)342-5510
Dr. John Baker, State Dir.

Northeast Louisiana University
Small Business Development Center
College of Business Administration, Rm. 2-57
Monroe, LA 71209
Phone: (318)342-1215
Fax: (318)342-1209
Dr. Paul Dunn, Dir.

Northeast Louisiana University
Small Business Development Center

College of Business Administration,
Rm. 2-57
Monroe, LA 71209
Phone: (318)342-5506
Fax: (318)342-5510
E-mail: brbaker@alpha.nlu.edu
Website: isbdc.net1.nlu.edu
Dr. John Baker, State Director

Northwestern State University
Small Business Development Center
College of Business Administration
Natchitoches, LA 71497
Phone: (318)357-5611
Fax: (318)357-6810
Mary Lynn Wilkerson, Dir.

Louisiana International Trade Center
SBDC
World Trade Center, Ste. 2926
2 Canal St.
New Orleans, LA 70130
Phone: (504)568-8222
Fax: (504)568-8228
Ruperto Chavarri, Dir.

Loyola University
Small Business Development Center
College of Business Administration
Box 134
New Orleans, LA 70118
Phone: (504)865-3474
Fax: (504)865-3496
Ronald Schroeder, Dir.

Southern University at New Orleans
Small Business Development Center
College of Business Administration
New Orleans, LA 70126
Phone: (504)286-5308
Fax: (504)286-5131
Jon Johnson, Dir.

University of New Orleans
Small Business Development Center
1600 Canal St., Ste. 620
New Orleans, LA 70112
Phone: (504)539-9292
Fax: (504)539-9205
Norma Grace, Dir.

Louisiana Tech University
Small Business Development Center
College of Business Administration
Box 10318, Tech Sta.
Ruston, LA 71272
Phone: (318)257-3537
Fax: (318)257-4253
Tracey Jeffers, Dir.

Louisiana State University at
Shreveport
Small Business Development Center
College of Business Administration
1 University Dr.
Shreveport, LA 71115
Phone: (318)797-5144
Fax: (318)797-5208
Peggy Cannon, Dir.

Nicholls State University
Small Business Development Center
College of Business Administration
PO Box 2015
Thibodaux, LA 70310
Phone: (504)448-4242
Fax: (504)448-4922
Weston Hull, Dir.

Maine

Androscoggin Valley Council of
Governments
Small Business Development Center
125 Manley Rd.
Auburn, ME 04210
Phone: (207)783-9186
Fax: (207)783-5211
Jane Mickeriz, Counselor

Coastal Enterprises Inc.
SBDC
Weston Bldg.
7 N. Chestnut St.
Augusta, ME 04330
Phone: (207)621-0245
Fax: (207)622-9739
Robert Chiozzi, Counselor

Eastern Maine Development Corp.
Small Business Development Center
1 Cumberland Pl., Ste. 300
PO Box 2579
Bangor, ME 04402-2579
Phone: (207)942-6389
Free: (800)339-6389
Fax: (207942-3548
Ron Loyd, Dir.

Belfast Satellite
Waldo County Development Corp.
SBDC
67 Church St.
Belfast, ME 04915
Phone: (207)942-6389
Free: (800)339-6389
Fax: (207)942-3548

Brunswick Satellite
Midcoast Council for Business
Development
SBDC
8 Lincoln St.
Brunswick, ME 04011
Phone: (207)882-4340

Northern Maine Development
Commission
Small Business Development Center
2 S. Main St.
PO Box 779
Caribou, ME 04736
Phone: (207)498-8736
Free: (800)427-8736
Fax: (207)498-3108
Rodney Thompson, Dir.

East Millinocket Satellite
Katahdin Regional Development
Corp.
SBDC
58 Main St.
East Millinocket, ME 04430
Phone: (207)746-5338
Fax: (207)746-9535

East Wilton Satellite
Robinhood Plaza
Rte. 2 & 4
East Wilton, ME 04234
Phone: (207)783-9186
Fax: (207)783-9186

Fort Kent Satellite
SBDC
Aroostook County Registry of Deeds
Elm and Hall Sts.
Fort Kent, ME 04743
Phone: (207)498-8736
Free: (800)427-8736
Fax: (207)498-3108

Houlton Satellite
SBDC
Superior Court House
Court St.
Houlton, ME 04730
Phone: (207)498-8736
Free: (800)427-8736
Fax: (207)498-3108

Lewiston Satellite
Business Information Center (BIC)
SBDC
Bates Mill Complex
35 Canal St.
Lewiston, ME 04240

Phone: (207)783-9186
Fax: (207)783-5211

Machias Satellite
Sunrise County Economic Council
(Calais Area)
SBDC
63 Main St.
PO Box 679
Machias, ME 04654
Phone: (207)454-2430
Fax: (207)255-0983

University of Southern Maine
Maine SBDC
96 Falmouth St.
PO Box 9300
Portland, ME 04104-9300
Phone: (207)780-4420
Fax: (207)780-4810
E-mail: msbdc@portland.maine.edu
Charles Davis, Dir.

University of Southern Maine
Small Business Development Center
15 Surrenden St.
PO Box 9300
Portland, ME 04103
Phone: (207)780-4420
Fax: (207)780-4810
E-mail: msbdc@portland.maine.edu
Website: www.usm.maine.edu/~sbdc
Charles Davis, Director

Rockland Satellite
SBDC
331 Main St.
Rockland, ME 04841
Phone: (207)882-4340
Fax: (207)882-4456

Rumford Satellite
River Valley Growth Council
Hotel Harris Bldg.
23 Hartford St.
Rumford, ME 04276
Phone: (207)783-9186
Fax: (207)783-5211

Biddeford Satellite
Biddeford-Saco Chamber of
Commerce and Industry
SBDC
110 Main St.
Saco, ME 04072
Phone: (207)282-1567
Fax: (207)282-3149

Southern Maine Regional Planning
Commission
Small Business Development Center
255 Main St.
PO Box Q
Sanford, ME 04073
Phone: (207)324-0316
Fax: (207)324-2958
Joseph Vitko, Dir.

Skowhegan Satellite
SBDC
Norridgewock Ave.
Skowhegan, ME 04976
Phone: (207)621-0245
Fax: (207)622-9739

South Paris Satellite
SBDC
166 Main St.
South Paris, ME 04281
Phone: (207)783-9186
Fax: (207)783-5211

Waterville Satellite
Thomas College
SBDC
Administrative Bldg. - Library
180 W. River Rd.
Waterville, ME 04901
Phone: (207)621-0245
Fax: (207)622-9739

Coastal Enterprises, Inc. (Wiscasset)
Small Business Development Center
Water St.
PO Box 268
Wiscasset, ME 04578
Phone: (207)882-4340
Fax: (207)882-4456
James Burbank, Dir.

York Satellite
York Chamber of Commerce
SBDC
449 Rte. 1
York, ME 03909
Phone: (207)363-4422
Fax: (207)324-2958

Maryland

Anne Arundel, Office of Economic
Development
SBDC
2666 Riva Rd., Ste. 200
Annapolis, MD 21401
Phone: (410)224-4205
Fax: (410)222-7415
Mike Fish, Consultant

Central Maryland
SBDC
1420 N. Charles St., Rm 142
Baltimore, MD 21201-5779
Phone: (410)837-4141
Fax: (410)837-4151
Barney Wilson, Executive Dir.

Maryland Department of Economic
and Employment Development
Small Business Development Center
Program Control Center
217 E. Redwood St., Ste. 936
Baltimore, MD 21202
Phone: (410)767-2000
Fax: (410)333-4460
A. Thomas McLamore, Director

Hartford County Economic
Development Office
SBDC
220 S. Main St.
Bel Air, MD 21014
Phone: (410)893-3837
Fax: (410)879-8043
Maurice Brown, Consultant

Maryland Small Business
Development Center
7100 Baltimore Ave., Ste. 401
College Park, MD 20740
Phone: (301)403-8300
Fax: (301)403-8303
James N. Graham, State Dir.

Maryland Small Business
Development Center
SBDC
7100 Baltimore Ave., Ste. 401
College Park, MD 20740
Phone: (301)403-8300
Fax: (301)403-8303
Website: www.mbs.umd.edu/sbdc
James M. Graham, Director

University of Maryland
SBDC
College of Business and Management
College Park, MD 20742-1815
Phone: (301)405-2144
Fax: (301)314-9152

Howard County Economic
Development Office
SBDC
6751 Gateway Dr., Ste. 500
Columbia, MD 21044
Phone: (410)313-6552
Fax: (410)313-6556
Ellin Dize, Consultant

Western Maryland Small Business
Development Center
Western Region, Inc.
3 Commerce Dr.
Cumberland, MD 21502
Phone: (301)724-6716
Free: (800)457-7232
Fax: (301)777-7504
Sam LaManna, Exec. Dir.

Cecil County Chamber of Commerce
SBDC
135 E. Main St.
Elkton, MD 21921
Phone: (410)392-0597
Fax: (410)392-6225
Maurice Brown, Consultant

Frederick Community College
SBDC
7932 Opossumtown Pike
Frederick, MD 21702
Phone: (301)846-2683
Fax: (301)846-2689
Mary Ann Garst, Program Dir.

Arundel Center N.
SBDC
101 Crain Hwy., NW, Rm. 110B
Glen Burnie, MD 21061
Phone: (410)766-1910
Fax: (410)766-1911
Mike Fish, Consultant

Community College at Saint Mary's
County
SBDC
PO Box 98, Great Mills Rd.
Great Mills, MD 20634
Phone: (301)868-6679
Fax: (301)868-7392
James Shepherd

Hagerstown Junior College
SBDC
Technology Innovation Center
11404 Robinwood Dr.
Hagerstown, MD 21740
Phone: (301)797-0327
Fax: (301)777-7504
Tonya Fleming Brockett, Dir.

Landover SBDC
7950 New Hampshire Ave., 2nd Fl.
Langley Park, MD 20783
Phone: (301)445-7324
Fax: (301)883-6479
Avon Evans, Consultant

Charles County Community College
Southern Maryland SBDC
SBDC
Mitchell Rd.
PO Box 910
LaPlata, MD 20646-0910
Phone: (301)934-7580
Free: (800)762-7232
Fax: (301)934-7681
Betsy Cooksey, Exec. Dir.

Garrett Community College
SBDC
Mosser Rd.
McHenry, MD 21541
Phone: (301)387-6666
Fax: (301)387-3096
Sandy Major, Business Analyst

Salisbury State University
Eastern Shore Region Small Business
Development Center
Power Professional Bldg., Ste. 170
Salisbury, MD 21801
Phone: (410)546-4325
Free: (800)999-7232
Fax: (410)548-5389
Marty Green, Exec. Dir.

Baltimore County Chamber of
Commerce
SBDC
102 W. Pennsylvania Ave., Ste. 402
Towson, MD 21204
Phone: (410)832-5866
Fax: (410)821-9901
John Casper, Consultant

Prince George's County Minority
Business Opportunities Commission
Suburban Washington Region Small
Business Development Center
1400 McCormick Dr., Ste. 282
Upper Marlboro, MD 20774
Phone: (301)883-6491
Fax: (301)883-6479
Avon Evans, Acting Executive Dir.

Carrol County Economic
Development Office
SBDC
125 N. Court St., Rm. 101
Westminster, MD 21157
Phone: (410)857-8166
Fax: (410)848-0003
Michael Fish, Consultant

Eastern Region - Upper Shore SBDC
PO Box 8

Wye Mills, MD 21679
Phone: (410)822-5400
Free: (800)762SBDC
Fax: (410)827-5286
Patricia Ann Marie Schaller,
Consultant

Massachusetts

International Trade Center
University of Massachusetts Amherst
SBDC
205 School of Management
Amherst, MA 01003-4935
Phone: (413)545-6301
Fax: (413)545-1273

University of Massachusetts
Massachusetts SBDC
205 School of Management
Amherst, MA 01003-4935
Phone: (413)545-6301
Fax: (413)545-1273
John Ciccarelli, State Dir.

University of Massachusetts
Small Business Development Center
School of Management, Rm. 205
Amherst, MA 01003-4935
Phone: (413)545-6301
Fax: (413)545-1273
Ms. Georgeanna Parhen, Acting State
Director

Massachusetts Export Center
World Trade Center, Ste. 315
Boston, MA 02210
Phone: (617)478-4133
Free: (800)478-4133
Fax: (617)478-4135
Paula Murphy, Dir.

Minority Business Assistance Center
SBDC
University of Massachusetts (Boston)
College of Management, 5th Fl.
Boston, MA 02125-3393
Phone: (617)287-7750
Fax: (617)287-7767
Hank Turner, Dir.

Boston College
Capital Formation Service
SBDC
Rahner House
96 College Rd.
Chestnut Hill, MA 02167
Phone: (617)552-4091
Fax: (617)552-2730
Don Reilley, Dir.

Metropolitan Boston Small Business
Development Center Regional Office
Rahner House
96 College Rd.
Chestnut Hill, MA 02167
Phone: (617)552-4091
Fax: (617)552-2730
Dr. Jack McKiernan, Regional Dir.

Southeastern Massachusetts Small
Business Development Center
Regional Office
200 Pocasset St.
PO Box 2785
Fall River, MA 02722
Phone: (508)673-9783
Fax: (508)674-1929
Clyde Mitchell, Regional Dir.

North Shore Massachusetts Small
Business Development Center
Regional Office
197 Essex St.
Salem, MA 01970
Phone: (508)741-6343
Fax: (508)741-6345
Frederick Young, Regional Dir.

Western Massachusetts Small
Business Development Center
Regional Office
101 State St., Ste. 424
Springfield, MA 01103
Phone: (413)737-6712
Fax: (413)737-2312
Dianne Fuller Doherty, Regional Dir.

Clark University
Central Massachusetts Small Business
Development Center Regional Office
Dana Commons
950 Main St.
Worcester, MA 01610
Phone: (508)793-7615
Fax: (508)793-8890
Laurence March, Regional Dir.

Michigan

Lenawee County Chamber of
Commerce
SBDC
202 N. Main St., Ste. A
Adrian, MI 49221-2713
Phone: (517)266-1488
Fax: (517)263-6065
Sally Pinchock, Dir.

Allegan County Economic Alliance
SBDC
Allegan Intermediate School Bldg.
2891 M-277
PO Box 277
Allegan, MI 49010-8042
Phone: (616)673-8442
Fax: (616)650-8042
Chuck Birr, Dir.

Ottawa County Economic
Development Office, Inc.
Small Business Development Center
6676 Lake Michigan Dr.
PO Box 539
Allendale, MI 49401-0539
Phone: (616)892-4120
Fax: (616)895-6670
Ken Rizzio, Dir.

Gratiot Area Chamber of Commerce
SBDC
110 W. Superior St.
PO Box 516
Alma, MI 48801-0516
Phone: (517)463-5525

Alpena Community College
SBDC
666 Johnson St.
Alpena, MI 49707
Phone: (517)356-9021
Fax: (517)354-7507
Carl Bourdelais, Dir.

MMTC SBDC
2901 Hubbard Rd.
PO Box 1485
Ann Arbor, MI 48106-1485
Phone: (313)769-4110
Fax: (313)769-4064
Bill Loomis, Dir.

Huron County Economic
Development Corp.
Small Business Development Center
Huron County Bldg., Rm. 303
250 E. Huron
Bad Axe, MI 48413
Phone: (517)269-6431
Fax: (517)269-7221
Carl Osentoski, Dir.

Battle Creek Area Chamber of
Commerce
SBDC
4 Riverwalk Centre
34 W. Jackson, Ste. A
Battle Creek, MI 49017

Phone: (616)962-4076
Fax: (616)962-4076
Kathy Perrett, Dir.

Bay Area Chamber of Commerce
SBDC
901 Saginaw
Bay City, MI 48708
Phone: (517)893-4567
Fax: (517)893-7016
Cheryl Hiner, Dir.

Lake Michigan College
Corporation and Community
Development Department
Small Business Development Center
2755 E. Napier
Benton Harbor, MI 49022-1899
Phone: (616)927-8179
Fax: (616)927-8103
Milton E. Richter, Dir.

Ferris State University
Small Business Development Center
330 Oak St.
West 115
Big Rapids, MI 49307
Phone: (616)592-3553
Fax: (616)592-3539
Lora Swenson, Dir.

Northern Lakes Economic Alliance
SBDC
1048 East Main St.
PO Box 8
Boyne City, MI 49712-0008
Phone: (616)582-6482
Fax: (616)582-3213
Thomas Johnson, Dir.

Livingston County Small Business
Development Center
131 S. Hyne
Brighton, MI 48116
Phone: (810)227-3556
Fax: (810)227-3080
Dennis Whitney, Dir.

Buchanan Chamber of Commerce
SBDC
119 Main St.
Buchanan, MI 49107
Phone: (616)695-3291
Fax: (616)695-4250
Marlene Gauer, Dir.

Tuscola County Economic
Development Corp.
Small Business Development Center

194 N. State St., Ste. 200
Caro, MI 48723
Phone: (517)673-2849
Fax: (517)673-2517
James McLoskey, Dir.

Branch County Economic Growth
Alliance
SBDC
20 Division St.
Coldwater, MI 49036
Phone: (517)278-4146
Fax: (517)278-8369
Joyce Elferdink, Dir.

University of Detroit-Mercy
Small Business Development Center
Commerce and Finance Bldg., Rm.
105
4001 W. McNichols
PO Box 19900
Detroit, MI 48219-0900
Phone: (313)993-1115
Fax: (313)993-1052
Ram Kesavan, Dir.

Wayne State University
Michigan Small Business
Development Center
2727 Second Ave., Ste. 107
Detroit, MI 48201
Phone: (313)964-1798
Fax: (313)964-3648
E-mail:
stateoffice@misbdc.wayne.edu.
Website: www.bizserve.com/sbdc
Ronald R. Hall, State Director

Wayne State University
2727 2nd Ave., Rm. 121
Detroit, MI 48201
Phone: (313)577-4850
Fax: (313)577-8933
Kevin Lauderdale, Dir.

Wayne State University
Michigan SBDC
2727 Second Ave., Ste. 107
Detroit, MI 48201
Phone: (313)964-1798
Fax: (313)964-3648
E-mail:
stateoffice@misbdc.wayne.edu
Ronald R. Hall, State Dir.

First Step, Inc.
Small Business Development Center
2415 14th Ave., S.
Escanaba, MI 49829

Phone: (906)786-9234
Fax: (906)786-4442
David Gillis, Dir.

Community Capital Development
Corp.
SBDC
Walter Ruether Center
711 N. Saginaw, Ste. 123
Flint, MI 48503
Phone: (810)239-5847
Fax: (810)239-5575
Kim Yarber, Dir.

Center For Continuing Education-
Macomb Community College
SBDC
32101 Caroline
Fraser, MI 48026
Phone: (810)296-3516
Fax: (810)293-0427

North Central Michigan College
SBDC
800 Livingston Blvd.
Gaylord, MI 49735
Phone: (517)731-0071

Association of Commerce and
Industry
SBDC
1 S. Harbor Ave.
PO Box 509
Grand Haven, MI 49417
Phone: (616)846-3153
Fax: (616)842-0379
Karen K. Benson, Dir.

Grand Valley State University
SBDC
Seidman School of Business, Ste.
718S
301 W. Fulton St.
Grand Rapids, MI 49504
Phone: (616)771-6693
Fax: (616)458-3872
Carol R. Lopucki, Dir.

The Right Place Program
SBDC
820 Monroe NW, Ste. 350
Grand Rapids, MI 49503-1423
Phone: (616)771-0571
Fax: (616)458-3768
Raymond P. DeWinkle, Dir.

Oceana County Economic
Development Corp.
SBDC

100 State St.
PO Box 168
Hart, MI 49420-0168
Phone: (616)873-7141
Fax: (616)873-5914
Charles Persenaire, Dir.

Hastings Industrial Incubator
SBDC
1035 E. State St.
Hastings, MI 49058
Phone: (616)948-2305
Fax: (616)948-2947
Joe Rahn, Dir.

Greater Gratiot Development, Inc.
Small Business Center
136 S. Main
Ithaca, MI 48847
Phone: (517)875-2083
Fax: (517)875-2990
Don Schurr, Dir.

Jackson Business Development
Center
SBDC
414 N. Jackson St.
Jackson, MI 49201
Phone: (517)787-0442
Fax: (517)787-3960
Duane Miller, Dir.

Kalamazoo College
Small Business Development Center
Stryker Center for Management
Studies
1327 Academy St.
Kalamazoo, MI 49006-3200
Phone: (616)337-7350
Fax: (616)337-7415
Carl R. Shook, Dir.

Lansing Community College
Small Business Development Center
Continental Bldg.
333 N. Washington Sq.
PO Box 40010
Lansing, MI 48901-7210
Phone: (517)483-1921
Fax: (517)483-9803
Deleski Smith, Dir.

Lapeer Development Corp.
Small Business Development Center
449 McCormick Dr.
Lapeer, MI 48446
Phone: (810)667-0080
Fax: (810)667-3541
Patricia Crawford Lucas, Dir.

Midland Chamber of Commerce
SBDC
300 Rodd St.
Midland, MI 48640
Phone: (517)839-9901
Fax: (517)835-3701
Sam Boeke, Dir.

Genesis Center for Entrepreneurial
Development
SBDC
111 Conant Ave.
Monroe, MI 48161
Phone: (313)243-5947
Fax: (313)242-0009
Dani Topolski, Dir.

Macomb County Business Assistance
Network
Small Business Development Center
115 S. Groesbeck Hwy.
Mt. Clemens, MI 48043
Phone: (810)469-5118
Fax: (810)469-6787
Donald L. Morandi, Dir.

Central Michigan University
Small Business Development Center
256 Applied Business Studies
Complex
Mt. Pleasant, MI 48859
Phone: (517)774-3270
Fax: (517)774-7992
Charles Fitzpatrick, Dir.

Muskegon Economic Growth
Alliance
Small Business Development Center
230 Terrace Plz.
PO Box 1087
Muskegon, MI 49443-1087
Phone: (616)722-3751
Fax: (616)728-7251
Mert Johnson, Dir.

Harbor County Chamber of
Commerce
SBDC
3 W. Buffalo
New Buffalo, MI 49117
Phone: (616)469-5409
Fax: (616)469-2257

Greater Niles Economic Development
Fund
SBDC
1105 N. Front St.
Niles, MI 49120
Phone: (616)683-1833

Fax: (616)683-7515
Chris Brynes, Dir.

Huron Shores Campus
SBDC
5800 Skeel Ave.
Oscoda, MI 48750
Phone: (517)739-1445
Fax: (517)739-1161
Dave Wentworth, Dir.

St. Clair County Community Small
Business Development Center
800 Military St., Ste. 320
Port Huron, MI 48060-5015
Phone: (810)982-9511
Fax: (810)982-9531
Todd Brian, Dir.

Kirtland Community College
SBDC
10775 N. St. Helen Rd.
Roscommon, MI 48653
Phone: (517)275-5121
Fax: (517)275-8745
John Loiacano, Dir.

Saginaw County Chamber of
Commerce
SBDC
901 S. Washington Ave.
Saginaw, MI 48601
Phone: (517)752-7161
Fax: (517)752-9055
James Bockelman, Dir.

Saginaw Future, Inc.
Small Business Development Center
301 E. Genesee, 3rd Fl.
Saginaw, MI 48607
Phone: (517)754-8222
Fax: (517)754-1715
Matthew Hufnagel, Dir.

Washtenaw Community College
SBDC
740 Woodland
Saline, MI 48176
Phone: (313)944-1016
Fax: (313)944-0165
Kathleen Woodard, Dir.

West Shore Community College
Small Business Development Center
Business and Industrial Development
Institute
3000 N. Stiles Rd.
PO Box 277
Scottville, MI 49454-0277

Phone: (616)845-6211
Fax: (616)845-0207
Mark Bergstrom, Dir.

South Haven Chamber of Commerce
SBDC
300 Broadway
South Haven, MI 49090
Phone: (616)637-5171
Fax: (616)639-1570
Larry King, Dir.

Downriver Small Business
Development Center
15100 Northline Rd.
Southgate, MI 48195
Phone: (313)281-0700
Fax: (313)281-3418
Paula Boase, Dir.

Arenac County Extension Service
SBDC
County Bldg.
PO Box 745
Standish, MI 48658
Phone: (517)846-4111

Sterling Heights Area Chamber of
Commerce
Small Business Development Center
12900 Hall Rd., Ste. 110
Sterling Heights, MI 48313
Phone: (810)731-5400
Fax: (810)731-3521
Lillian Adams-Yanssens, Dir.

Northwest Michigan Council of
Governments
Small Business Development Center
2200 Dendrinos Dr.
PO Box 506
Traverse City, MI 49685-0506
Phone: (616)929-5000
Fax: (616)929-5017
Richard J. Beldin, Dir.

Northwestern Michigan College
Small Business Development Center
Center for Business and Industry
1701 E. Front St.
Traverse City, MI 49686
Phone: (616)922-1717
Fax: (616)922-1722
Cheryl Troop, Dir.

Traverse Bay Economic Development
Corp.
Small Business Development Center
202 E. Grandview Pkwy.

PO Box 387
Traverse City, MI 49684
Phone: (616)946-1596
Fax: (616)946-2565
Charles Blankcnship, Dir.

Traverse City Area Chamber of
Commerce
Small Business Development Center
202 E. Grandview Pkwy.
PO Box 387
Traverse City, MI 49684
Phone: (616)947-5075
Fax: (616)946-2565
Matthew Meadors, Dir.

Oakland Count Small Business
Development Center
SOC Bldg.
4555 Corporate Dr., Ste. 201
PO Box 7085
Troy, MI 48098
Phone: (810)641-0088
Fax: (810)267-3809
Daniel V. Belknap, Dir.

Saginaw Valley State University
Small Business Development Center
7400 Bay Rd.
University Center, MI 48710-0001
Phone: (517)791-7746
Fax: (517)249-1955
Christine Greve, Dir.

Macomb Community College
SBDC
14500 12 Mile Rd.
Warren, MI 48093
Phone: (810)445-7348
Fax: (810)445-7316
Geary Maiurini, Dir.

Warren-Center Line Sterling Heights
Chamber of Commerce
SBDC
30500 Van Dyke, No.118
Warren, MI 48093
Phone: (313)751-3939
Fax: (313)751-3995
Janet E. Masi, Dir.

Warren - Centerline - Sterling Heights
Chamber of Commerce
Small Business Development Center
30500 Van Dyke, Ste. 118
Warren, MI 48093
Phone: (313)751-3939
Fax: (313)751-3995
Janet Masi, Dir.

Minnesota

Northwest Technical College
SBDC
905 Grant Ave., SE
Bemidji, MN 56601
Phone: (218)755-4286
Fax: (218)755-4289
Susan Kozojed, Dir.

Normandale Community College
(Bloomington)
Small Business Development Center
9700 France Ave. S
Bloomington, MN 55431
Phone: (612)832-6398
Fax: (612)832-6352
Scott Harding, Dir.

Central Lakes College
Small Business Development Center
501 W. College Dr.
Brainerd, MN 56401
Phone: (218)825-2028
Fax: (218)828-2053
Pamela Thomsen, Dir.

University of Minnesota at Duluth
Small Business Development Center
School of Business and Economics,
Rm. 150
10 University Dr.
Duluth, MN 55812-2496
Phone: (218)726-8758
Fax: (218)726-6338
Lee Jensen, Dir.

Itasca Development Corp.
Grand Rapids Small Business
Development Center
19 NE 3rd St.
Grand Rapids, MN 55744
Phone: (218)327-2241
Fax: (218)327-2242
Kirk Bustrom, Dir.

Hibbing Community College
Small Business Development Center
1515 E. 25th St.
Hibbing, MN 55746
Phone: (218)262-6703
Fax: (218)262-6717
Jim Antilla, Dir.

Rainy River Community College
Small Business Development Center
1501 Hwy. 71
International Falls, MN 56649
Phone: (218)285-2255

Fax: (218)285-2239
Tom West, Dir.

Region Nine Development
Commission
SBDC
410 Jackson St.
PO Box 3367
Mankato, MN 56002-3367
Phone: (507)389-8863
Fax: (507)387-7105
Jill Miller, Dir.

Southwest State University
Small Business Development Center
Science and Technical Resource
Center, Ste. 105
1501 State St.
Marshall, MN 56258
Phone: (507)537-7386
Fax: (507)387-7105
Jack Hawk, Dir.

Minnesota Project Innovation
Small Business Development Center
111 3rd Ave. S., Stc. 100
Minneapolis, MN 55401
Phone: (612)347-6751
Fax: (612)338-3483
Pat Dillon, Dir.

University of St. Thomas
SBDC
Mail Stop 25H 225
Ste. MPL 100
Minneapolis, MN 55403
Phone: (612)962-4500
Fax: (612)962-4810
Gregg Schneider, Dir.

Moorhead State University
Small Business Development Center
1104 7th Ave. S.
MSU Box 303
Moorhead, MN 56563
Phone: (218)236-2289
Fax: (218)236-2280
Len Sliwoski, Dir.

Owatonna Incubator, Inc.
SBDC
560 Dunnell Dr., Ste. 203
PO Box 505
Owatonna, MN 55060
Phone: (507)451-0517
Fax: (507)455-2788
Ken Henrickson, Dir.

Pine Technical College
Small Business Development Center

1100 4th St.
Pine City, MN 55063
Phone: (320)629-7340
Fax: (320)629-7603
John Sparling, Dir.

Hennepin Technical College
SBDC
1820 N. Xenium Ln.
Plymouth, MN 55441
Phone: (612)550-7218
Fax: (612)550-7272
Danelle Wolf, Dir.

Pottery Business and Tech. Center
Small Business Development Center
2000 Pottery Pl. Dr., Ste. 339
Red Wing, MN 55066
Phone: (612)388-4079
Fax: (612)385-2251
Marv Bollum, Dir.

Rochester Community and Tech.
College
Small Business Development Center
Riverland Hall
851 30th Ave. SE
Rochester, MN 55904
Phone: (507)285-7425
Fax: (507)285-7110
Michelle Pyfferoen, Dir.

Dakota County Technical College
Small Business Development Center
1300 E. 145th St.
Rosemount, MN 55068
Phone: (612)423-8262
Fax: (612)322-5156
Tom Trutna, Dir.

Dakota County Technical College
SBDC
1300 145th St. E.
Rosemount, MN 55068
Phone: (612)423-8262
Fax: (612)423-8761
Tom Trutna, Dir.

Southeast Minnesota Development
Corp.
SBDC
111 W. Jessie St.
PO Box 684
Rushford, MN 55971
Phone: (507)864-7557
Fax: (507)864-2091
Terry Erickson, Dir.

St. Cloud State University
Small Business Development Center

720 4th Ave. S.
St. Cloud, MN 56301-3761
Phone: (320)255-4842
Fax: (320)255-4957
Dawn Jensen-Ragnier, Dir.

Department of Trade and Economic
Development
Minnesota SBDC
500 Metro Sq.
121 7th Pl. E.
St. Paul, MN 55101-2146
Phone: (612)297-5770
Fax: (612)296-1290
Mary Kruger, State Dir.

Minnesota Department of Trade and
Economic Development
Small Business Development Center
500 Metro Square
121 7th. Pl. E
St. Paul, MN 55101-2146
Phone: (612)297-5770
Free: (800)657-3858
Fax: (612)296-1290
Website: www.dted.state.mn.us
Mary Kruger, State Director

Minnesota Technology, Inc.
Small Business Development Center
Olcott Plaza Bldg., Ste. 140
820 N. 9th St.
Virginia, MN 55792
Phone: (218)741-4241
Fax: (218)741-4249
John Freeland, Dir.

Wadena Chamber of Commerce
SBDC
222 2nd St., SE
Wadena, MN 56482
Phone: (218)631-1502
Fax: (218)631-2396
Paul Kinn, Dir.

Century College
SBDC
3300 Century Ave., N., Ste. 200-D
White Bear Lake, MN 55110-1894
Phone: (612)773-1794
Fax: (612)779-5802
Ernie Brodtmann, Dir.

Mississippi

Northeast Mississippi Community
College
SBDC
Holiday Hall, 2nd Fl.

Cunningham Blvd.
Booneville, MS 38829
Phone: (601)720-7448
Fax: (601)720-7464
Kenny Holt, Dir.

Delta State University
Small Business Development Center
PO Box 3235 DSU
Cleveland, MS 38733
Phone: (601)846-4236
Fax: (601)846-4235
David Holman, Dir.

East Central Community College
SBDC
Broad St.
PO Box 129
Decatur, MS 39327
Phone: (601)635-2111
Fax: (601)635-4031
Ronald Westbrook, Dir.

Jones County Junior College
SBDC
900 Court St.
Ellisville, MS 39437
Phone: (601)477-4165
Fax: (601)477-4166
Gary Suddith, Dir.

Mississippi Gulf Coast Community
College
SBDC
Jackson County Campus
PO Box 100
Gautier, MS 39553
Phone: (601)497-7723
Fax: (601)497-7788
Janice Mabry, Dir.

Mississippi Delta Community College
Small Business Development Center
PO Box 5607
Greenville, MS 38704-5607
Phone: (601)378-8183
Fax: (601)378-5349
Chuck Herring, Dir.

MS Delta Community College
SBDC
PO Box 5607
Greenville, MS 38704-5607
Phone: (601)378-8183
Fax: (601)378-5349
Chuck Herring, Dir.

Mississippi Contract Procurement
Center
SBDC

3015 12th St.
PO Box 610
Gulfport, MS 39502-0610
Phone: (601)864-2961
Fax: (601)864-2969
C. W. "Skip" Ryland, Exec. Dir.

Pearl River Community College
Small Business Development Center
5448 U.S. Hwy. 49 S.
Hattiesburg, MS 39401
Phone: (601)544-0030
Fax: (601)544-9149
Heidi McDuffie, Dir.

Mississippi Valley State University
Affiliate SBDC
PO Box 992
Itta Bena, MS 38941
Phone: (601)254-3601
Fax: (601)254-6704
Dr. Jim Breyley, Dir.

Jackson State University
Small Business Development Center
Jackson Enterprise Center, Ste. A-1
931 Hwy. 80 W
Box 43
Jackson, MS 39204
Phone: (601)968-2795
Fax: (601)968-2796
Henry Thomas, Dir.

University of Southern Mississippi
Small Business Development Center
136 Beach Park Pl.
Long Beach, MS 39560
Phone: (601)865-4578
Fax: (601)865-4581
Lucy Betcher, Dir.

Alcorn State University
SBDC
552 West St.
PO Box 90
Lorman, MS 39096-9402
Phone: (601)877-6684
Fax: (601)877-6256
Sharon Witty, Dir.

Meridian Community College
Small Business Development Center
910 Hwy. 19 N
Meridian, MS 39307
Phone: (601)482-7445
Fax: (601)482-5803
Mac Hodges, Dir.

Mississippi State University
Small Business Development Center

1 Research Bldg., Ste 201
PO Drawer 5288
Mississippi State, MS 39762
Phone: (601)325-8684
Fax: (601)325-4016
Sonny Fisher, Dir.

Copiah-Lincoln Community College
Small Business Development Center
11 County Line Circle
Natchez, MS 39120
Phone: (601)445-5254
Fax: (601)446-1221
Bob D. Russ, Dir.

Hinds Community College
Small Business Development Center/
International Trade Center
1500 Raymond Lake Rd., 2nd Fl.
Raymond, MS 39154
Phone: (601)857-3536
Fax: (601)857-3474
Marguerite Wall, Dir.

Holmes Community College
SBDC
412 W. Ridgeland Ave.
Ridgeland, MS 39157
Phone: (601)853-0827
Fax: (601)853-0844
John Deddens, Dir.

Northwest Mississippi Community
College
SBDC
DeSoto Ctr.
5197 W.E. Ross Pkwy.
Southaven, MS 38671
Phone: (601)280-7648
Fax: (601)280-7648
Jody Dunning, Dir.

Southwest Mississippi Community
College
SBDC
College Dr.
Summit, MS 39666
Phone: (601)276-3890
Fax: (601)276-3883
Kathryn Durham, Dir.

Itawamba Community College
Small Business Development Center
653 Eason Blvd.
Tupelo, MS 38801
Phone: (601)680-8515
Fax: (601)680-8547
Rex Hollingsworth, Dir.

University of Mississippi
Small Business Development Center
Old Chemistry Bldg., Ste. 216
University, MS 38677
Phone: (601)232-5001
Free: (800)725-7232
Fax: (601)232-5650
E-mail: msbdc@olemiss.edu
Website: www.olemiss.edu/depts/
mssbdc
Walter "Doug" Gurley, Jr., Director

University of Mississippi
SBDC
Old Chemistry Bldg., Ste. 216
University, MS 38677
Phone: (601)232-5001
Fax: (601)232-5650
Walter D. Gurley, Jr., Dir.

University of Mississippi
Mississippi SBDC
N.C.P.A., Rm. 1082
University, MS 38677
Phone: (601)234-2120
Fax: (601)232-4220
Michael Vanderlip, Dir.

Missouri

Camden County
SBDC Extension Center
113 Kansas
PO Box 1405
Camdenton, MO 65020
Phone: (573)882-0344
Fax: (573)884-4297
Jackie Rasmussen, B&I Spec.

Missouri PAC - Southeastern
Missouri State University
SBDC
222 N. Pacific
Cape Girardeau, MO 63701
Phone: (573)290-5965
Fax: (573)651-5005
George Williams, Dir.

Southeast Missouri State University
Small Business Development Center
University Plaza
MS 5925
Cape Girardeau, MO 63701
Phone: (573)290-5965
Fax: (573)651-5005
E-mail: sbdc-cg@ext.missouri.edu
Frank "Buz" Sutherland, Dir.

Chillicothe City Hall
SBDC
715 Washington St.
Chillicothe, MO 64601-2229
Phone: (660)646-6920
Fax: (660)646-6811
Nanette Anderjaska, Dir.

East Central Missouri/St. Louis
County
Extension Center
121 S. Meramac, Ste. 501
Clayton, MO 63105
Phone: (314)889-2911
Fax: (314)854-6147
Carole Leriche-Price, B&I Specialist

Boone County Extension Center
SBDC
1012 N. Hwy. UU
Columbia, MO 65203
Phone: (573)445-9792
Fax: (573)445-9807
Mr. Casey Venters, B&I Specialist

MO PAC-Central Region
University of Missouri-Columbia
SBDC
University Pl., Ste. 1800
1205 University Ave.
Columbia, MO 65211
Phone: (573)882-3597
Fax: (573)884-4297
E-mail: mopcol@ext.missouri.edu
Morris Hudson, Dir.

University of Missouri
Missouri SBDC System
1205 University Ave., Ste. 300
Columbia, MO 65211
Phone: (573)882-0344
Fax: (573)884-4297
E-mail: sbdc-mso@ext.missouri.edu
Max E. Summers, State Dir.

University of Missouri—Columbia
Small Business Development Center
University Pl., Ste. 1800
1205 University Ave.
Columbia, MO 65211
Phone: (573)882-7096
Fax: (573)882-6156
E-mail: sbdc-c@ext.missouri.edu
Frank Siebert, Dir.

University of Missouri—Columbia
Small Business Development Center
300 University Pl.
Columbia, MO 65211

Phone: (573)882-0344
Fax: (573)884-4297
Max E. Summers, State Director

Hannibal Satellite Center
Hannibal, MO 63401
Phone: (816)385-6550
Fax: (816)385-6568

Jefferson County
Courthouse, Annex No. 203
Extension Center
Courthouse, Annex 203
725 Maple St.
PO Box 497
Hillsboro, MO 63050
Phone: (573)789-5391
Fax: (573)789-5059

Cape Girardeau County
SBDC Extension Center
815 Hwy. 25S
PO Box 408
Jackson, MO 63755
Phone: (573)243-3581
Fax: (573)243-1606
Richard Sparks, B&I Specialist

Cole County Extension Center
SBDC
2436 Tanner Bridge Rd.
Jefferson City, MO 65101
Phone: (573)634-2824
Fax: (573)634-5463
Mr. Chris Bouchard, B&I Specialist

Missouri Southern State College
Small Business Development Center
Matthews Hall, Ste. 107
3950 Newman Rd.
Joplin, MO 64801-1595
Phone: (417)625-9313
Fax: (417)625-9782
E-mail: sbdc-j@ext.missouri.edu
Jim Krudwig, Dir.

Rockhurst College
Small Business Development Center
1100 Rockhurst Rd.
VanAckeren Hall, Rm. 205
Kansas City, MO 64110-2508
Phone: (816)501-4572
Fax: (816)501-4646
Rhonda Gerke, Dir.

Truman State University
Small Business Development Center
100 E. Norman
Kirksville, MO 63501-4419

Phone: (816)785-4307
Fax: (816)785-4357
E-mail: sbdc-k@ext.missouri.edu
Glen Giboney, Dir.

Thomas Hill Enterprise Center
SBDC
1409 N. Prospect Dr.
PO Box 246
Macon, MO 63552
Phone: (816)385-6550
Fax: (816)562-3071
Jane Vanderham, Dir.

Northwest Missouri State University
Small Business Development Center
423 N. Market St.
Maryville, MO 64468-1614
Phone: (660)562-1701
Fax: (660)582-3071
Brad Anderson, Dir.

Audrain County Extension Center
SBDC
Courthouse, 4th Fl.
101 Jefferson
Mexico, MO 65265
Phone: (573)581-3231
Fax: (573)581-2766
Virgil Woolridge, B&I Specialist

Randolph County
Extension Center
417 E. Urbandale
Moberly, MO 65270
Phone: (816)263-3534
Fax: (816)263-1874
Ray Marshall, B&I Specialist

Mineral Area College
SBDC
PO Box 1000
Park Hills, MO 63601-1000
Phone: (573)431-4593
Fax: (573)431-2144
E-mail: sbdc-fr@ext.missouri.edu
Eugene Cherry, Dir.

Telecommunications Community
Resource Center
Longhead Learning Center
Small Business Development Center
1121 Victory Ln.
3019 Fair St.
Poplar Bluff, MO 63901
Phone: (573)840-9450
Fax: (573)840-9456
Judy Moss, Dir.

Washington County SBDC
102 N. Missouri
Potosi, MO 63664
Phone: (573)438-2671
Fax: (573)438-2079
LaDonna McCuan, B&I Specialist

Center for Technology Transfer and
Economic Development
Nagogami Ter., Bldg. 1, Rm. 104
Rolla, MO 65401-0249
Phone: (573)341-4559
Fax: (573)346-2694
Fred Goss, Dir.

Phelps County
SBDC Extension Center
Courthouse
200 N. Main
PO Box 725
Rolla, MO 65401
Phone: (573)364-3147
Fax: (573)364-0436
Paul Cretin, B&I Specialist

University of Missouri at Rolla
SBDC
Nagogami Terrace, Bldg. 1, Rm. 104
Rolla, MO 65401-0249
Phone: (573)341-4559
Fax: (573)341-6495
E-mail: sbdc-rt@ext.missouri.edu
Fred Goss, Dir.

Missouri PAC - Eastern Region
SBDC
3830 Washington Ave.
St. Louis, MO 63108
Phone: (314)534-4413
Fax: (314)534-3237
E-mail:
MOPSTL@EXT.MISSOURI.EDU
Ken Konchel, Dir.

St. Louis County
Extension Center
207 Marillac, UMSL
8001 Natural Bridge Rd.
St. Louis, MO 63121
Phone: (314)553-5944
John Henschke, Specialist

St. Louis University
Small Business State University
SBDC
3750 Lindell Blvd.
St. Louis, MO 63108-3412
Phone: (314)977-7232
Fax: (314)977-7241

E-mail: sbdc-stl@ext.missouri.edu
Virginia Campbell, Dir.

St. Louis / St. Charles County
Economic Council
SBDC Extension Center
260 Brown Rd.
St. Peters, MO 63376
Phone: (314)970-3000
Fax: (314)274-3310
Tim Wathen, B&I Specialist

Pettis County
Extension Center
1012A Thompson Blvd.
Sedalia. MO 65301
Phone: (816)827-0591
Fax: (816)827-4888
Betty Lorton, B&I Specialist

Southwest Missouri State University
Center for Business Research
Small Business Development Center
901 S. National
Box 88
Springfield, MO 65804-0089
Phone: (417)836-5685
Fax: (417)836-7666
Jane Peterson, Dir.

Franklin County
SBDC Extension Center
414 E. Main
PO Box 71
Union, MO 63084
Phone: (573)583-5141
Fax: (573)583-5145
Rebecca How, B&I Specialist

Central Missouri State University
SBDC
Grinstead, No. 9
Warrensburg, MO 64093-5037
Phone: (816)543-4402
Fax: (816)543-8159
Wes Savage, Coordinator

Central Missouri State University
Center for Technology
Grinstead, No. 75
Warrensburg, MO 64093-5037
Phone: (816)543-4402
Fax: (816)747-1653
Cindy Tanck, Coordinator

Howell County
SBDC Extension Center
217 S. Aid Ave.
West Plains, MO 65775

Phone: (417)256-2391
Fax: (417)256-8569
Mick Gilliam, B&I Specialist

Montana

Montana Tradepost Authority
Small Business Development Center
2722 3rd Ave., Ste. W300
115 N. Broadway, 2nd Fl.
Billings, MT 59101
Phone: (406)256-6871
Fax: (406)256-6877
Tom McKerlick, Contact

Bozeman Small Business
Development Center
222 E. Main St., Ste. 102
Bozeman, MT 59715
Phone: (406)587-3113
Fax: (406)587-9565
Michele DuBose, Contact

Butte Small Business Development
Center
305 W. Mercury, Ste. 211
Butte, MT 59701
Phone: (406)782-7333
Fax: (406)782-9675
John Donovan, Contact

High Plains Development Authority
Great Falls SBDC
710 1st. Ave. N.
PO Box 2568
Great Falls, MT 59403
Phone: (406)454-1934
Fax: (406)454-2995
Suzie David

Havre Small Business Development
Center
PO Box 170
Havre, MT 59501
Phone: (406)265-9226
Fax: (406)265-5602
Randy Hanson, Contact

Montana Department of Commerce
Small Business Development Center
1424 9th Ave.
Helena, MT 59620
Phone: (406)444-4780
Fax: (406)444-1872
E-mail: rkloser@mt.gov
Ralph Kloser, State Director

Montana Department of Commerce
Montana SBDC

1424 9th Ave.
PO Box 200505
Helena, MT 59620
Phone: (406)444-2463
Fax: (406)444-1872
Ralph Kloser, State Dir.

Kalispell Small Business
Development Center
PO Box 8300
Kalispell, MT 59901
Phone: (406)758-5412
Fax: (406)758-6582
Dan Manning, Contact

Missoula Small Business
Development Center
127 N. Higgins, 3rd Fl.
Missoula, MT 59802
Phone: (406)728-9234
Fax: (406)721-4584
Brett George, Contact

Sidney Small Business Development
Center
123 W. Main
Sidney, MT 59270
Phone: (406)482-5024
Fax: (406)482-5306
Dwayne Heintz, Contact

Nebraska

Chadron State College
SBDC
Administration Bldg.
1000 Main St.
Chadron, NE 69337
Phone: (308)432-6282
Fax: (308)432-6430
Cliff Hanson, Dir.

University of Nebraska at Kearney
SBDC
Welch Hall
19th St. and College Dr.
Kearney, NE 68849-3035
Phone: (308)865-8344
Fax: (308)865-8153
Susan Jensen, Dir.

University of Nebraska at Lincoln
SBDC
1135 M St., No. 200
11th and Cornhusker Hwy.
Lincoln, NE 68521
Phone: (402)472-3358
Fax: (402)472-3363
Cliff Mosteller, Dir.

Mid-Plains Community College
SBDC
416 N. Jeffers, Rm. 26
North Platte, NE 69101
Phone: (308)534-5115
Fax: (308)534-5117
Dean Kurth, Dir.

Nebraska Small Business
Development Center
Omaha Business and Technology
Center
2505 N. 24 St., Ste. 101
Omaha, NE 68110
Phone: (402)595-3511
Fax: (402)595-3524
Tom McCabe, Dir.

University of Nebraska at Omaha
Nebraska Business Development
Center
College of Business Administration,
Rm. 407
60th & Dodge Sts.
CBA Rm. 407
Omaha, NE 68182
Phone: (402)554-2521
Fax: (402)554-3747
Robert Bernier, State Dir.

University of Nebraska at Omaha
Nebraska Small Business
Development Center
CBA Rm. 407
60th & Dodge Streets
Omaha, NE 68182-0248
Phone: (402)554-2521
Fax: (402)554-3473
Website: www.nbdc.unomaha.edu
Robert Bernier, State Director

University of Nebraska at Omaha
Peter Kiewit Conference Center
SBDC
1313 Farnam-on-the-Mall, Ste. 132
Omaha, NE 68182-0248
Phone: (402)595-2381
Fax: (402)595-2385
Nate Brei, Dir.

Peru State College
SBDC
T.J. Majors Hall, Rm. 248
Peru, NE 68421
Phone: (402)872-2274
Fax: (402)872-2422
Jerry Brazil, Dir.

Western Nebraska Community
College
SBDC
Nebraska Public Power Bldg., Rm.
408
1721 Broadway
Scottsbluff, NE 69361
Phone: (308)635-7513
Fax: (308)635-6596
Ingrid Battershell, Dir.

Wayne State College
SBDC
Gardner Hall
1111 Main St.
Wayne, NE 68787
Phone: (402)375-7575
Fax: (402)375-7574
Loren Kucera, Dir.

Nevada

Carson City Chamber of Commerce
Small Business Development Center
1900 S. Carson St., Ste. 100
Carson City, NV 89701
Phone: (702)882-1565
Fax: (702)882-4179
Larry Osborne, Dir.

Great Basin College
Small Business Development Center
1500 College Pkwy.
Elko, NV 89801
Phone: (702)753-2205
Fax: (702)753-2242
John Pryor, Dir.

Incline Village Chamber of
Commerce
SBDC
969 Tahoe Blvd.
Incline Village, NV 89451
Phone: (702)831-4440
Fax: (702)832-1605
Sheri Woods, Exec. Dir.

Las Vegas SBDC
SBDC
3720 Howard Hughes Pkwy., Ste. 130
Las Vegas, NV 89109
Phone: (702)734-7575
Fax: (702)734-7633
Robert Holland, Bus. Dev. Specialist

University of Nevada at Las Vegas
Small Business Development Center
4505 Maryland Pkwy.
Box 456011

Las Vegas, NV 89154-6011
Phone: (702)895-0852
Fax: (702)895-4095
Nancy Buist, Business Development
Specialist

North Las Vegas Small Business
Development Center
19 W. Brooks Ave., Ste. B
North Las Vegas, NV 89030
Phone: (702)399-6300
Fax: (702)895-4095
Janis Stevenson, Business
Development Specialist

Nevada Small Business Development
Center
University of Nevada at Reno
College of Business Administration/
032
Business Bldg., Rm. 411
Mail Stop 032
Reno, NV 89557-0100
Phone: (702)784-1717
Fax: (702)784-4337
Website: www.scs.unr.edu/nfbdc
Sam Males, State Director

University of Nevada at Reno
Small Business Development Center
College of Business Administration
Nazir Ansari Business Bldg., Rm. 411
Reno, NV 89557-0100
Phone: (702)784-1717
Fax: (702)784-4337
E-mail: nsbdc@scs.unr.edu
Sam Males, Dir.

Tri-County Development Authority
Small Business Development Center
50 W. 4th St.
PO Box 820
Winnemucca, NV 89446
Phone: (702)623-5777
Fax: (702)623-5999
Teri Williams, Dir.

New Hampshire

University of New Hampshire
Small Business Development Center
108 McConnell Hall
15 College Rd.
Durham, NH 03824-3593
Phone: (603)862-2200
Fax: (603)862-4876
Mary Collins, State Dir.

University of New Hampshire
Small Business Development Center
108 McConnell Hall
Durham, NH 03824-3593
Phone: (603)862-2200
Fax: (603)862-4876
E-mail: mec@christa.unh.edu
Website: www.mv.com/ipusers/
nhsbdc
Mary Collins, State Director

Keene State College
Small Business Development Center
Mail Stop 210
Keene, NH 03435-2101
Phone: (603)358-2602
Fax: (603)358-2612
Gary Cloutier, Regional Mgr.

Littleton Small Business
Development Center
120 Main St.
Littleton, NH 03561
Phone: (603)444-1053
Fax: (603)444-5463
Liz Ward, Regional Mgr.

Manchester Small Business
Development Center
1000 Elm St., 14th Fl.
Manchester, NH 03101
Phone: (603)624-2000
Fax: (603)634-2449
Bob Ebberson, Regional Mgr.

Office of Economic Initiatives
SBDC
1000 Elm St., 14th Fl.
Manchester, NH 03101
Phone: (603)634-2796
E-mail: ahj@hopper.unh.edu
Amy Jennings, Dir.

New Hampshire Small Business
Development Center
1 Indian Head Plz., Ste. 510
Nashua, NH 03060
Phone: (603)886-1233
Fax: (603)598-1164
Bob Wilburn, Regional Mgr.

Plymouth State College
Small Business Development Center
Outreach Center, MSC24A
Plymouth, NH 03264-1595
Phone: (603)535-2523
Fax: (603)535-2850
Janice Kitchen, Regional Mgr.

SBDC
18 S. Main St., Ste. 3A
Rochester, NH 03867
Phone: (603)330-1929
Fax: (603)330-1948

New Jersey

Greater Atlantic City Chamber of
Commerce
Small Business Development Center
1301 Atlantic Ave.
Atlantic City, NJ 08401
Phone: (609)345-5600
Fax: (609)345-1666
William R. McGinley, Dir.

Rutgers University at Camden
Small Business Development Center
227 Penn St., 3rd Fl., Rm. 334
Camden, NJ 08102
Phone: (609)757-6221
Fax: (609)225-6231
Patricia Peacock, Dir.

Brookdale Community College
Small Business Development Center
Newman Springs Rd.
Lincroft, NJ 07738
Phone: (732)842-1900
Fax: (732)842-0203
Larry Novick, Dir.

New Jersey Small Business
Development Center
Rutgers Graduate School of
Management
49 Bleeker St.
University Heights
Newark, NJ 07102-1993
Phone: (973)353-1927
Fax: (973)353-1110
Website: www.nj.com/njsbdc
Brenda B. Hopper, State Director

Rutgers University
New Jersey SBDC
Graduate School of Management
49 Bleeker St.
Newark, NJ 07102
Phone: (973)353-5950
Fax: (973)353-1110
Brenda B. Hopper, State Dir.

Bergen County Community College
SBDC
400 Paramus Rd., Rm. A333
Paramus, NJ 07652-1595
Phone: (201)447-7841

Fax: (201)447-7495
Melody Irvin, Dir.

Mercer County Community College
Small Business Development Center
West Windsor Campus
1200 Old Trenton Rd.
PO Box B
Trenton, NJ 08690
Phone: (609)586-4800
Fax: (609)890-6338
Herb Spiegel, Dir.

Kean College
Small Business Development Center
East Campus, Rm. 242
Union, NJ 07083
Phone: (908)527-2946
Fax: (908)527-2960
Mira Kostak, Dir.

Warren County Community College
Small Business Development Center
Skylands 475
Rte. 57 W.
Washington, NJ 07882-9605
Phone: (908)689-9620
Fax: (908)689-2247
James Smith, Dir.

New Mexico

New Mexico State University at
Alamogordo
Small Business Development Center
2230 Lawrence Blvd.
Alamogordo, NM 88310
Phone: (505)434-5272
Fax: (505)439-3643
Dwight Harp, Dir.

Albuquerque Technical-Vocational
Institute
Small Business Development Center
525 Buena Vista SE
Albuquerque, NM 87106
Phone: (505)224-4246
Fax: (505)224-4251
Ray Garcia, Dir.

South Valley SBDC
SBDC
70 4th St. SW, Ste. A
Albuquerque, NM 87102
Phone: (505)248-0132
Fax: (505)248-0127
Steven Becerra, Dir.

New Mexico State University at
Carlsbad
Small Business Development Center
301 S. Canal St.
PO Box 1090
Carlsbad, NM 88220
Phone: (505)887-6562
Fax: (505)885-0818
Larry Coalson, Dir.

Clovis Community College
Small Business Development Center
417 Schepps Blvd.
Clovis, NM 88101
Phone: (505)769-4136
Fax: (505)769-4190
Sandra Taylor-Smith

Northern New Mexico Community
College
Small Business Development Center
1002 N. Onate St.
Espanola, NM 87532
Phone: (505)747-2236
Fax: (505)757-2234
Ralph Prather, Dir.

San Juan College
Small Business Development Center
4601 College Blvd.
Farmington, NM 87402
Phone: (505)599-0528
Fax: (505)599-0385
Cal Tingey, Dir.

University of New Mexico at Gallup
Small Business Development Center
103 W. Hwy. 66
Gallup, NM 87305
Phone: (505)722-2220
Fax: (505)863-6006
Elsie Sanchez, Dir.

New Mexico State University at
Grants
Small Business Development Center
709 E. Roosevelt Ave.
Grants, NM 87020
Phone: (505)287-8221
Fax: (505)287-2125
Clemente Sanchez, Dir.

New Mexico Junior College
Small Business Development Center
5317 Lovington Hwy.
Hobbs, NM 88240
Phone: (505)392-5549
Fax: (505)392-2527
Don Leach, Dir.

Dona Ana Branch Community
College
Small Business Development Center
3400 S. Espina St.
Dept. 3DA, Box 30001
Las Cruces, NM 88003-0001
Phone: (505)527-7601
Fax: (505)527-7515
Terry Sullivan, Dir.

Luna Vocational-Technical Institute
Small Business Development Center
Camp Luna Site
Hot Springs Blvd.
PO Box 1510
Las Vegas, NM 87701
Phone: (505)454-2595
Fax: (505)454-2588
Don Bustos, Dir.

University of New Mexico at Los
Alamos
Small Business Development Center
901 18th St., No. 18
PO Box 715
Los Alamos, NM 87544
Phone: (505)662-0001
Fax: (505)662-0099
Jay Wechsler, Interim Dir.

University of New Mexico at
Valencia
Small Business Development Center
280 La Entrada
Los Lunas, NM 87031
Phone: (505)925-8980
Fax: (505)925-8987
David Ashley, Dir.

Eastern New Mexico University at
Roswell
Small Business Development Center
57 University Ave.
PO Box 6000
Roswell, NM 88201-6000
Phone: (505)624-7133
Fax: (505)624-7132
Eugene D. Simmons, Dir.

Santa Fe Community College
New Mexico Small Business
Development Center
6401 Richards Ave.
Santa Fe, NM 87505
Phone: (505)428-1343
Free: (800)281-7232
Fax: (505)428-1469
J. Roy Miller, State Director

Santa Fe Community College
New Mexico SBDC
6401 Richards Ave.
Santa Fe, NM 87505
Phone: (505)438-1362
Free: (800)281-SBDC
Fax: (505)471-1469
Roy Miller, State Dir.

Western New Mexico University
Small Business Development Center
PO Box 2672
Silver City, NM 88062
Phone: (505)538-6320
Fax: (505)538-6341
Linda K. Jones, Dir.

Mesa Technical College
Small Business Development Center
911 S. 10th St.
Tucumcari, NM 88401
Phone: (505)461-4413
Fax: (505)461-1901
Carl Reiney, Dir.

New York

State University of New York
New York Small Business
Development Center
State University Plz., Rm. S-523
Albany, NY 12246
Phone: (518)443-5398
Free: (800)732-SBDC
Fax: (518)465-4992
Website: www.smallbiz.suny.edu/
nysbdc.htm
James L. King, Director

State University of New York at
Albany
Small Business Development Center
Draper Hall, Rm. 107
135 Western Ave.
Albany, NY 12222
Phone: (518)442-5577
Fax: (518)442-5582
Peter George III, Dir.

State University of New York (Suny)
New York SBDC
Suny Plaza, S-523
Albany, NY 12246
Phone: (518)443-5398
Free: (800)732-SBDC
Fax: (518)465-4992
E-mail: kingjl@cc.sunycentral.edu
James L. King, State Dir.

Binghamton University
Small Business Development Center
PO Box 6000
Binghamton, NY 13902-6000
Phone: (607)777-4024
Fax: (607)777-4029
E-mail: sbdcbu@spectra.net
Joanne Bauman, Dir.

State University of New York
Small Business Development Center
74 N. Main St.
Brockport, NY 14420
Phone: (716)637-6660
Fax: (716)637-2102
Wilfred Bordeau, Dir.

Bronx Community College
Small Business Development Center
McCracken Hall, Rm. 14
W. 181st St. & University Ave.
Bronx, NY 10453
Phone: (718)563-3570
Fax: (718)563-3572
Adi Israeli, Dir.

Bronx Outreach Center
Con Edison
SBDC
560 Cortlandt Ave.
Bronx, NY 10451
Phone: (718)563-9204
David Bradley

Downtown Brooklyn Outreach Center
Kingsborough Community College
SBDC
395 Flatbush Ave., Extension Rm.
413
Brooklyn, NY 11201
Phone: (718)260-9783
Fax: (718)260-9797
Stuart Harker, Assoc. Dir.

Kingsborough Community College
Small Business Development Center
2001 Oriental Blvd., Bldg. T4, Rm.
4204
Manhattan Beach
Brooklyn, NY 11235
Phone: (718)368-4619
Fax: (718)368-4629
Edward O'Brien, Dir.

State University of New York at
Buffalo
Small Business Development Center
Bacon Hall 117
1300 Elmwood Ave.

Buffalo, NY 14222
Phone: (716)878-4030
Fax: (716)878-4067
Susan McCartney, Dir.

Canton Outreach Center (SUNY)
Jefferson Community College
SBDC
Canton, NY 13617
Phone: (315)386-7312
Fax: (315)386-7945

Cobleskill Outreach Center
SBDC
SUNY Cobleskill
Warner Hall, Rm. 218
Cobleskill, NY 12043
Phone: (518)234-5528
Fax: (518)234-5272
Peter Desmond, Business Advisor

Corning Community College
Small Business Development Center
24 Denison Pkwy. W
Corning, NY 14830
Phone: (607)962-9461
Free: (800)358-7171
Fax: (607)936-6642
Bonnie Gestwicki, Dir.

Mercy College/Westchester Outreach
Center
SBDC
555 Broadway
Dobbs Ferry, NY 10522-1189
Phone: (914)674-7485
Fax: (914)693-4996
Tom Milton, Coordinator

State University of New York at
Farmingdale
Small Business Development Center
Campus Commons Bldg.
2350 Route 110
Farmingdale, NY 11735
Phone: (516)420-2765
Fax: (516)293-5343
Joseph Schwartz, Dir.

Dutchess Outreach Center
SBDC
Fishkill Extension Center
2600 Rte. 9, Unit 90
Fishkill, NY 12524-2001
Phone: (914)897-2607
Fax: (914)897-4653

Suny Geneseo Outreach Center
SBDC
South Hall, No. 111

1 College Circle
Geneseo, NY 14454
Phone: (716)245-5429
Fax: (716)245-5430
Charles VanArsdale, Dir.

Geneva Outreach Center
SBDC
122 N. Genesee St.
Geneva, NY 14456
Phone: (315)781-1253
Sandy Bordeau, Administrative Dir.

Hempstead Outreach Center
SBDC
269 Fulton Ave.
Hempstead, NY 11550
Phone: (516)564-8672
Fax: (516)481-4938
Lloyd Clarke, Asst. Dir.

York College/City University of New
York
Small Business Development Center
Science Bldg., Rm. 107
94-50 159th St.
Jamaica, NY 11451
Phone: (718)262-2880
Fax: (718)262-2881
James A. Heyliger

Jamestown Community College
Small Business Development Center
525 Falconer St.
PO Box 20
Jamestown, NY 14702-0020
Phone: (716)665-5754
Free: (800)522-7232
Fax: (716)665-6733
Irene Dobies, Dir.

Kingston Small Business
Development Center
1 Development Ct.
Kingston, NY 12401
Phone: (914)339-0025
Fax: (914)339-1631
Patricia La Susa, Dir.

Baruch College
Mid-Town Outreach Center
SBDC
360 Park Ave. S., Rm. 1101
New York, NY 10010
Phone: (212)802-6620
Fax: (212)802-6613
Cheryl Fenton, Dir.

East Harlem Outreach Center
SBDC

145 E. 116th St., 3rd Fl.
New York, NY 10029
Phone: (212)346-1900
Fax: (212)534-4576
Anthony Sanchez, Coordinator

Harlem Outreach Center
SBDC
163 W. 125th St., Rm. 1307
New York, NY 10027
Phone: (212)346-1900
Fax: (212)534-4576
Anthony Sanchez, Coordinator

Mid-Town Outreach Ctr.
Baruch College
SBDC
360 Park Ave. S. Rm. 1101
New York, NY 10010
Phone: (212)802-6620
Fax: (212)802-6613
Barrie Phillip, Coordinator

Pace University
Small Business Development Center
1 Pace Plz., Rm. W483
New York, NY 10038
Phone: (212)346-1900
Fax: (212)346-1613
Ira Davidson, Dir.

Niagara Falls Satellite Office
SBDC/International Trade Center
Carborundum Center
345 3rd St.
Niagara Falls, NY 14303-1117
Phone: (716)285-4793
Fax: (716)285-4797

SUNY at Oswego
Operation Oswego County
SBDC
44 W. Bridge St.
Oswego, NY 13126
Phone: (315)343-1545
Fax: (315)343-1546

Clinton Community College
SBDC
Lake Shore Rd., Rte. 9 S.
136 Clinton Point Dr.
Plattsburgh, NY 12901
Phone: (518)562-4260
Fax: (518)563-9759
Merry Gwynn, Coordinator

Suffolk County Community College
Riverhead Outreach Center
SBDC
Orient Bldg., Rm. 132

Riverhead, NY 11901
Phone: (516)369-1409
Fax: (516)369-3255
Al Falkowski, Contact

SUNY at Brockport
SBDC
Sibley Bldg.
228 E. Main St.
Rochester, NY 14604
Phone: (716)232-7310
Fax: (716)637-2182

Niagara County Community College
at Sanborn
Small Business Development Center
3111 Saunders Settlement Rd.
Sanborn, NY 14132
Phone: (716)693-1910
Fax: (716)731-3595
Richard Gorko, Dir.

Long Island University at
Southhampton/Southampton Outreach
Center
SBDC
Abney Peak, Montauk Hwy.
Southampton, NY 11968
Phone: (516)287-0059
Fax: (516)287-8287
George Tulmany, Business Advisor

College of Staten Island
SBDC
Bldg. 1A, Rm. 111
2800 Victory Blvd.
Staten Island, NY 10314-9806
Phone: (718)982-2560
Fax: (718)982-2323
Dr. Martin Schwartz, Dir.

SUNY at Stony Brook
SBDC
Harriman Hall, Rm. 103
Stony Brook, NY 11794-3775
Phone: (516)632-9070
Fax: (516)632-7176
Judith McEvoy, Dir.

Rockland Community College
Small Business Development Center
145 College Rd.
Suffern, NY 10901-3620
Phone: (914)356-0370
Fax: (914)356-0381
Thomas J. Morley, Dir.

Onondaga Community College
Small Business Development Center
Excell Bldg., Rm. 108

4969 Onondaga Rd.
Syracuse, NY 13215-1944
Phone: (315)498-6070
Fax: (315)492-3704
Robert Varney, Dir.

Manufacturing Field Office
SBDC
Rensselaer Technology Park
385 Jordan Rd.
Troy, NY 12180-7602
Phone: (518)286-1014
Fax: (518)286-1006
Bill Brigham, Dir.

State University Institute of
Technology
Small Business Development Center
PO Box 3050
Utica, NY 13504-3050
Phone: (315)792-7546
Fax: (315)792-7554
David Mallen, Dir.

SUNY Institute of Technology at
Utica/Rome
SBDC
PO Box 3050
Utica, NY 13504-3050
Phone: (315)792-7546
Fax: (315)792-7554
David Mallen, Dir.

Jefferson Community College
Small Business Development Center
Coffeen St.
Watertown, NY 13601
Phone: (315)782-9262
Fax: (315)782-0901
John F. Tanner, Dir.

SBDC Outreach Small Business
Resource Center
222 Bloomingdale Rd., 3rd Fl.
White Plains, NY 10605-1500
Phone: (914)644-4116
Fax: (914)644-2184
Kathleen Cassels, Coordinator

North Carolina

Asheville SBTDC
Haywood St.
PO Box 2570
Asheville, NC 28805
Phone: (704)251-6025
Fax: (704)251-6025

Appalachian State University
Small Business and Technology
Development Center (Northwestern
Region)
Walker College of Business
2123 Raley Hall
Boone, NC 28608
Phone: (704)262-2492
Fax: (704)262-2027
Bill Parrish, Regional Dir.

University of North Carolina at
Chapel Hill
Central Carolina Regional Small
Business Development Center
608 Airport Rd., Ste. B
Chapel Hill, NC 27514
Phone: (919)962-0389
Fax: (919)962-3291
Dan Parks, Dir.

University of North Carolina at
Charlotte
Small Business and Technology
Development Center (Southern
Piedmont Region)
The Ben Craig Center
8701 Mallard Creek Rd.
Charlotte, NC 28262
Phone: (704)548-1090
Fax: (704)548-9050
George McAllister, Dir.

Western Carolina University
Small Business and Technology
Development Center (Western
Region)
Center for Improving Mountain
Living
Bird Bldg.
Cullowhee, NC 28723
Phone: (704)227-7494
Fax: (704)227-7422
Allan Steinburg, Dir.

Elizabeth City State University
Small Business and Technology
Development Center (Northeastern
Region)
1704 Weeksville Rd.
PO Box 874
Elizabeth City, NC 27909
Phone: (919)335-3247
Fax: (919)335-3648
Wauna Dooms, Dir.

Fayetteville State University
Cape Fear Small Business and
Technology Development Center

PO Box 1334
Fayetteville, NC 28302
Phone: (910)486-1727
Fax: (910)486-1949
Dr. Sid Gautam, Regional Dir.

North Carolina A&T State University
Northern Piedmont Small Business
and Technology Development Center
(Eastern Region)
C. H. Moore Agricultural Research
Center
1601 E. Market St.
PO Box D-22
Greensboro, NC 27411
Phone: (910)334-7005
Fax: (910)334-7073
Cynthia Clemons, Dir.

East Carolina University
Small Business and Technology
Development Center (Eastern Region)
Willis Bldg.
300 East 1st St.
Greenville, NC 27858-4353
Phone: (919)328-6157
Fax: (919)328-6992
Walter Fitts, Dir.

Catawba Valley Region
SBTDC
514 Hwy. 321 NW, Ste. A
Hickory, NC 28601
Phone: (704)345-1110
Fax: (704)326-9117
Rand Riedrich, Dir.

Pembroke State University
Office of Economic Development and
SBTDC
SBDC
Pembroke, NC 28372
Phone: (910)521-6603
Fax: (910)521-6550

NC Small Business and Technology
Development Center
University of North Carolina
333 Fayetteville Steet Mall, Ste. 1150
Raleigh, NC 27601-1742
Phone: (919)715-7272
Free: (800)2580-UNC
Fax: (919)715-7777
Website: www.sbtdc.org
Scott R. Daugherty, Executive
Director

North Carolina SBTDC
SBDC

333 Fayette St. Mall, Ste. 1150
Raleigh, NC 27601
Phone: (919)715-7272
Fax: (919)715-7777
Scott R. Daugherty, Executive Dir.

North Carolina State University
Capital Region
SBTDC
MCI Small Business Resource Center
800 S. Salisbury St.
Raleigh, NC 27601
Phone: (919)715-0520
Fax: (919)715-0518
Mike Seibert, Dir.

North Carolina Wesleyan College
SBTDC
3400 N. Wesleyan Blvd.
Rocky Mount, NC 27804
Phone: (919)985-5130
Fax: (919)977-3701

University of North Carolina at
Wilmington
Small Business and Technology
Development Center (Southeast
Region)
601 S. College Rd.
Cameron Hall, Rm. 131
Wilmington, NC 28403
Phone: (910)395-3744
Fax: (910)350-3990
Mike Bradley, Dir.

University of North Carolina at
Wilmington
Southeastern Region
SBTDC
601 S. College Rd.
Wilmington, NC 28403
Phone: (910)395-3744
Fax: (910)350-3014
Dr. Warren Guiko, Acting Dir.

Winston-Salem State University
Northwestern Piedmont Region Small
Business and Technology Center
PO Box 13025
Winston Salem, NC 27110
Phone: (910)750-2030
Fax: (910)750-2031
Bill Dowe, Dir.

North Dakota

Bismarck Regional Small Business
Development Center
700 E. Main Ave., 2nd Fl.

Bismarck, ND 58502
Phone: (701)328-5865
Fax: (701)250-4304
Jan M. Peterson, Regional Dir.

Devils Lake Outreach Center
SBDC
417 5th St.
Devils Lake, ND 58301
Free: (800)445-7232
Gordon Synder, Regional Dir.

Dickinson Regional Small Business
Development Center
Small Business Development Center
314 3rd Ave. W
Drawer L
Dickinson, ND 58602
Phone: (701)227-2096
Fax: (701)225-0049
Bryan Vendsel, Regional Dir.

Procurement Assistance Center
SBDC
PO Box 1309
Fargo, ND 58107-1309
Phone: (701)237-9678
Free: (800)698-5726
Fax: (701)237-9734
Eric Nelson

Tri-county Economic Development
Corp.
Fargo Regional Small Business
Development Center
657 2nd Ave. N, Rm. 279
PO Box 1309
Fargo, ND 58103
Phone: (701)237-0986
Fax: (701)237-9734
Jon Grinager, Regional Mgr.

Grafton Outreach Center
Red River Regional Planning Council
SBDC
PO Box 633
Grafton, ND 58237
Free: (800)445-7232
Gordon Snyder, Regional Dir.

Grand Forks Regional Small Business
Development Center
202 N. 3rd St., Ste. 200
The Hemmp Center
Grand Forks, ND 58203
Phone: (701)772-8502
Fax: (701)772-9238
Gordon Snyder, Regional Dir.

University of North Dakota
North Dakota Small Business
Development Center
118 Gamble Hall, UND
P O Box 7308
Grand Forks, ND 58202-7308
Phone: (701)777-3700
Free: (800)445-7232
Fax: (701)777-3225
Walter Kearns, State Director

University of North Dakota
North Dakota SBDC
118 Gamble Hall
University Station, Box 7308
Grand Forks, ND 58202-7308
Phone: (701)777-3700
Fax: (701)777-3225
Walter "Wally" Kearns, State Dir.

Jamestown Outreach Center
North Dakota Small Business
Development Center
210 10th St. SE
PO Box 1530
Jamestown, ND 58402
Phone: (701)252-9243
Fax: (701)251-2488
Jon Grinager, Regional Dir.

Jamestown Outreach Ctr.
SBDC
210 10th St.
S.E.P.O Box 1530
Jamestown, ND 58402
Phone: (701)252-9243
Fax: (701)251-2488
Jon Grinager, Regional Dir.

Minot Regional Small Business
Development Center
SBDC
900 N. Broadway, Ste. 300
Minot, ND 58703
Phone: (701)852-8861
Fax: (701)858-3831
Brian Argabright, Regional Dir.

Williston Outreach Center
SBDC
PO Box 2047
Williston, ND 58801
Free: (800)445-7232
Bryan Vendsel, Regional Dir.

Ohio

Akron Regional Development Board
Small Business Development Center

1 Cascade Plz., 8th Fl.
Akron, OH 44308-1192
Phone: (330)379-3170
Fax: (330)379-3164
Charles Smith, Dir.

Women's Entrepreneurial Growth
Organization
Small Business Development Center
Buckingham Bldg., Rm. 55
PO Box 544
Akron, OH 44309
Phone: (330)972-5179
Fax: (330)972-5513
Dr. Penny Marquette, Exec. Dir.

Women's Network
SBDC
1540 West Market St., Ste. 100
Akron, OH 44313
Phone: (330)864-5636
Fax: (330)884-6526
Marlene Miller, Dir.

Enterprise Development Corp.
SBDC
900 E. State St.
Athens, OH 45701
Phone: (614)592-1188
Fax: (614)593-8283
Karen Patton, Dir.

Ohio University Innovation Center
Small Business Development Center
Enterprise & Technical Bldg., Rm. 155
20 East Circle Dr.
Athens, OH 45701
Phone: (614)593-1797
Fax: (614)593-1795
Debra McBride, Dir.

WSOS Community Action
Commission, Inc.
Wood County SBDC
121 E. Wooster St.
PO Box 539
Bowling Green, OH 43402
Phone: (419)352-3817
Fax: (419)353-3291
Pat Fligor, Dir.

Kent State University/Stark Campus
SBDC
6000 Frank Ave., NW
Canton, OH 44720
Phone: (330)499-9600
Fax: (330)494-6121
Annette Chunko, Contact

Women's Business Development
Center
SBDC
2400 Cleveland Ave., NW
Canton, OH 44709
Phone: (330)453-3867
Fax: (330)773-2992

Wright State University—Lake
Campus
Small Business Development Center
West Central Office
7600 State Rte. 703
Celina, OH 45882
Phone: (419)586-0355
Free: (800)237-1477
Fax: (419)586-0358
Tom Knapke, Dir.

Clermont County Chamber of
Commerce
Clermont County Area SBDC
4440 Glen Este-Withamsville Rd.
Cincinnati, OH 45245
Phone: (513)753-7141
Fax: (513)753-7146
Matt VanSant, Dir.

University of Cincinnati
SBDC
1111 Edison Ave.
Cincinnati, OH 45216-2265
Phone: (513)948-2051
Fax: (513)948-2109
Mark Sauter, Dir.

Greater Cleveland Growth
Association
Small Business Development Center
200 Tower City Center
50 Public Sq.
Cleveland, OH 44113-2291
Phone: (216)621-1294
Fax: (216)621-4617
JoAnn Uhlik, Dir.

Northern Ohio Manufacturing
SBDC
Prospect Park Bldg.
4600 Prospect Ave.
Cleveland, OH 44103-4314
Phone: (216)432-5300
Fax: (216)361-2900
Gretchen Faro, Dir.

Central Ohio Manufacturing
SBDC
1250 Arthur E. Adams Dr.
Columbus, OH 43221

Phone: (614)688-5136
Fax: (614)688-5001

Department of Development
Ohio SBDC
77 S. High St., 28th Fl.
Columbus, OH 43216-1001
Phone: (614)466-2711
Fax: (614)466-0829
Holly I. Schick, State Dir.

Greater Columbus Area Chamber of
Commerce
Central Ohio SBDC
37 N. High St.
Columbus, OH 43215-3065
Phone: (614)225-6910
Fax: (614)469-8250
Linda Steward, Dir.

Ohio Department of Development
Small Business Development Center
77 S. High St., 28th Fl.
Columbus, OH 43215-6108
Phone: (614)466-2711
Free: (800)848-1300
Fax: (614)466-0829
Holly I. Schick, State Director

Dayton Area Chamber of Commerce
Small Business Development Center
Chamber Plz.
5th & Main Sts.
Dayton, OH 45402-2400
Phone: (937)226-8239
Fax: (937)226-8254
Harry Bumgarner, Dir.

Wright State University/Dayton
SBDC
Center for Small Business Assistance
College of Business
Rike Hall, Rm. 120C
Dayton, OH 45435
Phone: (937)873-3503
Dr. Mike Body, Dir.

Northwest Private Industry Council
SBDC
197-2-B1 Park Island Ave.
Defiance, OH 43512
Phone: (419)784-6270
Fax: (419)782-6273
Don Wright, Dir.

Northwest Technical College
Small Business Development Center
1935 E. 2nd St., Ste. D
Defiance, OH 43512

Phone: (419)784-3777
Fax: (419)782-4649
Don Wright, Dir.

Terra Community College
Small Business Development Center
North Central Fremont Office
1220 Cedar St.
Fremont, OH 43420
Phone: (419)334-8400
Fax: (419)334-9414
Joe Wilson, Dir.

Enterprise Center
Small Business Development Center
129 E. Main St.
PO Box 756
Hillsboro, OH 45133
Phone: (937)393-9599
Fax: (937)393-8159
Bill Grunkemeyer, Interim Dir.

Ashtabula County Economic
Development Council, Inc.
Small Business Development Center
36 W. Walnut St.
Jefferson, OH 44047
Phone: (216)576-9134
Fax: (216)576-5003
Sarah Bogardus, Dir.

Kent State University Partnership
SBDC
College of Business Administration,
Rm. 300A
Summit and Terrace
Kent, OH 44242
Phone: (330)672-2772
Fax: (330)672-2448
Linda Yost, Dir.

EMTEC/Southern Area
Manufacturing
SBDC
3155 Research Park, Ste. 206
Kettering, OH 45420
Phone: (513)258-6180
Fax: (513)258-8189
Harry Bumgarner, Dir.

Lake County Economic Development
Center
SBDC
Lakeland Community College
7750 Clocktower Dr.
Kirtland, OH 44080
Phone: (216)951-1290
Fax: (216)951-7336
Cathy Haworth, Dir.

Lima Technical College
Small Business Development Center
West Central Office
545 W. Market St., Ste. 305
Lima, OH 45801-4717
Phone: (419)229-5320
Fax: (419)229-5424
Gerald J. Biedenharn, Dir.

Lorain County Chamber of
Commerce
SBDC
6100 S. Boadway
Lorain, OH 44053
Phone: (216)233-6500
Dennis Jones, Dir.

Mid-Ohio Small Business
Development Center
246 E. 4th St.
PO Box 1208
Mansfield, OH 44901
Phone: (419)521-2655
Free: (800)366-7232
Fax: (419)522-6811
Barbara Harmony, Dir.

Marietta College
SBDC
213 Fourth St., 2nd Fl.
Marietta, OH 45750
Phone: (614)376-4832
Fax: (614)376-4832
Emerson Shimp, Dir.

Marion Area Chamber of Commerce
SBDC
206 S. Prospect St.
Marion, OH 43302
Phone: (614)387-0188
Fax: (614)387-7722
Lynn Lovell, Dir.

Tuscarawas SBDC
300 University Dr., NE
Kent State University
300 University Dr., NE
New Philadelphia, OH 44663-9447
Phone: (330)339-3391
Fax: (330)339-2637
Tom Farbizo, Dir.

Miami University
Small Business Development Center
Department of Decision Sciences
336 Upham Hall
Oxford, OH 45056
Phone: (513)529-4841
Fax: (513)529-1469
Dr. Michael Broida, Dir.

Upper Valley Joint Vocational School
Small Business Development Center
8811 Career Dr.
N. Country Rd., 25A
Piqua, OH 45356
Phone: (937)778-8419
Free: (800)589-6963
Fax: (937)778-9237
Jon Heffner, Dir.

Ohio Valley Minority Business
Association
SBDC
1208 Waller St.
PO Box 847
Portsmouth, OH 45662
Phone: (614)353-8395
Fax: (614)353-3695
Clemmy Womack, Dir.

Department of Development
CIC of Belmont County
Small Business Development Center
100 E. Main St.
St. Clairsville, OH 43950
Phone: (614)695-9678
Fax: (614)695-1536
Mike Campbell, Dir.

Kent State University/Salem Campus
SBDC
2491 State Rte. 45 S.
Salem, OH 44460
Phone: (330)332-0361
Fax: (330)332-9256
Deanne Taylor, Dir.

Lawrence County Chamber of
Commerce
Small Business Development Center
U.S. Rte. 52 & Solida Rd.
PO Box 488
South Point, OH 45680
Phone: (740)894-3838
Fax: (740)894-3836
Lou-Ann Walden, Dir.

Springfield Small Business
Development Center
300 E. Auburn Ave.
Springfield, OH 45505
Phone: (937)322-7821
Fax: (937)322-7824
Ed Levanthal, Dir.

Greater Steubenville Chamber of
Commerce
Jefferson County Small Business
Development Center

630 Market St.
PO Box 278
Steubenville, OH 43952
Phone: (614)282-6226
Fax: (614)282-6285
Tim McFadden, Dir.

Toledo Small Business Development
Center
300 Madison Ave., Ste. 200
Toledo, OH 43604-1575
Phone: (419)243-8191
Fax: (419)241-8302
Wendy Gramza, Dir.

Youngstown/Warren SBDC
Region Chamber of Commerce
180 E. Market St., Ste. 225
Warren, OH 44482
Phone: (330)393-2565
Jim Rowlands, Mgr.

Youngstown State University
SBDC
241 Federal Plaza W.
Youngstown, OH 44503
Phone: (330)746-3350
Fax: (330)746-3324
Patricia Veisz, Mgr.

Zanesville Area Chamber of
Commerce
Mid-East Small Business
Development Center
217 N. 5th St.
Zanesville, OH 43701
Phone: (614)452-4868
Fax: (614)454-2963
Bonnie J. Winnett, Dir.

Oklahoma

East Central University
Small Business Development Center
1036 E. 10th St.
Ada, OK 74820
Phone: (405)436-3190
Fax: (405)436-3190
Frank Vater

Northwestern Oklahoma State
University
Small Business Development Center
709 Oklahoma Blvd.
Alva, OK 73717
Phone: (405)327-8608
Fax: (405)327-0560
Clance Doelling, Dir.

Southeastern Oklahoma State
University
Small Business Development Center
517 University
Station A, Box 2584
Durant, OK 74701
Phone: (580)924-0277
Free: (800)522-6154
Fax: (580)920-7471
E-mail: gpennington@sosu.edu
Dr. Grady Pennington, State Director

Southeastern Oklahoma State
University
Oklahoma SBDC
517 University
Station A, Box 2584
Durant, OK 74701
Phone: (405)924-0277
Free: (800)522-6154
Fax: (405)920-7471
Dr. Grady Pennington, State Dir.

Phillips University
Small Business Development Center
100 S. University Ave.
Enid, OK 73701
Phone: (405)242-7989
Fax: (405)237-1607
Bill Gregory, Coordinator

Langston University Center
Small Business Development Center
Minority Assistance Center
Hwy. 33 E.
Langston, OK 73050
Phone: (405)466-3256
Fax: (405)466-2909
Robert Allen, Dir.

Lawton Satellite
Small Business Development Center
American National Bank Bldg.
601 SW D Ave., Ste. 209
Lawton, OK 73501
Phone: (405)248-4946
Fax: (405)355-3560
Jim Elliot, Business Development
Specialists

Northeastern Oklahoma A&M
Miami Satellite
SBDC
Dyer Hall, Rm. 307
215 I St.
Miami, OK 74354
Phone: (918)540-0575
Fax: (918)540-0575

Hugh Simon, Business Development
Specialist

Rose State College
SBDC
Procurement Speciality Center
6420 Southeast 15th St.
Midwest City, OK 73110
Phone: (405)733-7348
Fax: (405)733-7495
Judy Robbins, Dir.

University of Central Oklahoma
Small Business Development Center
115 Park Ave.
Oklahoma City, OK 73102-9005
Phone: (405)232-1968
Fax: (405)232-1967
E-mail: sbdc@aix1.ucok.edu
Website: www.osbdc.org/osbdc.htm
Susan Urbach, Director

Carl Albert College
Small Business Development Center
1507 S. McKenna
Poteau, OK 74953
Phone: (918)647-4019
Fax: (918)647-1218
Dean Qualls, Dir.

Northeastern Oklahoma State
University
Small Business Development Center
Oklahoma Small Business
Development Center
Tahlequah, OK 74464
Phone: (918)458-0802
Fax: (918)458-2105
Danielle Coursey, Business
Development Specialist

Tulsa Satellite
Small Business Development Center
State Office Bldg.
616 S. Boston, Ste. 100
Tulsa, OK 74119
Phone: (918)583-2600
Fax: (918)599-6173
Jeff Horvath, Dir.

Southwestern Oklahoma State
University
Small Business Development Center
100 Campus Dr.
Weatherford, OK 73096
Phone: (405)774-1040
Fax: (405)774-7091
Chuck Felz, Dir.

Oregon

Linn-Benton Community College
Small Business Development Center
6500 SW Pacific Blvd.
Albany, OR 97321
Phone: (541)917-4923
Fax: (541)917-4445
Dennis Sargent, Dir.

Southern Oregon State College/
Ashland
Small Business Development Center
Regional Services Institute
Ashland, OR 97520
Phone: (541)482-5838
Fax: (541)482-1115
Liz Shelby, Dir.

Central Oregon Community College
Small Business Development Center
2600 NW College Way
Bend, OR 97701
Phone: (541)383-7290
Fax: (541)317-3445
Bob Newhart, Dir.

Southwestern Oregon Community
College
Small Business Development Center
2110 Newmark Ave.
Coos Bay, OR 97420
Phone: (541)888-7100
Fax: (541)888-7113
Jon Richards, Dir.

Columbia Gorge Community College
SBDC
400 E. Scenic Dr., Ste. 257
The Dalles, OR 97058
Phone: (541)298-3118
Fax: (541)298-3119
Mr. Bob Cole, Dir.

Lane Community College
Oregon SBDC
44 W. Broadway, Ste. 501
Eugene, OR 97401-3021
Phone: (541)726-2250
Fax: (541)345-6006
Dr. Edward, Cutler, State Dir.

Lane Community College
Oregon SBDC
44 W. Broadway St., Ste. 501
Eugene, OR 97401-3021
Phone: (541)726-2250
Fax: (541)345-6006
Website: www.efn.org/~osbdcn
Dr. Edward Cutler, State Director

Rogue Community College
Small Business Development Center
214 SW 4th St.
Grants Pass, OR 97526
Phone: (541)471-3515
Fax: (541)471-3589
Lee Merritt, Dir.

Mount Hood Community College
Small Business Development Center
323 NE Roberts St.
Gresham, OR 97030
Phone: (503)667-7658
Fax: (503)666-1140
Don King, Dir.

Oregon Institute of Technology
Small Business Development Center
3201 Campus Dr. S. 314
Klamath Falls, OR 97601
Phone: (541)885-1760
Fax: (541)885-1855
Jamie Albert, Dir.

Eastern Oregon State College
Small Business Development Center
Regional Services Institute
1410 L Ave.
La Grande, OR 97850
Phone: (541)962-3391
Free: (800)452-8639
Fax: (541)962-3668
John Prosnik, Dir.

Oregon Coast Community College
Small Business Development Center
4157 NW Hwy. 101, Ste. 123
PO Box 419
Lincoln City, OR 97367
Phone: (541)994-4166
Fax: (541)996-4958
Guy Faust, Contact

Southern Oregon State College/
Medford
Small Business Development Center
Regional Services Institute
332 W. 6th St.
Medford, OR 97501
Phone: (541)772-3478
Fax: (541)734-4813
Liz Shelby, Dir.

Clackamas Community College
Small Business Development Center
7616 SE Harmony Rd.
Milwaukie, OR 97222
Phone: (503)656-4447
Fax: (503)652-0389
Jan Stennick, Dir.

Treasure Valley Community College
Small Business Development Center
650 College Blvd.
Ontario, OR 97914
Phone: (541)889-6493
Fax: (541)881-2743
Kathy Simko, Dir.

Blue Mountain Community College
Small Business Development Center
37 SE Dorion
Pendleton, OR 97801
Phone: (541)276-6233
Fax: (541)276-6819
Gerald Wood, Dir.

Portland Community College
Small Business Development Center
2701 NW Vaughn St., No. 499
Portland, OR 97209
Phone: (503)978-5080
Fax: (503)228-6350
Robert Keyser, Dir.

Portland Community College
Small Business International Trade
Program
121 SW Salmon St., Ste. 210
Portland, OR 97204
Phone: (503)274-7482
Fax: (503)228-6350
Tom Niland, Dir.

Umpqua Community College
Small Business Development Center
744 SE Rose
Roseburg, OR 97470
Phone: (541)672-2535
Fax: (541)672-3679
Terry Swagerty, Dir.

Chemeketa Community College
Small Business Development Center
365 Ferry St. SE
Salem, OR 97301
Phone: (503)399-5088
Fax: (503)581-6017
Tom Nelson, Dir.

Clatsop Community College
Small Business Development Center
1761 N. Holladay
Seaside, OR 97138
Phone: (503)738-3347
Fax: (503)738-7843
Lori Martin, Dir.

Tillamook Bay Community College
Small Business Development Center

401 B Main St.
Tillamook, OR 97141
Phone: (503)842-2551
Fax: (503)842-2555
Kathy Wilkcs, Dir.

Pennsylvania

Lehigh University
Small Business Development Center
Rauch Business Ctr., No. 37
621 Taylor St.
Bethlehem, PA 18015
Phone: (610)758-3980
Fax: (610)758-5205
Dr. Larry A. Strain, Dir.

Clarion University of Pennsylvania
Small Business Development Center
Dana Still Bldg., Rm. 102
Clarion, PA 16214
Phone: (814)226-2060
Fax: (814)226-2636
Dr. Woodrow Yeaney, Dir.

Bucks County SBDC Outreach Center
2 E. Court St.
Doylestown, PA 18901
Phone: (215)230-7150
Bruce Love, Dir.

Gannon University
Small Business Development Center
120 W. 9th St.
Erie, PA 16501
Phone: (814)871-7714
Fax: (814)871-7383
Ernie Post, Dir.

Kutztown University
Small Business Development Center
2986 N. 2nd St.
Harrisburg, PA 17110
Phone: (717)720-4230
Fax: (717)720-4262
Katherine Wilson, Dir.

Indiana University of Pennsylvania
SBDC
208 Eberly College of Business
Indiana, PA 15705
Phone: (412)357-7915
Fax: (412)357-5985
Dr. Tony Palamone, Dir.

St. Vincent College
Small Business Development Center
Alfred Hall, 4th Fl.
300 Fraser Purchase Rd.

Latrobe, PA 15650
Phone: (412)537-4572
Fax: (412)537-0919
Jack Fabean, Dir.

Bucknell University
Small Business Development Center
126 Dana Engineering Bldg., 1st Fl.
Lewisburg, PA 17837
Phone: (717)524-1249
Fax: (717)524-1768
Charles Knisely, Dir.

St. Francis College
Small Business Development Center
Business Resource Center
Loretto, PA 15940
Phone: (814)472-3200
Fax: (814)472-3202
Edward Huttenhower, Dir.

LaSalle University
Small Business Development Center
1900 W. Olney Ave.
Box 365
Philadelphia, PA 19141
Phone: (215)951-1416
Fax: (215)951-1597
Andrew Lamas, Dir.

Temple University
Small Business Development Center
1510 Cecil B. Moore Ave.
Philadelphia, PA 19121
Phone: (215)204-7282
Fax: (215)204-4554
Geraldine Perkins, Dir.

University Of Pennsylvania
Pennsylvania SBDC
The Wharton School
423 Vance Hall
3733 Spruce St.
Philadelphia, PA 19104-6374
Phone: (215)898-1219
Fax: (215)573-2135
E-mail:
ghiggins@sec1.wharton.upenn.edu
Gregory L. Higgins, Jr., State Dir.

University of Pennsylvania
Small Business Development Center
The Wharton School
423 Vance Hall
3733 Spruce St.
Philadelphia, PA 19104-6374
Phone: (215)898-1219
Fax: (215)573-2135

E-mail:
pasbdc@atcwharton.upenn.edu
Website: www.libertynet.org/pasbdc
Gregory L. Higgins, Jr., State
Director

Duquesne University
Small Business Development Center
Rockwell Hall, Rm. 10, Concourse
600 Forbes Ave.
Pittsburgh, PA 15282
Phone: (412)396-6233
Fax: (412)396-5884
Dr. Mary T. McKinney, Dir.

University of Pittsburgh
Small Business Development Center
The Joseph M. Katz Graduate School
of Business
208 Bellefield Hall
315 S. Bellefield Ave.
Pittsburgh, PA 15213
Phone: (412)648-1544
Fax: (412)648-1636
Ann Dugan, Dir.

University of Scranton
Small Business Development Center
St. Thomas Hall, Rm. 588
Scranton, PA 18510
Phone: (717)941-7588
Fax: (717)941-4053
Elaine M. Tweedy, Dir.

West Chester University
SBDC
319 Anderson Hall
211 Carter Dr.
West Chester, PA 19383
Phone: (610)436-2162
Fax: (610)436-2577

Wilkes University
Small Business Development Center
Hollenback Hall
192 S. Franklin St.
Wilkes Barre, PA 18766-0001
Phone: (717)831-4340
Free: (800)572-4444
Fax: (717)824-2245
Jeffrey Alves, Dir.

Puerto Rico

Puerto Rico Small Business
Development Center
Edificio Union Plaza, Ste. 701
416 Ponce de Leon Ave.
Hato Rey, PR 00918

Phone: (787)763-6811
Fax: (787)763-4629

Small Business Development Center
Edificio Union Plaza, Ste. 701
416 Ponce de Leon Ave.
Hato Rey, PR 00918
Phone: (787)763-6811
Fax: (787)763-4629
Carmen Marti, State Dir.

University of Puerto Rico at
Mayaguez
Small Business Development Center
Mayaguez Campus
Box 5253, College Station
Mayaguez, PR 00681
Phone: (809)834-3790
Fax: (809)834-3790
Carmen Marti, Executive Director

Rhode Island

Northern Rhode Island Chamber of
Commerce
SBDC
6 Blackstone Valley Pl., Ste. 105
Lincoln, RI 02865-1105
Phone: (401)334-1000
Fax: (401)334-1009
Shelia Hoogeboom, Program Mgr.

Newport County Chamber of
Commerce
E. Bay Small Business Development
Center
45 Valley Rd.
Middletown, RI 02842-6377
Phone: (401)849-6900
Fax: (401)841-0570
Samuel Carr, Program Mgr.

Fishing Community Program Office
SBDC
PO Box 178
Narragansett, RI 02882
Phone: (401)783-2466
Angela Caporelli, Program Mgr.

South County SBDC
QP/D Industrial Park
35 Belver Ave., Rm. 212
North Kingstown, RI 02852-7556
Phone: (401)294-1227
Fax: (401)294-6897
Elizabeth Kroll, Program Mgr.

Bryant College
Small Business Development Center

30 Exchange Terrace, 4th Fl.
Providence, RI 02903-1793
Phone: (401)831-1330
Fax: (401)274-5410
Ann Marie Marshall, Case Mgr.

Enterprise Community SBDC/BIC
550 Broad St.
Providence, RI 02907
Phone: (401)272-1083
Fax: (401)272-1186
Simon Goudiaby, Program Mgr.

Bell Atlantic Telecommunications
Center
1150 Douglas Pke.
Smithfield, RI 02917-1284
Phone: (401)232-0220
Fax: (401)232-0242
Kate Dolan, Managing Dir.

Bryant College
Export Assistance Center
SBDC
1150 Douglas Pike
Smithfield, RI 02917
Phone: (401)232-6407
Fax: (401)232-6416
Raymond Fogarty, Dir.

Bryant College
Rhode Island Small Business
Development Center
1150 Douglas Pke.
Smithfield, RI 02917-1284
Phone: (401)232-6111
Fax: (401)232-6933
Website: www.ri-sbdc.com
Richard Brussard, State Director

Bryant College
Rhode Island SBDC
1150 Douglas Pike
Smithfield, RI 02917-1284
Phone: (401)232-6111
Fax: (401)232-6933
Douglas H. Jobling, State Dir.

Entrepreneurship Training Program
Bryant College
SBDC
1150 Douglas Pike
Smithfield, RI 02917-1284
Phone: (401)232-6115
Fax: (401)232-6933
Sydney Okashige, Program Mgr.

Bristol County Chamber of
Commerce
SBDC

PO Box 250
Warren, RI 02885-0250
Phone: (401)245-0750
Fax: (401)245-0110
Samuel Carr, Program Mgr.

Central Rhode Island Chamber of
Commerce
SBDC
3288 Post Rd.
Warwick, RI 02886-7151
Phone: (401)732-1100
Fax: (401)732-1107
Mr. Elizabeth Kroll, Program Mgr.

South Carolina

University of South Carolina at Aiken
Aiken Small Business Development
Center
171 University Pkwy.
Box 9
Aiken, SC 29801
Phone: (803)641-3646
Fax: (803)641-3647
Jackie Moore, Area Mgr.

University of South Carolina at
Beaufort
Small Business Development Center
800 Carteret St.
Beaufort, SC 29902
Phone: (803)521-4143
Fax: (803)521-4142
Martin Goodman, Area Mgr.

Clemson University
Small Business Development Center
College of Business and Public
Affairs
425 Sirrine Hall
Box 341392
Clemson, SC 29634-1392
Phone: (803)656-3227
Fax: (803)656-4869
Becky Hobart, Regional Dir.

Small Business Development Center
University of South Carolina
College of Business Administration
Hipp Bldg.
1710 College St.
Columbia, SC 29208
Phone: (803)777-4907
Fax: (803)777-4403
Website: sbdcweb.badm.sc.edu
John Lenti, State Director

University of South Carolina
Small Business Development Center
College of Business Administration
Columbia, SC 29208
Phone: (803)777-5118
Fax: (803)777-4403
James Brazell, Dir.

University of South Carolina
College of Business Administration
South Carolina SBDC
Hipp Bldg.
1710 College St.
Columbia, SC 29208
Phone: (803)777-4907
Fax: (803)777-4403
John Lenti, State Director

Coastal Carolina College
Small Business Development Center
School of Business Administration
PO Box 261954
Conway, SC 29526-6054
Phone: (803)349-2170
Fax: (803)349-2455
Tim Lowery, Area Mgr.

Florence-Darlington Technical
College
Small Business Development Center
PO Box 100548
Florence, SC 29501-0548
Phone: (803)661-8256
Fax: (803)661-8041
David Raines, Area Mgr.

Greenville Manufacturing Field
Office
SBDC
53 E. Antrim Dr.
Greenville, SC 29607
Phone: (803)271-3005

University Center
Upstate Area Office Small Business
Development Center
216 S. Pleasantburg Dr., Rm. 140
Greenville, SC 29607
Phone: (864)250-8894
Fax: (864)250-8897

Upper Savannah Council of
Government
Small Business Development Center
Exchange Building
222 Phoenix St., Ste. 200
PO Box 1366
Greenwood, SC 29648
Phone: (803)941-8071

Fax: (803)941-8090
George Long, Area Mgr.

University of South Carolina at Hilton
Head
Small Business Development Center
1 College Center Dr.
10 Office Park Rd.
Hilton Head, SC 29928-7535
Phone: (803)785-3995
Fax: (803)785-3995
Pat Cameron, Consultant

Charleston SBDC
5900 Core Dr., Ste. 104
North Charleston, SC 29406
Phone: (803)740-6160
Fax: (803)740-1607
Merry Boone, Area Mgr.

South Carolina State College
Small Business Development Center
School of Business Administration
Algernon Belcher Hall
300 College Ave.
Campus Box 7176
Orangeburg, SC 29117
Phone: (803)536-8445
Fax: (803)536-8066
John Gadson, Regional Dir.

Winthrop University
Winthrop Regional Small Business
Development Center
College of Business Administration
118 Thurmond Bldg.
Rock Hill, SC 29733
Phone: (803)323-2283
Fax: (803)323-4281
Nate Barber, Regional Dir.

Spartanburg Chamber of Commerce
Small Business Development Center
105 Pine St.
PO Box 1636
Spartanburg, SC 29304
Phone: (803)594-5080
Fax: (803)594-5055
John Keagle, Area Mgr.

South Dakota

Aberdeen Small Business
Development Center (Northeast
Region)
620 15th Ave., SE
Aberdeen, SD 57401
Phone: (605)626-2565
Fax: (605)626-2667
Belinda Engelhart, Regional Dir.

Pierre Small Business Development
Center
105 S. Euclid, Ste. C
Pierre, SD 57501
Phone: (605)773-5941
Fax: (605)773-5942
Greg Sund, Dir.

Rapid City Small Business
Development Center (Western
Region)
444 N. Mount Rushmore Rd., Rm.
208
Rapid City, SD 57701
Phone: (605)394-5311
Fax: (605)394-6140
Carl Gustafson, Regional Dir.

Sioux Falls Region
SBDC
405 S. 3rd Ave., Ste. 101
Sioux Falls, SD 57104
Phone: (605)367-5757
Fax: (605)367-5755
Wade Bruin, Regional Dir.

University of South Dakota
South Dakota SBDC
School of Business
414 E. Clark
Vermillion, SD 57069
Phone: (605)677-5498
Fax: (605)677-5272
E-mail: sbdc@sundance.usd.edu
Robert E. Ashley, Jr., State Dir.

University of South Dakota
Small Business Development Center
School of Business
414 E. Clark St.
Vermillion, SD 57069-2390
Phone: (605)677-5287
Fax: (605)677-5427
Steve Tracy, Jr., Acting State Director

Watertown Small Business
Development Center
124 1st. Ave., NW
PO Box 1207
Watertown, SD 57201
Phone: (605)886-7224
Fax: (605)882-5049
Belinda Engelhart, Regional Dir.

Tennessee

Chattanooga State Technical
Community College
SBDC
100 Cherokee Blvd., No. 202

Chattanooga, TN 37405-3878
Phone: (423)752-1774
Fax: (423)752-1925
Donna Marsh, Specialist

Southeast Tennessee Development
District
Small Business Development Center
25 Cherokee Blvd.
PO Box 4757
Chattanooga, TN 37405-0757
Phone: (423)266-5781
Fax: (423)267-7705
Sherri Bishop, Dir.

Austin Peay State University
Small Business Development Center
College of Business
Clarksville, TN 37044
Phone: (615)648-7764
Fax: (615)648-5985
John Volker, Dir.

Cleveland State Community College
Small Business Development Center
PO Box 3570
Cleveland, TN 37320-3570
Phone: (423)478-6247
Fax: (423)478-6251
Don Green, Dir.

Small Business Development Center
(Columbia)
Maury County Chamber of
Commerce Bldg.
106 W. 6th St.
PO Box 8069
Columbia, TN 38402-8069
Phone: (615)898-2745
Fax: (615)893-7089
Eugene Osekowsky, Small Business
Specialist

Tennessee Technological University
SBDC
College of Business Administration
PO Box 5023
Cookeville, TN 38505
Phone: (931)372-3648
Fax: (931)372-6249
Dorothy Vaden, Senior Small Bus.
Specialist

Dyersburg State Community College
Small Business Development Center
1510 Lake Rd.
Dyersburg, TN 38024-2450
Phone: (901)286-3201
Fax: (901)286-3271
Bob Wylie

Four Lakes Regional Industrial
Development Authority
SBDC
PO Box 63
Hartsville, TN 37074-0063
Phone: (615)374-9521
Fax: (615)374-4608
Dorothy Vaden, Senior Small Bus.
Specialist

Jackson State Community College
Small Business Development Center
McWherter Center, Rm. 213
2046 N. Parkway St.
Jackson, TN 38301-3797
Phone: (901)424-5389
Fax: (901)425-2641
David L. Brown

Lambuth University
SBDC
705 Lambuth Blvd.
Jackson, TN 38301
Phone: (901)425-3326
Fax: (901)425-3327
Phillip Ramsey, SB Specialist

East Tennessee State University
College of Business
SBDC
PO Box 70625
Johnson City, TN 37614-0625
Phone: (423)929-5630
Fax: (423)461-7080
Bob Justice, Dir.

Knoxville Area Chamber Partnership
International Trade Center
SBDC
Historic City Hall
601 W. Summit Hill Dr.
Knoxville, TN 37902-2011
Phone: (423)632-2990
Fax: (423)521-6367
Richard Vogler, IT Specialist

Pellissippi State Technical
Community College
Small Business Development Center
Historic City Hall
601 W. Summit Hill Dr.
Knoxville, TN 37902-2011
Phone: (423)632-2980
Fax: (423)971-4439
Teri Brahams, Consortium Dir.

University of Memphis
Tennessee Small Business
Development Center

South Campus, Bldg. 1, Rm. 101
Campass Box 526324
Memphis, TN 38152-0001
Phone: (901)678-2500
Fax: (901)678-4072
E-mail: gmickle@cc.memphis.edu
Website: www.tsbdc.memphis.edu
Dr. Kenneth J. Burns, State Director

University of Memphis
International Trade Center
SBDC
320 S. Dudley St.
Memphis, TN 38152-0001
Phone: (901)678-4174
Fax: (901)678-4072
Philip Johnson, Dir.

University of Memphis
Tennessee SBDC
320 S. Dudley St.
Building No. 1
Memphis, TN 38152
Phone: (901)678-2500
Fax: (901)678-4072
Dr. Kenneth J. Burns, State Dir.

Walters State Community College
Tennessee Small Business
Development Center
500 S. Davy Crockett Pkwy.
Morristown, TN 37813
Phone: (423)585-2675
Fax: (423)585-2679
Jack Tucker, Dir.

Middle Tennessee State University
Small Business Development Center
Chamber of Commerce Bldg.
501 Memorial Blvd.
PO Box 487
Murfreesboro, TN 37129-0001
Phone: (615)898-2745
Fax: (615)890-7600
Patrick Geho, Dir.

Tennessee State University
Small Business Development Center
College of Business
330 10th Ave. N.
Nashville, TN 37203-3401
Phone: (615)963-7179
Fax: (615)963-7160
Billy E. Lowe, Dir.

Texas

Abilene Christian University
Small Business Development Center

College of Business Administration
648 E. Hwy. 80
Abilene, TX 79601
Phone: (915)670-0300
Fax: (915)670-0311
Judy Wilhelm, Dir.

Sul Ross State University
Big Bend SBDC Satellite
PO Box C-47, Rm. 319
Alpine, TX 79832
Phone: (915)837-8694
Fax: (915)837-8104
Michael Levine, Dir.

Alvin Community College
Small Business Development Center
3110 Mustang Rd.
Alvin, TX 77511-4898
Phone: (713)388-4686
Fax: (713)388-4903
Gina Mattei, Dir.

West Texas A&M University
Small Business Development Center
T. Boone Pickens School of Business
1800 S. Washington, Ste. 209
Amarillo, TX 79102
Phone: (806)372-5151
Fax: (806)372-5261
Don Taylor, Dir.

Trinity Valley Community College
Small Business Development Center
500 S. Prairieville
Athens, TX 75751
Phone: (903)675-7403
Free: (800)335-7232
Fax: (903)675-5199
Judy Loden, Dir.

Lower Colorado River Authority
Small Business Development Center
3701 Lake Austin Blvd.
PO Box 220
Austin, TX 78703
Phone: (512)473-3510
Fax: (512)473-3285
Larry Lucero, Dir.

Lee College
Small Business Development Center
Rundell Hall
PO Box 818
Baytown, TX 77522-0818
Phone: (281)425-6309
Fax: (713)425-6309
Tommy Hathaway, Dir.

Lamar University
Small Business Development Center
855 Florida Ave.
Beaumont, TX 77705
Phone: (409)880-2367
Fax: (409)880-2201
Gene Arnold, Dir.

Bonham Satellite
Small Business Development Center
Sam Rayburn Library, Bldg. 2
1201 E. 9th St.
Bonham, TX 75418
Phone: (903)583-7565
Fax: (903)583-6706
Darroll Martin, Coordinator

Blinn College
Small Business Development Center
902 College Ave.
Brenham, TX 77833
Phone: (409)830-4137
Fax: (409)830-4135
Phillis Nelson, Dir.

Brazos Valley Small Business
Development Center
Small Business Development Center
4001 E. 29th St., Ste. 175
PO Box 3695
Bryan, TX 77805-3695
Phone: (409)260-5222
Fax: (409)260-5229
Sam Harwell, Dir.

Greater Corpus Christi Business
Alliance
Small Business Development Center
1201 N. Shoreline
Corpus Christi, TX 78401
Phone: (512)881-1847
Fax: (512)882-4256
Rudy Ortiz, Dir.

Navarro Small Business Development
Center
120 N. 12th St.
Corsicana, TX 75110
Phone: (903)874-0658
Free: (800)320-7232
Fax: (903)874-4187
Leon Allard, Dir.

Dallas County Community College
North Texas SBDC
1402 Corinth St.
Dallas, TX 75215
Phone: (800)350-7232

Fax: (214)860-5813
Elizabeth (Liz) Klimback, Regional
Dir.

International Assistance Center
SBDC
2050 Stemmons Fwy.
PO Box 420451
Dallas, TX 75258
Phone: (214)747-1300
Free: (800)337-7232
Fax: (214)748-5774
Beth Huddleston, Dir.

Bill J. Priest Institute for Economic
Development
North Texas-Dallas Small Business
Development Center
1402 Corinth St.
Dallas, TX 75215
Phone: (214)860-5842
Free: (800)348-7232
Fax: (214)860-5881
Pamela Speraw, Dir.

Technology Assistance Center
SBDC
1402 Corinth St.
Dallas, TX 75215
Phone: (800)355-7232
Fax: (214)860-5881
Pamela Speraw, Dir.

Texas Center for Government
Contracting and Technology
Assistance
Small Business Development Center
1402 Corinth St.
Dallas, TX 75215
Phone: (214)860-5841
Fax: (214)860-5881
Gerald Chandler, Dir.

Grayson County College
Small Business Development Center
6101 Grayson Dr.
Denison, TX 75020
Phone: (903)463-8787
Free: (800)316-7232
Fax: (903)463-5437
Cynthia Flowers-Whitfield, Dir.

Denton Small Business Development
Center
PO Drawer P
Denton, TX 76201
Phone: (254)380-1849
Fax: (254)382-0040
Carolyn Birkhead, Coordinator

Best Southwest
SBDC
214 S, Main, Ste. 102A
Duncanville, TX 75116
Phone: (214)709-5878
Free: (800)317-7232
Fax: (214)709-6089
Herb Kamm, Dir.

Best Southwest Small Business
Development Center
214 S. Main, Ste. 102A
Duncanville, TX 75116
Phone: (972)709-5878
Free: (800)317-7232
Fax: (972)709-6089
Neil Small, Dir.

University of Texas—Pan American
Small Business Development Center
1201 W. University Dr., Rm. BA-124
Center for Entrepreneurship &
Economic Development
Edinburg, TX 78539-2999
Phone: (956)316-2610
Fax: (956)316-2612
Juan Garcia, Dir.

El Paso Community College
Small Business Development Center
103 Montana Ave., Ste. 202
El Paso, TX 79902-3929
Phone: (915)831-4410
Fax: (915)831-4625
Roque R. Segura, Dir.

Small Business Development Center
for Enterprise Excellence
SBDC
7300 Jack Newell Blvd., S.
Fort Worth, TX 76118
Phone: (817)272-5930
Fax: (817)272-5932
Jo An Weddle, Dir.

Tarrant County Junior College
Small Business Development Center
Mary Owen Center, Rm. 163
1500 Houston St.
Ft. Worth, TX 76102
Phone: (817)871-2068
Fax: (817)871-0031
David Edmonds, Dir.

North Central Texas College
Small Business Development Center
1525 W. California
Gainesville, TX 76240
Phone: (254)668-4220

Free: (800)351-7232
Fax: (254)668-6049
Cathy Keeler, Dir.

Galveston College
Small Business Development Center
4015 Avenue Q
Galveston, TX 77550
Phone: (409)740-7380
Fax: (409)740-7381
Georgette Peterson, Dir.

Western Bank and Trust Satellite
SBDC
PO Box 461545
Garland, TX 75046
Phone: (214)860-5850
Fax: (214)860-5857
Al Salgado, Dir.

Grand Prairie Satellite
SBDC
Chamber of Commerce
900 Conover Dr.
Grand Prairie, TX 75053
Phone: (214)860-5850
Fax: (214)860-5857
Al Salgado, Dir.

Houston Community College System
Small Business Development Center
10450 Stancliff, Ste. 100
Houston, TX 77099
Phone: (281)933-7932
Fax: (281)568-3690
Joe Harper, Dir.

Houston International Trade Center
Small Business Development Center
1100 Louisiana, Ste. 500
Houston, TX 77002
Phone: (713)752-8404
Fax: (713)756-1500
Mr. Carlos Lopez, Dir.

North Harris Montgomery
Community College District
Small Business Development Center
250 N. Sam Houston Pkwy. E.
Houston, TX 77060
Phone: (281)260-3174
Fax: (713)591-3513
Kay Hamilton, Dir.

University of Houston
Southeastern Texas Small Business
Development Center
1100 Louisiana, Ste. 500
Houston, TX 77002

Phone: (713)752-8444
Fax: (713)756-1500
Website: smbizsolutions.2uh.edu
Dr. Elizabeth Gatewood,m Director

University of Houston
Texas Information Procurement
Service
Small Business Development Center
1100 Louisiana, Ste. 500
Houston, TX 77002
Phone: (713)752-8477
Fax: (713)756-1515
Jacqueline Taylor, Dir.

University of Houston
Texas Manufacturing Assistance
Center (Gulf Coast)
1100 Louisiana, Ste. 500
Houston, TX 77002
Phone: (713)752-8440
Fax: (713)756-1500
Roy Serpa, Regional Dir.

University of Houston
Southeastern Texas SBDC
1100 Louisiana, Ste. 500
Houston, TX 77002
Phone: (713)752-8444
Fax: (713)756-1500
J.E. "Ted" Cadou, Reg. Dir.

Sam Houston State University
Small Business Development Center
843 S. Sam Houston Ave.
PO Box 2058
Huntsville, TX 77341-3738
Phone: (409)294-3737
Fax: (409)294-3612
Bob Barragan, Dir.

Kingsville Chamber of Commerce
Small Business Development Center
635 E. King
Kingsville, TX 78363
Phone: (512)595-5088
Fax: (512)592-0866
Marco Garza, Dir.

Brazosport College
Small Business Development Center
500 College Dr.
Lake Jackson, TX 77566
Phone: (409)266-3380
Fax: (409)265-3482
Patricia Leyendecker, Dir.

Laredo Development Foundation
Small Business Development Center

Division of Business Administration
616 Leal St.
Laredo, TX 78041
Phone: (956)722-0563
Fax: (956)722-6247
Araceli Lozano, Acting Dir.

Kilgore College
SBDC
Triple Creek Shopping Plaza
110 Triple Creek Dr., Ste. 70
Longview, TX 75601
Phone: (903)757-5857
Free: (800)338-7232
Fax: (903)753-7920
Brad Bunt, Dir.

Texas Tech University
Northwestern Texas SBDC
Spectrum Plaza
2579 S. Loop 289, Ste. 114
Lubbock, TX 79423
Phone: (806)745-3973
Fax: (806)745-6207
E-mail: odbea@ttacs.ttu.edu
Craig Bean, Regional Dir.

Angelina Community College
Small Business Development Center
Hwy. 59 S.
PO Box 1768
Lufkin, TX 75902
Phone: (409)639-1887
Fax: (409)639-3863
Brian McClain, Dir.

Midlothian SBDC
330 N. 8th St., Ste. 203
Midlothian, TX 76065-0609
Phone: (214)775-4336
Fax: (214)775-4337

Northeast Texarkana
Small Business Development Center
PO Box 1307
Mt. Pleasant, TX 75455
Phone: (903)572-1911
Free: (800)357-7232
Fax: (903)572-0598
Bob Wall, Dir.

University of Texas—Permian Basin
Small Business Development Center
College of Management
4901 E. University Blvd.
Odessa, TX 79762
Phone: (915)552-2455
Fax: (915)552-2433
Arthur L. Connor III, Dir.

Paris Junior College
Small Business Development Center
2400 Clarksville St.
Paris, TX 75460
Phone: (903)784-1802
Fax: (903)784-1801
Pat Bell, Dir.

Courtyard Center for Professional and
Economic Development
Collin Small Business Development
Center
4800 Preston Park Blvd., Ste. A126
Box 15
Plano, TX 75093
Phone: (972)985-3770
Fax: (972)985-3775
Chris Jones, Dir.

Angelo State University
Small Business Development Center
2610 West Ave. N.
Campus Box 10910
San Angelo, TX 76909
Phone: (915)942-2098
Fax: (915)942-2096
Harlan Bruha, Dir.

University of Texas (Downtown San
Antonio)
South Texas Border SBDC
1222 N. Main, Ste. 450
San Antonio, TX 78212
Phone: (210)458-2450
Fax: (210)458-2464
E-mail: rmckinle@utsadt.utsa.edu
Robert McKinley, Regional Dir.

University of Texas at San Antonio
International Trade Center
SBDC
1222 N. Main, Ste. 450
San Antonio, TX 78212
Phone: (210)458-2470
Fax: (210)458-2464
Sara Jackson, Dir.

University of Texas at San Antonio
Small Business Development Center
1222 N. Main St., Ste. 450
San Antonio, TX 78212
Phone: (210)458-2458
Fax: (210)458-2464
Judith Ingalls, Dir.

Houston Community College System
Small Business Development Center
13600 Murphy Rd.
Stafford, TX 77477

Phone: (713)499-4870
Fax: (713)499-8194
Ted Charlesworth, Acting Dir.

Tarleton State University
Small Business Development Center
College of Business Administration
Box T-0650
Stephenville, TX 76402
Phone: (817)968-9330
Fax: (817)968-9329
Jim Choate, Dir.

College of the Mainland
Small Business Development Center
1200 Amburn Rd.
Texas City, TX 77591
Phone: (409)938-1211
Free: (800)246-7232
Fax: (409)938-7578
Elizabeth Boudreau, Dir.

Tyler Junior College
Small Business Development Center
1530 South SW Loop 323, Ste. 100
Tyler, TX 75701
Phone: (903)510-2975
Fax: (903)510-2978
Frank Viso, Dir.

Middle Rio Grande Development
Council
Small Business Development Center
209 N. Getty St.
Uvalde, TX 78801
Phone: (830)278-2527
Fax: (830)278-2929
Sheri Rutledge, Dir.

University of Houston—Victoria
Small Business Development Center
700 Main Center, Ste. 102
Victoria, TX 77901
Phone: (512)575-8944
Fax: (512)575-8852
Carole Parks, Dir.

McLennan Community College
Small Business Development Center
401 Franklin
Waco, TX 76708
Phone: (254)714-0077
Free: (800)349-7232
Fax: (254)714-1668
Lu Billings, Dir.

LCRA Coastal Plains
SBDC
PO Box 148

Wharton, TX 77488
Phone: (409)532-1007
Fax: (409)532-0056
Lynn Polson, Dir.

Midwestern State University
Small Business Development Center
3410 Taft Blvd.
Wichita Falls, TX 76308
Phone: (817)397-4373
Fax: (817)397-4374
Tim Thomas, Dir.

Utah

Southern Utah University
Small Business Development Center
351 W. Center
Cedar City, UT 84720
Phone: (435)586-5400
Fax: (435)586-5493
Derek Snow, Dir.

Snow College
Small Business Development Center
345 West 100 North
Ephraim, UT 84627
Phone: (435)283-7472
Fax: (435)283-6913
Russell Johnson, Dir.

Utah State University
Small Business Development Center
East Campus Bldg., Rm. 124
Logan, UT 84322
Phone: (435)797-2277
Fax: (435)797-3317
Franklin C. Prante, Dir.

Weber State University
Small Business Development Center
School of Business and Economics
Ogden, UT 84408-3815
Phone: (435)626-6070
Fax: (435)626-7423
Bruce Davis, Dir.

Utah Valley State College
Utah Small Business Development
Center
800 West 200 South
Orem, UT 84058
Phone: (435)222-8230
Fax: (435)225-1229
Chuck Cozzens, Contact

South Eastern Utah AOG
Small Business Development Center
Price Center
PO Box 1106

Price, UT 84501
Phone: (435)637-5444
Fax: (435)637-7336
Dennis Rigby, Dir.

Utah State University Extension
Office
SBDC
987 E. Lagoon St.
Roosevelt, UT 84066
Phone: (435)722-2294
Fax: (435)789-3689
Mark Holmes, Dir.

Dixie College
Small Business Development Center
225 South 700 East
St. George, UT 84770-3876
Phone: (435)652-7751
Fax: (435)652-7870
Jill Ellis, Dir.

Salt Lake City Small Business
Development Center
Salt Lake Community College
1623 S State St.
Salt Lake City, UT 84115
Phone: (801)957-3480
Fax: (801)957-3489
Mike Finnerty, State Director

Salt Lake Community College
SBDC
1623 S. State St.
Salt Lake City, UT 84115
Phone: (801)957-3480
Fax: (801)957-3489
Mike Finnerty, State Dir.

Salt Lake Community College
SBDC
1623 S. State St.
Salt Lake City, UT 84115
Phone: (801)957-3480
Fax: (801)957-3489
Pamela Hunt, Dir.

Salt Lake Community College
Sandy SBDC
8811 South 700 East
Sandy, UT 84070
Phone: (435)255-5878
Fax: (435)255-6393
Barry Bartlett, Dir.

Vermont

Brattleboro Development Credit
Corp.
SBDC

72 Cotton Mill Hill
PO Box 1177
Brattleboro, VT 05301-1177
Phone: (802257-7731
Fax: (802258-3886
William McGrath, Executive V.P.

Greater Burlington Industrial Corp.
Northwestern Vermont Small
Business Development Center
PO Box 786
Burlington, VT 05402-0786
Phone: (802)658-9228
Fax: (802)860-1899
Thomas D. Schroeder, Specialist

Addison County Economic
Development Corp.
SBDC
RD4, Box 1309A
Middlebury, VT 05753
Phone: (802)388-7953
Fax: (802)388-8066
James Stewart, Exec. Dir.

Central Vermont Economic
Development Center
SBDC
PO Box 1439
Montpelier, VT 05601-1439
Phone: (802)223-4654
Fax: (802)223-4655
Donald Rowan, Exec. Dir.

Lamoille Economic Development
Corp.
SBDC
Sunset Dr.
PO Box 455
Morrisville, VT 05661-0455
Phone: (802)888-4542
Chris D'Elia, Executive Dir.

Bennington County Industrial Corp.
SBDC
PO Box 357
North Bennington, VT 05257-0357
Phone: (802)442-8975
Fax: (802)442-1101
Chris Hunsinger, Executive Dir.

Lake Champlain Islands Chamber of
Commerce
SBDC
PO Box 213
North Hero, VT 05474-0213
Phone: (802)372-5683
Fax: (802)372-6104
Barbara Mooney, Exec. Dir.

Vermont Small Business
Development Center
Vermont Technical College
PO Box 422
Randolph Center, VT 05060-0422
Phone: (802)728-9101
Free: (800)464-SBDC
Fax: (802)728-3026
Website: www.vtsbdc.org
Donald L. Kelpinski, State Director

Vermont Technical College
Small Business Development Center
PO Box 422
Randolph Center, VT 05060-0422
Phone: (802)728-9101
Free: (800)464-7232
Fax: (802)728-3026
Donald L. Kelpinski, State Dir.

Rutland Economic Development
Corp.
Southwestern Vermont Small
Business Development Center
256 N. Main St.
Rutland, VT 05701-0039
Phone: (802)773-9147
Fax: (802)773-2772
Wendy Wilton, Regional Dir.

Franklin County Industrial
Development Corp.
SBDC
PO Box 1099
St. Albans, VT 05478-1099
Phone: (802)524-2194
Fax: (802)527-5258
Timothy J. Soule, Executive Dir.

Northeastern Vermont Small Business
Development Center
44 Main St.
PO Box 630
St. Johnsbury, VT 05819-0630
Phone: (802)748-1014
Fax: (802)748-1223
Charles E. Carter, Exec. Dir.

Springfield Development Corp.
Southeastern Vermont Small Business
Development Center
PO Box 58
Springfield, VT 05156-0058
Phone: (802)885-2071
Fax: (802)885-3027
Steve Casabona, Specialist

Green Mountain Economic
Development Corporation
SBDC

PO Box 246
White River Jct., VT 05001-0246
Phone: (802)295-3710
Fax: (802)295-3779
Lenae Quillen-Blume, SBDC
Specialist

Virgin Islands

University of the Virgin Islands
(Charlotte Amalie)
Small Business Development Center
8000 Nisky Center, Ste. 202
Charlotte Amalie, VI 00802-5804
Phone: (809)776-3206
Fax: (809)775-3756
Ian Hodge, Assoc. State Dir.

University of the Virgin Islands
Small Business Development Center
Sunshine Mall
No.1 Estate Cane, Ste. 104
Frederiksted, VI 00840
Phone: (809)692-5270
Fax: (809)692-5629
Chester Williams, State Dir.

University of the Virgin Islands
Small Business Development Center
8000 Nisky Center, Ste. 202
Charlotte Amalie
St. Thomas, VI 00802-5804
Phone: (809)776-3206
Fax: (809)775-3756
Chester Williams, Director

Virginia

Virginia Highlands SBDC
Rte. 382
PO Box 828
Abingdon, VA 24212
Phone: (540676-5615
Fax: (540628-7576
Jim Tilley, Dir.

Arlington Small Business
Development Center
George Mason University, Arlington
Campus
4001 N. Fairfax Dr., Ste. 450
Arlington, VA 22203-1640
Phone: (703)993-8129
Fax: (703)430-7293
Paul Hall, Dir.

Virginia Eastern Shore Corp.
SBDC
36076 Lankford Hwy.

PO Box 395
Belle Haven, VA 23306
Phone: (757)442-7179
Fax: (757)442-7181

Mount Empire Community College
Southwest Small Business
Development Center
Drawer 700, Rte. 23, S.
Big Stone Gap, VA 24219
Phone: (540)523-6529
Fax: (540)523-2400
Tim Blankenbecler, Dir.

Central Virginia Small Business
Development Center
918 Emmet St., N., Ste. 200
Charlottesville, VA 22903-4878
Phone: (804)295-8198
Fax: (804)295-7066
Robert A. Hamilton, Jr., Dir.

Hampton Roads Chamber of
Commerce
SBDC
400 Volvo Pkwy.
PO Box 1776
Chesapeake, VA 23320
Phone: (757)664-2590
Fax: (757)548-1835
William J. Holoran, Jr., Dir.

George Mason University
Northern Virginia Small Business
Development Center
4031 University Dr., Ste. 200
Fairfax, VA 22030
Phone: (703)277-7700
Fax: (703)993-2126
Michael Kehoe, Exec. Dir.

Longwood College (Farmville)
Small Business Development Center
515 Main St.
Farmville, VA 23909
Phone: (804)395-2086
Fax: (804)395-2359
Gerald L. Hughes, Jr., Exec. Dir.

Rappahannock Region Small
Business Development Center
1301 College Ave.
Seacobeck Hall, Rm. 102
Fredericksburg, VA 22401
Phone: (540)654-1060
Fax: (540)654-1070
Jeffrey R. Sneddon, Exec. Dir.

Hampton Roads Inc.
Small Business Development Center

525 Butler Farm Rd., Ste. 102
Hampton, VA 23666
Phone: (757)825-2957
Fax: (757)825-2960
James Carroll, Dir.

James Madison University
Small Business Development Center
College of Business
Zane Showker Hall, Rm. 527
PO Box MSC 0206
Harrisonburg, VA 22807
Phone: (540)568-3227
Fax: (540)568-3106
Karen Wigginton, Dir.

Lynchburg Regional Small Business
Development Center
147 Mill Ridge Rd.
Lynchburg, VA 24502-4341
Phone: (804)582-6170
Free: (800)876-7232
Fax: (804)582-6106
Barry Lyons, Dir.

Flory Small Business Development
Center
10311 Sudley Manor Dr.
Manassas, VA 20109-2962
Phone: (703)335-2500
Linda Decker, Dir.

SBDC Satellite Office of Longwood
PO Box 709
115 Broad St.
Martinsville, VA 24114
Phone: (540)632-4462
Fax: (540)632-5059
Ken Copeland, Dir.

Lord Fairfax Community College
SBDC
173 Skirmisher Ln.
PO Box 47
Middletown, VA 22645
Phone: (540)869-6649
Fax: (540)868-7002
Robert Crosen, Dir.

Small Business Development Center
of Hampton Roads, Inc. (Norfolk)
420 Bank St.
PO Box 327
Norfolk, VA 23501
Phone: (757)664-2528
Fax: (757)622-5563
Warren Snyder, Dir.

New River Valley
SBDC

600-H Norwood St.
PO Box 3726
Radford, VA 24141
Phone: (540)831-6056
Fax: (540)831-6057
David Shanks, Dir.

Southwest Virginia Community
College
Southwest Small Business
Development Center
PO Box SVCC, Rte. 19
Richlands, VA 24641
Phone: (540)964-7345
Fax: (540)964-5788
Jim Boyd. Dir.

Department of Business Assistance
Small Business Development Center
707 East Main St. Ste. 300
Richmond, VA 23219
Phone: (804)371-8253
Fax: (804)225-3384
Website: www.vdba.org
Dr. Robert D. Smith, State
Coordinator

Department of Business Assistance
Virginia SBDC
707 E. Main St., Ste. 300
Richmond, VA 23219
Phone: (804)371-8253
Fax: (804)225-3384
Bob Wilburn, State Dir.

Greater Richmond Small Business
Development Center
1 N. 5th St., Ste. 510
Richmond, VA 23219
Phone: (804)648-7838
Free: (800)646-SBDC
Fax: (804)648-7849
Charlie Meacham, Dir.

Virginia Small Business Development
Center
Commonwealth of Virginia
Department of Economic
Development
901 E Byrd St., Ste. 1400
Richmond, VA 23219
Phone: (804)371-8253
Fax: (804)225-3384
Robert D. Wilburn, State Director

Regional Chamber Small Business
Development Center
Western Virginia SBDC Consortium
212 S. Jefferson St.

Roanoke, VA 24011
Phone: (540)983-0717
Fax: (540)983-0723
Ian Webb, Dir.

South Boston Satellite Office of
Longwood
Small Business Development Center
515 Broad St.
PO Box 1116
South Boston, VA 24592
Phone: (804)575-0044
Fax: (804)572-1762
Vincent Decker, Dir.

Loudoun County Small Business
Development Center
Satellite Office of Northern Virginia
207 E. Holly Ave., Ste. 214
Sterling, VA 20164
Phone: (703)430-7222
Fax: (703)430-7258
Ted London, Dir.

Warsaw Small Business Development
Center
Satellite Office of Rappahannock
5559 W. Richmond Rd.
PO Box 490
Warsaw, VA 22572
Phone: (804)333-0286
Free: (800)524-8915
Fax: (804)333-0187
John Clickener, Dir.

Wytheville Community College
Wytheville Small Business
Development Center
1000 E. Main St.
Wytheville, VA 24382
Phone: (540)223-4798
Free: (800)468-1195
Fax: (540)223-4716
Rob Edwards, Dir.

Washington

Bellevue Small Business
Development Center
Bellevue Community College
3000 Landerholm Circle SE
Bellevue, WA 98007-6484
Phone: (425)643-2888
Fax: (425)649-3113
Bill Huenefeld, Business Dev.
Specialist

Western Washington University
Small Business Development Center

College of Business and Economics
308 Parks Hall
Bellingham, WA 98225-9073
Phone: (360)650-4831
Fax: (360)650-4844
Tom Dorr, Business Dev. Specialist

Centralia Community College
Small Business Development Center
600 W. Locust St.
Centralia, WA 98531
Phone: (360)736-9391
Fax: (360)730-7504
Joanne Baria, Business Dev.
Specialist

Columbia Basin College—TRIDEC
Small Business Development Center
901 N. Colorado
Kennewick, WA 99336
Phone: (509)735-6222
Fax: (509)735-6609
Blake Escudier, Business Dev.
Specialist

Edmonds Community College
Small Business Development Center
20000 68th Ave. W.
Lynnwood, WA 98036
Phone: (425)640-1435
Fax: (425)640-1532
Jack Wicks, Business Dev. Specialist

Big Bend Community College
Small Business Development Center
7662 Chanute St.
Moses Lake, WA 98837-3299
Phone: (509)762-6306
Fax: (509)762-6329
Ed Baroch, Business Dev. Specialist

Skagit Valley College
Small Business Development Center
2405 College Way
Mount Vernon, WA 98273
Phone: (360)428-1282
Fax: (360)336-6116
Peter Stroosma, Business Dev.
Specialist

Wenatchee Valley College
SBDC
PO Box 741
Okanogan, WA 98840
Phone: (509)826-5107
Fax: (509)826-1812
John Rayburn, Business Dev.
Specialist

South Puget Sound Community
College
Small Business Development Center
721 Columbia St. SW
Olympia, WA 98501
Phone: (360)753-5616
Fax: (360)586-5493
Douglas Hammel, Business Dev.
Specialist

Washington State University
Small Business Development Center
College of Business & Economics
501 Johnson Tower
Pullman, WA 99164-4851
Phone: (509)335-1576
Fax: (509)335-0949
Website: www.sbdc.wsu.edu
Carol Riesenberg, Acting State
Director

Washington State University
(Pullman)
Small Business Development Center
501 Johnson Tower
PO Box 644851
Pullman, WA 99164-4727
Phone: (509)335-1576
Fax: (509)335-0949
Carol Riesenberg, State Dir.

International Trade Institute
North Seattle Community College
Small Business Development Center
2001 6th Ave., Ste. 650
Seattle, WA 98121
Phone: (206)553-0052
Fax: (206)553-7253
Ann Tamura, IT Specialist

South Seattle Community College
Duwamish Industrial Education
Center
Small Business Development Center
6770 E. Marginal Way S
Seattle, WA 98108-3405
Phone: (206)768-6855
Fax: (206)764-5838
Henry Burton, Business Dev.
Specialist

Washington Small Business
Development Center (Seattle)
180 Nickerson, Ste. 207
Seattle, WA 98109
Phone: (206)464-5450
Fax: (206)464-6357
Warner Wong, Business Dev.
Specialist

Washington State University
(Spokane)
Small Business Development Center
665 North Riverpoint Blvd.
Spokane, WA 99202
Phone: (509)358-7894
Fax: (509)358-7896
Richard Thorpe, Business Dev.
Specialist

Washington Small Business
Development Center (Tacoma)
950 Pacific Ave., Ste. 300
PO Box 1933
Tacoma, WA 98401-1933
Phone: (253)272-7232
Fax: (253)597-7305
Neil Delisanti, Business Dev.
Specialist

Columbia River Economic
Development Council
Small Business Development Center
217 SE 136th Ave., Ste. 105
Vancouver, WA 98660
Phone: (360)260-6372
Fax: (360)260-6369
Janet Harte, Business Dev. Specialist

Port of Walla Walla SBDC
500 Tausick Way
Rte. 4, Box 174
Walla Walla, WA 99362
Phone: (509)527-4681
Fax: (509)525-3101
Rich Monacelli, Business Dev.
Specialist

Quest Small Business Development
Center
37 S. Wenatchee Ave., Ste. C
Industrial Bldg. 2, Ste. D.
Wenatchee, WA 98801-2443
Phone: (509)662-8016
Fax: (509)663-0455
Rich Reim, Business Dev. Specialist

Yakima Valley College
Small Business Development Center
PO Box 1647
Yakima, WA 98907
Phone: (509)454-3608
Fax: (509)454-4155
Audrey Rice, Business Dev.
Specialist

West Virginia

College of West Virginia
SBDC

PO Box AG
Beckley, WV 25802
Phone: (304)252-7885
Fax: (304)252-9584
Tom Hardiman, Program Mgr.

West Virginia Department Office
West Virginia SBDC
950 Kanawha Blvd. E., Ste. 200
Charleston, WV 25301
Phone: (304)558-2960
Free: (888)WVA-SBDC
Fax: (304)348-0127
Dr. Hazel Kroesser-Palmer, State-Dir.

West Virginia Development Office
Small Business Development Center
950 Kanawha Blvd. E., 2nd Floor
Charleston, WV 25301
Phone: (304)558-2960
Fax: (304)558-0127
Dr. Hazel Kroesser, State Director

Fairmont State College (Elkins
Satellite)
SBDC
10 Eleventh St., Ste. 1
Elkins, WV 26241
Phone: (304)637-7205
Fax: (304)637-4902
James Martin, Business Analyst

Fairmont State College
Small Business Development Center
1000 Technology Dr., Ste. 1120
Fairmont, WV 26554
Phone: (304)367-2712
Fax: (304)367-2717
Jack Kirby, Program Mgr.

Marshall University
Small Business Development Center
1050 4th Ave.
Huntington, WV 25755-2126
Phone: (304)696-6246
Fax: (304)696-6277
Edna McClain, Program Mgr.

West Virginia Institute of Technology
Small Business Development Center
Engineering Bldg., Rm. 102
Montgomery, WV 25136
Phone: (304)442-5501
Fax: (304)442-3307
James Epling, Program Mgr.

West Virginia University
Fairmont State College Satellite
Small Business Development Center

PO Box 6025
Morgantown, WV 26506-6025
Phone: (304)293-5839
Fax: (304)293-7061
Sharon Stratton, Business Analyst

West Virginia University
(Parkersburg)
Small Business Development Center
Rte. 5, Box 167-A
Parkersburg, WV 26101
Phone: (304)424-8277
Fax: (3040424-8315
Greg Hill, Program Mgr.

Shepherd College
Small Business Development Center
120 N. Princess St.
Shepherdstown, WV 25443
Phone: (304)876-5261
Fax: (304)876-5467
Fred Baer, Program Mgr.

West Virginia Northern Community
College
Small Business Development Center
1701 Market St.
College Sq.
Wheeling, WV 26003
Phone: (304)233-5900
Fax: (304)232-0965
Ron Trevellini, Program Mgr.

Wisconsin

University of Wisconsin—Eau Claire
Small Business Development Center
Schneider Hall, Rm. 113
PO Box 4004
Eau Claire, WI 54702-4004
Phone: (715)836-5811
Fax: (715)836-5263
Fred Waedt, Dir.

University of Wisconsin—Green Bay
Small Business Development Center
Wood Hall, Rm. 480
2420 Nicolet Dr.
Green Bay, WI 54311
Phone: (920)465-2089
Fax: (920)465-2552
Jan Thornton, Dir.

University of Wisconsin—Parkside
Small Business Development Center
Tallent Hall, Rm. 284
900 Wood Rd.
Kenosha, WI 53141-2000
Phone: (414)595-2189

Fax: (414)595-2471
Patricia Deutsch, Dir.

University of Wisconsin—La Crosse
Small Business Development Center
North Hall, Rm. 120
1701 Farwell St.
La Crosse, WI 54601
Phone: (608)785-8782
Fax: (608)785-6919
Jan Gallagher, Dir.

University of Wisconsin
Wisconsin SBDC
432 N. Lake St., Rm. 423
Madison, WI 53706
Phone: (608)263-7794
Fax: (608)263-7830
Erica McIntire, State Dir.

University of Wisconsin—Extension
Small Business Development Center
432 N. Lake St., Rm. 423
Madison, WI 53706-1498
Phone: (608)263-7794
Fax: (608)262-3878
Website: www.vwex.edu/sbdc
Erica Kauten, State Director

University of Wisconsin—Madison
Small Business Development Center
975 University Ave., Rm. 3260
Grainger Hall
Madison, WI 53706
Phone: (608)263-2221
Fax: (608)263-0818
Neil Lerner, Dir.

University of Wisconsin—Milwaukee
Small Business Development Center
161 W. Wisconsin Ave., Ste. 600
Milwaukee, WI 53203
Phone: (414)227-3240
Fax: (414)227-3142
Sara Thompson, Dir.

University of Wisconsin—Oshkosh
Small Business Development Center
800 Algoma Blvd.
Oshkosh, WI 54901
Phone: (920)424-1453
Fax: (920)424-7413
John Mozingo, Dir.

University of Wisconsin—Stevens
Point
Small Business Development Center
Old Main Bldg., Rm. 103
Stevens Point, WI 54481

Phone: (715)346-3838
Fax: (715)346-4045
Vicki Lobermeier, Acting Dir.

University of Wisconsin—Superior
Small Business Development Center
1800 Grand Ave.
Superior, WI 54880-2898
Phone: (715)394-8352
Fax: (715)394-8592
Laura Urban, Dir.

University of Wisconsin—
Whitewater
Small Business Development Center
2000 Carlson Bldg.
Whitewater, WI 53190
Phone: (414)472-3217
Fax: (414)472-5692
Carla Lenk, Dir.

University of Wisconsin at
Whitewater
Wisconsin Innovation Service Center
SBDC
416 McCutchen Hall
Whitewater, WI 53190
Phone: (414)472-1365
Fax: (414)472-1600
E-mail: malewicd@uwwvax.uww.edu
Debra Malewicki, Dir.

Wisconsin Innovation Service Center
SBDC
University of Wisconsin at
Whitewater
402 McCutchan Hall
Whitewater, WI 53190
Phone: (414)472-1365
Fax: (414)472-1600
Debra Malewicki, Dir.

Wyoming

Casper Small Business Development
Center
Region III
111 W. 2nd St., Ste. 502
Casper, WY 82601
Phone: (307)234-6683
Free: (800)348-5207
Fax: (307)577-7014
Leonard Holler, Dir.

Cheyenne SBDC
Region IV
1400 E. College Dr.
Cheyenne, WY 82007-3298
Phone: (307)632-6141

Free: (800)348-5208
Fax: (307)632-6061
Arlene Soto, Regional Dir.

Wyoming Small Business
Development Center
State Office
University of Wyoming
PO Box 3622
Laramie, WY 82071-3622
Phone: (307)766-3505
Free: (800)348-5194
Fax: (307)766-3406
Diane Wolverton, State Dir.

Wyoming Small Business
Development Center
University of Wyoming
PO Box 3922
Laramie, WY 82071-3922
Phone: (307)766-3505
Free: (800)348-5194
Fax: (307)766-3406
Diane Wolverton, State Director

Northwest Community College
Small Business Development Center
Region II
146 South Bent St.
John Dewitt Student Center
Powell, WY 82435
Phone: (307)754-2139
Free: (800)348-5203
Fax: (307)754-0368
Dwane Heintz, Dir.

Rock Springs Small Business
Development Center
Region I
PO Box 1168
Rock Springs, WY 82902
Phone: (307)352-6894
Free: (800)348-5205
Fax: (307)352-6876

SERVICE CORPS OF RETIRED EXECUTIVES (SCORE) OFFICES

This section contains a listing of all SCORE offices organized alphabetically by state/U.S. territory name, then by city, then by agency name.

Alabama

SCORE Office (Northeast Alabama)
c/o Chamber of Commerce
1330 Quintard Ave.
Anniston, AL 36202
Phone: (256)237-3536

SCORE Office (North Alabama)
901 South 15th St, Rm. 201
Birmingham, AL 35294-2060
Phone: (205)934-6868
Fax: (205)934-0538

SCORE Office (Baldwin County)
c/o Eastern Shore Chamber of
Commerce
29750 Larry Dee Cawyer Dr.
Daphne, AL 36526
Phone: (334)928-5838

SCORE Office (Shoals)
Florence, AL 35630
Phone: (256)760-9067

SCORE Office (Mobile)
600 S Court St.
Mobile, AL 36104
Phone: (334)240-6868
Fax: (334)240-6869

SCORE Office (Alabama Capitol
City)
600 S. Court St.
Montgomery, AL 36104
Phone: (334)240-6868
Fax: (334)240-6869

SCORE Office (East Alabama)
601 Ave. A
Opelika, AL 36801
Phone: (334)745-4861
Email: score636@hotmail.com
Website: www.angelfire.com/sc/
score636/

SCORE Office (Tuscaloosa)
2200 University Blvd.
Tuscaloosa, AL 35402
Phone: (205)758-7588

Alaska

SCORE Office (Anchorage)
c/o il SBA/#67
222 W. 8th Ave.
Anchorage, AK 99513-7559
Phone: (907)271-4022
Fax: (907)271-4545

Arizona

SCORE Office (Lake Havasu)
10 S. Acoma Blvd.
Lake Havasu City, AZ 86403
Phone: (5200453-5951
Email: SCORE@ctaz.com
Website: www.scorearizona.org/
lake_havasu/

SCORE Office (East Valley)
Federal Bldg., Rm. 104
26 N. MacDonald St.
Mesa, AZ 85201
Phone: (602)379-3100
Fax: (602)379-3143
Email: 402@aol.com
Website: www.scorearizona.org/
mesa/

SCORE Office (Phoenix)
2828 N. Central Ave., Ste. 800
Central & One Thomas
Phoenix, AZ 85004
Phone: (602)640-2329
Fax: (602)640-2360
Email: e-mail@SCORE-phoenix.org
Website: www.score-phoenix.org/

SCORE Office (Prescott Arizona)
1228 Willow Creek Rd., Ste. 2
Prescott, AZ 86301
Phone: (520)778-7438
Fax: (520)778-0812
Email: score@northlink.com
Website: www.scorearizona.org/
prescott/

SCORE Office (Tucson)
110 E. Pennington St.
Tucson, AZ 85702
Phone: (520)670-5008
Fax: (520)670-5011
Email: score@azstarnet.com
Website: www.scorearizona.org/
tucson/

SCORE Office (Yuma)
281 W. 24th St., Ste. 116
Yuma, AZ 85364
Phone: (520)314-0480

Email: score@C2i2.com
Website: www.scorearizona.org/yuma

Arkansas

SCORE Office (South Central)
201 N. Jackson Ave.
El Dorado, AR 71730-5803
Phone: (870)863-6113
Fax: (870)863-6115

SCORE Office (Ozark)
Fayetteville, AR 72701
Phone: (501)442-7619

SCORE Office (Northwest Arkansas)
Glenn Haven Dr., No. 4
Ft. Smith, AR 72901
Phone: (501)783-3556

SCORE Office (Garland County)
Grand & Ouachita
PO Box 6012
Hot Springs Village, AR 71902
Phone: (501)321-1700

SCORE Office (Little Rock)
2120 Riverfront Dr., Rm. 100
Little Rock, AR 72202-1747
Phone: (501)324-5893
Fax: (501)324-5199

SCORE Office (Southeast Arkansas)
121 W. 6th
Pine Bluff, AR 71601
Phone: (870)535-7189
Fax: (870)535-1643

California

SCORE Office (Golden Empire)
1706 Chester Ave., No. 200
Bakersfield, CA 93301
Phone: (805)322-5881
Fax: (805)322-5663

SCORE Office (Greater Chico Area)
1324 Mangrove St., Ste. 114
Chico, CA 95926
Phone: (916)342-8932
Fax: (916)342-8932

SCORE Office (Concord)
2151-A Salvio St., Ste. B
Concord, CA 94520
Phone: (510)685-1181
Fax: (510)685-5623

SCORE Office (Covina)
935 W. Badillo St.
Covina, CA 91723

Phone: (818)967-4191
Fax: (818)966-9660

SCORE Office (Rancho Cucamonga)
8280 Utica, Ste. 160
Cucamonga, CA 91730
Phone: (909)987-1012
Fax: (909)987-5917

SCORE Office (Culver City)
PO Box 707
Culver City, CA 90232-0707
Phone: (310)287-3850
Fax: (310)287-1350

SCORE Office (Danville)
380 Diablo Rd., Ste. 103
Danville, CA 94526
Phone: (510)837-4400

SCORE Office (Downey)
11131 Brookshire Ave.
Downey, CA 90241
Phone: (310)923-2191
Fax: (310)864-0461

SCORE Office (El Cajon)
109 Rea Ave.
El Cajon, CA 92020
Phone: (619)444-1327
Fax: (619)440-6164

SCORE Office (El Centro)
1100 Main St.
El Centro, CA 92243
Phone: (619)352-3681
Fax: (619)352-3246

SCORE Office (Escondido)
720 N. Broadway
Escondido, CA 92025
Phone: (619)745-2125
Fax: (619)745-1183

SCORE Office (Fairfield)
1111 Webster St.
Fairfield, CA 94533
Phone: (707)425-4625
Fax: (707)425-0826

SCORE Office (Fontana)
17009 Valley Blvd., Ste. B
Fontana, CA 92335
Phone: (909)822-4433
Fax: (909)822-6238

SCORE Office (Foster City)
1125 E. Hillsdale Blvd.
Foster City, CA 94404
Phone: (415)573-7600
Fax: (415)573-5201

ORGANIZATIONS, AGENCIES, & CONSULTANTS

SCORE Office (Fremont)
2201 Walnut Ave., Ste. 110
Fremont, CA 94538
Phone: (510)795-2244
Fax: (510)795-2240

SCORE Office (Central California)
2719 N. Air Fresno Dr., Ste. 200
Fresno, CA 93727-1547
Phone: (559)487-5605
Fax: (559)487-5636

SCORE Office (Gardena)
1204 W. Gardena Blvd.
Gardena, CA 90247
Phone: (310)532-9905
Fax: (310)515-4893

SCORE Office (Lompoc)
330 N. Brand Blvd., Ste. 190
Glendale, CA 91203-2304
Phone: (818)552-3206
Fax: (818)552-3323

SCORE Office (Los Angeles)
330 N. Brand Blvd., Ste. 190
Glendale, CA 91203-2304
Phone: (818)552-3206
Fax: (818)552-3323

SCORE Office (Glendora)
131 E. Foothill Blvd.
Glendora, CA 91740
Phone: (818)963-4128
Fax: (818)914-4822

SCORE Office (Grover Beach)
177 S. 8th St.
Grover Beach, CA 93433
Phone: (805)489-9091
Fax: (805)489-9091

SCORE Office (Hawthorne)
12477 Hawthorne Blvd.
Hawthorne, CA 90250
Phone: (310)676-1163
Fax: (310)676-7661

SCORE Office (Hayward)
22300 Foothill Blvd., Ste. 303
Hayward, CA 94541
Phone: (510)537-2424

SCORE Office (Hemet)
1700 E. Florida Ave.
Hemet, CA 92544-4679
Phone: (909)652-4390
Fax: (909)929-8543

SCORE Office (Hesperia)
16367 Main St.

PO Box 403656
Hesperia, CA 92340
Phone: (619)244-2135

SCORE Office (Holloster)
321 San Felipe Rd., No. 11
Hollister, CA 95023

SCORE Office (Hollywood)
7018 Hollywood Blvd.
Hollywood, CA 90028
Phone: (213)469-8311
Fax: (213)469-2805

SCORE Office (Indio)
82503 Hwy. 111
PO Drawer TTT
Indio, CA 92202
Phone: (619)347-0676

SCORE Office (Inglewood)
330 Queen St.
Inglewood, CA 90301
Phone: (818)552-3206

SCORE Office (La Puente)
218 N. Grendanda St. D.
La Puente, CA 91744
Phone: (818)330-3216
Fax: (818)330-9524

SCORE Office (La Verne)
2078 Bonita Ave.
La Verne, CA 91750
Phone: (909)593-5265
Fax: (714)929-8475

SCORE Office (Lake Elsinore)
132 W. Graham Ave.
Lake Elsinore, CA 92530
Phone: (909)674-2577

SCORE Office (Lakeport)
PO Box 295
Lakeport, CA 95453
Phone: (707)263-5092

SCORE Office (Lakewood)
5445 E. Del Amo Blvd., Ste. 2
Lakewood, CA 90714
Phone: (213)920-7737

SCORE Office (Long Beach)
1 World Trade Center
Long Beach, CA 90831

SCORE Office (Los Alamitos)
901 W. Civic Center Dr., Ste. 160
Los Alamitos, CA 90720

SCORE Office (Los Altos)
321 University Ave.

Los Altos, CA 94022
Phone: (415)948-1455

SCORE Office (Manhattan Beach)
PO Box 3007
Manhattan Beach, CA 90266
Phone: (310)545-5313
Fax: (310)545-7203

SCORE Office (Merced)
1632 N. St.
Merced, CA 95340
Phone: (209)725-3800
Fax: (209)383-4959

SCORE Office (Milpitas)
75 S. Milpitas Blvd., Ste. 205
Milpitas, CA 95035
Phone: (408)262-2613
Fax: (408)262-2823

SCORE Office (Yosemite)
c/o SCEDCO
1012 11th St., Ste. 300
Modesto, CA 95354
Phone: (209)521-9333

SCORE Office (Montclair)
5220 Benito Ave.
Montclair, CA 91763

SCORE Office (Monterey Bay)
380 Alvarado St.
PO Box 1770
Monterey, CA 93940-1770
Phone: (408)649-1770

SCORE Office (Moreno Valley)
25480 Alessandro
Moreno Valley, CA 92553

SCORE Office (Morgan Hill)
25 W. 1st St.
PO Box 786
Morgan Hill, CA 95038
Phone: (408)779-9444
Fax: (408)778-1786

SCORE Office (Morro Bay)
880 Main St.
Morro Bay, CA 93442
Phone: (805)772-4467

SCORE Office (Mountain View)
580 Castro St.
Mountain View, CA 94041
Phone: (415)968-8378
Fax: (415)968-5668

SCORE Office (Napa)
1556 1st St.

Napa, CA 94559
Phone: (707)226-7455
Fax: (707)226-1171

SCORE Office (North Hollywood)
5019 Lankershim Blvd.
North Hollywood, CA 91601
Phone: (818)552-3206

SCORE Office (Northridge)
8801 Reseda Blvd.
Northridge, CA 91324
Phone: (818)349-5676

SCORE Office (Novato)
807 De Long Ave.
Novato, CA 94945
Phone: (415)897-1164
Fax: (415)898-9097

SCORE Office (East Bay)
519 17th St.
Oakland, CA 94612
Phone: (510)273-6611
Fax: (510)273-6015
Email: webmaster@eastbayscore.org
Website: www.eastbayscore.org

SCORE Office (Oceanside)
928 N. Coast Hwy.
Oceanside, CA 92054
Phone: (619)722-1534

SCORE Office (Ontario)
121 West B. St.
Ontario, CA 91762
Fax: (714)984-6439

SCORE Office (Oxnard)
PO Box 867
Oxnard, CA 93032
Phone: (805)385-8860
Fax: (805)487-1763

SCORE Office (Pacifica)
450 Dundee Way, Ste. 2
Pacifica, CA 94044
Phone: (415)355-4122

SCORE Office (Palm Desert)
72990 Hwy. 111
Palm Desert, CA 92260
Phone: (619)346-6111
Fax: (619)346-3463

SCORE Office (Palm Springs)
650 E. Tahquitz Canyon Way Ste. D
Palm Springs, CA 92262-6706
Phone: (760)320-6682
Fax: (760)323-9426

SCORE Office (Lakeside)
2150 Low Tree
Palmdale, CA 93551
Phone: (805)948-4518
Fax: (805)949-1212

SCORE Office (Palo Alto)
325 Forest Ave.
Palo Alto, CA 94301
Phone: (415)324-3121
Fax: (415)324-1215

SCORE Office (Pasadena)
117 E. Colorado Blvd., Ste. 100
Pasadena, CA 91105
Phone: (818)795-3355
Fax: (818)795-5663

SCORE Office (Paso Robles)
1225 Park St.
Paso Robles, CA 93446-2234
Phone: (805)238-0506
Fax: (805)238-0527

SCORE Office (Petaluma)
799 Baywood Dr., Ste. 3
Petaluma, CA 94954
Phone: (707)762-2785
Fax: (707)762-4721

SCORE Office (Pico Rivera)
9122 E. Washington Blvd.
Pico Rivera, CA 90660

SCORE Office (Pittsburg)
2700 E. Leland Rd.
Pittsburg, CA 94565
Phone: (510)439-2181
Fax: (510)427-1599

SCORE Office (Pleasanton)
777 Peters Ave.
Pleasanton, CA 94566
Phone: (510)846-9697

SCORE Office (Monterey Park)
485 N. Garey
Pomona, CA 91769

SCORE Office (Pomona)
485 N. Garey Ave.
Pomona, CA 91766
Phone: (909)622-1256

SCORE Office (Antelope Valley)
4511 West Ave. M-4
Quartz Hill, CA 93536
Phone: (805)272-0087
Email: avscore@ptw.com
Website: www.score.av.org/

SCORE Office (Shasta)
c/o Cascade SBDC
737 Auditorium Dr.
Redding, CA 96099
Phone: (916)225-2770

SCORE Office (Redwood City)
1675 Broadway
Redwood City, CA 94063
Phone: (415)364-1722
Fax: (415)364-1729

SCORE Office (Richmond)
3925 MacDonald Ave.
Richmond, CA 94805

SCORE Office (Ridgecrest)
PO Box 771
Ridgecrest, CA 93555
Phone: (619)375-8331
Fax: (619)375-0365

SCORE Office (Riverside)
3685 Main St., Ste. 350
Riverside, CA 92501
Phone: (909)683-7100

SCORE Office (Sacramento)
9845 Horn Rd., 260-B
Sacramento, CA 95827
Phone: (916)361-2322
Fax: (916)361-2164
Email: sacchapter@directcon.net

SCORE Office (Salinas)
c/o. Salinas Chamber of Commerce
PO Box 1170
Salinas, CA 93902
Phone: (408)424-7611
Fax: (408)424-8639

SCORE Office (Inland Empire)
777 E. Rialto Ave.
Purchasing
San Bernardino, CA 92415-0760
Phone: (909)386-8278

SCORE Office (San Carlos)
San Carlos Chamber of Commerce
PO Box 1086
San Carlos, CA 94070
Phone: (415)593-1068
Fax: (415)593-9108

SCORE Office (Encinitas)
550 W. C St., Ste. 550
San Diego, CA 92101-3540
Phone: (619)557-7272
Fax: (619)557-5894

SCORE Office (San Diego)
550 West C. St., Ste. 550
San Diego, CA 92101-3540
Phone: (619)557-7272
Fax: (619)557-5894
Website: www.score-sandiego.org

SCORE Office (Menlo Park)
1100 Merrill St.
San Francisco, CA 94105
Phone: (415)325-2818
Fax: (415)325-0920

SCORE Office (San Francisco)
455 Market St., 6th Fl.
San Francisco, CA 94105
Phone: (415)744-6827
Fax: (415)744-6750
Email: sfscore@sfscore.
Website: www.sfscore.com

SCORE Office (San Gabriel)
401 W. Las Tunas Dr.
San Gabriel, CA 91776
Phone: (818)576-2525
Fax: (818)289-2901

SCORE Office (San Jose)
Deanza College
208 S. 1st. St., Ste. 137
San Jose, CA 95113
Phone: (408)288-8479
Fax: (408)535-5541

SCORE Office (Santa Clara County)
280 S. 1st St., Rm. 137
San Jose, CA 95113
Phone: (408)288-8479
Fax: (408)535-5541
Email: svscore@Prodigy.net
Website: www.svscore.org

SCORE Office (San Luis Obispo)
3566 S. Hiquera, No. 104
San Luis Obispo, CA 93401
Phone: (805)547-0779

SCORE Office (San Mateo)
1021 S. El Camino, 2nd Fl.
San Mateo, CA 94402
Phone: (415)341-5679

SCORE Office (San Pedro)
390 W. 7th St.
San Pedro, CA 90731
Phone: (310)832-7272

SCORE Office (Orange County)
200 W. Santa Anna Blvd., Ste. 700
Santa Ana, CA 92701

Phone: (714)550-7369
Fax: (714)550-0191
Website: www.score114.org

SCORE Office (Santa Barbara)
3227 State St.
Santa Barbara, CA 93130
Phone: (805)563-0084

SCORE Office (Central Coast)
509 W. Morrison Ave.
Santa Maria, CA 93454
Phone: (805)347-7755

SCORE Office (Santa Maria)
614 S. Broadway
Santa Maria, CA 93454-5111
Phone: (805)925-2403
Fax: (805)928-7559

SCORE Office (Santa Monica)
501 Colorado, Ste. 150
Santa Monica, CA 90401
Phone: (310)393-9825
Fax: (3100394-1868

SCORE Office (Santa Rosa)
777 Sonoma Ave., Rm. 115E
Santa Rosa, CA 95404
Phone: (707)571-8342
Fax: (707)541-0331
Website: www.pressdemo.com/
community/score/score.html

SCORE Office (Scotts Valley)
4 Camp Evers Ln.
Scotts Valley, CA 95066
Phone: (408)438-1010
Fax: (408)438-6544

SCORE Office (Simi Valley)
40 W. Cochran St., Ste. 100
Simi Valley, CA 93065
Phone: (805)526-3900
Fax: (805)526-6234

SCORE Office (Sonoma)
453 1st St. E
Sonoma, CA 95476
Phone: (707)996-1033

SCORE Office (Los Banos)
222 S. Shepard St.
Sonora, CA 95370
Phone: (209)532-4212

SCORE Office (Tuolumne County)
39 North Washington St.
Sonora, CA 95370
Phone: (209)588-0128
Email: score@mlode.com

SCORE Office (South San Francisco)
445 Market St., Ste. 6th Fl.
South San Francisco, CA 94105
Phone: (415)744-6827
Fax: (415)744-6812

SCORE Office (Stockton)
401 N. San Joaquin St., Rm. 215
Stockton, CA 95202
Phone: (209)946-6293

SCORE Office (Taft)
314 4th St.
Taft, CA 93268
Phone: (805)765-2165
Fax: (805)765-6639

SCORE Office (Conejo Valley)
625 W. Hillcrest Dr.
Thousand Oaks, CA 91360
Phone: (805)499-1993
Fax: (805)498-7264

SCORE Office (Torrance)
c/o Torrance Chamber of Commerce
3400 Torrance Blvd., Ste. 100
Torrance, CA 90503
Phone: (310)540-5858
Fax: (310)540-7662

SCORE Office (Truckee)
PO Box 2757
Truckee, CA 96160
Phone: (916)587-2757
Fax: (916)587-2439

SCORE Office (Visalia)
c/o Tulare County E.D.C.
113 S. M St.
Tulare, CA 93274
Phone: (209)627-0766
Fax: (209)627-8149

SCORE Office (Upland)
c/o Upland Chamber of Commerce
433 N. 2nd Ave.
Upland, CA 91786
Phone: (909)931-4108

SCORE Office (Vallejo)
2 Florida St.
Vallejo, CA 94590
Phone: (707)644-5551
Fax: (707)644-5590

SCORE Office (Van Nuys)
14540 Victory Blvd.
Van Nuys, CA 91411
Phone: (818)989-0300
Fax: (818)989-3836

SCORE Office (Ventura)
5700 Ralston St., Ste. 310
Ventura, CA 93001
Phone: (805)658-2688
Fax: (805)658-2252
Email: scoreven@jps.net
Website: www.jps.net/scoreven

SCORE Office (Vista)
201 E. Washington St.
Vista, CA 92084
Phone: (619)726-1122
Fax: (619)226-8654

SCORE Office (Watsonville)
PO Box 1748
Watsonville, CA 95077
Phone: (408)724-3849
Fax: (408)728-5300

SCORE Office (West Covina)
c/o West Covina Chamber of
Commerce
811 S. Sunset Ave.
West Covina, CA 91790
Phone: (818)338-8496
Fax: (818)960-0511

SCORE Office (Westlake)
c/o Westlake Chamber of Commerce
30893 Thousand Oaks Blvd.
Westlake Village, CA 91362
Phone: (805)496-5630
Fax: (818)991-1754

Colorado

SCORE Office (Colorado Springs)
2 N. Cascade Ave., Ste. 110
Colorado Springs, CO 80903
Phone: (719)636-3074
Website: www.cscc.org/score02/
index.html

SCORE Office (Denver)
US Custom's House, 4th Fl.
721 19th St.
Denver, CO 80201-0660
Phone: (303)844-3985
Fax: (303)844-6490
Email: score62@csn.net
Website: www.sni.net/score62

SCORE Office (Tri-River)
1102 Grand Ave.
Glenwood Springs, CO 81601
Phone: (970)945-6589

SCORE Office (Grand Junction)
c/o Dennett K. Ela

2591 B & 3/4 Rd.
Grand Junction, CO 81503
Phone: (970)243-5242

SCORE Office (Gunnison)
608 N. 11th
Gunnison, CO 81230
Phone: (303)641-4422

SCORE Office (Montrose)
1214 Peppertree Dr.
Montrose, CO 81401
Phone: (970)249-6080

SCORE Office (Pagosa Springs)
PO Box 4381
Pagosa Springs, CO 81157
Phone: (970)731-4890

SCORE Office (Rifle)
0854 W. Battlement Pky., Apt. C106
Parachute, CO 81635
Phone: (970)285-9390

SCORE Office (Pueblo)
c/o Chamber of Commerce
302 N. Santa Fe
Pueblo, CO 81003
Phone: (719)542-1704
Fax: (719)542-1624
Email: mackey@iex.net
Website: www.pueblo.org/score

SCORE Office (Ridgway)
143 Poplar Pl.
Ridgway, CO 81432

SCORE Office (Silverton)
PO Box 480
Silverton, CO 81433
Phone: (303)387-5430

SCORE Office (Minturn)
PO Box 2066
Vail, CO 81658
Phone: (970)476-1224

Connecticut

SCORE Office (Greater Bridgeport)
230 Park Ave.
Bridgeport, CT 06601-0999
Phone: (203)576-4369
Fax: (203)576-4388

SCORE Office (Bristol)
10 Main St. 1st. Fl.
Bristol, CT 06010
Phone: (203)584-4718
Fax: (203)584-4722

SCORE office (Greater Danbury)
246 Federal Rd.
Unit LL2, Ste. 7
Brookfield, CT 06804
Phone: (203)775-1151

SCORE Office (Greater Danbury)
246 Federal Rd., Unit LL2, Ste. 7
Brookfield, CT 06804
Phone: (203)775-1151

SCORE Office (Eastern Connecticut)
Administration Bldg., Rm. 313
PO 625
61 Main St. (Chapter 579)
Groton, CT 06475
Phone: (203)388-9508

SCORE Office (Greater Hartford
County)
330 Main St.
Hartford, CT 06106
Phone: (860)548-1749
Fax: (860)240-4659
Website: www.score56.org

SCORE Office (Manchester)
20 Hartford Rd.
Manchester, CT 06040
Phone: (203)646-2223
Fax: (203)646-5871

SCORE Office (New Britain)
185 Main St., Ste. 431
New Britain, CT 06051
Phone: (203)827-4492
Fax: (203)827-4480

SCORE Office (New Haven)
25 Science Pk., Bldg. 25, Rm. 366
New Haven, CT 06511
Phone: (203)865-7645

SCORE Office (Fairfield County)
24 Beldon Ave., 5th Fl.
Norwalk, CT 06850
Phone: (203)847-7348
Fax: (203)849-9308

SCORE Office (Old Saybrook)
146 Main St.
Old Saybrook, CT 06475
Phone: (860)388-9508

SCORE Office (Simsbury)
Box 244
Simsbury, CT 06070
Phone: (203)651-7307
Fax: (203)651-1933

SCORE Office (Torrington)
23 North Rd.
Torrington, CT 06791
Phone: (203)482-6586

Delaware

SCORE Office (Dover)
Treadway Towers
PO Box 576
Dover, DE 19903
Phone: (302)678-0892
Fax: (302)678-0189

SCORE Office (Lewes)
PO Box 1
Lewes, DE 19958
Phone: (302)645-8073
Fax: (302)645-8412

SCORE Office (Milford)
204 NE Front St.
Milford, DE 19963
Phone: (302)422-3301

SCORE Office (Wilmington)
824 Market St., Ste. 610
Wilmington, DE 19801
Phone: (302)573-6652
Fax: (302)573-6092
Website: www.scoredelaware.com

District of Columbia

SCORE Office (George Mason
University)
409 3rd St. SW, 4th Fl.
Washington, DC 20024
Free: (800)634-0245

SCORE Office (Washington DC)
1110 Vermont Ave. NW, 9th Fl.
Washington, DC 20043
Phone: (202)606-4000
Fax: (202)606-4225
Email: dcscore@hotmail.com
Website: www.scoredc.org/

Florida

SCORE Office (Desota County
Chamber of Commerce)
16 South Velucia Ave.
Arcadia, FL 34266
Phone: (941)494-4033

SCORE Office (Suncoast/Pinellas)
Airport Business Ctr.
4707 - 140th Ave. N, No. 311

Clearwater, FL 33755
Phone: (813)532-6800
Fax: (813)532-6800

SCORE Office (DeLand)
336 N. Woodland Blvd.
DeLand, FL 32720
Phone: (904)734-4331
Fax: (904)734-4333

SCORE Office (South Palm Beach)
1050 S. Federal Hwy., Ste. 132
Delray Beach, FL 33483
Phone: (561)278-7752
Fax: (561)278-0288

SCORE Office (Ft. Lauderdale)
Federal Bldg., Ste. 123
299 E. Broward Blvd.
Ft. Lauderdale, FL 33301
Phone: (954)356-7263
Fax: (954)356-7145

SCORE Office (Southwest Florida)
The Renaissance
8695 College Pky., Ste. 345 & 346
Ft. Myers, FL 33919
Phone: (941)489-2935
Fax: (941)489-1170

SCORE Office (Treasure Coast)
Professional Center, Ste. 2
3220 S. US, No. 1
Ft. Pierce, FL 34982
Phone: (561)489-0548

SCORE Office (Gainesville)
101 SE 2nd Pl., Ste. 104
Gainesville, FL 32601
Phone: (904)375-8278

SCORE Office (Hialeah Dade
Chamber)
59 W. 5th St.
Hialeah, FL 33010
Phone: (305)887-1515
Fax: (305)887-2453

SCORE Office (Daytona Beach)
921 Nova Rd., Ste. A
Holly Hills, FL 32117
Phone: (904)255-6889
Fax: (904)255-0229
Email: score87@dbeach.com

SCORE Office (South Broward)
3475 Sheridian St., Ste. 203
Hollywood, FL 33021
Phone: (305)966-8415

SCORE Office (Citrus County)
5 Poplar Ct.
Homosassa, FL 34446
Phone: (352)382-1037

SCORE Office (Jacksonville)
7825 Baymeadows Way, Ste. 100-B
Jacksonville, FL 32256
Phone: (904)443-1911
Fax: (904)443-1980
Email: scorejax@juno.com
Website: www.scorejax.org/

SCORE Office (Jacksonville
Satellite)
3 Independent Dr.
Jacksonville, FL 32256
Phone: (904)366-6600
Fax: (904)632-0617

SCORE Office (Central Florida)
5410 S. Florida Ave., No. 3
Lakeland, FL 33801
Phone: (941)687-5783
Fax: (941)687-6225

SCORE Office (Lakeland)
100 Lake Morton Dr.
Lakeland, FL 33801
Phone: (941)686-2168

SCORE Office (St. Petersburg)
800 W. Bay Dr., Ste. 505
Largo, FL 33712
Phone: (813)585-4571

SCORE Office (Leesburg)
9501 US Hwy. 441
Leesburg, FL 34788-8751
Phone: (352)365-3556
Fax: (352)365-3501

SCORE Office (Cocoa)
1600 Farno Rd., Unit 205
Melbourne, FL 32935
Phone: (407)254-2288

SCORE Office (Melbourne)
Melbourne Professional Complex
1600 Sarno, Ste. 205
Melbourne, FL 32935
Phone: (407)254-2288
Fax: (407)245-2288

SCORE Office (Merritt Island)
1600 Sarno Rd., Ste. 205
Melbourne, FL 32935
Phone: (407)254-2288
Fax: (407)254-2288

SCORE Office (Space Coast)
Melbourn Professional Complex
1600 Sarno, Ste. 205
Melbourne, FL 32935
Phone: (407)254-2288
Fax: (407)254-2288

SCORE Office (Dade)
49 NW 5th St.
Miami, FL 33128
Phone: (305)371-6889
Fax: (305)374-1882
Email: score@netrox.net
Website: www.netrox.net/~score/

SCORE Office (Naples of Collier)
International College
2654 Tamiami Trl. E
Naples, FL 34112
Phone: (941)417-1280
Fax: (941)417-1281
Email: score@naples.net
Website: www.naples.net/clubs/score/
index.htm

SCORE Office (Pasco County)
6014 US Hwy. 19, Ste. 302
New Port Richey, FL 34652
Phone: (813)842-4638

SCORE Office (Southeast Volusia)
115 Canal St.
New Smyrna Beach, FL 32168
Phone: (904)428-2449
Fax: (904)423-3512

SCORE Office (Ocala)
110 E. Silver Springs Blvd.
Ocala, FL 34470
Phone: (352)629-5959
Clay County SCORE Office
Clay County Chamber of Commerce
1734 Kingsdey Ave.
PO Box 1441
Orange Park, FL 32073
Phone: (904)264-2651
Fax: (904)269-0363

SCORE Office (Orlando)
80 N. Hughey Ave.
Rm. 445 Federal Bldg.
Orlando, FL 32801
Phone: (407)648-6476
Fax: (407)648-6425

SCORE Office (Emerald Coast)
19 W. Garden St., No. 325
Pensacola, FL 32501
Phone: (904)444-2060
Fax: (904)444-2070

SCORE Office (Charlotte County)
201 W. Marion Ave., Ste. 211
Punta Gorda, FL 33950
Phone: (941)575-1818
Email: score@gls3c.com
Website: www.charlotte-florida.com/
business/scorepg01.htm

SCORE Office (St. Augustine)
1 Riberia St.
St. Augustine, FL 32084
Phone: (904)829-5681
Fax: (904)829-6477

SCORE Office (Bradenton)
2801 Fruitville, Ste. 280
Sarasota, FL 34237
Phone: (813)955-1029

SCORE Office (Manasota)
2801 Fruitville Rd., Ste. 280
Sarasota, FL 34237
Phone: (941)955-1029
Fax: (941)955-5581
Email: score116@gte.net
Website: www.score-suncoast.org/

SCORE Office (Tallahassee)
c/o Leon County Library
200 W. Park Ave.
Tallahassee, FL 32302
Phone: (850)487-2665

SCORE Office (Hillsborough)
4732 Dale Mabry Hwy. N, Ste. 400
Tampa, FL 33614-6509
Phone: (813)870-0125

SCORE Office (Lake Sumter)
c/o First Union National Bank
122 E. Main St.
Tavares, FL 32778-3810
Phone: (352)365-3556

SCORE Office (Titusville)
2000 S. Washington Ave.
Titusville, FL 32780
Phone: (407)267-3036
Fax: (407)264-0127

SCORE Office (Venice)
257 N. Tamiami Trl.
Venice, FL 34285
Phone: (941)488-2236
Fax: (941)484-5903

SCORE Office (Palm Beach)
500 Australian Ave. S, Ste. 100
West Palm Beach, FL 33401
Phone: (561)833-1672
Fax: (561)833-1712

SCORE Office (Wildwood)
103 N. Webster St.
Wildwood, FL 34785

Georgia

SCORE Office (Atlanta)
Harris Tower, Suite 1900
233 Peachtree Rd., NE
Atlanta, GA 30309
Phone: (404)347-2442
Fax: (404)347-1227

SCORE Office (Augusta)
3126 Oxford Rd.
Augusta, GA 30909
Phone: (706)869-9100

SCORE Office (Columbus)
School Bldg.
PO Box 40
Columbus, GA 31901
Phone: (706)327-3654

SCORE Office (Dalton-Whitfield)
305 S. Thorton Ave.
Dalton, GA 30720
Phone: (706)279-3383

SCORE Office (Gainesville)
PO Box 374
Gainesville, GA 30503
Phone: (770)532-6206
Fax: (770)535-8419

SCORE Office (Macon)
711 Grand Bldg.
Macon, GA 31201
Phone: (912)751-6160

SCORE Office (Brunswick)
4 Glen Ave.
St. Simons Island, GA 31520
Phone: (912)265-0620
Fax: (912)265-0629

SCORE Office (Savannah)
111 E. Liberty St., Ste. 103
Savannah, GA 31401
Phone: (912)652-4335
Fax: (912)652-4184
Email: infosubcommitteeresav.org
Website: www.coastalempire.com/
score/index.htm

Guam

SCORE Office (Guam)
Pacific News Bldg., Rm. 103
238 Archbishop Flores St.

Agana, GU 96910-5100
Phone: (671)472-7308

Hawaii

SCORE Office (Hawaii, Inc.)
1111 Bishop St., Ste. 204
PO Box 50207
Honolulu, HI 96813
Phone: (808)522-8132
Fax: (808)522-8135
Email: hnlscore@juno.com

SCORE Office (Kahului)
c/o Chamber of Commerce
250 Alamaha, Unit N16A
Kahului, HI 96732
Phone: (808)871-7711

SCORE Office (Maui, Inc.)
590 E. Lipoa Pkwy., Ste. 227
Kihei, HI 96753
Phone: (808)875-2380

Idaho

SCORE Office (Treasure Valley)
1020 Main St., No. 290
Boise, ID 83702
Phone: (208)334-1696
Fax: (208)334-9353

SCORE Office (Eastern Idaho)
2300 N. Yellowstone, Ste. 119
Idaho Falls, ID 83401
Phone: (208)523-1022
Fax: (208)528-7127

Illinois

SCORE Office (Fox Valley)
40 W. Downer Pl.
PO Box 277
Aurora, IL 60506
Phone: (630)897-9214
Fax: (630)897-7002

SCORE Office (Greater Belvidere)
419 S. State St.
Belvidere, IL 61008
Phone: (815)544-4357
Fax: (815)547-7654

SCORE Office (Bensenville)
1050 Busse Hwy. Suite 100
Bensenville, IL 60106
Phone: (708)350-2944
Fax: (708)350-2979

SCORE Office (Central Illinois)
402 N. Hershey Rd.
Bloomington, IL 61704
Phone: (309)644-0549
Fax: (309)663-8270
Email: webmaster@central-illinois-score.org
Website: www.central-illinois-score.org/

SCORE Office (Southern Illinois)
150 E. Pleasant Hill Rd.
Box 1
Carbondale, IL 62901
Phone: (618)453-6654
Fax: (618)453-5040

SCORE Office (Chicago)
Northwest Atrium Ctr.
500 W. Madison St., No. 1250
Chicago, IL 60661
Phone: (312)353-7724
Fax: (312)886-5688
Website: www.mcs.net/~bic/

SCORE Office (Chicago—Oliver Harvey College)
Pullman Bldg.
1000 E. 11th St., 7th Fl.
Chicago, IL 60628
Fax: (312)468-8086

SCORE Office (Danville)
28 W. N. Street
Danville, IL 61832
Phone: (217)442-7232
Fax: (217)442-6228

SCORE Office (Decatur)
Milliken University
1184 W. Main St.
Decatur, IL 62522
Phone: (217)424-6297
Fax: (217)424-3993
Email: charding@mail.millikin.edu
Website: www.millikin.edu/academics/Tabor/score.html

SCORE Office (Downers Grove)
925 Curtis
Downers Grove, IL 60515
Phone: (708)968-4050
Fax: (708)968-8368

SCORE Office (Elgin)
24 E. Chicago, 3rd Fl.
PO Box 648
Elgin, IL 60120
Phone: (847)741-5660
Fax: (847)741-5677

SCORE Office (Freeport Area)
26 S. Galena Ave.
Freeport, IL 61032
Phone: (815)233-1350
Fax: (815)235-4038

SCORE Office (Galesburg)
292 E. Simmons St.
PO Box 749
Galesburg, IL 61401
Phone: (309)343-1194
Fax: (309)343-1195

SCORE Office (Glen Ellyn)
500 Pennsylvania
Glen Ellyn, IL 60137
Phone: (708)469-0907
Fax: (708)469-0426

SCORE Office (Greater Alton)
Alden Hall
5800 Godfrey Rd.
Godfrey, IL 62035-2466
Phone: (618)467-2280
Fax: (618)466-8289
Website: www.altonweb.com/score/

SCORE Office (Grayslake)
19351 W. Washington St.
Grayslake, IL 60030
Phone: (708)223-3633
Fax: (708)223-9371

SCORE Office (Harrisburg)
303 S. Commercial
Harrisburg, IL 62946-1528
Phone: (618)252-8528
Fax: (618)252-0210

SCORE Office (Joliet)
100 N. Chicago
Joliet, IL 60432
Phone: (815)727-5371
Fax: (815)727-5374

SCORE Office (Kankakee)
101 S. Schuyler Ave.
Kankakee, IL 60901
Phone: (815)933-0376
Fax: (815)933-0380

SCORE Office (Macomb)
216 Seal Hall, Rm. 214
Macomb, IL 61455
Phone: (309)298-1128
Fax: (309)298-2520

SCORE Office (Matteson)
210 Lincoln Mall
Matteson, IL 60443

Phone: (708)709-3750
Fax: (708)503-9322

SCORE Office (Mattoon)
1701 Wabash Ave.
Mattoon, IL 61938
Phone: (217)235-5661
Fax: (217)234-6544

SCORE Office (Quad Cities)
c/o Chamber of Commerce
622 19th St.
Moline, IL 61265
Phone: (309)797-0082
Fax: (309)757-5435
Email: score@qconline.com
Website: www.qconline.com/
business/score/

SCORE Office (Naperville)
131 W. Jefferson Ave.
Naperville, IL 60540
Phone: (708)355-4141
Fax: (708)355-8355

SCORE Office (Northbrook)
2002 Walters Ave.
Northbrook, IL 60062
Phone: (847)498-5555
Fax: (847)498-5510

SCORE Office (Palos Hills)
10900 S. 88th Ave.
Palos Hills, IL 60465
Phone: (847)974-5468
Fax: (847)974-0078

SCORE Office (Peoria)
c/o Peoria Chamber of Commerce
124 SW Adams, Ste. 300
Peoria, IL 61602
Phone: (309)676-0755
Fax: (309)676-7534

SCORE Office (Prospect Heights)
1375 Wolf Rd.
Prospect Heights, IL 60070
Phone: (847)537-8660
Fax: (847)537-7138

SCORE Office (Quincy Tri-State)
c/o Chamber of Commerce
300 Civic Center Plz., Ste. 245
Quincy, IL 62301
Phone: (217)222-8093
Fax: (217)222-3033

SCORE Office (River Grove)
2000 5th Ave.
River Grove, IL 60171

Phone: (708)456-0300
Fax: (708)583-3121

SCORE Office (Northern Illinois)
515 N. Court St.
Rockford, IL 61103
Phone: (815)962-0122
Fax: (815)962-0122

SCORE Office (St. Charles)
103 N. 1st Ave.
St. Charles, IL 60174-1982
Phone: (847)584-8384
Fax: (847)584-6065

SCORE Office (Springfield)
511 W. Capitol Ave., Ste. 302
Springfield, IL 62704
Phone: (217)492-4416
Fax: (217)492-4867

SCORE Office (Sycamore)
112 Somunak St.
Sycamore, IL 60178
Phone: (815)895-3456
Fax: (815)895-0125

SCORE Office (University)
Hwy. 50 & Stuenkel Rd. Ste. C3305
University Park, IL 60466
Phone: (708)534-5000
Fax: (708)534-8457

Indiana

SCORE Office (Anderson)
c/o Chamber of Commerce
205 W. 11th St.
Anderson, IN 46015
Phone: (317)642-0264

SCORE Office (Bloomington)
Star Center
216 W. Allen
Bloomington, IN 47403
Phone: (812)335-7334
Email: wtfische@indiana.edu
Website:
www.brainfreezemedia.com/
score527/

SCORE Office (South East Indiana)
c/o Chamber of Commerce
500 Franklin St.
Box 29
Columbus, IN 47201
Phone: (812)379-4457

SCORE Office (Corydon)
310 N. Elm St.
Corydon, IN 47112

Phone: (812)738-2137
Fax: (812)738-6438

SCORE Office (Crown Point)
Old Courthouse Sq. Ste. 206
PO Box 43
Crown Point, IN 46307
Phone: (219)663-1800

SCORE Office (Elkhart)
418 S. Main St.
Elkhart, IN 46515
Phone: (219)293-1531
Fax: (219)294-1859

SCORE Office (Evansville)
1100 W. Lloyd Expy., Ste. 105
Evansville, IN 47708
Phone: (812)426-6144

SCORE Office (Fort Wayne)
1300 S. Harrison St.
Ft. Wayne, IN 46802
Phone: (219)422-2601
Fax: (219)422-2601

SCORE Office (Gary)
973 W. 6th Ave., Rm. 326
Gary, IN 46402
Phone: (219)882-3918

SCORE Office (Hammond)
7034 Indianapolis Blvd.
Hammond, IN 46324
Phone: (219)931-1000
Fax: (219)845-9548

SCORE Office (Indianapolis)
429 N. Pennsylvania St., Ste. 100
Indianapolis, IN 46204-1873
Phone: (317)226-7264
Fax: (317)226-7259
Email: inscore@indy.net
Website: www.score-
indianapolis.org/

SCORE Office (Jasper)
PO Box 307
Jasper, IN 47547-0307
Phone: (812)482-6866

SCORE Office (Kokomo/Howard
Counties)
106 N. Washington St.
Kokomo, IN 46901
Phone: (765)457-5301
Fax: (765)452-4564

SCORE Office (Logansport)
c/o Logansport County Chamber of
Commerce

300 E. Broadway, Ste. 103
Logansport, IN 46947
Phone: (219)753-6388

SCORE Office (Madison)
301 E. Main St.
Madison, IN 47250
Phone: (812)265-3135
Fax: (812)265-2923

SCORE Office (Marengo)
Rt. 1 Box 224D
Marengo, IN 47140
Fax: (812)365-2793

SCORE Office (Marion/Grant
Counties)
215 S. Adams
Marion, IN 46952
Phone: (765)664-5107

SCORE Office (Merrillville)
255 W. 80th Pl.
Merrillville, IN 46410
Phone: (219)769-8180
Fax: (219)736-6223

SCORE Office (Michigan City)
200 E. Michigan Blvd.
Michigan City, IN 46360
Phone: (219)874-6221
Fax: (219)873-1204

SCORE Office (South Central
Indiana)
4100 Charleston Rd.
New Albany, IN 47150-9538
Phone: (812)945-0066

SCORE Office (Rensselaer)
104 W. Washington
Rensselaer, IN 47978

SCORE Office (Salem)
210 N. Main St.
Salem, IN 47167
Phone: (812)883-4303
Fax: (812)883-1467

SCORE Office (South Bend)
300 N. Michigan St.
South Bend, IN 46601
Phone: (219)282-4350
Email: chair@southbend-score.org
Website: www.southbend-score.org/

SCORE Office (Valparaiso)
150 Lincolnway
Valparaiso, IN 46383
Phone: (219)462-1105
Fax: (219)469-5710

SCORE Office (Vincennes)
27 N. 3rd
PO Box 553
Vincennes, IN 47591
Phone: (812)882-6440
Fax: (812)882-6441

SCORE Office (Wabash)
PO Box 371
Wabash, IN 46992
Phone: (219)563-1168
Fax: (219)563-6920

Iowa

SCORE Office (Burlington)
Federal Bldg.
300 N. Main St.
Burlington, IA 52601
Phone: (319)752-2967

SCORE Office (Cedar Rapids)
Lattner Bldg., Ste. 200
215-4th Avenue, SE, No. 200
Cedar Rapids, IA 52401-1806
Phone: (319)362-6405
Fax: (319)362-7861

SCORE Office (Illowa)
333 4th Ave. S
Clinton, IA 52732
Phone: (319)242-5702

SCORE Office (Council Bluffs)
7 N. 6th St.
Council Bluffs, IA 51502
Phone: (712)325-1000

SCORE Office (Northeast Iowa)
3404 285th St.
Cresco, IA 52136
Phone: (319)547-3377

SCORE Office (Des Moines)
Federal Bldg., Rm. 749
210 Walnut St.
Des Moines, IA 50309-2186
Phone: (515)284-4760

SCORE Office (Ft. Dodge)
Federal Bldg., Rm. 436
205 S. 8th St.
Ft. Dodge, IA 50501
Phone: (515)955-2622

SCORE Office (Independence)
110 1st. St. East
Independence, IA 50644
Phone: (319)334-7178
Fax: (319)334-7179

SCORE Office (Iowa City)
210 Federal Bldg.
PO Box 1853
Iowa City, IA 52240-1853
Phone: (319)338-1662

SCORE Office (Keokuk)
401 Main St.
Pierce Bldg., No. 1
Keokuk, IA 52632
Phone: (319)524-5055

SCORE Office (Central Iowa)
Fisher Community College
709 S. Center
Marshalltown, IA 50158
Phone: (515)753-6645

SCORE Office (River City)
15 West State St.
Mason City, IA 50401
Phone: (515)423-5724

SCORE Office (South Central)
SBDC, Indian Hills Community
College
525 Grandview Ave.
Ottumwa, IA 52501
Phone: (515)683-5127
Fax: (515)683-5263

SCORE Office (Dubuque)
10250 Sundown Rd.
Peosta, IA 52068
Phone: (319)556-5110

SCORE Office (Southwest Iowa)
c/o Chamber of Commerce
614 W. Sheridan
Shenandoah, IA 51601
Phone: (712)246-3260

SCORE Office (Sioux City)
Federal Bldg.
320 6th St.
Sioux City, IA 51101
Phone: (712)277-2324
Fax: (712)277-2325

SCORE Office (Iowa Lakes)
122 W. 5th St.
Spencer, IA 51301
Phone: (712)262-3059

SCORE Office (Vista)
c/o Storm Lake Chamber of
Commerce
119 W. 6th St.
Storm Lake, IA 50588
Phone: (712)732-3780

SCORE Office (Waterloo)
c/o Chamber of Commerce
215 E. 4th
Waterloo, IA 50703
Phone: (319)233-8431

Kansas

SCORE Office (Southwest Kansas)
501 W. Spruce
Dodge City, KS 67801
Phone: (316)227-3119

SCORE Office (Emporia)
811 Homewood
Emporia, KS 66801
Phone: (316)342-1600

SCORE Office (Golden Belt)
1307 Williams
Great Bend, KS 67530
Phone: (316)792-2401

SCORE Office (Hays)
c/o Empire Bank
PO Box 400
Hays, KS 67601
Phone: (913)625-6595

SCORE Office (Hutchinson)
1 E. 9th St.
Hutchinson, KS 67501
Phone: (316)665-8468
Fax: (316)665-7619

SCORE Office (Southeast Kansas)
404 Westminster Pl.
PO Box 886
Independence, KS 67301
Phone: (316)331-4741

SCORE Office (McPherson)
306 N. Main
PO Box 616
McPherson, KS 67460
Phone: (316)241-3303

SCORE Office (Salina)
120 Ash St.
Salina, KS 67401
Phone: (785)243-4290
Fax: (785)243-1833

SCORE Office (Topeka)
1700 College
Topeka, KS 66621
Phone: (785)231-1010

SCORE Office (Wichita)
c/o SBA
100 E. English, Ste. 510

Wichita, KS 67202
Phone: (316)269-6273
Fax: (316)269-6499

SCORE Office (Ark Valley)
c/o Winfield Chamber of Commerce
205 E. 9th St.
Winfield, KS 67156
Phone: (316)221-1617

Kentucky

SCORE Office (Ashland)
PO Box 830
Ashland, KY 41105
Phone: (606)329-8011
Fax: (606)325-4607

SCORE Office (Bowling Green)
812 State St.
PO Box 51
Bowling Green, KY 42101
Phone: (502)781-3200
Fax: (502)843-0458

SCORE Office (Tri-Lakes)
508 Barbee Way
Danville, KY 40422-1548
Phone: (606)231-9902

SCORE Office (Glasgow)
301 W. Main St.
Glasgow, KY 42141
Phone: (502)651-3161
Fax: (502)651-3122

SCORE Office (Hazard)
B & I Technical Center
100 Airport Gardens Rd.
Hazard, KY 41701
Phone: (606)439-5856
Fax: (606)439-1808

SCORE Office (Lexington)
410 W. Vine St., Ste. 290, Civic C
Lexington, KY 40507
Phone: (606)231-9902
Fax: (606)253-3190
Email: scorelex@uky.campus.mci.net

SCORE Office (Louisville)
188 Federal Office Bldg.
600 Dr. Martin L. King Jr. Pl.
Louisville, KY 40202
Phone: (502)582-5976

SCORE Office (Madisonville)
257 N. Main
Madisonville, KY 42431
Phone: (502)825-1399
Fax: (502)825-1396

SCORE Office (Paducah)
Federal Office Bldg.
501 Broadway, Rm. B-36
Paducah, KY 42001
Phone: (502)442-5685

Louisiana

SCORE Office (Central Louisiana)
802 3rd St.
Alexandria, LA 71309
Phone: (318)442-6671

SCORE Office (Baton Rouge)
564 Laurel St.
PO Box 3217
Baton Rouge, LA 70801
Phone: (504)381-7130
Fax: (504)336-4306

SCORE Office (North Shore)
2 W. Thomas
Hammond, LA 70401
Phone: (504)345-4457
Fax: (504)345-4749

SCORE Office (Lafayette)
804 St. Mary Blvd.
Lafayette, LA 70505-1307
Phone: (318)233-2705
Fax: (318)234-8671
Email: score302@aol.com

SCORE Office (Lake Charles)
120 W. Pujo St.
Lake Charles, LA 70601
Phone: (318)433-3632

SCORE Office (New Orleans)
365 Canal St., Ste. 3100
New Orleans, LA 70130
Phone: (504)589-2356
Fax: (504)589-2339

SCORE Office (Shreveport)
400 Edwards St.
Shreveport, LA 71101
Phone: (318)677-2536
Fax: (318)677-2541

Maine

SCORE Office (Augusta)
40 Western Ave.
Augusta, ME 04330
Phone: (207)622-8509

SCORE Office (Bangor)
Peabody Hall, Rm. 229
One College Cir.

Bangor, ME 04401
Phone: (207)941-9707

SCORE Office (Central & Northern
Arroostock)
111 High St.
Caribou, ME 04736
Phone: (207)492-8010
Fax: (207)492-8010

SCORE Office (Penquis)
South St.
Dover Foxcroft, ME 04426
Phone: (207)564-7021

SCORE Office (Maine Coastal)
Mill Mall
Box 1105
Ellsworth, ME 04605-1105
Phone: (207)667-5800
Email: score@arcadia.net

SCORE Office (Lewiston-Auburn)
BIC of Maine-Bates Mill Complex
35 Canal St.
Lewiston, ME 04240-7764
Phone: (207)782-3708
Fax: (207)783-7745

SCORE Office (Portland)
66 Pearl St., Rm. 210
Portland, ME 04101
Phone: (207)772-1147
Fax: (207)772-5581
Email: Score53@score.maine.org
Website: www.score.maine.org/
chapter53/

SCORE Office (Western Mountains)
c/o Oxford Federal Credit Union
255 River St.
PO Box 252
Rumford, ME 04257-0252
Phone: (207)369-9976

SCORE Office (Oxford Hills)
166 Main St.
South Paris, ME 04281
Phone: (207)743-0499

Maryland

SCORE Office (Southern Maryland)
2525 Riva Rd., Ste. 110
Annapolis, MD 21401
Phone: (410)266-9553
Fax: (410)573-0981
Email: score390@aol.com
Website: members.aol.com/score390/
index.htm

SCORE Office (Baltimore)
The City Crescent Bldg., 6th Fl.
10 S. Howard St.
Baltimore, MD 21201
Phone: (410)962-2233
Fax: (410)962-1805

SCORE Office (Bel Air)
108 S. Bond St.
Bel Air, MD 21014
Phone: (410)838-2020
Fax: (410)893-4715

SCORE Office (Bethesda)
7910 Woodmont Ave., Ste. 1204
Bethesda, MD 20814
Phone: (301)652-4900
Fax: (301)657-1973

SCORE Office (Bowie)
6670 Race Track Rd.
Bowie, MD 20715
Phone: (301)262-0920
Fax: (301)262-0921

SCORE Office (Dorchester County)
203 Sunburst Hwy.
Cambridge, MD 21613
Phone: (410)228-3575

SCORE Office (Upper Shore)
c/o Talbout County Chamber of
Commerce
210 Marlboro Ave.
Easton, MD 21601
Phone: (410)822-4606
Fax: (410)822-7922

SCORE Office (Frederick County)
c/o Frederick County Chamber of
Commerce
43A S. Market St.
Frederick, MD 21701
Phone: (301)662-8723
Fax: (301)846-4427

SCORE Office (Gaithersburg)
9 Park Ave.
Gaithersburg, MD 20877
Phone: (301)840-1400
Fax: (301)963-3918

SCORE Office (Glen Burnie)
103 Crain Hwy. SE
Glen Burnie, MD 21061
Phone: (410)766-8282
Fax: (410)766-9722

SCORE Office (Hagerstown)
111 W. Washington St.

Hagerstown, MD 21740
Phone: (301)739-2015
Fax: (301)739-1278

SCORE Office (Laurel)
7901 Sandy Spring Rd. Ste. 501
Laurel, MD 20707
Phone: (301)725-4000
Fax: (301)725-0776

SCORE Office (Salisbury)
c/o Chamber of Commerce
300 E. Main St.
Salisbury, MD 21801
Phone: (410)749-0185
Fax: (410)860-9925

Massachusetts

SCORE Office (NE Massachusetts)
Danvers Savings Bank
100 Cummings Ctr., Ste. 101 K
Beverly, MA 01923
Phone: (978)922-9441
Website: www1.shore.net/~score/

SCORE Office (Boston)
10 Causeway St., Rm. 265
Boston, MA 02222-1093
Phone: (617)565-5591
Fax: (617)565-5598
Email: boston-score-
20@worldnet.att.net
Website: www.scoreboston.org/

SCORE office (Bristol/Plymouth
County)
53 N. 6th St., Federal Bldg.
Bristol, MA 02740
Phone: (508)994-5093

SCORE Office (SE Massachusetts)
60 School St.
Brockton, MA 02401
Phone: (508)587-2673
Fax: (508)587-1340
Website:
www.metrosouthchamber.com/
score.html

SCORE Office (North Adams)
820 N. State Rd.
Cheshire, MA 01225
Phone: (413)743-5100

SCORE Office (Clinton Satellite)
1 Green St.
Clinton, MA 01510
Fax: (508)368-7689

SCORE Office (Greenfield)
PO Box 898
Greenfield, MA 01302
Phone: (413)773-5463
Fax: (413)773-7008

SCORE Office (Haverhill)
87 Winter St.
Haverhill, MA 01830
Phone: (508)373-5663
Fax: (508)373-8060

SCORE Office (Hudson Satellite)
PO Box 578
Hudson, MA 01749
Phone: (508)568-0360
Fax: (508)568-0360

SCORE Office (Cape Cod)
Independence Pk., Ste. 5B
270 Communications Way
Hyannis, MA 02601
Phone: (508)775-4884
Fax: (508)790-2540

SCORE Office (Lawrence)
264 Essex St.
Lawrence, MA 01840
Phone: (508)686-0900
Fax: (508)794-9953

SCORE Office (Leominster Satellite)
110 Erdman Way
Leominster, MA 01453
Phone: (508)840-4300
Fax: (508)840-4896

SCORE Office (Bristol/Plymouth
Counties)
53 N. 6th St., Federal Bldg.
New Bedford, MA 02740
Phone: (508)994-5093

SCORE Office (Newburyport)
29 State St.
Newburyport, MA 01950
Phone: (617)462-6680

SCORE Office (Pittsfield)
66 West St.
Pittsfield, MA 01201
Phone: (413)499-2485

SCORE Office (Haverhill-Salem)
32 Derby Sq.
Salem, MA 01970
Phone: (508)745-0330
Fax: (508)745-3855

SCORE Office (Springfield)
1350 Main St.

Federal Bldg.
Springfield, MA 01103
Phone: (413)785-0314

SCORE Office (Carver)
12 Taunton Green, Ste. 201
Taunton, MA 02780
Phone: (508)824-4068
Fax: (508)824-4069

SCORE Office (Worcester)
33 Waldo St.
Worcester, MA 01608
Phone: (508)753-2929
Fax: (508)754-8560

Michigan

SCORE Office (Allegan)
PO Box 338
Allegan. MI 49010
Phone: (616)673-2479

SCORE Office (Ann Arbor)
425 S. Main St., Ste. 103
Ann Arbor, MI 48104
Phone: (313)665-4433

SCORE Office (Battle Creek)
34 W. Jackson Ste. 4A
Battle Creek, MI 49017-3505
Phone: (616)962-4076
Fax: (616)962-6309

SCORE Office (Cadillac)
222 Lake St.
Cadillac, MI 49601
Phone: (616)775-9776
Fax: (616)768-4255

SCORE Office (Detroit)
477 Michigan Ave., Rm. 515
Detroit, MI 48226
Phone: (313)226-7947
Fax: (313)226-3448

SCORE Office (Flint)
708 Root Rd., Rm. 308
Flint, MI 48503
Phone: (810)233-6846

SCORE Office (Grand Rapids)
c/o Grand Rapids Chamber of
Commerce
111 Pearl St. NW
Grand Rapids, MI 49503-2831
Phone: (616)771-0305
Fax: (616)771-0328
Email: scoreone@iserv.net
Website: www.iserv.net/~scoreone/

SCORE Office (Holland)
480 State St.
Holland, MI 49423
Phone: (616)396-9472

SCORE Office (Jackson)
209 East Washington
PO Box 80
Jackson, MI 49204
Phone: (517)782-8221
Fax: (517)782-0061

SCORE Office (Kalamazoo)
345 W. Michigan Ave.
Kalamazoo, MI 49007
Phone: (616)381-5382
Fax: (616)384-0096
Email: score@nucleus.net

SCORE Office (Lansing)
117 E. Allegan
PO Box 14030
Lansing, MI 48901
Phone: (517)487-6340
Fax: (517)484-6910

SCORE Office (Livonia)
15401 Farmington Rd.
Livonia, MI 48154
Phone: (313)427-2122
Fax: (313)427-6055

SCORE Office (Madison Heights)
26345 John R
Madison Heights, MI 48071
Phone: (810)542-5010
Fax: (810)542-6821

SCORE Office (Monroe)
111 E. 1st
Monroe, MI 48161
Phone: (313)242-3366
Fax: (313)242-7253

SCORE Office (Mt. Clemens)
58 S/B Gratiot
Mt. Clemens, MI 48043
Phone: (810)463-1528
Fax: (810)463-6541

SCORE Office (Muskegon)
PO Box 1087
230 Terrace Plz.
Muskegon, MI 49443
Phone: (616)722-3751
Fax: (616)728-7251

SCORE Office (Petoskey)
401 E. Mitchell St.
Petoskey, MI 49770
Phone: (616)347-4150

SCORE Office (Pontiac)
Executive Office Bldg.
1200 N. Telegraph Rd.
Pontiac, MI 48341
Phone: (810)975-9555

SCORE Office (Pontiac)
PO Box 430025
Pontiac, MI 48343
Phone: (810)335-9600

SCORE Office (Port Huron)
920 Pinegrove Ave.
Port Huron, MI 48060
Phone: (810)985-7101

SCORE Office (Rochester)
71 Walnut Ste. 110
Rochester, MI 48307
Phone: (810)651-6700
Fax: (810)651-5270

SCORE Office (Saginaw)
901 S. Washington Ave.
Saginaw, MI 48601
Phone: (517)752-7161
Fax: (517)752-9055

SCORE Office (Upper Peninsula)
c/o Chamber of Commerce
2581 I-75 Business Spur
Sault Ste. Marie, MI 49783
Phone: (906)632-3301

SCORE Office (Southfield)
21000 W. 10 Mile Rd.
Southfield, MI 48075
Phone: (810)204-3050
Fax: (810)204-3099

SCORE Office (Traverse City)
202 E. Grandview Pkwy.
PO Box 387
Traverse City, MI 49685
Phone: (616)947-5075
Fax: (616)946-2565

SCORE Office (Warren)
30500 Van Dyke, Ste. 118
Warren, MI 48093
Phone: (810)751-3939

Minnesota

SCORE Office (Aitkin)
Aitkin, MN 56431
Phone: (218741-3906

SCORE Office (Albert Lea)
202 N. Broadway Ave.

Albert Lea, MN 56007
Phone: (507)373-7487

SCORE Office (Austin)
PO Box 864
Austin, MN 55912
Phone: (507)437-4561
Fax: (507)437-4869

SCORE Office (South Metro)
Ames Business Ctr.
2500 W. County Rd., No. 42
Burnsville, MN 55337
Phone: (612)898-5645
Fax: (612)435-6972
Email: southmetro@scoreminn.org
Website: www.scoreminn.org/
southmetro/

SCORE Office (Duluth)
1717 Minnesota Ave.
Duluth, MN 55802
Phone: (218)727-8286
Fax: (218)727-3113
Email: duluth@scoreminn.org
Website: www.scoreminn.org

SCORE Office (Fairmont)
PO Box 826
Fairmont, MN 56031
Phone: (507)235-5547
Fax: (507)235-8411

SCORE Office (Southwest
Minnesota)
112 Riverfront St.
Box 999
Mankato, MN 56001
Phone: (507)345-4519
Fax: (507)345-4451
Website: www.scoreminn.org/

SCORE Office (Minneapolis)
North Plaza Bldg., Ste. 51
5217 Wayzata Blvd.
Minneapolis, MN 55416
Phone: (612)591-0539
Fax: (612)544-0436
Website: www.scoreminn.org/

SCORE Office (Owatonna)
PO Box 331
Owatonna, MN 55060
Phone: (507)451-7970
Fax: (507)451-7972

SCORE Office (Red Wing)
2000 W. Main St., Ste. 324
Red Wing, MN 55066
Phone: (612)388-4079

SCORE Office (Southeastern
Minnesota)
220 S. Broadway, Ste. 100
Rochester, MN 55901
Phone: (507)288-1122
Fax: (507)282-8960
Website: www.scoreminn.org/

SCORE Office (Brainerd)
St. Cloud, MN 56301
SCORE Office (Central Area)
1527 Northway Dr.
St. Cloud, MN 56301
Phone: (320)240-1332
Fax: (320)255-9050
Website: www.scoreminn.org/

SCORE Office (St. Paul)
350 St. Peter St., No. 295
Lowry Professional Bldg.
St. Paul, MN 55102
Phone: (651)223-5010
Fax: (651)223-5048
Website: www.scoreminn.org/

SCORE Office (Winona)
Box 870
Winona, MN 55987
Phone: (507)452-2272
Fax: (507)454-8814

SCORE Office (Worthington)
1121 3rd Ave.
Worthington, MN 56187
Phone: (507)372-2919
Fax: (507)372-2827

Mississippi

SCORE Office (Delta)
c/o Greenville Chamber of Commerce
915 Washington Ave.
PO Box 933
Greenville, MS 38701
Phone: (601)378-3141

SCORE Office (Gulfcoast)
1 Government Plaza
2909 13th St., Ste. 203
Gulfport, MS 39501
Phone: (228)863-0054

SCORE Office (Jackson)
1st Jackson Center, Ste. 400
101 W. Capitol St.
Jackson, MS 39201
Phone: (601)965-5533

SCORE Office (Meridian)
5220 16th Ave.

Meridian, MS 39305
Phone: (601)482-4412

Missouri

SCORE Office (Lake of the Ozark)
University Extension
113 Kansas St.
PO Box 1405
Camdenton, MO 65020
Phone: (573)346-2644
Fax: (573)346-2694
Email: score@cdoc.net
Website: sites.cdoc.net/score/

Chamber of Commerce (Cape
Girardeau)
c/o Chamber of Commerce
PO Box 98
Cape Girardeau, MO 63702-0098
Phone: (314)335-3312

SCORE Office (Mid-Missouri)
1705 Halstead Ct.
Columbia, MO 65203
Phone: (573)874-1132

SCORE Office (Ozark-Gateway)
1486 Glassy Rd.
Cuba, MO 65453-1640
Phone: (573)885-4954

SCORE Office (Kansas City)
323 W. 8th St., Ste. 104
Kansas City, MO 64105
Phone: (816)374-6675
Fax: (816)374-6692
Email: SCOREBIC@AOL.COM
Website: www.crn.org/score/

SCORE Office (Sedalia)
Lucas Place
323 W. 8th St., Ste.104
Kansas City, MO 64105
Phone: (816)374-6675

SCORE office (Tri-Lakes)
c/o Dwayne Shoemaker
PO Box 1148
Kimberling, MO 65686
Phone: (417)739-3041

SCORE Office (Tri-Lakes)
HCRI Box 85
Lampe, MO 65681
Phone: (417)858-6798

SCORE Office (Mexico)
c/o Mexico Chamber of Commerce
111 N. Washington St.

Mexico, MO 65265
Phone: (314)581-2765

SCORE Office (Southeast Missouri)
Rte. 1, Box 280
Neelyville, MO 63954
Phone: (573)989-3577

SCORE office (Poplar Bluff Area)
c/o James W. Carson
806 Emma St.
Poplar Bluff, MO 63901
Phone: (573)686-8892

SCORE Office (St. Joseph)
c/o Chamber of Commerce
3003 Frederick Ave.
St. Joseph, MO 64506
Phone: (816)232-4461

SCORE Office (St. Louis)
815 Olive St., Rm. 242
St. Louis, MO 63101-1569
Phone: (314)539-6970
Fax: (314)539-3785
Email: info@stlscore.org
Website: www.stlscore.org/

SCORE Office (Lewis & Clark)
425 Spencer Rd.
St. Peters, MO 63376
Phone: (314)928-2900
Fax: (314)928-2900
Email: score01@mail.win.org

SCORE Office (Springfield)
620 S. Glenstone, Ste. 110
Springfield, MO 65802-3200
Phone: (417)864-7670
Fax: (417)864-4108

SCORE office (Southeast Kansas)
1206 W. First St.
Webb City, MO 64870
Phone: (417)673-3984

Montana

SCORE Office (Billings)
815 S. 27th St.
Billings, MT 59101
Phone: (406)245-4111

SCORE Office (Bozeman)
1205 E. Main St.
Bozeman, MT 59715
Phone: (406)586-5421

SCORE Office (Butte)
1000 George St.

Butte, MT 59701
Phone: (406)723-3177

SCORE Office (Great Falls)
710 First Ave. N
Great Falls, MT 59401
Phone: (406)761-4434
Email: scoregtf@in.tch.com

SCORE office (Havre, Montana)
518 First St.
Havre, MT 59501
Phone: (406)265-4383

SCORE Office (Helena)
Federal Bldg.
301 S. Park
Helena, MT 59626-0054
Phone: (406)441-1081

SCORE Office (Kalispell)
2 Main St.
Kalispell, MT 59901
Phone: (406)756-5271
Fax: (406)752-6665

SCORE Office (Missoula)
c/o Safe Shop Tools
723 Ronan
Missoula, MT 59806
Phone: (406)327-8806
Email: score@safeshop.com
Website: missoula.bigsky.net/score/

Nebraska

SCORE Office (Columbus)
Columbus, NE 68601
Phone: (402)564-2769

SCORE Office (North Platte)
414 E. 16th St.
Cozad, NE 69130
Phone: (308)784-2590

SCORE Office (Fremont)
c/o Chamber of Commerce
92 W. 5th St.
Fremont, NE 68025
Phone: (402)721-2641

SCORE office (Hastings)
Hastings, NE 68901
Phone: (402)463-3447

SCORE Office (Lincoln)
8800 O St.
Lincoln, NE 68520
Phone: (402)437-2409

SCORE Office (Panhandle)
150549 CR 30
Minatare, NE 69356
Phone: (308)632-2133
Website: www.tandt.com/SCORE

SCORE Office (Norfolk)
3209 S. 48th Ave.
Norfolk, NE 68106
Phone: (402)564-2769

SCORE Office (North Platte)
3301 W. 2nd St.
North Platte, NE 69101
Phone: (308)532-4466

SCORE Office (Omaha)
11145 Mill Valley Rd.
Omaha, NE 68154
Phone: (402)221-3606
Fax: (402)221-3680
Email: infoctr@ne.uswest.net
Website: www.tandt.com/score/

Nevada

SCORE Office (Incline Village)
969 Tahoe Blvd.
Incline Village, NV 89451
Phone: (702)831-7327
Fax: (702)832-1605

SCORE Office (Carson City)
301 E. Stewart
PO Box 7527
Las Vegas, NV 89125
Phone: (702)388-6104

SCORE Office (Las Vegas)
300 Las Vegas Blvd. S, Ste. 1100
Las Vegas, NV 89101
Phone: (702)388-6104

SCORE Office (Northern Nevada)
SBDC, College of Business
Administration
Univ. of Nevada
Reno, NV 89557-0100
Phone: (702)784-4436
Fax: (702)784-4337

New Hampshire

SCORE Office (North Country)
PO Box 34
Berlin, NH 03570
Phone: (603)752-1090

SCORE Office (Concord)
143 N. Main St., Rm. 202A

PO Box 1258
Concord, NH 03301
Phone: (603)225-1400
Fax: (603)225-1409

SCORE Office (Dover)
299 Central Ave.
Dover, NH 03820
Phone: (603)742-2218
Fax: (603)749-6317

SCORE Office (Monadnock)
34 Mechanic St.
Keene, NH 03431-3421
Phone: (603)352-0320

SCORE Office (Lakes Region)
67 Water St., Ste. 105
Laconia, NH 03246
Phone: (603)524-9168

SCORE Office (Upper Valley)
Citizens Bank Bldg., Rm. 310
20 W. Park St.
Lebanon, NH 03766
Phone: (603)448-3491
Fax: (603)448-1908
Email: billt@valley.net
Website: www.valley.net/~score/

SCORE Office (Merrimack Valley)
275 Chestnut St., Rm. 618
Manchester, NH 03103
Phone: (603)666-7561
Fax: (603)666-7925

SCORE office (Mt. Washington
Valley)
PO Box 1066
North Conway, NH 03818
Phone: (603)383-0800

SCORE Office (Seacoast)
195 Commerce Way, Unit-A
Portsmouth, NH 03801-3251
Phone: (603)433-0575

New Jersey

SCORE Office (Somerset)
Paritan Valley Community College,
Rte. 28
Branchburg, NJ 08807
Phone: (908)218-8874
Email: nj-score@grizbiz.com.
Website: www.nj-score.org/

SCORE Office (Chester)
c/o John C. Apelian, Chair
5 Old Mill Rd.

Chester, NJ 07930
Phone: (908)879-7080

SCORE Office (Greater Princeton)
4 A George Washington Dr.
Cranbury, NJ 08512
Phone: (609)520-1776

SCORE Office (Freehold)
36 W. Main St.
Freehold, NJ 07728
Phone: (908)462-3030
Fax: (908)462-2123

SCORE office (North West)
Picantinny Innovation Ctr.
3159 Schrader Rd.
Hamburg, NJ 07419
Phone: (973)209-8525
Fax: (973)209-7252
Email: nj-score@grizbiz.com
Website: www.nj-score.org/

SCORE Office (Monmouth)
c/o Brookdale Community College
Career Services
765 Newman Springs Rd.
Lincroft, NJ 07738
Phone: (908)224-2573
Email: nj-score@grizbiz.com
Website: www.nj-score.org/

SCORE Office (Manalapan)
125 Symmes Dr.
Manalapan, NJ 07726
Phone: (908)431-7220

SCORE Office (Jersey City)
2 Gateway Ctr., 4th Fl.
Newark, NJ 07102
Phone: (973)645-3982
Fax: (973)645-2375

SCORE Office (Newark)
2 Gateway Center, 15th Fl.
Newark, NJ 07102-5553
Phone: (973)645-3982
Fax: (973)645-2375
Email: nj-score@grizbiz.com
Website: www.nj-score.org

SCORE Office (Bergen County)
327 E. Ridgewood Ave.
Paramus, NJ 07652
Phone: (201)599-6090
Email: nj-score@grizbiz.com
Website: www.nj-score.org/

SCORE Office (Pennsauken)
c/o United Jersey Bank

4900 Rte. 70
Pennsauken, NJ 08109
Phone: (609)486-3421

SCORE Office (Southern New
Jersey)
c/o United Jersey Bank
4900 Rte. 70
Pennsauken, NJ 08109
Phone: (609)486-3421
Email: nj-score@grizbiz.com
Website: www.nj-score.org/

SCORE office (Greater Princeton)
216 Rockingham Row
Princeton Forrestal Village
Princeton, NJ 08540
Phone: (609)520-1776
Fax: (609)520-9107
Email: nj-score@grizbiz.com
Website: www.nj-score.org/

SCORE Office (Shrewsbury)
Hwy. 35
Shrewsbury, NJ 07702
Phone: (908)842-5995
Fax: (908)219-6140

SCORE Office (Ocean County)
33 Washington St.
Toms River, NJ 08754
Phone: (732)505-6033
Email: nj-score@grizbiz.com
Website: www.nj-score.org/

SCORE Office (Wall)
2700 Allaire Rd.
Wall, NJ 07719
Phone: (908)449-8877

SCORE Office (Wayne)
2055 Hamburg Tpke.
Wayne, NJ 07470
Phone: (201)831-7788
Fax: (201)831-9112

New Mexico

SCORE Office (Albuquerque)
c/o TVI Workforce Training Center
525 Buena Vista, SE
Albuquerque, NM 87106
Phone: (505)272-7999
Fax: (505)272-7963

SCORE Office (Las Cruces)
Loretto Towne Center
505 S. Main St., Ste. 125
Las Cruces, NM 88001
Phone: (505)523-5627

Fax: (505)524-2101
Email: score.397@zianet.com

SCORE Office (Roswell)
Federal Bldg., Rm. 237
Roswell, NM 88201
Phone: (505)625-2112
Fax: (505)623-2545

SCORE Office (Santa Fe)
Montoya Federal Bldg.
120 Federal Place, Rm. 307
Santa Fe, NM 87501
Phone: (505)988-6302
Fax: (505)988-6300

New York

SCORE Office (Northeast)
c/o Albany College Chamber of
Commerce
1 Computer Dr. S
Albany, NY 12205
Phone: (518)446-1118
Fax: (518)446-1228

SCORE Office (Auburn)
c/o Chamber of Commerce
30 South St.
PO Box 675
Auburn, NY 13021
Phone: (315)252-7291

SCORE Office (South Tier
Binghamton)
Metro Center, 2nd Fl.
49 Court St.
PO Box 995
Binghamton, NY 13902
Phone: (607)772-8860

SCORE Office (Queens County City)
12055 Queens Blvd., Rm. 333
Borough Hall, NY 11424
Phone: (718)263-8961

SCORE Office (Buffalo)
Federal Bldg., Rm. 1311
111 W. Huron St.
Buffalo, NY 14202
Phone: (716)551-4301
Website: www2.pcom.net/score/
buf45.html

SCORE Office (Canandaigua)
Chamber of Commerce Bldg.
113 S. Main St.
Canandaigua, NY 14424
Phone: (716)394-4400
Fax: (716)394-4546

SCORE Office (Chemung)
c/o Small Business Administration
333 E. Water St., 4th Fl.
Elmira, NY 14901
Phone: (607)734-3358

SCORE Office (Geneva)
Chamber of Commerce Bldg.
PO Box 587
Geneva, NY 14456
Phone: (315)789-1776
Fax: (315)789-3993

SCORE Office (Glens Falls)
84 Broad St.
Glens Falls, NY 12801
Phone: (518)798-8463
Fax: (518)745-1433

SCORE Office (Orange County)
c/o Chamber of Commerce
40 Matthews St.
Goshen, NY 10924
Phone: (914)294-8080
Fax: (914)294-6121

SCORE Office (Huntington Area)
c/o Chamber of Commerce
151 W. Carver St.
Huntington, NY 11743
Phone: (516)423-6100

SCORE Office (Tompkins County)
c/o Tompkins Chamber of Commerce
904 E. Shore Dr.
Ithaca, NY 14850
Phone: (607)273-7080

SCORE Office (Long Island City)
120-55 Queens Blvd.
Jamaica, NY 11424
Phone: (718)263-8961
Fax: (718)263-9032

SCORE Office (Chatauqua)
101 W. 5th St.
Jamestown, NY 14701
Phone: (716)484-1103

SCORE Office (Westchester)
2 Caradon Ln.
Katonah, NY 10536
Phone: (914)948-3907
Fax: (914)948-4645
Email: score@w-w-w.com
Website: w-w-w.com/score/

SCORE Office (Queens County)
Queens Borough Hall
120-55 Queens Blvd. Rm. 333

Kew Gardens, NY 11424
Phone: (718)263-8961
Fax: (718)263-9032

SCORE Office (Brookhaven)
3233 Rte. 112
Medford, NY 11763
Phone: (516)451-6563
Fax: (516)451-6925

SCORE Office (Melville)
35 Pinelawn Rd., Rm. 207-W
Melville, NY 11747
Phone: (516)454-0771

SCORE Office (Nassau County)
c/o Dept. of Commerce & Industry
400 County Seat Dr., No. 140
Mineola, NY 11501
Phone: (516)571-3303
Email: Counse1998@aol.com
Website: members.aol.com/
Counse1998/Default.htm

SCORE Office (Mt. Vernon)
4 N. 7th Ave.
Mt. Vernon, NY 10550
Phone: (914)667-7500

SCORE Office (New York)
26 Federal Plz., Rm. 3100
New York, NY 10278
Phone: (212)264-4507
Fax: (212)264-4963
Email: score1000@erols.com
Website: users.erols.com/score-nyc/

SCORE Office (Newburgh)
47 Grand St.
Newburgh, NY 12550
Phone: (914)562-5100

SCORE Office (Owego)
188 Front St.
Owego, NY 13827
Phone: (607)687-2020

SCORE Office (Peekskill)
1 S. Division St.
Peekskill, NY 10566
Phone: (914)737-3600
Fax: (914)737-0541

SCORE Office (Penn Yan)
2375 Rte. 14A
Penn Yan, NY 14527
Phone: (315)536-3111

SCORE Office (Dutchess)
c/o Chamber of Commerce
110 Main St.

Poughkeepsie, NY 12601
Phone: (914)454-1700

SCORE Office (Rochester)
601 Keating Federal Bldg., Rm. 410
100 State St.
Rochester, NY 14614
Phone: (716)263-6473
Fax: (716)263-3146
Website: www.ggw.org/score/

SCORE Office (Saranac Lake)
30 Main St.
Saranac Lake, NY 12983
Phone: (315)448-0415

SCORE Office (Suffolk)
286 Main St.
Setauket, NY 11733
Phone: (516)751-3886

SCORE Office (Staten Island)
c/o Chamber of Commerce
130 Bay St.
Staten Island, NY 10301
Phone: (718)727-1221

SCORE Office (Ulster)
c/o Ulster County Community
College
Clinton Bldg., Rm. 107
Stone Ridge, NY 12484
Phone: (914)687-5035
Fax: (914)687-5015
Website: www.scoreulster.org/

SCORE Office (Syracuse)
401 S. Salina, 5th Fl.
Syracuse, NY 13202
Phone: (315)471-9393

SCORE Office (Utica)
SUNY Institute of Technology, Route
12
Utica, NY 13504-3050
Phone: (315)792-7553

SCORE Office (Watertown)
518 Davidson St.
Watertown, NY 13601
Phone: (315)788-1200
Fax: (315)788-8251

SCORE Office (Westchester)
350 Main St.
White Plains, NY 10601
Phone: (914)948-3907
Fax: (914)948-4645

North Carolina

SCORE office (Asheboro)
c/o Asheboro/Randolph Chamber of
Commerce
317 E. Dixie Dr.
Asheboro, NC 27203
Free: (336)626-2626
Fax: (336)626-7077

SCORE Office (Asheville)
Federal Bldg., Rm. 259
151 Patton
Asheville, NC 28801-5770
Phone: (828)271-4786
Fax: (828)271-4009

SCORE Office (Chapel Hill)
c/o Chapel Hill/Carboro C of C
104 S. Estes Dr.
PO Box 2897
Chapel Hill, NC 27514
Phone: (919)967-7075

SCORE Office (Coastal Plains)
PO Box 2897
Chapel Hill, NC 27515
Phone: (919)967-7075
Fax: (919)968-6874

SCORE Office (Charlotte)
200 N. College St., Ste. A-2015
Charlotte, NC 28202
Phone: (704)344-6576
Fax: (704)344-6769
Email:
CharlotteSCORE47@AOL.com
Website: www.charweb.org/business/
score/

SCORE Office (Durham)
411 W. Chapel Hill St.
Durham, NC 27707
Phone: (919)541-2171

SCORE Office (Gastonia)
PO Box 2168
Gastonia, NC 28053
Phone: (704)864-2621
Fax: (704)854-8723

SCORE Office (Greensboro)
400 W. Market St., Ste. 103
Greensboro, NC 27401-2241
Phone: (910)333-5399

SCORE Office (Henderson)
PO Box 917
Henderson, NC 27536
Phone: (919)492-2061
Fax: (919)430-0460

SCORE Office (Hendersonville)
Federal Bldg., Rm. 108
W. 4th Ave. & Church St.
Hendersonville, NC 28792
Phone: (828)693-8702
Email: score@circle.net
Website: www.wncguide.com/score/
Welcome.html

SCORE Office (Unifour)
PO Box 1828
Hickory, NC 28603
Phone: (704)328-6111

SCORE Office (High Point)
c/o High Point Chamber of
Commerce
1101 N. Main St.
High Point, NC 27262
Phone: (336)882-8625
Fax: (336)889-9499

SCORE Office (Outer Banks)
c/o Outer Banks Chamber of
Commerce
Collington Rd. and Mustain
Kill Devil Hills, NC 27948
Phone: (252)441-8144

SCORE Office (Down East)
312 S. Front St., Ste. 6
New Bern, NC 28560
Phone: (252)633-6688
Fax: (252)633-9608

SCORE Office (Kinston)
PO Box 95
New Bern, NC 28561
Phone: (919)633-6688

SCORE Office (Raleigh)
Century Post Office Bldg., Ste. 306
300 Federal St. Mall
Raleigh, NC 27601
Phone: (919)856-4739
Email: jendres@ibm.net
Website: www.intrex.net/score96/
score96.htm

SCORE Office (Sanford)
1801 Nash St.
Sanford, NC 27330
Phone: (919)774-6442
Fax: (919)776-8739

SCORE Office (Sandhills Area)
c/o Sand Hills Area Chamber of
Commerce
1480 Hwy. 15-501
PO Box 458

Southern Pines, NC 28387
Phone: (910)692-3926

SCORE Office (Wilmington)
Corps of Engineers Bldg.
96 Darlington Ave., Ste. 207
Wilmington, NC 28403
Phone: (910)815-4576
Fax: (910)815-4658

North Dakota

SCORE Office (Bismarck-Mandan)
700 E. Main Ave., 2nd Fl.
PO Box 5509
Bismarck, ND 58506-5509
Phone: (701)250-4303

SCORE Office (Fargo)
657 2nd Ave., Rm. 225
Fargo, ND 58108-3083
Phone: (701)239-5677

SCORE Office (Upper Red River)
4275 Technology Dr., Rm. 156
Grand Forks, ND 58202-8372
Phone: (701)777-3051

SCORE Office (Minot)
100 1st St. SW
Minot, ND 58701-3846
Phone: (701)852-6883
Fax: (701)852-6905

Ohio

SCORE Office (Akron)
c/o Regional Dev. Board
1 Cascade Plz., 7th Fl.
Akron, OH 44308
Phone: (330)379-3163
Fax: (330)379-3164

SCORE Office (Ashland)
Gill Center
47 W. Main St.
Ashland, OH 44805
Phone: (419)281-4584

SCORE Office (Canton)
116 Cleveland Ave. NW, Ste. 601
Canton, OH 44702-1720
Phone: (330)453-6047

SCORE Office (Chillicothe)
165 S. Paint St.
Chillicothe, OH 45601
Phone: (614)772-4530

SCORE Office (Cincinnati)
Ameritrust Bldg., Rm. 850

525 Vine St.
Cincinnati, OH 45202
Phone: (513)684-2812
Fax: (513)684-3251
Website: www.score.chapter34.org/

SCORE Office (Cleveland)
Eaton Center, Ste. 620
1100 Superior Ave.
Cleveland, OH 44114-2507
Phone: (216)522-4194
Fax: (216)522-4844

SCORE Office (Columbus)
2 Nationwide Plz., Ste. 1400
Columbus, OH 43215-2542
Phone: (614)469-2357
Fax: (614)469-2391
Email: info@scorecolumbus.org
Website: www.scorecolumbus.org/

SCORE Office (Dayton)
Dayton Federal Bldg., Rm. 505
200 W. Second St.
Dayton, OH 45402-1430
Phone: (513)225-2887
Fax: (513)225-7667

SCORE Office (Defiance)
615 W. 3rd St.
PO Box 130
Defiance, OH 43512
Phone: (419)782-7946

SCORE Office (Findlay)
123 E. Main Cross St.
PO Box 923
Findlay, OH 45840
Phone: (419)422-3314

SCORE Office (Lima)
147 N. Main St.
Lima, OH 45801
Phone: (419)222-6045
Fax: (419)229-0266

SCORE Office (Mansfield)
c/o Chamber of Commerce
55 N. Mulberry St.
Mansfield, OH 44902
Phone: (419)522-3211

SCORE Office (Marietta)
Thomas Hall
Marietta, OH 45750
Phone: (614)373-0268

SCORE Office (Medina)
County Administrative Bldg.
144 N. Broadway

Medina, OH 44256
Phone: (216)764-8650

SCORE Office (Licking County)
50 W. Locust St.
Newark, OH 43055
Phone: (614)345-7458

SCORE Office (Salem)
2491 State Rte. 45 S
Salem, OH 44460
Phone: (216)332-0361

SCORE Office (Tiffin)
62 S. Washington St.
Tiffin, OH 44883
Phone: (419)447-4141
Fax: (419)447-5141

SCORE Office (Toledo)
608 Madison Ave, Ste. 910
Toledo, OH 43624
Phone: (419)259-7598
Fax: (419)259-6460

SCORE Office (Heart of Ohio)
377 W. Liberty St.
Wooster, OH 44691
Phone: (330)262-5735
Fax: (330)262-5745

SCORE Office (Youngstown)
306 Williamson Hall
Youngstown, OH 44555
Phone: (330)746-2687

Oklahoma

SCORE Office (Anadarko)
PO Box 366
Anadarko, OK 73005
Phone: (405)247-6651

SCORE Office (Ardmore)
410 W. Main
Ardmore, OK 73401
Phone: (580)226-2620

SCORE Office (Northeast Oklahoma)
210 S. Main
Grove, OK 74344
Phone: (918)787-2796
Fax: (918)787-2796
Email: Score595@greencis.net

SCORE Office (Lawton)
4500 W. Lee Blvd., Bldg. 100, Ste.
107
Lawton, OK 73505
Phone: (580)353-8727
Fax: (580)250-5677

SCORE Office (Oklahoma City)
c/o SBA, Oklahoma Tower Bldg.
210 Park Ave., No. 1300
Oklahoma City, OK 73102
Phone: (405)231-5163
Fax: (405)231-4876
Email: score212@usa.net

SCORE Office (Stillwater)
439 S. Main
Stillwater, OK 74074
Phone: (405)372-5573
Fax: (405)372-4316

SCORE Office (Tulsa)
616 S. Boston, Ste. 406
Tulsa, OK 74119
Phone: (918)581-7462
Fax: (918)581-6908
Website: www.ionet.net/~tulscore/

Oregon

SCORE Office (Bend)
c/o Bend Chamber of Commerce
63085 N. Hwy. 97
Bend, OR 97701
Phone: (541)923-2849
Fax: (541)330-6900

SCORE Office (Willamette)
1401 Willamette St.
PO Box 1107
Eugene, OR 97401-4003
Phone: (541)465-6600
Fax: (541)484-4942

SCORE Office (Florence)
3149 Oak St.
Florence, OR 97439
Phone: (503)997-8444
Fax: (503)997-8448

SCORE Office (Southern Oregon)
33 N. Central Ave., Ste. 216
Medford, OR 97501
Phone: (541)776-4220
Email: pgr134f@prodigy.com

SCORE Office (Portland)
1515 SW 5th Ave., Ste. 1050
Portland, OR 97201
Phone: (503)326-3441
Fax: (503)326-2808
Email: gr134@prodigy.com

SCORE Office (Salem)
c/o Key Bank
416 State St. (corner of Liberty)

Salem, OR 97301
Phone: (503)370-2896

Pennsylvania

SCORE Office (Altoona-Blair)
c/o Altoona-Blair Chamber of
Commerce
1212 12th Ave.
Altoona, PA 16601-3493
Phone: (814)943-8151

SCORE Office (Lehigh Valley)
Rauch Bldg. 37
Lehigh University
621 Taylor St.
Bethlehem, PA 18015
Phone: (610)758-4496
Fax: (610)758-5205

SCORE Office (Butler County)
100 N. Main St.
PO Box 1082
Butler, PA 16003
Phone: (412)283-2222
Fax: (412)283-0224

SCORE Office (Harrisburg)
4211 Trindle Rd.
Camp Hill, PA 17011
Phone: (717)761-4304
Fax: (717)761-4315

SCORE Office (Cumberland Valley)
c/o Chambersburg Chamber of
Commerce
75 S. 2nd St.
Chambersburg, PA 17201
Phone: (717)264-2935

SCORE Office (Monroe County-
Stroudsburg)
556 Main St.
East Stroudsburg, PA 18301
Phone: (717)421-4433

SCORE Office (Erie)
120 W. 9th St.
Erie, PA 16501
Phone: (814)871-5650
Fax: (814)871-7530

SCORE Office (Bucks County)
c/o Chamber of Commerce
409 Hood Blvd.
Fairless Hills, PA 19030
Phone: (215)943-8850
Fax: (215)943-7404

SCORE Office (Hanover)
146 Broadway

Hanover, PA 17331
Phone: (717)637-6130
Fax: (717)637-9127

SCORE Office (Harrisburg)
100 Chestnut, Ste. 309
Harrisburg, PA 17101
Phone: (717)782-3874

SCORE Office (East Montgomery
County)
Baederwood Shopping Center
1653 The Fairways, Ste. 204
Jenkintown, PA 19046
Phone: (215)885-3027

SCORE Office (Kittanning)
c/o Kittanning Chamber of Commerce
2 Butler Rd.
Kittanning, PA 16201
Phone: (412)543-1305
Fax: (412)543-6206

SCORE Office (Lancaster)
118 W. Chestnut St.
Lancaster, PA 17603
Phone: (717)397-3092

SCORE Office (Westmoreland
County)
300 Fraser Purchase Rd.
Latrobe, PA 15650-2690
Phone: (412)539-7505
Fax: (412)539-1850

SCORE Office (Lebanon)
252 N. 8th St.
PO Box 899
Lebanon, PA 17042-0899
Phone: (717)273-3727
Fax: (717)273-7940

SCORE Office (Lewistown)
c/o Lewistown Chamber of
Commerce
3 W. Monument Sq., Ste. 204
Lewistown, PA 17044
Phone: (717)248-6713
Fax: (717)248-6714

SCORE Office (Delaware County)
602 E. Baltimore Pike
Media, PA 19063
Phone: (610)565-3677
Fax: (610)565-1606

SCORE Office (Milton Area)
112 S. Front St.
Milton, PA 17847
Phone: (717)742-7341
Fax: (717)792-2008

SCORE Office (Mon-Valley)
435 Donner Ave.
Monessen, PA 15062
Phone: (412)684-4277
Fax: (412)684-7688

SCORE Office (Monroeville)
William Penn Plaza
2790 Mosside Blvd., Ste. 295
Monroeville, PA 15146
Phone: (412)856-0622
Fax: (412)856-1030

SCORE Office (Airport Area)
986 Brodhead Rd.
Moon Township, PA 15108-2398
Phone: (412)264-6270
Fax: (412)264-1575

SCORE Office (Northeast)
8601 E. Roosevelt Blvd.
Philadelphia, PA 19152
Phone: (215)332-3400
Fax: (215)332-6050

SCORE Office (Philadelphia)
1315 Walnut St., Ste. 500
Philadelphia, PA 19107
Phone: (215)790-5050
Fax: (215)790-5057
Email: score46@bellatlantic.net
Website: www.pgweb.net/score46/

SCORE Office (Pittsburgh)
1000 Liberty Ave., Rm. 1122
Pittsburgh, PA 15222
Phone: (412)395-6560
Fax: (412)395-6562

SCORE Office (Tri-County)
801 N. Charlotte St.
Pottstown, PA 19464
Phone: (610)327-2673

SCORE Office (Reading)
c/o Reading Chamber of Commerce
601 Penn St.
Reading, PA 19601
Phone: (610)376-3497

SCORE Office (Scranton)
Oppenheim Bldg.
116 N. Washington Ave., Ste. 650
Scranton, PA 18503
Phone: (717)347-4611
Fax: (717)347-4611

SCORE Office (Central
Pennsylvania)
200 Innovation Blvd., Ste. 242-B

State College, PA 16803
Phone: (814)234-9415
Fax: (814)238-9686
Website: countrystore.org/business/
score.htm

SCORE Office (Monroe-Stroudsburg)
556 Main St.
Stroudsburg, PA 18360
Phone: (717)421-4433

SCORE Office (Uniontown)
Federal Bldg.
Pittsburg St.
PO Box 2065 DTS
Uniontown, PA 15401
Phone: (412)437-4222
Email: uniontownscore@lcsys.net

SCORE Office (Warren County)
315 2nd Ave.
Warren, PA 16365
Phone: (814)723-9017

SCORE Office (Waynesboro)
323 E. Main St.
Waynesboro, PA 17268
Phone: (717)762-7123
Fax: (717)962-7124

SCORE Office (Chester County)
Government Service Center, Ste. 281
601 Westtown Rd.
West Chester, PA 19382-4538
Phone: (610)344-6910
Fax: (610)344-6919
Email: score@locke.ccil.org

SCORE Office (Wilkes-Barre)
7 N. Wilkes-Barre Blvd.
Wilkes Barre, PA 18702-5241
Phone: (717)826-6502
Fax: (717)826-6287

SCORE Office (North Central
Pennsylvania)
240 W. 3rd St., Rm. 227
PO Box 725
Williamsport, PA 17703
Phone: (717)322-3720
Fax: (717)322-1607
Email: score234@mail.csrlink.net
Website: www.lycoming.org/score/

SCORE Office (York)
Cyber Center
2101 Pennsylvania Ave.
York, PA 17404
Phone: (717)845-8830
Fax: (717)854-9333

Puerto Rico

SCORE Office (Puerto Rico & Virgin
Islands)
SBA Resource Center, Sacred Heart
University
PO Box 12383-96
San Juan, PR 00914-0383
Phone: (787)726-8040
Fax: (787)726-8135

Rhode Island

SCORE Office (Barrington)
281 County Rd.
Barrington, RI 02806
Phone: (401)247-1920
Fax: (401)247-3763

SCORE Office (Woonsocket)
640 Washington Hwy.
Lincoln, RI 02865
Phone: (401)334-1000
Fax: (401)334-1009

SCORE Office (Wickford)
8045 Post Rd.
North Kingstown, RI 02852
Phone: (401)295-5566
Fax: (401)295-8987

SCORE Office (J.G.E. Knight)
380 Westminster St.
Providence, RI 02903
Phone: (401)528-4571
Fax: (401)528-4539
Email: feedback@ch13.score.org.
Website: chapters.score.org/ch13

SCORE Office (Warwick)
3288 Post Rd.
Warwick, RI 02886
Phone: (401)732-1100
Fax: (401)732-1101

SCORE Office (Westerly)
74 Post Rd.
Westerly, RI 02891
Phone: (401)596-7761
Free: (800)732-7636
Fax: (401)596-2190

South Carolina

SCORE Office (Aiken)
PO Box 892
Aiken, SC 29802
Phone: (803)641-1111
Free: (800)542-4536
Fax: (803)641-4174

SCORE Office (Anderson)
Anderson Mall
3130 N. Main St.
Anderson, SC 29621
Phone: (864)224-0453

SCORE Office (Coastal)
284 King St.
Charleston, SC 29401
Phone: (803)727-4778
Fax: (803)853-2529

SCORE Office (Midlands)
Strom Thurmond Bldg., Rm. 358
1835 Assembly St., Rm 358
Columbia, SC 29201
Phone: (803)765-5131
Fax: (803)765-5962
Website: www.scoremidlands.org/

SCORE Office (Piedmont)
Federal Bldg., Rm. B-02
300 E. Washington St.
Greenville, SC 29601
Phone: (864)271-3638

SCORE Office (Greenwood)
PO Drawer 1467
Greenwood, SC 29648
Phone: (864)223-8357

SCORE Office (Hilton Head Island)
c/o Paul Kopelcheck
52 Savannah Trail
Hilton Head, SC 29926
Phone: (803)785-7107
Fax: (803)785-7110

SCORE Office (Grand Strand)
937 Broadway
Myrtle Beach, SC 29577
Phone: (803)918-1079
Fax: (803)918-1083
Email: score381@aol.com

SCORE Office (Spartanburg)
PO Box 1636
Spartanburg, SC 29304
Phone: (864)594-5000
Fax: (864)594-5055

South Dakota

SCORE Office (West River)
Rushmore Plz. Civic Ctr.
444 Mount Rushmore Rd., No. 209
Rapid City, SD 57701
Phone: (605)394-5311
Email: score@gwtc.net

SCORE Office (Sioux Falls)
First Financial Center
110 S. Phillips Ave., Ste. 200
Sioux Falls, SD 57104-6727
Phone: (605)330-4231
Fax: (605)330-4231

Tennessee

SCORE Office (Chattanooga)
Federal Bldg., Rm. 26
900 Georgia Ave.
Chattanooga, TN 37402
Phone: (423)752-5190
Fax: (423)752-5335

SCORE Office (Cleveland)
PO Box 2275
Cleveland, TN 37320
Phone: (423)472-6587
Fax: (423)472-2019

SCORE Office (Upper Cumberland
Center)
1225 S. Willow Ave.
Cookeville, TN 38501
Phone: (615)432-4111
Fax: (615)432-6010

SCORE Office (Unicoi County)
PO Box 713
Erwin, TN 37650
Phone: (423)743-3000
Fax: (423)743-0942

SCORE Office (Greeneville)
115 Academy St.
Greeneville, TN 37743
Phone: (423)638-4111
Fax: (423)638-5345

SCORE Office (Jackson)
c/o Chamber of Commerce
194 Auditorium St.
Jackson, TN 38301
Phone: (901)423-2200

SCORE Office (Northeast Tennessee)
1st Tennessee Bank Bldg.
2710 S. Roan St., Ste. 584
Johnson City, TN 37601
Phone: (423)929-7686
Fax: (423)461-8052

SCORE Office (Kingsport)
c/o Chamber of Commerce
151 E. Main St.
Kingsport, TN 37662
Phone: (423)392-8805

SCORE Office (Greater Knoxville)
Farragot Bldg., Ste. 224
530 S. Gay St.
Knoxville, TN 37902
Phone: (423)545-4203
Email: scoreknox@ntown.com
Website: www.scoreknox.org/

SCORE Office (Maryville)
201 S. Washington St.
Maryville, TN 37804-5728
Phone: (423)983-2241
Free: (800)525-6834
Fax: (423)984-1386

SCORE Office (Memphis)
Federal Bldg., Ste. 390
167 N. Main St.
Memphis, TN 38103
Phone: (901)544-3588

SCORE Office (Nashville)
50 Vantage Way, Ste. 201
Nashville, TN 37228-1500
Phone: (615)736-7621

Texas

SCORE Office (Abilene)
2106 Federal Post Office and Court
Bldg.
Abilene, TX 79601
Phone: (915)677-1857

SCORE Office (Austin)
2501 S. Congress
Austin, TX 78701
Phone: (512)442-7235
Fax: (512)442-7528

SCORE Office (Golden Triangle)
450 Boyd St.
Beaumont, TX 77704
Phone: (409)838-6581
Fax: (409)833-6718

SCORE Office (Brownsville)
3505 Boca Chica Blvd., Ste. 305
Brownsville, TX 78521
Phone: (210)541-4508

SCORE Office (Brazos Valley)
c/o Victoria Bank & Trust
3000 Briarcrest, Ste. 302
Bryan, TX 77802
Phone: (409)776-8876
Email:
102633.2612@compuserve.com

SCORE Office (Cleburne)
Watergarden Pl., 9th Fl., Ste. 400
Cleburne, TX 76031
Phone: (817)871-6002

SCORE Office (Corpus Christi)
651 Upper North Broadway, Ste. 654
Corpus Christi, TX 78477
Phone: (512)888-4322
Fax: (512)888-3418

SCORE Office (Dallas)
c/o Comerica Bank, 2nd Fl.
6260 E. Mockingbird
Dallas, TX 75214-2619
Phone: (214)828-2471
Fax: (214)821-8033

SCORE Office (El Paso)
c/o Business Information Center,
Greater El Paso Chamber of
Commerce
10 Civic Center Plaza
El Paso, TX 79901
Phone: (915)534-0541
Fax: (915)534-0513

SCORE Office (Bedford)
100 E. 15th St., Ste. 400
Ft. Worth, TX 76102
Phone: (817)871-6002

SCORE Office (Ft. Worth)
100 E. 15th St., No. 24
Ft. Worth, TX 76102
Phone: (817)871-6002
Fax: (817)871-6031
Email: fwbac@onramp.net

SCORE Office (Garland)
2734 W. Kingsley Rd.
Garland, TX 75041
Phone: (214)271-9224

SCORE Office (Granbury Chamber
of Commerce)
416 S. Morgan
Granbury, TX 76048
Phone: (817)573-1622
Fax: (817)573-0805

SCORE Office (Lower Rio Grande
Valley)
222 E. Van Buren, Ste. 500
Harlingen, TX 78550
Phone: (956)427-8533
Fax: (956)427-8537

SCORE Office (Houston)
9301 Southwest Fwy., Ste. 550

Houston, TX 77074
Phone: (713)773-6565
Fax: (713)773-6550

SCORE Office (Irving)
3333 N. MacArthur Blvd., Ste. 100
Irving, TX 75062
Phone: (214)252-8484
Fax: (214)252-6710

SCORE Office (Lubbock)
1205 Texas Ave., Rm. 411D
Lubbock, TX 79401
Phone: (806)472-7462
Fax: (806)472-7487

SCORE Office (Midland)
Post Office Annex
200 E. Wall St., Rm. P121
Midland, TX 79701
Phone: (915)687-2649

SCORE Office (Orange)
1012 Green Ave.
Orange, TX 77630-5620
Phone: (409)883-3536
Free: (800)528-4906
Fax: (409)886-3247

SCORE Office (Plano)
1200 E. 15th St.
PO Drawer 940287
Plano, TX 75094-0287
Phone: (214)424-7547
Fax: (214)422-5182

SCORE Office (Port Arthur)
4749 Twin City Hwy., Ste. 300
Port Arthur, TX 77642
Phone: (409)963-1107
Fax: (409)963-3322

SCORE Office (Richardson)
411 Belle Grove
Richardson, TX 75080
Phone: (214)234-4141
Free: (800)777-8001
Fax: (214)680-9103

SCORE Office (San Antonio)
c/o SBA
Federal Bldg., Rm. A527
727 E. Durango
San Antonio, TX 78206
Phone: (210)472-5931
Fax: (210)472-5935

SCORE Office (Texarkana State
College)
819 State Line Ave.

Texarkana, TX 75501
Phone: (903)792-7191
Fax: (903)793-4304

SCORE Office (East Texas)
RTDC
1530 SSW Loop 323, Ste. 100
Tyler, TX 75701
Phone: (903)510-2975
Fax: (903)510-2978

SCORE Office (Waco)
401 Franklin Ave.
Waco, TX 76701
Phone: (817)754-8898
Fax: (817)756-0776
Website: www.brc-waco.com/

SCORE Office (Wichita Falls)
Hamilton Bldg.
900 8th St.
Wichita Falls, TX 76307
Phone: (940)723-2741
Fax: (940)723-8773

Utah

SCORE Office (Northern Utah)
c/o Cache Valley Chamber of
Commerce
160 N. Main
Logan, UT 84321
Phone: (435)752-2161

SCORE Office (Ogden)
1701 E. Windsor Dr.
Ogden, UT 84604
Phone: (801)226-0881
Email: score158@netscape.net

SCORE Office (Central Utah)
1071 E. Windsor Dr.
Provo, UT 84604
Phone: (801)226-0881

SCORE Office (Southern Utah)
c/o Dixie College
225 South 700 East
St. George, UT 84770
Phone: (801)652-7741

SCORE Office (Salt Lake)
169 E. 100 S.
Salt Lake City, UT 84111
Phone: (801)364-1331
Fax: (801)364-1310

Vermont

SCORE Office (Champlain Valley)
Winston Prouty Federal Bldg.

11 Lincoln St., Rm. 106
Essex Junction, VT 05452
Phone: (802)951-6762

SCORE Office (Montpelier)
c/o SBA
87 State St., Rm. 205
PO Box 605
Montpelier, VT 05601
Phone: (802)828-4422
Fax: (802)828-4485

SCORE Office (Marble Valley)
256 N. Main St.
Rutland, VT 05701-2413
Phone: (802)773-9147

SCORE Office (Northeast Kingdom)
c/o NCIC
20 Main St.
PO Box 904
St. Johnsbury, VT 05819
Phone: (802)748-5101

Virgin Islands

SCORE Office (St. Croix)
United Plaza Shopping Center
PO Box 4010, Christiansted
St. Croix, VI 00822
Phone: (809)778-5380

SCORE Office (St. Thomas-St. John)
Federal Bldg., Rm. 21
Veterans Dr.
St. Thomas, VI 00801
Phone: (809)774-8530

Virginia

SCORE Office (Arlington)
2009 N. 14th St., Ste. 111
Arlington, VA 22201
Phone: (703)525-2400

SCORE Office (Blacksburg)
141 Jackson St.
Blacksburg, VA 24060
Phone: (540)552-4061

SCORE Office (Bristol)
20 Volunteer Pkwy.
Bristol, VA 24203
Phone: (540)989-4850

SCORE Office (Central Virginia)
1001 E. Market St., Ste. 101
Charlottesville, VA 22902
Phone: (804)295-6712
Fax: (804)295-7066

SCORE Office (Alleghany Satellite)
241 W. Main St.
Covington, VA 24426
Phone: (540)962-2178
Fax: (540)962-2179

SCORE Office (Central Fairfax)
3975 University Dr., Ste. 350
Fairfax, VA 22030
Phone: (703)591-2450

SCORE Office (Falls Church)
PO Box 491
Falls Church, VA 22040
Phone: (703)532-1050
Fax: (703)237-7904

SCORE Office (Glenns)
Glenns Campus
Box 287
Glenns, VA 23149
Phone: (804)693-9650

SCORE Office (Peninsula)
c/o Peninsula Chamber of Commerce
6 Manhattan Sq.
PO Box 7269
Hampton, VA 23666
Phone: (757)766-2000
Fax: (757)865-0339
Email: score100@seva.net

SCORE Office (Tri-Cities)
c/o Chamber of Commerce
108 N. Main St.
Hopewell, VA 23860
Phone: (804)458-5536

SCORE Office (Lynchburg)
Federal Bldg.
1100 Main St.
Lynchburg, VA 24504-1714
Phone: (804)846-3235

SCORE Office (Greater Prince
William)
8963 Center St
Manassas, VA 20110
Phone: (703)368-4813
Fax: (703)368-4733

SCORE Office (Martinsville)
115 Broad St.
Martinsville, VA 24112-0709
Phone: (540)632-6401
Fax: (540)632-5059

SCORE Office (Hampton Roads)
Federal Bldg., Rm. 737
200 Grandby St.

Norfolk, VA 23510
Phone: (757)441-3733
Fax: (757)441-3733
Email: scorehr60@juno.com

SCORE Office (Norfolk)
Federal Bldg., Rm. 737
200 Granby St.
Norfolk, VA 23510
Phone: (757)441-3733
Fax: (757)441-3733

SCORE Office (Virginia Beach)
Chamber of Commerce
200 Grandby St., Rm 737
Norfolk, VA 23510
Phone: (804)441-3733

SCORE Office (Radford)
1126 Norwood St.
Radford, VA 24141
Phone: (540)639-2202

SCORE Office (Richmond)
Federal Bldg.
400 N. 8th St., Ste. 1150
PO Box 10126
Richmond, VA 23240-0126
Phone: (804)771-2400
Fax: (804)771-8018
Email: scorechapter12@yahoo.com
Website: www.cvco.org/score/

SCORE Office (Roanoke)
Federal Bldg., Rm. 716
250 Franklin Rd.
Roanoke, VA 24011
Phone: (540)857-2834
Fax: (540)857-2043
Email: scorerva@juno.com
Website: hometown.aol.com/scorerv/
Index.html

SCORE Office (Fairfax)
8391 Old Courthouse Rd., Ste. 300
Vienna, VA 22182
Phone: (703)749-0400

SCORE Office (Greater Vienna)
513 Maple Ave. West
Vienna, VA 22180
Phone: (703)281-1333
Fax: (703)242-1482

SCORE Office (Shenandoah Valley)
c/o Waynesboro Chamber of
Commerce
301 W. Main St.
Waynesboro, VA 22980
Phone: (540)949-8203

Fax: (540)949-7740
Email: score427@intelos.net

SCORE Office (Williamsburg)
c/o Chamber of Commerce
201 Penniman Rd.
Williamsburg, VA 23185
Phone: (757)229-6511
Email: wacc@williamsburgcc.com

SCORE Office (Northern Virginia)
c/o Winchester-Frederick Chamber of
Commerce
1360 S. Pleasant Valley Rd.
Winchester, VA 22601
Phone: (540)662-4118

Washington

SCORE Office (Gray's Harbor)
506 Duffy St.
Aberdeen, WA 98520
Phone: (360)532-1924
Fax: (360)533-7945

SCORE Office (Bellingham)
101 E. Holly St.
Bellingham, WA 98225
Phone: (360)676-3307

SCORE Office (Everett)
2702 Hoyt Ave.
Everett, WA 98201-3556
Phone: (206)259-8000

SCORE Office (Gig Harbor)
3125 Judson St.
Gig Harbor, WA 98335
Phone: (206)851-6865

SCORE Office (Kennewick)
PO Box 6986
Kennewick, WA 99336
Phone: (509)736-0510

SCORE Office (Puyallup)
322 2nd St. SW
PO Box 1298
Puyallup, WA 98371
Phone: (206)845-6755
Fax: (206)848-6164

SCORE Office (Seattle)
1200 6th Ave., Ste. 1700
Seattle, WA 98101
Phone: (206)553-7320
Fax: (206)553-7044
Email: score55@aol.com
Website: www.scn.org/civic/score-
online/index55.html

SCORE Office (Spokane)
801 W. Riverside Ave., No. 240
Spokane, WA 99201
Phone: (509)353-2820
Fax: (509)353-2600
Email: score@dmi.net
Website: www.dmi.net/score/

SCORE Office (Clover Park)
PO Box 1933
Tacoma, WA 98401-1933
Phone: (206)627-2175

SCORE Office (Tacoma)
1101 Pacific Ave.
Tacoma, WA 98402
Phone: (253)274-1288
Fax: (253)274-1289

SCORE Office (Fort Vancouver)
1701 Broadway, S-1
Vancouver, WA 98663
Phone: (360)699-1079

SCORE Office (Walla Walla)
500 Tausick Way
Walla Walla, WA 99362
Phone: (509)527-4681

SCORE Office (Mid-Columbia)
1113 S. 14th Ave.
Yakima, WA 98907
Phone: (509)574-4944
Fax: (509)574-2943
Website: www.ellensburg.com/
~score/

West Virginia

SCORE Office (Charleston)
1116 Smith St.
Charleston, WV 25301
Phone: (304)347-5463
Email: score256@juno.com

SCORE Office (Virginia Street)
1116 Smith St., Ste. 302
Charleston, WV 25301
Phone: (304)347-5463

SCORE Office (Marion County)
PO Box 208
Fairmont, WV 26555-0208
Phone: (304)363-0486

SCORE Office (Upper Monongahela
Valley)
1000 Technology Dr., Ste. 1111
Fairmont, WV 26555
Phone: (304)363-0486
Email: score537@hotmail.com

SCORE Office (Huntington)
1101 6th Ave., Ste. 220
Huntington, WV 25701-2309
Phone: (304)523-4092

SCORE Office (Wheeling)
1310 Market St.
Wheeling, WV 26003
Phone: (304)233-2575
Fax: (304)233-1320

Wisconsin

SCORE Office (Fox Cities)
227 S. Walnut St.
Appleton, WI 54913
Phone: (920)734-7101
Fax: (920)734-7161

SCORE Office (Beloit)
136 W. Grand Ave., Ste. 100
PO Box 717
Beloit, WI 53511
Phone: (608)365-8835
Fax: (608)365-9170

SCORE Office (Eau Claire)
Federal Bldg., Rm. B11
510 S. Barstow St.
Eau Claire, WI 54701
Phone: (715)834-1573
Email: score@ecol.net
Website: www.ecol.net/~score/

SCORE Office (Fond du Lac)
207 N. Main St.
Fond du Lac, WI 54935
Phone: (414)921-9500
Fax: (414)921-9559

SCORE Office (Green Bay)
835 Potts Ave.
Green Bay, WI 54304
Phone: (414)496-8930
Fax: (414)496-6009

SCORE Office (Janesville)
20 S. Main St., Ste. 11
PO Box 8008
Janesville, WI 53547
Phone: (608)757-3160
Fax: (608)757-3170

SCORE Office (La Crosse)
712 Main St.
La Crosse, WI 54602-0219
Phone: (608)784-4880

SCORE Office (Madison)
c/o MG&E Innovation Ctr.

505 S. Rosa Rd.
Madison, WI 53719
Phone: (608)441-2820

SCORE Office (Manitowoc)
1515 Memorial Dr.
PO Box 903
Manitowoc, WI 54221-0903
Phone: (414)684-5575
Fax: (414)684-1915

SCORE Office (Milwaukee)
310 W. Wisconsin Ave., Ste. 425
Milwaukee, WI 53203
Phone: (414)297-3942
Fax: (414)297-1377

SCORE Office (Central Wisconsin)
1224 Lindbergh Ave.
Stevens Point, WI 54481
Phone: (715)344-7729

SCORE Office (Superior)
Superior Business Center Inc.
1423 N. 8th St.
Superior, WI 54880
Phone: (715)394-7388
Fax: (715)393-7414

SCORE Office (Waukesha)
223 Wisconsin Ave.
Waukesha, WI 53186-4926
Phone: (414)542-4249

SCORE Office (Wausau)
300 3rd St., Ste. 200
Wausau, WI 54402-6190
Phone: (715)845-6231

SCORE Office (Wisconsin Rapids)
2240 Kingston Rd.
Wisconsin Rapids, WI 54494
Phone: (715)423-1830

Wyoming

SCORE Office (Casper)
Federal Bldg., No. 2215
100 East B St.
Casper, WY 82602
Phone: (307)261-6529
Fax: (307)261-6530

VENTURE CAPITAL & FINANCING COMPANIES

This section contains a listing of financing and loan companies in the United States and Canada. These listings are arranged alphabetically by country, state/territory/ province, then by city, then by organization name.

CANADA

Manitoba

Manitoba Department of Industry,
Trade and Tourism
Small Business Services
Entrepreneurial Development
240 Graham Ave., Rm. 250
PO Box 2609
Winnipeg, MB R3C 4B3
Phone: (204)984-0037
Free: (800)665-2019
Fax: (204)983-3852
A matching loan guarantee program
that will promote the success of new
business start-ups by ensuring that
entrepreneurs have a comprehensive
business plan, by offering business
training and counseling, and by
providing access to funding up to
$10,000 via a loan guarantee through
a number of existing financial
institutions.

Ontario

Industry Canada
Small Business Loans Administration
Small Business Loan Administration
235 Queen St., 8th Fl., E.
Ottawa, ON K1A 0H5
Phone: (613)954-5540
Fax: (613)952-0290

Quebec

Societe de Developpement Industriel
du Quebec
Small Business Revival Program
1200 Route de Egliase
Bureau 500
Ste. Foy, PQ G1V 5A3
Phone: (418)643-5172
Free: (800)461-AIDE
Fax: (418)528-2063

Allows businesses facing temporary difficulties to obtain financial assistance aimed at reinforcing their financial structures.

Saskatchewan

Saskatchewan Department of Economic and Cooperative Development
Investment Programs Branch
1919 Saskatchewan Dr.
Regina, SK S4P 3V7
Phone: (306)787-1605
Fax: (306)787-1620
Promotes the formation of venture capital corporations by employees of a small business, to provide equity capital for the expansion of existing facilities or establishment of new businesses. Federal and provincial tax credits are available to the investor.

UNITED STATES

Alabama

21st Century Health Ventures
One Health South Pkwy.
Birmingham, AL 35243
Phone: (256)268-6250
Fax: (256)970-8928
W. Barry McRae
Preferred Investment Size: $5,000,000. Investment Types: First stage, second stage and leveraged buyout. Industry Preferences: Medical/Health related. Geographic Preferences: Entire U.S.

FHL Capital Corp.
Email: fhl@scott.net
600 20th Street North
Suite 350
Birmingham, AL 35203
Phone: (205)328-3098
Fax: (205)323-0001
Kevin Keck, Vice President
Preferred Investment Size: Between $500,000 and $1,000,000. Investment Types: Mezzanine, leveraged buyout, and special situations. Geographic Preferences: Southeast.

Harbert Management Corp.
One Riverchase Pkwy. South

Birmingham, AL 35244
Phone: (205)987-5500
Fax: (205)987-5707
Charles P. Shook, IV, Investment Director
Preferred Investment Size: $5,000,000 to $25,000,000. Investment Types: Leveraged buyout, special situations and industry roll ups. Industry Preferences: Oil and gas not considered. Geographic Preferences: Entire U.S.

Jefferson Capital Fund
1901 Sixth Avenue North
Suite 1510
Birmingham, AL 35203
Phone: (205)324-7709
Fax: (205)252-7783
Lana E. Sellers, Managing Director
Preferred Investment Size: $500,000 to $5,000,000. Investment Types: Leveraged buyout, special situations and control block purchases. Industry Preferences: Telephone communications; consumer leisure and recreational products; consumer and industrial, medical and catalog specialty distribution; industrial products and equipment; medical/health related; publishing and education related. Geographic Preferences: Northeast, Southeast, Gulf states, and Middle Atlantic.

Jefferson County Community Development
Planning and Community Development
805 N. 22nd St.
Birmingham, AL 35203
Phone: (205)325-5761
Fax: (205)325-5095
Provides loans for purchasing real estate, construction, working capital, or machinery and equipment.

Private Capital Corp.
101 Brookwood Place
Suite 410
Birmingham, AL 35209
Phone: (205)879-2722
Fax: (205)879-5121
Preferred Investment Size: $1,000,000 to $5,000,000. Investment

Types: Startup, first stage, second stage, mezzanine, leveraged buyout, and special situations. Industry Preferences: Communications; computer related; consumer food and beverage products; communication, computer, industrial, and medical product distribution; electronic components and instrumentation; energy/natural resources; medical/health related; education; and finance and insurance. Geographic Preferences: Southeast.

FJC Growth Capital Corp.
200 W. Side Sq., Ste. 340
Huntsville, AL 35801
Phone: (256)922-2918
Fax: (256)922-2909
William B. Noojin
Preferred Investment Size: Between $100,000 and $500,000. Investment Types: Second stage. Industry Preferences: Hotel and resort, restaurant, and electronic equipment. Does not consider turnarounds, startups, real estate development and agriculture. Geographic Preferences: Southeast.

Hickory Venture Capital Corp.
Email: hvcc@hvcc.com
301 Washington Street NW
Suite 301
Huntsville, AL 35801
Phone: (256)539-1931
Fax: (256)539-5130
Preferred Investment Size: $1,000,000. Investment Types: First stage, second stage, mezzanine, and leverage buyout. Industry Preferences: Communications, computer-related, electronic components and instrumentation, energy/natural resources, genetic engineering, industrial products and equipment, medical/health related and transportation. Geographic Preferences: Southeast, Southwest, Midwest, Gulf states and Middle Atlantic.

Alabama Capital Corp.
16 Midtown Park E.
Mobile, AL 36606
Phone: (334)476-0700

Fax: (334)476-0026
David C. DeLaney, President
Preferred Investment Size: $400,000.
Investment Policies: Asset based
loans with equity. Investment Types:
Seed, early, expansion, later stages.
Industry Preferences: Diversified.
Geographic Preferences: Southeast.

First SBIC of Alabama
16 Midtown Park E.
Mobile, AL 36606
Phone: (334)476-0700
Fax: (334)476-0026
David C. DeLaney, President
Preferred Investment Size: $400,000.
Investment Policies: Asset based
Loans with equity. Investment Types:
Seed, early, expansion, later stages.
Industry Preferences: Diversified.
Geographic Preferences: Southeast.

Small Business Clinic of Alabama/
AG Bartholomew & Associates
4255 Knollgate Road
Montgomery, AL 36116
Phone: (334)284-3640
Preferred Investment Size: $100,000
to $5,000,000. Investment Types:
Startup, first stage, second stage,
leveraged buyout, and special
situations. Industry Preferences:
Communications, computer related,
consumer, distribution, industrial
products and equipment, medical/
health related, education, finance and
insurance, real estate, specialty
consulting, and transportation.
Geographic Preferences: Southeast.

Southern Development Council
Email: sdci@sdcinc.org
4101 C Wall St.
Montgomery, AL 36106
Phone: (334)244-1801
Free: (800)499-3034
Fax: (334)244-1421
Statewide nonprofit financial
packaging corporation. Helps small
businesses arrange financing.

Alaska

Alaska Department of Commerce and
Economic Development
Division of Investments

Email:
investments@commerce.state.ak.us
3601 C St., Ste. 724
Anchorage, AK 99503
Phone: (907)269-8150
Fax: (907)269-8147
Offers a program that assists purchasers to assume existing small business
loans.

Alaska Department of Commerce and
Economic Development (Anchorage)
Industrial Development and Export
Authority
480 W. Tudor Rd.
Anchorage, AK 99503-6690
Phone: (907)269-3000
Fax: (907)269-3044
Assists businesses in securing long-
term financing for capital invest-
ments, such as the acquisition of
equipment or the construction of a
new plant, at moderate interest rates.

Calista Corp.
601 W. 5th Ave., Ste. 200
Anchorage, AK 99501-2226
Phone: (907)279-5516
Fax: (907)272-5060
A minority enterprise small business
investment corporation. No industry
preference.

Alaska Department of Commerce and
Economic Development (Juneau)
Division of Investments
Email:
investments@commerce.state.ak.us
PO Box 34159
Juneau, AK 99803-4159
Phone: (907)465-2510
Free: (800)478-LOAN
Fax: (907)465-2103
Offers a program that assists purchas-
ers to assume existing small business
loans.

Alaska Department of Natural
Resources
Division of Agriculture
1800 Glenn Hwy., Ste. 12
Palmer, AK 99645
Phone: (907)745-7200
Fax: (907)745-7112
Provides loans for farm development,
general farm operations, chattel, and
land clearing. Resident farmers,

homesteaders, partnerships, and
corporations are eligible.

Arizona

McKellar & Co.
311 East Rose Lane
Phoenix, AZ 85012-1243
Phone: (602)277-1800
Fax: (602)277-0429
Winston P. McKellar, President
Preferred Investment Size: $250,000
to $5,000,000. Investment Types:
First stage, second stage, mezzanine,
leveraged buyout and special situa-
tions. Industry Preferences: Diversi-
fied. Geographic Preferences: Entire
U.S.

Miller Capital Corp.
4909 East McDowell Rd.
Phoenix, AZ 85008
Phone: (602)225-0504
Fax: (602)225-9024
Rudy R. Miller, Chairman and
President
Preferred Investment Size:
$1,000,000 to $5,000,000. Investment
Types: First stage, second stage,
mezzanine, and special situations.
Industry Preferences: Communica-
tions, computer related, and distribu-
tion. Geographic Preferences: Entire
U.S.

Southwest Venture Capital Network
One East Camelback Rd.
Box 60756
Suite 1100
Phoenix, AZ 85082-0756
Phone: (602)263-2390
Preferred Investment Size: $100,000
to $250,000. Investment Types: Seed,
startup, first and second stage.
Industry Preferences: Diversified.
Geographic Preferences: Southwest,
Rocky Mountains.

Arizona Growth Partners
Email: jock@valleyventures.com
6617 N. Scottsdale Rd., Ste. 104
Scottsdale, AZ 85250
Phone: (602)661-6600
Fax: (602)661-6262
Venture capital firm. Industry
preferences include high technology,

medical, biotechnology, and computer industries.

Gwynn Financial Services
Email: gwynnd@primenet.com
7373 E. Doubletree Ranch Rd.
Suite 700
Scottsdale, AZ 85258
Phone: (602)948-5005
Fax: (602)948-3339
Preferred Investment Size: $250,000 to $5 million. Investment Types: First stage, second stage, mezzanine and special situations. Industry Preferences: Communications, computer related, consumer, distribution, electronic components and instrumentation, energy/natural resources, genetic engineering, industrial products and equipment, medical/heath related, agriculture, education, and finance. Geographic Preferences: Northwest, Southwest, Rocky Mountains, West Coast.

Valley Ventures
6617155 North Scottsdale Rd.
Suite 104
Scottsdale, AZ 85250-5412
Phone: (602)661-6600
Fax: (602)661-6262
Preferred Investment Size: $500,000 to $1,000,000. Investment Types: Second stage, mezzanine, and leveraged buyout. Industry Preferences: Diversified. Retailing, real estate, and professional services not considered. Geographic Preferences: Southwest, Rocky Mountains, and Southern California.

W.B. McKee Securities Inc.
7702 East Doubletree Ranch Rd.
Suite 230
Scottsdale, AZ 85258
Phone: (602)368-0333
Fax: (602)607-7446
William B. McKee, Chairman
Preferred Investment Size: $1,000,000 to $5,000,000. Investment Types: Second stage, mezzanine, and leveraged buyout. Industry Preferences: Communications, computer related, consumer, distribution, electronic components and instrumen-

tation, energy/natural resources, genetic engineering, industrial products and equipment, medical and health related, finance, and transportation. Geographic Preferences: Entire U.S.

Coronado Venture Fund
PO Box 65420
Tucson, AZ 85728-5420
Phone: (520)577-3764
Fax: (520)299-8491
Preferred Investment Size: $100,000. Investment Types: Seed, startup, first and second stage. Industry Preferences: Communications, computer related, electronic components and instrumentation, genetic engineering, industrial products and equipment, medical and health related. Geographic Preferences: No preference for later stage financing. Southwest for seed and startup financing.

Arkansas

Arkansas Development Finance Authority
PO Box 8023
Little Rock, AR 72203-8023
Phone: (501)682-5900
Fax: (501)682-5859
Provides bond financing to small borrowers, who may otherwise be excluded from the bond market due to high costs, by using umbrella bond issues. Can provide interim financing for approved projects awaiting a bond issuance.

Roher Capital Group, LLC
Email: mroher@worldnet.att.net
21405 Walnut Grove Trail
Little Rock, AR 72223
Phone: (501)821-2885
Fax: (501)218-2513
Preferred Investment Size: $1,000,000 to $20,000,000. Investment Types: Second stage, mezzanine, leveraged buyout, special situations, control block purchases, and industry roll ups. Industry Preferences: Communications, distribution, energy/natural resources, and industrial products and equip-

ment. Geographic Preferences: United States and Canada.

Small Business Investment Capital, Inc.
12103 Interstate 30
PO Box 3627
Little Rock, AR 72203
Phone: (501)455-6599
Fax: (501)455-6556
Charles E. Toland, President
Preferred Investment Size: Up to $230,000. Investment Policies: Loans. Investment Types: Start-ups and debt consolidation. Industry Preferences: Supermarkets. Geographic Preferences: Arkansas, Oklahoma, Texas, Louisiana.

California

Calsafe Capital Corp.
245 E. Main St., Ste. 107
Alhambra, CA 91801
Phone: (626)289-3400
Fax: (626)300-8025
A minority enterprise small business investment company. Diversified industry preference.

Ally Finance Corp.
9100 Wilshire Blvd., Ste. 408
Beverly Hills, CA 90212
Phone: (760)241-7025
Fax: (760)241-8232
A small business investment corporation. No industry preference.

Developers Equity Capital Corp.
447 S. Robertson Blvd. Ste. 101
Beverly Hills, CA 90211
Phone: (310)550-7552
Fax: (310)550-7529
Preferred Investment Size: $100,000 to $500,000. Investment Types: Seed, startup, and leverage buyout. Industry Preferences: Diversified. Geographic Preferences: Within two hours of office.

BioVentures West LLC
Email: bobrobb123@msn.com
2131 Palomar Airport Rd.
Carlsbad, CA 92009
Phone: (760)431-5104
Fax: (760)431-5105
Robert Robb, President

Preferred Investment Size: $100,000 to $1,000,000. Investment Types: Seed, research and development, and startup. Industry Preferences: Genetic engineering, industrial products and equipment, and medical/health related. Geographic Preferences: West Coast.

Makenna Delaney & Sullivan, L.L.C.
Email: rs@venturefinance.com
5973 Avenida Encinas, Ste. 216
Carlsbad, CA 92008
Phone: (760)931-2500
Fax: (760)931-2503
Robert Sullivan, CEO
Preferred Investment Size: $500,000 to $5,000,000. Investment Types: Early and later stages, leveraged buyout, and private placements. Industry Preferences: Diversified. Geographic Preferences: National and Canada.

First SBIC of California (Costa Mesa)
3029 Harbor Blvd.
Costa Mesa, CA 92626
Fax: (714)668-6099
A small business investment corporation and venture capital company. No industry preference.

Oxford Ventures, Inc.
650 Town Center Dr., Ste. 810
Costa Mesa, CA 92626
Phone: (714)754-5719
Fax: (714)754-6802

Westar Capital (Costa Mesa)
949 South Coast Dr., Ste. 650
Costa Mesa, CA 92626
Phone: (714)481-5160
Fax: (714)481-5166
Alan Sellers, General Partner
Preferred Investment Size: $3,000,000 to $10,000,000. Investment Types: Leveraged buyouts, special situations, control block purchases, and industry roll ups. Industry Preferences: Diversified technology. Does not consider sports, real estate, oil and gas, hospitality, gaming, or airlines. Geographic Preferences: Northwest, Southwest, Rocky Mountains, and West Coast.

Fulcrum Venture Capital Corp.
300 Corp. Pointe, Ste. 380
Culver City, CA 90230
Phone: (310)645-1271
Fax: (310)645-1272
A minority enterprise small business investment corporation. No industry preference.

Alpine Technology Ventures
Email: carol@alpineventures.com
20300 Stevens Creek Boulevard, Ste. 495
Cupertino, CA 95014
Phone: (408)725-1810
Fax: (408)725-1207
Preferred Investment Size: $500,000 to $6,000,000. Investment Types: Seed, startup, research and development, first and second stage, and mezzanine. Industry Preferences: Communications, computer related, distribution, electronic components and instrumentation, industrial products and equipment. Biotechnology and healthcare not considered. Geographic Preferences: California.

Bay Partners
10600 N. De Anza Blvd.
Cupertino, CA 95014-2031
Phone: (408)725-2444
Fax: (408)446-4502
Preferred Investment Size: $1,000,000 to $5,000,000. Investment Types: Seed, startup, first and second stage. Industry Preferences: Communications and computer related. Geographic Preferences: Northeast, Northwest, Southwest, West Coast.

Horn Venture Partners
20300 Stevens Creek Blvd., Ste. 330
Cupertino, CA 95014
Phone: (408)725-0774
Fax: (408)725-0327
Areas of interest include information technology, life sciences, specialty retail and consumer products, restaurant, and biotechnology industries.

Novus Ventures
20111 Stevens Creek Blvd., Ste. 130
Cupertino, CA 95014
Phone: (408)252-3900

Fax: (408)252-1713
Dan Tompkins, Managing General Partner
Preferred Investment Size: $250,000 to $1 Million. Investment Types: First and second stage. Industry Preferences: Information technology. Geographic Preferences: Western U.S.

Sundance Venture Partners, L.P.
10600 North de Anza Blvd., Ste. 215
Cupertino, CA 95014
Phone: (408)257-8100
Preferred Investment Size: $100,000 to $250,000. Investment Types: First and second stage, mezzanine, leveraged buyout, special situations, and subordinated debt with warrants. Industry Preferences: No preference. Geographic Preferences: Southwest and West Coast.

Pacific Mezzanine Fund, L.P.
2200 Powell St., Ste. 1250
Emeryville, CA 94608
Phone: (510)595-9800
Fax: (510)595-9801
David C. Woodward, General Partner
Preferred Investment Size: $2 to $5 Million. Investment Policies: Loans with equity features. Investment Types: Expansion, later stage. Industry Preferences: Diversified. Geographic Preferences: Western U.S.

BankAmerica Ventures
950 Tower Ln., Ste. 700
Foster City, CA 94404
Phone: (650)378-6000
Fax: (650)378-6040
Anchie Y. Kuo, Managing Director
Preferred Investment Size: $1,000,000 to $12,000,000. Investment Types: Startup, first and second stage, and mezzanine. Industry Preferences: Communications, computer related, medical product distribution, electronic components and instrumentation, genetic engineering, and medical/health related. Retail, real estate, and oil and gas exploration not considered. Geographic Preferences: No preference.

First American Capital Funding, Inc.
10840 Warner Ave., Ste. 202
Fountain Valley, CA 92708
Phone: (714)965-7190
Fax: (714)965-7193
A minority enterprise small business
investment corporation. No industry
preference.

Opportunity Capital Partners
2201 Walnut Ave.,Ste. 210
Fremont, CA 94538
Phone: (510)795-7000
Fax: (510)494-5439
Peter Thompson, Managing Partner
Preferred Investment Size: $750,000
to $2,500,000. Investment Types:
Second stage, mezzanine, leveraged
buyouts, and industry roll ups.
Industry Preferences: Communications, consumer franchise businesses,
electronics, industrial products,
medical/health related, and transportation. Geographic Preferences: No
preference.

Opportunity Capital Partners
2201 Walnut Ave., Ste. 210
Fremont, CA 94538
Phone: (510)795-7000
Fax: (510)494-5439
Peter Thompson, Managing Partner
Preferred Investment Size: $750,000
to $2,500,000. Investment Types:
Second stage, mezzanine, leveraged
buyout, and industry roll ups. Industry
Preferences: Communications,
franchise businesses, electronic
components, industrial equipment and
machinery, and medical/health
related. Geographic Preferences:
Entire U.S.

San Joaquin Business Investment
Group, Inc.
1900 Mariposa Mall, Ste. 100
Fresno, CA 93721
Phone: (209)233-3580
Fax: (209)233-3709
A minority enterprise small business
investment company. Diversified
industry preference.

Magna Pacific Investments
330 N. Brand Blvd., Ste. 670
Glendale, CA 91203

Phone: (818)547-0809
Fax: (818)547-9303
A minority enterprise small business
investment company. Diversified
industry preference.

Brentwood Venture Capital
1920 Main St., Ste. 820
Irvine, CA 92614
Phone: (949)251-1010
Fax: (949)251-1011
Preferred Investment Size:
$2,000,000 to $5,000,000. Investment
Types: Seed, startup, first and second
stage, and mezzanine. Industry
Preferences: Electronics and medical/
health related. Geographic Preferences: Entire U.S. for later-stage, and
within two hours of office for start-
ups.

Crosspoint Venture Partners (Irvine)
Email: partners@crosspointvc.com
18552 MacArthur Blvd.
Irvine, CA 92612
Phone: (949)852-1611
Fax: (949)852-9804
Preferred Investment Size: $100,000
to $5,000,000. Investment Types:
Seed and startup. Industry Prefer-
ences: Communications, computer
related, and communications and
medical product distribution. Geo-
graphic Preferences: Northwest,
Southwest, Rocky Mountains, and
West Coast.

DSV Partners
1920 Main St., Ste. 820
Irvine, CA 92614
Phone: (949)475-4242
Fax: (949)475-1950
Preferred Investment Size:
$1,000,000 maximum. Investment
Types: Startup and first stage.
Industry Preferences: Diversified.
Real estate not considered. Geo-
graphic Preferences: Entire U.S.

Ventana Growth Funds (Irvine)
Email: ventana@ventanaglobal.com
18881 Von Karman Ave., Ste. 1150
Irvine, CA 92612
Phone: (949)476-2204
Fax: (949)752-0223
Carlos de Rivas, Managing Director

Preferred Investment Size: $250,000
to $5,000,000. Investment Types:
First and second stage, and mezzanine. Industry Preferences: Diversified technology. Geographic Preferences: Southwest.

Centex Securities Inc.
Email: regraves1@aol.com
1020 Prospect Street, Ste. 200
La Jolla, CA 92037
Phone: (619)456-8200
Douglas Gale
Preferred Investment Size:
$5,000,000 to $50,000,000. Investment Types: First and second stage,
mezzanine, leveraged buyout, special
situations, and control block purchases. Industry Preferences: Diversified. Geographic Preferences: No
preference.

Domain Associates
28202 Cabot Road, Ste. 200
Laguna Niguel, CA 92677
Phone: (949)347-2446
Fax: (949)347-9720
Preferred Investment Size:
$1,000,000 to $20,000,000. Invest-
ment Types: Seed, first stage and
second stage. Industry Preferences:
Electronics, genetic engineering, and
medical/health related. Geographic
Preferences: Entire U.S.

Cascade Communications Ventures
60 East Sir Francis Drake Blvd., Ste.
300
Larkspur, CA 94939
Phone: (415)925-6500
Fax: (415)925-6501
Preferred Investment Size:
$1,000,000 to $5,000,000. Investment
Types: Leveraged buyout and special
situations. Industry Preferences:
Communications. Geographic
Preferences: Entire U.S.

South Bay Capital Corporation
5325 E. Pacific Coast Hwy.
Long Beach, CA 90804
Phone: (562)597-3285
Fax: (562)498-7167
John Wang, Manager

Aspen Ventures
1000 Fremont Ave., Ste. 200

Los Altos, CA 94024
Phone: (650)917-5670
Fax: (650)917-5677
Alexander Cilento, Partner
Preferred Investment Size: $500,000
to $3,000,000. Investment Policies:
Equity. Investment Types: Seed,
research and development, startup,
first and second stage, special
situations. Industry Preferences:
Communications, computer related,
electronic components and instrumen-
tation. Geographic Preferences:
Northeast, Southwest, and West
Coast.

AVI Management Partners
1 1st St., Ste. 2
Los Altos, CA 94022
Phone: (650)949-9862
Fax: (650)949-8510
Brian J. Grossi, General Partner
Preferred Investment Size: $100,000
to $3 million. Investment Policies:
Equity Only. Investment Types: Seed,
startup, first and second stage, and
special situations. Industry Prefer-
ences: High technology and electronic
deals only. Geographic Preferences:
West Coast, Silicon Valley/San
Francisco Bay area.

HMS Capital Partners
1 1st St., Ste. 6
Los Altos, CA 94022
Phone: (650)917-0390
Fax: (650)917-0394
Preferred Investment Size: $100,000
to $500,000. Investment Types: Seed,
startup, first stage, and leveraged
buyout. Industry Preferences:
Communications, computer related,
electronics, and industrial products.
Geographic Preferences: No preference.

MBW Management, Inc. (Los Altos)
350 2nd St., Ste. 4
Los Altos, CA 94022
Phone: (650)941-2392
Fax: (650)941-2865

Bank of America National Trust and
Savings Association
PO Box 60049
Los Angeles, CA 90060-0049

Phone: (714)973-8495
Venture capital firm preferring
investments of $1 million-$3 million.
Diversified industry preference.

Bastion Capital Corp.
Email: ga@bastioncapital.com
1999 Avenue of the Stars, Ste. 2960
Los Angeles, CA 90067
Phone: (310)788-5700
Fax: (310)277-7582
James Villanueva, Vice President
Preferred Investment Size:
$5,000,000 to $10,000,000. Invest-
ment Types: Leveraged buyout,
special situations and control block
purchases. Industry Preferences:
Diversified. Real estate not consid-
ered. Geographic Preferences: Entire
U.S. and Canada.

Best Finance Corp.
4929 W. Wilshire Blvd., Ste. 407
Los Angeles, CA 90010
Phone: (213)937-1636
Fax: (213)937-6393
Vincent Lee, General Manager
Preferred Investment Size: $50,000.
Investment Policies: Loans and/or
equity. Investment Types: Purchase,
seed, expansion. Industry Preferences:
Diversified. Geographic Preferences:
California.

Brentwood Associates (Los Angeles)
11150 Santa Monica Blvd., Ste. 1200
Los Angeles, CA 90025
Phone: (310)477-7678
Fax: (310)477-1868
Preferred Investment Size:
$2,000,000 to $5,000,000. Investment
Types: Seed, startup, first and second
stage, and mezzanine. Industry
Preferences: Electronics and medical/
health related. Geographic Preferences: Entire U.S. for later-stage, and
within two hours of office for start-
ups.

BT Corp.
300 S. Grand Ave.
Los Angeles, CA 90071
Phone: (213)620-8200
Fax: (213)620-8484
A small business investment com-
pany.

Charterway Investment Corp.
One Wilshire Bldg., No.1600
Los Angeles, CA 90017-3317
Phone: (213)689-9107
Fax: (213)890-1968
A minority enterprise small business
investment corporation. No industry
preference.

Davis Group
PO Box 69953
Los Angeles, CA 90069-0953
Phone: (310)659-6327
Fax: (310)659-6337
Roger W. Davis, Chairman
Preferred Investment Size: $100,000
minimum. Investment Types: Early
stages, leveraged buyouts, and special
situations. Industry Preferences:
Diversified. Geographic Preferences:
National.

Far East Capital Corp.
977 N. Broadway, Ste.401
Los Angeles, CA 90012
Phone: (213)687-1361
Fax: (213)626-7497
Tom C. Wang, Vice President and
Manager
Preferred Investment Size: $100,000
to $250,000. Investment Types:
Second stage. Geographic Prefer-
ences: Within two hours of office.

Kline Hawkes California SBIC, LP
11726 San Vicente Blvd., Ste. 300
Los Angeles, CA 90049
Phone: (310)442-4700
Fax: (310)442-4707
Robert M. Freiland, Partner
Preferred Investment Size:
$1,000,000 to $10,000,000. Invest-
ment Types: Second stage, leveraged
buyout, special situations, and
intergenerational buyouts. Industry
Preferences: Diversified technology.
Geographic Preferences: Northwest,
Southwest, and California.

Lawrence Financial Group
701 Teakwood
PO Box 491773
Los Angeles, CA 90049
Phone: (310)471-4060
Fax: (310)472-3155
Preferred Investment Size: $100,000

to $1,000,000. Investment Types: Late stages. Industry Preferences: Diversified. Geographic Preferences: West Coast.

Peregrine Ventures
PO Box 491760
Los Angeles, CA 90049
Phone: (310)458-1441
Fax: (310)394-0771
Venture capital firm providing start-up, first stage, and leveraged buyout financing. Areas of interest include communications and health.

Riordan Lewis & Haden
300 S. Grand Ave., 29th Fl.
Los Angeles, CA 90071
Phone: (213)229-8500
Fax: (213)229-8597
Preferred Investment Size: $2,000,000 to $20,000,000. Investment Types: Leveraged buyouts, and special situations. Industry Preferences: Diversified. Geographic Preferences: West Coast, within two hours of office.

The Seideler Companies, Inc.
515 S. Figueroa St., 11th Fl.
Los Angeles, CA 90071-3396
Phone: (213)624-4232
Fax: (213)623-1131

Triune Capital
1888 Century Park East, Ste. 1900
Los Angeles, CA 90067
Phone: (310)284-6800
Fax: (310)284-3290
Preferred Investment Size: $1,000,000 to $5,000,000. Investment Types: Late stage and special situations. Industry Preferences: Diversified technology. Geographic Preferences: West Coast.

Wedbush Capital Partners
1000 Wilshire Blvd., Ste. 900
Los Angeles, CA 90017
Phone: (213)688-4545
Fax: (213)688-6642
Preferred Investment Size: $250,000 to $500,000. Investment Types: Later stages, and leveraged buyouts. Industry Preferences: Diversified computer technology, consumer

related, distribution, and healthcare. Geographic Preferences: West Coast.

August Capital
2480 Sand Hill Road, Ste. 101
Menlo Park, CA 94025
Phone: (650)234-9900
Fax: (650)234-9910
Andrew S. Rappaport, General Partner
Preferred Investment Size: $1,000,000 to $5,000,000. Investment Types: Startup, first stage and special situations. Industry Preferences: Communications, computer related, distribution, and electronic components and instrumentation. Real estate, finance and insurance not considered. Geographic Preferences: Northwest, Southwest, Rocky Mountains and West Coast.

Baccharis Capital Inc.
2420 Sand Hill Road, Ste. 100
Menlo Park, CA 94025
Phone: (650)324-6844
Fax: (650)854-3025
Michelle von Roedelbronn
Preferred Investment Size: $250,000 to $1,000,000. Investment Types: Startup, first stage and second stage, mezzanine and special situations. Industry Preferences: Diversified. Geographic Preferences: West Coast.

Benchmark Capital
Email: creynolds@benchmark.com
2480 Sand Hill Road, Ste. 200
Menlo Park, CA 94025
Phone: (650)854-8180
Fax: (650)854-8183
Preferred Investment Size: $1,000,000 to $5,000,000. Investment Types: Seed, research and development, startup, first and second stage, and special situations. Industry Preferences: Communications, computer related, and electronic components and instrumentation. Medical/health related, environmental, and biotechnology not considered. Geographic Preferences: Southwest and West Coast.

Bessemer Venture Partners (Menlo Park)
535 Middlefield Rd., Ste. 245
Menlo Park, CA 94025
Phone: (650)853-7000
Fax: (650)853-7001

Brentwood Associates (Menlo Park)
3000 Sandhill Rd., Ste. 260
Menlo Park, CA 94025
Phone: (650)854-7691
Fax: (650)854-9513

The Cambria Group
724 Oak Grove Ave., Ste. 120
Menlo Park, CA 94025
Phone: (650)329-8600
Fax: (650)329-8601
Paul L. Davies, III
Preferred Investment Size: $500,000 to $1,000,000. Investment Types: Second stage, mezzanine, leveraged buyout, special situations, and control block purchases. Industry Preferences: Diversified. Computer related and biotechnology not considered. Geographic Preferences: Entire U.S.

Canaan Partners
2884 Sand Hill Rd., Ste. 115
Menlo Park, CA 94025
Phone: (650)854-8092
Fax: (650)854-8127
Preferred Investment Size: $1,00,000 to $5,000,000. Investment Types: First and second stage, mezzanine, leverage buyout, acquisition financing. Geographic Preferences: No preference.

Capstone Ventures
Email: gfischer@capstonevc.com
3000 Sand Hill Rd., Building One, Ste. 290
Menlo Park, CA 94025
Phone: (650)854-2523
Fax: (650)854-9010
Eugene J. Fischer
Preferred Investment Size: $500,000 to $5,000,000. Investment Types: Startup, and first and second stage. Industry Preferences: Diversified high technology. Geographic Preferences: Midwest, Rocky Mountains, and West Coast.

Comdisco Venture Group (Silicon Valley)
3000 Sand Hill Rd., Bldg. 1, Ste. 155
Menlo Park, CA 94025
Phone: (415)854-9484
Fax: (415)854-4026
Preferred Investment Size: $250,000 to $500,000. Investment Types: Seed, startup, first and second stage, receivables, loans, and equipment leases. Industry Preferences: Diversified. Geographic Preferences: No preference.

Commtech International
535 Middlefield Rd., Ste. 200
Menlo Park, CA 94025
Phone: (650)328-0190
Fax: (650)328-6442
Preferred Investment Size: $100,000 to $250,000. Investment Types: Seed, startup, research and development. Industry Preferences: Diversified. Geographic Preferences: West Coast.

Compass Technology Partners
1550 El Camino Real, Ste. 275
Menlo Park, CA 94025-4111
Phone: (650)322-7595
Fax: (650)322-0588
David G. Arscott, General Partner
Preferred Investment Size: $250,000 to $1,000,000. Investment Types: Mezzanine, leveraged buyout, and special situations. Industry Preferences: Diversified high technology. Geographic Preferences: National.

Convergence Partners
3000 Sand Hill Rd., Ste. 235
Menlo Park, CA 94025
Phone: (650)854-3010
Fax: (650)854-3015
Preferred Investment Size: $100,000 to $5,000,000. Investment Types: Seed, startup, research and development, early and late stage, and mezzanine. Industry Preferences: Communications, computer related, electronic components and instrumentation, and interactive media. Geographic Preferences: National.

Cornerstone Ventures
750 Menlo Ave., Ste. 350
Menlo Park, CA 94025

Phone: (650)473-9780
Fax: (650)473-9784
Preferred Investment Size: $1,000,000 to $5,000,000. Investment Types: Second stage, mezzanine, leveraged buyout, special situations, and control block purchases. Industry Preferences: Diversified technology. Geographic Preferences: Southwest, West Coast, and Western Canada.

Dakota Capital
Email: info@dakota.com
PO Box 1025
Menlo Park, CA 94025
Phone: (650)853-0600
Fax: (650)851-4899
Stephen A. Meyer, General Partner
Preferred Investment Size: $250,000 to $1,000,000. Investment Types: Early and later stages, and special situations. Industry Preferences: Diversified computer and communications technology, education, and publishing. Geographic Preferences: National.

El Dorado Ventures (Cupertino)
2400 Sand Hill Rd., Ste. 100
Menlo Park, CA 94025
Phone: (650)854-1200
Fax: (650)854-1202
Preferred Investment Size: $500,000 to $5,000,000. Investment Types: Seed, startup, first and second stage. Industry Preferences: Communications, computer related, electronics, and industrial products and equipment. Geographic Preferences: West Coast.

Glenwood Management
3000 Sand Hill Rd., Bldg. 4, Ste. 230
Menlo Park, CA 94025
Phone: (650)854-8070
Fax: (650)854-4961
Venture capital supplier. Areas of interest include high technology and biomedical industries.

Glynn Ventures
3000 Sand Hill Rd., Bldg. 4, Ste. 225
Menlo Park, CA 94025
Phone: (650)854-2215
John W. Glynn, Jr., General Partner
Preferred Investment Size: $250,000

to $500,000. Investment Types: Later stages. Industry Preferences: Diversified computer and communications technology, and consumer services. Geographic Preferences: East and West Coast.

Institutional Venture Partners
Email: litesci@ivp.com
3000 Sand Hill Rd., Bldg. 2, Ste. 290
Menlo Park, CA 94025
Phone: (650)854-0132
Fax: (650)854-5762
Preferred Investment Size: $500,000 to $5,000,000. Investment Types: Seed, startup, first and second stage, mezzanine, and special situations. Industry Preferences: Diversified. Geographic Preferences: Entire U.S.

Interwest Partners (Menlo Park)
3000 Sand Hill Rd., Bldg. 3, Ste. 255
Menlo Park, CA 94025-7112
Phone: (650)854-8585
Fax: (650)854-4706
Preferred Investment Size: $1,000,000 to $17,500,000. Investment Types: Seed, research and development, startup, first and second stage, mezzanine, and special situations. Industry Preferences: Diversified. Oil and gas exploration and real estate not considered. Geographic Preferences: Entire U.S.

Kleiner Perkins Caufield & Byers (Menlo Park)
2750 Sand Hill Rd.
Menlo Park, CA 94025
Phone: (650)233-2750
Fax: (650)233-0300
Provides seed, start-up, second and third-round, and bridge financing to companies on the West Coast. Preferred industries of investment include electronics, computers, software, telecommunications, biotechnology, medical devices, and pharmaceuticals.

Matrix Partners
2500 Sand Hill Rd., Ste. 113
Menlo Park, CA 94025
Phone: (650)854-3131
Fax: (650)854-3296
Preferred Investment Size: $500,000

to $5,000,000. Investment Types: Startup, first and second stage, and leveraged buyout. Industry Preferences: Communications, computer related, and electronic components and instrumentation. Geographic Preferences: Entire U.S.

Mayfield Fund
2800 Sand Hill Rd.
Menlo Park, CA 94025
Phone: (650)854-5560
Fax: (650)854-5712
Preferred Investment Size: $250,000 to $5,000,000. Investment Types: Seed, startup, first and second stage. Industry Preferences: Diversified technology. Real estate, oil and gas, and motion pictures not considered. Geographic Preferences: Northwest, East Coast, Rocky Mountains, and West Coast.

McCown De Leeuw and Co. (Menlo Park)
3000 Sand Hill Rd., Bldg. 3, Ste. 290
Menlo Park, CA 94025-7111
Phone: (650)854-6000
Fax: (650)854-0853
David E. De Leeuw, Managing Member
Preferred Investment Size: $20,000,000 minimum. Investment Types: Leveraged buyout, special situations, and recapitalization. Industry Preferences: Diversified. Geographic Preferences: Entire U.S.

Medicus Venture Partners
Email: fred@medicusvc.com
2882 Sand Hill Rd., Ste. 116
Menlo Park, CA 94025
Phone: (650)854-7100
Fax: (650)854-5700
Fred Dotzler, General Partner
Preferred Investment Size: $100,000 to $5,000,000. Investment Types: Early stages. Industry Preferences: Genetic engineering and healthcare industry. Geographic Preferences: Western U.S.

Menlo Ventures
3000 Sand Hill Rd., Bldg. 4, Ste. 100
Menlo Park, CA 94025
Phone: (650)854-8540

Fax: (650)854-7059
H. DuBose Montgomery, General Partner and Managing Director
Venture capital supplier. Provides start-up and expansion financing to companies with experienced management teams, distinctive product lines, and large growing markets. Primary interest is in technology-oriented, service, consumer products, and distribution companies. Investments range from $1,000,000 to $2 million; also provides capital for leveraged buy outs.

Merrill Pickard Anderson & Eyre
2480 Sand Hill Rd., Ste. 200
Menlo Park, CA 94025
Phone: (650)854-8600
Fax: (650)854-8183
Preferred Investment Size: $5,000,000 maximum. Investment Types: Seed, startup, first and second stage. Industry Preferences: Diversified technology. Geographic Preferences: No preference.

New Enterprise Associates (Menlo Park)
2490 Sand Hill Road
Menlo Park, CA 94025
Phone: (650)854-9499
Fax: (650)854-9397
Frank A. Bonsal, Jr., Founding Partner
Preferred Investment Size: $100,000 to $5,000,000. Investment Types: Seed, startup, first and second stage, mezzanine, and incubator. Industry Preferences: Diversified technology. Geographic Preferences: No preference.

New Enterprise Associates (San Francisco)
2490 Sand Hill Road
Menlo Park, CA 94025
Phone: (650)854-9499
Fax: (650)854-9397
Venture capital supplier. Concentrates in technology-based industries that have the potential for product innovation, rapid growth, and high profit margins.

Paragon Venture Partners
3000 Sand Hill Rd., Bldg. 1, Ste. 275
Menlo Park, CA 94025
Phone: (650)854-8000
Fax: (650)854-7260
Private venture capital firm. Maximum investment is $500,000.

Pathfinder Venture Capital Funds (Menlo Park)
Email: jahrens620@aol.com
3000 Sand Hill Rd., Bldg. 1, Ste. 290
Menlo Park, CA 94025
Phone: (650)854-2523
Fax: (650)854-9010
Jack K. Ahrens, II, Investment Officer
Preferred Investment Size: $250,000 to $500,000. Investment Types: Seed, startup, first and second stage, mezzanine, leveraged buyout, and special situations. Industry Preferences: Diversified technology. Geographic Preferences: Entire U.S. and Canada.

Ritter Partners
3000 Sandhill Rd. Bldg.1, Ste. 190
Menlo Park, CA 94025
Phone: (650)854-1555
Fax: (650)854-5015
William C. Edwards, President

Sequoia Capital
Email: sequoia@sequioacap.com
3000 Sand Hill Rd., Bldg. 4, Ste. 280
Menlo Park, CA 94025
Phone: (415)854-3927
Fax: (415)854-2977
Private venture capital partnership with $700 million under management. Provides financing for all stages of development of wellmanaged companies with exceptional growth prospects in fast-growth industries. Past investments have been made in computers and peripherals, communications, health care, biotechnology, and medical instruments and devices. Investments range from $100,000 for early stage companies to $1 million for late stage accelerates.

Sierra Ventures
3000 Sand Hill Rd., Bldg. 4, Ste. 210
Menlo Park, CA 94025
Phone: (650)854-1000

Fax: (650)854-5593
Preferred Investment Size:
$1,000,000 maximum. Investment
Types: Seed, startup, first and second
stage, and leveraged buyout. Industry
Preferences: Diversified. Geographic
Preferences: East and West Coast.

Sigma Partners
Email: info@sigmapartners.com
2884 Sand Hill Rd., Ste. 121
Menlo Park, CA 94025-7022
Phone: (650)854-1300
Fax: (650)854-1323
Robert E. Devoli, Partner
Independent venture capital partnership. Prefers to invest in the following
areas: communications, computer
hardware, computer software,
manufacturing, medical equipment,
and semiconductor capital equipment.
Avoids investing in construction,
hotels, leasing, motion pictures, and
natural resources. Minimum initial
commitment is $2,000,000.

Sprout Group (Menlo Park)
3000 Sand Hill Rd.
Bldg. 4, Ste. 270
Menlo Park, CA 94025
Phone: (650)854-1550
Fax: (650)234-2779

TA Associates (Menlo Park)
70 Willow Rd., Ste. 100
Menlo Park, CA 94025
Phone: (650)328-1210
Fax: (650)326-4933
Michael C. Child, Managing Director
Private venture capital firm. Prefers
technology companies and leveraged
buy outs. Provides $5 million in
investments. No geographical
preference.

Technology Venture Investors
2480 Sand Hill Rd., Ste. 101
Menlo Park, CA 94025
Phone: (650)854-7472
Fax: (650)854-4187
Private venture capital partnership.
Primary interest is in technology
companies with minimum investment
of $1 million.

Thompson Clive Inc.
Email: mail@tcvc.com

3000 Sand Hill Rd., Bldg. 1, Ste. 185
Menlo Park, CA 94025-7102
Phone: (650)854-0314
Fax: (650)854-0670
Greg Ennis
Preferred Investment Size: $500,000
to $1,000,000. Investment Types:
Early and later stages, and special
situations. Industry Preferences:
Diversified computer and communi-
cations technology, electronic
instrumentation, genetic engineering,
and education. Geographic Prefer-
ences: National and Western Canada.

Trinity Ventures Ltd.
3000 Sand Hill Rd., Bldg. 1, Ste. 240
Menlo Park, CA 94025
Phone: (650)854-9500
Fax: (650)854-9501
Noel J. Fenton, General Partner
Preferred Investment Size:
$1,000,000 maximum. Investment
Types: Startup, first and second stage,
mezzanine, and leveraged buyout.
Industry Preferences: Communica-
tions, computer related, and consumer
products, services, food and beverage,
restaurants, and retailing. Geographic
Preferences: Northwest, Southwest,
Midwest, Rocky Mountains, and West
Coast.

U.S. Venture Partners
2180 Sand Hill Rd., Ste. 300
Menlo Park, CA 94025
Phone: (415)854-9080
Fax: (415)854-3018
William K. Bowes, Jr., General
Partner
Preferred Investment Size: $500,000
to $5,000,000. Investment Types:
Seed, research and development,
startup, first and second stage, and
mezzanine. Industry Preferences:
Communications, computer related,
consumer products and services,
distribution, electronics, and medical/
health related. Geographic Preferences: Northwest and West Coast.

USVP-Schlein Marketing Fund
2180 Sand Hill Rd., Ste. 300
Menlo Park, CA 94025
Phone: (415)854-9080

Fax: (415)854-3018
Venture capital fund. Prefers specialty
retailing/consumer products companies.

Venrock Associates
2497 Sand Hill Rd., Ste. 200
Menlo Park, CA 94025
Phone: (650)561-9580
Fax: (650)561-9180
Ted H. McCourtney, Managing
General Partner
Preferred Investment Size:
$2,000,000 to $10,000,000. Investment Types: Seed, research and
development, startup, first and second
stage. Industry Preferences: Diversified. Geographic Preferences: No
preference.

Brad Peery Capital Inc.
145 Chapel Pkwy.
Mill Valley, CA 94941
Phone: (415)389-0625
Fax: (415)389-1336
Brad Peery, Chairman
Prefers communications and com-
puter related industry. No geographi-
cal preference.

Hall, Capital Management
26161 Lapaz Rd., Ste. E
Mission Viejo, CA 92691
Phone: (714)707-5096
Fax: (714)707-5121
A small business investment corporation. No industry preference. Provides
capital for small and medium-sized
companies through participation in
private placements of subordinated
debt, preferred, and common stock.
Offers growth-acquisition and later-
stage venture capital.

ABC Capital Funding
917 Waittier Blvd.
Montebello, CA 90640
Phone: (213)725-7890
Fax: (213)725-7115
A minority enterprise small business
investment corporation. No industry
preference.

LaiLai Capital Corp.
223 E. Garvey Ave., Ste. 228
Monterey-Park, CA 91754
Phone: (626)288-0704

Fax: (626)288-4101
A minority enterprise small business investment company. Diversified industry preference.

Myriad Capital, Inc.
701 S. Atlantic Blvd., Ste. 302
Monterey Park, CA 91754-3242
Phone: (626)570-4548
Fax: (626)570-9570
A minority enterprise small business investment corporation. Prefers investing in production and manufacturing industries.

Marwit Capital LLC
180 Newport Center Dr., Ste. 200
Newport Beach, CA 92660
Phone: (714)640-6234
Fax: (714)720-8077
Matthew L. Witte, President and CEO
A small business investment corporation. Provides financing for leveraged buyouts, mergers, acquisitions, and expansion stages. Investments are in the $500,000 to $5 million range. Does not provide financing for startups or real estate ventures.

Nu Capital Access Group, Ltd.
7677 Oakport St., Ste. 105
Oakland, CA 94621
Phone: (510)635-7345
Fax: (510)635-7068
Preferred Investment Size: $500,000 to $2,500,000. Investment Types: Early and later stages, and special situations. Industry Preferences: Diversified consumer products and services, food and industrial product distribution. Geographic Preferences: Western U.S.

Inman and Bowman
4 Orinda Way, Bldg. D, Ste. 150
Orinda, CA 94563
Phone: (510)253-1611
Fax: (510)253-9037
Preferred Investment Size: $500,000 to $1,000,000. Investment Types: Startup, first and second stage. Industry Preferences: Diversified technology. Geographic Preferences: West Coast.

Accel Partners (San Francisco)
428 University Ave.

Palo Alto, CA 94301
Phone: (650)614-4800
Fax: (650)614-4880
Preferred Investment Size: $100,000 minimum. Investment Types: Seed, research and development, startup, first and second stage, mezzanine, leveraged buyout, special situations and control block purchases. Industry Preferences: Communications, computer related, and electronic components and instrumentation. Geographic Preferences: No preference.

Advanced Technology Ventures
485 Ramona St.,Ste. 200
Palo Alto, CA 94301
Phone: (650)321-8601
Fax: (650)321-0934

Asset Management Associates Inc.
Email: postmaster@assetman.com
2275 E. Bayshore, Ste. 150
Palo Alto, CA 94303
Phone: (650)494-7400
Fax: (650)856-1826
Preferred Investment Size: $750,000 to $2,000,000. Investment Types: Seed, startup, and first stage. Industry Preferences: High technology. Geographic Preferences: Northeast, West Coast.

Campbell Venture Management
375 California St.
Palo Alto, CA 94308
Phone: (650)941-2068
Fax: (650)857-0303

Charter Ventures
525 University Avenue, Ste. 1500
Palo Alto, CA 94301
Phone: (415)325-6953
Fax: (415)325-4762
Preferred Investment Size: $250,000 maximum. Investment Types: Seed, startup, first and second stage, mezzanine, leveraged buyout, and special situations. Industry Preferences: Diversified. Geographic Preferences: No preference.

Communications Ventures
505 Hamilton Avenue, Ste. 305
Palo Alto, CA 94301
Phone: (650)325-9600

Fax: (650)325-9608
Preferred Investment Size: $500,000 to $5,000,000. Investment Types: Seed. Industry Preferences: Communications. Geographic Preferences: No preference.

Greylock Management (Palo Alto)
755 Page Mill Rd., Ste. A-100
Palo Alto, CA 94304-1018
Phone: (650)493-5525
Fax: (650)493-5575
Venture capital firm providing all stages of financing. Areas of interest include computer software, communications, health, biotechnology, publishing, and specialty retail.

MK Global Ventures
2471 E. Bayshore Rd., Ste. 520
Palo Alto, CA 94303
Phone: (650)424-0151
Fax: (650)494-2753

Norwest Venture Capital (Palo Alto)
245 Lytton Ave., Ste. 250
Palo Alto, CA 94301-1426
Phone: (650)321-8000
Fax: (650)321-8010
Charles B. Lennin, Partner
Preferred Investment Size: $2,000,000 to $3,000,000. Investment Types: Seed, startup, first and second stage, mezzanine, leveraged buyout, and special situations. Industry Preferences: Diversified. Geographic Preferences: No preference.

Oak Investment Partners (Menlo Park)
525 University Avenue, Ste. 1300
Palo Alto, CA 94301
Phone: (650)614-3700
Fax: (650)328-6345
Preferred Investment Size: $250,000 to $5,000,000. Investment Types: Seed, startup, first stage, leveraged buyout, and special situations. Industry Preferences: Communications, computer related, consumer restaurants and retailing, electronics, genetic engineering, and medical/health related. Geographic Preferences: No preference.

Patricof & Co. Ventures, Inc. (Palo Alto)
2100 Geng Rd., Ste. 150
Palo Alto, CA 94303
Phone: (650)494-9944
Fax: (650)494-6751
Preferred Investment Size: $5,000,000 to $25,000,000. Investment Types: Seed, startup, first and second stage, mezzanine, and leveraged buyout. Industry Preferences: Diversified. Geographic Preferences: No preference.

Summit Partners (Palo Alto)
499 Hamilton Ave., Ste. 200
Palo Alto, CA 94301
Phone: (650)321-1166
Fax: (650)321-1188
Preferred Investment Size: $5,000,000 maximum. Investment Types: First and second stage, mezzanine, leveraged buyout, special situations, and control block purchases. Industry Preferences: Diversified. Geographic Preferences: Entire U.S. and Canada.

Sutter Hill Ventures
Email: shv@shv.com
755 Page Mill Rd., Ste. A-200
Palo Alto, CA 94304
Phone: (650)493-5600
Fax: (650)858-1854
Preferred Investment Size: $100,000 to $2,000,000. Investment Types: Seed, startup, first and second stage, and purchase of secondary positions. Industry Preferences: Diversified. Geographic Preferences: Entire U.S.

Vanguard Venture Partners
525 University Ave., Ste. 600
Palo Alto, CA 94301
Phone: (650)321-2900
Fax: (650)321-2902
Laura F. Gwosden, Chief Financial Officer
Preferred Investment Size: $250,000 to $5,000,000. Investment Types: Early stages. Industry Preferences: Diversified computer and communications technology, genetic engineering, and healthcare. Geographic Preferences: National.

Venture Growth Associates
2479 East Bayshore St., Ste. 710
Palo Alto, CA 94303
Phone: (650)855-9100
Fax: (650)855 9104
James R. Berdell, Managing Partner
Preferred Investment Size: $1,000,000 to $5,000,000. Investment Types: Early and later stages, and special situations. Industry Preferences: Diversified technology, finance and insurance. Geographic Preferences: West Coast.

Jafco America Ventures, Inc. (San Francisco)
505 Hamilton Ste. 310
Palto Alto, CA 94301
Phone: (650)463-8800
Fax: (650)463-8801
Preferred Investment Size: $1,000,000 to $5,000,000. Investment Types: First and second stage and mezzanine. Industry Preferences: Diversified technology. Geographic Preferences: Entire U.S.

BankAmerica Ventures (Pasadena)
155 N. Lake Ave., Ste. 1010
Pasadena, CA 91109
Phone: (626)578-5474
Fax: (626)440-9931

First SBIC of California (Pasadena)
155 N. Lake Ave., Ste. 1010
Pasadena, CA 91109
Fax: (818)440-9931
A small business investment company.

Idealab Capital Partners
Email: venture.info@icp.com
130 West Union Street
Pasadena, CA 91103
Phone: (626)535-2870
Fax: (626)535-2881
Jim Armstrong
Preferred Investment Size: $500,000 to $4,000,000. Investment Types: Early stages. Industry Preferences: Data communications, Internet, retailing, and computer distribution. Geographic Preferences: National.

Access Venture Partners
4133 Mohr Avenue, Ste. H
Pleasanton, CA 94566

Phone: (925)426-9574
Fax: (925)462-4398
V. Frank Mendecino, II, Managing Director
Preferred Investment Size: $250,000 to $5 million. Investment Types: Seed, startup, first stage, and special situations. Industry Preferences: Diversified. Real estate, oil and gas, motion pictures, and consulting services not considered. Geographic Preferences: Northwest, Southwest, Midwest, Rocky Mountains, and West Coast.

Hallador Venture Partners, L.L.C.
Email: chris@hallador.com
740 University Ave., Ste. 110
Sacramento, CA 95825-6710
Phone: (916)920-0191
Fax: (916)920-5188
Chris L. Branscum, Managing Director
Preferred Investment Size: $250,000 to $1,000,000. Investment Types: Early and later stages. Industry Preferences: Diversified computer and communications technology, and electronic semiconductors. Geographic Preferences: Western U.S.

The Money Store Investment Corp.
3301 "C" St., Ste. 100 M
Sacramento, CA 95816
Phone: (916)446-5000
Free: (800)639-1102
Fax: (916)443-2399
Non-bank lender providing start-up and expansion financing.

Forward Ventures
Email: fleming@forwardventure.com
9255 Towne Centre Dr.
San Diego, CA 92121
Phone: (619)677-6077
Fax: (619)452-8799
Standish M. Fleming, Partner
Preferred Investment Size: $250,000 to $5,000,000. Investment Types: Seed, research and development, startup, and first stage. Industry Preferences: Genetic engineering and medical/health related. Geographic Preferences: West Coast.

Idanta Partners Ltd.
4660 La Jolla Village Dr., Ste. 850

San Diego, CA 92122
Phone: (619)452-9690
Fax: (619)452-2013
Preferred Investment Size: $500,000.
Investment Types: Seed, startup, first
and second stage. Industry Prefer-
ences: Diversified. Geographic
Preferences: Entire U.S.

Sorrento Associates, Inc.
4370 LaJolla Village Dr., Ste. 1040
San Diego, CA 92122
Phone: (619)452-3100
Fax: (619)452-7607
Robert M. Jaffe, President
Preferred Investment Size: $500,000
TO $7,000,000. Investment Policies:
Equity only. Investment Types: Seed,
early, expansion, later stages. Industry
Preferences: Medicine, health,
communications, electronics, special
retail. Geographic Preferences: West
Coast.

21ST Century Internet Venture
Partners
Two South Park
2nd Floor
San Francisco, CA 94107
Phone: (415)512-1221
Fax: (415)512-2650
Robert Reid, Associate
Preferred Investment Size:
$5,000,000 maximum. Investment
Types: Seed, research and develop-
ment, startup, first and second stage,
mezzanine, leveraged buyout, and
special situations. Industry Prefer-
ences: Diversified. Geographic
Preferences: Entire U.S. and Canada.

Acacia Venture Partners
101 California St., Ste. 3160
San Francisco, CA 94111
Phone: (415)433-4200
Fax: (415)433-4250
Preferred Investment Size:
$2,000,000 to $10,000,000. Invest-
ment Types: Seed, startup, first and
second stage, mezzanine and lever-
aged buyout. Industry Preferences:
Computer, and medical/health related.
Geographic Preferences: Entire U.S.

Alta Partners
Email: alta@altapartners.com

One Embarcadero Center, Ste. 4050
San Francisco, CA 94111
Phone: (415)362-4022
Fax: (415)362-6178
Jean Deleage, Partner
Preferred Investment Size:
$1,000,000 to $10,000,000. Investment Types: Seed, startup, first and
second stage, and mezzanine. Industry
Preferences: Communications,
computer related, distribution,
electronic components and instrumentation, genetic engineering, industrial
products and equipment, medical/
health related. Real estate, oil and
natural gas exploration, and environmental not considered. Geographic
Preferences: West Coast and California.

American Realty and Construction
1489 Webster St., Ste. 218
San Francisco, CA 94115-3767
Phone: (415)928-6600
Fax: (415)928-6363
A minority enterprise small business
investment corporation. No industry
preference.

Bangert Dawes Reade Davis & Thom
Email: bdrdt@pacbell.net
220 Montgomery Street, Ste. 424
San Francisco, CA 94104
Phone: (415)954-9900
Fax: (415)954-9901
K. Deane Reade, President
Preferred Investment Size: $500,000
to $5,000,000. Investment Types:
Second stage, mezzanine, leveraged
buyout and special situations.
Industry Preferences: Diversified.
Geographic Preferences: No prefer-
ence.

Bentley Capital
592 Vallejo St. Ste. 2
San Francisco, CA 94133
Phone: (415)362-2868
Fax: (415)398-8209
A minority enterprise small business
investment company. Diversified
industry preference.

Berkeley International Capital Corp.
650 California St., Ste. 2800
San Francisco, CA 94108-2609

Phone: (415)249-0450
Fax: (415)392-3929
Arthur I. Trueger, Chairman
Preferred Investment Size:
$3,000,000 to $15,000,000. Investment Types: Second stage, mezzanine, leveraged buyout and special
situations. Industry Preferences:
Communications, computer related,
distribution, electronic components
and instrumentation, industrial
products and equipment, and medical/
health related. Geographic Preferences: Entire U.S.

Bluewater Capital Management Inc.
50 California St., Ste. 3200
San Francisco, CA 94111
Phone: (415)362-5007
Fax: (415)788-6763
Adam L. Rothstein
Preferred Investment Size:
$1,000,000 to $25,000,000. Investment Types: Second stage, mezzanine, leveraged buyout, special
situations, and control block purchases. Industry Preferences: Diversified high technology. Geographic
Preferences: No preference.

Bryan and Edwards Partnership (San
Francisco)
600 Montgomery St., 35th Fl.
San Francisco, CA 94111-2854
Phone: (415)421-9990
Fax: (415)421-0471
A small business investment corpora-
tion. No industry preference.

Burr, Egan, Deleage, and Co. (San
Francisco)
1 Embarcadero Center, Ste. 4050
San Francisco, CA 94111
Phone: (415)362-4022
Fax: (415)362-6178
Private venture capital supplier.
Invests start-up, expansion, and
acquisitions capital nationwide.
Principal concerns are strength of the
management team; large, rapidly
expanding markets; and unique
products for services. Past investments have been made in the fields of
biotechnology and pharmaceuticals,
cable TV, chemicals/plastics, commu-

nications, software, computer systems and peripherals, distributorships, radio common carriers, electronics and electrical components, environmental control, health services, medical devices and instrumentation, and radio and cellular telecommunications. Primarily interested in medical, electronics, and media industries.

Burrill & Company
120 Montgomery St., Ste. 1370
San Francisco, CA 94104
Phone: (415)743-3160
Fax: (415)743-3161
David Collier, Managing Director
Preferred Investment Size: $500,000 to $5,000,000. Investment Types: Startup, first and second stage, and mezzanine. Industry Preferences: Diversified. Geographic Preferences: No preference.

CMEA Ventures
235 Montgomery St., Ste. 920
San Francisco, CA 94401
Phone: (415)352-1520
Fax: (415)352-1524
Thomas R. Baruch, General Partner
Preferred Investment Size: $100,000 to $1,000,000. Investment Types: Seed, startup, first and second stage. Industry Preferences: Diversified high technology. Geographic Preferences: No preference.

Dominion Ventures, Inc.
44 Montgomery St., Ste. 4200
San Francisco, CA 94104
Phone: (415)362-4890
Fax: (415)394-9245
Preferred Investment Size: $1,000,000 to $10,000,000. Investment Types: First and second stage, mezzanine, leveraged buyout, and equity or secured debt. Industry Preferences: Diversified. Geographic Preferences: No preference.

Dynasty Capital Services LLC
258 11th Avenue, Suite 1000
San Francisco, CA 94118
Contact: Randolph L. Tom
Phone: (415)387-7700
Fax: (415)387-2750
Email: dynasty@dynastycap.com

Website: www.dynastycap.com
Provides financial and advisory services to entrepreneurs and emerging companies, including obtaining capital through financial investors and strategic partnerships. Focuses on high technology, Internet and communications companies. Extensive experience in financing and managing multi-million dollar transactions.

Eucalyptus Venture Management, L.L.C.
1 Bush Street, 12th Fl.
San Francisco, CA 94104
Phone: (415)439-3590
Fax: (415)439-3621
Bruce E. Crocker
Preferred Investment Size: $1,000,000 to $5,000,000. Investment Types: Early and later stages. Industry Preferences: Diversified computer and communications technology, and healthcare industry. Geographic Preferences: National.

Eurolink International
Email: vallee@eurolink.com
690 Market St., Ste. 702
San Francisco, CA 94104
Phone: (415)398-6352
Fax: (415)398-6355
Private venture capital supplier. Provides all stages of financing.

G C and H Partners
1 Maritime Plz., 20th Fl.
San Francisco, CA 94111
Phone: (415)693-2000
Fax: (415)951-3699
A small business investment corporation. No industry preference.

Gatx Capital
Four Embarcadero Center, Ste. 2200
San Francisco, CA 94904
Phone: (415)955-3200
Fax: (415)955-3449
Preferred Investment Size: $500,000 to $5,000,000. Investment Types: Early and later stages, and leveraged buyouts. Industry Preferences: Diversified technologies, forestry, and agriculture. Geographic Preferences: National and Canada.

Hambrecht and Quist (San Francisco)
1 Bush St.
San Francisco, CA 94104
Phone: (415)439-3300
Fax: (415)677-7747
Prefers to invest in computer technology, environmental technology, and biotechnology. Investments from $500,000.

Heller First Capital Corp.
50 Beale Ste. 1600
San Francisco, CA 94105
Phone: (415)356-1300
Fax: (415)356-1301
Non-bank lender providing start-up and expansion financing.

Jupiter Partners
600 Montgomery St., 35th Fl.
San Francisco, CA 94111
Phone: (415)421-9990
Fax: (415)421-0471
A small business investment company. Prefers to invest in electronic manufacturing industry.

Montgomery Securities
600 Montgomery St., 21st Fl.
San Francisco, CA 94111-2702
Phone: (415)627-2454
Fax: (415)249-5516
Private venture capital and investment banking firm. Diversified, but will not invest in real estate or energy-related industries. Involved in both start-up and later-stage financing.

Morgan Stanley Venture Capital Fund L.P.
555 California St., Ste. 2200
San Francisco, CA 94104
Phone: (415)576-2345
Fax: (415)576-2099
Venture capital firm providing second and third stage and buyout financing. Areas of interest include information technology and health care products/services.

NC Berkowitz & Co.
Email: nathaniels@yahoo.com
1095 Market Street
San Francisco, CA 94103
Phone: (415)255-9781
Fax: (415)255-9392
Nathaniel Berkowitz

Preferred Investment Size: $100,000 to $250,000. Investment Types: Seed, startup, first stage, leveraged buyout, and special situations. Industry Preferences: Diversified. Geographic Preferences: Entire U.S.

Newbury Ventures
535 Pacific Ave., 2nd Fl.
San Francisco, CA 94133
Phone: (415)296-7408
Fax: (415)296-7416
Preferred Investment Size: $500,000 to $1,000,000. Investment Types: Early and later stages, and leveraged buyout. Industry Preferences: Diversified high technology. Geographic Preferences: Eastern and Western U.S. and Canada.

Positive Enterprises, Inc.
1489 Webster St., Ste. 228
San Francisco, CA 94115
Phone: (415)885-6600
Fax: (415)928-6363
A minority enterprise small business investment company. Diversified industry preference.

Quest Ventures (San Francisco)
Email: ruby@crownadvisors.com
333 Bush St., Ste. 1750
San Francisco, CA 94104
Phone: (415)782-1414
Fax: (415)782-1415
Preferred Investment Size: $100,000 maximum. Investment Types: Seed and special situations. Industry Preferences: Diversified. Geographic Preferences: No preference.

Robertson-Stephens Co.
555 California St., Ste. 2600
San Francisco, CA 94104
Phone: (415)781-9700
Fax: (415)781-2556
Private venture capital firm. Considers investments in any attractive merging-growth area, including product and service companies. Key preferences include health care, communications and technology, biotechnology, software, and information services. Maximum investment is $5 million.

Rosewood Capital, L.P.
One Maritime Plaza, Ste. 1330
San Francisco, CA 94111-3503
Phone: (415)362-5526
Fax: (415)362-1192
Preferred Investment Size: $1,000,000 to $3,000,000. Investment Policies: Equity. Investment Types: Later stages, leveraged buyout, and special situations. Industry Preferences: Consumer and Internet related. Geographic Preferences: National.

Taylor & Turner
268 Bush St., Penthouse 10
San Francisco, CA 94104-3402
Phone: (415)398-6325
Fax: (415)398-3220
Preferred Investment Size: $100,000 to $500,000. Investment Types: Early stages and special situations. Industry Preferences: Diversified technology and education. Geographic Preferences: West Coast.

Ticonderoga Capital Inc.
555 California St., No. 4950
San Francisco, CA 94104
Phone: (415)296-7900
Fax: (415)296-8956
Preferred Investment Size: $5,000,000 maximum. Investment Types: Second stage, mezzanine, leveraged buyout, and consolidation strategies. Industry Preferences: Diversified. Geographic Preferences: Entire U.S. and Canada.

VK Ventures
600 California St., Ste.1700
San Francisco, CA 94111
Phone: (415)391-5600
Fax: (415)397-2744
David D. Horwich, Senior Vice President
Preferred Investment Size: $100,000 to $250,000. Investment Types: Second stage, mezzanine, and leveraged buyout. Industry Preferences: Diversified. Geographic Preferences: West Coast.

Volpe, Welty and Co.
1 Maritime Plz., 11th Fl.
San Francisco, CA 94111
Phone: (415)956-8120

Fax: (415)986-6754
Prefers investing with companies involved in entertainment, multi-media, computer-aided software engineering, gaming, software tools, biotechnology, and health care industries.

Walden Group of Venture Capital Funds
750 Battery St., Seventh Floor
San Francisco, CA 94111
Phone: (415)391-7225
Fax: (415)391-7262
Arthur Berliner
Preferred Investment Size: $1,000,000 to $7,000,000. Investment Types: Seed, startup, first and second stage. Industry Preferences: Diversified technology. Geographic Preferences: Entire U.S.

Weiss, Peck and Greer Venture Partners L.P. (San Francisco)
555 California St., Ste. 3130
San Francisco, CA 94104
Phone: (415)622-6864
Fax: (415)989-5108
Peter Nich, General Partner
Preferred Investment Size: $500,000 to $2,000,000. Investment Types: Seed, startup, first and second stage, and mezzanine. Industry Preferences: Diversified technology. Geographic Preferences: No preference.

Allied Business Investors, Inc.
301 W. Valley Blvd. Ste. 208
San Gabriel, CA 91776
Phone: (626)289-0186
Fax: (626)289-2369
Jack Hong, President
Preferred Investment Size: $50,000.
Investment Policies: Loans only.
Investment Types: Early stage.
Industry Preferences: Diversified.
Geographic Preferences: Los Angeles.

Acer Technology Ventures
2641 Orchard Pkwy.
San Jose, CA 95134
Phone: (408)433-4945
Fax: (408)433-5230
Ronald Chwang, President and CEO
Preferred Investment Size: $500,000 to $5,000,000. Investment Types:

Seed, startup, first and second stage. Industry Preferences: Diversified. Geographic Preferences: Entire U.S. and Canada.

2M Invest Inc.
Email: 2minfo@2minvest.com
1875 South Grant Street
Suite 750
San Mateo, CA 94402
Phone: (650)655-3765
Fax: (650)372-9107
Preferred Investment Size: $500,000 to $5 million. Investment Types: Startup. Industry Preferences: Communications, computer related, electronic components and instrumentation. Non-information technology companies not considered. Geographic Preferences: West Coast.

Dougery & Wilder (San Mateo)
155 Bovet Rd., Ste. 350
San Mateo, CA 94402-3113
Phone: (415)566-5220
Fax: (415)358-8706
Venture capital supplier. Areas of interest include computers systems and software, communications, and medical/biotechnology industries.

Drysdale Enterprises
Email: drysdale@aol.com
177 Bovet Rd., Ste. 600
San Mateo, CA 94402
Phone: (650)341-6336
Fax: (650)341-1329
Preferred Investment Size: $500,000 to $5,000,000. Investment Types: First and second stage, mezzanine, leveraged buyout, and special situations. Industry Preferences: Diversified. Geographic Preferences: West Coast.

Technology Funding
2000 Alameda de las Pulgas, Ste. 250
San Mateo, CA 94403
Phone: (415)345-2200
Fax: (415)345-1797
Peter F. Bernardoni, Partner
Small business investment corporation. Provides primarily late firststage, early second-stage, and mezzanine equity financing. Also offers secured debt with equity participation to

venture capital backed companies. Investments range from $250,000 to $500,000.

Phoenix Growth Capital Corp.
Email: nnelson@phxa.com
2401 Kerner Blvd.
San Rafael, CA 94901
Phone: (415)485-4569
Fax: (415)485-4663
Preferred Investment Size: $250,000 to $1,000,000. Investment Types: First and second stage, and mezzanine. Industry Preferences: Communications, computer related, consumer retailing, distribution, electronics, genetic engineering, medical/health related, education, publishing, and transportation. Geographic Preferences: Entire U.S.

Redleaf Venture Management
Email: nancy@redleaf.com
14395 Saratoga Ave., Ste. 130
Saratoga, CA 95070
Phone: (408)868-0800
Fax: (408)868-0810
Robert von Goeben, Director
Preferred Investment Size: $1,000,000 to $4,000,000. Investment Policies: Equity. Investment Types: Early and late stage. Industry Preferences: Internet business related. Geographic Preferences: Northwest and Silicon Valley.

Buttonwood Capital Inc.
15250 Ventura Blvd., Ste. 520
Sherman Oaks, CA 94103
Phone: (818)981-2210
Fax: (818)981-2223
Curtice A. Cornell, Managing Director
Preferred Investment Size: $1,000,000 to $5,000,000. Investment Types: Second stage and leveraged buyout. Industry Preferences: Diversified high technology. Biotechnology not considered. Geographic Preferences: Entire U.S. and Canada.

Astar Capital Corp.
9537 E. Gidley St.
Temple City, CA 91780
Phone: (818)350-1211
Fax: (818)350-0868
George Hsu, President

Spectra Enterprise Associates
PO Box 7688
Thousand Oaks, CA 91359-7688
Phone: (818)865-0213
Fax: (818)865-1309
Venture capital partnership. Areas of interest include information, computer, semiconductor, software, life sciences, and wireless industries.

National Investment Management, Inc.
Email: robins621@aol.com
2601 Airport Dr., Ste. 210
Torrance, CA 90505
Phone: (310)784-7600
Fax: (310)784-7605
Preferred Investment Size: $1,000,000 to $5,000,000. Investment Types: Leveraged buyout. Industry Preferences: Consumer products and retailing, distribution, industrial products and equipment, medical/health related, and publishing. Real estate deals not considered. Geographic Preferences: Entire U.S.

Round Table Capital Corp.
2175 N. California Blvd., Ste. 400
Walnut Creek, CA 94596
Phone: (925)274-1700
Fax: (925)974-3978
A small business investment corporation. No industry preference.

Sandton Financial Group
21550 Oxnard St., Ste. 300
Woodland Hills, CA 91367
Phone: (818)702-9283
Preferred Investment Size: $100,000 to $250,000. Investment Types: Early and later stages, and special situations. Industry Preferences: No preference. Geographic Preferences: National and Canada.

Crosspoint Venture Partners
Email: partners@crosspointvc.com
2925 Woodside Rd.
Woodside, CA 94062
Phone: (650)851-7600
Fax: (650)851-7661
Preferred Investment Size: $100,000 to $5,000,000. Investment Types: Seed and startup. Industry Preferences: Communications, computer

related, and communications and medical product distribution. Geographic Preferences: Northwest, Southwest, Rocky Mountains, and West Coast.

Colorado

Opus Capital
1113 Spruce St., Ste. 406
Boulder, CO 80302
Phone: (303)443-1023
Fax: (303)443-0986

Sequel Venture Partners
Email: tom@sequelvc.com
4430 Arapahoe Ave., Ste. 220
Boulder, CO 80303
Phone: (303)546-0400
Fax: (303)546-9728
Kinney Johnson, Partner
Preferred Investment Size: $100,000 to $5,000,000. Investment Types: Seed, startup, and early stage. Industry Preferences: Diversified technology. Geographic Preferences: Within two hours of office.

New Venture Resources
5875 Lehman Dr., Ste. 201C
Colorado Springs, CO 80918
Phone: (719)598-9272
Fax: (719)598-9272
Jeffrey M. Cooper
Preferred Investment Size: $100,000 to $250,000. Investment Types: Seed and startup. Industry Preferences: Diversified technology. Geographic Preferences: Southwest.

Capital Health Management
2084 S. Milwaukee St.
Denver, CO 80210
Fax: (303)692-9656

The Centennial Funds
1428 15th St.
Denver, CO 80202-1318
Phone: (303)405-7500
Fax: (303)405-7575
Preferred Investment Size: $250,000 to $5,000,000. Investment Types: Seed, startup, first and second stage, and national consolidations. Industry Preferences: Diversified. Geographic Preferences: No preference.

Colorado Housing and Finance Authority
1981 Blake St.
Denver, CO 80202-1272
Phone: (303)297-2432
Fax: (303)297-2615
Operates financing programs for small and minority businesses.

Colorado Office of Business Development
1625 Broadway, Ste. 1710
Denver, CO 80202
Phone: (303)892-3840
Fax: (303)892-3848
Provides loans to new and expanding businesses.

UBD Capital, Inc.
1700 Broadway
Denver, CO 80274
Phone: (303)863-4857
A small business investment company. Diversified industry preference.

Wolf Ventures
50 South Steele St., Ste. 777
Denver, CO 80209
Phone: (303)321-4800
Fax: (303)321-4848
David O. Wolf
Preferred Investment Size: $500,000 to $3,000,000. Investment Types: Later stage and special situations. Industry Preferences: Diversified. Geographic Preferences: Within two hours of office.

Century Capital Group
6530 South Yosemite St.
Englewood, CO 80111-5128
Phone: (303)796-2600
Fax: (303)796-2612
Preferred Investment Size: $100,000 to $250,000. Investment Types: Late stage, leveraged buyout, and special situations. Industry Preferences: Diversified. Geographic Preferences: Rocky Mountain area and Canada.

The Columbine Venture Funds
5460 S. Quebec St., Ste. 270
Englewood, CO 80111
Phone: (303)694-3222
Fax: (303)694-9007
Preferred Investment Size: $100,000 to $250,000. Investment Types: Seed,

research and development, startup, and first stage. Industry Preferences: Diversified technology. Geographic Preferences: Southwest, Rocky Mountains, and West Coast.

Holden Capital, L.L.C.
Email: block@vailsys.com
6300 South Syracruse Way, Ste. 484
Englewood, CO 80111
Phone: (303)694-0268
Fax: (303)694-1707
Preferred Investment Size: $250,000 to $5,000,000. Investment Types: Early and late stage, and leveraged buyout. Industry Preferences: Diversified. Geographic Preferences: National.

Investment Securities of Colorado, Inc.
4605 Denice Dr.
Englewood, CO 80111
Phone: (303)796-9192
Preferred Investment Size: $100,000 to $300,000. Investment Types: Seed and startup. Industry Preferences: Healthcare industry. Geographic Preferences: Rocky Mountain area.

Kinship Partners
Email: block@vailsys.com
6300 S. Syracuse Way, Ste. 484
Englewood, CO 80111
Phone: (303)694-0268
Fax: (303)694-1707
Preferred Investment Size: $250,000 to $1,000,000. Investment Types: Seed, startup, and early stage. Industry Preferences: Diversified computer and communication technology, specialty retailing, genetic engineering, and healthcare. Geographic Preferences: Within two hours of office.

Boranco Management, L.L.C.
1528 Hillside Dr.
Fort Collins, CO 80524-1969
Phone: (970)221-2297
Fax: (970)221-4787
Preferred Investment Size: $100,000. Investment Types: Late stage. Industry Preferences: Agricultural and animal biotechnology. Geographic Preferences: Within two hours of office.

Chase Capital Partners
108 S. Frontage Road W., Ste. 307
Vail, CO 81657
Phone: (970)476-7700
Fax: (970)476-7900
Preferred Investment Size:
$5,000,000 to $100,000,000. Investment Types: Startup, first and second stage, mezzanine, leveraged buyout, and special situations. Industry Preferences: Diversified. Geographic Preferences: Entire U.S. and Canada.

Connecticut

AB SBIC, Inc.
275 School House Rd.
Cheshire, CT 06410
Phone: (203)272-0203
Fax: (203)250-2954
A small business investment company. Prefers to invest in grocery stores.

James B Kobak & Co.
Four Mansfield Place
Darien, CT 06820
Phone: (203)656-3471
Fax: (203)655-2905
Preferred Investment Size: $100,000 maximum. Investment Types: Early stage. Industry Preferences: Publishing. Geographic Preferences: National.

James B. Kobak and Co.
Four Mansfield Place
Darien, CT 06820
Fax: (203)655-2905
Venture capital supplier and consultant. Provides assistance to new ventures in the communications field through conceptualization, planning, organization, raising money, and control of actual operations. Special interest is in magazine publishing.

Marcon Capital Corp.
10 John St.
Fairfield, CT 06490-1437
Fax: (203)259-9428
A small business investment corporation; secured lending preferred.

Consumer Venture Partners
Email: lcummin@consumer-venture.com

3 Pickwick Plz.
Greenwich, CT 06830
Phone: (203)629-8800
Fax: (203)629-2019
Linda Cummin, Business Manager
Preferred Investment Size: $500,000 to $5,000,000. Investment Types: Startup, first and second stage, and leveraged buyout. Industry Preferences: Internet related, consumer related, consumer and food distribution, education, and publishing. Geographic Preferences: Entire U.S.

Regulus International Capital Co., Inc.
140 Greenwich Ave.
Greenwich, CT 06830
Phone: (203)625-9700
Fax: (203)625-9706
Preferred Investment Size: $100,000. Investment Types: Early stage. Industry Preferences: Software, packaging and printing, chemicals and materials, and publishing. Geographic Preferences: National.

Northeast Ventures
One State St., Ste. 1720
Hartford, CT 06103
Phone: (860)547-1414
Fax: (860)246-8755
Preferred Investment Size: $5,000,000 maximum. Investment Types: Secondary. Industry Preferences: Diversified technology and education. Geographic Preferences: National.

Bio-Investigations, Ltd.
32 Country Way
PO Box 4041
Madison, CT 06443
Phone: (203)421-3697
Stewart B. Rosenberg, President
Preferred Investment Size: $100,000 to $500,000. Investment Types: Diversified early and late stage. Industry Preferences: Communications, computers, consumer, distribution, electronics, natural resources, genetic engineering, industrial products, and healthcare. Geographic Preferences: National.

Summit Capital Markets
38 Sylvan Rd.
Madison, CT 06443
Phone: (203)245-6870
Fax: (203)245-6865
Rockwell D. Marsh, Managing Partner
Preferred Investment Size: $250,000 to $5,000,000. Investment Types: Late stage and buyouts. Industry Preferences: Consumer products, industrial products, electronics, and pharmaceuticals. Geographic Preferences: East Coast.

Windward Holdings.
38 Sylvan Rd.
Madison, CT 06443
Phone: (203)245-6870
Fax: (203)245-6865
Preferred Investment Size: $250,000 to $1,000,000. Investment Types: Late stage and special situations. Industry Preferences: Diversified distribution, electronics, and industrial products. Geographic Preferences: East Coast.

Advanced Materials Partners, Inc.
Email: wkb@amplink.com
45 Pine St.
PO Box 1022
New Canaan, CT 06840
Phone: (203)966-6415
Fax: (203)966-8448
Preferred Investment Size: $500,000 to $5,000,000. Investment Types: Diversified early and late stage. Industry Preferences: Diversified. Geographic Preferences: National.

FRE Capital Partners, LP
36 Grove St.
New Canaan, CT 06840
Phone: (203)966-2800
Fax: (203)966-3109
A small business investment company. Diversified industry preference.

RFE Investment Partners
36 Grove St.
New Canaan, CT 06840
Phone: (203)966-2800
Fax: (203)966-3109
James A. Parsons, General Partner
Preferred Investment Size:

$5,000,000 to $25,000,000. Investment Policies: Prefer equity investments. Investment Types: Later stage, expansion, acquisitions. Industry Preferences: Diversified. Geographic Preferences: Entire U.S.

Cove Associates, Ltd.
19 Pine Hill Ave.
Norwalk, CT 06855
Phone: (203)866-5251
Fax: (203)866-4099
Preferred Investment Size: $500,000 to $5,000,000. Investment Types: Later stage and leveraged buyout. Industry Preferences: Internet related, consumer products and services, and food and beverage products. Geographic Preferences: National.

Connecticut Innovations, Inc.
Email: stephaniemitchell@ctinnovations.com
999 West St.
Rocky Hill, CT 06033
Phone: (860)563-5851
Fax: (860)563-4877
Preferred Investment Size: $100,000 minimum. Investment Types: Early and late stage. Industry Preferences: Diversified technology. Geographic Preferences: Connecticut.

Canaan Partners
105 Rowayton Ave.
Rowayton, CT 06853
Phone: (203)855-0400
Fax: (203)854-9117
Preferred Investment Size: $1,000,000 to $5,000,000. Investment Types: First and second stage, mezzanine, leveraged buyout, and acquisition financing. Industry Preferences: Diversified. Geographic Preferences: No preference.

First Connecticut Capital
1000 Bridgeport Ave.
Shelton, CT 06484
Phone: (203)944-5400
Free: (800)401-3222
Fax: (203)944-5405
A small business investment corporation.

Landmark Partners, Inc.
760 Hopmeadow St.

PO Box 188
Simsbury, CT 06070-0188
Phone: (860)651-9760
Fax: (860)651-8890
James P. McConnell, Partner
Preferred Investment Size: $500,000 to $5,000,000. Investment Types: Special situations. Industry Preferences: Communications. Geographic Preferences: National.

Baxter Associates, Inc.
PO Box 1333
Stamford, CT 06904
Phone: (203)323-3143
Fax: (203)348-0622
Preferred Investment Size: $100,000 to $500,000. Investment Types: Early and late stage. Industry Preferences: Radio and TV, franchise businesses, industrial and medical product distribution, chemicals and materials, genetic engineering, and specialty consulting. Geographic Preferences: National.

Collinson, Howe, and Lennox, LLC
1055 Washington Blvd. 5th Fl.
Stamford, CT 06901
Phone: (203)324-7700
Fax: (203)324-3636

Saugatuck Capital Co.
1 Canterbury Green
Stamford, CT 06901
Phone: (203)348-6669
Fax: (203)324-6995
Preferred Investment Size: $5,000,000 maximum. Investment Types: Second stage, mezzanine, leveraged buyout, special situations, and buyout or acquisition. Industry Preferences: Diversified. Geographic Preferences: Entire U.S.

Soundview Technology Group
22 Gatehouse Rd.
Stamford, CT 06902
Phone: (203)462-7200
Fax: (203)462-7350
Brian Bristol, Managing Director
Preferred Investment Size: $100,000 to $500,000. Investment Types: Late stage and mezzanine. Industry Preferences: Diversified information technology. Geographic Preferences: United States and Canada.

TSG Ventures, L.L.C.
177 Broad St., 12th Fl.
Stamford, CT 06901
Phone: (203)406-1500
Fax: (203)406-1590
Cleveland A. Christophe, Managing Partner
Preferred Investment Size: $5,000,000 to $10,000,000. Investment Types: Second stage and leveraged buyout. Industry Preferences: Diversified. Geographic Preferences: Entire U.S. and Canada.

Xerox Venture Capital (Stamford)
Email: xerox.com
Headquarters
800 Long Ridge Rd.
Stamford, CT 06904
Phone: (203)968-3000
Venture capital subsidiary of operating company. Prefers to invest in document processing industries.

The SBIC of Connecticut, Inc.
2 Corpoate Dr., Ste. 203
Trumbull, CT 06611
Phone: (203)261-0011
Fax: (203)459-1563
A small business investment corporation. No industry preference.

Marketcorp Venture Associates, L.P. (MCV)
274 Riverside Ave.
Westport, CT 06880
Phone: (203)226-2413
Fax: (203)222-6546
E. Bulkeley Griswold, General Partner
Preferred Investment Size: $250,000 to $1,000,000. Investment Types: First and second stage, mezzanine, and leveraged buyout. Industry Preferences: Consumer products and services. Geographic Preferences: Entire U.S.

Oak Investment Partners (Westport)
1 Gorham Island
Westport, CT 06880
Phone: (203)226-8346
Fax: (203)227-0372
Preferred Investment Size: $250,000 to $5,000,000. Investment Types: Seed, startup, first stage, leveraged

buyout, and special situations. Industry Preferences: Diversified technology. Geographic Preferences: No preference.

Oxford Bioscience Partners
315 Post Rd. W.
Westport, CT 06880-5200
Phone: (203)341-3300
Fax: (203)341-3300
William Greenman
Preferred Investment Size: $500,000 to $5,000,000. Investment Types: Seed, research and development, startup, first and second stage, and mezzanine. Industry Preferences: Genetic engineering and medical/health related. Geographic Preferences: Entire U.S.

Prince Ventures (Westport)
25 Ford Rd.
Westport, CT 06880
Phone: (203)227-8332
Fax: (203)226-5302
Preferred Investment Size: $500,000 to $1,000,000. Investment Types: Seed, startup, first and second stage, and leveraged buyout. Industry Preferences: Genetic engineering and medical/health related. Geographic Preferences: No preference.

Delaware

Delaware Economic Development Authority
99 Kings Hwy.
Dover, DE 19901
Phone: (302)739-4271
Free: (800)441-8846
Fax: (302)739-5749
Provides financing to new and expanding businesses at interest rates below the prime rate by issuing industrial revenue bonds (IRBs). Manufacturing and agricultural projects are eligible.

Blue Rock Capital.
5803 Kennett Pike, Ste. A
Wilmington, DE 19807
Phone: (302)426-0981
Fax: (302)426-0982
Preferred Investment Size: $250,000 to $3,000,000. Investment Types:

Early stage. Industry Preferences: Communication, computer, semiconductors, and education. Geographic Preferences: Northeast.

Delaware Innovation Fund
100 West 10th St., Ste. 413
Wilmington, DE 19801
Phone: (302)777-1616
Fax: (302)777-1620
David J. Freschman, President
Preferred Investment Size: $100,000 to $500,000. Investment Types: Early stage. Industry Preferences: Diversified technology. Geographic Preferences: Delaware.

PNC Capital Corp.
300 Delaware Ave., Ste. 304
Wilmington, DE 19801
Phone: (302)427-5895
Gary J. Zentner, President
Preferred Investment Size: $2 to $8 million. Investment Policies: Loans and/or equity. Investment Types: Expansion, later stage. Industry Preferences: No real estate or tax-oriented investments. Geographic Preferences: Northeast.

District of Columbia

Allied Capital Corp.
1919 Pennsylvania Ave., NW
Washington, DC 20006-3434
Phone: (202)331-2444
Fax: (202)659-2053
Preferred Investment Size: $3,000,000 to $25,000,000. Investment Types: Second stage, mezzanine, leveraged buyout, special situations, industry roll ups. Industry Preferences: Diversified. Geographic Preferences: No preference.

Atlantic Coastal Ventures, L.P.
3101 South St., N.W.
Washington, DC 20007
Phone: (202)293-1166
Fax: (202)293-1181
Preferred Investment Size: $1,000,000 to $2,000,000. Investment Types: Early and late stage. Industry Preferences: Communication and computer related. Geographic Preferences: East Coast.

Calvert Social Investment Fund
1918 18th St. NW, Ste. 22
Washington, DC 20009
Phone: (202)986-4272
Fax: (202)986-6950
Private venture capital partnership focusing on Mid-Atlantic companies involved in socially or environmentally beneficial products or services.

Columbia Capital Group, Inc.
1660 L St., N.W., Ste. 308
Washington, DC 20036
Phone: (202)775-8815
Fax: (202)223-0544
Erica Batie, Director of Investments
Preferred Investment Size: $100,000 to $250,000. Investment Types: Early and late stage, and mezzanine. Industry Preferences: Communication and computer related, consumer products and services, and education. Geographic Preferences: Washington, DC.

Helio Capital, Inc.
666 11th St., NW, Ste. 900
Washington, DC 20001
Phone: (202)272-3617
Fax: (202)504-2247
A minority enterprise small business investment corporation. No industry preference.

MultiMedia Broadcast Investment Corp.
Email: mbic@mmbic.com
3101 South Street NW
Washington, DC 20007
Phone: (202)293-1166
Fax: (202)293-1181
Preferred Investment Size: $100,000 to $1,000,000. Investment Types: Mezzanine, leveraged buyout, and special situations. Industry Preferences: Communications, computer scanning, and electronics equipment distribution. Geographic Preferences: No preference.

Plaza Street Capital, L.P.
Email: mfaber@mintz.com
701 Pennsylvania Ave. NW
Washington, DC 20004
Phone: (202)434-7319
Preferred Investment Size: $500,000

to $5,000,000. Investment Types: Early and late stage. Industry Preferences: Communication and computer related, consumer, distribution, electronics, genetic engineering, medical, and agriculture. Geographic Preferences: National.

Wachtel & Co., Inc.
1101 4th St., N.W.
Washington, DC 20005-5680
Phone: (202)898-1144
Preferred Investment Size: $100,000 to $250,000. Investment Types: Early and late stage. Industry Preferences: Diversified. Geographic Preferences: East Coast.

Florida

Sigma Capital Corp.
22668 Caravelle Circle
Boca Raton, FL 33433
Phone: (561368-9783
Preferred Investment Size: $250,000 to $1,000,000. Investment Types: Early and late stage. Industry Preferences: Diversified communication and computer, consumer products and services, distribution, electronics, genetic engineering, finance, and real estate. Geographic Preferences: Southeast.

North American Business Development Co., L.L.C.
312 SE 17th St., Ste.300
Ft. Lauderdale, FL 33316
Phone: (954)463-0681
Fax: (954)527-0904
PIS $2,000,000 to $16,000,000. Investment Types: Leveraged buyout, special situations, control block purchases, industry roll ups, and small business with growth potential. Industry Preferences: No preference. Geographic Preferences: Southeast and Midwest.

Adventure Capital Corp.
Email: corp@adventurecapital.com
PO Box 370531
Miami, FL 33137
Phone: (305)530-0046
Fax: (305)350-6826
Jeffrey M. Stoller, President

Preferred Investment Size: $100,000. Investment Types: Early stage. Industry Preferences: Communication and computer related, and consumer products and services. Geographic Preferences: National.

BAC Investment Corp.
6600 NW 27th Ave.
Miami, FL 33147
Fax: (305)693-7450
A minority enterprise small business investment company. Diversified industry preference.

J and D Capital Corp.
12747 Biscayne Blvd.
North Miami, FL 33181
Phone: (305)893-0303
Fax: (305)891-2338
A small business investment corporation. No industry preference.

PMC Investment Corp.
AmeriFirst Bank Bldg., 2nd Fl. S
18301 Biscayne Blvd.
North Miami Beach, FL 33160
Fax: (305)933-9410

Western Financial Capital Corp. (North Miami Beach)
AmeriFirst Bank Bldg., 2nd Fl. S
18301 Biscayne Blvd.
North Miami Beach, FL 33160
Fax: (305)933-9410
A small business investment company.

Bailey Capital
205 Worth Avenue, Ste. 201
Palm Beach, FL 33480
Phone: (561)366-9223
Fax: (561)833-5825
Preferred Investment Size: $250,000 to $1,000,000. Investment Types: Early and late stage. Industry Preferences: No preference. Geographic Preferences: Southeast.

Henry & Co.
8201 Peters Rd., Ste. 1000
Plantation, FL 33324
Phone: (954)797-7400
Preferred Investment Size: $500,000 to $1,000,000. Investment Types: Early stage. Industry Preferences: Healthcare industry. Geographic Preferences: West Coast.

Venture Capital Management Corp.
PO Box 2626
Satellite Beach, FL 32937
Phone: (407)777-1969
Preferred Investment Size: $100,000 to $250,000. Investment Types: Early and late stage. Industry Preferences: Diversified. Geographic Preferences: National.

Florida High Technology and Industry Council
Collins Bldg.
107 W. Gaines St., Rm. 315
Tallahassee, FL 32399-2000
Phone: (850)487-3136
Fax: (850)487-3014
Provides financing for research and development for high-tech businesses.

Financial Capital Resources, Inc.
3001 North Rocky Point Drive East, Ste. 200
Tampa, FL 33607
Phone: (813)281-5486
Preferred Investment Size: $1,000,000 to $5,000,000. Investment Types: Leveraged buyout. Industry Preferences: Financial services. Geographic Preferences: National.

Florida Venture Partners, Inc.
325 Florida Bank Plaza
100 W. Kennedy Blvd.
Tampa, FL 33602
Phone: (813)229-2294
Fax: (813)229-2028
Preferred Investment Size: $1,000,000 to $5,000,000. Investment Types: Startup, first and second stage. Industry Preferences: Diversified. Geographic Preferences: Southeast.

Market Capital Corp.
1102 N. 28th St.
PO Box 31667
Tampa, FL 33605
Fax: (813)248-9106
A small business investment corporation. Grocery industry preferred.

South Atlantic Venture Fund
Email: venture@southatlantic.com
614 W. Bay St.
Tampa, FL 33606-2704
Phone: (813)253-2500
Fax: (813)253-2360

Donald W. Burtonm Chairman and Managing Director
Preferred Investment Size: $1,500,000 to $7,500,000. Investment Types: Startup, first and second stage, mezzanine, special situations, and control block purchases. Industry Preferences: Diversified. Geographic Preferences: Southeast, Middle Atlantic, and Texas.

Allied Financial Services Corp. (Vero Beach)
Executive Office Center, Ste. 300
2770 N. Indian River Blvd.
Vero Beach, FL 32960
Phone: (561)778-5556
Fax: (561)569-9303
A minority enterprise small business investment company.

LM Capital Corp.
120 South Olive, Ste. 400
West Palm Beach, FL 33401
Phone: (561)833-9700
Fax: (561)655-6587
Preferred Investment Size: $1,000,000 to $5,000,000. Investment Types: Leveraged buyout. Industry Preferences: Diversified consumer products and services.

Georgia

Venture First Associates
4811 Thornwood Dr.
Acworth, GA 30102
Phone: (770)928-3733
Fax: (770)928-6455
Preferred Investment Size: $500,000 to $5,000,000. Investment Types: Seed, startup, first and second stage. Industry Preferences: Diversified technology and consumer products and services. Geographic Preferences: Southeast.

Cordova Capital
2500 North Winds Pkwy., Ste. 475
Alpharetta, GA 30004
Phone: (678)942-0300
Fax: (678)942-0301
Charles E. Adair, General Partner
Preferred Investment Size: $1,000,000 to $5,000,000. Investment Policies: Equity and/or debt. Invest-

ment Types: Second stage and mezzanine. Industry Preferences: Diversified. Geographic Preferences: Southeast.

Advanced Technology Development Fund
1000 Abernathy Rd., Ste. 1420
Atlanta, GA 30328
Phone: (770)668-2333
Fax: (770)668-2330
Venture capital firm providing start-up, first stage, second stage expansion, purchase or secondary positions, and buyout or acquisition financing. Areas of interest include information processing, health care and specialized mobile radio.

Alliance Technology Ventures
Email: info@atv.com
3343 Peachtree Rd., N.E.
East Tower, Ste. 1140
Atlanta, GA 30326
Phone: (404)816-4791
Fax: (404)816-4891
Preferred Investment Size: $250,000 to $1,000,000. Investment Types: Early and late stage. Industry Preferences: Diversified technology. Geographic Preferences: Southeast.

Arete Ventures, L.L.C.
115 Perimeter Center Pl., Ste. 640
Atlanta, GA 30346
Phone: (770)399-1660
Fax: (770)399-1664
Preferred Investment Size: $500,000 to $5,000,000. Investment Types: Startup, first and second stage, and leveraged buyout. Industry Preferences: Electric and gas utility industry. Geographic Preferences: No preference.

CGW Southeast Partners
12 Piedmont Center, Ste. 210
Atlanta, GA 30305
Phone: (404)816-3255
Fax: (404)816-3258
Richard L. Cravey, Managing Partner
Preferred Investment Size: $3,000,000 to $7,000,000. Investment Types: Leveraged buyout. Industry Preferences: Diversified. Geographic Preferences: Southeastern U.S. and Canada.

EGL Holdings, Inc.
3495 Piedmont Rd., Bldg. 10, Ste. 412
Atlanta, GA 30305
Phone: (404)949-8300
Fax: (404)949-8311
Salvatore A. Massaro, Partner
Preferred Investment Size: $1,000,000 to $2,000,000. Investment Types: Mezzanine, leveraged buyout, industry roll ups, and development capital. Industry Preferences: Diversified. Geographic Preferences: Southeast and East Coast.

Equity Capital Partners, Inc.
Email: ecp@mindspring.com
4330 Georgetown Sq., Ste. 502
Atlanta, GA 30338
Phone: (770)458-9966
Fax: (770)451-4408
Katie Goodman, Marketing Associate
Preferred Investment Size: $750,000 to $4,000,000. Investment Types: Late stage, recaps, and industry roll ups. Industry Preferences: Diversified communication and computer technology, consumer products and services, distribution, electronics, and publishing. Geographic Preferences: Southeast, Southwest, Midwest, and East Coast.

Equity South Advisors
1790 The Lenox Bldg.
3399 Peachtree Rd., NE
Atlanta, GA 30326
Phone: (404)237-6222
Fax: (404)261-1578
Douglas L. Diamond, Managing Director
Preferred Investment Size: $2,000,000 to $3,000,000. Investment Types: Mezzanine, leveraged buyout, and control block purchases. Industry Preferences: Diversified. Geographic Preferences: Northeast, Southeast, Southwest, and East Coast.

Frontline Capital, Inc.
3475 Lenox Rd., Ste. 400
Atlanta, GA 30326
Phone: (404)240-7280
Fax: (404)240-7281
Preferred Investment Size: $500,000 to $5,000,000. Investment Types:

Early stage. Industry Preferences: Diversified communication and computer technology, consumer products and services, distribution, electronics, and publishing. Geographic Preferences: Southeast.

Georgia Department of Community Affairs
Community and Economic Development Division
60 Executive Park South NE
Atlanta, GA 30329-2231
Phone: (404)679-4940
Fax: (404)679-0669
Provides assistance in applying for state and federal grants.

Green Capital Investors L.P.
3343 Peachtree Rd., Ste. 1420
Atlanta, GA 30326
Phone: (404)261-1187
Fax: (404)266-8677
Venture capital firm providing purchase or secondary positions and buyout or acquisition financing.

Noro-Moseley Partners
4200 Northside Pkwy., Bldg. 9
Atlanta, GA 30327
Phone: (404)233-1966
Fax: (404)239-9280
Preferred Investment Size: $1,000,000 to $5,000,000. Investment Types: Startup, first and second stage, mezzanine, leveraged buyout, special situations, and control block purchases. Industry Preferences: No preference. Geographic Preferences: Southeast.

Premier HealthCare
Email: BoxBenjamin@convene.com
3414 Peachtree Rd., Ste. 238
Atlanta, GA 30326
Phone: (404)816-0049
Fax: (404)816-0248
Venture capital firm providing start-up, first stage, second stage expansion, late stage expansion, purchase or secondary positions, and buyout or acquisition financing. Areas of interest include health care.

Renaissance Capital Corp.
34 Peachtree St. NW, Ste. 2230

Atlanta, GA 30303
Phone: (404)658-9061
Fax: (404)658-9064
Preferred Investment Size: $200,000 to $450,000. Investment Types: Second stage, mezzanine, and leveraged buyout. Industry Preferences: Diversified. Geographic Preferences: Southeast.

River Capital, Inc.
Two Midtown Plaza
1360 Peachtree St. NE, Ste. 1430
Atlanta, GA 30309
Phone: (404)873-2166
Fax: (404)873-2158
Jerry D. Wethington
Preferred Investment Size: $1,000,000 to $15,000,000. Investment Types: Mezzanine and leveraged buyout. Industry Preferences: Diversified. Geographic Preferences: Southeast, Southwest, East Coast, Midwest, Gulf States, and Middle Atlantic.

Seaboard Management Corp.
3400 Peachtree Rd. NE, Ste. 741
Atlanta, GA 30326
Phone: (404)239-6270
Fax: (404)239-6284
Venture capital firm providing first stage and second stage expansion financing. Areas of interest include manufacturing and telecommunications.

UPS Strategic Enterprise Fund
Email: unk1jpc@is.ups.com
55 Glenlake Pkwy., N.E.
Atlanta, GA 30328
Phone: (404)828-7082
Fax: (404)828-8088
Preferred Investment Size: $100,000 to $1,000,000. Investment Types: Early and late stage. Industry Preferences: Diversified communication and computer technology, distribution, electronics, and transportation. Geographic Preferences: United States and Canada.

Johnson Industries, Inc. (Rockville)
105 13th St.
Columbus, GA 31901
Phone: (706)641-3140

Fax: (706)641-3159
Haywood Miller, Manager
Preferred Investment Size: $1,000,000. Investment Policies: Subordinated debt with warrant. Investment Types: Expansion, later stage. Industry Preferences: Diversified. Geographic Preferences: National.

First Growth Capital, Inc.
Best Western Plz.
I-75 Georgia 42N Exit 63
Forsyth, GA 31029
Phone: (912)994-9260
Free: (800)447-3241
Fax: (912)994-9260
A minority enterprise small business investment company. Diversified industry preference.

North Riverside Capital Corp.
Email: Tom.Barry.Mighty.com
50 Technology Park/Atlanta
Norcross, GA 30092
Phone: (770)446-5556
Fax: (770)446-8627
A small business investment corporation. No industry preference.

Hawaii

Hawaii Agriculture Department
PO Box 22159
Honolulu, HI 96823-2159
Phone: (808)973-9600
Fax: (808)973-9613
Provides information and advice in such areas as marketing, production, and labeling. Administers loan programs, including the New Farmer Loan Program, the Emergency Loan Program, and the Aquaculture Loan Program.

Hawaii Department of Business, Economic Development, and Tourism
Financial Assistance Branch
1 Capital District Bldg.
250 S. Hotel St., Ste. 503
PO Box 2359
Honolulu, HI 96804
Phone: (808)586-2576
Fax: (808)587-3832
Provides loans to small businesses, including the Hawaii Capital Loan

Program and the Hawaii Innovation Development Loan Program.

Pacific Century SBIC
130 Merchant St.
Honolulu, HI 96813
Phone: (808)537-8286
Fax: (808)537-8557
Preferred Investment Size: $100,000 to $250,000. Investment Types: Second stage, mezzanine, leveraged buyout, and special situations. Industry Preferences: Computer related, communications, consumer related, distribution, electronics, genetic engineering, and medical/health related. Geographic Preferences: Hawaii.

Pacific Venture Capital Ltd.
222 S. Vineyard St., No. PH-1
Honolulu, HI 96813-2445
Phone: (808)521-6502
Free: (800)455-1888
Fax: (808)521-6541
A minority enterprise small business investment corporation.

Illinois

Open Prairie Ventures
Email: inquire@openprairie.com
115 North Neil St., Ste. 209
Champaign, IL 61820
Phone: (217)351-7000
Fax: (217)351-7051
Dennis D. Spice, Managing Member
Preferred Investment Size: $250,000 to $3,000,000. Investment Types: Seed and startup. Industry Preferences: Diversified communication and computer technology, distribution, electronics, and genetic engineering. Geographic Preferences: Midwest.

ABN AMRO Capital Private Equity
208 S. La Salle St., 10th Fl.
Chicago, IL 60604
Phone: (312)855-7079
Fax: (312)553-6648
David Bogetz, Managing Director
Preferred Investment Size: $1,000,000 maximum. Investment Types: First and second stage, mezzanine, leveraged buyout, and

special situations. Industry Preferences: Diversified. Geographic Preferences: Entire U.S.

Alpha Capital Partners, Ltd.
Email: acp@alphacapital.com
122 S. Michigan Ave., Ste. 1700
Chicago, IL 60603
Phone: (312)322-9800
Fax: (312)322-9808
Preferred Investment Size: $500,000 maximum. Investment Types: First and second stage, leveraged buyout, and special situations. Industry Preferences: Diversified. Geographic Preferences: Midwest.

Ameritech Development Corp.
30 S. Wacker Dr., 37th Fl.
Chicago, IL 60606
Phone: (312)750-5083
Fax: (312)609-0244
Craig Lee, Director
Preferred Investment Size: $500,000 to $1,000,000. Investment Types: Startup, first and second stage. Industry Preferences: Communications, computer related, and electronics. Geographic Preferences: Entire U.S.

Apex Investment Partners
Email: apex@apexvc.com
233 South Wacker Pkwy., Ste. 9500
Chicago, IL 60606
Phone: (312)258-0320
Fax: (312)258-0592
Preferred Investment Size: $500,000 to $7,000,000. Investment Types: Early and late stage. Industry Preferences: Diversified communication and computer technology, consumer products and services, distribution, electronics, and education. Geographic Preferences: United States and Canada.

Arch Venture Partners
8735 West Higgins Rd., Ste. 235
Chicago, IL 60631
Phone: (773)380-6600
Fax: (773)380-6606
Steven Lazarus, Managing Director
Preferred Investment Size: $100,000 to $1,000,000. Investment Types: Early stage. Industry Preferences:

Diversified communication and computer technology, electronics, and genetic engineering. Geographic Preferences: National.

Batterson, Johnson and Wang Venture Partners
Email: bvp@vcapital.com
303 W. Madison St., Ste. 1110
Chicago, IL 60606-3309
Phone: (312)269-0300
Fax: (312)269-0021
Preferred Investment Size: $100,000 to $1,000,000. Investment Types: Seed, startup, first and second stage, mezzanine, and leveraged buyout. Industry Preferences: Diversified. Geographic Preferences: Entire U.S.

William Blair Capital Partners, L.L.C.
Email: privateequity@wmblair.com
222 W. Adams St., Ste. 1300
Chicago, IL 60606
Phone: (312)364-8250
Fax: (312)236-1042
Maureen Maddy, Office Manager
Preferred Investment Size: $2,000,000 to $30,000,000. Investment Types: First and second stage, and leveraged buyout. Industry Preferences: Communications, computer related, consumer, electronics, energy/natural resources, genetic engineering, and medical/health related. Geographic Preferences: Entire U.S.

Brinson Partners, Inc.
209 S. LaSalle, Ste. 114
Chicago, IL 60604-1295
Phone: (312)220-7100
Fax: (312)220-7110
Terry Gould, Executive Director
Preferred Investment Size: $1,000,000 to $2,000,000. Investment Types: First and second stage, and leveraged buyout. Industry Preferences: Diversified. Geographic Preferences: No preference.

Business Ventures, Inc.
20 N. Wacker Dr., Ste. 1741
Chicago, IL 60606-2904
Phone: (312)346-1580
Fax: (312)346-6693
A small business investment corpora-

tion. No industry preference; considers only ventures in the Chicago area.

Capital Health Venture Partners
20 N. Wacker Dr. Ste. 2200
Chicago, IL 60606
Phone: (312)782-7560
Fax: (312)726-2290
Investments limited to early stage medical, biotech, and health care related companies.

The Capital Strategy Management Co.
233 South Wacker Pkwy.
Box 06334
Chicago, IL 60606
Phone: (312)444-1170
Preferred Investment Size: $200,000 to $10,000,000. Investment Types: Early and late stage, leveraged buyout, and special situations. Industry Preferences: Diversified communication and computer technology, consumer products and services, distribution, electronics, and education. Geographic Preferences: Within two hours of office.

The Combined Fund, Inc.
7936 S. Cottage Grove
Chicago, IL 60619
Phone: (773)371-7030
Fax: (773)371-7035
A minority enterprise small business investment company. Diversified industry preference.

Continental Illinois Venture Corp.
231 S. LaSalle St., Seventh Fl.
Chicago, IL 60697
Phone: (312)828-8021
Fax: (312)987-0763
Gregory W. Wilson, Managing Director
Preferred Investment Size: $5,000,000 maximum. Investment Types: Leveraged buyout, special situations, control block purchases, industry consolidation. Industry Preferences: Diversified. Geographic Preferences: Entire U.S.

Environmental Private Equity Fund II, L.P.
233 South Wacker Pkwy., Ste. 9500

First Analysis Corp.
Chicago, IL 60606-3103
Phone: (312)258-1400
Fax: (312)258-0334
Preferred Investment Size: $250,000 to $5,000,000. Investment Types: Early and late stage, leveraged buyout, and special situations. Industry Preferences: Diversified communication and computer technology, consumer products and services, electronics, and natural resources. Geographic Preferences: National.

Essex Woodlands Health Ventures, L.P.
190 S. LaSalle St., Ste. 2800
Chicago, IL 60603
Phone: (312)444-6040
Fax: (312)444-6034
Marc S. Sandroff, Managing Director
Preferred Investment Size: $1,000,000 to $12,000,000. Investment Types: Startup and first stage. Industry Preferences: Healthcare. Geographic Preferences: No preference.

First Analysis Corp.
233 S. Wacker Dr., Ste. 9500
Chicago, IL 60606
Phone: (312)258-1400
Fax: (312)258-0334
Bret Maxwell, Managing Director
Preferred Investment Size: $1,000,000 to $10,000,000. Investment Types: Startup, first and second stage, leveraged buyout, special situations, and industry roll ups. Industry Preferences: Diversified. Geographic Preferences: No preference.

Frontenac Co.
135 S. LaSalle St., Ste.3800
Chicago, IL 60603
Phone: (312)368-0044
Fax: (312)368-9520
Preferred Investment Size: $10,000,000 to $50,000,000. Investment Types: Leveraged buyout and industry roll ups. Industry Preferences: Diversified. Geographic Preferences: Entire U.S.

GTCR Golder Rauner, LLC
6100 Sears Tower
Chicago, IL 60606
Phone: (312)382-2200
Fax: (312)382-2201
Bruce V. Rauner
Preferred Investment Size: $10,000,000 maximum. Investment Types: Leveraged buyout, special situations, and industry consolidations. Industry Preferences: Diversified. Geographic Preferences: No preference.

IEG Venture Management, Inc.
70 West Madison
Chicago, IL 60602
Phone: (312)644-0890
Fax: (312)454-0369
Preferred Investment Size: $100,000 to $500,000. Investment Types: Seed, startup, first and second stage. Industry Preferences: Diversified. Geographic Preferences: Midwest.

Illinois Development Finance Authority
Sears Tower
233 S. Wacker Dr., Ste. 5310
Chicago, IL 60606
Phone: (312)793-5586
Fax: (312)793-6347
Provides bond, venture capital, and direct loan programs.

JK&B Capital
Email: gspencer@jkbcapital.com
205 North Michigan Ave., Ste. 808
Chicago, IL 60601
Phone: (312)946-1200
Preferred Investment Size: $500,000 to $5,000,000. Investment Types: Early and late stage, and mezzanine. Industry Preferences: Diversified communication and computer technology, consumer products and services, distribution, electronics, and finance and insurance. Geographic Preferences: National.

Linc Capital, Inc.
Email: bdemars@linccap.com
303 East Wacker Pkwy., Ste. 1000
Chicago, IL 60601
Phone: (312)946-1000
Fax: (312)938-4290

Martin E. Zimmerman, Chairman
Preferred Investment Size: $250,000
to $5,000,000. Investment Types:
Early and late stage, mezzanine, and
special situations. Industry Preferences: Diversified communication
and computer technology, distribution, electronics, and finance and
insurance. Geographic Preferences:
National.

Madison Dearborn Partners, Inc.
Email: invest@mdcp.com
3 1st National Plz., Ste. 3800
Chicago, IL 60602
Phone: (312)895-1000
Fax: (312)895-1001
Preferred Investment Size:
$20,000,000 to $200,000,000.
Investment Types: Leveraged buyout,
special situations, control block
purchases, and industry roll ups.
Industry Preferences: Diversified.
Geographic Preferences: Entire U.S.
and Canada.

Mesirow Capital Partners SBIC, Ltd.
350 N. Clark St.
Chicago, IL 60610
Phone: (312)595-6099
Fax: (312)595-6211
Thomas E. Galuhn, Senior Managing
Director
Preferred Investment Size:
$1,000,000 to $5,000,000. Investment
Types: Second stage, mezzanine,
leveraged buyout, and later-stage
financing. Industry Preferences:
Diversified. Geographic Preferences:
Entire U.S.

Polestar Capital, Inc.
180 N. Michigan Ave., Ste. 1905
Chicago, IL 60601
Phone: (312)984-9090
Fax: (312)984-9877
Preferred Investment Size: $250,000
to $1,000,000. Investment Policies:
Primarily equity. Investment Types:
Early to later stages. Industry Prefer-
ences: Diversified. Geographic
Preferences: Entire U.S.

Prince Ventures (Chicago)
10 S. Wacker Dr., Ste. 2575
Chicago, IL 60606-7407

Phone: (312)454-1408
Fax: (312)454-9125
Preferred Investment Size: $500,000
to $1,000,000. Investment Types:
Seed, startup, first and second stage,
leveraged buyout. Industry Preferences: Genetic engineering and
medical/health related. Geographic
Preferences: No preference.

Shorebank Capital Corp.
7936 S. Cottage Grove
Chicago, IL 60619
Phone: (773)371-7030
Fax: (773)371-7035
A minority enterprise small business
investment corporation providing
second stage, buyout, and acquisition
financing to companies in the
Midwest. Diversified industry
preference.

Third Coast Capital
Email: manic@earthlink.com
900 North Franklin St., Ste. 850
Chicago, IL 60610
Phone: (312)337-3303
Fax: (312)337-2567
Preferred Investment Size: $500,000
to $5,000,000. Investment Policies:
Venture leasing. Investment Types:
Early and late stage, and special
situations. Industry Preferences:
Diversified communication and
computer technology, consumer
franchise businesses, distribution,
electronics, and finance and insur-
ance. Geographic Preferences:
National.

Wind Point Partners (Chicago)
676 N. Michigan Ave., No. 3300
Chicago, IL 60611
Phone: (312)649-4000
Preferred Investment Size:
$1,000,000 to $5,000,000. Investment
Types: Startup, first stage, leveraged
buyout, and special situations.
Industry Preferences: Diversified.
Geographic Preferences: Midwest.

Marquette Venture Partners
520 Lake Cook Rd., Ste. 450
Deerfield, IL 60015
Phone: (847)940-1700
Fax: (847)940-1724

Preferred Investment Size: $500,000
to $5,000,000. Investment Types:
Startup, first and second stage.
Industry Preferences: Diversified.
Geographic Preferences: Entire U.S.

Evanston Business Investment Corp.
Email: t-parkinson@nwu.com
1840 Oak Avenue
Evanston, IL 60201
Phone: (847)866-1840
Fax: (847)866-1808
Preferred Investment Size: $250,000
to $500,000. Investment Types: Early
stage. Industry Preferences: Diversified communication and computer
technology, consumer products and
services, distribution, electronics, and
education. Geographic Preferences:
Within two hours of office.

The Cerulean Fund/WGC Associates,
Inc.
Email: walnet@aol.com
1701 E. Lake Ave., Ste. 170
Glenview, IL 60025
Phone: (847)657-8002
Fax: (847)657-8168
Walter G. Cornett, III, Managing
Director
Preferred Investment Size:
$3,000,000 to $50,000,000. Invest-
ment Types: Leveraged buyout,
special situations, control block
purchases, and consolidation. Industry
Preferences: Diversified. Geographic
Preferences: Midwest, entire U.S. for
leverage buyouts or consolidations.

Tower Ventures, Inc.
Sears Tower, BSC 23-27
3333 Beverly Holtman St., Ste.
AC254A
Hoffman Estates, IL 60179
Fax: (847)906-0164
A minority enterprise small business
investment company. Diversified
industry preference.

Ventana Financial Resources, Inc.
249 Market Square
Lake Forest, IL 60045
Phone: (847)234-3434
Preferred Investment Size: $100,000
to $1,000,000. Investment Types:
Early and late stage, and mezzanine.

Industry Preferences: Diversified communication and computer technology, consumer products and services, distribution, electronics, natural resources, genetic engineering, and healthcare. Geographic Preferences: Midwest, Southeast, and Southwest.

Allstate Private Equity
3075 Sanders Rd., Ste. G5D
Northbrook, IL 60062-7127
Phone: (847)402-8247
Fax: (847)402-0880
William E. Engbers, Director
Preferred Investment Size: $5,000,000 maximum. Investment Types: Startup, first and second stage, mezzanine, leveraged buyout, and special situations. Industry Preferences: Diversified. Geographic Preferences: Entire U.S.

Graystone Venture Partners, L.L.C.
One Northfield Plaza, Ste. 530
Northfield, IL 60093
Phone: (847)446-9460
Fax: (847)446-9470
Mathew B. McCall, Vice President
Preferred Investment Size: $250,000 to $3,000,000. Investment Types: Early and late stage. Industry Preferences: Diversified communication and computer technology, consumer products and services, distribution, electronics, genetic engineering, and education. Geographic Preferences: National.

Caterpillar Venture Capital, Inc.
100 NE Adams St.
Peoria, IL 61629
Phone: (309)675-1000
Fax: (309)675-4457
Venture capital subsidiary of operating firm.

Cilcorp Ventures, Inc.
300 Hamilton Blvd., Ste. 300
Peoria, IL 61602
Phone: (309)675-8850
Fax: (309)675-8800
Invests in environmental services only.

Comdisco Ventures Group
(Rosemont)
6111 N. River Rd.
Rosemont, IL 60018
Phone: (847)698-3000
Free: (800)321-1111
Fax: (847)518-5440
Preferred Investment Size: $250,000 to $500,000. Investment Types: Seed, startup, first and second stage, receivables, loans, and equipment leases. Industry Preferences: Diversified. Geographic Preferences: No preference.

Indiana

Cambridge Ventures, L.P.
8440 Woodfield Crossing Blvd., No. 315
Indianapolis, IN 46240
Phone: (317)469-3927
Fax: (317)469-3926
Jean Wojtowicz, President
Preferred Investment Size: $100,000 maximum. Investment Types: Second stage, mezzanine, and leveraged buyout. Industry Preferences: No preference. Geographic Preferences: Midwest, within 200 miles of office.

CID Equity Partners
One American Square, Ste. 2850
Box 82074
Indianapolis, IN 46282
Phone: (317)269-2350
Fax: (317)269-2355
Chris Gough, Associate
Preferred Investment Size: $1,000,000 to $5,000,000. Investment Types: Early and late stage, and special situations. Industry Preferences: Diversified communication and computer technology, distribution, electronics, genetic engineering, natural resources, and finance and insurance. Geographic Preferences: Midwest.

Circle Ventures, Inc.
26 N. Arsenal Ave.
Indianapolis, IN 46201-3808
Phone: (317)636-7242
Fax: (317)637-7581
A small business investment corpora-

tion. Prefers second-stage, leveraged buy out, and growth financings. Geographical preference is Indianapolis.

Indiana Business Modernization and Technology Corp.
1 N. Capitol Ave., Ste. 925
Indianapolis, IN 46204
Phone: (317)635-3058
Free: (800)877-5182
Fax: (317)231-7095
Invests in and counsels applied research ventures.

Indiana Development Finance Authority
1 N. Capitol Ave., Ste. 320
Indianapolis, IN 46204
Phone: (317)233-4332
Fax: (317)232-6786
Administers the Ag Finance, Export Finance, Loan Guarantee, and Industrial Development Bond Financing Programs.

Tier 4 Partners, L.L.C.
2421 Production Pkwy., Ste. 111
Indianapolis, IN 46241
Phone: (317)244-7429
Fax: (317)244-6401
David A. Shaw, CEO
Preferred Investment Size: $250,000 to $1,000,000. Investment Types: Early and late stage, and leveraged buyout. Industry Preferences: No preference. Geographic Preferences: Midwest, East and West Coast.

First Source Capital Corp.
100 North Michigan St.
PO Box 1602
South Bend, IN 46601
Phone: (219)235-2180
Fax: (219)235-2227
Eugene L. Cavanaugh, Vice President
Preferred Investment Size: $200,000 maximum. Investment Types: Second stage, mezzanine, leveraged buyout, and special situations. Industry Preferences: Diversified. Geographic Preferences: Midwest.

Thomas Lowe Ventures
3600 McGill St., Ste. 300
PO Box 3688
South Bend, IN 46628

Phone: (219)232-0300
Fax: (219)232-0500
Venture capital firm preferring to invest in the toy industry.

Iowa

Allsop Venture Partners (Cedar Rapids)
2750 1st Ave. NE, Ste. 210
Cedar Rapids, IA 52402
Phone: (319)363-8971
Fax: (319)363-9519

InvestAmerica Investment Advisors, Inc.
101 2nd St. SE, Ste. 800
Cedar Rapids, IA 52401
Phone: (319)363-8249
Fax: (319)363-9683
Preferred Investment Size: $750,000 to $2,000,000. Investment Types: First and second stage, leveraged buyout, and special situations. Industry Preferences: Diversified. Geographic Preferences: Entire U.S.

Marshall Venture Capital
118 Third Avenue S.E., Ste. 837
Cedar Rapids, IA 52401
Phone: (319)368-6675
Fax: (319)363-9515
Preferred Investment Size: $250,000 to $750,000. Investment Policies: Equity. Investment Types: Early and late stage, and special situations. Industry Preferences: Diversified communication and computer technology, consumer products and services, distribution, electronics, animal biotechnology, healthcare, and education. Geographic Preferences: National.

Equity Dinamics
2116 Financial Center
Des Moines, IA 50309
Phone: (515)244-5746
Fax: (515)244-2346
Joe Dunham, Vice President
Preferred Investment Size: $250,000 to $5,000,000. Investment Policies: Equity. Investment Types: Early and late stage, and special situations. Industry Preferences: Diversified communication and computer

technology, electronics, genetic engineering, and healthcare. Geographic Preferences: National.

Iowa Department of Economic Development
Iowa New Jobs Training Program
150 Des Moines St.
Des Moines, IA 50309
Phone: (515)281-9328
Fax: (515)281-9033
Reimburses new or expanding companies for up to 50 percent of new employees' salaries and benefits for up to one year of on-the-job training. Coordinated through the state's 15 community colleges.

Iowa Department of Economic Development
Division of Financial Assistance
200 E. Grand Ave.
Des Moines, IA 50309
Phone: (515)242-4819
Fax: (515)242-4819
Bestows grants from the U.S. Department of Housing and Urban Development to help finance community improvements and job-generating expansions. Funds are primarily awarded on a competitive basis.

Iowa Department of Economic Development
International Division
200 E. Grand Ave.
Des Moines, IA 50309
Phone: (515)242-4700
Fax: (515)242-4918
Provides funding to qualified exporters of Iowa-manufactured and processed products.

Iowa Department of Economic Development
Bureau of Business Finance
Iowa Dept. of Economic Development
Self-Employment Loan Program
Des Moines, IA 50309
Phone: (515)242-4793
Fax: (515)242-4749
Provides low-interest loans for low-income entrepreneurs who are expanding or starting a new business.

Iowa Finance Authority
100 E. Grand Ave., Ste. 250
Des Moines, IA 50309
Phone: (515)242-4990
Fax: (515)242-4957
Provides loans to new and expanding small businesses. Funds may be used to purchase land, construction, building improvements, or equipment; loans cannot be used for working capital, inventory, or operations.

Pappajohn Capital Resources
2116 Financial Center
Des Moines, IA 50309
Phone: (515)244-5746
Fax: (515)244-2346
Joe Dunham, President
Preferred Investment Size: $100,000 to $250,000. Investment Policies: Equity. Investment Types: Early and late stage, and special situations. Industry Preferences: Diversified communication and computer technology, electronics, genetic engineering, and healthcare. Geographic Preferences: National.

Kansas

Allsop Venture Partners (Overland Park)
6602 W. 131st. St.
Overland Park, KS 66209
Phone: (913)338-0820
Fax: (913)681-5535

Enterprise Capital Management, Inc.
7400 West 110th St., Ste. 560
Overland Park, KS 66210
Phone: (913)327-8500
Fax: (913)327-8505
Preferred Investment Size: $500,000 to $1,000,000. Investment Types: Late stage and special situations. Geographic Preferences: Midwest.

Kansas Venture Capital, Inc. (Overland Park)
Email: jdalton@kvci.com
6700 Antioch Plz., Ste. 460
Overland Park, KS 66204
Phone: (913)262-7117
Fax: (913)262-3509
John S. Dalton, President
Preferred Investment Size: $250,000

to $1,500,000. Investment Types: First and second stage, mezzanine, leveraged buyout, turnaround, and recapitalization. Industry Preferences: Diversified. Real estate, oil and gas, and finance and insurance not considered. Geographic Preferences: Kansas.

Kansas City Equity Partners
4200 Somerset Dr., Ste. 101
Prairie Village, KS 66208
Fax: (913)649-2125
Paul H. Henson, Manager
Preferred Investment Size: $500,000 to $2 million. Investment Policies: Equity. Investment Types: Seed, early stage, expansion. Industry Preferences: Diversified. Geographic Preferences: Midwest.

Kansas Department of Housing and Commerce
Division of Community Development
700 SW Harrison, Ste. 1300
Topeka, KS 66603
Phone: (785)296-3485
Fax: (785)296-0186
Administers Community Development Block Grants and the enterprise zone program, in which businesses receive tax credits and exemptions for locating in targeted areas.

Kansas Development Finance Authority
700 SW Jackson
Jayhawk Tower, Ste. 1000
Topeka, KS 66603
Phone: (785)296-6747
Fax: (785)296-6810
Dedicated to improving access to capital financing to business enterprises through the issuance of bonds.

Kansas Technology Enterprise Corp.
Email: ktec@ktec.com
214 SW 6th, 1st Fl.
Topeka, KS 66603-3719
Phone: (785)296-5272
Fax: (785)296-1160
Preferred Investment Size: $50,000 to $500,000. Investment Types: Early stage. Industry Preferences: Diversified communication and computer technology, electronics, genetic

engineering, and healthcare. Geographic Preferences: Within two hours of office.

Kentucky

Kentucky Cabinet for Economic Development
Financial Incentives Department
Capitol Plaza Tower
500 Mero St., 24th Fl.
Frankfort, KY 40601
Phone: (502)564-4554
Fax: (502)564-7697
Provides loans to supplement private financing. Offers two major programs: issuance of industrial revenue bonds; and second mortgage loans to private firms in participation with other lenders. Also has a Crafts Guaranteed Loan Program providing loans up to $20,000 to qualified craftspersons, and a Commonwealth Venture Capital Program, encouraging the establishment or expansion of small business and industry.

Mountain Ventures, Inc.
362 Old Whitley Rd.
PO Box 1738
London, KY 40743-1738
Phone: (606)864-5175
Fax: (606)864-5194
A small business investment corporation. No industry preference; geographic area limited to southeast Kentucky.

Chrysalis Ventures, L.L.C.
Email:
bobsany@chrysalisventures.com
1850 National City Tower
Louisville, KY 40202
Phone: (502)583-7644
Fax: (502)583-7648
Preferred Investment Size: $500,000 to $5,000,000. Investment Types: Early and late stage. Industry Preferences: Diversified communication and computer technology, distribution, healthcare, and education. Geographic Preferences: Southeast and Midwest.

Equal Opportunity Finance, Inc.
420 S. Hurstbourne Pkwy., Ste. 201

Louisville, KY 40222-8002
Phone: (502)423-1943
Fax: (502)423-1945
A minority enterprise small business investment corporation. No industry preference; geographic areas limited to Indiana, Kentucky, Ohio, and West Virginia.

Humana Venture Capital
Email: gemont@humana.com
500 West Main St.
Louisville, KY 40202
Phone: (502)580-3922
Fax: (502)580-2051
George Emont, Director
Preferred Investment Size: $500,000 to $5,000,000. Investment Types: Early and late stage. Industry Preferences: Healthcare. Geographic Preferences: National.

Management Alternatives, Inc.
Summit Capital Group, Inc.
418 Knightsbridge Rd., Ste. 2
Louisville, KY 40206
Phone: (502)897-7733
Fax: (502)897-5838
Preferred Investment Size: $100,000 to $250,000. Investment Types: Early and late stage, and special situations. Industry Preferences: Communications, computer services, consumer products and services, distribution, forestry and fishing, and healthcare. Geographic Preferences: United States and Canada.

Louisiana

Bank One Equity Investors, Inc.
451 Florida St.
Baton Rouge, LA 70801
Phone: (504)332-4421
Fax: (504)332-7377
Preferred Investment Size: $1,000,000 to $15,000,000. Investment Types: First and second stage, mezzanine, leveraged buyout, and special situations. Industry Preferences: Diversified. Geographic Preferences: Southeast, Southwest, and Gulf states.

Louisiana Department of Economic Development

Email:
marketing@mail.lded.state.la.us
PO Box 94185
Baton Rouge, LA 70804-9185
Phone: (504)342-3000
Fax: (504)342-5389

S.C.D.F. Investment Corp., Inc.
PO Box 3885
Lafayette, LA 70502
Phone: (318)232-7672
Fax: (318)232-5094
A minority enterprise small business
investment corporation. No industry
preference.

Advantage Capital Partners
LLE Tower
909 Poydras St., Ste. 2230
New Orleans, LA 70112
Phone: (504)522-4850
Fax: (504)522-4950
Steven T. Stull, President and
Managing Director
Preferred Investment Size:
$1,000,000 to $6,000,000. Investment
Types: Early and late stage, and
special situations. Industry Prefer-
ences: Diversified. Geographic
Preferences: North and Southeast,
Midwest, and Gulf States.

First Commerce Capital, Inc.
201 St. Charles Ave., 16th Fl.
PO Box 60279
New Orleans, LA 70170
Phone: (504)623-1600
Fax: (504)623-1779
William Harper, Manager
Preferred Investment Size: $1 to $2
million. Investment Policies: Loans,
equity. Investment Types: Later stage,
acquisition, buyouts. Industry
Preferences: Manufacturing
healthcare, retail, wholesale/distribu-
tion. Geographic Preferences: Gulf
South region.

Maine

Finance Authority of Maine
Email: info@samemaine.com
83 Western Ave.
PO Box 949
Augusta, ME 04332-0949
Phone: (207)623-3263

Fax: (800)623-0095
Assists business development and job
creation through direct loans, loan
guarantee programs, and project
grants.

Maine Capital Corp.
Email: info@norhtatlantacapital.com
70 Center St.
Portland, ME 04101
Phone: (207)772-1001
Fax: (207)772-3257
A small business investment corpora-
tion. No industry preference.

The Maine Merchant Bank, L.L.C.
Two Monument Square
Portland, ME 04101
Phone: (207)772-8141
Fax: (207)761-4464
Douglas H. Bagin, President
Preferred Investment Size: $500,000
minimum. Investment Policies:
Equity. Investment Types: Late stage,
and leveraged buyout. Industry
Preferences: No preference. Geo-
graphic Preferences: Midwest and
eastern U.S.

Maryland

ABS Ventures (Baltimore)
1 South St., Ste. 2150
Baltimore, MD 21202
Phone: (410)895-3895
Fax: (410)895-3899
Preferred Investment Size: $500,000
maximum. Investment Types: Startup,
first and second stage, and mezzanine.
Industry Preferences: Communications, computer related, genetic
engineering, and medical/health
related. Geographic Preferences:
Entire U.S.

American Security Capital Corp., Inc.
100 S. Charles St., 8th Fl.
Baltimore, MD 21201
Fax: (410)547-4990
A small business investment com-
pany. Diversified industry preference.

Anthem Capital, L.P.
16 S. Calvert St., Ste. 800
Baltimore, MD 21202-1305
Phone: (410)625-1510

Fax: (410)625-1735
Preferred Investment Size: $500,000
to $1,000,000. Investment Types:
Early and later stage. Industry
Preferences: Diversified. Geographic
Preferences: Maryland.

Armata Partners
Email: armata@digen.com
300 East Lombard St.
Baltimore, MD 21202
Phone: (410)727-4495
Preferred Investment Size: $100,000
to $500,000. Investment Types:
Mezzanine, leveraged buyout, and
special situations. Industry Preferences: Internet related, restaurants,
and education. Geographic Preferences: Southeast.

Catalyst Ventures
1119 St. Paul St.
Baltimore, MD 21202
Phone: (410)244-0123
Fax: (410)752-7721
Preferred Investment Size: $500,000
maximum. Investment Policies:
Equity. Investment Types: Research
and development, and early stage.
Industry Preferences: Data communi-
cations, and medical related. Geo-
graphic Preferences: Middle Atlantic.

Maryland Department of Business
and Economic Development
Financing Programs Division
217 E. Redwood St.,10th Fl.
Baltimore, MD 21202-3316
Phone: (410)767-0095
Free: (800)333-6995
Fax: (410)333-1836
Provides short-term financing for
government contracts and longterm
financing for equipment and working
capital. Also operates a surety bond
guarantee program for small businesses and an equity participation
investment program for potential
minority franchises.

Maryland Venture Capital Trust
Email:
rblank@mdbusiness.state.md.us
217 E. Redwood St., Ste. 2212
Baltimore, MD 21202
Phone: (410)767-6358

Fax: (410)333-6931
Preferred Investment Size:
$1,000,000 to $5,000,000. Investment
Types: Seed, startup, first and second
stage. Geographic Preferences:
Maryland.

New Enterprise Associates
(Baltimore)
1119 St. Paul St.
Baltimore, MD 21202
Phone: (410)244-0115
Fax: (410)752-7721
Frank A. Bonsal, Jr., Founding
Partner
Preferred Investment Size: $100,000
to $5,000,000. Investment Types:
Seed, startup, first and second stage,
mezzanine, and incubator. Industry
Preferences: Diversified. Geographic
Preferences: Entire U.S.

T. Rowe Price Threshold Partnerships
100 E. Pratt St.
Baltimore, MD 21202
Phone: (410)345-2000
Douglas O. Hickman, Managing
Director
Preferred Investment Size:
$2,000,000 to $3,000,000. Investment
Types: Mezzanine, special situations,
expansion financing, and established
growing companies. Industry Prefer-
ences: Diversified. Geographic
Preferences: Entire U.S.

Triad Investor's Corp.
300 E. Joppa Rd., Ste. 1111
Baltimore, MD 21286
Phone: (410)828-6497
Fax: (410)337-7312
Barbara P. Melera, President
Preferred Investment Size: $100,000
to $1,000,000. Investment Types:
Seed, research and development,
startup, first and second stage.
Industry Preferences: Communica-
tions, computer related, electronics,
energy/natural resources, genetic
engineering, medical and health
related. Geographic Preferences:
Middle Atlantic.

Security Financial and Investment
Corp.
7720 Wisconsin Ave., Ste. 207

Bethesda, MD 20814
Phone: (301)951-4288
Fax: (301)951-9282
A minority enterprise small business
investment corporation. No industry
preference.

Syncom Capital Corp.
8401 Coalville Rd.-Ste. 300
Silver Spring, MD 20910
Phone: (301)608-3203
Fax: (301)608-3307
A minority enterprise small business
investment corporation. Areas of
interest include telecommunications
and media.

Grotech Capital Group
9690 Deereco Rd.,Ste. 800
Timonium, MD 21093
Phone: (410)560-2000
Fax: (410)560-1910
Frank A. Adams, President and CEO
Preferred Investment Size:
$1,000,000 to $5,000,000. Investment
Types: First and second stage,
mezzanine, leveraged buyouts, and
special situations. Industry Prefer-
ences: Diversified. Geographic
Preferences: Southeast and Middle
Atlantic.

Massachusetts

Adams, Harkness & Hill, Inc.
60 State St.
Boston, MA 02109
Phone: (617)371-3900
Tim McMahan, Managing Director
Preferred Investment Size: $500,000
to $1,000,000. Investment Types:
Late stage. Industry Preferences:
Computer, consumer, electronics,
genetic engineering, industrial
products and equipment, and medical.
Geographic Preferences: National.

Advent International
75 State St., 24th Fl.
Boston, MA 02109
Phone: (617)951-9400
Fax: (617)951-0566
Preferred Investment Size:
$1,000,000 to $2,000,000. Investment
Types: Startup, first and second stage,
mezzanine, leveraged buyout, special

situations, recaps, and acquisitions.
Industry Preferences: Diversified.
Geographic Preferences: Entire U.S.
and Canada.

American Research and Development
30 Federal St.
Boston, MA 02110-2508
Phone: (617)423-7500
Fax: (617)423-9655
Maureen A. White, Administrative
Manager
Preferred Investment Size: $100,000
to $1,000,000. Investment Types:
Seed, startup, first and second stage,
and special situations. Industry
Preferences: Diversified technology.
Geographic Preferences: Northeast.

Aspen Ventures (Boston)
1 Post Office Square, Ste. 3320
Boston, MA 02109
Fax: (617)426-2181
Venture capital supplier. Provides
start-up and early stage financing to
companies in high-growth industries
such as biotechnology, communications, electronics, and health care.

Atlas Venture
222 Berkeley St.
Boston, MA 02116
Phone: (617)859-9290
Fax: (617)859-9292
Preferred Investment Size: $500,000
to $5,000,000. Investment Types:
Seed, research and development, first
and second stage, mezzanine, and
expansion. Industry Preferences:
Communications, computer, genetic
engineering, medical and health
related. Geographic Preferences:
Entire U.S. and Canada.

Bain Capital Fund (Boston)
2 Copley Pl.
Boston, MA 02116
Phone: (617)572-3000
Fax: (617)572-3274
Private venture capital firm. No
industry preference, but avoids
investing in high-tech industries.
Minimum investment is $500,000.

BancBoston Capital/BancBoston
Ventures
Email: cannovicki@bkb.com

175 Federal St., 10th Fl.
Mail code 75-10-01
Boston, MA 02110
Phone: (617)434-2509
Fax: (617)434-1153
Frederick M. Fritz, President and Managing Director
Preferred Investment Size: $1,000,000 to $3,000,000. Investment Types: First and second stage, mezzanine, leveraged buyouts, special situations, and minority buyouts. Industry Preferences: Diversified. Geographic Preferences: Entire U.S. and Atlantic provinces of Canada.

Boston Capital Ventures
Email: info@bcv.com
Old City Hall
45 School St.
Boston, MA 02108
Phone: (617)227-6550
Fax: (617)227-3847
Alexander Wilmerding
Preferred Investment Size: $250,000 to $8,000,000. Investment Types: Startup, first and second stage. Industry Preferences: Diversified. Geographic Preferences: Entire U.S.

Boston Financial & Equity Corp.
Email: debbie@bfec.com
20 Overland St.
PO Box 15071
Boston, MA 02215
Phone: (617)267-2900
Fax: (617)437-7601
Deborah J. Monosson, Senior Vice President
Preferred Investment Size: $100,000 to $1,500,000. Investment Types: Early and late stage. Industry Preferences: Diversified. Geographic Preferences: National.

Boston Millennia Partners
30 Rowes Wharf
Boston, MA 02110
Phone: (617)428-5150
Fax: (617)428-5160
Dana Callow, Managing General Partner
Preferred Investment Size: $1,000,000 to $15,000,000. Investment Policies: Equity. Investment Types: Early and late stage. Industry

Preferences: Communication, computer related, consumer services, natural resources, genetic engineering, medical, and education. Geographic Preferences: National.

Bristol Investment Trust
842A Beacon St.
Boston, MA 02215-3199
Phone: (617)566-5212
Fax: (617)267-0932
Preferred Investment Size: $100,000 minimum. Investment Policies: Equity. Investment Types: Early and late stage. Industry Preferences: Restaurants, retailing, consumer distribution, medical/health, and real estate. Geographic Preferences: Northeast.

Burr, Egan, Deleage, and Co.
(Boston)
1 Post Office Sq., Ste. 3800
Boston, MA 02109
Phone: (617)482-8020
Fax: (617)482-1944
Preferred Investment Size: $1,000,000 to $5,000,000. Investment Types: No preference. Industry Preferences: Communications, computer, and medical/health related. Geographic Preferences: Entire U.S.

Cambridge/Samsung Partners
One Exeter Plaza
Ninth Fl.
Boston, MA 02116
Phone: (617)262-4440
Fax: (617)262-5562
Lee M. Lambert, Managing Director
Preferred Investment Size: $100,000 minimum. Investment Policies: Equity. Investment Types: Early stage. Industry Preferences: No preference. Geographic Preferences: National.

Chestnut Partners, Inc.
Email: chestnut@chestnutp.com
One Financial Center, 28th Floor
Boston, MA 02111
Phone: (617)832-8600
Fax: (617)832-8610
Drew Zalkind, Vice President
Preferred Investment Size: $100,000 to $1,000,000. Investment Types:

Seed, research and development, startup, and first stage. Industry Preferences: Diversified. Geographic Preferences: No preference.

Claflin Capital Management, Inc.
Email: venutre@clafcap.com
77 Franklin St., Second Fl.
Boston, MA 02110
Phone: (617)426-6505
Fax: (617)482-0016
Preferred Investment Size: $100,000 to $170,000. Investment Types: Seed, startup, and first stage. Industry Preferences: Diversified. Geographic Preferences: Northeast.

Commonwealth Enterprise Fund, Inc.
10 Post Office Sq., Ste. 1090
Boston, MA 02109
Phone: (617)482-1881
Fax: (617)482-7129
A minority enterprise small business investment corporation. No industry preference, but clients must be located in Massachusetts.

Copley Venture Partners
600 Atlantic Ave., 13th Fl.
Boston, MA 02210
Phone: (617)722-6030
Fax: (617)523-7739

Corning Capital
121 High Street
Boston, MA 02110
Phone: (617)338-2656
Preferred Investment Size: $100,000 to $500,000. Investment Policies: Equity. Investment Types: Early and late stage. Industry Preferences: Diversified technology. Geographic Preferences: National.

Downer & Co.
Email: cdowner@downer.com
211 Congress St.
Boston, MA 02110
Phone: (617)482-6200
Fax: (617)482-6201
Charles W. Downer
Preferred Investment Size: $250,000 to $500,000. Investment Types: Early and late stage. Industry Preferences: Computer related, retailing, distribution, electronics, and healthcare.

Geographic Preferences: Northeastern U.S. and Canada.

Eastech Management Co., Inc.
30 Federal St.
Boston, MA 02110
Phone: (617)423-1096
Fax: (617)695-2699
Michael H. Shanahan, Partner
Preferred Investment Size: $250,000 to $1,000,000. Investment Types: Seed, startup, first and second stage. Industry Preferences: Communications, computer, electronics, and industrial controls and sensors. Geographic Preferences: Northeast.

Fidelity Ventures
82 Devonshire St., Mail Zone R25C
Boston, MA 02109
Phone: (617)563-9160
Fax: (617)476-5015
Neal Yanofsky, Vice President
Preferred Investment Size: $500,000 to $5,000,000. Investment Types: Startup, first and second stage, leveraged buyout, and special situations. Industry Preferences: Diversified. Geographic Preferences: Northeast.

Greylock Management Corp. (Boston)
1 Federal St.
Boston, MA 02110
Phone: (617)423-5525
Fax: (617)482-0059
David B. Aronoff
Preferred Investment Size: $500,000 to $5,000,000. Investment Types: Startup, first and second stage, mezzanine, leveraged buyout, and special situations. Industry Preferences: Diversified. Geographic Preferences: No preference.

Harbourvest Partners, LLC
1 Financial Center, 44th Fl.
Boston, MA 02111
Phone: (617)348-3707
Fax: (617)350-0305
Kevin Delbridge
Preferred Investment Size: $5,000,000 maximum. Investment Types: First and second stage, mezzanine, and leveraged buyout.

Also invests in other funds and partnerships. Industry Preferences: Diversified. Geographic Preferences: No preference.

Harvard Management Co., Inc.
600 Atlantic Ave.
Boston, MA 02210
Phone: (617)523-4400
Free: (800)723-0044
Fax: (617)523-1283
Diversified venture capital firm. Minimum investment is $1 million.

Highland Capital Partners
Email: info@hcp.com
2 International Pl.
Boston, MA 02110
Phone: (617)531-1500
Fax: (617)531-1550
Preferred Investment Size: $500,000 to $5,000,000. Investment Types: Seed, research and development, startup, first and second stage, mezzanine, special situations, control block purchases, and consolidations. Industry Preferences: Communications, computer, genetic engineering, and medical/health related. Geographic Preferences: Entire U.S.

Liberty Ventures Corp.
Email: @1liberty.com
1 Liberty Sq.
Boston, MA 02109
Phone: (617)423-1765
Free: (800)423-1766
Fax: (617)338-4362
Venture capital partnership. Provides start-up, early stage, and expansion financing to companies that are pioneering applications of proven technology; also will consider nontechnology-based companies with strong management teams and plans for expansion. Investments range from $500,000 to $1 million, with a $6 million maximum.

M/C Venture Partners
75 State St.,Ste. 2500
Boston, MA 02109
Phone: (617)345-7200
Fax: (617)345-7201
Matthew J. Rubins

Preferred Investment Size: $5,000,000 to $25,000,000. Investment Types: Startup, first and second stage, and industry roll ups. Industry Preferences: Communications. Geographic Preferences: Entire U.S. and Canada.

Massachusetts Business Development Corp.
50 Milk St., 16th Fl.
Boston, MA 02109
Phone: (617)350-8877
Fax: (617)350-0052
Provides assistance to businesses and individuals attempting to utilize federal, state, and local loan finance programs.

Massachusetts Capital Resources Co.
420 Boylston St.
Boston, MA 02116
Phone: (617)536-3900
Fax: (617)536-7930
William J. Torpey, Jr., President
Preferred Investment Size: $250,000 to $1,000,000. Investment Policies: Equity. Investment Types: Late stage. Industry Preferences: No preference. Geographic Preferences: Northeast.

Massachusetts Community Development Finance Corp.
10 Post Office Sq., Ste. 1090
Boston, MA 02109
Phone: (617)482-9141
Fax: (617)482-7129
Provides financing for small businesses and for commercial, industrial, and residential business developments through community development corporations (CDCs) in depressed areas of Massachusetts. Three investment programs are offered: the Venture Capital Investment Program, the Community Development Program, and the Small Loan Guarantee Program.

Massachusetts Industrial Finance Agency
75 Federal St., 10th Fl.
Boston, MA 02110
Phone: (617)451-2477
Free: (800)445-8030
Fax: (617)451-3429

Promotes expansion, renovation, and modernization of small businesses through the use of investment incentives.

Massachusetts Technology Development Corp. (MTDC)
Email: jhodgman@mtdc.com
148 State St.
Boston, MA 02109
Phone: (617)723-4920
Fax: (617)723-5983
John F. Hodgman, President
Preferred Investment Size: $100,000 to $500,000. Investment Types: Seed, startup, first and second stage. Industry Preferences: Diversified. Geographic Preferences: Northeast.

Medallion Financial Corp.
45 Newbury St., Rm. 207
Boston, MA 02116
Phone: (617)536-0344
Fax: (617)536-5750
A minority enterprise small business investment corporation. Specializes in taxicabs and taxicab medallion loans.

Media Communication Partners
75 State St., Ste. 2500
Boston, MA 02109
Phone: (617)345-7200
Fax: (617)345-7201
A small business investment company. Diversified industry preference.

Northeast Small Business Investment Corp.
130 New Market Square
Boston, MA 02118
Phone: (617)445-0101
Fax: (617)442-1013
A small business investment corporation. No industry preference.

OneLiberty Ventures
One Liberty Square
Boston, MA 02109
Phone: (617)423-1765
Fax: (617)338-4362
Edwin M. Kania, Jr., General Partner
Preferred Investment Size: $500,000 to $5,000,000. Investment Policies: Equity. Investment Types: Early and late stage. Industry Preferences: Diversified technology. Geographic

Preferences: United States and Canada.

Pioneer Capital Corp.
60 State St.
Boston, MA 02109
Phone: (617)422-4947
Fax: (617)742-7315
C.W. Dick, Partner
Preferred Investment Size: $500,000 to $5,000,000. Investment Types: Seed, startup, first and second stage, mezzanine, and leveraged buyout. Industry Preferences: Diversified. Geographic Preferences: East Coast.

P.R. Venture Partners, L.P.
100 Federal St., 37th Fl.
Boston, MA 02110
Phone: (617)357-9600
Fax: (617)357-9601
Venture capital firm providing early stage financing. Areas of interest include health care, information, and food.

Private Equity Management
10 Liberty Sq., 5th Fl.
Boston, MA 02109
Phone: (617)345-9440
Fax: (617)345-9878

Spray Venture Partners
One Walnut St.
Boston, MA 02108
Phone: (617)305-4140
Fax: (617)305-4144
Preferred Investment Size: $50,000 to $4,000,000. Investment Policies: Equity. Investment Types: Early and late stage. Industry Preferences: Medical and health related, and genetic engineering. Geographic Preferences: National.

Summit Partners
600 Atlantic Ave., Ste. 2800
Boston, MA 02210-2227
Phone: (617)824-1000
Fax: (617)824-1100
Preferred Investment Size: $5,000,000 maximum. Investment Types: First and second stage, mezzanine, leveraged buyout, special situations, and control block purchases. Industry Preferences: Diversi-

fied. Geographic Preferences: Entire U.S. and Canada.

TA Associates, Inc. (Boston)
High Street Tower
125 High St., Ste. 2500
Boston, MA 02110
Phone: (617)574-6700
Fax: (617)574-6728
Preferred Investment Size: $5,000,000 maximum. Investment Types: Leveraged buyout, special situations, control block purchases, and all stages of business. Industry Preferences: Diversified. Geographic Preferences: No preference.

TVM Techno Venture Management
Email: info@tvmvc.com
101 Arch St., Ste. 1950
Boston, MA 02110
Phone: (617)345-9320
Fax: (617)345-9377
John J. DiBello, Partner, Chief Financial Officer and Chi
Venture capital firm providing early stage financing as well as mezzanine and foreign market entry. Areas of interest include high technology such as software, communications, medical, and biotechnology industries. Preferred investment size is $1 million to $3.5 million.

UST Capital Corp.
40 Court St.
Boston, MA 02108
Phone: (617)726-7000
Free: (800)441-8782
Fax: (617)726-7369
A small business investment company. Diversified industry preference.

Venture Capital Fund of New England
Email: kjdvcfne3@aol.com
160 Federal St., 23rd Fl.
Boston, MA 02110
Phone: (617)439-4646
Fax: (617)439-4652
Kevin J. Dougherty, General Partner
Preferred Investment Size: $250,000 to $1,000,000. Investment Types: Startup, first and second stage. Industry Preferences: Diversified. Geographic Preferences: Northeast, New England.

MDT Advisers, Inc.
125 Cambridge Park Dr.
Cambridge, MA 02140-2314
Phone: (617)234-2200
Fax: (617)234-2210
Michael E.A. O'Malley
Preferred Investment Size: $500,000
to $5,000,000. Investment Types:
Startup, first and second stage,
mezzanine, leveraged buyout, special
situations, and secondaries. Industry
Preferences: Diversified. Geographic
Preferences: No preference.

Zero Stage Capital
Email: zerostage@aol.com
101 Main St., 17th Fl.
Cambridge, MA 02142
Phone: (617)876-5355
Fax: (617)876-1248
Paul Kelley, Managing General
Partner
Preferred Investment Size: $50,000 to
$1,000,000. Investment Types: Early
and later stage. Industry Preferences:
Diversified technology. Geographic
Preferences: Northeast.

Zero Stage Capital Co., Inc.
Email: bjohnson@zerostage.com
101 Main St., 17th Fl.
Cambridge, MA 02142
Phone: (617)876-5355
Fax: (617)876-1248
Venture capital firm. Industry
preferences include high-technology
start-up companies located in the
northeastern U.S.

Boston College Capital Formation
Service
96 College Rd.
Rahner House
Chestnut Hill, MA 02167
Phone: (617)552-4091
Fax: (617)552-2730

Capital Formation Service
Boston College
96 College Rd., Rahner House
Chestnut Hill, MA 02167
Phone: (617)552-4091
Fax: (617)552-2730
Provides assistance to clients requir-
ing financing from nonconventional
sources, such as quasi-public financ-

ing programs; state, federal, and local
programs; venture capital; and private
investors.

Atlantic Capital
164 Cushing Highway
Cohasset, MA 02025
Phone: (617)383-9449
Fax: (617)383-6040
Preferred Investment Size: $100,000
to $500,000. Investment Policies:
Equity. Investment Types: Early
stage. Industry Preferences: Diversi-
fied. Geographic Preferences:
National.

Seacoast Capital Partners
Email: gdeli@seacoastcapital.com
55 Ferncroft Rd.
Danvers, MA 01923
Phone: (978)750-1300
Preferred Investment Size:
$2,000,000 to $15,000,000. Invest-
ment Policies: Loans and equity
investments. Investment Types:
Expansion, later stage. Industry
Preferences: Diversified. Geographic
Preferences: National.

Sage Management Group
Email: sagemgt@capecod.net
44 South Street
PO Box 2026
East Dennis, MA 02641
Phone: (508)385-7172
Fax: (508)385-7272
Preferred Investment Size: $500,000
to $1,000,000. Investment Policies:
Equity. Investment Types: Early and
late stage. Industry Preferences:
Diversified technology. Geographic
Preferences: National.

Argonauts MESBIC Corp.
929 Worcester Rd.
Framingham, MA 01701
Phone: (617)697-0501
A minority enterprise small business
investment company. Diversified
industry preference.

Applied Technology
1 Cranberry Hill
Lexington, MA 02421-7397
Phone: (617)862-8622
Fax: (617)862-8367

Preferred Investment Size: $100,000
to $2,000,000. Investment Types:
Seed, startup, first and second stage.
Industry Preferences: Diversified.
Geographic Preferences: Entire U.S.

Business Achievement Corp.
1172 Beacon St.
Newton, MA 02161
Phone: (617)965-0550
Fax: (617)969-2671
A small business investment corpora-
tion. No industry preference.

New England MESBIC Inc.
530 Turnpike St.
North Andover, MA 01845-5812

Analog Devices, Inc.
1 Technology Way
PO Box 9106
Norwood, MA 02062-9106
Phone: (781)329-4700
Free: (800)262-5643
Venture capital supplier. Prefers to
invest in industries involved in analog
devices.

Advanced Technology Ventures
(Boston)
Email: info@atv-ventures.com
281 Winter St., Ste. 350
Waltham, MA 02154
Phone: (781)290-0707
Fax: (781)684-0045
Preferred Investment Size:
$2,000,000 to $8,000,000. Investment
Types: Startup, first stage, second
stage, and mezzanine. Industry
Preferences: Diversified. Geographic
Preferences: No preference.

Charles River Ventures
1000 Winter St., Ste. 02451
Waltham, MA 02154
Phone: (781)487-7060
Fax: (781)487-7065
Richard M. Burnes, Jr., General
Partner
Preferred Investment Size:
$1,000,000 to $6,000,000. Investment
Types: Seed, startup, first and second
stage. Industry Preferences: Commu-
nications, computer, and electronics.
Geographic Preferences: No prefer-
ence.

Comdisco Venture Group (Waltham)
Totton Pond Office Center
400-1 Totten Pond Rd.
Waltham, MA 02154
Phone: (617)672-0250
Fax: (617)398-8099

Hambro International Equity Partners
(Boston)
404 Wyman, Ste. 365
Waltham, MA 02154
Fax: (617)290-0999
Private venture firm. Seeks to invest
in software, electronics and instrumentation, biotechnology, retailing,
direct marketing of consumer goods,
and environmental industries.

Matrix Partners
Bay Colony Corporate Center
1000 Winter St., Ste.4500
Waltham, MA 02154
Phone: (781)890-2244
Fax: (781)890-2288
Preferred Investment Size: $500,000
to $5,000,000. Investment Types:
Startup, first and second stage, and
leveraged buyout. Industry Prefer-
ences: Diversified. Geographic
Preferences: Entire U.S.

North Bridge Venture Partners
Email: eta@nbvp.com
404 Wyman St. Ste. 365
Waltham, MA 02154
Phone: (781)290-0004
Fax: (781)290-0999
Preferred Investment Size: $100,000
to $6,000,000. Investment Types:
Seed, research and development,
startup, first and second stage.
Industry Preferences: Communica-
tions, computer related, distribution,
and electronics. Geographic Prefer-
ences: Entire U.S.

Ampersand Ventures
Email: info@ampersandventures.com
55 William St., Ste. 240
Wellesley, MA 02482
Phone: (617)239-0700
Fax: (617)239-0824
Paul C. Zigman, Partner
Preferred Investment Size:
$1,000,000 to $5,000,000. Investment
Types: Startup, first and second stage,
mezzanine, leveraged buyout, and

special situations. Industry Preferences: Diversified. Geographic
Preferences: No preference.

Battery Ventures (Boston)
20 Williams St., Ste. 200
Wellesley, MA 02481
Phone: (781)996-1000
Fax: (781)996-1001
David A. Hartwig, Associate
Preferred Investment Size:
$1,000,000 to $10,000,000. Investment Types: Seed, startup, first and
second stage, mezzanine, and
leveraged buyout. Industry Preferences: Communications, computer,
computer and communications
distribution. Geographic Preferences:
No preference.

Commonwealth Capital Ventures,
L.P.
20 William St.
Wellesley, MA 02481
Phone: (781)237-7373
Fax: (781)235-8627
Preferred Investment Size: $500,000
to $5,000,000. Investment Policies:
Equity. Investment Types: Early and
late stage. Industry Preferences:
Diversified communication and
computer technology, consumer
products and services, retailing,
distribution, electronics, medical and
health related. Geographic Preferences: New England.

Geneva Middle Market Investors,
L.P.
70 Walnut St.
Wellesley, MA 02181
Fax: (617)239-8064
James J. Goodman, Manager

Northwest Venture Capitol
40 William St., Ste. 305
Wellesley, MA 02181
Phone: (781)237-5870
Fax: (781)237-6270

Bessemer Venture Partners
(Wellesley Hills)
Email: bob@bvpny.com
83 Walnut St.
Wellesley Hills, MA 02181
Phone: (617)237-6050
Fax: (617)235-7068

Palmer Science Corp.
200 Unicorn Park Dr.
Woburn, MA 01801
Phone: (781)933-5445
Fax: (781)933-0698
Preferred Investment Size: $250,000
to $1,000,000. Investment Types:
Startup, first and second stage, and
special situations. Industry Prefer-
ences: Communications, computer,
energy/natural resources, industrial,
education, finance, and publishing.
Geographic Preferences: Northeast,
Southeast, Southwest, East Coast,
Midwest, and Middle Atlantic.

Michigan

Arbor Partners, L.L.C.
Email: jburr@arborpartners.com
130 South First St.
Ann Arbor, MI 48104
Phone: (734)668-9000
Preferred Investment Size: $500,000
to $10,000,000. Investment Policies:
Equity. Investment Types: Early and
late stage. Industry Preferences:
Diversified technology. Geographic
Preferences: National.

Enterprise Development Fund
Email: edf@edfvc.com
425 North Main St.
Ann Arbor, MI 48104
Phone: (734)663-3213
Fax: (734)663-7358
Mary L. Campbell, General Partner
Preferred Investment Size:
$1,000,000 to $2,000,000. Investment
Policies: Equity. Investment Types:
Early and late stage. Industry
Preferences: Diversified technology.
Geographic Preferences: Great Lakes
region.

White Pines Management, L.L.C.
Email: ibund@whitepines.com
2401 Plymouth Rd., Ste. B
Ann Arbor, MI 48105
Phone: (734)747-9401
Fax: (734)747-9704
Preferred Investment Size:
$1,000,000 to $4,000,000. Investment
Types: Second stage, mezzanine,
leveraged buyout, and special
situations. Industry Preferences:

Diversified. Geographic Preferences: Southeast and Midwest.

Demery Seed Capital Fund
3707 W. Maple Rd.
Bloomfield Hills, MI 48301
Phone: (248)433-1722
Fax: (248)644-4526
Invests in start-up companies in Michigan.

Wellmax, Inc.
6905 Telegraph Rd., Ste. 330
Bloomfield Hills, MI 48301
Phone: (248)646-3554
Fax: (248)646-6220
Preferred Investment Size: $100,000. Investment Policies: Equity. Investment Types: Early and late stage and special situations. Industry Preferences: Diversified. Geographic Preferences: Midwest.

Dearborn Capital Corp.
PO Box 1729
Dearborn, MI 48126
Phone: (313)337-8577
Fax: (313)248-1252
A minority enterprise small business investment corporation. Loans to minority-owned, operated, and controlled suppliers to Ford Motor Company, Dearborn Capital Corporation's parent.

Motor Enterprises, Inc.
3044 W. Grand Blvd.
Detroit, MI 48202
Phone: (313)556-4273
Fax: (313)974-4854
A minority enterprise small business investment corporation. Prefers automotive-related industries.

Venture Funding, Ltd.
Fisher Bldg.
3011 West Grand Blvd., Ste. 321
Detroit, MI 48202
Phone: (313)871-3606
Fax: (313)873-4935
Monis Schuster, Vice President
Preferred Investment Size: $250,000 to $500,000. Investment Policies: Equity. Investment Types: Startup and special situations. Industry Preferences: Diversified. Geographic Preferences: National.

Liberty Bidco Investment Corp.
30833 Northwestern Highway, Ste. 211
Farmington Hills, MI 48334
Phone: (248)626-6070
Fax: (248)626-6072
James Zabriskie, Vice President
Preferred Investment Size: $250,000 to $2,000,000. Investment Types: Late stage and special situations. Industry Preferences: Diversified. Geographic Preferences: United States and Ontario.

Metro-Detroit Investment Co.
30777 Northwestern Hwy., Ste. 300
Farmington Hills, MI 48334-2549
Phone: (248)851-6300
Fax: (248)851-9551
A minority enterprise small business investment corporation. Food store industry preferred.

The Capital Fund
6412 Centurion Dr., Ste. 150
Lansing, MI 48917
Phone: (517)323-7772
Fax: (517)323-1999
A small business investment company. Provides expansion financing.

State Treasurer's Office
Alternative Investments Division
PO Box 15128
Lansing, MI 48901
Phone: (517)373-4330
Fax: (517)335-3668

Minnesota

Development Corp. of Austin
Email: dca@smig.net
1900 Eight Ave., N.W.
Austin, MN 55912
Phone: (507)433-0346
Fax: (507)433-0361
Preferred Investment Size: $100,000. Investment Types: Startup and early stage. Industry Preferences: Diversified industrial products and equipment. Geographic Preferences: Minnesota.

Ceridian Corp.
8100 34th Ave. S
Bloomington, MN 55425-1640
Phone: (612)853-8100

Northeast Ventures Corp.
802 Alworth Bldg.
Duluth, MN 55802
Phone: (218)722-9915
Fax: (218)722-9871
Greg Sandbulte, President
Preferred Investment Size: $100,000 to $500,000. Investment Policies: Equity. Investment Types: Startup, early and late stage. Industry Preferences: No preference. Geographic Preferences: Midwest.

St. Paul Venture Capital, Inc.
10400 Vicking Dr., Ste. 550
Eden Prairie, MN 55344
Phone: (612)995-7474
Fax: (612)995-7475
Barb Shronts
Preferred Investment Size: $500,000 to $2,000,000. Investment Types: Startup, early and late stage. Industry Preferences: Diversified. Geographic Preferences: National.

Cherry Tree Investments, Inc.
7601 France Ave. S., Ste 225
Edina, MN 55435
Phone: (612)893-9012
Fax: (612)893-9036
Preferred Investment Size: $100,000 to $5,000,000. Investment Types: Seed, startup, first and second stage, mezzanine, and management buyout. Industry Preferences: Diversified. Geographic Preferences: Midwest.

Affinity Capital Management
1900 Foshay Tower
821 Marquette
Minneapolis, MN 55402
Phone: (612)904-2305
Fax: (612)204-0913
Preferred Investment Size: $250,000 to $1,100,000. Investment Types: Seed, research and development, startup, first and second stage, and mezzanine. Industry Preferences: Medical/Health related. Geographic Preferences: Midwest.

Artesian Capital
Email: artesian@artesian.com
Foshay Tower
821 Marquette Ave., Ste. 1700
Minneapolis, MN 55402

Phone: (612)334-5600
Fax: (612)334-5601
Frank B. Bennett, President
Preferred Investment Size: $100,000
to $500,000. Investment Types: Seed,
research and development, and
startup. Industry Preferences: Diversified. Geographic Preferences:
Midwest.

Capital Dimensions Inc.
7831 Glenroy Rd., Ste. 480
Minneapolis, MN 55439-3132
Phone: (612)831-2025
Fax: (612)831-2945
A minority enterprise small business
investment corporation. No industry
preference.

Coral Ventures
60 S. 6th St., Ste. 3510
Minneapolis, MN 55402
Phone: (612)335-8666
Fax: (612)335-8668
Mark C. Headrick, Senior Associate
Preferred Investment Size: $100,000
to $8,000,000. Investment Types:
Seed, research and development,
startup, first and second stage, and
mezzanine. Industry Preferences:
Diversified technology. Geographic
Preferences: No preference.

Crawford Capital Corp.
713 Interchange Tower
600 S. Hwy. 169
Minneapolis, MN 55426
Phone: (612)544-2221
Fax: (612)544-5885
Venture capital firm providing
financing for firm's own venture fund
limited partnerships. Areas of interest
include medical, software, and
technology industries.

Crescendo Venture Management,
L.L.C.
800 LaSalle Ave., Ste. 2250
Minneapolis, MN 55402
Phone: (612)607-2800
Fax: (612)607-2801
Jeffrey R. Tollefson, Vice President
Preferred Investment Size: $250,000
to $5,000,000. Investment Types:
Startup, early and late stage. Industry
Preferences: Diversified information

technology. Geographic Preferences:
National.

Gideon Hixon Venture
Email: bkwhitney@gideonhixon.com
1900 Foshay Tower
821 Marquette Ave.
Minneapolis, MN 55402
Phone: (612)904-2314
Fax: (612)204-0913
Preferred Investment Size: $100,000
to $1,000,000. Investment Policies:
Equity. Investment Types: Startup,
early and late stage. Industry Preferences: Diversified communication
and computer technology, education,
finance and insurance, and publishing.
Geographic Preferences: Minnesota.

Milestone Growth Fund, Inc.
401 2nd Ave. S., Ste. 1032
Minneapolis, MN 55401-2310
Phone: (612)338-0090
Esperanza Guerrero-Anderson,
President and CEO
Preferred Investment Size: $200,000
to $500,000. Investment Types:
Second stage. Industry Preferences:
Communication, computer, distribu-
tion, electronics, genetic engineering,
and industrial products and equip-
ment. Geographic Preferences:
Middle Atlantic.

Norwest Equity Partners V, L.P.
2800 Piper Jaffray Tower
222 S. 9th St.
Minneapolis, MN 55402-3388
Phone: (612)667-1650
Fax: (612)667-1660
Charles B. Lennin, Partner
Preferred Investment Size:
$2,000,000 to $3,000,000. Investment
Policies: Equity. Investment Types:
Start-up, expansion, later stage.
Industry Preferences: Diversified.
Geographic Preferences: National.

Norwest Venture Capital
2800 Piper Jaffray Tower
222 S. 9th St.
Minneapolis, MN 55402-3388
Phone: (612)667-1650
Fax: (612)667-1660
Charles B. Lennin, Partner
Preferred Investment Size:

$2,000,000 to $3,000,000. Investment
Types: Seed, startup, first and second
stage, mezzanine, leveraged buyout,
and special situations. Industry
Preferences: Diversified. Geographic
Preferences: Entire U.S.

Oak Investment Partners
(Minneapolis)
4550 Norwest Center
90 S. 7th St., Ste. 4550
Minneapolis, MN 55402
Phone: (612)339-9322
Fax: (612)337-8017
Preferred Investment Size: $250,000
to $5,000,000. Investment Types:
Seed, startup, first stage, leveraged
buyout, and special situations.
Industry Preferences: Communications, computer related, consumer
restaurants and retailing, electronics,
and medical/health related. Geographic Preferences: Entire U.S.

Pathfinder Venture Capital Funds
(Minneapolis)
Email: jahrens620@aol.com
7300 Metro Blvd., Ste. 585
Minneapolis, MN 55439
Phone: (612)835-1121
Fax: (612)835-8389
Jack K. Ahrens, II, Investment Officer
Preferred Investment Size: $250,000
to $500,000. Investment Types: Seed,
startup, first and second stage,
mezzanine, leveraged buyouts, and
special situations. Industry Prefer-
ences: Diversified. Geographic
Preferences: Entire U.S. and Canada.

Piper Jaffray Ventures, Inc.
222 S. 9th St.
Minneapolis, MN 55402
Phone: (612)342-5686
Fax: (612)337-8514
Preferred Investment Size:
$1,000,000 to $5,000,000. Investment
Types: First and second stage, and
mezzaninc. Industry Preferences:
Computer and medical/health related.
Geographic Preferences: Entire U.S.

University Technology Center, Inc.
Email: utec@pro-ns.net
1313 5th St. SE
Minneapolis, MN 55414

Phone: (612)379-3800
Fax: (612)379-3875
Venture capital firm providing start-up, first stage, initial expansion and acquisition financing. Areas of interest include environment, consumer products, industrial products, transportation and diversified industry.

Wellspring Corp.
4530 IDS Center
Minneapolis, MN 55402
Phone: (612)338-0704
Fax: (612)338-0744
Venture capital firm providing acquisition and leveraged buyout financing. Areas of interest include marine transportation equipment and weighing and measuring equipment manufacturing.

The Food Fund, L.P.
5720 Smatana Dr., Ste. 300
Minnetonka, MN 55343
Phone: (612)939-3950
Fax: (612)939-8106
John Trucano, Managing General Partner
Preferred Investment Size: $100,000 to $250,000. Investment Types: Startup, first and second stage, leveraged buyout, and special situations. Industry Preferences: Consumer food and beverage products. Geographic Preferences: Entire U.S.

Medical Innovation Partners, Inc.
Opus Center
9900 Bren Rd. E
Minnetonka, MN 55343-9667
Phone: (612)931-0154
Fax: (612)931-0003
Mark B. Knudson, Ph.D., Managing Partner
Preferred Investment Size: $100,000 to $5,000,000. Investment Types: Seed, startup, and first stage. Industry Preferences: Medical technology and healthcare. Geographic Preferences: Northwest and Midwest.

Quest Venture Partners
730 E. Lake St.
Wayzata, MN 55391-1769

Phone: (612)473-8367
Fax: (612)473-4702
Venture capital firm providing second stage and bridge financing. Areas of interest include communications, computer products and medical/health care.

Mississippi

Delta Foundation
Email: deltafdn@tednfo.com
819 Main St.
Greenville, MS 38701
Phone: (601)335-5291
Fax: (601)335-5295
A minority enterprise small business investment corporation. No industry preference.

Mississippi Department of Economic and Community Development
Mississippi Business Finance Corp.
1200 Walter Sillers Bldg.
PO Box 849
Jackson, MS 39205
Phone: (601)359-3552
Fax: (601)359-2832
Administers the SBA(503) Loan and the Mississippi Small Business Loan Guarantee.

Missouri

Bankers Capital Corp.
3100 Gillham Rd.
Kansas City, MO 64109
Phone: (816)531-1600
Fax: (816)531-1334
Lee Glasnapp, Vice President
Preferred Investment Size: $100,000 to $250,000. Investment Types: Leveraged buyout. Industry Preferences: Consumer product and electronics distribution, and industrial equipment and machinery. Geographic Preferences: Midwest.

Capital for Business, Inc. (Kansas City)
1000 Walnut St., 18th Fl.
Kansas City, MO 64106
Phone: (816)234-2357
Fax: (816)234-2333
Bart S. Bergman, President
Preferred Investment Size: $500,000 to $5,000,000. Investment Types:

Mezzanine, leveraged buyout, special situations, control block purchases, and management buyouts. Industry Preferences: Diversified. Geographic Preferences: Midwest.

CFB Venture Fund II, Inc.
1000 Walnut St., 18th Fl.
Kansas City, MO 64106
Phone: (816)234-2357
Fax: (816)234-2333
A small business investment company. Diversified industry preference.

InvestAmerica Investment Advisors, Inc. (Kansas City)
Commerce Tower
911 Main St., Ste. 2424
Kansas City, MO 64105
Phone: (816)842-0114
Fax: (816)471-7339
Preferred Investment Size: $750,000 to $2,000,000. Investment Types: First and second stage, leveraged buyout, and special situations. Industry Preferences: Diversified. Geographic Preferences: Entire U.S.

InvestAmerica Investment Advisors, Inc. (Kansas City)
Commerce Tower
911 Main St., Ste. 2424
Kansas City, MO 64105
Phone: (816)842-0114
Fax: (816)471-7339
Preferred Investment Size: $750,000 to $2,000,000. Investment Types: First and second stage, leveraged buyout, and special situations. Industry Preferences: Diversified. Geographic Preferences: Entire U.S.

United Missouri Capital Corp.
PO Box 419226
Kansas City, MO 64141
Phone: (816)860-7914
Fax: (816)860-7143
A small business investment corporation. No industry preference.

Midland Bank
740 NW Blue Pkwy.
Lees Summit, MO 64086-5707
Phone: (816)524-8000
Fax: (816)525-8624
A small business investment company. Diversified industry preference.

Allsop Venture Partners (St. Louis)
55 W. Port Plz., Ste. 575
St. Louis, MO 63146
Phone: (314)434-1688
Fax: (314)434-6560

Bome Investors, Inc.
8000 Maryland Ave., Ste. 1190
St. Louis, MO 63105
Phone: (314)721-5707
Fax: (314)721-5135
Gregory R. Johnson
Preferred Investment Size: $500,000
to $1,000,000. Investment Types:
Startup, early and late stage. Industry
Preferences: Diversified. Geographic
Preferences: Midwest.

Capital for Business, Inc. (St. Louis)
11 S. Meramec, Ste. 1430
St. Louis, MO 63105
Phone: (314)746-7427
Fax: (314)746-8739
Bart S. Bergman, President
Preferred Investment Size: $500,000
to $5,000,000. Investment Types:
Mezzanine, leveraged buyout, special
situations, control block purchases,
and management buyouts. Industry
Preferences: Diversified. Geographic
Preferences: Midwest.

CFB Venture Fund I, Inc.
11 S. Meramec, Ste. 1430
St. Louis, MO 63105
Phone: (314)746-7427
Fax: (314)746-8739
A small business investment com-
pany. Diversified industry preference.

Gateway Venture Associates L.P.
8000 Maryland Ave., Ste. 1190
St. Louis, MO 63105
Phone: (314)721-5707
Fax: (314)721-5135
John S. McCarthy, Managing General
Partner
Preferred Investment Size: $250,000
to $1,000,000. Investment Types:
Second stage, mezzanine, leveraged
buyout, special situations, control
block purchases. Industry Prefer-
ences: Communications, computer
related, and hospital and other
institutional management. Geographic
Preferences: Entire U.S.

GE Capital, Small Business Corp.
635 Maryville Center Dr., Ste. 120
St. Louis, MO 63141
Phone: (314)205-3500
Free: (800)447-2025
Fax: (314)205-3699
Non-bank lender providing start-up
and expansion financing.

Montana

Bozeman Technology Incubator, Inc.
Email: grg@mcn.net
1320 Manley Rd.
Bozeman, MT 59715
Phone: (406)585-0665
Fax: (406)585-0723
Preferred Investment Size: $100,000
to $250,000. Investment Policies:
Equity. Investment Types: Startup,
early and late stage. Industry Prefer-
ences: Software. Geographic Prefer-
ences: Rocky Mountains.

Montana Board of Investments
Office of Development Finance
PO Box 200126
555 Fuller Ave.
Helena, MT 59620-0126
Phone: (406)444-0001
Fax: (406)449-6579
Provides investments to businesses
that will bring long-term benefits to
the Montana economy.

Montana Department of Commerce
Economic Development Division
1424 9th Ave.
Helena, MT 59620-0501
Phone: (406)444-4780
Fax: (406)444-1872
Provides financial analysis, financial
planning, loan packaging, industrial
revenue bonding, state and private
capital sources, and business tax
incentives.

Nebraska

Nebraska Investment Finance
Authority
1230 "O" St., Ste. 200
Lincoln, NE 68508
Phone: (402)434-3900
Free: (800)204-6432
Fax: (402)434-3921

Provides lower cost financing for
manufacturing facilities, certain farm
property, and health care and residential development. Also established a
Small Industrial Development Bond
Program to help small Nebraska-
based companies (those with fewer
than 100 employees or less than $2.5
million in gross salaries).

Heartland Capital Fund, Ltd.
Email: hrtlndcptl@aol.com
11930 Arbor St., Ste. 201
Omaha, NE 68144
Phone: (402)333-8840
Fax: (402)333-8944
John G. Gustafson, Vice President
Preferred Investment Size: $500,000
to $2,000,000. Investment Policies:
Equity. Investment Types: Early and
late stage. Industry Preferences:
Diversified technology. Geographic
Preferences: Southwest and Midwest.

Nevada

Nevada Department of Business and
Industry
Bond Division
1665 Hot Springs Rd., Ste. 100
Carson City, NV 89706
Phone: (702)687-4250
Fax: (702)687-4266
Issues up to $100 million in bonds to
fund venture capital projects in
Nevada; helps companies expand or
build new facilities through the use of
tax-exempt financing.

Atlanta Investment Co., Inc.
Call Box 10,001
Incline Village, NV 89450
Phone: (702)833-1836
Fax: (702)833-1890
L. Mark Newman, Chairman of the
Board
Preferred Investment Size:
$2,000,000. Investment Policies:
Equity. Investment Types: Expansion,
later stage. Industry Preferences:
Technology. Geographic Preferences:
National.

Development Financial Institute of
Nevada, L.P.
PO Box 11464

Las Vegas, NV 89111-1464
Phone: (702)732-4966
Fax: (702)735-2912
Paula Rushiddin, Managing Partner
Preferred Investment Size: $100,000
to $1,000,000. Investment Types:
Startup, early and late stage. Industry
Preferences: Diversified technology
and retailing. Geographic Preferences:
United States and Western Canada.

New Hampshire

Business Finance Authority of the
State of New Hampshire
Email: bfa@enterwebb.com
4 Park St., Ste. 302
Concord, NH 03301-6313
Phone: (603)271-2391
Fax: (603)271-2396
Works to foster economic development and promote the creation of
employment in the state of New
Hampshire. Provides guarantees on
loans to businesses made by banks
and local development organizations;
guarantees on portions of loans
guaranteed in part by the U.S. Small
Business Administration; cash
reserves on loans made by state banks
to businesses with annual revenues
less than or equal to $5,000,000; and
opportunities for local development
organizations to acquire additional
funds for the purpose of promoting
and developing business within the
state.

New Jersey

MidMark Capital, L.P.
Email: mfinlay@midmarkassoc.com
466 Southern Blvd.
Chatham, NJ 07928
Phone: (973)822-2999
Fax: (973)822-8911
Matthew W. Finlay, Vice President
Preferred Investment Size:
$1,000,000 to $5,000,000. Investment
Policies: Equity. Investment Types:
Expansion, later stage. Industry
Preferences: Diversified, communica-
tion, manufacturing, retail/service.
Geographic Preferences: National.

Transpac Capital Corp.
1037 Rte. 46 E
Clifton, NJ 07013
Phone: (973)470-8855
Fax: (973)470-8827
A minority enterprise small business
investment company. Diversified
industry preference.

Monmouth Capital Corp.
125 Wyckoff Rd.
PNC Bldg.
PO Box 335
Eatontown, NJ 07724
Phone: (732)542-4927
Fax: (732)542-1106
A small business investment corpora-
tion. No industry preference.

Capital Circulation Corp.
2035 Lemoine Ave., 2nd Fl.
Ft. Lee, NJ 07024
Phone: (201)947-8637
Fax: (201)585-1965
A minority enterprise small business
investment company. Diversified
industry preference.

Taroco Capital Corp.
716 Jersey Ave.
Jersey City, NJ 07310-1306
Phone: (201)798-5000
Fax: (201)798-4322
A minority enterprise small business
investment corporation. Focuses on
Chinese-Americans.

Edison Venture Fund
Email: info@edisonadventure.com
1009 Lenox Dr., Ste. 4
Lawrenceville, NJ 08648
Phone: (609)896-1900
Fax: (609)896-0066
Preferred Investment Size:
$1,000,000 to $6,000,000. Investment
Types: First and second stage,
mezzanine, leveraged buyout, and
industry rollups. Industry Preferences:
Diversified. Geographic Preferences:
Northeast and Middle Atlantic.

Tappan Zee Capital Corp. (New
Jersey)
201 Lower Notch Rd.
PO Box 416
Little Falls, NJ 07424
Phone: (973)256-8280

Fax: (973)256-2841
Jeffrey Birnberg, President
Preferred Investment Size: $100,000
to $250,000. Investment Types:
Leveraged buyout, debt, and debt
with equity secured. Industry Preferences: Consumer products, food and
beverage products, franchise businesses, restaurants, distribution of
communications and electronics
equipment. Geographic Preferences:
Within two hours of office.

The CIT Group/Equity Investments,
Inc.
Email: cweiler@citigroup.com
650 CIT Dr.
Livingston, NJ 07039
Phone: (973)740-5435
Fax: (973)740-5555
Colby W. Collier, Managing Director
Preferred Investment Size:
$1,000,000 to $5,000,000. Investment
Types: First and second stage,
mezzanine, and leveraged buyout.
Industry Preferences: Radio and TV,
consumer products and retailing,
biotechnology research, chemicals
and materials, plastics, and manufac-
turing. Geographic Preferences:
Entire U.S.

ESLO Capital Corp.
212 Wright St.
Newark, NJ 07114
Phone: (973)242-4488
Fax: (973)643-6062
Leo Katz, President
Preferred Investment Size: $100,000.
Investment Policies: Loans. Invest-
ment Types: Start-ups, early stage.
Industry Preferences: Business
services, manufacturing. Geographic
Preferences: Northeast.

Rutgers Minority Investment Co.
180 University Ave., 3rd Fl.
Newark, NJ 07102
Phone: (973)353-5627
A minority enterprise small business
investment corporation. No industry
preference.

Westford Technology Ventures, L.P.
17 Academy St.
Newark, NJ 07102

Phone: (973)624-2131
Fax: (973)624-2008
Preferred Investment Size: $250,000
to $500,000. Investment Types:
Startup, early and late stage. Industry
Preferences: Diversified communica-
tion and computer technology,
electronics, industrial products and
equipment. Geographic Preferences:
Eastern U.S.

Accel Partners
1 Palmer Sq.
Princeton, NJ 08542
Phone: (609)683-4500
Fax: (609)683-0384

Accel Partners (Princeton)
1 Palmer Sq.
Princeton, NJ 08542
Phone: (609)683-4500
Fax: (609)683-0384
Venture capital firm. Telecommunications, software, and health care
industries preferred. Minimum
investment of $100,000 required.

Carnegie Hill Co.
202 Carnegie Center, Ste. 103
Princeton, NJ 08540
Phone: (609)520-0500
Fax: (609)520-1160

DSV Partners (Princeton)
221 Nassau St.
Princeton, NJ 08542
Phone: (609)924-6420
Fax: (609)683-0174
Preferred Investment Size:
$1,000,000 maximum. Investment
Types: Startup and first stage.
Industry Preferences: Diversified.
Geographic Preferences: Entire U.S.

Johnston Associates, Inc.
Email: jaincorp@aol.com
181 Cherry Valley Rd.
Princeton, NJ 08540
Phone: (609)924-3131
Fax: (609)683-7524
Preferred Investment Size: $500,000
to $3,000,000. Investment Types:
Seed, startup, and leveraged buyout.
Industry Preferences: Science and
healthcare industry. Geographic
Preferences: Northeast.

NJS Partners, Inc.
18 Willow Ave.
Randolph, NJ 07869
Preferred Investment Size: $100,000.
Investment Types: Seed, early stage,
and special situations. Industry
Preferences: Diversified. Geographic
Preferences: National.

Capital Express, L.L.C.
Genesis Direct
100 Plaza Pkwy.
Secaucus, NJ 07094
Phone: (201)583-3635
Fax: (201)583-3634
Niles Cohen
Preferred Investment Size: $250,000
to $2,000,000. Investment Policies:
Equity. Investment Types: Early and
late stage. Industry Preferences:
Internet and consumer related.
Geographic Preferences: East Coast.

Early Stage Enterprises
995 Route 518
Skillman, NJ 08558
Phone: (609)921-8896
Fax: (609)921-8703
Ronald R. Hahn, Managing Director
Preferred Investment Size: $100,000
to $1,000,000. Investment Types:
Seed, early and late stage. Industry
Preferences: Diversified. Geographic
Preferences: Within two hours of
office.

BCI Advisors, Inc.
Email: geninfo@bciadvisors.com
Glenpointe Center W.
Teaneck, NJ 07666
Phone: (201)836-3900
Fax: (201)836-6368
Preferred Investment Size:
$3,000,000 to $20,000,000. Invest-
ment Types: Second stage and
mezzanine. Industry Preferences:
Diversified. Geographic Preferences:
Entire U.S.

Demuth, Folger and Wetherill
300 Frank W. Burr, 5th Floor
Teaneck, NJ 07666
Phone: (201)836-6000
Fax: (201)836-5666
Venture capital firm with preferences
for technology, services, and health
care investments.

Demuth, Folger & Wetherill
Glenpointe Center E., 5th Fl.
Teaneck, NJ 07666
Phone: (201)836-6000
Fax: (201)836-5666
Donald F. DeMuth, General Partner
Preferred Investment Size:
$1,000,000 to $5,000,000. Investment
Policies: Equity. Investment Types:
Later stage. Industry Preferences:
Healthcare, computer, communica-
tion, diversified. Geographic Prefer-
ences: National.

New Jersey Commission on Science
and Technology
Email: njcst@scitech.state.nj.us
28 W. State St.
PO Box 832
Trenton, NJ 08625-0832
Phone: (609)984-1671
Fax: (609)292-5920
Awards bridge grants to small
companies that have received seed
money under the Federal State
Business Innovation Research
programs and works to improve the
scientific and technical research
capabilities within the state. Also
provides management and technical
assistance and other services to small,
technology-oriented companies.

New Jersey Department of
Agriculture
Division of Rural Resources
John Fitch Plz., CN 330
Trenton, NJ 08625
Phone: (609)292-5532
Fax: (609)633-7229
Fosters the agricultural economic
development of rural areas of the state
through financial assistance for
farmers and agribusinesses.

New Jersey Economic Development
Authority
PO Box 990
Trenton, NJ 08625-0990
Phone: (609)292-1800
Fax: (609)292-0368
Arranges low-interest, long-term
financing for manufacturing facilities,
land acquisition, and business
equipment and machinery purchases.
Also issues taxable bonds to provide

financing for manufacturing, distribution, warehousing, research, commercial, office, and service uses.

First Princeton Capital Corp.
One Garret Mountain Plaza, 9th Fl.
West Paterson, NJ 07424
Phone: (973)278-8111
Fax: (973)278-4290
Preferred Investment Size: $250,000 to $2,000,000. Investment Types: Early stage, mezzanine, and leveraged buyout. Industry Preferences: Diversified. Geographic Preferences: Northeast and East Coast.

Edelson Technology Partners
300 Tice Blvd.
Woodcliff Lake, NJ 07675
Phone: (201)930-9898
Fax: (201)930-8899
Harry Edelson, Managing Partner
Preferred Investment Size: Seed, startup, first and second stage, and mezzanine. Industry Preferences: Diversified. Geographic Preferences: No preference.

New Mexico

Associated Southwest Investors, Inc.
1650 University NE, Ste.200
Albuquerque, NM 87102
Phone: (505)247-4050
Fax: (505)247-4050
A minority enterprise small business investment corporation. No industry preference.

High Desert Ventures, Inc.
6101 Imparata St., N.E.
Ste. 1721
Albuquerque, NM 87111
Phone: (505)797-3330
Preferred Investment Size: $500,000 to $2,500,000. Investment Types: Startup and early stage. Industry Preferences: Diversified. Geographic Preferences: Northeast and Southwest.

New Business Capital Fund, Ltd.
5805 Torreon, N.E.
Albuquerque, NM 87109
Phone: (505)822-8445
Preferred Investment Size: $100,000.

Investment Policies: Equity. Investment Types: Seed and startup. Industry Preferences: Diversified. Geographic Preferences: New Mexico.

Industrial Development Corp. of Lea County
Email: edclea@leaconet.com
PO Box 1376
Hobbs, NM 88240
Phone: (505)397-2039
Free: (800)443-2236
Fax: (505)392-2300
Certified development company.

Ads Capital Corp.
142 Lincoln Ave., Ste. 500
Santa Fe, NM 87501
Fax: (505)983-2887
Venture capital supplier. Prefers to invest in manufacturing or distribution companies.

New Mexico Economic Development Department
Technology Enterprise Division
1100 St. Francis Dr.
Santa Fe, NM 87503
Phone: (505)827-0300
Free: (800)374-3061
Fax: (505)827-3061
Provides state funds to advanced-technology business ventures that are close to the commercial stage.

New Mexico Economic Development Department
Economic Development Division
1100 St. Francis Dr.
Santa Fe, NM 87503
Phone: (505)827-0300
Free: (800)374-3061
Fax: (505)827-0328
Provides start-up or expansion loans for businesses that are established in or are new to New Mexico.

New Mexico Labor Department
Job Training Division
Aspen Plz.
1596 Pacheco St.
PO Box 4218
Santa Fe, NM 87502
Phone: (505)827-6827
Fax: (505)827-6812
Provides new and expanding indus-

tries with state-sponsored funds to train a New Mexican workforce.

New York

Fleet Bank
69 St.
Albany, NY 12207
Phone: (518)447-4115
Fax: (518)447-4043
Venture capital supplier. No industry preference. Typical investment is between $500,000 and $1 million.

New York State Science & Technology Foundation
Small Business Technology Investment Fund
Email: jvanwie@empire.state.ny.us
99 Washington Ave., Ste. 1731
Albany, NY 12210
Phone: (518)473-9741
Fax: (518)473-6876
Preferred Investment Size: $100,000 to $250,000. Investment Types: Startup, early and late stage. Industry Preferences: Diversified technology. Geographic Preferences: New York state.

NYBDC Capital Corp.
41 State St.
PO Box 738
Albany, NY 12201
Phone: (518)463-2268
Fax: (518)463-0240
A small business investment corporation.

Vega Capital Corp.
80 Business Park Dr.
Armonk, NY 10504
Phone: (914)273-1025
Fax: (914)273-1028
Preferred Investment Size: $100,000 to $250,000. Investment Types: Second stage, mezzanine, leveraged buyout, special situations, and collateralized loans. Industry Preferences: Diversified. Geographic Preferences: Northeast, Southeast, and Middle Atlantic.

Triad Capital Corp. of New York
305 7th Avenue, 20th Fl.
Bronx, NY 10001
Phone: (212)243-7360

Fax: (212)243-7647
A minority enterprise small business investment corporation. No industry preference.

First New York Management Co.
1 Metrotech Center N, 11th Fl.
Brooklyn, NY 11201
Phone: (718)797-5990
Fax: (718)722-3533
A small business investment corporation. No industry preference.

M & T Capital Corporation
1 Fountain Plz., 3rd Fl.
Buffalo, NY 14203-1495
Phone: (716)848-3800
Fax: (716)848-3150
A small business investment corporation providing equity financing for small to mid-size companies for expansion activities, acquisitions, recapitalizations, and buyouts. Initial investments range from $500,000 $2 million. Prefers businesses located in the Northeast and Midwest.

Rand Capital Corp.
2200 Rand Bldg.
Buffalo, NY 14203
Phone: (716)853-0802
Fax: (716)854-8480
Allen F. Grum, President and CEO
Preferred Investment Size: $100,000 to $500,000. Investment Types: First and second stage, mezzanine, and leveraged buyout. Industry Preferences: Diversified. Geographic Preferences: Northeast.

Tessler and Cloherty, Inc.
155 Main St.
Cold Spring, NY 10516
Phone: (914)265-4244
Fax: (914)265-4158
Anne Saunders, Manager
Preferred Investment Size: $250,000 to $1,000,000. Investment Types: First and second stage, leveraged buyouts, and special situations. Industry Preferences: Precious metals. Does not consider real estate, publishing, or consumer related. Geographic Preferences: Entire U.S.

Esquire Capital Corp.
69 Veterans Memorial Hwy.

Commack, NY 11725
Phone: (516)462-6946
Fax: (516)864-8152
A minority enterprise small business investment company. Diversified industry preference.

Pan Pac Capital Corp.
121 E. Industry Ct.
Deer Park, NY 11729
Fax: (516)586-7505
A minority enterprise small business investment corporation. No industry preference.

First County Capital, Inc.
135-14 Northern Blvd., 2nd Fl.
Flushing, NY 11354
Phone: (718)461-1778
Fax: (718)461-1835
A minority enterprise small business investment company. Diversified industry preference.

Flushing Capital Corp.
39-06 Union St., Rm.202
Flushing, NY 11354
Phone: (718)886-5866
Fax: (718)939-7761
A minority enterprise small business investment company. Diversified industry preference.

Herbert Young Securities, Inc.
98 Cuttermill Rd.
Great Neck, NY 11021
Phone: (516)487-8300
Fax: (516)487-8319
Herbert D. Levine, President
Preferred Investment Size: $100,000 to $5,000,000. Investment Types: Early and late stage. Industry Preferences: Diversified communications and computer technology, consumer products and services, electronics, genetic engineering, healthcare, and real estate. Geographic Preferences: National.

Sterling/Carl Marks Capital, Inc.
175 Great Neck Rd.
Great Neck, NY 11021
Phone: (516)482-7374
Fax: (516)487-0781
Preferred Investment Size: $250,000 to $1,000,000. Investment Types: Second stage and mezzanine. Industry

Preferences: Consumer related; distribution of electronics equipment, food and industrial products; and industrial equipment and machinery. Geographic Preferences: Northeast.

Situation Ventures Corp.
56-20 59th St.
Maspeth, NY 11378
Phone: (718)894-2000
Fax: (718)326-4642
Sam Hollander, President
Preferred Investment Size: $100,000. Investment Policies: Loans and/or equity. Industry Preferences: Manufacturing, service, retail. Geographic Preferences: New York metro area.

KOCO Capital Co., L.P.
111 Radio Cir.
Mt. Kisco, NY 10549
Phone: (914)242-2324
Fax: (914)241-7476
Albert Pastino, President
Preferred Investment Size: $2 to $3 million. Investment Policies: Equity and debt with warrants. Investment Types: Expansion. Industry Preferences: Healthcare, media, basic manufacturing. Geographic Preferences: Mid-Atlantic.

Tappan Zee Capital Corp. (New York)
120 N. Main St.
New City, NY 10956
A small business investment company.

Aberlyn Holding Co., Inc.
500 Fifth Ave.
New York, NY 10110
Phone: (212)391-7750
Fax: (212)391-7762
Lawrence Hoffman, Chairman and CEO
Preferred Investment Size: $500,000 to $5,000,000. Investment Types: Startup, early and late stage. Industry Preferences: Diversified computer technology, food and beverage products, genetic engineering, and healthcare. Geographic Preferences: National.

The Argentum Group
The Chyrsler Bldg.

405 Lexington Ave.
New York, NY 10174
Phone: (212)949-6262
Fax: (212)949-8294
Walter H. Barandiaran
Preferred Investment Size:
$1,000,000 to $5,000,000. Investment
Types: Second stage, mezzanine,
leveraged buyout, and special
situations. Industry Preferences:
Diversified. Geographic Preferences:
Entire U.S.

Asian American Capital Corp.
44 Wall St.
New York, NY 10005
Phone: (212)315-2600
Howard H. Lin, President

Bedford Capital Corp.
18 East 48th St., Ste. 1800
New York, NY 10017
Phone: (212)688-5700
Fax: (212)754-4699
Ross M. Patten, Managing Director
Preferred Investment Size: $250,000
to $5,000,000. Investment Types:
Early and late stage, and leveraged
buyout. Industry Preferences:
Diversified. Geographic Preferences:
East Coast and Midwest.

Bloom & Co.
950 Third Ave.
New York, NY 10022
Phone: (212)838-1858
Fax: (212)838-1843
Jack S. Bloom, President
Preferred Investment Size: $500,000
to $3,000,000. Investment Types:
Startup, early and late stage. Industry
Preferences: No preference. Geo-
graphic Preferences: Within two
hours of office.

Bradford Ventures Ltd.
1 Rockefeller Plaza, Ste. 1722
New York, NY 10020
Phone: (212)218-6900
Fax: (212)218-6901
Venture capital firm. No industry
preference.

BT Capital Partners, Inc.
130 Liberty St., 34th Fl.
New York, NY 10006
Phone: (212)250-5563

Fax: (212)669-1749
Preferred Investment Size:
$5,000,000 maximum. Investment
Types: Second stage, mezzanine,
leveraged buyouts, and special
situations. Industry Preferences:
Diversified. Geographic Preferences:
No preference.

The Business Loan Center
645 Madison Ave., 18th Fl.
New York, NY 10022
Phone: (212)751-5626
Fax: (212)751-9345
A small business loan company.

Capital Investors and Management
Corp.
212 Canal St., Ste. 611
New York, NY 10013-4155
Phone: (212)964-2480
Fax: (212)349-9160
A minority enterprise small business
investment corporation. No industry
preference.

CB Commercial, Inc.
560 Lexington Ave.,20th Fl.
New York, NY 10022
Phone: (212)207-6119
Fax: (212)207-6095
A small business investment com-
pany. Diversified industry preference.

CBIC Oppenheimer
425 Lexington Ave., 5th Fl.
New York, NY 10017
Phone: (212)856-4000
Fax: (212)697-1554
A small business investment com-
pany. Diversified industry preference.

Chase Capital Partners
380 Madison Ave., 12th Fl.
New York, NY 10017-2070
Phone: (212)622-3060
Fax: (212)622-3101
Preferred Investment Size:
$5,000,000 to $100,000,000. Invest-
ment Types: Startup, first and second
stage, mezzanine, leveraged buyout,
and special situations. Industry
Preferences: Diversified. Geographic
Preferences: Entire U.S. and Canada.

Citicorp Venture Capital Ltd. (New
York City)
399 Park Ave., 14th Fl./Zone 4

New York, NY 10043
Phone: (212)559-1127
Fax: (212)888-2940
Preferred Investment Size:
$5,000,000 maximum. Investment
Types: Leveraged buyout. Industry
Preferences: Diversified. Geographic
Preferences: No preference.

CMNY Capital II, LP
135 E. 57th St.
New York, NY 10022
Phone: (212)909-8428
Fax: (212)980-2630
Preferred Investment Size: $250,000
to $500,000. Investment Types: First
and second stage, mezzanine,
leveraged buyout, special situations,
and turnarounds. Industry Preferences: Diversified. Geographic
Preferences: No preference.

Cohen & Co., L.L.C.
Email: nlcohen@aol.com
800 Third Ave.
New York, NY 10022
Phone: (212)317-2250
Fax: (212)317-2255
Neil L. Cohen, President
Preferred Investment Size: $500,000
to $5,000,000. Investment Types:
Startup, early and late stage. Industry
Preferences: Communications,
consumer, distribution, electronics,
energy, and healthcare. Geographic
Preferences: National.

Concord Partners
535 Madison Ave.
New York, NY 10022
Phone: (212)906-7100
Fax: (212)906-8690
Venture capital partnership. Diversified in terms of stage of development,
industry classification, and geographic location. Areas of special
interest include computer software,
electronics, environmental services,
biopharmaceuticals, health care, and
oil and gas.

Cornerstone Equity Investors, L.L.C.
717 5th Ave., Ste. 1100
New York, NY 10022
Phone: (212)753-0901
Fax: (212)826-6798

Mark Rossi, Senior Managing
Director
Preferred Investment Size:
$5,000,000 maximum. Investment
Types: Leveraged buyout, later stage
equity, and special situations. Industry
Preferences: Diversified. Geographic
Preferences: No preference.

Credit Suisse First Boston
11 Madison Ave.
New York, NY 10010
Phone: (212)909-2000
Investment banker. Provides financing to the oil and gas pipeline,
hydroelectric, medical technology,
consumer products, electronics,
aerospace, and telecommunications
industries. Supplies capital for
leveraged buy outs.

Creditanstalt SBIC
245 Park Ave., 27th Fl.
New York, NY 10167
Fax: (212)856-1699
Dennis O'Dowd, President

CW Group, Inc.
1041 3rd Ave., 2nd fl.
New York, NY 10021
Phone: (212)308-5266
Fax: (212)644-0354
Walter Channing, Jr., Managing
General Partner
Preferred Investment Size: $100,000
to $5,000,000. Investment Types:
Seed, research and development,
startup, first and second stage, special
situations, and control block pur-
chases. Industry Preferences: Special-
ize in the medical/health business.
Geographic Preferences: Entire U.S.

DAEDHIE
1261 Broadway, Rm. 405
New York, NY 10001
Fax: (212)684-6474
A minority enterprise small business
investment company. Diversified
industry preference.

DNC Capital Group
55 5th Ave., 15th Fl.
New York, NY 10003
Phone: (212)206-6041
Fax: (212)727-0563

Small business investment corporation interested in financing acquisitions in the real estate industry.

East Coast Venture Capital, Inc.
313 W. 53rd St., 3rd Fl.
New York, NY 10019
Phone: (212)245-6460
Fax: (212)265-2962
A minority enterprise small business
investment company. Diversified
industry preference.

East River Ventures, L.P.
645 Madison Ave., 22nd Fl.
New York, NY 10022
Phone: (212)644-6211
Fax: (212)644-5498
Alicia B. Lindgren
Preferred Investment Size: $500,000
to $5,000,000. Investment Types:
Early and late stage, and mezzanine.
Industry Preferences: Diversified
communication and computer
technology, consumer services, and
medical. Geographic Preferences:
National.

Edwards Capital Co.
437 Madison Ave., 38th Fl.
New York, NY 10022
Phone: (212)682-3300
Fax: (212)328-2121
A small business investment corpora-
tion. Transportation industry pre-
ferred.

Elf Aquitain, Inc.
280 Park Ave., 36th Fl. W
New York, NY 10017-1216
Phone: (212)922-3000
Free: (800)922-0027
Fax: (212)922-3001

Elk Associates Funding Corp.
747 3rd Ave., Ste. 4C
New York, NY 10017
Phone: (212)355-2449
Fax: (212)759-3338
Preferred Investment Size: $100,000
to $1,000,000. Investment Types:
Second stage and leveraged buyout.
Industry Preferences: Radio and TV,
consumer franchise businesses, hotel
and resort areas, and transportation.
Geographic Preferences: Southeast
and Midwest.

Elron Technologies, Inc.
666 5th Ave., 37th Fl.
New York, NY 10103
Phone: (212)541-2443
Fax: (212)541-2448
Venture capital supplier. Provides
incubation and start-up financing to
high-technology companies.

Empire State Capital Corp.
170 Broadway, Ste. 1200
New York, NY 10038
Phone: (212)513-1799
Fax: (212)513-1892
A minority enterprise small business
investment company. Diversified
industry preference.

Empire State Development Corp.
633 3rd Ave.
New York, NY 10017
Phone: (212)803-3100
Participates in a broad range of
initiatives. Addresses the needs of the
state in six areas, including downtown
development, industrial development,
minority business development,
university research and development,
and planning and special projects.

EOS Partners, L.P.
Email: mfirst@eospartners.com
320 Park Ave., 22nd Fl.
New York, NY 10022
Phone: (212)832-5800
Fax: (212)832-5815
Mark L. First, Manager
Preferred Investment Size:
$3,000,000. Investment Policies:
Equity and equity-oriented debt.
Investment Types: Expansion, later
stage. Industry Preferences: Diversi-
fied. Geographic Preferences: United
States and Canada.

Euclid Partners
Email: graham@euclidpartners.com
45 Rockefeller Plaza, Ste. 907
New York, NY 10111
Phone: (212)218-6880
Fax: (212)218-6877
Preferred Investment Size: $500,000
to $5,000,000. Investment Types:
Startup, first and second stage.
Industry Preferences: Data communi-
cations, computer services, genetic

engineering, and medical/health related. Geographic Preferences: No preference.

Evergreen Capital Partners, Inc.
Email: rysmith@evergreencapital.com
150 East 58th St.
New York, NY 10155
Phone: (212)813-0758
Fax: (212)759-0486
Preferred Investment Size: $500,000 to $5,000,000. Investment Types: Early and late stage, and special situations. Industry Preferences: Diversified. Geographic Preferences: National.

The Exeter Group
Email: exeter@usa.net
10 E. 53rd St.
New York, NY 10022
Phone: (212)872-1172
Fax: (212)872-1198
Karen J. Watai, Partner
Preferred Investment Size: $1,000,000 to $12,000,000. Investment Policies: Loans and equity investments. Investment Types: Expansion, later stage. Industry Preferences: Diversified. Geographic Preferences: National.

Exim Capital Corp.
241 5th Ave., 3rd Fl.
New York, NY 10016
Phone: (212)683-3375
Fax: (212)689-4118
A minority enterprise small business investment corporation. No industry preference.

Fair Capital Corp.
212 Canal St., Ste. 611
New York, NY 10013
Phone: (212)964-2480
Fax: (212)349-9160
A minority enterprise small business investment corporation. No industry preference.

First Charter Partners, Inc.
405 Park Avenue
New York, NY 10022
Phone: (212)644-9700
Fax: (212)644-5483
Eric Gilchrest, President

Preferred Investment Size: $500,000 to $5,000,000. Investment Types: Late stage and special situations. Industry Preferences: Diversified. Geographic Preferences: United States and Canada.

First Wall Street SBIC, LP
26 Broadway, Ste. 2310
New York, NY 10004
Fax: (212)742-3776
A small business investment company. Diversified industry preference.

Franklin Holding Corp.
450 Park Ave.
New York, NY 10022
Phone: (212)486-2323
Fax: (212)755-5451
A small business investment corporation. No industry preference; no start-ups.

Fredericks Michael and Co.
2 Wall St., 4th Fl.
New York, NY 10005
Phone: (212)732-1600
Fax: (212)732-1872
Private venture capital supplier. Provides start-up and early stage financing, and supplies capital for buy outs and acquisitions.

Fresh Start Venture Capital Corp.
313 W. 53rd St., 3rd Fl.
New York, NY 10019
Phone: (212)265-2249
Fax: (212)265-2962
A minority enterprise small business investment corporation. No industry preference.

Furman Selz SBIC, L.P.
230 Park Ave.
New York, NY 10169
Phone: (212)309-8200
Fax: (212)692-9608
Brian Friedman, Manager
Preferred Investment Size: $2 to $6 million. Investment Policies: Equity. Investment Types: Expansion, later stage, no start-ups. Industry Preferences: Diversified. Geographic Preferences: National.

Generation Partners
551 Fifth Ave., Ste. 3100

New York, NY 10176
Phone: (212)450-8507
Fax: (212)450-8550
Preferred Investment Size: $1,000,000. Investment Types: Startup, early and late stage. Industry Preferences: Diversified communications and computer technology, consumer products and services, and industrial products and equipment. Geographic Preferences: United States and Canada.

The Growth Group
400 Park Ave., 14th Fl.
New York, NY 10022
Phone: (212)486-7722
Fax: (212)888-8856
Preferred Investment Size: $1,000,000 to $5,000,000. Investment Types: Startup, early and late stage. Industry Preferences: No preference. Geographic Preferences: United States and Canada.

Hambro International Equity Partners (New York)
650 Madison Ave., 21st Floor
New York, NY 10022
Phone: (212)223-7400
Fax: (212)223-0305
Preferred Investment Size: $2,500,000 to $5,000,000. Investment Types: First and second stage, and special situations. Industry Preferences: Genetic engineering, chemicals and materials, and medical/health related. Geographic Preferences: Entire U.S.

Hanam Capital Corp.
38 W.32nd St.,Rm.1512
New York, NY 10001
Phone: (212)564-5225
Fax: (212)564-5307
A minority enterprise small business investment company. Diversified industry preference.

Harvest Partners, Inc.
280 Park Ave, Third Fl.
New York, NY 10017
Phone: (212)549-6300
Fax: (212)812-0100
Preferred Investment Size: $8,000,000 to $12,000,000. Invest-

ment Types: Leveraged buyout. Industry Preferences: Consumer products and services, communications, distribution, fiberoptics, and medical/health related. Geographic Preferences: No preference.

Harvest Partners, Inc. (New York)
280 Park Ave., 33rd Fl.
New York, NY 10017
Phone: (212)549-6300
Fax: (212)812-0100
Harvey P. Mallement, Managing Partner
Preferred Investment Size: $8,000,000 to $12,000,000. Investment Types: Leveraged buyout. Industry Preferences: Diversified. Geographic Preferences: No preference.

Holding Capital Group, Inc.
10 E. 53rd St., 30th Fl.
New York, NY 10022
Phone: (212)486-6670
Fax: (212)486-0843
James W. Donaghy, President
Preferred Investment Size: $5,000,000. Investment Types: Leveraged buyout. Industry Preferences: No preference. Geographic Preferences: Entire U.S.

IBJS Capital Corp.
1 State St.
New York, NY 10004
Phone: (212)858-2019
Fax: (212)858-2768
George Zombeck, Chief Operations Officer
Preferred Investment Size: $2,000,000 maximum. Investment Types: Mezzanine, leveraged buyout, and special situations. Industry Preferences: Consumer products and services, and chemicals and materials. Geographic Preferences: Entire U.S.

Inclusive Ventures, L.L.C.
14 Wall St., 26th Fl.
New York, NY 10005
Phone: (212)619-4000
Fax: (212)619-7202
Preferred Investment Size: $100,000 to $250,000. Investment Types: Seed and startup. Industry Preferences:

Diversified computer technology. Geographic Preferences: National.

InterEquity Capital Partners, L.P.
Email: iecp@aol.com
220 5th Ave.
New York, NY 10001
Phone: (212)779-2022
Fax: (212)779-2103
Preferred Investment Size: $250,000 to $500,000. Investment Types: first and second stage, mezzanine, leveraged buyout, and special situations. Industry Preferences: Diversified. Geographic Preferences: Entire U.S.

Investor International (U.S.), Inc.
320 Park Ave., 33 Fl.
New York, NY 10022
Phone: (212)508-0900
Fax: (212)508-0901

Jafco America Ventures, Inc. (New York)
2 World Financial Center, Bldg. B, 17th Fl.
225 Liberty St.
New York, NY 10281-1196
Fax: (212)667-1004
Venture capital firm. Provides middle- to later-stage financing to technology-oriented companies.

Jardine Capital Corp.
105 Lafayette St., Unit 204
New York, NY 10013
Phone: (212)941-0993
Fax: (212)941-0998
Lawrence Wong, President
Preferred Investment Size: $360,000. Investment Policies: Loans and/or equity. Investment Types: Expansion. Industry Preferences: Diversified. Geographic Preferences: North/South.

Josephberg, Grosz and Co., Inc.
810 Seventh Ave., 27th Fl.
New York, NY 10019
Phone: (212)974-9926
Fax: (212)397-5832
Preferred Investment Size: $1,000,000 to $5,000,000. Investment Types: Seed, research and development, startup, first and second stage, mezzanine, and leveraged buyout.

Industry Preferences: Diversified. Geographic Preferences: Entire U.S.

J.P. Morgan Capital Corp.
60 Wall St.
New York, NY 10260-0060
Phone: (212)648-9000
Fax: (212)648-5002
Lincoln E. Frank, Chief Operational Officer
Preferred Investment Size: $5,000,000 maximum. Investment Types: Second stage and special situations. Industry Preferences: Diversified. Geographic Preferences: Entire U.S. and Canada.

Kwiat Capital Corp.
579 5th Ave.
New York, NY 10017
Phone: (212)223-1111
Fax: (212)223-2796
A small business investment corporation. No industry preference.

LandMark, Inc.
115 E. 69th Ave.
New York, NY 10021
Phone: (212)794-6060
Fax: (212)794-6169
Venture capital partnership.

Lawrence, Smith, and Horey
515 Madison Ave., 29th Fl.
New York, NY 10022
Phone: (212)826-9080
Fax: (212)759-2561
Venture capital firm. Prefers to invest in health care, software, and fragmented industries that grow by acquisition.

Loeb Partners Corp.
61 Broadway, Ste. 2450
New York, NY 10006
Phone: (212)483-7000
Fax: (212)425-7090
Preferred Investment Size: $100,000 to $1,000,000. Investment Types: Startup, early and late stage. Industry Preferences: Diversified. Geographic Preferences: National.

McCown, De Leeuw and Co. (New York)
65 E. 55th St., 36th Fl.
New York, NY 10022

Phone: (212)355-5500
Fax: (212)355-6283

Medallion Funding Corp.
437 Madison Ave., 38th Fl.
New York, NY 10022
Phone: (212)682-3300
Fax: (212)328-2121
A minority enterprise small business investment corporation. Transportation industry preferred.

Mercury Capital, L.P.
650 Madison Ave., Ste. 2600
New York, NY 10022
Phone: (212)838-0888
Fax: (212)838-7598
David W. Elenowitz, Manager

Morgan Stanley Venture Partners (New York)
Email: msventures@ms.com
1221 Avenue of the Americas, 33rd Fl.
New York, NY 10020
Phone: (212)762-7900
Fax: (212)762-8424
David Hammer, Associate
Preferred Investment Size: $3,000,000 to $40,000,000. Investment Types: Second stage, mezzanine, industry roll ups, and growth buyouts. Industry Preferences: Communications, computer related, computer and electronics distribution, electronics, and medical/health related. Geographic Preferences: Entire U.S. and Canada.

NatWest USA Capital Corp.
175 Water St., 27th Fl.
New York, NY 10038
Phone: (212)602-4000
Fax: (212)602-3393
A small business investment company. Diversified industry preference.

Nazem and Co.
Email: nazem@msn.com
645 Madison Ave., 12th Fl.
New York, NY 10022
Phone: (212)371-7900
Fax: (212)371-2150
Fred F. Nazem, Managing General Partner
Preferred Investment Size: $500,000 to $5,000,000. Investment Types: Seed, startup, first and second stage,

mezzanine, and special situations. Industry Preferences: Diversified. Geographic Preferences: No preference.

Needham Capital Management, L.L.C.
445 Park Ave.
New York, NY 10022
Phone: (212)371-8300
Fax: (212)371-1450
Chad W. Keck, Manager
Preferred Investment Size: $1,000,000 to $5,000,000. Investment Policies: Equity. Investment Types: Later stage. Industry Preferences: Diversified technology. Geographic Preferences: National.

Norwood Venture Corp.
Email: nvc@mail.idt.net
1430 Broadway, Ste. 1607
New York, NY 10018
Phone: (212)869-5075
Fax: (212)869-5331
Preferred Investment Size: $250,000. Investment Types: Mezzanine, leveraged buyout, and special situations. Industry Preferences: No preference. Geographic Preferences: No preference.

Paribas Principal, Inc.
787 7th Ave.
New York, NY 10019
Phone: (212)841-2115
Fax: (212)841-3558
Preferred Investment Size: $5,000,000. Investment Types: Leveraged buyout, special situations, and control block purchases. Industry Preferences: Diversified. Geographic Preferences: Entire U.S.

Patricof & Co. Ventures, Inc. (New York)
445 Park Ave.
New York, NY 10022
Phone: (212)753-6300
Fax: (212)319-6155
Preferred Investment Size: $5,000,000 to $25,000,000. Investment Types: Seed, startup, first and second stage, mezzanine, and leveraged buyout. Industry Preferences: Diversified. Geographic Preferences: No preference.

Pierre Funding Corp.
805 3rd Ave., 6th Fl.
New York, NY 10022
Phone: (212)888-1515
Fax: (212)688-4252
A minority enterprise small business investment corporation. No industry preference.

Prospect Street Ventures
Email: wkohler@prospectstreet.com
10 East 40th St., 44th Fl.
New York, NY 10016
Phone: (212)448-0702
Fax: (212)448-9652
Edward Ryeom, Vice President
Preferred Investment Size: $1,000,000 to $3,000,000. Investment Types: Early and later stage. Industry Preferences: No preference. Geographic Preferences: East and West Coast.

Pyramid Ventures, Inc.
130 Liberty St., 25th Fl.
New York, NY 10006
Phone: (212)250-9571
Fax: (212)250-7651
A small business investment company. Diversified industry preference.

R and R Financial Corp.
1370 Broadway
New York, NY 10018
Phone: (212)356-1400
Free: (800)999-4800
Fax: (212)356-0900
A small business investment corporation. No industry preference.

Rothschild Ventures, Inc.
1251 Avenue of the Americas, 51st Fl.
New York, NY 10020
Phone: (212)403-3500
Fax: (212)403-3652
Scott T. Jones, Senior Vice President
Preferred Investment Size: $500,000 to $5,000,000. Investment Types: Seed, research and development, startup, first and second stage, mezzanine, and leveraged buyout. Industry Preferences: Diversified. Geographic Preferences: Entire U.S. and Canada.

Sandler Capital Management
767 Fifth Ave., 45th Fl.
New York, NY 10153
Phone: (212)754-8100
Fax: (212)826-0280
Preferred Investment Size: $500,000
to $5,000,000. Investment Policies:
Equity. Investment Types: No
preference. Industry Preferences:
Diversified communication and
computer technology, consumer
products and services, education, and
publishing. Geographic Preferences:
United States and Canada.

767 Limited Partnership
767 3rd Ave., 7th Fl.
New York, NY 10017
Phone: (212)838-7776
Fax: (212)593-0734
A small business investment corpora-
tion. No industry preference.

Sixty Wall Street SBIC Fund, L.P.
60 Wall St.
New York, NY 10260
Phone: (212)648-7778
Fax: (212)648-5032
David Cromwell

Sprout Group (New York City)
Email: info@sproutgroup.com
277 Park Ave.
New York, NY 10172
Phone: (212)892-3600
Fax: (212)892-3444
Patrick J. Boroian, General Partner
Preferred Investment Size: $500,000
to $5,000,000. Investment Types:
Seed, startup, first and second stage,
mezzanine, leveraged buyout, and
special situations. Industry Prefer-
ences: Diversified technology.
Geographic Preferences: Entire U.S.
and Atlantic provinces of Canada.

TCW Capital
200 Park Ave., Ste. 2200
New York, NY 10166
Phone: (212)297-4000
Fax: (212)297-4024
Venture capital fund. Companies with
sales of $25 to $100 million preferred.
Will provide up to $20 million in
later-stage financing for recapitalizations, restructuring management buy
outs, and general corporate purposes.

399 Venture Partners
399 Park Ave., 14th Fl./ Zone 4
New York, NY 10043
Phone: (212)559-1127
Fax: (212)888-2940
A small business investment com-
pany. Diversified industry preference.

Trusty Capital, Inc.
350 5th Ave., Ste. 2026
New York, NY 10118
Phone: (212)629-3011
Fax: (212)629-3019
A minority enterprise small business
investment company. Diversified
industry preference.

UBS Partners, Inc.
299 Park Ave., 34th Fl.
New York, NY 10171
Phone: (212)821-6490
Fax: (212)821-6333
Justin S. Maccarone, President

United Capital Investment Corp.
60 E. 42nd St., Ste. 1515
New York, NY 10165
Phone: (212)682-7210
Fax: (212)573-6352
A minority enterprise small business
investment company. Diversified
industry preference.

Venture Capital Fund of America,
Inc.
Email: vcfa@mindspring.com
509 Madison Ave., Ste. 812
New York, NY 10022
Phone: (212)838-5577
Fax: (212)838-7614
Dayton T. Carr, General Partner
Preferred Investment Size: $100,000
to $1,000,000. Investment Types:
Secondary partnership interests.
Industry Preferences: Does not
consider tax shelters, real estate, or
direct investments in companies.
Geographic Preferences: Entire U.S.

Venture Opportunities Corp.
Email: jerryvoc@aol.com
150 E. 58th St., 16th Floor
New York, NY 10155
Phone: (212)832-3737
Fax: (212)980-6603
A. Fred March, President
Preferred Investment Size: $100,000

maximum. Investment Types: Startup,
first and second stage, mezzanine,
leveraged buyout, and special
situations. Industry Preferences:
Diversified. Geographic Preferences:
Entire U.S.

Warburg Pincus Ventures, Inc.
466 Lexington Ave.
New York, NY 10017
Phone: (212)878-0600
Fax: (212)878-9351
Preferred Investment Size:
$1,000,000 to $5,000,000. Investment
Types: Seed, startup, first and second
stage, mezzanine, leveraged buyouts,
and special situations. Industry
Preferences: Diversified. Geographic
Preferences: No preference.

Weiss, Peck and Greer Venture
Partners L.P.
1 New York Plz.
New York, NY 10004
Phone: (212)908-9500
Fax: (212)908-9652

Welsh, Carson, Anderson, & Stowe
320 Park Ave., Ste. 2500
New York, NY 10022-6815
Phone: (212)893-9500
Fax: (212)893-9575
Patrick J. Welsh, General Partner
Preferred Investment Size:
$10,000,000 for leveraged buyout.
Investment Types: Leveraged buyout
and special situations. Industry
Preferences: Computer related and
medical/health related. Geographic
Preferences: Entire U.S.

J. H. Whitney and Co. (New York)
630 Fifth Ave. Ste. 3225
New York, NY 10111
Phone: (212)332-2400
Fax: (212)332-2422
James R. Matthews, Vice President
Preferred Investment Size:
$1,000,000 to $5,000,000. Investment
Types: First and second stage,
mezzanine, and leveraged buyout.
Industry Preferences: No industry
preference. Geographic Preferences:
Entire U.S.

Winthrop Ventures
74 Trinity Place, Ste. 600

New York, NY 10006
Phone: (212)422-0100
Cyrus Brown
Preferred Investment Size: $500,000
to $5,000,000. Investment Types:
Startup, early and late stage. Industry
Preferences: Diversified. Geographic
Preferences: National.

Wolfensohn Partners, L.P. (New
York)
590 Madison Ave., 32nd Fl.
New York, NY 10022
Phone: (212)849-8120
Fax: (212)849-8171
Jonathan E. Gold, Associate
$500,000 to $5,000,000. Investment
Types: Seed, research and develop-
ment, startup, first and second stage,
and special situations. Industry
Preferences: Diversified. Geographic
Preferences: No preference.

International Paper Capital
Formation, Inc. (Purchase)
Email: comm@ipaper.com
2 Manhattanville Rd.
Purchase, NY 10577-2196
Phone: (914)397-1500
Fax: (914)397-1909
A minority enterprise small business
investment company.

Ibero-American Investors Corp.
104 Scio St.
Rochester, NY 14604-2552
Phone: (716)262-3440
Fax: (716)262-3441
A minority enterprise small business
investment corporation. No industry
preference.

Gabelli Multimedia Partners
Email: fsommer@gabelli.com
One Corporate Center
Rye, NY 10580
Phone: (914)921-5395
Fax: (914)921-5031
Preferred Investment Size: $250,000
to $500,000. Investment Policies:
Equity. Investment Types: Startup,
early and late stage. Industry Prefer-
ences: Diversified communications.
Geographic Preferences: Northeast.

Northwood Ventures LLC
Email: northwdven@aol.com

485 Underhill Blvd., Ste. 205
Syosset, NY 11791
Phone: (516)364-5544
Fax: (516)364-0879
Henry T. Wilson, Managing Director
Preferred Investment Size:
$1,000,000 to $6,000,000. Investment
Types: First and second stage,
leveraged buyout, special situations,
and industry roll ups. Industry
Preferences: Diversified. Geographic
Preferences: Entire U.S.

Exponential Business Development
Co.
Email: dirksonn@aol.com
216 Walton St.
Syracuse, NY 13202-1227
Phone: (315)474-4500
Fax: (315)474-4682
Dirk E. Sonneborn, Partner
Preferred Investment Size: $100,000
to $250,000. Investment Types:
Startup, early and late stage. Industry
Preferences: No preference. Geo-
graphic Preferences: Northeast.

TLC Funding Corp.
660 White Plains Rd.
Tarrytown, NY 10591
Phone: (914)332-5200
Fax: (914)332-5660
A small business investment corpora-
tion. No industry preference.

Bessemer Venture Partners
(Westbury)
Email: bob@bvpny.com
1400 Old Country Rd., Ste. 407
Westbury, NY 11590
Phone: (516)997-2300
Fax: (516)997-2371
Preferred Investment Size: $500,000
maximum. Investment Types: Seed,
research and development, startup,
first and second stage, leveraged
buyout, special situations, and control
block purchases. Industry Preferences: No preference. Geographic
Preferences: Entire U.S.

SBP Technology
106 Corporate Park
White Plains, NY 10604
Phone: (914)694-2280
Fax: (914)694-2286

Winfield Capital Corp.
237 Mamaroneck Ave.
White Plains, NY 10605
Phone: (914)949-2600
Fax: (914)949-7195
A small business investment corpora-
tion. No industry preference.

North Carolina

First Union Capital Partners
1 1st Union Center
Charlotte, NC 28288-0732
Phone: (704)374-4656
Fax: (704)374-6711
L. Watts Hamrick, III, Partner
Preferred Investment Size:
$1,000,000 to $5,000,000. Investment
Types: First and second stage,
mezzanine, leveraged buyout, special
situations, and control block purchases. Industry Preferences: Diversified. Geographic Preferences: No
preference.

Kitty Hawk Capital
2700 Coltsgate Rd., Ste. 202
Charlotte, NC 28211
Phone: (704)362-3909
Fax: (704)362-2774
Preferred Investment Size: $500,000
to $5,000,000. Investment Types:
Startup, first and second stage.
Industry Preferences: Diversified.
Geographic Preferences: Southeast.

NationsBanc Leveraged Capital
Group
100 N. Tryon St., 10th Fl.
Charlotte, NC 28255
Phone: (704)386-8063
Fax: (704)386-6432
Doug Williamson, Managing Director
Preferred Investment Size:
$3,000,000 to $5,000,000. Investment
Policies: Equity, sub debt with
warrants. Investment Types: Later
stage, expansion. Industry Prefer-
ences: Diversified. Geographic
Preferences: National.

Ruddick Investment Co.
1800 Two First Union Center
Charlotte, NC 28282
Phone: (704)372-5404
Fax: (704)372-6409

Richard N. Brigden
Preferred Investment Size: $250,000
to $1,000,000. Investment Types:
Early and late stage. Industry Prefer-
ences: Diversified. Geographic
Preferences: Southeast.

Southeastern Publishing Ventures Inc.
528 E. Blvd.
Charlotte, NC 28203
Phone: (704)373-0051
Fax: (704)343-0170
Private venture capital firm. Diversi-
fied industry preference.

The Aurora Funds, Inc.
2525 Meridian Pkwy., Ste. 220
Durham, NC 27713
Phone: (919)484-0400
Fax: (919)484-0444
Preferred Investment Size: $250,000
to $1,000,000. Investment Types:
Startup, early and late stage. Industry
Preferences: Diversified. Geographic
Preferences: Eastern United States.

Center for Community Self-Help
North Carolina's Development Bank
PO Box 3619
301 W. Maine St.
Durham, NC 27701
Phone: (919)956-4400
Free: (800)476-7428
Fax: (919)956-4600
Statewide, private-sector financial
institution providing technical
assistance and financing to small
businesses, non-profit organizations,
and low-income homebuyers in North
Carolina.

The North Carolina Enterprise Fund,
L.P.
3600 Glenwood Ave., Ste. 107
Raleigh, NC 27612
Phone: (919)781-2691
Fax: (919)783-9195
Charles T. Closson, President and
CEO
Preferred Investment Size:
$1,000,000 to $2,000,000. Investment
Policies: Equity. Investment Types:
Startup, early and late stage. Industry
Preferences: Diversified. Real estate,
natural resources, and energy not
considered. Geographic Preferences:
North Carolina.

Atlantic Venture Partners (Winston
Salem)
380 Knollwood St., No. 410
Winston Salem, NC 27103
Phone: (910)721-1800
Fax: (910)748-1208
Private venture capital partnership.
Prefers to invest in manufacturing,
distribution, and service industries.

North Dakota

Bank of North Dakota
Small Business Loan Program
700 E. Main Ave.
PO Box 5509
Bismarck, ND 58506-5509
Phone: (701)328-5600
Free: (800)472-2166
Fax: (701)328-5632
Assists new and existing businesses in
securing competitive financing with
reasonable terms and conditions.

Dakota Certified Development Corp.
406 Main Ave., Ste. 404
Fargo, ND 58103
Phone: (701)293-8892
Fax: (701)293-7819
Administers the 504 Loan Program.

Fargo Cass County Economic
Development Corp.
Email: info@fedc.com
406 Main Ave., Ste. 404
Fargo, ND 58103
Phone: (701)237-6132
Fax: (701)293-7819
Certified development company that
lends to small and medium-sized
businesses at fixed rates.

North Dakota SBIC, L.P.
406 Main Ave., Ste. 404
Fargo, ND 58103
Phone: (701)298-0003
Fax: (701)293-7819
David R. Schroeder, Manager

Ohio

River Capital Corp. (Cleveland)
2544 Chamberlain Rd.
Akron, OH 44333
Phone: (330)864-8836
Fax: (216)781-2821
A small business investment corpora-
tion. No industry preference.

River Cities Capital Funds
221 E. 4th St., Ste. 2250
Cincinnati, OH 45202
Phone: (513)621-9700
Fax: (513)579-8939
Preferred Investment Size:
$1,000,000 to $6,000,000. Investment
Policies: Equity investments. Invest-
ment Types: Early stage, expansion,
later stage. Industry Preferences:
Diversified. Geographic Preferences:
Southeast and Midwest.

Walnut Capital Partners
312 Walnut St., Ste. 1151
Cincinnati, OH 45202
Phone: (513)651-3300
Fax: (513)241-1321
Lawrence H. Horwitz
Preferred Investment Size: $500,000
to $5,000,000. Investment Types:
Early and late stage, and special
situations. Industry Preferences:
Consumer products and services, and
business marketing and services.
Does not consider high technology.
Geographic Preferences: United
States and Canada.

Brantley Venture Partners
20600 Chagrin Blvd., Ste. 1150
Cleveland, OH 44122
Phone: (216)283-4800
Fax: (216)283-5324
Kevin J. Cook, Associate
Preferred Investment Size:
$1,000,000 to $5,000,000. Investment
Types: Industry roll ups and lever-
aged build ups. Industry Preferences:
Diversified. Geographic Preferences:
Entire U.S.

Clarion Capital Corp.
1801 E. 9th St., Ste. 1120
Cleveland, OH 44114
Phone: (216)687-1096
Fax: (216)694-3545
Preferred Investment Size: $250,000
to $500,000. Investment Types: First
and second stage, leveraged buyout,
and private placements. Industry
Preferences: Diversified. Geographic
Preferences: East Coast, Midwest, and
West Coast.

Crystal Internet Venture Fund, L.P.
Email: civf@worldnet.att.net
1120 Chester Ave., Ste. 418
Cleveland, OH 44114
Phone: (216)263-5515
Fax: (216)349-1119
Joseph Tzeng, Managing Director
Preferred Investment Size: $750,000
to $4,000,000. Investment Policies:
Equity. Investment Types: Seed, early
and late stage. Industry Preferences:
Diversified communications and
computer technology. Geographic
Preferences: National.

Gries Investment Co.
1801 E. 9th St., Ste. 1600
Cleveland, OH 44114-3110
Phone: (216)861-1146
Fax: (216)861-0106
A small business investment corpora-
tion. No industry preference.

Key Equity Capital Corp.
127 Public Sq., 28th Fl.
Cleveland, OH 44114
Phone: (216)689-5776
Fax: (216)689-3204
Sean P. Ward, Vice President
Preferred Investment Size:
$5,000,000 to $50,000,000. Investment Policies: Willing to make equity
investments. Investment Types: Later
stage. Industry Preferences: Diversified. Geographic Preferences:
National.

Morgenthaler Ventures
Terminal Tower
50 Public Square, Ste. 2700
Cleveland, OH 44113
Phone: (216)621-3070
Fax: (216)621-2817
Gary J. Morgenthaler, Managing
Partner
Preferred Investment Size:
$1,000,000 to $12,000,000. Invest-
ment Types: Startup, first and second
stage, leveraged buyout, special
situations, and industry roll ups.
Industry Preferences: Diversified.
Geographic Preferences: Entire U.S.
and Canada.

National City Capital
Email: nccap@aol.com

1965 E. 6th St.
Cleveland, OH 44114
Phone: (216)575-2491
Fax: (216)575-9965
Carl E. Baldassarre, Managing
Director
Preferred Investment Size:
$1,000,000 to $15,000,000. Invest-
ment Types: Second stage, mezza-
nine, leveraged buyout, special
situations, industry roll ups, manage-
ment buyouts, consolidations plays.
Industry Preferences: Diversified.
Geographic Preferences: Northeast,
Southeast, East Coast, Midwest,
Middle Atlantic.

Primus Venture Partners, Inc.
Email: info@primusventure.com
5900 LanderBrook Dr. Ste. 200
Cleveland, OH 44124-4020
Phone: (440)684-7300
Fax: (440)684-7342
Jeffrey J. Milius, Investment Manager
Preferred Investment Size:
$5,000,000 maximum. Investment
Types: First and second stage, startup,
and leveraged buyout. Industry
Preferences: Diversified. Geographic
Preferences: Entire U.S.

Society Venture Capital Corp.
127 Public Sq. 6th Fl.
Cleveland, OH 44114
Phone: (216)689-5776
Fax: (216)689-3204
A small business investment corpora-
tion. Prefers to invest in manufactur-
ing and service industries.

Tomlinson Industries
13700 Broadway Ave.
Cleveland, OH 44125-1992
Phone: (216)587-3400
Free: (800)526-9634
Fax: (216)587-0733
A small business investment corpora-
tion. Miniature supermarket industry
preferred.

Banc One Capital Partners
(Columbus)
150 E. Gay St., 24th Fl.
Columbus, OH 43215
Phone: (614)217-1100
Fax: (614)217-0192

Suzanne B. Kriscunas, Managing
Director
Preferred Investment Size:
$5,000,000 to $15,000,000. Invest-
ment Types: Later stage, leveraged
buyout, and special situations.
Industry Preferences: Diversified.
Geographic Preferences: Entire U.S.

Scientific Advances, Inc.
601 W. 5th Ave.
Columbus, OH 43201
Phone: (614)424-7005
Fax: (614)424-4874
Venture capital partnership interested
in natural gas related industries.

Interprise Ohio
8 N. Maine St.
Dayton, OH 45402
Phone: (937)461-6164
Fax: (937)222-7035
A minority enterprise small business
investment corporation. Diversified
industries.

Capital Technology Group, L.L.C.
Email: lws@capitaltech.com
400 Metro Place North, Ste. 300
Dublin, OH 43017
Phone: (614)792-6066
Fax: (614)792-6070
Daniel D. Oglevee, Associate
Preferred Investment Size: $250,000
to $1,000,000. Investment Types:
Seed, early and late stage. Industry
Preferences: Diversified electronics,
alternative energy, and Internet
related. Geographic Preferences:
National.

Seed One
Park Pl.
10 W. Streetsboro St.
Hudson, OH 44236
Phone: (330)650-2338
Fax: (330)650-4946
Private venture capital firm. No
industry preference. Equity financing
only.

Fifth Third Bank of Northwestern
Ohio, N.A.
606 Madison Ave.
Toledo, OH 43604
Phone: (419)259-7141
Fax: (419)259-7134

A small business investment corporation. No industry preference.

Northwest Ohio Venture Fund
Email: bwalsh@novf.com
4159 Holland-Sylvania R., Ste. 202
Toledo, OH 43623
Phone: (419)824-8144
Fax: (419)882-2035
Barry P. Walsh, Managing Partner
Preferred Investment Size: $250,000
to $1,000,000. Investment Types:
Seed, early and late stage. Industry
Preferences: Diversified. Does not
consider oil and gas exploration or
real estate. Geographic Preferences:
Midwest.

Lubrizol Performance Products Co.
29400 Lakeland Blvd.
Wickliffe, OH 44092
Phone: (440)943-4200
Fax: (440)943-5337
Venture capital supplier. Provides
seed capital and later-stage expansion
financing to emerging companies in
the biological, chemical, and material
sciences whose technology is applicable to and related to the production
and marketing of specialty and fine
chemicals.

Cactus Capital Co.
6660 High St., Office 1-B
Worthington, OH 43085
Phone: (614)436-4060
Fax: (614)436-4060
A minority enterprise small business
investment company. Diversified
industry preference.

Oklahoma

Southwestern Oklahoma
Development Authority
PO Box 569
Burns Flat, OK 73624
Phone: (405)562-4884
Free: (800)627-4882
Fax: (405)562-4880

Langston University
Minority Business Assistance Center
Hwy. 33 E.
PO Box 667
Langston, OK 73050
Phone: (405)466-3256
Fax: (405)466-2909

BancFirst Investment Corp.
1100 N. Broadway
PO Box 26788
Oklahoma City, OK 73106-0788
Phone: (405)270-1000
Fax: (405)270-1089
T. Kent Faison, Manager
Preferred Investment Size: Up to
$500,000. Investment Policies: Loans
and/or equity. Investment Types:
Early stage, expansion. Industry
Preferences: Diversified. Geographic
Preferences: Oklahoma.

Oklahoma Department of Commerce
Business Development Division
PO Box 26980
Oklahoma City, OK 73126-0980
Phone: (405)815-6552
Fax: (405)815-5142
Helps companies gain access to
capital needed for growth. Provides
financial specialists to help businesses
analyze their financing needs and to
work closely with local economic
development staff to help package
proposals for their companies. Also
responsible for assisting in the
development of new loan and
investment programs.

Oklahoma Development Finance
Authority
301 NW 63rd St., Ste. 225
Oklahoma City, OK 73116-7906
Phone: (405)848-9761
Fax: (405)848-3314
Issues tax-exempt industrial development bonds for manufacturing firms.

Oklahoma Industrial Finance
Authority
301 NW 63rd., Ste. 225
Oklahoma City, OK 73116-7906
Phone: (405)842-1145
Fax: (405)848-3314
Provides financing for manufacturing
projects involving the purchase of
land, buildings, and stationary
equipment.

Oklahoma State Treasurer's Office
Agriculture/Small Business Linked
Deposit Programs
Email: Treas@oklaosF.state.ok.us
2300 N. Lincoln Blvd.

Oklahoma City, OK 73105
Phone: (405)521-3191
Fax: (405)521-4994
Provides reduced loan rates for
Oklahoma's farming, ranching, and
small business communities.

Rees/Source Ventures, Inc.
4045 NE 64th St. Ste. 410
Oklahoma City, OK 73116
Phone: (405)843-8049
Fax: (405)843-8048
Venture capital firm providing seed,
start-up, first-stage, and second-stage
financing. Prefers to make investments in the $250,000 to $500,000
range to companies within a three-
mile radius of Oklahoma City. Areas
of interest include recreation and
leisure, environmental products and
services, packaging machinery and
materials, energy-related technologies, printing and publishing, manufacturing and automation, information
processing and software, and specialty chemicals industries. Will not
consider the following industries: oil,
gas, or mineral exploration; real
estate; motion pictures; and consulting services.

Alliance Business Investment Co.
(Tulsa)
320 South Boston Ste.1000
Tulsa, OK 74103-3703
Phone: (918)584-3581
Fax: (918)582-3403
A small business investment corporation. Provides later-stage financing
for basic industries.

Chisholm Private Capital, Inc.
10830 E. 45th St., Ste. 307
Tulsa, OK 74146
Phone: (918)663-2500
Fax: (918)663-1140
James Bode, General Partner
Preferred Investment Size: $250,000
to $1,000,000. Investment Types:
Startup, early and late stage. Industry
Preferences: Diversified communications and computer, consumer
products and retailing, electronics,
alternative energy, and medical.
Geographic Preferences: Southwest.

Davis, Tuttle Venture Partners, L.P.
(Tulsa)
320 S. Boston Ste.,1000
Tulsa, OK 74103-3703
Phone: (918)584-7272
Fax: (918)582-3403
Preferred Investment Size:
$1,000,000 to $5,000,000. Investment
Types: First and second stage,
mezzanine, and leveraged buyout.
Industry Preferences: Diversified.
Geographic Preferences: Southwest.

RBC Ventures
2627 East 21st St.
Tulsa, OK 74114
Phone: (918)744-5607
Fax: (918)743-8630
K.Y. Vargas, Vice President
Preferred Investment Size: $250,000
to $5,000,000. Investment Policies:
Equity. Investment Types: Late stage
and special situations. Industry
Preferences: Diversified transporta-
tion. Geographic Preferences:
Southwest.

Oregon

Olympic Venture Partners (Lake
Oswego)
Email: info@ovp.com
340 Oswego Pointe Dr., Ste. 200
Lake Oswego, OR 97034
Phone: (503)697-8766
Fax: (503)697-8863
Preferred Investment Size: $500,000
to $5,000,000. Investment Types:
Seed, startup, first and second stage.
Industry Preferences: Communica-
tions, computer related, electronics,
genetic engineering, and medical
health related. Geographic Prefer-
ences: Western U.S.

Orien Ventures
300 Oswego Pointe Dr., Ste. 100
Lake Oswego, OR 97034
Phone: (503)699-1680
Fax: (503)699-1681
Preferred Investment Size: $500,000
to $1,000,000. Investment Types:
Startup, first and second stage, and
mezzanine. Industry Preferences:
Diversified. Geographic Preferences:
No preference.

Northern Pacific Capital Corp.
PO Box 1658
Portland, OR 97205
Phone: (503)241-1255
Fax: (503)299-6653
A small business investment com-
pany. Diversified industry preference.

Orca Capital
1200 N.W. Naito Pkwy., Ste. 500
Portland, OR 97209
Phone: (503)227-3055
Fax: (503)248-1713
Norman B. Duffett, President
Preferred Investment Size:
$1,000,000. Investment Types: Early
and late stage, and special situations.
Industry Preferences: Diversified
communications and computer,
consumer food and beverage products, distribution, electronics,
education, and publishing. Geographic Preferences: Northwest.

Oregon Resource and Technology
Development Fund
4370 NE Halsey St., Ste. 233
Portland, OR 97213-1566
Phone: (503)282-4462
Fax: (503)282-2976
State chartered venture capital fund.
Provides investment capital for early
stage business finance and applied
research and development projects
that leads to commercially viable
products.

Shaw Venture Partners
400 SW 6th Ave., Ste. 1100
Portland, OR 97204-1636
Phone: (503)228-4884
Fax: (503)227-2471
Preferred Investment Size: $250,000
to $750,000. Investment Types: Seed,
startup, first and second stage,
leveraged buyout, and special
situations. Industry Preferences:
Diversified. Geographic Preferences:
Northwest and West Coast.

U.S. Bancorp Capital Corp.
PO Box 8837
Portland, OR 97208
Phone: (503)275-6111
Fax: (503)275-7565
A small business investment com-

pany. Diversified industry preference.

Oregon Economic Development
Department
Business Finance Section
775 Summer St. NE
Salem, OR 97310
Phone: (503)986-0160
Fax: (503)581-5115
Structures and issues loans to manu-
facturing, processing, and tourism-
related small businesses.

Tektronix Development Co.
PO Box 1000, Mail Sta. 63-862
Wilsonville, OR 97070
Phone: (503)685-4233
Fax: (503)685-3754
Venture capital firm interested in high
tech, opto electronics and measure-
ment systems investment.

Pennsylvania

Mid-Atlantic Venture Funds
Email: thebeste@net.bfp.org
125 Goodman Dr.
Bethlehem, PA 18015
Phone: (610)865-6550
Fax: (610)865-6427
Glen R. Bressner
Preferred Investment Size: $250,000
to $1,000,000. Investment Types:
Seed, research and development,
startup, first and second stage,
leveraged buyout. Industry Prefer-
ences: Diversified. Geographic
Preferences: Middle Atlantic.

Pennsylvania Department of
Community and Economic
Development
Governor's Response Team
100 Pine St., Ste. 100
Harrisburg, PA 17101
Phone: (717)787-8199
Fax: (717)772-5419
Works with individual companies to
find buildings or sites for start-up or
expansion projects; contacts manufacturers to make them aware of financial and technical assistance available,
to assist with difficulties, and to learn
of future plans for expansions or
cutbacks.

Pennsylvania Department of
Community and Economic
Development
Bureau of Bonds
Email: abrennan@doc.state.pa.us
Office of Program Management
466 Forum Bldg.
Harrisburg, PA 17120
Phone: (717)783-1109
Fax: (717)787-0879
Preserves existing jobs and creates
new jobs by assisting and promoting
employee ownership in existing
enterprises which are experiencing
layoffs or would otherwise close.

Pennsylvania Department of
Community and Economic
Development
Bureau of Bonds
Email: abrennan@doc.state.pa.us
466 Forum Bldg.
Harrisburg, PA 17120
Phone: (717)783-1109
Fax: (717)787-0879
Financing for projects approved
through the Program are borrowed
from private sources, and can be used
to acquire land, buildings, machinery,
and equipment. Borrowers must
create a minimum number of new
jobs within three years of the loan's
closing.

Enterprise Venture Capital Corp. of
Pennsylvania
111 Market St.
Johnstown, PA 15901
Phone: (814)535-7597
Fax: (814)535-8677
A small business investment corporation. No industry preference. Geographic preference is two-hour
driving radius of Johnstown, Pennsylvania.

Foster Management Co.
1018 W. 9th Ave.
King of Prussia, PA 19406
Phone: (610)992-7650
Fax: (610)992-3390
Private venture capital supplier. Not
restricted to specific industries or
geographic locations; diversified with
investments in the health care,
transportation, broadcasting, commu-

nications, energy, and home furnishings industries. Investments range
from $2 million to $15 million.

Patricof & Co. Ventures, Inc.
Executive Terrace Bldg.
455 S. Gulph Rd., Ste. 410
King of Prussia, PA 19406
Phone: (610)265-0286
Fax: (610)265-4959
Venture capital firm providing mid-
to later stage financing.

Core States Enterprise Fund
1345 Chestnut St., F.C. 1-8-12-1
Philadelphia, PA 19107
Phone: (215)973-6519
Fax: (215)973-6900
Venture capital supplier. Invests with
any industry except real estate or
construction. Minimum investment is
$1 million.

Fidelcor Capital Corp.
Fidelity Bldg., 11th Fl.
123 S. Broad St.
Philadelphia, PA 19109
Phone: (215)985-3722
Fax: (215)985-7282
A small business investment com-
pany. Diversified industry preference.

Ben Franklin Technology Center of
Southeastern Pennsylvania
University City Science Center
3624 Market St.
Philadelphia, PA 19104
Phone: (215)382-0380
Fax: (215)387-6050
Public venture capital fund interested
in technology industries.

Keystone Venture Capital
1601 Market St., Ste.2500
Philadelphia, PA 19103
Phone: (215)241-1200
Fax: (215)241-1211
Preferred Investment Size: $500,000
to $1,000,000. Investment Types:
First and second stage, mezzanine,
and leveraged buyout. Industry
Preferences: Diversified. Geographic
Preferences: Middle Atlantic.

Penn Janney Fund, Inc.
1801 Market St., 11th Fl.
Philadelphia, PA 19103

Phone: (215)665-4447
Fax: (215)665-0820
Richard M. Fox, President
Preferred Investment Size: $250,000
to $1,000,000. Investment Types:
Second stage, mezzanine, leveraged
buyout, and special situations.
Industry Preferences: Diversified.
Geographic Preferences: Northeast,
West Coast, and Middle Atlantic.

Philadelphia Ventures, Inc.
The Bellevue
200 S. Broad St.
Philadelphia, PA 19102
Phone: (215)732-4445
Fax: (215)732-4644
Walter M. Aikman, Managing
Director
Preferred Investment Size: $500,000
maximum. Investment Types: Startup,
first and second stage, mezzanine, and
leveraged buyout. Industry Prefer-
ences: Diversified technology.
Geographic Preferences: Entire U.S.

PNC Corporate Finance
(Philadelphia)
1600 Market St., 21st Fl.
Philadelphia, PA 19103
Phone: (215)585-6282
Fax: (215)585-5525
Small business investment company.

Fostin Capital Corp.
681 Andersen Dr.
Pittsburgh, PA 15220
Phone: (412)928-1400
Fax: (412)928-9635
Venture capital corporation.

Loyalhanna Venture Funds
221 7th St., Ste. 302
Pittsburgh, PA 15238
Phone: (412)820-7035
Fax: (412)820-7036
Preferred Investment Size: $100,000
to $1,000,000. Investment Types:
First and second stage. Industry
Preferences: No preference. Geo-
graphic Preferences: Entire U.S.

Pennsylvania Growth Fund
5850 Ellsworth Ave., Ste. 303
Pittsburgh, PA 15232
Phone: (412)661-1000
Fax: (412)361-0676

Barry Lhomer, Partner
Preferred Investment Size: $300,000
to $2,000,000. Investment Types:
Late stage and special situations.
Industry Preferences: Diversified.
High technology not considered.
Geographic Preferences: Middle
Atlantic.

PNC Equity Management Corp.
3150 CNG Tower
625 Liberty Ave.
Pittsburgh, PA 15222
Phone: (412)762-7035
Fax: (412)762-6233
Robert Daley, Associate
Preferred Investment Size:
$2,000,000 to $20,000,000. Invest-
ment Types: Second stage, mezza-
nine, leveraged buyout, and industry
roll ups. Industry Preferences:
Diversified. Geographic Preferences:
Eastern U.S. and Midwest.

Meridian Venture Partners (Radnor)
Email: mvpart@ix.netcom.com
The Radnor Court Bldg., Ste. 140
259 Radnor-Chester Rd.
Radnor, PA 19087
Phone: (610)254-2999
Fax: (610)254-2996
Joseph A. Hawke, Associate
Preferred Investment Size:
$1,000,000 to $5,000,000. Investment
Types: Second stage, leveraged
buyout, and special situations.
Industry Preferences: Diversified.
Geographic Preferences: East Coast
and Middle Atlantic.

First Union Capital Market
600 Penn St.
Reading, PA 19602
Phone: (610)655-1437
Fax: (610)655-1437
Small business investment corpora-
tion.

TDH
919 Conestoga Rd., Bldg. 1, Ste. 301
Rosemont, PA 19010
Phone: (610)526-9970
Fax: (610)526-9971
J.B. Doherty, Managing General
Partner
Preferred Investment Size:

$1,000,000 to $5,000,000. Investment
Types: Startup, first and second stage,
mezzanine, and leveraged buyout.
Industry Preferences: Diversified.
Geographic Preferences: Eastern U.S.
and Midwest.

S.R. One, Ltd.
Four Tower Bridge
200 Barr Harbor Dr., Ste. 250
W. Conshohocken, PA 19428-2977
Phone: (610)567-1000
Fax: (610)567-1039
Preferred Investment Size: $100,000
to $3,000,000. Investment Types:
Seed, startup, first and second stage,
leveraged buyout, and mezzanine.
Industry Preferences: Healthcare and
life sciences. Geographic Preferences:
No preference.

First SBIC of California
(Washington)
PO Box 512
Washington, PA 15301
Fax: (412)223-8290
A small business investment com-
pany.

Aloe Investment Corp.
200 Eagle Rd., Ste. 308
Wayne, PA 19087
Phone: (610)254-9403
Fax: (610)254-9404
Preferred Investment Size: $100,000
minimum. Investment Types: Startup,
early and late stage. Industry Preferences: Diversified communications
and computer, consumer products,
education and publishing. Geographic
Preferences: Within two hours of
office.

CIP Capital, L.P.
435 Devon Port Dr., Bld. 300
Wayne, PA 19087
Phone: (610)964-7860
Fax: (610)964-8136
Joseph M. Corr, President
Preferred Investment Size: $250,000
to $1,000,000. Investment Types:
First and second stage, leveraged
buyout, and special situations.
Industry Preferences: Diversified.
Geographic Preferences: Entire U.S.

Greater Philadelphia Venture Capital
Corp.
351 East Conestoga Rd.
Wayne, PA 19087
Phone: (610)688-6829
Fax: (610)254-8958
Fred Choate, Manager
Preferred Investment Size: $100,000
to $250,000. Investment Types: Early
and late stage, and special situations.
Industry Preferences: Diversified.
Geographic Preferences: Middle
Atlantic.

Safeguard Scientifics, Inc.
800 The Safeguard Bldg.
435 Devon Park Dr.
Wayne, PA 19087
Phone: (888)733-1200
Fax: (610)293-0601
Private venture capital fund. Areas of
interest include biotechnology, health
care, information services, and high
technology industries.

The Sandhurst Venture Fund, L.P.
351 E. Constoga Rd.
Wayne, PA 19087
Phone: (610)254-8900
Fax: (610)254-8958
Preferred Investment Size: $500,000
to $1,000,000. Investment Types:
Second stage and leveraged buyout.
Industry Preferences: Computer
stores, disposable medical/health
related, and industrial products.
Geographic Preferences: East Coast
and Middle Atlantic.

Rockhill Ventures, Inc.
Email: hsbroderso@aol.com
100 Front St., Ste. 1350
West Conshohocken, PA 19428
Phone: (610)940-0300
Fax: (610)940-0301
Preferred Investment Size: $100,000
to $5,000,000. Investment Types:
Seed, research and development,
startup, first and second stage, virtual
company strategy. Industry Prefer-
ences: Genetic engineering and
medical/health related. Geographic
Preferences: Eastern U.S.

Puerto Rico

Advent-Morro Equity Partners
Banco Popular Bldg.
206 Tetuan St., Ste. 903
San Juan, PR 00902
Phone: (787)725-5285
Fax: (787)721-1735
Cyril L. Meduna, General Partner
Preferred Investment Size: $500,000
to $1,000,000. Investment Types:
Early and late stage, and special
situations. Industry Preferences:
Diversified. Retail not considered.
Geographic Preferences: Southeast
and East Coast.

North America Investment Corp.
Mercantil Plaza, Ste. 813
PO Box 191831
San Juan, PR 00919-1813
Phone: (787)754-6177
Fax: (787)754-6181
Marcelino D. Pastrana-Torres,
President
Preferred Investment Size: $100,000
to $250,000. Investment Types:
Second stage. Industry Preferences:
Consumer products and retailing,
consumer distribution, industrial
equipment, therapeutic equipment,
real estate, and transportation.
Geographic Preferences: Puerto Rico.

Rhode Island

Domestic Capital Corp.
815 Reservoir Ave.
Cranston, RI 02910
Phone: (401)946-3310
Fax: (401)943-6708
A small business investment corpora-
tion. No industry preference.

Fairway Capital Corp.
285 Governor St.
Providence, RI 02906
Phone: (401)861-4600
Fax: (401)861-0530
A small business investment com-
pany. Diversified industry preference.

Fleet Equity Partners
Email: fep@fleetequity.com
50 Kennedy Plaza, 12th Fl.
Providence, RI 02903
Phone: (401)278-6770

Fax: (401)278-6387
Rory B. Smith, General Partner
Preferred Investment Size:
$5,000,000 to $25,000,000. Investment Policies: Equity. Investment
Types: Leverage buyouts, expansion.
Industry Preferences: Media/commu-
nications, healthcare, printing,
manufacturing. Geographic Preferences: National.

Fleet Equity Partners (Providence)
Email: fep@fleetequity.com
50 Kennedy Plaza
RI MO F12C
Providence, RI 02903
Phone: (401)278-6770
Fax: (401)278-6387
Roby B. Smith, General Partner
Preferred Investment Size:
$5,000,000 to $25,000,000. Invest-
ment Types: Leveraged buyout,
special situations, and management
buyouts. Industry Preferences:
Diversified. Geographic Preferences:
Entire U.S.

Moneta Capital Corp.
285 Governor St.
Providence, RI 02906
Phone: (401)861-4600
Fax: (401)861-0530
A small business investment corpora-
tion. No industry preference.

Rhode Island Economic Development
Corp.
Rhode Island Port Operations
Division
1 W. Exchange
Providence, RI 02903
Phone: (401)277-2601
Fax: (401)277-2102
Provides financing through tax-
exempt revenue bonds.

Rhode Island Economic Development
Corp.
Rhode Island Industrial-Recreational
Building Authority
1 W. Exchange
Providence, RI 02903
Phone: (401)222-2601
Fax: (401)222-2102
Issues mortgage insurance on
financing obtained through other
financial institutions.

Rhode Island Economic Development
Corp.
Rhode Island Partnership for Science
and Technology
1 W. Exchange
Providence, RI 02903
Phone: (401)222-2601
Fax: (401)222-2102
Offers grants to businesses for applied
research with a potential for profitable
commercialization. Research must be
conducted in conjunction with
universities, colleges, or hospitals.
Also has a program which provides
consulting services and grants to
applicants of the Federal Small
Business Innovation Research
Program.

Rhode Island Economic Development
Corp.
Ocean State Business Development
Authority
1 W. Exchange
Providence, RI 02903
Phone: (401)222-2601
Fax: (401)222-2102
Private, nonprofit corporation
certified by the Small Business
Administration to administer the
SBA(504) loan program.

Rhode Island Office of the General
Treasurer
Business Investment Fund
Email: treasury@treasury.state.ri.us
40 Fountain St., 8th Fl.
Providence, RI 02903-1855
Phone: (401)222-2287
Free: (800)752-8088
Fax: (401)222-6141
Provides fixed-rate loans in coopera-
tion with the U.S. Small Business
Administration and local banks.

Richmond Square Capital Corp.
1 Richmond Sq.
Providence, RI 02906
Phone: (401)521-3000
Fax: (401)751-8997
A small business investment com-
pany. Diversified industry preference.

Wallace Capital Corp.
170 Westminster St., Ste.1200
Providence, RI 02903
Fax: (401)273-9648

A small business investment company. Diversified industry preference.

South Carolina

Charleston Capital Corp.
111 Church St.
PO Box 328
Charleston, SC 29402
Phone: (843)723-6464
Fax: (843)723-1228
Small business investment corporation preferring secured loans. Assists the southeastern U.S. only.

Lowcountry Investment Corp.
4401 Piggly Wiggly Dr.
PO Box 118047
Charleston, SC 29423
Phone: (803)554-9880
Fax: (803)745-2730
A small business investment corporation. Diversified industry preference.

Capital Insights, L.L.C.
Email: jwarner@capitalinsights.com
PO Box 27162
Greenville, SC 29616-2162
Phone: (864)242-6832
Fax: (864)242-6755
Preferred Investment Size: $500,000 to $5,000,000. Investment Policies: Equity. Investment Types: Early and late stage. Industry Preferences: No preference. Geographic Preferences: Southeast.

Floco Investment Co., Inc.
PO Box 1629
Lake City, SC 29560
Phone: (843)389-2731
Fax: (843)389-4199
A small business investment corporation. Invests only in grocery stores.

South Dakota

South Dakota Department of Agriculture
Office of Rural Development
Foss Bldg.
523 E. Capitol
Pierre, SD 57501-3182
Phone: (605)773-3375
Free: (800)228-5254
Fax: (605)773-5926
Provides loans, administered and

serviced through local lenders, that are intended to supplement existing credit.

South Dakota Development Corp.
SBA 504 Loan Program
711 E. Wells Ave.
Pierre, SD 57501-3369
Phone: (605)773-5032
Free: (800)872-6190
Fax: (605)773-3256
Offers subordinated mortgage financing to healthy and expanding small businesses.

South Dakota Governor's Office of Economic Development
Economic Development Finance Authority
711 E. Wells Ave.
Pierre, SD 57501-3369
Phone: (605)773-5032
Free: (800)872-6190
Fax: (605)773-3256
Pools tax-exempt or taxable development bonds to construct any site, structure, facility, service, or utility for the storage, distribution, or manufacture of industrial, agricultural, or nonagricultural products, machinery, or equipment.

South Dakota Governor's Office of Economic Development
Revolving Economic Development and Initiative Fund
711 E. Wells Ave.
Pierre, SD 57501-3369
Phone: (605)773-5032
Free: (800)872-6190
Fax: (605)773-3256
Provides low-interest revolving loans for the creation of primary jobs, capital investment, and the diversification of the state's economy. Costs eligible for participation include land and the associated site improvements; construction, acquisition, and renovation of buildings; fees, services and other costs associated with construction; the purchase and installation of machinery and equipment; and trade receivables, inventory, and work-inprogress inventory.

Tennessee

Valley Capital Corp.
Krystal Bldg.
100 W. Martin Luther King Blvd., Ste. 212
Chattanooga, TN 37402
Phone: (423)265-1557
Fax: (423)265-1588
Preferred Investment Size: $100,000 to $350,000. Investment Types: Second stage, mezzanine, and leveraged buyout. Industry Preferences: Diversified. Geographic Preferences: Southeast.

Coleman Swenson-Hoffman, Booth Inc.
237 2nd Ave. S
Franklin, TN 37064-2649
Phone: (615)791-9462
Fax: (615)791-9636
Larry H. Coleman, Ph.D., Managing Partner
Preferred Investment Size: $1,000,000 to $7,000,000. Investment Types: Seed, startup, first and second stage. Industry Preferences: Healthcare related. Geographic Preferences: No preference.

Capital Services & Resources, Inc.
5159 Wheelis Dr., Ste. 106
Memphis, TN 38117
Phone: (901)761-2156
Fax: (907)767-0060
Charles Y. Bancroft, Treasurer
Preferred Investment Size: $100,000 to $250,000. Investment Policies: Equity. Investment Types: Late stage and special situations. Industry Preferences: Diversified. Geographic Preferences: United States and Canada.

Chickasaw Capital Corp.
8354 Championship Dr., Ste. 203
Memphis, TN 38125
Phone: (901)748-0214
Fax: (901)748-3135
A minority enterprise small business investment corporation. No industry preference.

Flemming Companies
4681 Burbank
Memphis, TN 38118

Phone: (901)794-8660
Fax: (901)797-3987
A small business investment corporation.

Gulf Pacific
5100 Poplar Ave., No. 427
Memphis, TN 38137-0401
Phone: (901)767-3400
Free: (800)456-1867
Fax: (901)680-7033
A minority enterprise small business investment corporation.

International Paper Capital
Formation, Inc.
6400 Poplar Ave.
Tower 2, 4th Fl., Rm. 130
Memphis, TN 38197
Phone: (901)763-6217
Fax: (901)763-6076
A minority enterprise small business investment corporation. Diversified industry preference. Involvement includes expansion, refinancing, and acquisitions, but no start-up projects. Requires a minimum investment of $50,000 to $300,000.

Union Platters Bank
158 Madison Ave.
Memphis, TN 38103-0708
Phone: (901)524-5700
Free: (800)821-9979
Fax: (901)524-5713
A small business investment corporation.

West Tennessee Venture Capital
Corp.
Tennessee Valley Center for Minority
Economics Dev.
5 N. 3rd St., Ste. 2000
Memphis, TN 38103-2610
Phone: (901)523-1884
Fax: (901)527-6091
A minority enterprise small business investment corporation.

Equitas L.P.
2000 Glen Echo Rd., Ste. 101
PO Box 158838
Nashville, TN 37215-8838
Phone: (615)383-8673
Fax: (615)383-8693
Preferred Investment Size: $500.000.
Investment Types: Later stage.

Industry Preferences: Diversified.
Geographic Preferences: Southeast and East Coast.

Massey Burch Capital Corp.
Email: tcalton@masseyburch.com
310 25th Ave. N, Ste. 103
Nashville, TN 37203
Phone: (615)329-9448
Fax: (615)329-9237
Lucious E. Burch, IV, Partner
Preferred Investment Size: $500,000 to $2,000,000. Investment Types: Seed, startup, first and second stage. Industry Preferences: Communication and computer related. Geographic Preferences: Southern U.S. and Middle Atlantic.

Sirrom Capital Corp.
500 Church St., Ste. 200
Nashville, TN 37219
Phone: (615)256-0701
Fax: (615)726-1208
Kathy Harris, Vice President
Preferred Investment Size: $500,000 to $5,000,000. Investment Types: Mezzanine and leveraged buyout. Industry Preferences: Diversified. Geographic Preferences: No preference.

Tennessee Department of Economic
and Community Development
Grants Program Management Section
Rachel Jackson Bldg., 6th Fl.
320 6th Ave. N.
Nashville, TN 37243-0405
Phone: (615)741-6201
Free: (800)342-8470
Fax: (615)741-5070
Administers grant money for the community development block grant program, the Appalachian Regional Commission, and the Economic Development Administration.

Texas

Phillips-Smith Specialty Retail Group
Email: pssrg@aol.com
5080 Spectrum Dr., Ste. 805 W
Addison, TX 75001
Phone: (972)387-0725
Fax: (972)458-2560
G. Michael Machens, General Partner

Preferred Investment Size:
$1,000,000 to $5,000,000. Investment Types: Seed, startup, first and second stage, mezzanine, and leveraged buyout. Industry Preferences: Retail related. Geographic Preferences: Entire U.S.

Austin Ventures, L.P.
Email: info@ausven.com
114 W. 7th St., Ste. 1300
Austin, TX 78701
Phone: (512)485-1900
Fax: (512)476-3952
Joseph C. Aragona, General Partner
Preferred Investment Size:
$1,000,000 to $2,000,000. Investment Types: Seed, startup, first and second stage, leveraged buyout, and special situations. Industry Preferences: Diversified. Geographic Preferences: Southwest and Texas.

The Capital Network
Email: davidg@ati.utexas.edu
3925 West Braker Lane, Ste. 406
Austin, TX 78759-5321
Phone: (512)305-0826
Fax: (512)305-0836
Preferred Investment Size: $100,000.
Investment Types: Seed, early and late stage, and special situations. Industry Preferences: Diversified. Geographic Preferences: United States and Canada.

Huber Capital Ventures
11917 Oak Knoll, Ste. G
Austin, TX 78759
Phone: (512)258-8668
Fax: (512)258-9091
Venture capital firm providing short-term working capital funding for specific projects. Areas of interest include small capitalization companies in manufacturing, wholesaling, and technical services.

Texas Department of Economic
Development
Finance Office
PO Box 12728
Austin, TX 78711
Phone: (512)936-0281
Fax: (512)936-0520
Administers several programs that

benefit small businesses, including those authorized under the Industrial Development Corporation Act of 1979 and the Rural Development Act, as well as the state industrial revenue bond program.

Alliance Enterprise Corp. (Dallas)
Email: mesbic@gan.net
12655 N. Central Expy., Ste 710
Dallas, TX 75243
Phone: (972)991-1597
Fax: (972)991-1647
A minority enterprise small business investment company. Diversified industry preference.

Arkoma Venture Partners
Email: joelf@arkomavp.com
5950 Berkshire Lane, Ste. 1400
Dallas, TX 75225
Phone: (214)739-3515
Fax: (214)739-3572
Joel Fontenot, Executive Vice President
Preferred Investment Size: $500,000 to $5,000,000. Investment Policies: Equity. Investment Types: Seed, early and late stage, and leveraged buyout. Industry Preferences: Diversified communications and computer, distribution, electronics, and industrial products and equipment. Geographic Preferences: National.

Banc One Capital Partners (Dallas)
3811 Turtle Creek Blvd., Ste. 1600
Dallas, TX 75219
Phone: (214)979-0650
Fax: (214)979-0769
Suzanne B. Kriscunas, Managing Director
Preferred Investment Size: $5,000,000 to$15,000,000. Investment Types: Second stage, mezzanine, leveraged buyout, special situations, recaps, and expansion financing for mature companies. Industry Preferences: Food, industrial, and medical product distribution; medical/health related; education; and transportation. Geographic Preferences: Entire U.S.

Capital Southwest Corp.
12900 Preston Rd., Ste. 700

Dallas, TX 75230
Phone: (972)233-8242
Fax: (972)233-7362
Preferred Investment Size: $1,000,000 to $6,000,000. Investment Types: First and second stage, leveraged buyout, special situations, and control block purchases. Industry Preferences: Diversified. Geographic Preferences: Entire U.S.

Diamond A. Ford Corp.
200 Crescent Court, Ste. 1350
Dallas, TX 75201
Phone: (214)871-5177
Fax: (214)871-5199
A small business investment company. Diversified industry preference.

Erickson Capital Group, Inc.
5950 Berkshire Lane, Ste. 1100
Dallas, TX 75225
Phone: (214)365-6060
Fax: (214)365-6001
Venture capital firm providing seed, start-up, first and second stage, and expansion financing. Areas of interest include health care.

Gaekeke Landers
3710 Rawlins St., Ste. 100
Dallas, TX 75219
Phone: (214)528-8883
Fax: (214)528-8058
Venture capital firm providing acquisition, start-up, and leverage equity financing. Areas of interest include real estate.

Hook Partners
Email: dhook@hookpartners.com
13760 Noel Rd., Ste. 805
Dallas, TX 75240
Phone: (972)991-5457
Fax: (972)991-5458
David J. Hook
Preferred Investment Size: $100,000 maximum. Investment Types: Seed, research and development, startup, and first stage. Industry Preferences: Diversified. Geographic Preferences: Southwest and West Coast.

Interwest Partners (Dallas)
2 Galleria Tower
13455 Noel Rd., Ste. 1670
Dallas, TX 75240

Phone: (972)392-7279
Fax: (972)490-6348

Kahala Investments, Inc.
8214 Westchester Dr., Ste. 715
Dallas, TX 75225
Phone: (214)987-0077
Fax: (214)987-2332
Lee R. Slaughter, Jr., President
Preferred Investment Size: $100,000 maximum. Investment Types: Mezzanine, leveraged buyout, special situations, control block purchases, industry roll ups, and private equity. Industry Preferences: Diversified. Geographic Preferences: Southeast and Southwest.

Mapleleaf Capital, Ltd.
3 Forest Plz., Ste.935
12221 Merit Dr.
Dallas, TX 75251-2248
Phone: (972)239-5650
Fax: (972)701-0024
A small business investment company. Diversified industry preference.

May Financial Corp.
8333 Douglas Ave., Ste. 400
Lock Box 82
Dallas, TX 75225
Phone: (214)987-5200
Free: (800)767-4397
Fax: (214)987-1994
Brokerage firm working with a venture capital firm. Prefers food, oil and gas, and electronics industries.

Merchant Banking Group Ltd.
PO Box 763189
Dallas, TX 75376
Phone: (214)337-5490
Fax: (214)337-5497
Venture capital firm providing leveraged buyout financing. Areas of interest include basic manufacturing and distribution.

MESBIC Ventures Holding Co.
12655 N. Central Expy., Ste. 710
Dallas, TX 75243
Phone: (972)991-1597
Fax: (972)991-1647
Linda Roach, Senior Vice President
Preferred Investment Size: Up to $1,000,000. Investment Policies: Loans and/or equity. Investment

Types: Expansion, later stage.
Industry Preferences: Diversified.
Geographic Preferences: Southwest.

MSI Capital Corp.
6500 Greenville Ave., Ste. 350
Dallas, TX 75206-1012
Phone: (214)265-1801
Fax: (214)265-1804
No industry preference.

NationsBank Capital Investors
901 Main St., 22nd Fl.
Dallas, TX 75202-2911
Phone: (214)508-0900
Fax: (214)508-0604
Doug Williamson, Managing Director
Preferred Investment Size:
$3,000,000 to $5,000,000. Investment
Types: Second stage, mezzanine,
leveraged buyout, recaps, manage-
ment buyouts, and expansion.
Industry Preferences: Diversified.
Geographic Preferences: Entire U.S.

NCNB Texas Venture Group, Inc.
901 Maine, 22nd Fl.
Dallas, TX 75202
Phone: (214)508-0900
Fax: (214)508-0985
Venture capital firm providing
expansion and leveraged buyout
financing. Areas of interest include
medical products and services, energy
service, environmental, specialty
retail, transportation, general manufacturing, and communications.

North Texas MESBIC, Inc.
9500 Forest Lane, Ste. 430
Dallas, TX 75243
Phone: (214)221-3565
Fax: (214)221-3566
Preferred Investment Size: $100,000
to $250,000. Investment Types:
Second stage, mezzanine, and
leveraged buyout. Industry Preferences: Consumer food and beverage
products, restaurants, retailing,
consumer and food distribution.
Geographic Preferences: Southwest.

PMC Capital, Inc.
Attn: Andy Rosemore
17290 Preston Rd., 3rd Fl.
Dallas, TX 75252-5618

Phone: (972)349-3200
Free: (800)486-3223
Fax: (972)349-3265
A small business investment corpora-
tion, minority enterprise small
business investment corporation, and
SBA guaranteed lender. No industry
preferred.

Pro-Med Investment Corp.
17290 Preston Rd., 3rd Fl.
Dallas, TX 75252
Phone: (972)349-3200
Fax: (972)349-3265
A minority enterprise small business
investment company. Diversified
industry preference.

Sevin Rosen Funds
Email: info@srfunds.com
13455 Noel Rd., Ste. 1670
Dallas, TX 75240
Phone: (972)702-1100
Fax: (972)702-1103
Stephen L. Domenik, Partner
Preferred Investment Size:
$1,000,000 to $10,000,000. Invest-
ment Types: Seed, research and
development, startup, and first stage.
Industry Preferences: Diversified
technology. Geographic Preferences:
Entire U.S.

Stratford Capital Partners, L.P.
Email: stratcap@hmtf.com
200 Crescent Ct., Ste. 1600
Dallas, TX 75201
Phone: (214)740-7377
Fax: (214)720-7888
Michael D. Brown, Managing Partner
Preferred Investment Size:
$3,000,000 to $9,000,000. Investment
Policies: Equity, sub debt with equity.
Investment Types: Expansion, later
stage, acquisition. Industry Prefer-
ences: Manufacturing, distribution,
diversified. Geographic Preferences:
National.

Sullivan Enterprises
9130 Markville Dr.
PO Box 743803
Dallas, TX 75374-3803
Phone: (972)414-5690
Venture capital firm providing
refinancings and expansion, mezza-

nine, and leveraged buyouts financing. Areas of interest include manufacturing, service, retailing, wholesale
and distribution.

Sunwestern Investment Group
12221 Merit Dr., Ste. 935
Dallas, TX 75251
Phone: (972)239-5650
Fax: (972)701-0024
Preferred Investment Size: $500,000
to $1,000,000. Investment Types:
Second stage, leveraged buyout, and
special situations. Industry Prefer-
ences: Diversified. Geographic
Preferences: Southwest and West
Coast.

Tower Ventures, Inc.
12655 N. Central Expy., Ste. 710
Dallas, TX 75243
Fax: (972)991-1647
Donald R. Lawhorne, President
Preferred Investment Size: Up to
$500,000. Investment Policies: Loans
and/or equity. Investment Types:
Early stage, expansion, later stage.

Western Financial Capital Corp.
17290 Preston Rd., 3rd Fl.
Dallas, TX 75252
Phone: (972)349-3200
Fax: (972)349-3265
A small business investment com-
pany. Provides financing to the
medical industry.

Wingate Partners
750 N. St. Paul St., Ste. 1200
Dallas, TX 75201
Phone: (214)720-1313
Fax: (214)871-8799
Preferred Investment Size:
$5,000,000 maximum. Investment
Types: Leveraged buyout and control
block purchases. Industry Prefer-
ences: Diversified. Geographic
Preferences: Entire U.S. and Canada.

HCT Capital Corp.
4916 Camp Bowie Blvd., Ste. 200
Ft. Worth, TX 76107
Phone: (817)763-8706
Fax: (817)377-8049
A small business investment com-
pany. Diversified industry preference.

SBIC Partners, L.P.
201 Main St., Ste. 2302
Ft. Worth, TX 76102
Phone: (817)339-7020
Fax: (817)729-3226
Gregory Forrest, Manager
Preferred Investment Size: $2 to $5
million. Investment Policies: Equity.
Investment Types: Expansion, later
stage. Industry Preferences: Diversi-
fied. Geographic Preferences:
National.

Acorn Ventures, Inc.
3000 Richmond Ave., Ste. 360
Houston, TX 77098
Phone: (713)807-7200
No industry preference.

Alliance Business Investment Co.
(Houston)
1221 McKinney Ste.3100
Houston, TX 77010
Phone: (713)659-3131
Fax: (713)659-8070
A small business investment corpora-
tion.

Aspen Capital Ltd.
55 Waugh, Ste. 710
Houston, TX 77007
Phone: (713)880-4494
Fax: (713)880-5294
A small business investment corpora-
tion. No industry preference.

The Catalyst Group
Email: herman@the-catalyst-
group.com
3 Riverway, Ste. 770
Houston, TX 77056
Phone: (713)623-8133
Fax: (713)623-0473
Preferred Investment Size: $500,000
to $5,000,000. Investment Types:
Second stage, mezzanine, leveraged
buyout, and control block purchases.
Industry Preferences: Diversified.
Geographic Preferences: No prefer-
ence.

Chase Bank of Texas
PO Box 2558
Houston, TX 77252-8032
Phone: (713)216-4553
A small business investment corpora-
tion. No industry preference.

Chen's Financial Group, Inc.
10101 Southwest Fwy., Ste. 370
Houston, TX 77074
Phone: (713)772-8868
Fax: (713)772-2168
A minority enterprise small business
investment corporation. Areas of
interest include real estate, franchise
restaurants, banking, and import/
export industries.

Criterion Ventures
1330 Post Oak Blvd., Ste. 1525
Houston, TX 77056
Phone: (713)627-9200
Fax: (713)627-9292
Venture capital fund. Raises venture
capital. Interested in companies
headquartered in the Sunbelt region.
Areas of interest include telecommunications, biomedical, and specialty
retail.

Cureton & Co., Inc.
Email: chipcur@aol.com
1100 Louisiana, Ste. 3250
Houston, TX 77002
Phone: (713)658-9806
Fax: (713)658-0476
Stewart Cureton, President
Preferred Investment Size:
$1,000,000 to $25,000,000. Invest-
ment Types: First and second stage,
leveraged buyout, and special
situations. Industry Preferences:
Diversified. Geographic Preferences:
Southwest.

Davis, Tuttle Venture Partners
(Dallas)
8 Greenway Plaza, Ste. 1020
Houston, TX 77046
Phone: (713)993-0440
Fax: (713)621-2297
Preferred Investment Size:
$1,000,000 to $5,000,000. Investment
Types: First and second stage,
mezzanine, and leveraged buyout.
Industry Preferences: Diversified.
Geographic Preferences: Southwest.

High Technology Associates
1775 St. James Pl., Ste. 105
Houston, TX 77056
Phone: (713)963-9300
Fax: (713)963-8341

Venture capital firm providing second
stage and expansion financing. Areas
of interest include biotechnology,
chemicals, food processing and food
processing machinery. Particularly
interested in companies willing to
establish operations in the Northern
Netherlands.

Houston Partners, SBIC
401 Louisiana, 8th Fl.
Houston, TX 77002
Phone: (713)222-8600
Fax: (713)222-8932
A small business investment com-
pany. Diversified industry preference.

MESBIC Financial Corp. of Houston
9130 North Fwy., Ste. 203
Houston, TX 77037
Fax: (281)447-4222
Atillio Galli, President
Preferred Investment Size: $100,000
to $1 million. Investment Policies:
Loans and equity investments.
Investment Types: Consolidated debt
& preferred stock with warrants.
Industry Preferences: Diversified - no
real estate or gas and oil. Geographic
Preferences: Houston.

Payne Webber, Inc.
700 Louisiana St., Ste.3800
Houston, TX 77002
Fax: (713)236-3133

Penzoil
PO Box 2967
Houston, TX 77252
Phone: (713)546-8910
Fax: (713)546-4154
A small business investment com-
pany. Diversified industry preference.

Triad Ventures
AM Fund
4600 Post Oak Place, Ste. 100
Houston, TX 77027
Phone: (713)627-9111
Fax: (713)627-9119
Preferred Investment Size: $250,000
maximum. Investment Types: First
and second stage, and mezzanine.
Industry Preferences: No preference.
Geographic Preferences: Southwest
and Texas.

UNCO Ventures, Inc.
3000 Richmond Ave. Ste. 360
Houston, TX 77098
Phone: (713)807-7200
A small business investment company. Diversified industry preference.

United Oriental Capital Corp.
908 Town and Country Blvd., Ste. 310
Houston, TX 77024-2207
Phone: (713)461-3909
Fax: (713)465-7559
A minority enterprise small business investment corporation. No industry preference.

Ventex Management, Inc.
1001 Fannin St., Ste. 1095
Houston, TX 77002
Phone: (713)659-7870
Fax: (713)659-7855
Preferred Investment Size: $1,000,000 to $5,000,000. Investment Types: Second stage, mezzanine, leveraged buyout, and special situations. Industry Preferences: Diversified. Geographic Preferences: Southwest.

First Capital Group Management Co., L.C.
750 East Mulberry St., Ste. 305
PO Box 15616
San Antonio, TX 78212
Phone: (210)736-4233
Fax: (210)736-5449
Jeffrey P. Blanchard, Managing Partner
Preferred Investment Size: $500,000 to $5,000,000. Investment Types: Second stage, mezzanine, leveraged buyout, and special situations. Industry Preferences: Diversified. Geographic Preferences: Southwest.

Southwest Venture Partners/Hixven Partners
Email: swvp@aol.com
16414 San Pedro, Ste. 345
San Antonio, TX 78232
Phone: (210)402-1200
Fax: (210)402-1221
Preferred Investment Size: $500,000 to $5,000,000. Investment Types: Startup, first and second stage.

Industry Preferences: Diversified. Geographic Preferences: Southwest and Gulf states.

Norwest Bank & Trust
1 O'Connor Plz.
Victoria, TX 77902
Phone: (512)573-5151
Fax: (512)574-5236
A small business investment company. Diversified industry preference.

Woodlands Venture Partners
2170 Buckthorne Pl., Ste. 170
The Woodlands, TX 77380
Phone: (281)367-9999
Fax: (281)298-1295
Venture capital firm providing start-up, first stage, second stage and seed financing. Areas of interest include medical/biotechnology only.

Utah

Deseret Certified Development Corp. (Orem)
228 N. Orem Blvd.
Orem, UT 84057-5011
Phone: (801)221-7772
Fax: (801)221-7775
Maintains an SBA(504) loan program, designed for community development and job creation, and an intermediary loan program, through Farmer's Home Administration.

Deseret Certified Development Corp. (Midvale)
Email: deseretcdc@aol.com
2595 East 3300 South
Salt Lake City, UT 84109
Phone: (801)474-3232
Fax: (801)566-1532
Maintains an SBA(504) loan program, designed for community development and job creation, and an intermediary loan program, through Farmer's Home Administration.

First Security Business Investment Corp.
15 East 100 South, Ste. 100
Salt Lake City, UT 84111
Phone: (801)246-5688
Fax: (801)246-5740
Preferred Investment Size: $250,000.
Investment Policies: Loans and/or

equity. Investment Types: Expansion, later stage. Industry Preferences: Diversified. Geographic Preferences: West Coast.

Travis Capital, Inc.
Email: ntravis@traviscapital.com
39 Market St., Ste. 200
Salt Lake City, UT 84101
Phone: (801)355-4321
Fax: (801)521-9142
Elliot R. Travis, President
Preferred Investment Size: $1,000,000 to $5,000,000. Investment Types: Early and late stage, and leveraged buyout. Industry Preferences: Diversified communications and computer, consumer products and services, publishing, and transportation. Geographic Preferences: National.

Utah Technology Finance Corp.
177 E., 100 S.
Salt Lake City, UT 84111
Phone: (801)364-4346
Fax: (801)741-4249
Assists the start-up and growth of emerging technology-based businesses and products.

Utah Ventures II, L.P.
423 Wakara Way, Ste. 206
Salt Lake City, UT 84108
Phone: (801)583-5922
Fax: (801)583-4105
James C. Dreyfous, Managing General Partner
Preferred Investment Size: $100,000 to $3,000,000. Investment Types: Seed, startup, first and second stage. Industry Preferences: Diversified technology. Geographic Preferences: Northwest, Southwest, Rocky Mountains, and West Coast.

Wasatch Venture Corp.
Email: mail@wasatchvc.com
1 S. Main St., Ste. 1400
Salt Lake City, UT 84133
Phone: (801)524-8939
Fax: (801)524-8941
Todd Stevens, Manager
Preferred Investment Size: $250,000 to $2,000,000. Investment Policies: Equity and debt. Investment Types:

Early stage. Industry Preferences: High technology. Geographic Preferences: Western U.S.

Vermont

Vermont Economic Development Authority
58 E. State St.
Montpelier, VT 05602
Phone: (802)828-5627
Fax: (802)828-5474
Several financial programs to assist small and medium-sized manufacturing firms in the state.

Vermont Economic Development Authority
Vermont Job Start
58 E. State St.
Montpelier, VT 05602
Phone: (802)828-5627
Fax: (802)828-5474
A state-funded economic opportunity program aimed at increasing self-employment by low-income Vermonters.

Green Mountain Capital, L.P.
RD 1, Box 1503
Waterbury, VT 05676
Phone: (802)244-8981
Fax: (802)244-8990
Michael Sweatman, President
Preferred Investment Size: $100,000 to $500,000. Investment Types: Second stage and mezzanine. Industry Preferences: No preference. Geographic Preferences: Northeast.

Virgin Islands

Tri-Island Economic Development Council, Inc.
PO Box 838
St. Thomas, VI 00804-0838
Provides counseling, information, referrals, and management and technical assistance to help strengthen existing businesses and expand the rate of development of new businesses.

Virginia

Continental SBIC
PO Box 3723

Arlington, VA 22203
Phone: (703)527-5200
Fax: (703)527-3700
Michael W. Jones, Senior Vice President
Preferred Investment Size: $100,000 to $1,000,000. Investment Types: Second stage, mezzanine, leveraged buyout, and special situations. Industry Preferences: Diversified. Geographic Preferences: Northeast, Southeast, Middle Atlantic, and Central Canada.

East West United Investment Co.
1568 Spring Hill Rd., Ste. 100
McLean, VA 22102
Phone: (703)442-0150
Fax: (703)442-0156
A minority enterprise small business investment company. Diversified industry preference.

East West United Investment Co. (Mc Lean)
1568 Spring Hill Rd., Ste. 100
McLean, VA 22102
Phone: (703)442-0150
Fax: (703)442-0156
Dung Bui, President

Spacevest
Email: spacevest@spacevest.com
11911 Freedom Dr., Ste. 500
Reston, VA 20190
Phone: (703)904-9800
Fax: (703)904-0571
Roger P. Widing, Managing Director
Preferred Investment Size: $500,000 to $5,000,000. Investment Policies: Equity. Investment Types: Early and late stage. Industry Preferences: Diversified. Geographic Preferences: National.

Ewing, Monroe, Bemiss and Co.
Email: embco@embco.com
901 E. Cary St., Ste. 1510
Richmond, VA 23219
Phone: (804)780-1900
Fax: (804)780-1901
A small business investment corporation. No industry preference.

Virginia Small Business Financing Authority
PO Box 446

Richmond, VA 23218-0446
Phone: (804)371-8254
Fax: (804)225-3384
Assists small businesses in obtaining financing for development and expansion.

Walnut Capital Corp. (Vienna)
8000 Towers Crescent Dr., Ste.1070
Vienna, VA 22182
Phone: (703)448-3771
Fax: (703)448-7751
Preferred Investment Size: $100,000 to $500,000. Investment Types: Startup, first and second stage, mezzanine, and leveraged buyout. Industry Preferences: Diversified. Geographic Preferences: No preference.

Washington

Cable and Howse Ventures (Bellevue)
777 108th Ave. NE, Ste. 2300
Bellevue, WA 98004
Phone: (425)646-3035
Fax: (425)646-3041
Venture capital investor. Provides start-up and early stage financing to enterprises in the western United States, although a national perspective is maintained. Interests lie in proprietary or patentable technology. Investments range from $50,000 to $2 million.

Pacific Northwest Partners SBIC, L.P.
City Center Bellevue
500-108th Ave. NE, Ste. 800
Bellevue, WA 98004
Phone: (425)646-7357
Fax: (425)646-7356
Preferred Investment Size: $5,000,000 maximum. Investment Policies: Private equity investments. Investment Types: Seed Through later stage. Industry Preferences: Diversified, retail, healthcare, technology. Geographic Preferences: Pacific Northwest.

Columbia Basin Ventures, L.L.C.
8911 Grandridge Blvd., Ste. A
Kennewick, WA 99336
Phone: (509)783-4227
Fax: (509)783-4612

Richard J. Reisinger, Vice President
Preferred Investment Size: $100,000
to $500,000. Investment Types: Early
and late stage. Industry Preferences:
Diversified. Geographic Preferences:
Eastern Washington.

Materia Venture Associates, L.P.
3435 Carillon Pointe
Kirkland, WA 98033-7354
Phone: (425)822-4100
Fax: (425)827-4086
Preferred Investment Size: $250,000
to $1,000,000. Investment Types:
Startup, first and second stage, and
mezzanine. Industry Preferences:
Advanced industrial products and
equipment. Geographic Preferences:
Entire U.S.

Olympic Venture Partners (Kirkland)
Email: info@ovp.com
2420 Carillon Pt.
Kirkland, WA 98033
Phone: (425)889-9192
Fax: (425)889-0152
Preferred Investment Size: $500,000
to $5,000,000. Investment Types:
Seed, startup, first and second stage.
Industry Preferences: Diversified
technology. Geographic Preferences:
Western U.S. and Canada.

Washington Department of
Community, Trade and Economic
Development
Community Development Finance
(CDF) Program
906 Columbia St. SW
PO Box 48300
Olympia, WA 98504-8300
Phone: (360)753-7426
Fax: (360)586-3582
Helps businesses and industries
secure needed financing by combin-
ing private financial loans with
federal and state loans.

Washington Department of
Community, Trade and Economic
Development
Development Loan Fund
906 Columbia St. SW
PO Box 48300
Olympia, WA 98504-8300
Phone: (360)753-7426

Fax: (360)586-3582
Provides capital for businesses in
distressed areas to create new jobs,
particularly for low and moderate
income persons.

Phoenix Partners
Email: djohnsto@interserv.com
1000 2nd Ave., Ste. 3600
Seattle, WA 98104
Phone: (206)624-8968
Fax: (206)624-1907
William B. Horne, Chief Financial
Officer
Preferred Investment Size: $500,000
to $2,000,000. Investment Types:
Seed, research and development,
startup, first and second stage, and
mezzanine. Industry Preferences:
Diversified. Geographic Preferences:
No preference.

Tredegar Investments
701 Fifth Ave., Ste. 6501
Seattle, WA 98104
Phone: (206)652-9240
Fax: (206)652-9259
Steven M. Johnson, President
Preferred Investment Size: $250,000
to $5,000,000. Investment Policies:
Equity. Investment Types: Seed, early
and late stage. Industry Preferences:
Diversified technology. Geographic
Preferences: National.

Voyager Capital
Email: info@voyagercap.com
800 5th St., Ste. 98103
Seattle, WA 98103
Phone: (206)470-1180
Fax: (206)470-1185
Erik Benson, Senior Associate
Preferred Investment Size: $500,000
to $4,000,000. Investment Policies:
Equity. Investment Types: Startup,
early and late stage. Industry Prefer-
ences: Diversified communications
and computer related. Geographic
Preferences: West Coast and Western
Canada.

Washington Department of
Community, Trade and Economic
Development
Industrial Revenue Bonds
2001 6th Ave., Ste. 2600

Seattle, WA 98121
Phone: (206)464-7143
Fax: (206)464-7222
Issued to finance the acquisition,
construction, enlargement, or improvement of industrial development
facilities.

West Virginia

Shenandoah Venture Capital L.P.
208 Capital St., Ste. 300
Charleston, WV 25301
Phone: (304)344-1796
Fax: (304)344-1798
Thomas E. Loehr, President

West Virginia Development Office
West Virginia Economic
Development Authority
1018 Kanawha Blvd., E., Ste. 501
Charleston, WV 25301-2827
Phone: (304)558-3650
Fax: (304)558-0206
Provides low-interest loans for land or
building acquisition, building
construction, and equipment pur-
chases.

WestVen Ltd. Partnership
208 Capitol St., Ste. 300
Charleston, WV 25301
Phone: (304)344-1794
Fax: (304)344-1798
Thomas E. Loehr, President
Preferred Investment Size: $500,000.
Investment Policies: Combination of
debt and equity. Investment Types:
Expansion, early stage, spin-off.
Industry Preferences: Wood products,
computer industry, manufacturing.
Geographic Preferences: West
Virginia, Ohio, Pennsylvania,
Virginia, Maryland.

Wisconsin

Impact Seven, Inc.
Email: impact@win.bright.net
651 Garfield Street
Almena, WI 54805-9900
Phone: (715)357-3334
Fax: (715)357-6233
Provides equity investment.

Madison Development Corp.
550 W. Washington Ave.

Madison, WI 53703
Phone: (608)256-2799
Fax: (608)256-1560
Provides loans of up to $150,000 to eligible businesses in Dane County for working capital, inventory, equipment, leasehold improvements, and business real estate.

Venture Investors Management, L.L.C.
Email: roger@ventureinvestors.com
University Research Park
565 Science Dr.,Ste.A
Madison, WI 53711-1071
Phone: (414)298-3070
Fax: (608)238-5120
Scott Button, Investment Analyst
Preferred Investment Size: $250,000 to $1,000,000. Investment Types: Seed, startup, first and second stage, mezzanine, and special situations. Industry Preferences: Diversified. Geographic Preferences: Southeast and Midwest.

Venture Investors of Wisconsin, Inc. (Madison)
Email: vi@ventureinvestors.com
565 Science Dr., Ste. A
Madison, WI 53711-1071
Phone: (608)233-3070
Fax: (608)238-5120
Venture capital firm providing early-stage financing to Wisconsinbased companies with strong management teams. Areas of interest include biotechnology, software, analytical instruments, medical products, consumer products, and publishing industries.

Wisconsin Business Development Finance Corp.
Email: wbdfc@waun.tdsnet.com
PO Box 2717
Madison, WI 53701
Phone: (608)258-8830
Fax: (608)258-1664
Provides small business financing for the purchase of land, buildings, machinery, equipment, and the construction and modernization of facilities.

Wisconsin Department of Commerce
Wisconsin Development Fund
Bureau of Business Finance
201 W. Washington Ave.
Madison, WI 53707
Phone: (608)266-1018
Free: (800)HELP-BUS
Fax: (608)264-6151

Wisconsin Housing and Economic Development Authority
Venture Capital Fund
201 W. Washington Ave., Ste. 700
Madison, WI 53701
Phone: (608)266-7884
Free: (800)334-6873
Fax: (608)267-1099
Invests in new and existing businesses that are developing new products.

Wisconsin Innovation Network Foundation
PO Box 71
Madison, WI 53701-0071
Phone: (608)256-8348
Fax: (608)256-0333
Seeks to join people with marketing and sales ideas to those willing to finance them. Acts as a resource center for financing information; offers networking opportunities for business professionals, entrepreneurs, and small business owners at regular monthly meetings.

Capital Investment, Inc.
Email: dmayer@capitalinvestmentsinc.com
1009 W. Glen Oaks Ln., Ste. 103
Mequon, WI 53092
Phone: (414)241-0303
Fax: (414)241-8451
Preferred Investment Size: $500,000 to $1 million. Investment Policies: Subordinated debt with warrant. Investment Types: Expansion, later stage. Industry Preferences: Diversified. Geographic Preferences: Midwest and Southwest.

Capital Investments, Inc.
Email: dmayer@capitalinvestmentsinc.com
1009 West Glen Oaks Lane, Ste. 103
Mequon, WI 53092
Phone: (414)241-0303
Fax: (414)241-8451

Preferred Investment Size: $500,000 to $1,000,000. Investment Types: Second stage, mezzanine, and leveraged buyout. Industry Preferences: Diversified. Geographic Preferences: Southwest and Midwest.

Banc One Venture Corp. (Milwaukee)
111 E. Wisconsin Ave.
Milwaukee, WI 53202
Free: (800)947-1111
H. Wayne Foreman, President
Preferred Investment Size: $1 to $10 million. Investment Types: Later stage, expansion, LBO, MBO. Industry Preferences: Publishing, distribution, manufacturing, mail-order. Geographic Preferences: National.

Future Value Venture, Inc.
2821 North 4th St., Ste. 526
Milwaukee, WI 53212-2300
Phone: (414)264-2252
Fax: (414)264-2253
William Beckett, President
Preferred Investment Size: $100,000 to $250,000. Investment Types: First and second stage, and mezzanine. Industry Preferences: No preference. Geographic Preferences: Entire U.S.

Horizon Partners, Ltd.
225 E. Mason St., 6th Fl.
Milwaukee, WI 53202
Phone: (414)271-2200
Fax: (414)271-4016
Preferred Investment Size: $1,000,000 to $5,000,000. Investment Types: Mezzanine. Industry Preferences: Consumer products and services, consumer distribution, electronic components, chemicals and materials, and publishing. Geographic Preferences: Midwest.

Lubar and Co., Inc.
700 N. Water St., Ste. 1200
Milwaukee, WI 53202
Phone: (414)291-9000
Fax: (414)291-9061
David J. Lubar, Partner
Preferred Investment Size: $500,000 to $5,000,000. Investment Types: Second stage, leveraged buyout, special situations, and control block

purchases. Industry Preferences: Diversified. Geographic Preferences: Midwest.

M & I Ventures Corp.
770 N. Water St.
Milwaukee, WI 53202
Phone: (414)765-7910
Free: (800)342-2265
Fax: (414)765-7850
Diane Lau, Marketing Administrator
Preferred Investment Size: $1,000,000 to $5,000,000. Investment Types: Mezzanine and leveraged buyout. Industry Preferences: Diversified. Geographic Preferences: Midwest.

Wisconsin Venture Capital Fund
700 N. Water St., Ste. 1200
Milwaukee, WI 53202
Phone: (414)291-9000
Fax: (414)291-9061

Wind Point Partners
420 3 Mile, Apt. B4
Racine, WI 53402
Phone: (414)639-3113
Fax: (414)639-3417
Venture capital firm.

Bando-McGlocklin SBIC
W239 N. 1700 Busse Rd.
Waukesha, WI 53188
Phone: (414)523-4300
Fax: (414)523-4193
George Schonath, Chief Executive Officer
Preferred Investment Size: $3,000,000. Investment Policies: Loans. Investment Types: Early stage, expansion, later stage. Industry Preferences: Diversified. Geographic Preferences: Midwest.

Wyoming

Frontier Certified Development Co.
PO Box 3599
Casper, WY 82602
Phone: (307)234-5351
Free: (800)934-5351
Fax: (307)234-0501
Created by the Wyoming Industrial Development Corporation to provide expansion financing for Wyoming business.

Wyoming Industrial Development Corp.
PO Box 3599
Casper, WY 82602
Phone: (307)234-5351
Free: (800)934-5351
Fax: (307)234-0501
Administers SBA 7(A) and SBA(502) programs. Purchases the guaranteed portion of U.S. Small Business Administration and Farmers Home Administration Loans to small businesses to pool into a common fund that enables small businesses to obtain loans at more reasonable rates and terms.

Wyoming Department of Commerce
Economic and Community Development Division
Barrett Bldg.
2301 Central Ave.
Cheyenne, WY 82002
Phone: (307)777-6303
Fax: (307)777-6005

Appendix C - Glossary of Small Business Terms

Glossary of Small Business Terms

Absolute liability
Liability that is incurred due to product defects or negligent actions. Manufacturers or retail establishments are held responsible, even though the defect or action may not have been intentional or negligent.

ACE
See Active Corps of Executives

Accident and health benefits
Benefits offered to employees and their families in order to offset the costs associated with accidental death, accidental injury, or sickness.

Account statement
A record of transactions, including payments, new debt, and deposits, incurred during a defined period of time.

Accounting system
System capturing the costs of all employees and/or machinery included in business expenses.

Accounts payable
See Trade credit

Accounts receivable
Unpaid accounts which arise from unsettled claims and transactions from the sale of a company's products or services to its customers.

Active Corps of Executives (ACE)
(See also Service Corps of Retired Executives)
A group of volunteers for a management assistance program of the U.S. Small Business Administration; volunteers provide one-on-one counseling and teach workshops and seminars for small firms.

ADA
See Americans with Disabilities Act

Adaptation
The process whereby an invention is modified to meet the needs of users.

Adaptive engineering
The process whereby an invention is modified to meet the manufacturing and commercial requirements of a targeted market.

Adverse selection
The tendency for higher-risk individuals to purchase health care and more comprehensive plans, resulting in increased costs.

Advertising
A marketing tool used to capture public attention and influence purchasing decisions for a product or service. Utilizes various forms of media to generate consumer response, such as flyers, magazines, newspapers, radio, and television.

Age discrimination
The denial of the rights and privileges of employment based solely on the age of an individual.

Agency costs
Costs incurred to insure that the lender or investor maintains control over assets while allowing the borrower or entrepreneur to use them. Monitoring and information costs are the two major types of agency costs.

Agribusiness
The production and sale of commodities and products from the commercial farming industry.

America Online
(See also Prodigy)
An online service which is accessible by computer modem. The service features Internet access, bulletin boards, online periodicals, electronic mail, and other services for subscribers.

Americans with Disabilities Act (ADA)
Law designed to ensure equal access and opportunity to handicapped persons.

Annual report

(See also Securities and Exchange Commission)
Yearly financial report prepared by a business that adheres to the requirements set forth by the Securities and Exchange Commission (SEC).

Antitrust immunity

(See also Collective ratemaking)
Exemption from prosecution under antitrust laws. In the transportation industry, firms with antitrust immunity are permitted—under certain conditions—to set schedules and sometimes prices for the public benefit.

Applied research

Scientific study targeted for use in a product or process.

Asians

A minority category used by the U.S. Bureau of the Census to represent a diverse group that includes Aleuts, Eskimos, American Indians, Asian Indians, Chinese, Japanese, Koreans, Vietnamese, Filipinos, Hawaiians, and other Pacific Islanders.

Assets

Anything of value owned by a company.

Audit

The verification of accounting records and business procedures conducted by an outside accounting service.

Average cost

Total production costs divided by the quantity produced.

Balance Sheet

A financial statement listing the total assets and liabilities of a company at a given time.

Bankruptcy

(See also Chapter 7 of the 1978 Bankruptcy Act; Chapter 11 of the 1978 Bankruptcy Act)
The condition in which a business cannot meet its debt obligations and petitions a federal district court either for reorganization of its debts (Chapter 11) or for liquidation of its assets (Chapter 7).

Basic research

Theoretical scientific exploration not targeted to application.

Basket clause

A provision specifying the amount of public pension funds that may be placed in investments not included on a state's legal list (see separate citation).

BBS

See Bulletin Board Service

BDC

See Business development corporation

Benefit

Various services, such health care, flextime, day care, insurance, and vacation, offered to employees as part of a hiring package. Typically subsidized in whole or in part by the business.

BIDCO

See Business and industrial development company

Billing cycle

A system designed to evenly distribute customer billing throughout the month, preventing clerical backlogs.

Birth

See Business birth

Blue chip security

A low-risk, low-yield security representing an interest in a very stable company.

Blue sky laws

A general term that denotes various states' laws regulating securities.

Bond

(See also General obligation bond; Taxable bonds; Treasury bonds)
A written instrument executed by a bidder or contractor (the principal) and a second party (the surety or sureties) to assure fulfillment of the principal's obligations to a third party (the obligee or government) identified in the bond. If the principal's obligations are not met, the bond assures payment to the extent stipulated of any loss sustained by the obligee.

Bonding requirements

Terms contained in a bond (see separate citation).

Bonus

An amount of money paid to an employee as a reward for achieving certain business goals or objectives.

Brainstorming

A group session where employees contribute their ideas for solving a problem or meeting a company objective without fear of retribution or ridicule.

Brand name

The part of a brand, trademark, or service mark that can be spoken. It can be a word, letter, or group of words or letters.

Bridge financing

A short-term loan made in expectation of intermediate-term or long-term financing. Can be used when a company plans to go public in the near future.

Broker

One who matches resources available for innovation with those who need them.

Budget

An estimate of the spending necessary to complete a project or offer a service in comparison to cash-on-hand and expected earnings for the coming year, with an emphasis on cost control.

Bulletin Board Service (BBS)

An online service enabling users to communicate with each other about specific topics.

Business birth

The formation of a new establishment or enterprise. The appearance of a new establishment or enterprise in the Small Business Data Base (see separate citation).

Business conditions

Outside factors that can affect the financial performance of a business.

Business contractions

The number of establishments that have decreased in employment during a specified time.

Business cycle

A period of economic recession and recovery. These cycles vary in duration.

Business death

The voluntary or involuntary closure of a firm or establishment. The disappearance of an establishment or enterprise from the Small Business Data Base (see separate citation).

Business development corporation (BDC)

A business financing agency, usually composed of the financial institutions in an area or state, organized to assist in financing businesses unable to obtain assistance through normal channels; the risk is spread among various members of the business development corporation, and interest rates may vary somewhat from those charged by member institutions. A venture capital firm in which shares of ownership are publicly held and to which the Investment Act of 1940 applies.

Business dissolution

For enumeration purposes, the absence of a business that was present in the prior time period from any current record.

Business entry

See Business birth

Business ethics

Moral values and principles espoused by members of the business community as a guide to fair and honest business practices.

Business exit

See Business death

Business expansions

The number of establishments that added employees during a specified time.

Business failure

Closure of a business causing a loss to at least one creditor.

Business format franchising

(See also Franchising)

The purchase of the name, trademark, and an ongoing business plan of the parent corporation or franchisor by the franchisee.

Business and industrial development company (BIDCO)

A private, for-profit financing corporation chartered by the state to provide both equity and long-term debt capital to small business owners (see separate citations for equity and debt capital).

Business license

A legal authorization issued by municipal and state governments and required for business operations.

Business name
(See also Business license; Trademark)
Enterprises must register their business names with local governments usually on a "doing business as" (DBA) form. (This name is sometimes referred to as a "fictional name.") The procedure is part of the business licensing process and prevents any other business from using that same name for a similar business in the same locality.

Business norms
See Financial ratios

Business permit
See Business license

Business plan
A document that spells out a company's expected course of action for a specified period, usually including a detailed listing and analysis of risks and uncertainties. For the small business, it should examine the proposed products, the market, the industry, the management policies, the marketing policies, production needs, and financial needs. Frequently, it is used as a prospectus for potential investors and lenders.

Business proposal
See Business plan

Business service firm
An establishment primarily engaged in rendering services to other business organizations on a fee or contract basis.

Business start
For enumeration purposes, a business with a name or similar designation that did not exist in a prior time period.

Cafeteria plan
See Flexible benefit plan

Capacity
Level of a firm's, industry's, or nation's output corresponding to full practical utilization of available resources.

Capital
Assets less liabilities, representing the ownership interest in a business. A stock of accumulated goods, especially at a specified time and in contrast to income received during a specified time period. Accumulated goods devoted to production. Accumulated possessions calculated to bring income.

Capital expenditure
Expenses incurred by a business for improvements that will depreciate over time.

Capital gain
The monetary difference between the purchase price and the selling price of capital. Capital gains are taxed at a rate of 28% by the federal government.

Capital intensity
(See also Debt capital; Equity midrisk venture capital; Informal capital; Internal capital; Owner's capital; Secondhand capital; Seed capital; Venture capital)
The relative importance of capital in the production process, usually expressed as the ratio of capital to labor but also sometimes as the ratio of capital to output.

Capital resource
The equipment, facilities and labor used to create products and services.

Caribbean Basin Initiative
An interdisciplinary program to support commerce among the businesses in the nations of the Caribbean Basin and the United States. Agencies involved include: the Agency for International Development, the U.S. Small Business Administration, the International Trade Administration of the U.S. Department of Commerce, and various private sector groups.

Catastrophic care
Medical and other services for acute and long-term illnesses that cost more than insurance coverage limits or that cost the amount most families may be expected to pay with their own resources.

CDC
See Certified development corporation

CD-ROM
Compact disc with read-only memory used to store large amounts of digitized data.

Certified development corporation (CDC)
A local area or statewide corporation or authority (for profit or nonprofit) that packages U.S. Small Business Administration (SBA), bank, state, and/or private money into financial assistance for existing business capital improvements. The SBA holds the second lien on its maximum share of 40 percent involvement. Each state has

at least one certified development corporation. This program is called the SBA 504 Program.

Certified lenders
Banks that participate in the SBA guaranteed loan program (see separate citation). Such banks must have a good track record with the U.S. Small Business Administration (SBA) and must agree to certain conditions set forth by the agency. In return, the SBA agrees to process any guaranteed loan application within three business days.

Champion
An advocate for the development of an innovation.

Channel of distribution
The means used to transport merchandise from the manufacturer to the consumer.

Chapter 7 of the 1978 Bankruptcy Act
Provides for a court-appointed trustee who is responsible for liquidating a company's assets in order to settle outstanding debts.

Chapter 11 of the 1978 Bankruptcy Act
Allows the business owners to retain control of the company while working with their creditors to reorganize their finances and establish better business practices to prevent liquidation of assets.

Closely held corporation
A corporation in which the shares are held by a few persons, usually officers, employees, or others close to the management; these shares are rarely offered to the public.

Code of Federal Regulations
Codification of general and permanent rules of the federal government published in the Federal Register.

Code sharing
See Computer code sharing

Coinsurance
(See also Cost sharing)
Upon meeting the deductible payment, health insurance participants may be required to make additional health care cost-sharing payments. Coinsurance is a payment of a fixed percentage of the cost of each service; copayment is usually a fixed amount to be paid with each service.

Collateral
Securities, evidence of deposit, or other property pledged by a borrower to secure repayment of a loan.

Collective ratemaking
(See also Antitrust immunity)
The establishment of uniform charges for services by a group of businesses in the same industry.

Commercial insurance plan
See Underwriting

Commercial loans
Short-term renewable loans used to finance specific capital needs of a business.

Commercialization
The final stage of the innovation process, including production and distribution.

Common stock
The most frequently used instrument for purchasing ownership in private or public companies. Common stock generally carries the right to vote on certain corporate actions and may pay dividends, although it rarely does in venture investments. In liquidation, common stockholders are the last to share in the proceeds from the sale of a corporation's assets; bondholders and preferred shareholders have priority. Common stock is often used in first-round start-up financing.

Community development corporation
A corporation established to develop economic programs for a community and, in most cases, to provide financial support for such development.

Competitor
A business whose product or service is marketed for the same purpose/use and to the same consumer group as the product or service of another.

Computer code sharing
An arrangement whereby flights of a regional airline are identified by the two-letter code of a major carrier in the computer reservation system to help direct passengers to new regional carriers.

Consignment
A merchandising agreement, usually referring to second-hand shops, where the dealer pays the owner of an item a percentage of the profit when the item is sold.

Consortium

A coalition of organizations such as banks and corporations for ventures requiring large capital resources.

Consultant

An individual that is paid by a business to provide advice and expertise in a particular area.

Consumer price index

A measure of the fluctuation in prices between two points in time.

Consumer research

Research conducted by a business to obtain information about existing or potential consumer markets.

Continuation coverage

Health coverage offered for a specified period of time to employees who leave their jobs and to their widows, divorced spouses, or dependents.

Contractions

See Business contractions

Convertible preferred stock

A class of stock that pays a reasonable dividend and is convertible into common stock (see separate citation). Generally the convertible feature may only be exercised after being held for a stated period of time. This arrangement is usually considered second-round financing when a company needs equity to maintain its cash flow.

Convertible securities

A feature of certain bonds, debentures, or preferred stocks that allows them to be exchanged by the owner for another class of securities at a future date and in accordance with any other terms of the issue.

Copayment

See Coinsurance

Copyright

A legal form of protection available to creators and authors to safeguard their works from unlawful use or claim of ownership by others. Copyrights may be acquired for works of art, sculpture, music, and published or unpublished manuscripts. All copyrights should be registered at the Copyright Office of the Library of Congress.

Corporate financial ratios

(See also Industry financial ratios)

The relationship between key figures found in a company's financial statement expressed as a numeric value. Used to evaluate risk and company performance. Also known as Financial averages, Operating ratios, and Business ratios.

Corporation

A legal entity, chartered by a state or the federal government, recognized as a separate entity having its own rights, privileges, and liabilities distinct from those of its members.

Cost containment

Actions taken by employers and insurers to curtail rising health care costs; for example, increasing employee cost sharing (see separate citation), requiring second opinions, or preadmission screening.

Cost sharing

The requirement that health care consumers contribute to their own medical care costs through deductibles and coinsurance (see separate citations). Cost sharing does not include the amounts paid in premiums. It is used to control utilization of services; for example, requiring a fixed amount to be paid with each health care service.

Cottage industry

(See also Home-based business)

Businesses based in the home in which the family members are the labor force and family-owned equipment is used to process the goods.

Credit Rating

A letter or number calculated by an organization (such as Dun & Bradstreet) to represent the ability and disposition of a business to meet its financial obligations.

Customer service

Various techniques used to ensure the satisfaction of a customer.

Cyclical peak

The upper turning point in a business cycle.

Cyclical trough

The lower turning point in a business cycle.

DBA

See Business name

Death

See Business death

Debenture

A certificate given as acknowledgment of a debt (see separate citation) secured by the general credit of the issuing corporation. A bond, usually without security, issued by a corporation and sometimes convertible to common stock.

Debt

(See also Long-term debt; Mid-term debt; Securitized debt; Short-term debt)

Something owed by one person to another. Financing in which a company receives capital that must be repaid; no ownership is transferred.

Debt capital

Business financing that normally requires periodic interest payments and repayment of the principal within a specified time.

Debt financing

See Debt capital

Debt securities

Loans such as bonds and notes that provide a specified rate of return for a specified period of time.

Deductible

A set amount that an individual must pay before any benefits are received.

Demand shock absorbers

A term used to describe the role that some small firms play by expanding their output levels to accommodate a transient surge in demand.

Demographics

Statistics on various markets, including age, income, and education, used to target specific products or services to appropriate consumer groups.

Demonstration

Showing that a product or process has been modified sufficiently to meet the needs of users.

Deregulation

The lifting of government restrictions; for example, the lifting of government restrictions on the entry of new businesses, the expansion of services, and the setting of prices in particular industries.

Desktop Publishing

Using personal computers and specialized software to produce camera-ready copy for publications.

Disaster loans

Various types of physical and economic assistance available to individuals and businesses through the U.S. Small Business Administration (SBA). This is the only SBA loan program available for residential purposes.

Discrimination

The denial of the rights and privileges of employment based on factors such as age, race, religion, or gender.

Diseconomies of scale

The condition in which the costs of production increase faster than the volume of production.

Dissolution

See Business dissolution

Distribution

Delivering a product or process to the user.

Distributor

One who delivers merchandise to the user.

Diversified company

A company whose products and services are used by several different markets.

Doing business as (DBA)

See Business name

Dow Jones

An information services company that publishes the Wall Street Journal and other sources of financial information.

Dow Jones Industrial Average

An indicator of stock market performance.

Earned income

A tax term that refers to wages and salaries earned by the recipient, as opposed to monies earned through interest and dividends.

Economic efficiency

The use of productive resources to the fullest practical extent in the provision of the set of goods and services that is most preferred by purchasers in the economy.

Economic indicators

Statistics used to express the state of the economy. These include the length of the average work week, the rate of unemployment, and stock prices.

Economically disadvantaged
See Socially and economically disadvantaged

Economies of scale
See Scale economies

EEOC
See Equal Employment Opportunity Commission

8(a) Program
A program authorized by the Small Business Act that directs federal contracts to small businesses owned and operated by socially and economically disadvantaged individuals.

Electronic mail (e-mail)
The electronic transmission of mail via phone lines.

E-mail
See Electronic mail

Employee leasing.
A contract by which employers arrange to have their workers hired by a leasing company and then leased back to them for a management fee. The leasing company typically assumes the administrative burden of payroll and provides a benefit package to the workers.

Employee tenure
The length of time an employee works for a particular employer.

Employer identification number
The business equivalent of a social security number. Assigned by the U.S. Internal Revenue Service.

Enterprise
An aggregation of all establishments owned by a parent company. An enterprise may consist of a single, independent establishment or include subsidiaries and other branches under the same ownership and control.

Enterprise zone
A designated area, usually found in inner cities and other areas with significant unemployment, where businesses receive tax credits and other incentives to entice them to establish operations there.

Entrepreneur
A person who takes the risk of organizing and operating a new business venture.

Entry
See Business entry

Equal Employment Opportunity Commission (EEOC)
A federal agency that ensures nondiscrimination in the hiring and firing practices of a business.

Equal opportunity employer
An employer who adheres to the standards set by the Equal Employment Opportunity Commission (see separate citation).

Equity
(See also Common Stock; Equity midrisk venture capital)
The ownership interest. Financing in which partial or total ownership of a company is surrendered in exchange for capital. An investor's financial return comes from dividend payments and from growth in the net worth of the business.

Equity capital
See Equity; Equity midrisk venture capital

Equity financing
See Equity; Equity midrisk venture capital

Equity midrisk venture capital
An unsecured investment in a company. Usually a purchase of ownership interest in a company that occurs in the later stages of a company's development.

Equity partnership
A limited partnership arrangement for providing start-up and seed capital to businesses.

Equity securities
See Equity

Equity-type
Debt financing subordinated to conventional debt.

Establishment
A single-location business unit that may be independent (a single-establishment enterprise) or owned by a parent enterprise.

Establishment and Enterprise Microdata File
See U.S. Establishment and Enterprise Microdata File

Establishment birth
See Business birth

Establishment Longitudinal Microdata File
See U.S. Establishment Longitudinal Microdata File

Ethics
See Business ethics

Evaluation
Determining the potential success of translating an invention into a product or process.

Exit
See Business exit

Experience rating
See Underwriting

Export
A product sold outside of the country.

Export license
A general or specific license granted by the U.S. Department of Commerce required of anyone wishing to export goods. Some restricted articles need approval from the U.S. Departments of State, Defense, or Energy.

Failure
See Business failure

Fair share agreement
(See also Franchising)
An agreement reached between a franchisor and a minority business organization to extend business ownership to minorities by either reducing the amount of capital required or by setting aside certain marketing areas for minority business owners.

Feasibility study
A study to determine the likelihood that a proposed product or development will fulfill the objectives of a particular investor.

Federal Trade Commission (FTC)
Federal agency that promotes free enterprise and competition within the U.S.

Federal Trade Mark Act of 1946
See Lanham Act

Fictional name
See Business name

Fiduciary
An individual or group that hold assets in trust for a beneficiary.

Financial analysis
The techniques used to determine money needs in a business. Techniques include ratio analysis, calculation of return on investment, guides for measuring profitability, and break-even analysis to determine ultimate success.

Financial intermediary
A financial institution that acts as the intermediary between borrowers and lenders. Banks, savings and loan associations, finance companies, and venture capital companies are major financial intermediaries in the United States.

Financial ratios
See Corporate financial ratios; Industry financial ratios

Financial statement
A written record of business finances, including balance sheets and profit and loss statements.

Financing
See First-stage financing; Second-stage financing; Third-stage financing

First-stage financing
(See also Second-stage financing; Third-stage financing)
Financing provided to companies that have expended their initial capital, and require funds to start full-scale manufacturing and sales. Also known as First-round financing.

Fiscal year
Any twelve-month period used by businesses for accounting purposes.

504 Program
See Certified development corporation

Flexible benefit plan
A plan that offers a choice among cash and/or qualified benefits such as group term life insurance, accident and health insurance, group legal services, dependent care assistance, and vacations.

FOB
See Free on board

Format franchising
See Business format franchising; Franchising

401(k) plan
A financial plan where employees contribute a percentage of their earnings to a fund that is invested in stocks, bonds, or money markets for the purpose of saving money for retirement.

Four Ps
Marketing terms referring to Product, Price, Place, and Promotion.

Franchising
A form of licensing by which the owner—the franchisor—distributes or markets a product, method, or service through affiliated dealers called franchisees. The product, method, or service being marketed is identified by a brand name, and the franchisor maintains control over the marketing methods employed. The franchisee is often given exclusive access to a defined geographic area.

Free on board (FOB)
A pricing term indicating that the quoted price includes the cost of loading goods into transport vessels at a specified place.

Frictional unemployment
See Unemployment

FTC
See Federal Trade Commission

Fulfillment
The systems necessary for accurate delivery of an ordered item, including subscriptions and direct marketing.

Full-time workers
Generally, those who work a regular schedule of more than 35 hours per week.

Garment registration number
A number that must appear on every garment sold in the U.S. to indicate the manufacturer of the garment, which may or may not be the same as the label under which the garment is sold. The U.S. Federal Trade Commission assigns and regulates garment registration numbers.

Gatekeeper
A key contact point for entry into a network.

GDP
See Gross domestic product

General obligation bond
A municipal bond secured by the taxing power of the municipality. The Tax Reform Act of 1986 limits the purposes for which such bonds may be issued and establishes volume limits on the extent of their issuance.

GNP
See Gross national product

Good Housekeeping Seal
Seal appearing on products that signifies the fulfillment of the standards set by the Good Housekeeping Institute to protect consumer interests.

Goods sector
All businesses producing tangible goods, including agriculture, mining, construction, and manufacturing businesses.

GPO
See Gross product originating

Gross domestic product (GDP)
The part of the nation's gross national product (see separate citation) generated by private business using resources from within the country.

Gross national product (GNP)
The most comprehensive single measure of aggregate economic output. Represents the market value of the total output of goods and services produced by a nation's economy.

Gross product originating (GPO)
A measure of business output estimated from the income or production side using employee compensation, profit income, net interest, capital consumption, and indirect business taxes.

HAL
See Handicapped assistance loan program

Handicapped assistance loan program (HAL)
Low-interest direct loan program through the U.S. Small Business Administration (SBA) for handicapped persons. The SBA requires that these persons demonstrate that their disability is such that it is impossible for them to secure employment, thus making it necessary to go into their own business to make a living.

Health maintenance organization (HMO)

Organization of physicians and other health care professionals that provides health services to subscribers and their dependents on a prepaid basis.

Health provider

An individual or institution that gives medical care. Under Medicare, an institutional provider is a hospital, skilled nursing facility, home health agency, or provider of certain physical therapy services.

Hispanic

A person of Cuban, Mexican, Puerto Rican, Latin American (Central or South American), European Spanish, or other Spanish-speaking origin or ancestry.

HMO

See Health maintenance organization

Home-based business

(See also Cottage industry)

A business with an operating address that is also a residential address (usually the residential address of the proprietor).

Hub-and-spoke system

A system in which flights of an airline from many different cities (the spokes) converge at a single airport (the hub). After allowing passengers sufficient time to make connections, planes then depart for different cities.

Human Resources Management

A business program designed to oversee recruiting, pay, benefits, and other issues related to the company's work force, including planning to determine the optimal use of labor to increase production, thereby increasing profit.

Idea

An original concept for a new product or process.

Import

Products produced outside the country in which they are consumed.

Income

Money or its equivalent, earned or accrued, resulting from the sale of goods and services.

Income statement

A financial statement that lists the profits and losses of a company at a given time.

Incorporation

The filing of a certificate of incorporation with a state's secretary of state, thereby limiting the business owner's liability.

Incubator

A facility designed to encourage entrepreneurship and minimize obstacles to new business formation and growth, particularly for high-technology firms, by housing a number of fledgling enterprises that share an array of services, such as meeting areas, secretarial services, accounting, research library, on-site financial and management counseling, and word processing facilities.

Independent contractor

An individual considered self-employed (see separate citation) and responsible for paying Social Security taxes and income taxes on earnings.

Indirect health coverage

Health insurance obtained through another individual's health care plan; for example, a spouse's employer-sponsored plan.

Industrial development authority

The financial arm of a state or other political subdivision established for the purpose of financing economic development in an area, usually through loans to nonprofit organizations, which in turn provide facilities for manufacturing and other industrial operations.

Industry financial ratios

(See also Corporate financial ratios)

Corporate financial ratios averaged for a specified industry. These are used for comparison purposes and reveal industry trends and identify differences between the performance of a specific company and the performance of its industry. Also known as Industrial averages, Industry ratios, Financial averages, and Business or Industrial norms.

Inflation

Increases in volume of currency and credit, generally resulting in a sharp and continuing rise in price levels.

Informal capital

Financing from informal, unorganized sources; includes informal debt capital such as trade credit or loans from friends and relatives and equity capital from informal investors.

Initial public offering (IPO)
A corporation's first offering of stock to the public.

Innovation
The introduction of a new idea into the marketplace in the form of a new product or service or an improvement in organization or process.

Intellectual property
Any idea or work that can be considered proprietary in nature and is thus protected from infringement by others.

Internal capital
Debt or equity financing obtained from the owner or through retained business earnings.

Internet
A government-designed computer network that contains large amounts of information and is accessible through various vendors for a fee.

Intrapreneurship
The state of employing entrepreneurial principles to nonentrepreneurial situations.

Invention
The tangible form of a technological idea, which could include a laboratory prototype, drawings, formulas, etc.

IPO
See Initial public offering

Job description
The duties and responsibilities required in a particular position.

Job tenure
A period of time during which an individual is continuously employed in the same job.

Joint marketing agreements
Agreements between regional and major airlines, often involving the coordination of flight schedules, fares, and baggage transfer. These agreements help regional carriers operate at lower cost.

Joint venture
Venture in which two or more people combine efforts in a particular business enterprise, usually a single transaction or a limited activity, and agree to share the profits and losses jointly or in proportion to their contributions.

Keogh plan
Designed for self-employed persons and unincorporated businesses as a tax-deferred pension account.

Labor force
Civilians considered eligible for employment who are also willing and able to work.

Labor force participation rate
The civilian labor force as a percentage of the civilian population.

Labor intensity
(See also Capital intensity)
The relative importance of labor in the production process, usually measured as the capital-labor ratio; i.e., the ratio of units of capital (typically, dollars of tangible assets) to the number of employees. The higher the capital-labor ratio exhibited by a firm or industry, the lower the capital intensity of that firm or industry is said to be.

Labor surplus area
An area in which there exists a high unemployment rate. In procurement (see separate citation), extra points are given to firms in counties that are designated a labor surplus area; this information is requested on procurement bid sheets.

Labor union
An organization of similarly-skilled workers who collectively bargain with management over the conditions of employment.

Laboratory prototype
See Prototype

LAN
See Local Area Network

Lanham Act
Refers to the Federal Trade Mark Act of 1946. Protects registered trademarks, trade names, and other service marks used in commerce.

Large business-dominated industry
Industry in which a minimum of 60 percent of employment or sales is in firms with more than 500 workers.

LBO
See Leveraged buy-out

Leader pricing

A reduction in the price of a good or service in order to generate more sales of that good or service.

Legal list

A list of securities selected by a state in which certain institutions and fiduciaries (such as pension funds, insurance companies, and banks) may invest. Securities not on the list are not eligible for investment. Legal lists typically restrict investments to high quality securities meeting certain specifications. Generally, investment is limited to U.S. securities and investment-grade blue chip securities (see separate citation).

Leveraged buy-out (LBO)

The purchase of a business or a division of a corporation through a highly leveraged financing package.

Liability

An obligation or duty to perform a service or an act. Also defined as money owed.

License

(See also Business license)

A legal agreement granting to another the right to use a technological innovation.

Limited partnerships

See Venture capital limited partnerships

Liquidity

The ability to convert a security into cash promptly.

Loans

See Commercial loans; Disaster loans; SBA direct loans; SBA guaranteed loans; SBA special lending institution categories

Local Area Network (LAN)

Computer networks contained within a single building or small area; used to facilitate the sharing of information.

Local development corporation

An organization, usually made up of local citizens of a community, designed to improve the economy of the area by inducing business and industry to locate and expand there. A local development corporation establishes a capability to finance local growth.

Long-haul rates

Rates charged by a transporter in which the distance traveled is more than 800 miles.

Long-term debt

An obligation that matures in a period that exceeds five years.

Low-grade bond

A corporate bond that is rated below investment grade by the major rating agencies (Standard and Poor's, Moody's).

Macro-efficiency

(See also Economic efficiency)

Efficiency as it pertains to the operation of markets and market systems.

Managed care

A cost-effective health care program initiated by employers whereby low-cost health care is made available to the employees in return for exclusive patronage to program doctors.

Management Assistance Programs

See SBA Management Assistance Programs

Management and technical assistance

A term used by many programs to mean business (as opposed to technological) assistance.

Mandated benefits

Specific treatments, providers, or individuals required by law to be included in commercial health plans.

Market evaluation

The use of market information to determine the sales potential of a specific product or process.

Market failure

The situation in which the workings of a competitive market do not produce the best results from the point of view of the entire society.

Market information

Data of any type that can be used for market evaluation, which could include demographic data, technology forecasting, regulatory changes, etc.

Market research

A systematic collection, analysis, and reporting of data about the market and its preferences, opinions, trends, and plans; used for corporate decision-making.

Market share

In a particular market, the percentage of sales of a specific product.

Marketing
Promotion of goods or services through various media.

Master Establishment List (MEL)
A list of firms in the United States developed by the U.S. Small Business Administration; firms can be selected by industry, region, state, standard metropolitan statistical area (see separate citation), county, and zip code.

Maturity
(See also Term)
The date upon which the principal or stated value of a bond or other indebtedness becomes due and payable.

Medicaid (Title XIX)
A federally aided, state-operated and administered program that provides medical benefits for certain low-income persons in need of health and medical care who are eligible for one of the government's welfare cash payment programs, including the aged, the blind, the disabled, and members of families with dependent children where one parent is absent, incapacitated, or unemployed.

Medicare (Title XVIII)
A nationwide health insurance program for disabled and aged persons. Health insurance is available to insured persons without regard to income. Monies from payroll taxes cover hospital insurance and monies from general revenues and beneficiary premiums pay for supplementary medical insurance.

MEL
See Master Establishment List

MESBIC
See Minority enterprise small business investment corporation

MET
See Multiple employer trust

Metropolitan statistical area (MSA)
A means used by the government to define large population centers that may transverse different governmental jurisdictions. For example, the Washington, D.C. MSA includes the District of Columbia and contiguous parts of Maryland and Virginia because all of these geopolitical areas comprise one population and economic operating unit.

Mezzanine financing
See Third-stage financing

Micro-efficiency
(See also Economic efficiency)
Efficiency as it pertains to the operation of individual firms.

Microdata
Information on the characteristics of an individual business firm.

Mid-term debt
An obligation that matures within one to five years.

Midrisk venture capital
See Equity midrisk venture capital

Minimum premium plan
A combination approach to funding an insurance plan aimed primarily at premium tax savings. The employer self-funds a fixed percentage of estimated monthly claims and the insurance company insures the excess.

Minimum wage
The lowest hourly wage allowed by the federal government.

Minority Business Development Agency
Contracts with private firms throughout the nation to sponsor Minority Business Development Centers which provide minority firms with advice and technical assistance on a fee basis.

Minority Enterprise Small Business Investment Corporation (MESBIC)
A federally funded private venture capital firm licensed by the U.S. Small Business Administration to provide capital to minority-owned businesses (see separate citation).

Minority-owned business
Businesses owned by those who are socially or economically disadvantaged (see separate citation).

Mom and Pop business
A small store or enterprise having limited capital, principally employing family members.

Moonlighter
A wage-and-salary worker with a side business.

MSA
See Metropolitan statistical area

Multi-employer plan
A health plan to which more than one employer is required to contribute and that may be maintained through a collective bargaining agreement and required to meet standards prescribed by the U.S. Department of Labor.

Multi-level marketing
A system of selling in which you sign up other people to assist you and they, in turn, recruit others to help them. Some entrepreneurs have built successful companies on this concept because the main focus of their activities is their product and product sales.

Multimedia
The use of several types of media to promote a product or service. Also, refers to the use of several different types of media (sight, sound, pictures, text) in a CD-ROM (see separate citation) product.

Multiple employer trust (MET)
A self-funded benefit plan generally geared toward small employers sharing a common interest.

NAFTA
See North American Free Trade Agreement

NASDAQ
See National Association of Securities Dealers Automated Quotations

National Association of Securities Dealers Automated Quotations
Provides price quotes on over-the-counter securities as well as securities listed on the New York Stock Exchange.

National income
Aggregate earnings of labor and property arising from the production of goods and services in a nation's economy.

Net assets
See Net worth

Net income
The amount remaining from earnings and profits after all expenses and costs have been met or deducted. Also known as Net earnings.

Net profit
Money earned after production and overhead expenses (see separate citations) have been deducted.

Net worth
(See also Capital)
The difference between a company's total assets and its total liabilities.

Network
A chain of interconnected individuals or organizations sharing information and/or services.

New York Stock Exchange (NYSE)
The oldest stock exchange in the U.S. Allows for trading in stocks, bonds, warrants, options, and rights that meet listing requirements.

Niche
A career or business for which a person is well-suited. Also, a product which fulfills one need of a particular market segment, often with little or no competition.

Nodes
One workstation in a network, either local area or wide area (see separate citations).

Nonbank bank
A bank that either accepts deposits or makes loans, but not both. Used to create many new branch banks.

Noncompetitive awards
A method of contracting whereby the federal government negotiates with only one contractor to supply a product or service.

Nonmember bank
A state-regulated bank that does not belong to the federal bank system.

Nonprofit
An organization that has no shareholders, does not distribute profits, and is without federal and state tax liabilities.

Norms
See Financial ratios

North American Free Trade Agreement (NAFTA)
Passed in 1993, NAFTA eliminates trade barriers among businesses in the U.S., Canada, and Mexico.

NYSE
See New York Stock Exchange

Occupational Safety & Health Administration (OSHA)
Federal agency that regulates health and safety standards within the workplace.

Optimal firm size
The business size at which the production cost per unit of output (average cost) is, in the long run, at its minimum.

Organizational chart
A hierarchical chart tracking the chain of command within an organization.

OSHA
See Occupational Safety & Health Administration

Overhead
Expenses, such as employee benefits and building utilities, incurred by a business that are unrelated to the actual product or service sold.

Owner's capital
Debt or equity funds provided by the owner(s) of a business; sources of owner's capital are personal savings, sales of assets, or loans from financial institutions.

P & L
See Profit and loss statement

Part-time workers
Normally, those who work less than 35 hours per week. The Tax Reform Act indicated that part-time workers who work less than 17.5 hours per week may be excluded from health plans for purposes of complying with federal nondiscrimination rules.

Part-year workers
Those who work less than 50 weeks per year.

Partnership
Two or more parties who enter into a legal relationship to conduct business for profit. Defined by the U.S. Internal Revenue Code as joint ventures, syndicates, groups, pools, and other associations of two or more persons organized for profit that are not specifically classified in the IRS code as corporations or proprietorships.

Patent
A grant made by the government assuring an inventor the sole right to make, use, and sell an invention for a period of 17 years.

PC
See Professional corporation

Peak
See Cyclical peak

Pension
A series of payments made monthly, semiannually, annually, or at other specified intervals during the lifetime of the pensioner for distribution upon retirement. The term is sometimes used to denote the portion of the retirement allowance financed by the employer's contributions.

Pension fund
A fund established to provide for the payment of pension benefits; the collective contributions made by all of the parties to the pension plan.

Performance appraisal
An established set of objective criteria, based on job description and requirements, that is used to evaluate the performance of an employee in a specific job.

Permit
See Business license

Plan
See Business plan

Pooling
An arrangement for employers to achieve efficiencies and lower health costs by joining together to purchase group health insurance or self-insurance.

PPO
See Preferred provider organization

Preferred lenders program
See SBA special lending institution categories

Preferred provider organization (PPO)
A contractual arrangement with a health care services organization that agrees to discount its health care rates in return for faster payment and/or a patient base.

Premiums
The amount of money paid to an insurer for health insurance under a policy. The premium is generally paid periodically (e.g., monthly), and often is split between the employer and the employee. Unlike deductibles and coinsurance or copayments, premiums are paid for coverage whether or not benefits are actually used.

Prime-age workers
Employees 25 to 54 years of age.

Prime contract

A contract awarded directly by the U.S. Federal Government.

Private company

See Closely held corporation

Private placement

A method of raising capital by offering for sale an investment or business to a small group of investors (generally avoiding registration with the Securities and Exchange Commission or state securities registration agencies). Also known as Private financing or Private offering.

Pro forma

The use of hypothetical figures in financial statements to represent future expenditures, debts, and other potential financial expenses.

Proactive

Taking the initiative to solve problems and anticipate future events before they happen, instead of reacting to an already existing problem or waiting for a difficult situation to occur.

Procurement

(See also 8(a) Program; Small business set asides)

A contract from an agency of the federal government for goods or services from a small business.

Prodigy

(See also America Online)

An online service which is accessible by computer modem. The service features Internet access, bulletin boards, online periodicals, electronic mail, and other services for subscribers.

Product development

The stage of the innovation process where research is translated into a product or process through evaluation, adaptation, and demonstration.

Product franchising

An arrangement for a franchisee to use the name and to produce the product line of the franchisor or parent corporation.

Production

The manufacture of a product.

Production prototype

See Prototype

Productivity

A measurement of the number of goods produced during a specific amount of time.

Professional corporation (PC)

Organized by members of a profession such as medicine, dentistry, or law for the purpose of conducting their professional activities as a corporation. Liability of a member or shareholder is limited in the same manner as in a business corporation.

Profit and loss statement (P & L)

The summary of the incomes (total revenues) and costs of a company's operation during a specific period of time. Also known as Income and expense statement.

Proposal

See Business plan

Proprietorship

The most common legal form of business ownership; about 85 percent of all small businesses are proprietorships. The liability of the owner is unlimited in this form of ownership.

Prospective payment system

A cost-containment measure included in the Social Security Amendments of 1983 whereby Medicare payments to hospitals are based on established prices, rather than on cost reimbursement.

Prototype

A model that demonstrates the validity of the concept of an invention (laboratory prototype); a model that meets the needs of the manufacturing process and the user (production prototype).

Prudent investor rule or standard

A legal doctrine that requires fiduciaries to make investments using the prudence, diligence, and intelligence that would be used by a prudent person in making similar investments. Because fiduciaries make investments on behalf of third-party beneficiaries, the standard results in very conservative investments. Until recently, most state regulations required the fiduciary to apply this standard to each investment. Newer, more progressive regulations permit fiduciaries to apply this standard to the portfolio taken as a whole, thereby allowing a fiduciary to balance a portfolio with higher-yield, higher-risk investments. In states with more progressive regulations, practically every type of security is eligible for inclusion in the portfolio of investments made by a fiduciary, provided that the portfolio investments, in their totality, are those of a prudent person.

Public equity markets
Organized markets for trading in equity shares such as common stocks, preferred stocks, and warrants. Includes markets for both regularly traded and nonregularly traded securities.

Public offering
General solicitation for participation in an investment opportunity. Interstate public offerings are supervised by the U.S. Securities and Exchange Commission (see separate citation).

Quality control
The process by which a product is checked and tested to ensure consistent standards of high quality.

Rate of return
(See also Yield)
The yield obtained on a security or other investment based on its purchase price or its current market price. The total rate of return is current income plus or minus capital appreciation or depreciation.

Real property
Includes the land and all that is contained on it.

Realignment
See Resource realignment

Recession
Contraction of economic activity occurring between the peak and trough (see separate citations) of a business cycle.

Regulated market
A market in which the government controls the forces of supply and demand, such as who may enter and what price may be charged.

Regulation D
A vehicle by which small businesses make small offerings and private placements of securities with limited disclosure requirements. It was designed to ease the burdens imposed on small businesses utilizing this method of capital formation.

Regulatory Flexibility Act
An act requiring federal agencies to evaluate the impact of their regulations on small businesses before the regulations are issued and to consider less burdensome alternatives.

Research
The initial stage of the innovation process, which includes idea generation and invention.

Research and development financing
A tax-advantaged partnership set up to finance product development for start-ups as well as more mature companies.

Resource mobility
The ease with which labor and capital move from firm to firm or from industry to industry.

Resource realignment
The adjustment of productive resources to interindustry changes in demand.

Resources
The sources of support or help in the innovation process, including sources of financing, technical evaluation, market evaluation, management and business assistance, etc.

Retained business earnings
Business profits that are retained by the business rather than being distributed to the shareholders as dividends.

Revolving credit
An agreement with a lending institution for an amount of money, which cannot exceed a set maximum, over a specified period of time. Each time the borrower repays a portion of the loan, the amount of the repayment may be borrowed yet again.

Risk capital
See Venture capital

Risk management
The act of identifying potential sources of financial loss and taking action to minimize their negative impact.

Routing
The sequence of steps necessary to complete a product during production.

S corporations
See Sub chapter S corporations

SBA
See Small Business Administration

SBA direct loans
Loans made directly by the U.S. Small Business Administration (SBA); monies come from funds appropriated specifically for this purpose. In general, SBA direct loans carry interest rates slightly lower than those in the private financial markets and are available only to applicants unable to secure private financing or an SBA guaranteed loan.

SBA 504 Program
See Certified development corporation

SBA guaranteed loans
Loans made by lending institutions in which the U.S. Small Business Administration (SBA) will pay a prior agreed-upon percentage of the outstanding principal in the event the borrower of the loan defaults. The terms of the loan and the interest rate are negotiated between the borrower and the lending institution, within set parameters.

SBA loans
See Disaster loans; SBA direct loans; SBA guaranteed loans; SBA special lending institution categories

SBA Management Assistance Programs
(See also Active Corps of Executives; Service Corps of Retired Executives; Small business institutes program)
Classes, workshops, counseling, and publications offered by the U.S. Small Business Administration.

SBA special lending institution categories.
U.S. Small Business Administration (SBA) loan program in which the SBA promises certified banks a 72-hour turnaround period in giving its approval for a loan, and in which preferred lenders in a pilot program are allowed to write SBA loans without seeking prior SBA approval.

SBDB
See Small Business Data Base

SBDC
See Small business development centers

SBI
See Small business institutes program

SBIC
See Small business investment corporation

SBIR Program
See Small Business Innovation Development Act of 1982

Scale economies
The decline of the production cost per unit of output (average cost) as the volume of output increases.

Scale efficiency
The reduction in unit cost available to a firm when producing at a higher output volume.

SCORE
See Service Corps of Retired Executives

SEC
See Securities and Exchange Commission

SECA
See Self-Employment Contributions Act

Second-stage financing
(See also First-stage financing; Third-stage financing)
Working capital for the initial expansion of a company that is producing, shipping, and has growing accounts receivable and inventories. Also known as Second-round financing.

Secondary market
A market established for the purchase and sale of outstanding securities following their initial distribution.

Secondary worker
Any worker in a family other than the person who is the primary source of income for the family.

Secondhand capital
Previously used and subsequently resold capital equipment (e.g., buildings and machinery).

Securities and Exchange Commission (SEC)
Federal agency charged with regulating the trade of securities to prevent unethical practices in the investor market.

Securitized debt
A marketing technique that converts long-term loans to marketable securities.

Seed capital
Venture financing provided in the early stages of the innovation process, usually during product development.

Self-employed person
One who works for a profit or fees in his or her own business, profession, or trade, or who operates a farm.

Self-Employment Contributions Act (SECA)
Federal law that governs the self-employment tax (see separate citation).

Self-employment income
Income covered by Social Security if a business earns a net income of at least $400.00 during the year. Taxes are paid on earnings that exceed $400.00.

Self-employment retirement plan
See Keogh plan

Self-employment tax
Required tax imposed on self-employed individuals for the provision of Social Security and Medicare. The tax must be paid quarterly with estimated income tax statements.

Self-funding
A health benefit plan in which a firm uses its own funds to pay claims, rather than transferring the financial risks of paying claims to an outside insurer in exchange for premium payments.

Service Corps of Retired Executives (SCORE)
(See also Active Corps of Executives)
Volunteers for the SBA Management Assistance Program who provide one-on-one counseling and teach workshops and seminars for small firms.

Service firm
See Business service firm

Service sector
Broadly defined, all U.S. industries that produce intangibles, including the five major industry divisions of transportation, communications, and utilities; wholesale trade; retail trade; finance, insurance, and real estate; and services.

Set asides
See Small business set asides

Short-haul service
A type of transportation service in which the transporter supplies service between cities where the maximum distance is no more than 200 miles.

Short-term debt
An obligation that matures in one year.

SIC codes
See Standard Industrial Classification codes

Single-establishment enterprise
See Establishment

Small business
An enterprise that is independently owned and operated, is not dominant in its field, and employs fewer than 500 people. For SBA purposes, the U.S. Small Business Administration (SBA) considers various other factors (such as gross annual sales) in determining size of a business.

Small Business Administration (SBA)
An independent federal agency that provides assistance with loans, management, and advocating interests before other federal agencies.

Small Business Data Base
(See also U.S. Establishment and Enterprise Microdata File; U.S. Establishment Longitudinal Microdata File)
A collection of microdata (see separate citation) files on individual firms developed and maintained by the U.S. Small Business Administration.

Small business development centers (SBDC)
Centers that provide support services to small businesses, such as individual counseling, SBA advice, seminars and conferences, and other learning center activities. Most services are free of charge, or available at minimal cost.

Small business development corporation
See Certified development corporation

Small business-dominated industry
Industry in which a minimum of 60 percent of employment or sales is in firms with fewer than 500 employees.

Small Business Innovation Development Act of 1982
Federal statute requiring federal agencies with large extramural research and development budgets to allocate a certain percentage of these funds to small research and development firms. The program, called the Small Business Innovation Research (SBIR) Program, is designed to stimulate technological innovation and make greater use of small businesses in meeting national innovation needs.

Small business institutes (SBI) program
Cooperative arrangements made by U.S. Small Business Administration district offices and local colleges and universities to provide small business firms with graduate students to counsel them without charge.

Small business investment corporation (SBIC)
A privately owned company licensed and funded through the U.S. Small Business Administration and private sector sources to provide equity or debt capital to small businesses.

Small business set asides
Procurement (see separate citation) opportunities required by law to be on all contracts under $10,000 or a certain percentage of an agency's total procurement expenditure.

Smaller firms
For U.S. Department of Commerce purposes, those firms not included in the Fortune 1000.

SMSA
See Metropolitan statistical area

Socially and economically disadvantaged
Individuals who have been subjected to racial or ethnic prejudice or cultural bias without regard to their qualities as individuals, and whose abilities to compete are impaired because of diminished opportunities to obtain capital and credit.

Sole proprietorship
An unincorporated, one-owner business, farm, or professional practice.

Special lending institution categories
See SBA special lending institution categories

Standard Industrial Classification (SIC) codes
Four-digit codes established by the U.S. Federal Government to categorize businesses by type of economic activity; the first two digits correspond to major groups such as construction and manufacturing, while the last two digits correspond to subgroups such as home construction or highway construction.

Standard metropolitan statistical area (SMSA)
See Metropolitan statistical area

Start-up
A new business, at the earliest stages of development and financing.

Start-up costs
Costs incurred before a business can commence operations.

Start-up financing
Financing provided to companies that have either completed product development and initial marketing or have been in business for less than one year but have not yet sold their product commercially.

Stock
(See also Common stock; Convertible preferred stock)
A certificate of equity ownership in a business.

Stop-loss coverage
Insurance for a self-insured plan that reimburses the company for any losses it might incur in its health claims beyond a specified amount.

Strategic planning
Projected growth and development of a business to establish a guiding direction for the future. Also used to determine which market segments to explore for optimal sales of products or services.

Structural unemployment
See Unemployment

Sub chapter S corporations
Corporations that are considered noncorporate for tax purposes but legally remain corporations.

Subcontract
A contract between a prime contractor and a subcontractor, or between subcontractors, to furnish supplies or services for performance of a prime contract (see separate citation) or a subcontract.

Surety bonds
Bonds providing reimbursement to an individual, company, or the government if a firm fails to complete a contract. The U.S. Small Business Administration guarantees surety bonds in a program much like the SBA guaranteed loan program (see separate citation).

Swing loan
See Bridge financing

Target market
The clients or customers sought for a business' product or service.

Targeted Jobs Tax Credit
Federal legislation enacted in 1978 that provides a tax credit to an employer who hires structurally unemployed individuals.

Tax number
(See also Employer identification number)
A number assigned to a business by a state revenue department that enables the business to buy goods without paying sales tax.

Taxable bonds
An interest-bearing certificate of public or private indebtedness. Bonds are issued by public agencies to finance economic development.

Technical assistance
See Management and technical assistance

Technical evaluation
Assessment of technological feasibility.

Technology
The method in which a firm combines and utilizes labor and capital resources to produce goods or services; the application of science for commercial or industrial purposes.

Technology transfer
The movement of information about a technology or intellectual property from one party to another for use.

Tenure
See Employee tenure

Term
(See also Maturity)
The length of time for which a loan is made.

Terms of a note
The conditions or limits of a note; includes the interest rate per annum, the due date, and transferability and convertibility features, if any.

Third-party administrator
An outside company responsible for handling claims and performing administrative tasks associated with health insurance plan maintenance.

Third-stage financing
(See also First-stage financing; Second-stage financing)
Financing provided for the major expansion of a company whose sales volume is increasing and that is breaking even or profitable. These funds are used for further plant expansion, marketing, working capital, or development of an improved product. Also known as Third-round or Mezzanine financing.

Time deposit
A bank deposit that cannot be withdrawn before a specified future time.

Time management
Skills and scheduling techniques used to maximize productivity.

Trade credit
Credit extended by suppliers of raw materials or finished products. In an accounting statement, trade credit is referred to as "accounts payable."

Trade name
The name under which a company conducts business, or by which its business, goods, or services are identified. It may or may not be registered as a trademark.

Trade periodical
A publication with a specific focus on one or more aspects of business and industry.

Trade secret
Competitive advantage gained by a business through the use of a unique manufacturing process or formula.

Trade show
An exhibition of goods or services used in a particular industry. Typically held inexhibition centers where exhibitors rent space to display their merchandise.

Trademark
A graphic symbol, device, or slogan that identifies a business. A business has property rights to its trademark from the inception of its use, but it is still prudent to register all trademarks with the Trademark Office of the U.S. Department of Commerce.

Translation
See Product development

Treasury bills
Investment tender issued by the Federal Reserve Bank in amounts of $10,000 that mature in 91 to 182 days.

Treasury bonds

Long-term notes with maturity dates of not less than seven and not more than twenty-five years.

Treasury notes

Short-term notes maturing in less than seven years.

Trend

A statistical measurement used to track changes that occur over time.

Trough

See Cyclical trough

UCC

See Uniform Commercial Code

UL

See Underwriters Laboratories

Underwriters Laboratories (UL)

One of several private firms that tests products and processes to determine their safety. Although various firms can provide this kind of testing service, many local and insurance codes specify UL certification.

Underwriting

A process by which an insurer determines whether or not and on what basis it will accept an application for insurance. In an experience-rated plan, premiums are based on a firm's or group's past claims; factors other than prior claims are used for community-rated or manually rated plans.

Unfair competition

Refers to business practices, usually unethical, such as using unlicensed products, pirating merchandise, or misleading the public through false advertising, which give the offending business an unequitable advantage over others.

Unfunded accrued liability

The excess of total liabilities, both present and prospective, over present and prospective assets.

Unemployment

The joblessness of individuals who are willing to work, who are legally and physically able to work, and who are seeking work. Unemployment may represent the temporary joblessness of a worker between jobs (frictional unemployment) or the joblessness of a worker whose skills are not suitable for jobs available in the labor market (structural unemployment).

Uniform Commercial Code (UCC)

A code of laws governing commercial transactions across the U.S., except Louisiana. Their purpose is to bring uniformity to financial transactions.

Uniform product code (UPC symbol)

A computer-readable label comprised of ten digits and stripes that encodes what a product is and how much it costs. The first five digits are assigned by the Uniform Product Code Council, and the last five digits by the individual manufacturer.

Unit cost

See Average cost

UPC symbol

See Uniform product code

U.S. Establishment and Enterprise Microdata (USEEM) File

A cross-sectional database containing information on employment, sales, and location for individual enterprises and establishments with employees that have a Dun & Bradstreet credit rating.

U.S. Establishment Longitudinal Microdata (USELM) File

A database containing longitudinally linked sample microdata on establishments drawn from the U.S. Establishment and Enterprise Microdata file (see separate citation).

U.S. Small Business Administration 504 Program

See Certified development corporation

USEEM

See U.S. Establishment and Enterprise Microdata File

USELM

See U.S. Establishment Longitudinal Microdata File

VCN

See Venture capital network

Venture capital

(See also Equity; Equity midrisk venture capital)

Money used to support new or unusual business ventures that exhibit above-average growth rates, significant potential for market expansion, and are in need of additional financing to sustain growth or further research and development; equity or equity-type financing traditionally provided at the commercialization stage, increasingly available prior to commercialization.

Venture capital company

A company organized to provide seed capital to a business in its formation stage, or in its first or second stage of expansion. Funding is obtained through public or private pension funds, commercial banks and bank holding companies, small business investment corporations licensed by the U.S. Small Business Administration, private venture capital firms, insurance companies, investment management companies, bank trust departments, industrial companies seeking to diversify their investment, and investment bankers acting as intermediaries for other investors or directly investing on their own behalf.

Venture capital limited partnerships

Designed for business development, these partnerships are an institutional mechanism for providing capital for young, technology-oriented businesses. The investors' money is pooled and invested in money market assets until venture investments have been selected. The general partners are experienced investment managers who select and invest the equity and debt securities of firms with high growth potential and the ability to go public in the near future.

Venture capital network (VCN)

A computer database that matches investors with entrepreneurs.

WAN

See Wide Area Network

Wide Area Network (WAN)

Computer networks linking systems throughout a state or around the world in order to facilitate the sharing of information.

Withholding

Federal, state, social security, and unemployment taxes withheld by the employer from employees' wages; employers are liable for these taxes and the corporate umbrella and bankruptcy will not exonerate an employer from paying back payroll withholding. Employers should escrow these funds in a separate account and disperse them quarterly to withholding authorities.

Workers' compensation

A state-mandated form of insurance covering workers injured in job-related accidents. In some states, the state is the insurer; in other states, insurance must be acquired from commercial insurance firms. Insurance rates are based on a number of factors, including salaries, firm history, and risk of occupation.

Working capital

Refers to a firm's short-term investment of current assets, including cash, short-term securities, accounts receivable, and inventories.

Yield

(See also Rate of return)

The rate of income returned on an investment, expressed as a percentage. Income yield is obtained by dividing the current dollar income by the current market price of the security. Net yield or yield to maturity is the current income yield minus any premium above par or plus any discount from par in purchase price, with the adjustment spread over the period from the date of purchase to the date of maturity.

Appendix D -
Cumulative Index

Cumulative Index

Listings in this index are arranged alphabetically by business plan type (in bold), then alphabetically by business plan name. Users are provided with the volume number on which the plan begins.